Oxford Primary Dictionary for Eastern Africa

OXFORD
UNIVERSITY PRESS

Great Clarendon Street, Oxford, OX2 6DP, United Kingdom

Oxford University Press is a department of the University of Oxford. It furthers the University's objective of excellence in research, scholarship, and education by publishing worldwide. Oxford is a registered trade mark of Oxford University Press in the UK and in certain other countries

First published 2016
2020 2019 2018 2017 2016
10 9 8 7 6 5 4 3 2 1

This dictionary includes some words which have or are asserted to have proprietary status as trademarks or otherwise. Their inclusion does not imply that they have acquired for legal purposes a non-proprietary or general significance nor any other judgement concerning their legal status. In cases where the editorial staff have some evidence that a word has proprietary status this is indicated in the entry for that word but no judgement concerning the legal status of such words is made or implied thereby

Links to third party websites are provided by Oxford in good faith and for information only. Oxford disclaims any responsibility for the materials contained in any third party website referenced in this work

The British National Corpus is a collaborative project involving Oxford University Press, Longman, Chambers, the Universities of Oxford and Lancaster and the British Library

ISBN: 978 0 19 442095 2

ACKNOWLEDGEMENTS

Edited by: Victoria Bull

Consultant: Florence Waeni

We would like to thank the following for their permission to reproduce photographs and illustrations:
Alamy Ltd.: p137; Corel: p77, p337, p356, p77; Hemera Technologies Inc.: p22, p26, p43, p61, p67, p69, p77, p130, p154, p198, p202, p221, p232, p239, p243, p244, p252, p267, p281, p291, p311, p314, p317, p331, p346, p381; JB Illustrations: p27; KJA-artists.com: p29; Paul Mirocha/Wiley: p183; Phil Schramm/Meiklejohn Illustrations: p311, p379; Photodisc/Getty: p249; Shutterstock: p61; Stockbyte/Getty: p220.

Illustrations: Lorna Barnard, Jeremy Bays, Anna Brookes, David Burroughs, Martin Cox, Mark Dunn, David Eaton, Angelika Elsebach, Gay Galsworthy, Margaret Heath, Robert Hichens, Karen Hiscock, Margaret Jones, Bennie Kruger, Richard Lewington, Martin Lonsdale/Hardlines, Vanessa Luff, Kevin Maddison, Julien Marais, Ian McCaughrean, Coral Mula, Martin Shovel, Technical Graphics Department OUP, Oxford Illustrators, Harry Venning, Margaret Wellbank, Graham White, Leigh-Anne Wolfaardt, Michael Woods

Study pages A2–3 adapted from Oxford Primary Dictionary © Oxford University Press

Typeset by Sharon McTeir, Creative Publishing Services
Printed in China

CONTENTS

GUIDE TO THE DICTIONARY

Finding words and phrases

The **2000 keywords** (= the most important words to learn) are clearly marked.

Idioms and **phrasal verbs** (which have a special meaning) are shown below the main words.

easy 🔑 /ˈiːzi/ *adjective* **(easier, easiest)** **1** If something is easy, you can do or understand it without any difficulty: *The homework was very easy.* **take it easy; take things easy** to not worry or work too much: *After my exams I'm going to take it easy for a few days.*

Words with the **same meaning**, but different parts of speech, have different numbers.

Related words are shown below the main word.

instant[1] /ˈɪnstənt/ *adjective* **1** that happens very quickly; immediate: *The film was an instant success.* **2** quick and easy to prepare: *an instant meal* ▶ **instantly** *adverb* immediately; at once: *I asked him a question and he replied instantly.*

instant[2] /ˈɪnstənt/ *noun* a very short time; a moment: *She thought for an instant before she answered.*

Grammar

The **part of speech** (for example verb, noun or adjective)

The **forms of a verb**. We show the he/she form, the –ing form, the past tense (and the past participle of irregular verbs).

catch 🔑 /kætʃ/ *verb* (**catches, catching, caught** /kɔːt/, **has caught**) **1** to take and hold something that is moving: *He threw the ball to me and I caught it.*

Plurals. To make the plural of most nouns, you add –s (for example *girl – girls*). For all other nouns we give you full information.

Some nouns have a completely different **plural form** or there is a change in the spelling.

leaf 🔑 /liːf/ *noun* (*plural* **leaves** /liːvz/) one of the flat green parts that grow on a plant or tree: *The leaves turn red in autumn.*

Some nouns are **always plural**.

clothes 🔑 /kləʊðz/ *noun* (plural) things like trousers, shirts and coats that you wear to cover your body: *She was wearing new clothes.* ◇ *Take off those wet clothes.*

Sometimes a noun has no plural form and is not used with a or an.

information 🔑 /ˌɪnfəˈmeɪʃn/ *noun* (no plural) what you tell someone; facts: *Can you give me some information about buses to Meru?* ➲ Look at the verb **inform**.

Nouns with no plural form often have notes giving extra information about grammar.

❖ **GRAMMAR**

Be careful! You cannot say 'an information'. You can say 'some information' or 'a piece of information': *She gave me an interesting piece of information.*

Comparative and **superlative** forms are given, unless they are formed with **more** or **most**.

busy 🔑 /ˈbɪzi/ *adjective* **(busier, busiest)** **1** with a lot of things that you must do;

Understanding and using words

Pronunciation and **stress** tell you how to say the word.

What the word **means**

Related words help you to build your vocabulary.

Opposites and words with the **same meaning** are given. **Examples** help you to understand a word and show you how it is used.

bus stop /ˈbʌs stɒp/ *noun* a place where buses stop and people get on and off

elephant /ˈelɪfənt/ *noun* a very big wild animal from Africa or Asia, with a long nose (called a **trunk**) that hangs down

expensive 🔑 /ɪkˈspensɪv/ *adjective* Something that is expensive costs a lot of money: *expensive clothes* SAME MEANING **dear** OPPOSITE **inexpensive**

Notes

These notes show you the **difference** between two words.

high[1] 🔑 /haɪ/ *adjective* (**higher, highest**)

❖ **high** or **tall**?

We use **tall**, not **high**, to talk about people: *How tall are you?* ◇ *He's 1.72 metres tall.*

Word family boxes show you groups of words that are based on the same form.

able 🔑 /ˈeɪbl/ *adjective*

❖ **WORD FAMILY**

able: OPPOSITE **unable**
ability: OPPOSITE **inability**

Word building notes show you related words to help you build your vocabulary.

cat 🔑 /kæt/ *noun*

❖ **WORD BUILDING**

A young cat is called a **kitten**. A young lion or tiger is called a **cub**.

Spelling boxes help you to remember how to spell a word correctly.

accommodation /əˌkɒməˈdeɪʃn/ *noun*

❖ **SPELLING**

Remember! You spell **accommodation** with **cc** and **mm**.

Pronunciation boxes help you to understand how to say a word correctly.

trough /trɒf/ *noun*

❖ **PRONUNCIATION**

Trough sounds like **off**.

Grammar notes tell you more about grammar.

trousers 🔑 /ˈtraʊzəz/ *noun* (plural) a

❖ **GRAMMAR**

Be careful! You cannot say 'a trousers'. You can say **a pair of trousers**: *I bought a new pair of trousers.*

Speaking. These notes show you a word or phrase that is common in speech.

inflate /ɪnˈfleɪt/ *verb* (**inflates, inflating,**

❖ **SPEAKING**

It is more usual to say **blow up** or **pump up**.

DICTIONARY QUIZ

This quiz shows you how your Oxford dictionary can help you. You will find the answers to all these questions in the dictionary.

Finding what you want

1 Finding a word

Put these words into alphabetical order:

coconut argue prize vegetable open shepherd

---

2 Finding what a word means

1 What is a **squirrel**?
2 What is **bronze** made from?
3 How many meanings does **trunk** have?
4 The part of your leg above your knee is called your **calf**. True or false?

3 Finding the grammar

1 Is the word **lung** a noun, a verb or an adjective?
2 What is the past tense of the verb **break**?
3 What is the plural of **party**?
4 Can you say 'Please give me an **advice**'?

4 Finding how to say a word

Match the word on the left with a word that sounds like it (rhymes) on the right:

1 whole	i who
2 dumb	ii young
3 tongue	iii water
4 through	iv drum
5 daughter	v hole

5 Checking your spelling

Use the notes at these words to check if the spelling is correct.

1 accomodation
2 committee
3 until
4 decieve
5 fourty

Building your vocabulary

The notes in the dictionary will help you learn more words.

1 Word families

Fill in the missing words

Noun	Verb	Adjective
		weak
	satisfy	
	enjoy	
memory		

2 Word Building

Look at the notes at the word in **bold** to help you answer these questions.

1 What is the word for a bad **dream**?
2 A crocodile is a **reptile**. True or false?
3 A doctor who **operates** is called a ________________
4 What is the word for a book of **maps**?
5 A young **goat** is called a foal. True or false?

3 Finding opposites

Find the opposite of these words in the word square.
One has been done for you.

awake before fit first cheap do up freeze wet

L	A	F	T	E	R
D	S	I	D	R	Y
U	L	L	D	U	K
N	E	T	E	N	T
D	E	M	A	F	H
O	P	T	R	I	A
G	L	A	S	T	W

See page A24 to check all your answers.

PHONETIC SYMBOLS

Vowels

iː	see	/siː/	ʌ	cup	/kʌp/
i	happy	/ˈhæpi/	ɜː	bird	/bɜːd/
ɪ	sit	/sɪt/	ə	about	/əˈbaʊt/
e	ten	/ten/	eɪ	say	/seɪ/
æ	cat	/kæt/	əʊ	go	/gəʊ/
ɑː	father	/ˈfɑːðə(r)/	aɪ	my	/maɪ/
ɒ	got	/gɒt/	aʊ	now	/naʊ/
ɔː	saw	/sɔː/	ɔɪ	boy	/bɔɪ/
ʊ	put	/pʊt/	ɪə	near	/nɪə(r)/
u	actual	/ˈæktʃuəl/	eə	hair	/heə(r)/
uː	too	/tuː/	ʊə	pure	/pjʊə(r)/

Consonants

p	pen	/pen/	f	fall	/fɔːl/	h	hat	/hæt/
b	bad	/bæd/	v	van	/væn/	m	man	/mæn/
t	tea	/tiː/	θ	thin	/θɪn/	n	no	/nəʊ/
d	did	/dɪd/	ð	this	/ðɪs/	ŋ	sing	/sɪŋ/
k	cat	/kæt/	s	see	/siː/	l	leg	/leg/
g	get	/get/	z	zoo	/zuː/	r	red	/red/
tʃ	chain	/tʃeɪn/	ʃ	shoe	/ʃuː/	j	yes	/jes/
dʒ	jam	/dʒæm/	ʒ	vision	/ˈvɪʒn/	w	wet	/wet/

(ˈ) shows the strong stress: it is in front of the part of the word that you say most strongly, for example **because** /bɪˈkɒz/.

(ˌ) shows a weaker stress. Some words have a part that is said with a weaker stress as well as a strong stress, for example **conversation** /ˌkɒnvəˈseɪʃn/.

(r) at the end of a word means that you say this sound only when the next word begins with a vowel sound.

Some words, for example **at** and **must**, have two pronunciations. We give the usual pronunciation first. The second pronunciation must be used when the word is stressed, and is also often used when the word is at the end of a sentence. For example:

This book is for /fə(r)/ *Karimi.* *Who is this book for?* /fɔː(r)/

Symbols and abbreviations used in the dictionary

ℹ tells you that there is something important to remember about this word.

➲ tells you about a note or picture on another page, or about a related word that you should look at.

etc. means 'and so on' and tells you that there are other things in the list that we have not named.

Aa

A, a /eɪ/ *noun* (*plural* **A's, a's** /eɪz/) the first letter of the English alphabet: *'Apple' begins with an 'A'.*

a /ə; eɪ/ *article* **1** one or any: *Would you like a drink?* ◇ *A dog has four legs.* ◇ *He's a teacher.* **2** each, or for each: *She phones her mother three times a week.* ◇ *These sweets cost 150 shillings a packet.*

> ❖ **a or an?**
>
> You use **an**, not **a**, in front of a word that starts with the sound of a, e, i, o or u. Be careful! It is the sound that is important, not the spelling. Look at these examples: *a box* ◇ *an apple* ◇ *a singer* ◇ *an hour* ◇ *a university* ◇ *an MP*

abandon /əˈbændən/ *verb* (**abandons, abandoning, abandoned** /əˈbændənd/) **1** to leave someone or something completely: *He abandoned his shoe in the deep mud.* **2** to stop doing something before it is finished: *When the storm started, we abandoned our game.*

abbreviate /əˈbriːvieɪt/ *verb* (**abbreviates, abbreviating, abbreviated**) to make a word shorter by not saying or writing some of the letters: *The word 'telephone' is often abbreviated to 'phone'.*

abbreviation /əˌbriːviˈeɪʃn/ *noun* a short form of a word: *TV is an abbreviation for 'television'.*

ability /əˈbɪləti/ *noun* (*plural* **abilities**) the power and knowledge to do something: *She has the ability to pass the exam, but she must work harder.*

able /ˈeɪbl/ *adjective*
be able to to have the power and knowledge to do something: *Will you be able to come to the party?* ◇ *Is Ereng able to swim?* ➲ Look at **can**[1].

> ❖ **WORD FAMILY**
>
> **able**: OPPOSITE **unable**
> **ability**: OPPOSITE **inability**

aboard /əˈbɔːd/ *adverb, preposition* on or onto a ship, train, bus or plane: *Are all the passengers aboard?* ◇ *Welcome aboard flight 603 to Nairobi.*

abolish /əˈbɒlɪʃ/ *verb* (**abolishes, abolishing, abolished** /əˈbɒlɪʃt/) to stop or end something by law: *The Americans abolished slavery in 1863.* ▸ **abolition** /ˌæbəˈlɪʃn/ *noun* (no plural): *the abolition of hunting*

about /əˈbaʊt/ *preposition, adverb* **1** a little more or less than; a little before or after: *She's about 12 years old.* ◇ *I arrived at about two o'clock.* **2** of; on the subject of: *It's a book about cats.* ◇ *We talked about the problem.* ◇ *What are you thinking about?* **3** in or to different places or in different directions: *The children were running about in the road.* ◇ *There were books lying about on the floor.* **4** almost: *Dinner is about ready.* **5** in a place; here: *Is your mother about? I want to see her.*
be about to to be going to do something very soon: *The film is about to start.*

above /əˈbʌv/ *preposition, adverb* **1** in or to a higher place; higher than someone or something: *I looked up at the sky above.* ◇ *The office is above a shop.* OPPOSITE **below** ➲ picture on page A6 **2** more than a number or price: *This game is for children aged ten and above.* OPPOSITE **below, under**
above all more than any other thing; what is most important: *He's handsome and intelligent and, above all, he's kind!*

abroad /əˈbrɔːd/ *adverb* in or to another country: *She lives abroad.* ◇ *She went abroad to study.*

absence /ˈæbsəns/ *noun* (no plural) a time when a person or thing is not there: *Bigogo is doing Kendi's job in her absence.*

absent /ˈæbsənt/ *adjective* not there; away: *He was absent from school yesterday.* OPPOSITE **present**

absent-minded /ˌæbsənt ˈmaɪndɪd/ *adjective* often forgetting things because you are thinking about something else SAME MEANING **forgetful**

absolute /ˈæbsəluːt/ *adjective* complete: *I've never played the guitar before. I'm an absolute beginner.*

absolutely /ˈæbsəluːtli/ *adverb* completely: *You're absolutely right.*

absorb /əbˈsɔːb; əbˈzɔːb/ *verb* (**absorbs, absorbing, absorbed** /əbˈsɔːbd; əbˈzɔːbd/) to take in something like liquid or heat, and hold it: *The dry ground absorbed all the rain.*

abstain /əbˈsteɪn/ *verb* (**abstains, abstaining, abstained** /əbˈsteɪnd/) to stop yourself from doing something: *The doctor told him to abstain from (eating) sugar.* ▸ **abstinence** /ˈæbstɪnəns/ *noun* (no plural): *The doctor advised total abstinence from dairy produce.*

abstract /ˈæbstrækt/ *adjective* **1** about an idea, not a real thing: *abstract thought* **2** not like a real thing: *abstract paintings*

absurd /əbˈsɜːd/ *adjective* so silly that it makes you laugh: *You look absurd in that hat!*

abuse[1] /əˈbjuːz/ *verb* (**abuses**, **abusing**, **abused** /əˈbjuːzd/) **1** to use something in a wrong or bad way: *The manager often abuses her power.* **2** to be cruel or unkind to someone: *They abused their workers.* **3** to say rude things to someone

abuse[2] /əˈbjuːs/ *noun* (no plural) **1** using something in a wrong or bad way: *drug abuse* **2** being cruel or unkind to someone: *child abuse* **3** rude words: *The driver shouted abuse.*

acacia /əˈkeɪʃə/ *noun* a kind of tree that grows in hot places, with small leaves and often with a flat top

acacia

accelerate /əkˈseləreɪt/ *verb* (**accelerates**, **accelerating**, **accelerated** /əkˈseləreɪtɪd/) to go faster: *The driver accelerated to overtake the bus.* ▸ **acceleration** /əkˌseləˈreɪʃn/ *noun* (no plural): *This car has excellent acceleration.*

accent /ˈæksent/ *noun* **1** the way a person from a certain place or country speaks a language: *She speaks English with an American accent.* **2** saying one word or part of a word more strongly than another: *In the word 'because', the accent is on the second part of the word.*

accept /əkˈsept/ *verb* (**accepts**, **accepting**, **accepted**)
1 to say 'yes' when someone asks you to have or do something: *I accepted the invitation to his house.* ◇ *Please accept this present.* **2** to believe that something is true: *Odoi cannot accept that he failed.*

> ❖ **SPELLING**
>
> Remember! **Accept** and **except** sound nearly the same but do not mean the same.

acceptable /əkˈseptəbl/ *adjective* allowed by most people; good enough: *It's not acceptable to make so many mistakes.*

access[1] /ˈækses/ *noun* (no plural) a way to go into a place or to use something: *The flying doctor visits villages that have no access to a hospital.* ◇ *Do you have access to a computer at school?*

access[2] /ˈækses/ *verb* (**accesses**, **accessing**, **accessed** /ˈæksest/) to find information on a computer: *Click on the icon to access a file.*

accident /ˈæksɪdənt/ *noun* something that happens by chance: *I had an accident on the way to school – I fell over and cut my knee.* ◇ *I'm sorry I broke your watch – it was an accident.*
by accident by chance; not because you have planned it: *I took Awino's book by accident. I thought it was mine.*

accidental /ˌæksɪˈdentl/ *adjective* If something is **accidental**, it happens by chance: *accidental damage* ▸ **accidentally** /ˌæksɪˈdentəli/ *adverb*: *He accidentally broke the window.*

accommodation /əˌkɒməˈdeɪʃn/ *noun* (no plural) a place to stay or live: *It is difficult to find cheap accommodation in Mombasa.*

> ❖ **GRAMMAR**
>
> Be careful! You cannot say 'an accommodation'. You can use other phrases instead: *I'll help you find somewhere to live.*

> ❖ **SPELLING**
>
> Remember! You spell **accommodation** with **cc** and **mm**.

accompany /əˈkʌmpəni/ *verb* (**accompanies**, **accompanying**, **accompanied** /əˈkʌmpənid/, **has accompanied**) **1** to go with someone to a place: *Two teachers accompanied the class on their walk.* **2** to happen at the same time as something else: *Thunder is usually accompanied by lightning.* **3** to play music while someone sings or plays another instrument: *You sing and I'll accompany you on the guitar.*

accord /əˈkɔːd/ *noun* (no plural)
of your own accord because you want to, not because someone has asked you to: *She left the club of her own accord.*

according to /əˈkɔːdɪŋ tə/ *preposition* as someone or something says: *According to Karimi, this film is really good.* ◇ *It's going to rain today, according to the newspaper.*

account /əˈkaʊnt/ *noun* **1** words that someone says or writes about something that happened: *He gave the police an account of the car accident.* **2** an amount of money that you keep in a bank: *I paid the money into my bank account.* ◇ *I'd like to open an account* (= start keeping money in the bank). ◇ *a current account* (= one that you can take money out of at any time) **3 accounts** (plural) lists of all the money that a person or business receives and pays: *Who keeps* (= does) *the accounts for your father's business?*

on no account; not on any account not for any reason: *On no account must you open this door.*

take account of something; take something into account to remember something when you are thinking about other things: *Opiyo is always last, but you must take his age into account – he is much younger than the other children.*

accountable /ə'kaʊntəbl/ *adjective* expected to give an explanation of your actions; responsible: *She is too young to be held accountable for what she did.* ▸ **accountability** /əˌkaʊntə'bɪləti/ *noun* (no plural): *The new law requires greater accountability from the police.*

accountant /ə'kaʊntənt/ *noun* a person whose job is to make lists of all the money that people or businesses receive and pay: *Juma is an accountant.*

accurate /'ækjərət/ *adjective* exactly right; with no mistakes: *He gave an accurate description of the thief.* OPPOSITE **inaccurate** ▸ **accurately** *adverb*: *The map was accurately drawn.*

accuse 🔑 /ə'kju:z/ *verb* (**accuses, accusing, accused** /ə'kju:zd/) to say that someone has done something wrong: *The police accused the woman of stealing.* ◇ *He was accused of murder.* ▸ **accusation** /ˌækju'zeɪʃn/ *noun*: *The accusations were not true.*

the accused /ə'kju:zd/ *noun* (no plural) (in a court of law) the person who is said to have done something wrong: *The jury found the accused guilty of theft.* SAME MEANING **respondent**

ache[1] /eɪk/ *verb* (**aches, aching, ached** /eɪkt/) to give you pain: *My legs ached after the long walk.*

ache[2] /eɪk/ *noun* a pain that lasts for a long time: *I've got a headache.* ◇ *She's got toothache.* ◇ *stomach ache* ◇ *earache*

> ❖ **GRAMMAR**
>
> We often use **ache** with a part of the body.
>
> We usually use **ache** without 'a' or 'an': *I've got backache.* But we always say 'a headache': *I've got a terrible headache.*

achieve 🔑 /ə'tʃi:v/ *verb* (**achieves, achieving, achieved** /ə'tʃi:vd/) to do or finish something well after trying hard: *He worked hard and achieved his aim of becoming a doctor.*

achievement /ə'tʃi:vmənt/ *noun* something that someone has done after trying hard: *Winning an Olympic gold medal was his greatest achievement.*

acid 🔑 /'æsɪd/ *noun* a liquid that can burn things: *The acid burned a hole in his shirt.*

acid rain /ˌæsɪd 'reɪn/ *noun* (no plural) rain that has chemicals in it from factories, etc. It can damage trees, rivers and buildings.

acknowledge /ək'nɒlɪdʒ/ *verb* (**acknowledges, acknowledging, acknowledged** /ək'nɒlɪdʒd/) **1** to agree that something is true: *He acknowledged that he had made a mistake.* **2** to say or write that you have received something: *She never acknowledged my letter.*

acquaintance /ə'kweɪntəns/ *noun* a person that you know a little: *Teta has many friends and acquaintances.*

acquire /ə'kwaɪə(r)/ *verb* (**acquires, acquiring, acquired** /ə'kwaɪəd/) to get or buy something: *He acquired some English from listening to pop songs.*

acquit /ə'kwɪt/ *verb* (**acquits, acquitting, acquitted**) to say that someone has not done wrong and is not guilty: *The jury acquitted him of murder.*

acre /'eɪkə(r)/ *noun* a measure of land (=0.405 of a hectare): *a farm of 40 acres*

acrobat /'ækrəbæt/ *noun* a person who does difficult movements of the body, or walks on high ropes ▸ **acrobatic** /ˌækrə'bætɪk/ *adjective* performing difficult movements of the body: *She's an acrobatic dancer.*

across 🔑 /ə'krɒs/ *adverb, preposition* **1** from one side to the other side of something: *We walked across the field.* ➲ picture on page A7 **2** on the other side of something: *There is a bank across the road.* **3** from side to side: *The river is two kilometres across.*

act[1] /ækt/ *verb* (**acts, acting, acted**) **1** to do something, or behave in a certain way: *Doctors acted quickly to save the boy's life after the accident.* ◇ *Stop acting like a baby!* **2** to pretend to be someone else in a play, film or television programme: *Who's acting the part of the wicked queen?*
act as something to do the job of another person, usually for a short time: *She acted as our teacher while Mrs Mundia was ill.*

❖ **WORD FAMILY**
act acting actor actress

act[2] /ækt/ *noun* **1** something that you do: *It was an act of kindness to offer them food.* **2** one part of a play: *This play has five acts.* **3** a law that a government makes: *Children have a right to education, according to the Children's Act.*
in the act of while doing something wrong: *I caught him in the act of stealing the money.*

acting /ˈæktɪŋ/ *noun* (no plural) being in plays or films: *Have you ever done any acting?*

action /ˈækʃn/ *noun* **1** (no plural) doing things: *Now is the time for action!* **2** (*plural* **actions**) something that you do: *The little girl copied her mother's actions.* **3** (no plural) exciting things that happen: *I like films with a lot of action.*
in action doing something; working: *We watched the machine in action.*

active /ˈæktɪv/ *adjective* **1** If you are active, you are always busy and able to do a lot of things: *My grandmother is 65 and she's still very active.* **2** A sentence is active when the person or thing doing the action is the subject of the verb: *In the sentence 'A girl broke the window', the verb is active.* ❶ You can also say 'The verb is **in the active**.' OPPOSITE **passive**

activity /ækˈtɪvəti/ *noun* **1** (no plural) a lot of things happening and people doing things: *On the day of the festival there was a lot of activity in the streets.* **2** (*plural* **activities**) something that you do: *Fishing is one of his favourite activities.*

actor /ˈæktə(r)/ *noun* a person who acts in plays, films or television programmes: *He is one of the country's leading actors.*

actress /ˈæktrəs/ *noun* (*plural* **actresses**) a woman who acts in plays, films or television programmes: *A well-known actress played the leading role.*

actual /ˈæktʃuəl/ *adjective* that really happened; real: *We thought the bus would cost about 150 shillings, but the actual fare was much more.*

actually /ˈæktʃuəli/ *adverb* **1** really; in fact: *We thought it was going to rain, but actually it was sunny all day.* **2** a word that you use to disagree politely or when you say something new: *'Let's go later.' 'Actually, I think we should go now.'*

AD /ˌeɪ ˈdiː/ **AD** in a date shows that it was after Christ was born: *AD 1066* ◇ *Paper was invented in the second century AD.* ❶ **AD** is from the Latin 'Anno Domini' meaning 'in the year of the Lord'. ➲ Look at **BC**.

ad /æd/ *short for* ADVERTISEMENT

adapt /əˈdæpt/ *verb* (**adapts, adapting, adapted**) **1** to change the way that you do things because you are in a new situation: *He has adapted very well to being at a new school.* **2** to change something so that you can use it in a different way: *The car was adapted for use as a taxi.*

add /æd/ *verb* (**adds, adding, added**) **1** to put something with something else: *Mix the flour with the milk and then add the eggs.* ◇ *Add your name to the list.* **2** to put numbers together: *If you add 2 and 5 together, you get 7.* OPPOSITE **subtract** **3** to say something more: *'Go away – and don't come back again,' she added.* ➲ Look at **addition**.

addict /ˈædɪkt/ *noun* **1** a person who cannot stop wanting something that is very bad for them: *He admitted that he was a drug addict.* **2** a person who is very interested in something and spends a lot of their free time on it: *Many boys are computer game addicts.* ▶ **addiction** /əˈdɪkʃn/ *noun*: *the problem of teenage drug addiction*

addicted /əˈdɪktɪd/ *adjective* not able to stop wanting something that is bad for you: *He is addicted to drugs.*

addition /əˈdɪʃn/ *noun* **1** (no plural) putting numbers together: *We learnt addition and subtraction at primary school.* **2** (*plural* **additions**) a thing or person that you add to other things or people: *They have a new addition to their family* (= a new baby). ➲ Look at **add**.
in addition also: *She plays the guitar, and in addition she writes her own songs.*
in addition to something as well as: *He speaks five languages in addition to English.*

additional /əˈdɪʃənl/ *adjective* added; extra: *There is a small additional charge for lunch.*

address[1] /əˈdres/ *noun* (*plural* **addresses**) **1** the number of the house and the name of the street and town where someone lives or works: *Their address is 18 Mashundu Road, Nairobi.* ◇ *Are you still living at that address?* ➲ picture on page A14 **2** a number used as an address in order to receive letters or parcels: *My address is PO Box 70532, 00200 Nairobi.* **3** a group of words or symbols that tells you where you can find someone or something using a computer: *What's your email address?* ◇ *a web address*

❖ **SPELLING**

Remember! You spell **address** with **dd** and **ss**.

address[2] /əˈdres/ *verb* (**addresses**, **addressing**, **addressed** /əˈdrest/) to write on a letter or parcel the name and address of the person you are sending it to: *The letter was addressed to Rono Odenda.*

address book /əˈdres bʊk/ *noun* **1** a book in which you keep addresses and phone numbers **2** a computer file where you store email and Internet addresses

adequate /ˈædɪkwət/ *adjective* enough for what you need: *They are very poor and do not have adequate food or clothing.* OPPOSITE **inadequate**

adjective /ˈædʒɪktɪv/ *noun* a word that you use with a noun, that tells you more about it: *In the sentence 'This soup is hot', 'hot' is an adjective.*

adjudicator /əˈdʒuːdɪkeɪtə(r)/ *noun* a person who judges a competition: *She was an adjudicator in the music festival.* ▸ **adjudicate** /əˈdʒuːdɪkeɪt/ *verb* (**adjudicates**, **adjudicating**, **adjudicated**): *Who is adjudicating at this year's contest?*

adjust /əˈdʒʌst/ *verb* (**adjusts**, **adjusting**, **adjusted**) to make a small change to something, to make it better: *You can adjust the height of this chair.*

administration /ədˌmɪnɪˈstreɪʃn/ *noun* (no plural) controlling or managing something, for example a business, an office or a school: *There's a lot of work involved in the administration of a school.*

administrator /ədˈmɪnɪstreɪtə(r)/ *noun* a person whose job is to control or manage something, for example a business, an office or a school

admire /ədˈmaɪə(r)/ *verb* (**admires**, **admiring**, **admired** /ədˈmaɪəd/) to think or say that someone or something is very good: *I really admire you for working so hard.* ◇ *They were admiring the view from the top of the hill.* ▸ **admiration** /ˌædməˈreɪʃn/ *noun* (no plural): *I have great admiration for her writing.*

admission /ədˈmɪʃn/ *noun* **1** (no plural) letting someone go into a place: *There is no admission to the park after 6 p.m.* **2** (no plural) accepting someone into a school, club, etc: *He passed the test and gained admission to the school of his choice.* **3** (no plural) the money that you pay to go into a place: *Admission to the stadium is 200 shillings.* **4** a statement that admits that something is true: *Malika's admission that she had lied proved her brother's innocence.*

admit /ədˈmɪt/ *verb* (**admits**, **admitting**, **admitted**) **1** to say that you have done something wrong: *He admitted stealing the money.* ◇ *I admit that I made a mistake.* OPPOSITE **deny** **2** to let someone or something go into a place: *This ticket admits one person to the museum.*

adopt /əˈdɒpt/ *verb* (**adopts**, **adopting**, **adopted**) to take the child of another person into your family to become your own child: *They adopted Kisoso after his parents died.*

adore /əˈdɔː(r)/ *verb* (**adores**, **adoring**, **adored** /əˈdɔːd/) to love someone or something very much: *She adores her grandchildren.*

adult /ˈædʌlt/ *noun* a person or an animal that has grown to the full size; not a child: *Adults as well as children will enjoy this film.* ▸ **adult** *adjective*: *She was born in France, but has spent her adult life in Kenya.*

advance[1] /ədˈvɑːns/ *noun* (no plural) **in advance** before something happens: *We paid for the tickets in advance.*

advance[2] /ədˈvɑːns/ *verb* (**advances**, **advancing**, **advanced** /ədˈvɑːnst/) to develop and become better: *Technology has advanced rapidly in recent years.*

advanced /ədˈvɑːnst/ *adjective* at a high level; difficult: *an advanced English class* ◇ *The language in the textbook was too advanced for the pupils.*

advantage /ədˈvɑːntɪdʒ/ *noun* something that helps you or that is useful: *When you're travelling in West Africa, it's a great advantage if you speak French.* ◇ *One advantage of solar power is that it's cheap.* OPPOSITE **disadvantage**

take advantage of something to use something to help yourself: *Buy now and take advantage of these special prices!*

adventure 🔑 /əd'ventʃə(r)/ *noun* something exciting that you do or that happens to you: *She wrote a book about her adventures as a journalist.*

adventurous /əd'ventʃərəs/ *adjective* An **adventurous** person likes to do exciting, dangerous things.

adverb /'ædvɜːb/ *noun* a word that tells you how, when or where something happens: *In the sentence 'Please speak slowly', 'slowly' is an adverb.*

advert 🔑 /'ædvɜːt/ *short for* ADVERTISEMENT

advertise /'ædvətaɪz/ *verb* (**advertises, advertising, advertised** /'ædvətaɪzd/) to give people information in newspapers, on television, on the wall, on the Internet, etc. about jobs, things to buy or events to go to: *That drink is advertised on the radio.* ◇ *My parents sold our car by advertising it in the newspaper.* ▶ **advertiser** /'ædvətaɪzə(r)/ *noun* a person or company that **advertises**: *Advertisers like to persuade us that we need new things.*

advertisement 🔑 /əd'vɜːtɪsmənt/ *noun* information in a newspaper, on television, on the wall, on the Internet, etc. that tells you about a job, something to buy or an event to go to: *I saw an advertisement for a cheap laptop in the paper.* ℹ The short form is **advert** or **ad**.

advertising /'ædvətaɪzɪŋ/ *noun* (no plural) telling people about things to buy: *He works in advertising.* ◇ *The magazine gets a lot of money from advertising.*

advice 🔑 /əd'vaɪs/ *noun* (no plural) words that you say to help someone decide what to do: *He will give you advice about where to go.*

take someone's advice to do what someone says you should do: *I took the doctor's advice and stayed in bed.*

> ❖ **GRAMMAR**
>
> Be careful! You cannot say 'an advice'. You can say 'some advice' or 'a piece of advice': *I need some advice.* ◇ *Let me give you a piece of advice.*

advise 🔑 /əd'vaɪz/ *verb* (**advises, advising, advised** /əd'vaɪzd/) to tell someone what you think they should do: *The doctor advised him to stop eating sweets.*

> ❖ **SPELLING**
>
> Remember! You spell the verb **advise** and the noun **advice**.

advocate /'ædvəkət/ *noun* (in a court of law) a person who says someone has not done something wrong

aerials

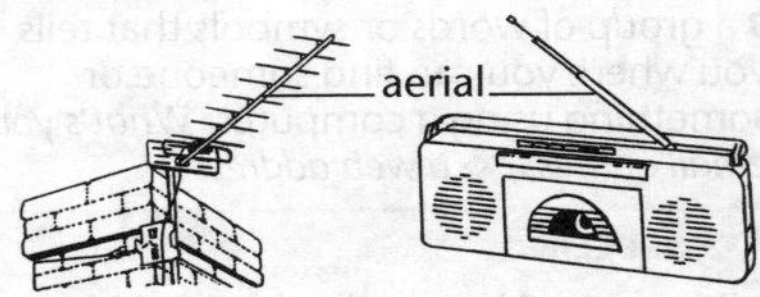

aerial /'eəriəl/ *noun* a wire that receives radio or television signals

aeroplane /'eərəpleɪn/ *noun* a machine that has wings and can fly ➲ Look at **plane**.

aerosol /'eərəsɒl/ *noun* a can with liquid in it. You press a button to make the liquid come out in a lot of very small drops: *an aerosol spray*

affair /ə'feə(r)/ *noun* **1** something that happens; an event: *The wedding was a very quiet affair.* **2** something that you need to do or think about; business: *Don't worry about that – it's not your affair.* ◇ *foreign affairs*

affect 🔑 /ə'fekt/ *verb* (**affects, affecting, affected**) to make something different: *Poor diet can affect your health.*

affection /ə'fekʃn/ *noun* (no plural) the feeling of loving or liking someone: *She has great affection for her aunt.*

affectionate /ə'fekʃənət/ *adjective* that feels or shows love: *She gave him an affectionate kiss.* ▶ **affectionately** *adverb*: *He smiled at his son affectionately.*

afford 🔑 /ə'fɔːd/ *verb* (**affords, affording, afforded**)

can afford something If you **can afford something**, you have enough money to pay for it: *I can't afford a new bike.*

afraid 🔑 /ə'freɪd/ *adjective* If you are afraid of something, it makes you feel fear: *Some people are afraid of snakes.* ◇ *I was afraid to open the door.*

I'm afraid ... a polite way of saying that you are sorry: *I'm afraid I've lost your key.* ◇ *I'm afraid that I can't help you.*

African /'æfrɪkən/ *adjective* connected with Africa: *Kiswahili is an African language.* ◇ *the East African Community*

▸ **African** *noun* a person from Africa: *Young Africans want to travel.*

after[1] 🔑 /ˈɑːftə(r)/ *preposition* **1** later than someone or something: *Nafula arrived after dinner.* ◇ *After doing my homework, I went out.* **2** behind or following someone or something: *Ten comes after nine.* ◇ *Close the door after you.* OPPOSITE **before, in front of** **3** trying to get or catch someone or something: *The police officer ran after her.*
after all **1** when you thought something different would happen: *I was worried about the exam, but it wasn't difficult after all.* **2** do not forget: *She doesn't understand. After all, she's only two.*

after[2] 🔑 /ˈɑːftə(r)/ *conjunction, adverb* at a time later than someone or something: *He arrived after the lesson had started.* ◇ *Hawa left at ten o'clock and I left soon after.*

afternoon 🔑 /ˌɑːftəˈnuːn/ *noun* the part of a day between midday and the evening: *We had lunch and in the afternoon we went for a walk.* ◇ *I saw Robi this afternoon.* ◇ *Yesterday afternoon I went shopping.* ◇ *I'll see you on Monday afternoon.*

afterwards 🔑 /ˈɑːftəwədz/ *adverb* later: *We played football and did our homework afterwards.*

again 🔑 /əˈgen/ *adverb* **1** one more time; once more: *Could you say that again, please?* ◇ *I will never see him again.* **2** in the way that someone or something was before: *You'll soon feel well again.*
again and again many times: *I've told you again and again not to do that!*

against 🔑 /əˈgenst/ *preposition* **1** on the other side in a game, fight, etc: *They played against a football team from another village.* **2** If you are against something, you do not like it: *Many people are against the plan.* **3** next to and touching someone or something: *Put the cupboard against the wall.* ➲ picture on page A6 **4** to prevent something from happening: *Have you had an injection against the disease?*

age 🔑 /eɪdʒ/ *noun* **1** (*plural* **ages**) the amount of time that someone or something has been in the world: *I started school at the age of 3.* ◇ *She is seven years of age.* **2** (no plural) being old: *Her hair was grey with age.* **3** (*plural* **ages**) a certain time in history: *The Stone Age is a time when people used stone tools.* **4** **ages** (plural) a very long time: *She has lived here for ages.*

> ❖ **SPEAKING**
>
> When you want to ask about someone's age, you usually say 'How old are you?'
>
> To say your age, you say **I am 12**, or **I'm 12 years old** (BUT NOT: *I'm twelve years*).

aged 🔑 /eɪdʒd/ *adjective* at the age of: *They have two sons, aged five and six.*

agency /ˈeɪdʒənsi/ *noun* (*plural* **agencies**) the work or office of someone who does business for others: *A travel agency arranges travel for people.*

agenda /əˈdʒendə/ *noun* a list of all the things to be talked about in a meeting: *The next item on the agenda is the school sports day.*

agent /ˈeɪdʒənt/ *noun* a person who does business for another person or for a company: *A music agent tries to find work for musicians.* ◇ *a travel agent*

age-set /ˈeɪdʒ set/ *noun* (in some societies) a group of boys or girls who are of a similar age: *Kamau and Nduku belong to the same age-set.*

aggressive /əˈgresɪv/ *adjective* If you are **aggressive**, you are ready to argue or fight: *Watching violence on TV makes some children aggressive.*

> ❖ **SPELLING**
>
> Remember! We spell **aggressive** with **gg** and **ss**.

ago 🔑 /əˈgəʊ/ *adverb* before now; in the past: *She started school two months ago.* ◇ *He left school a long time ago.*
long ago a very long time in the past: *Long ago there were no cars or planes.*

agony /ˈægəni/ *noun* (no plural) very great pain: *He screamed in agony.*

agree 🔑 /əˈgriː/ *verb* (**agrees, agreeing, agreed** /əˈgriːd/) **1** to have the same idea as another person about something: *I'm afraid I don't agree.* ◇ *I agree with you.* **2** to say 'yes' when someone asks you to do something: *Chebet agreed to give me the money.* OPPOSITE **refuse** **3** to decide something with another person: *Hawa and I agreed to meet later.*

> ❖ **WORD FAMILY**
>
> **agree**: OPPOSITE **disagree**
> **agreement**: OPPOSITE **disagreement**

agreement 🔑 /əˈgriːmənt/ *noun* **1** (*plural* **agreements**) a plan or decision that two or more people or countries have made together: *There is a trade agreement* *between the two countries* (= they have agreed to buy things from and sell things to each other). **2** (no plural) having the same ideas as someone or something: *We talked about which film to see, but there was not much agreement.*

agriculture /ˈæɡrɪkʌltʃə(r)/ *noun* (no plural) keeping animals and growing plants for food; farming: *Many people are employed in agriculture.* ▶ **agricultural** /ˌæɡrɪˈkʌltʃərəl/ *adjective*: *The shop sells agricultural tools.*

ahead 🔑 /əˈhed/ *adverb* **1** in front of someone or something: *We could see a light ahead of us.* **2** into the future: *We must look ahead and make a plan.* **3** doing better than other people: *Moraa is ahead of the others in her class.*
go ahead do something that you want to do; start to do something: *'Can I borrow your bicycle?' 'Yes, go ahead.'*

aid /eɪd/ *noun* (no plural) help, or something that gives help: *He walks with the aid of a stick.* ◇ *The government sent aid to the victims of the floods.* ◇ *a hearing aid* (= a small thing that you put in your ear so you can hear better)
in aid of someone or **something** to get money for someone or something: *The concert was in aid of the hospital.*

AIDS /eɪdz/ *noun* (no plural) a very serious illness that stops the body protecting itself against other diseases. **AIDS** stands for 'Acquired Immune Deficiency Syndrome': *the AIDS virus* ◇ *He contracted AIDS last year.* ➲ Look at **HIV**.

aim[1] 🔑 /eɪm/ *verb* (**aims, aiming, aimed** /eɪmd/) **1** to point something, for example a gun, at someone or something that you want to hit: *The farmer aimed his gun at the lion and fired.* **2** to want or plan to do something: *He's aiming to leave at nine o'clock.* **3** to plan something for a certain person or group: *This book is aimed at teenagers.*

aim[2] 🔑 /eɪm/ *noun* something that you want and plan to do: *Boke's aim is to run faster than anyone in her class.*

air 🔑 /eə(r)/ *noun* (no plural) **1** what you take in through your nose and mouth when you breathe: *Let's go out for some fresh air.* **2** the space around and above things: *He threw the ball up in the air.*
by air in a plane: *It's more expensive to travel by air than by train.*
on the air on the radio or on television: *The programme will go on the air next month.*

airbase /ˈeəbeɪs/ *noun* an airport for aircraft used by soldiers: *a military airbase*

airborne /ˈeəbɔːn/ *adjective* flying in the air: *Tuberculosis is an airborne disease.*

air conditioning /ˈeə kəndɪʃnɪŋ/ *noun* (no plural) a way of keeping the air in a building or car cool and dry ▶ **air-conditioned** /ˈeə kəndɪʃnd/ *adjective* with **air conditioning**: *an air-conditioned office*

aircraft 🔑 /ˈeəkrɑːft/ *noun* (*plural* **aircraft**) a vehicle that can fly, for example a plane: *The government has invested in military aircraft.*

air force /ˈeə fɔːs/ *noun* the aircraft that a country uses for fighting, and the people who fly them

airline /ˈeəlaɪn/ *noun* a company with planes that carry people or goods: *KQ is a Kenyan airline.*

airmail /ˈeəmeɪl/ *noun* (no plural) a way of sending letters and parcels by plane: *an airmail letter*

airport 🔑 /ˈeəpɔːt/ *noun* a place where people get on and off planes, with buildings where passengers can wait: *I'll meet you at the airport.*

airstrip /ˈeəstrɪp/ *noun* a piece of land where planes can take off and land

aisle /aɪl/ *noun* a way between lines of seats, for example in a church, a theatre or a plane

alarm[1] /əˈlɑːm/ *noun* **1** (no plural) a sudden feeling of fear: *He heard a noise, and jumped out of bed in alarm.* **2** (*plural* **alarms**) something that tells you about danger, for example by making a loud noise: *When the thieves broke the window, the alarm went off.* **3** (*plural* **alarms**) an alarm clock: *I set the alarm for 6 a.m.*

alarm[2] /əˈlɑːm/ *verb* (**alarms, alarming, alarmed** /əˈlɑːmd/) to make someone or something suddenly feel worried or afraid: *She was alarmed to hear that Wasike was ill.* ◇ *The noise alarmed the bird and it flew away.*

alarm clock /əˈlɑːm klɒk/ *noun* a clock that makes a noise to wake you up

alarm clock

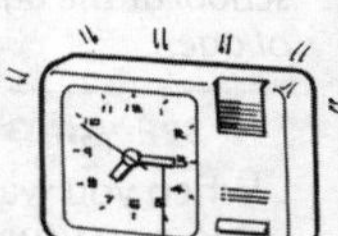

album /ˈælbəm/ *noun* **1** a collection of music or songs that are usually on one CD or on the internet:

Have you heard this album? ➲ Look at **single²**. **2** a book with empty pages where you can put photographs, stamps, etc: *a photograph album*

alcohol 🔑 /ˈælkəhɒl/ *noun* (no plural) **1** the liquid in drinks, for example wine or beer, that can make people feel drunk: *This beer is low in alcohol.* **2** drinks like wine or beer: *My father doesn't drink alcohol.*

alcoholic¹ 🔑 /ˌælkəˈhɒlɪk/ *adjective* containing alcohol: *an alcoholic drink*

alcoholic² /ˌælkəˈhɒlɪk/ *noun* a person who drinks too much alcohol and can't stop

alert¹ /əˈlɜːt/ *adjective* awake and ready to do things: *A good driver is always alert.*

alert² /əˈlɜːt/ *noun* a warning of danger: *a malaria alert*

algebra /ˈældʒɪbrə/ *noun* (no plural) a type of mathematics in which letters and symbols are used for numbers

alien /ˈeɪliən/ *noun* **1** a person who comes from another country or place **2** a person or an animal that comes from another planet in space

alight /əˈlaɪt/ *adjective* on fire; burning: *A fire started in the kitchen and soon the whole house was alight.*
set something alight to make something start to burn: *The petrol was set alight by a cigarette.*

alike /əˈlaɪk/ *adjective* almost the same; not different: *The two sisters are very alike.* ▸ **alike** *adverb* in the same way: *The twins always dress alike* (= wear the same clothes).

alive 🔑 /əˈlaɪv/ *adjective* living; not dead: *Are your grandparents alive?*

all¹ 🔑 /ɔːl/ *adjective, pronoun* **1** every one of a group: *All cats are animals but not all animals are cats.* ◇ *They invited sixty people to the wedding, but not all of them came.* ◇ *Are you all listening?* **2** every part of something; the whole of something: *She's eaten all the bread.* ◇ *It rained all day.*

all² 🔑 /ɔːl/ *adverb* completely: *She lives all alone.* ◇ *He was dressed all in black.*
all along from the beginning: *I knew all along that she was lying.*

alliance /əˈlaɪəns/ *noun* an agreement between countries or people to work together and help each other: *An alliance was formed among the East African countries.*

alligator

alligator /ˈælɪgeɪtə(r)/ *noun* a big long animal with sharp teeth. Alligators live in and near rivers. ➲ Look at **crocodile**.

allow 🔑 /əˈlaʊ/ *verb* (**allows, allowing, allowed** /əˈlaʊd/) to say that someone can have or do something: *We were allowed to used calculators during the maths exam.* ◇ *The teacher allowed me to leave the class early.* ➲ Look at **forbid**.

all right 🔑 (also **alright**) /ˌɔːl ˈraɪt/ *adjective* **1** good or good enough: *Is everything all right?* **2** well; not hurt: *I was ill, but I'm all right now.* **3** yes, I agree: *'Let's go home now.' 'All right.'*

ally /ˈælaɪ/ *noun* (*plural* **allies**) a person or country that agrees to help another person or country, especially at a difficult time

almost 🔑 /ˈɔːlməʊst/ *adverb* nearly; not quite: *It's almost three o'clock.* ◇ *I almost fell into the river!*

aloe /ˈæləʊ/ *noun* a plant with thick leaves with sharp points that grows in hot countries

aloe

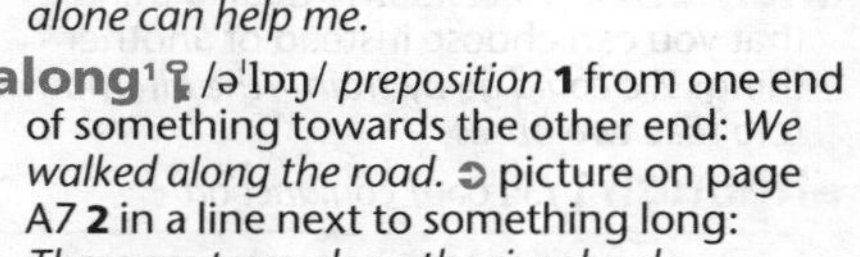

alone 🔑 /əˈləʊn/ *adverb* **1** without any other person: *My grandmother lives alone.* **2** only: *You alone can help me.*

along¹ 🔑 /əˈlɒŋ/ *preposition* **1** from one end of something towards the other end: *We walked along the road.* ➲ picture on page A7 **2** in a line next to something long: *There are trees along the river bank.*

along² 🔑 /əˈlɒŋ/ *adverb* **1** forward: *He drove along very slowly.* **2** with me, you, etc: *We're going to the cinema. Why don't you come along too?*

alongside /əˌlɒŋˈsaɪd/ *preposition* next to something: *Put your bicycle alongside mine.*

aloud /əˈlaʊd/ *adverb* speaking so that other people can hear: *I read the story aloud to my sister.*

alphabet 🔑 /ˈælfəbet/ *noun* all the letters of a language: *The English alphabet starts with A and ends with Z.*

alphabetical /ˌælfəˈbetɪkl/ *adjective* in the order of the alphabet: *Put these words in alphabetical order* (= with words beginning with A first, then B, then C, then D, etc.) ▶ **alphabetically** /ˌælfəˈbetɪkli/ *adverb*: *The books are listed alphabetically.*

already ⚷ /ɔːlˈredi/ *adverb* before now or before then: *'Would you like something to eat.' 'No, thank you – I've already eaten.'* ◇ *We ran to the station but the bus had already left.*

❖ **already** or **yet**?

Yet means the same as **already**, but you only use it in negative sentences and in questions: *I have finished this book already.* ◇ *I haven't finished this book yet.* ◇ *Have you finished the book yet?*

alright = **all right**

also ⚷ /ˈɔːlsəʊ/ *adverb* as well; too: *She's the fastest runner in the school and she's also very clever.*

alter /ˈɔːltə(r)/ *verb* (**alters, altering, altered** /ˈɔːltəd/) to make something different; to change: *We had to alter our plans.*

alteration /ˌɔːltəˈreɪʃn/ *noun* a small change.

alternate /ɔːlˈtɜːnət/ *adjective* (of two things) happening one after the other regularly: *I buy milk on alternate days* (= Monday I buy it, Tuesday I don't, Wednesday I do, Thursday I don't, etc.)

alternative[1] /ɔːlˈtɜːnətɪv/ *adjective* different; other: *The main road is closed so we'll have to use an alternative route.*

alternative[2] /ɔːlˈtɜːnətɪv/ *noun* a thing that you can choose instead of another thing: *We could go by train – the alternative is to take two buses.*

although ⚷ /ɔːlˈðəʊ/ *conjunction*

❖ **PRONUNCIATION**

Although ends with the same sound as **go**.

1 in spite of something; though: *Although she was ill, she went to school.* ➲ Note at **spite**. **2** but: *I think he's from Tunisia, although I'm not sure.*

altitude /ˈæltɪtjuːd/ *noun* **1** (no plural) how high something is above sea level: *The plane is flying at an altitude of 10 000 metres.* **2** (*plural* **altitudes**) a place that is high above sea level: *It can be very cool at higher altitudes.*

alto /ˈæltəʊ/ *noun* (*plural* **altos**) the second highest singing voice; a person with this voice: *Are you a soprano or an alto?*

altogether /ˌɔːltəˈgeðə(r)/ *adverb* **1** counting everything or everybody: *Pembe gave me 100 shillings and Shayo gave me 50, so I've got 150 shillings altogether.* **2** completely: *I don't altogether agree with you.*

aluminium /ˌæljəˈmɪniəm/ *noun* (no plural) a light metal with a silver colour: *an aluminium saucepan*

always ⚷ /ˈɔːlweɪz/ *adverb* **1** at all times; every time: *I have always lived in this town.* ◇ *The bus is always late.* **2** for ever: *I will always remember that day.* **3** again and again: *My sister is always borrowing my clothes!*

a.m. /ˌeɪ ˈem/ You use **a.m.** after a time to show that it is between midnight and midday. **A.m.** is from the Latin 'ante meridiem': *School starts at 8 a.m.*

❖ **WORD BUILDING**

We use **p.m.** for times between midday and midnight.

am *form of* BE

amateur /ˈæmətə(r)/ *noun* a person who does something because they enjoy it, not for money or for a job ▶ **amateur** *adjective*: *an amateur photographer* ➲ Look at **professional**.

amaze /əˈmeɪz/ *verb* (**amazes, amazing, amazed** /əˈmeɪzd/) to make someone very surprised: *Deng amazed me by remembering my birthday.*

amazed /əˈmeɪzd/ *adjective* If you are **amazed**, you are very surprised: *I was amazed to see Shema – I thought he was in hospital.*

amazement /əˈmeɪzmənt/ *noun* (no plural) great surprise: *She looked at me in amazement.*

amazing /əˈmeɪzɪŋ/ *adjective* If something is **amazing**, it surprises you very much: *She told us an amazing story.* ▶ **amazingly** *adverb*: *The game is amazingly simple to play.*

ambassador /æmˈbæsədə(r)/ *noun* an important person who goes to another country and works there for the government of their own country: *the Kenyan Ambassador to the United States*

❖ **WORD BUILDING**

An ambassador works in an **embassy**.

ambition /æmˈbɪʃn/ *noun* **1** (no plural) a very strong wish to do well: *Malika* *is intelligent, but she has no ambition.* **2** (*plural* **ambitions**) something that you want to do: *My ambition is to become a doctor.*

ambitious /æmˈbɪʃəs/ *adjective* A person who is **ambitious** wants to do well.

ambulance /ˈæmbjələns/ *noun* a special vehicle that takes people who are ill or hurt to hospital

amiss /əˈmɪs/ *adjective* wrong: *When we heard the screaming, we knew something was amiss.*

ammunition /ˌæmjəˈnɪʃn/ *noun* (no plural) things that you throw, or fire from a gun, to hurt or damage people or things: *The plane was carrying ammunition to the soldiers.*

among ⚷ /əˈmʌŋ/ (also **amongst** /əˈmʌŋst/) *preposition* **1** in the middle of: *The house stands among the trees.* ➲ picture on page A6 **2** for or by more than two things or people: *He divided the money amongst his six children.*

> ❖ **among** or **between**?
>
> We use **among** when we are talking about more than two people or things. If there are only two people or things, we use **between**: *You're among friends here.* ◇ *I was standing between Njoki and Tanei.*

amount[1] ⚷ /əˈmaʊnt/ *noun* how much there is of something: *He spent a large amount of money.*

amount[2] /əˈmaʊnt/ *verb* (**amounts**, **amounting**, **amounted**)
amount to something to make a certain amount when you put everything together: *The cost of the repairs amounted to 5 000 shillings.*

amp /æmp/ *noun* a measure of electricity: *a 13 amp plug*

amphibian /æmˈfɪbiən/ *noun* an animal that can live on the land and in water: *Frogs and toads are amphibians.*

amplifier /ˈæmplɪfaɪə(r)/ *noun* an electrical machine that makes sounds louder: *He turned up the volume on the amplifier so that everyone could hear.*

amuse ⚷ /əˈmjuːz/ *verb* (**amuses**, **amusing**, **amused** /əˈmjuːzd/) **1** to make someone smile or laugh: *Kamal's joke did not amuse his mother.* **2** to keep someone happy and busy: *We played games to amuse ourselves on the long journey.*

amusement /əˈmjuːzmənt/ *noun* (no plural) the feeling that you have when something makes you laugh or smile: *We watched in amusement as the dog chased its tail.*

amusing ⚷ /əˈmjuːzɪŋ/ *adjective* Something that is amusing makes you smile or laugh: *It was an amusing story.*

an ⚷ /ən; æn/ *article* **1** one or any: *I ate an apple.* **2** each, or for each: *The car was going at 60 kilometres an hour.* ➲ Note at **a**.

anaemia /əˈniːmiə/ *noun* (no plural) a medical condition in which there are not enough red **cells** (= the smallest parts of any living thing) in the blood ▸ **anaemic** /əˈniːmɪk/ *adjective*: *My brother is anaemic.*

anaesthetic /ˌænəsˈθetɪk/ *noun* something that a doctor gives you so that you will not feel pain in an operation: *The doctor gave him an anaesthetic before she stitched the wound.*

ancestor /ˈænsestə(r)/ *noun* a person in your family who lived a long time before you: *My ancestors came from West Africa.*

anchor /ˈæŋkə(r)/ *noun* **1** a heavy metal thing that you drop into the water from a boat to stop the boat moving away **2** a person who presents a radio or TV report as it happens: *Our news anchor reports live from Mwanza.*

anchor

ancient ⚷ /ˈeɪnʃənt/ *adjective* very old; from a time long ago: *We saw ancient buildings at Fort Jesus.*

and ⚷ /ənd; ænd/ *conjunction* a word that joins words or parts of sentences together: *day and night* ◇ *They sang and danced.* ◇ *The cat was black and white.*

angel /ˈeɪndʒl/ *noun* a spirit who carries messages from God. In pictures, angels usually have wings: *God sent an angel to talk to Gideon.*

anger ⚷ /ˈæŋgə(r)/ *noun* (no plural) the strong feeling that you have when you are not pleased about something: *He was filled with anger when he saw the man trying to steal his car.*

> ❖ **WORD FAMILY**
>
> **anger** **angry** **angrily**

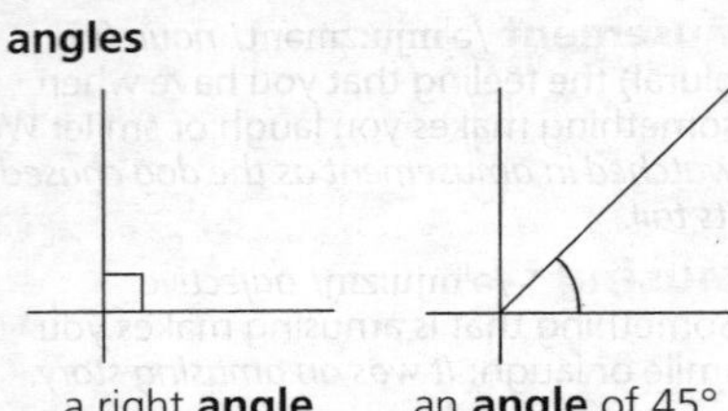

angle 🔑 /ˈæŋgl/ *noun* the space between two lines that meet: *The angle is 40 degrees.*

angry 🔑 /ˈæŋgri/ *adjective* (**angrier, angriest**) If you are angry, you feel or show anger: *My father was angry with me when I got home late.* ▶ **angrily** 🔑 /ˈæŋgrəli/ *adverb*: *'Someone has taken my book!' she shouted angrily.*

animal 🔑 /ˈænɪml/ *noun* **1** any living thing that is not a plant: *the animal kingdom* **2** any living thing that can move and feel, but is not a person, a bird, a fish or an insect: *Cats, sheep and rats are animals.*

> ❖ **WORD BUILDING**
>
> There are many different types of animal. Here are some of them: **cows**, **lions** and **monkeys**. How many others do you know?

ankle /ˈæŋkl/ *noun* the part of your leg where it joins your foot ➲ picture on page A13

anniversary /ˌænɪˈvɜːsəri/ *noun* (*plural* **anniversaries**) a day when you remember something special that happened on the same day in another year: *Today is their 25th wedding anniversary.*

announce 🔑 /əˈnaʊns/ *verb* (**announces, announcing, announced** /əˈnaʊnst/) to tell a lot of people about something important: *The teacher announced the winner of the competition.*

> ❖ **WORD FAMILY**
>
> **announce announcement announcer**

announcement /əˈnaʊnsmənt/ *noun* important information that someone tells a lot of people: *I have an important announcement to make.*

announcer /əˈnaʊnsə(r)/ *noun* a person whose job is to tell us about programmes on radio or television: *The announcer introduced the next programme.*

annoy 🔑 /əˈnɔɪ/ *verb* (**annoys, annoying, annoyed** /əˈnɔɪd/) to make someone a little angry: *My brother annoys me when he leaves his clothes all over the floor.*

annoyance /əˈnɔɪəns/ *noun* (no plural) the feeling of being a little angry: *She could not hide her annoyance when I arrived late.*

annoyed 🔑 /əˈnɔɪd/ *adjective* a little angry: *I was annoyed when he forgot to return my book.* ◇ *My father is annoyed with me.*

annoying 🔑 /əˈnɔɪɪŋ/ *adjective* If a person or thing is annoying, they make you a little angry: *It's annoying when people don't listen to you.*

annual /ˈænjuəl/ *adjective* **1** that happens or comes once every year: *There is an annual meeting in June.* **2** for one year: *What is his annual income* (= How much money does he get for one year's work)? ▶ **annually** *adverb*: *The company makes 50 000 cars annually.*

anonymous /əˈnɒnɪməs/ *adjective* **1** If a person is **anonymous**, other people do not know their name: *He made an anonymous call to the police.* **2** If something is **anonymous**, you do not know who did, gave or made it: *She received an anonymous letter.*

another 🔑 /əˈnʌðə(r)/ *adjective, pronoun* **1** one more thing or person: *Would you like another drink?* ◇ *I like these cakes – can I have another?* **2** a different thing or person: *I can't see you tomorrow – can we meet another day?* ◇ *I've read this book. Do you have another?*

answer[1] 🔑 /ˈɑːnsə(r)/ *verb* (**answers, answering, answered** /ˈɑːnsəd/)

> ❖ **PRONUNCIATION**
>
> **Answer** sounds like **dancer**.

1 to say or write something when someone has asked a question: *I asked him if he was hungry but he didn't answer.* ◇ *I couldn't answer all the exam questions.* **2** to write a letter to someone who has written to you: *She did not answer my letter.*
answer the door to open the door when someone knocks or rings: *Can you answer the door, please?*
answer the telephone to pick up the telephone when it rings, and speak

answer[2] 🔑 /ˈɑːnsə(r)/ *noun* **1** something that you say or write when you answer someone: *I asked Nafula a question but she didn't give me an answer.* ◇ *Have you had an answer to your letter?* **2** a way of stopping a problem: *If you are tired, the answer is to go to bed early!*

answerphone /ˈɑːnsəfəʊn/ (also **answering machine** /ˈɑːnsərɪŋ məʃiːn/) *noun* a machine that answers the telephone for you and keeps messages so that you can listen to them later: *I left a message on the answerphone.*

ant /ænt/ *noun* a very small insect that lives in big groups ➲ Picture at **insect**.

antelope /ˈæntɪləʊp/ *noun* a wild animal with long horns and long thin legs, that can run fast

antenatal /ˌæntiˈneɪtl/ *adjective* for women who are **pregnant** (= have babies growing in them): *an antenatal clinic* ◇ *antenatal care*

anthem /ˈænθəm/ *noun* a song that you sing on special occasions: *the national anthem* (= the special song of a country)

anthrax /ˈænθræks/ *noun* (no plural) a serious illness of cattle, sheep and sometimes people. **Anthrax** harms the **lungs** (= the parts inside your body that you use for breathing) and skin.

anti- /ˈænti/ *prefix* **anti** at the beginning of a word often means 'against': *an anti-smoking campaign* ◇ *an anti-corruption police unit*

antibiotic /ˌæntibaɪˈɒtɪk/ *noun* a medicine that fights illness in your body: *The doctor gave me antibiotics for my chest infection.*

antibody /ˈæntibɒdi/ *noun* (*plural* **antibodies**) a substance that the body produces in the blood to fight disease, or as a reaction when certain substances are put into the body

anticipate /ænˈtɪsɪpeɪt/ *verb* (**anticipates, anticipating, anticipated**) to think that something will happen and be ready for it: *We didn't anticipate so many problems.*

anticlockwise /ˌæntɪˈklɒkwaɪz/ *adjective, adverb* in the opposite direction to the hands of a clock: *Turn the handle anticlockwise.* OPPOSITE **clockwise**

antique /ænˈtiːk/ *noun* an old thing that is worth a lot of money: *These chairs are antiques.* ▶ **antique** *adjective*: *an antique vase*

antiseptic /ˌæntiˈseptɪk/ *noun* a liquid or cream that kills **germs** (= small living things that can make you ill): *Put some antiseptic on that cut.* ➲ Look at **disinfectant**. ▶ **antiseptic** *adjective*: *antiseptic cream*

antivirus /ˈæntivaɪrəs/ *adjective* designed to find and destroy computer **viruses** (= programs that stop your computer working properly): *antivirus software*

anxiety /æŋˈzaɪəti/ *noun* (*plural* **anxieties**) a feeling of worry and fear: *Waiting for exam results is a time of great anxiety.*

anxious /ˈæŋkʃəs/ *adjective* **1** worried and afraid: *She's anxious because her daughter hasn't arrived yet.* **2** If you are **anxious** to do something, you want to do it very much: *My family are anxious to meet you.* ▶ **anxiously** *adverb*: *We waited anxiously.*

any[1] 🔑 /ˈeni/ *adjective, pronoun* **1** a word that you use instead of 'some' in questions and after 'not' and 'if': *Have you got any money?* ◇ *I don't speak any French.* ◇ *She asked if I had any milk.* ◇ *He needed medicine but there wasn't any.* ➲ Note at **some**. **2** used for saying that it does not matter which thing or person you choose: *Come any day next week.* ◇ *Take any book you want.*

any[2] 🔑 /ˈeni/ *adverb* used in questions and after 'not' to make an adjective or adverb stronger: *I can't walk any faster.*

anybody /ˈenibɒdi/ = **anyone**

anyhow /ˈenihaʊ/ = **anyway**

anyone 🔑 /ˈeniwʌn/ (also **anybody**) *pronoun* **1** any person: *Did you see anyone you know?* ◇ *There wasn't anybody there.* **2** no special person: *Anyone* (= all people) *can play this game.*

anything 🔑 /ˈeniθɪŋ/ *pronoun* **1** a thing of any kind: *Is there anything in that box?* ◇ *I can't see anything.* **2** no special thing: *'What would you like to drink?' 'Oh, anything. I don't mind.'*

anything else something more: *'Would you like anything else?' asked the waitress.*

anything like the same as someone or something in any way: *She isn't anything like her sister.*

anyway 🔑 /ˈeniweɪ/ (also **anyhow**) *adverb* **1** a word that you use when you give a second reason for something: *I don't want to see the film and anyway I haven't got any money.* **2** no matter what is true; however: *It was very expensive but she bought it anyway.* **3** a word that you use when you start to talk about something different: *That's what Katee said. Anyway, how are you?*

anywhere 🔑 /ˈeniweə(r)/ *adverb* **1** at, in or to any place: *Are you going anywhere* *nice?* ◇ *I can't find my pen anywhere.* **2** no special place: *'Where shall I sit?' 'Oh, anywhere – it doesn't matter.'*

AOB /ˌeɪ əʊ ˈbiː/ *noun* (no plural) extra things that are talked about at the end of a meeting ℹ **AOB** is short for 'any other business'.

apart 🔑 /əˈpɑːt/ *adverb* **1** away from the others; away from each other: *The two houses are 500 metres apart.* ◇ *My mother and father live apart now.* **2** into parts: *He took my radio apart to repair it.*
apart from someone or **something** if you do not count someone or something: *There were ten people in the room, apart from me.* ◇ *I like all vegetables apart from carrots.*

apartment 🔑 /əˈpɑːtmənt/ *noun* a group of rooms for living in, usually on one floor of a building SAME MEANING **flat**

ape /eɪp/ *noun* an animal like a big **monkey** with no tail: *Gorillas and chimpanzees are apes.*

apologize /əˈpɒlədʒaɪz/ *verb* (**apologizes, apologizing, apologized** /əˈpɒlədʒaɪzd/) to say that you are sorry about something that you have done: *I apologized to Egesa for losing his book.*

apology /əˈpɒlədʒi/ *noun* (*plural* **apologies**) words that you say or write to show that you are sorry about something you have done: *Please accept my apologies.*

apostrophe /əˈpɒstrəfi/ *noun* the sign (') that you use in writing to show that you have left a letter out of a word, for example in 'I'm' (I am). You also use it to show that something belongs to someone or something: 'the boy's leg'. ➲ Look at page A17.

app /æp/ *noun* a computer program that is designed to do a particular job, especially one that lets you see information about a particular subject, play games, etc. on your mobile phone: *I've got a dictionary app on my phone.*

appalling /əˈpɔːlɪŋ/ *adjective* very bad; terrible: *The prisoners were living in appalling conditions.*

apparent /əˈpærənt/ *adjective* easy to see or understand; clear: *It was apparent that she did not like him.*

apparently 🔑 /əˈpærəntli/ *adverb* **1** You use apparently to talk about what another person said, when you do not know if it is true: *Apparently, her father has a new job in Kigali.* **2** it seems: *He went to school today, so apparently he's feeling better.*

appeal¹ /əˈpiːl/ *verb* (**appeals, appealing, appealed** /əˈpiːld/) to ask in a serious way for something that you want very much: *They appealed for food and clothing.*
appeal to someone to please or interest someone: *Living in a big city doesn't appeal to me.*

appeal² /əˈpiːl/ *noun* asking for something in a serious way: *They made an appeal for help.*

appear 🔑 /əˈpɪə(r)/ *verb* (**appears, appearing, appeared** /əˈpɪəd/) **1** to come and be seen: *The sun suddenly appeared from behind a cloud.* ◇ *We waited for an hour but he didn't appear.* OPPOSITE **disappear** **2** to seem: *It appears that I was wrong.*

appearance 🔑 /əˈpɪərəns/ *noun* **1** the coming of someone or something; when someone or something is seen: *Nakato's appearance at the meeting surprised everybody.* **2** what someone or something looks like: *Her new glasses change her appearance.*

appendix /əˈpendɪks/ *noun* **1** (*plural* **appendixes**) a small tube inside your body near your stomach: *She went into hospital to have her appendix out* (= removed). **2** (*plural* **appendices** /əˈpendɪsiːz/) a section at the end of a book or document that gives extra information

appetite /ˈæpɪtaɪt/ *noun* the feeling that you want to eat: *Swimming always gives me an appetite* (= makes me hungry).

applaud /əˈplɔːd/ *verb* (**applauds, applauding, applauded**) **1** to make a noise by hitting your hands together to show that you like something: *We all applauded loudly at the end of the song.* **2** to say or show that you like something that someone has done: *We applauded her decision to go to college.*

applause /əˈplɔːz/ *noun* (no plural) when a lot of people hit their hands together to show that they like something: *loud applause*

apple 🔑 /ˈæpl/ *noun* a hard round fruit: *She peeled an apple.*

apple

core pip

appliance /əˈplaɪəns/ *noun* a useful machine for doing something in the house: *Washing machines and irons are electrical appliances.*

applicant /ˈæplɪkənt/ *noun* a person who asks for a job, a place at a university, etc:

There were six applicants for the job. ℹ The verb is **apply**.

application /ˌæplɪˈkeɪʃn/ *noun* writing to ask for something, for example a job: *Applications should be made in writing.*

application form /ˌæplɪˈkeɪʃn fɔːm/ *noun* a special piece of paper that you write on when you are trying to get something, for example a job: *To become a member, fill in an application form.*

apply ⚷ /əˈplaɪ/ *verb* (**applies**, **applying**, **applied** /əˈplaɪd/, **has applied**) **1** to write to ask for something: *Ali has applied for a place at university.* **2** to be about or be important to someone or something: *This notice applies to all children over the age of twelve.*

❖ **WORD FAMILY**

apply **application** **applicant**

appoint /əˈpɔɪnt/ *verb* (**appoints**, **appointing**, **appointed**) to choose someone for a job: *The school has appointed a new maths teacher.*

appointment /əˈpɔɪntmənt/ *noun* a time that you have fixed to meet someone: *I've got an appointment with the doctor at ten o'clock.*

appreciate /əˈpriːʃieɪt/ *verb* (**appreciates**, **appreciating**, **appreciated**) **1** to understand and enjoy something: *I didn't appreciate poetry when I was younger.* **2** to understand something: *I appreciate your problem, but I can't help you.* **3** to be pleased about something that someone has done for you: *Thank you for your help. I really appreciate it.*

appreciation /əˌpriːʃiˈeɪʃn/ *noun* (no plural) **1** the feeling of being pleased about something that someone has done for you: *We gave her some flowers to show our appreciation for her hard work.* **2** understanding and enjoyment of something: *She shows little appreciation of good music.*

apprentice /əˈprentɪs/ *noun* a young person who is learning to do a job: *Mwita is an apprentice electrician.*

approach[1] /əˈprəʊtʃ/ *verb* (**approaches**, **approaching**, **approached** /əˈprəʊtʃt/) to come near or nearer to someone or something: *When you approach the village, you will see a big house on your right.* ◇ *The exams were approaching.*

approach[2] /əˈprəʊtʃ/ *noun* **1** (no plural) the act of coming near or nearer to someone or something: *The children fell silent at the approach of their teacher.* **2** (*plural* **approaches**) a way of doing something: *This is a new approach to treating AIDS.*

appropriate ⚷ /əˈprəʊpriət/ *adjective* right for that time, place or person; suitable: *A book would be an appropriate gift for a quiet girl like Sarika.* OPPOSITE **inappropriate**

approval ⚷ /əˈpruːvl/ *noun* (no plural) showing or saying that someone or something is good or right: *She desperately wanted to win her father's approval.* OPPOSITE **disapproval**

approve ⚷ /əˈpruːv/ *verb* (**approves**, **approving**, **approved** /əˈpruːvd/) to think or say that something or someone is good or right: *My parents don't approve of my friends.* OPPOSITE **disapprove**

approximate /əˈprɒksɪmət/ *adjective* almost correct but not exact: *The approximate time of arrival is three o'clock.*

approximately /əˈprɒksɪmətli/ *adverb* about; not exactly: *I live approximately two kilometres from the station.*

apricot /ˈeɪprɪkɒt/ *noun* a small soft yellow fruit with a large hard seed inside

April ⚷ /ˈeɪprəl/ *noun* the fourth month of the year

apron /ˈeɪprən/ *noun* a thing that you wear over the front of your clothes to keep them clean, for example when you are cooking: *My mother put on an apron to wash the dishes.*

arbitrate /ˈɑːbɪtreɪt/ *verb* (**arbitrate**, **arbitrating**, **arbitrated**) to officially settle an argument between people or groups: *A governor was asked to arbitrate in the dispute.* ▸ **arbitrator** /ˈɑːbɪtreɪtə(r)/ *noun* a person who is chosen to settle an argument: *an independent arbitrator*

arch /ɑːtʃ/ *noun* (*plural* **arches**) a part of a bridge, building or wall that is in the shape of a half circle

archaeology /ˌɑːkiˈɒlədʒi/ *noun* (no plural) the study of very old things like buildings and objects that are found in the ground ▸ **archaeologist** /ˌɑːkiˈɒlədʒɪst/ *noun* a person who studies or knows a lot about **archaeology**: *Archaeologists discovered a skull at Olduvai Gorge in 1959.*

archbishop /ˌɑːtʃˈbɪʃəp/ *noun* a very important priest in the Christian church:

The Archbishop of Nairobi visited the local church.

architect /ˈɑːkɪtekt/ *noun* a person whose job is to plan buildings: *The house was designed by a famous architect.*

architecture /ˈɑːkɪtektʃə(r)/ *noun* (no plural) **1** planning and making buildings **2** the shape of buildings: *Do you like modern architecture?*

are *form of* BE

area /ˈeəriə/ *noun* **1** a part of a town, a country or the world: *Do you live in this area?* **2** the size of a flat place. If a room is three metres wide and four metres long, it has an area of twelve square metres: *Calculate the area of the triangle.* **3** a space that you use for something special: *There is a practice area for athletes.*

arena /əˈriːnə/ *noun* a place with seats around it where you can watch sports or concerts

aren't /ɑːnt/ *short for* ARE NOT

argue /ˈɑːgjuː/ *verb* (**argues, arguing, argued** /ˈɑːgjuːd/) **1** to talk angrily with someone because you do not agree: *They often argue about money.* ◇ *I often argue with my brother.* **2** to say why you think something is right or wrong: *Ngenzi argued that it would be unfair to report the boy to the police.*

argument /ˈɑːgjəmənt/ *noun* an angry talk between people with different ideas: *They had an argument about which game to play.* ◇ *I had an argument with my cousin.*

arid /ˈærɪd/ *adjective* very dry; with little or no rain: *Do you know the arid lands of northern Kenya?*

arise /əˈraɪz/ *verb* (**arises, arising, arose** /əˈrəʊz/, **has arisen** /əˈrɪzn/) to begin to exist; to happen: *A storm arose during the night.* ◇ *Are there any matters arising from the last meeting* (= things which were talked about last time that must be talked about again)*?*

arithmetic /əˈrɪθmətɪk/ *noun* (no plural) working with numbers to find the answer to a sum

arm /ɑːm/ *noun* the part of your body from your shoulder to your hand: *Put your arms in the air.* ◇ *He was carrying a book under his arm.* ➲ picture on page A13

arm in arm with your arm holding another person's arm: *The two friends walked arm in arm.*

armchair /ˈɑːmtʃeə(r)/ *noun* a soft chair with parts where you can put your arms: *She was asleep in an armchair.*

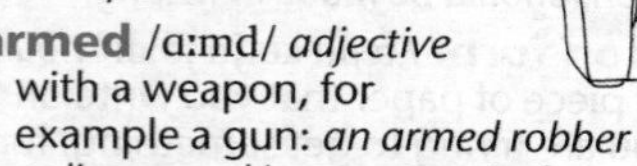

armed /ɑːmd/ *adjective* with a weapon, for example a gun: *an armed robber* ◇ *Are the police armed in your country?*

the armed forces /ði ˌɑːmd ˈfɔːsɪz/ *noun* (plural) the army, air force and navy: *The armed forces protect our country.*

armour /ˈɑːmə(r)/ *noun* (no plural) metal clothes that men wore long ago to cover their bodies when they were fighting: *a suit of armour*

arms /ɑːmz/ *noun* (plural) guns, bombs and other weapons for fighting

army /ˈɑːmi/ *noun* (*plural* **armies**) a large group of soldiers who fight on land in a war: *He joined the army when he was 17.*

around /əˈraʊnd/ *preposition, adverb* **1** in or to different places or in different directions: *The children were running around the house.* ◇ *We walked around for an hour looking for the street.* ◇ *Her clothes were lying around the room.* **2** on or to all sides of something, often in a circle: *We sat around the table.* ◇ *He ran around the track.* ◇ *There is a fence around the farm.* **3** in the opposite direction or in another direction: *Turn around and go back the way you came.* **4** a little more or less than; a little before or after: *We met at around seven o'clock.* **5** in a place; near here: *Is there a bank around here?* ◇ *Is Malika around? I want to speak to her.*

arrange /əˈreɪndʒ/ *verb* (**arranges, arranging, arranged** /əˈreɪndʒd/) **1** to make a plan for the future: *I have arranged to meet Deng at six o'clock.* ◇ *We arranged a big party for Mr Dando's birthday.* **2** to put things in a certain order or place: *Arrange the chairs in a circle.*

arrangement /əˈreɪndʒmənt/ *noun* **1** something that you plan or agree for the future: *They are making the arrangements for their wedding.* **2** a group of things put together so that they look nice: *a beautiful flower arrangement*

arrest[1] /əˈrest/ *verb* (**arrests, arresting, arrested**) When the police arrest someone, they make that person a prisoner because they think that they have done something wrong: *The thief was arrested yesterday.*

arrest² /ə'rest/ *noun* the act of arresting someone: *The police made five arrests.* **be under arrest** to be a prisoner of the police: *The suspect was under arrest.*

arrival /ə'raɪvl/ *noun* coming to a place: *My brother met me at the bus station on my arrival.* OPPOSITE **departure**

arrive 🔑 /ə'raɪv/ *verb* (**arrives, arriving, arrived** /ə'raɪvd/) **1** to get to a place: *What time will we arrive in Dar es Salaam?* ◇ *Has my letter arrived?* OPPOSITE **leave, depart** **2** to come or happen: *The rainy season arrived early.*

arrogant /'ærəgənt/ *adjective* A person who is **arrogant** thinks that they are better or more important than other people.

arrows

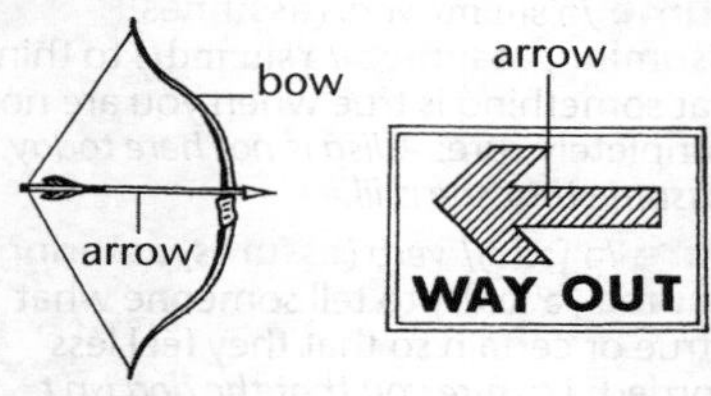

arrow 🔑 /'ærəʊ/ *noun* **1** a long thin piece of wood or metal with a point at one end. You shoot an arrow from a **bow**: *He fired an arrow at the target.* **2** a sign in the shape of an arrow, that shows where something is or where you should go: *Follow the arrows.*

arrowroot /'ærəru:t/ *noun* (no plural) a plant with roots that you can eat or make into flour

art 🔑 /ɑ:t/ *noun* **1** (no plural) making beautiful things, like paintings and drawings: *He was good at art and painted many pictures.* **2** (no plural) beautiful things like paintings and drawings that someone has made: *Do you like modern art?* **3 the arts** (plural) things like films, plays and literature: *How much money does the government spend on the arts?*

❖ **WORD FAMILY**
art artist artistic

artefact /'ɑ:tɪfækt/ *noun* an object that is made by a person: *The National Museum has collections of historical and cultural artefacts.*

article 🔑 /'ɑ:tɪkl/ *noun* **1** a piece of writing in a newspaper or magazine: *Did you read the article about tourism in yesterday's newspaper?* **2** a thing: *Many of the articles in the shop are half-price.* ◇ *articles of clothing* (= things like skirts, socks and shirts) **3** The words 'a', 'an' and 'the' are called articles.

artificial 🔑 /ˌɑ:tɪ'fɪʃl/ *adjective* made by people; not natural: *After the accident, the boy was fitted with an artificial leg.*

artisan /ˌɑ:tɪ'zæn/ *noun* a worker who is good at making things: *juakali artisans*

artist 🔑 /'ɑ:tɪst/ *noun* a person who paints or draws pictures: *Ali is a good artist.*

artistic 🔑 /ɑ:'tɪstɪk/ *adjective* good at painting, drawing or making beautiful things: *He's very artistic.*

as 🔑 /əz; æz/ *conjunction, preposition* **1** while; at the same time that something is happening: *As I was going out, the telephone rang.* **2** because: *She didn't go to school as she was ill.* **3** in the same way; like: *Please do as I tell you!* **4** in the job of: *She works as a supervisor in a big company.* **as ... as** words that you use to compare people or things; the same amount: *Bigogo is as tall as his father.* ◇ *I don't work as hard as you.*

ash /æʃ/ *noun* (no plural) the grey stuff that you see after something has burned: *ash from the fire*

ashamed 🔑 /ə'ʃeɪmd/ *adjective* sorry and unhappy about something that you have done, or unhappy because you are not as good as other people in some way: *I was ashamed about lying to my parents.* ◇ *She was ashamed of her son's behaviour.*

ashore /ə'ʃɔ:(r)/ *adverb* onto the land: *We left the boat and went ashore.*

ashtray /'æʃtreɪ/ *noun* a small dish for cigarette ash and the ends of cigarettes: *The waiter emptied the ashtray.*

aside /ə'saɪd/ *adverb* on or to one side; away: *He put the letter aside quickly.*

ask 🔑 /ɑ:sk/ *verb* (**asks, asking, asked** /ɑ:skt/) **1** to try to get an answer by using a question: *I asked him what the time was.* ◇ *'What's your name?' she asked.* ◇ *Achal asked the teacher a question.* ◇ *I asked if I could go home early.* **2** to say that you would like someone to do something for you: *I asked Kirezi to help me cook.* **3** to invite someone: *Shayo has asked me to his house on Saturday.* **ask for someone** to say that you want to speak to someone: *Phone this number and ask for Mrs Emoto.*

ask for something to say that you want someone to give you something: *He asked his parents for a bicycle.*

askari *noun* an East African soldier, police officer, guard, etc: *The askari was stationed at the entrance to the building.*

asleep 🔑 /əˈsliːp/ *adjective* sleeping: *The baby is asleep in bed.* OPPOSITE **awake**
fall asleep to start sleeping: *He fell asleep under a tree.*

aspect /ˈæspekt/ *noun* one part of a problem, idea, etc: *Spelling is one of the most difficult aspects of learning English.*

aspirin /ˈæsprɪn/ *noun* a medicine that stops pain: *I took two aspirins* (= two tablets of aspirin) *for my headache.*

assassinate /əˈsæsɪneɪt/ *verb* (**assassinates, assassinating, assassinated**) to kill an important or a famous person: *President Sadat was assassinated in 1981.* ▸ **assassination** /əˌsæsɪˈneɪʃn/ *noun* the killing of an important or famous person: *an assassination attempt*

assault /əˈsɔːlt/ *verb* (**assaults, assaulting, assaulted**) to suddenly start fighting or hurting someone: *He assaulted a police officer.* ▸ **assault** *noun*: *an assault on an old lady*

assemble /əˈsembl/ *verb* (**assembles, assembling, assembled** /əˈsembld/) **1** to come together or bring people or things together in a group: *All the students were asked to assemble in the main hall.* ◇ *Assemble all the pieces before you start.* **2** to fit the parts of something together: *The shelves are easy to assemble.*

assembly /əˈsembli/ *noun* (*plural* **assemblies**) a meeting of a big group of people for a special reason: *Our school assembly* (= a meeting of all the pupils and teachers in the school) *is at 7.30 in the morning.*

assertive /əˈsɜːtɪv/ *adjective* saying what you think clearly and firmly: *You should try to be more assertive.* ▸ **assertiveness** /əˈsɜːtɪvnəs/ *noun* (no plural): *Assertiveness is an important life skill.*

assess /əˈses/ *verb* (**assesses, assessing, assessed** /əˈsest/) to judge how good, bad or important something is: *A nurse will assess the patient's needs.* ▸ **assessment** /əˈsesmənt/ *noun*: *Students have written exams and other forms of assessment.*

assist /əˈsɪst/ *verb* (**assists, assisting, assisted**) to help someone: *The driver assisted her with her bags.* ❶ **Help** is the word that we usually use.

assistance /əˈsɪstəns/ *noun* (no plural) help: *The school offers assistance in finding a sponsor.*

assistant /əˈsɪstənt/ *noun* a person who helps: *Ms Njoro is not here today. Would you like to speak to her assistant?* ➲ Look at **shop assistant**.

associate /əˈsəʊʃieɪt/ *verb* (**associates, associating, associated**) to put two ideas together in your mind: *We usually associate Egypt with desert and pyramids.*

association /əˌsəʊʃiˈeɪʃn/ *noun* a group of people who join or work together for a special reason: *the Primary Teachers' Association*

assume /əˈsjuːm/ *verb* (**assumes, assuming, assumed** /əˈsjuːmd/) to think that something is true when you are not completely sure: *Adisa is not here today, so I assume that she is ill.*

assure /əˈʃɔː(r)/ *verb* (**assures, assuring, assured** /əˈʃɔːd/) to tell someone what is true or certain so that they feel less worried: *I assure you that the dog isn't dangerous.*

asteroid /ˈæstərɔɪd/ *noun* one of the very large rocks or small planets that move around the sun

astonish /əˈstɒnɪʃ/ *verb* (**astonishes, astonishing, astonished** /əˈstɒnɪʃt/) to surprise someone very much: *The news astonished everyone.*

astonished /əˈstɒnɪʃt/ *adjective* very surprised: *I was astonished to hear that Fatma was getting married.*

astonishing /əˈstɒnɪʃɪŋ/ *adjective* If something is **astonishing**, it surprises you very much: *astonishing news*

astonishment /əˈstɒnɪʃmənt/ *noun* (no plural) great surprise: *He looked at me in astonishment when I told him the news.*

astronaut /ˈæstrənɔːt/ *noun* a person who works and travels in space

astronomer /əˈstrɒnəmə(r)/ *noun* a person who studies or knows a lot about the sun, moon, planets and stars

astronomy /əˈstrɒnəmi/ *noun* (no plural) the study of the sun, moon, planets and stars

at 🔑 /ət; æt/ *preposition* **1** a word that shows where someone or something is: *They are at school.* ◇ *Ajuma is at home.* ◇ *The answer is at the back of the book.* **2** a word that shows when: *I go to bed at ten o'clock.* ◇ *At night you can see the stars.* ➲ Look at page A8. **3** towards someone or something: *Look at the picture.* ◇ *I smiled at her.* ◇ *Someone threw an egg at the President.* **4** a word that shows what someone is doing or what is happening: *The two countries are at war.* **5** a word that shows how much, how fast, etc: *I bought two pencils at 10 shillings each.* **6** a word that shows how well someone or something does something: *I'm not very good at art.* **7** because of something: *We laughed at his jokes.* **8** the symbol @ which is used in email addresses ➲ Note at **dot**.

ate *form of* EAT

athlete /ˈæθliːt/ *noun* a person who is good at sports like running, jumping or throwing: *Athletes from all over the world go to the Olympic Games.*

athletics /æθˈletɪks/ *noun* (no plural) sports like running, jumping or throwing

atlas /ˈætləs/ *noun* (*plural* **atlases**) a book of maps: *an atlas of the world*

ATM /ˌeɪ tiː ˈem/ the abbreviation for 'automated teller machine' SAME MEANING **cash machine**

ATM card /ˌeɪ tiː ˈem kɑːd/ *noun* a plastic card that you use to get money from a cash machine

atmosphere ⚷ /ˈætməsfɪə(r)/ *noun* **1** (no plural) all the gases around the earth: *the earth's atmosphere* **2** the air in a place: *a cool atmosphere* **3** the feeling that places or people give you: *Our classroom has a friendly atmosphere.*

atom /ˈætəm/ *noun* one of the very small things that everything is made of: *Water is made of atoms of hydrogen and oxygen.* ➲ Look at **molecule**.

atomic /əˈtɒmɪk/ *adjective* **1** of or about **atoms**: *atomic physics* **2** using the great power that is made by breaking **atoms**: *an atomic bomb* ◇ *atomic energy*

attach ⚷ /əˈtætʃ/ *verb* (**attaches**, **attaching**, **attached** /əˈtætʃt/) to join or fix one thing to another thing: *I attached the photo to the letter.*
be attached to someone or **something** to like someone or something very much: *I think he's very attached to you.*

attachment /əˈtætʃmənt/ *noun* something that you send to someone by email: *Send your story as an email attachment to this address.*

attack[1] ⚷ /əˈtæk/ *verb* (**attacks**, **attacking**, **attacked** /əˈtækt/) to start fighting or hurting someone or something: *The army attacked the town.* ◇ *The old man was attacked and his money was stolen.* ▶ **attacker** /əˈtækə(r)/ *noun*: *She escaped from her attackers and called the police.*

attack[2] ⚷ /əˈtæk/ *noun* **1** trying to hurt someone or something: *There was an attack on the President.* **2** a time when you are ill: *She had a bad attack of flu.*

attempt ⚷ /əˈtempt/ *verb* (**attempts**, **attempting**, **attempted**) to try to do something: *He attempted to swim across the river.* ❶ **Try** is the word that we usually use. ▶ **attempt** *noun*: *She made no attempt to help me.*

attend /əˈtend/ *verb* (**attends**, **attending**, **attended**) to go to or be at a place where something is happening: *Did you attend the meeting?*

attention ⚷ /əˈtenʃn/ *noun* (no plural) looking or listening carefully and with interest: *Can I have your attention, please* (= please listen to me)*?*
pay attention to look or listen carefully: *Please pay attention to what I am saying.*

attitude ⚷ /ˈætɪtjuːd/ *noun* the way you think or feel about something: *I like her cheerfulness and positive attitude.*

attorney general /əˌtɜːni ˈdʒenrəl/ *noun* (*plural* **attorneys general** *or* **attorney generals**) the person whose job is to advise the government about legal matters

attract ⚷ /əˈtrækt/ *verb* (**attracts**, **attracting**, **attracted**) **1** to make someone or something come nearer: *The birds were attracted by the smell of fish.* **2** to make someone like someone or something: *The sandy beaches were what attracted me to the area.*

> ❖ **WORD FAMILY**
> **attract** **attraction**
> **attractive**: OPPOSITE **unattractive**

attraction /əˈtrækʃn/ *noun* **1** (*plural* **attractions**) something that people like and feel interested in: *Tanzania has a lot of tourist attractions, like Mount Kilimanjaro and the Serengeti National Park.* **2** (no plural) liking someone or something very much; being liked very much: *What is the attraction of living in the city?*

attractive ⚷ /əˈtræktɪv/ *adjective* **1** A person who is attractive is nice to look at: *He's very attractive.* **2** Something that is attractive pleases you or interests you: *That's an attractive idea.*

auction /ˈɔːkʃn/ *noun* a sale where each thing is sold to the person who will give the most money for it: *The house was sold at auction.* ▶ **auction** *verb* (**auctions**, **auctioning**, **auctioned** /ˈɔːkʃnd/) to sell something at an auction: *The star's dresses were auctioned for charity.*

audience /ˈɔːdiəns/ *noun* all the people who are watching or listening to a play, concert, speech, the TV, etc: *There were only about 200 people in the audience.*

audit /ˈɔːdɪt/ *verb* (**audits**, **auditing**, **audited**) to officially examine the financial records of a company

audition /ɔːˈdɪʃn/ *noun* a short performance you do if you want to be chosen to act in a play, sing in a concert, etc: *Auditions for the school choir will be held on Friday.*

auditor /ˈɔːdɪtə(r)/ *noun* a person whose job is to examine the financial records of a company: *The auditors' report will be sent to the directors.*

auditorium /ˌɔːdɪˈtɔːriəm/ *noun* (*plural* **auditoriums** *or* **auditoria** /ˌɔːdɪˈtɔːriə/) the part of a theatre or hall where people sit: *The auditorium was full.*

August /ˈɔːgəst/ *noun* the eighth month of the year: *Schools are closed in August.*

aunt /ɑːnt/ *noun*

> ❖ **PRONUNCIATION**
>
> **Aunt** sounds like **plant**.

the sister of your mother or father, or the wife of your uncle: *I went to visit my aunt and uncle.* ❶ **Auntie** and **aunty** /ˈɑːnti/ are informal words for aunt.

authentic /ɔːˈθentɪk/ *adjective* real and true: *He says that the painting is by a famous artist, but I don't believe that it's authentic.*

author /ˈɔːθə(r)/ *noun* a person who writes books or stories: *Who is your favourite author?*

authority /ɔːˈθɒrəti/ *noun* **1** (no plural) the power to tell people what they must do: *The police have the authority to stop cars.* **2** (*plural* **authorities**) a group of people that tell other people what they must do: *the city authorities* ◇ *a local authority*

autobiography /ˌɔːtəbaɪˈɒgrəfi/ *noun* (*plural* **autobiographies**) a book that a person has written about their life: *In his autobiography, he describes the village he grew up in.*

autograph /ˈɔːtəgrɑːf/ *noun* a famous person's name, that they have written: *He asked the singer for her autograph.*

automatic /ˌɔːtəˈmætɪk/ *adjective* **1** If a machine is **automatic**, it can work by itself, without people controlling it: *an automatic washing machine* **2** done without thinking: *Breathing is automatic.* ▶ **automatically** /ˌɔːtəˈmætɪkli/ *adverb*: *The security door closes automatically.*

autumn /ˈɔːtəm/ *noun* in cool countries, the part of the year between summer and winter: *In autumn, the leaves begin to fall from the trees.*

available /əˈveɪləbl/ *adjective* ready for you to use, have or see: *I'm sorry – the doctor is not available this afternoon.* ◇ *These sweets are available at most supermarkets.*

avenue /ˈævənjuː/ *noun* a wide road or street: *The shop is in Nile Avenue.*

average /ˈævərɪdʒ/ *noun* **1** (*plural* **averages**) the number you get when you add two or more figures together and divide the total by the number of figures you added: *The average of 2, 3 and 7 is 4* (2+3+7= 12, and 12÷3=4). **2** (no plural) what is ordinary or usual: *Sarika's work at school is above average* (= better than the average). ▶ **average** *adjective*: *The average age of the students is 19.*

avert /əˈvɜːt/ *verb* (**averts**, **averting**, **averted**) to stop something bad from happening: *We could not avert the accident.*

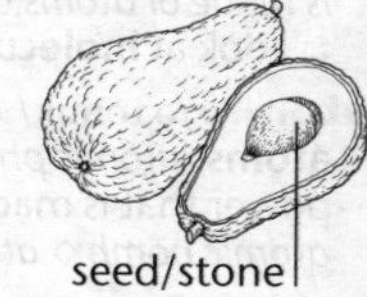

avocado /ˌævəˈkɑːdəʊ/ *noun* (*plural* **avocados**) a soft green fruit with a hard skin and a large seed

avoid /əˈvɔɪd/ *verb* (**avoids**, **avoiding**, **avoided**) **1** to stay away or go away from someone or something: *We crossed the road to avoid the big dog.* **2** to stop something from happening; to try not to do something: *You should avoid wasting water.*

awake /əˈweɪk/ *adjective* not sleeping: *The children are still awake.* OPPOSITE **asleep**

award[1] /əˈwɔːd/ *noun* a prize or money that you give to someone who has done something very well: *The company won a national award.*

award² /əˈwɔːd/ *verb* (**awards, awarding, awarded**) to give a prize or money to someone: *He was awarded first prize in the writing competition.*

aware /əˈweə(r)/ *adjective* If you are aware of something, you know about it: *I was aware that someone was watching me.* ◇ *He's aware of the problem.* OPPOSITE **unaware**

away /əˈweɪ/ *adverb* **1** to or in another place: *She ran away.* ◇ *He put his books away.* **2** from a place: *The sea is two kilometres away.* **3** not here: *Awino is away from school today because she is ill.* **4** in the future: *The holiday is only three weeks away.*

awesome /ˈɔːsəm/ *adjective* very good, big or strong and sometimes frightening: *The caves are an awesome sight.*

awful /ˈɔːfl/ *adjective* very bad: *The pain was awful.*

awfully /ˈɔːfli/ *adverb* very: *It was awfully hot.* ◇ *I'm awfully sorry!*

awkward /ˈɔːkwəd/ *adjective* **1** difficult to do or use: *This big box will be awkward to carry.* **2** not comfortable: *I felt awkward on my first day at work because I didn't know anyone.* **3** difficult to please: *My son is very awkward. He never likes the food I give him.* **4** not able to move your body in an easy way: *He's very awkward when he dances.*

axe /æks/ *noun* a tool for cutting wood: *He chopped down the tree with an axe.*

Bb

B, b /biː/ *noun* (*plural* **B's, b's** /biːz/) the second letter of the English alphabet: *'Ball' begins with a 'B'.*

baboon /bəˈbuːn/ *noun* a large **monkey** (= an animal with a long tail that can climb trees) with big teeth

baboon

baby /ˈbeɪbi/ *noun* (*plural* **babies**) a very young child: *She is going to have a baby.*

babysit /ˈbeɪbisɪt/ *verb* (**babysits, babysitting, babysat** /ˈbeɪbisæt/) to look after a child for a short time when the parents are not there: *She babysat for her neighbours last night.*

bachelor /ˈbætʃələ(r)/ *noun* **1** a man who has never married **2** a person who has a university **degree** (= they have finished their course and passed all their exams): *a Bachelor of Science*

back¹ /bæk/ *noun* **1** the part that is behind or farthest from the front: *The answers are at the back of the book.* ◇ *We sat at the back of the bus.* **2** the part of a person or an animal between the neck and the bottom: *He lay on his back and looked up at the sky.* ➲ picture on page A13

back to front

back to front with the back part in front: *You've put your jumper on back to front.*

behind someone's back when someone is not there, so that they do not know about it: *Don't talk about Fatma behind her back.*

back

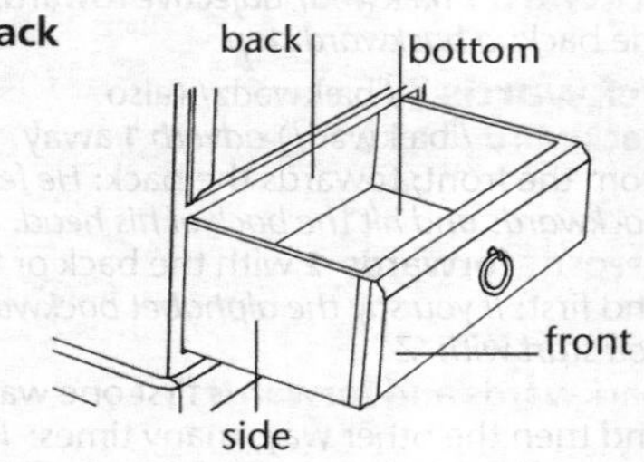

back² /bæk/ *adjective* away from the front: *the back door* ◇ *the back page* (= the last page in a book, newspaper, etc.)

back³ /bæk/ *adverb* **1** away from the front: *Can you all move back, please?* ◇ *I looked back to see if she was coming.* OPPOSITE **forward** **2** in or to the place where someone or something was before: *I'll be back* (= I will return) *at six o'clock.* ◇ *Give the book back to me when you've read it.* ◇ *We walked to the lake and back.* **3** as a way of returning or answering something: *He paid me the money back.* ◇ *I wrote her a letter, but she didn't write back.* ◇ *I was out when she phoned, so I phoned her back.* **4** to an earlier time: *If you travel west, you will need to put your watch back during the journey.* OPPOSITE **forward**

back and forth first one way and then the other, many times: *She travels back and forth between Nairobi and Kisumu.*

back[4] 🔑 /bæk/ *verb* (**backs, backing, backed** /bækt/) **1** to move backwards or make something move backwards: *She backed the car into a parking space.* **2** to say that you think that someone or something is right or the best: *They are backing their school team.*

back away to move away backwards: *Ngenzi backed away from the big dog.*

back out to not do something that you promised or agreed to do: *Kamal backed out of the game.*

back up to make a copy of information in your computer that you do not want to lose: *Back up your work regularly.*

backbone /ˈbækbəʊn/ *noun* the line of bones down the back of your body SAME MEANING **spine**

background /ˈbækgraʊnd/ *noun* the things at the back in a picture: *This is a photo of my house with the mountains in the background.* OPPOSITE **foreground**

backstroke /ˈbækstrəʊk/ *noun* (no plural) a way of swimming on your back

backward /ˈbækwəd/ *adjective* towards the back: *a backward step*

backwards 🔑 /ˈbækwədz/ (also **backward** /ˈbækwəd/) *adverb* **1** away from the front; towards the back: *He fell backwards and hit the back of his head.* OPPOSITE **forwards** **2** with the back or the end first: *If you say the alphabet backwards, you start with 'Z'.*

backwards and forwards first one way and then the other way, many times: *The dog ran backwards and forwards.*

bacon /ˈbeɪkən/ *noun* (no plural) long thin pieces of meat from a pig, that are prepared using salt or smoke: *We had bacon and eggs for breakfast.* ➲ Note at **pig**.

bacteria /bækˈtɪəriə/ *noun* (plural) very small things that live in air, water, earth, plants and animals. Some **bacteria** can make us ill.

bad 🔑 /bæd/ *adjective* (**worse, worst**) **1** not good or nice: *The weather was very bad.* ◇ *He's had some bad news.* ◇ *a bad smell* **2** serious: *She had a bad accident.* **3** not done or made well: *bad driving* **4** not able to work or do something well: *My eyesight is bad.* ◇ *He's a bad driver.* **5** too old to eat; not fresh: *bad eggs*

bad at something If you are **bad at something**, you cannot do it well: *I'm very bad at sports.*

bad for you If something is **bad for you**, it can make you ill: *Too much sugar is bad for you.*

go bad to become too old to eat: *This fish has gone bad.*

not bad quite good: *'What was the film like?' 'Not bad.'*

too bad words that you use to say that you cannot change something: *'I want to go out.' 'Too bad – you can't!'*

badge /bædʒ/ *noun* a small thing made of metal, plastic or cloth that you wear on your clothes. A **badge** can show that you belong to a school, club, etc. or it can have words or a picture on it: *Teta sewed a badge on her Scout's uniform.* ◇ *All the nurses wear name badges.*

badly 🔑 /ˈbædli/ *adverb* (**worse, worst**) **1** in a bad way; not well: *She played badly.* ◇ *These clothes are badly made.* **2** very much: *He was badly hurt in the accident.* ◇ *I badly need a holiday.*

badminton /ˈbædmɪntən/ *noun* (no plural) a game for two or four players who try to hit a kind of light ball with feathers on it (called a **shuttlecock**) over a high net, using **rackets** (= pieces of equipment that you hold in your hand): *Do you want to play badminton?*

bad-tempered 🔑 /ˌbæd ˈtempəd/ *adjective* often angry: *He's bad-tempered in the mornings.*

bag 🔑 /bæg/ *noun* a thing made of cloth, paper, leather, etc, for holding and carrying things: *He put a spare shirt in his bag.* ◇ *a plastic shopping bag* ➲ Look at **carrier bag, handbag**. ➲ Picture at **container**.

baggy /ˈbægi/ *adjective* (**baggier, baggiest**) If clothes are **baggy**, they are big and loose: *He was wearing baggy trousers.*

bake /beɪk/ *verb* (**bakes, baking, baked** /beɪkt/) to cook food in an oven: *She baked him a cake.*

baker /ˈbeɪkə(r)/ *noun* a person who makes and sells bread and cakes: *The baker sold fresh bread.*

> ❖ **WORD BUILDING**
> A shop that sells bread and cakes is called a **baker's** or a **bakery**.

baking powder /ˈbeɪkɪŋ paʊdə(r)/ *noun* (no plural) soft white powder that we use to make cakes rise

balance[1] 🔑 /ˈbæləns/ *noun* **1** (no plural) the ability to keep steady with an equal amount of weight on each side of your body: *Athletes need a good sense of balance.* **2** (no plural) when two things are the same, so that one is not bigger or more important, for example: *You need a balance between work and play.* **3** (*plural* **balances**) how much money you have or must pay after you have spent or paid some: *The machine costs 10 000 shillings. You can pay 1 000 now and the balance (= 9 000) over six months.*
keep your balance to stay steady without falling: *He tried to keep his balance on the ice.*
lose your balance to be unable to stay steady; to fall: *She lost her balance and fell off her bike.*

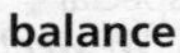

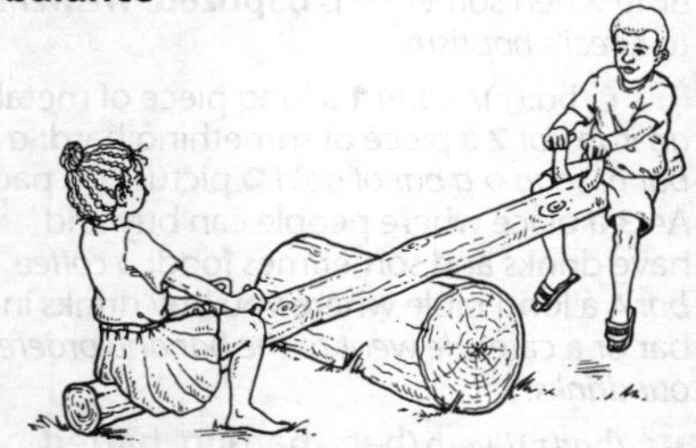
They are trying to **balance** on the see-saw.

balance[2] /ˈbæləns/ *verb* (**balances, balancing, balanced** /ˈbælənst/) to make yourself or something stay without falling to one side or the other: *She balanced on one leg.* ◇ *He balanced the bag on his head.*

balcony /ˈbælkəni/ *noun* (*plural* **balconies**) a small place on the outside wall of a building, above the ground, where you can stand or sit: *She watched the game from the balcony.*

bald /bɔːld/ *adjective* with no hair or not much hair: *My dad is going* (= becoming) *bald.*

ball 🔑 /bɔːl/ *noun* **1** a round thing that you use in games and sports: *Throw the ball to me.* ◇ *a football* ◇ *a tennis ball* ◇ *Volleyball is my favourite ball game.* ➲ Picture at cricket. **2** any round thing: *a ball of string* ➲ picture on page A4

ballet /ˈbæleɪ/ *noun* a kind of dancing that tells a story with music but no words: *We saw a ballet.* ◇ *Do you like ballet?*

ballet dancer /ˈbæleɪ dɑːnsə(r)/ *noun* a person who dances in **ballets**

balloons

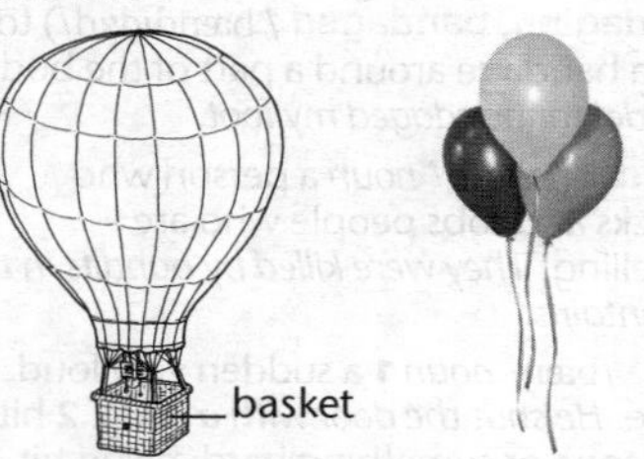

balloon /bəˈluːn/ *noun* **1** a very big bag that you fill with gas or air so that it can fly. People ride in a container (called a **basket**) under it: *I would like to go up in a balloon.* **2** a small coloured rubber thing that you fill with air or gas and use as a toy or for decoration: *They hung balloons around the room for the party.*

ballot /ˈbælət/ *noun* when people choose someone or something by writing secretly on a piece of paper: *We held a ballot to choose a new chairperson.*

ballpoint /ˈbɔːlpɔɪnt/ *noun* a pen that has a very small ball at the end: *Fill in the form with a ballpoint pen.* SAME MEANING **Biro**

bamboo /ˌbæmˈbuː/ *noun* (*plural* **bamboos**) a tall plant that grows in hot countries. We use it for making furniture etc: *a bamboo chair*

ban /bæn/ *verb* (**bans, banning, banned** /bænd/) to say that something must stop or must not happen: *The film was banned* (= people were not allowed to see it).
▸ **ban** *noun*: *The school has put a ban on sweets in the classroom.*

banana /bəˈnɑːnə/ *noun* a long fruit with yellow or green skin

banana

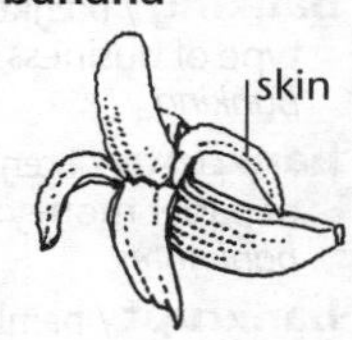

band 🔑 /bænd/ *noun* **1** a group of people who play music together: *He plays in a rock band.*

SAME MEANING **group** **2** a thin flat piece of material that you put around something: *I put a rubber band round the letters to keep them together.*

bandage¹ /ˈbændɪdʒ/ *noun* a long piece of white cloth that you put around a part of the body that is hurt: *Make sure the bandage isn't too tight.*

bandage² /ˈbændɪdʒ/ *verb* (**bandages**, **bandaging**, **bandaged** /ˈbændɪdʒd/) to put a bandage around a part of the body: *The doctor bandaged my foot.*

bandit /ˈbændɪt/ *noun* a person who attacks and robs people who are travelling: *They were killed by bandits in the mountains.*

bang¹ /bæŋ/ *noun* **1** a sudden very loud noise: *He shut the door with a bang.* **2** hitting someone or something hard; being hit hard: *He fell and got a bang on the head.*

bang² /bæŋ/ *verb* (**bangs**, **banging**, **banged** /bæŋd/) to make a loud noise by hitting something hard or by closing something: *He banged his head on the ceiling.* ◇ *Don't bang the door!*

bangle /ˈbæŋɡl/ *noun* a piece of jewellery like a large ring that you wear round your arm: *She wore silver bangles on each wrist.*

bangles

bank ⚷ /bæŋk/ *noun* **1** a place that keeps money safe for people: *I've got 5 000 shillings in the bank.*

❖ **WORD BUILDING**

If you have a bank **account**, you can **save** money, **pay** money **in** (or **deposit** it), or **draw** it **out** (or **withdraw** it). At a bank, you can also **exchange** the money of one country for the money of another. If you want to **borrow** money, a bank may **lend** it to you.

2 the land along the side of a river: *I climbed out of the boat onto the bank.*

banking /ˈbæŋkɪŋ/ *noun* (no plural) the type of business done in banks: *a career in banking*

banknote /ˈbæŋknəʊt/ *noun* a piece of paper money: *These are Ugandan banknotes.*

bankrupt /ˈbæŋkrʌpt/ *adjective* not able to pay the money that you should pay to people: *His business went* (= became) *bankrupt.*

bank statement /ˈbæŋk steɪtmənt/ *noun* a list of the amounts of money that go into and come out of your bank account

bank teller /ˈbæŋk telə(r)/ *noun* the person who gives or takes money in a bank

banner /ˈbænə(r)/ *noun* a long piece of cloth with words on it. People carry banners to show what they think: *The banner said 'Stop the war'.*

baobab /ˈbeɪəʊbæb/ *noun* a kind of tree with a very thick main part (called a **trunk**): *We sat under a baobab tree.*

baobab

baptize /bæpˈtaɪz/ *verb* (**baptizes**, **baptizing**, **baptized** /bæpˈtaɪzd/) to put water on someone or put someone in water, and give them a name, to show that they belong to the Christian Church: *The children were baptized in church on Sunday.* ▶ **baptism** /ˈbæptɪzəm/ *noun* a special time when someone is **baptized**: *We went to Kirezi's baptism.*

bar¹ ⚷ /bɑː(r)/ *noun* **1** a long piece of metal: *an iron bar* **2** a piece of something hard: *a bar of soap* ◇ *a bar of gold* ➲ picture on page A4 **3** a place where people can buy and have drinks and sometimes food: *a coffee bar* **4** a long table where you buy drinks in a bar or a cafe: *He went to the bar and ordered our drinks.*

bar² /bɑː(r)/ *verb* (**bars**, **barring**, **barred** /bɑːd/) **1** to put something across a place so that people cannot pass: *A line of police barred the road.* **2** to say that someone must not do something or go somewhere: *The teacher barred him from the club for fighting.*

baraza *noun* (East African English) a public meeting to discuss important things: *The chief held a baraza to discuss rising insecurity.*

barbecue /ˈbɑːbɪkjuː/ *noun* a party where you cook food on a fire outside: *We had a barbecue on the beach.* ▶ **barbecue** *verb* (**barbecues**, **barbecuing**, **barbecued** /ˈbɑːbɪkjuːd/) to cook food on a fire outside: *barbecued meats*

barbed wire /ˌbɑːbd ˈwaɪə(r)/ *noun* (no plural) wire with a lot of sharp points on it. Some fences are made of **barbed wire**.

barbed wire

barber /ˈbɑːbə(r)/ *noun* a person whose job is to cut people's hair: *I went to the barber's* (= the barber's shop) *to have my hair cut.*

bar chart /ˈbɑː tʃɑːt/ = **bar graph**

bare /beə(r)/ *adjective* **1** with no clothes or anything else covering it: *He had bare feet* (= he wasn't wearing shoes or socks). ◇ *The walls were bare* (= with no pictures on them). **2** empty: *Everyone was buying sugar and soon the shelves were bare.*

barefoot /ˈbeəfʊt/ *adjective, adverb* with no shoes or socks on your feet: *a barefoot little boy* ◇ *The children ran barefoot.*

barely /ˈbeəli/ *adverb* almost not; only just: *She barely ate anything.*

bargain[1] /ˈbɑːgən/ *noun* something that is cheaper than usual: *This book was a bargain – it only cost 200 shillings.*

bargain[2] /ˈbɑːgən/ *verb* (**bargains, bargaining, bargained** /ˈbɑːgənd/) to talk with someone about the right price for something: *I think she'll sell the bracelet for less if you bargain with her.*

barge /bɑːdʒ/ *noun* a long boat with a flat bottom for carrying things or people on rivers or **canals** (= artificial rivers)

bar graph /ˈbɑː grɑːf/ (also **bar chart**) *noun* a picture that uses narrow columns of different heights to show how numbers, amounts, etc. are different from each other

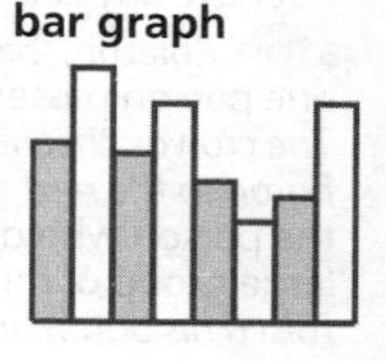

bar graph

bark[1] /bɑːk/ *noun* **1** (no plural) the stuff that covers the outside of a tree **2** (*plural* **barks**) the short loud sound that a dog makes: *His dog has a very loud bark.*

bark[2] /bɑːk/ *verb* (**barks, barking, barked** /bɑːkt/) If a dog **barks**, it makes short loud sounds: *The dog always barks at people it doesn't know.*

barley /ˈbɑːli/ *noun* (no plural) a plant that we use for food and for making beer and some other drinks

barman /ˈbɑːmən/ *noun* (*plural* **barmen** /ˈbɑːmən/) a man who sells drinks in a bar

barn /bɑːn/ *noun* a large building on a farm where you keep crops or animals

barometer /bəˈrɒmɪtə(r)/ *noun* an instrument that helps us to know what the weather will be: *The weather station has barometers, thermometers and a rain gauge.*

barracks /ˈbærəks/ *noun* (plural) a building or group of buildings where soldiers live: *an army barracks*

barrel /ˈbærəl/ *noun* **1** a big container for liquids, with round sides and flat ends: *a barrel of oil* **2** the long metal part of a gun that a bullet goes through

barricade /ˌbærɪˈkeɪd/ *noun* a wall of things that people build quickly to stop other people going somewhere: *There was a barricade of lorries across the road.* ▶ **barricade** *verb* (**barricades, barricading, barricaded**) to stop people going somewhere by building a **barricade**: *He barricaded the door to keep the police out.*

barrier /ˈbæriə(r)/ *noun* a fence or gate that stops you going somewhere: *The car crashed into the safety barrier at the side of the road.*

barrow = **wheelbarrow**

barter /ˈbɑːtə(r)/ *verb* (**barters, bartering, bartered** /ˈbɑːtəd/) to exchange things for other things without using money: *She bartered baskets for pots.*

base[1] 🔑 /beɪs/ *noun* **1** the bottom part of something; the part that something stands on: *The basket has a flat base.* **2** the place that you start from and go back to: *She travels all over the country but Kisii is her base* (= the place where she lives). ◇ *an army base*

base[2] 🔑 /beɪs/ *verb* (**bases, basing, based** /beɪst/)

base something on something to make something, using another thing as an important part: *The film is based on a true story.*

baseball /ˈbeɪsbɔːl/ *noun* **1** (no plural) a game for two teams of nine players who try to hit a ball with a **bat** (= a piece of wood) on a large field: *We played baseball in the park.* **2** (*plural* **baseballs**) a ball for playing this game

basement /ˈbeɪsmənt/ *noun* the part of a building that is under the ground: *Kitchen goods are sold in the basement.*

bases *plural of* BASIS

bash /bæʃ/ *verb* (**bashes, bashing, bashed** /bæʃt/) to hit someone or something very hard: *I fell and bashed my knee.*

basic 🔑 /ˈbeɪsɪk/ *adjective* most important and necessary; simple: *A person's basic needs are food, clothes and a place to live.*

basically /ˈbeɪsɪkli/ *adverb* mostly; mainly: *Basically, I agree with you.*

basin /ˈbeɪsn/ *noun* a round bowl for cooking or mixing food: *Put the eggs in the basin and beat well.* ➲ Look at **washbasin**.

basis ⚷ /ˈbeɪsɪs/ *noun* (*plural* **bases** /ˈbeɪsiːz/) the most important part or idea, from which something grows: *Her notes formed the basis of a book.*

basket /ˈbɑːskɪt/ *noun* a container made of thin sticks or thin pieces of plastic or metal, that you use for holding or carrying things: *a shopping basket* ◇ *a bread basket* ➲ Picture at **balloon**. ➲ Look at **waste-paper basket**.

basket

basketball

They are playing **basketball**.

basketball /ˈbɑːskɪtbɔːl/ *noun* **1** (no plural) a game for two teams of five players who try to throw a ball into a high net **2** (*plural* **basketballs**) a ball for playing this game

bass /beɪs/ *noun* (*plural* **basses**) the lowest male singing voice; a man with this voice. ▶ **bass** *adjective* with a deep sound: *She plays the bass guitar.* ◇ *a bass drum*

bat /bæt/ *noun* **1** a piece of wood for hitting the ball in a game like **cricket** or **table tennis**: *a baseball bat* ➲ Picture at **cricket**. **2** an animal like a mouse with wings. **Bats** come out and fly at night.

bat

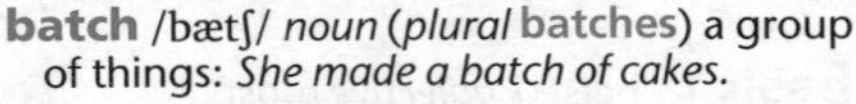

batch /bætʃ/ *noun* (*plural* **batches**) a group of things: *She made a batch of cakes.*

bath ⚷ /bɑːθ/ *noun* (*plural* **baths** /bɑːðz/) **1** a large container that you fill with water and sit in to wash your body: *I filled the bath with hot water.* **2** washing your body in a bath: *I had a bath this morning.*

bathe /beɪð/ *verb* (**bathes, bathing, bathed** /beɪðd/) **1** to wash a part of your body carefully: *He bathed the cut on his finger.* **2** to swim in the sea or in a lake or river: *On hot days we often bathe in the lake.* ℹ It is more usual to say **go swimming**.

bathroom ⚷ /ˈbɑːθruːm/ *noun* a room where you can wash and have a bath or shower: *Wash your hands in the bathroom.*

batik

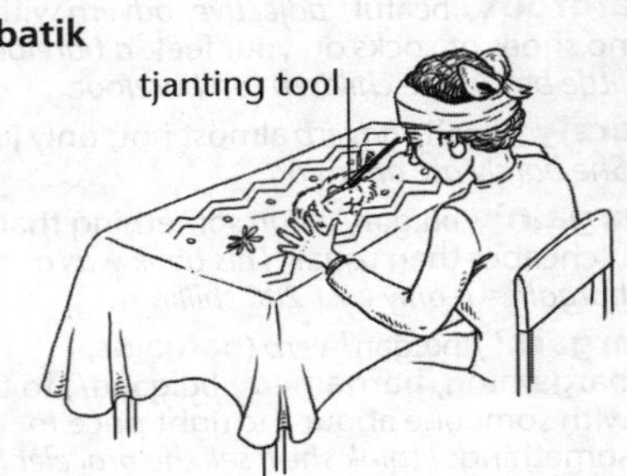

batik /bəˈtiːk/ *noun* a way of printing patterns on cloth using **wax** (= a substance made from fat or oil) on the parts that will not have any colour: *batik scarves*

baton /ˈbætɒn; ˈbætõ/ *noun* **1** a stick that one person passes to another in a race: *The crowds cheered as Kamau handed the baton to the next runner.* **2** a stick used by the person who directs an **orchestra** (= a large group of musicians): *The conductor raised his baton and the concert began.*

batter /ˈbætə(r)/ *noun* (no plural) a thick liquid made of flour, eggs and milk. We use it for making cakes, etc: *Pour the batter into the baking tin.*

battery /ˈbætri/ *noun* (*plural* **batteries**) a thing that gives electricity. You put **batteries** inside things like toys and radios to make them work: *My torch needs a new battery.*

batteries

battle¹ /ˈbætl/ *noun* **1** a fight between armies in a war: *Thousands of men were killed in battle.* **2** trying very hard to do something difficult: *a battle against the illness*

battle² /ˈbætl/ *verb* (**battles, battling, battled** /ˈbætld/) to try very hard to do something difficult: *The doctors battled to save her life.*

battlefield /ˈbætlfiːld/ *noun* a place where armies fight in a war

bauxite /ˈbɔːksaɪt/ *noun* (no plural) a kind of clay from which we get **aluminium** (= a light metal)

bay

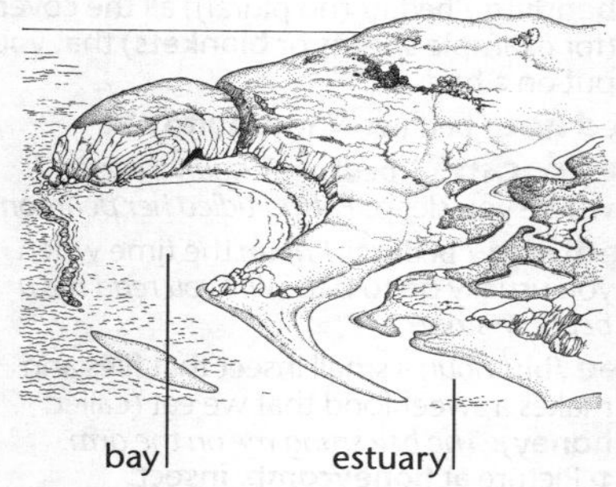

bay /beɪ/ *noun* (*plural* **bays**) a part of the coast where the land goes in to form a curve: *There was a ship in the bay.*

bazaar /bəˈzɑː(r)/ *noun* a market in Asia or Africa

BC /ˌbiː ˈsiː/ short for 'Before Christ'. **BC** in a date shows it was before Christ was born: *Julius Caesar died in 44 BC.* ➲ Look at **AD**.

be 🔑 /bi; biː/ *verb* **1** a word that you use when you name or describe someone or something: *I'm* (= I am) *Pembe.* ◇ *Grass is green.* ◇ *Are you hot?* ◇ *Juma is a doctor.* ◇ *Where were you yesterday?* ◇ *It is six o'clock.* **2** to happen: *Her birthday was in May.* **3** a word that you use with another verb: *'What are you doing?' 'I am reading.'* **4** a word that you use with part of another verb to show that something happens to someone or something: *A lot of tea is grown in East Africa.* ◇ *The airport was built in 1970.* **5** a word that shows that something must or will happen: *A new factory is to be built in Konza.*

beach 🔑 /biːtʃ/ *noun* (*plural* **beaches**) a piece of land next to the sea that is covered with sand or stones: *We played on the sandy beach.*

bead /biːd/ *noun* a small ball of wood, glass or plastic with a hole in the middle. **Beads** are put on a string to make jewellery: *She wore a necklace made of big colourful beads.*

beak /biːk/ *noun* the hard pointed part of a bird's mouth ➲ Picture at **bird**, **pelican**.

beam /biːm/ *noun* **1** a long heavy piece of wood that holds up a roof or ceiling: *The house had thick old beams.* **2** a line of light: *the beams of a car's headlights*

bean

bean /biːn/ *noun* the long thin part of some plants, or the seeds inside it, that we use as food: *We ate rice and beans for lunch.*

bear[1] 🔑 /beə(r)/ *verb* (**bears, bearing, bore** /bɔː(r)/, **has borne** /bɔːn/) **1** to have pain or problems without complaining: *The pain was difficult to bear.* **2** to hold someone or something up so that they do not fall: *The rope is too thin to bear your weight.*

can't bear something to hate something: *I can't bear this music.* ◇ *He can't bear having nothing to do.*

be

present tense		*short forms*	*negative short forms*
I	**am**	I**'m**	I**'m not**
you	**are**	you**'re**	you **aren't**
he/she/it	**is**	he**'s**/she**'s**/it**'s**	he/she/it **isn't**
we	**are**	we**'re**	we **aren't**
you	**are**	you**'re**	you **aren't**
they	**are**	they**'re**	they **aren't**

past tense		
I	**was**	*present participle* **being**
you	**were**	
he/she/it	**was**	*past participle* **been**
we	**were**	
you	**were**	
they	**were**	

bear² /beə(r)/ *noun* a big wild animal with thick fur: *Bears and wolves live in the forest.* ➲ Look at **teddy bear**.

bear

beard 🔑 /bɪəd/ *noun* the hair on a man's chin and cheeks: *He has got a beard.*

beast /bi:st/ *noun* a big animal ℹ **Animal** is the word that we usually use.

beat¹ 🔑 /bi:t/ *noun* a sound that comes again and again: *We heard the beat of the drums.* ➲ Look at **heartbeat**.

beat² 🔑 /bi:t/ *verb* (**beats, beating, beat, has beaten** /ˈbi:tn/) **1** to win a fight or game against a person or group of people: *Odoi always beats me at wrestling* ◇ *Our team was beaten.* **2** to hit someone or something very hard many times: *She beats her dog with a stick.* ◇ *The rain was beating on the roof.* **3** to make the same sound or movement many times: *His heart was beating fast.*

beautiful 🔑 /ˈbju:təfl/ *adjective* very nice to see, hear or smell; attractive: *Those flowers are beautiful.* ◇ *What a beautiful song!*

> ❖ **WORD BUILDING**
>
> When we talk about people, we usually use **beautiful** and **pretty** for women and girls, and **handsome** and **good-looking** for men and boys.

beauty 🔑 /ˈbju:ti/ *noun* (no plural) being beautiful: *the beauty of the mountains*

because 🔑 /bɪˈkɒz/ *conjunction* for the reason that: *He was angry because I was late.*
because of something as a result of something: *We stayed at home because of the rain.*

beckon /ˈbekən/ *verb* (**beckons, beckoning, beckoned** /ˈbekənd/) to move your finger to show you want someone to come nearer: *She beckoned me over to speak to her.*

become 🔑 /bɪˈkʌm/ *verb* (**becomes, becoming, became** /bɪˈkeɪm/, **has become**) to grow or change and begin to be something: *She became a doctor in 1982.* ◇ *The weather is becoming cooler.*
become of someone or **something** to happen to someone or something: *What became of Shema? I haven't seen him for years.*

bed 🔑 /bed/ *noun* **1** a thing that you sleep on: *I was tired, so I went to bed.* ◇ *The children are in bed.* **2** the bottom of a river or the sea: *Stones lie on the river bed.*
make the bed to put the covers on a bed so that it is tidy and ready for someone to sleep in: *Make your bed before you go to school.*

bedclothes /ˈbedkləʊðz/ *noun* (plural) (also **bedding** /ˈbedɪŋ/ (no plural)) all the covers (for example **sheets** or **blankets**) that you put on a bed

bed net /ˈbed net/ = **mosquito net**

bedroom 🔑 /ˈbedru:m/ *noun* a room where you sleep: *Fatma tidied her bedroom.*

bedtime /ˈbedtaɪm/ *noun* the time when you usually go to bed: *Will you read me a bedtime story?*

bee /bi:/ *noun* a small insect that flies and makes a sweet food that we eat (called **honey**): *The bee stung me on the arm.* ➲ Picture at **honeycomb, insect**.

beef /bi:f/ *noun* (no plural) meat from a cow: *roast beef* ➲ Note at **cow**.

beehive /ˈbi:haɪv/ (also **hive** /haɪv/) *noun* a box where bees live: *The farmer harvested honey from the beehives.*

beekeeping /ˈbi: ki:pɪŋ/ *noun* (no plural) owning and keeping bees for their honey and for the stuff that is used for making candles (called **wax**) ▸ **beekeeper** /ˈbi: ki:pə(r)/ *noun*: *Beekeepers need special clothes to protect themselves.*

been 🔑 **1** *form of* BE **2** *form of* GO¹
have been to to have gone to a place and come back: *Have you ever been to Lake Victoria?*

> ❖ **been** or **gone**?
>
> If someone has **been** to a place, they have travelled there and come back again: *I've been to Mombasa three times.*
>
> If someone has **gone** to a place they have travelled there and they are there now: *Malika isn't here. She's gone to Zanzibar.*

beer 🔑 /bɪə(r)/ *noun* **1** (no plural) an alcoholic drink made from grain: *My uncle drinks beer.* **2** (*plural* **beers**) a glass, bottle or can of beer: *Three beers, please.*

beetle /ˈbi:tl/ *noun* an insect with hard wings and a shiny body ➲ Picture at **insect**.

before¹ 🔑 /bɪˈfɔ:(r)/ *preposition* **1** earlier than someone or something: *He arrived before me.* ◇ *I lived in Nakuru before coming to Malindi.* **2** in front of someone or something: *B comes before C in the alphabet.* OPPOSITE **after**

before² 🔑 /bɪˈfɔː(r)/ *adverb* at an earlier time; in the past: *I have never met them before.* ◇ *I've seen that man before.*

before³ 🔑 /bɪˈfɔː(r)/ *conjunction* earlier than the time that: *I said goodbye before I left.*

beforehand /bɪˈfɔːhænd/ *adverb* at an earlier time than something: *Tell me beforehand if you are going to be late.*

beg /beg/ *verb* (**begs**, **begging**, **begged** /begd/) **1** to ask for money or food because you are very poor: *There was an old man begging in the street.* **2** to ask someone for something in a very strong way: *She begged me to stay with her.* ◇ *He begged for help.*

I beg your pardon **1** I am sorry: *'You've taken my seat.' 'Oh, I beg your pardon.'* **2** What did you say?: *'I beg your pardon? I didn't hear what you said.'*

beggar /ˈbegə(r)/ *noun* a person who asks other people for money or food: *There were beggars on the streets.*

begin 🔑 /bɪˈgɪn/ *verb* (**begins**, **beginning**, **began** /bɪˈgæn/, **has begun** /bɪˈgʌn/) to start to do something or start to happen: *The film begins at 7.30.* ◇ *I'm beginning to feel cold.* ◇ *The name Juma begins with a 'J'.* OPPOSITE **end**, **finish**

to begin with at first; at the beginning: *To begin with he was afraid of the water, but he soon learnt to swim.*

beginner /bɪˈgɪnə(r)/ *noun* a person who is starting to do or learn something: *She is in the beginners' class.*

beginning 🔑 /bɪˈgɪnɪŋ/ *noun* the time or place where something starts; the first part of something: *I didn't see the beginning of the film.* OPPOSITE **end**

begun *form of* BEGIN

behalf /bɪˈhɑːf/ *noun*

on behalf of someone; **on someone's behalf** for someone; in the place of someone: *Mr Kairu is away, so I am writing to you on his behalf.*

behave 🔑 /bɪˈheɪv/ *verb* (**behaves**, **behaving**, **behaved** /bɪˈheɪvd/) to do and say things in a certain way when you are with other people: *They behaved very kindly towards me.*

behave yourself to be good; to do and say the right things: *Did the children behave themselves?*

behaviour 🔑 /bɪˈheɪvjə(r)/ *noun* (no plural) the way you are; the way that you do and say things when you are with other people: *The teacher was pleased with the children's good behaviour.*

behind 🔑 /bɪˈhaɪnd/ *preposition*, *adverb* **1** at or to the back of someone or something: *I hid behind the wall.* ◇ *I went in front and Mwita followed behind.* ➲ picture on page A6 **2** slower or less good than someone or something; slower or less good than you should be: *She is behind with her work because she is often ill.* **3** in the place where you were before: *I got off the bus but left my suitcase behind* (= on the bus).

being¹ *form of* BE

being² /ˈbiːɪŋ/ *noun* a person or living thing: *The creature looked like a being from another planet.*

belief 🔑 /bɪˈliːf/ *noun* a sure feeling that something is true or real: *his belief in God* ➲ Look at **disbelief**.

believable /bɪˈliːvəbl/ *adjective* that you can believe: *Her explanation sounded believable.* OPPOSITE **unbelievable**

believe 🔑 /bɪˈliːv/ *verb* (**believes**, **believing**, **believed** /bɪˈliːvd/) to feel sure that something is true or right; to feel sure that what someone says is true: *She says she didn't take the money. Do you believe her?* ◇ *Long ago, people believed that the earth was flat.*

believe in someone or **something** to feel sure that someone or something is real: *Do you believe in ghosts?*

bell 🔑 /bel/ *noun* a metal thing that makes a sound when something hits or touches it: *The church bells were ringing.* ◇ *I rang the bell and he answered the door.*

bell

belly /ˈbeli/ *noun* (*plural* **bellies**) the part of your body between your chest and your legs; your stomach: *I ate so much that my belly ached.*

belong 🔑 /bɪˈlɒŋ/ *verb* (**belongs**, **belonging**, **belonged** /bɪˈlɒŋd/) to have its right or usual place: *That chair belongs in my room.*

belong to someone to be someone's: *'Who does this pen belong to?' 'It belongs to me.'*

belong to something to be in a group, club, etc: *He belongs to the school football club.*

belongings /bɪˈlɒŋɪŋz/ *noun* (plural) the things that you own: *They lost all their belongings in the fire.*

below /bɪˈləʊ/ *preposition, adverb* **1** in or to a lower place than someone or something: *From the hill we could see the village below.* ◇ *Your mouth is below your nose.* ◇ *Do not write below this line.* OPPOSITE **above** **2** less than a number or price: *The temperature was below zero.* ➲ picture on page A6

belt /belt/ *noun* a long piece of leather or cloth that you wear around the middle of your body: *I need a belt to keep these trousers up.* ➲ Picture at **suit**[1]. ➲ Look at **safety belt**, **seat belt**.

belt

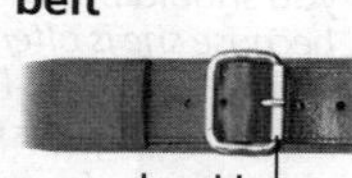

bench /bentʃ/ *noun* (*plural* **benches** /ˈbentʃɪz/) **1** a long seat made of wood or metal, usually outside **2** a long table where someone works, for example a person who makes things from wood: *The carpenter cleared his bench.*

bench

bend

She is **bending** a spoon. He is **bending** down.

bend[1] /bend/ *verb* (**bends**, **bending**, **bent** /bent/, **has bent**) to become curved; to make something that was straight into a curved shape: *Bend your legs!* ◇ *She couldn't bend the metal bar.*
bend down; **bend over** to move your body forward and down: *She bent down to put on her shoes.*

bend[2] /bend/ *noun* a part of a road or river that is not straight: *Drive slowly – there's a bend in the road.*

beneath /bɪˈniːθ/ *preposition, adverb* in or to a lower place than someone or something: *The boat sank beneath the waves.* ◇ *From the tower they looked down on the city beneath.* OPPOSITE **above**

❖ **SPEAKING**

Under and **below** are the words that we usually use.

benefit[1] /ˈbenɪfɪt/ *noun* something that is good or helpful: *What are the benefits of learning another language?* ◇ *I did it for your benefit* (= to help you).

benefit[2] /ˈbenɪfɪt/ *verb* (**benefits**, **benefiting**, **benefited**) to be good or helpful in some way: *The new railway line will benefit several towns.*
benefit from something to get something good or useful from something: *She will benefit from a rest.*

bent *form of* BEND[1]

berry /ˈberi/ *noun* (*plural* **berries**) a small soft fruit with seeds in it: *a strawberry* ◇ *These monkeys eat leaves, nuts and berries.*

berth /bɜːθ/ *noun* **1** a place where a ship can stop and stay: *The port has berths for ten ships.* **2** a place to sleep on a ship or train: *a cabin with three berths*

beside /bɪˈsaɪd/ *preposition* at the side of someone or something; next to someone or something: *Come and sit beside me.* ➲ picture on page A6

besides[1] /bɪˈsaɪdz/ *preposition* as well as someone or something; if you do not count someone or something: *There were four people in the room, besides me and Achal.* ◇ *Besides playing football, Ereng plays hockey and basketball.*

besides[2] /bɪˈsaɪdz/ *adverb* also: *I don't like this shirt. Besides, it's too expensive.*

best[1] /best/ *adjective* (**good**, **better**, **best**) better than all others: *This is the best stew I have ever eaten!* ◇ *Adisa is my best friend.* OPPOSITE **worst**

best[2] /best/ *adverb* **1** most well: *I work best in the morning.* **2** more than all others; most: *Which picture do you like best?* OPPOSITE **least**

best[3] /best/ *noun* (no plural) the person or thing that is better than all others: *Opiyo and Kisoso are good at running but Rono is the best.*
all the best words that you use when you say goodbye to someone, to wish them success: *All the best! Do keep in touch!*
do your best to do all that you can: *I don't know if I can finish the work today, but I'll do my best.*

best man /ˌbest ˈmæn/ *noun* (no plural) the man at a wedding who helps the man who is getting married (the **bridegroom**)

bet /bet/ *verb* (**bets**, **betting**, **bet**, **has bet**) to say what you think will happen. If you are right, you win money, but if you are wrong, you lose money: *I bet you 10 shillings that our team will win.*
I bet I am sure: *I bet it will rain today.* ◇ *I bet you can't climb that tree.* ▶ **bet** *noun*: *I lost the bet.*

betray /bɪˈtreɪ/ *verb* (**betrays**, **betraying**, **betrayed** /bɪˈtreɪd/) to do something that harms someone who trusted you or who was your friend: *The guards betrayed the king and let the enemy into the palace.*

better¹ 🔑 /ˈbetə(r)/ *adjective* (**good**, **better**, **best**) **1** of a higher standard or quality: *This book is better than that one.* **2** less ill: *I was ill yesterday, but I feel better now.* OPPOSITE **worse**

better² 🔑 /ˈbetə(r)/ *adverb* more well: *You speak French better than I do.*
better off happier, richer, etc: *You look ill – you would be better off in bed.*
had better ought to; should: *You had better go now if you want to catch the train.*

between 🔑 /bɪˈtwiːn/ *preposition* **1** in the space in the middle of two things or people: *The letter B comes between A and C.* ◇ *I sat between Katee and Wasike.* ➲ picture on page A6 **2** to and from two places: *The boat sails between Zanzibar and Dar es Salaam.* **3** more than one thing but less than another thing: *The children are all between three and seven years old.* **4** after one time and before the next time: *I will meet you between 4.00 and 4.30.* **5** for or by two or more people or things: *We shared the food between us* (= each of us had some food). **6** a word that you use when you compare two people or things: *What is the difference between the two vehicles?* ➲ Note at **among**.
in between in the middle of two things, people, times, etc: *I found my shoe in between two rocks.* ◇ *We played two games, with a short break in between.*

beware /bɪˈweə(r)/ *verb*
beware of someone or **something** to be careful because someone or something is dangerous: *Beware of the dog!* (= words written on a sign)

bewildered /bɪˈwɪldəd/ *adjective* If you are **bewildered**, you do not understand something or you do not know what to do: *He was bewildered by all the noises of the big city.*

beyond 🔑 /bɪˈjɒnd/ *preposition*, *adverb* on the other side of something; further than something: *The road continues beyond Eldoret.* ◇ *We could see the lake and the mountains beyond.*

bhang /bæŋ/ *noun* (no plural) the leaves and flower tops of a special plant, used as a drug

bib /bɪb/ *noun* a piece of cloth or plastic that a baby wears under its chin when it is eating

the Bible /ˈbaɪbl/ *noun* (no plural) the book of great religious importance to the Christian or Jewish religions ▶ **biblical** /ˈbɪblɪkl/ *adjective*: *The children listened to biblical stories.*

bicycle

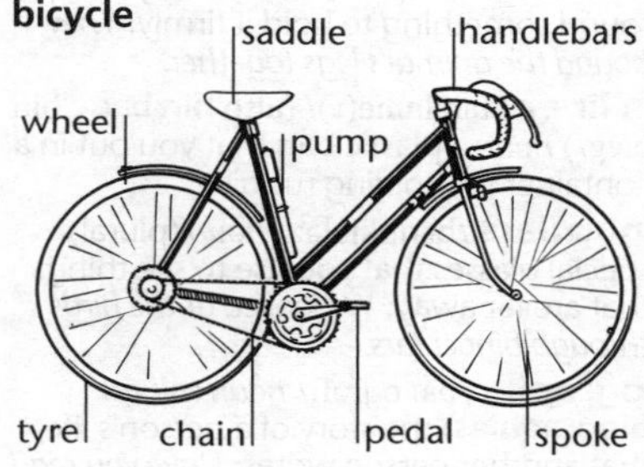

bicycle 🔑 /ˈbaɪsɪk(ə)l/ *noun* a machine with two wheels. You sit on a bicycle and move your legs to make the wheels turn: *Can you ride a bicycle?* ℹ The short form is **bike**.

> ❖ **WORD BUILDING**
>
> **Cycle** means to travel by bicycle.

bid¹ /bɪd/ *verb* (**bids**, **bidding**, **bid**, **has bid**) to offer some money because you want to buy something: *He bid a lot of money for the oxen, but it was not enough.*

bid² /bɪd/ *noun* an offer of money for something that you want to buy: *They made a bid of 800 000 shillings for the piece of land.*

big 🔑 /bɪg/ *adjective* (**bigger**, **biggest**) **1** not small; large: *Mombasa is a big city.* ◇ *This shirt is too big for me.* ◇ *How big is your flat?* OPPOSITE **small** ➲ picture on page A5 **2** great or important: *a big problem* **3** older: *Boke is my big sister.* OPPOSITE **little**

bike /baɪk/ *noun* a bicycle or a motorbike: *I go to school by bike.*

bilharzia /bɪlˈhɑːtsiə/ *noun* (no plural) a serious illness that you get from dirty water

bill 🔑 /bɪl/ *noun* **1** a piece of paper that shows how much money you must pay for something: *We have to pay our electricity bill this week.* **2** a plan for a possible new law: *MPs debated a new bill about education.*

billboard /ˈbɪlbɔːd/ *noun* a big sign beside a road for advertising something

billion 🔑 /ˈbɪliən/ *number* 1 000 000 000; one thousand million: *five billion shillings* ◇ *There are billions of people in the world.*

billionth /ˈbɪliənθ/ *adjective, adverb, noun* 1 000 000 000th; each of one billion equal parts of something

bin /bɪn/ *noun* **1** a thing that you put rubbish in: *I threw the empty bag in the bin.* ➲ Look at **dustbin**. **2** a thing with a lid that you keep things in: *a bread bin*

bind /baɪnd/ *verb* (**binds, binding, bound** /baʊnd/, **has bound**) to tie string or rope round something to hold it firmly: *They bound the animal's legs together.*

bin liner /ˈbɪn laɪnə(r)/ (also **bin bag** /ˈbɪn bæg/) *noun* a plastic bag that you put in a container for holding rubbish

binoculars /bɪˈnɒkjələz/ *noun* (plural) special glasses that you use to see things that are far away: *We looked at the birds through binoculars.*

biography /baɪˈɒgrəfi/ *noun* (*plural* **biographies**) the story of a person's life, that another person writes: *Have you read the biography of Nelson Mandela?* ➲ Look at **autobiography**.

biology 🔑 /baɪˈɒlədʒi/ *noun* (no plural) the study of the life of animals and plants: *Biology is my favourite subject at school.*
▸ **biologist** /baɪˈɒlədʒɪst/ *noun* a person who studies or knows a lot about biology

bird

bird 🔑 /bɜːd/ *noun* an animal with feathers and wings: *Ostriches and vultures are birds.*

> ❖ **WORD BUILDING**
>
> Most birds can **fly** and **sing**. They build **nests** and **lay eggs**.
>
> There are many different types of bird. Here are some of them: **crow, eagle, flamingo, ostrich, parrot, vulture.** Do you know any others?

bird of prey /ˌbɜːd əv ˈpreɪ/ *noun* (*plural* **birds of prey**) a bird that catches and eats small birds and animals: *Eagles are birds of prey.*

Biro™ /ˈbaɪrəʊ/ *noun* (*plural* **Biros**) a pen that has a very small ball at the end. ℹ **Biro** is a trademark. ➲ Picture at **pen**.

birr /biː(r)/ *noun* (*plural* **birr**) money that people use in Ethiopia: *A hundred cents make one birr.*

birth 🔑 /bɜːθ/ *noun* the time when a baby comes out of its mother; being born: *the birth of a baby* ◇ *What's your date of birth* (= the date when you were born)*?*
give birth to have a baby: *My aunt gave birth to her second child last week.*

birthday 🔑 /ˈbɜːθdeɪ/ *noun* (*plural* **birthdays**) the day each year that is the same as the date when you were born: *My birthday is on January 2nd.* ◇ *She gave him a birthday present.*

> ❖ **SPEAKING**
>
> When it is a person's birthday, we say **Happy Birthday!** or **Many happy returns!**

biscuit 🔑 /ˈbɪskɪt/ *noun* a kind of small thin dry cake: *He bought a packet of biscuits.* ◇ *Would you like a chocolate biscuit?*

bishop /ˈbɪʃəp/ *noun* an important priest in the Christian church, who looks after all the churches in a large area

bit 🔑 /bɪt/ *noun* **1** a small piece or amount of something: *Would you like a bit of cake?* ◇ *Some bits of the film were very funny.* **2** a unit of information that is stored in the memory of a computer: *a 64-bit computer*
a bit 1 a little: *You look a bit tired.* ➲ Note at **very**[1]. **2** a short time: *Let's wait a bit.*
a bit of a rather a: *It's a bit of a long way to the station.*
bit by bit slowly or a little at a time: *Bit by bit, I started to feel better.*
come to bits or **fall to bits** to break into small pieces: *The cake fell to bits when I tried to cut it.*

bite[1] 🔑 /baɪt/ *verb* (**bites, biting, bit** /bɪt/, **has bitten** /ˈbɪtn/) **1** to cut something with your teeth: *That dog bit my leg!* **2** If an insect or snake bites you, it hurts you by pushing a small sharp part into your skin: *My brother was bitten by a snake.*
bite off more than you can chew to try to do too much

bite[2] 🔑 /baɪt/ *noun* **1** a piece of food that you can put in your mouth: *He took a bite of the potato.* **2** a painful place on your skin made by an insect or an animal: *a snake bite*

bitter 🔑 /ˈbɪtə(r)/ *adjective* **1** with a sharp unpleasant taste, like very strong coffee; not sweet: *Bitter medicine is hard to swallow.*

2 angry and sad about something that has happened: *He felt very bitter about missing the trip.* **3** very cold: *a bitter wind*

black[1] /blæk/ *adjective* (**blacker**, **blackest**) **1** with the colour of the sky at night: *A black dog ran down the path.* ➲ Note at **hair**. **2** with dark skin: *Nelson Mandela was the first black president of South Africa.* **3** without milk: *He prefers black coffee.*

black[2] /blæk/ *noun* **1** (no plural) the colour of the sky at night: *She was dressed in black.* **2** (*plural* **blacks**) a person with dark skin

black and white with the colours black, white and grey only: *The film was made in black and white.*

blackberry /ˈblækbəri/ *noun* (*plural* **blackberries**) a small soft black fruit that grows on a bush

blackberries

blackboard /ˈblækbɔːd/ (also **chalkboard**) *noun* a dark board that a teacher writes on with **chalk** (= a white substance): *Look at the blackboard.*

blackcurrant /ˌblækˈkʌrənt/ *noun* a small round black fruit that grows on a bush

blackmail /ˈblækmeɪl/ *noun* (no plural) saying that you will tell something bad about someone if they do not give you money or do something for you ▶ **blackmail** *verb* (**blackmails**, **blackmailing**, **blackmailed** /ˈblækmeɪld/): *She blackmailed him into giving her all his savings.*

blackout /ˈblækaʊt/ *noun* a time when there is no electricity and therefore no light or power: *We couldn't do our lessons during the blackout.*

blade /bleɪd/ *noun* **1** the flat sharp part of a knife or another thing that cuts: *He sharpened the blade of his knife.* **2** a long thin leaf of plants like grass: *a blade of grass*

blame /bleɪm/ *verb* (**blames**, **blaming**, **blamed** /bleɪmd/) to say that a certain person or thing made something bad happen: *The teacher blamed me for the accident.* ▶ **blame** *noun* (no plural): *Hawa took the blame for the mistake* (= said that she made it happen).

blank /blæŋk/ *adjective* **1** with no writing, pictures or anything else on it: *Use a blank piece of paper.* **2** If your face is **blank**, it shows no feelings or understanding: *I asked her a question, but she just gave me a blank look.*

blanket /ˈblæŋkɪt/ *noun* a thick cover that you put on a bed: *It's cold tonight. Can I have another blanket?*

blast[1] /blɑːst/ *noun* **1** an explosion: *A bomb exploded and two people were killed in the blast.* **2** a sudden movement of air: *There was a blast of cold air.* **3** a sudden loud sound: *He blew a blast on his trumpet.*

blast[2] /blɑːst/ *verb* (**blasts**, **blasting**, **blasted**) to make a hole in something with an explosion: *They blasted through the mountain to make a tunnel.*

blast furnace /ˈblɑːst fɜːnəs/ *noun* a machine with a very hot fire in a closed place for getting metal from rock or earth (**ore**)

blast-off /ˈblɑːst ɒf/ *noun* (no plural) the time when a vehicle that travels into space (a **spacecraft**) leaves the ground: *Blast-off is in 30 seconds.*

blaze /bleɪz/ *noun* a large strong fire: *The firefighters put out the blaze.* ▶ **blaze** *verb* (**blazes**, **blazing**, **blazed** /bleɪzd/) to burn strongly and brightly: *A blazing fire kept us warm.*

blazer /ˈbleɪzə(r)/ *noun* a jacket. Blazers sometimes show which school or club you belong to.

bleach /bliːtʃ/ *noun* (no plural) a chemical that you use to clean things or to remove colour from things like cloth ▶ **bleach** *verb* (**bleaches** /ˈbliːtʃɪz/, **bleaching**, **bleached** /bliːtʃt/): *bleached cotton*

bleak /bliːk/ *adjective* (**bleaker**, **bleakest**) **1** cold and grey: *It was bleak on top of the mountain.* **2** bad; without much hope: *The country's future looked bleak.*

bleat /bliːt/ *noun* the sound that a sheep makes ▶ **bleat** *verb* (**bleats**, **bleating**, **bleated** /ˈbliːtɪd/): *I could hear sheep bleating.*

bleed /bliːd/ *verb* (**bleeds**, **bleeding**, **bled** /bled/, **has bled**) to lose blood: *I have cut my hand and it is bleeding.*

blend /blend/ *verb* (**blends**, **blending**, **blended**) **1** to mix: *Blend the sugar and the butter together.* **2** to look or sound good together: *These colours blend very well.* ▶ **blend** *noun* a mixture of things: *This is a blend of two different kinds of coffee.*

bless /bles/ *verb* (**blesses**, **blessing**, **blessed** /blest/) to ask God to help and protect someone or something: *The priest blessed the young couple.*

Bless you! words that you say to someone when they **sneeze** (= make a loud noise through their nose)

blew *form of* BLOW[1]

blind[1] /blaɪnd/ *adjective* not able to see: *The blind man had a white stick to help him.* ◇ *My grandfather is going* (= becoming) *blind.* ▸ **blindness** /ˈblaɪndnəs/ *noun* (no plural) being blind: *Some diseases can cause blindness.*

❖ **WORD BUILDING**

People who cannot see very well are sometimes described as **partially sighted** or **visually impaired** rather than **blind**.

blind[2] /blaɪnd/ *noun* a piece of cloth or other material that you pull down to cover a window

blind

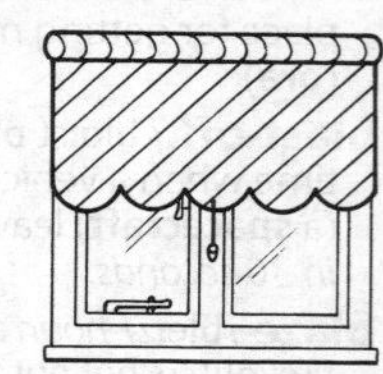

blindfold /ˈblaɪndfəʊld/ *noun* a piece of cloth that you put over someone's eyes so that they cannot see ▸ **blindfold** *verb* (**blindfolds, blindfolding, blindfolded**): *The prisoner was blindfolded.*

bling /blɪŋ/ (also **bling-bling** /ˌblɪŋ ˈblɪŋ/) *noun* (no plural) expensive shiny jewellery

blink /blɪŋk/ *verb* (**blinks, blinking, blinked** /blɪŋkt/) to shut and open your eyes very quickly: *She blinked in the bright sunlight.*

blister /ˈblɪstə(r)/ *noun* a small painful place on your skin, that is full of liquid. Rubbing or burning can cause blisters: *My new shoes gave me blisters.*

blob /blɒb/ *noun* a small amount of a thick liquid: *There are blobs of paint on the floor.*

block[1] 🔑 /blɒk/ *noun* **1** a big heavy piece of something, with flat sides: *a block of wood* ◇ *The bridge is made of concrete blocks.* **2** a big building with a lot of offices or flats inside: *an office block* ◇ *a block of flats* **3** a group of buildings with streets all round it: *We drove round the block looking for the hotel.* **4** a thing that stops someone or something from moving forward: *The police set up a roadblock on the bridge.*

block[2] 🔑 /blɒk/ *verb* (**blocks, blocking, blocked** /blɒkt/) to stop someone or something from moving forward: *A fallen tree blocked the road.*

block capitals /ˌblɒk ˈkæpɪtlz/ *noun* (plural) big letters such as 'ABC' rather than 'abc': *Write your name in block capitals.*

blog /blɒg/ *noun* a personal record that someone puts on their website saying what they do every day and what they think about things ▸ **blog** *verb* (**blogs, blogging, blogged** /blɒgd/) to write a **blog**: *She blogs a lot about music and films.* ▸ **blogger** /ˈblɒgə(r)/ *noun* a person who writes a **blog**

blond /blɒnd/ *adjective* (**blonder, blondest**) with light-coloured hair: *He's a small blond boy.* ◇ *Her sister has blonde hair.*

❖ **SPELLING**

The spelling **blonde** is used for girls and women.

▸ **blonde** /blɒnd/ *noun* a woman who has **blonde** hair: *She's a blonde.*

blood 🔑 /blʌd/ *noun* (no plural) the red liquid inside your body: *He lost a lot of blood in the accident.* ◇ *a blood cell* ◇ *a blood sample*

blood group /ˈblʌd gruːp/ *noun* one of the several different types of human blood: *'What blood group are you?' 'O.'*

bloodstream /ˈblʌdstriːm/ *noun* (no plural) the blood as it flows through the body: *They injected the drug straight into her bloodstream.*

blood test /ˈblʌd test/ *noun* a test that doctors do to find out more about someone's health

bloody /ˈblʌdi/ *adjective* (**bloodier, bloodiest**) **1** covered with blood: *a bloody nose* **2** with a lot of killing: *It was a bloody war.*

bloom /bluːm/ *verb* (**blooms, blooming, bloomed** /bluːmd/) **1** to have flowers: *The roses are blooming now.* **2** to become healthy, happy or confident: *The children bloomed after their holiday by the sea.*

blossom /ˈblɒsəm/ *noun* (no plural) the flowers on a tree or bush: *orange blossom* ▸ **blossom** *verb* (**blossoms, blossoming, blossomed** /ˈblɒsəmd/) to have flowers: *The orange trees are blossoming.*

blouse /blaʊz/ *noun* a piece of clothing like a shirt that a woman or girl wears on the top part of her body: *She wore a pale yellow blouse and a long green skirt.*

blow[1] 🔑 /bləʊ/ *verb* (**blows, blowing, blew** /bluː/, **has blown** /bləʊn/) **1** When air or wind blows, it moves: *The wind was blowing from the sea.* **2** to move something through the air: *The wind* *blew my hat off.* **3** to send air out from your mouth: *She blew on her tea to cool it.* **4** to send air out from your mouth into a musical instrument, etc. to make a noise: *The referee blew his whistle.*

blow up **1** to explode; to make something explode, for example with a bomb: *The plane blew up.* ◇ *They blew up the station.* **2** to fill something with air: *I blew up the tyre on my bicycle.*

blow² /bləʊ/ *noun* **1** a hard hit from someone's hand, a weapon, etc: *He felt a blow on the back of his head and he fell.* **2** something that happens suddenly and that makes you very unhappy: *Her father's death was a terrible blow to her.*

blue 🔑 /bluː/ *adjective* (**bluer**, **bluest**) with the colour of a clear sky when the sun shines: *He wore a bright blue shirt.* ◇ *dark blue* ▶ **blue** *noun*: *She was dressed in blue.*

blunt /blʌnt/ *adjective* (**blunter**, **bluntest**) **1** with an edge or point that is not sharp: *This pencil is blunt.* **2** If you are **blunt**, you say what you think in a way that is not polite: *She was very blunt and told me that she did not like my plan.*

blur /blɜː(r)/ *verb* (**blurs**, **blurring**, **blurred** /blɜːd/) to make something less clear: *If you move while you are taking the photo, it will be blurred.* ▶ **blur** *noun* something that you cannot see clearly or remember well: *Without my glasses their faces were just a blur.*

blush /blʌʃ/ *verb* (**blushes**, **blushing**, **blushed** /blʌʃt/) If you **blush**, your face suddenly becomes red because you are shy, etc: *She blushed when everyone looked at her.*

boar /bɔː(r)/ *noun* **1** a male pig **2** a wild pig

board¹ 🔑 /bɔːd/ *noun* **1** a long thin flat piece of wood: *I nailed a board across the broken window.* **2** a flat piece of wood, etc. that you use for a special purpose: *There is a list of names on the board.* ◇ *an ironing board* ➲ Look at **noticeboard**, **whiteboard**. **3** a group of people who have a special job, for example controlling a company: *the board of directors*

on board on a ship or a plane: *How many passengers are on board?*

board² /bɔːd/ *verb* (**boards**, **boarding**, **boarded**) to get on a ship, bus, train or plane: *We boarded the plane at Kisumu International Airport.* ◇ *Flight BA065 to London is now boarding* (= is ready for passengers to get on).

boarding card /ˈbɔːdɪŋ kɑːd/ (also **boarding pass** /ˈbɔːdɪŋ pɑːs/) *noun* a card that you must show when you get on a plane or a ship: *Please have your boarding card ready.*

boarding school /ˈbɔːdɪŋ skuːl/ *noun* a school where the pupils live

boast /bəʊst/ *verb* (**boasts**, **boasting**, **boasted**) to talk in a way that shows you are too proud of something that you have or something that you can do: *He boasted that he was the fastest runner in the school.*

boats

boat 🔑 /bəʊt/ *noun* a small ship for travelling on water: *a fishing boat* ◇ *We travelled by boat.*

bodaboda *noun* (East African English) a bicycle or motorcycle taxi: *There were boys on bodabodas riding on Kampala's streets.*

body 🔑 /ˈbɒdi/ *noun* (*plural* **bodies**) **1** all of a person or an animal: *Arms, legs, hands and feet are all parts of the body.* ◇ *the human body* **2** the part of a person that is not their legs, arms or head: *She had injuries to the head and body.* **3** a dead person: *The police found a body.*

bodyguard /ˈbɒdigɑːd/ *noun* a person or group of people whose job is to keep an important person safe: *The President's bodyguards all carry guns.*

boil¹ 🔑 /bɔɪl/ *verb* (**boils**, **boiling**, **boiled** /bɔɪld/) **1** When a liquid boils, it becomes very hot and makes steam and bubbles: *Water boils at 100 degrees Celsius.* **2** to heat a liquid until it boils: *I boiled some water for the rice.* **3** to cook something in very hot water: *Boil the potatoes until they are soft.*

boil over to boil and flow over the sides of a pan: *Don't let the stew boil over.*

boil² /bɔɪl/ *noun* a small, painful spot under your skin, with a red or yellow top

boiler /ˈbɔɪlə(r)/ *noun* a big metal container that heats water

boiling /ˈbɔɪlɪŋ/ *adjective* very hot: *I'm boiling.*

boiling point /ˈbɔɪlɪŋ pɔɪnt/ *noun* (no plural) the temperature that water boils at: *The boiling point of water is 100°C.*

bold /bəʊld/ *adjective* (**bolder, boldest**) **1** brave and not afraid: *It was very bold of you to ask for more money.* **2** (used about a type of writing or printing) with thick, dark letters: *Make the important text **bold**.* ▶ **boldly** *adverb*: *He boldly said that he disagreed.* ▶ **boldness** *noun* (no plural): *He was surprised by the boldness of the question.*

bolt /bəʊlt/ *noun* **1** a piece of metal that you move across to lock a door: *He slid back the bolt on the door.* **2** a thick metal pin that you use with another piece of metal (a **nut**) to fix things together ▶ **bolt** *verb* (**bolts, bolting, bolted**) to lock a door by putting a **bolt** across it: *Don't forget to bolt the door.*

boma *noun* (East African English) an area with a fence around it to keep people or animals safe: *The animals were kept in the boma at night.*

bomb¹ 🔑 /bɒm/ *noun*

> ❖ **PRONUNCIATION**
> We do not say the 'b' at the end of **bomb**.

a thing that explodes and hurts or damages people or things: *A bomb went off* (= exploded) *at the bus station.*

bomb² 🔑 /bɒm/ *verb* (**bombs, bombing, bombed** /bɒmd/) to attack people or a place with bombs: *The city was bombed.*

bondage /ˈbɒndɪdʒ/ *noun* (no plural) the state of being a prisoner or a **slave** (= a person who must work for another person for no money): *The slaves longed to escape from bondage.*

bone 🔑 /bəʊn/ *noun* one of the hard white parts inside the body of a person or an animal: *She broke a bone in her foot.* ◇ *This fish has a lot of bones in it.* ▶ **bony** /ˈbəʊni/ *adjective* (**bonier, boniest**) very thin: *a tall bony man*

bonfire /ˈbɒnfaɪə(r)/ *noun* a big fire that you make outside: *We lit a bonfire at Scout camp.*

bonnet /ˈbɒnɪt/ *noun* the front part of a car that covers the engine ➲ Picture at **car**.

book¹ 🔑 /bʊk/ *noun* a thing that you read or write in, that has a lot of pieces of paper joined together inside a cover: *I am reading a book by Meja Mwangi.* ◇ *Put your exercise books away.*

book² 🔑 /bʊk/ *verb* (**books, booking, booked** /bʊkt/) to ask someone to keep something for you so that you can use it later: *We booked tickets for the concert.* ◇ *The hotel is fully booked* (= all the rooms are full).

book in to tell the person at the desk in a hotel that you have arrived: *We arrived late and booked straight in to the hotel.*

bookcase

bookcase /ˈbʊkkeɪs/ *noun* a piece of furniture that you put books in

booking /ˈbʊkɪŋ/ *noun* asking someone to keep something for you so that you can use it later: *When did you make your booking?*

booking office /ˈbʊkɪŋ ɒfɪs/ *noun* a place where you buy tickets: *There was a long queue at the booking office.*

booklet /ˈbʊklət/ *noun* a small thin book: *Look at the instruction booklet if you need help.*

bookmark /ˈbʊkmɑːk/ *noun* **1** a piece of card that you put between the pages of a book so that you can find the same place again **2** a record of the address of an Internet file that you store on your computer ▶ **bookmark** *verb* (**bookmarks, bookmarking, bookmarked**): *Do you want to bookmark this site?*

bookshelf /ˈbʊkʃelf/ *noun* (*plural* **bookshelves** /ˈbʊkʃelvz/) a shelf that you keep books on

bookshop /ˈbʊkʃɒp/ *noun* a shop that sells books ➲ Note at **library**.

boom /buːm/ *verb* (**booms, booming, boomed** /buːmd/) to make a loud deep sound: *We heard the guns booming in the distance.*

boots

boot 🔑 /buːt/ *noun* **1** a shoe that covers your foot and sometimes part of your leg: *The guard had a new pair of boots.* **2** the part of a car where you can put bags and boxes, usually at the back: *Put your luggage in the boot.* ➲ Picture at **car**.

border /ˈbɔːdə(r)/ *noun* **1** a line between two countries: *You need a passport to cross the border.* **2** a line along the edge of something: *white material with a blue border*

bore¹ *form of* BEAR¹

bore² /bɔː(r)/ *verb* (**bores, boring, bored** /bɔːd/) **1** If something **bores** you, it makes you feel tired because it is not interesting: *He bores everyone with his complaining.* **2** to make a hole by pushing a tool into something: *They bored a deep hole in the ground.*

bored /bɔːd/ *adjective* not interested; unhappy because you have nothing interesting to do: *I get bored on long bus journeys.*

> ❖ **bored** or **boring**?
>
> If you have nothing to do, or if what you are doing does not interest you, then you are **bored**: *Njoki was so bored she went home.*
>
> The person or thing that makes you feel like this is **boring**: *The film was very boring.*

boring /ˈbɔːrɪŋ/ *adjective* not interesting: *That lesson was boring!*

born /bɔːn/ *verb*
be born start your life: *I was born in 1997.* ◇ *Where were you born?*

borne *form of* BEAR¹

borrow or lend?

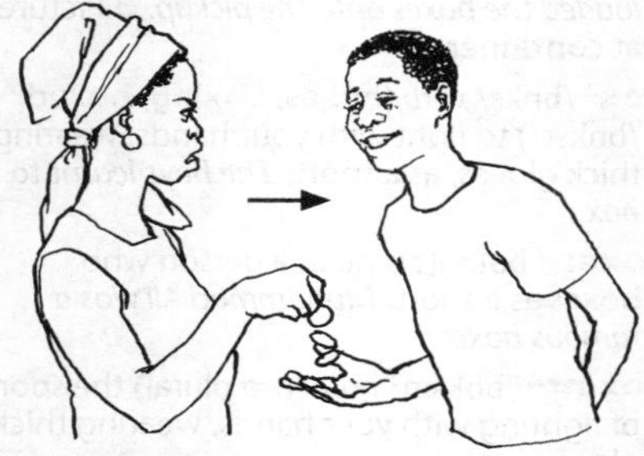

She is **lending** her son some money. He is **borrowing** some money from his mother.

borrow /ˈbɒrəʊ/ *verb* (**borrows, borrowing, borrowed** /ˈbɒrəʊd/) to take and use something that you will give back after a short time: *I borrowed some books from the library.*

boss /bɒs/ *noun* (*plural* **bosses**) a person who controls a place where people work and tells people what they must do: *I asked my boss for the morning off.*

bossy /ˈbɒsi/ *adjective* (**bossier, bossiest**) A **bossy** person likes to tell other people what to do: *My sister is very bossy.*

both /bəʊθ/ *adjective, pronoun* the two; not only one but also the other: *Hold it in both hands.* ◇ *Both her brothers are doctors.* ◇ *Both of us like swimming.* ◇ *We both like swimming.*

> ❖ **GRAMMAR**
>
> You use **both of** with **us, you** and **them.**

both … and not only … but also: *Both Kiswahili and English are official languages in Tanzania.*

bother¹ /ˈbɒðə(r)/ *verb* (**bothers, bothering, bothered** /ˈbɒðəd/) **1** to do something that gives you extra work or that takes extra time: *Don't bother to wash the dishes – I'll do it later.* **2** to annoy or worry someone, especially when they are doing something else: *Don't bother me now – I'm busy!* ◇ *Is this music bothering you?* ◇ *I'm sorry to bother you, but could you open the door for me?*
can't be bothered If you **can't be bothered** to do something, you do not want to do it because it is too much work: *I can't be bothered to do my homework now.*

bother² /ˈbɒðə(r)/ *noun* (no plural) trouble or difficulty: *'Thanks for your help!' 'It was no bother.'*

bottle /ˈbɒtl/ *noun* a tall round glass or plastic container for liquids, with a thin part at the top: *They drank two bottles of water.*

bottle

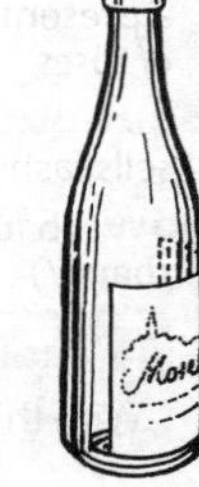

bottom¹ /ˈbɒtəm/ *noun* **1** the lowest part of something: *They live at the bottom of the hill.* ◇ *The book was at the bottom of my bag.* OPPOSITE **top** ➲ Picture at **back¹**. **2** the last part of something; the end: *The bank is at the bottom of the road.* OPPOSITE **top** **3** the part of your body that you sit on: *She fell on her bottom.* ➲ picture on page A13

bottom² /ˈbɒtəm/ *adjective* lowest: *Put the book on the bottom shelf.* OPPOSITE **top**

bougainvillea /ˌbuːɡənˈvɪliə/ *noun* a plant with bright red, purple or white flowers that climbs up walls or trees

bought *form of* BUY

boulder /ˈbəʊldə(r)/ *noun* a very big rock: *A huge boulder rolled down the hill.*

bounce

bounce /baʊns/ *verb* (**bounces**, **bouncing**, **bounced** /ˈbaʊnst/) **1** When a ball **bounces**, it moves away quickly after it hits something hard: *The ball bounced off the wall.* **2** to make a ball do this: *The boy was bouncing a ball.* **3** to jump up and down a lot: *The children were bouncing up and down to the music.*

bound[1] *form of* BIND

bound[2] /baʊnd/ *adjective*
bound for going to a place: *This ship is bound for Egypt.*
bound to certain to do something: *She works very hard, so she is bound to pass the exam.*

boundary /ˈbaʊndri/ *noun* (*plural* **boundaries**) a line between two places: *This fence is the boundary between the two farms.*

bouquet /buˈkeɪ/ *noun*

> ❖ **PRONUNCIATION**
> The end of **bouquet** sounds like **pay**.

a group of flowers that you give or get as a present: *The bride carried a huge bouquet of roses.*

boutique /buːˈtiːk/ *noun* a small shop that sells fashionable clothes or expensive gifts

bow[1] /baʊ/ *verb* (**bows**, **bowing**, **bowed** /baʊd/)

> ❖ **PRONUNCIATION**
> With this meaning, **bow** sounds like **now**.

to bend your head or body forward to show respect: *The actors bowed at the end of the play.* ▶ **bow** *noun*: *He gave a bow and left the room.*

bow[2] /baʊ/ *noun*

> ❖ **PRONUNCIATION**
> With this meaning, **bow** sounds like **now**.

the front end of a boat OPPOSITE **stern**

bow[3] /bəʊ/ *noun*

> ❖ **PRONUNCIATION**
> With this meaning, **bow** sounds like **go**.

bow

1 a kind of knot with two round parts, that you use when you are tying shoes, etc: *Tie your shoelaces in a bow.* **2** a curved piece of wood with a string between the two ends. You use a bow to send **arrows** (= long pieces of wood or metal) through the air. ➲ Picture at **arrow**. **3** a long thin piece of wood with strong strings along it. You use it to play a **violin** or another musical instrument that has strings. ➲ Picture at **zeze**.

bowl[1] 🔑 /bəʊl/ *noun* a deep round dish or container: *a sugar bowl* ◇ *I drank a bowl of soup.*

bowl

bowl[2] /bəʊl/ *verb* (**bowls**, **bowling**, **bowled** /bəʊld/) to throw a ball so that someone can hit it in a game of **cricket**

box[1] 🔑 /bɒks/ *noun* (*plural* **boxes**) a container with straight sides. A box often has a lid: *Put the books in a cardboard box.* ◇ *a box of oranges* ◇ *a box of matches* ◇ *We loaded the boxes onto the pickup.* ➲ Picture at **container**.

box[2] /bɒks/ *verb* (**boxes**, **boxing**, **boxed** /bɒkst/) to fight with your hands, wearing thick gloves, as a sport: *The boys learnt to box.*

boxer /ˈbɒksə(r)/ *noun* a person who boxes as a sport: *Muhammad Ali was a famous boxer.*

boxing /ˈbɒksɪŋ/ *noun* (no plural) the sport of fighting with your hands, wearing thick gloves

box office /ˈbɒks ɒfɪs/ *noun* a place where you buy tickets in a theatre or cinema

boy 🔑 /bɔɪ/ *noun* (*plural* **boys**) a male child; a young man: *They have two children, a boy and a girl.*

boycott /ˈbɔɪkɒt/ *verb* (**boycotts**, **boycotting**, **boycotted**) to refuse to do something or buy something: *Several countries boycotted the Olympic Games as a protest.* ▶ **boycott** *noun*: *a trade boycott*

boyfriend /ˈbɔɪfrend/ *noun* a boy or man who is someone's special friend: *She had a coffee with her boyfriend.*

bra /brɑː/ *noun* a thing that a woman wears under her other clothes to cover and support her **breasts** (= the two soft round parts of a woman's body)

bracelet /ˈbreɪslət/ *noun* a pretty piece of metal, wood or plastic that you wear around your arm

bracelet

brackets /ˈbrækɪts/ *noun* (plural) marks like these ( ) that you use in writing: *(This sentence is written in brackets.)*

brain /breɪn/ *noun* the part inside the head of a person or an animal that thinks and feels: *The brain controls the rest of the body.*

brake /breɪk/ *noun* a thing that you move to make a car, bicycle, etc. go slower or stop: *I put my foot on the brake.* ▶ **brake** *verb* (**brakes**, **braking**, **braked** /breɪkt/) to use a brake: *A child ran into the road and the driver braked suddenly.*

branch /brɑːntʃ/ *noun* (*plural* **branches**) **1** one of the parts of a tree that grow out from the thick main part (the **trunk**): *He climbed the tree and sat on a branch.* ➲ Picture at **tree**. **2** an office or a shop that is part of a big company: *This bank has branches all over the country.*

brand /brænd/ *noun* the name of a thing you buy that a certain company makes: *'Coke' is a famous brand of soft drink.*

brand new /ˌbrænd ˈnjuː/ *adjective* completely new: *a brand new car*

brass /brɑːs/ *noun* (no plural) a yellow metal: *a brass door handle*

brave /breɪv/ *adjective* (**braver**, **bravest**) ready to do dangerous or difficult things without fear: *It was brave of her to go into the burning building.* ▶ **bravely** *adverb*: *He fought bravely in the war.* ▶ **bravery** /ˈbreɪvəri/ *noun* (no plural) being brave

bray /breɪ/ *noun* the noise that a **donkey** (= an animal like a small horse with long ears) makes ▶ **bray** (**brays**, **braying**, **brayed** /breɪd/) *verb*: *The donkey brayed loudly.*

bread /bred/ *noun* (no plural) food made from flour and cooked in an oven: *I bought a loaf of bread.*

breadcrumbs /ˈbredkrʌmz/ *noun* (plural) very small pieces of bread that you use in cooking

breadth /bredθ/ *noun* how far it is from one side of something to the other: *We measured the length and breadth of the room.* SAME MEANING **width** ❶ The adjective is **broad**.

break[1] /breɪk/ *verb* (**breaks**, **breaking**, **broke** /brəʊk/, **has broken** /ˈbrəʊkən/) **1** to make something go into smaller pieces by dropping it, hitting it, etc: *He broke the window.* ◇ *She has broken her arm.* **2** to go into smaller pieces by falling, hitting, etc: *I dropped the cup and it broke.* **3** to stop working; to damage something so that it stops working: *The radio is broken.* ◇ *You've broken my pen.*

break down **1** If a machine or car **breaks down**, it stops working: *He was late because his car broke down.* **2** If a person **breaks down**, they start to cry: *He broke down when he heard the news.*

break in; break into something to go into a place by breaking a door or window so that you can steal something: *Thieves broke into the building.*

break off to take away a piece of something by breaking it: *He broke off a piece of bread and ate it.*

break out **1** to start suddenly: *A fire broke out last night.* **2** to get free from a place like a prison: *Four prisoners broke out of the jail last night.*

break up **1** to start the school holidays: *We break up in two weeks.* **2** If someone you are talking to on a mobile phone is **breaking up**, you can no longer hear them clearly: *Sorry, I can't hear you - you're breaking up.*

break up; break up with someone to stop being with someone, for example a husband or wife, boyfriend or girlfriend: *Her parents broke up last year.*

break[2] /breɪk/ *noun* **1** a short time when you stop doing something: *We worked all day without a break.* **2** a place where something opens or has broken: *There was a break in the clouds.*

breakdown /ˈbreɪkdaʊn/ *noun* a time when a machine, car, etc. stops working: *He (= his car) had a breakdown.*

breakfast /ˈbrekfəst/ *noun* the first meal of the day: *I had breakfast at seven o'clock.* ➲ Note at **meal**.

breast /brest/ *noun* **1** one of the two soft round parts of a woman's body that can give milk: *She put the baby to her breast.* **2** the front part of a bird's body

breaststroke /ˈbreststrəʊk/ *noun* (no plural) a way of swimming on your front

breath ⚷ /breθ/ *noun* taking in or letting out air through your nose and mouth: *Take a deep breath.*
hold your breath to stop breathing for a short time: *Can you hold your breath and swim underwater?*
out of breath breathing very quickly: *She was out of breath after running.*

breathe ⚷ /bri:ð/ *verb* (**breathes, breathing, breathed** /bri:ðd/) to take in and let out air through your nose and mouth: *The doctor told me to breathe in and then breathe out again slowly.*

breathless /ˈbreθləs/ *adjective* If you are **breathless**, you are breathing quickly or with difficulty.

breed[1] /bri:d/ *verb* (**breeds, breeding, bred** /bred/, **has bred**) **1** to make young animals: *Birds breed in the spring.* **2** to keep animals to make young ones: *They breed goats on their farm.*

breed[2] /bri:d/ *noun* a particular kind of animal: *There are many different breeds of cattle.*

breeze /bri:z/ *noun* a light wind: *We enjoyed the cool evening breeze.*

brewery /ˈbru:əri/ *noun* (*plural* **breweries**) a place where beer is made

bribe /braɪb/ *noun* money or a present that you give to someone to make them do something: *It is wrong to offer or accept bribes.* ▸ **bribe** *verb* (**bribes, bribing, bribed** /braɪbd/) to give a bribe to someone: *The prisoner bribed the guard to let him go free.*

bribery /ˈbraɪbəri/ *noun* (no plural) giving someone money or a present to make them do something: *They were accused of bribery.*

brick ⚷ /brɪk/ *noun* a small block made of hard **clay** (= a type of earth), with two long sides and two short sides. Bricks are used for building: *a brick wall*

bricklayer /ˈbrɪkleɪə(r)/ *noun* a person whose job is to build things with bricks

bride /braɪd/ *noun* a woman on the day of her wedding: *The bride wore a beautiful white dress.*

bridegroom /ˈbraɪdgru:m/ *noun* a man on the day of his wedding: *I enjoyed the bridegroom's speech.*

bridesmaid /ˈbraɪdzmeɪd/ *noun* a girl or woman who helps a **bride** at her wedding: *Njoki asked her sister to be her bridesmaid.*

bridge

bridge ⚷ /brɪdʒ/ *noun* a thing that is built over a road, railway or river so that people, trains or cars can cross it: *We walked over the bridge.*

brief ⚷ /bri:f/ *adjective* (**briefer, briefest**) short or quick: *He made a brief telephone call.*
in brief in a few words: *Here is the news in brief* (words said on a radio or television programme). ▸ **briefly** *adverb*: *We stopped work briefly for a drink.*

briefcase

briefcase /ˈbri:fkeɪs/ *noun* a flat case for carrying papers in

brigade /brɪˈgeɪd/ *noun* a large group of soldiers that forms a unit in an army

bright ⚷ /braɪt/ *adjective* (**brighter, brightest**) **1** with a lot of light: *It was a bright sunny day.* ◇ *That lamp is very bright.* **2** with a strong colour: *He wore a bright yellow shirt.* **3** clever: *She is the brightest child in the class.*
▸ **brightly** ⚷ *adverb*: *She likes brightly coloured clothes.* ▸ **brightness** /ˈbraɪtnəs/ *noun* (no plural): *the brightness of the sun*

brighten /ˈbraɪtn/ (also **brighten up**) *verb* (**brightens, brightening, brightened** /ˈbraɪtnd/) to become brighter or happier; to make something brighter: *These flowers will brighten the room up.* ◇ *Her face brightened when she heard the good news.*

brilliant /ˈbrɪliənt/ *adjective* **1** with a lot of light; very bright: *brilliant sunshine* **2** very intelligent: *a brilliant student* **3** very good; excellent: *The film was brilliant!*
▸ **brilliance** /ˈbrɪliəns/ *noun* (no plural): *the brilliance of the light* ▸ **brilliantly** *adverb*: *She played brilliantly.*

brim /brɪm/ *noun* **1** the edge around the top of something like a cup, bowl or glass: *The cup was filled to the brim.* **2** the wide part around the bottom of a hat: *She wore a straw hat with a wide brim.*

bring, fetch or **take**?

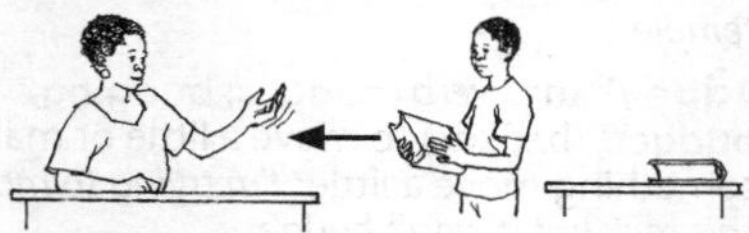

Bring the book.

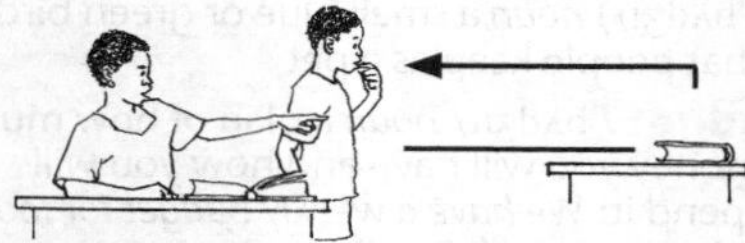

Fetch the book.

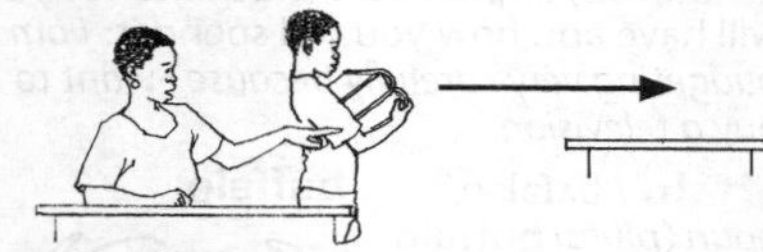

Take the books.

bring 🔑 /brɪŋ/ *verb* (**brings, bringing, brought** /brɔːt/, **has brought**) **1** to come to a place with someone or something: *Can you bring me a glass of water?* ◇ *Bring your brother with you next time you come.* **2** to make something happen: *Money doesn't always bring happiness.*

bring back 1 to return something: *I have brought back the book you lent me.* **2** to make you remember something: *These old photos bring back lots of memories.*

bring someone up to look after a child until they are grown up: *He was brought up by his aunt after his parents died.*

bring something up 1 to be sick, so that food comes up from your stomach and out of your mouth **2** to start to talk about something: *Can you bring up this problem at the next meeting?*

bristle /ˈbrɪsl/ *noun* a short thick hair like the hair on a brush

brittle /ˈbrɪtl/ *adjective* Something that is **brittle** is hard but breaks easily: *This glass is very brittle.*

broad 🔑 /brɔːd/ *adjective* (**broader, broadest**) large from one side to the other; wide: *a broad river* ℹ The noun is **breadth**. OPPOSITE **narrow**

broadband /ˈbrɔːdbænd/ *noun* (no plural) If you have **broadband**, you can send and receive a lot of information over the Internet very quickly.

broadcast /ˈbrɔːdkɑːst/ *verb* (**broadcasts, broadcasting, broadcast, has broadcast**) to send out sound or pictures by radio or television: *The news is broadcast every night at 9 p.m.*
▸ **broadcast** *noun* something that is sent out by radio or television: *a news broadcast* ▸ **broadcaster** /ˈbrɔːdkɑːstə(r)/ *noun* a person whose job is to talk on radio or television

brochure /ˈbrəʊʃə(r)/ *noun* a thin book with pictures and information about something: *a travel brochure*

broke[1] (also **broken**) *forms of* BREAK[1]

broke[2] /brəʊk/ *adjective* having no money: *I can't come out with you today — I'm broke.*

broken 🔑 /ˈbrəʊkən/ *adjective* in pieces or not working: *a broken window* ◇ *'What's the time?' 'I don't know – my watch is broken.'*

bronze /brɒnz/ *noun* (no plural) a brown metal made from copper and tin: *The athlete won a bronze medal.*

brooch /brəʊtʃ/ *noun* (*plural* **brooches**) a pretty thing with a pin at the back that you wear on your clothes: *She pinned a large brooch on her collar.*

broom /bruːm/ *noun* a brush, often with a long handle, that you use for sweeping

brooms

brother 🔑 /ˈbrʌðə(r)/ *noun* Your brother is a man or boy who has the same parents as you: *My younger brother is called Egesa.* ◇ *Karimi and Bigogo are brothers.*

brother-in-law /ˈbrʌðər ɪn lɔː/ *noun* (*plural* **brothers-in-law**) **1** the brother of someone's wife or husband **2** the husband of someone's sister

brought *form of* BRING

brow /braʊ/ *noun* **1** the part of your face above your eyes SAME MEANING **forehead 2** = **eyebrow**

brown 🔑 /braʊn/ *adjective* (**browner, brownest**) with the colour of coffee: *He* *has brown eyes.* ▸ **brown** *noun* the colour of coffee

browser /ˈbraʊzə(r)/ *noun* a computer program that lets you look at pages on the Internet ▸ **browse** /braʊz/ *verb* (**browses, browsing, browsed** /braʊzd/) to look at information on the Internet: *He sat browsing the Web.*

bruise /bru:z/ *noun* a dark mark on your skin that comes after something hits it: *He was covered in bruises after the accident.* ▸ **bruise** *verb* (**bruises, bruising, bruised** /bru:zd/): *He fell and bruised his leg.*

brushes

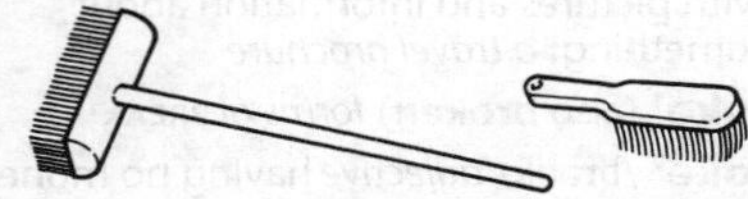

brush¹ 🔑 /brʌʃ/ *noun* (*plural* **brushes**) a thing that you use for sweeping, cleaning, painting, etc: *She fetched a brush and swept the floor.* ➲ Look at **paintbrush**, **toothbrush**.

brush² 🔑 /brʌʃ/ *verb* (**brushes, brushing, brushed** /brʌʃt/) to use a brush to do something: *I brush my teeth twice a day.*

Brussels sprout /ˌbrʌslz ˈspraʊt/ = **sprout¹**

brutal /ˈbru:tl/ *adjective* very cruel: *a brutal murder* ▸ **brutally** /ˈbru:təli/ *adverb*: *She was brutally attacked.*

bubble¹ 🔑 /ˈbʌbl/ *noun* a small ball of air or gas inside a liquid: *We saw bubbles on the surface of the water.*

bubble² /ˈbʌbl/ *verb* (**bubbles, bubbling, bubbled** /ˈbʌbld/) to make a lot of bubbles: *When water boils, it bubbles.*

buck /bʌk/ *noun* **1** a type of **antelope** (= a wild animal with long horns and long thin legs) **2** a male rabbit

bucket /ˈbʌkɪt/ *noun* a round metal or plastic container with a handle: *He filled the bucket with water.*

bucket

buckle /ˈbʌkl/ *noun* a metal or plastic thing on the end of a belt or other flat piece of material that you use for joining it to the other end

bud /bʌd/ *noun* a leaf or flower before it opens: *There are buds on the trees in spring.* ➲ Picture at **plant¹**.

Buddhist /ˈbʊdɪst/ *noun* a person who follows the religion of Buddhism, which was started in India by Buddha: *He is a Buddhist.* ▸ **Buddhist** *adjective*: *a Buddhist temple*

budge /bʌdʒ/ *verb* (**budges, budging, budged** /bʌdʒd/) to move a little or make something move a little: *I'm trying to move this rock but it won't budge.*

budgerigar /ˈbʌdʒərigɑ:(r)/ (also **budgie** /ˈbʌdʒi/) *noun* a small blue or green bird that people keep as a pet

budget /ˈbʌdʒɪt/ *noun* a plan of how much money you will have and how you will spend it: *We have a weekly budget for food.* ▸ **budget** *verb* (**budgets, budgeting, budgeted**) to plan how much money you will have and how you will spend it: *I am budgeting very carefully because I want to buy a television.*

buffalo /ˈbʌfələʊ/ *noun* (*plural* **buffalo** *or* **buffaloes**) a large wild cow with long horns

buffalo

bug /bʌg/ *noun* **1** a small insect **2** an illness that is not serious: *I've caught a bug.*

buibui *noun* (East African English) a long black dress and a piece of black cloth that covers the head showing only the face or eyes, that some Muslim women wear

build 🔑 /bɪld/ *verb* (**builds, building, built** /bɪlt/, **has built**) to make something by putting parts together: *He built a wall in front of the house.* ◇ *The bridge is built of stone.*

builder /ˈbɪldə(r)/ *noun* a person whose job is to make buildings

building 🔑 /ˈbɪldɪŋ/ *noun* a thing with a roof and walls. Houses, schools, churches and shops are all buildings: *There are a lot of new buildings in this town.*

building society /ˈbɪldɪŋ səsaɪəti/ *noun* (*plural* **building societies**) a kind of bank that lends you money when you want to buy a house or flat

built *form of* BUILD

bulb /bʌlb/ *noun*
1 (also **light bulb**) the glass part of an electric lamp that gives light: *Use a 60-watt light bulb in this lamp.* **2** a round thing that some plants grow from: *an onion bulb*

bulbs

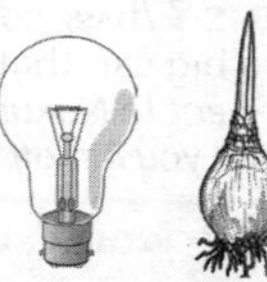

light bulb plant bulb

bulge /bʌldʒ/ *verb* (**bulges**, **bulging**, **bulged** /bʌldʒd/) to become bigger than usual; to go out in a round shape from something that is usually flat: *My stomach is bulging – I have eaten too much.* ▶ **bulge** *noun* a round part that goes out from something that is usually flat: *a bulge in the wall*

bulk /bʌlk/ *noun* (no plural) most of something: *The bulk of the work has been completed.*
in bulk in large quantities: *It's cheaper to buy in bulk.*

bulky /ˈbʌlki/ *adjective* (**bulkier**, **bulkiest**) big, heavy and difficult to carry: *She had a bulky bag full of books.*

bull /bʊl/ *noun* the male of the cow and of some other animals ➲ Look at **cow**.

bulldozer /ˈbʊldəʊzə(r)/ *noun* a big heavy machine that moves earth and makes land flat

bulldozer

bullet /ˈbʊlɪt/ *noun* a small piece of metal that shoots out of a gun: *The bullet hit him in the leg.*

bully /ˈbʊli/ *noun* (*plural* **bullies**) a person who hurts or frightens a weaker person: *Bullies will be punished.* ▶ **bully** *verb* (**bullies**, **bullying**, **bullied** /ˈbʊlid/, **has bullied**) to hurt or frighten a weaker person: *She was bullied by older girls.*

bum /bʌm/ *noun* the part of your body that you sit on

> ❖ **SPEAKING**
>
> Be careful! Some people think the word **bum** is quite rude. **Bottom** is the more usual word.

bump[1] /bʌmp/ *verb* (**bumps**, **bumping**, **bumped** /bʌmpt/) **1** to hit someone or something when you are moving: *She bumped into a chair.* **2** to hit a part of your body against something hard: *I bumped my head on the low ceiling.*
bump into someone to meet someone by chance: *I bumped into Kendi today.*

bump[2] /bʌmp/ *noun* **1** the action or sound of something hitting a hard surface: *He fell and hit the ground with a bump.* **2** a small round fat place on your body where you have hit it: *I've got a bump on my head.* **3** a small part on something flat that is higher than the rest: *The car hit a bump in the road.*

bumper /ˈbʌmpə(r)/ *noun* a bar on the front and back of a car, lorry, etc. It helps to protect the car if it hits something. ➲ Picture at **car**.

bumpy /ˈbʌmpi/ *adjective* (**bumpier**, **bumpiest**) **1** with a lot of **bumps**: *a bumpy road* **2** that shakes you: *We had a very bumpy journey in an old bus.* OPPOSITE **smooth**

bunch /bʌntʃ/ *noun* (*plural* **bunches**) a group of things that grow together or that you tie or hold together: *a bunch of bananas* ◇ *a bunch of keys* ➲ picture on page A4

bundle /ˈbʌndl/ *noun* a group of things that you tie or wrap together: *a bundle of old newspapers* ➲ picture on page A13

bungalow /ˈbʌŋgələʊ/ *noun* a house that has only one floor, with no upstairs rooms

bunk /bʌŋk/ *noun*
1 (also **bunk bed** /ˈbʌŋk bed/) one of a pair of single beds built one on top of the other: *I slept on the top bunk bed and my sister slept on the bottom one.* **2** a narrow bed that is fixed to a wall, on a ship, train, etc.

bunk beds

buoy /bɔɪ/ *noun* (*plural* **buoys**) a thing that floats in the sea to show ships where there are dangerous places

burger /ˈbɜːgə(r)/ *noun* meat cut into very small pieces and made into a flat round shape, that you cook and eat between two pieces of bread

burglar /ˈbɜːglə(r)/ *noun* a person who goes into a building to steal things ➲ Note at **thief**.

burglary /ˈbɜːgləri/ *noun* (*plural* **burglaries**) going into a house to steal things: *There were two burglaries in this street last week.*

burgle /ˈbɜːɡl/ *verb* (**burgles, burgling, burgled** /ˈbɜːɡld/) to go into a building to steal things: *Our house was burgled.*

burial /ˈberiəl/ *noun* the time when a dead body is put in the ground ❶ The verb is **bury**.

buried (also **buries**) *form of* BURY

burn[1] 🔑 /bɜːn/ *verb* (**burns, burning, burnt** /bɜːnt/ *or* **burned** /bɜːnd/, **has burnt** *or* **has burned**) **1** to make flames and heat; be on fire: *Paper burns easily.* ◇ *She escaped from the burning building.* **2** to harm or destroy someone or something with fire or heat: *I burnt my fingers on a match.* ◇ *We burned the wood on the fire.*
burn down to burn, or make a building burn, until there is nothing left: *Their house burnt down.*

burn[2] /bɜːn/ *noun* a place on your body where fire or heat has hurt it: *I have got a burn on my arm from the cooker.*

burp /bɜːp/ *verb* (**burps, burping, burped** /bɜːpt/) to make a noise from your mouth when air suddenly comes up from your stomach: *He burped loudly.* ▸ **burp** *noun*: *a loud burp*

burrow /ˈbʌrəʊ/ *noun* a hole in the ground where some animals live: *Rabbits live in burrows.*

burst[1] 🔑 /bɜːst/ *verb* (**bursts, bursting, burst, has burst**) **1** to break open suddenly because there is too much inside; to make something break open suddenly: *The bag was so full that it burst.* ◇ *He burst the balloon.* **2** to go or come suddenly: *Kirezi burst into the room.*
burst into something to start doing something suddenly: *He read the letter and burst into tears* (= started to cry). ◇ *The car burst into flames* (= started to burn).
burst out laughing to suddenly start to laugh: *When she saw my hat, she burst out laughing.*

burst[2] /bɜːst/ *noun* something that happens suddenly and quickly: *a burst of activity*

bury 🔑 /ˈberi/ *verb* (**buries, burying, buried** /ˈberid/, **has buried**)

> ❖ **PRONUNCIATION**
>
> **Bury** sounds the same as **berry**.

1 to put a dead body in the ground: *People cried when the chief was buried.* ❶ The noun is **burial**. **2** to put something in the ground or under something: *The dog buried a bone then dug it up again.*

bus 🔑 /bʌs/ *noun* (*plural* **buses**) a thing like a big car, that carries a lot of people: *We went to Nakuru on the bus/by bus.* ◇ *Where do you get off the bus?*

> ❖ **WORD BUILDING**
>
> You **get on** and **get off** a bus at a **bus stop**. The place where most buses start is called a **bus station**. The **bus conductor** takes your money and may give you a ticket.
>
> Remember that we travel **by bus** or **on the bus**.

bush 🔑 /bʊʃ/ *noun* **1 the bush** (no plural) wild country that is not used for farming or building: *A gazelle ran into the bush.* **2** (*plural* **bushes**) a plant like a small tree with a lot of branches: *a cotton bush*

business 🔑 /ˈbɪznəs/ *noun* **1** (no plural) buying and selling things: *I want to go into business when I leave school.* ◇ *Business is not very good this year.* **2** (*plural* **businesses**) a place where people sell or make things or provide services, for example a shop or factory: *He owns a small business in Arusha.*
it's none of your business or **mind your own business** words that you use when you do not want to tell someone about something that is private: *'Where are you going?' 'Mind your own business!'*
on business because of your work: *Mrs Gitau is in Uganda on business.*

businessman /ˈbɪznəsmən/ (*plural* **businessmen** /ˈbɪznəsmen/), **businesswoman** /ˈbɪznəswʊmən/ (*plural* **businesswomen** /ˈbɪznəswɪmɪn/) *noun* a person who works in business, especially in a top position

> ❖ **WORD BUILDING**
>
> We say **business person** /ˈbɪznəs pɜːsn/ when we want to refer to either a man or a woman. The plural is **business people** /ˈbɪznəs piːpl/.

bus stop /ˈbʌs stɒp/ *noun* a place where buses stop and people get on and off

busy 🔑 /ˈbɪzi/ *adjective* (**busier, busiest**) **1** with a lot of things that you must do; working or not free: *Mr Ochom can't see you now – he's busy.* **2** with a lot of things happening: *I had a busy morning.* ▸ **busily** /ˈbɪzɪli/ *adverb*: *He was busily writing a letter.*

but[1] 🔑 /bət; bʌt/ *conjunction* a word that you use to show something different: *He worked hard but he didn't pass the exam.* ◇ *The teacher is strict but fair.*

but[2] /bət; bʌt/ *preposition* except: *She does nothing but study.*

butcher /ˈbʊtʃə(r)/ *noun* a person who cuts and sells meat

> ❖ **WORD BUILDING**
>
> A shop that sells meat is called a **butcher's**.

butter 🔑 /ˈbʌtə(r)/ *noun* (no plural) soft yellow food that is made from milk. You put it on bread or use it in cooking: *Fry the onions in butter.*

butterfly /ˈbʌtəflaɪ/ *noun* (*plural* **butterflies**) an insect with big coloured wings

butterfly

button 🔑 /ˈbʌtn/ *noun* **1** a small round thing on clothes. You push it through a small hole (a **buttonhole** /ˈbʌtnhəʊl/) to hold clothes together: *I sewed a button on my shirt.* **2** a small thing on a machine, that you push: *Press this button to ring the bell.*

button

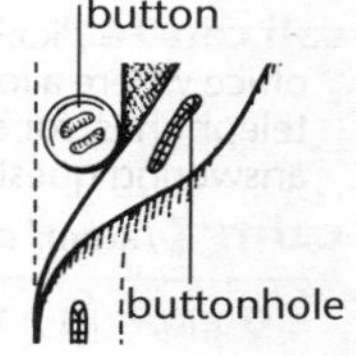

buy 🔑 /baɪ/ *verb* (**buys, buying, bought** /bɔːt/, **has bought**)

> ❖ **PRONUNCIATION**
>
> **Buy** and **by** sound the same.

to give money to get something: *I bought a new watch.* ◇ *He bought the bike from a friend.* ➲ Look at **sell**.

buzz /bʌz/ *verb* (**buzzes, buzzing, buzzed** /bʌzd/) to make a sound like bees ▸ **buzz** *noun* (*plural* **buzzes**): *There was a loud buzz of insects in the garden.*

by[1] 🔑 /baɪ/ *preposition* **1** very near: *The telephone is by the door.* ◇ *They live by the sea.* **2** from one side of someone or something to the other; past: *He walked by me without speaking.* **3** not later than: *I must finish this work by six o'clock.* **4** a word that shows who or what did something: *Who is the book by?* (= Who wrote it?) ◇ *She was caught by the police.* **5** using something: *I go to school by train.* **6** a word that shows how: *You operate the machine by turning the handle.* **7** a word that shows how you measure something: *We buy material by the metre.* **8** a word that shows which part: *She took me by the hand.*

by[2] 🔑 /baɪ/ *adverb* past: *She ran by without saying hello.*

bye 🔑 /baɪ/ (also **bye-bye** /ˌbaɪ ˈbaɪ/) *exclamation* goodbye: *Bye! See you tomorrow.*

by-product /ˈbaɪ prɒdʌkt/ *noun* something that is made during the making of something else: *When plastic burns, it produces dangerous by-products.*

bystander /ˈbaɪstændə(r)/ *noun* a person who is standing near and sees something happen: *Two innocent bystanders were hurt in the robbery.*

byte /baɪt/ *noun* a unit of information in a computer

Cc

C, c /siː/ *noun* (*plural* **C's, c's** /siːz/) **1** the third letter of the English alphabet: *'Car' begins with a 'C'.* **2** *short for* **CELSIUS, CENTIGRADE**

cab /kæb/ *noun* **1** = **taxi** **2** the part of a lorry, train or bus where the driver sits

cabbage /ˈkæbɪdʒ/ *noun* a large round vegetable with thick green leaves: *Cabbages are easy to grow.*

cabin /ˈkæbɪn/ *noun* **1** a small bedroom on a ship **2** a part of an aircraft: *The passengers in the first-class cabin were asleep.* **3** a small simple house made of wood: *We stayed in a log cabin by the lake.*

cabinet /ˈkæbɪnət/ *noun* **1** (*plural* **cabinets**) a piece of furniture that you can keep things in: *a bathroom cabinet* **2** (no plural) a group of the most important people in the government

cable /ˈkeɪbl/ *noun* **1** a wire that carries electricity or messages: *Telephone cables run under the road.* **2** a very strong thick rope or wire

cactus /ˈkæktəs/ *noun* (*plural* **cactuses** *or* **cacti** /ˈkæktaɪ/) a plant with a lot of sharp points that grows in hot dry places

cafe /ˈkæfeɪ/ *noun* a place where you can have a drink and something to eat: *The two friends met in a cafe.*

cage /keɪdʒ/ *noun* a place with bars round it where animals or birds are kept so that they cannot escape

cage

cake 🔑 /keɪk/ *noun* sweet food that you make from flour, eggs, sugar and butter, and cook in the oven: *She baked a chocolate cake.* ◇ *Would you like a piece of cake?*

calabash /ˈkæləbæʃ/ *noun* (*plural* **calabashes**) a container that is made from the hard, dried skin of a large fruit (a **gourd**)

calabash

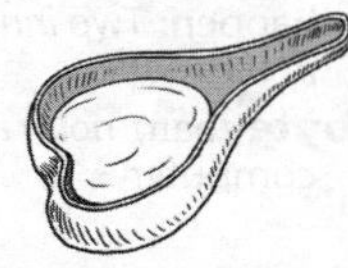

calculate 🔑 /ˈkælkjuleɪt/ *verb* (**calculates**, **calculating**, **calculated**) to find the answer by using mathematics: *Can you calculate how much the vegetables will cost?*

calculation /ˌkælkjuˈleɪʃn/ *noun* finding an answer by using mathematics: *A computer can do very difficult calculations.*

calculator /ˈkælkjuleɪtə(r)/ *noun* a small electronic machine that adds, **subtracts**, multiplies and divides numbers: *He used a pocket calculator to find the total cost.*

calendar /ˈkæləndə(r)/ *noun* a list of the days, weeks and months of one year: *Look at the calendar and tell me what day of the week December 2nd is this year.*

calf /kɑːf/ *noun* (*plural* **calves** /kɑːvz/) **1** a young cow ➲ Picture at **cow**. **2** the back of your leg, below your knee ➲ picture on page A13

call¹ 🔑 /kɔːl/ *noun* **1** a loud cry or shout: *We heard a call for help.* **2** using the telephone: *I'll give you a call later.* **3** a short visit to someone: *We paid a call on Mrs Lugadya.*

call² 🔑 /kɔːl/ *verb* (**calls**, **calling**, **called** /kɔːld/) **1** to speak loudly and clearly so that someone who is far away can hear you: *'Breakfast is ready,' she called.* ◇ *She called out the names of the winners.* **2** to ask someone to come: *someone call the police!* **3** to give a name to someone or something: *They called the baby Moraa.* **4** to telephone someone: *I'll call you later.* ◇ *Who's calling, please?*

be called to have as a name: *'What is your teacher called?' 'She's called Mrs Mtenga.'*

call someone back to telephone someone again: *I can't talk now – I'll call you back later.*

call for someone to go to someone's house on your way to a place so that they can come with you: *Chebet usually calls for me in the morning and we walk to school together.*

call in to make a short visit: *I'll call in to see you this evening.*

call something off to say that something that you have planned will not happen: *We called off the race because it was raining.*

call on or **upon someone** to ask someone to speak

call someone or **something to order** to ask people to be quiet so that a meeting can start

call box /ˈkɔːl bɒks/ *noun* (*plural* **call boxes**) a kind of small building in the street or in a public place that has a telephone in it

call centre /ˈkɔːl sentə(r)/ *noun* an office where a lot of people work using telephones, for example taking orders or answering questions

calm¹ 🔑 /kɑːm/ *adjective* (**calmer**, **calmest**)

> ❖ **PRONUNCIATION**
>
> **Calm** sounds like **arm**.

1 quiet, and not excited or afraid: *Try to keep calm – there's no danger.* **2** without much wind: *calm weather* **3** without big waves: *calm sea* ▸ **calmly** *adverb*: *He spoke calmly about the accident.*

calm² 🔑 /kɑːm/ *verb* (**calms**, **calming**, **calmed** /kɑːmd/)

calm down to become less afraid or excited; to make someone less afraid or excited: *Calm down and tell me what happened.*

calorie /ˈkæləri/ *noun* Food that has a lot of **calories** in it can make you fat.

calves *plural of* CALF

came *form of* COME

camel /ˈkæml/ *noun* a large animal with one or two round parts (called **humps**) on its back. **Camels** carry people and things in the desert.

camera 🔑 /ˈkæmərə/ *noun* a thing that you use for taking photographs or moving pictures: *I need a new battery for my camera.*

camp[1] 🔑 /kæmp/ *noun* a place where people live in tents for a short time: *Let's return to camp.*

camp[2] 🔑 /kæmp/ *verb* (**camps, camping, camped** /kæmpt/) to live in a tent for a short time: *Some Girl Guides were camping on the hill.*

❖ GRAMMAR

It is more usual to say **go camping** when you mean that you are living in a tent on holiday: *We went camping by the lake.*

campaign /kæmˈpeɪn/ *noun* a plan to get a special result: *They held a campaign to reduce road accidents.*

camping 🔑 /ˈkæmpɪŋ/ *noun* (no plural) living in a tent for a short time: *Camping isn't much fun when it rains.*

campsite /ˈkæmpsaɪt/ *noun* a place where you can camp

can[1] 🔑 /kən; kæn/ *modal verb* **1** to be able to; to be strong enough, clever enough, etc: *She can speak three languages.* ◇ *Can you play tennis?* **2** to be allowed to: *You can go now.* ◇ *Can I have some more porridge, please?* ◇ *The doctor says she can't go back to school yet.* **3** a word that you use when you ask someone to do something: *Can you tell me the time, please?* **4** to be possible or likely: *It can be very cold in the mountains at night.* **5** a word that you use with verbs like *'see', 'hear', 'smell'* and *'taste'*: *I can smell something burning.* ◇ *'What's that noise?' 'I can't hear anything.'*

❖ GRAMMAR

The negative form of **can** is **cannot** or the short form **can't**: *She can't swim.*

The past tense of **can** is **could**: *We could hear people shouting.*

You use **be able to**, NOT **can**, to make the future tense: *You will be able to see it if you stand on this chair.*

can[2] 🔑 /kæn/ *noun* **1** a container used for carrying liquid: *an oil can* ➲ Picture at **spray**[1]. **2** a metal container for food or drink that keeps it fresh: *a can of beans* ◇ *Two cans of lemonade, please.* SAME MEANING **tin** ➲ Picture at **container**.

canal /kəˈnæl/ *noun* a deep cut that is made through the land and filled with water so that boats can travel on it: *the Suez Canal*

cancel /ˈkænsl/ *verb* (**cancels, cancelling, cancelled** /ˈkænsld/) to say that something that you have planned will not happen: *The singer was ill, so the concert was cancelled.*

cancellation /ˌkænsəˈleɪʃn/ *noun* a decision that a planned activity or event will not happen: *The cancellation of the President's visit was disappointing.*

cancer /ˈkænsə(r)/ *noun* a very dangerous illness that makes some **cells** (= very small parts of the body) grow too fast: *Smoking can cause cancer.*

candidate /ˈkændɪdət/ *noun* **1** a person who wants to be chosen for something: *When the director leaves, there will be a lot of candidates for her job.* **2** a person who takes an examination: *There are 12 candidates for the exam today.*

candle /ˈkændl/ *noun* a long round piece of **wax** (= solid oil or fat) with a string in the middle that burns to give light

candle

candlestick /ˈkændlstɪk/ *noun* a thing that holds a **candle**

cane /keɪn/ *noun* the long central part of some plants: *sugar cane* ◇ *a cane chair*

canned /kænd/ *adjective* in a can: *canned drinks*

cannot 🔑 /ˈkænɒt/ ➲ Look at **can**[1].

canoe /kəˈnuː/ *noun* a light narrow boat that you use on rivers. You move it through the water with a piece of wood (called a **paddle**).

canoe

ℹ When you talk about using a canoe, you often say **go canoeing**: *We went canoeing on the river.*

canopy /ˈkænəpi/ *noun* (*plural* **canopies**) a cover that hangs or spreads above something: *The king sat under a purple canopy.* ◇ *the canopy of a rainforest* (= the thick layer of branches and leaves that covers the top)

can't /kɑːnt/ = **cannot**

canteen /kæn'tiːn/ *noun* the place where people eat when they are at school or work

canvas /'kænvəs/ *noun* (no plural) strong heavy cloth. Tents and sails are often made of **canvas**, and it is also used for painting pictures on.

cap /kæp/ *noun* **1** a soft hat: *a baseball cap* **2** a thing that covers the top of a bottle or tube: *Put the cap back on the bottle.* ➲ Picture at **container**.

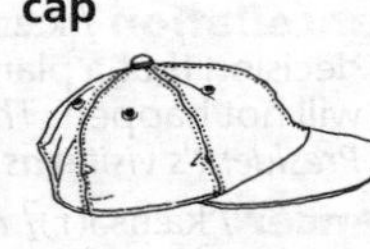

capable ⚷ /'keɪpəbl/ *adjective* **1** able to do something: *You are capable of passing the exam if you work harder.* **2** able to do things well: *He's a capable student.* OPPOSITE **incapable**

capacity /kə'pæsəti/ *noun* (*plural* **capacities**) how much a container can hold: *a tank with a capacity of 1 000 litres* ◇ *The game was watched by a capacity crowd* (= all the space was full).

cape /keɪp/ *noun* **1** a piece of clothing that covers your body and arms but does not have sleeves **2** a high part of the land that goes out into the sea: *the Cape of Good Hope*

capital ⚷ /'kæpɪtl/ *noun* **1** the most important city in a country, where the government is: *Addis Ababa is the capital of Ethiopia.* **2** (also **capital letter** /ˌkæpɪtl 'letə(r)/) a big letter of the alphabet: *A, B and C are capitals; a, b and c are small letters.* ◇ *Names of people and places begin with a capital letter.* ❶ Look at page A17.

capsize /kæp'saɪz/ *verb* (**capsizes, capsizing, capsized** /kæp'saɪzd/) to turn over in the water: *During the storm, the boat capsized.*

captain /'kæptɪn/ *noun* **1** the person who is in charge of a ship or an aircraft: *The captain sent a message by radio for help.* **2** the leader of a group of people: *He's the captain of the school football team.*

caption /'kæpʃn/ *noun* the words above or below a picture in a book or newspaper, that tell you about it

captive /'kæptɪv/ *noun* a person who is not free; a prisoner

captivity /kæp'tɪvəti/ *noun* (no plural) **in captivity** kept in a place that you cannot leave: *Wild animals are often unhappy in captivity* (= in a cage, for example).

capture /'kæptʃə(r)/ *verb* (**captures, capturing, captured** /'kæptʃəd/) to catch someone and keep them somewhere so that they cannot leave: *The police captured the robbers.* ▶ **capture** *noun* (no plural): *This information led to the capture of the thieves.*

car ⚷ /kɑː(r)/ *noun* a vehicle with four wheels, usually with enough space for four or five people: *She travels to work by car.*

caravan /'kærəvæn/ *noun* a group of people and animals that travel together, especially across the desert

carbohydrate /ˌkɑːbəʊ'haɪdreɪt/ *noun* one of the things in food, for example sugar, that gives your body energy: *Bread and rice contain carbohydrates.*

carbon /'kɑːbən/ *noun* (no plural) the chemical that coal and diamonds are made of and that is in all living things

car

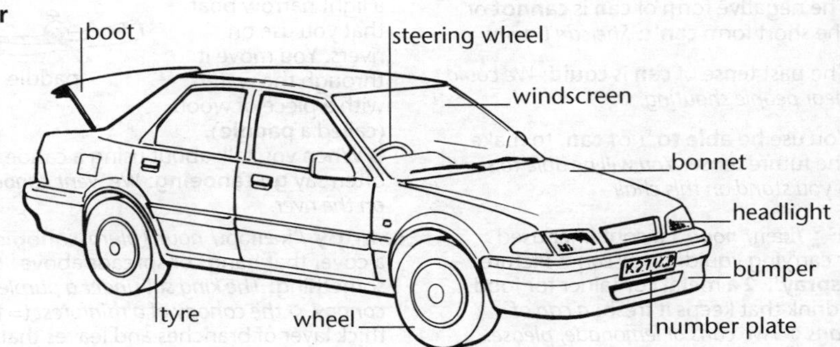

carbon dioxide /ˌkɑːbən daɪˈɒksaɪd/ *noun* (no plural) a gas that has no colour or smell and that people and animals breathe out

cards

jack queen king ace joker

hearts
clubs
spades
diamonds

pack of cards — cards — suits

card /kɑːd/ *noun* **1** (no plural) thick stiff paper: *a piece of card* **2** (*plural* **cards**) a piece of card with a picture on it: *We send Christmas cards and birthday cards to our friends.* **3** (*plural* **cards**) a small piece of card or plastic that has information on it: *a membership card* ➲ Look at **credit card**. **4** (*plural* **cards**) (also **playing cards** /ˈpleɪɪŋ kɑːdz/) one of a set of 52 cards called a **pack of cards** that you use to play games: *Let's have a game of cards.* ◇ *They often play cards in the evening.*

❖ **WORD BUILDING**

Each pack has four sets (called **suits**) of thirteen cards: **hearts**, **clubs**, **diamonds** and **spades**. Each set of cards has an **ace**, a **jack**, a **queen**, a **king** and nine other cards numbered from 2-10. There is one extra card that is used in some games, called a **joker**.

cardboard /ˈkɑːdbɔːd/ *noun* (no plural) very thick paper that is used for making boxes, etc: *Put the books in a cardboard box.*

cardigan /ˈkɑːdɪgən/ *noun* a piece of clothing like a jacket, that is usually made of wool

cardinal /ˈkɑːdɪnl/ *noun* an important priest in the Roman Catholic church

cardinal points /ˌkɑːdɪnl ˈpɔɪnts/ *noun* (plural) the four main points of the **compass** (= an instrument for finding direction): *North, south, east and west are the cardinal points of the compass.* ➲ Picture at **compass**.

care¹ /keə(r)/ *noun* (no plural) thinking about what you are doing so that you do not make a mistake or break something: *Wash these glasses with care!*

care of someone ➲ Look at **c/o**.

take care be careful: *Take care when you cross the road.*

take care of someone or **something** to look after someone or something; to do what is necessary: *Nakato is taking care of her sister's baby today.* ◇ *I'll take care of the shopping if you do the cleaning.*

❖ **WORD FAMILY**

care *noun*, **care** *verb*
careful: OPPOSITE **careless**

care² /keə(r)/ *verb* (**cares**, **caring**, **cared** /keəd/) to think that it is important: *The only thing he cares about is money.* ◇ *I don't care who wins – I'm not interested in football.*

care for someone or **something** **1** to do the things for someone that they need: *After the accident, her parents cared for her until she was better.* **2** to like someone or something: *I don't care for classical music.*

❖ **SPEAKING**

You use expressions like **I don't care**, **who cares?** and **I couldn't care less** when you feel a little angry and want to be rude.

career /kəˈrɪə(r)/ *noun* a job that you learn to do and then do for many years: *He had a long career in teaching.*

careful /ˈkeəfl/ *adjective* If you are careful, you think about what you are doing so that you do not make a mistake or have an accident: *Careful! The plate is very hot.* ◇ *Be careful with those glasses.* ▸ **carefully** /ˈkeəfəli/ *adverb*: *Please listen carefully.*

careless /ˈkeələs/ *adjective* If you are careless, you do not think enough about what you are doing, and so you make mistakes: *Careless drivers can cause accidents.* ▸ **carelessly** *adverb*: *She carelessly threw her coat on the floor.* ▸ **carelessness** /ˈkeələsnəs/ *noun* (no plural) being careless

caretaker /ˈkeəteɪkə(r)/ *noun* a person whose job is to look after a large building like a school or a block of flats

cargo /ˈkɑːɡəʊ/ *noun* (*plural* **cargoes**) the things that a ship or a plane carries: *a cargo of wheat*

carjacker /ˈkɑːdʒækə(r)/ *noun* a person who makes the driver of a car give them the car or take them somewhere: *The driver was forced to hand over his keys to the carjacker.* ➲ Look at **hijack**.
▸ **carjacking** /ˈkɑːdʒækɪŋ/ *noun*: *Carjacking is a serious crime.*

carnivore /ˈkɑːnɪvɔː(r)/ *noun* any animal that eats meat

car park /ˈkɑː pɑːk/ *noun* a piece of land or a building where you can put your car for a time

carpenter /ˈkɑːpəntə(r)/ *noun* a person who makes things from wood
▸ **carpentry** /ˈkɑːpəntri/ *noun* (no plural) making things from wood

carpet 🔑 /ˈkɑːpɪt/ *noun* a soft covering for a floor that is often made of wool: *There was a thick, soft carpet on the bedroom floor.*

carriage /ˈkærɪdʒ/ *noun* one of the parts of a train where people sit: *The carriages at the back of the train were empty.* ➲ Picture at **train**[1].

carried *form of* CARRY

carrier bag /ˈkæriə bæɡ/ (also **carrier**) *noun* a large bag made from plastic or paper that you use for carrying shopping

carrot /ˈkærət/ *noun* a long thin orange vegetable

carrot

carry 🔑 /ˈkæri/ *verb* (**carries**, **carrying**, **carried** /ˈkærid/) **1** to hold something and take it to another place or keep it with you: *He carried the bag to my room.* ◇ *I can't carry this box – it's too heavy.* ◇ *Do the police carry guns in your country?*

> ❖ **carry** or **wear**?
>
> Be careful! You use **wear**, not **carry**, to talk about having clothes on your body: *She is wearing a red dress and carrying a black bag.*

2 to move people or things: *Special fast trains carry people to the city centre.*
carry on to continue doing something: *Carry on with your work.* ◇ *If you carry on to the end of this road, you'll see the shop.*
carry out to do or finish what you have planned: *The swimming pool was closed while they carried out the repairs.*

cart /kɑːt/ *noun* a wooden vehicle with wheels that an animal usually pulls: *an ox cart*

carton /ˈkɑːtn/ *noun* a container made of cardboard or plastic: *a carton of milk* ➲ Picture at **container**.

cartoon /kɑːˈtuːn/ *noun* **1** a funny drawing, for example in a newspaper or magazine **2** a television or cinema film made with drawings, not pictures of real people and places: *a Disney cartoon*

cartridge /ˈkɑːtrɪdʒ/ *noun* a container that holds something that you use in a machine, for example film for a camera or ink for printing

carve /kɑːv/ *verb* (**carves**, **carving**, **carved** /kɑːvd/) **1** to cut wood or stone to make a picture or shape: *Her father carved a little elephant for her out of wood.* **2** to cut meat into thin pieces after you have cooked it

carving /ˈkɑːvɪŋ/ *noun* a shape or pattern made by cutting wood or stone: *Tourists bought wood carvings at the market.*

case 🔑 /keɪs/ *noun* **1** a container like a box for keeping something in: *Put the camera back in its case.* ➲ Look at **briefcase**, **suitcase**. **2** an example of something: *There were four cases of this disease in the school last month.* **3** something that happens or something that is true: *'My bicycle's broken.' 'Well, in that case you'll have to walk.'* **4** a question that people in a court of law must decide about: *The case will be heard next week.* **5** a problem that the police must find an answer to: *The police are dealing with a difficult murder case.*
in any case words that you use when you give a second reason for something: *I don't want to see the film, and in any case I'm too busy.*
in case because something might happen: *Take some money in case you need it.*

> ❖ **in case** or **if**?
>
> These do not mean the same. Look at these sentences: *You should take two pencils in case one breaks.* ◇ *If one pencil breaks, ask the teacher for another.*

cash[1] 🔑 /kæʃ/ *noun* (no plural) money in coins and notes: *How would you like to pay, cash or cheque?*

cash[2] /kæʃ/ *verb* (**cashes**, **cashing**, **cashed** /kæʃt/) to give a cheque and get money for it: *I'd like to cash a cheque, please.*

cash crop /ˈkæʃ krɒp/ *noun* plants that you grow to sell, not to use yourself

cashew /ˈkæʃuː/ (also **cashew nut** /ˈkæʃuː nʌt/) *noun* a curved nut that you can cook and eat

cashier /kæˈʃɪə(r)/ *noun* the person who gives or takes money in a bank

cash machine /ˈkæʃ məʃiːn/ (also **ATM**) *noun* a machine that you can get money from with a special plastic card

cassava

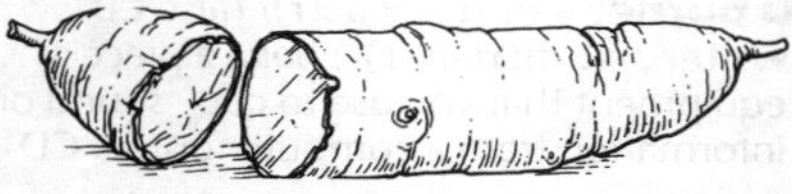

cassava /kəˈsɑːvə/ *noun* (no plural) a plant with fat roots, or the flour that we make from these roots

cassette /kəˈset/ *noun* a plastic box with special tape inside for storing and playing sound, music or moving pictures: *Put on* (= play) *the cassette.*

❖ **SPELLING**

Remember! You spell **cassette** with **ss** and **tt**.

cassette deck /kəˈset dek/ *noun* the part of a machine that can put (**record**) sound or music on tapes or play them

cassette player /kəˈset pleɪə(r)/ (also **cassette recorder** /kəˈset rɪˌkɔːdə(r)/) *noun* a machine that can put (**record**) sound or music on tape and play it again later

castle 🔑 /ˈkɑːsl/ *noun*

❖ **PRONUNCIATION**

Castle sounds like **parcel** because we do not say the 't'.

a large old building that was built to keep people safe from their enemies: *There was a ruined castle on the hill.*

casual /ˈkæʒuəl/ *adjective* **1** showing that you are not worried about something; relaxed: *She gave us a casual wave as she passed.* **2** not for serious or important times: *You should not wear casual clothes to a wedding.* ▸ **casually** /ˈkæʒuəli/ *adverb*: *They chatted casually on the phone.*

casualty /ˈkæʒuəlti/ *noun* (*plural* **casualties**) a person who is hurt or killed in an accident or a war: *After the accident the casualties were taken to hospital.*

casualty department /ˈkæʒuəlti dɪpɑːtmənt/ (also **casualty** no plural) *noun* the place in a hospital where doctors help people who have been hurt in an accident

cats

cat 🔑 /kæt/ *noun* **1** an animal that people keep in their house to catch mice and other small animals: *The cat has had kittens.* **2** the name of a group of large wild animals: *the big cats, such as lions and tigers*

❖ **WORD BUILDING**

A young cat is called a **kitten**. A young lion or tiger is called a **cub**.

let the cat out of the bag to tell a secret by mistake

catalogue /ˈkætəlɒg/ *noun* a list of all the things that you can buy or see somewhere: *an online catalogue*

catch 🔑 /kætʃ/ *verb* (**catches**, **catching**, **caught** /kɔːt/, **has caught**) **1** to take and hold something that is moving: *He threw the ball to me and I caught it.* **2** to find and hold someone or something: *They caught a fish in the river.* ◇ *The man ran so fast that the police couldn't catch him.* **3** to see someone when they are doing something wrong: *They caught the thief stealing the money.* **4** to be early enough for a bus, train, etc. that is going to leave: *You should run if you want to catch the bus.* OPPOSITE **miss** **5** to get an illness: *She caught a cold.* **6** to become stuck in or on something: *I caught my fingers in the door.*

catch fire to start to burn: *The house caught fire.*

catch up to do something quickly so that you are not behind others: *If you miss a lesson, you can work at home to catch up.* ◇ *Quick! Run and catch them up.*

catchy /ˈkætʃi/ *adjective* (**catchier**, **catchiest**) If a song or a tune is **catchy**, it is easy to remember.

caterpillar /ˈkætəpɪlə(r)/ *noun* a small animal with a long body and a lot of legs. A **caterpillar** later becomes an insect with coloured wings (a **butterfly** or a **moth**).

caterpillar

catfish /ˈkætfɪʃ/ *noun* (*plural* **catfish**) a large fish with long stiff hairs round its mouth

cathedral /kəˈθiːdrəl/ *noun* a big important church: *All Saints' Cathedral*

Catholic /ˈkæθəlɪk/ = **Roman Catholic**

cattle /ˈkætl/ *noun* (plural) cows and bulls: *a herd* (= a group) *of cattle*

catwalk /ˈkætwɔːk/ *noun* the long stage that models walk on during a fashion show: *Tall and beautiful models paraded gracefully down the catwalk.*

caught *form of* CATCH

cauliflower /ˈkɒliflaʊə(r)/ *noun* a large vegetable with green leaves outside and a hard white part in the middle

cauliflower

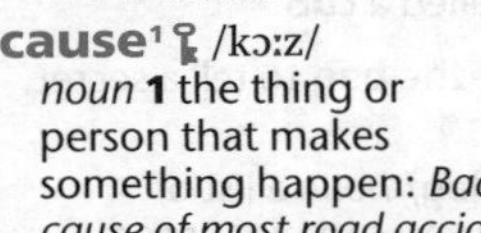

cause¹ /kɔːz/ *noun* **1** the thing or person that makes something happen: *Bad driving is the cause of most road accidents.* **2** something that people care about and want to help: *They gave the money to a good cause – it was used to build a new hospital.*

cause² /kɔːz/ *verb* (**causes**, **causing**, **caused** /kɔːzd/) to be the reason why something happens: *Who caused the accident?* ◇ *The fire was caused by an electrical fault.*

caution /ˈkɔːʃn/ *noun* (no plural) great care: *Caution! Wet floor.*

cautious /ˈkɔːʃəs/ *adjective* careful because there may be danger: *He has always been cautious about driving at night.* ▶ **cautiously** *adverb* with care: *Cautiously, he pushed open the door.*

cave /keɪv/ *noun* a large hole in the side of a mountain or under the ground: *Thousands of years ago, people lived in caves.*

CCTV /ˌsiː siː tiː ˈviː/ *noun* (no plural) a television system used in a public place, such as a shop, to protect it from crime ℹ **CCTV** is short for 'closed-circuit television'.

CD /ˌsiː ˈdiː/ *noun* a small round piece of plastic. You play it on a special machine called a **CD player**: *Have you heard her new CD?* ℹ **CD** is short for 'compact disc'.

CD

CD burner /ˌsiː ˈdiː bɜːnə(r)/ (also **CD writer** /ˌsiː ˈdiː raɪtə(r)/) *noun* a piece of equipment that you use to copy sound or information from a computer onto a CD

CD-ROM /ˌsiː diː ˈrɒm/ *noun* a CD that you can store a lot of information, sound and pictures on, to use on a computer ℹ **CD-ROM** is short for 'compact disc read-only memory'.

ceiling

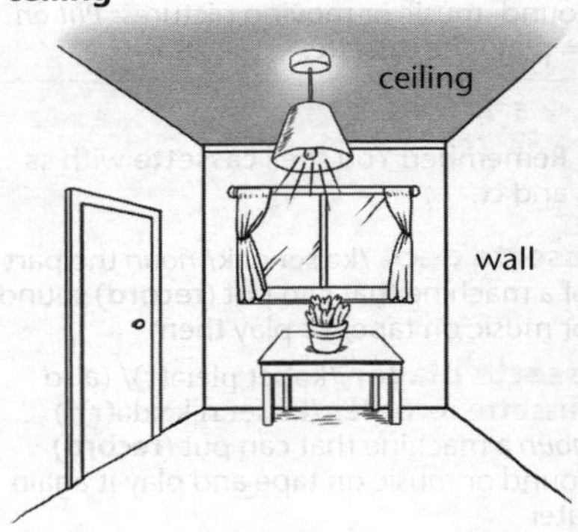

ceiling /ˈsiːlɪŋ/ *noun*

> ❖ **PRONUNCIATION**
>
> The first part of **ceiling** sounds like **seal**. When **c** comes in front of **e** or **i** we say it like **s**. Some other words like this are **cement**, **niece**, **receive** and **society**.

the part of a room over your head

celebrate /ˈselɪbreɪt/ *verb* (**celebrates**, **celebrating**, **celebrated**) to enjoy yourself because you have a special reason to be happy: *If you pass your exams, we'll go out to celebrate.*

celebration /ˌseləˈbreɪʃn/ *noun* a time when you enjoy yourself because you have a special reason to be happy: *birthday celebrations*

celebrity /sə'lebrəti/ *noun* (*plural* **celebrities**) a famous person

cell /sel/ *noun* **1** a small room where a prisoner lives: *The prisoners were locked in their cells.* **2** the smallest living part of any plant or animal: *white blood cells*

cellar /'selə(r)/ *noun* a room in the part of a building that is under the ground: *The wine was stored in a cellar.*

cell phone /'selfəʊn/ = **mobile phone**

Celsius /'selsiəs/ *noun* (no plural) a way of measuring temperature. Water freezes at 0 degrees **Celsius** and boils at 100 degrees **Celsius**. ℹ The short way of writing **Celsius** s 'C'. : *Normal body temperature is 37° C.* ➔ Look at **centigrade**.

cement /sɪ'ment/ *noun* (no plural) grey powder that becomes hard like stone when you mix it with water and leave it to dry. Cement is used in building.

cemetery /'semətri/ *noun* (*plural* **cemeteries**) an area of ground where dead people are put under the earth

cent /sent/ *noun* money that people use in some countries. There are 100 cents in a **shilling**: *Can you lend me fifty cents?* ◇ *I found a fifty-cent coin.*

centigrade /'sentɪgreɪd/ = **Celsius** ℹ The short way of writing **centigrade** is 'C'.

centilitre /'sentɪli:tə(r)/ *noun* a measure of liquid. There are 100 centilitres in a **litre**. ℹ The short way of writing 'centilitre' is **cl**: *250 cl*

centimetre /'sentɪmi:tə(r)/ *noun* a measure of length. There are 100 centimetres in a **metre**. ℹ The short way of writing 'centimetre' is **cm**: *My ruler is 30 cm long.*

centipede /'sentɪpi:d/ *noun* a small creature like an insect, with many legs

centipede

central /'sentrəl/ *adjective* in the middle part: *He works in central Nairobi.*

centre /'sentə(r)/ *noun* **1** the part in the middle: *We went to the city centre.* ◇ *The flower has a yellow centre with white petals.* **2** a place where people come to do something special: *a shopping centre* ◇ *They're building a new training centre.*

century /'sentʃəri/ *noun* (*plural* **centuries**) **1** 100 years: *The library has been there for more than a century.* **2** a time of 100 years, that we use in dates: *the beginning of the twenty-first century*

cereal /'sɪəriəl/ *noun* **1** (*plural* **cereals**) a plant that farmers grow so that we can eat the seed: *Wheat and maize are cereals.* **2** (no plural) a food made from grain, that you can eat for breakfast: *a bowl of cereal*

ceremony /'serəməni/ *noun* (*plural* **ceremonies**) a time when you do something special and important: *We watched the opening ceremony of the Olympic Games.* ◇ *a wedding ceremony*

certain /'sɜ:tn/ *adjective* **1** without any doubt; sure: *I am certain that I have seen her before.* ◇ *It's not certain that they will come.* OPPOSITE **uncertain** **2** used for talking about a particular thing or person without saying what or who they are: *It's cheaper to travel at certain times.*

for certain without any doubt: *I don't know for certain where she is.*

make certain to check something so that you are sure about it: *Please make certain that the door is locked.*

certainly /'sɜ:tnli/ *adverb* **1** without any doubt: *She is certainly the best swimmer in the team.* **2** yes: *'Will you open the door for me, please?' 'Certainly.'*

certainly not no: *'Can I borrow your bicycle?' 'Certainly not!'*

certificate /sə'tɪfɪkət/ *noun* an important piece of paper that shows that something is true: *Your birth certificate shows when and where you were born.*

chain¹ /tʃeɪn/ *noun* metal rings that are joined together: *Round her neck she wore a gold chain.* ◇ *My bicycle chain is broken.*

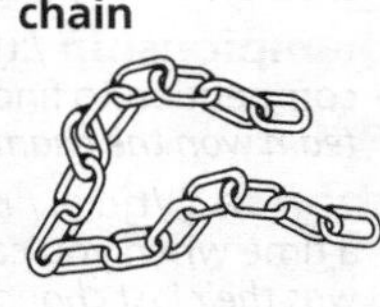
chain

chain² /tʃeɪn/ *verb* (**chains, chaining, chained** /tʃeɪnd/) to attach someone or something to a place with a chain: *The dog was chained to the fence.*

chair /tʃeə(r)/ *noun* **1** a piece of furniture with four legs, a seat and a back that one person can sit on: *There's a table and four chairs in the room.* **2** a person who controls a meeting: *She took the chair in the meeting.* ➔ Note on page 53.

❖ **WORD BUILDING**

You can also say **chairman**/ˈtʃeəmən/, **chairwoman**/ˈtʃeəwʊmən/ or **chairperson**/ˈtʃeəpɜːsn/ for the person who controls a meeting.

chalk /tʃɔːk/ *noun* (no plural) **1** soft white rock: *The cliffs are made of chalk.* **2** a piece of this rock that you use for writing on a board: *a packet of chalk*

chalkboard /ˈtʃɔːkbɔːd/ = **blackboard**

challenge¹ 🔑 /ˈtʃælɪndʒ/ *noun* a new or difficult thing that makes you try hard: *Climbing the mountain will be a real challenge.*

challenge² /ˈtʃælɪndʒ/ *verb* (**challenges, challenging, challenged** /ˈtʃælɪndʒd/) to ask someone to play a game with you or fight with you to see who wins: *The boxer challenged the world champion to a fight.*

chamber /ˈtʃeɪmbə(r)/ *noun* a room that is used for a particular purpose: *He visited the judge in his chambers.*

chameleon /kəˈmiːliən/ *noun* a **lizard** (= a small animal with rough skin) with a long tongue and large eyes. Chameleons can change colour.

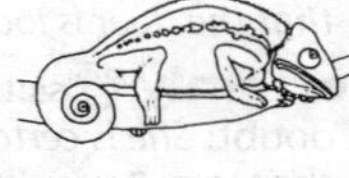
chameleon

❖ **PRONUNCIATION**

ch at the beginning of this word sounds just like **k**.

champion /ˈtʃæmpiən/ *noun* a person who is the best at a sport or game: *a chess champion* ◇ *the world champion*

championship /ˈtʃæmpiənʃɪp/ *noun* a competition to find the **champion**: *Our team won the championship this year.*

chance 🔑 /tʃɑːns/ *noun* **1** (*plural* **chances**) a time when you can do something: *It was their last chance to escape.* ◇ *I haven't had a chance to write to Ajuma today. I'll do it tomorrow.* **2** (*plural* **chances**) a possibility that something may happen: *He has a good chance of passing the exam because he has worked hard.* **3** (no plural) something that happens that you cannot control SAME MEANING **luck**

by chance not because you have planned it: *We met by chance at the station.*

take a chance to do something when it is possible that something bad may happen because of it: *We took a chance on the weather and planned a long walk.*

change¹ 🔑 /tʃeɪndʒ/ *verb* (**changes, changing, changed** /tʃeɪndʒd/) **1** to become different: *She has changed a lot – she looks much older.* ◇ *Water changes into ice when it gets very cold.* **2** to make something different: *Nduku changes her hairstyle often.* **3** to put or take something in place of another thing: *My new watch didn't work, so I took it back to the shop and changed it.* ◇ *I went to the bank to change my dollars into Tanzanian shillings.* ◇ *Can you change a 100 shilling note please? I need some 10 shilling coins.* **4** to put on different clothes: *I must change before I go out.* ℹ You can also say **get changed**: *I must get changed before I go out.* **5** to get off a bus or train and get on another one: *I have to change buses in Nairobi.*

change² 🔑 /tʃeɪndʒ/ *noun* **1** (no plural) money that you get when you have paid too much: *I gave the shop assistant twenty shillings. The sweets cost twelve shillings, so he gave me eight shillings change.* **2** (no plural) small pieces of money; coins: *I haven't got any change.* **3** (*plural* **changes**) a thing that is different now: *The new government has made a lot of changes.*

for a change because you want something different: *I usually drink tea, but today I had coffee for a change.*

channel /ˈtʃænl/ *noun* **1** a narrow place where water can go: *We dug a channel from the river to the field.* **2** a television station: *Which channel are you watching?*

chapatti /tʃəˈpɑːti/ *noun* a kind of flat bread

chapel /ˈtʃæpl/ *noun* a room or a small church where Christians go to speak to God (to **pray**)

chapter /ˈtʃæptə(r)/ *noun* one of the parts of a book: *You start reading a book at the beginning of Chapter 1.*

character 🔑 /ˈkærəktə(r)/ *noun*

❖ **PRONUNCIATION**

ch at the beginning of this word sounds just like **k**.

1 (no plural) the way a person or thing is: *He has a strong character.* ◇ *The new factory will change the character of the village.* **2** (*plural* **characters**) a person in a play, book or film: *The main character in the novel is a twelve-year-old boy.*

characteristic 🔑 /ˌkærəktəˈrɪstɪk/ *noun* a quality that someone or something has: *The chief characteristic of fish is that they live in water.*

charcoal /ˈtʃɑːkəʊl/ *noun* (no plural) black stuff that we make by burning wood. You use **charcoal** as a fuel or for drawing.

charge[1] 🔑 /tʃɑːdʒ/ *verb* (**charges**, **charging**, **charged** /tʃɑːdʒd/) **1** to ask someone to pay a certain price for something: *He charged me 300 shillings for the bus ride.* **2** to say that someone has done something wrong: *The police have charged him with murder.* **3** to move quickly and with a lot of force: *The bull charged.* ◇ *The children charged into the room.* **4** to put electricity into something: *I need to charge my phone.*

charge[2] 🔑 /tʃɑːdʒ/ *noun* **1** the money that you must pay for something: *There is an extra charge if you travel at night.* **2** a statement that someone has done something wrong: *a charge of murder* **be in charge of someone** or **something** to look after or control someone or something: *Ali is in charge of his baby brother while his mother is out.* ◇ *The head teacher is in charge of the school.*

charger /ˈtʃɑːdʒə(r)/ *noun* a piece of equipment that you use to put electricity into something: *a mobile phone charger*

charge sheet /ˈtʃɑːdʒ ʃiːt/ *noun* an official list of the names of people who have done something wrong

charity 🔑 /ˈtʃærəti/ *noun* **1** (*plural* **charities**) a group of people who collect money to help people who need it: *The Red Cross is a charity.* **2** (no plural) being kind and helping other people

charm[1] /tʃɑːm/ *noun* **1** (no plural) being able to make people like you: *Tanei has great charm.* **2** (*plural* **charms**) a small thing that you wear because you think it will bring good luck: *She wears a necklace with a lucky charm on it.*

charm[2] /tʃɑːm/ *verb* (**charms**, **charming**, **charmed** /tʃɑːmd/) to make someone like you: *The baby charmed everybody with her smile.*

charming /ˈtʃɑːmɪŋ/ *adjective* beautiful; attractive: *a charming smile*

chart /tʃɑːt/ *noun* **1** a drawing that gives information about something: *a temperature chart* **2 the charts** (plural) a list of the songs or CDs that have sold the most in a particular week: *Her last album topped the charts* (= sold more copies than all the others).

charter /ˈtʃɑːtə(r)/ *noun* **1** the renting of a ship, plane, etc. for a particular purpose or group of people: *The new charter airline flies to holiday destinations.* **2** a written statement describing the beliefs or aims of an organization or the rights of a particular group of people: *the United Nations Charter*

chase 🔑 /tʃeɪs/ *verb* (**chases**, **chasing**, **chased** /tʃeɪst/) to run behind someone or something and try to catch them: *We saw a cheetah chasing an antelope.* ◇ *The police chased after the thief but he escaped.* ▶ **chase** 🔑 *noun*: *The film includes an exciting car chase.*

chastity /ˈtʃæstəti/ *noun* (no plural) the state of not having sex with anyone or only having sex with the person you are married to

chat[1] /tʃæt/ *noun* **1** a friendly talk: *Let's have a chat about it later.* **2** communication between people on the Internet: *Fans are invited to an online chat.*

chat[2] /tʃæt/ *verb* (**chats**, **chatting**, **chatted**) **1** to talk in a friendly way: *The two friends chatted for hours.* **2** to exchange messages with other people on the Internet: *He's been on the computer all morning, chatting with his friends.*

chatter /ˈtʃætə(r)/ *verb* (**chatters**, **chattering**, **chattered** /ˈtʃætəd/) to talk quickly about things that are not very important: *Stop chattering and finish your work.*

cheap 🔑 /tʃiːp/ *adjective* (**cheaper**, **cheapest**) Something that is cheap does not cost a lot of money: *Buses are cheaper than trains.* ◇ *That restaurant is very good and quite cheap.* OPPOSITE **dear**

cheat 🔑 /tʃiːt/ *verb* (**cheats**, **cheating**, **cheated**) to do something that is not honest or fair: *She cheated in the exam – she copied her friend's work.* ▶ **cheat** *noun* a person who cheats

check[1] 🔑 /tʃek/ *verb* (**checks**, **checking**, **checked** /tʃekt/) to look at something to see that it is right, good, safe, etc: *When I checked the address I realized that I was in the wrong street.* ◇ *Check that all the windows are closed before you leave.* **check in** to tell the person at the desk in a hotel or an airport that you have arrived: *I have to check in an hour before my flight.* **check out** to pay your bill at a hotel and leave

check² 🔑 /tʃek/ *noun* **1** a look to see that everything is right, good, safe, etc: *Have a quick check to see that you haven't forgotten anything.* **2** a pattern of squares: *Do you prefer checks or stripes?*

checked /tʃekt/ *adjective* with a pattern of squares: *He wore a checked shirt.*

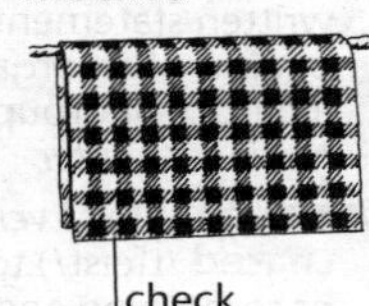

checkout /ˈtʃekaʊt/ *noun* one of the places in a large shop where you pay for the things you are buying: *supermarket checkouts*

check-up /ˈtʃek ʌp/ *noun* an examination by a doctor to see if you are well

cheek 🔑 /tʃiːk/ *noun* **1** (*plural* **cheeks**) one of the two round parts of your face under your eyes: *Tears rolled down her cheeks.* ➲ picture on page A13 **2** (no plural) doing something without caring that it will make other people angry or unhappy: *What a cheek! Someone has taken my seat!*

cheeky /ˈtʃiːki/ *adjective* (**cheekier, cheekiest**) not polite: *Don't be so cheeky!* ◇ *You must not be cheeky to a teacher.*

cheer¹ /tʃɪə(r)/ *verb* (**cheers, cheering, cheered** /tʃɪəd/) to shout to show that you are pleased: *The crowd cheered loudly when the President arrived.*

cheer up to make someone happier; to become happier: *We gave Achal some flowers to cheer her up.* ◇ *Cheer up! You will feel better soon.*

cheer² /tʃɪə(r)/ *noun* a shout that shows that you are pleased: *The crowd gave a cheer as the singer came onto the stage.*

three cheers for … Hip, hip, hooray! words that you shout when someone has done something good: *Three cheers for the winner! Hip, hip, hooray!*

cheerful /ˈtʃɪəfl/ *adjective* happy: *a cheerful smile* ◇ *You don't look very cheerful today. What's the matter?*

cheers /tʃɪəz/ *exclamation* a word that you say to someone when you have a drink together: *'Cheers!' she said, raising her glass.*

> ❖ **SPEAKING**
>
> People sometimes say **cheers** instead of **thank you** or **goodbye**.

cheese 🔑 /tʃiːz/ *noun* (no plural) yellow or white food made from milk: *bread and cheese*

cheetah

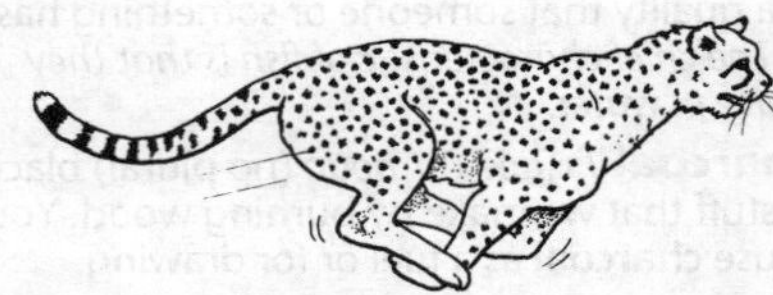

cheetah /ˈtʃiːtə/ *noun* a wild animal like a big cat with black spots. **Cheetahs** can run very fast.

chef /ʃef/ *noun* a professional cook, especially the head cook in a restaurant or hotel

chemical¹ 🔑 /ˈkemɪkl/ *adjective* of chemistry or used in chemistry: *a chemical experiment*

chemical² 🔑 /ˈkemɪkl/ *noun*

> ❖ **PRONUNCIATION**
>
> **ch** at the beginning of this word sounds just like **k**.

a solid or liquid substance that is used or produced in a chemical process: *Chemicals can harm the environment.*

chemist /ˈkemɪst/ *noun*

> ❖ **PRONUNCIATION**
>
> **ch** at the beginning of this word sounds just like **k**.

1 (also **pharmacist**) a person who makes and sells medicines: *The chemist told me to take all the tablets.*

> ❖ **WORD BUILDING**
>
> The shop where a chemist works is called a **chemist's** or a **pharmacy**. It sells things like **soap** and **perfume** as well as **medicines**.

2 a person who studies chemistry or who makes chemicals

chemistry 🔑 /ˈkemɪstri/ *noun* (no plural)

> ❖ **PRONUNCIATION**
>
> **ch** at the beginning of this word sounds just like **k**.

the science that studies gases, liquids and solids to find out what they are and what they do: *My favourite subjects are chemistry and biology.*

cheque 🔑 /tʃek/ *noun*

> ❖ **PRONUNCIATION**
>
> **Cheque** sounds the same as **check**.

a piece of paper from a bank that you can write on and use to pay for things: *I gave him a cheque for 5 000 shillings.* ◇ *Can I pay by cheque?*

chequebook /ˈtʃekbʊk/ *noun* a book of cheques

cherry /ˈtʃeri/ *noun* (*plural* **cherries**) a small round red or black fruit

cherry

chess /tʃes/ *noun* (no plural) a game that two people play with pieces called **chessmen** on a board that has black and white squares on it (called a **chessboard**)

chest 🔑 /tʃest/ *noun* **1** the top part of the front part of your body: *She hugged the baby to her chest.* ➲ picture on page A13 **2** a large strong box with a lid: *We packed all our books into a chest.*

chest

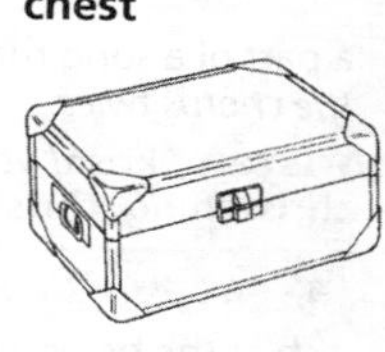

chest of drawers /ˌtʃest əv ˈdrɔːz/ *noun* (*plural* **chests of drawers**) a piece of furniture like a box with parts that you can pull out (**drawers**). A **chest of drawers** is usually used for keeping clothes in.

chew /tʃuː/ *verb* (**chews**, **chewing**, **chewed** /tʃuːd/) to use your teeth to make food soft: *You should chew your food thoroughly.*

chewing gum /ˈtʃuːɪŋ ɡʌm/ *noun* (no plural) sweet stuff that you can chew for a long time

chick /tʃɪk/ *noun* a young bird, especially a young chicken: *The hen had ten chicks.*

chickens

chicken 🔑 /ˈtʃɪkɪn/ *noun* **1** (*plural* **chickens**) a bird that people keep on farms for its eggs and meat: *Chickens were running around the yard.*

❖ **WORD BUILDING**

A female chicken is called a **hen** and a male chicken is called a **cock**. A young chicken is a **chick**.

2 (no plural) meat from a chicken: *roast chicken*

chickenpox /ˈtʃɪkɪnpɒks/ *noun* (no plural) an illness, especially of children. When you have **chickenpox** you feel very hot and get red spots on your skin that make you want to scratch.

chief[1] 🔑 /tʃiːf/ *adjective* most important: *The lion is the zebra's chief enemy.*

chief[2] 🔑 /tʃiːf/ *noun* the leader or ruler of a group of people: *the chief of a tribe*

the Chief Justice /ˌtʃiːf ˈdʒʌstɪs/ *noun* (no plural) the head of the Judiciary of Kenya

chiefly /ˈtʃiːfli/ *adverb* mostly; mainly: *The rain fell chiefly in the north of the country.*

child 🔑 /tʃaɪld/ *noun* (*plural* **children** /ˈtʃɪldrən/) **1** a boy or girl: *There are 30 children in the class.* **2** a daughter or son: *One of her children got married last year.*

childhood /ˈtʃaɪldhʊd/ *noun* (no plural) the time when you are a child: *She had a happy childhood.*

childish /ˈtʃaɪldɪʃ/ *adjective* like a child: *Don't be so childish! It's only a game.*

chill[1] /tʃɪl/ *verb* (**chills**, **chilling**, **chilled** /tʃɪld/) **1** to make something very cold: *Chill the lemonade in the fridge for an hour before serving.* **2** (also **chill out**) to relax and not feel angry or nervous: *I study all week so on Sundays I just chill out.*

chill[2] /tʃɪl/ *noun* (no plural) an unpleasant cold feeling: *There's a chill in the air.* ◇ *A chill of fear went down my spine.*

chilli /ˈtʃɪli/ *noun* (*plural* **chillies**) a small red vegetable that tastes very hot. We often use it dried or as powder.

chilly /ˈtʃɪli/ *adjective* (**chillier**, **chilliest**) cold: *a chilly night*

chime /tʃaɪm/ *verb* (**chimes**, **chiming**, **chimed** /tʃaɪmd/) to make the sound that a bell makes: *The clock chimed midnight.*

chimney /ˈtʃɪmni/ *noun* (*plural* **chimneys**) a large pipe over a fire that lets smoke go outside into the air

chimpanzee /ˌtʃɪmpænˈziː/ *noun* an animal like a **monkey** with dark hair and no tail

chimpanzee

chin 🔑 /tʃɪn/ *noun* the part of your face below your mouth: *She rested her chin on her hands.* ➲ picture on page A13

china /ˈtʃaɪnə/ *noun* (no plural) a hard white material made from earth, or things like plates and cups that are made from this: *a china cup*

chip[1] /tʃɪp/ *noun* **1** a small piece of wood, stone or other material that has broken off a larger piece **2** a piece of potato cooked in oil: *We had chicken and chips for lunch.* **3** = **microchip**

chip[2] /tʃɪp/ *verb* (**chips, chipping, chipped** /tʃɪpt/) to break a small piece from something: *I chipped a cup.*

chirp /tʃɜːp/ *noun* the short high sound that a small bird makes ▶ **chirp** *verb* (**chirps, chirping, chirped** /tʃɜːpt/) to make this sound

chocolate 🔑 /ˈtʃɒklət/ *noun* **1** (no plural) dark brown sweet food that is made from **cocoa** (= a powder made from seeds): *Do you like chocolate?* **2** (*plural* **chocolates**) a sweet made of chocolate: *She gave her mother a box of chocolates.*

choice 🔑 /tʃɔɪs/ *noun* **1** (*plural* **choices**) deciding which one: *You made the right choice.* **2** (no plural) the chance to choose: *We have no choice. We must go immediately.* **3** (no plural) the number of things that you can choose from: *There is a big choice of vegetables in the market.*

choir /ˈkwaɪə(r)/ *noun*

> ❖ **PRONUNCIATION**
>
> **ch** at the beginning of this word sounds just like **k**.

a big group of people who sing together: *a school choir* ◇ *the church choir*

choke /tʃəʊk/ *verb* (**chokes, choking, choked** /tʃəʊkt/) to not be able to breathe because something is in your throat: *He was choking on a fish bone.*

cholera /ˈkɒlərə/ *noun* (no plural)

> ❖ **PRONUNCIATION**
>
> **ch** at the beginning of this word sounds just like **k**.

a dangerous illness that gives you stomach pains and makes you **vomit** (= bring food up through your mouth). You can get it from dirty food and water: *an outbreak of cholera*

choose 🔑 /tʃuːz/ *verb* (**chooses, choosing, chose** /tʃəʊz/, **has chosen** /ˈtʃəʊzn/) to take the thing or person that you like best: *Robi chose a yellow and blue dress.* ❶ The noun is **choice**.

chop[1] /tʃɒp/ *verb* (**chops, chopping, chopped** /tʃɒpt/) to cut something with a knife or an axe: *We chopped some wood.* ◇ *Chop the meat up into small pieces.*

chop[2] /tʃɒp/ *noun* a thick slice of meat with a piece of bone in it: *a mutton chop*

chore /tʃɔː(r)/ *noun* a job that you must do: *On Saturdays I help Mum with the washing and other chores.*

chorus /ˈkɔːrəs/ *noun* (*plural* **choruses**)

> ❖ **PRONUNCIATION**
>
> **ch** at the beginning of this word sounds just like **k**.

a part of a song that you repeat: *We sang the chorus twice.*

christen /ˈkrɪsn/ *verb* (**christens, christening, christened** /ˈkrɪsnd/)

> ❖ **PRONUNCIATION**
>
> **ch** at the beginning of this word sounds just like **k**.

to give a first name to a baby and make them a member of the Christian church in a special ceremony: *The baby was christened Ereng.*

christening /ˈkrɪsnɪŋ/ *noun* the ceremony when a baby is christened

Christian /ˈkrɪstʃən/ *noun*

> ❖ **PRONUNCIATION**
>
> **ch** at the beginning of this word sounds just like **k**.

a person who believes in Jesus Christ and what he taught ▶ **Christian** *adjective*: *the Christian church*

Christianity /ˌkrɪstiˈænəti/ *noun* (no plural) the religion that follows what Jesus Christ taught

Christmas /ˈkrɪsməs/ (*plural* **Christmases**) (also **Xmas**) *noun*

> ❖ **PRONUNCIATION**
>
> **ch** at the beginning of this word sounds just like **k**.

the special time when Christians remember the birth of Christ: *Merry Christmas!* ➲ Look at **Xmas**.

church 🔑 /tʃɜːtʃ/ *noun* (*plural* **churches**) a building where Christians go to sing and to speak to God (to **pray**): *They go to church every Sunday.*

churchyard /ˈtʃɜːtʃjɑːd/ *noun* a piece of land around a church

cigar /sɪˈɡɑː(r)/ *noun* a roll of dried leaves (called **tobacco**) that some people smoke. **Cigars** are larger than cigarettes.

cigarette 🔑 /ˌsɪɡəˈret/ *noun* a thin tube of white paper filled with dried leaves (called **tobacco**) that some people smoke: *Cigarettes are harmful to your health.*

cinema 🔑 /ˈsɪnəmə/ *noun* a place where you go to see a film: *Let's go to the cinema.*

circle 🔑 /ˈsɜːkl/ *noun* a round shape: *There are 360 degrees in a circle.* ➲ picture on page A12

circle graph /ˈsɜːkl ɡrɑːf/ = **pie chart**

circular /ˈsɜːkjələ(r)/ *adjective* with the shape of a circle; round: *A wheel is circular.*

circulate /ˈsɜːkjəleɪt/ *verb* (**circulates, circulating, circulated**) to move round: *Blood circulates in our bodies.*

circumference /səˈkʌmfərəns/ *noun* the distance around a circle ➲ picture on page A12

circumstances /ˈsɜːkəmstənsɪz/ *noun* (plural) the facts that are true when something happens
in or **under the circumstances** because things are as they are: *My father was ill, so under the circumstances I decided to stay at home.*
under no circumstances not at all; never: *Under no circumstances should you go out alone at night.*

circumstantial /ˌsɜːkəmˈstænʃl/ *adjective* (in law) containing information that suggests that something is true but does not prove it: *The case was based largely on circumstantial evidence.*

circus /ˈsɜːkəs/ *noun* (*plural* **circuses**) a show in a big tent, with a performance by a group of people and trained animals

citizen /ˈsɪtɪzn/ *noun* a person who belongs to a country or a town: *a Kenyan citizen*

citizenship /ˈsɪtɪzənʃɪp/ *noun* (no plural) when you are a member of a particular country: *I hold Kenyan citizenship.*

city 🔑 /ˈsɪti/ *noun* (*plural* **cities**) a big and important town: *The museum is in the city centre.* ◇ *the city of Kampala* ➲ Note at **town**.

civil /ˈsɪvl/ *adjective* connected with the people of a country: *civil rights*

civilian /səˈvɪliən/ *noun* a person who is not a soldier: *Two soldiers and one civilian were hurt in the blast.*

civilization /ˌsɪvəlaɪˈzeɪʃn/ *noun* the way people live together in a certain place at a certain time: *ancient civilizations*

the civil service /ðə ˌsɪvl ˈsɜːvɪs/ *noun* (no plural) the people who work for the government

civil war /ˌsɪvl ˈwɔː(r)/ *noun* a war between groups of people in one country

cl *short for* CENTILITRE

claim[1] /kleɪm/ *verb* (**claims, claiming, claimed** /kleɪmd/) **1** to ask for something because it is yours: *If nobody claims the camera you found, you can keep it.* **2** to say that something is true: *Kamau claims that he did the work without help.*

claim[2] /kleɪm/ *noun* **1** saying that something is true: *Nobody believed his claim that he had found the money on the street.* **2** something you ask for because you think you have a right to it: *The workers are making a claim for better pay.*

clan /klæn/ *noun* a group of people who all have the same **ancestors** (= the people in your family who lived a long time before you): *He became clan chief after his father's death.*

clang /klæŋ/ *noun* the loud sound that metal makes when you hit it with something: *The gates shut with a clang.*

clap /klæp/ *verb* (**claps, clapping, clapped** /klæpt/) to hit your hands together to make a noise, usually to show that you like something: *At the end of the concert the audience clapped loudly.* ► **clap** *noun* the sound that you make when you hit your hands together: *Let's have a big clap for the performers!*

clash /klæʃ/ *verb* (**clashes, clashing, clashed** /klæʃt/) **1** to fight or argue: *Police clashed with football fans outside the stadium last Saturday.* **2** to be at the same time: *The match clashed with my swimming lesson, so I couldn't watch it.* **3** If colours **clash**, they do not look nice together: *Your tie clashes with your shirt!*

class 🔑 /klɑːs/ *noun* (*plural* **classes**) **1** a group of children or students who learn together: *The whole class passed the exam.* ◇ *There is a new girl in my class.* **2** the time when you learn something with a teacher: *Classes begin at nine o'clock.* ◇ *You mustn't eat in class.* **3** a group of people or things that are the same in some way: *There are* *many different classes of animals.* **4** how good, comfortable, etc. something is: *It costs more to travel first class.*

classic /ˈklæsɪk/ *noun* a book that is so good that people read it for many years after it was written

classical /ˈklæsɪkl/ *adjective* **1** in a style that people have used for a long time because they think it is good: *classical music* **2** connected with ancient Greece or Rome: *classical Greek architecture*

classmate /ˈklɑːsmeɪt/ *noun* a person who is in the same class as you at school or college

classroom /ˈklɑːsruːm/ *noun* a room where you have lessons in a school

clatter /ˈklætə(r)/ *noun* (no plural) a loud noise that hard things make when they hit each other: *the clatter of dishes*

clause /klɔːz/ *noun* a part of a sentence that has a verb in it: *The sentence 'After we had finished eating, we went out.' contains two clauses.*

claw /klɔː/ *noun* one of the hard pointed parts on the feet of some animals and birds: *Cats have sharp claws.* ➲ Picture at **bird**, **cat**, **crab**.

clay /kleɪ/ *noun* (no plural) a kind of heavy earth that becomes hard when it is dry: *clay pots and tiles*

clean¹ 🔑 /kliːn/ *adjective* (**cleaner**, **cleanest**) not dirty: *clean clothes* ◇ *Are your hands clean?*

clean² 🔑 /kliːn/ *verb* (**cleans**, **cleaning**, **cleaned** /kliːnd/) to take away the dirt or marks from something; to make something clean: *Deng helped his mother to clean the kitchen.* ◇ *Don't forget to clean your teeth before you go to bed.* ▸ **clean** *noun* (no plural): *The car needs a clean.*

cleanliness /ˈklenlinəs/ *noun* (no plural) being clean; keeping things clean

clear¹ 🔑 /klɪə(r)/ *adjective* (**clearer**, **clearest**) **1** easy to see, hear or understand: *She spoke in a loud clear voice.* ◇ *This photograph is very clear.* ◇ *It's clear that Egesa is not happy.* **2** that you can see through: *clear glass* **3** with nothing in the way; empty: *The roads were very clear.* **4** bright; without clouds: *a clear day* ◇ *a clear sky*

clear² 🔑 /klɪə(r)/ *verb* (**clears**, **clearing**, **cleared** /klɪəd/) **1** to take things away from a place because you do not need them there: *They cleared the rocks from the path.* ◇ *When you have finished your meal, clear the table.* **2** to become clear: *It rained in the morning, but in the afternoon the sky cleared.*

clear off to go away: *He got angry and told them to clear off.*

clear out to take everything out of a cupboard, room, etc. so that you can clean it and make it tidy

clear up to make a place clean and tidy: *She helped me to clear up after the meal.*

clearance /ˈklɪərəns/ *noun* (no plural) official permission for someone to do something: *The pilot was waiting for clearance to leave the airport.*

clearing /ˈklɪərɪŋ/ *noun* a small area without trees in the middle of a forest: *We camped in a clearing in the forest.*

clearly 🔑 /ˈklɪəli/ *adverb* **1** in a way that is easy to see, hear or understand: *Please speak louder – I can't hear you very clearly.* ◇ *The notes explain very clearly what you have to do.* **2** without any doubt: *She is clearly very intelligent.*

clerk /klɑːk/ *noun* a person in an office or bank whose job is to do written work or to look after accounts

clever 🔑 /ˈklevə(r)/ *adjective* (**cleverer**, **cleverest**) able to learn, understand or do something quickly and well: *She's a clever pupil.* ▸ **cleverly** *adverb*: *The book is cleverly written.*

click¹ /klɪk/ *noun* **1** a short sharp sound: *I heard a click as someone switched the light on.* **2** pressing a button on a computer mouse: *You can do this with a click of the mouse.*

click² /klɪk/ *verb* (**clicks**, **clicking**, **clicked** /klɪkt/) **1** to make a short sharp sound: *The door clicked shut.* **2** to press a button on a computer mouse: *To open a file, click on the menu.* ◇ *Click the OK button to start.*

client /ˈklaɪənt/ *noun* a person who pays another person, for example a lawyer, for help or advice

cliff

cliff /klɪf/ *noun* the high steep side of a hill by the sea

climate 🔑 /ˈklaɪmət/ *noun* the sort of weather that a place has: *Coffee will not grow in a cold climate.*

climate change /ˈklaɪmət tʃeɪndʒ/ *noun* (no plural) changes in the earth's weather, especially the increase in temperature that is caused by the increase of certain gases in the atmosphere

climb 🔑 /klaɪm/ *verb* (**climbs**, **climbing**, **climbed** /klaɪmd/)

> ❖ **PRONUNCIATION**
>
> **Climb** sounds like **time** because we do not say the 'b'.

1 to go up or down, walking or using your hands and feet: *The cat climbed to the top of the tree.* ◇ *They climbed the mountain.* **2** to move to or from a place when it is not easy to do it: *The children climbed through a hole in the fence.* **3** to move to a higher place: *The road climbs steeply.* ► **climb** *noun*: *It was a long climb from the village to the top of the mountain.*

climber /ˈklaɪmə(r)/ *noun* a person who goes up and down mountains or rocks as a sport: *a rock climber*

cling /klɪŋ/ *verb* (**clings**, **clinging**, **clung** /klʌŋ/, **has clung**) to hold or stick tightly to someone or something: *The child cried and clung to her mother.* ◇ *His wet clothes clung to his body.*

clinic /ˈklɪnɪk/ *noun* a place where you can go to get special help from a doctor

clip[1] /klɪp/ *noun* a small piece of metal or plastic for holding things together: *a paper clip*

clip[2] /klɪp/ *verb* (**clips**, **clipping**, **clipped** /klɪpt/) to join something to another thing with a clip: *I clipped the photo to the letter.*

clip art /ˈklɪp ɑːt/ *noun* (no plural) pictures that are stored in computer programs or on websites for you to copy and add to your own documents

cloak /kləʊk/ *noun* a very loose coat that has no sleeves

cloak

cloakroom /ˈkləʊkruːm/ *noun* **1** a place in a building where you can leave your coat or bag **2** a toilet in a public building

clock

watch

clock 🔑 /klɒk/ *noun* a thing that shows you what time it is. It stands in a room or hangs on a wall: *an alarm clock by my bed*

> ❖ **WORD BUILDING**
>
> A thing that shows the time and that you wear on your wrist is called a **watch**.
>
> You say that a clock or watch is **fast** if it shows a time that is later than the real time. You say that it is **slow** if it shows a time that is earlier than the real time.

clockwise /ˈklɒkwaɪz/ *adjective, adverb* in the direction that the hands of a clock move: *Turn the handle clockwise.* OPPOSITE **anticlockwise**

clone /kləʊn/ *noun* an exact copy of a plant or animal that is produced from one of its cells by scientific methods ► **clone** *verb* (**clones**, **cloning**, **cloned** /kləʊnd/): *A team from the UK were the first to clone an animal successfully.*

close[1] 🔑 /kləʊs/ *adjective, adverb* (**closer**, **closest**)

> ❖ **PRONUNCIATION**
>
> **Close** (adjective and adverb) ends with an 's' sound like **dose**.

1 near: *We live close to the river.* ◇ *You're too close to the fire.* **2** If people are close, they like or love each other very much: *I'm very close to my sister.* ◇ *Kamal and I are close friends.* **3** with only a very small difference: *'Did Katee win the race?' 'No, but it was very close.'* **4** careful: *Keep a close watch on the children.*
close together with not much space between them: *Stand closer together.*

close[2] 🔑 /kləʊz/ *verb* (**closes**, **closing**, **closed** /kləʊzd/)

> ❖ **PRONUNCIATION**
>
> **Close** (verb) ends with a 'z' sound like **nose** or **doze**.

1 to shut: *Please close the window.* ◇ *Close your eyes!* ◇ *The door closed quietly.*

2 to stop being open, so that people cannot go there: *The banks close at 2 p.m.* OPPOSITE **open**
close down to shut and stop working; to make something shut and stop working: *The shop closed down when the owner died.*

closed /kləʊzd/ *adjective* not open; shut: *The shops are closed on Sundays.*

closely /kləʊsli/ *adverb* in a close way: *We watched her closely.*

cloth /klɒθ/ *noun* **1** (no plural) material that is made of wool, cotton, etc. and that we use for making clothes and other things: *The skirt is made of thick woollen cloth.* ℹ **Material** is the word that we usually use. **2** (*plural* **cloths**) a piece of cloth that you use for a special job: *a tablecloth* (= for covering a table) ◇ *Wipe the floor with a cloth.*

clothes /kləʊðz/ *noun* (plural) things like trousers, shirts and coats that you wear to cover your body: *She was wearing new clothes.* ◇ *Take off those wet clothes.*

clothes line /ˈkləʊðz laɪn/ *noun* a thin rope that you hang clothes on so that they can dry

clothing /ˈkləʊðɪŋ/ *noun* (no plural) clothes: *They sell skirts, trousers and other items of clothing.*

cloud /klaʊd/ *noun* **1** a white or grey shape in the sky that is made of small drops of water: *Look at those dark clouds. It's going to rain.* **2** dust or smoke that looks like a cloud: *Clouds of smoke filled the sky.*

cloudy /ˈklaʊdi/ *adjective* (**cloudier**, **cloudiest**) with a lot of clouds: *a cloudy sky* ◇ *It's a cloudy day.*

clove /kləʊv/ *noun* the dried **bud** (= young flower) of a kind of tree. **Cloves** have a strong taste and we use them in cooking.

clown /klaʊn/ *noun* a person who wears funny clothes and a big red nose and makes people laugh

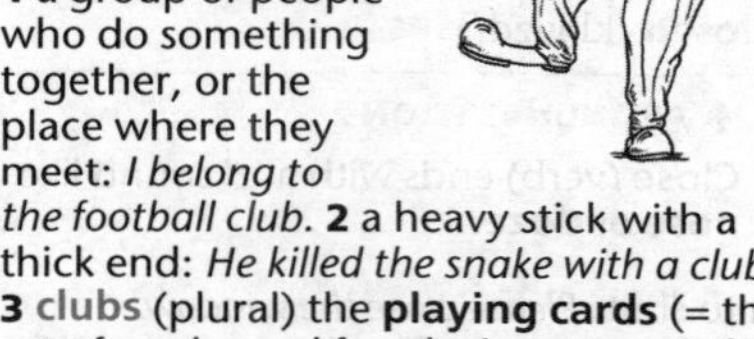
clown

club¹ /klʌb/ *noun* **1** a group of people who do something together, or the place where they meet: *I belong to the football club.* **2** a heavy stick with a thick end: *He killed the snake with a club.* **3** **clubs** (plural) the **playing cards** (= the set of cards used for playing games) that have the shape ♣ on them: *the three of clubs*

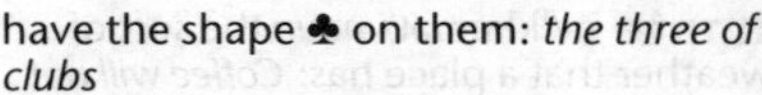

club² /klʌb/ *verb* (**clubs**, **clubbing**, **clubbed** /klʌbd/)
club together to give money so that a group of people can buy something: *We all clubbed together to buy Awino and Mwita a wedding present.*

clue /kluː/ *noun* something that helps to find the answer to a problem, or to know the truth: *The police have found a clue that may help them to catch the murderer.*
not have a clue to know nothing about something: *'What's his name?' 'I haven't a clue.'*

clumsy /ˈklʌmzi/ *adjective* (**clumsier**, **clumsiest**) If you are **clumsy**, you often drop things or do things badly because you do not move in an easy or careful way: *I'm so clumsy! I've just broken a glass.* ▶ **clumsily** /ˈklʌmzəli/ *adverb*: *He clumsily knocked the cup off the table.*

clung *form of* CLING

clutch /klʌtʃ/ *verb* (**clutches**, **clutching**, **clutched** /klʌtʃt/) to hold something tightly: *The child clutched my hand.*

cm *short for* CENTIMETRE

Co. /kəʊ/ *short for* COMPANY

c/o /ˌsiː ˈəʊ/ You use **c/o** (short for 'care of') when you are writing to someone who is staying at another person's house: *Miss Kendi Gombe, c/o Mrs Boke Malaba*

coach¹ /kəʊtʃ/ *noun* (*plural* **coaches**) **1** a person who teaches a sport: *a football coach* **2** a bus for taking people on long journeys **3** one of the parts of a train where people sit

coach² /kəʊtʃ/ *verb* (**coaches**, **coaching**, **coached** /kəʊtʃt/) to teach someone: *She is coaching the Kenyan team for the Olympics.*

coal /kəʊl/ *noun* (no plural) hard black stuff that comes from under the ground and gives heat when you burn it: *Put some more coal on the fire.*

coarse /kɔːs/ *adjective* (**coarser**, **coarsest**) made of thick pieces so that it is not smooth: *coarse sand* ◇ *coarse material* OPPOSITE **fine**

coast /kəʊst/ *noun* the part of the land that is next to the sea: *Their village is near the coast.* ◇ *Zanzibar is off the east coast of Africa.* ▶ **coastal** /ˈkəʊstl/ *adjective*: *There was heavy rain in the coastal areas.*

coastguard /ˈkəʊstɡɑːd/ *noun* a person

whose job is to watch the sea and ships and help people who are in danger

coastline /ˈkəʊstlaɪn/ *noun* the edge of the land next to the sea: *a rocky coastline*

coat[1] 🔑 /kəʊt/ *noun* **1** a piece of clothing that you wear over your other clothes when you go outside in cold weather or rain: *Put your coat on – it's cold today.* **2** the hair or fur that covers an animal: *A zebra has a striped coat.*

coat[2] /kəʊt/ *verb* (**coats, coating, coated**) to put a thin covering of something over another thing: *Their shoes were coated with mud.*

coat hanger /ˈkəʊt hæŋə(r)/ (also **hanger**) *noun* a piece of wood, metal or plastic with a hook, for hanging clothes on

coat hanger

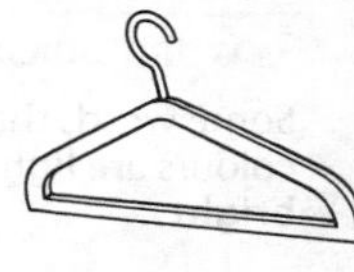

cobra /ˈkəʊbrə/ *noun* a dangerous snake that can make its neck big

cobra

cobweb /ˈkɒbweb/ *noun* a net that a spider makes to catch insects

cocaine /kəʊˈkeɪn/ *noun* (no plural) a very strong drug that can be dangerous

cock /kɒk/ *noun* **1** a male bird **2** a male chicken ➲ Picture at **chicken**.

cockpit /ˈkɒkpɪt/ *noun* the part of a plane where the pilot sits

cockroach /ˈkɒkrəʊtʃ/ *noun* (*plural* **cockroaches**) a large, brown insect that often lives inside buildings

cocoa /ˈkəʊkəʊ/ *noun* (no plural) **1** a brown powder from the seeds (called **cocoa beans**) of a tree, that is used to make chocolate **2** a drink made from this powder: *Would you like a cup of cocoa?*

coconut /ˈkəʊkənʌt/ *noun* a very large brown nut that grows on trees. **Coconuts** are brown and hard on the outside, and they have sweet white food and liquid inside.

coconut

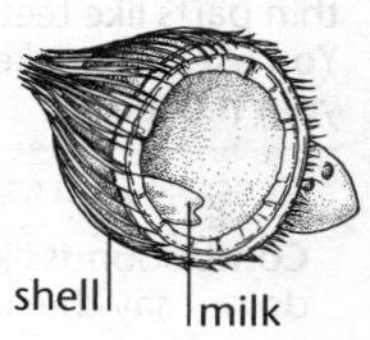

cocoon /kəˈkuːn/ *noun* a covering of silk threads that some insects make to protect themselves while they change into adults: *Caterpillars spin cocoons before they change into butterflies or moths.*

cod /kɒd/ *noun* (*plural* **cod**) a fish that lives in the sea and that you can eat

code /kəʊd/ *noun* **1** a way of writing secret messages, using letters, numbers or special signs: *The list of names was written in code.* **2** a group of numbers or letters that helps you find something: *What's the code* (= the telephone number) *for Goma?* **3** a set of rules for a group of people: *the Highway Code* (= rules for people who are driving on the road) ◇ *a strict code of conduct* (= rules of behaviour)

coffee 🔑 /ˈkɒfi/ *noun* **1** (no plural) brown powder made from the seeds (called **coffee beans**) of a tree that grows in hot countries. You use it for making a drink: *He is a coffee farmer.* **2** (no plural) a drink of hot water mixed with this powder: *Would you like coffee or tea?* ◇ *a cup of coffee* **3** (*plural* **coffees**) a cup of this drink: *Two coffees, please.*

> ❖ **WORD BUILDING**
>
> **White** coffee has milk in it and **black** coffee has no milk.

coffee table /ˈkɒfi teɪbl/ *noun* a small low table

coffin /ˈkɒfɪn/ *noun* a box that you put a dead person's body in

coil[1] /kɔɪl/ *noun* a long piece of rope or wire that goes round in circles: *a coil of rope*

coil[2] /kɔɪl/ *verb* (**coils, coiling, coiled** /kɔɪld/) to make something into a lot of circles that are joined together: *The snake coiled itself round a branch.*

coin 🔑 /kɔɪn/ *noun* a round piece of money made of metal: *a pound coin*

coincidence /kəʊˈɪnsɪdəns/ *noun* when things happen at the same time or in the same place by chance: *What a coincidence! I was thinking about you when you phoned!*

cola /ˈkəʊlə/ *noun* **1** (no plural) a sweet brown drink with bubbles in it **2** (*plural* **colas**) a glass, bottle or can of **cola**

cold[1] 🔑 /kəʊld/ *adjective* (**colder, coldest**) **1** not hot or warm; with a low temperature. Ice and snow are cold: *Put your coat on – it's cold outside.* ◇ *I'm cold. Will you put the radiator on?* ◇ *hot and cold water* **2** not friendly or kind: *a cold person* ➲ Look at **warm**[1]. ▸ **coldly** *adverb* in an unfriendly way: *She looked at me coldly.*

cold² /kəʊld/ *noun* **1** (no plural) cold weather: *Don't go out in the cold.* OPPOSITE **heat** **2** (*plural* **colds**) a common illness when your throat hurts and you often cannot breathe through your nose: *I've got a cold.*
catch a cold to become ill with a cold: *Come in out of the rain, or you'll catch a cold.*

collapse /kəˈlæps/ *verb* (**collapses, collapsing, collapsed** /kəˈlæpst/) to fall down suddenly: *The building collapsed in the earthquake.* ◇ *She collapsed in the street and she was taken to hospital.* ▶ **collapse** *noun*: *the collapse of the bridge*

collar /ˈkɒlə(r)/ *noun* **1** the part of your clothes that goes round your neck: *The collar of his shirt was dirty.* **2** a band that you put round the neck of a dog or cat: *Put a collar and lead on your dog.*

collar

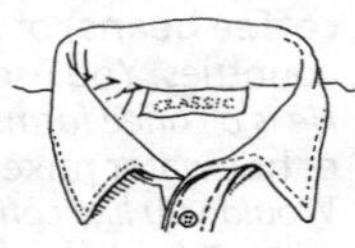

colleague /ˈkɒliːg/ *noun* a person who works with you: *Mr Odoi is a colleague of my father's.*

collect /kəˈlekt/ *verb* (**collect, collecting, collected**) **1** to take things from different people or places and put them together: *The waiter collected the dirty glasses.* **2** to bring together things that are the same in some way, to study or enjoy them: *My friend collects stamps.* **3** to go and bring someone or something from a place: *She went to collect the parcel from the post office.*

collection /kəˈlekʃn/ *noun* a group of things that someone has brought together: *The museum has a large collection of carvings.* ◇ *a stamp collection*

collector /kəˈlektə(r)/ *noun* a person who collects things as a hobby or as a job: *a stamp collector* ◇ *a ticket collector at a railway station*

college /ˈkɒlɪdʒ/ *noun* a place where people go to study more difficult subjects after they have left school: *She's going to college next year.* ◇ *My brother is at college.*

collide /kəˈlaɪd/ *verb* (**collides, colliding, collided**) to move towards each other and hit each other: *The two trucks collided.* ◇ *The pickup collided with a bus.* SAME MEANING **crash**

collision /kəˈlɪʒn/ *noun* when things or people **collide**: *The driver of the car was killed in the collision.* SAME MEANING **crash**

colon /ˈkəʊlən/ *noun* a mark (:) that you use in writing, for example before a list ➲ Look at page A17.

colonel /ˈkɜːnl/ *noun* an officer in the army

colony /ˈkɒləni/ *noun* (*plural* **colonies**) a country that is ruled by another country: *Kenya was once a British colony.*

colour¹ /ˈkʌlə(r)/ *noun* Red, blue, yellow and green are all colours: *'What colour are your new shoes?' 'Black.'*
off colour not well; ill: *She was feeling off colour yesterday and stayed at home.*

> ❖ **WORD BUILDING**
>
> Some words that we use to talk about colours are **light, pale, dark, deep** and **bright**.

colour² /ˈkʌlə(r)/ *verb* (**colours, colouring, coloured** /ˈkʌləd/) to put colours on something: *The children coloured their pictures with crayons.*

> ❖ **WORD FAMILY**
>
> **colour** *noun*, **colour** *verb*
> **coloured** **colourful**

coloured /ˈkʌləd/ *adjective* with a colour: *She was wearing a brightly coloured sweater.* ◇ *coloured paper*

colourful /ˈkʌləfl/ *adjective* with a lot of bright colours: *a colourful dress*

column /ˈkɒləm/ *noun* **1** a tall piece of stone that is part of a building: *There were columns on either side of the door.* **2** a long thin piece of writing on one side or part of a page: *Each page of this dictionary has two columns.*

comb¹ /kəʊm/ *noun* a flat piece of metal or plastic with a line of thin parts like teeth. You use it to make your hair tidy.

combs

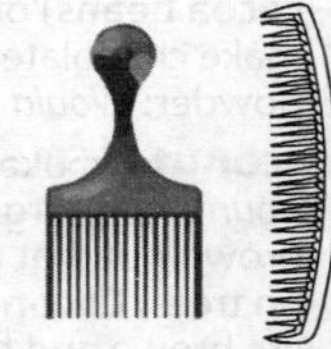

> ❖ **PRONUNCIATION**
>
> **Comb** sounds like **home** because we do not say the 'b'.

comb² /kəʊm/ *verb* (**combs, combing, combed** /kəʊmd/) to make your hair tidy with a **comb**: *Have you combed your hair?*

combination 🔑 /ˌkɒmbɪˈneɪʃn/ *noun* two or more things mixed together: *The building is a combination of new and old styles.*

combine 🔑 /kəmˈbaɪn/ *verb* (**combined, combining, combined** /kəmˈbaɪnd/) to join or mix together: *The two schools combined and moved to a larger building.* ◇ *Combine the eggs and flour in a bowl.*

come 🔑 /kʌm/ *verb* (**comes, coming, came** /keɪm/, **has come**) **1** to move towards the person who is speaking or the place that you are talking about: *Come here, please.* ◇ *The dog came when I called him.* ◇ *I'm sorry, but I can't come to the match.* **2** to arrive: *If you go along that road, you will come to the river.* ◇ *A letter came for you this morning.* **3** to be or happen: *June comes after May.* **4** to go with the person who is speaking: *I'm going to the cinema. Do you want to come?*

how come ...? why or how.?: *How come you're here so early?*

to come in the future: *I'll be very busy in the months to come.*

come across something to find something when you are not looking for it: *I came across these old photos.*

come apart to break into pieces: *These old shoes are coming apart.*

come back to return: *I'm going to out now and I'm coming back this evening.*

come down to fall or become lower: *The price of oil is coming down.*

come from something or **somewhere** **1** to be made from something: *Wool comes from sheep.* **2** The place that you come from is where you were born or where you live: *I come from Mombasa.* ◇ *Where do you come from?*

come in to enter a place: *Come in and sit down.*

come off something to be removed from something: *The handle has come off my new cup.*

come on! or **come along!** words that you use for telling someone to hurry or to try harder: *Come on! We'll be late!*

come out to appear: *The rain stopped and the sun came out.* ◇ *This book came out in 2016.*

come up with something to find an answer: *Have you come up with a good plan yet?*

comedian /kəˈmiːdiən/ *noun* a person whose job is to make people laugh

comedy /ˈkɒmədi/ *noun* (*plural* **comedies**) a funny play or film

comet /ˈkɒmɪt/ *noun* an object in space that moves around the sun and looks like a bright star with a tail

comfort[1] /ˈkʌmfət/ *noun* **1** (no plural) having everything your body needs; being without pain or problems: *They have enough money to live in comfort.* **2** (*plural* **comforts**) a person or thing that helps you or makes life better: *Her children were a comfort to her when she was ill.*

> ❖ **WORD FAMILY**
>
> **comfort** *noun*, **comfort** *verb*
> **comfortable**: OPPOSITE **uncomfortable**

comfort[2] /ˈkʌmfət/ *verb* (**comforts, comforting, comforted**) to make someone feel less unhappy or worried: *A mother was comforting her crying child.*

comfortable 🔑 /ˈkʌmftəbl/ *adjective* **1** nice to sit in, to be in, or to wear: *This is a very comfortable bed.* ◇ *Wear comfortable shoes.* **2** with no pain or worry: *Sit down and make yourself comfortable.*
▸ **comfortably** /ˈkʌmftəbli/ *adverb*: *He was sitting comfortably in the armchair.*

comic[1] /ˈkɒmɪk/ (also **comical** /ˈkɒmɪkl/) *adjective* funny: *She told a comic story.*

comic[2] /ˈkɒmɪk/ *noun* a magazine for children, with pictures that tell a story

comic strip /ˈkɒmɪk strɪp/ *noun* a short series of pictures that tell a funny story, for example in a newspaper

comma /ˈkɒmə/ *noun* a mark (,) that you use in writing to make a short stop in a sentence ➲ Look at page A17.

command[1] 🔑 /kəˈmɑːnd/ *noun* **1** (*plural* **commands**) words that tell you that you must do something: *The soldiers must obey their general's commands.* **2** (no plural) the power to tell people what to do: *Who is in command of this ship?*

command[2] /kəˈmɑːnd/ *verb* (**commands, commanding, commanded**) to tell someone that they must do something: *He commanded us to leave immediately.*
ℹ **Order** is the word that we usually use.

comment[1] 🔑 /ˈkɒment/ *noun* words that you say about something to show what you think: *She made some interesting comments about the film.*

comment[2] 🔑 /ˈkɒment/ *verb* (**comments, commenting, commented**) to say what you think about something: *She made helpful comments on my work.*

commentary /ˈkɒməntri/ *noun* (*plural* **commentaries**) words that someone says about something that is happening: *We listened to the radio commentary on the football match.*

commentator /ˈkɒmənteɪtə(r)/ *noun* a person who gives a **commentary** on radio or television: *a sports commentator*

commerce /ˈkɒmɜːs/ *noun* (no plural) the work of buying and selling things

commercial[1] /kəˈmɜːʃl/ *adjective* for or about buying and selling things: *a commercial vehicle*

commercial[2] /kəˈmɜːʃl/ *noun* a short film on television or radio that helps to sell something: *a TV commercial*

commissioner /kəˈmɪʃənə(r)/ *noun* an important person who works for the government: *They appointed a new County Commissioner.*

commit /kəˈmɪt/ *verb* (**commits, committing, committed**) to do something bad: *This man has committed a very serious crime.*

committal bundle /kəˈmɪtl bʌndl/ *noun* a collection of documents that someone accused of a crime must take with them to court

committee /kəˈmɪti/ *noun* a group of people that other people choose to plan or organize something: *The members of the club elect a new committee every year.*

> ❖ **SPELLING**
> Remember! You spell **committee** with **mm, tt** and **ee.**

common 🔑 /ˈkɒmən/ *adjective* **1** (**commoner, commonest**) that you often see or that often happens: *Mohammed is a common name in many countries.* OPPOSITE **rare** **2** that everybody in a group does or has: *People in East Africa have Kiswahili as a common language.* ▸ **common** *noun*
have something in common to be like someone in a certain way, or have the same interests as someone: *Kirezi and I are good friends. We have a lot in common.* ◇ *I don't know why they like each other – they've got nothing in common.*

common market /ˌkɒmən ˈmɑːkɪt/ *noun* a group of countries that have agreed to pay lower taxes when they do business with each other: *COMESA is the name for the Common Market for Eastern and Southern Africa.*

common sense /ˌkɒmən ˈsens/ *noun* (no plural) the ability to do the right thing and not make stupid mistakes, because of what you know about the world: *Robi's got no common sense. She left her money on the table and it was stolen.*

communal /kəˈmjuːnl/ *adjective* If something is **communal**, all the members of a group can use it.

communicate 🔑 /kəˈmjuːnɪkeɪt/ *verb* (**communicates, communicating, communicated**) to talk or write to someone: *The pilots communicate with the airport by radio.*

communication 🔑 /kəˌmjuːnɪˈkeɪʃn/ *noun* **1** (no plural) talking or writing to someone: *Communication is difficult when two people don't speak the same language.* **2 communications** (plural) ways of sending information or moving from one place to another: *There are good communications with the islands.*

community 🔑 /kəˈmjuːnəti/ *noun* (*plural* **communities**) **1** the people who live in a place: *Life in a small farming community is very different from life in a big city.* **2** a group of people who join together, for example because they have the same interests or religion: *the Asian community in Tanzania*

commute /kəˈmjuːt/ *verb* (**commutes, commuting, commuted**) to travel a long way from home to work every day: *She lives in the countryside and commutes to Nairobi.* ▸ **commuter** /kəˈmjuːtə(r)/ *noun* a person who commutes

companion /kəmˈpæniən/ *noun* a person who is with another person

company 🔑 /ˈkʌmpəni/ *noun* **1** (*plural* **companies**) a group of people who work to make or sell things: *an advertising company* ❶ The short form is **Co. 2** (no plural) being with other people: *She lives alone so she likes company at weekends.*
keep someone company to be or go with someone: *Please stay and keep me company for a while.*

comparative /kəmˈpærətɪv/ *noun* in the form of an adjective or adverb that shows more of something: *The comparative of 'bad' is 'worse'.* ▶ **comparative** *adjective*: *'Longer' is the comparative form of 'long'.*

compare 🔑 /kəmˈpeə(r)/ *verb* (**compares, comparing, compared** /kəmˈpeəd/) to think about or look at people or things together so that you can see how they are different: *We compared prices in Nairobi and Mombasa and found that Mombasa was cheaper.* ◇ *Compare your answers with those at the back of the book.*
compared to or **with** if you compare someone or something: *Shayo is quite small, compared with his friends.*

comparison 🔑 /kəmˈpærɪsn/ *noun* seeing or understanding how things are different or the same: *We made a comparison of prices in three different towns.*
in or **by comparison with someone** or **something** if you see or think about someone or something together with another person or thing: *Uganda is a small country in comparison with Sudan.*

compartment /kəmˈpɑːtmənt/ *noun* **1** one of the sections which a part of a train is divided into: *He found an empty first-class compartment.* **2** a separate part inside a box or bag: *The suitcase had a secret compartment at the back.*

compass

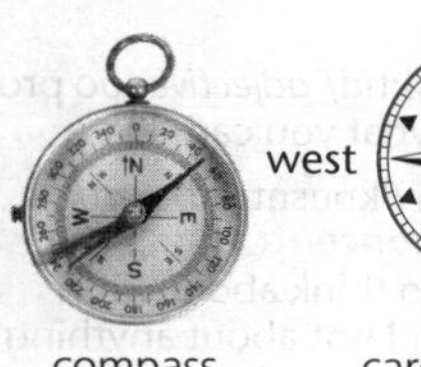

compass

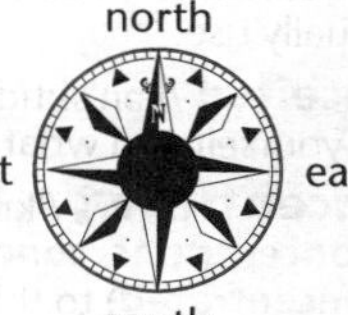

cardinal points

compass /ˈkʌmpəs/ *noun* (*plural* **compasses**) a thing with a needle that always shows where north is

compensation /ˌkɒmpenˈseɪʃn/ *noun* (no plural) money that you pay because you hurt someone, or lose or break something: *She received 800 000 shillings in compensation for her injuries.*

compete /kəmˈpiːt/ *verb* (**competes, competing, competed**) to try to win a race or competition: *Teams from many countries compete in the World Cup.*

competent /ˈkɒmpɪtənt/ *adjective* good at something: *He's a very competent footballer.* OPPOSITE **incompetent**
▶ **competence** /ˈkɒmpɪtəns/ *noun* (no plural): *She has a high level of competence in English.*

competition 🔑 /ˌkɒmpəˈtɪʃn/ *noun* **1** (*plural* **competitions**) a game or test that people try to win: *I entered the painting competition and won first prize.* **2** (no plural) trying to win or be best: *We were in competition with a team from another school.*

competitive /kəmˈpetətɪv/ *adjective* wanting to win or be best: *Do you play competitive sports?*

competitor /kəmˈpetɪtə(r)/ *noun* a person who is trying to win a competition: *There are ten competitors in the first race.*

compile /kəmˈpaɪl/ *verb* (**compiles, compiling, compiled** /kəmˈpaɪld/) to collect information and arrange it in a list or book: *We compiled a list of useful websites.*

complain 🔑 /kəmˈpleɪn/ *verb* (**complains, complaining, complained** /kəmˈpleɪnd/) to say that you do not like something; to say that you are unhappy or angry about something: *Sarika complained that she was too tired to walk any further.* ◇ *She was complaining about the weather.*

complainant /kəmˈpleɪnənt/ *noun* = **plaintiff**

complaint 🔑 /kəmˈpleɪnt/ *noun* when you say that you do not like something: *We made a complaint to the hotel manager about the dirty rooms.*

complete[1] 🔑 /kəmˈpliːt/ *adjective* **1** with none of its parts missing: *I've got a complete set of teeth.* OPPOSITE **incomplete** **2** finished: *The work is complete.* OPPOSITE **incomplete** **3** in every way; total: *Their visit was a complete surprise.*

complete[2] 🔑 /kəmˈpliːt/ *verb* (**completes, completing, completed**) to finish doing or making something: *She was at university for two years but she did not complete her studies.* ◇ *When will the new building be completed?*

completely 🔑 /kəmˈpliːtli/ *adverb* totally; in every way: *The money has disappeared completely.* ◇ *I completely forgot that it was your birthday!*

complex[1] /ˈkɒmpleks/ *adjective* difficult to understand because it has a lot of different parts: *a complex problem* OPPOSITE **simple**

complex² /ˈkɒmpleks/ *noun* (*plural* **complexes**) a group of buildings: *a sports complex*

complicated 🔑 /ˈkɒmplɪkeɪtɪd/ *adjective* difficult to understand because it has a lot of different parts: *I can't explain how to play the game. It's too complicated.* OPPOSITE **simple**

compliment¹ /ˈkɒmplɪmənt/ *noun* **pay someone a compliment** to say something nice about someone: *I know she likes me because she's always paying me compliments.*

compliment² /ˈkɒmplɪment/ *verb* (**compliments, complimenting, complimented**) to say something nice about someone: *They complimented Nafula on her cooking.*

compose /kəmˈpəʊz/ *verb* (**composes, composing, composed** /kəmˈpəʊzd/) to write something, especially music: *Mr Mugambi has composed a school song.* **be composed of something** to be made of something; to have something as parts: *Water is composed of oxygen and hydrogen.*

composer /kəmˈpəʊzə(r)/ *noun* a person who writes music: *'Malaika' was written by Kenyan composer Fadhili William.*

composition /ˌkɒmpəˈzɪʃn/ *noun* a piece of writing or music

compound /ˈkɒmpaʊnd/ *noun* **1** a group of buildings with a wall or a fence round it: *a school compound* **2** something that is made of two or more parts: *Salt is a chemical compound.* **3** a word or expression that is made from other words: *'Fingernail' and 'waiting room' are compounds.*

comprehension /ˌkɒmprɪˈhenʃn/ *noun* (no plural) understanding something that you hear or read: *a test in listening comprehension*

compromise /ˈkɒmprəmaɪz/ *noun* an agreement with another person or group, when you both do part of what the other person or group wants: *After long talks, the workers and management reached a compromise.*

compulsory /kəmˈpʌlsəri/ *adjective* If something is **compulsory**, you must do it: *It's compulsory to study English at my school, but joining the English club is optional.* OPPOSITE **optional**

computer

computer 🔑 /kəmˈpjuːtə(r)/ *noun* a machine that stores information and finds answers very quickly: *The information is processed by computer.*

computer game /kəmˈpjuːtə geɪm/ *noun* a game that you play on a computer

computer program /kəmˈpjuːtə prəʊgræm/ *noun* information that tells a computer what to do

computer programmer /kəmˌpjuːtə ˈprəʊgræmə(r)/ *noun* a person who writes computer programs

computing /kəmˈpjuːtɪŋ/ *noun* (no plural) using computers to do work: *She is studying computing at college.*

conceal /kənˈsiːl/ *verb* (**conceals, concealing, concealed** /kənˈsiːld/) to hide something: *They concealed the bomb in a suitcase.* ℹ **Hide** is the word that we usually use.

conceited /kənˈsiːtɪd/ *adjective* too proud of yourself and what you can do

concentrate 🔑 /ˈkɒnsntreɪt/ *verb* (**concentrates, concentrating, concentrated**) to think about what you are doing and not about anything else: *Stop looking out of the window and concentrate on your work!*

concentration /ˌkɒnsnˈtreɪʃn/ *noun* (no plural) the ability to give all your attention to something: *Concentration is very difficult when there's so much noise.*

concern¹ 🔑 /kənˈsɜːn/ *verb* (**concerns, concerning, concerned** /kənˈsɜːnd/) **1** to be important or interesting to someone: *This notice concerns all passengers travelling to Kampala.* **2** to worry someone: *It concerns me that she is always late.* **3** to be about something: *The story concerns a boy and his dog.*

concern² /kənˈsɜːn/ *noun* **1** (no plural) worry: *When Wasike didn't return, there* *was concern for his safety.* **2** (*plural* **concerns**) something that is important or interesting to someone: *Her problems are not my concern.*

concerned /kən'sɜ:nd/ *adjective* worried: *They are very concerned about their son's illness.*

concerning /kən'sɜ:nɪŋ/ *preposition* about: *Thank you for your letter concerning the date of the next meeting.*

concert 🔑 /'kɒnsət/ *noun* music played for a lot of people: *a school concert*

conclusion 🔑 /kən'klu:ʒn/ *noun* what you believe or decide after thinking carefully: *We came to the conclusion* (= we decided) *that you were right.*

concrete /'kɒŋkri:t/ *noun* (no plural) hard grey material used for building things: *a concrete path*

condemn /kən'dem/ *verb* (**condemns, condemning, condemned** /kən'demd/) **1** to say that someone must be punished in a certain way: *The murderer was condemned to death.* **2** to say strongly that someone or something is bad or wrong: *Many people condemned the council's decision.*

condense /kən'dens/ *verb* (**condenses, condensing, condensed** /kən'denst/) **1** to change or make something change from gas into liquid: *Steam condenses into water when it cools.* **2** If a liquid **condenses** or you **condense** it, it becomes thicker and stronger because it has lost some of its water: *Condense the soup by boiling it for several minutes.*

condition 🔑 /kən'dɪʃn/ *noun* **1** (no plural) how a person, an animal or a thing is: *The car was in good condition, so he bought it.* **2** (*plural* **conditions**) something that must happen before another thing can happen: *One of the conditions of the job is that he agrees to work on Saturdays.* **3 conditions** (plural) how things are around you: *The prisoners lived in terrible conditions.*
on condition that only if: *You can watch the football match on condition that you do your homework first.*

condolence /kən'dəʊləns/ *noun* an expression of how sorry you feel for someone whose relative or friend has just died: *We sent our condolences to his wife and family.*

conducive /kən'dju:sɪv/ *adjective* helping or making something happen: *The warm afternoon was conducive to sleep.*

conduct /kən'dʌkt/ *verb* (**conducts, conducting, conducted**) **1** to stand in front of a group of musicians and control what they do: *Mr Odoi conducted the school band.* **2** to show someone where to go: *She conducted us on a tour of the factory.*

conductor /kən'dʌktə(r)/ *noun* **1** a person who stands in front of a group of musicians and controls what they do **2** a person who collects money from passengers on a bus

cones

cone

pine cone

ice cream cone

cone /kəʊn/ *noun* **1** a shape with one flat round end and one pointed end **2** the hard fruit of **pine** or **fir** trees: *a pine cone*

confederation /kənˌfedə'reɪʃn/ *noun* a large group of smaller groups that have joined together

conference /'kɒnfərəns/ *noun* a time when many people meet to talk about a special thing: *an international conference*

confess /kən'fes/ *verb* (**confesses, confessing, confessed** /kən'fest/) to say that you have done something wrong: *She confessed that she had stolen the money.* ◇ *He confessed to the crime.*

confession /kən'feʃn/ *noun* when you say that you have done something wrong: *She made a confession to the police.*

confidence 🔑 /'kɒnfɪdəns/ *noun* (no plural) the feeling that you can do something well: *She answered the questions with confidence.*
have confidence in someone to feel sure that someone will do something well: *I'm sure you'll pass the exam. I have great confidence in you.*
in confidence If someone tells you something in confidence, it is a secret.

confident 🔑 /'kɒnfɪdənt/ *adjective* sure that you can do something well, or that something will happen: *I'm confident that our team will win.*

confirm /kən'fɜ:m/ *verb* (**confirms, confirming, confirmed** /kən'fɜ:md/)

to say that something is true or that something will happen: *The police confirmed that the dead man was murdered.*

confirmation /ˌkɒnfəˈmeɪʃn/ *noun* (no plural) saying that something is true or will happen

conflict /ˈkɒnflɪkt/ *noun* a fight or an argument ➲ Look at **resolution**.

confuse 🔑 /kənˈfjuːz/ *verb* (**confuses, confusing, confused** /kənˈfjuːzd/) **1** to mix someone's ideas, so that they cannot think clearly or understand: *They confused me by asking so many questions.* **2** to think that one thing or person is another thing or person: *Don't confuse the word 'weather' with 'whether'.* ▶ **confusing** /kənˈfjuːzɪŋ/ *adjective* difficult to understand: *This map is very confusing.*

confused 🔑 /kənˈfjuːzd/ *adjective* not able to think clearly: *I got confused and took the wrong books to school.*

confusion /kənˈfjuːʒn/ *noun* (no plural) not being able to think clearly or understand something: *He didn't speak any English and he looked at me in confusion when I asked him a question.*

congested /kənˈdʒestɪd/ *adjective* so full of something that nothing can move: *The street was congested with cars.* ▶ **congestion** /kənˈdʒestʃən/ *noun* (no plural): *traffic congestion*

congratulate /kənˈɡrætʃuleɪt/ *verb* (**congratulates, congratulating, congratulated**) to tell someone that you are pleased about something that they have done: *I congratulated Teta on passing her exam.*

congratulations /kənˌɡrætʃuˈleɪʃnz/ *noun* (plural) something you say to someone when you are pleased about something they have done: *Congratulations! You've won first prize.*

congress /ˈkɒŋɡres/ *noun* (*plural* **congresses**) a meeting of many people to talk about important things: *He gave a speech at an international teachers' congress.*

conifer /ˈkɒnɪfə(r)/ *noun* a tree with thin sharp leaves that stays green all the year. Conifers have **cones** (= hard brown fruit). ▶ **coniferous** /kəˈnɪfərəs/ *adjective* having **cones** ➲ Look at **evergreen**.

conjunction /kənˈdʒʌŋkʃn/ *noun* a word that joins other words or parts of a sentence: *'And', 'or' and 'but' are conjunctions.*

connect 🔑 /kəˈnekt/ *verb* (**connects, connecting, connected**) to join one thing to another thing: *This wire connects the light to the switch.* ◇ *The two cities are connected by a highway.* ▶ **connector** /kəˈnektə(r)/ *noun* a thing that links two or more things together: *a cable connector*

connection 🔑 /kəˈnekʃn/ *noun* **1** the way that one thing is joined to or affected by another: *There is a problem with our Internet connection.* ◇ *Is there a connection between crime and poverty?* **2** a train, plane or bus that leaves a place soon after another arrives, so that people can change from one to the other: *The bus was late, so I missed my connection.*
in connection with something about something: *The police want to talk to him in connection with the robbery.*

conscience /ˈkɒnʃəns/ *noun* the feeling inside you about what is right and wrong: *He has a guilty conscience* (= he feels that he has done something wrong).

conscious 🔑 /ˈkɒnʃəs/ *adjective* **1** awake and able to think: *The patient was conscious during the operation.* OPPOSITE **unconscious** **2** If you are conscious of something, you know about it: *I was conscious that he was watching me.*

consciousness /ˈkɒnʃəsnəs/ *noun* (no plural)
lose consciousness to stop being conscious: *As she fell, she hit her head and lost consciousness.*

consent /kənˈsent/ *noun* (no plural) agreeing to let someone do something: *Her parents gave their consent to the operation.*

consequence /ˈkɒnsɪkwəns/ *noun* what happens because of something: *As a consequence of the recent landslides, 400 people have no homes.* ◇ *The mistake had terrible consequences.*

consequently /ˈkɒnsɪkwəntli/ *adverb* because of that; therefore: *He didn't do any work, and consequently failed the exam.*

conservation /ˌkɒnsəˈveɪʃn/ *noun* (no plural) taking good care of the world and its trees, lakes, plants, and animals: *the conservation of the rain forests* ❶ Look at the verb **conserve**.

conserve /kənˈsɜːv/ *verb* (**conserves, conserving, conserved** /kənˈsɜːvd/) to not waste something: *We must conserve water.* ❶ Look at the noun **conservation**.

consider 🔑 /kənˈsɪdə(r)/ *verb* (**considers,**

considering, considered /kən'sɪdəd/) **1** to think carefully about something: *I'm considering going to work with my uncle.* ◇ *We must consider what to do next.* **2** to think that something is true: *I consider her to be a good teacher.* **3** to think about the feelings of other people when you do something: *He spent all his money on a car without considering what his family thought.*

considerable /kən'sɪdərəbl/ *adjective* great or large: *The car cost a considerable amount of money.* ▶ **considerably** /kən'sɪdərəbli/ *adverb*: *Burundi is considerably smaller than Tanzania.*

considerate /kən'sɪdərət/ *adjective* A person who is **considerate** is kind, and thinks and cares about other people: *Please be more considerate and don't play loud music late at night.* OPPOSITE **inconsiderate**

consideration /kənˌsɪdə'reɪʃn/ *noun* (no plural) **1** thinking carefully about something: *After a lot of consideration, she decided not to leave the team.* **2** being kind, and caring about other people's feelings: *He shows no consideration for anybody else.*

take something into consideration to think carefully about something when you are deciding: *Age will be taken into consideration when the winner is chosen.*

consist ⚷ /kən'sɪst/ *verb* (**consists, consisting, consisted**)

consist of something to be made of something; to have something as parts: *Water consists of hydrogen and oxygen.*

consistent /kən'sɪstənt/ *adjective* always the same: *His work isn't very consistent – sometimes it's good and sometimes it's terrible!* OPPOSITE **inconsistent**

consonant /'kɒnsənənt/ *noun* any letter of the alphabet that is not *a, e, i, o* or *u*: *In the word 'time' , the letters 't' and 'm' are consonants.* ➲ Look at **vowel**.

constable /'kʌnstəbl/ *noun* an ordinary police officer: *Constable Mwaura will handle the case.*

constant /'kɒnstənt/ *adjective* Something that is **constant** happens all the time: *the constant noise of traffic* ▶ **constantly** *adverb*: *She talked constantly all evening.*

constituency /kən'stɪtjuənsi/ *noun* (*plural* **constituencies**) a town or an area that chooses one **Member of Parliament** (= a person in the government): *Kacheliba constituency*

constitution /ˌkɒnstɪ'tju:ʃn/ *noun* the laws of a country: *the Kenyan constitution*

construct /kən'strʌkt/ *verb* (**constructs, constructing, constructed**) to build something: *The bridge was constructed out of stone.* ℹ **Build** is the word that we usually use.

construction /kən'strʌkʃn/ *noun* **1** (no plural) building something: *Work has begun on the construction of a new railway.* **2** (*plural* **constructions**) something that people have built: *The house was a simple wooden construction.*

consult /kən'sʌlt/ *verb* (**consults, consulting, consulted**) to ask someone or look in a book when you want to know something: *If the pain doesn't go away, you should consult a doctor.*

consume /kən'sju:m/ *verb* (**consumes, consuming, consumed** /kən'sju:md/) to eat, drink or use something: *This car consumes a lot of petrol.*

consumer /kən'sju:mə(r)/ *noun* **1** a person who buys things: *Consumers want clean and fresh vegetables.* **2** a person or an animal that eats or uses something ➲ Look at **food chain**.

consumption /kən'sʌmpʃn/ *noun* (no plural) eating, drinking or using something: *This car has a high petrol consumption* (= it uses a lot of petrol).

contact[1] ⚷ /'kɒntækt/ *noun* (no plural) meeting, talking to or writing to someone: *Until Moraa started work at the airport, she didn't have much contact with people from other countries.* ◇ *Are you still in contact with your old friends from school?* ◇ *Doctors come into contact with* (= meet) *a lot of people.*

contact[2] ⚷ /'kɒntækt/ *verb* (**contacts, contacting, contacted**) to telephone or write to someone, or go to see them: *If you see this man, please contact the police.*

contact lens /'kɒntækt lenz/ *noun* (*plural* **contact lenses**) a small round piece of thin plastic that you wear in your eye so that you can see better

contagious /kən'teɪdʒəs/ *adjective* A **contagious** disease passes from one person to another if they touch each other: *Measles is a contagious disease.* ➲ Look at **infectious**.

contain ⚷ /kən'teɪn/ *verb* (**contains, containing, contained** /kən'teɪnd/) to have something inside it: *This box contains pens and pencils.* ◇ *Chocolate contains a lot of sugar.*

containers

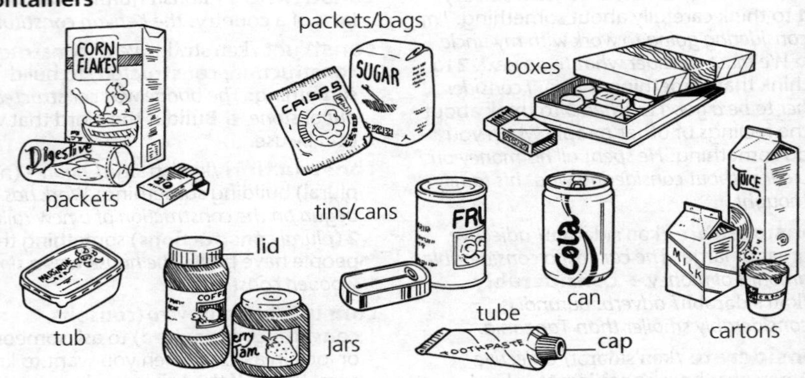

container /kən'teɪnə(r)/ *noun* a thing that you can put other things in. Boxes, bottles and bags are all containers.

contaminate /kən'tæmɪneɪt/ *verb* (**contaminates, contaminating, contaminated** /kən'tæmɪneɪtɪd/) to add a substance which will make something dirty or harmful: *The river was contaminated by poisonous chemicals.* ▶ **contamination** /kən,tæmɪ'neɪʃn/ *noun* (no plural): *environmental contamination*

content /kən'tent/ *adjective* happy with what you have: *She is not content with the money she has – she wants more.*

contented /kən'tentɪd/ *adjective* happy: *The baby gave a contented smile.* OPPOSITE **discontented**

contents /'kɒntents/ *noun* (plural) what is inside something: *I poured the contents of the bottle into a bowl.* ◇ *The contents page of a book tells you what is in it.*

contest /'kɒntest/ *noun* a game or competition that people try to win: *a boxing contest*

contestant /kən'testənt/ *noun* a person who tries to win a **contest**: *There are six contestants in the race.*

context /'kɒntekst/ *noun* the words that come before and after another word or a sentence: *You can often understand the meaning of a word by looking at its context.*

continent /'kɒntɪnənt/ *noun* one of the seven big pieces of land in the world, for example Africa, Asia or Europe ▶ **continental** /,kɒntɪ'nentl/ *adjective*: *The tournament included continental champions from Africa, Asia and Oceania.*

continual /kən'tɪnjuəl/ *adjective* that happens often: *We have had continual problems with this machine.* ▶ **continually** /kən'tɪnjuəli/ *adverb*: *He is continually late for work.*

continue /kən'tɪnju:/ *verb* (**continues, continuing, continued** /kən'tɪnju:d/) **1** to not stop happening or doing something: *We continued working until five o'clock.* ◇ *The rain continued all afternoon.* **2** to start again after stopping: *Let's have lunch now and continue the meeting this afternoon.* **3** to go further: *We continued along the path until we came to the river.*

continuous /kən'tɪnjuəs/ *adjective* Something that is continuous goes on and does not stop: *a continuous line* ◇ *a continuous noise* ▶ **continuously** *adverb*: *It rained continuously for five hours.*

contract[1] /'kɒntrækt/ *noun* a piece of paper that says that someone agrees to do something: *The company has signed a contract to build the new road.*

contract[2] /kən'trækt/ *verb* (**contracts, contracting, contracted**) **1** to become smaller: *Glass contracts as it cools.* OPPOSITE **expand** **2** to get an illness, especially a serious one: *to contract pneumonia*

contraction /kən'trækʃn/ *noun* the process of becoming or making something become smaller or shorter: *the expansion and contraction of metal*

contradict /,kɒntrə'dɪkt/ *verb* (**contradicts, contradicting, contradicted**) to say that something is wrong or not true: *'This is my book, not yours!' he shouted, and nobody dared to contradict him.*

contrary[1] /ˈkɒntrəri/ *noun* (no plural)
on the contrary the opposite is true: *'You look ill.' 'On the contrary, I feel fine!'*

contrary[2] /ˈkɒntrəri/ *adjective*
contrary to something very different from something; opposite to something: *He didn't stay in bed, contrary to the doctor's orders.*

contrast[1] /kənˈtrɑːst/ *verb* (**contrasts, contrasting, contrasted**) to look at or think about two or more things together and see the differences between them: *The book contrasts life today with life 100 years ago.*

contrast[2] /ˈkɒntrɑːst/ *noun* a difference between things that you can see clearly: *There is a big contrast between the weather in Tanzania and in Egypt.*

contribute /kənˈtrɪbjuːt/ *verb* (**contributes, contributing, contributed**) to give something when other people are giving too: *We contributed 100 shillings each to the fund.*

contribution /ˌkɒntrɪˈbjuːʃn/ *noun* something that you give when other people are giving too: *We are sending contributions of food and toys to children in poor regions.*

control[1] /kənˈtrəʊl/ *noun* **1** (no plural) the power to make people or things do what you want: *As head of the company, he has control over how much workers are paid.* **2 controls** (plural) the parts of a machine that you press or move to make it work: *He checked the controls of the plane.* **3** (no plural) (also **control key**) a computer key that you sometimes need to press at the same time as another key: *Press Control and C to copy something.*
in control able to direct or manage a situation: *A teacher must be in control of the class.*
lose control to be unable to make people or things do what you want: *The driver lost control and the bus went into the river.*
out of control If something is **out of control**, you cannot stop it or make it do what you want: *The truck went out of control and crashed.*
under control If something is **under control**, it is doing what you want it to do: *The fire is under control.*

control[2] /kənˈtrəʊl/ *verb* (**controls, controlling, controlled** /kənˈtrəʊld/) to make people or things do what you want: *He couldn't control his feelings and started to cry.* ◇ *This switch controls the speed.* ▸ **controller** /kənˈtrəʊlə(r)/ *noun* a person who controls something: *an air traffic controller*

control tower /kənˈtrəʊl taʊə(r)/ *noun* a building at an airport where the movements of aircraft are controlled

convenience /kənˈviːniəns/ *noun* (no plural) being easy to use; making things easy: *For convenience, the books are kept in alphabetical order.*

convenient /kənˈviːniənt/ *adjective* **1** easy to use or go to: *The bus stop is very convenient – it's outside my house.* **2** easy for someone or something; suitable: *Let's meet on Friday. What's the most convenient time for you?* OPPOSITE **inconvenient**
▸ **conveniently** *adverb*: *We live conveniently close to the school.*

convent /ˈkɒnvənt/ *noun* a place where religious women (called **nuns**) live, work and speak to God (**pray**)

conversation /ˌkɒnvəˈseɪʃn/ *noun* a talk: *She had a long conversation with her friend.*

conversion /kənˈvɜːʃn/ *noun* changing something into another thing: *the conversion of the sun's heat to electricity*

convert /kənˈvɜːt/ *verb* (**converts, converting, converted**) to change into another thing: *They converted the offices into a school.*

convict /kənˈvɪkt/ *verb* (**convicts, convicting, convicted**) to decide in a court of law that someone has done something wrong: *She was convicted of murder and sent to prison.*

convince /kənˈvɪns/ *verb* (**convinces, convincing, convinced** /kənˈvɪnst/) to make someone believe something: *I couldn't convince him that I was right.*

convinced /kənˈvɪnst/ *adjective* certain: *I'm convinced that I have seen her somewhere before.*

cook[1] /kʊk/ *verb* (**cooks, cooking, cooked** /kʊkt/) to make food ready to eat by heating it: *My father cooked the dinner.* ◇ *I am learning to cook.*

> ❖ **WORD BUILDING**
>
> There are many words for ways of cooking food. Look at **bake, boil, fry, grill, roast** and **stew**.

cook[2] /kʊk/ *noun* a person who cooks: *She works as a cook.* ◇ *He is a good cook.*

cooker 🔑 /ˈkʊkə(r)/ *noun* a thing that you use in a kitchen for cooking food. It has an **oven** for cooking food inside it and places for heating pans on the top: *an electric cooker*

cookery /ˈkʊkəri/ *noun* (no plural) making food ready to eat, often as a subject that you can study: *cookery lessons*

cooking 🔑 /ˈkʊkɪŋ/ *noun* (no plural) **1** making food ready to eat: *Who does the cooking in your family?* **2** what you cook: *He misses his mother's cooking when he's away.*

cool¹ 🔑 /kuːl/ *adjective* (**cooler, coolest**) **1** a little cold; not warm: *cool water* ◇ *I'd like a cool drink.* **2** calm; not excited: *She always manages to remain cool under pressure.* **3** very good or fashionable: *Those are cool shoes!* **4** People say **Cool!** to show that they think something is a good idea: *'We're going to play football tomorrow.' 'Cool!'*

cool² /kuːl/ *verb* (**cools, cooling, cooled** /kuːld/) to make something less hot; to become less hot: *We let the food cool a little before we started eating.*
cool down 1 to become less hot: *We swam in the river to cool down after our long walk.* **2** to become less excited or angry

cooperate /kəʊˈɒpəreɪt/ *verb* (**cooperates, cooperating, cooperated**)

> ❖ **PRONUNCIATION**
> We say **coop-** in 2 parts: 'co' (like **go**) and 'op'.

to work together with someone else in a helpful way: *The two companies are cooperating with each other.*

cooperation /kəʊˌɒpəˈreɪʃn/ *noun* (no plural) help: *Thank you for your cooperation.*

cooperative¹ /kəʊˈɒpərətɪv/ *adjective* happy to help: *The police asked her a lot of questions and she was very cooperative.*

cooperative² /kəʊˈɒpərətɪv/ *noun* a business that is owned and run by all the people who work in it

cope /kəʊp/ *verb* (**copes, coping, coped** /kəʊpt/)
cope with someone or **something** to do something well although it is difficult: *She has four young children. I don't know how she copes with them!*

copied *form of* COPY²

copies 1 *plural of* COPY¹ **2** *form of* COPY²

copper /ˈkɒpə(r)/ *noun* (no plural) a metal with a colour between brown and red: *copper wire*

copy¹ 🔑 /ˈkɒpi/ *noun* (*plural* **copies**) **1** a thing that is made to look exactly like another thing: *This is a copy of a famous painting.* ◇ *The secretary made two copies of the letter.* **2** one book or newspaper: *Two million copies of the newspaper are sold every day.*

copy² 🔑 /ˈkɒpi/ *verb* (**copies, copying, copied** /ˈkɒpid/, **has copied**) **1** to write or draw something so that it is exactly the same as another thing: *The teacher asked us to copy the list of words into our books.* **2** to try to look or do the same as another person: *Odoi always copies what his brother does.*

coral /ˈkɒrəl/ *noun* (no plural) a hard red, pink or white substance that forms in the sea from the bones of very small sea animals

cord /kɔːd/ *noun* strong thick string

core /kɔː(r)/ *noun* the middle part of some kinds of fruit, where the seeds are: *an apple core*

core

cork /kɔːk/ *noun*
1 (no plural) light soft stuff that comes from the outside of a special tree **2** (*plural* **corks**) a round piece of **cork** that you put in a bottle to close it ➲ Picture at **corkscrew**.

corkscrew /ˈkɔːkskruː/ *noun* a thing that you use for taking corks out of bottles

corkscrew

corn /kɔːn/ *noun* (no plural) **1** the seeds of plants like **wheat 2** a small painful place on your foot

corner

The lamp is **in** the corner.
The bank is **on** the corner.

corner 🔑 /ˈkɔːnə(r)/ *noun* a place where two lines, walls or roads meet

corporal /ˈkɔːpərəl/ *noun* a person at a low level in the army or the police

corporation /ˌkɔːpəˈreɪʃn/ *noun* a big company: *the Kenya Broadcasting Corporation*

corpse /kɔːps/ *noun* the body of a dead person

correct¹ 🔑 /kəˈrekt/ *adjective* right or true; with no mistakes: *All your answers were correct.* ◇ *What is the correct time, please?* OPPOSITE **incorrect** ▶ **correctly** 🔑 *adverb*: *Have I spelt your name correctly?*

correct² 🔑 /kəˈrekt/ *verb* (**corrects, correcting, corrected**) to show where the mistakes are in something and make it right: *The class did the exercises and the teacher corrected them.* ◇ *Please correct me if I make a mistake.*

correction /kəˈrekʃn/ *noun* the right word or answer that is put in the place of what was wrong: *When the teacher gave my homework back to me it was full of corrections.*

correspond /ˌkɒrəˈspɒnd/ *verb* (**corresponds, corresponding, corresponded**) to be the same, or almost the same: *Does the name on the envelope correspond with the name inside the letter?*

correspondence /ˌkɒrəˈspɒndəns/ *noun* (no plural) writing letters; the letters that someone writes or receives: *Her secretary reads all her correspondence.*

corridor /ˈkɒrɪdɔː(r)/ *noun* a long narrow part inside a building with rooms on each side of it

corrupt¹ /kəˈrʌpt/ *adjective* doing illegal or dishonest things for money: *Corrupt officials accepted bribes.*

corrupt² /kəˈrʌpt/ *verb* (**corrupts, corrupting, corrupted**) to make someone do illegal or dishonest things: *Power can corrupt people.*

corruption /kəˈrʌpʃn/ *noun* (no plural) doing illegal or dishonest things for money

cosmetics /kɒzˈmetɪks/ *noun* (plural) special powders or creams that you use on your face or hair to make yourself more beautiful

cost¹ 🔑 /kɒst/ *noun* **1** the money that you must pay for something: *The cost of the repairs was very high.* **2** what you lose or give to have another thing: *He saved the child at the cost of his own life.*
at all costs no matter what you must do to make it happen: *We must win at all costs.*

cost² 🔑 /kɒst/ *verb* (**costs, costing, cost, has cost**) **1** to have the price of: *This shirt cost 500 shillings.* ◇ *How much did the book cost?* **2** to make you lose something: *One mistake cost him the match.*

costly /ˈkɒstli/ *adjective* (**costlier, costliest**) expensive: *The repairs will be very costly.*

costume /ˈkɒstjuːm/ *noun* the special clothes that people wear in a country or at a certain time: *The actors wore beautiful costumes.* ◇ *traditional tribal costume* ➲ Look at **swimming costume**.

cosy /ˈkəʊzi/ *adjective* (**cosier, cosiest**) warm and comfortable: *a cosy room*

cot /kɒt/ *noun* a baby's bed with high sides

cot

cotton 🔑 /ˈkɒtn/ *noun* (no plural) cloth or thread that is made from the soft white stuff on the seeds of a special plant: *a cotton shirt* ◇ *a reel of cotton* ➲ Picture at **reel**.

cotton wool /ˌkɒtn ˈwʊl/ *noun* (no plural) soft light stuff made from cotton: *The nurse cleaned the cut with cotton wool.*

couch /kaʊtʃ/ *noun* (*plural* **couches**) a long comfortable seat for two or more people to sit on: *They sat next to each other on the couch.* ➲ Look at **sofa**.

cough¹ 🔑 /kɒf/ *verb* (**coughs, coughing, coughed** /kɒft/) to send air out of your throat with a sudden loud noise: *The smoke made me cough.*

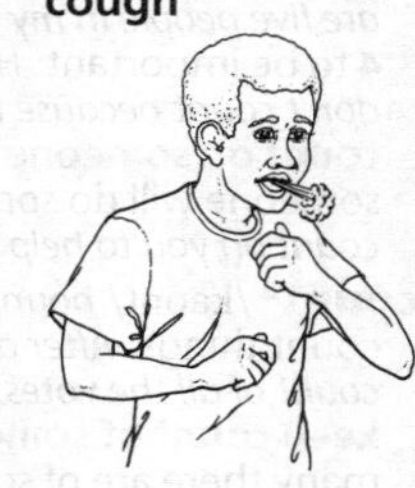
cough

cough² 🔑 /kɒf/ *noun* when you send air out of your throat with a sudden loud noise: *I've got a bad cough.* ◇ *He gave a little cough before he started to speak.*

> ❖ **PRONUNCIATION**
> **Cough** sounds like **off**.

could /kʊd/ *modal verb*

> ❖ **PRONUNCIATION**
> **Could** sounds like **good**.

1 the word for 'can' in the past tense: *He could run very fast when he was young.* ◇ *I could hear the birds singing.* **2** a word that shows what will perhaps happen or what is possible: *It could rain tomorrow.* ◇ *I don't know where Chebet is. She could be in the kitchen.* ◇ *You could be doing your homework while you wait for tea.* **3** a word that you use to ask something in a polite way: *Could you open the door?* ◇ *Could I have another drink, please?* ➲ Look at **modal verb**.

couldn't /ˈkʊdnt/ *short for* COULD NOT: *It was dark and I couldn't see anything.*

could've /ˈkʊdəv/ *short for* COULD HAVE: *I could've gone with them, but I didn't want to.*

council /ˈkaʊnsl/ *noun* a group of people who are chosen to work together and to make rules and decide things: *The county council is planning to build a new road.*

councillor /ˈkaʊnsələ(r)/ *noun* a member of a **council**: *Five new councillors were elected.*

counsellor /ˈkaʊnsələ(r)/ *noun* a person whose job is to give people advice with problems: *If you're having problems, you can talk to a counsellor.*

count[1] /kaʊnt/ *verb* (**counts, counting, counted**) **1** to say numbers one after the other in the right order: *The children are learning to count from one to ten.* **2** to look at people or things to see how many there are: *I have counted the chairs – there are 32.* **3** to include someone or something: *There are five people in my family, counting me.* **4** to be important: *He said that my ideas don't count because I'm only a child!*
count on someone to feel sure that someone will do something for you: *Can I count on you to help me?*

count[2] /kaʊnt/ *noun* a time when you count things: *After an election there is a count of all the votes.*
keep count of something to know how many there are of something: *Try to keep count of the number of tickets you have sold.*
lose count of something to not know how many there are of something

countable /ˈkaʊntəbl/ *adjective* **Countable** nouns are ones that you can use in the plural or with *a* or *an*, for example *chair* and *idea*. OPPOSITE **uncountable**

counter /ˈkaʊntə(r)/ *noun* **1** a long high table in a shop, bank or bar, that is between the people who work there and the people who want to buy things: *I put my money on the counter.* **2** a small round thing that you use when you play some games

counterfoil /ˈkaʊntəfɔɪl/ *noun* the part of a ticket that you keep when you give the other part to someone else

countless /ˈkaʊntləs/ *adjective* very many: *I have tried to telephone him countless times.*

country /ˈkʌntri/ *noun* **1** (*plural* **countries**) an area of land with its own people and government: *Uganda, Tanzania and Kenya are countries.* **2 the country** (no plural) land that is not in a town: *Do you live in the town or the country?*

countryside /ˈkʌntrisaɪd/ *noun* (no plural) land with fields, woods, farms, etc, that is away from towns: *She has lived in the countryside all her life.*

county /ˈkaʊnti/ *noun* (*plural* **counties**) an area of a country which has its own local government: *Turkana County*

county council /ˌkaʊnti ˈkaʊnsl/ *noun* a group of people elected to the local government of a **county**: *a member of Lamu County Council*

couple /ˈkʌpl/ *noun* two people who are married: *A young couple live next door.*
a couple of 1 two: *I invited a couple of friends to lunch.* **2** a few: *I'll be back in a couple of minutes.*

courage /ˈkʌrɪdʒ/ *noun* (no plural) not being afraid, or not showing that you are afraid, when you do something dangerous or difficult: *She showed great courage when she went into the burning building to save the child.* ► **courageous** /kəˈreɪdʒəs/ *adjective* brave: *a courageous young man*

course /kɔːs/ *noun* **1** a set of lessons on a certain subject: *He's taking a course in computer programming.* **2** the direction that something moves in: *We followed the course of the river.* **3** one part of a meal: *I had chicken for the main course.* **4** a piece of ground for some kinds of sport: *a golf course* ◇ *a racecourse* (= where you go to see horses race) **5** the time when something is happening: *During the course of the evening I began to feel more and more ill.*
change course to start to go in a different direction: *The plane had to change course because of the storm.*

of course certainly: *Of course I'll help you.* ◇ *'Can I borrow a pen?' 'Of course you can.'* ◇ *'Are you angry with me?' 'Of course not!'*

court 🔑 /kɔːt/ *noun* **1** a place where people (a **judge** or **jury**) decide if a person has done something wrong, and what the punishment will be: *The man will appear in court tomorrow.* **2** a piece of ground where you can play a certain sport: *a tennis court*

courteous /ˈkɜːtiəs/ *adjective* polite and pleasant: *The hotel staff are friendly and courteous.*

court of law /ˌkɔːt əv ˈlɔː/ *noun* (*plural* **courts of law**) (also **courtroom** /ˈkɔːtruːm/) a place where people (a **judge** or **jury**) decide if a person has done something wrong, and what the punishment will be

courtyard /ˈkɔːtjɑːd/ *noun* an open space without a roof, inside a building or between buildings

cousin 🔑 /ˈkʌzn/ *noun* the child of your aunt or uncle

cover¹ 🔑 /ˈkʌvə(r)/ *verb* (**covers, covering, covered** /ˈkʌvəd/) to put one thing over another thing to hide it or to keep it safe or warm: *Cover the floor with newspaper before you start painting.* ◇ *She covered her head with a scarf.*
be covered with or **in something** to have something all over yourself or itself: *The floor was covered in mud.*

cover² 🔑 /ˈkʌvə(r)/ *noun* **1** a thing that you put over another thing, for example to keep it safe: *The computer has a plastic cover.* **2** the outside part of a book or magazine: *The book had a picture of a footballer on the cover.*

covering 🔑 /ˈkʌvərɪŋ/ *noun* something that covers another thing: *There was a thick covering of dust on the floor.*

cow

cow 🔑 /kaʊ/ *noun* a big female farm animal that gives milk

> ❖ **WORD BUILDING**
> The male is called a **bull** and a young cow is called a **calf**. Meat from a cow is called **beef** and meat from a calf is called **veal**.

coward /ˈkaʊəd/ *noun* a person who is afraid when there is danger or a problem

cowpea /ˈkaʊpiː/ *noun* a kind of bean that is white with a black spot

coxswain /ˈkɒksn/ *noun* the person who controls the direction of a boat

crab /kræb/ *noun* an animal that lives in and near the sea. It has a hard shell and ten legs.

crab

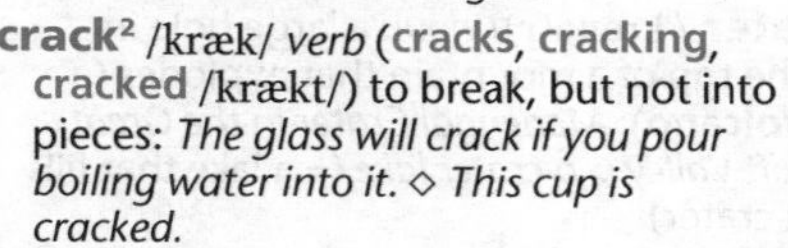

crack¹ /kræk/ *noun* **1** a thin line on something where it is nearly broken: *There's a crack in this glass.* **2** a sudden loud noise: *There was a loud crack of thunder as the storm began.*

crack² /kræk/ *verb* (**cracks, cracking, cracked** /krækt/) to break, but not into pieces: *The glass will crack if you pour boiling water into it.* ◇ *This cup is cracked.*

crackle /ˈkrækl/ *verb* (**crackles, crackling, crackled** /ˈkrækld/) to make a lot of short sharp sounds: *Dry wood crackles when you burn it.*

cradle /ˈkreɪdl/ *noun* a bed for a baby

craft /krɑːft/ *noun* a job in which you need skill with your hands to make things: *Pottery and weaving are crafts.*

craftsman /ˈkrɑːftsmən/ *noun* (*plural* **craftsmen** /ˈkrɑːftsmən/), **craftswoman** /ˈkrɑːftswʊmən/ (*plural* **craftswomen** /ˈkrɑːftswɪmɪn/) a person who is good at making things

> ❖ **WORD BUILDING**
> We say **craftsperson** /ˈkrɑːftspɜːsn/ when we want to refer to either a man or a woman. The plural is **craftspeople** /ˈkrɑːftspiːpl/.

cram /kræm/ *verb* (**crams, cramming, crammed** /kræmd/) **1** to push too many people or things into something: *She crammed her clothes into a bag.* **2** to study very hard and learn a lot in a short time: *She's cramming for her exams.*

crane /kreɪn/ *noun* a big machine with a long part for lifting heavy things

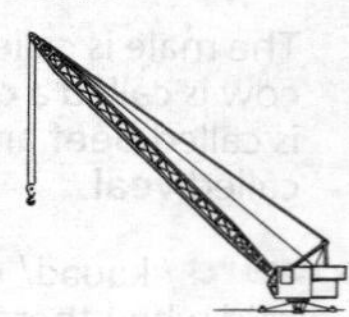

crash[1] 🔑 /kræʃ/ *noun* (*plural* **crashes**) **1** an accident when something that is moving hits another thing: *He was injured in a car crash.* **2** a loud noise when something falls or hits another thing: *I heard a crash as the tree fell.*

crash[2] 🔑 /kræʃ/ *verb* (**crashes, crashing, crashed** /kræʃt/) **1** to have an accident; to hit something: *The bus crashed into a tree.* **2** to make something hit another thing: *My uncle crashed his car.* **3** to fall or hit something with a loud noise: *A tree crashed through the window.*

crash helmet /ˈkræʃ helmɪt/ *noun* a hard hat that you wear when you ride a motorbike to keep your head safe

crate /kreɪt/ *noun* a big box for carrying bottles or other things

crater /ˈkreɪtə(r)/ *noun* a large hole in the top of a mountain that explodes (a **volcano**): *Menengai Crater in the Great Rift Valley* ◇ *a crater lake* (= a lake that fills a crater)

crawl[1] /krɔːl/ *verb* (**crawls, crawling, crawled** /krɔːld/) **1** to move slowly on your hands and knees: *Babies crawl before they can walk.* **2** to move slowly with the body close to the ground: *An insect crawled across the floor.*

crawl[2] /krɔːl/ *noun* (no plural) a way of swimming on your front

crayon /ˈkreɪən/ *noun* a soft thick coloured pencil: *The children were drawing pictures with crayons.*

crazy 🔑 /ˈkreɪzi/ *adjective* (**crazier, craziest**) mad or very stupid: *You must be crazy to ride a bike at night with no lights.*
crazy about someone or **something** If you are **crazy about** someone or something, you like them very much: *He's crazy about her.* ◇ *She's crazy about football.*
go crazy become very angry or excited: *My mother will go crazy if I get home late.*

creak /kriːk/ *verb* (**creaks, creaking, creaked** /kriːkt/) to make a noise like a door that needs oil, or like an old wooden floor when you walk on it ▸ **creak** *noun*: *The door opened with a creak.*

cream[1] 🔑 /kriːm/ *noun* **1** (no plural) the thick liquid on the top of milk: *Would you like cream in your coffee?* **2** (*plural* **creams**) a thick liquid that you put on your skin: *She put antiseptic cream on the cut.*

cream[2] 🔑 /kriːm/ *adjective* with a colour between white and yellow: *She was wearing a cream dress.*

creamery /ˈkriːməri/ *noun* (*plural* **creameries**) a place where we make milk into butter and cheese

creamy /ˈkriːmi/ *adjective* (**creamier, creamiest**) **1** with cream in it: *a creamy sauce* **2** like cream: *a creamy colour*

crease /kriːs/ *verb* (**creases, creasing, creased** /kriːst/) **1** to make untidy lines in paper or cloth by not being careful with it: *Don't sit on my jacket – you'll crease it.* **2** to become full of untidy lines: *This shirt creases easily.* ▸ **crease** *noun*: *You need to iron this shirt – it's full of creases.*

create 🔑 /kriˈeɪt/ *verb* (**creates, creating, created**) to make something new: *Do you believe that God created the world?* ◇ *The company has created a new kind of engine.*

creation /kriˈeɪʃn/ *noun* **1** (no plural) making something new: *the creation of the world* **2** (*plural* **creations**) a new thing that someone has made: *The new pictures were the creations of the children.*

creative /kriˈeɪtɪv/ *adjective* A person who is **creative** has a lot of new ideas or is good at making new things: *Young children are very creative.* ◇ *creative thinking* (= thinking about things in a new way)

creative arts /kriˌeɪtɪv ˈɑːts/ *noun* (plural) things like painting and drawing, acting, dancing and playing music

creator /kriˈeɪtə(r)/ *noun* a person who makes something new: *Walt Disney was the creator of Mickey Mouse.*

creature /ˈkriːtʃə(r)/ *noun* any living thing that is not a plant: *birds, fish and other creatures* ◇ *This story is about creatures from another planet.*

credit[1] /ˈkredɪt/ *noun* (no plural) **1** buying something and paying for it later: *He bought the pickup on credit over two years.* **2** saying that someone or something is good: *I did all the work but Kisoso got all the credit for it!*

credit[2] /ˈkredɪt/ *verb* (**credits, crediting, credited**) to add money to someone's bank account: *Ten thousand shillings has been credited to his account.*

credit card 🔑 /ˈkredɪt kɑːd/ *noun* a plastic card from a bank that you can use to buy something and pay for it later: *Can I pay by credit card?*

creep /kriːp/ *verb* (**creeps, creeping, crept** /krept/, **has crept**) to move quietly and carefully so that nobody hears or sees you; to move along close to the ground: *The cat crept towards the bird.* ◇ *I crept into the room where the children were sleeping.*

crescent /ˈkreznt/ *noun* the shape of the moon when it is less than half a circle ➲ picture on page A12

crew /kruː/ *noun* all the people who work on a ship or a plane: *The crew welcomed the passengers on board.*

cricket /ˈkrɪkɪt/ *noun* **1** (*plural* **crickets**) a small brown insect that makes a loud noise **2** (no plural) a game for two teams of eleven players who try to hit a small hard ball with a **bat** on a large field: *We watched a cricket match.* ▶ **cricketer** /ˈkrɪkɪtə(r)/ *noun* a person who plays cricket

cried *form of* CRY[1]

cries **1** *form of* CRY[1] **2** *plural of* CRY[2]

crime 🔑 /kraɪm/ *noun* something that someone does that is against the law: *Murder and robbery are serious crimes.*

> ❖ **WORD BUILDING**
>
> There are many different types of crimes. Here are some of them: **burglary, kidnap, mugging, murder, robbery** and **theft**.

criminal[1] 🔑 /ˈkrɪmɪnl/ *noun* a person who does something that is against the law: *The police failed to catch the criminals.*

criminal[2] 🔑 /ˈkrɪmɪnl/ *adjective* **1** against the law: *Stealing is a criminal act.* **2** of crime: *She studied criminal law.*

crimson /ˈkrɪmzn/ *adjective* with a dark red colour, like blood

cripple /ˈkrɪpl/ *verb* (**cripples, crippling, crippled** /ˈkrɪpld/) to hurt your legs or back badly so that you cannot walk: *She was crippled in an accident.*

crisis 🔑 /ˈkraɪsɪs/ *noun* (*plural* **crises** /ˈkraɪsiːz/) a time when something very dangerous or serious happens: *a political crisis*

crisp[1] /krɪsp/ *adjective* (**crisper, crispest**) **1** hard and dry: *The bread stayed in the oven too long and went crisp.* **2** fresh and not soft: *crisp apples*

crisp[2] /krɪsp/ *noun* a very thin piece of potato cooked in hot oil: *a packet of crisps*

critic /ˈkrɪtɪk/ *noun* **1** a person who says that someone or something is wrong or bad: *critics of the government* **2** a person who writes about a book, film or play and says if they like it or not: *The critics liked his new film.*

critical /ˈkrɪtɪkl/ *adjective* **1** If you are **critical** of someone or something, you say that they are wrong or bad: *They were very critical of my work.* **2** very serious or dangerous: *a critical illness* ▶ **critically** /ˈkrɪtɪkli/ *adverb*: *She's critically ill.*

critical thinking /ˌkrɪtɪkl ˈθɪŋkɪŋ/ *noun* (no plural) the process of thinking about information in a careful way: *The school encourages critical thinking and problem-solving.*

criticism 🔑 /ˈkrɪtɪsɪzəm/ *noun* what you think is bad about someone or something: *I listened to all their criticisms of my plan.*

criticize /ˈkrɪtɪsaɪz/ *verb* (**criticizes, criticizing, criticized** /ˈkrɪtɪsaɪzd/) to say that someone or something is wrong or bad: *He criticizes everything I do!*

croak /krəʊk/ *noun* the noise that a frog makes ▶ **croak** *verb* (**croaks, croaking, croaked** /krəʊkt/): *A frog croaked by the pond.*

crockery /ˈkrɒkəri/ *noun* (no plural) plates, cups and dishes: *She washed the crockery in hot water.*

crocodile /ˈkrɒkədaɪl/ *noun* a big long animal with sharp teeth and a strong tail. **Crocodiles** live in rivers: *A crocodile is a reptile.*

crooked /ˈkrʊkɪd/ *adjective* not straight: *She has crooked teeth.* ➲ Picture at **straight**[1].

crop /krɒp/ *noun* all the plants of one kind that a farmer grows at the same time: *There was a good crop of potatoes last year.* ◇ *Rain is good for the crops.*

crop rotation /ˈkrɒp rəʊteɪʃn/ *noun* (no plural) growing a different **crop** on a piece of land each year so that the soil stays healthy

cross[1] 🔑 /krɒs/ *noun* (*plural* **crosses**) **1** a mark like + or X: *The cross on the map shows where I live.* **2** something with the shape + or X: *She wears a cross around her neck.*

cross[2] 🔑 /krɒs/ *verb* (**crosses, crossing, crossed** /krɒst/) **1** to go from one side of something to the other: *Be careful when you cross the road.* **2** to put one thing over another thing: *She sat down and crossed her legs.*
cross out to draw a line through a word or words, for example because you have made a mistake: *I crossed the word out and wrote it again.*

cross[3] /krɒs/ *adjective* angry: *I was cross with her because she was late.*

crossbar /ˈkrɒsbɑː(r)/ *noun* the piece of wood over the top of a goal ➲ Picture at **goal**.

cross-country /ˌkrɒs ˈkʌntri/ *adjective* across fields; not using roads: *cross-country running*

cross-examine /ˌkrɒs ɪɡˈzæmɪn/ *verb* (**cross-examines, cross-examining, cross-examined** /ˌkrɒs ɪɡˈzæmɪnd/) to ask someone many questions, especially in court: *The witness was cross-examined for over two hours.*

crossing /ˈkrɒsɪŋ/ *noun* a place where cars must stop for people to cross the road

crossroads /ˈkrɒsrəʊdz/ *noun* (*plural* **crossroads**) a place where two roads cross each other

crossword /ˈkrɒswɜːd/ (also **crossword puzzle** /ˈkrɒswɜːd pʌzl/) *noun* a game where you write words in squares

crossword

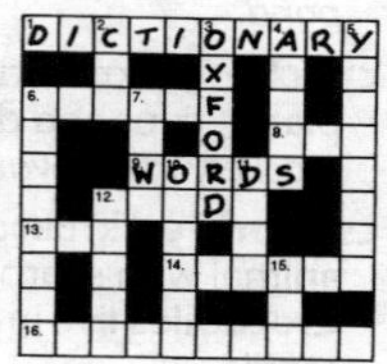

crouch /kraʊtʃ/ *verb* (**crouches, crouching, crouched** /kraʊtʃt/) to bend your knees and back so that your body is close to the ground: *I crouched under the table to hide.*

crow[1] /krəʊ/ *noun* a black or mostly black bird that makes a loud noise

crow[2] /krəʊ/ *verb* (**crows, crowing, crowed** /krəʊd/) to make a loud noise like a **cock** (= a male chicken) makes early in the morning

crowd[1] 🔑 /kraʊd/ *noun* a lot of people together: *There was a large crowd at the football match.* ➲ picture on page A4

crowd[2] /kraʊd/ *verb* (**crowds, crowding, crowded**) to come together in a big group: *The journalists crowded round the Prime Minister.*

crowded 🔑 /ˈkraʊdɪd/ *adjective* full of people: *The streets were very crowded.* ◇ *a crowded bus*

crown[1] /kraʊn/ *noun* a special thing that a king or queen wears on his or her head at important times

crown[2] /kraʊn/ *verb* (**crowns, crowning, crowned** /kraʊnd/) to put a crown on the head of a new king or queen: *Elizabeth II was crowned in 1953.*

crucial /ˈkruːʃl/ *adjective* very important: *a crucial moment*

cruel 🔑 /ˈkruːəl/ *adjective* (**crueller, cruellest**) A person who is cruel is unkind and likes to hurt other people or animals: *He is cruel to his children.* ▶ **cruelly** /ˈkruːəli/ *adverb* in a cruel way: *He was cruelly treated as a child.*

cruelty /ˈkruːəlti/ *noun* (no plural) being cruel: *I can't bear cruelty to animals.*

cruise /kruːz/ *noun* a holiday in which you travel on a ship and visit different places: *They went round the world on a luxury cruise.* ◇ *a cruise ship*

crumb /krʌm/ *noun*

> ❖ **PRONUNCIATION**
> **Crumb** sounds like **come**.

a very small piece of bread, cake or biscuit: *She brushed the cake crumbs off the table.*

crumble /ˈkrʌmbl/ *verb* (**crumbles, crumbling, crumbled** /ˈkrʌmbld/) to break into very small pieces: *The old stone walls are crumbling.*

crunch /krʌntʃ/ *verb* (**crunches, crunching, crunched** /krʌntʃt/) **1** to make a loud noise when you eat something that is hard: *The dog was crunching a bone.* **2** to make a noise like this when you press it hard: *The pebbles crunched under our feet as we walked.*

crush /krʌʃ/ *verb* (**crushes, crushing, crushed** /krʌʃt/) to press something very hard so that you break or damage it: *She sat on my hat and crushed it.*

crust /krʌst/ *noun* the hard part on the outside of bread ▶ **crusty** *adjective* (**crustier, crustiest**) with a hard crust: *crusty bread*

crutch /krʌtʃ/ *noun* (*plural* **crutches**) a long stick that you put under your arm to help you walk when you have hurt your leg: *He broke his leg and now he's on crutches* (= he walks using crutches).

cry[1] /kraɪ/ *verb* (**cries, crying, cried** /kraɪd/, **has cried**) **1** to have drops of water falling from your eyes, usually because you are unhappy: *The baby cries a lot.* **2** to shout or make a loud noise: *'Help!' he cried.* ◇ *She cried out in pain.*

cry[2] /kraɪ/ *noun* (*plural* **cries**) a loud noise that you make to show pain, fear or excitement: *We heard her cries and ran to help.*

crystal /ˈkrɪstl/ *noun* **1** a kind of rock that looks like glass **2** a shape that some chemicals make when they are solid: *salt crystals*

cub /kʌb/ *noun* a young animal such as a **lion**, **bear** or **wolf**

cube /kju:b/ *noun* a shape like a box with six square sides all the same size: *an ice cube* ➲ picture on page A12 ▶ **cubic** /ˈkju:bɪk/ *adjective*: *a cubic metre* (= a space like a cube that is one metre long on each side)

cucumber

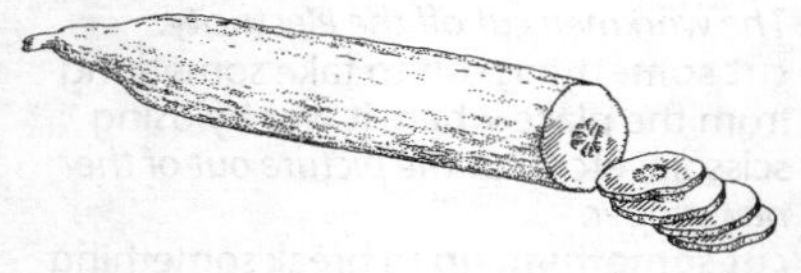

cucumber /ˈkju:kʌmbə(r)/ *noun* a long vegetable with a green skin

cuddle /ˈkʌdl/ *verb* (**cuddles, cuddling, cuddled** /ˈkʌdld/) to hold someone or something in your arms to show love: *He cuddled his baby.* ▶ **cuddle** *noun*: *I gave her a cuddle.*

cuff /kʌf/ *noun* the end part of a sleeve, near your hand

culprit /ˈkʌlprɪt/ *noun* a person who has done something wrong: *The police soon found the culprits.*

cultivate /ˈkʌltɪveɪt/ *verb* (**cultivates, cultivating, cultivated**) **1** to use land for growing plants: *Only a small area of the island was cultivated.* **2** to keep and care for plants ▶ **cultivation** /ˌkʌltɪˈveɪʃn/ *noun* (no plural): *cultivation of the land*

cultural /ˈkʌltʃərəl/ *adjective* **1** about the art, ideas and way of life of a group of people: *There are many cultural differences between Tanzania and Britain.* **2** about things like art, music or theatre: *The festival was packed with cultural events.*

culture /ˈkʌltʃə(r)/ *noun* the art, ideas and way of life of a group of people: *She taught us about the culture of the Maasai.*

cunning /ˈkʌnɪŋ/ *adjective* clever; good at making people believe something that is not true: *Their plan was quite cunning.*

cup /kʌp/ *noun* **1** a small round container with a handle, that you can drink from: *a cup and saucer* **2** a large metal thing like a cup, that you get for winning in a sport: *She's won several cups for swimming.*

cup

cupboard /ˈkʌbəd/ *noun*

❖ **PRONUNCIATION**

We do not say the 'p' in **cupboard**.

a piece of furniture with shelves and doors, where you keep things like clothes or food: *Put the clothes in the cupboard.*

cure[1] /kjʊə(r)/ *verb* (**cures, curing, cured** /kjʊəd/) **1** to make an ill person well again: *The doctors can't cure her.* **2** to make an illness go away: *Can this disease be cured?*

cure[2] /kjʊə(r)/ *noun* something that makes an illness go away: *a cure for cancer*

curiosity /ˌkjʊəriˈɒsəti/ *noun* (no plural) wanting to know about things: *I was full of curiosity about her letter.*

curious /ˈkjʊəriəs/ *adjective* **1** If you are **curious**, you want to know about something: *I am curious to know where she found the money.* **2** strange or unusual: *a curious noise* ▶ **curiously** *adverb*: *'Where is he?' she asked curiously.*

curl[1] /kɜ:l/ *noun* a piece of hair in a round shape: *The baby's hair was a mass of curls.*

curl² /kɜːl/ *verb* (**curls, curling, curled** /kɜːld/) to bend into a round or **curved** shape: *The leaves were brown and curled.*
curl up to put your arms, legs and head close to your body: *The cat curled up and went to sleep.*

curly /ˈkɜːli/ *adjective* (**curlier, curliest**) with a lot of curls: *He's got curly hair.*
OPPOSITE **straight**

currant /ˈkʌrənt/ *noun* **1** a very small sweet black dried fruit: *I made a currant cake.* **2** a small soft fruit: *blackcurrants*

currency /ˈkʌrənsi/ *noun* (*plural* **currencies**) the money that a country uses: *The currency of Ethiopia is the birr.*

current¹ /ˈkʌrənt/ *adjective* Something that is **current** is happening or used now: *current fashions* ▶ **currently** *adverb* now: *We are currently living in Narok.*

current² /ˈkʌrənt/ *noun* **1** air or water that is moving: *It is dangerous to swim here because of the strong current.* **2** electricity that is going through a wire: *electric current*

curriculum vitae /kəˌrɪkjələm ˈviːtaɪ/ = **CV**

curry /ˈkʌri/ *noun* (*plural* **curries**) meat or vegetables cooked with spices. You often eat **curry** with rice.

curse /kɜːs/ *noun* words that wish for something bad to happen to someone: *People say that there is a curse on this house.*

cursor /ˈkɜːsə(r)/ *noun* a small sign that moves on a computer screen and shows where you are working: *Place the cursor on the icon and click.*

curtain /ˈkɜːtn/ *noun* a piece of cloth that you use to cover a window, etc: *Could you open the curtains, please?* ◇ *a pair of curtains*

curtains

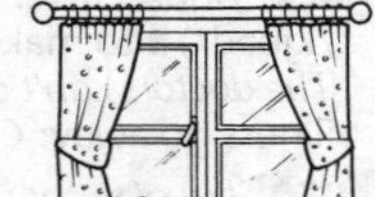

curtain-raiser /ˈkɜːtn reɪzə(r)/ *noun* a short act before the main play in a theatre

curve¹ /kɜːv/ *noun* a line that is not straight; a bend: *The road went round in a curve.*

curve

curve² /kɜːv/ *verb* (**curves, curving, curved** /kɜːvd/) to make a round shape; to bend: *The road curves to the right.* ▶ **curved** /kɜːvd/ *adjective*: *a curved line*

cushion /ˈkʊʃn/ *noun* a bag filled with something soft. You put it on a chair and sit on it or rest your body against it.

custody /ˈkʌstədi/ *noun* (no plural) A person in custody is kept in prison until they are taken to court.

custom /ˈkʌstəm/ *noun* something that a group of people usually do: *It is a custom in Japan to leave your shoes outside a house.*

customer /ˈkʌstəmə(r)/ *noun* a person who buys things from a shop

customs /ˈkʌstəmz/ *noun* (plural) the place at an airport or a port where you must show what you have brought with you from another country: *a customs officer*

cut¹ /kʌt/ *verb* (**cuts, cutting, cut, has cut**) **1** to break or make a hole in something with a knife, scissors, etc: *I cut the string and opened the parcel.* ◇ *I cut the mango in half* (= into two parts). ◇ *She cut her finger on some broken glass.* **2** to take one piece from something bigger: *Can you cut me a piece of that meat, please?* **3** to make something shorter with a knife, scissors, etc: *Have you had your hair cut?* **4** to remove writing or pictures from a computer document so that you can put them somewhere else: *You can* ***cut and paste*** *the diagram into your essay.*
be cut off to be kept alone, away from other people: *Our village was cut off by the floods.*
cut down to use, do or buy less of something: *The doctor told me to cut down on sugar.*
cut something down to cut something so that it falls down: *We cut down the tree.*
cut something off to stop something: *The workmen cut off the electricity.*
cut something out to take something from the place where it was by using scissors, etc: *I cut the picture out of the newspaper.*
cut something up to break something into pieces with a knife or scissors: *He cut up the meat on his plate.*

cut² /kʌt/ *noun* a place where something has been cut: *I have a cut on my leg.*

cute /kjuːt/ *adjective* (**cuter, cutest**) pretty: *What a cute little baby!*

cutlery /ˈkʌtləri/ *noun* (no plural) knives, forks and spoons: *Where do you keep the cutlery?*

CV /ˌsiː ˈviː/ *noun* a list of the education and the jobs that you have had, that you send when you are trying to get a new job: *Send a full CV with your job application.* ℹ CV is short for **curriculum vitae**.

cycle¹ /ˈsaɪkl/ *noun* a bicycle: *a cycle shop*

cycle² /ˈsaɪkl/ *verb* (**cycles**, **cycling**, **cycled** /ˈsaɪkld/) to ride a bicycle: *I cycle to school every day.*

cyclist /ˈsaɪklɪst/ *noun* a person who rides a bicycle: *He's a keen cyclist* (= he likes cycling).

cyclone /ˈsaɪkləʊn/ *noun* a very strong wind that moves in a circle and causes a storm: *The cyclone struck the village.*

cylinder /ˈsɪlɪndə(r)/ *noun* a long round shape, like a tube or a tin of food ➲ picture on page A12 ▸ **cylindrical** /sɪˈlɪndrɪkl/ *adjective* with this shape

cypress /ˈsaɪprəs/ *noun* (*plural* **cypresses**) a tall straight tree that does not lose its leaves

Dd

D, d /diː/ *noun* (*plural* **D's**, **d's** /diːz/) the fourth letter of the English alphabet: *'Dog' begins with a 'D'.*

dab /dæb/ *verb* (**dabs**, **dabbing**, **dabbed** /dæbd/) to touch something lightly and quickly: *She dabbed the cut with cotton wool.*

dad /dæd/ *noun* father: *Hello, Dad.* ◇ *This is my dad.* ℹ Children sometimes use the word **daddy** /ˈdædi/.

daft /dɑːft/ *adjective* (**dafter**, **daftest**) silly; stupid: *I think you're daft to work for nothing!* ◇ *Don't be daft!*

dagger /ˈdæɡə(r)/ *noun* a short pointed knife that people use as a weapon

dagger

daily /ˈdeɪli/ *adjective*, *adverb* that happens or comes every day or once a day: *There are daily flights between Dar es Salaam and Entebbe.* ◇ *a daily newspaper* ◇ *The museum is open daily from 9 to 6.*

dainty /ˈdeɪnti/ *adjective* (**daintier**, **daintiest**) small and pretty: *a dainty little girl*

dairy /ˈdeəri/ *noun* (*plural* **dairies**) a place where milk is kept or where food like butter and cheese is made

> ❖ **SPELLING**
>
> Be careful! We spell **dairy** with **ai** and **diary** with **ia**.

daladala /ˌdʌləˈdʌlə/ *noun* (in Tanzania) a small bus that is used as a taxi

dam

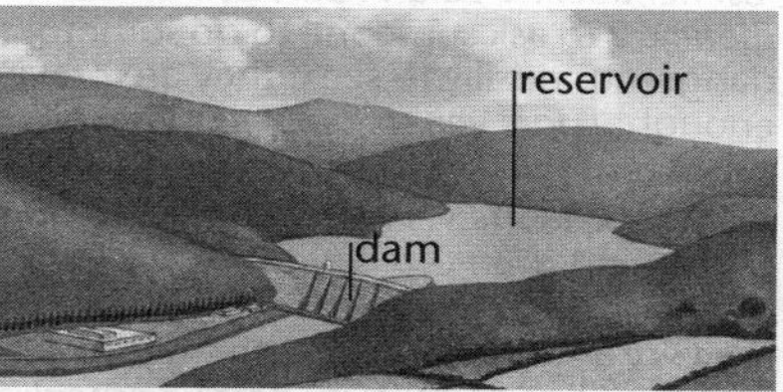

dam /dæm/ *noun* a wall that is built across a river to hold the water back

damage¹ /ˈdæmɪdʒ/ *verb* (**damages**, **damaging**, **damaged** /ˈdæmɪdʒd/) to break or harm something: *The house was badly damaged by fire.*

damage² /ˈdæmɪdʒ/ *noun* **1** (no plural) harm or injury to something: *Hungry insects caused a lot of damage to the crops.* **2 damages** (plural) money that you can ask for if someone damages something of yours or hurts you: *After the accident, Malika was awarded 350 000 shillings in damages.*

damn /dæm/ *exclamation* a rude word that people sometimes use when they are angry: *Damn! I've lost my key!*

damp /dæmp/ *adjective* (**damper**, **dampest**) a little wet: *a cold damp house*

dance¹ /dɑːns/ *verb* (**dances**, **dancing**, **danced** /dɑːnst/) to move your body to music: *Deng dances well.* ◇ *I danced with her all night.* ▸ **dancing** /ˈdɑːnsɪŋ/ *noun* (no plural) moving to music: *The dancing went on all night.*

dance² /dɑːns/ *noun* **1** movements that you do to music: *She stood up and did a little dance.* **2** a party where people dance: *My parents are going to a dance.*

dancer /ˈdɑːnsə(r)/ *noun* a person who dances: *I'm not a very good dancer.* ➲ Look at **ballet dancer**.

danger /ˈdeɪndʒə(r)/ *noun* **1** (no plural) the possibility that something bad may happen: *You may be in danger if you travel alone at late at night.* **2** (*plural* **dangers**) a person or thing that may bring harm or trouble: *Smoking is a danger to health.*

dangerous /ˈdeɪndʒərəs/ *adjective* A person or thing that is dangerous may hurt you: *It's dangerous to drive a car at night without any lights.* ◇ *a dangerous illness* ▸ **dangerously** /ˈdeɪndʒərəsli/ *adverb*: *She drives dangerously.*

dare /deə(r)/ *verb* (**dares, daring, dared** /deəd/) **1** to be brave enough to do something: *I daren't tell Nakato that I've lost her book.* ◇ *I didn't dare ask for more money.* **2** to ask someone to do something dangerous or silly to see if they are brave enough: *I dare you to jump off that wall!*
don't you dare words that you use for telling someone very strongly not to do something: *Don't you dare read my letters!*
how dare you words that show you are very angry about something that someone has done: *How dare you speak to me like that!*

daring /ˈdeərɪŋ/ *adjective* not afraid to do dangerous things

dark¹ /dɑːk/ *adjective* (**darker, darkest**) **1** with no light, or not much light: *It was so dark that I couldn't see anything.* ◇ *What time does it get dark tonight?* OPPOSITE **light** **2** A dark colour is nearer to black than to white: *a dark green skirt* ◇ *He's got dark brown eyes.* OPPOSITE **light, pale** **3** A person who is dark has brown or black hair or skin: *a thin, dark woman* OPPOSITE **fair**

dark² /dɑːk/ *noun* (no plural) where there is no light: *Cats can see in the dark.* ◇ *Are you afraid of the dark?*
after dark after the sun goes down: *Don't go out alone after dark.*
before dark before the sun goes down: *Make sure you get home before dark.*

darkness /ˈdɑːknəs/ *noun* (no plural) where there is no light
in darkness with no light: *The whole house was in darkness.*

darling /ˈdɑːlɪŋ/ *noun* a name that you call someone that you love: *Are you all right, darling?*

dart /dɑːt/ *verb* (**darts, darting, darted**) to move quickly and suddenly: *He darted across the road.*

dash¹ /dæʃ/ *verb* (**dashes, dashing, dashed** /dæʃt/) to run quickly: *I dashed into a shop when it started to rain.* ◇ *I must dash – I'm late for school.*

dash² /dæʃ/ *noun* (*plural* **dashes**) **1** a mark (–) that you use in writing ➲ Look at page A17. **2** a sudden short run: *The robber made a dash for the door.*

dashboard /ˈdæʃbɔːd/ *noun* the part of a car in front of the driver where most of the switches and controls are

data /ˈdeɪtə/ *noun* (plural) facts or information: *We are studying the data that we have collected.*

date /deɪt/ *noun* **1** the number of the day, the month and sometimes the year: *'What's the date today?' 'The first of February.'* ◇ *Today's date is 11 May 2016.* ◇ *What is your date of birth?* ❶ Look at page A11. **2** a small sweet brown fruit
out of date **1** not modern: *The machinery they use is completely out of date.* **2** too old, so that you cannot use it: *This ticket is out of date.*
up to date **1** modern: *The factory is full of up-to-date equipment.* **2** with the newest information: *Is this list of names up to date?*

daughter /ˈdɔːtə(r)/ *noun*

> ❖ **PRONUNCIATION**
> **Daughter** sounds like **water**.

a girl or woman who is someone's child: *They have two daughters and a son.*

daughter-in-law /ˈdɔːtər ɪn lɔː/ *noun* (*plural* **daughters-in-law**) the wife of someone's son

dawn /dɔːn/ *noun* the time when the sun comes up

day /deɪ/ *noun* (*plural* **days**) **1** a time of 24 hours from midnight to the next midnight: *There are seven days in a week.* ◇ *I went to Masaka for a few days.* ◇ *'What day is it today?' 'Tuesday.'* ➲ Look at **daily**. **2** the time when it is light outside: *Most people work during the day and sleep at night.* **3** a time in the past: *In my grandparents' day, there were no computers.*
one day **1** on a certain day in the past: *One day, a letter arrived.* ❶ We often use **one day** at the beginning of a story. **2** at some time in the future: *I hope to visit Canada one day.*
some day at some time in the future: *Some day I'll be rich and famous.*
the day after tomorrow not tomorrow, but the next day
the day before yesterday not yesterday, but the day before

the other day a few days ago: *I went to Kisumu the other day.*
these days now: *A lot of people work with computers these days.*

daylight /ˈdeɪlaɪt/ *noun* (no plural) the light from the sun during the day: *These colours look different in daylight.*

day off /ˌdeɪ ˈɒf/ *noun* (*plural* **days off**) a day when someone does not go to school or work

daytime /ˈdeɪtaɪm/ *noun* (no plural) the time when it is day and not night: *I prefer to study in the daytime and relax in the evening.* OPPOSITE **night-time**

dazzle /ˈdæzl/ *verb* (**dazzles**, **dazzling**, **dazzled** /ˈdæzld/) If a light **dazzles** you, it shines brightly in your eyes so that you cannot see for a short time: *I was dazzled by the car's lights.*

dead[1] /ded/ *adjective* **1** not living: *All my grandparents are dead.* ◇ *Throw away those dead flowers.* ➲ Look at **death**. **2** very quiet: *This town is dead: everywhere is closed after ten o'clock at night.* ▸ **the dead** /ðə ˈded/ *noun* (plural) dead people

dead[2] /ded/ *adverb* completely or very: *I'm dead tired.*

dead end /ˌded ˈend/ *noun* a street that is only open at one end

deadline /ˈdedlaɪn/ *noun* a day or time before which you must do something: *The deadline for finishing this essay is next Tuesday.*

deadly[1] /ˈdedli/ *adjective* (**deadlier**, **deadliest**) Something that is **deadly** may kill people or other living things: *a deadly virus*

deadly[2] /ˈdedli/ *adverb* extremely: *I'm deadly serious.*

deaf /def/ *adjective* not able to hear: *When did he start to go deaf?* ▸ **the deaf** /ðə ˈdef/ *noun* (plural) people who are cannot hear

deafen /ˈdefn/ *verb* (**deafens**, **deafening**, **deafened** /ˈdefnd/) to make a very loud noise so that someone cannot hear well: *We were deafened by the sound of a plane flying overhead.*

deafness /ˈdefnəs/ *noun* (no plural) being deaf

deal[1] /diːl/ *verb* (**deals**, **dealing**, **dealt** /delt/, **has dealt**)
deal in something to buy and sell something in business: *We deal in insurance.*
deal out to give something to each person: *I dealt out the cards for the game.*
deal with something **1** to look after something and do what is necessary: *I am too busy to deal with this problem now.* **2** to tell about something: *The first chapter of the book deals with letter-writing.*

deal[2] /diːl/ *noun* an agreement, usually about buying, selling or working: *Let's make a deal – I'll help you today if you help me tomorrow.*
a good deal or **a great deal** a lot; much: *He's visited a good deal of the country.* ◇ *We ate a great deal.*

dealer /ˈdiːlə(r)/ *noun* a person who buys and sells things: *He's a car dealer.*

dear /dɪə(r)/ *adjective* (**dearer**, **dearest**) **1** a word that you use before a person's name at the beginning of a letter: *Dear Mr Kamau, …* ◇ *Dear Sir or Madam, …* **2** that you love very much: *She was a dear friend.* **3** that costs a lot of money; expensive: *Those radios are too dear.* OPPOSITE **cheap**

death /deθ/ *noun* when a life finishes: *He became manager of the company after his father's death.* ◇ *There are thousands of deaths in car accidents every year.* ➲ Look at **dead**[1].

deathly /ˈdeθli/ (**deathlier**, **deathliest**) *adjective* like death: *There was a deathly silence.*

debate /dɪˈbeɪt/ *noun* a public meeting where people talk about something important ▸ **debate** *verb* (**debates**, **debating**, **debated**): *Parliament is debating the new law.*

debit /ˈdebɪt/ *noun* an amount of money paid out of a bank account: *Can I pay by **debit card** (= a plastic card that takes money directly from your account)?*

debt /det/ *noun*

> ❖ **PRONUNCIATION**
>
> **Debt** sounds like **let**, because we do not say the 'b'.

money that you must pay back to someone: *The company borrowed a lot of money and it still has debts.*
in debt If you are **in debt**, you must pay money to someone.

debut (also **début**) /ˈdeɪbjuː/ *noun* the first time an actor or sports player performs in public: *She made her debut in Mombasa in 2014.*

decay /dɪˈkeɪ/ *verb* (**decays**, **decaying**, **decayed** /dɪˈkeɪd/) to become bad or fall to pieces: *If you don't clean your teeth, they will decay.* ▸ **decay** *noun* (no plural): *tooth decay*

deceive /dɪˈsiːv/ *verb* (**deceives**, **deceiving**, **deceived** /dɪˈsiːvd/) to make someone believe something that is not true: *Egesa's story didn't deceive me – I knew it was a lie.* ◇ *He deceived me into thinking he was a police officer.*

> ❖ **SPELLING**
> Remember! When the sound is /iː/, there is a spelling rule: **i before e, except after c**, so you spell **deceive** with **ei** (not **ie**).

December ⚷ /dɪˈsembə(r)/ *noun* the twelfth month of the year: *Christmas is in December.*

decent /ˈdiːsnt/ *adjective* **1** good enough; right: *You can't wear jeans to the wedding – put on some decent clothes.* **2** honest and good: *decent people*

decide ⚷ /dɪˈsaɪd/ *verb* (**decides**, **deciding**, **decided**) to choose something after thinking: *I can't decide what colour to paint my room.* ◇ *I've decided to save up for a new bike.* ◇ *She decided that she didn't want to come.* ℹ The noun is **decision**.

deciduous /dɪˈsɪdʒuəs/ *adjective* A **deciduous** tree loses its leaves in the cold or dry season. ➲ Look at **evergreen**.

decimal /ˈdesɪml/ *noun* a part of a number, written after a small mark (called a **decimal point**), for example 0.75

> ❖ **SPEAKING**
> We say '0.75' as 'zero point seven five'.

decision ⚷ /dɪˈsɪʒn/ *noun* choosing something after thinking; deciding: *I must make a decision about what I'm going to do when I leave school.* ℹ The verb is **decide**.

decision-making /dɪˈsɪʒn meɪkɪŋ/ *noun* (no plural) deciding about something important, especially with other people: *All the class should be involved in the decision-making process.*

deck /dek/ *noun* the floor of a ship

declare ⚷ /dɪˈkleə(r)/ *verb* (**declares**, **declaring**, **declared** /dɪˈkleəd/) **1** to say very clearly what you think or what you will do, often to a lot of people: *He declared that he was not a thief.* ◇ *The government has declared war on terrorism.* **2** In an airport or port you declare things that you have bought in another country so that you can pay tax on them: *Have you anything to declare?* ▸ **declaration** /ˌdekləˈreɪʃn/ *noun*: *a declaration of independence*

decorate ⚷ /ˈdekəreɪt/ *verb* (**decorates**, **decorating**, **decorated**) to make something look nicer by adding beautiful things to it or by painting it: *We decorated the room with flowers.* ◇ *The hotel is closed because they're decorating the rooms.*

decorations /ˌdekəˈreɪʃnz/ *noun* (plural) beautiful things that you add to something to make it look nicer

decrease /dɪˈkriːs/ *verb* (**decreases**, **decreasing**, **decreased** /dɪˈkriːst/) to become smaller or less; to make something smaller or less: *The number of people in the village has decreased from 200 to 100.* OPPOSITE **increase** ▸ **decrease** /ˈdiːkriːs/ *noun*: *There was a decrease in the number of people living in the village.* OPPOSITE **increase**

deep ⚷ /diːp/ *adjective* (**deeper**, **deepest**) **1** Something that is deep goes down a long way: *Be careful: the water is very deep.* ◇ *There were deep cuts in his face.* OPPOSITE **shallow** ➲ picture on page A5 **2** You use 'deep' to say or ask how far something is from the top to the bottom: *The hole was about six metres deep and three metres wide.* **3** A deep colour is strong and dark: *She has deep brown eyes.* OPPOSITE **pale**, **light** **4** A deep sound is low and strong: *He has a deep voice.* **5** Deep feelings are very strong: *deep sadness* **6** If you are in a deep sleep, it is difficult for someone to wake you up: *She was in such a deep sleep that she didn't hear me calling her.* ℹ The noun is **depth**.

deeply ⚷ /ˈdiːpli/ *adverb* strongly or completely: *He is sleeping very deeply.*

defeat ⚷ /dɪˈfiːt/ *verb* (**defeats**, **defeating**, **defeated**) to win a fight or game against a person or group of people: *Kenya defeated Ghana in the final.* ℹ **Beat** is the word that we usually use. ▸ **defeat** *noun* losing a game, a fight or a war

defence /dɪˈfens/ *noun* (no plural) **1** fighting against people who attack, or keeping away dangerous people or things: *They fought the war in defence of their country.* **2** (also **the defence**) the players who try to stop another person or team scoring goals or points in a game:

The attacking players made the defence work very hard.

defence lawyer /dɪˌfens ˈlɔːjə(r)/ *noun* a person whose job is to prove in a court of law that someone did not do something wrong: *The defence lawyer claimed that the witness was lying.*

defend /dɪˈfend/ *verb* (**defends, defending, defended**) **1** to fight to keep away people or things that attack: *They defended the city against the enemy.* **2** to say that someone has not done something wrong: *My sister defended me when my father said I was lazy.* ◇ *He had a lawyer to defend him in court.* **3** to try to stop another person or team scoring goals or points in a game

defendant /dɪˈfendənt/ = **respondent**

defender /dɪˈfendə(r)/ *noun* a player who must stop the other team from scoring in football and other games

deficient /dɪˈfɪʃnt/ *adjective* not having enough of something ▶ **deficiency** /dɪˈfɪʃnsi/ *noun*: *Vitamin deficiency can cause illness.*

defied (also **defies**) *form of* DEFY

define /dɪˈfaɪn/ *verb* (**defines, defining, defined** /dɪˈfaɪnd/) to say what a word means: *How do you define 'rich'?*

definite ⚷ /ˈdefɪnət/ *adjective* sure; certain: *I want a definite answer, 'yes' or 'no'.* ◇ *They might be able to find you a sponsor but it's not definite.*

definitely ⚷ /ˈdefɪnətli/ *adverb* certainly: *I am definitely going to the match this afternoon – I have already bought my ticket.*

> ❖ **SPELLING**
>
> Remember! You spell **definitely** with two **i** s in the middle.

definition /ˌdefɪˈnɪʃn/ *noun* a group of words that tell you what another word means

defy /dɪˈfaɪ/ *verb* (**defies, defying, defied** /dɪˈfaɪd/, **has defied**) If you **defy** someone or something, you do something that they say you should not do: *She defied her parents and stayed out all night.*

degree ⚷ /dɪˈgriː/ *noun* **1** a measurement of temperature: *Water boils at 100 degrees Celsius (100° C).* **2** a measurement of angles: *There are 90 degrees (90°) in a right angle.* **3** Universities and colleges give degrees to students who have completed special courses there: *She has a degree in Mathematics.*

dehydrate /ˌdiːhaɪˈdreɪt/ *verb* (**dehydrates, dehydrating, dehydrated**) **1** to remove all the water from something: *Dehydrated vegetables can be stored for months.* **2** to lose too much water from your body

delay[1] /dɪˈleɪ/ *noun* (*plural* **delays**) a time when someone or something is late: *There was a long delay at the airport.*
without delay immediately: *You must pay the money without delay.*

delay[2] /dɪˈleɪ/ *verb* (**delays, delaying, delayed** /dɪˈleɪd/) **1** to make someone or something late: *My flight was delayed for two hours because of the bad weather.* **2** to not do something until a later time: *I delayed my visit to Hawa because she was ill.*

deliberate /dɪˈlɪbərət/ *adjective* that you want and plan to do, and do not do by mistake: *'Do you think it was an accident?' 'No, I'm sure it was deliberate.'*

deliberately ⚷ /dɪˈlɪbərətli/ *adverb* If you do something deliberately, you wanted or planned to do it: *The police think that someone started the fire deliberately.*

delicate /ˈdelɪkət/ *adjective* **1** If something is **delicate**, you can break or damage it very easily: *This old book is very delicate.* **2** pretty and fine; not strong: *delicate colours like pale pink and pale blue* ◇ *She had long, delicate fingers.*

delicious /dɪˈlɪʃəs/ *adjective* very good to eat: *This soup is delicious.*

delight[1] /dɪˈlaɪt/ *verb* (**delights, delighting, delighted**) to make someone very pleased or happy

delight[2] /dɪˈlaɪt/ *noun* (no plural) great happiness

delighted /dɪˈlaɪtɪd/ *adjective* very pleased: *I'm delighted to meet you.*

delightful /dɪˈlaɪtfl/ *adjective* very nice; attractive

delinquent /dɪˈlɪŋkwənt/ *adjective* behaving badly and often breaking the law: *She worked in a school for troubled or delinquent children.* ▶ **delinquent** *noun*: *young delinquents*

deliver ⚷ /dɪˈlɪvə(r)/ *verb* (**delivers, delivering, delivered** /dɪˈlɪvəd/) to take something to the place where it must go: *The messenger delivered two large parcels* *to the office.* ▶ **delivery** /dɪˈlɪvəri/ *noun* (*plural* **deliveries**): *We are waiting for a delivery of bread.*

delta /ˈdeltə/ *noun* an area of flat land where a river divides into many smaller rivers as it goes into the sea: *the Niger Delta*

demand[1] /dɪˈmɑːnd/ *verb* (**demands, demanding, demanded**) to say strongly that you must have something: *The workers are demanding more money.* ◇ *She demanded to see the manager.*

demand[2] /dɪˈmɑːnd/ *noun* saying strongly that you must have something: *a demand for higher pay*
in demand wanted by a lot of people: *I'm in demand today – I've had eight phone calls!*

democracy /dɪˈmɒkrəsi/ *noun* (*plural* **democracies**) **1** a system of government where the people choose their leader (by **voting**) **2** a country with a government that the people choose: *Kenya is a democracy.*

democrat /ˈdeməkræt/ *noun* a person who wants **democracy**

democratic /ˌdeməˈkrætɪk/ *adjective* If a country, etc. is **democratic**, all the people in it can choose its leaders or decide about the way it is organized.

demolish /dɪˈmɒlɪʃ/ *verb* (**demolishes, demolishing, demolished** /dɪˈmɒlɪʃt/) to break a building so that it falls down: *They demolished six houses.*
▶ **demolition** /ˌdeməˈlɪʃn/ *noun* (no plural): *The demolition of the factory will make room for more houses.*

demonstrate /ˈdemənstreɪt/ *verb* (**demonstrates, demonstrating, demonstrated**) **1** to show something clearly: *He demonstrated how to operate the machine.* **2** to walk or stand in public with a group of people to show that you have strong feelings about something: *Crowds demonstrated against the war.*

demonstration /ˌdemənˈstreɪʃn/ *noun* **1** a group of people walking or standing together in public to show that they have strong feelings about something: *There were demonstrations in the streets of the capital today.* **2** showing how to do something, or how something works: *He gave us a cookery demonstration.*

den /den/ *noun* the place where a wild animal lives

denied, denies *forms of* DENY

denim /ˈdenɪm/ *noun* (no plural) strong cotton material that is used for making jeans and other clothes. **Denim** is often blue: *a denim jacket*

denomination /dɪˌnɒmɪˈneɪʃn/ *noun* a religious group

dense /dens/ *adjective* (**denser, densest**) **1** with a lot of things or people close together: *dense forests* **2** thick and difficult to see through: *dense smoke* ▶ **densely** /ˈdensli/ *adverb*: *The area is densely populated.*

dent

He **dented** the side of his car.

dent /dent/ *noun* a place in something flat, especially metal, that comes when you hit it or press it hard: *There's a big dent in the side of my car.* ▶ **dent** *verb* (**dents, denting, dented**) to hit something and make a **dent** in it: *I dropped the tin and dented it.*

dentist /ˈdentɪst/ *noun* a person whose job is to look after your teeth ℹ When we talk about visiting the dentist, we say **go to the dentist's**: *I've got toothache so I'm going to the dentist's.* ➲ Note at **tooth**.

deny /dɪˈnaɪ/ *verb* (**denies, denying, denied** /dɪˈnaɪd/, **has denied**) to say that something is not true: *He denied that he had stolen the phone.* ◇ *They denied breaking the window.* OPPOSITE **admit**

depart /dɪˈpɑːt/ *verb* (**departs, departing, departed**) to leave a place: *The train will depart in 5 minutes.* OPPOSITE **arrive**
ℹ **Leave** is the word that we usually use.
ℹ The noun is **departure**.

department /dɪˈpɑːtmənt/ *noun* one of the parts of a university, school, government, shop, big company, etc: *The book department is on the second floor.* ◇ *Professor Mulindwa is the head of the English department.*

department store /dɪˈpɑːtmənt stɔː(r)/ *noun* a big shop that sells a lot of different things

departure /dɪˈpɑːtʃə(r)/ *noun* leaving a place: *The board inside the airport shows arrivals and departures.* ◇ *the departure lounge.* OPPOSITE **arrival** ❶ The verb is **depart**

depend ⚷ /dɪˈpend/ *verb* (**depends, depending, depended**)
depend on someone or **something** **1** to trust someone; to feel sure that someone or something will do what you want: *I know I can depend on you to help me.* **2** to need someone or something: *She depends on her parents for money while she's at college.*
it depends or **that depends** words that you use to show that something is not certain: *'Do you want to go for a swim tomorrow?' 'It depends on how much homework we have.* ◇ *'Can you lend me some money?' 'That depends. How much do you want?'*

dependence /dɪˈpendəns/ *noun* (no plural) **1** the state of needing someone or something: *his dependence on his parents* **2** the state of being unable to live without something: *drug dependence*

dependent /dɪˈpendənt/ *adjective* If you are **dependent** on someone or something, you need them: *A baby is completely dependent on its parents.*

deposit[1] /dɪˈpɒzɪt/ *noun* **1** money that you pay to show that you want something and that you will pay the rest later: *My parents paid a deposit on a holiday.* **2** money that you pay into a bank: *I'd like to make a deposit, please.* ◇ *a deposit form* **3** extra money that you pay when you rent something. You get it back if you do not damage or lose what you have rented.

deposit[2] /dɪˈpɒzɪt/ *verb* (**deposits, depositing, deposited**) to put something somewhere to keep it safe: *The money was deposited in the bank.*

depress /dɪˈpres/ *verb* (**depresses, depressing, depressed** /dɪˈprest/) to make someone feel unhappy: *Seeing sick children really depresses me.*

> ❖ **WORD FAMILY**
> **depress depressed depressing depression**

depressed /dɪˈprest/ *adjective* If you are **depressed**, you are very unhappy: *He's been very depressed since his mother died.*

depressing /dɪˈpresɪŋ/ *adjective* Something that is **depressing** makes you very unhappy: *The stories in the newspaper are always so depressing.*

depression /dɪˈpreʃn/ *noun* (no plural) a feeling of unhappiness that lasts a long time

depth /depθ/ *noun* how deep something is; how far it is from the top of something to the bottom: *What is the depth of the pool?* ◇ *The hole was 2 metres in depth.*

deputy /ˈdepjəti/ *noun* (*plural* **deputies**) the person in a company, school, etc, who does the work of the leader when they are not there: *You can speak to the deputy head teacher if the head is not available.*

derivative /dɪˈrɪvətɪv/ *noun* a word that is made from another word: *'Sadness' is a derivative of 'sad'.*

descend /dɪˈsend/ *verb* (**descends, descending, descended**) to go down: *The plane started to descend.* ➲ Look at **descent**.

> ❖ **SPEAKING**
> It is more usual to say **go down**.

descendant /dɪˈsendənt/ *noun* Someone's **descendants** are their children, their children's children (**grandchildren**) and everybody in their family who lives after them: *Kabaka Mutebi II is a descendant of Kabaka Mwanga.*

descent /dɪˈsent/ *noun* going down: *The plane began its descent to Arusha Airport.* ➲ Look at **descend**.

describe ⚷ /dɪˈskraɪb/ *verb* (**describes, describing, described** /dɪˈskraɪbd/) to say what someone or something is like or what happened: *Can you describe the man you saw?* ◇ *She described the accident to the police.* ❶ The noun is **description**.

description ⚷ /dɪˈskrɪpʃn/ *noun* words that tell what someone or something is like or what happened: *I have given the police a description of the thief.* ❶ The verb is **describe**.

desert[1] ⚷ /ˈdezət/ *noun* a large area of land that is usually covered with sand. Deserts are very dry and not many plants can grow there: *the Sahara Desert*

> ❖ **SPELLING**
> Remember! You spell **desert** with one **s**.

desert[2] /dɪˈzɜːt/ *verb* (**deserts, deserting, deserted**) to leave a person or place when it is wrong to go: *He deserted his wife and children.*

deserted /dɪˈzɜːtɪd/ *adjective* empty, because all the people have left: *At night the streets are deserted.*

desert island /ˌdezət ˈaɪlənd/ *noun* an island where nobody lives, in a hot part of the world

deserve /dɪˈzɜːv/ *verb* (**deserves, deserving, deserved** /dɪˈzɜːvd/) to be good or bad enough to have something: *You have worked very hard and you deserve a rest.* ◇ *They stole money from old people, so they deserve to go to prison.*

design[1] 🔑 /dɪˈzaɪn/ *verb* (**designs, designing, designed** /dɪˈzaɪnd/)

❖ **PRONUNCIATION**

The end part of **design** sounds like **nine**.

to draw a plan that shows how to make something: *He designed his own house.*

design[2] 🔑 /dɪˈzaɪn/ *noun* **1** a drawing that shows how to make something: *Have you seen the designs for the new cars?* **2** lines, shapes and colours on something: *His shirt has a design of blue and green squares on it.*

designer /dɪˈzaɪnə(r)/ *noun* a person whose job is to make drawings that show how something will be made: *a fashion designer*

desire 🔑 /dɪˈzaɪə(r)/ *noun* a feeling of wanting something very much: *a desire for peace* ▶ **desire** /dɪˈzaɪə(r)/ *verb* (**desires, desiring, desired** /dɪˈzaɪəd/): *The shop had every toy you could desire.*

❖ **SPEAKING**

It is more usual to say **want** or **would like**.

desk 🔑 /desk/ *noun* **1** a table, often with drawers, where you sit to write or work: *She sat at a desk to write a story.* **2** a table or place in a building where someone gives information, etc: *Ask at the information desk.*

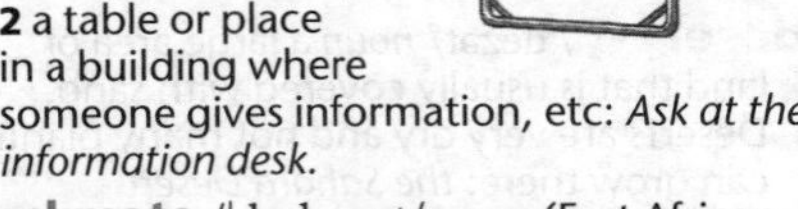

desk

deskmate /ˈdeskmeɪt/ *noun* (East African English) a person who sits next to you in class at school: *I get on well with my deskmate.*

desktop /ˈdesktɒp/ *noun* **1** a computer screen where you can see symbols (called **icons**) showing the programs that you can use **2** (also **desktop computer**) /ˌdesktɒp kəmˈpjuːtə(r)/ a computer that can fit on a desk

despair /dɪˈspeə(r)/ *noun* (no plural) a feeling of not having hope: *He was in despair because he had no money and nowhere to live.*

desperate /ˈdespərət/ *adjective* **1** If you are **desperate**, you have no hope and you are ready to do anything to get what you want: *She is so desperate for food that she will eat anything now.* **2** very serious: *The injured man was in desperate need of a doctor.* ▶ **desperately** *adverb*: *He is desperately unhappy.*

desperation /ˌdespəˈreɪʃn/ *noun* (no plural) the feeling of having no hope, that makes you do anything to get what you want: *In desperation, she sold her fridge to get money for food.*

despise /dɪˈspaɪz/ *verb* (**despises, despising, despised** /dɪˈspaɪzd/) to hate someone or something very much: *I despise people who tell lies.*

despite /dɪˈspaɪt/ *preposition* although something is true; not noticing or not caring about something: *We decided to go out despite the bad weather.*

dessert /dɪˈzɜːt/ *noun* something sweet that you eat at the end of a meal: *We had ice cream for dessert.*

❖ **SPELLING**

Remember! You spell **dessert** with **ss**.

dessertspoon /dɪˈzɜːtspuːn/ *noun* a spoon that you use for eating **desserts**

destination /ˌdestɪˈneɪʃn/ *noun* the place where someone or something is going: *They were very tired when they finally reached their destination.*

destroy 🔑 /dɪˈstrɔɪ/ *verb* (**destroys, destroying, destroyed** /dɪˈstrɔɪd/) to break something completely so that you cannot use it again or so that it is gone: *The house was destroyed by fire.* ℹ The noun is **destruction**.

destruction /dɪˈstrʌkʃn/ *noun* (no plural) breaking something completely so that you cannot use it again or so that it is gone: *the destruction of the crops by insects* ℹ The verb is **destroy**.

detached /dɪˈtætʃt/ *adjective* A **detached** house stands alone and is not joined to any other house.

detail 🔑 /ˈdiːteɪl/ *noun* **1** one of the very small parts that make the whole of

something: *Tell me quickly what happened – I don't need to know all the details.* **2 details** (plural) information about something: *For more details, please phone this number.*
in detail with all the small parts: *Tell me about your plan in detail.*

detective /dɪˈtektɪv/ *noun* a person whose job is to find out who did a crime. **Detectives** are usually police officers.

detergent /dɪˈtɜːdʒənt/ *noun* a powder or liquid that you use for washing things

determination 🔑 /dɪˌtɜːmɪˈneɪʃn/ *noun* (no plural) being certain that you want to do something: *She has shown great determination to succeed.*

determined 🔑 /dɪˈtɜːmɪnd/ *adjective* very certain that you want do something: *She is determined to win.*

detest /dɪˈtest/ *verb* (**detests, detesting, detested**) to hate someone or something very much: *I detest spiders.*

detour /ˈdiːtʊə(r)/ *noun* a longer way to a place when you cannot go by the usual way: *The bridge was closed so we had to make a detour.*

develop 🔑 /dɪˈveləp/ *verb* (**develops, developing, developed** /dɪˈveləpt/) **1** to become bigger or more complete; to make something bigger or more complete: *Children develop into adults.* **2** to begin to have something: *She developed the disease at the age of 27.* **3** When a photograph is developed, special chemicals are used on the film so that you can see the picture.

developing country /dɪˌveləpɪŋ ˈkʌntri/ *noun* a country that is poor and is just starting to have modern industries

development 🔑 /dɪˈveləpmənt/ *noun* **1** (no plural) becoming bigger or more complete; growing: *We are studying the development of babies in their first year of life.* **2** (*plural* **developments**) something new that happens: *There are new developments in science almost every day.* **3** (*plural* **developments**) a piece of land with new buildings on it: *housing developments*

device /dɪˈvaɪs/ *noun* a tool or machine that you use for doing a special job: *a device for opening tins*

devil /ˈdevl/ *noun* **1 the Devil** (no plural) the most powerful evil spirit, in the Christian religion **2** an evil being or spirit

devote /dɪˈvəʊt/ *verb* (**devotes, devoting, devoted**) to give a lot of time or energy to something: *She devoted her life to helping the poor.*

devoted /dɪˈvəʊtɪd/ *adjective* If you are **devoted** to someone or something, you love them very much: *Egesa is devoted to his wife and children.*

dew /djuː/ *noun* (no plural) small drops of water that form on plants and grass in the night: *In the morning, the grass was wet with dew.*

diagnose /ˈdaɪəgnəʊz/ *verb* (**diagnoses, diagnosing, diagnosed** /ˈdaɪəgnəʊzd/) to discover what is causing an illness: *She was diagnosed with malaria.*

diagnosis /ˌdaɪəgˈnəʊsɪs/ *noun* (*plural* **diagnoses** /ˌdaɪəgˈnəʊsiːz/) finding out what is causing an illness: *The doctor made a diagnosis quickly.*

diagonal /daɪˈægənl/ *adjective* If you draw a **diagonal** line from one corner of a square to another, you make two triangles. ➲ picture on page A12

diagram 🔑 /ˈdaɪəgræm/ *noun* a picture that explains something: *This diagram shows all the parts of an engine.*

dial[1] /ˈdaɪəl/ *noun* a circle with numbers or letters on it. Some telephones and clocks have dials.

dial[2] /ˈdaɪəl/ *verb* (**dials, dialling, dialled** /ˈdaɪəld/) to make a telephone call by pushing buttons or moving a dial: *You have dialled the wrong number.*

dialogue /ˈdaɪəlɒg/ *noun* words that people say to each other in a book, play or film

diameter /daɪˈæmɪtə(r)/ *noun* a straight line across a circle, through the centre ➲ picture on page A12

diamond 🔑 /ˈdaɪəmənd/ *noun* **1** a hard stone that looks like clear glass and is very expensive: *South Africa is famous for its diamond mines.* ◇ *a diamond necklace* **2** the shape ♦ **3 diamonds** (plural) the **playing cards** (= the set of cards used for playing games) that have red shapes like diamonds on them: *Have you got the eight of diamonds?*

diarrhoea /ˌdaɪəˈrɪə/ *noun* an illness that makes you pass waste material (**faeces**) from your body very often and in a more liquid form than usual

diary /ˈdaɪəri/ *noun* (*plural* **diaries**) **1** a book where you write what you are going

to do: *I'll look in my diary to see if I'm free tomorrow.* **2** a book where you write what you have done each day
keep a diary to write in a diary every day

> ❖ **SPELLING**
> Be careful! We spell **diary** with **ia** and **dairy** with **ai**.

dice /daɪs/ *noun* (*plural* **dice**) a small piece of wood or plastic with spots on the sides for playing games: *Throw the dice.*

dice

dictate /dɪkˈteɪt/ *verb* (**dictates, dictating, dictated**) **1** to say words so that another person can write them: *She dictated a letter to the children.* ❶ The noun is **dictation**. **2** to tell someone that they must do something: *You can't dictate to me where I should go.* ➲ Look at **dictator**.

dictation /dɪkˈteɪʃn/ *noun* words that you say so that another person can write them: *We had a dictation in English today* (= a test when we wrote what the teacher said). ❶ The verb is **dictate**.

dictator /dɪkˈteɪtə(r)/ *noun* a person who has complete control of a country

dictionary 🔑 /ˈdɪkʃənri/ *noun* (*plural* **dictionaries**) a book that gives words from A to Z and explains what each word means: *Look it up in your dictionary.*

did *form of* DO¹

didn't /ˈdɪdnt/ = **did not**

die 🔑 /daɪ/ *verb* (**dies, dying, died** /daɪd/, **has died**) to stop living: *People, animals and plants die if they don't have water.*
die down to slowly become less strong: *The storm died down.*
die of something to stop living because of an illness: *She died of a heart attack.*

diesel /ˈdiːzl/ *noun* **1** (no plural) a type of oil that is used in some engines instead of petrol: *a diesel engine* **2** (*plural* **diesels**) a vehicle that uses **diesel**

diet /ˈdaɪət/ *noun* **1** the food that you usually eat: *It is important to have a healthy diet.* **2** special foods that you eat when you are ill or when you want to get thinner
be or **go on a diet** to eat only special foods because you want to get thinner

difference 🔑 /ˈdɪfrəns/ *noun* the way that one thing is not the same as another thing: *There is a big difference between the female mosquito and the male.* ◇ *What's the difference in price between these two bikes?* OPPOSITE **similarity**
make a difference to change something: *Your help has made a big difference – I understand the work much better now.*
make no difference to not change anything; to not be important: *It makes no difference which bus you catch – the price of the ticket is the same.*
tell the difference to see how one thing or person is different from another: *Teta looks exactly like her sister – I can't tell the difference (between them).*

different 🔑 /ˈdɪfrənt/ *adjective* **1** not the same: *These two shoes are different sizes!* ◇ *Pembe is very different from his brother.* **2** many and not the same: *They grow fifteen different sorts of fruit.* ▶ **differently** *adverb*: *He's very quiet at home but he behaves differently at school.*

difficult 🔑 /ˈdɪfɪkəlt/ *adjective* **1** not easy to do or understand: *a difficult problem* ◇ *The exam was very difficult.* ◇ *It's difficult to learn a new language.* OPPOSITE **easy, simple** **2** A person who is difficult is not easy to please or will not do what you want: *She's a very difficult child.*

difficulty 🔑 /ˈdɪfɪkəlti/ *noun* (*plural* **difficulties**) a problem; something that is not easy to do or understand: *I have difficulty understanding his accent.*
with difficulty not easily: *My grandfather walks with difficulty now.*

dig 🔑 /dɪg/ *verb* (**digs, digging, dug** /dʌg/, **has dug**) to move earth and make a hole in the ground: *You need to dig the garden before you plant the seeds.* ◇ *They dug a tunnel through the mountain for the new railway.*
dig up to take something from the ground by digging: *They dug up some old coins in their field.*

dig

digest /daɪˈdʒest/ *verb* (**digests, digesting, digested**) to change food in your stomach so that your body can use it ▶ **digestion** /daɪˈdʒestʃən/ *noun* (no plural): *Fresh fruit is good for the digestion.*

digit *noun* /ˈdɪdʒɪt/ any of the numbers from 0 to 9: *a six-digit telephone number*

digital /ˈdɪdʒɪtl/ *adjective* **1** A **digital** clock or watch shows the time in numbers. **2** using an electronic system that changes sounds or pictures into numbers before it stores or sends them: *a digital camera*

digital television /ˌdɪdʒɪtl ˈtelɪvɪʒn/ *noun* (no plural) a way of sending and receiving television programmes using **digital** signals

dignified /ˈdɪɡnɪfaɪd/ *adjective* calm, quiet and serious: *a dignified old lady*

dignity /ˈdɪɡnəti/ *noun* (no plural) calm and serious behaviour that makes other people respect you: *She spoke to him with quiet dignity.*

diligent /ˈdɪlɪdʒənt/ *adjective* showing care and effort in your work or duties: *a diligent student* ▸ **diligence** /ˈdɪlɪdʒəns/ *noun* (no plural): *She shows great diligence in her work.*

dilute /daɪˈljuːt/ *verb* (**dilutes**, **diluting**, **diluted**) to add water to another liquid: *Dilute this paint before you use it.*

dim /dɪm/ *adjective* (**dimmer**, **dimmest**) not bright or clear: *The light was so dim that we couldn't see anything.* ▸ **dimly** *adverb*: *The room was dimly lit.*

dinghy /ˈdɪŋi/ *noun* (*plural* **dinghies**) a small boat

dining room /ˈdaɪnɪŋ ruːm/ *noun* a room where people eat

dinner /ˈdɪnə(r)/ *noun* the largest meal of the day. You usually have dinner in the evening: *What time do you have dinner?* ◇ *What's for dinner?* ➲ Note at **meal**.

dinosaur /ˈdaɪnəsɔː(r)/ *noun* a big wild animal that lived a very long time ago

dip /dɪp/ *verb* (**dips**, **dipping**, **dipped** /dɪpt/) to put something into a liquid for a short time and then take it out again: *Dip your hand in the water to see how hot it is.*

dinosaur

diploma /dɪˈpləʊmə/ *noun* a piece of paper that shows you have passed an examination or finished special studies: *a teaching diploma*

diplomat /ˈdɪpləmæt/ *noun* a person whose job is to speak and do things for their country in another country ▸ **diplomatic** /ˌdɪpləˈmætɪk/ *adjective*: *diplomatic talks*

direct[1] /dəˈrekt/ *adjective, adverb* **1** as straight as possible, without turning or stopping: *Which is the most direct way to the town centre from here?* ◇ *You can fly direct from Entebbe to Kigali.* ◇ *The 7.30 bus goes direct to Kampala.* **2** from one person or thing to another person or thing with nobody or nothing between them: *You should keep this plant out of direct sunlight.* ➲ Look at **indirect**.

direct[2] /dəˈrekt/ *verb* (**directs**, **directing**, **directed**) **1** to tell someone how to get to a place: *The police officer directed us to the passport office.* **2** to tell or show someone how to do something; to control someone or something: *He has directed many plays at the National Theatre.*

direction /dəˈrekʃn/ *noun* where a person or thing is going or looking: *They got lost because they went in the wrong direction.*

directions /dəˈrekʃnz/ *noun* (plural) words that tell you how to get to a place or how to do something: *I couldn't find the school so I asked a woman for directions.* ◇ *I didn't read the directions on the packet before I took the medicine.*

directly /dəˈrektli/ *adverb* **1** exactly; in a direct way: *The teacher was looking directly at me.* ◇ *The post office is directly opposite the bank.* **2** immediately: *They left directly after breakfast.*

director /dəˈrektə(r)/ *noun* **1** a person who controls a business or a group of people **2** a person who controls a film or play, for example by telling the actors what to do

direct speech /dəˌrekt ˈspiːtʃ/ *noun* (no plural) the exact words that someone said ➲ Look at **reported speech**.

dirt /dɜːt/ *noun* (no plural) stuff that is not clean, for example mud or dust: *The children came into the house covered in dirt.*

dirty /ˈdɜːti/ *adjective* (**dirtier**, **dirtiest**) not clean: *Your hands are dirty – go and wash them!*

dis- /dɪs/ *prefix* You can add **dis-** to the beginning of some words to give them the opposite meaning: *disagree* (= not agree) ◇ *dishonest* (= not honest)

disability /ˌdɪsəˈbɪləti/ *noun* (*plural* **disabilities**) something that makes you unable to use a part of your body well

disable /dɪsˈeɪbl/ *verb* (**disables**, **disabling**, **disabled** /dɪsˈeɪbld/) to make you unable to use a part of your body well

disabled /dɪsˈeɪbld/ *adjective* not able to use a part of your body well: *Kamau is disabled – he injured his legs in an accident.* ▸ **the disabled** *noun* (plural) people who are disabled

disadvantage 🔑 /ˌdɪsədˈvɑːntɪdʒ/ *noun* a problem that makes something difficult or less good: *One of the disadvantages of living by a main road is the noise.* OPPOSITE **advantage**

disagree 🔑 /ˌdɪsəˈɡriː/ *verb* (**disagrees**, **disagreeing**, **disagreed** /ˌdɪsəˈɡriːd/) to say that another person's idea is wrong; to not agree: *I said it was a good film, but Shema disagreed with me.* ◇ *My sister and I disagree about everything!*

disagreement 🔑 /ˌdɪsəˈɡriːmənt/ *noun* a talk between people with different ideas; an argument: *My parents sometimes have disagreements about money.* OPPOSITE **agreement**

disappear 🔑 /ˌdɪsəˈpɪə(r)/ *verb* (**disappears**, **disappearing**, **disappeared** /ˌdɪsəˈpɪəd/) If a person or thing disappears, they go away so people cannot see them: *The sun disappeared behind the clouds.* ◇ *The police are looking for a woman who disappeared on Sunday.* OPPOSITE **appear** ▸ **disappearance** /ˌdɪsəˈpɪərəns/ *noun*: *Everybody was worried about the child's disappearance.*

> ❖ **SPELLING**
> Remember! You spell **disappear** with **s** and **pp**.

disappoint 🔑 /ˌdɪsəˈpɔɪnt/ *verb* (**disappoints**, **disappointing**, **disappointed**) to make you sad because what you wanted did not happen: *I'm sorry to disappoint you, but you haven't won the prize.*

disappointed 🔑 /ˌdɪsəˈpɔɪntɪd/ *adjective* If you are disappointed, you feel sad because what you wanted did not happen: *Teta was disappointed when she didn't win the prize.*

> ❖ **SPELLING**
> Remember! You spell **disappointed** with **s** and **pp**.

disappointing 🔑 /ˌdɪsəˈpɔɪntɪŋ/ *adjective* If something is disappointing, it makes you feel sad because it is not as good as you hoped: *disappointing exam results*

disappointment 🔑 /ˌdɪsəˈpɔɪntmənt/ *noun* **1** (no plural) a feeling of sadness because what you wanted did not happen: *She couldn't hide her disappointment when she lost the match.* **2** (*plural* **disappointments**) something that makes you sad because it is not what you hoped: *The new cafe was a disappointment – the food was terrible.*

disapproval /ˌdɪsəˈpruːvl/ *noun* (no plural) a feeling that something is bad or that someone is behaving badly: *She shook her head in disapproval.* OPPOSITE **approval**

disapprove /ˌdɪsəˈpruːv/ *verb* (**disapproves**, **disapproving**, **disapproved** /ˌdɪsəˈpruːvd/) to think that someone or something is bad: *Kamau's parents disapproved of his new friend.* OPPOSITE **approve**

> ❖ **SPELLING**
> Remember! You spell **disapprove** with **s** and **pp**.

disaster 🔑 /dɪˈzɑːstə(r)/ *noun* **1** something very bad that happens and that may hurt a lot of people: *Floods and earthquakes are disasters.* **2** something that is very bad: *The match was a disaster! Our team lost 10–0!*

disastrous /dɪˈzɑːstrəs/ *adjective* very bad; that causes great trouble: *The heavy rain brought disastrous floods.*

disbelief /ˌdɪsbɪˈliːf/ *noun* (no plural) a feeling that you do not believe something: *'It can't be true!' he shouted in disbelief.*

disc /dɪsk/ *noun* a round flat thing ➲ Look at **hard disk**.

disciple /dɪˈsaɪpl/ *noun* a person who follows a religious leader

discipline /ˈdɪsəplɪn/ *noun* (no plural) teaching you to control yourself and follow rules: *Children learn discipline at school.* ▸ **discipline** *verb* (**disciplines**, **disciplining**, **disciplined** /ˈdɪsəplɪnd/): *You must discipline yourself to work harder.*

disc jockey /ˈdɪsk dʒɒki/ *noun* (*plural* **disc jockeys**) a person who plays records on the radio or in a club ❶ The short form is **DJ**.

disco /ˈdɪskəʊ/ *noun* (*plural* **discos**) a place where people dance and listen to music

disconnect /ˌdɪskəˈnekt/ *verb* (**disconnects**, **disconnecting**, **disconnected**) to stop electricity, water, etc: *Your phone will be disconnected if you don't pay the bill.*

discontented /ˌdɪskənˈtentɪd/ *adjective* not happy: *Karimi is discontented with his part in the play.* OPPOSITE **contented**

discount /ˈdɪskaʊnt/ *noun* money that someone takes away from the price of something to make it cheaper: *The company is offering a 50% discount on travel this week.*

discourage /dɪsˈkʌrɪdʒ/ *verb* (**discourages**, **discouraging**, **discouraged** /dɪsˈkʌrɪdʒd/) to make someone not want to do something: *Kirezi's parents tried to discourage her from leaving school.* OPPOSITE **encourage**

discover 🔑 /dɪˈskʌvə(r)/ *verb* (**discovers**, **discovering**, **discovered** /dɪˈskʌvəd/) to find or learn something for the first time: *Who first discovered America?* ◇ *I was in the shop when I discovered that I didn't have any money.*

discovery /dɪˈskʌvəri/ *noun* (*plural* **discoveries**) finding or learning something for the first time: *Scientists have made an important new discovery.*

discriminate /dɪˈskrɪmɪneɪt/ *verb* (**discriminates**, **discriminating**, **discriminated**) to treat one person or a group in a different way to others: *This company discriminates against women – it pays them less than men for doing the same work.* ▸ **discrimination** /dɪˌskrɪmɪˈneɪʃn/ *noun* (no plural): *religious discrimination* (= treating someone in an unfair way because their religion is not the same as yours)

discus /ˈdɪskəs/ *noun* (no plural) the event or sport of throwing a heavy round flat object (called a **discus**) as far as possible

discus

discus

discuss 🔑 /dɪˈskʌs/ *verb* (**discusses**, **discussing**, **discussed** /dɪˈskʌst/) to talk about something: *I discussed the problem with my parents.*

discussion 🔑 /dɪˈskʌʃn/ *noun* talking about something seriously: *We had an interesting discussion about the trip.*

disease 🔑 /dɪˈziːz/ *noun* an illness: *Cholera and malaria are diseases.*

disembark /ˌdɪsɪmˈbɑːk/ *verb* (**disembarks**, **disembarking**, **disembarked** /ˌdɪsɪmˈbɑːkt/) to get off a ship or a plane OPPOSITE **embark**

disgrace /dɪsˈɡreɪs/ *noun* (no plural) when other people stop thinking well of you, because you have done something bad: *He's in disgrace because he stole money from his brother.*

disgraceful /dɪsˈɡreɪsfl/ *adjective* Something that is **disgraceful** is very bad and makes you feel shame: *The way the football fans behaved was disgraceful.*

disguise[1] /dɪsˈɡaɪz/ *verb* (**disguises**, **disguising**, **disguised** /dɪsˈɡaɪzd/) to make someone or something different so that people will not know who or what they are: *They disguised themselves as guards and escaped from the prison.*

disguise[2] /dɪsˈɡaɪz/ *noun* things that you wear so that people do not know who you are: *We went to the party in disguise.*

disgust[1] 🔑 /dɪsˈɡʌst/ *noun* (no plural) a strong feeling of not liking something: *They covered their faces in disgust when they smelt the dead elephant.*

disgust[2] 🔑 /dɪsˈɡʌst/ *verb* (**disgusts**, **disgusting**, **disgusted**) to make someone have a strong feeling of not liking something: *Cruelty towards animals disgusts me.*

disgusted 🔑 /dɪsˈɡʌstɪd/ *adjective* If you are disgusted, you have a strong feeling of not liking something: *I was disgusted to find a rat in the house.*

disgusting 🔑 /dɪsˈɡʌstɪŋ/ *adjective* very bad: *What a disgusting smell!* SAME MEANING **revolting**, **vile**

dish 🔑 /dɪʃ/ *noun* (*plural* **dishes**) **1** a container for food. You can use a dish to cook food in an oven, or to put food on the table: *They helped themselves from a large dish of rice.* **2** a part of a meal: *We had a fish dish and a vegetable dish.* **3 the dishes** (plural) all the plates, bowls, cups, etc. that you must wash after a meal: *I'll wash the dishes.*

dishonest 🔑 /dɪsˈɒnɪst/ *adjective* A person who is dishonest says things that are not true, or steals or cheats: *Beware* *of dishonest traders selling fake goods.* OPPOSITE **honest**

dishonour¹ /dɪsˈɒnə(r)/ *noun* (no plural) a loss of respect because you have done something bad: *Her cheating in exams has brought dishonour on the school.*

dishonour² /dɪsˈɒnə(r)/ *verb* (**dishonours, dishonouring, dishonoured** /dɪsˈɒnəd/) to refuse to keep a promise: *a dishonoured cheque* (= one that will not be paid)

disinfect /ˌdɪsɪnˈfekt/ *verb* (**disinfects, disinfecting, disinfected**) to clean something very well with a special liquid: *Wash the dustbin and disinfect it regularly.*

disinfectant /ˌdɪsɪnˈfektənt/ *noun* a liquid that you use for cleaning something very well: *The hospital smelt strongly of disinfectant.*

disk 🔑 /dɪsk/ *noun* a flat thing that stores information for computers: *a hard disk*

disk drive /ˈdɪsk draɪv/ *noun* the part of a computer where you can put a disk ➲ Picture at **computer**.

dislike /dɪsˈlaɪk/ *verb* (**dislikes, disliking, disliked** /dɪsˈlaɪkt/) to not like someone or something: *I dislike getting up early.* ▶ **dislike** *noun* a feeling of not liking someone or something: *I have a strong dislike of snakes.*

disloyal /dɪsˈlɔɪəl/ *adjective* A person who is **disloyal** does not support their friends, family or country. OPPOSITE **loyal**

dismal /ˈdɪzməl/ *adjective* that makes you feel sad; not bright: *dark, dismal buildings*

dismay /dɪsˈmeɪ/ *noun* (no plural) a strong feeling of surprise and worry: *Kamal looked at me in dismay when I told him about the accident.* ▶ **dismayed** /dɪsˈmeɪd/ *adjective*: *I was dismayed to find that someone had stolen my bike.*

dismiss /dɪsˈmɪs/ *verb* (**dismisses, dismissing, dismissed** /dɪsˈmɪst/) **1** to make someone leave their job: *He was dismissed for stealing money from the company.*

> ❖ **SPEAKING**
> **Sack** and **fire** are the words that we usually use.

2 to allow someone to leave a place: *The lesson finished and the teacher dismissed the class.*

disobedient /ˌdɪsəˈbiːdiənt/ *adjective* A person who is **disobedient** does not do what someone tells them to do: *a disobedient child* OPPOSITE **obedient**

▶ **disobedience** /ˌdɪsəˈbiːdiəns/ *noun* (no plural) not doing what someone tells you to do OPPOSITE **obedience**

disobey /ˌdɪsəˈbeɪ/ *verb* (**disobeys, disobeying, disobeyed** /ˌdɪsəˈbeɪd/) to not do what someone tells you to do: *She disobeyed her parents and went out with her friends.* OPPOSITE **obey**

disorderly /dɪsˈɔːdəli/ *adjective* **1** untidy **2** behaving badly OPPOSITE **orderly**

dispensary /dɪˈspensəri/ *noun* (**dispensaries**) a place where you can get medicine

display¹ /dɪˈspleɪ/ *verb* (**displays, displaying, displayed** /dɪˈspleɪd/) to show something so that people can see it: *Our pictures were displayed on the wall.*

display² /dɪˈspleɪ/ *noun* (*plural* **displays**) something that people look at: *a display of traditional dancing*
on display in a place where people can look at it: *The paintings are on display in the museum.*

disposable /dɪˈspəʊzəbl/ *adjective* made to be thrown away after you have used it: *disposable gloves*

dispose /dɪˈspəʊz/ *verb* (**disposes, disposing, disposed** /dɪˈspəʊzd/)
dispose of something to throw something away or give something away because you do not want it: *Where can I dispose of this rubbish?* ▶ **disposal** /dɪˈspəʊzl/ *noun* (no plural): *the disposal of nuclear waste*

dispute /dɪˈspjuːt/ *noun* an angry talk between people with different ideas: *There was a dispute about which driver caused the accident.*

dissatisfied /ˌdɪsˈsætɪsfaɪd/ *adjective* not pleased with something: *I am very dissatisfied with your work.* OPPOSITE **satisfied**

distance 🔑 /ˈdɪstəns/ *noun* **1** how far it is from one place to another place: *It's a short distance from my house to the station.* ◇ *We usually measure distance in kilometres or miles.* **2** a place that is far from someone or something: *From a distance, he looks quite young.*
in the distance far away: *I could see a light in the distance.*

distant /ˈdɪstənt/ *adjective* far away in space or time: *distant countries*

distinct /dɪˈstɪŋkt/ *adjective* **1** easy to hear, see or smell; clear: *There is a distinct smell* *of burning in this room.* **2** clearly different: *The African and the Indian elephant are two distinct species.* ▸ **distinctly** *adverb* clearly: *I distinctly heard him say his name was Rono.*

distinguish /dɪˈstɪŋɡwɪʃ/ *verb* (**distinguishes**, **distinguishing**, **distinguished** /dɪˈstɪŋɡwɪʃt/) to see, hear, etc. the difference between two things or people: *Some people can't distinguish between me and my twin sister.* ◇ *Can you distinguish a South African accent from an English one?*

distinguished /dɪˈstɪŋɡwɪʃt/ *adjective* famous or important: *a distinguished actor*

distract /dɪˈstrækt/ *verb* (**distracts**, **distracting**, **distracted**) If a person or thing **distracts** you, they stop you thinking about what you are doing: *The noise distracted me from my homework.*

distress /dɪˈstres/ *noun* (no plural) **1** a strong feeling of pain or sadness **2** being in danger and needing help: *a ship in distress*

distressing /dɪˈstresɪŋ/ *adjective* making you feel sad or upset: *I've just heard some distressing news.*

distribute /dɪˈstrɪbjuːt/ *verb* (**distributes**, **distributing**, **distributed**) to give or send things to each person: *New books are distributed on the first day of school.* ▸ **distribution** /ˌdɪstrɪˈbjuːʃn/ *noun* (no plural): *the distribution of newspapers*

district /ˈdɪstrɪkt/ *noun* a part of a country or town: *Ruvuma district is in Southern Tanzania.*

disturb 🔑 /dɪˈstɜːb/ *verb* (**disturbs**, **disturbing**, **disturbed** /dɪˈstɜːbd/) **1** to stop someone doing something, for example thinking, working or sleeping: *My brother always disturbs me when I'm trying to do my homework.* ◇ *Do not disturb* (= a notice that you put on a door to tell people not to come in). **2** to worry someone: *We were disturbed by the news that our teacher was ill.*

disturbance /dɪˈstɜːbəns/ *noun* **1** a thing that stops you doing something, for example thinking, working or sleeping **2** when a group of people fight or make a lot of noise and trouble: *The football fans were causing a disturbance outside the stadium.*

ditch /dɪtʃ/ *noun* (*plural* **ditches**) a long narrow hole at the side of a road or field that carries away water

dive /daɪv/ *verb* (**dives**, **diving**, **dived** /daɪvd/) **1** to jump into water with your arms and head first: *Ali dived into the pool.* **2** to go under water: *The birds were diving for fish.* **3** to move or jump quickly: *Opiyo dived for the ball.* ▸ **diving** /ˈdaɪvɪŋ/ *noun* (no plural) the sport of jumping into water or swimming underwater

diversion /daɪˈvɜːʃn/ *noun* a way that you must go when the usual way is closed: *There was a diversion around Elgon Road because of a road accident.*

divert /daɪˈvɜːt/ *verb* (**diverts**, **diverting**, **diverted**) to make something go a different way: *Our flight was diverted to another airport because of the bad weather.*

divide 🔑 /dɪˈvaɪd/ *verb* (**divides**, **dividing**, **divided**) **1** to share or cut something into smaller parts: *The teacher divided the class into groups of three.* ◇ *The book is divided into ten chapters.* **2** to go into parts: *When the road divides, go left.* **3** to find out how many times one number goes into a bigger number: *36 divided by 4 is 9* (36 ÷ 4 = 9). ⓘ The noun is **division**.

divine /dɪˈvaɪn/ *adjective* of, like or from God or a god: *a divine message*

division 🔑 /dɪˈvɪʒn/ *noun* **1** (no plural) sharing or cutting something into parts: *the division of the class into four groups* **2** (no plural) finding out how many times one number goes into a bigger number: *the division sign* ÷ **3** (*plural* **divisions**) one of the parts of a big company: *He works in the sales division.* ⓘ The verb is **divide**.

divorce /dɪˈvɔːs/ *noun* the end of a marriage by law: *She is getting a divorce.* ▸ **divorce** *verb* (**divorces**, **divorcing**, **divorced** /dɪˈvɔːst/): *He divorced his wife.* ⓘ We often say **get divorced**: *They got divorced last year.* ▸ **divorced** /dɪˈvɔːst/ *adjective*: *He's not married – he's divorced.*

dizzy /ˈdɪzi/ *adjective* (**dizzier**, **dizziest**) If you feel **dizzy**, you feel that everything is turning round and round and that you are going to fall: *The room was very hot and I started to feel dizzy.*

DJ /ˈdiː dʒeɪ/ *short for* DISC JOCKEY

do[1] /duː; də/ *verb* **1** a word that you use with another verb to make a question: *Do you want a drink?* ◇ *Did you ask Achal to come with us?* **2** a word that you use with another verb when you are saying 'not': *I like watching football but I don't* (= do not) *like playing it.* **3** a word that you use in place of saying something again: *She doesn't speak English, but I do* (= I speak English). **4** a word that you use before another verb to make its meaning stronger: *You do look nice!* ➲ Look at the table below.

do[2] /duː/ *verb* (**does** /dʌz/, **doing**, **did** /dɪd/, **has done** /dʌn/) **1** to carry out an action: *What are you doing?* ◇ *She did the cooking.* ◇ *What did you do with my key?* (= where did you put it?) **2** to finish something; to find the answer: *I have done my homework.* ◇ *I can't do this sum – it's too difficult.* **3** to have a job or to study something: *'Tell me what he does.' 'He's a doctor.'* ◇ *She's doing Economics at Makerere University.* **4** to be good enough; to be enough: *I couldn't find any rope, but will this string do?* ➲ Look at the table below.

be or **have to do with someone** or **something** to be connected with someone or something: *I'm not sure what his job is – I think it's something to do with computers.* ◇ *Don't read that letter. It has nothing to do with you!*

could do with something to want or need something: *I could do with a drink.*

do up 1 to fasten something: *Do up the buttons on your shirt.* OPPOSITE **undo 2** to clean and repair something to make it look newer: *They bought an old house and now they are doing it up.*

dock /dɒk/ *noun* a place by the sea or a river where ships go so that people can move things on and off them or repair them

doctor /ˈdɒktə(r)/ *noun* **1** a person whose job is to make sick people well again: *Doctor Baucha sees patients every morning.* **2** a person who has the highest degree from a university ❶ When you write 'Doctor' as part of a person's name the short form is **Dr**: *Dr Oloo*

document /ˈdɒkjumənt/ *noun* **1** a paper with important information on it: *a legal document* **2** a computer file with writing in it: *Save changes to your document before closing it.*

documentary /ˌdɒkjuˈmentri/ *noun* (*plural* **documentaries**) a film about true things: *I watched an interesting documentary about lions on TV last night.*

dodge /dɒdʒ/ *verb* (**dodges**, **dodging**, **dodged** /dɒdʒd/) to move quickly to avoid something or someone: *He ran across the busy road, dodging the cars.*

does *form of* DO[1]

doesn't /ˈdʌznt/ = **does not**

dog /dɒg/ *noun* an animal that many people keep to do work or as a pet: *Keep your dog on a lead.*

❖ **WORD BUILDING**

A young dog is called a **puppy**.

dog-eared /ˈdɒg ɪəd/ *adjective* A **dog-eared** book has untidy corners and edges because it has been used a lot.

doll /dɒl/ *noun* a toy like a very small person

dollar /ˈdɒlə(r)/ *noun* money that people use in the USA, Zimbabwe and some other countries. There are 100 **cents** in a dollar. ❶ We say: *This shirt costs 30 dollars* but we write **$**: *This shirt costs $30.*

dolphin

dolphin /ˈdɒlfɪn/ *noun* an intelligent animal that lives in the sea

do

present tense		*negative short forms*		*past tense* **did**
I	**do**	I	**don't**	
you	**do**	you	**don't**	*present participle* **doing**
he/she/it	**does**	he/she/it	**doesn't**	
we	**do**	we	**don't**	*past participle* **done**
you	**do**	you	**don't**	
they	**do**	they	**don't**	

dome /dəʊm/ *noun* the round roof of a building

domestic /də'mestɪk/ *adjective* **1** of or about the home or family: *Cooking and cleaning are domestic jobs.* ◇ *Many cats and dogs are domestic animals* (= animals that live in your home with you). **2** of or inside a country: *a domestic flight* (= to a place in the same country)

domestic help /dəˌmestɪk 'help/ (also **domestic worker** /dəˌmestɪk 'wɜːkə(r)/) = **house help**

dominate /'dɒmɪneɪt/ *verb* (**dominates, dominating, dominated**) to control someone or something because you are stronger or more important: *He dominates his younger brother.*

donate /dəʊ'neɪt/ *verb* (**donates, donating, donated**) to give something to people who need it: *The company donated one million shillings to the hospital.*
▸ **donation** /dəʊ'neɪʃn/ *noun* something that you give to people who need it: *a donation of clothes*

done *form of* DO[1]

donkey /'dɒŋki/ *noun* (*plural* **donkeys**) an animal like a small horse with long ears

donkey

donor /'dəʊnə(r)/ *noun* a person who gives something to help someone: *a blood donor*

don't /dəʊnt/ = **do not**

door ⚷ /dɔː(r)/ *noun* the way into a building or room; a piece of wood, glass or metal that you use to open and close the way in to a building, room, cupboard, car, etc: *Can you close the door, please?* ◇ *Nakato knocked on the door.* ◇ *There is someone at the door.*

> ❖ **WORD BUILDING**
>
> A house often has a **front door** and a **back door**.

answer the door to open the door when someone knocks or rings the bell
next door in the next house, room or building: *Karimi lives next door to us.*
out of doors outside; not in a building: *Farmers spend a lot of time out of doors.*

doorbell /'dɔːbel/ *noun* a bell outside a house that you ring to tell people inside that you want to go in

doorstep /'dɔːstep/ *noun* a step in front of a door outside a building: *She left the parcel on her aunt's doorstep.*

doorway /'dɔːweɪ/ *noun* an opening for going into a building or room: *Katee was waiting in the doorway when they arrived.*

dormitory /'dɔːmətri/ *noun* (*plural* **dormitories**) a big bedroom for a lot of people, for example in a school

dose /dəʊs/ *noun* an amount of medicine that you take at one time: *Take a large dose of medicine before you go to bed.*
▸ **dosage** /'dəʊsɪdʒ/ *noun* the amount of a medicine that you should take over a period of time: *The recommended dosage is one tablet every four hours.*

dot /dɒt/ *noun* a small round mark: *The letter 'i' has a dot over it.*
on the dot at exactly the right time: *Please be here at nine o'clock on the dot.*

> ❖ **SPEAKING**
>
> We use **dot** when we say a person's email address. For the address **nuru@mutai.co.ke** we say 'Nuru **at** mutai **dot** co **dot** k e'.

dotted line /ˌdɒtɪd 'laɪn/ *noun* a line of small round marks that sometimes shows where you have to write something: *Please sign* (= write your name) *on the dotted line.* ➲ Picture at **wavy**.

double[1] ⚷ /'dʌbl/ *adjective*

> ❖ **PRONUNCIATION**
>
> **Double** sounds like **bubble**.

1 two times as much or as many; twice as much or as many: *They get paid double wages for working nights.* **2** with two parts that are the same: *double doors* **3** for two people: *a double bed* ◇ *a double room* **4** You use 'double' before a letter or a number to show that it comes two times: *'How do you spell your name, Mr Ninsiima?' 'N, I, N, S, double I, M, A'* ◇ *The phone number is double four nine five one* (44951). ➲ Look at **single[1]**.

double[2] /'dʌbl/ *verb* (**doubles, doubling, doubled** /'dʌbld/) to make something twice as much or as many; to become twice as much or as many: *The price has doubled: last year it was 500 shillings and this year it's 1000.*

doubt¹ /daʊt/ *noun*

> ❖ **PRONUNCIATION**
>
> **Doubt** sounds like **out** because we do not say the 'b'.

a feeling that you are not sure about something: *She says the story is true but I have my doubts about it.*
in doubt not sure: *If you are in doubt, ask your teacher.*
no doubt I am sure: *Egesa isn't here yet, but no doubt he will come later.*

doubt² /daʊt/ *verb* (**doubts, doubting, doubted**) to not feel sure about something; to think that something is probably not true or probably will not happen: *I doubt if he will come.*

doubtful /ˈdaʊtfl/ *adjective* not certain or not likely: *It is doubtful whether he will walk again.*

doubtless /ˈdaʊtləs/ *adverb* almost certainly: *Doubtless she'll be late!*

dough /dəʊ/ *noun* (no plural)

> ❖ **PRONUNCIATION**
>
> **Dough** sounds like **no.**

flour, water and other things mixed together, for making bread, etc.

doughnut /ˈdəʊnʌt/ *noun* a small round cake that is cooked in oil

doughnut

dove /dʌv/ *noun* a bird that is often used as a sign of peace

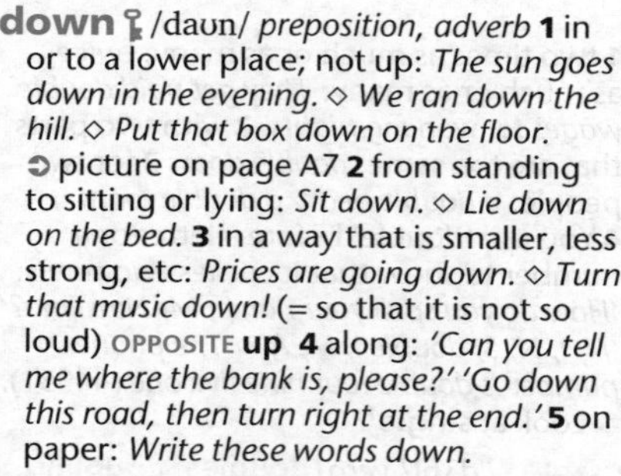

down /daʊn/ *preposition, adverb* **1** in or to a lower place; not up: *The sun goes down in the evening.* ◇ *We ran down the hill.* ◇ *Put that box down on the floor.* ➲ picture on page A7 **2** from standing to sitting or lying: *Sit down.* ◇ *Lie down on the bed.* **3** in a way that is smaller, less strong, etc: *Prices are going down.* ◇ *Turn that music down!* (= so that it is not so loud) OPPOSITE **up** **4** along: *'Can you tell me where the bank is, please?' 'Go down this road, then turn right at the end.'* **5** on paper: *Write these words down.*

downhill /ˌdaʊnˈhɪl/ *adverb* down, towards the bottom of a hill: *My bicycle can go fast downhill.* OPPOSITE **uphill**

download /ˌdaʊnˈləʊd/ *verb* (**downloads, downloading, downloaded**) If you **download** something from the Internet, you make a copy of it on your own computer. OPPOSITE **upload**

downpour /ˈdaʊnpɔː(r)/ *noun* a heavy fall of rain that often starts suddenly: *The boys were cold and wet from the sudden downpour.*

downstairs /ˌdaʊnˈsteəz/ *adverb* to or on a lower floor of a building: *I ran downstairs and out of the building.* ▸ **downstairs** *adjective*: *She lives in the downstairs flat.* OPPOSITE **upstairs**

downwards /ˈdaʊnwədz/ (also **downward** /ˈdaʊnwəd/) *adverb* down; towards a lower place or towards the ground: *She was lying face downward on the grass.* OPPOSITE **upwards**

doze /dəʊz/ *verb* (**dozes, dozing, dozed** /dəʊzd/) to sleep lightly for a short time: *My grandfather was dozing in his armchair.*
doze off to start dozing: *I dozed off in front of the television.* ▸ **doze** *noun*: *She had a doze after lunch.*

dozen /ˈdʌzn/ *noun* (*plural* **dozen**) twelve: *a dozen red roses* ◇ *two dozen boxes* ◇ *half a dozen eggs*
dozens of a lot of: *They've invited dozens of people to the wedding.*

Dr *short for* DOCTOR

drag

drag /dræg/ *verb* (**drags, dragging, dragged** /drægd/) **1** to pull something along the ground slowly, often because it is heavy: *He couldn't lift the log, so he dragged it along the path.* **2** If something **drags**, it seems to go slowly because it is not interesting: *Time drags when you're waiting for a bus.*

dragon /ˈdrægən/ *noun* a big dangerous animal with fire in its mouth, that you find only in stories

dragon

drain[1] /dreɪn/ *noun* a pipe that carries away dirty water from a building: *The drain is blocked.*

drain[2] /dreɪn/ *verb* (**drains, draining, drained** /dreɪnd/) **1** to let liquid flow away from something, so that it becomes dry: *Boil the rice in water and then drain it.* **2** to become dry because liquid is flowing away: *Let the dishes drain.* **3** to flow away: *The water drained away slowly.*

drama /ˈdrɑːmə/ *noun* **1** (*plural* **dramas**) a story that you watch in the theatre or on television, or listen to on the radio: *a TV drama* **2** (no plural) the study of plays and acting: *She liked drama at school.* **3** (*plural* **dramas**) an exciting thing that happens: *There was a big drama at school when one of the teachers fell in the river!*

dramatic /drəˈmætɪk/ *adjective* **1** of plays or the theatre: *a dramatic society* **2** sudden, great or exciting: *The finish of the race was very dramatic.*
▸ **dramatically** /drəˈmætɪkli/ *adverb*: *Prices went up dramatically.*

dramatist /ˈdræmətɪst/ *noun* a person who writes plays

dramatize /ˈdræmətaɪz/ *verb* (**dramatizes, dramatizing, dramatized** /ˈdræmətaɪzd/) **1** to show a story or an idea as a play or film **2** to make something seem more exciting or important than it really is: *It's only a little scratch – don't dramatize.*

drank *form of* DRINK[1]

draught /drɑːft/ *noun* cold air that comes into a room: *Can you shut the window? I can feel a draught.* ▸ **draughty** /ˈdrɑːfti/ *adjective* (**draughtier, draughtiest**): *a draughty house*

draughts /drɑːfts/ *noun* (plural) a game that two people play with round flat pieces on a board that has black and white squares on it: *Do you want a game of draughts?*

draw[1] ⚷ /drɔː/ *verb* (**draws, drawing, drew** /druː/, **has drawn** /drɔːn/)

> ❖ **PRONUNCIATION**
> **Draw** and **drawer** both sound like **more**.

1 to make a picture with a pencil, pen, etc: *She drew a picture of a horse.* ◇ *He has drawn a car.* ◇ *My sister draws well.* ➲ Look at **drawing**. **2** to pull or take something from a place: *He drew a knife from his pocket.* **3** to move or come: *The train drew into the station.* **4** to pull something to make it move: *The plough was drawn by two oxen.* **5** to end a game with the same number of points for both players or teams: *Ghana and Morocco drew in last Saturday's match.* **6** to open or close curtains: *I switched on the light and drew the curtains.*
draw out to take money out of a bank: *She drew out all her money and bought a ticket to London.*
draw up to come to a place and stop: *A taxi drew up outside the house.*
draw something up to write something: *They drew up a list of people who they wanted to invite to the conference.*

draw[2] /drɔː/ *noun* the result of a game when both players or teams have the same number of points: *The football match ended in a 1–1 draw.*

drawer

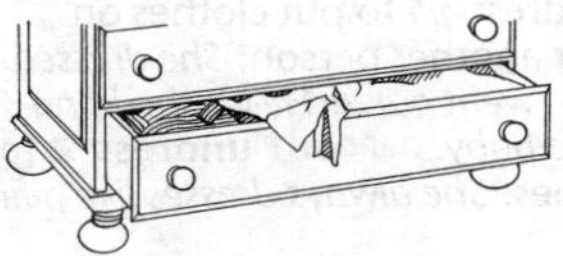

drawer ⚷ /drɔː(r)/ *noun* a thing like a box that you can pull out from a cupboard, desk, etc: *Your crayons are in the bottom drawer.*

drawing ⚷ /ˈdrɔːɪŋ/ *noun* **1** (*plural* **drawings**) a picture made with a pencil, pen, etc. **2** (no plural) making pictures with a pencil, pen, etc: *Karimi is very good at drawing.* ➲ Look at **draw**[1].

drawing pin /ˈdrɔːɪŋ pɪn/ *noun* a short pin with a flat round top, that you use for attaching paper to a wall or board: *I put the poster up with drawing pins.* ➲ Picture at **pin**[1].

drawn *form of* DRAW[1]

dread /dred/ *verb* (**dreads, dreading, dreaded**) to be very afraid of something: *I'm dreading the long journey as I get very sick on buses.*

dreadful /ˈdredfl/ *adjective* very bad: *I had a dreadful journey – my bus was twelve hours late!*

dreadfully /ˈdredfəli/ *adverb* very: *I'm dreadfully sorry, but I must go now.*

dream[1] ⚷ /driːm/ *verb* (**dreams, dreaming, dreamt** /dremt/ *or* **dreamed** /driːmd/, **has dreamt** *or* **has dreamed**)

1 to have a picture or an idea in your mind when you are asleep: *I dreamt about you last night.* ◇ *I dreamt that I met the president.* **2** to hope for something nice in the future: *She dreams of becoming a famous actress.*

dream² /dri:m/ *noun* **1** pictures or ideas in your mind when you are asleep: *I had a dream about school last night.*

> ❖ **WORD BUILDING**
>
> A bad or frightening dream is called a **nightmare**.

2 something nice that you hope for: *His dream is to go to New York.*

dress¹ /dres/ *noun* **1** (*plural* **dresses**) a piece of clothing with a top part and a skirt, that a woman or girl wears: *She's wearing a pretty blue dress.* **2** (no plural) clothes: *The group of dancers wore national dress.*

dress² /dres/ *verb* (**dresses, dressing, dressed** /drest/) **1** to put clothes on yourself or another person: *She dressed quickly and went out.* ◇ *He washed and dressed the baby.* OPPOSITE **undress** **2** to wear clothes: *She always dresses like a film star.*

dressed in something wearing something: *He was dressed in black.*

dress up **1** to put on your best clothes: *They dressed up to go to the wedding.* **2** to put on special clothes for fun, so that you look like another person or a thing: *The children dressed up as animals.*

get dressed to put on your clothes: *I got up, got dressed and ran to school.* OPPOSITE **get undressed**

dressing /ˈdresɪŋ/ *noun* a thing for covering a part of your body that is hurt: *You should put a dressing on that cut.*

dressing table /ˈdresɪŋ teɪbl/ *noun* a piece of bedroom furniture like a table with drawers and a mirror

drew *form of* DRAW¹

dribble /ˈdrɪbl/ *verb* (**dribbles, dribbling, dribbled** /ˈdrɪbld/) **1** to make a ball move along with small kicks **2** If someone **dribbles**, liquid runs out of their mouth.

dried *form of* DRY²

drier /ˈdraɪə(r)/ *noun* **1** *form of* DRY¹ **2** = **dryer**

dries *form of* DRY²

driest *form of* DRY¹

drift /drɪft/ *verb* (**drifts, drifting, drifted**) to move slowly in the air or on water: *The empty boat drifted along on the sea.* ◇ *The balloon drifted away.*

drill /drɪl/ *noun* a tool that you use for making holes: *They used a big drill to break up the road.* ▶ **drill** *verb* (**drills, drilling, drilled** /drɪld/) to make a hole using a drill: *He was drilling a hole in a piece of wood.*

drink¹ /drɪŋk/ *verb* (**drinks, drinking, drank** /dræŋk/, **has drunk** /drʌŋk/) **1** to take in liquid, for example water, milk or coffee, through your mouth: *What do you want to drink?* ◇ *She was drinking a cup of tea.* **2** to drink alcohol: *'Would you like some wine?' 'No, thank you. I don't drink.'*

drink² /drɪŋk/ *noun* **1** liquid, for example water, milk or coffee, that you take in through your mouth: *Would you like a drink?* ◇ *Can I have a drink of water?* **2** drink with alcohol in it, for example beer or wine: *There was lots of food and drink at the wedding.*

drip /drɪp/ *verb* (**drips, dripping, dripped** /drɪpt/) **1** to fall slowly in small drops: *Water was dripping through the roof.* **2** to have liquid falling from it in small drops ▶ **drip** *noun*: *Put a bucket under the hole to catch the drips.*

drip

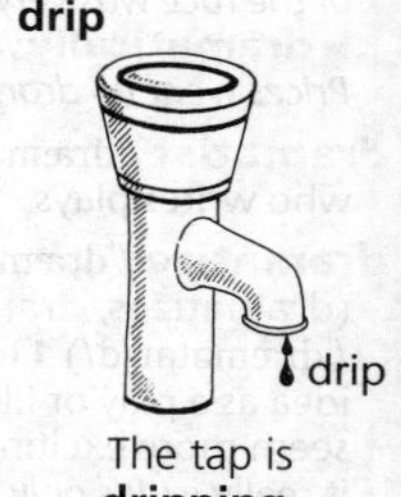

The tap is **dripping**.

drive¹ /draɪv/ *verb* (**drives, driving, drove** /drəʊv/, **has driven** /ˈdrɪvn/) **1** to control a car, bus, etc. and make it go where you want to go: *Can you drive?* ◇ *Don't drive too fast!* **2** to take someone to a place in a car: *My uncle drove us to school in his pickup.*

drive² /draɪv/ *noun* **1** a journey in a car: *It's a long drive from Nakuru to Ahero.* **2** the part of a computer that reads and stores information: *the hard drive* ◇ *a CD drive*

drive-in /ˈdraɪv ɪn/ *noun* a place where you can go to eat or to watch a film while you are sitting in your car

driver /ˈdraɪvə(r)/ *noun* a person who controls a car, bus, train, etc: *Karimi is a good driver.* ◇ *a taxi driver*

driving /ˈdraɪvɪŋ/ *noun* (no plural) controlling a car, bus, etc: *Driving at night can be dangerous.*

driving licence /ˈdraɪvɪŋ laɪsns/ *noun* a piece of paper that shows that someone is allowed to drive a car, etc.

driving test /ˈdraɪvɪŋ test/ *noun* a test that someone has to pass before they get their **driving licence**

drizzle /ˈdrɪzl/ *noun* (no plural) very light rain ▸ **drizzle** *verb* (**drizzles, drizzling, drizzled** /ˈdrɪzld/): *It was drizzling outside.*

drone /drəʊn/ *noun* a male **bee** that does not work

droop /druːp/ *verb* (**droops, drooping, drooped** /druːpt/) to bend or hang down: *Flowers droop if they don't get water.*

drop[1] /drɒp/ *verb* (**drops, dropping, dropped** /drɒpt/) **1** to let something fall: *I dropped my watch and it broke.* **2** to fall: *The glass dropped from her hands.* **3** to become lower or less: *The temperature has dropped.* **4** to stop a car and let someone get out: *Could you drop me at the next corner?* **5** to stop doing something: *I'm going to drop music at school next year.*

drop in to visit someone who does not know that you are coming: *I dropped in to see my aunt while I was in town.*

drop off to fall asleep: *She dropped off in class.*

drop out to stop doing something with a group of people: *I dropped out of the football team when my father got ill.*

drop[2] /drɒp/ *noun* **1** a very small amount of liquid: *a drop of water* ➲ picture on page A12 **2** a fall; going down: *a drop in temperature* ◇ *a drop in prices*

drought /draʊt/ *noun* a long time when there is not enough rain: *Thousands of people died in the drought.*

drove *form of* DRIVE[1]

drown /draʊn/ *verb* (**drowns, drowning, drowned** /draʊnd/) to die under water because you cannot breathe; to make a person or animal die in this way: *The boy fell in the river and drowned.*

drowsy /ˈdraʊzi/ *adjective* (**drowsier, drowsiest**) feeling tired and wanting to sleep: *The heat made him very drowsy.*

drug /drʌg/ *noun* **1** something that makes you better when you are ill: *They are looking for a drug that can cure AIDS.* **2** something that people eat, smoke or put into their body with a special needle, because it makes them feel happy or excited. In many countries it is against the law to use drugs: *She takes drugs.*

drum[1] /drʌm/ *noun* **1** a musical instrument that you hit with sticks or with your hands: *He sometimes plays the drum for hours.* **2** a big round container for oil: *an oil drum*

drums

drum[2] /drʌm/ *verb* (**drums, drumming, drummed** /drʌmd/) to play a **drum**

drumbeat /ˈdrʌmbiːt/ *noun* the sound that a **drum** makes when someone hits it again and again

drummer /ˈdrʌmə(r)/ *noun* a person who plays a **drum**

drunk[1] /drʌŋk/ *adjective* If a person is drunk, they have drunk too much alcohol.

drunk[2] *form of* DRINK[1]

dry[1] /draɪ/ *adjective* (**drier, driest**) **1** with no liquid in it or on it; not wet: *The washing isn't dry yet.* ➲ picture on page A5 **2** with no rain: *dry weather* ◇ *the dry season* OPPOSITE **wet**

dry[2] /draɪ/ *verb* (**dries, drying, dried** /draɪd/, **has dried**) **1** to become dry: *Our clothes were drying in the sun.* **2** to make something dry: *Dry your hands on this towel.*

dry out to become completely dry: *Leave your shoes in the sun to dry out.*

dry up 1 to become completely dry: *There was no rain for several months and all the rivers dried up.* **2** to dry things like plates, spoons and forks with a towel after you have washed them: *If I wash the dishes, could you dry up?*

> ❖ **GRAMMAR**
>
> You can also say **do the drying-up**.

dry-clean /ˌdraɪ ˈkliːn/ *verb* (**dry-cleans, dry-cleaning, dry-cleaned** /ˌdraɪ ˈkliːnd/) to make clothes clean by using chemicals, not water: *I had my suit dry-cleaned.*

dry-cleaner's /ˌdraɪ ˈkliːnəz/ *noun* a shop where clothes and other things are **dry-cleaned**

dryer (also **drier**) /ˈdraɪə(r)/ *noun* a machine for drying something: *Take the clothes out of the washing machine and put them in the dryer.* ◇ *a hairdryer*

duchess /ˈdʌtʃəs/ *noun* (*plural* **duchesses**) a woman who has a special title or is the wife of a **duke**

duck¹ /dʌk/ *noun* a bird that lives on and near water

> ❖ **WORD BUILDING**
>
> A young duck is called a **duckling**.

duck² /dʌk/ *verb* (**ducks**, **ducking**, **ducked** /dʌkt/) to move your head down quickly, so that something does not hit you or so that someone does not see you: *He saw the stone coming towards him and ducked.*

duckling /ˈdʌklɪŋ/ *noun* a young duck

due /dju:/ *adjective* **1** If something is **due** at a certain time, you expect it to happen or come then: *What time is the bus due?* ◇ *The new road is due to open in April.* **2** If an amount of money is **due**, you must pay it: *The rent is due at the beginning of the month.*
due for something ready for something: *The car is due for a service.*
due to something because of something: *The accident was due to bad driving.*

duet /djuˈet/ *noun* music for two people to sing or play on musical instruments: *Moraa and Juma sang a duet.*

dug *form of* DIG

duke /dju:k/ *noun* a man who has a special title

dull /dʌl/ *adjective* (**duller**, **dullest**) **1** not bright: *It was a dull, cloudy day.* **2** not strong or loud: *a dull pain* **3** not interesting or exciting: *Life is never dull in a big city.*

dumb /dʌm/ *adjective*

> ❖ **PRONUNCIATION**
>
> **Dumb** sounds like **drum**.

not able to speak: *She was born deaf and dumb.*

dump /dʌmp/ *verb* (**dumps**, **dumping**, **dumped** /dʌmpt/) **1** to take something to a place and leave it there because you do not want it: *They dumped their rubbish by the side of the road.* **2** to put something down without being careful: *Don't dump your clothes on the floor!* ▶ **dump** *noun* a place where you can take and leave things that you do not want

dune /dju:n/ *noun* a small hill of sand near the sea or in a desert

dung /dʌŋ/ *noun* (no plural) waste material from the bodies of large animals: *Cattle dung is a valuable fertilizer.*

dungarees /ˌdʌŋgəˈri:z/ *noun* (plural) trousers with a part that covers the top of your body: *a new pair of dungarees*

dung beetle /ˈdʌŋ bi:tl/ *noun* a large insect that feeds on waste material from animals (**dung**)

duration /djuˈreɪʃn/ *noun* (no plural) the length of time that something lasts: *The duration of the journey was 11 hours.*

during 🔑 /ˈdjʊərɪŋ/ *preposition* **1** all the time that something is happening: *The sun gives us light during the day.* **2** at some time while something else is happening: *She died during the night.* ◇ *I fell asleep during the film.*

dusk /dʌsk/ *noun* (no plural) the time in the evening when it is nearly dark

dust¹ 🔑 /dʌst/ *noun* (no plural) dry dirt that is like powder: *The old table was covered in dust.*

dust² /dʌst/ *verb* (**dusts**, **dusting**, **dusted**) to take dust off something with a cloth: *I dusted the furniture.*

dustbin /ˈdʌstbɪn/ *noun* a thing that you put rubbish in

dustbin

duster /ˈdʌstə(r)/ *noun* a cloth that you use for taking the dust off furniture

dustman /ˈdʌstmən/ *noun* (*plural* **dustmen** /ˈdʌstmən/) a person whose job is to take away rubbish from outside people's houses

dusty /ˈdʌsti/ *adjective* (**dustier**, **dustiest**) covered with dust: *The shelf was dusty.*

duty 🔑 /ˈdju:ti/ *noun* (*plural* **duties**) **1** something that you must do because it is part of your job or because you think it is right: *One of the duties of a secretary is to type letters.* ◇ *It's your duty to look after your parents when they get older.* **2** money (a **tax**) that you pay to the government when you bring things into a country from another country
off duty not working: *The police officer was off duty.*

on duty working: *Some nurses at the hospital are on duty all night.*

duty-free /ˌdjuːti ˈfriː/ *adjective, adverb* that you can bring into a country without paying money to the government. You can buy **duty-free** goods on planes or ships and at airports.

DVD /ˌdiː viː ˈdiː/ *noun* a small plastic disk that you record films and music on. You can play a **DVD** on a computer or a special machine (called a **DVD player**): *Is the film available* ***on DVD****?*

DVD burner /ˌdiːviːˈdiː bɜːnə(r)/ (also **DVD writer** /ˌdiːviːˈdiː raɪtə(r)/) *noun* a piece of equipment that you use to record from a computer onto a DVD

dwarf /dwɔːf/ *noun* (*plural* **dwarfs, dwarves** /dwɔːvz/) a person who is much smaller than the usual size

dye /daɪ/ *noun* stuff that you use to change the colour of something, for example cloth or hair ▶ **dye** *verb* (**dyes, dyeing, dyed** /daɪd/) to change the colour of something: *We dyed the cloth red.*

dying *form of* DIE

be dying for something to want to have something very much: *It's so hot! I'm dying for a drink.*

be dying to to want to do something very much: *My brother is dying to meet you.*

dysentery /ˈdɪsəntriː/ *noun* (no plural) a serious illness that gives you very bad **diarrhoea** (= an illness that makes you want to go to the toilet very often)

Ee

E, e /iː/ *noun* (*plural* **E's, e's** /iːz/) the fifth letter of the English alphabet: *'Egg' begins with an 'E'.*

e- /iː/ *prefix* using the Internet: *e-learning* ◇ *e-commerce*

each /iːtʃ/ *adjective, pronoun* every person or thing in a group: *Each pupil has to give a short talk to the class.* ◇ *He gave a present to each of the children.* ◇ *These envelopes cost 10 shillings each* (= for one).

each other /ˌiːtʃ ˈʌðə(r)/ *pronoun* words that show that someone does the same thing as another person: *Robi and Malika looked at each other* (= Robi looked at Malika and Malika looked at Robi).

eager /ˈiːgə(r)/ *adjective* If you are **eager** to do something, you want to do it very much: *We were all eager to hear the president's speech.* ▶ **eagerly** *adverb*: *The crowd were waiting eagerly for the match to begin.*

eagle /ˈiːgl/ *noun* a large bird that catches and eats small birds and animals

eagle

ear /ɪə(r)/ *noun* **1** one of the two parts of a person or an animal that are used for hearing: *Elephants have big ears.* ➲ picture on page A13 ➲ Picture at **elephant**. **2** the top part of a plant that produces grain: *an ear of wheat* ➲ Picture at **wheat**.

have an ear for something to be able to recognize and copy sounds well: *Hawa has an ear for music and sings beautifully.*

early /ˈɜːli/ *adjective, adverb* (**earlier, earliest**) **1** before the usual or right time: *The train arrived ten minutes early.* ◇ *I was early for the lesson.* **2** near the beginning of a time: *the early afternoon* ◇ *She was in her early twenties* (= between the ages of 20 and about 23 or 24). ◇ *I have to get up early tomorrow.* OPPOSITE **late**

an early night an evening when you go to bed earlier than usual

earn /ɜːn/ *verb* (**earns, earning, earned** /ɜːnd/) **1** to get money by working: *How much do teachers earn in your country?* ◇ *He earns about 10 000 shillings a month.* **2** to get something because you have worked well or done something good: *You've earned a rest!*

earnings /ˈɜːnɪŋz/ *noun* (plural) money that you get for working

earphones /ˈɪəfəʊnz/ *noun* (plural) things that you put over or in your ears for listening to a radio, CD, etc.

earring /ˈɪərɪŋ/ *noun* a pretty thing that you wear on your ear

earth /ɜːθ/ *noun* (no plural) **1** this world; the planet that we live on: *The moon travels round the earth.* **2** what you grow plants in; soil: *Cover the seeds with earth.*

on earth You use 'on earth' in questions with words like 'how' and 'what' when you are very surprised or do not know what the answer will be: *Where on earth is Rono? He's two hours late!* ◇ *What on earth are you doing?*

earthquake /ˈɜːθkweɪk/ *noun* a sudden strong shaking of the ground

ease /iːz/ *noun* (no plural)
with ease with no difficulty: *She answered the questions with ease.*

easily 🔑 /ˈiːzəli/ *adverb* with no difficulty: *The cinema was almost empty so we easily found a seat.*

east 🔑 /iːst/ *noun* (no plural) **1** where the sun comes up in the morning: *Which way is east?* ➲ Picture at **compass**. **2 the far east** (no plural) the countries of Asia, for example China and Japan: *He's travelled a lot in the far east.* ▶ **east** *adjective, adverb*: *Tanzania is on the east coast of Africa.* ◇ *an east wind* (= that comes from the east) ◇ *We travelled east from Kisumu to Nakuru.*

East Coast Fever /ˌiːst kəʊst ˈfiːvə(r)/ *noun* (no plural) a serious illness that cattle get from small insects (called **ticks**)

Easter /ˈiːstə(r)/ *noun* (no plural) a Sunday in March or April and the days around it, when Christians think about Christ coming back to life

eastern 🔑 /ˈiːstən/ *adjective* in or of the east part of a place: *eastern Kenya*

easy 🔑 /ˈiːzi/ *adjective* (**easier, easiest**)
1 If something is easy, you can do or understand it without any difficulty: *The homework was very easy.* ◇ *Kiswahili is an easy language to learn.* **2** without problems or pain: *He has had an easy life.*
OPPOSITE **difficult**, **hard**
take it easy; take things easy to not worry or work too much: *After my exams I'm going to take it easy for a few days.*

❖ **WORD FAMILY**
easy easily ease

eat 🔑 /iːt/ *verb* (**eats, eating, ate** /et/, **has eaten** /ˈiːtn/) to take in food through your mouth: *Have you eaten all the bread?* ◇ *Do you want something to eat?*

Ebola fever /iːˈbəʊlə fiːvə(r)/ *noun* (no plural) a very dangerous illness that makes you feel very hot and makes you **bleed** (= lose blood) inside your body

e-book /ˈiː bʊk/ *noun* a book that you read on a computer or an electronic machine (called an **e-reader**)

echo /ˈekəʊ/ *noun* (*plural* **echoes** /ˈekəʊz/) a sound that a wall sends back so that you hear it again ▶ **echo** *verb* (**echoes, echoing, echoed** /ˈekəʊd/): *His footsteps echoed in the empty hall.*

eclipse

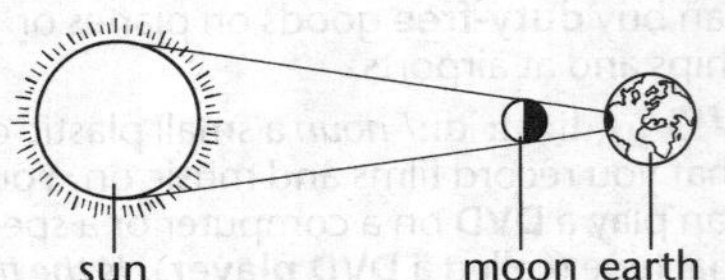

eclipse /iˈklɪps/ *noun* **1** a time when the moon comes between the earth and the sun so that we cannot see the sun's light **2** a time when the earth comes between the sun and the moon so that we cannot see the moon's light

ecology /iˈkɒlədʒi/ *noun* (no plural) the study of the connection between living things and everything around them ▶ **ecological** /ˌiːkəˈlɒdʒɪkl/ *adjective*: *The destruction of the rain forests is causing serious ecological problems.* ▶ **ecologist** /iˈkɒlədʒɪst/ *noun* a person who studies or knows a lot about **ecology**

economic /ˌiːkəˈnɒmɪk/ *adjective* about the way that a country spends its money and makes, buys and sells things: *The country is in serious economic difficulties.*

economical /ˌiːkəˈnɒmɪkl/ *adjective* If something is **economical**, it does not cost a lot of money to use it: *This car is economical to run* (= it does not use a lot of petrol).

economics /ˌiːkəˈnɒmɪks/ *noun* (no plural) the study of the way that countries spend money and make, buy and sell things

economist /ɪˈkɒnəmɪst/ *noun* a person who studies or knows a lot about **economics**

economy /ɪˈkɒnəmi/ *noun* (*plural* **economies**) **1** the way that a country spends its money and makes, buys and sells things: *the economies of Kenya and Tanzania* **2** using money or things well and carefully: *For reasons of economy, turn off the light when you leave the room.*

❖ **WORD FAMILY**
economy economics economist economic economical

edge 🔑 /edʒ/ *noun* the part along the end or side of something: *Don't sit on the edge of your chair – you might fall!*

edition /ɪˈdɪʃn/ *noun* one form of a book, magazine or newspaper: *The story was in the Sunday edition of the newspaper.*

editor /ˈedɪtə(r)/ *noun* a person whose job is to prepare or control a magazine, newspaper, book or film

educate 🔑 /ˈedʒukeɪt/ *verb* (**educates**, **educating**, **educated**) to teach someone about things like reading, writing and mathematics at school or college: *Where was she educated?* ❶ The noun is **education**.

educated /ˈedʒukeɪtɪd/ *adjective* A person who is **educated** has studied and learnt a lot of things to a high standard: *She is a highly educated woman.*

education 🔑 /ˌedʒuˈkeɪʃn/ *noun* (no plural) teaching someone about things like reading, writing and mathematics at school or college: *He had a good education.* ◇ *The government spends a lot of money on education.* ❶ The verb is **educate**. ▸ **educational** /ˌedʒuˈkeɪʃənl/ *adjective*: *an educational visit to a factory*

eel /iːl/ *noun* a long fish that looks like a snake

effect 🔑 /ɪˈfekt/ *noun* a change that happens because of something: *We are studying the effects of heat on different metals.*
have an effect on something to make something change: *His problems had a bad effect on his health.*

effective /ɪˈfektɪv/ *adjective* Something that is **effective** works well: *Running is an effective way of keeping fit.*

efficient /ɪˈfɪʃnt/ *adjective* A person or thing that is **efficient** works well and in the best way, without wasting time or materials: *Our secretary is very efficient.* OPPOSITE **inefficient** ▸ **efficiency** /ɪˈfɪʃnsi/ *noun* (no plural) being efficient ▸ **efficiently** *adverb*: *You must use your time more efficiently.*

effort 🔑 /ˈefət/ *noun* trying hard to do something; hard work: *Thank you for all your efforts.*
make an effort to try hard to do something: *He made an effort to arrive on time.*

e.g. /ˌiː ˈdʒiː/ *short for* for example: *She travels to a lot of European countries, e.g. England, Spain and France.*

egg 🔑 /eg/ *noun* **1** a round or almost round (**oval**) thing that has a baby bird, fish, insect or snake inside it: *The nest contained three eggs.* **2** an egg from a chicken that we eat: *I like boiled eggs.*

egg

egg cup /ˈeg kʌp/ *noun* a small cup that holds a boiled egg while you are eating it ➲ Picture at **egg**.

eight 🔑 /eɪt/ *number* 8

eighteen 🔑 /ˌeɪˈtiːn/ *number* 18

eighteenth /ˌeɪˈtiːnθ/ *adjective, adverb, noun* 18th

eighth 🔑 /eɪtθ/ *adjective, adverb, noun* **1** 8th **2** one of eight equal parts of something; ⅛

eightieth /ˈeɪtiəθ/ *adjective, adverb, noun* 80th

eighty 🔑 /ˈeɪti/ *number* **1** 80 **2 the eighties** (plural) the numbers, years or temperature between 80 and 89
in your eighties between the ages of 80 and 89: *a man in his eighties*

either[1] 🔑 /ˈaɪðə(r); ˈiːðə(r)/ *adjective, pronoun* **1** one of two things or people: *There is fish and meat. You can have either.* ◇ *Either of us will help you.* **2** each: *There are trees along either side of the road.*

either[2] 🔑 /ˈaɪðə(r); ˈiːðə(r)/ *adverb* (used in sentences with 'not') also: *Kamau can't swim and I can't (swim) either.*
either ... or words that show two different things or people that you can choose: *You can have either tea or coffee.* ◇ *I'll see you either tomorrow or Thursday.*

eject /iˈdʒekt/ *verb* (**ejects**, **ejecting**, **ejected**) to press a button to remove a CD, DVD, etc. from a machine

elaborate /ɪˈlæbərət/ *adjective* not simple; with a lot of different parts: *Her kanga has a very elaborate pattern on it.*

elastic /ɪˈlæstɪk/ *noun* (no plural) material that becomes longer when you pull it and then goes back to its usual size: *His trousers have elastic in the top to stop them falling down.* ▸ **elastic** *adjective*: *elastic material*

elastic band /ɪˌlæstɪk ˈbænd/ *noun* a thin circle of rubber that you use for holding things together

elbow /ˈelbəʊ/ *noun* the part in the middle of your arm where it bends ➲ picture on page A13

elder¹ /ˈeldə(r)/ *adjective* older of two people: *My elder brother is at university.*

elder² /ˈeldə(r)/ *noun* an older member of a village or **clan** (= a special group of people), who makes decisions, gives advice, etc: *The village elders met to settle the dispute.*

elderly /ˈeldəli/ *adjective* quite old: *She is elderly and can't hear very well.*

eldest /ˈeldɪst/ *adjective* oldest of three or more people: *Their eldest son is at university but the other two are at school.*

elect /ɪˈlekt/ *verb* (**elects, electing, elected**) to choose someone to be a leader by voting: *A new president was elected last year.*

election 🔑 /ɪˈlekʃn/ *noun* a time when people choose someone to be a leader by voting: *The election will be held on Wednesday.*

electric 🔑 /ɪˈlektrɪk/ *adjective* using electricity to make it work: *an electric drill* ◇ *an electric guitar* ➲ Picture at **guitar**.

electrical 🔑 /ɪˈlektrɪkl/ *adjective* of or using electricity: *an electrical engineer*

electrician /ɪˌlekˈtrɪʃn/ *noun* a person whose job is to work with electricity: *This light isn't working – we need an electrician to mend it.*

electricity 🔑 /ɪˌlekˈtrɪsəti/ *noun* (no plural) power that comes through wires. Electricity can make heat and light and makes things work.

> ❖ **WORD FAMILY**
> **electricity electric electrical electrician**

electronic 🔑 /ɪˌlekˈtrɒnɪk/ *adjective* **Electronic** equipment includes things like computers and televisions. They use electricity and very small electrical parts (called **microchips** and **transistors**) to make them work: *an electronic calculator*

electronics /ɪˌlekˈtrɒnɪks/ *noun* (no plural) the technology that is used to make things like computers and televisions: *the electronics industry*

elegant /ˈelɪɡənt/ *adjective* with a beautiful style or shape: *She looked very elegant in her best clothes.*

element /ˈelɪmənt/ *noun* a simple chemical, for example iron or gold: *Water is made of the elements hydrogen and oxygen.*

elementary /ˌelɪˈmentri/ *adjective* for people who are beginning; not difficult to do or understand: *an elementary dictionary*

elephant

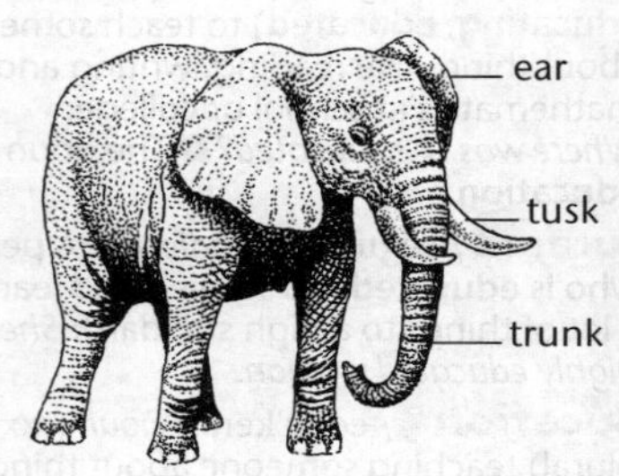

elephant /ˈelɪfənt/ *noun* a very big wild animal from Africa or Asia, with a long nose (called a **trunk**) that hangs down

eleven 🔑 /ɪˈlevn/ *number* 11

eleventh /ɪˈlevnθ/ *adjective, adverb, noun* 11th

eliminate /ɪˈlɪmɪneɪt/ *verb* (**eliminates, eliminating, eliminated** /ɪˈlɪmɪneɪtɪd/) to remove or get rid of something or someone: *The organization is working hard to eliminate child labour.*

else 🔑 /els/ *adverb* **1** more; extra: *What else would you like?* ◇ *Is anyone else coming with us?* **2** different; other: *If you don't like it here we can go somewhere else.* ◇ *It's not mine – it must be someone else's.* ◇ *There was nothing else to eat so we had eggs again.*

> ❖ **GRAMMAR**
> You use **else** after words like **anybody**, **nothing** and **somewhere**, and after question words like **where** and **who**.

or else if not, then: *Go now, or else you'll be late.*

elsewhere /elsˈweə(r)/ *adverb* in or to another place: *He can't find a job in Thika so he's looking elsewhere for work.*

email 🔑 (also **e-mail**) /ˈiːmeɪl/ *noun* **1** (no plural) a way of sending messages from one computer to another: *You can contact us by email.* ◇ *What is your email address?* **2** (*plural* **emails**) a message that you write on one computer and send to another: *I'll send you an email.*
▸ **email** (also **e-mail**) *verb* (**emails, emailing, emailed** /ˈiːmeɪld/): *She emails her parents every week.*

embark /ɪmˈbɑːk/ *verb* (**embarks**, **embarking**, **embarked** /ɪmˈbɑːkt/) to get on a ship OPPOSITE **disembark**

embarrass /ɪmˈbærəs/ *verb* (**embarrasses**, **embarrassing**, **embarrassed** /ɪmˈbærəst/) to make someone feel shy or worried about what other people think of them: *Odoi embarrassed his friends by singing very loudly on the bus.*

embarrassed /ɪmˈbærəst/ *adjective* If you are embarrassed, you feel shy or worried about what other people think of you: *Everyone laughed when I fell off my chair – I was really embarrassed!*

> ❖ SPELLING
> Remember! You spell **embarrassed** with **rr** and **ss**.

embarrassing /ɪmˈbærəsɪŋ/ *adjective* Something that is embarrassing makes you feel shy or worried about what other people will think: *I couldn't remember her name – it was so embarrassing!*

embarrassment /ɪmˈbærəsmənt/ *noun* the feeling that you have when you are embarrassed; a person or thing that embarrasses you: *He hid his face in embarrassment.*

embassy /ˈembəsi/ *noun* (*plural* **embassies**) a place where people work whose job is to speak and act for their government in another country: *To get a visa to travel to America, you should apply to the American embassy.*

embezzle /ɪmˈbezl/ *verb* (**embezzles**, **embezzling**, **embezzled** /ɪmˈbezld/) to steal money that belongs to the person you work for ▸ **embezzlement** /ɪmˈbezlmənt/ *noun* (no plural): *She was found guilty of embezzlement.*

embroider /ɪmˈbrɔɪdə(r)/ *verb* (**embroiders**, **embroidering**, **embroidered** /ɪmˈbrɔɪdəd/) to make pictures or patterns with thread on cloth ▸ **embroidered** /ɪmˈbrɔɪdəd/ *adjective*: *an embroidered blouse*

embroidery /ɪmˈbrɔɪdəri/ *noun* (no plural) patterns that are made on cloth with thread

emerald /ˈemərəld/ *noun* a very valuable green stone: *an emerald ring* ▸ **emerald** (also **emerald green**) *adjective* bright green in colour

emerge /ɪˈmɜːdʒ/ *verb* (**emerges**, **emerging**, **emerged** /ɪˈmɜːdʒd/) to come out from a place: *The moon emerged from behind the clouds.*

emergency /ɪˈmɜːdʒənsi/ *noun* (*plural* **emergencies**) a sudden dangerous situation, when people must help quickly: *Come quickly, doctor! It's an emergency!* ◇ *I can lend you some money in an emergency.*

emigrate /ˈemɪɡreɪt/ *verb* (**emigrates**, **emigrating**, **emigrated**) to leave your country to live in another country: *They emigrated to Britain in the 1960s to find work.* ▸ **emigration** /ˌemɪˈɡreɪʃn/ *noun* (no plural)

emoticon /ɪˈməʊtɪkɒn/ *noun* a symbol that shows your feelings when you send an email or text message. For example, :-) represents a smiling face.

emotion /ɪˈməʊʃn/ *noun* a strong feeling, for example love or anger: *His voice was filled with emotion.*

emotional /ɪˈməʊʃənl/ *adjective* **1** about feelings: *She's got emotional problems – her friend has gone away.* **2** If you are **emotional**, you have strong feelings and you show them: *He got very emotional when we said goodbye.*

empathize /ˈempəθaɪz/ *verb* (**empathizes**, **empathizing**, **empathized** /ˈempəθaɪzd/)
empathize with someone to be able to understand how other people feel: *He's a good teacher because he empathizes with his pupils.*

empathy /ˈempəθi/ *noun* (no plural) the ability to understand how other people feel

emperor /ˈempərə(r)/ *noun* a man who rules a group of countries (called an **empire**): *Emperor Haile Selassie of Ethiopia* ➲ Look at **empress**.

emphasize /ˈemfəsaɪz/ *verb* (**emphasizes**, **emphasizing**, **emphasized** /ˈemfəsaɪzd/) to say something strongly to show that it is important: *She emphasized the importance of hard work.* ▸ **emphasis** /ˈemfəsɪs/ *noun* (*plural* **emphases** /ˈemfəsiːz/): *Our school places a lot of emphasis on science.*

empire /ˈempaɪə(r)/ *noun* a group of countries that is controlled by one country: *the Roman Empire*

employ /ɪmˈplɔɪ/ *verb* (**employs**, **employing**, **employed** /ɪmˈplɔɪd/) to pay someone to do work for you: *The factory employs 800 workers.* ➲ Look at **unemployed**.

❖ **WORD FAMILY**
employ **employer** **employee**
employment: OPPOSITE **unemployment**
unemployed

employee /ɪmˈplɔɪiː/ *noun* a person who is paid to work: *This company treats its employees very well.*

employer /ɪmˈplɔɪə(r)/ *noun* a person or company that pays other people to do work

employment /ɪmˈplɔɪmənt/ *noun* (no plural) having a job that you are paid to do: *He went to Kitale and found employment as a taxi driver.* OPPOSITE **unemployment**

empress /ˈemprəs/ *noun* (*plural* **empresses**) a woman who rules a group of countries (called an **empire**), or the wife of an emperor

empty[1] /ˈempti/ *adjective* (**emptier**, **emptiest**) with nothing or nobody inside or on it: *My glass is empty.* ◇ *The cinema was almost empty.* ➲ Picture at **full**.

empty[2] /ˈempti/ *verb* (**empties**, **emptying**, **emptied** /ˈemptid/, **has emptied**) **1** to take everything out of something: *The waiter emptied the ashtrays.* ◇ *We emptied our bags out onto the floor.* **2** to become empty: *The film finished and the cinema started to empty.*

enable /ɪˈneɪbl/ *verb* (**enables**, **enabling**, **enabled** /ɪˈneɪbld/) to make it possible for someone to do something: *Your help enabled me to pass my exam.*

enclose /ɪnˈkləʊz/ *verb* (**encloses**, **enclosing**, **enclosed** /ɪnˈkləʊzd/) **1** to put something inside a letter or parcel: *I enclose a map and instructions how to get here.* **2** to put something, for example a wall or fence, around a place on all sides: *The prison is enclosed by a high wall.*

enclosure /ɪnˈkləʊʒə(r)/ *noun* land inside a wall or fence: *a cattle enclosure*

encourage /ɪnˈkʌrɪdʒ/ *verb* (**encourages**, **encouraging**, **encouraged** /ɪnˈkʌrɪdʒd/) to give someone hope or help so that they do something or continue doing something: *We encouraged him to write a letter to the newspaper.* OPPOSITE **discourage**
▸ **encouraging** /ɪnˈkʌrɪdʒɪŋ/ *adjective*: *Kaburo's school report is very encouraging.*

encouragement /ɪnˈkʌrɪdʒmənt/ *noun* (no plural) giving someone hope or help so that they do something or continue doing something: *Kendi's parents gave her a lot of encouragement when she was taking her exams.*

encyclopedia /ɪnˌsaɪkləˈpiːdiə/ *noun* (*plural* **encyclopedias**) a book or set of books that gives information about a lot of different things from A to Z: *an encyclopedia of world history*

end[1] /end/ *noun* the furthest or last part of something: *Turn right at the end of the street.* ◇ *They were sitting at the other end of the room.* ◇ *She's getting married at the end of June.*
come to an end to finish: *The holiday was coming to an end and we started to think about going back to school.*
end to end in a line with the ends touching: *They put the tables end to end.*
for … on end for a very long time: *He practises heading the ball for hours on end.*
in the end finally; at last: *I looked for the keys for hours and in the end I found them in the drawer.*
make ends meet to have enough money for your needs: *After her husband died it was difficult to make ends meet.*
put an end to something to stop something happening: *We must put an end to this terrible war.*

❖ **WORD FAMILY**
end *noun*, **end** *verb*
ending **endless**

end[2] /end/ *verb* (**ends**, **ending**, **ended**) **1** to stop: *What time does the film end?* ◇ *The road ends here.* ◇ *Most adverbs in English end in '-ly'.* ◇ *The match ended in a draw.* **2** to finish something: *We ended the meeting with a song.*
end up to finally be in a place or doing something when you did not plan it: *If she continues to steal, she'll end up in prison.* ◇ *He ended up as a teacher.*

endanger /ɪnˈdeɪndʒə(r)/ *verb* (**endangers**, **endangering**, **endangered** /ɪnˈdeɪndʒəd/) to cause danger for someone or something: *Smoking can endanger your health.*

endangered /ɪnˈdeɪndʒəd/ *adjective* If animals or plants are **endangered**, soon there might be none left in the world: *The black rhino is an endangered species.*

ending /ˈendɪŋ/ *noun* the last part of something, for example a word, story or film: *All these words have the same ending: criticize, organize and realize.* ◇ *The film has a happy ending.*

endless /ˈendləs/ *adjective* never stopping or finishing; very long: *The journey seemed endless.* ▶ **endlessly** *adverb*: *He talks endlessly about nothing.*

endure /ɪnˈdjʊə(r)/ *verb* (**endures, enduring, endured** /ɪnˈdjʊəd/)
1 to suffer something that is painful or uncomfortable: *She endured the cold without complaining.*
SAME MEANING **bear** **2** to continue: *The girls' friendship endured for many years.*
▶ **endurance** /ɪnˈdjʊərəns/ *noun* (no plural) the ability to continue doing something difficult for a long time: *Running a marathon is a real test of endurance.*

enemy /ˈenəmi/ *noun* **1** (*plural* **enemies**) a person who hates you: *He was a kind man with no enemies.* **2 the enemy** (no plural) the army or country that your country is fighting against in a war: *The enemy is attacking from the north.*
make enemies to do things that make people hate you: *In business, you often make enemies.*

energetic /ˌenəˈdʒetɪk/ *adjective* full of energy so that you can do a lot of things

energy /ˈenədʒi/ *noun* (no plural) **1** the power that your body has to do things: *He ran out of energy at the end of the race.* **2** the power from electricity, gas, coal, etc. that is used to make machines work and to make heat and light: *It is important to try to save energy.* ◇ *solar energy*

engaged /ɪnˈɡeɪdʒd/ *adjective* **1** If two people are **engaged**, they have agreed to get married: *Fatma is engaged to Shayo.* ◇ *They got engaged last year.* **2** (used about a telephone) being used: *I tried to phone him but his number was engaged.*

engagement /ɪnˈɡeɪdʒmənt/ *noun* an agreement to marry someone

engine /ˈendʒɪn/ *noun* **1** a machine that makes things move: *a car engine* **2** the front part of a train which pulls the rest
➲ Picture at **train**[1].

engineer /ˌendʒɪˈnɪə(r)/ *noun* a person whose job is to plan, make or repair things like machines, roads or bridges: *My brother is an electrical engineer.*

engineering /ˌendʒɪˈnɪərɪŋ/ *noun* (no plural) planning and making things like machines, roads or bridges: *She's studying engineering at college.*

enjoy /ɪnˈdʒɔɪ/ *verb* (**enjoys, enjoying, enjoyed** /ɪnˈdʒɔɪd/) to like something very much: *I enjoy playing football.* ◇ *Did you enjoy your dinner?*
enjoy yourself to have a happy time; to have fun: *I really enjoyed myself yesterday. Did you?*

❖ **WORD FAMILY**
enjoy enjoyment enjoyable

enjoyable /ɪnˈdʒɔɪəbl/ *adjective* Something that is enjoyable makes you happy: *Thank you for a very enjoyable day.*

enjoyment /ɪnˈdʒɔɪmənt/ *noun* (no plural) a feeling of enjoying something; pleasure: *I get a lot of enjoyment from reading.*

enlarge /ɪnˈlɑːdʒ/ *verb* (**enlarges, enlarging, enlarged** /ɪnˈlɑːdʒd/) to make something bigger: *We had the photograph enlarged.* ▶ **enlargement** /ɪnˈlɑːdʒmənt/ *noun* a photograph that someone has made bigger

enormous /ɪˈnɔːməs/ *adjective* very big: *an enormous dog*

enormously /ɪˈnɔːməsli/ *adverb* very or very much: *I enjoyed myself enormously on holiday.*

enough /ɪˈnʌf/ *adjective, adverb, pronoun*

❖ **PRONUNCIATION**
Enough sounds like **stuff**.

as much or as many as you need: *There isn't enough food for ten people.* ◇ *You're too thin – you don't eat enough.* ◇ *Is she old enough to get married?*

enquire (also **inquire**) /ɪnˈkwaɪə(r)/ *verb* (**enquires, enquiring, enquired** /ɪnˈkwaɪəd/) to ask: *I enquired about buses to Kisumu.* ◇ *'Are you hungry?' he enquired.*
ⓘ **Ask** is the word that we usually use.
enquire into something to try to find out more about something that happened: *The police are enquiring into the murder.*

enquiry (also **inquiry**) /ɪnˈkwaɪəri/ *noun* (*plural* **enquiries, inquiries**) a question that you ask about something: *The police are making enquiries about the robbery.*

enrich /ɪnˈrɪtʃ/ *verb* (**enriches, enriching, enriched** /ɪnˈrɪtʃt/) to make something better: *Reading enriches our lives.* ◇ *The flour is enriched with vitamins.*

enrol /ɪnˈrəʊl/ *verb* (**enrols, enrolling, enrolled** /ɪnˈrəʊld/) to join a group, for example a school, college, course or club.

You usually pay money (a **fee**) when you enrol: *I've enrolled for the French Club.*

ensure /ɪn'ʃɔː(r)/ *verb* (**ensures, ensuring, ensured** /ɪn'ʃɔːd/) to make certain: *Please ensure that all the lights are switched off before you leave.*

enter 🔑 /'entə(r)/ *verb* (**enters, entering, entered** /'entəd/) **1** to come or go into a place: *They stopped talking when she entered the room.* ◇ *Do not enter without knocking.*

❖ **SPEAKING**
In this sense, it is more usual to say **go in** or **come in**.

2 to write a name or other information: *Please enter your name, address and date of birth at the bottom of the form.* **3** to give your name to someone because you want to do something like take an examination or run in a race: *I entered a competition and won 5 000 shillings.*

❖ **WORD FAMILY**
enter entrance entry

enterprise /'entəpraɪz/ *noun* a plan to do something new and difficult, often to get money: *a business enterprise*

entertain 🔑 /ˌentə'teɪn/ *verb* (**entertains, entertaining, entertained** /ˌentə'teɪnd/) **1** to make someone have a good time: *She entertained us all with her funny stories.* **2** to give food and drink to visitors in your house: *We're entertaining friends this afternoon.*

entertainer /ˌentə'teɪnə(r)/ *noun* a person whose job is to help people have a good time, by singing, dancing, telling jokes, etc.

entertaining /ˌentə'teɪnɪŋ/ *adjective* funny or interesting: *The play was really entertaining.*

entertainment 🔑 /ˌentə'teɪnmənt/ *noun* (no plural) anything that entertains people, for example films, plays or concerts: *There isn't much entertainment for young people in this town.*

enthusiasm 🔑 /ɪn'θjuːziæzəm/ *noun* (no plural) a strong feeling of wanting to do something or liking something: *They didn't show much enthusiasm when I asked them to help me with the shopping.*

enthusiastic 🔑 /ɪnˌθjuːzi'æstɪk/ *adjective* full of excitement and interest in something: *She's very enthusiastic about her new school.*

entire /ɪn'taɪə(r)/ *adjective* whole or complete; with no parts missing: *He spent the entire day trying to repair the engine.*

entirely /ɪn'taɪəli/ *adverb* completely: *She looks entirely different from her sister.* ◇ *I entirely agree with you.*

entrance 🔑 /'entrəns/ *noun* **1** (*plural* **entrances**) where you go into a place: *I'll meet you at the entrance to the museum.* **2** (*plural* **entrances**) coming or going into a place: *He made his entrance onto the stage.* **3** (no plural) the right to go into a place: *Entrance to the museum costs 2 000 Tanzanian shillings.*

entry /'entri/ *noun* **1** (no plural) the right to go into a place: *You can't go into that room – there's a sign on the door that says 'No Entry'.* **2** (no plural) going into a place: *The thief gained entry* (= went in) *through a window.* **3** (*plural* **entries**) a person or thing that is in a competition: *The standard of the entries this year was very high.*

envelope /'envələʊp/ *noun* a paper cover for a letter: *Have you written his address on the envelope?* ➲ picture on page A15

envied, envies *form of* envy

envious /'enviəs/ *adjective* wanting what someone else has: *She's envious of her sister's success.*

environment 🔑 /ɪn'vaɪrənmənt/ *noun* **1** everything around you: *The children need a happy home environment.* **2 the environment** (no plural) the air, water, land, animals and plants around us: *We must do more to protect the environment.* ▸ **environmental** /ɪnˌvaɪrən'mentl/ *adjective*: *We talked about pollution and other environmental problems.*

envy /'envi/ *noun* (no plural) a sad or angry feeling of wanting what another person has: *I was filled with envy when I saw her new bike.* ▸ **envy** *verb* (**envies, envying, envied** /'envid/, **has envied**): *I envy you! You always seem so happy!*

epidemic /ˌepɪ'demɪk/ *noun* a disease that many people in a place have at the same time: *The cholera epidemic has claimed thousands of victims.*

episode /'epɪsəʊd/ *noun* a programme on radio or television that is part of a longer story: *You can see the final episode of the series on Monday.*

equal[1] 🔑 /'iːkwəl/ *adjective* the same; as big, as much or as good as another: *The women were demanding equal pay for equal* *work.* ◇ *I tried to give everyone an equal amount of food.*

❖ **WORD FAMILY**

equal *adjective*, **equal** *verb*
equally **equality** **equalize**

equal[2] /ˈiːkwəl/ *verb* (**equals**, **equalling**, **equalled** /ˈiːkwəld/) **1** to be exactly the same amount as something: *Two plus two equals four* (2+2=4). **2** to be as good as someone or something: *He ran the race in 19.32 seconds, equalling the world record.*

equality /ɪˈkwɒləti/ *noun* (no plural) being the same or having the same rights: *In some countries black people are still fighting for equality.*

equalize /ˈiːkwəlaɪz/ *verb* (**equalizes**, **equalizing**, **equalized** /ˈiːkwəlaɪzd/) to make things exactly the same amount or number: *Thika United FC equalized in the second half of the game.*

equally /ˈiːkwəli/ *adverb* **1** in equal parts: *Don't eat all the stew yourself – share it out equally!* **2** in the same way: *He's equally good at running and football.*

equation /ɪˈkweɪʒn/ *noun* (in mathematics) a statement that two quantities are equal: *2x + 5 = 11 is an equation.*

equator /ɪˈkweɪtə(r)/ *noun* (no plural) the line on maps around the middle of the world. Countries near the **equator** are very hot.

equip /ɪˈkwɪp/ *verb* (**equips**, **equipping**, **equipped** /ɪˈkwɪpt/) to give someone, or put in a place, all the things that are needed for doing something: *The bus is equipped with a rack for carrying luggage on the roof.* ◇ *The kitchen is well equipped.*

equipment /ɪˈkwɪpmənt/ *noun* (no plural) special things that you need for doing something: *sports equipment*

❖ **GRAMMAR**

Be careful! You cannot say 'an equipment' or 'equipments'. You can say 'some equipment' or 'a piece of equipment'.

-er /ə(r)/ *suffix* letters that make an adjective or adverb mean 'more': *wider* ◇ *bigger* ◇ *You must work harder.* ➲ Look at **-est**.

erase /ɪˈreɪz/ *verb* (**erases**, **erasing**, **erased** /ɪˈreɪzd/) to remove a pencil mark, writing on a board, etc: *The teacher asked me to erase the sums on the chalkboard.*

❖ **SPEAKING**

We usually use **rub out**.

eraser /ɪˈreɪzə(r)/ = **rubber**

e-reader /ˈiː riːdə(r)/ *noun* an electronic machine with a screen that you use for reading **e-books**

erect /ɪˈrekt/ *verb* (**erects**, **erecting**, **erected**) to build something: *New school buildings were erected last year.*

erode /ɪˈrəʊd/ *verb* (**erodes**, **eroding**, **eroded**) **1** to destroy something very slowly: *If there is no vegetation, wind and rain will erode the soil.* ◇ *Over the years, the weather has eroded the rock away.* **2** When something **erodes**, the wind and rain destroy it slowly: *Gabions were placed on the hillside to prevent the soil from eroding.* ▶ **erosion** /ɪˈrəʊʒn/ *noun* (no plural): *soil erosion*

error /ˈerə(r)/ *noun* a thing that is done wrong; a mistake: *The letter was sent to the wrong address because of a computer error.*

erupt /ɪˈrʌpt/ *verb* (**erupts**, **erupting**, **erupted**) When a **volcano** (= a mountain with a hole in the top) **erupts**, smoke, fire and **lava** (= hot liquid rock) suddenly come out: *The volcano erupted and buried the village.* ▶ **eruption** /ɪˈrʌpʃn/ *noun*: *a volcanic eruption*

escalator /ˈeskəleɪtə(r)/ *noun* stairs that move and carry people up and down

escape[1] /ɪˈskeɪp/ *verb* (**escapes**, **escaping**, **escaped** /ɪˈskeɪpt/) **1** to get free from someone or something: *The bird escaped from the cage.* ◇ *The prisoner escaped, but he was caught.* **2** If a liquid or gas escapes, it comes out of a place.

escape[2] /ɪˈskeɪp/ *noun* **1** (*plural* **escapes**) escaping from a place or a dangerous or unpleasant situation: *As soon as he turned his back, she would **make** her **escape**.* **2** (no plural) (also **escape key**) a computer key that you press to stop doing something or leave a program: *Press Escape to get back to the menu.*

escort[1] /ˈeskɔːt/ *noun* one or more people or vehicles that go with someone to protect them: *The President always travels with an armed escort.*

escort[2] /ɪˈskɔːt/ *verb* (**escorts**, **escorting**, **escorted**) to go with someone, for example to make sure that they arrive somewhere: *The police escorted him out of the building.*

esikuti (also **isikuti**) *noun* (East African English) a quick dance with a lot of movement

especially ⚷ /ɪˈspeʃəli/ *adverb* **1** very; more than usual or more than others: *I like bright colours, especially red.* ◇ *I like a lot of sports, but I especially enjoy athletics.* **2** for a particular person or thing: *I made this food especially for you.*

essay /ˈeseɪ/ *noun* a short piece of writing about a subject: *We had to write an essay on volcanoes.*

essential /ɪˈsenʃl/ *adjective* If something is **essential**, you must have or do it: *It is essential that you work hard for this exam.*

-est /ɪst/ *suffix* letters that make an adjective or adverb mean 'most': *widest* ◇ *biggest* ◇ *Who works hardest?* ➲ Look at **-er**.

establish /ɪˈstæblɪʃ/ *verb* (**establishes, establishing, established** /ɪˈstæblɪʃt/) to start something new: *This company was established in 1852.*

estate /ɪˈsteɪt/ *noun* **1** land with a lot of houses or factories on it: *We live on a housing estate.* ◇ *an industrial estate* **2** a large piece of land in the country that one person or family owns

estate agent /ɪˈsteɪt eɪdʒənt/ *noun* a person whose job is to sell buildings and land for other people

estimate[1] /ˈestɪmeɪt/ *verb* (**estimates, estimating, estimated**) to say how much you think something will cost, how big something is, how long it will take to do something, etc: *The builders estimated that it would take a week to repair the roof.*

estimate[2] /ˈestɪmət/ *noun* a guess about the size or cost of something: *The estimate for repairing the roof was 3 000 shillings.*

estuary /ˈestʃuəri/ *noun* (*plural* **estuaries**) the wide part of a river where it goes into the sea: *the estuary of the river Gambia*

etc. ⚷ /etˈsetərə/ You use 'etc.' at the end of a list to show that there are other things but you are not going to name them all: *I bought coffee, meat, oil, etc. at the market.*

ethics /ˈeθɪks/ *noun* (plural) beliefs about what is right or correct: *The medical profession has its own code of ethics.*

ethnic /ˈeθnɪk/ *adjective* of or from another country or race: *There are a lot of different ethnic groups in East Africa.*

eucalyptus /juːkəˈlɪptəs/ *noun* (*plural* **eucalyptus** *or* **eucalyptuses**) a tall tree with leaves that produce oil with a strong smell, that is used in medicine

eulogy /ˈjuːlədʒi/ *noun* (*plural* **eulogies**) a speech that says good things about someone who has died: *He gave the eulogy at my aunt's funeral.*

evacuate /ɪˈvækjueɪt/ *verb* (**evacuates, evacuating, evacuated**) to take people away from a dangerous place to a safer place: *The area near the factory was evacuated after the explosion.* ▸ **evacuation** /ɪˌvækjuˈeɪʃn/ *noun*: *the evacuation of cities during the war*

evaporate /ɪˈvæpəreɪt/ *verb* (**evaporates, evaporating, evaporated**) If a liquid **evaporates**, it changes into a gas: *Water evaporates if you heat it.* ▸ **evaporation** /ɪˌvæpəˈreɪʃn/ *noun* (no plural): *Heat and wind can cause evaporation.*

eve /iːv/ *noun* the day before a special day: *24 December is Christmas Eve.* ◇ *I visited my grandmother on New Year's Eve* (= 31 December).

even[1] ⚷ /ˈiːvn/ *adverb* **1** a word that you use to say that something is surprising: *The game is so easy that even a child can play it.* ◇ *He didn't laugh – he didn't even smile.* **2** a word that you use to make another word stronger: *That car is big, but this one is even bigger.*
even if it does not change anything if: *Even if you run, you won't catch the bus.*
even so although that is true: *I didn't have any lunch today, but even so I'm not hungry.*
even though although: *I went to the shamba, even though I was tired.*

even[2] /ˈiːvn/ *adjective* **1** flat and smooth: *I fell over because the floor wasn't even.* OPPOSITE **uneven** **2** the same; equal: *We've won one game each, so we're even.* **3 Even** numbers can be divided exactly by two: *4, 6 and 8 are even numbers.* OPPOSITE **odd**
get even with someone hurt someone who has hurt you

evening ⚷ /ˈiːvnɪŋ/ *noun* the part of the day between the afternoon and when you go to bed: *What are you doing this evening?* ◇ *We studied all day and in the evening we relaxed.* ◇ *Bigogo came on Monday evening.*

event ⚷ /ɪˈvent/ *noun* **1** something important that happens: *My sister's wedding was a big event for our family.* **2** a race or competition: *The next event will be the high jump.*

eventful /ɪ'ventfl/ *adjective* full of important, exciting or dangerous things happening: *2015 was an eventful year for our school.*

eventually ⚿ /ɪ'ventʃuəli/ *adverb* after a long time: *I waited for him for three hours, and eventually he came.*

ever ⚿ /'evə(r)/ *adverb* at any time: *'Have you ever been to Marsabit?' 'No, I haven't.'* ◇ *Do you ever see Malika?*
ever since in all the time since: *I have known Katee ever since we were children.*
ever so; ever such a very: *I'm ever so hot.* ◇ *It's ever such a good film.*
for ever for all time; always: *I will love you for ever.*

evergreen /'evəgri:n/ *noun* a tree that has green leaves all the year ➲ Look at **deciduous.**

every ⚿ /'evri/ *adjective* **1** all of the people or things in a group: *She knows every pupil in the school.* ◇ *Every time I ask him to play with us, he says no.* **2** once in each: *He phones every evening.*
every now and then; every now and again; every so often sometimes, but not often: *I see Ali every now and then.*
every other one, not the next, but the next, and so on: *She comes every other day* (= for example on Monday, Wednesday and Friday but not on Tuesday or Thursday).

everybody ⚿ /'evribɒdi/ = **everyone**

everyday /'evrideɪ/ *adjective* normal; not special: *The Internet has become part of everyday life.*

everyone ⚿ /'evriwʌn/ (also **everybody**) *pronoun* each person; all people: *Everyone at school likes my shoes.* ◇ *If everybody is here then we can start.*

everything ⚿ /'evriθɪŋ/ *pronoun* each thing; all things: *Everything in that shop is very expensive.*

everywhere ⚿ /'evriweə(r)/ *adverb* in all places or to all places: *I've looked everywhere for my pen, but I can't find it.*

evidence ⚿ /'evɪdəns/ *noun* (no plural) a thing that makes you believe that something has happened or that helps you know who did something: *The police searched the room, looking for evidence.* ◇ *a piece of evidence*
give evidence to tell what you know about someone or something in a court of law: *The man who saw the accident will give evidence in court.*

> ❖ **GRAMMAR**
>
> Be careful! You cannot say 'an evidence' or 'evidences'. You can say 'a piece of evidence'.

evident /'evɪdənt/ *adjective* easy to see or understand: *It was evident that he was lying, because he didn't look at me when he was speaking.*

evidently /'evɪdəntli/ *adverb* clearly: *She was evidently very upset.*

evil ⚿ /'i:vl/ *adjective* very bad: *an evil person*

ewe /ju:/ *noun* a female sheep

exact ⚿ /ɪg'zækt/ *adjective* completely correct; without any mistakes: *Have you got the exact time?*

exactly ⚿ /ɪg'zæktli/ *adverb* **1** You use 'exactly' when you are asking for or giving information that is completely correct: *Can you tell me exactly what happened?* ◇ *It cost 500 shillings exactly.* **2** just: *This shirt is exactly what I wanted.* **3** You use 'exactly' to agree with someone: *'So you've never met this man before?' 'Exactly.'*

exaggerate ⚿ /ɪg'zædʒəreɪt/ *verb* (**exaggerates, exaggerating, exaggerated**) to say that something is bigger, better, worse, etc. than it really is: *Don't exaggerate! I was only two minutes late, not twenty.* ▸ **exaggeration** /ɪg,zædʒə'reɪʃn/ *noun*: *It's an exaggeration to say he never does any work – he sometimes does a little.*

> ❖ **SPELLING**
>
> Remember! You spell **exaggerate** with **gg**.

exam ⚿ /ɪg'zæm/ *noun* a test of what you know or can do: *We've got an exam in English next week.*

> ❖ **WORD BUILDING**
>
> You **sit** or **take** an exam. If you do well, you **pass** and if you do badly, you **fail**: *I took an exam at the end of the year.* ◇ *Did she pass all her exams?*

examination ⚿ /ɪg,zæmɪ'neɪʃn/ *noun* **1** looking carefully at someone or something: *She went into hospital for an examination.* **2** = **exam**

examine ⚿ /ɪg'zæmɪn/ *verb* (**examines, examining, examined** /ɪg'zæmɪnd/) **1** to look carefully at something or someone: *I had my chest examined by the doctor.* ◇ *The* *detective examined the room for clues.* **2** to ask questions to find out what someone knows or what they can do: *You will be examined on everything you have learnt this year.*

examiner /ɪɡˈzæmɪnə(r)/ *noun* a person who tests someone in an exam

example 🔑 /ɪɡˈzɑːmpl/ *noun* something that shows what other things of the same kind are like: *This dictionary gives many examples of how words are used in sentences.*
for example let me give you an example: *Many different kinds of crop are grown in the region, for example maize, wheat and coffee.* ❶ The short form is **e.g.**

excavate /ˈekskəveɪt/ *verb* (**excavates**, **excavating**, **excavated** /ˈekskəveɪtɪd/) to dig in the ground to look for old objects that have been there for a long time; to find something in this way: *Pottery and weapons were excavated from the burial site.* ▸ **excavation** /ˌekskəˈveɪʃn/ *noun*: *Excavations on the site revealed the remains of a building.*

exceed /ɪkˈsiːd/ *verb* (**exceeds**, **exceeding**, **exceeded**) to do or be more than something: *The price will not exceed 200 shillings.*

excel /ɪkˈsel/ *verb* (**excels**, **excelling**, **excelled** /ɪkˈseld/) to be very good at doing something: *Nduku excels at sports.*

excellent 🔑 /ˈeksələnt/ *adjective* very good: *She speaks excellent French.*

except 🔑 /ɪkˈsept/ *preposition* but not: *The shop is open every day except Sunday.* ◇ *Everyone went to the park except for me.*
except that apart from the fact that: *I don't know what he looks like, except that he's very tall.*

exception /ɪkˈsepʃn/ *noun* a person or thing that is not the same as the others: *Most of his family are tall but he is an exception.*
with the exception of someone or **something** if you do not count someone or something: *I like all sports with the exception of swimming.*

exceptional /ɪkˈsepʃənl/ *adjective* **1** not usual: *It's exceptional to have so much rain at this time of year.* **2** very good: *She is going to be an exceptional athlete.* ▸ **exceptionally** /ɪkˈsepʃənəli/ *adverb*: *He was an exceptionally good student.*

exchange[1] 🔑 /ɪksˈtʃeɪndʒ/ *verb* (**exchanges**, **exchanging**, **exchanged** /ɪksˈtʃeɪndʒd/) to give one thing and get another thing for it: *My new radio didn't work so I exchanged it for another one.* ◇ *We exchanged addresses before saying goodbye.*

exchange[2] 🔑 /ɪksˈtʃeɪndʒ/ *noun*
in exchange for something If you get one thing **in exchange for** another thing, you give one thing and get another thing for it: *He worked for them in exchange for a room in their house.*

exchange rate /ɪksˈtʃeɪndʒ reɪt/ *noun* how much money from one country you can buy with money from another country: *The exchange rate in Tanzania is about 1300 shillings to one dollar.*

excite /ɪkˈsaɪt/ *verb* (**excites**, **exciting**, **excited**) to make someone have strong feelings of happiness or interest so that they are not calm: *Please don't excite the children too much or they won't sleep.*

> ❖ **WORD FAMILY**
> **excite** **exciting** **excited** **excitement**

excited 🔑 /ɪkˈsaɪtɪd/ *adjective* not calm, for example because you are happy about something that is going to happen: *He's getting very excited about the trip.*

excitement 🔑 /ɪkˈsaɪtmənt/ *noun* (no plural) a strong feeling of happiness or interest: *There was great excitement in the stadium before the match began.*

exciting 🔑 /ɪkˈsaɪtɪŋ/ *adjective* Something that is exciting makes you have strong feelings of happiness or interest: *an exciting film* ◇ *She's got a very exciting life – she travels all over the world and meets lots of famous people.*

exclaim /ɪkˈskleɪm/ *verb* (**exclaims**, **exclaiming**, **exclaimed** /ɪkˈskleɪmd/) to say something suddenly and loudly because you are surprised, angry, etc: *'I don't believe it!' she exclaimed.* ▸ **exclamation** /ˌekskləˈmeɪʃn/ *noun* a word or phrase that you use because you are surprised, angry, etc: *He gave an exclamation of amazement.* SAME MEANING **interjection**

exclamation mark /ˌekskləˈmeɪʃn mɑːk/ *noun* a mark (!) that you use in writing to show loud or strong words, or surprise ➲ Look at page A17.

exclude /ɪkˈskluːd/ *verb* (**excludes**, **excluding**, **excluded**) to shut or keep a person or thing out: *We cannot exclude the* *students from the meeting. Their ideas are important.* ➲ Look at **include**.

excluding 🔑 /ɪkˈskluːdɪŋ/ *preposition* without; if you do not count: *It costs 2 500 shillings, excluding tax.* ➲ Look at **including**.

excursion /ɪkˈskɜːʃn/ *noun* a short journey to see something interesting or to enjoy yourself: *We're going on an excursion to the coast on Sunday.*

excuse¹ 🔑 /ɪkˈskjuːs/ *noun*

> ❖ **PRONUNCIATION**
>
> **Excuse** (noun) ends with an 's' sound like **juice**.

words you say or write to explain why you have done something wrong: *You're late! What's your excuse this time?*

excuse² 🔑 /ɪkˈskjuːz/ *verb* (**excuses**, **excusing**, **excused** /ɪkˈskjuːzd/)

> ❖ **PRONUNCIATION**
>
> **Excuse** (verb) ends with a 'z' sound like **shoes** or **choose**.

to say that it is not important that a person has done something wrong: *Please excuse us for being late.*
excuse me You use 'excuse me' when you want to stop someone who is speaking, or when you want to speak to someone you don't know. You can also use 'excuse me' to say that you are sorry: *Excuse me, could you tell me the time, please?* ◇ *Did I stand on your foot? Excuse me.*

execute /ˈeksɪkjuːt/ *verb* (**executes**, **executing**, **executed**) to kill someone to punish them ▸ **execution** /ˌeksɪˈkjuːʃn/ *noun*: *the execution of prisoners*

executive /ɪɡˈzekjʊtɪv/ *noun* a person who has an important position in a business

exercise¹ 🔑 /ˈeksəsaɪz/ *noun* **1** (*plural* **exercises**) a piece of work that you do to learn something: *The teacher asked us to do exercises 1 and 2 for homework.* **2** (no plural) moving your body to keep it strong and well: *Swimming is very good exercise.* **3** (*plural* **exercises**) a special movement that you do to keep your body strong and well: *Touch your toes and stand up 20 times. This exercise is good for your legs, stomach and back.*

exercise² /ˈeksəsaɪz/ *verb* (**exercises**, **exercising**, **exercised** /ˈeksəsaɪzd/) to move your body to keep it strong and well: *They exercise in the field every morning.*

exercise book /ˈeksəsaɪz bʊk/ *noun* a small book that you use at school for writing in

exhaust¹ /ɪɡˈzɔːst/ *verb* (**exhausts**, **exhausting**, **exhausted**) to make someone very tired: *The long journey exhausted us.* ▸ **exhausted** /ɪɡˈzɔːstɪd/ *adjective* very tired: *I'm exhausted – I think I'll go to bed.* ▸ **exhausting** /ɪɡˈzɔːstɪŋ/ *adjective* making you very tired: *Looking after young children can be exhausting.*

exhaust² /ɪɡˈzɔːst/ *noun* a pipe that takes gas out from an engine, for example on a car

exhibit /ɪɡˈzɪbɪt/ *verb* (**exhibits**, **exhibiting**, **exhibited**) to show something in a public place for people to look at: *The carvings were exhibited in a local art gallery.* ▸ **exhibitor** /ɪɡˈzɪbɪtə(r)/ *noun* a person who shows their work to the public: *Over 50 exhibitors took part in the craft show.*

exhibition 🔑 /ˌeksɪˈbɪʃn/ *noun* a group of things in a place so that people can look at them: *an exhibition of paintings by local children*

exile /ˈeksaɪl/ *noun* **1** (no plural) having to live away from your own country, for example as a punishment: *The former president spent the last years of his life in exile.* **2** (*plural* **exiles**) a person who must live away from their own country

exist 🔑 /ɪɡˈzɪst/ *verb* (**exists**, **existing**, **existed**) to be real; to live: *Does life exist on other planets?* ◇ *That word does not exist.*

existence /ɪɡˈzɪstəns/ *noun* (no plural) being real; existing: *Do you believe in the existence of God?*

exit /ˈeksɪt/ *noun* a way out of a building: *Where is the exit?*
make an exit to go out of a place: *He made a quick exit.*

exotic /ɪɡˈzɒtɪk/ *adjective* strange or interesting because it comes from another country: *exotic fruits*

expand /ɪkˈspænd/ *verb* (**expands**, **expanding**, **expanded**) to become bigger or to make something bigger: *Metals expand when they are heated.* OPPOSITE **contract** ▸ **expansion** /ɪkˈspænʃn/ *noun* (no plural) getting bigger: *The company needs bigger offices because of the expansion.*

expect 🔑 /ɪk'spekt/ *verb* (**expects, expecting, expected**) **1** to think that someone or something will come or that something will happen: *I expect she'll be late. She usually is.* ◇ *Everyone expected Ethiopia to win the game, but they lost 3-0.* ◇ *She's expecting* (= she is going to have) *a baby in June.* **2** to think that something is probably true: *They haven't had lunch yet, so I expect they're hungry.* **3** If you are expected to do something, you must do it: *I am expected to attend every lesson.*
I expect so You say 'I expect so' when you think that something will happen or that something is true: *'Is Sarika coming?' 'Oh yes, I expect so.'*

expedition /ˌekspə'dɪʃn/ *noun* a journey to find or do something special: *They went on an expedition to climb Mt. Kilimanjaro.*

expel /ɪk'spel/ *verb* (**expels, expelling, expelled** /ɪk'speld/) to send someone away from a school or club: *The boys were expelled from school for fighting.*

expenditure /ɪk'spendɪtʃə(r)/ *noun* (no plural) the act of spending money; the amount of money that is spent: *The cricket club has increased its expenditure this year.*

expense /ɪk'spens/ *noun* **1** the cost of something: *Having a car is a big expense.* **2 expenses** (plural) money that you spend on a certain thing: *travel expenses*
at someone's expense If you do something **at someone's expense**, they pay for it: *dinner at the company's expense*

expensive 🔑 /ɪk'spensɪv/ *adjective* Something that is expensive costs a lot of money: *expensive clothes*
SAME MEANING **dear** OPPOSITE **inexpensive**

experience[1] 🔑 /ɪk'spɪəriəns/ *noun* **1** (no plural) knowing about something because you have seen it or done it: *She has four years' teaching experience.* ◇ *Does he have much experience of working with children?* **2** (*plural* **experiences**) something that has happened to you: *He wrote a book about his experiences in prison.*

experience[2] 🔑 /ɪk'spɪəriəns/ *verb* (**experiences, experiencing, experienced** /ɪk'spɪəriənst/) to have something happen to you; to feel: *She's never experienced failure before.*

experienced /ɪk'spɪəriənst/ *adjective* If you are **experienced**, you know about something because you have done it many times before: *She's an experienced swimmer.* OPPOSITE **inexperienced**

experiment 🔑 /ɪk'sperɪmənt/ *noun* You do an experiment to find out what will happen or to see if something is true: *They are doing experiments to find out if the drug is safe for humans.* ▶ **experiment** *verb* (**experiments, experimenting, experimented**): *I don't think it's right to experiment on animals.*

expert 🔑 /'ekspɜːt/ *noun* a person who knows a lot about something: *He's an expert on metals.* ◇ *a computer expert*

expire /ɪk'spaɪə(r)/ *verb* (**expires, expiring, expired** /ɪk'spaɪəd/) (used about an official document or agreement) to come to the end of the time when you can use it: *My passport has expired.*
SAME MEANING **run out**

explain 🔑 /ɪk'spleɪn/ *verb* (**explains, explaining, explained** /ɪk'spleɪnd/) **1** to tell someone about something so that they understand it: *The teacher usually explains the new words to us.* ◇ *He explained how to use the machine.* **2** to give a reason for something: *I explained why we needed the money.* ❶ The noun is **explanation**.

explanation 🔑 /ˌeksplə'neɪʃn/ *noun* telling someone about something so that they understand it, or giving a reason for something: *What explanation did they give for being late?* ❶ The verb is **explain**.

explode 🔑 /ɪk'spləʊd/ *verb* (**explodes, exploding, exploded**) to burst suddenly with a very loud noise: *A bomb exploded in the city, killing two people.*

> ❖ **WORD FAMILY**
> **explode explosion explosive**

exploit /ɪk'splɔɪt/ *verb* (**exploits, exploiting, exploited**) to treat someone badly to get what you want: *People who work for that company are exploited – they work long hours for very little money.* ▶ **exploitation** /ˌeksplɔɪ'teɪʃn/ *noun* (no plural): *the exploitation of children*

explore 🔑 /ɪk'splɔː(r)/ *verb* (**explores, exploring, explored** /ɪk'splɔːd/) to travel around a new place to learn about it: *The boys found an old, empty building and went inside to explore.* ▶ **exploration** /ˌeksplə'reɪʃn/ *noun* (no plural): *the exploration of space*

explorer /ɪk'splɔːrə(r)/ *noun* a person who travels around a new place to learn about it: *The first European explorers arrived in Africa in the 15th century.*

explosion 🔑 /ɪk'spləʊʒn/ *noun* bursting suddenly with a very loud noise: *There was an explosion and pieces of glass flew everywhere.*

explosive[1] /ɪk'spləʊsɪv/ *adjective* Something that is **explosive** can cause an explosion: *an explosive gas*

explosive[2] /ɪk'spləʊsɪv/ *noun* a substance that can make things burst suddenly with a very loud noise: *Dynamite is an explosive.*

export[1] /ɪk'spɔːt/ *verb* (**exports, exporting, exported**) to sell things to another country: *Kenya exports coffee to Britain.* OPPOSITE **import** ▶ **exporter** /ek'spɔːtə(r)/ *noun* a person, company or country that **exports** things: *the world's biggest exporter of oil* OPPOSITE **importer**

export[2] /'ekspɔːt/ *noun* **1** (no plural) selling things to another country: *These cars are made for export.* **2** (*plural* **exports**) something that you sell to another country: *The country's biggest exports are tea and cotton.* OPPOSITE **import**

expose /ɪk'spəʊz/ *verb* (**exposes, exposing, exposed** /ɪk'spəʊzd/) to show something that is usually covered or hidden: *A baby's skin should not be exposed to the sun for too long.* ◇ *The newspaper exposed his terrible secret.*

express[1] /ɪk'spres/ *verb* (**expresses, expressing, expressed** /ɪk'sprest/) to say or show how you think or feel: *She expressed her ideas well.*

express[2] /ɪk'spres/ *adjective* that goes or is sent very quickly: *an express letter* ▶ **express** *adverb*: *I sent the parcel express.*

express[3] /ɪk'spres/ *noun* (*plural* **expresses**) (also **express train**) a fast train that does not stop at all stations

expression 🔑 /ɪk'spreʃn/ *noun* **1** a word or group of words; a way of saying something: *The expression 'to drop off' means 'to fall asleep'.* **2** the look on your face that shows how you feel: *an expression of surprise*

extend /ɪk'stend/ *verb* (**extends, extending, extended**) **1** to make something longer or bigger: *The company has extended the contract for another six months.* **2** to continue or stretch: *The park extends as far as the river.*

extension /ɪk'stenʃn/ *noun* **1** a part that you add to something to make it bigger: *They've built an extension on the back of the house.* **2** one of the telephones in a building that is connected to the main telephone: *Can I have extension 4110, please?*

extent /ɪk'stent/ *noun* (no plural) how big something is: *I didn't know the full extent of the problem* (= how big it was) *until he explained it to me.*

to a certain extent; to some extent used to show that you do not think something is completely true: *I agree with you to a certain extent.*

exterior /ɪk'stɪəriə(r)/ *noun* the outside part: *We painted the exterior of the house white.* ▶ **exterior** *adjective*: *an exterior door* OPPOSITE **interior**

external /ɪk'stɜːnl/ *adjective* on, of or from the outside: *external walls* OPPOSITE **internal** ▶ **externally** /ɪk'stɜːnəli/ *adverb* on the outside

extinct /ɪk'stɪŋkt/ *adjective* If a type of animal or plant is **extinct**, it does not exist now: *Dinosaurs became extinct millions of years ago.*

extra 🔑 /'ekstrə/ *adjective, adverb* more than what is usual: *I have put an extra blanket on your bed because it's cold tonight.* ◇ *The room costs 600 shillings and you have to pay extra for breakfast.* ◇ *The football match went into extra time.*

extract /ɪk'strækt/ *verb* (**extracts, extracting, extracted**) to take something out: *The dentist said that her tooth had to be extracted.*

extraordinarily /ɪk'strɔːdnrəli/ *adverb* extremely: *She's extraordinarily clever.*

extraordinary /ɪk'strɔːdnri/ *adjective* very unusual or strange: *I had an extraordinary dream last night – I dreamt that I could fly.* ◇ *Have you seen that extraordinary building with the pink roof?*

extravagant /ɪk'strævəgənt/ *adjective* **1** If you are **extravagant**, you spend too much money. **2** Something that is **extravagant** costs too much money: *He buys her a lot of extravagant presents.*

extreme 🔑 /ɪk'striːm/ *adjective* **1** very great or strong: *the extreme cold of the Arctic* **2** as far away as possible: *They came from the extreme north of Uganda.* **3** If you say that a person is extreme, you mean that their ideas are too strong.

extremely 🔑 /ɪk'striːmli/ *adverb* very: *He's extremely good-looking.*

eye 🔑 /aɪ/ *noun* one of the two parts in your head that you see with: *She's got*

beautiful eyes. ◇ *Open your eyes!*
catch someone's eye 1 If you **catch someone's eye**, you make them look at you: *Try to catch the waiter's eye the next time he comes this way.* **2** If something **catches your eye**, you see it suddenly: *Her bright yellow clothes caught my eye.*
in someone's eyes as someone thinks: *Nafula is 42, but in her mother's eyes, she's still a little girl!*
keep an eye on someone or **something** to look after or watch someone or something: *Keep an eye on your money at the market – there are thieves around.*
see eye to eye with someone to agree with someone: *Mr Masagazi doesn't always see eye to eye with his neighbours.*

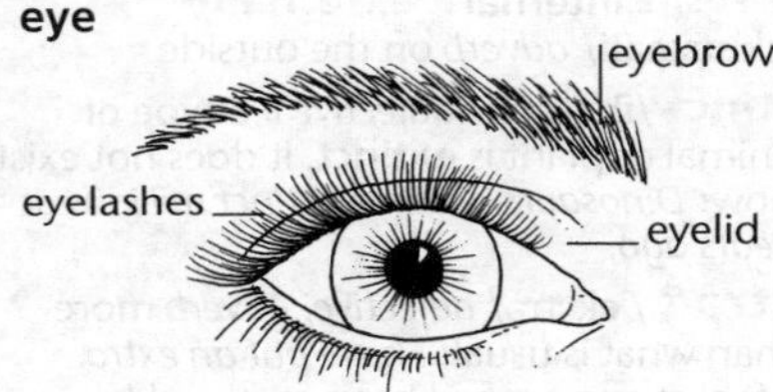

eyebrow /ˈaɪbraʊ/ (also **brow**) *noun* one of the two lines of hair above your eyes

eyelash /ˈaɪlæʃ/ *noun* (*plural* **eyelashes**) one of the hairs that grow in a line on your **eyelid**: *She's got beautiful long eyelashes.*

eyelid /ˈaɪlɪd/ *noun* the piece of skin that can move to close your eye

eyesight /ˈaɪsaɪt/ *noun* (no plural) the power to see: *Your eyesight is very good.*

F, f /ef/ *noun* **1** (*plural* **F's, f's** /efs/) the sixth letter of the English alphabet: *'Father' begins with an 'F'.* **2** **F** *short for* FAHRENHEIT

fable /ˈfeɪbl/ *noun* a short story, usually about animals, that teaches people something

fabric /ˈfæbrɪk/ *noun* cloth that is used for making things such as clothes and curtains: *Use silk or cotton fabric to make the dress.*

fabulous /ˈfæbjʊləs/ *adjective* very good; wonderful: *The food smells fabulous!*

face[1] 🔑 /feɪs/ *noun* **1** the front part of your head: *Have you washed your face?* ◇ *She had a smile on her face.* **2** the front or one side of something: *a clock face* ◇ *He put the cards face down on the table.*
face to face If two people are **face to face**, they are looking straight at each other: *They stood face to face.*
keep a straight face to not smile or laugh when something is funny: *I couldn't keep a straight face when he dropped his watch in the soup!*
make or **pull a face** to move your mouth and eyes to show that you do not like something: *She made a face when she saw what I had made for dinner.*

face[2] 🔑 /feɪs/ *verb* (**faces, facing, faced** /feɪst/) **1** to have the face or the front towards something: *Can you all face the front of the class, please?* ◇ *My bedroom faces the garden.* **2** to be brave enough to meet someone unfriendly or do something difficult: *I can't face seeing him – I know he'll be angry.*
face the music to accept the bad results of something you have done: *They all ran off and left me to face the music.*
let's face it we must agree that it is true: *Let's face it – you're not very good at football.*

facial /ˈfeɪʃl/ *adjective* connected with a person's face: *The actor showed his emotions through his facial expression.*

facilities /fəˈsɪlətiz/ *noun* (plural) things in a place for you to use: *Our school has very good sports facilities.*

fact 🔑 /fækt/ *noun* something that you know has happened or is true: *It's a fact that the earth travels around the sun.*
in fact; in actual fact words that you use to show that something is true; really: *I thought she was Moroccan, but in actual fact she's from Algeria.* ◇ *I think I saw him – I'm certain, in fact.*

factor /ˈfæktə(r)/ *noun* one of the things that causes or affects something: *Price was a major factor in his choice of a new phone.*

factory 🔑 /ˈfæktəri/ *noun* (*plural* **factories**) a place where people make things, usually with machines: *He works at the car factory.*

fade /feɪd/ *verb* (**fades, fading, faded**) to become less bright in colour: *Will this shirt fade when I wash it?* ◇ *faded jeans*

faeces /ˈfiːsiːz/ *noun* (plural) solid waste material that you pass from your body

Fahrenheit /ˈfærənhaɪt/ *noun* (no plural) a way of measuring temperature. Water freezes at 32 degrees Fahrenheit and boils at 212 degrees Fahrenheit. ℹ The short way of writing 'Fahrenheit' is **F**: *32 degrees F*

fail[1] 🔑 /feɪl/ *verb* (**fails, failing, failed** /feɪld/) **1** to not pass an exam or test: *She failed her maths test again.* ◇ *How many students failed last term?* **2** to try to do something but not be able to do it: *He played quite well but failed to win the match.* OPPOSITE **succeed** **3** to not do something that you should do: *The driver failed to stop at a red light.*

fail[2] /feɪl/ *noun* (no plural)
without fail certainly: *Be there at twelve o'clock without fail!*

failure 🔑 /ˈfeɪljə(r)/ *noun* **1** (no plural) not being successful: *The search for the missing children ended in failure.* **2** (*plural* **failures**) a person or thing that does not do well: *I felt that I was a failure because I didn't pass the exam.* OPPOSITE **success**

faint[1] /feɪnt/ *adjective* (**fainter, faintest**) **1** not clear or strong: *We could hear the faint sound of music in the distance.* **2** If you feel **faint**, you feel that you are going to fall, for example because you are ill or tired.

faint[2] /feɪnt/ *verb* (**faints, fainting, fainted**) to fall down suddenly, for example because you are weak, ill or shocked: *She almost fainted when she saw the blood on her leg.*

fair[1] 🔑 /feə(r)/ *adjective* (**fairer, fairest**) **1** Someone or something that is fair treats people equally or in the right way: *a fair teacher* ◇ *It's not fair! I have to go to bed but you can stay up and watch TV!* ◇ *That's a fair price for a new phone.* OPPOSITE **unfair** **2** with a light colour: *He's got fair skin.* ◇ *He is fair-skinned.* OPPOSITE **dark** **3** quite good or quite large: *They've invited a fair number of people to their wedding.*
fair play equal treatment of both/all sides according to the rules: *The referee is there to ensure fair play during the match.*

fair[2] /feə(r)/ *noun* a place outside where you can ride on big machines and play games to win prizes: *We're going to the fair this weekend.*

fairly 🔑 /ˈfeəli/ *adverb* **1** in a way that is right and honest: *This company treats its workers fairly.* OPPOSITE **unfairly** **2** quite; not very: *She speaks French fairly well.* ◇ *I'm fairly certain it was him.* ➲ Note at **very**[1].

fairness /ˈfeənəs/ *noun* (no plural) treating people equally or in the right way

fairy /ˈfeəri/ *noun* (*plural* **fairies**) a very small person in stories. Fairies have wings and can do magic.

fairy tale /ˈfeəri teɪl/ (also **fairy story** /ˈfeəri stɔːri/) *noun* a story for children that is about magic

faith /feɪθ/ *noun* **1** (no plural) feeling sure that someone or something is good, right, honest, etc: *I've got great faith in your ability to pass the exam* (= I'm sure that you can do it). **2** (*plural* **faiths**) a religion: *the Muslim faith*

faithful /ˈfeɪθfl/ *adjective* always ready to help your friends and to do what you have promised to do: *a faithful friend*

faithfully /ˈfeɪθfəli/ *adverb*
Yours faithfully words that you write at the end of a formal letter, before your name

fake[1] /feɪk/ *noun* a copy of something, made to trick people: *This painting is not really by Picasso – it's a fake.* ▶ **fake** *adjective*: *a fake thousand-shilling note* OPPOSITE **genuine, real**

fake[2] /feɪk/ *verb* (**fakes, faking, faked** /feɪkt/) **1** to pretend you are feeling something when you are not: *Odoi had already heard the news, but he faked surprise when I told him.* **2** to copy something to trick people

fall[1] 🔑 /fɔːl/ *verb* (**falls, falling, fell** /fel/, **has fallen** /ˈfɔːlən/) **1** to go down quickly; to drop: *The book fell off the table.* ◇ *She fell down the steps and broke her arm.* **2** (also **fall over**) to suddenly stop standing: *He slipped on the mud and fell.* ◇ *I fell over and hurt my leg.* **3** to become lower or less: *In the desert the temperature falls at night.* ◇ *Prices have fallen again.* OPPOSITE **rise** **4** to come or happen: *Darkness was falling.*
fall apart to break into pieces: *The chair fell apart when I sat on it.*
fall asleep to start sleeping: *She was so tired that she fell asleep in the armchair.*
fall behind to become slower than others, or to not do something when you should do it: *She's falling behind in class because she doesn't do her homework.*
fall for someone to start to love someone: *He has fallen for someone he met on holiday.*

fall out with someone to argue with someone so that you stop being friends: *Opiyo has fallen out with his best friend.*
fall through If a plan **falls through**, it does not happen.

fall² 🔑 /fɔːl/ *noun* **1** a sudden drop from a higher place to a lower place: *He had a fall from his bicycle.* **2** becoming lower or less: *a fall in the price of oil* **3 falls** (plural) a place where water falls from a high place to a low place: *the Victoria Falls*

false /fɔːls/ *adjective* **1** not true; wrong: *A spider has eight legs – true or false?* ◇ *She gave a false name to the police.* **2** not real or not natural: *People who have lost their own teeth wear false teeth* (= teeth that are made of plastic). ➲ Note at **tooth**.

false alarm /ˌfɔːls əˈlɑːm/ *noun* a warning about something bad that does not happen: *Everyone thought there was a fire, but it was just a false alarm.*

fame /feɪm/ *noun* (no plural) being known by many people ℹ The adjective is **famous**.

familiar 🔑 /fəˈmɪliə(r)/ *adjective* that you know well: *I heard a familiar voice in the next room.* OPPOSITE **unfamiliar**, **unknown**
be familiar with something know something well: *I'm not familiar with this area.*

family 🔑 /ˈfæməli/ *noun* (*plural* **families**) **1** parents and children: *How many people are there in your family?* ◇ *My family are all very tall.* ◇ *His family lives on a farm.* ◇ *Nduku was the first family member to attend college.*

> ❖ **WORD BUILDING**
>
> Sometimes **family** means not just parents and children but other people too, for example **grandparents**, **aunts**, **uncles** and **cousins**.

2 a group of plants or animals: *Lions belong to the cat family.*

family tree /ˌfæməli ˈtriː/ *noun* a plan that shows all the people in a family

famine /ˈfæmɪn/ *noun* A **famine** happens when there is not enough food in a country: *Thousands of people died in the famine.*

famous 🔑 /ˈfeɪməs/ *adjective* known by many people: *Oxford is famous for its university.* ◇ *Henry Rono was a famous athlete.* OPPOSITE **unknown** ℹ The noun is **fame**.

fan¹ /fæn/ *noun* **1** a thing that moves the air to make you cooler: *an electric fan on the ceiling* **2** a person who likes someone or something, for example a singer or a sport, very much: *She was a fan of Sauti Sol.* ◇ *football fans*

fans

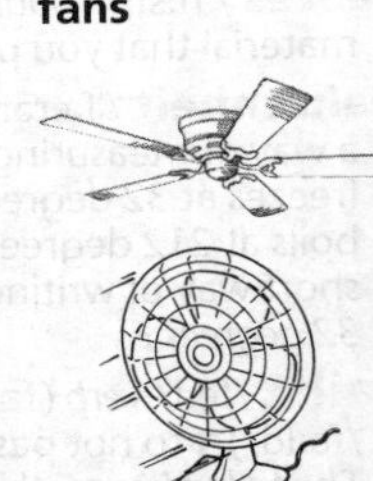

fan² /fæn/ *verb* (**fans**, **fanning**, **fanned** /fænd/) to make someone or something cooler by moving the air: *I fanned my face with the newspaper.*

fancy¹ /ˈfænsi/ *verb* (**fancies**, **fancying**, **fancied** /ˈfænsid/, **has fancied**) **1** to feel that you would like something: *Do you fancy a drink?* **2** a word that shows you are surprised: *Fancy seeing you here!*

fancy² /ˈfænsi/ *adjective* (**fancier**, **fanciest**) not simple or ordinary: *She wore a very fancy hat to the wedding.*

fantastic /fænˈtæstɪk/ *adjective* **1** very good; wonderful: *We had a fantastic holiday.* **2** strange or difficult to believe: *He told us fantastic stories about his adventures.*

fantasy /ˈfæntəsi/ *noun* (*plural* **fantasies**) something nice that you think about and that you hope will happen, although it is unlikely

far¹ 🔑 /fɑː(r)/ *adjective* (**farther** /ˈfɑːðə(r)/ *or* **further** /ˈfɜːðə(r)/, **farthest** /ˈfɑːðɪst/ *or* **furthest** /ˈfɜːðɪst/) **1** a long way away: *Let' walk – it's not far.* OPPOSITE **near** **2** other: *They live on the far side of town.*

far² 🔑 /fɑː(r)/ *adverb* (**farther** /ˈfɑːðə(r)/ *or* **further** /ˈfɜːðə(r)/, **farthest** /ˈfɑːðɪst/ *or* **furthest** /ˈfɜːðɪst/) **1** a long way: *My house isn't far from the school.* ◇ *It's too far to wal in one day.* ◇ *I walked much farther than you.* ◇ *If we sit too far away from the screen I won't be able to see the film.* **2** You use 'far' to ask about the distance from one place to another place: *How far is it to Dar es Salaam from here?*

> ❖ **GRAMMAR**
>
> We usually use 'far' only in questions and negative sentences, and after 'too' and 'so'. In other sentences we use **a long way**: *It's a long way to walk – let's take the bus.*

3 very much: *He's far taller than his brother.* ◇ *That's far too expensive.*
as far as to a place: *We walked as far as the village and then came back.*
as far as I know words that you use when you think something is true but you are not certain: *As far as I know, she's well, but I haven't seen her for a long time.*
by far You use 'by far' to show that a person or thing is much better, bigger, etc. than anyone or anything else: *She's by far the best player in the team.*
far apart If two things or people are **far apart**, they are a long way from each other: *I don't see him very often because we live too far apart.*
far from not at all: *I'm far from certain.*
so far until now: *So far the work has been easy.*

fare /feə(r)/ *noun* the money that you pay to travel by bus, train, plane, etc: *How much is the train fare to Kisii?*

farewell /ˌfeəˈwel/ *noun* saying goodbye: *We are having a farewell party for Ali because he is going to live in Australia.*

farm 🔑 /fɑːm/ *noun* land and buildings where people keep animals and grow crops: *They work on a farm.* ◇ *farm animals* ▸ **farm** *verb* (**farms**, **farming**, **farmed** /fɑːmd/): *He farms in the north of the country.*

farmer 🔑 /ˈfɑːmə(r)/ *noun* a person who owns or looks after a farm

farmhouse /ˈfɑːmhaʊs/ *noun* the house on a farm where the farmer lives

farming 🔑 /ˈfɑːmɪŋ/ *noun* (no plural) managing a farm or working on it: *Sheep farming is hard work.*

farmyard /ˈfɑːmjɑːd/ *noun* the outside space near the main house on a farm, with buildings or walls around it

farther, farthest 🔑 *form of* FAR[1]

fascinating /ˈfæsɪneɪtɪŋ/ *adjective* very interesting: *She told us fascinating stories about her journey through the mountains.*

fashion 🔑 /ˈfæʃn/ *noun* **1** (*plural* **fashions**) a way of dressing or doing something that people like and try to copy for a short time: *She loves African fashion and colour.* ◇ *We saw the latest designs at a fashion show.* **2** (no plural) the way you do something: *He spoke in a very strange fashion.*
in fashion If something is **in fashion**, people like it at the moment: *What style of clothes are in fashion at the moment?*
out of fashion If something is **out of fashion**, people do not like it at the moment: *Bright colours have gone out of fashion.*

fashionable 🔑 /ˈfæʃnəbl/ *adjective* in the newest fashion: *She was wearing a fashionable black hat.*
OPPOSITE **unfashionable, old-fashioned**
▸ **fashionably** /ˈfæʃnəbli/ *adverb*: *He was fashionably dressed.*

fashion designer /ˈfæʃn dɪzaɪnə(r)/ *noun* a person whose job is to design clothes

fast[1] 🔑 /fɑːst/ *adjective* (**faster**, **fastest**) **1** A person or thing that is fast can move quickly: *a fast car* **2** If a clock or watch is fast, it shows a time that is later than the real time: *My watch is five minutes fast.*
OPPOSITE **slow** ➲ Note at **clock**.

fast[2] 🔑 /fɑːst/ *adverb* (**faster**, **fastest**) quickly: *Don't talk so fast – I can't understand what you're saying.*
OPPOSITE **slowly**
fast asleep sleeping very well: *The baby was fast asleep.*

fast[3] /fɑːst/ *verb* (**fasts**, **fasting**, **fasted**) to not eat food for a certain time: *Muslims fast during Ramadhan.*

fasten 🔑 /ˈfɑːsn/ *verb* (**fastens**, **fastening**, **fastened** /ˈfɑːsnd/) **1** to close something so that it will not come open: *Please fasten your seat belts.* ◇ *Can you fasten this suitcase for me?* **2** to join one thing to another thing: *Fasten this badge to your jacket.* OPPOSITE **unfasten**

fast food /ˌfɑːst ˈfuːd/ *noun* (no plural) hot food that is cooked very quickly in special restaurants and that you can take away to eat

fat[1] 🔑 /fæt/ *adjective* (**fatter**, **fattest**) with a large round body: *You'll get fat if you eat too much.* OPPOSITE **thin**

fat[2] 🔑 /fæt/ *noun* **1** (no plural) the soft white substance under the skins of animals and people: *Cut the fat off the meat.* **2** (*plural* **fats**) oil that you use for cooking: *Heat some fat in a frying pan.*

fatal /ˈfeɪtl/ *adjective* **1** Something that is **fatal** causes death: *a fatal car accident* **2** Something that is **fatal** has very bad results: *I made the fatal mistake of not reading the exam question properly.*
▸ **fatally** /ˈfeɪtəli/ *adverb*: *She was fatally injured in the crash.*

fate /feɪt/ *noun* **1** (no plural) the power that some people believe controls everything that happens **2** (*plural* **fates**) what will happen to someone or something: *What will be the fate of the prisoners?*

father 🔑 /ˈfɑːðə(r)/ *noun* a man who has a child: *Where do your mother and father live?* ➲ Look at **dad**.

father-in-law /ˈfɑːðər ɪn lɔː/ *noun* (*plural* **fathers-in-law**) the father of someone's husband or wife

fatigue /fəˈtiːg/ *noun* (no plural) a feeling of being extremely tired: *I was dropping with fatigue and could not keep my eyes open.*

fault 🔑 /fɔːlt/ *noun* **1** (no plural) If something bad is your fault, you made it happen: *It's my fault that we're late.* **2** (*plural* **faults**) something that is wrong or bad in a person or thing: *There is a serious fault in the machine.*

faulty /ˈfɔːlti/ *adjective* not working well: *This light doesn't work – the switch is faulty.*

favour 🔑 /ˈfeɪvə(r)/ *noun* something that you do to help someone: *Would you do me a favour and open the door?* ◇ *Could I ask you a favour – will you take me to the station this evening?*
be in favour of something to like or agree with something: *Are you in favour of school uniform?*

favourable /ˈfeɪvərəbl/ *adjective* good, suitable or acceptable: *She made a favourable impression on his parents.*

favourite[1] 🔑 /ˈfeɪvərɪt/ *adjective* Your favourite person or thing is the one that you like more than any other: *What's your favourite food?*

favourite[2] 🔑 /ˈfeɪvərɪt/ *noun* **1** a person or thing that you like more than any other: *I like all chocolates but these are my favourites.* **2** a file from the Internet that you have stored on your computer so that you can find it again quickly: *I've added this site to my favourites.*
SAME MEANING **bookmark**

fax /fæks/ *verb* (**faxes, faxing, faxed** /fækst/) to send a copy of something like a letter or picture using telephone lines and a machine called a **fax machine**: *The drawings were faxed from New York.* ▸ **fax** *noun* (*plural* **faxes**) a copy of something that is sent by a fax machine

fear[1] 🔑 /fɪə(r)/ *noun* the feeling that you have when you think that something bad might happen: *I have a terrible fear of dogs.*

fear[2] /fɪə(r)/ *verb* (**fears, fearing, feared** /fɪəd/) **1** to be afraid of someone or something: *We all fear illness and death.* **2** to feel that something bad might happen: *I fear we will be late.*

> ❖ **SPEAKING**
> It is more usual to say **be afraid (of)** or **be frightened (of)**.

fearful /ˈfɪəfl/ *adjective* afraid or worried about something: *They were fearful they would be late and miss the trip.*

feast /fiːst/ *noun* a large special meal for a lot of people: *a wedding feast*

feat /fiːt/ *noun* something you do that is clever, difficult or dangerous: *Breaking the world record was an amazing feat.*

feather 🔑 /ˈfeðə(r)/ *noun* Birds have feathers on their bodies to keep them warm and to help them fly: *The owl fluffed up its feathers.*

feather

feature 🔑 /ˈfiːtʃə(r)/ *noun* **1** an important part of something: *Pictures are a feature of this dictionary.* **2 features** (plural) the parts of the face, for example the eyes, nose or mouth: *He has strong, handsome features.* **3** an important piece of writing in a magazine or newspaper, or a programme on TV: *The magazine has a special feature on volcanoes on the centre pages.*

February 🔑 /ˈfebruəri/ *noun* the second month of the year: *February is the shortest month of the year.*

fed *form of* FEED

federal /ˈfedərəl/ *adjective* A **federal** country has several smaller countries or states that are joined together: *the Federal Government of the United States*

federation /ˌfedəˈreɪʃn/ *noun* a group of states or companies that work together

fed up /ˌfed ˈʌp/ *adjective* unhappy or bored because you have had or done too much of something: *I'm fed up with waiting for Hawa – let's go without her.*

fee /fiː/ *noun* **1** money that you pay to someone for special work: *The lawyer's fee was very high.* **2** money that you pay to do something, for example to join a club: *How much is the entrance fee?* **3 fees** (plural) the money that you pay for lessons at college or university: *Who pays your college fees?*

feeble /ˈfiːbl/ *adjective* (**feebler, feeblest**) not strong; weak: *a feeble old man*

feed 🔑 /fiːd/ *verb* (**feeds, feeding, fed**

/fed/, **has fed**) to give food to a person or an animal: *The baby's crying – I'll go and feed her.*

feeder road /ˈfiːdə rəʊd/ *noun* a small road that joins places to the main road system

feel ⚷ /fiːl/ *verb* (**feels**, **feeling**, **felt** /felt/, **has felt**) **1** to know something because your body tells you: *How do you feel?* ◇ *I don't feel well.* ◇ *I'm feeling tired.* ◇ *He felt someone touch his arm.* **2** to be rough, smooth, wet, dry, etc. when you touch it: *The water felt cold.* ◇ *A snake's skin looks wet but feels dry if you touch it.* **3** to think; to believe: *I feel that we should talk about this.* **4** to touch something to learn about it: *Feel this wool – it's really soft.*

feel for something If you **feel for something**, you try to get something you cannot see with your hands: *She felt in her pocket for her money.*

feel like to want something: *Do you feel like a cup of tea?* ◇ *I don't feel like studying tonight.*

feeling ⚷ /ˈfiːlɪŋ/ *noun* **1** (*plural* **feelings**) something that you feel inside yourself, like happiness or anger: *a feeling of sadness* **2** (no plural) the ability to feel in your body: *I was so cold that I had no feeling in my feet.* **3** (*plural* **feelings**) an idea that you are not certain about: *I have a feeling she isn't telling the truth.*

hurt someone's feelings to do or say something that makes someone sad: *Don't tell him you don't like his shirt – you'll hurt his feelings.*

feet *plural of* FOOT

fell *form of* FALL[1]

fellow[1] /ˈfeləʊ/ *noun* a man: *What is that fellow doing?*

fellow[2] /ˈfeləʊ/ *adjective* a word that you use to talk about people who are the same as you: *She doesn't know many of her fellow students.*

felony /ˈfeləni/ *noun* (*plural* **felonies**) a serious crime

felt *form of* FEEL

felt-tip pen /ˌfelt tɪp ˈpen/ (also **felt-pen** /ˌfelt ˈpen/) *noun* a pen with a soft point

female ⚷ /ˈfiːmeɪl/ *adjective* A female animal or person belongs to the sex that can have babies: *a female student* ▸ **female** *noun*: *That elephant is a female.* ➲ Look at **male**.

feminine /ˈfemənɪn/ *adjective* of or like a woman; right for a woman: *feminine clothes* ➲ Look at **masculine**.

fence ⚷ /fens/ *noun* a thing like a wall that is made of pieces of wood or metal. Fences are put round gardens and fields: *He jumped over the fence.*

ferocious /fəˈrəʊʃəs/ *adjective* very angry and wild: *A rhinoceros is a ferocious animal.*

ferry /ˈferi/ *noun* (*plural* **ferries**) a boat that takes people or things on short journeys across a river or sea: *We travelled to Kisumu by ferry.* ▸ **ferry** *verb* (**ferries**, **ferrying**, **ferried** /ˈferid/, **has ferried**) to take people or things across a river or sea: *Could you ferry us across to the island?*

fertile /ˈfɜːtaɪl/ *adjective* where plants grow well: *fertile soil* OPPOSITE **infertile**

fertilize /ˈfɜːtəlaɪz/ *verb* (**fertilizes**, **fertilizing**, **fertilized** /ˈfɜːtəlaɪzd/) to give plants food to make them grow better ▸ **fertilization** /ˌfɜːtəlaɪˈzeɪʃn/ *noun* (no plural): *fertilization of the soil*

fertilizer /ˈfɜːtəlaɪzə(r)/ *noun* food for plants

festival ⚷ /ˈfestɪvl/ *noun* **1** a time when people do special things because they are happy about something: *Christmas is an important Christian festival.* **2** a time when there are a lot of plays, concerts, etc. in one place: *a festival of music and dance*

fetch /fetʃ/ *verb* (**fetches**, **fetching**, **fetched** /fetʃt/) **1** to go and bring back someone or something: *Can you fetch me the books from the bookcase?* ◇ *I went to fetch my brother from school.* ➲ Look at **bring**. **2** If something **fetches** a certain price, someone pays this price for it: *That old cow won't fetch much.*

fever /ˈfiːvə(r)/ *noun* If you have a **fever**, your body is too hot because you are ill. ▸ **feverish** /ˈfiːvərɪʃ/ *adjective* If you are **feverish**, your body is too hot because you are ill.

few ⚷ /fjuː/ *adjective, pronoun* (**fewer**, **fewest**) not many: *Few people live to the age of 100.* ◇ *There are fewer buses in the evenings.*

a few some but not many: *Only a few people came to the meeting.* ◇ *She has written a lot of books, but I have only read a few of them.*

quite a few quite a lot: *I have read quite a few of her books.*

> ❖ **few** or **a few**?
>
> Be careful! **Few** and **a few** are not the same. Look at these examples: *I've only been at the school a short time and I have few* (= not many) *friends.* ◇ *I've only been at the school a short time and already I have a few* (= some) *friends.*
>
> Look also at **little**.

fiancé /fiˈɒnseɪ/ *noun* A woman's **fiancé** is the man she is going to marry: *My aunt introduced her fiancé Shema. They've just got engaged.*

fiancée /fiˈɒnseɪ/ *noun* A man's **fiancée** is the woman he is going to marry.

fib /fɪb/ *noun* something you say that you know is not true; a small lie: *Don't tell fibs!*
▸ **fib** *verb* (**fibs, fibbing, fibbed** /fɪbd/): *I was fibbing when I said I liked her hat.*
▸ **fibber** /ˈfɪbə(r)/ *noun* a person who tells fibs

fibre /ˈfaɪbə(r)/ *noun* **1** (no plural) the part of your food that helps to move other food through your body and keep you healthy: *Dried fruits are high in fibre.* **2** (*plural* **fibres**) one of the many thin threads in a material: *cotton fibres*

fiction /ˈfɪkʃn/ *noun* (no plural) stories that someone writes and that are not true: *I enjoy reading fiction.*

fiddle /ˈfɪdl/ *verb* (**fiddles, fiddling, fiddled** /ˈfɪdld/) to touch something a lot with your fingers: *Stop fiddling with your pen and do some work!*

fidget /ˈfɪdʒɪt/ *verb* (**fidgets, fidgeting, fidgeted**) to keep moving your body, hands or feet because you are nervous, excited or bored

field 🔑 /fiːld/ *noun* **1** a piece of land where people grow crops: *a field of maize* **2** one thing that you study: *Dr Ereng is one of the most famous scientists in his field.* **3** a piece of land used for something special: *a football field* ◇ *an airfield* (= a place where planes land and take off) **4** a place where people find oil, coal, gold, etc: *the oilfields of Saudi Arabia*

field event /ˈfiːld ɪvent/ *noun* a sport, such as jumping or throwing, that is not a race and does not involve running ➲ Look at **track event**.

fierce /fɪəs/ *adjective* (**fiercer, fiercest**) **1** angry and wild: *a fierce dog* **2** very strong: *the fierce heat of the sun*

fifteen 🔑 /ˌfɪfˈtiːn/ *number* 15

fifteenth /ˌfɪfˈtiːnθ/ *adjective, adverb, noun* 15th

fifth /fɪfθ/ *adjective, adverb, noun* **1** 5th **2** one of five equal parts of something; $^1/_5$

fiftieth /ˈfɪftiəθ/ *adjective, adverb, noun* 50th

fifty 🔑 /ˈfɪfti/ *number* **1** 50
2 the fifties (plural) the numbers, years or temperature between 50 and 59: *He was born in the fifties* (= in the 1950s).
in your fifties between the ages of 50 and 59

fig /fɪɡ/ *noun* a soft sweet fruit that is full of small seeds

fight[1] 🔑 /faɪt/ *verb* (**fights, fighting, fought** /fɔːt/, **has fought**) **1** When people fight, they try to hurt or kill each other using their hands, knives or guns: *Why are the children fighting?* **2** to try very hard to stop something: *He fought against the illness for two years.* **3** to talk in an angry way; to argue: *My parents were fighting about money.*
fight tooth and nail to try very hard to get what you want
fight for something to try hard to do or to get something: *The workers are fighting for better pay.*

fight[2] 🔑 /faɪt/ *noun* an act of fighting: *There was a fight outside the restaurant.*

fighter /ˈfaɪtə(r)/ *noun* **1** a person who fights as a sport **2** a small fast plane that shoots at other planes in a war

figure 🔑 /ˈfɪɡə(r)/ *noun* **1** one of the symbols (0 – 9) that we use to show numbers: *Shall I write the numbers in words or figures?* **2** an amount or price: *What are the sales figures for last month?* **3** the shape of a person's body: *She's got a good figure.* **4** a shape of a person that you cannot see clearly: *I saw a tall figure outside the window.* **5 figures** (plural) working with numbers to find an answer: *I'm not very good with figures.*
figure of speech words that you use in an unusual way to make your meaning stronger: *I didn't really mean that she was mad – it was just a figure of speech.*

file[1] 🔑 /faɪl/ *noun*
1 a box or cover for keeping papers in: *There is a pile of files on his desk.*

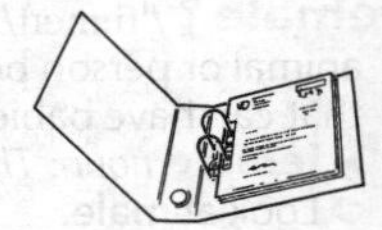
file

2 a collection of information on a computer: *Give your file a name.* **3** a tool with rough sides that you use for making things smooth: *a nail file*
in single file in a line with each person following the one in front: *The children walked into the hall in single file.*

file² /faɪl/ *verb* (**files, filing, filed** /faɪld/) **1** to put papers into a file: *Can you file these letters, please?* **2** to walk in a line, one behind the other: *The pupils filed into the classroom.* **3** to make something smooth with a file: *She filed her nails.*

fill 🔑 /fɪl/ *verb* (**fills, filling, filled** /fɪld/) **1** to make something full: *Can you fill this jug with water, please?* ➲ Look at **tooth**. **2** to become full: *His eyes filled with tears.*
fill in to write facts or answers in the spaces that have been left for them: *She gave me a form and told me to fill it in.*
fill up to become or make something completely full: *He filled up his glass.*

film¹ 🔑 /fɪlm/ *noun* **1** moving pictures that you see at a cinema or on television: *There's a good film on at the cinema this week.* **2** the special thin plastic that you use in some cameras for taking photographs: *I bought a roll of black and white film.*

film² 🔑 /fɪlm/ *verb* (**films, filming, filmed** /fɪlmd/) to use a camera to make moving pictures of a story, news, etc: *A TV company are filming outside my house.*

filter /ˈfɪltə(r)/ *noun* a thing used for holding back the solid parts in a liquid or gas: *a coffee filter* ▶ **filter** *verb* (**filters, filtering, filtered** /ˈfɪltəd/): *You should filter the water before you drink it.*

filthy /ˈfɪlθi/ *adjective* (**filthier, filthiest**) very dirty: *Go and wash your hands. They're filthy!*

fin /fɪn/ *noun* one of the thin flat parts on a fish that help it to swim ➲ Picture at **fish¹**, **shark**.

final¹ 🔑 /ˈfaɪnl/ *adjective* last; at the end: *The final word in this dictionary is 'zoom'.*

final² 🔑 /ˈfaɪnl/ *noun* **1** the last game in a competition to decide who wins: *She reached the final of the 100m.* **2** **finals** (plural) the last exams that you take at university: *He sits his finals next year.*

finally 🔑 /ˈfaɪnəli/ *adverb* **1** after a long time; in the end: *After a long wait the bus finally arrived.* **2** You use 'finally' before saying the last thing in a list: *And finally, I'd like to thank my parents for all their help.*

finance¹ /ˈfaɪnæns/ *noun* **1** (no plural) money; planning how to get, save and use money for a business, country, etc: *the Minister of Finance* **2** **finances** (plural) the money you have that you can spend: *His finances aren't very good* (= He hasn't got much money).

finance² /ˈfaɪnæns/ *verb* (**finances, financing, financed** /ˈfaɪnænst/) to give money to pay for something: *The building was financed by the government.*

financial 🔑 /faɪˈnænʃl/ *adjective* of or about money: *financial problems*

find 🔑 /faɪnd/ *verb* (**finds, finding, found** /faʊnd/, **has found**) **1** to see or get something after looking or trying: *I can't find my glasses.* ◇ *She hasn't found a gift for her sister yet.* ◇ *Can you find me a good book to read?* **2** to see or get something that you did not expect: *I found some money in the street.* ◇ *I woke up and found myself in hospital.* **3** to think or have an idea about something because you have felt, tried, seen it, etc: *I didn't find that book very interesting.* ◇ *He finds it difficult to sleep at night.*
find out to discover something, for example by asking or studying: *Can you find out what time the train leaves?* ◇ *Has she found out that you broke the window?*

findings /ˈfaɪndɪŋz/ *noun* (plural) the things you discover as a result of doing research into something: *Explain your findings to the rest of the class.*

fine¹ 🔑 /faɪn/ *adjective* (**finer, finest**) **1** well or happy: *'How are you?' 'Fine thanks. And you?'* **2** good enough; OK: *'Let's meet on Monday.' 'Fine.'* ◇ *'Do you want some more milk in your coffee?' 'No, that's fine.'* **3** beautiful or of good quality: *There's a fine view from the top floor of the building.* ◇ *That was one of Rono's finest races.* **4** in very thin pieces: *fine thread* OPPOSITE **thick** **5** in very small pieces: *Salt is finer than sugar.* OPPOSITE **coarse**

fine² /faɪn/ *noun* money that you must pay because you have done something wrong: *You'll get a fine if you park your car there.* ▶ **fine** *verb* (**fines, fining, fined** /faɪnd/) to make someone pay a fine: *He was fined 2 000 shillings for stealing.*

finger 🔑 /ˈfɪŋgə(r)/ *noun* one of the five parts at the end of each hand: *She wears a ring on her little* (= smallest) *finger.*
➲ picture on page A13
keep your fingers crossed to hope that

someone or something will be successful: *I'll keep my fingers crossed for you in your exams.*

fingernail /ˈfɪŋɡəneɪl/ *noun* the **nail** (= hard part) at the end of your finger ➲ picture on page A13

fingerprint /ˈfɪŋɡəprɪnt/ *noun* the mark that a finger makes when it touches something: *The police found his fingerprints on the gun.*

finish[1] /ˈfɪnɪʃ/ *verb* (**finishes, finishing, finished** /ˈfɪnɪʃt/) **1** to stop happening: *School finishes at four o'clock.* **2** to stop doing something; to come to the end of something: *I finish work at half past five.* ◇ *Hurry up and finish your dinner!* ◇ *Have you finished cleaning your room?* OPPOSITE **begin, start**
finish off to do or eat the last part of something: *He finished off the milk.*
finish with something to not want or need something any more: *Can I read this book when you've finished with it?*

finish[2] /ˈfɪnɪʃ/ *noun* (*plural* **finishes**) the last part of something; the end: *the finish of a race* OPPOSITE **start**

finishing line /ˈfɪnɪʃɪŋ laɪn/ *noun* the line across a sports track that marks the end of a race: *Everyone cheered as Egesa crossed the finishing line.*

fir /fɜː(r)/ (also **fir tree**) *noun* a tall tree with thin sharp leaves (called **needles**) that usually grows in cold countries

fir

fir cone

fire[1] /ˈfaɪə(r)/ *noun* **1** the heat and bright light that comes from burning things: *Many animals are afraid of fire.* ◇ *There was a big fire at the factory last night.* **2** burning wood or coal that you use for keeping a place warm or for cooking: *They lit a fire to keep warm.* **3** a thing that uses electricity or gas to keep a room warm: *Switch on the fire.*
catch fire to start to burn: *She dropped a match and the chair caught fire.*
on fire burning: *My house is on fire!*
put out a fire to stop something from burning: *We put out the fire with buckets of water.*
set fire to something; set something on fire to make something start to burn: *Someone set the house on fire.*

fire[2] /ˈfaɪə(r)/ *verb* (**fires, firing, fired** /ˈfaɪəd/) **1** to shoot with a gun: *The soldiers fired at the enemy.* **2** to tell someone to leave their job: *He was fired because he was always late for work.*

fire alarm /ˈfaɪər əlɑːm/ *noun* a bell that rings to tell people that there is a fire

fire brigade /ˈfaɪə brɪɡeɪd/ *noun* a group of people whose job is to stop fires: *Call the fire brigade!*

fire engine /ˈfaɪər endʒɪn/ *noun* a vehicle that takes people and equipment to stop fires

fire escape /ˈfaɪər ɪskeɪp/ *noun* stairs on the outside of a building where people can leave quickly when there is a fire inside

fire extinguisher /ˈfaɪər ɪkstɪŋɡwɪʃə(r)/ *noun* a metal container full of chemicals for stopping a fire

fire extinguisher

firefighter /ˈfaɪəfaɪtə(r)/ *noun* a person whose job is to stop fires

fireman /ˈfaɪəmən/ *noun* (*plural* **firemen** /ˈfaɪəmən/) a man whose job is to stop fires

fireplace /ˈfaɪəpleɪs/ *noun* the place in a room where you can have a fire to make the room warm

fire station /ˈfaɪə steɪʃn/ *noun* a building where **fire engines** are kept

firewood /ˈfaɪəwʊd/ *noun* (no plural) wood that we burn on fires

firework /ˈfaɪəwɜːk/ *noun* a container with special powder in it that sends out coloured lights and smoke or makes a loud noise when you burn it: *We watched a firework display in the park.*

firm[1] /fɜːm/ *adjective* (**firmer, firmest**) **1** Something that is firm is quite hard or does not move easily: *Wait until the glue is firm.* ◇ *The shelf isn't very firm, so don't put too many books on it.* **2** showing that you will not change your ideas: *She's very firm with her children* (= she makes them do what she wants). ◇ *a firm promise*
▶ **firmly** *adverb*: *Nail the pieces of wood together firmly.*

firm[2] /fɜːm/ *noun* a group of people working together in a business; a company: *My father works for a building firm.*

first[1] 🔑 /fɜːst/ *adjective* before all the others: *January is the first month of the year.* OPPOSITE **last**

first[2] 🔑 /fɜːst/ *adverb* **1** before all the others: *I arrived at the house first.* **2** for the first time: *I first met Njoki in 2015.* **3** before doing anything else: *First fry the onions, then add the potatoes.* OPPOSITE **last**

at first at the beginning: *At first she was afraid of the water, but she soon learnt to swim.*

first of all before anything else: *I'm going to cook dinner, but first of all I need to buy some food.*

first[3] 🔑 /fɜːst/ *noun* (no plural) a person or thing that comes earliest or before all others: *I was the first to arrive at the party.* ◇ *Today is the first of May (May 1st).* OPPOSITE **last**

first aid /ˌfɜːst ˈeɪd/ *noun* (no plural) quick simple help that you give to a person who is hurt, before a doctor comes: *a first aid kit/course*

firstborn /ˈfɜːstbɔːn/ *noun* a person's first child: *Pembe was their firstborn, soon followed by a little sister.*

first class /ˌfɜːst ˈklɑːs/ *noun* (no plural) the part of a train, plane, etc. that it is more expensive to travel in: *I got a seat in first class.* ▶ **first class** /ˌfɜːst ˈklɑːs/ *adjective, adverb*: *a first-class ticket* ◇ *It costs more to travel first class.* ➲ Look at **second class**.

firstly /ˈfɜːstli/ *adverb* a word that you use when you are giving the first thing in a list: *We were angry firstly because he didn't come, and secondly because he didn't telephone.*

first name /ˈfɜːst neɪm/ *noun* the name that your parents choose for you when you are born: *'What is Mr Mwangi's first name?' 'Opiyo.'* ➲ Note at **name**[1].

fir tree /ˈfɜː triː/ = **fir**

fish

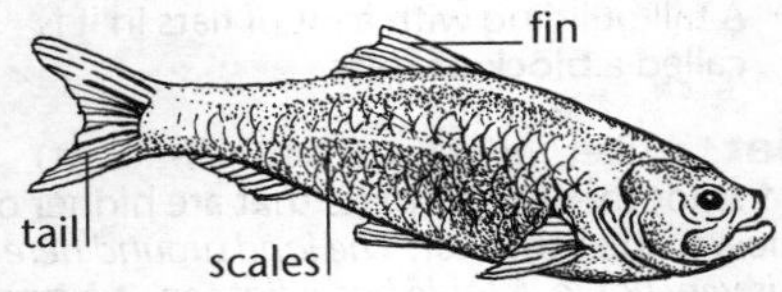

fish[1] 🔑 /fɪʃ/ *noun* (*plural* **fish** *or* **fishes**) an animal that lives and breathes in water and uses its tail and **fins** (= thin flat parts) for swimming: *I caught a big fish.* ◇ *We had fish for dinner.*

fish[2] 🔑 /fɪʃ/ *verb* (**fishes, fishing, fished** /fɪʃt/) to try to catch fish

> ❖ **GRAMMAR**
> When you talk about spending time fishing as a sport, you often say **go fishing**: *I go fishing at weekends.*

▶ **fishing** *noun* (no plural) catching fish

fisherman /ˈfɪʃəmən/ *noun* (*plural* **fishermen** /ˈfɪʃəmən/) a person who catches fish as a job or sport

fishmonger /ˈfɪʃmʌŋɡə(r)/ *noun* a person who sells fish

> ❖ **WORD BUILDING**
> A shop that sells fish is called a **fishmonger's**.

fist /fɪst/ *noun* a hand with the fingers closed tightly: *She banged on the door with her fist.*

fist

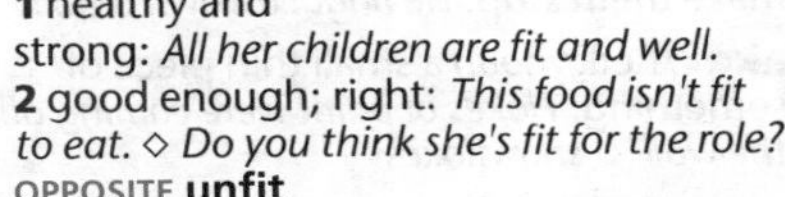

fit[1] 🔑 /fɪt/ *adjective* (**fitter, fittest**) **1** healthy and strong: *All her children are fit and well.* **2** good enough; right: *This food isn't fit to eat.* ◇ *Do you think she's fit for the role?* OPPOSITE **unfit**

fit[2] 🔑 /fɪt/ *verb* (**fits, fitting, fitted**) **1** to be the right size and shape for someone or something: *These shoes don't fit me – they're too tight.* ◇ *This key doesn't fit the lock.* **2** to put something in the right place: *Can you fit these pieces of the puzzle together?*

fit in 1 to have space for someone or something: *We can't fit in any more chairs.* **2** to have time to do something or see someone: *He plays lots of sport so it's hard to fit in studying.*

fit[3] /fɪt/ *noun* **1** a sudden illness when someone may fall down and make violent movements **2** doing something suddenly that you cannot stop: *He was so funny – we were in fits of laughter.* ◇ *I had a coughing fit.*

fitness /ˈfɪtnəs/ *noun* (no plural) being healthy and strong

five 🔑 /faɪv/ *number* 5

fix 🔑 /fɪks/ *verb* (**fixes, fixing, fixed** /fɪkst/) **1** to put something in a place so that it will not move: *We fixed the shelf to the wall.* **2** to repair something: *The light isn't working – can you fix it?* **3** to decide something; to make a plan for something: *We fixed a date for the concert.*

fixed /fɪkst/ *adjective* Something that is fixed does not change or move: *a fixed price*

fixture /ˈfɪkstʃə(r)/ *noun* a sports event that is arranged for a particular date: *a fixture list*

fizz /fɪz/ *verb* (**fizzes, fizzing, fizzed** /fɪzd/) If a drink **fizzes**, it makes a lot of small bubbles.

fizzy /ˈfɪzi/ *adjective* (**fizzier, fizziest**) A **fizzy** drink has many small bubbles of gas in it: *Do you like fizzy drinks?* ➲ Look at **still²**.

flag¹ /flæg/ *noun* a piece of cloth with a special pattern on it joined to a stick (called a **flagpole**). Every country has its own flag.

flag

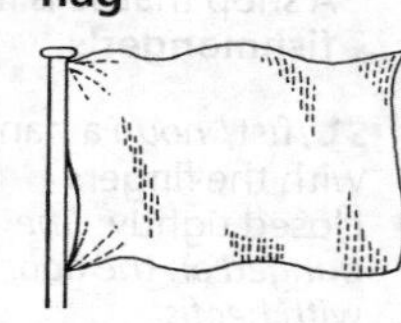

flag² /flæg/ *verb* (**flags, flagging, flagged** /flægd/)
flag down to wave to someone in a car to make them stop: *He flagged down a taxi.*

flake¹ /fleɪk/ *noun* a small thin piece of something: *Flakes of paint were coming off the wall.* ◇ *snowflakes*

flake² /fleɪk/ *verb* (**flakes, flaking, flaked** /fleɪkt/) to come off in small thin pieces: *Paint was flaking off the wall.*

flame /fleɪm/ *noun* a hot bright pointed piece of fire: *The flames were growing higher and higher.* ➲ Picture at **candle**.
in flames burning: *The house was in flames.*

flamingo /fləˈmɪŋgəʊ/ *noun* (*plural* **flamingos** *or* **flamingoes**) a large pink and red bird that has long legs and stands in water

flamingo

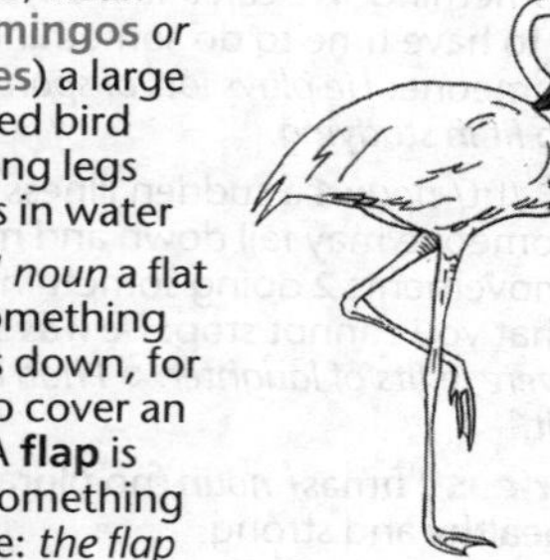

flap¹ /flæp/ *noun* a flat piece of something that hangs down, for example to cover an opening. A **flap** is joined to something by one side: *the flap of an envelope*

flap² /flæp/ *verb* (**flaps, flapping, flapped** /flæpt/) to move quickly up and down or from side to side: *Birds flap their wings when they fly.* ◇ *The sails of the boat flapped in the wind.*

flare /fleə(r)/ *verb* (**flares, flaring, flared** /fleəd/)
flare up If a fire **flares up**, it suddenly burns more brightly or strongly.

flash¹ /flæʃ/ *verb* (**flashes, flashing, flashed** /flæʃt/) **1** to send out a bright light that comes and goes quickly: *The police car's lights flashed on and off.* **2** to make something send out a sudden bright light: *She flashed a torch into the dark room.* **3** to come and go very quickly: *I saw something flash past the window.*

flash² /flæʃ/ *noun* (*plural* **flashes**) **1** a bright light that comes and goes quickly: *a flash of lightning* **2** a bright light that you use with a camera for taking photographs
in a flash very quickly: *Wait for me – I'll be back in a flash.*

flash drive = **memory stick**

flash flood /ˌflæʃ ˈflʌd/ *noun* a large amount of water that covers the land suddenly and quickly after very heavy rain

flasks

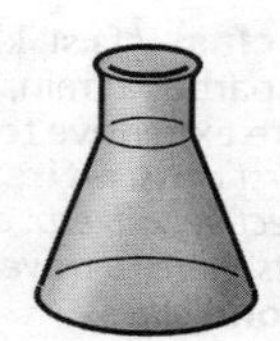

flask /flɑːsk/ *noun* **1** a type of container used for keeping a liquid hot or cold: *a flask of tea/coffee* **2** a bottle with a narrow top, used in scientific work

flat¹ /flæt/ (also **apartment**) *noun* a group of rooms for living in. A flat is usually on one floor of a house or big building: *We live in a first-floor flat.*

❖ **WORD BUILDING**

A tall building with a lot of flats in it is called a **block of flats**.

flat² /flæt/ *adjective* (**flatter, flattest**) **1** smooth, with no parts that are higher or lower than the rest: *The land around here is very flat.* ◇ *A table has a flat top.* **2** A tyre that is flat does not have enough air inside it: *My bicycle has a flat tyre.*

flat³ /flæt/ *adverb* with no parts that are higher or lower than the rest: *He lay flat on his back on the floor.*

flat-screen /ˌflæt ˈskriːn/ *adjective* A **flat-screen** television or computer has a thin flat screen.

flatten /ˈflætn/ *verb* (**flattens, flattening, flattened** /ˈflætnd/) to make something flat: *I sat on the box and flattened it.*

flatter /ˈflætə(r)/ *verb* (**flatters, flattering, flattered** /ˈflætəd/) **1** to try to please someone by saying too many nice things about them that are not completely true **2** If you are **flattered** by something, you like it because it makes you feel important: *I felt flattered when she asked for my advice.*

flattering /ˈflætərɪŋ/ *adjective* making someone look or seem attractive or important: *That dress is very flattering.* ◇ *Thank you for your flattering remarks.*

flattery /ˈflætəri/ *noun* (no plural) saying nice things about someone to please them

flavour 🔑 /ˈfleɪvə(r)/ *noun* the taste of food: *This stew doesn't have much flavour.* ▶ **flavour** *verb* (**flavours, flavouring, flavoured** /ˈfleɪvəd/): *rice flavoured with spices*

flea /fliː/ *noun* a very small insect without wings that can jump and that lives on and bites animals and people: *Our cat has got fleas.*

flea

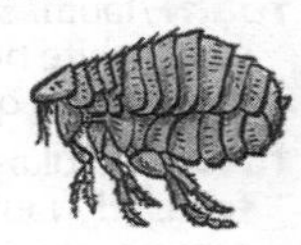

flee /fliː/ *verb* (**flees, fleeing, fled** /fled/, **has fled**) to run away from something bad or dangerous: *During the war, thousands of people fled the country.*

fleet /fliːt/ *noun* a big group of ships

flesh /fleʃ/ *noun* (no plural) the soft part of your body under your skin

❖ **WORD BUILDING**

The flesh of an animal that we eat is called **meat**.

flew *form of* FLY²

flex /fleks/ *noun* (*plural* **flexes**) a long piece of wire covered with plastic that brings electricity to things like lamps, irons, etc.

flexible /ˈfleksəbl/ *adjective* **1** that can bend easily without breaking **2** that can change easily: *It's not important to me when we go – my plans are quite flexible.*

flies 1 *plural of* FLY¹ **2** *form of* FLY²

flight 🔑 /flaɪt/ *noun* **1** (*plural* **flights**) a journey in a plane: *Our flight from Entebbe leaves at 10 a.m.* ◇ *a direct flight from Nairobi to Arusha* **2** (no plural) flying: *Have you ever seen an eagle in flight?* **3** (*plural* **flights**) a group of steps: *They carried the sofa up two flights of stairs.*

flight attendant /ˈflaɪt ətendənt/ *noun* a person whose job is to serve and take care of passengers on a plane

fling /flɪŋ/ *verb* (**flings, flinging, flung** /flʌŋ/, **has flung**) to throw something strongly or without care: *She flung a book and it hit me.*

flip-flop = **slipper**

flirt /flɜːt/ *verb* (**flirts, flirting, flirted**) to show someone that you are attracted to them: *Who was that boy she was flirting with?* ▶ **flirt** *noun* a person who **flirts** a lot

float 🔑 /fləʊt/ *verb* (**floats, floating, floated**) **1** to stay on top of a liquid: *Wood floats on water.* OPPOSITE **sink 2** to move slowly in the air: *Clouds were floating across the sky.*

flock /flɒk/ *noun* a group of birds or animals: *a flock of sheep and goats*

flood

flood¹ 🔑 /flʌd/ *noun* **1** When there is a flood, a lot of water covers the land: *Many homes were destroyed in the flood.* **2** a lot of something: *My dad had a flood of cards when he was in hospital.*

flood² /flʌd/ *verb* (**floods, flooding, flooded**) to fill or cover a place with water; to be covered with water: *Large areas of land have been flooded.*

floor 🔑 /flɔː(r)/ *noun* **1** the part of a room that you walk on: *There weren't any chairs so we sat on the floor.* **2** all the rooms at the same height in a building: *I live on the top floor.* ◇ *Our hotel room was on the sixth floor.*

florist /ˈflɒrɪst/ *noun* a person who sells flowers ➲ Note on page 132.

❖ **WORD BUILDING**

A shop that sells flowers is called a **florist's**.

flour /ˈflaʊə(r)/ *noun* (no plural)

❖ **PRONUNCIATION**

Flour and **flower** both sound the same (like **our** or **power**).

soft white or brown powder that we use to make bread, cakes, etc: *Rub the butter into the flour.*

flourish /ˈflʌrɪʃ/ *verb* (**flourishes, flourishing, flourished** /ˈflʌrɪʃt/) **1** to grow well: *The garden flourished after all the rain.* **2** to become strong or successful: *Their business is flourishing.*

flow[1] /fləʊ/ *verb* (**flows, flowing, flowed** /fləʊd/) to move along like a river: *This river flows into Lake Victoria.* ◇ *Her tears began to flow.*

flow[2] /fləʊ/ *noun* (no plural) a steady continuous movement: *I used a handkerchief to stop the flow of blood.*

flower /ˈflaʊə(r)/ *noun* the brightly coloured part of a plant that comes before the seeds or fruit: *The plant has a beautiful red flower.* ◇ *There was an attractive flower setting on every table.* ◇ *a flower garden/show* ➲ Picture at **plant**[1].

flower bed /ˈflaʊə bed/ *noun* a piece of ground in a garden or park where flowers are grown: *a garden with beautifully kept flower beds*

flowery /ˈflaʊəri/ (also **flowered** /ˈflaʊəd/) *adjective* with a pattern of flowers on it: *a flowery dress*

flown *form of* FLY[2]

flu /fluː/ *noun* (no plural) an illness like a bad cold that makes your body sore and very hot: *I think I've got flu.*

fluent /ˈfluːənt/ *adjective* **1** able to speak easily and correctly: *Malika is fluent in English and French.* **2** spoken easily and correctly: *He speaks fluent German.* ▶ **fluently** *adverb*: *She speaks five languages fluently.*

fluff /flʌf/ *noun* (no plural) soft light stuff that comes off wool, animals, etc.

fluid /ˈfluːɪd/ *noun* anything that can flow; a liquid: *Water is a fluid.* ◇ *body fluids*

flung *form of* FLING

flush /flʌʃ/ *verb* (**flushes, flushing, flushed** /flʌʃt/) to clean something by sending water through it: *Please flush the toilet.*

flute /fluːt/ *noun* a musical instrument with holes, that you hold out to the side and blow

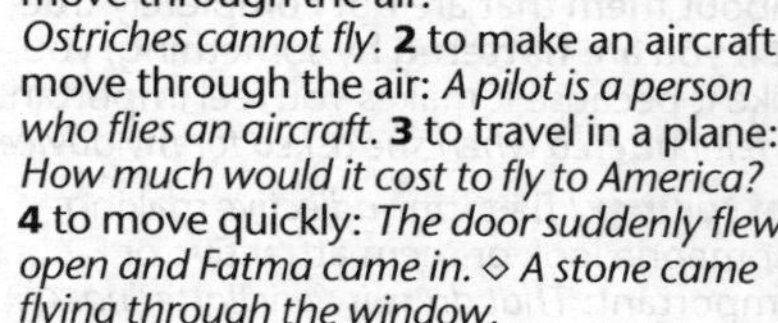

fly[1] /flaɪ/ *noun* (*plural* **flies**) a small insect with two wings

fly[2] /flaɪ/ *verb* (**flies, flying, flew** /fluː/, **has flown** /fləʊn/) **1** to move through the air: *Ostriches cannot fly.* **2** to make an aircraft move through the air: *A pilot is a person who flies an aircraft.* **3** to travel in a plane: *How much would it cost to fly to America?* **4** to move quickly: *The door suddenly flew open and Fatma came in.* ◇ *A stone came flying through the window.*

flying /ˈflaɪɪŋ/ *adjective* able to fly: *flying insects*

flying saucer /ˌflaɪɪŋ ˈsɔːsə(r)/ *noun* a flying object that some people think they have seen, and that may come from another planet

flyover /ˈflaɪəʊvə(r)/ *noun* a bridge that carries a road over other roads

foal /fəʊl/ *noun* a young horse

foam /fəʊm/ *noun* (no plural) a lot of very small white bubbles that you see when you move liquid quickly

focus[1] /ˈfəʊkəs/ *verb* (**focuses, focusing, focused** /ˈfəʊkəst/) to move parts of a camera, etc. so that you can see things through it clearly

focus[2] /ˈfəʊkəs/ *noun* (no plural)
in focus If a photograph is **in focus**, it is clear.
out of focus If a photograph is **out of focus**, it is not clear: *Your face is out of focus in this photo.*

foetus /ˈfiːtəs/ *noun* (*plural* **foetuses** /ˈfiːtəsɪz/) a young human or animal that is still growing inside its mother's body

fog /fɒg/ *noun* (no plural) thick cloud which forms close to the ground and which is difficult to see through: *Thick fog is making driving dangerous.* ▶ **foggy** /ˈfɒgi/ *adjective* (**foggier, foggiest**): *a foggy morning*

foil /fɔɪl/ *noun* (no plural) metal that is very thin like paper. **Foil** is often used for covering food.

fold[1] /fəʊld/ *verb* (**folds, folding, folded**) **1** (also **fold up**) to bend something so that one part is on top of another part: *I folded the letter and put it in the envelope.* ◇ *Fold up your clothes.* OPPOSITE **unfold** **2** to be able to be made smaller to be carried or stored

more easily: *This table folds up flat.*
fold your arms If you **fold your arms**, you cross them in front of your chest.

fold

fold a letter **fold** your arms

fold² /fəʊld/ *noun* a line that is made when you bend cloth or paper

folder /ˈfəʊldə(r)/ *noun* a cover made of cardboard or plastic for keeping papers in

folding /ˈfəʊldɪŋ/ *adjective* that can be made flat: *a folding bed*

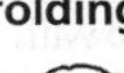

folding

a **folding** chair

foliage /ˈfəʊliɪdʒ/ *noun* (no plural) all the leaves of a tree or plant

folk /fəʊk/ *noun* (plural) people: *There are a lot of old folk living in this village.*

folk dance /ˈfəʊk dɑːns/ *noun* an old dance of the people of a particular place

folk song /ˈfəʊk sɒŋ/ *noun* an old song of the people of a particular place

follow /ˈfɒləʊ/ *verb* (**follows, following, followed** /ˈfɒləʊd/) **1** to come or go after someone or something: *Follow me and I'll show you the way.* ◇ *I think that car is following us!* **2** to go along a road, path, etc: *Follow this road for about a kilometre and then turn right.* **3** to do what someone says you should do: *Did you follow my advice?* **4** to understand something: *Has everyone followed the lesson so far?* **5** to regularly read the messages that someone writes on an Internet site: *I don't follow celebrities on Twitter any more.*
as follows as you will now hear or read: *The dates of the meetings will be as follows: 21 March, 3 April, 19 April.*

follower /ˈfɒləʊə(r)/ *noun* **1** a person who follows or supports a person or belief **2** a person who regularly read the messages that someone writes on an Internet site: *He has hundreds of followers on Twitter.*

following /ˈfɒləʊɪŋ/ *adjective* next: *I came back from my uncle's on Sunday and went to school on the following day.*

follow-up /ˈfɒləʊ ʌp/ *noun* something that is done to continue or develop something: *The book is a follow-up to her excellent television series.* ▶ **follow-up** *adjective*: *follow-up treatment at the local hospital*

fond /fɒnd/ *adjective* (**fonder, fondest**)
be fond of someone or **something** like someone or something a lot: *They are very fond of their uncle.*

font /fɒnt/ *noun* the size and style of a set of letters that are used in printing or on a computer screen

food /fuːd/ *noun* (no plural) People and animals eat food so that they can live and grow: *Let's go and get some food – I'm hungry.* ◇ *They gave the cows food and water.*

food chain /ˈfuːd tʃeɪn/ *noun* (no plural) when one type of living thing eats another type, which eats another type and so on: *Small fish are low on the food chain* (= they only eat plants, but they are eaten by larger fish, which are eaten by birds and so on).

foodstuff /ˈfuːdstʌf/ *noun* anything that is used as food: *There is a good supply of basic foodstuffs.*

food chain

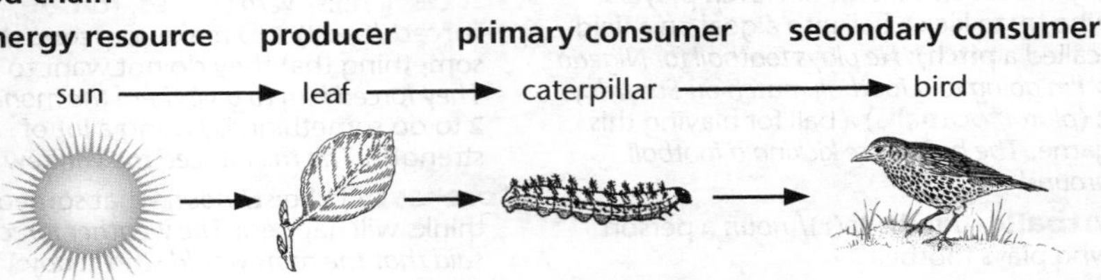

fool[1] /fu:l/ *noun* a person who is silly or who does something silly: *You fool! You forgot to lock the door!*
make a fool of yourself to do something that makes you look silly: *He made a fool of himself in the match today.*

fool[2] /fu:l/ *verb* (**fools**, **fooling**, **fooled** /fu:ld/) to make someone think something that is not true; to trick someone: *You can't fool me! I know you're lying!*
fool about; **fool around** to do silly things: *Stop fooling about with that knife.*

foolish /ˈfu:lɪʃ/ *adjective* stupid; silly: *a foolish mistake* ▸ **foolishly** *adverb*: *I foolishly forgot to bring any money.*

foot /fʊt/ *noun* **1** (*plural* **feet** /fi:t/) the part of your leg that you stand on: *I've been walking all day and my feet hurt.* ➲ picture on page A13 **2** (*plural* **foot** *or* **feet**) a measure of length (= 30.48 centimetres). There are twelve **inches** in a foot, and three feet in a **yard**: *'How tall are you?' 'Five foot six'* (= five feet and six inches). ❶ The short way of writing 'foot' is **ft. 3** (no plural) the lowest part; the bottom: *She was standing at the foot of the stairs.*
on foot walking: *Shall we go by car or on foot?*
put your feet up to rest: *If you're tired, put your feet up and listen to the radio.*
put your foot down to say strongly that something must or must not happen: *My father put his foot down and said I had to study every evening.*

football

The boys are playing **football**.

football /ˈfʊtbɔ:l/ *noun* **1** (no plural) a game for two teams of eleven players who try to kick a ball into a goal on a field (called a **pitch**): *He plays football for Nigeria.* ◇ *I'm going to a football match on Saturday.* **2** (*plural* **footballs**) a ball for playing this game: *The boys were kicking a football around.*

footballer /ˈfʊtbɔ:lə(r)/ *noun* a person who plays football

footpath /ˈfʊtpɑ:θ/ *noun* a path in the countryside for people to walk on

footprint /ˈfʊtprɪnt/ *noun* a mark that your foot or shoe makes on the ground

footstep /ˈfʊtstep/ *noun* the sound of a person walking: *I heard footsteps, and then a knock on the door.*

for[1] /fə(r); fɔ:(r)/ *preposition* **1** a word that shows who will get or have something: *These flowers are for you.* **2** a word that shows how something is used or why something is done: *We had fish for dinner.* ◇ *Take this medicine for your cold.* ◇ *He was sent to prison for murder.* **3** a word that shows how long: *She has lived here for 20 years.* ➲ Note at **since**[1]. **4** a word that shows how far: *We walked for two kilometres.* **5** a word that shows where a person or thing is going: *Is this the bus for Moshi?* **6** a word that shows the person or thing you are talking about: *It's time for us to go.* **7** a word that shows how much something is: *I bought this book for 200 shillings.* **8** a word that shows that you like an idea: *Some people were for the strike and others were against it.* **9** on the side of someone or something: *He plays football for Italy.* **10** with the meaning of: *What is the word for 'table' in Kiswahili?*

for[2] /fə(r)/ *conjunction* because: *She was crying, for she knew they could never meet again.* ❶ **Because** and **as** are the words that we usually use.

forbid /fəˈbɪd/ *verb* (**forbids**, **forbidding**, **forbade** /fəˈbæd/, **has forbidden** /fəˈbɪdn/) to say that someone must not do something: *My parents have forbidden me to come home late.* ◇ *Photography is forbidden* (= not allowed) *inside the museum.* OPPOSITE **allow**

force[1] /fɔ:s/ *noun* **1** (no plural) power or strength: *He was killed by the force of the explosion.* **2** (*plural* **forces**) a group of people, for example police or soldiers, who do a special job: *the police force*
by force using a lot of strength, for example by pushing, pulling or hitting: *I lost the key so I had to open the door by force.*

force[2] /fɔ:s/ *verb* (**forces**, **forcing**, **forced** /fɔ:st/) **1** to make someone do something that they do not want to do: *They forced him to give them the money.* **2** to do something by using a lot of strength: *The thief forced the window open.*

forecast /ˈfɔ:kɑ:st/ *noun* what someone thinks will happen: *The weather forecast said that the rains would start today.*

foreground /ˈfɔːgraʊnd/ *noun* the part of a picture that seems nearest to you: *The man in the foreground is my father.* OPPOSITE **background**

forehead /ˈfɔːhed/ *noun* the part of your face above your eyes ➲ picture on page A13

foreign /ˈfɒrən/ *adjective* **1** of or from another country: *We've got some foreign students staying at our house.* ◇ *a foreign language* ◇ *the department for foreign affairs* ➲ Note at **strange**. **2** (used about an object) not being where it should be: *I had a foreign body* (= object) *in my eye.*

foreigner /ˈfɒrənə(r)/ *noun* a person from another country ➲ Note at **stranger**.

foreign exchange /ˌfɒrən ɪksˈtʃeɪndʒ/ *noun* the system of buying and selling money from a different country; the place where it is bought and sold

foreman /ˈfɔːmən/ *noun* (*plural* **foremen** /ˈfɔːmən/) a person in charge of a group of workers

forest /ˈfɒrɪst/ *noun* a big piece of land with a lot of trees: *We went for a walk in the forest.*

❖ **WORD BUILDING**

A forest is larger than a **wood**. A **jungle** is a forest in a very hot country.

forester /ˈfɒrɪstə(r)/ *noun* a person who works in a forest, looking after the trees

forever /fərˈevə(r)/ *adverb* **1** (also **for ever**) for all time; always: *I will love you forever.* **2** very often: *I can't read because he is forever asking me questions!*

forgave *form of* FORGIVE

forge /fɔːdʒ/ *verb* (**forges, forging, forged** /fɔːdʒd/) to make a copy of something because you want to trick people and make them think it is real: *He was put in prison for forging money.*

forgery /ˈfɔːdʒəri/ *noun* **1** (no plural) making a copy of something to trick people: *Forgery is a crime.* **2** (*plural* **forgeries**) a copy of something made to trick people: *They discovered the notes were forgeries.*

forget /fəˈget/ *verb* (**forgets, forgetting, forgot** /fəˈgɒt/, **has forgotten** /fəˈgɒtn/) **1** to not remember something; to not have something in your mind any more: *I've forgotten her name.* ◇ *Don't forget to feed the cat.* **2** to not bring something with you: *I couldn't see the film very well because I had forgotten my glasses.*

❖ **GRAMMAR**

Be careful! We do not use **forget** if we mention the place where we have left something: *I've forgotten my book.* ◇ *I've left my book at home.*

3 to stop thinking about something: *Forget about your exams and enjoy yourself!*

forgetful /fəˈgetfl/ *adjective* often forgetting things: *My dad is very forgetful – he's always leaving things on the bus!* SAME MEANING **absent-minded**

forgive /fəˈgɪv/ *verb* (**forgives, forgiving, forgave** /fəˈgeɪv/, **has forgiven** /fəˈgɪvn/) to stop being angry with someone for a bad thing that they did: *He never forgave me for forgetting his birthday.* ▶ **forgiveness** /fəˈgɪvnəs/ *noun* (no plural): *He begged forgiveness for what he had done.*

forks

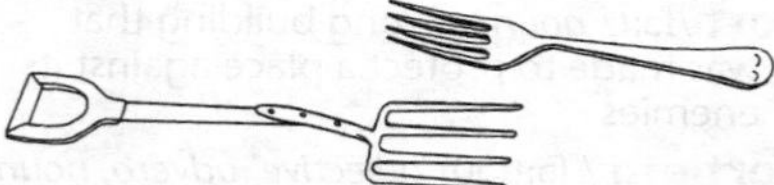

fork /fɔːk/ *noun* **1** a thing with long points at one end, that you use for putting food in your mouth: *He eats with a knife and fork.* **2** a large tool with points at one end, that you use for digging or moving soil: *She was digging the garden with a fork.* **3** a place where a road or river divides into two parts: *When you get to the fork in the road, go left.*

form¹ /fɔːm/ *noun* **1** a type of something: *Cars, trains and buses are all forms of transport.* **2** a piece of paper with spaces for you to answer questions: *You need to fill in this form to get a new passport.* ➲ Look at page A16. **3** the shape of a person or thing: *In the dark, we could just see her familiar form coming towards us.* **4** one of the ways you write or say a word: *'Forgot' is a form of 'forget'.* **5** a class in a secondary school: *Which form are you in?*

form² /fɔːm/ *verb* (**forms, forming, formed** /fɔːmd/) **1** to make something or give a shape to something: *We formed a line outside the cinema.* ◇ *In English we usually form the past tense by adding 'ed'.* **2** to grow; to take shape: *Ice forms when water freezes.* **3** to start a group, etc: *They formed a music club.*

formal ⚷ /ˈfɔːml/ *adjective* You use formal language or behave in a formal way at important or serious times and with people you do not know very well: *'Yours faithfully' is a formal way of ending a letter.* ◇ *He wore a suit and tie because it was a formal dinner.* OPPOSITE **informal** ▸ **formally** /ˈfɔːməli/ *adverb*: *He was dressed formally for his interview.*

former[1] /ˈfɔːmə(r)/ *adjective* of a time before now: *countries of the former Soviet Union*

the former[2] /ðə ˈfɔːmə(r)/ *noun* (no plural) the first of two things or people: *I have visited both Morocco and Tunisia, and I prefer the former.* ➲ Look at **latter**[2].

formerly /ˈfɔːməli/ *adverb* before this time: *Sri Lanka was formerly called Ceylon.*

formula /ˈfɔːmjulə/ *noun* (*plural* **formulae** /ˈfɔːmjuliː/, *or* **formulas**) **1** a group of letters, numbers or symbols that show a rule in mathematics or science: *The formula for finding the area of a circle is* πr^2. **2** a list of the substances that you need to make something: *a formula for a new drug*

fort /fɔːt/ *noun* a strong building that was made to protect a place against its enemies

fortieth /ˈfɔːtiəθ/ *adjective, adverb, noun* 40th

fortnight /ˈfɔːtnaɪt/ *noun* two weeks: *It took a fortnight for my letter to get there.* ▸ **fortnightly** *adjective, adverb* once in two weeks: *We have fortnightly meetings.*

fortress /ˈfɔːtrəs/ *noun* (*plural* **fortresses**) a large strong building that was made to protect a place against its enemies

fortunate /ˈfɔːtʃənət/ *adjective* lucky: *We were fortunate to have good weather for the match.* OPPOSITE **unfortunate** ▸ **fortunately** *adverb*: *There was an accident but fortunately nobody was hurt.* SAME MEANING luckily OPPOSITE **unfortunately**

fortune /ˈfɔːtʃuːn/ *noun* **1** (no plural) things that happen that you cannot control; luck: *I had the good fortune to win a prize.* **2** (*plural* **fortunes**) a lot of money: *He made a fortune selling cars.*
tell someone's fortune to say what will happen to someone in the future: *The old lady said she could tell my fortune by looking at my hand.*

forty ⚷ /ˈfɔːti/ *number* **1** 40 **2 the forties** (plural) the numbers, years or temperature between 40 and 49
in your forties between the ages of 40 and 49: *My mother is in her forties.*

> ❖ **SPELLING**
> Be careful! You spell **four** with a **u** but there is no **u** in **forty**.

forward[1] ⚷ /ˈfɔːwəd/ (also **forwards** /ˈfɔːwədz/) *adverb* **1** in the direction that is in front of you: *Move forwards to the front of the train.* OPPOSITE **back**, **backwards** **2** to a later time: *When you travel from Senegal to Tanzania, you need to put your watch forward.* OPPOSITE **back**
look forward to something wait for something with pleasure: *We're looking forward to seeing you again.*

forward[2] /ˈfɔːwəd/ *verb* (**forwards, forwarding, forwarded**) to send a letter to someone at their new address: *Could you forward all my post to me while I'm in London?*

fossil /ˈfɒsl/ *noun* a part of a dead plant or animal that has been in the ground for a very long time and has become hard

fought *form of* FIGHT[1]

foul[1] /faʊl/ *adjective* (**fouler, foulest**) dirty, or with a bad smell or taste: *What a foul smell!*

foul[2] /faʊl/ *noun* something you do that is against the rules of a game, for example football: *He was sent off the field for a foul against the goalkeeper.* ▸ **foul** *verb* (**fouls, fouling, fouled** /faʊld/): *Mariga was fouled twice.*

found[1] *form of* FIND

found[2] /faʊnd/ *verb* (**founds, founding, founded**) to start something, for example a school or business: *This school was founded in 1995.* ▸ **founder** *noun* a person who founds something

foundation /faʊnˈdeɪʃn/ *noun* **1** (no plural) starting a group, building, etc: *the foundation of a new school* **2 foundations** (plural) the strong parts of a building which you build first under the ground

fountain /ˈfaʊntən/ *noun* water that shoots up into the air and then falls down again

fountain

fountain pen /ˈfaʊntən pen/ *noun* a pen that you fill with a coloured liquid (called **ink**) ➲ Picture at **pen**.

four ⚷ /fɔː(r)/ *number* 4
on all fours with your hands and knees on

the ground: *We went through the tunnel on all fours.*

four-legged /ˌfɔː ˈlegɪd/ *adjective* with four legs: *A horse is a four-legged animal.*

fourteen /ˌfɔːˈtiːn/ *number* 14

fourteenth /ˌfɔːˈtiːnθ/ *adjective, adverb, noun* 14th

fourth /fɔːθ/ *adjective, adverb, noun* 4th

four-wheel drive

four-wheel drive /ˌfɔː wiːl ˈdraɪv/ *noun* a big car that can drive over rough ground

fowl /faʊl/ *noun* (*plural* **fowl** *or* **fowls**) a bird, especially a chicken, that people keep on farms

fox /fɒks/ *noun* (*plural* **foxes**) a wild animal that looks like a dog and has a long thick tail and red fur

fox

fraction /ˈfrækʃn/ *noun* **1** an exact part of a number: ¼ (= a quarter) *and* ⅓ (= a third) *are fractions.* **2** a very small part of something: *For a fraction of a second I thought you were my sister.*

fracture /ˈfræktʃə(r)/ *verb* (**fractures, fracturing, fractured** /ˈfræktʃəd/) to break a bone in your body: *She fell and fractured her leg.* ▸ **fracture** *noun*: *a fracture of the arm*

fragile /ˈfrædʒaɪl/ *adjective* A thing that is **fragile** breaks easily: *Be careful with those glasses. They're very fragile.*

fragment /ˈfrægmənt/ *noun* a very small piece that has broken off something: *The window broke and fragments of glass went everywhere.*

frail /freɪl/ *adjective* (**frailer, frailest**) not strong or healthy: *a frail old woman*

frame¹ /freɪm/ *noun* **1** a thin piece of wood or metal round the edge of a picture, window, mirror, etc: *The photos were in gold frames.* **2** strong pieces of wood or metal that give something its shape: *They made a shelter of plastic sheets on a wooden frame.*
frame of mind how you feel: *I'm not in the right frame of mind for singing.*
SAME MEANING **mood**

frame² /freɪm/ *verb* (**frames, framing, framed** /freɪmd/) to put a picture in a frame: *She had her daughter's photograph framed.*

framework /ˈfreɪmwɜːk/ *noun* the strong part of something that gives it shape: *The bridge has a steel framework.*

franc /fræŋk/ *noun* money that people use in Rwanda, Burundi and Djibouti: *A hundred centimes make one franc.* ◇ *The hotel costs 2 000 Rwandan francs per day with breakfast.*

frank /fræŋk/ *adjective* (**franker, frankest**) If you are **frank**, you say exactly what you think: *To be frank, I don't really like that shirt you're wearing.* ▸ **frankly** *adverb*: *Tell me frankly what you think of my work.*

fraud /frɔːd/ *noun* **1** (no plural) doing things that are not honest to get money: *Two of the company directors were sent to prison for fraud.* **2** (*plural* **frauds**) a person or thing that is not what they seem to be: *He said he was a police officer but I knew he was a fraud.*

freckles /ˈfreklz/ *noun* (plural) small light brown spots on a person's skin: *A lot of people with red hair have freckles.*

free¹ /friː/ *adjective, adverb* (**freer, freest**) **1** If you are free, you can go where you want and do what you want: *After five years in prison she was finally free.* **2** If something is free, you do not have to pay for it: *We've got some free tickets for the concert.* ◇ *Children under five travel free on buses.* **3** not busy: *Are you free this afternoon?* ◇ *I don't have much free time.* **4** not being used: *Excuse me, is this seat free?* **5** not fixed: *Take the free end of the rope in your left hand.*
free from something; free of something without something bad: *It's nice to be on holiday, free from all your worries.*
set free let a person or an animal go out of a prison or the place where they are kept: *We set the bird free and it flew away.*

free² /friː/ *verb* (**frees, freeing, freed** /friːd/) to make someone or something free: *He was freed after ten years in prison.*

freedom /ˈfriːdəm/ *noun* (no plural) being free: *They gave their children too much freedom.*

free kick /ˌfriː ˈkɪk/ *noun* (in football or **rugby**) a situation in which a player of one team is allowed to kick the ball because a member of the other team has done something wrong: *to take a free kick*

freeze 🔑 /friːz/ *verb* (**freezes, freezing, froze** /frəʊz/, **has frozen** /ˈfrəʊzn/) **1** to become hard because it is so cold. When water freezes, it becomes ice. OPPOSITE **thaw** **2** to make food very cold so that it stays fresh for a long time: *frozen food* OPPOSITE **thaw** **3** to stop suddenly and stay very still: *The cat froze when it saw the bird.*
freeze to death to be so cold that you die

freezer /ˈfriːzə(r)/ *noun* a big metal box for making food very cold, like ice, so that you can keep it for a long time

freezing /ˈfriːzɪŋ/ *adjective* very cold: *It's freezing at night in the desert.*

freezing point /ˈfriːzɪŋ pɔɪnt/ *noun* (no plural) the temperature that water freezes at

freight /freɪt/ *noun* (no plural) things that lorries, ships, trains and planes carry from one place to another: *a freight train*
➲ Note at **train**[1].

frequent /ˈfriːkwənt/ *adjective* Something that is frequent happens often: *How frequent is the Eldoret bus?* ▸ **frequently** *adverb* often: *Kendi is frequently late for school.*

fresh 🔑 /freʃ/ *adjective* (**fresher, freshest**) **1** made or picked not long ago; not old: *I love the smell of fresh bread.* ◇ *These beans are fresh – I picked them this morning.* **2** new or different: *fresh ideas* **3** not frozen or from a tin: *fresh fruit* **4** clean and cool: *Open the window and let some fresh air in.* ▸ **freshly** *adverb*: *freshly baked bread*

freshwater /ˈfreʃwɔːtə(r)/ *adjective* living in or having water that is not fresh: *freshwater fish* ◇ *a freshwater lake*

friction /ˈfrɪkʃn/ *noun* (no plural) when one thing rubs against another: *Oil reduces friction between the moving parts of an engine.*

Friday 🔑 /ˈfraɪdeɪ/ *noun* the sixth day of the week, next after Thursday

fridge /frɪdʒ/ *noun* a big metal box for keeping food and drink cold and fresh

fried *form of* FRY

friend 🔑 /frend/ *noun* **1** a person that you like and know very well: *Bigogo is my best friend.* ◇ *We are very good friends.* **2** a person who you communicate with on an Internet website: *How many friends have you got on Facebook?*
make friends with someone to become a friend of someone: *Have you made friends with any of the students in your class?*

> ❖ **WORD FAMILY**
> **friend** **friendship**
> **friendly**: OPPOSITE **unfriendly**

friendly 🔑 /ˈfrendli/ *adjective* (**friendlier, friendliest**) A person who is friendly is kind and helpful: *My neighbours are very friendly.*
be friendly with someone If you are friendly with someone, they are your friend: *Nakato is friendly with a girl who lives on the same estate.* ▸ **friendliness** /ˈfrendlines/ *noun* (no plural): *The people here are known for their friendliness.*

friendship 🔑 /ˈfrendʃɪp/ *noun* being friends with someone

fries *form of* FRY

fright /fraɪt/ *noun* a sudden feeling of fear: *Why didn't you knock on the door before you came in? You gave me a fright!*

frighten 🔑 /ˈfraɪtn/ *verb* (**frightens, frightening, frightened** /ˈfraɪtnd/) to make someone feel afraid: *Sorry, did I frighten you?*

frightened 🔑 /ˈfraɪtnd/ *adjective* If you are frightened, you are afraid of something: *He's frightened of spiders.*

> ❖ **WORD FAMILY**
> **frightened** **frightening** **frighten**
> **fright**

frightening 🔑 /ˈfraɪtnɪŋ/ *adjective* Something that is frightening makes you feel afraid: *That was the most frightening film I have ever seen.*

fringe /frɪndʒ/ *noun* **1** threads that hang from the edge of a piece of material **2** the edge of a place: *We live on the fringes of town.* **3** the short hair that hangs down above your eyes

fro /frəʊ/ *adverb*
to and fro first one way and then the other way, many times: *She travels to and fro between Mwingi and Kakunike.*

frog /frɒg/ *noun* a small animal that lives in and near water. **Frogs** have long back legs and they can jump.

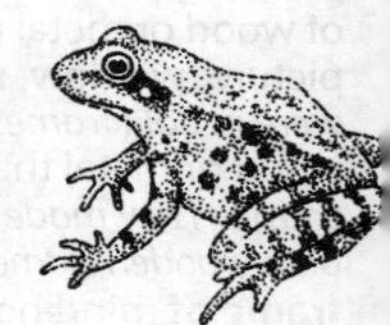
frog

from 🔑 /frəm; frɒm/ *preposition* **1** a word

that shows where something starts: *We travelled from Mumias to Butere.* ◇ *The tickets cost from 150 to 250 shillings.* **2** a word that shows where someone lives or was born: *I come from Uganda.* **3** a word that shows when someone or something starts: *The shop is open from 9.30 until 5.30.* **4** a word that shows who sent or gave something: *I had a letter from Kirezi.* ◇ *I borrowed a dress from my sister.* **5** a word that shows how far away something is: *The house is two kilometres from the village.* **6** a word that shows how something changes: *The sky changed from blue to grey.* **7** a word that shows what is used to make something: *Paper is made from wood.* **8** a word that shows difference: *My book is different from yours.* **9** a word that shows why: *Children are dying from this disease.* **10** a word that shows the place where you find something: *He took the money from my bag.*

front /frʌnt/ *noun* the side or part of something that faces forwards and that you usually see first: *The book has a picture of a lion on the front.* ◇ *Mum and Dad sat in the front of the car and we sat in the back.* ➲ Picture at **back**[1].

in front of someone or **something** **1** further forward than another person or thing: *Njoki was sitting in front of the television.* ➲ picture on page A6 **2** when other people are there: *Please don't talk about it in front of my parents.* ▸ **front** *adjective*: *the front door* ◇ *the front seat of a car*

frontier /ˈfrʌntiə(r)/ *noun* the line where one country joins another country

front-page /ˈfrʌnt peɪdʒ/ *adjective* interesting or important enough to appear on the front page of a newspaper: *The president's visit made front-page news.*

frost /frɒst/ *noun* in cold countries, ice like white powder that covers the ground when the weather is very cold: *There was a frost last night.* ▸ **frosty** *adjective* (**frostier**, **frostiest**): *a frosty morning*

frown /fraʊn/ *verb* (**frowns**, **frowning**, **frowned** /fraʊnd/) You frown when you are worried, angry or thinking hard, by making lines appear above your nose: *Katee frowned at me when I came in. 'You're late,' he said.* ▸ **frown** *noun*: *She looked at me with a frown.*

froze, **frozen** *forms of* FREEZE

frozen food /ˌfrəʊzn ˈfuːd/ *noun* (no plural) food that is very cold, like ice, when you buy it. You keep frozen food in a **freezer**.

fruit /fruːt/ *noun* (no plural) the part of a plant or tree that holds the seeds and that you can eat. Bananas, oranges and apples are kinds of fruit.

> ❖ **GRAMMAR**
>
> Be careful! We do not usually say 'a fruit'. We say 'a piece of fruit' or 'some fruit': *Would you like a piece of fruit?* ◇ *'Would you like some fruit?' 'Yes please – I'll have a banana.'*

frustrating /frʌˈstreɪtɪŋ/ *adjective* If something is **frustrating**, it makes you angry because you cannot do what you want to do: *It's very frustrating when you can't say what you mean in a foreign language.*

fry /fraɪ/ *verb* (**fries**, **frying**, **fried** /fraɪd/, **has fried**) to cook something or to be cooked in hot oil: *Fry the onions in butter.* ◇ *We ate fried eggs for lunch.*

frying pan /ˈfraɪɪŋ pæn/ *noun* a flat metal container with a long handle that you use for frying food

frying pan

handle

ft *short for* FOOT

fuel /ˈfjuːəl/ *noun* (no plural) anything that you burn to make heat or power. Wood, coal and oil are kinds of fuel: *He put fuel in the car.*

-ful /fəl/ *suffix* **1** full of: *graceful* ◇ *hopeful* ◇ *beautiful* **2** an amount that fills something: *a spoonful of sugar*

fulfil /fʊlˈfɪl/ *verb* (**fulfils**, **fulfilling**, **fulfilled** /fʊlˈfɪld/) to do what you have planned or promised to do: *Sarika fulfilled her dream of travelling around the world.*

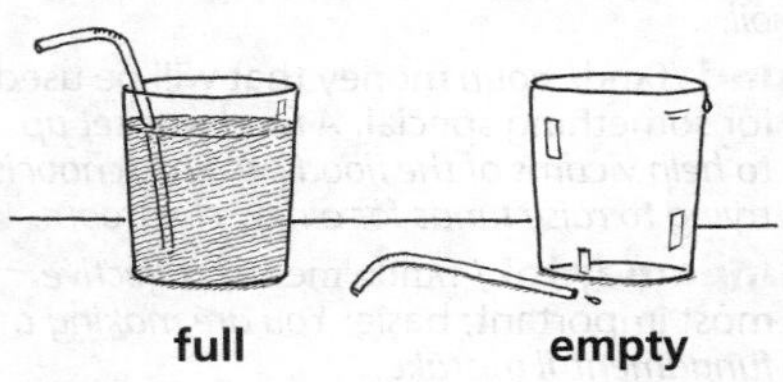

full /fʊl/ *adjective* (**fuller**, **fullest**) **1** with a lot of people or things in it, so that

there is no more space: *My glass is full.* ◇ *The bus was full so we waited for the next one.* ◇ *These socks are full of holes.* **2** complete; with nothing missing: *Please tell me the full story.* **3** as much, big, etc. as possible: *The matatu was travelling at full speed.*
full up with no space for anything or anyone else: *'Would you like anything else to eat?' 'No thank you, I'm full up.'*
in full completely; with nothing missing: *Please write your name in full.*

full moon /ˌfʊl ˈmuːn/ *noun* the time when you can see all of the moon

full stop /ˌfʊl ˈstɒp/ *noun* a mark (.) that you use in writing to show the end of a sentence, or after the short form of a word ➲ Look at page A17.

full-time /ˌfʊl ˈtaɪm/ *adjective, adverb* for all the normal working hours of the day or week: *My mother has a full-time job.* ◇ *Does he work full-time?* ➲ Look at **part-time**.

fully 🔑 /ˈfʊli/ *adverb* completely; totally: *'Do you have a room for tonight, please?' 'No, I'm sorry, we're fully booked.'*

fumes /fjuːmz/ *noun* (plural) smoke or gases that smell bad and can be dangerous

fun 🔑 /fʌn/ *noun* (no plural) something that you enjoy; pleasure: *Cooking is fun if you don't have to do it every day.* ◇ *We had great fun at the beach.* ◇ *Have fun!* (= enjoy yourself!)
for fun to enjoy yourself: *I don't enter races – I run just for fun.*
make fun of someone to laugh about someone in an unkind way: *The other children make fun of him because he wears glasses.*

function¹ /ˈfʌŋkʃn/ *noun* the special work that a person or thing does: *The function of the heart is to send blood round the body.*

function² /ˈfʌŋkʃn/ *verb* (**functions, functioning, functioned** /ˈfʌŋkʃnd/) to work: *The engine will not function without oil.*

fund /fʌnd/ *noun* money that will be used for something special: *A fund was set up to help victims of the floods.* ◇ *The school is trying to raise funds for a new classroom.*

fundamental /ˌfʌndəˈmentl/ *adjective* most important; basic: *You are making a fundamental mistake.*

fundraiser /ˈfʌndreɪzə(r)/ *noun* a person whose job is to find ways of collecting money for a charity or an organization
▸ **fundraising** /ˈfʌndreɪzɪŋ/ *noun* (no plural): *The theatre ran a successful fundraising event.*

funeral /ˈfjuːnərəl/ *noun* the ceremony when a dead person is buried or burned

fungus /ˈfʌŋgəs/ *noun* (*plural* **fungi** /ˈfʌŋgiː; ˈfʌŋgaɪ/) any plant without leaves, flowers or green colouring, that grows on other plants or on other surfaces: *Mushrooms are fungi.*

funnel /ˈfʌnl/ *noun* **1** a tube that is wide at the top to help you pour things into bottles **2** a large pipe on a ship or railway engine that smoke comes out of

funny 🔑 /ˈfʌni/ *adjective* (**funnier, funniest**) **1** A person or thing that is funny makes you laugh or smile: *a funny story* **2** strange or surprising: *There's a funny smell in this room.*

fur 🔑 /fɜː(r)/ *noun* the soft thick hair on some animals: *The cat carefully licked its fur.* ▸ **furry** /ˈfɜːri/ *adjective* (**furrier, furriest**): *a furry animal*

furious /ˈfjʊəriəs/ *adjective* very angry: *My parents were furious with me when I came home late again.*

furnace /ˈfɜːnɪs/ *noun* a very hot fire in a closed place, used for heating metals, making glass, etc.

furnished /ˈfɜːnɪʃt/ *adjective* with furniture already in it: *We live in a furnished flat.* OPPOSITE **unfurnished**

furniture 🔑 /ˈfɜːnɪtʃə(r)/ *noun* (no plural) tables, chairs, beds, etc: *They've bought some furniture for their new house.* ◇ *All the furniture is new.* ◇ *The only piece of furniture in the room was a large bed.*

> ❖ **GRAMMAR**
>
> Be careful! You cannot say 'a furniture' or 'furnitures'. You can say 'a piece of furniture' or 'some furniture'.

furrow /ˈfʌrəʊ/ *noun* a long cut that a **plough** (= a machine used on farms for digging and turning over the soil) makes in the soil

further 🔑 /ˈfɜːðə(r)/ *adjective, adverb* **1** more far: *Which is further from here – Cape Town or Cairo?* ◇ *We couldn't go any further because the road was closed.* **2** more; extra: *Do you have any further questions?*

further education /ˌfɜːðər edʒuˈkeɪʃn/ *noun* (no plural) studying that you do after you finish secondary school

furthest 🔑 *form of* FAR[1]

fuse /fjuːz/ *noun* a small piece of wire that stops too much electricity going through something: *Plugs usually have fuses in them.*

fuss[1] /fʌs/ *noun* (no plural) a lot of excitement or worry about small things that are not important: *He makes a fuss when I'm five minutes late.*
make a fuss of someone to be kind to someone; to do a lot of small things for someone: *I like visiting my grandfather because he always makes a fuss of me.*

fuss[2] /fʌs/ *verb* (**fusses, fussing, fussed** /fʌst/) to worry and get excited about a lot of small things that are not important: *Stop fussing!*

fussy /ˈfʌsi/ *adjective* (**fussier, fussiest**) A **fussy** person cares a lot about small things that are not important, and is difficult to please: *Pembe is fussy about his food – he won't eat vegetables.*

future[1] 🔑 /ˈfjuːtʃə(r)/ *noun* (no plural) the time that will come: *Nobody knows what will happen in the future.* ◇ *The company's future is uncertain.*
in future after now: *You must work harder in future.* ➲ Look at **past[1]**, **present[2]**.

future[2] 🔑 /ˈfjuːtʃə(r)/ *adjective* of the time that will come: *Have you met Shayo's future wife?*

the future tense /ðə ˌfjuːtʃə ˈtens/ *noun* (no plural) the form of a verb that you use to talk about what will happen after now ➲ Look at **past tense**, **present tense**.

Gg

G, g /dʒiː/ *noun* (*plural* **G's, g's** /dʒiːz/) **1** the seventh letter of the English alphabet: *'Girl' begins with a 'G'.* **2** *short for* GRAM

gabion /ˈɡeɪbiən/ *noun* a container made of wire that you fill with large stones. We put **gabions** on the side of a hill to prevent rain washing away the soil.

Gacaca courts /ɡʌˈtʃɑːtʃɑː kɔːts/ *noun* (plural) a system of courts in Rwanda that are held in villages where bad things happened

gadget /ˈɡædʒɪt/ *noun* a small machine or tool: *Their kitchen is full of electrical gadgets.*

gain 🔑 /ɡeɪn/ *verb* (**gains, gaining, gained** /ɡeɪnd/) **1** to get more of something: *She gained useful experience from helping on the farm.* ◇ *I have gained a lot of weight.* **2** to get what you want or need: *The police are trying to gain more information about the robbery.*

galaxy /ˈɡæləksi/ *noun* (*plural* **galaxies**) a very large group of stars and planets

gale /ɡeɪl/ *noun* a very strong wind: *The trees were blown down in the gale.*

gallery /ˈɡæləri/ *noun* (*plural* **galleries**) a building or room where people can go to look at paintings

gallon /ˈɡælən/ *noun* a measure of liquid (= 4.5 litres). There are eight **pints** in a gallon: *a gallon of petrol* ➲ Look at **pint**.

gallop /ˈɡæləp/ *verb* (**gallops, galloping, galloped** /ˈɡæləpt/) When a horse **gallops**, it runs very fast: *The horses galloped round the field.* ▶ **gallop** *noun*: *I took the horse for a gallop.*

gamble /ˈɡæmbl/ *verb* (**gambles, gambling, gambled** /ˈɡæmbld/) **1** to try to win money by playing games that need luck: *He gambled a lot of money on the last race.* **2** to do something, although there is a chance that you might lose: *I gambled on running the first part of the race very fast.* ▶ **gamble** *noun* something that you do without knowing if you will win or lose ▶ **gambling** /ˈɡæmblɪŋ/ *noun* (no plural) playing games that need luck, to try to win money

gambler /ˈɡæmblə(r)/ *noun* a person who tries to win money by playing games that need luck

game 🔑 /ɡeɪm/ *noun* **1** (*plural* **games**) something you play that has rules: *Shall we have a game of football?* ◇ *We played a game of cards, and I won.* **2** (no plural) wild animals or birds: *He's a game ranger in a national park.* **3 games** (plural) sports that you play at school or in a competition: *the Olympic Games*

game reserve /ˈɡeɪm rɪzɜːv/ (also **game park** /ˈɡeɪm pɑːk/) *noun* a large area of land where wild animals can live safely

gang[1] /ɡæŋ/ *noun* **1** a group of people who do bad things together: *a street gang* **2** a group of friends who often meet: *The whole gang is coming to my house.* **3** a group of workers: *a gang of builders*

gang[2] /gæŋ/ *verb* (**gangs, ganging, ganged** /gæŋd/)
gang up on or **against someone** to join together against another person: *The other boys ganged up on Deng because he was much smaller than them.*

gangster /ˈgæŋstə(r)/ *noun* one of a group of dangerous criminals: *Al Capone was a famous Chicago gangster.*

gangway /ˈgæŋweɪ/ *noun* **1** a bridge from the side of a ship to the land so that people can go on and off **2** the long space between two rows of seats in a cinema, theatre, etc. SAME MEANING **aisle**

gaol = **jail**

gap /gæp/ *noun* a space in something or between two things; a space where something should be: *The sheep got out through a gap in the fence.* ◇ *Write the correct word in the gap.*

gape /geɪp/ *verb* (**gapes, gaping, gaped** /geɪpt/) to look at someone or something with your mouth open because you are surprised: *She gaped at him when he said he was getting married.*

gaping /ˈgeɪpɪŋ/ *adjective* wide open: *There was a gaping hole in the ground.*

garage /ˈgærɑːʒ/ *noun* **1** a building where you keep your car **2** a place where cars are repaired **3** a place where you can buy petrol

garden 🔑 /ˈgɑːdn/ *noun* **1** a piece of land by your house where you can grow flowers, fruit and vegetables: *He spent all his free time working in the garden.* **2 gardens** (plural) a public park: *Jeevanjee Gardens*

garlic

garlic /ˈgɑːlɪk/ *noun* (no plural) a plant like a small onion with a strong taste and smell, that you use in cooking

garnish /ˈgɑːnɪʃ/ (**garnishes, garnishing, garnished** /ˈgɑːnɪʃt/) *verb* to decorate a dish of food with a small amount of another food: *Garnish the soup with a little parsley before serving.* ▸ **garnish** *noun* (*plural* **garnishes**): *a tomato garnish*

gas 🔑 /gæs/ *noun* **1** (*plural* **gases**) anything that is like air: *Hydrogen and oxygen are gases.* **2** (no plural) a gas with a strong smell, that you burn to make heat: *a gas fire*

gasoline /ˈgæsəliːn/ = **petrol**

gasp /gɑːsp/ *verb* (**gasps, gasping, gasped** /gɑːspt/) to breathe in quickly and noisily through your mouth: *She gasped in surprise when she heard the news.* ◇ *He was gasping for air when they pulled him out of the water.* ▸ **gasp** *noun*: *a gasp of surprise*

gate

gate 🔑 /geɪt/ *noun* **1** a kind of door in a fence or wall outside: *We closed the gate to stop the cows getting out of the field.* **2** a door in an airport that you go through to reach the plane: *Please go to gate 15.*

gateway /ˈgeɪtweɪ/ *noun* a way in or out of a place that has a gate to close it

gather /ˈgæðə(r)/ *verb* (**gathers, gathering, gathered** /ˈgæðəd/) **1** to come together in a group; to meet: *A crowd gathered to watch the fight.* **2** to take things that are in different places and bring them together: *I gathered up all the books and papers and put them in my bag.* **3** to understand something: *I gather that you know my sister.*

gathering /ˈgæðərɪŋ/ *noun* a time when people come together: *There was a large gathering outside the palace.*

gauge[1] /geɪdʒ/ *noun* an instrument that measures how much of something there is: *Where is the petrol gauge in this car?*

gauge[2] /geɪdʒ/ *verb* (**gauges, gauging, gauged** /geɪdʒd/) to measure something: *The tests are used to gauge the ability of the pupils.*

gave *form of* GIVE

gavel /ˈgævl/ *noun* a small hammer that a person in charge of a meeting uses in order to get people's attention: *The judge banged her gavel on the desk and the court fell silent.*

gay /geɪ/ *adjective* **1** attracted to people of the same sex SAME MEANING **homosexual** **2** happy and full of fun ℹ We do not often use 'gay' to mean 'happy'.

gaze /geɪz/ *verb* (**gazes, gazing, gazed** /geɪzd/) to look at someone or something for a long time: *She sat and gazed out of the window.* ◇ *He was gazing at her.*

gazelle /gəˈzel/ *noun* (*plural* **gazelle** *or* **gazelles**) a kind of small **antelope**

gazelle

Gb *short for* GIGABYTE

gear /gɪə(r)/ *noun* **1** (*plural* **gears**) a set of wheels that work together in a machine to pass power from one part to another. The **gears** of a car or bicycle help to control it when it goes up and down hills and help it to go faster or slower: *You need to change gear to go round the corner.* **2** (no plural) special clothes or things that you need for a job or sport: *camping gear*

geese *plural of* GOOSE

gem /dʒem/ *noun* a beautiful stone that is very valuable SAME MEANING **jewel**

general[1] 🔑 /ˈdʒenrəl/ *adjective* **1** of, by or for most people or things: *Is this car park for general use?* **2** not in detail: *The back cover gives you a general idea of what the book is about.*

in general usually: *I don't eat much meat in general.*

general[2] /ˈdʒenrəl/ *noun* a very important officer in the army

general election /ˌdʒenrəl ɪˈlekʃn/ *noun* a time when people choose a new government: *Did you vote in the last general election?*

general knowledge /ˌdʒenrəl ˈnɒlɪdʒ/ *noun* (no plural) what you know about a lot of different things

generally 🔑 /ˈdʒenrəli/ *adverb* usually; mostly: *I generally get up at about six o'clock.*

generate /ˈdʒenəreɪt/ *verb* (**generates, generating, generated**) to make heat, electricity, etc: *Power stations generate electricity.*

generation /ˌdʒenəˈreɪʃn/ *noun* **1** the children, or the parents, or the grandmothers and grandfathers, in a family: *This photo shows three generations of my family.* **2** all the people who were born at about the same time: *The older and the younger generations listen to different music.*

generator /ˈdʒenəreɪtə(r)/ *noun* a machine that produces electricity

generosity /ˌdʒenəˈrɒsəti/ *noun* (no plural) liking to give things to other people

generous 🔑 /ˈdʒenərəs/ *adjective* **1** always ready to give things or to spend money: *She is very generous – she often buys me presents.* OPPOSITE **mean** **2** large: *generous amounts of food* ▸ **generously** *adverb*: *He always gives generously to charities.*

genetics /dʒəˈnetɪks/ *noun* (no plural) the study of the way that qualities that have been passed from parents to children control the development of living things

genius /ˈdʒiːniəs/ *noun* (*plural* **geniuses**) a very clever person: *Einstein was a genius.*

genocide /ˈdʒenəsaɪd/ *noun* (no plural) the murder of very many of the people of a race or religion

gentle 🔑 /ˈdʒentl/ *adjective* (**gentler, gentlest**) quiet and kind; not rough: *Be gentle with the baby.* ◇ *a gentle voice* ◇ *It was a hot day, but there was a gentle breeze* (= a soft wind). ▸ **gently** /ˈdʒentli/ *adverb*: *Close the door gently or you'll wake the children up.*

gentleman /ˈdʒentlmən/ *noun* (*plural* **gentlemen** /ˈdʒentlmən/) **1** a polite way of saying 'man': *There is a gentleman here to see you.* **2** a man who is polite and kind to other people ➲ Look at **lady**.

genuine /ˈdʒenjuɪn/ *adjective* real and true: *Those aren't genuine diamonds – they're pieces of glass!* OPPOSITE **fake** ▸ **genuinely** *adverb* really: *Do you think he's genuinely sorry?*

geography /dʒiˈɒgrəfi/ *noun* (no plural) the study of the earth and its countries, mountains, rivers, weather, etc. ▸ **geographical** /ˌdʒiːəˈgræfɪkl/ *adjective*: *geographical names* (= names of countries, seas, cities, etc.)

geology /dʒiˈɒlədʒi/ *noun* (no plural) the study of rocks and soil and how they were made ▸ **geologist** /dʒiˈɒlədʒɪst/ *noun* a person who studies or knows a lot about **geology**

geometry /dʒiˈɒmətri/ *noun* (no plural) the study of things like lines, angles and shapes

germ /dʒɜːm/ *noun* a very small living thing that can make you ill: *flu germs*

germinate /ˈdʒɜːmɪneɪt/ *verb* (**germinates, germinating, germinated**) If a seed **germinates**, it starts growing.

▸ **germination** /ˌdʒɜːmɪˈneɪʃn/ *noun* (no plural): *Keep the seeds free to encourage germination.*

gesture /ˈdʒestʃə(r)/ *noun* a movement of your head or hand to show how you feel or what you want

get 🔑 /get/ *verb* (**gets, getting, got** /gɒt/, **has got**) **1** to buy or take something: *Will you get some bread when you go shopping?* **2** to receive something: *I got a lot of presents for my birthday.* **3** to become: *He is getting fat.* ◇ *Mum got angry.* ◇ *It's getting cold.* **4** to go and bring back someone or something: *Sarika will get the children from school.* **5** to arrive somewhere: *We got to Kasese at ten o'clock.* **6** to start to have an illness: *I think I'm getting a cold.* **7** to understand or hear something: *I don't get the joke.* **8** a word that you use with part of another verb to show that something happens to someone or something: *She got caught by the police.* **9** to travel on a train, bus, etc: *I didn't walk – I got the bus.* **10** to make someone do something: *I got Kisoso to help me.*

get away with something to do something bad and not be punished for it: *He lied but he got away with it.*

get back to return: *When did you get back from your holiday?*

get in to come to a place: *My bus got in at 7.15.*

get in; get into something to climb into a car: *Opiyo got into the car.*

get off; get off something to leave a bus, train, bicycle, etc: *Where did you get off the bus?*

get on 1 words that you use to say or ask how well someone does something: *Moraa is getting on well at school.* ◇ *How did you get on in the exam?* **2** to become late: *I must go home – it's getting on.* **3** to become old: *My grandfather is getting on – he's nearly 60.*

get on; get onto something to climb onto a bus, train or bicycle: *I got on the train.*

get on with someone to live or work in a friendly way with someone: *We get on well with our neighbours.*

get on with something to continue doing something: *Stop talking and get on with your work!*

get out; get out of something to leave a car, etc: *I opened the door and got out.*

get out of something to not do something that you do not like: *I'll come swimming with you if I can get out of some of my chores today.*

get something out to take something from the place where it was: *She opened her bag and got out a pen.*

get over something to become well or happy again after you have been ill or sad: *He still hasn't got over his wife's death.*

get through to be able to speak to someone on the telephone; to be connected: *I tried to ring the police station but I couldn't get through.*

get through something 1 to use or finish a certain amount of something: *I got through a lot of work today.* **2** to pass an examination, etc: *She's worked hard and deserves to get through the exam.*

get together to meet; to come together in a group: *The whole family got together for Christmas.*

get up to stand up; to get out of bed: *What time do you usually get up?*

get up to something 1 to do something, usually something bad: *I must go and see what the children are getting up to.* **2** to come as far as a place in a book, etc: *I've got up to page 180.*

have got to have something: *She has got brown eyes.* ◇ *Have you got any money?*

have got to If you **have got to** do something, you must do it: *I have got to leave soon.*

geyser /ˈɡiːzə(r)/ *noun* a **spring** (= a place where water comes out of the ground) that sometimes sends very hot water or steam up into the air

ghee /ɡiː/ *noun* (no plural) liquid butter that we use in cooking

ghost /ɡəʊst/ *noun* the form of a dead person that a living person thinks they see: *Do you believe in ghosts?* ▸ **ghostly** *adjective* of or like a ghost: *ghostly noises*

giant[1] /ˈdʒaɪənt/ *noun* a very big tall person in stories

giant[2] /ˈdʒaɪənt/ *adjective* very big: *a giant insect*

gift 🔑 /ɡɪft/ *noun* **1** something that you give to or get from someone; a present: *wedding gifts* **2** something that you can do well or learn easily: *She has a gift for languages.*

gigabyte /ˈɡɪɡəbaɪt/ *noun* a measure of computer memory or information. There are about a thousand million **bytes** in a **gigabyte**. ℹ The short way of writing 'gigabyte' is **Gb**

gigantic /dʒaɪˈgæntɪk/ *adjective* very big

giggle /ˈgɪgl/ *verb* (**giggles, giggling, giggled** /ˈgɪgld/) to laugh in a silly way: *The children couldn't stop giggling.*
▶ **giggle** *noun*: *There was a giggle from the back of the class.*

gill /gɪl/ *noun* the part on each side of a fish that it breathes through

ginger /ˈdʒɪndʒə(r)/ *noun* (no plural) the root of a plant used in cooking. It has a very hot strong taste.

giraffe /dʒəˈrɑːf/ *noun* a big animal with a very long neck and long legs

giraffe

girl ⚷ /gɜːl/ *noun* a female child; a young woman: *There are thirty girls in the class.*

girlfriend ⚷ /ˈgɜːlfrend/ *noun* a girl or woman who is someone's special friend: *Have you met my brother's girlfriend?*

Girl Guide /ˌgɜːl ˈgaɪd/ (also **Guide**) *noun* a member of a special club for girls

githeri *noun* (no plural) (East African English) a dish of **maize** and **beans** cooked slowly in liquid and served hot: *We ate githeri for lunch.*

give ⚷ /gɪv/ *verb* (**gives, giving, gave** /geɪv/, **has given** /ˈgɪvn/) **1** to let someone have something: *She gave me a watch for my birthday.* ◇ *I gave my ticket to the man at the door.* ◇ *I gave Rono 1000 shillings for his old bike.* **2** to make someone have or feel something: *That noise is giving me a headache.* **3** to make a sound, movement, etc: *Awino gave me an angry look.* ◇ *He gave a shout.* ◇ *She gave her mother a kiss.*
give away to give something to someone without getting money for it: *I've given all my old clothes away.*
give someone back something; give something back to someone to return something to someone: *Can you give me back the book I lent you last week?* ◇ *I picked it up and gave it back to him.*
give in to say that you will do something that you do not want to do, or agree that you will not win: *I had to give in and ask for the answer to the puzzle.*
give something in to give work, etc. to someone: *The teacher asked us to give in our homework.*
give out to give something to many people: *Could you give out these books to the class, please?*
give up to stop trying to do something, because you know that you cannot do it: *I give up – what's the answer?*
give something up to stop doing or having something: *I'm trying to give up sweets.*
give up on someone to stop thinking someone will arrive, improve, etc: *Her work is very bad, but her teacher won't give up on her.*

glacier /ˈglæsiə(r)/ *noun* a large river of ice that moves slowly down a mountain

glad /glæd/ *adjective* happy; pleased: *He was glad to see us.* ◇ *I'm glad you're feeling better.* ▶ **gladly** *adverb* If you do something **gladly**, you are happy to do it: *I'll gladly help you.* ➲ Look at **happy, pleased**.

glance[1] /glɑːns/ *verb* (**glances, glancing, glanced** /glɑːnst/) to look quickly at someone or something: *Fatma glanced at her watch.*

glance[2] /glɑːns/ *noun* a quick look: *a glance at the newspaper*
at a glance with one look: *I could see at a glance that he was ill.*

gland /glænd/ *noun* one of the parts inside your body that produce chemicals for your body to use

glare[1] /gleə(r)/ *verb* (**glares, glaring, glared** /gleəd/) **1** to look angrily at someone: *He glared at the children.* **2** to shine with a strong light that hurts your eyes: *The sun glared down.*

glare[2] /gleə(r)/ *noun* **1** (no plural) strong light that hurts your eyes: *the glare of the car's headlights* **2** (*plural* **glares**) a long angry look: *I tried to say something, but he gave me a glare.*

glass ⚷ /glɑːs/ *noun* **1** (no plural) hard stuff that you can see through. Bottles and windows are made of glass: *I cut myself on some broken glass.* ◇ *a glass jar* **2** (*plural* **glasses**) a thing made of glass that you drink from: *a glass of orange juice* ◇ *a wine glass*

glasses

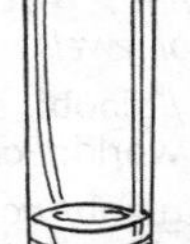

glasses ⚷ /ˈglɑːsɪz/ *noun* (plural) two pieces of special glass (called **lenses**) in a frame that people wear over their eyes to help them see better: *Does she wear glasses?* ➲ Look at **sunglasses**.

> ❖ **GRAMMAR**
> Be careful! You cannot say 'a glasses'. You can say 'a pair of glasses': *I need a new pair of glasses.* ◇ *I need (some) new glasses.*

gleam /gli:m/ *verb* (**gleams**, **gleaming**, **gleamed** /gli:md/) to shine with a soft light: *The lake gleamed in the moonlight.* ▸ **gleam** *noun*: *I could see a gleam of light through the trees.*

glide /glaɪd/ *verb* (**glides**, **gliding**, **glided**) to move smoothly and quietly: *The bird glided through the air.*

glider /ˈglaɪdə(r)/ *noun* a plane without an engine

gliding /ˈglaɪdɪŋ/ *noun* (no plural) flying in a plane without an engine as a sport: *I always wanted to go gliding.*

glimmer /ˈglɪmə(r)/ *verb* (**glimmers**, **glimmering**, **glimmered** /ˈglɪməd/) to shine with a small, weak light ▸ **glimmer** *noun*: *the glimmer of a candle*

glimpse[1] /glɪmps/ *verb* (**glimpses**, **glimpsing**, **glimpsed** /glɪmpst/) to see someone or something quickly, but not clearly: *I just glimpsed a plane between the clouds.*

glimpse[2] /glɪmps/ *noun*
catch a glimpse of someone or **something** to see someone or something quickly, but not clearly: *I caught a glimpse of myself in the mirror as I walked past.*

glisten /ˈglɪsn/ *verb* (**glistens**, **glistening**, **glistened** /ˈglɪsnd/) to shine because it is wet or smooth: *His eyes glistened with tears.*

glitter /ˈglɪtə(r)/ *verb* (**glitters**, **glittering**, **glittered** /ˈglɪtəd/) to shine brightly with a lot of small flashes of light: *The broken glass glittered in the sun.* ◇ *glittering diamonds* ▸ **glitter** *noun* (no plural): *the glitter of jewels*

global /ˈgləʊbl/ *adjective* of or about the whole world: *Pollution is a global problem.*

globe /gləʊb/ *noun* **1** a ball with a map of the world on it **2 the globe** (no plural) the earth: *He's travelled all over the globe.*

gloomy /ˈglu:mi/ *adjective* (**gloomier**, **gloomiest**) **1** dark and sad: *What a gloomy day!* **2** sad and without hope: *He's feeling very gloomy because they lost the match.* ▸ **gloomily** /ˈglu:mɪli/ *adverb*: *She stood looking gloomily out of the window at the rain.*

glorious /ˈglɔ:riəs/ *adjective* **1** wonderful or beautiful: *The weather was glorious.* **2** famous and full of glory: *a glorious history*

glory /ˈglɔ:ri/ *noun* (no plural) **1** fame and respect that you get when you do great things: *the glory of winning at the Olympics* **2** great beauty: *Dawn is the best time to see the forest in all its glory.*

glossy /ˈglɒsi/ *adjective* (**glossier**, **glossiest**) smooth and shiny: *glossy hair*

glove 🔑 /glʌv/ *noun* a thing that you wear to keep your hand warm or safe: *a pair of woollen gloves* ◇ *rubber gloves*

gloves

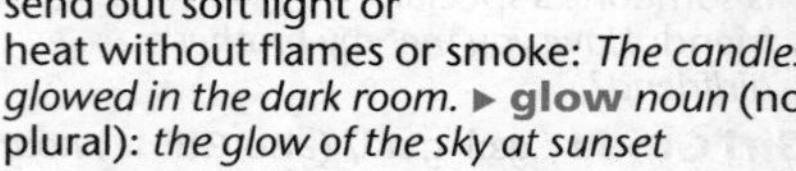

a pair of **gloves**

glow /gləʊ/ *verb* (**glows**, **glowing**, **glowed** /gləʊd/) to send out soft light or heat without flames or smoke: *The candles glowed in the dark room.* ▸ **glow** *noun* (no plural): *the glow of the sky at sunset*

glue[1] /glu:/ *noun* (no plural) a thick liquid that you use for sticking things together

glue[2] /glu:/ *verb* (**glues**, **gluing**, **glued** /glu:d/) to stick one thing to another thing with **glue**: *Glue the two pieces of wood together.*

gnaw /nɔ:/ *verb* (**gnaws**, **gnawing**, **gnawed** /nɔ:d/) to bite something for a long time: *The dog was gnawing a bone.*

go[1] 🔑 /gəʊ/ *verb* (**goes**, **going**, **went** /went/, **has gone** /gɒn/) **1** to move from one place to another: *I went to Arusha by bus.* ◇ *Her new car goes very fast.* ➲ Note at **been**. **2** to travel to a place to do something: *Boke has gone to school.* ◇ *Are you going to the meeting tomorrow?* ◇ *I'll go and make some coffee.* **3** to leave a place: *What time does the bus go?* ◇ *I must go now – it's four o'clock.* **4** to become: *Her hair has gone grey.* **5** to have as its place: *'Where do these plates go?' 'In that cupboard.'* **6** to lead to a place: *Does this road go to the lake?* **7** to work: *Nakato dropped the clock and now it doesn't go.* **8** to happen in a certain way: *How is your new class going?* ◇ *The week went very quickly.* **9** to disappear: *My headache has gone.* **10** to be or look good with something else: *Do these shoes go with my dress?* **11** to make a certain sound: *Cows go 'moo'.*

go after someone to chase or follow someone: *He's stolen my bag. Quick! Go after him!*
go ahead to begin or continue to do something: *'Can I borrow your pen?' 'Yes, go ahead.'*
go away to leave: *Go away! I'm doing my homework.* ◇ *They have gone away for a few days.*
go back to go again to a place where you were before; to return: *We're going back to school tomorrow.*
go by to pass: *The holidays went by very quickly.*
go down well to be something that people like: *The speech went down very well with the crowd.*
go in to enter a place: *Just knock and go in.*
go off 1 to explode: *A bomb went off in the station.* **2** When food or drink **goes off**, it becomes too old to eat or drink: *This meat has gone off – it smells horrible.*
go off someone or **something** to stop liking someone or something: *I've gone off cheese.*
go on 1 to happen: *What's going on?* **2** to continue; to not stop: *I went on reading.* **3** words that you use when you want someone to do something: *Oh, go on! Come to the playground with me!*
go out 1 to leave the place where you live or work: *I went out for a walk.* ◇ *We're going out tonight.* **2** to stop shining or burning: *The fire has gone out.*
go out with someone to have someone as a boyfriend or girlfriend: *She's going out with a boy from her college.*
go over something to look at or explain something carefully from the beginning to the end: *Go over your work before you give it to the teacher.*
go round 1 to be enough for everybody: *Is there enough cake to go round?* **2** to go to someone's home: *We're going round to Mwita's this evening.*
go through something 1 to look at or explain something carefully from the beginning to the end: *The teacher went through our homework.* **2** to suffer something: *She went through a difficult time when her husband was ill.*
go up to become higher or more: *The price of petrol has gone up again.*

go[2] /ɡəʊ/ *noun* (*plural* **goes**) the time when you can or should do something: *Get off the bike – it's my go!*
have a go to try to do something: *I'll have a go at mending your bike.*
in one go with one try: *There are too many books here to carry in one go.*

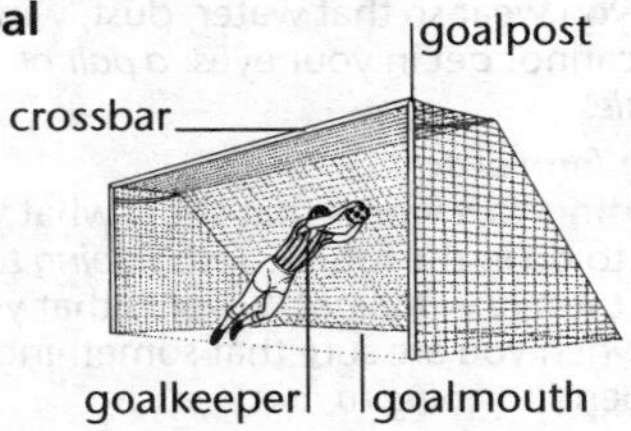

goal /ɡəʊl/ *noun* **1** the place where the ball must go to win a point in a game like football: *He kicked the ball into the goal.* **2** a point that a team wins in a game like football when the ball goes into the goal: *Tunisia won by three goals to two.* ◇ *Kisoso has scored another goal.*

goalkeeper /ˈɡəʊlkiːpə(r)/ *noun* a player in a game like football who must stop the ball from going into the goal ➲ Picture at **goal**.

goalmouth /ˈɡəʊlmaʊθ/ *noun* the area in front of the goal ➲ Picture at **goal**.

goalpost /ˈɡəʊlpəʊst/ *noun* one of the two posts that form the sides of a goal

goat /ɡəʊt/ *noun* an animal with horns. People keep **goats** for their milk.

goat

❖ **WORD BUILDING**

A young goat is called a **kid**.

god /ɡɒd/ *noun* **1** (*plural* **gods**) a being that people believe controls them and nature **2 God** (no plural) the one great being that Christians, Jews and Muslims believe made the world and controls everything

godchild /ˈɡɒdtʃaɪld/ *noun* (*plural* **godchildren** /ˈɡɒdtʃɪldrən/) (also **god-daughter** /ˈɡɒd dɔːtə(r)/; **godson** /ˈɡɒdsʌn/) a child who has an adult (called a **godparent**) who promises to help them and to teach them about the Christian religion

goddess /ˈɡɒdes/ *noun* (*plural* **goddesses**) a female god

godparent /ˈɡɒdpeərənt/ (also **godfather** /ˈɡɒdfɑːðə(r)/; **godmother** /ˈɡɒdmʌðə(r)/) *noun* a person that parents choose to help their child and teach them about the Christian religion

goes **1** *form of* GO[1] **2** *plural of* GO[2]

goggles /ˈgɒglz/ *noun* (plural) big glasses that you wear so that water, dust, wind, etc. cannot get in your eyes: *a pair of goggles*

going *form of* GO[1]
be going to **1** words that show what you plan to do in the future: *Teta's going to cook the dinner tonight.* **2** words that you use when you are sure that something will happen: *It's going to rain.*

go-kart /ˈgəʊ kɑːt/ *noun* a vehicle like a very small car with no roof or doors, used for racing

gold 🔑 /gəʊld/ *noun* (no plural) a yellow metal that is very valuable: *Is your ring made of gold?* ◇ *He wore a gold watch.*
▶ **gold** *adjective* with the colour of gold: *gold paint*

golden /ˈgəʊldən/ *adjective* **1** made of gold: *a golden crown* **2** with the colour of gold: *golden hair*

the golden rule /ðə ˌgəʊldən ˈruːl/ *noun* (no plural) the most important rule to remember

golf /gɒlf/ *noun* (no plural) a game that you play by hitting a small ball into holes with a long stick (called a **golf club**)

golf course /ˈgɒlf kɔːs/ *noun* a large piece of land, covered in grass, where people play **golf**

gomesi *noun* (*plural* **gomesi**) (East African English) a long dress that women in Uganda wear, with big sleeves and a wide piece of cloth round the middle (called a **sash**)

gone *form of* GO[1]

good[1] 🔑 /gʊd/ *adjective* (**better**, **best**)
1 that does what you want; done or made very well: *It's a good knife – it cuts very well.* ◇ *The film was really good.* **2** that you enjoy; nice: *Have a good evening!* ◇ *The weather was very good.* **3** able to do something well: *He's a good driver.* **4** kind, or doing the right thing: *It's good of you to help.* ◇ *The children were very good while you were out.* **5** right or suitable: *This is a good place to sit.* **6** big, long, complete, etc: *Take a good look at this photo.* **7** a word that you use when you are pleased: *Is everyone here? Good. Now let's begin.*
ℹ The adverb is **well**.
good at something able to do something well: *Opiyo is very good at boxing.*
good for you If something is **good for you**, it makes you well, happy, etc: *Fresh fruit and vegetables are good for you.*
Good for you! words that you say to someone when they have done something well

good[2] 🔑 /gʊd/ *noun* (no plural) something that is right or helpful: *They know the difference between good and bad.* ◇ *I'm telling you this for your own good.*
be no good; not be any good to not be useful: *These shoes aren't any good. They are too small.* ◇ *It's no good asking Mum for money – she hasn't got any.*
do someone good to make someone well or happy: *It will do you good to go to bed early tonight.*
for good for all time; for ever: *She is leaving for good.*

good afternoon /ˌgʊd ɑːftəˈnuːn/ *exclamation* words that you say when you see or speak to someone in the afternoon

> ❖ **SPEAKING**
> Often we just say **Afternoon**: *'Good afternoon, Mr Buke.' 'Afternoon, Chebet.'*

goodbye 🔑 /ˌgʊdˈbaɪ/ *exclamation* a word that you say when someone goes away, or when you go away: *Goodbye! See you tomorrow.*

good evening /ˌgʊd ˈiːvnɪŋ/ *exclamation* words that you say when you see or speak to someone in the evening

> ❖ **SPEAKING**
> Often we just say **Evening**: *'Good evening, Mr Muben.' 'Evening, Miss Njoro.'*

Good Friday /ˌgʊd ˈfraɪdeɪ/ *noun* the Friday before Easter when Christians remember the death of Christ

good-looking /ˌgʊd ˈlʊkɪŋ/ *adjective* nice to look at; attractive: *He's a good-looking boy.* ➲ Note at **beautiful**.

good morning /ˌgʊd ˈmɔːnɪŋ/ *exclamation* words that you say when you see or speak to someone in the morning

> ❖ **SPEAKING**
> Often we just say **Morning**: *'Good morning, Kendi.' 'Morning.'*

good-natured /ˌgʊd ˈneɪtʃəd/ *adjective* friendly and kind

goodness /ˈgʊdnəs/ *noun* (no plural) **1** something in food that is good for your health: *Fresh vegetables have a lot of* *goodness in them.* **2** being good or kind

for goodness' sake words that show anger: *For goodness' sake, hurry up!*

goodness; goodness me words that show surprise: *Goodness! What a big crowd!*

thank goodness words that show you are happy because a problem or danger has gone away: *Thank goodness it's stopped raining.*

goodnight /ˌgʊdˈnaɪt/ *exclamation* words that you say when you leave someone in the evening

goods 🔑 /gʊdz/ *noun* (plural) **1** things that you buy or sell: *That shop sells electrical goods.* **2** things that a train or lorry carries: *a goods train* ➲ Note at **train**[1].

good-tempered /ˌgʊd ˈtempəd/ *adjective* not often angry: *My dad is very good-tempered.*

google /ˈguːgl/ *verb* (**googles, googling, googled** /ˈguːgld/) to try to find something out by typing words into Google™, a computer program that searches the Internet for information: *When I got home I googled the band's name.*

goose /guːs/ *noun* (*plural* **geese** /giːs/) a big bird with a long neck. People keep **geese** on farms for their eggs and meat.

gorgeous /ˈgɔːdʒəs/ *adjective* very good; wonderful: *The weather was gorgeous!* ◇ *What a gorgeous dress!*

gorilla /gəˈrɪlə/ *noun* an animal like a very big black **monkey** with no tail

gorilla

gosh /gɒʃ/ *exclamation* a word that shows surprise: *Gosh! What a big house!*

gossip /ˈgɒsɪp/ *noun* (no plural) talk about other people that is often unkind: *Don't believe all the gossip you hear.* ▸ **gossip** *verb* (**gossips, gossiping, gossiped** /ˈgɒsɪpt/): *They were gossiping about Nafula's sister.*

got *form of* GET

gourd /gʊəd; gɔːd/ *noun* a large fruit that grows on the ground ❶ We use the hard, dried skin of a **gourd** as a container for water, food, etc. It can also be used as a **drum**. ➲ Look at **calabash**.

govern /ˈgʌvn/ *verb* (**governs, governing, governed** /ˈgʌvnd/) to control a country or part of a country: *Kenyatta governed Kenya until 1978.*

government 🔑 /ˈgʌvənmənt/ *noun* a group of people who control a country or a city: *The leaders of all the European governments will meet today in Brussels.* ◇ *The Government have discussed the plan.*

governor /ˈgʌvənə(r)/ *noun* **1** a person who controls part of a country **2** a person who controls a place like a prison or hospital

gown /gaʊn/ *noun* **1** a long dress that a woman wears at a special time: *She wore a white satin wedding gown.* **2** a long loose piece of clothing that people wear to do a special job. Judges and university teachers sometimes wear **gowns**.

grab /græb/ *verb* (**grabs, grabbing, grabbed** /græbd/) to take something in a rough and sudden way: *The thief grabbed her bag and ran away.*

grace /greɪs/ *noun* (no plural) **1** a beautiful way of moving: *She dances with grace.* **2** thanks to God that people say before or after they eat

graceful /ˈgreɪsfl/ *adjective* A person or thing that is **graceful** moves in a beautiful way: *a graceful dancer* ▸ **gracefully** /ˈgreɪsfəli/ *adverb*: *He moves very gracefully.*

grade[1] 🔑 /greɪd/ *noun* **1** how good something is; the level or quality of something: *Which grade of petrol does your car use?* **2** a number or letter that a teacher gives for your work to show how good it is: *She got very good grades in all her exams.*

grade[2] /greɪd/ *verb* (**grades, grading, graded**) to sort things or people into sizes, kinds, etc: *The eggs are graded by size.*

gradual /ˈgrædʒuəl/ *adjective* Something that is **gradual** happens slowly: *I am making gradual progress with my work.*

gradually /ˈgrædʒuəli/ *adverb* slowly, over a long period of time: *We all become gradually older.*

graduate[1] /ˈgrædʒuət/ *noun* a person who has finished studying at a university or college and who has passed their last exams: *a graduate of Makerere University*

graduate[2] /ˈgrædʒueɪt/ *verb* (**graduates, graduating, graduated**) to finish your

studies at a university or college and pass your last exams: *He graduated from Kenyatta University in 2015.*
▸ **graduation** /ˌgrædʒuˈeɪʃn/ *noun* (no plural): *My whole family came to my graduation.*

graffiti /grəˈfiːti/ *noun* (plural) funny, rude or angry words or pictures that people write or draw on walls: *The walls of the old building were covered with graffiti.*

graft /grɑːft/ *noun* **1** a piece of a living plant that is fixed onto another plant so that they will grow together **2** a piece of living skin, bone, etc. that is fixed onto a damaged part of someone's body in a medical operation: *a skin graft*

grain 🔑 /greɪn/ *noun* **1** (no plural) the seeds of a plant like **wheat** or rice that we eat: *The animals are fed on grain.* **2** (*plural* **grains**) a seed or a small hard piece of something: *grains of rice* ◇ *a grain of sand*

gram 🔑 (also **gramme**) /græm/ *noun* a measure of weight. There are 1 000 grams in a **kilogram**. ℹ The short way of writing 'gram' is **g**: *30 g of butter*

grammar 🔑 /ˈgræmə(r)/ *noun* (no plural) the rules that tell you how to put words together when you speak or write

❖ **SPELLING**
Remember! You spell **grammar** with **ar** at the end.

grammatical /grəˈmætɪkl/ *adjective* **1** of or about grammar: *What is the grammatical rule for making plurals in English?* **2** correct because it follows the rules of grammar: *The sentence 'They is happy' is not grammatical.* OPPOSITE **ungrammatical**
▸ **grammatically** /grəˈmætɪkli/ *adverb*: *The sentence is not grammatically correct.*

gramme = **gram**

gran /græn/ *noun* grandmother

grand /grænd/ *adjective* (**grander**, **grandest**) very big, important, rich, etc: *a grand house*

grandad /ˈgrændæd/ *noun* grandfather

grandchild /ˈgræntʃaɪld/ *noun* (*plural* **grandchildren** /ˈgræntʃɪldrən/) the child of someone's child

granddaughter 🔑 /ˈgrændɔːtə(r)/ *noun* the daughter of someone's child

grandfather 🔑 /ˈgrænfɑːðə(r)/ *noun* the father of your mother or father

grandma /ˈgrænmɑː/ *noun* grandmother

grandmother 🔑 /ˈgrænmʌðə(r)/ *noun* the mother of your mother or father

grandpa /ˈgrænpɑː/ *noun* grandfather

grandparent /ˈgrænpeərənt/ *noun* the mother or father of your mother or father: *We're going to stay with our grandparents.*

grandson 🔑 /ˈgrænsʌn/ *noun* the son of someone's child

grandstand /ˈgrændstænd/ *noun* lines of seats, with a roof over them, where you sit to watch a sport

granny (also **grannie**) /ˈgræni/ *noun* (*plural* **grannies**) grandmother

grant[1] /grɑːnt/ *noun* money that is given for a special reason: *The government gives grants to some young people so they can study at university.*

grant[2] /grɑːnt/ *verb* (**grants**, **granting**, **granted**) to give someone what they have asked for: *They granted him a visa to leave the country.*

grape /greɪp/ *noun* a small green or purple fruit that we eat or make into wine: *a bunch of grapes*

grapes

grapefruit /ˈgreɪpfruːt/ *noun* (*plural* **grapefruit** *or* **grapefruits**) a fruit that looks like a big orange, but is yellow

grapevine /ˈgreɪpvaɪn/ *noun*
on the grapevine the way that news is passed from one person to another: *I heard it on the grapevine that you won a prize.*

graph /grɑːf/ *noun* a picture that shows how numbers, amounts, etc. are different from each other

graph

grasp /grɑːsp/ *verb* (**grasps**, **grasping**, **grasped** /grɑːspt/) **1** to hold something tightly: *Awino grasped my arm to stop herself from falling.* **2** to understand something: *He could not grasp what I was saying.*
▸ **grasp** *noun* (no plural): *The ball fell from my grasp.*

grass 🔑 /grɑːs/ *noun* (no plural) a plant with thin green leaves that covers fields and gardens. Cows and sheep eat grass: *Don't walk on the grass.* ▸ **grassy** *adjective*

/ˈgrɑːsi/ (**grassier**, **grassiest**) covered with grass

grate /greɪt/ *verb* (**grates**, **grating**, **grated**) If you **grate** food, you rub it over a metal tool (called a **grater**) so that it is in very small pieces: *Can you grate some coconut?* ◇ *grated carrot*

grateful 🔑 /ˈgreɪtfl/ *adjective* If you are grateful, you feel or show thanks to someone: *We are grateful to you for the help you have given us.*
OPPOSITE **ungrateful**

gratitude /ˈgrætɪtjuːd/ *noun* (no plural) the feeling of being grateful: *We gave Shayo a present to show our gratitude for all his help.*

grave[1] /greɪv/ *adjective* (**graver**, **gravest**) very bad or serious ℹ **Serious** is the word that we usually use.

grave[2] /greɪv/ *noun* a hole in the ground where a dead person's body is put: *We put flowers on the grave.*

gravel /ˈgrævl/ *noun* (no plural) very small stones that are used for making roads

gravestone /ˈgreɪvstəʊn/ *noun* a piece of stone on a **grave** that shows the name of the dead person

graveyard /ˈgreɪvjɑːd/ *noun* a piece of land near a church where dead people are put in the ground

gravity /ˈgrævəti/ *noun* (no plural) the force that pulls everything towards the earth

gravy /ˈgreɪvi/ *noun* (no plural) a hot brown liquid that you eat with meat and vegetables

graze /greɪz/ *verb* (**grazes**, **grazing**, **grazed** /greɪzd/) **1** to eat grass: *The sheep were grazing in the fields.* **2** to hurt your skin by rubbing it against something rough: *He fell and grazed his arm.* ▸ **graze** *noun*: *She's got a graze on her knee.*

grease /griːs/ *noun* (no plural) fat from animals, or any thick stuff that is like oil: *You will need soap and hot water to get the grease off these plates.*

greasy /ˈgriːsi/ *adjective* (**greasier**, **greasiest**) with a lot of **grease** on or in it: *Greasy food is not good for you.* ◇ *greasy hair*

great 🔑 /greɪt/ *adjective* (**greater**, **greatest**) **1** very large or very much: *It's a great pleasure to meet you.* **2** important or special: *Samuel Wanjiru was a great runner.* **3** very; very good: *They are great friends.* ◇ *There's a great big dog in the garden!* **4** very good; wonderful: *I had a great weekend.* ◇ *It's great to see you!*
a great many very many: *He knows a great many people.*

great- /greɪt/ *prefix* a word that you put before other words to show some parts of a family. For example, your **great-grandmother** is the mother of your grandmother or grandfather, and your **great-grandson** is the son of your grandson or granddaughter.

greatly /ˈgreɪtli/ *adverb* very much: *I wasn't greatly surprised to see her.*

greed /griːd/ *noun* (no plural) the feeling that you want more of something than you need

greedy /ˈgriːdi/ *adjective* (**greedier**, **greediest**) A person who is **greedy** wants or takes more of something than they need: *She's so greedy – she's eaten the whole melon!*

green[1] 🔑 /griːn/ *adjective* (**greener**, **greenest**) with the colour of leaves and grass: *dark green*

green[2] /griːn/ *noun* **1** the colour of leaves and grass: *She was dressed in green.* **2** a place in the centre of a village that is covered with grass

greengrocer /ˈgriːngrəʊsə(r)/ *noun* a person who sells fruit and vegetables in a small shop (called a **greengrocer's** or a **greengrocery**)

greenhouse /ˈgriːnhaʊs/ *noun* (*plural* **greenhouses** /ˈgriːnhaʊzɪz/) a building made of glass, where plants grow

greet /griːt/ *verb* (**greets**, **greeting**, **greeted**) to say or do something when you meet someone: *He greeted me with a smile.*

greeting /ˈgriːtɪŋ/ *noun* **1** words that you say when you meet someone: *'Hello' and 'Good morning' are greetings.* **2** **greetings** (plural) words that you write to someone at a special time: *a greetings card* (= a card that you send at Christmas, on a birthday, etc.)

grew *form of* GROW

grey 🔑 /greɪ/ *adjective* (**greyer**, **greyest**) with a colour like black and white mixed together: *My grandmother has grey hair now.* ◇ *a grey-haired old man* ◇ *The sky was grey.* ▸ **grey** *noun*: He was dressed in grey.

grid /grɪd/ *noun* lines that cross each other to make squares, for example on a map

grief /griːf/ *noun* (no plural) great sadness

grieve /griːv/ *verb* (**grieves, grieving, grieved** /griːvd/) to feel great sadness: *She is grieving for her dead mother.*

grill¹ /grɪl/ *verb* (**grills, grilling, grilled** /grɪld/) to cook meat, fish, etc. on metal bars under or over heat: *grilled steak*

grill² /grɪl/ *noun* the part of a cooker, or a special metal thing, where you **grill** food

grin /grɪn/ *verb* (**grins, grinning, grinned** /grɪnd/) to have a big smile on your face: *She grinned at me.* ▶ **grin** *noun*: *He had a big grin on his face.*

grind /graɪnd/ *verb* (**grinds, grinding, ground** /graʊnd/, **has ground**) to make something into very small pieces or powder by crushing it: *They ground the wheat into flour.* ◇ *ground coffee*

grip /grɪp/ *verb* (**grips, gripping, gripped** /grɪpt/) to hold something tightly: *Nduku gripped my hand as we crossed the road.* ▶ **grip** *noun* (no plural): *He kept a tight grip on the rope.*

grit /grɪt/ *noun* (no plural) very small pieces of stone

groan /grəʊn/ *verb* (**groans, groaning, groaned** /grəʊnd/) to make a deep sad sound, for example because you are unhappy or in pain: *'I've got a headache,' he groaned.* ▶ **groan** *noun*: *'I've got toothache,' she said with a groan.*

grocer /ˈgrəʊsə(r)/ *noun* **1** a person who works in a shop that sells food and other things used in the home **2 grocer's** a shop that sells these things

groceries /ˈgrəʊsəriz/ *noun* (plural) food and other things for the home that you buy in packets, tins, bottles, etc.

groom /gruːm/ *noun* **1** a man on the day of his wedding SAME MEANING **bridegroom** **2** a person whose job is to look after horses

groove /gruːv/ *noun* a long thin cut in something hard

grope /grəʊp/ *verb* (**gropes, groping, groped** /grəʊpt/) to try to find something by using your hands, when you cannot see: *I groped in the dark for the door.*

ground¹ 🔑 /graʊnd/ *noun* **1** (no plural) the top part of the earth: *We sat on the ground and rested.* **2** (*plural* **grounds**) a piece of land that is used for something special: *a sports ground* ◇ *a playground* (= a place where children play) **3 grounds** (plural) the land around a large building: *the grounds of the hospital*

ground² *form of* GRIND

ground floor /ˌgraʊnd ˈflɔː(r)/ *noun* the part of a building that is at the same height as the street: *My office is on the ground floor.*

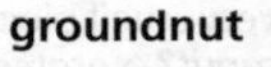

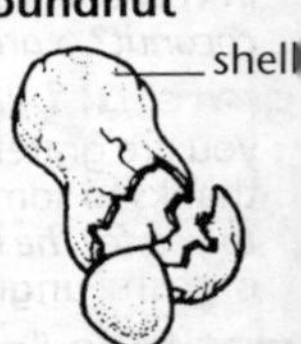

groundnut /ˈgraʊndnʌt/ (also **peanut**) *noun* a kind of nut that grows under the ground. You can eat **groundnuts** or use their oil.

group 🔑 /gruːp/ *noun* **1** a number of people or things together: *A group of people were standing outside the shop.* **2** people who play music together: *She sings in a group.* SAME MEANING **band**

grow 🔑 /grəʊ/ *verb* (**grows, growing, grew** /gruː/, **has grown** /grəʊn/) **1** to become bigger: *Children grow very quickly.* **2** When a plant grows somewhere, it lives there: *Oranges grow in warm countries.* **3** to plant something in the ground and look after it: *We grow potatoes and maize in our shamba.* **4** to let something grow: *Bigogo has grown a beard.* **5** to become: *It was growing dark.* ℹ In this sense, it is more usual to say **get** or **become**.

grow into something to get bigger and become something: *Kittens grow into cats.*

grow out of something to become too big to do or wear something: *She's grown out of her shoes.*

grow up to become an adult; to change from a child to a man or woman: *I want to be a doctor when I grow up.*

❖ WORD FAMILY

grow grower growth grown-up

grower /ˈgrəʊə(r)/ *noun* a person who plants something in the ground and looks after it: *tea growers*

growl /graʊl/ *verb* (**growls, growling, growled** /graʊld/) If an animal **growls**, it makes a low angry sound: *The dog growled at the stranger.* ▶ **growl** *noun*: *The dog gave a fierce growl.*

grown-up /ˈgrəʊn ʌp/ *noun* a man or woman, not a child; an adult: *Ask a grown-up to help you.* ▶ **grown-up** /ˌgrəʊn ˈʌp/ *adjective*: *She has a grown-up son.*

growth 🔑 /grəʊθ/ *noun* (no plural) getting bigger; growing: *the growth of a baby*

grubby /ˈgrʌbi/ *adjective* (**grubbier,**

grubbiest) dirty: *grubby hands*

grumble /ˈgrʌmbl/ *verb* (**grumbles, grumbling, grumbled** /ˈgrʌmbld/) to say many times that you do not like something: *My parents are always grumbling about prices.*

grumpy /ˈgrʌmpi/ *adjective* (**grumpier, grumpiest**) a little angry; bad-tempered: *She gets grumpy when she's tired.*

grunt /grʌnt/ *verb* (**grunts, grunting, grunted**) to make a short rough sound, like a pig makes ▶ **grunt** *noun*: *She didn't say anything – she just gave a grunt.*

guarantee¹ /ˌgærənˈtiː/ *noun* **1** a special promise on paper that a company will repair a thing you have bought, or give you a new one, if it goes wrong: *This watch has a two-year guarantee.* **2** a promise that something will happen: *I want a guarantee that you will do the work.*

guarantee² /ˌgærənˈtiː/ *verb* (**guarantees, guaranteeing, guaranteed** /ˌgærənˈtiːd/) **1** to say that you will repair a thing that someone buys, or give them a new one, if it goes wrong: *The television is guaranteed for three years.* **2** to promise something: *I can't guarantee that I will be able to help you, but I'll try.*

guard¹ /gɑːd/ *verb* (**guards, guarding, guarded**)

> ❖ **PRONUNCIATION**
>
> **Guard** sounds just like the beginning of **garden**. **Gu** at the beginning of a word in front of **a**, **e** or **i** sounds like **g**.

to keep someone or something safe from other people, or to stop someone from escaping: *The house was guarded by two large dogs.*

guard² /gɑːd/ *noun* a person who keeps someone or something safe from other people, or who stops someone from escaping: *There are guards outside the building.*

on guard guarding: *The soldiers were on guard outside the airport.*

guardian /ˈgɑːdiən/ *noun* a person who looks after a child, especially one whose parents have died

guava /ˈgwɑːvə/ *noun* (*plural* **guava** *or* **guavas**) a fruit that has yellow skin and is pink inside

guerrilla /gəˈrɪlə/ *noun* a person who is not in an army but who fights secretly against the government or an army

guess /ges/ *verb* (**guesses, guessing, guessed** /gest/) to give an answer when you do not know if it is right: *Can you guess how old he is?* ▶ **guess** *noun* (*plural* **guesses**): *If you don't know the answer, have a guess!*

guest /gest/ *noun* **1** a person that you invite to your home, to a party, etc: *There were 200 guests at the wedding.* ◇ *The governor was the **guest of honour** (= the most important person invited to the event) at the opening of the new sports centre.* **2** a person who is staying in a hotel: *Guests must leave their rooms by 10 a.m.*

guest house /ˈgest haʊs/ *noun* (*plural* **guest houses** /ˈgest haʊzɪz/) a small hotel

guidance /ˈgaɪdns/ *noun* (no plural) help and advice: *I want some guidance on how to revise for exams.*

guide¹ /gaɪd/ *noun* **1** a person who shows other people where to go and tells them about a place: *The guide took us round the town.* **2** (also **guidebook** /ˈgaɪdbʊk/) a book that tells you about a town, country, etc: *He writes travel guides.* **3** a book that tells you about something, or how to do something: *a guide to computing* **4** = **Girl Guide**

guide² /gaɪd/ *verb* (**guides, guiding, guided**) to show someone where to go or what to do: *He guided us through the busy streets to our hotel.*

guilt /gɪlt/ *noun* (no plural) **1** having done something wrong: *The police could not prove his guilt.* OPPOSITE **innocence** **2** the feeling that you have when you know that you have done something wrong: *She felt terrible guilt after stealing the money.*

guilty /ˈgɪlti/ *adjective* (**guiltier, guiltiest**) **1** If you are guilty, you have done something wrong: *He is guilty of stealing a watch.* OPPOSITE **innocent** **2** If you feel guilty, you feel that you have done something wrong: *I feel guilty about lying to her.*

guinea fowl /ˈgɪni faʊl/ *noun* (*plural* **guinea fowl**) a large bird that you can eat, with grey feathers and white spots

guinea fowl

guinea pig /ˈgɪni pɪg/ *noun* **1** a small animal that people keep as a pet **2** a person who is used in an experiment

guinea worm /ˈɡɪni wɜːm/ *noun* a long **worm** that lives under a person's skin

guitar /ɡɪˈtɑː(r)/ *noun* a musical instrument with strings: *I play the guitar in a band.* ▶ **guitarist** /ɡɪˈtɑːrɪst/ *noun* a person who plays the **guitar**

gulf /ɡʌlf/ *noun* a large area of sea that has land almost all the way around it: *the Gulf of Mexico*

gull /ɡʌl/ = **seagull**

gulp /ɡʌlp/ *verb* (**gulps**, **gulping**, **gulped** /ɡʌlpt/) to eat or drink something quickly: *He gulped down a cup of tea and left.* ▶ **gulp** *noun*: *She took a gulp of coffee.*

gum /ɡʌm/ *noun* **1** (*plural* **gums**) Your **gums** are the hard pink parts of your mouth that hold your teeth. **2** (no plural) thick liquid that you use for sticking pieces of paper together ➲ Look at **chewing gum**.

gumboot /ˈɡʌmbuːt/ *noun* one of a pair of long rubber boots that you wear to keep your feet and legs dry: *It's very muddy – you'll need your gumboots.*

gum tree /ˈɡʌm tri/ *noun* a tall tree that does not lose its leaves. It is also called a **eucalyptus** tree: *The children sat in the shade of a gum tree.*

gun ⚷ /ɡʌn/ *noun* a thing that shoots out pieces of metal (called **bullets**) to kill or hurt people or animals: *He pointed the gun at the bird and fired.*

gunman /ˈɡʌnmən/ *noun* (*plural* **gunmen** /ˈɡʌnmən/) a man who shoots another person with a gun

gunpowder /ˈɡʌnpaʊdə(r)/ *noun* (no plural) powder that explodes. It is used in guns and **fireworks**.

gunshot /ˈɡʌnʃɒt/ *noun* the sound a gun makes: *He called the police when he heard the gunshots.*

gush /ɡʌʃ/ *verb* (**gushes**, **gushing**, **gushed** /ɡʌʃt/) to flow out suddenly and strongly: *Blood was gushing from the cut in her leg.*

gust /ɡʌst/ *noun* a sudden strong wind: *A gust of wind blew his hat off.*

gutter /ˈɡʌtə(r)/ *noun* **1** a pipe under the edge of a roof to carry away water when it rains **2** the part at the edge of a road where water is carried away

guy /ɡaɪ/ *noun* a man: *He's a nice guy!*

gymnasium /dʒɪmˈneɪziəm/ *noun* a room where you do exercises for your body ℹ The short form is **gym**.

gymnastics /dʒɪmˈnæstɪks/ *noun* (plural) exercises for your body ℹ The short form is **gym**.

H, h /eɪtʃ/ *noun* (*plural* **H's**, **h's** /ˈeɪtʃɪz/) the eighth letter of the English alphabet: *'Hat' begins with an 'H'.*

habit ⚷ /ˈhæbɪt/ *noun* something that you do very often: *Being late every day is a bad habit.* ◇ *She's got a habit of touching her hair when she talks.*

habitat /ˈhæbɪtæt/ *noun* the natural place where a plant or an animal lives

had *form of* HAVE[1]

hadn't /ˈhædnt/ = **had not**

ha! ha! /ˌhɑː ˈhɑː/ *exclamation* words that you write to show that someone is laughing

hail /heɪl/ *noun* (no plural) small balls of ice (called **hailstones**) that fall like rain: *Hail was falling in the hills.*

hailstorm /ˈheɪlstɔːm/ *noun* a storm in which **hail** falls from the sky

hair ⚷ /heə(r)/ *noun* **1** (*plural* **hairs**) one of the long thin things that grow on the skin of people and animals: *There's a hair in my food.* **2** (no plural) all the hairs on a person's head :*She's got long hair.* ➲ Look at **hairy**. ➲ picture on page A13

❖ **WORD BUILDING**

You wash your hair with **shampoo** and make it tidy with a **comb** or a **hairbrush**. Some words that you can use to talk about the colour of a person's hair are **black, dark, brown, red, fair, blond** and **grey**.

hairbrush /ˈheəbrʌʃ/ *noun* (*plural* **hairbrushes**) a brush that you use to make your hair tidy

haircut /ˈheəkʌt/ *noun* **1** when someone cuts your hair: *I need a haircut.* **2** the way that your hair is cut: *I like your new haircut.*

hairdresser /ˈheədresə(r)/ *noun* a person whose job is to wash, cut and arrange hair

❖ **WORD BUILDING**

The place where a hairdresser works is called a **hairdresser's**: *I'm going to the hairdresser's to get my hair plaited.*

hairdryer (also **hairdrier**) /ˈheədraɪə(r)/ *noun* a machine that dries your hair by blowing hot air on it

hairless /ˈheələs/ *adjective* without hair OPPOSITE **hairy**

hairstyle /ˈheəstaɪl/ *noun* the way that your hair is cut and arranged

hairy /ˈheəri/ *adjective* (**hairier, hairiest**) covered with hair: *He has got hairy legs.* OPPOSITE **hairless**

half[1] 🔑 /hɑːf/ *noun, adjective, pronoun* (*plural* **halves** /hɑːvz/)

❖ **PRONUNCIATION**

Half sounds like **staff** because we do not say the 'l'.

one of two equal parts of something; ½: *Half of six is three.* ◇ *I lived in Britain for two and a half years.* ◇ *The journey takes an hour and a half.* ◇ *She gave me half of her food.* ◇ *No goals were scored in the first half* (= of a football match).
in half so that there are two equal parts: *Cut the melon in half.* ℹ The verb is **halve**.

half[2] 🔑 /hɑːf/ *adverb* 50%; partly: *The bottle is half empty.*
half past 30 minutes after an hour on the clock: *It's half past nine.* ➲ Look at page A10.

half-price /ˌhɑːf ˈpraɪs/ *adjective, adverb* for half the usual price: *I got a half-price ticket!* ◇ *Children travel half-price on this bus.*

half-time /ˌhɑːf ˈtaɪm/ *noun* (no plural) a short time in the middle of a game like football, when you are not playing

halfway /ˌhɑːfˈweɪ/ *adverb* in the middle: *They live halfway between Migori and Sirare.* ◇ *She went out halfway through the lesson.*

hall 🔑 /hɔːl/ *noun* **1** a big room or building where a lot of people meet: *a concert hall* ◇ *We did our exams in the school hall.* **2** the room in a house that is near the front door and has doors to other rooms: *You can leave your coat in the hall.*

hallo = **hello**

hallucination /həˌluːsɪˈneɪʃn/ *noun* when you see or hear something that is not really there

halt /hɔːlt/ *noun* (no plural)
come to a halt to stop: *The car came to a halt.*

halve /hɑːv/ *verb* (**halves, halving, halved** /hɑːvd/) to divide something into two parts that are the same: *There were two of us, so I halved the orange.* ℹ The noun is **half**.

halves *plural of* HALF[1]

ham /hæm/ *noun* (no plural) meat from a pig's leg that you can keep for a long time because salt or smoke was used to prepare it ➲ Note at **pig**.

hamburger /ˈhæmbɜːgə(r)/ *noun* meat cut into very small pieces and made into a flat round shape, that you eat between two pieces of bread: *A hamburger and chips, please.*

hammer

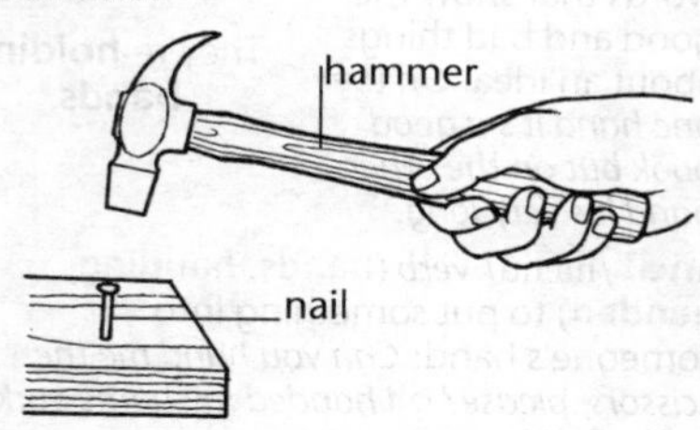

hammer[1] 🔑 /ˈhæmə(r)/ *noun* a tool with a handle and a heavy metal part, that you use for hitting **nails** (= small thin pieces of metal) into things

hammer[2] /ˈhæmə(r)/ *verb* (**hammers, hammering, hammered** /ˈhæməd/) **1** to hit something with a hammer: *I hammered the nail into the wood.* **2** to hit something hard: *He hammered on the door until someone opened it.*

hammock /ˈhæmək/ *noun* a bed made of cloth or rope that you hang up at the two ends

hammock

hand¹ 🔑 /hænd/ *noun* **1** the part at the end of your arm: *She held the letter in her hand.* ➲ picture on page A13 **2** one of the parts of a clock or watch that move to show the time ➲ Picture at **alarm clock**.
a hand some help: *Could you give me a hand with my homework?*
by hand without using a machine: *These shoes are made by hand.*
get out of hand to become difficult to control: *The party got out of hand.*
hand in hand with your hand in another person's hand
hands up 1 put one hand in the air if you can answer the question **2** put your hands in the air because someone has a gun
hold hands to have another person's hand in your hand
in good hands well looked after: *Don't worry – your son is in good hands.*
on hand near and ready to help: *There is a doctor on hand 24 hours a day.*
on the one hand ... on the other hand words that show the good and bad things about an idea: *On the one hand it's a good book but on the other hand it's very long.*

hold hands

They're **holding hands**.

hand² /hænd/ *verb* (**hands, handing, handed**) to put something into someone's hand: *Can you hand me the scissors, please?* ◇ *I handed my homework to the teacher.*
hand down to pass a thing, story, etc. from an older person to a younger one: *He never had new clothes – they were always handed down from his older brothers.*
hand in to give something to someone: *The teacher asked us to hand in our homework.*
hand out to give something to many people: *Please hand out these books.*
hand over to give something to someone: *'Hand over that knife!' said the police officer.*

handbag /ˈhændbæg/ *noun* a small bag for carrying things like money and keys

handball /ˈhændbɔːl/ *noun* (no plural) a game where two teams of seven players try to throw a ball into a goal

handcuffs /ˈhændkʌfs/ *noun* (plural) two metal rings with a chain that are put on a prisoner's arms so that they cannot use their hands

handful /ˈhændfʊl/ *noun* **1** as much as you can hold in one hand: *a handful of stones* **2** a small number: *Only a handful of people came to the meeting.*

handheld /ˌhændˈheld/ *adjective* small enough for you to hold in your hand: *a handheld computer*

handicap /ˈhændikæp/ *noun* something that stops you doing well: *a school for children with physical handicaps*
▸ **handicapped** /ˈhændikæpt/ *adjective* not able to use a part of your body well: *They have a handicapped son.*

handkerchief /ˈhæŋkətʃɪf/ (also **hanky, hankie**) *noun* a square piece of cloth or paper that you use for cleaning your nose

handles

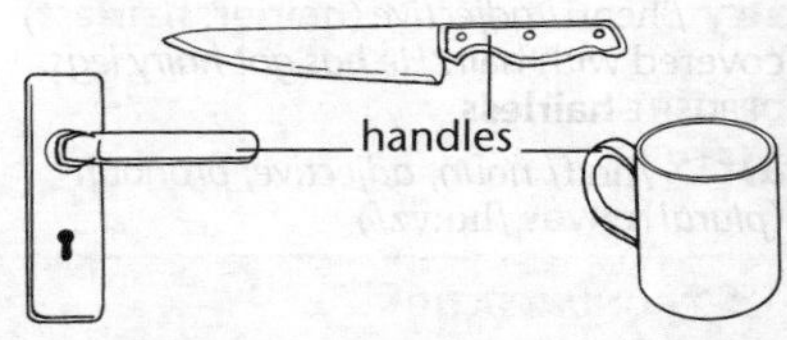

handle¹ 🔑 /ˈhændl/ *noun* the part of a thing that you hold in your hand: *I turned the handle and opened the door.* ◇ *Hold that knife by the handle.*

handle² 🔑 /ˈhændl/ *verb* (**handles, handling, handled** /ˈhændld/) **1** to touch something with your hands: *Please wash your hands before you handle the food.* **2** to control someone or something: *That dog is too big for a small child to handle.* **3** to look after something and do what is necessary: *Her secretary handles all letters.*

handlebars /ˈhændlbɑːz/ *noun* (plural) the part at the front of a bicycle or motorbike that you hold when you are riding it ➲ Picture at **bicycle**.

handmade /ˌhændˈmeɪd/ *adjective* made by a person, not by a machine: *handmade clothes*

handset /ˈhændset/ *noun* the part of a telephone that you use for speaking and listening: *mobile handsets*

handsome /ˈhænsəm/ *adjective* attractive: *a handsome man* SAME MEANING **good-looking** ➲ Note at **beautiful**.

handwriting /ˈhændraɪtɪŋ/ *noun* (no plural) the way you write: *Her handwriting is difficult to read.*

handy /ˈhændi/ *adjective* (**handier**, **handiest**) **1** useful: *This bag will be handy for carrying my books.* **2** near and easy to find or reach: *Have you got a pen handy?*
come in handy be useful: *Don't throw that box away – it might come in handy.*

hang 🔑 /hæŋ/ *verb* **1** (**hangs**, **hanging**, **hung** /hʌŋ/, **has hung**) to fix something, or to be fixed at the top, so that the lower part is free: *Hang your coat (up) on the hook.* ◇ *I hung the washing on the line to dry.* **2** (**hangs**, **hanging**, **hanged** /hæŋd/, **has hanged**) to kill someone by holding them above the ground by a rope around the neck: *He was hanged for murder.*
hang about; **hang around** to stay somewhere with nothing special to do: *My plane was late so I had to hang about in the airport all morning.*
hang on to wait: *Hang on – I'm not ready.*
hang on to something to hold something firmly: *Hang on to your purse.*
hang out to spend a lot of time in a place: *The local kids hang out in the park.*
hang up to end a phone call by putting the phone down or switching it off

hanger = **coat hanger**

hanky (also **hankie**) /ˈhæŋki/ *noun* (*plural* **hankies**) = **handkerchief**

happen 🔑 /ˈhæpən/ *verb* (**happens**, **happening**, **happened** /ˈhæpənd/) to take place: *How did the accident happen?* ◇ *Did you hear what happened to me yesterday?*
happen to to do something by chance: *I happened to meet Kendi yesterday.*

happily /ˈhæpɪli/ *adverb* **1** in a happy way **2** it is lucky that: *Happily, the accident was not serious.* OPPOSITE **unhappily**

happiness 🔑 /ˈhæpinəs/ *noun* (no plural) being happy OPPOSITE **unhappiness**

happy 🔑 /ˈhæpi/ *adjective* (**happier**, **happiest**) **1** If you are happy, you feel very pleased. People often laugh or smile when they are happy: *She looks very happy.* ◇ *That was one of the happiest days of my life.* OPPOSITE **unhappy**, **sad** **2** a word that you use to say that you hope someone will enjoy a special time: *Happy New Year!* ◇ *Happy Christmas!* ◇ *Happy Birthday!*
ℹ **Many happy returns (of the day)** means the same as **Happy Birthday.**

> ❖ **WORD FAMILY**
> **happy** **happiness** **happily**

harambee *noun* (no plural) a Kiswahili word that means 'pull together'. A **harambee** is a meeting held to raise money for something: *The school committee held a harambee to raise funds for two new classrooms.*

harbour /ˈhɑːbə(r)/ *noun* a place where ships can stay safely in the water

hard[1] 🔑 /hɑːd/ *adjective* (**harder**, **hardest**) **1** not soft; firm: *These apples are very hard.* ◇ *I couldn't sleep because the bed was too hard.* OPPOSITE **soft** **2** difficult to do or understand: *Training to be a dancer is hard work.* ◇ *The exam was very hard.* OPPOSITE **easy** **3** full of problems: *He's had a hard life.* OPPOSITE **easy** **4** not kind or gentle: *She is very hard on her children.* OPPOSITE **soft**

hard[2] 🔑 /hɑːd/ *adverb* (**harder**, **hardest**) **1** a lot: *She works very hard.* ◇ *You must try harder!* **2** strongly: *It's raining hard.* ◇ *She hit him hard.*

hardback /ˈhɑːdbæk/ *noun* a book with a hard cover ➲ Look at **paperback**.

hard disk /ˌhɑːd ˈdɪsk/ *noun* a plastic part inside a computer that stores information

harden /ˈhɑːdn/ *verb* (**hardens**, **hardening**, **hardened** /ˈhɑːdnd/) to become hard: *Wait for the cement to harden.*

hardly 🔑 /ˈhɑːdli/ *adverb* almost not; only just: *She spoke so quietly that I could hardly hear her.* ◇ *There's hardly any* (= almost no) *coffee left.*

hardware /ˈhɑːdweə(r)/ *noun* (no plural) **1** the parts of a computer system **2** tools and equipment that you use in the house and garden: *Dad bought a box of nails at the hardware shop.*

hardwood /ˈhɑːdwʊd/ *noun* hard heavy wood from a **deciduous** tree (= one that loses its leaves once a year): *Environmentalists called for an end to the trade in tropical hardwoods.*

hard-working /ˌhɑːd ˈwɜːkɪŋ/ *adjective* working a lot: *All the students here are very hard-working.* ◇ *hard-working nurses*

hare /heə(r)/ *noun* an animal like a big **rabbit** that can run very fast

harm¹ 🔑 /hɑːm/ *noun* (no plural) hurt or damage: *He may look fierce but he means no harm.*
come to harm to be hurt or damaged: *Make sure the children don't come to any harm.*
there is no harm in nothing bad will happen if you do something: *I don't know if she'll help you, but there's no harm in asking.*

harm² 🔑 /hɑːm/ *verb* (**harms**, **harming**, **harmed** /hɑːmd/) to hurt or damage someone or something: *The dog won't harm you.*

harmful 🔑 /ˈhɑːmfl/ *adjective* Something that is harmful can hurt or damage people or things: *Strong sunlight can be harmful to young babies.*

harmless /ˈhɑːmləs/ *adjective* not dangerous: *Don't be frightened – these insects are harmless.*

harmony /ˈhɑːməni/ *noun* **1** (no plural) having the same ideas, etc, with no arguments: *The different races live together in harmony.* **2** (*plural* **harmonies**) musical notes that sound nice together: *They sang in harmony.*

harsh /hɑːʃ/ *adjective* (**harsher**, **harshest**) **1** rough and unpleasant to see or hear: *a harsh voice* **2** not kind; cruel: *a harsh punishment* ▶ **harshly** *adverb*: *Crime is punished harshly.*

harvest /ˈhɑːvɪst/ *noun* **1** the time when fruit, grain or vegetables are ready to cut or pick: *Extra workers are needed at harvest time.* **2** all the fruit, grain or vegetables that are cut or picked: *We had a good harvest this year.* ▶ **harvest** *verb* (**harvests**, **harvesting**, **harvested**): *When does the farmer harvest his wheat?*

has *form of* HAVE¹

hash /hæʃ/ *noun* (*plural* **hashes**) the symbol #, especially one on a phone

hasn't /ˈhæznt/ = **has not**

haste /heɪst/ *noun* (no plural) doing things too quickly: *In his haste to get up, he knocked over the chair.*
in haste quickly; in a hurry: *The letter was written in haste.*

hasty /ˈheɪsti/ *adjective* (**hastier**, **hastiest**) **1** If you are **hasty**, you do something too quickly: *Don't be too hasty. This is a very important decision.* **2** said or done quickly: *We ate a hasty lunch, then left.* ▶ **hastily** /ˈheɪstɪli/ *adverb*: *He put the money hastily into his pocket.*

hats

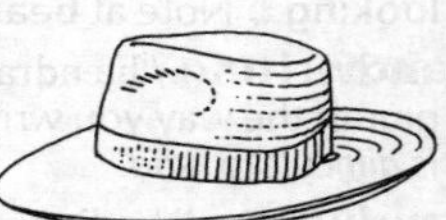

hat 🔑 /hæt/ *noun* a thing that you wear on your head: *She's wearing a hat.*

hatch /hætʃ/ *verb* (**hatches**, **hatching**, **hatched** /hætʃt/) When baby birds, insects, fish, etc. **hatch**, they come out of an egg.

hate¹ 🔑 /heɪt/ *verb* (**hates**, **hating**, **hated**) to have a very strong feeling of not liking someone or something: *Most cats hate water.* ◇ *I hate waiting for buses.*
OPPOSITE **love**

hate² 🔑 /heɪt/ (also **hatred** /ˈheɪtrɪd/) *noun* (no plural) a very strong feeling of not liking someone or something
OPPOSITE **love**

haul /hɔːl/ *verb* (**hauls**, **hauling**, **hauled** /hɔːld/) to pull something heavy: *They hauled the boat out of the river.*

haunt /hɔːnt/ *verb* (**haunts**, **haunting**, **haunted**) **1** If a **ghost** (= a spirit of a dead person) **haunts** a place, it visits it often: *A ghost haunts the village.* **2** If something sad or unpleasant **haunts** you, you often think of it: *Her unhappy face still haunts me.* ▶ **haunted** /ˈhɔːntɪd/ *adjective* often visited by **ghosts**: *a haunted house*

have¹ 🔑 /həv; hæv/ *verb* a word that you use with parts of other verbs to show that something happened or started in the past: *I have seen that man before.* ◇ *We have been here for two hours.* ◇ *When we arrived, Chebet had already left.* ➲ Look at the verb table below.

have² 🔑 /hæv/ *verb* (**has** /hæz/, **having**, **had** /hæd/, **has had**) **1** (also **have got**) to own or keep something: *She has lovely eyes.* ◇ *They have got a big farm.* ◇ *Do you have any brothers and sisters?* **2** to be ill with something; to feel something: *She has got a headache.* **3** to eat or drink something: *What time do you have breakfast?* **4** a word that shows that something happens to someone or something: *I had a shower.* ◇ *He has had an accident.* ◇ *Did you have a good*

have

present tense		*short forms*	*negative short forms*	
I	**have**	I**'ve**	I	**haven't**
you	**have**	you**'ve**	you	**haven't**
he/she/it	**has**	he**'s**/she**'s**/it**'s**	he/she/it	**hasn't**
we	**have**	we**'ve**	we	**haven't**
you	**have**	you**'ve**	you	**haven't**
they	**have**	they**'ve**	they	**haven't**

past tense **had** *present participle* **having** *past participle* **had**

journey? **5** (also **have got**) a word that you use with some nouns: *I have an idea.* ◇ *Have you got time to help me?*

have to; have got to used for saying that someone must do something or that something must happen: *I have to/ have got to go to school tomorrow.* ◇ *We don't have to/ haven't got to get up early tomorrow.* ◇ *Do we have to/ Have we got to pay for this now?*

have something done to let someone do something for you: *I had my hair cut yesterday.* ◇ *Have you had your car mended?*

haven't /ˈhævnt/ = **have not**

havoc /ˈhævək/ *noun* (no plural) a situation in which there is a lot of damage or trouble: *The storm caused havoc throughout the area.*

hawk /hɔːk/ *noun* a big bird that catches and eats other birds and small animals

hay /heɪ/ *noun* (no plural) dry grass that is used as food for farm animals

hay fever /ˈheɪ fiːvə(r)/ *noun* (no plural) an illness like a cold. Grass and other plants can cause **hay fever**.

hazard /ˈhæzəd/ *noun* a danger: *Animals are a hazard for drivers.*

hazardous /ˈhæzədəs/ *adjective* dangerous: *a hazardous journey*

he 🔑 /hiː/ *pronoun* the man or boy that the sentence is about: *I saw Mwita when he arrived.* ◇ *'Where is Shayo?' 'He's* (= he is) *at home.'*

head[1] 🔑 /hed/ *noun* **1** the part of your body above your neck, that has your eyes, ears, nose and mouth in it: *She turned her head to look at me.* ➲ picture on page A13 **2** what you use for thinking: *A strange thought came into his head.* **3** the top, front or most important part: *She sat at the head of the table.* **4** the most important person: *Mrs Ogonwe is head of the council.* **5 heads** (plural) the side of a coin that has the head of a person on it OPPOSITE **tails**

> ❖ **WORD BUILDING**
> You say **heads or tails** when you are throwing a coin in the air to decide something, for example who will start a game.

a head; per head for one person: *The meal cost 150 shillings a head.*

go to your head make you too pleased with yourself: *Winning a prize for his painting went to his head.*

head first with your head before the rest of your body: *She dived head first into the water.*

> ❖ **WORD BUILDING**
> You **nod** your head (move it up and down) to say 'yes' or to show that you agree, and you **shake** your head (move it from side to side) to say 'no' or to show that you disagree.

head[2] /hed/ *verb* (**heads, heading, headed**) **1** to be at the front or top of a group: *Adisa's name heads the list.* **2** to hit a ball with your head: *Okocha headed Nigeria's second goal.*

head for to go towards a place: *Let's head for home.*

headache /ˈhedeɪk/ *noun* a pain in your head: *I've got a headache.*

head boy /ˌhed ˈbɔɪ/ *noun* the boy who is chosen each year to speak or do things for the whole school

headgear /ˈhedgɪə(r)/ *noun* (no plural) anything that you wear on your head, for example a hat: *The boxers wore gloves and protective headgear.*

head girl /ˌhed ˈgɜːl/ *noun* the girl who is chosen each year to speak or do things for the whole school

heading /ˈhedɪŋ/ *noun* the words at the

top of a piece of writing to show what it is about; a title

headlight /ˈhedlaɪt/ (also **headlamp** /ˈhedlæmp/) *noun* one of the two big strong lights on the front of a car ➲ Picture at **car**.

headline /ˈhedlaɪn/ *noun* **1** words in big letters at the top of a newspaper story **2 the headlines** (plural) the most important news on radio or television: *Here are the news headlines.*

head-on /ˌhed ˈɒn/ *adjective* with the front of one car, train, etc. hitting the front of another: *a head-on collision*

headphones /ˈhedfəʊnz/ *noun* (plural) things that you put over your head and ears for listening to a radio, CD, etc.

headphones

headquarters /ˌhedˈkwɔːtəz/ *noun* (plural) the main offices where the leaders work: *The company's headquarters are in Arusha.* ℹ The short form is **HQ**.

headscarf /ˈhedskɑːf/ *noun* (*plural* **headscarves** /ˈhedskɑːvz/) a square piece of cloth that women wear to cover the head

head teacher /ˌhed ˈtiːtʃə(r)/ *noun* a person who is in charge of a school

> ❖ **WORD BUILDING**
>
> A man who is a head teacher is called a **headmaster** and a woman is called a **headmistress**.

headway /ˈhedweɪ/ *noun* (no plural) **make headway** go forward: *We haven't made much headway in our discussions.*

heal /hiːl/ *verb* (**heals, healing, healed** /hiːld/) to become well again; to make something well again: *The cut on his leg healed slowly.* ▸ **healing** /ˈhiːlɪŋ/ *noun* (no plural)

healer /ˈhiːlə(r)/ *noun* a person who uses natural medicines to make people well again: *Traditional healers play an important part in health care.*

health 🔑 /helθ/ *noun* (no plural) how well your body is; how you are: *Fresh fruit is good for your health.*

healthy 🔑 /ˈhelθi/ *adjective* (**healthier, healthiest**) **1** well; not ill: *healthy children* **2** that helps to make or keep you well: *healthy food* OPPOSITE **unhealthy**

heap[1] /hiːp/ *noun* **1** a lot of things on top of one another in an untidy way; a large amount of something: *She left her clothes in a heap on the floor.* **2 heaps** (plural) a lot: *Don't worry – we've got heaps of time.*

heap[2] /hiːp/ *verb* (**heaps, heaping, heaped** /hiːpt/) to put a lot of things on top of one another: *She heaped food onto my plate.*

hear 🔑 /hɪə(r)/ *verb* (**hears, hearing, heard** /hɜːd/, **has heard**)

> ❖ **PRONUNCIATION**
>
> **Hear** sounds just like **here**.

1 to get sounds with your ears: *Can you hear that noise?* ◊ *I heard someone laughing in the next room.* ◊ *Did you hear the teacher make the announcement?*

> ❖ **hear** or **listen**?
>
> **Hear** and **listen** are used in different ways. When you **hear** something, sounds come to your ears: *I heard the door close.*
>
> When you **listen** to something, you are trying to hear it: *I listen to the radio every morning.*

2 to learn about something with your ears: *Have you heard the news?*
hear from someone to get a letter or a phone call from someone: *Have you heard from your sister?*
hear of someone or **something** to know about someone or something: *Who is he? I've never heard of him.*
will not hear of something to refuse to allow something: *My father wouldn't hear of me going to art school.*

hearing /ˈhɪərɪŋ/ *noun* (no plural) the power to hear: *Speak louder – her hearing isn't very good.*

hearse /hɜːs/ *noun* a large car that carries a dead person to a **funeral** (= the time when they are buried or burned)

heart 🔑 /hɑːt/ *noun*

> ❖ **PRONUNCIATION**
>
> **Heart** sounds like **start**.

1 the part of a person's or animal's body that makes the blood go round inside: *Your heart beats faster when you run.* ➲ picture on page A13 **2** your feelings: *She has a kind heart.* **3** the centre; the middle part: *They live in the heart of* *the countryside.* **4** the shape ♥ **5 hearts** (plural) the **playing cards** (= the set of cards used for playing games) that have red shapes like hearts on them: *the six of hearts*

break someone's heart to make someone very sad: *It broke his heart when his wife died.*

by heart so that you know every word: *I have learnt the poem by heart.*

lose heart to stop hoping: *Don't lose heart – you can still win if you try.*

your heart sinks you suddenly feel unhappy: *My heart sank when I saw the first question on the exam paper.*

heart attack /ˈhɑːt ətæk/ *noun* a sudden dangerous illness, when your heart stops working properly: *She had a heart attack and died.*

heartbeat /ˈhɑːtbiːt/ *noun* the movement or sound of your heart as it pushes blood around your body: *The doctor listened to my heartbeat.*

heartless /ˈhɑːtləs/ *adjective* not kind; cruel

heat 🔑 /hiːt/ *noun* **1** (no plural) the feeling of something hot: *the heat of the sun* **2** (no plural) hot weather: *I love the heat.* OPPOSITE **cold** **3** (*plural* **heats**) one of the first parts of a race or competition: *The winner of this heat will run in the final.* ▶ **heat** (also **heat up**) *verb* (**heats, heating, heated**) to make something hot; to become hot: *I heated some water in a saucepan.* ◇ *Wait for the oven to heat up before you put the food in.*

heath /hiːθ/ *noun* a big piece of wild land where there are no farms

heatproof /ˈhiːtpruːf/ *adjective* Something **heatproof** cannot be damaged by heat: *Put the fish in a heatproof dish and cook it in the oven.*

heave /hiːv/ *verb* (**heaves, heaving, heaved** /hiːvd/) to lift or pull something heavy: *We heaved the suitcase up the stairs.*

heaven 🔑 /ˈhevn/ *noun* (no plural) Many people believe that God lives in heaven and that good people go to heaven when they die. ➲ Look at **hell**.

Good Heavens! words that you use to show surprise: *Good Heavens! I've won first prize!*

heavy 🔑 /ˈhevi/ *adjective* (**heavier, heaviest**) **1** with a lot of weight, so it is difficult to lift or move: *I can't carry this bag – it's too heavy.* **2** larger, stronger or more than usual: *heavy rain* ◇ *The traffic was very heavy this morning.* OPPOSITE **light** ▶ **heavily** /ˈhevəli/ *adverb*: *It was raining heavily.*

heavy

heavy metal /ˌhevi ˈmetl/ *noun* (no plural) a kind of very loud rock music

hectare /ˈhekteə(r)/ *noun* a measure of land. There are 10 000 **square metres** in a **hectare**.

hectic /ˈhektɪk/ *adjective* very busy: *I had a hectic day at work.*

he'd /hiːd/ **1** = **he had** **2** = **he would**

hedge /hedʒ/ *noun* a line of small trees that makes a kind of wall around a garden or field

heel /hiːl/ *noun* **1** the back part of your foot ➲ picture on page A13 **2** the back part of a shoe under the **heel** of your foot **3** the part of a sock that covers the **heel** of your foot

heifer /ˈhefə(r)/ *noun* a young female cow

height 🔑 /haɪt/ *noun*

> ❖ **PRONUNCIATION**
> **Height** sounds like **white**.

1 (*plural* **heights**) how far it is from the bottom to the top of someone or something: *What is the height of this mountain?* ◇ *The wall is two metres in height.* ◇ *She asked me my height, weight and age.* ➲ picture on page A12 **2** (*plural* **heights**) a high place: *I'm afraid of heights.* **3** (no plural) the strongest or most important part of something: *She was dressed in the height of fashion.*

heir /eə(r)/ *noun*

> ❖ **PRONUNCIATION**
> We do not say the 'h' in **heir** and **heiress**, so **heir** sounds the same as **air**.

a person who receives money, goods, etc. when another person dies: *Prince*

Charles is Queen Elizabeth's heir. ▸ **heiress** /ˈeəres/ *noun (plural* **heiresses***)* an **heir** who is a woman

held *form of* HOLD[1]

helicopter

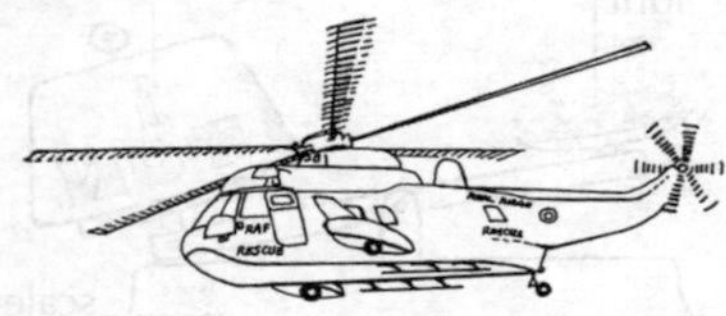

helicopter /ˈhelɪkɒptə(r)/ *noun* a kind of small aircraft that can go straight up in the air. It has long metal parts on top that turn to help it fly.

he'll /hiːl/ = **he will**

hell /hel/ *noun* (no plural) Some people believe that bad people go to **hell** when they die. ➲ Look at **heaven**.

hello 🔑 (also **hallo, hullo**) /həˈləʊ/ *exclamation* a word that you say when you meet someone or when you answer the telephone

helm /helm/ *noun* the handle or wheel that you turn to make a ship go the way that you want: *The captain remained at the helm all night.*

❖ **WORD BUILDING**

The person who is in charge of the helm is called a **helmsman**.

helmet /ˈhelmɪt/ *noun* a hard hat that keeps your head safe: *The motorcyclist survived the crash because he was wearing a helmet.*

helmsman /ˈhelmzmən/ *noun (plural* **helmsmen** /ˈhelmzmən/*)* a person who steers a boat or ship

help[1] 🔑 /help/ *verb* (**helps, helping, helped** /helpt/) **1** to do something useful for someone; to make someone's work easier: *Will you help me with the washing-up?* ◇ *She helped me to carry the box.* **2** a word that you shout when you are in danger: *Help! I can't swim!*
can't help If you **can't help** doing something, you cannot stop yourself doing it: *It was so funny that I couldn't help laughing.*
help yourself to take what you want: *Help yourself to a drink.* ◇ *'Can I have a drink?' 'Of course. Help yourself!'*

help[2] 🔑 /help/ *noun* (no plural) **1** helping someone: *Thank you for all your help.* ◇ *Do you need any help?* **2** a person or thing that helps: *He was a great help to me when I was ill.*

helpful 🔑 /ˈhelpfl/ *adjective* A person or thing that is helpful gives help: *The woman in the shop was very helpful.* ◇ *helpful advice* OPPOSITE **unhelpful**

helpless /ˈhelpləs/ *adjective* not able to do things without help: *Babies are totally helpless.*

hem /hem/ *noun* the bottom edge of something like a shirt or trousers, that is folded and sewn

hemisphere /ˈhemɪsfɪə(r)/ *noun* one half of the earth: *the northern/southern hemisphere*

hen /hen/ *noun* **1** a female bird that people keep on farms for its eggs ➲ Picture at **chicken**. **2** any female bird

❖ **WORD BUILDING**

A male bird is a **cock**.

hepatitis /ˌhepəˈtaɪtɪs/ *noun* (no plural) a serious illness of the **liver** (= the part inside the body that cleans the blood)

her[1] 🔑 /hɜː(r)/ *pronoun (plural* **them***)* a word that shows a woman or a girl: *Tell your mother that I'll see her tonight.* ◇ *I wrote to her yesterday.*

her[2] /hɜː(r)/ *adjective* belonging to the woman or girl that you have just talked about: *That's her book.* ◇ *Mrs Njehu has hurt her leg.* ➲ Look at **their**.

herb /hɜːb/ *noun* a plant that people use to make food taste good, or in medicine ▸ **herbal** /ˈhɜːbl/ *adjective*: *herbal medicine*

herbivore /ˈhɜːbɪvɔː(r)/ *noun* any animal that only eats plants

herd /hɜːd/ *noun* a big group of animals of the same kind: *a herd of cows* ◇ *a herd of elephants*

here 🔑 /hɪə(r)/ *adverb* in, at or to this place: *Your glasses are here.* ◇ *Come here, please.* ◇ *Here's my car.* ◇ *Where's Ngenzi? Oh, here he is.*
here and there in different places: *There were groups of people here and there along the beach.*
here goes words that you say before you do something exciting or dangerous: *'Here goes,' said Sarika, and jumped into the river.*

here you are words that you say when you give something to someone: *'Can I borrow a pen, please?' 'Yes, here you are.'*

here's /hɪəz/ = **here is**

hero /ˈhɪərəʊ/ *noun* (*plural* **heroes**) **1** a person who has done something brave or good: *Everybody said that Wasike was a hero after he rescued his sister from the fire.* **2** the most important man or boy in a book, play or film

heroic /həˈrəʊɪk/ *adjective* very brave

heroin /ˈherəʊɪn/ *noun* (no plural) a very strong drug that can be dangerous

heroine /ˈherəʊɪn/ *noun* **1** a woman who has done something brave or good **2** the most important woman or girl in a book, play or film

heron /ˈherən/ *noun* a large bird with long legs and a long neck, that lives near water

heron

hers /hɜːz/ *pronoun* something that belongs to her: *Kendi says this book is hers.* ◇ *Are these keys hers?*

herself /hɜːˈself/ *pronoun* (*plural* **themselves** /ðəmˈselvz/) **1** a word that shows the same woman or girl that you have just talked about: *She fell and hurt herself.* **2** a word that makes 'she' stronger: *'Who told you that Tanei was married?' 'She told me herself.'*
by herself **1** alone; without other people: *She lives by herself.* **2** without help: *She can carry the box by herself.*

he's /hiːz/ **1** = **he is** **2** = **he has**

hesitate /ˈhezɪteɪt/ *verb* (**hesitates, hesitating, hesitated**) to stop for a moment before you do or say something because you are not sure about it: *He hesitated before answering the question.*
▶ **hesitation** /ˌhezɪˈteɪʃn/ *noun* (no plural): *They agreed without hesitation.*

hexagon /ˈheksəgən/ *noun* a shape with six sides ▶ **hexagonal** /hekˈsægənl/ *adjective* with six sides: *a hexagonal box*

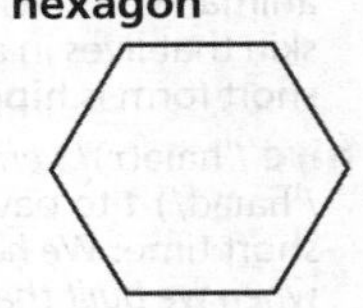

hexagon

hey /heɪ/ *exclamation* a word that you shout to make someone listen to you, or when you are surprised: *Hey! Where are you going?*

hi /haɪ/ *exclamation* a word that you say when you meet someone; hello: *Hi Ereng! How are you?*

hiccup (also **hiccough**) /ˈhɪkʌp/ *noun* a sudden noise that you make in your throat. You sometimes get **hiccups** when you have eaten or drunk too quickly.

hide¹ /haɪd/ *verb* (**hides, hiding, hid** /hɪd/, **has hidden** /ˈhɪdn/) **1** to put something where people cannot find it: *I hid the money under the bed.* **2** to be or to get in a place where people cannot see or find you: *Someone was hiding behind the door.* **3** to not tell or show something to someone: *She tried to hide her feelings.*

hide² /haɪd/ *noun* the skin of a large animal

hide-and-seek /ˌhaɪd n ˈsiːk/ *noun* (no plural) a game that children play. Some children hide and one child tries to find them.

hideous /ˈhɪdiəs/ *adjective* very ugly: *That shirt is hideous!*

hideout /ˈhaɪdaʊt/ *noun* a place where someone goes to hide

hiding /ˈhaɪdɪŋ/ *noun* (no plural)
be in hiding; go into hiding to be in, or to go into a place where people will not find you: *The prisoners escaped and went into hiding.*

high¹ /haɪ/ *adjective* (**higher, highest**) **1** Something that is high goes up a long way: *a high wall* ◇ *Mount Everest is the highest mountain in the world.* OPPOSITE **low** ℹ The noun is **height**. **2** You use 'high' to say or ask how far something is from the bottom to the top: *The table is 80 centimetres high.* ℹ The noun is **height**. ➲ picture on page A12

❖ **high** or **tall?**
We use **tall**, not **high**, to talk about people: *How tall are you?* ◇ *He's 1.72 metres tall.*

3 far from the ground: *a high shelf* OPPOSITE **low** **4** great; more than the usual level or amount: *The car was travelling at high speed.* ◇ *high temperatures* OPPOSITE **low** **5** A **high** sound is not deep: *I heard the high voice of a child.* OPPOSITE **low**

high² /haɪ/ *adverb* (**higher, highest**) a long way above the ground: *The plane flew high above the clouds.* OPPOSITE **low**

high and low everywhere: *I've looked high and low for my keys, but I can't find them anywhere.*

the high jump /ðə ˈhaɪ dʒʌmp/ *noun* (no plural) a sport where people jump over a high bar

highlands /ˈhaɪləndz/ *noun* (plural) the part of a country with hills and mountains: *the Kenyan Highlands*

highlight[1] /ˈhaɪlaɪt/ *noun* the best or most exciting part of something: *The highlight of the show was when everyone sang together.*

highlight[2] /ˈhaɪlaɪt/ *verb* (**highlights, highlighting, highlighted**) **1** to make something seem especially important so that people pay attention to it **2** to mark important words in a text with a different colour: *I have highlighted the main points in yellow.*

highlighter /ˈhaɪlaɪtə(r)/ *noun* a special pen that you use to mark words in a text in a bright colour

highly /ˈhaɪli/ *adverb* **1** very or very much: *Their children are highly intelligent.* **2** very well: *I think very highly of your work* (= I think it is very good).

Highness /ˈhaɪnəs/ *noun* (*plural* **Highnesses**) a word that you use when speaking to or about a royal person: *His Highness the Aga Khan*

high school /ˈhaɪ skuːl/ *noun* a kind of secondary school in some countries that you go to until you are 18 or 19 years old

highway /ˈhaɪweɪ/ *noun* a big road between towns ℹ **Highway** is used mostly in American English.

hijack /ˈhaɪdʒæk/ *verb* (**hijacks, hijacking, hijacked** /ˈhaɪdʒækt/) to take control of a plane or a car and make the pilot or driver take you somewhere ▸ **hijacker** /ˈhaɪdʒækə(r)/ *noun* a person who **hijacks** a plane or car ▸ **hijacking** /ˈhaɪdʒækɪŋ/ *noun*

hill /hɪl/ *noun* a high piece of land that is not as high as a mountain: *I pushed my bike up the hill.* ◇ *Their house is at the top of the hill.* ➲ Look at **uphill, downhill.** ▸ **hilly** /ˈhɪli/ *adjective* (**hillier, hilliest**) with a lot of hills: *The countryside is very hilly where I live.*

hillside /ˈhɪlsaɪd/ *noun* the side of a hill: *Our village was on the hillside overlooking the lake.*

him /hɪm/ *pronoun* (*plural* **them**) a word that shows a man or boy: *Where's Opiyo? I can't see him.* ◇ *I spoke to him yesterday.*

himself /hɪmˈself/ *pronoun* (*plural* **themselves** /ðəmˈselvz/) **1** a word that shows the same man or boy that you have just talked about: *Rono looked at himself in the mirror.* **2** a word that makes 'he' stronger: *Did he make this himself?*
by himself 1 alone; without other people: *Dad went shopping by himself.* **2** without help: *He did it by himself.*

Hindu /ˈhɪnduː/ *noun* a person who follows one of the religions of India (called **Hinduism**)

hinge /hɪndʒ/ *noun* a piece of metal that joins two sides of a box, door, etc. together so that it can open and close

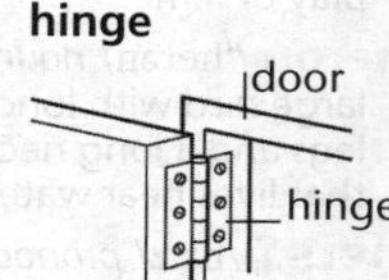

hint[1] /hɪnt/ *verb* (**hints, hinting, hinted**) to say something, but not in a direct way: *Nakato looked at her watch, hinting that she wanted to go home.*

hint[2] /hɪnt/ *noun* **1** something that you say, but not in a direct way: *When he said he had no money, it was a hint that he wanted to borrow some from you.* **2** a small amount of something: *There was a hint of anger in her voice.*

hip /hɪp/ *noun* the place where your leg joins the side of your body ➲ picture on page A13

hip hop /ˈhɪp hɒp/ *noun* (no plural) a type of modern music played on electronic instruments, with a regular beat and words that are spoken

hippopotamus /ˌhɪpəˈpɒtəməs/ *noun* (*plural* **hippopotamuses** *or* **hippopotami** /ˌhɪpəˈpɒtəmaɪ/) a large animal with thick skin that lives in and near water ℹ The short form is **hippo** /ˈhɪpəʊ/.

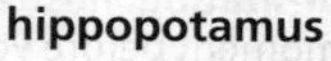

hire /ˈhaɪə(r)/ *verb* (**hires, hiring, hired** /ˈhaɪəd/) **1** to pay to use something for a short time: *We had to hire some machinery when we built the house.* **2** to pay someone to do a job for you: *We hired someone to mend the roof.*

hire out to let someone hire something from you: *They hire out trucks.* ▶ **hire** *noun* (no plural): *Have you got any boats for hire?*

his[1] 🔑 /hɪz/ *adjective* of him: *Wasike came with his sister.* ◇ *He has hurt his arm.*

his[2] 🔑 /hɪz/ *pronoun* something that belongs to him: *Are these books yours or his?*

hiss /hɪs/ *verb* (**hisses, hissing, hissed** /hɪst/) to make a noise like a very long **S**: *The cat hissed at me.* ▶ **hiss** *noun* (*plural* **hisses**): *the hiss of steam*

historic /hɪˈstɒrɪk/ *adjective* important in history: *It was a historic moment when man first walked on the moon.*

historical /hɪˈstɒrɪkl/ *adjective* of or about past times: *Mandela's release from prison was an important historical event.*

history 🔑 /ˈhɪstri/ *noun* (no plural) **1** the study of things that happened in the past: *History is my favourite subject at school.* **2** all the things that happened in the past: *It was an important moment in history.*

hit[1] 🔑 /hɪt/ *verb* (**hits, hitting, hit, has hit**) to touch someone or something hard: *He hit me on the head with a book.* ◇ *The car hit a wall.*

hit[2] 🔑 /hɪt/ *noun* **1** touching someone or something hard: *That was a good hit!* (in a game of cricket, baseball, etc.) **2** a person or a thing that a lot of people like: *This song was a hit last year.* **3** when you find something on the Internet: *The website gets a lot of hits from the USA.*

hitchhike /ˈhɪtʃhaɪk/ *verb* (**hitchhikes, hitchhiking, hitchhiked** /ˈhɪtʃhaɪkt/) (also **hitch** /hɪtʃ/) (**hitches, hitching, hitched** /hɪtʃt/) to travel by asking for free rides in cars and lorries: *We hitchhiked to the coast.* ▶ **hitchhiker** /ˈhɪtʃhaɪkə(r)/ *noun* a person who **hitchhikes**

HIV /ˌeɪtʃ aɪ ˈviː/ *noun* (no plural) a very small living thing (a **virus**) that can make a person get a very serious illness (called **AIDS**): *He is HIV positive* (= he has the virus in his body). ℹ **HIV** is short for 'human immunodeficiency virus'.

hive = **beehive**

hoard /hɔːd/ *noun* a secret store of something, for example food or money ▶ **hoard** *verb* (**hoards, hoarding, hoarded**) to save and keep things secretly: *The old man hoarded the money in a box under his bed.*

hoarse /hɔːs/ *adjective* If your voice is **hoarse**, it is rough and quiet, for example because you have a cold.

hoax /həʊks/ *noun* (*plural* **hoaxes**) a trick that makes someone believe something that is not true: *There wasn't really a bomb in the station – it was a hoax.*

hobby 🔑 /ˈhɒbi/ *noun* (*plural* **hobbies**) something that you like doing when you are not at school: *My hobbies are reading and football.*

hockey /ˈhɒki/ *noun* (no plural) a game for two teams of eleven players who hit a small ball with long curved sticks on a field (called a **pitch**)

hoe /həʊ/ *noun* a tool that you use for turning the soil and removing plants that you do not want ➲ Look at **jembe**.

hold[1] 🔑 /həʊld/ *verb* (**holds, holding, held** /held/, **has held**) **1** to have something in your hand or arms: *She was holding a rope.* ◇ *He held the baby in his arms.* **2** to keep something in a certain way: *Hold your hand up.* **3** to have space for a certain number or amount: *The car holds five people.* **4** to make something happen: *The meeting was held in the town hall.* **5** to have something: *He holds a Ugandan passport.*
hold someone or **something back** to stop someone or something from moving forwards: *The police held back the crowd.*
Hold it! Wait! Don't move!
hold on 1 to wait: *Hold on, I'm coming.* **2** to not stop holding something tightly: *The child held on to her mother's hand.*
hold up 1 to make someone or something late: *The bus was held up for two hours.* **2** to try to steal from a place, using a gun: *Two men held up a bank in Nairobi today.*

hold[2] 🔑 /həʊld/ *noun* (no plural) the part of a ship or a plane where you keep the goods
get hold of someone to find someone so that you can speak to them: *I'm trying to get hold of Ngenzi but he's not at home.*
get hold of something 1 to take something in your hands: *Can you get hold of* (= take and hold) *the other end of the table and help me move it?* **2** to find something: *I can't get hold of the book I need.*

hole 🔑 /həʊl/ *noun* an empty space or opening in something: *I'm going to dig a hole in the garden.* ◇ *They are filling in the holes in the road.* ◇ *My socks are full of holes.*

holiday 🔑 /ˈhɒlədeɪ/ *noun* a day or days when you do not go to work or school,

and when you may go and stay away from home: *The school holiday starts next week.* ◇ *The teacher gave us our holiday homework.*
on holiday not at work or school: *Mrs Gombe isn't here this week. She's on holiday.*

hollow /ˈhɒləʊ/ *adjective* with an empty space inside: *A drum is hollow.*

holy /ˈhəʊli/ *adjective* (**holier**, **holiest**)
1 very special because it is about God or a god: *The Bible is the holy book of Christians.* **2** A **holy** person lives a good and religious life.

home[1] 🔑 /həʊm/ *noun* **1** the place where you live: *Boke left home at the age of 18.* **2** a place where they look after people, for example children who have no parents, or old people: *The children's home looks after 100 children.*
at home in your house or flat: *I stayed at home yesterday.* ◇ *Is Njoki at home?*

home[2] 🔑 /həʊm/ *adverb* to the place where you live: *Let's go home.* ◇ *What time did you arrive home last night?*

❖ **GRAMMAR**

Be careful! We do not use **to** before **home**.

home[3] /həʊm/ *adjective* of your home or your country: *What is your home address?*

homeless /ˈhəʊmləs/ *adjective* If you are **homeless**, you have nowhere to live: *The floods made many people homeless.* ▸ **homelessness** /ˈhəʊmləsnəs/ *noun* (no plural): *Homelessness is increasing.*

home-made /ˌhəʊm ˈmeɪd/ *adjective* made in your house, not bought in a shop: *home-made bread*

homesick /ˈhəʊmsɪk/ *adjective* sad because you are away from home

homestead /ˈhəʊmsted/ *noun* a house with the land and buildings around it; a farm

homework /ˈhəʊmwɜːk/ *noun* (no plural) work that a teacher gives to you to do at home: *Have you done your science homework?* ➲ Note at **housework**.

homosexual /ˌhəʊməˈsekʃuəl/ *adjective* attracted to people of the same sex

honest 🔑 /ˈɒnɪst/ *adjective*
A person who is honest says what is true and does not steal or cheat: *She's a very honest person.* ◇ *Be honest – do you really like this dress?* OPPOSITE **dishonest** ▸ **honestly** *adverb*: *Try to answer the questions honestly.* ◇ *Honestly, I don't know where your money is.* ▸ **honesty** /ˈɒnəsti/ *noun* (no plural) being honest

❖ **PRONUNCIATION**

We do not say the 'h' in **honest**.

honey /ˈhʌni/ *noun* (no plural) the sweet food that bees make

honeycomb

bee

honeycomb /ˈhʌnikəʊm/ *noun* a thing made by bees, where they keep their eggs and honey

❖ **PRONUNCIATION**

We do not say the 'b' at the end of **honeycomb**.

honour /ˈɒnə(r)/ *noun* (no plural)

❖ **PRONUNCIATION**

We do not say the 'h' in **honour**.

1 something that makes you proud and pleased: *It was a great honour to be invited to meet the president.* **2** the respect from other people that a person or country gets because of something very good that they have done: *They are fighting for the honour of their country.*
in honour of someone to show that you respect someone: *There is a concert tonight in honour of our visitors.*

hood /hʊd/ *noun* the part of a coat or jacket that covers your head and neck

hoody (also **hoodie**) /ˈhʊdi/ *noun* (*plural* **hoodies**) a jacket made of warm, soft material, with long sleeves and a **hood**

hoof /huːf/ *noun* (*plural* **hoofs** *or* **hooves** /huːvz/) the hard part of the foot of cows, horses and some other animals ➲ Picture at **horse**.

hooks

hook 🔑 /hʊk/ *noun* a curved piece of metal or plastic for hanging things on, or for catching something: *Hang your coat on that hook.* ◇ *a fish hook*
off the hook If a telephone is **off the hook**, the part that you speak into (the **receiver**) is not in place so that the telephone will not ring.

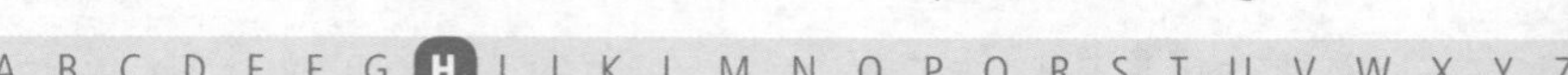

hooligan /ˈhuːlɪɡən/ *noun* a young person who behaves in a noisy way and fights other people: *football hooligans*

hooray (also **hurray** /həˈreɪ/, **hurrah** /həˈrɑː/) *exclamation* a word that you shout when you are very pleased about something: *Hooray! She's won!*

hoot /huːt/ *noun* the sound that an **owl** (= a type of bird) or a car's horn makes ▶ **hoot** *verb* (**hoots**, **hooting**, **hooted**) to make this sound: *The driver hooted at the dog.*

hooves *plural of* HOOF

hop /hɒp/ *verb* (**hops**, **hopping**, **hopped** /hɒpt/) **1** to jump on one foot **2** to jump with two or all feet together: *The frog hopped onto the stone.*

hope¹ 🔑 /həʊp/ *noun* **1** a feeling of wanting something to happen and thinking that it will: *He hasn't worked very hard so there is not much hope that he will pass the exam.* **2** a person or thing that gives you hope: *Can you help me? You're my only hope.*
give up hope to stop thinking that what you want will happen: *Don't give up hope. The letter may come tomorrow.*

hope² 🔑 /həʊp/ *verb* (**hopes**, **hoping**, **hoped** /həʊpt/) to want something that may happen: *I hope you have a nice holiday.* ◇ *I hope to see you tomorrow.* ◇ *We're hoping that you will come to the wedding.* ◇ *She's hoping for a letter from her friend.*
I hope not I do not want that to happen: *'Do you think we'll lose the match?' 'I hope not.'*
I hope so I want that to happen: *'Will you be at the wedding?' 'I'm not sure – I hope so.'*

hopeful /ˈhəʊpfl/ *adjective* If you are **hopeful**, you think that something that you want will happen: *I'm hopeful about getting a place on the team.*

hopefully /ˈhəʊpfəli/ *adverb* **1** I hope: *Hopefully he won't be late.* **2** hoping that what you want will happen: *My brother looked hopefully at my sweets.*

hopeless /ˈhəʊpləs/ *adjective* **1** useless: *It's hopeless trying to work when my brother is here – he's so noisy!* **2** very bad: *I'm hopeless at tennis.* ▶ **hopelessly** *adverb*: *We got hopelessly lost in the desert.*

horizon /həˈraɪzn/ *noun* the line between the earth or sea and the sky: *We could see a ship on the horizon.*

horizontal /ˌhɒrɪˈzɒntl/ *adjective* Something that is **horizontal** goes from side to side, not up and down: *a horizontal line* ➲ picture on page A12 ➲ Look at **vertical**.

horn 🔑 /hɔːn/ *noun* **1** one of the hard pointed things that some animals have on their heads: *A bull has long curved horns.* ➲ Picture at **buffalo**. **2** a thing in a car, ship, etc. that makes a loud sound to warn people: *Don't sound your horn late at night.* **3** a musical instrument that you blow: *He plays the horn.*

hornbill /ˈhɔːnbɪl/ *noun* a bird with a very big curved **beak** (= the hard pointed part of its mouth)

hornbill

horoscope /ˈhɒrəskəʊp/ *noun* something that tells you what will happen, using the planets and your date of birth: *Have you read your horoscope today?* (for example, in a newspaper)

horrible /ˈhɒrəbl/ *adjective* **1** very bad: *What horrible weather!* **2** Something that is **horrible** makes you feel afraid or shocked: *There was a horrible murder here last week.*

horrid /ˈhɒrɪd/ *adjective* very bad or unkind: *Don't be so horrid!*

horrify /ˈhɒrɪfaɪ/ *verb* (**horrifies**, **horrifying**, **horrified** /ˈhɒrɪfaɪd/, **has horrified**) to shock and frighten someone: *We were horrified by the photos of the car crash.*

horror /ˈhɒrə(r)/ *noun* (no plural) a feeling of fear or shock: *They watched in horror as the child ran in front of the bus.*

horror film /ˈhɒrə fɪlm/ *noun* a film that shows frightening things

horse

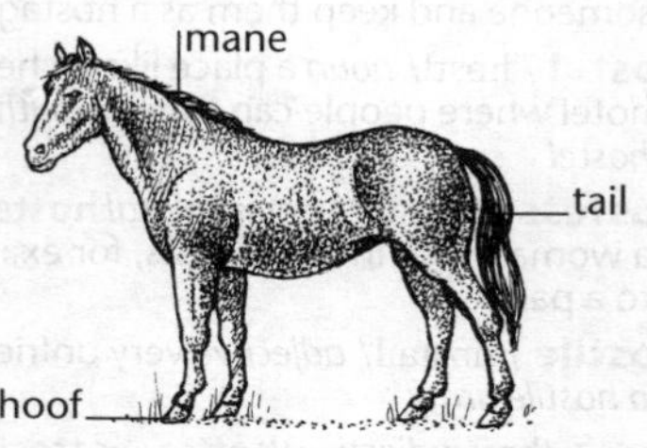

horse 🔑 /hɔːs/ *noun* a big animal that can carry people and pull heavy things: *Can you ride a horse?*

❖ **WORD BUILDING**

A young horse is called a **foal**.

horseback /ˈhɔːsbæk/ *noun*
on horseback sitting on a horse

horseshoe /ˈhɔːs ʃuː/ *noun* a piece of metal like a U that a horse wears on its foot

horticulture /ˈhɔːtɪkʌltʃə(r)/ *noun* (no plural) growing fruit, vegetables and flowers ▶ **horticultural** /ˌhɔːtɪˈkʌltʃərəl/ *adjective*: *Gardeners need lots of horticultural knowledge.*

hose /həʊz/ (also **hosepipe** /ˈhəʊzpaɪp/) *noun* a long soft tube that you use to bring water, for example in the garden or when there is a fire

hospital 🔑 /ˈhɒspɪtl/ *noun* a place where doctors and nurses look after people who are ill or hurt: *My brother is in hospital – he's broken his leg.* ◇ *The ambulance took her to hospital.*

❖ **WORD BUILDING**

A room in a hospital where people sleep is called a **ward**. A person who is staying in hospital is called a **patient**.

hospitality /ˌhɒspɪˈtæləti/ *noun* (no plural) being friendly to people who are visiting you, and looking after them well: *We thanked them for their hospitality.*

host /həʊst/ *noun* a person who invites guests, for example to a party: *The host offered me a drink.*

hostage /ˈhɒstɪdʒ/ *noun* a prisoner that you keep until people give you what you want: *The hijackers have freed all the hostages.*
hold someone hostage to keep someone as a hostage: *They held his daughter hostage until he paid them the money.*
take someone hostage to catch someone and keep them as a hostage

hostel /ˈhɒstl/ *noun* a place like a cheap hotel where people can stay: *a youth hostel*

hostess /ˈhəʊstəs/ *noun* (*plural* **hostesses**) a woman who invites guests, for example to a party

hostile /ˈhɒstaɪl/ *adjective* very unfriendly: *a hostile army*

hot 🔑 /hɒt/ *adjective* (**hotter**, **hottest**)
1 not cold. A fire is hot: *I'm hot. Can you open the window?* ◇ *It's hot today, isn't it?* ◇ *hot water* **2** Food that is hot has a strong, burning taste: *a hot curry*

hotel 🔑 /həʊˈtel/ *noun* a place where you pay to sleep and eat: *The journalists stayed at a hotel near the airport.*

hotline /ˈhɒtlaɪn/ *noun* a special telephone line that people can call to get advice or information: *For more information, phone our 24-hour hotline.*

hour 🔑 /ˈaʊə(r)/ *noun*

❖ **PRONUNCIATION**

Hour sounds just like **our** because we do not say the 'h'.

1 a measure of time. There are 60 **minutes** in an hour: *The journey took two hours.* ◇ *I've been waiting for an hour.* ◇ *half an hour* **2 hours** (plural) the time when someone is working, or when a shop or office is open: *The office hours are 8 a.m. to 5 p.m.*

hourly /ˈaʊəli/ *adjective, adverb* that happens or comes once an hour: *There is an hourly news report on the radio.* ◇ *Buses run hourly.*

house 🔑 /haʊs/ *noun* (*plural* **houses** /ˈhaʊzɪz/) **1** a building where a person or a family lives. A house has more than one floor: *How many rooms are there in your house?* ◇ *We're going to my grandmother's house tomorrow.* ➲ Look at **bungalow**, **flat**[1]. **2** a building for a special use: *a warehouse*

house help /ˈhaʊs help/ (also **domestic help, domestic worker**) *noun* a person whose job is to do the washing, cleaning, etc. in a house

house shoe /ˈhaʊs ʃuː/ *noun* a loose soft shoe that you wear in the house

house shoe

housewife /ˈhaʊswaɪf/ *noun* (*plural* **housewives** /ˈhaʊswaɪvz/) a woman who works for her family in the house

housework /ˈhaʊswɜːk/ *noun* (no plural) work that you do in your house, for example cleaning and washing

❖ **housework** or **homework**?

Be careful! Work that a teacher gives you to do at home is called **homework**.

housing /ˈhaʊzɪŋ/ *noun* (no plural) flats and houses for people to live in: *The government is spending a lot of money on new housing.*

housing estate /ˈhaʊzɪŋ ɪsteɪt/ *noun* a big group of houses that were built at the same time: *We live on a housing estate.*

hover /ˈhɒvə(r)/ *verb* (**hovers, hovering, hovered** /ˈhɒvəd/) to stay in the air in one place: *An eagle hovered above us.*

hovercraft /ˈhɒvəkrɑːft/ *noun* (*plural* **hovercraft**) a kind of boat that moves over the top of water on air that it pushes out

how 🔑 /haʊ/ *adverb* **1** in what way: *How does this machine work?* ◇ *She told me how to get to the station.* ◇ *Do you know how to spell 'elementary'?* **2** a word that you use to ask if someone is well: *'How is your sister?' 'She's very well, thank you.'*

> ❖ **SPEAKING**
> You use 'how' only when you are asking about someone's health. When you are asking someone to describe another person or a thing you use **what ... like?**: *'What is your sister like?' 'She's tall and has black hair.'*

3 a word that you use to ask if something is good: *How was the film?* **4** a word that you use to ask questions about amount, etc: *How old are you?* ◇ *How many brothers and sisters have you got?* ◇ *How much does this cost?* ◇ *How long have you lived here?* **5** a word that shows surprise or strong feeling: *How kind of you to help!*
how about ...? words that you use when you suggest something: *How about a drink?* ◇ *How about going for a walk?*
how are you? do you feel well?: *'How are you?' 'Fine, thanks.'*
how do you do? polite words that you say when you meet someone for the first time

> ❖ **SPEAKING**
> When someone says 'How do you do?', you also answer 'How do you do?'

however[1] 🔑 /haʊˈevə(r)/ *adverb* **1** it does not matter how: *I never win, however hard I try.* **2** a way of saying 'how' more strongly: *However did you find me?*

however[2] /haʊˈevə(r)/ *conjunction* but: *She's very clever. However, she's quite lazy.*

howl /haʊl/ *noun* a long loud sound, like a dog makes ▶ **howl** *verb* (**howls, howling, howled** /haʊld/): *The dogs howled all night.* ◇ *The wind howled around the house.*

HQ /ˌeɪtʃ ˈkjuː/ *short for* HEADQUARTERS

hug /hʌɡ/ *verb* (**hugs, hugging, hugged** /hʌɡd/) to put your arms around someone to show that you love them: *She hugged her parents and said goodbye.* ▶ **hug** *noun*: *He gave his brother a hug.*

huge 🔑 /hjuːdʒ/ *adjective* very big: *He caught a huge fish.*

hull /hʌl/ *noun* the bottom part of a ship that goes in the water: *a wooden/steel hull*

hullo = **hello**

hum /hʌm/ *verb* (**hums, humming, hummed** /hʌmd/) **1** to sing with your lips closed: *If you don't know the words of the song, hum it.* **2** to make a sound like bees

human[1] 🔑 /ˈhjuːmən/ *adjective* of or like people, not animals or machines: *the human body*

human[2] 🔑 /ˈhjuːmən/ (*also* **human being** /ˌhjuːmən ˈbiːɪŋ/) *noun* a person: *Human beings have lived on earth for thousands of years.*

the human race /ðə ˌhjuːmən ˈreɪs/ *noun* (no plural) all the people in the world

humble /ˈhʌmbl/ *adjective* A **humble** person does not think they are better or more important than other people: *Becoming rich and famous has not changed her – she is still very humble.*

humid /ˈhjuːmɪd/ *adjective* **Humid** weather is warm and wet: *The coast of East Africa has a hot and humid climate.* ▶ **humidity** /hjuːˈmɪdəti/ *noun* (no plural): *July is cooler, with lower humidity.*

humorous /ˈhjuːmərəs/ *adjective* A person or thing that is **humorous** makes you smile or laugh: *a humorous story*

humour 🔑 /ˈhjuːmə(r)/ *noun* (no plural) being funny: *a story full of humour*
have a sense of humour to be able to laugh and make other people laugh at funny things: *Rono has a good sense of humour.*

hump /hʌmp/ *noun* a round lump: *A camel has a hump on its back.*

humus /ˈhjuːməs/ *noun* (no plural) a substance made from dead leaves and plants that helps plants to grow

hundred 🔑 /ˈhʌndrəd/ *number* 100: *They invited a hundred people to the wedding.* ◇ *two hundred kilograms* ◇ *four hundred and twenty* ◇ *hundreds of people*

hundredth /ˈhʌndrədθ/ *adjective, adverb, noun* 100th

hung *form of* HANG

hunger /ˈhʌŋɡə(r)/ *noun* (no plural) the feeling that you want or need to eat

hungry /ˈhʌŋgri/ *adjective* (**hungrier, hungriest**) If you are hungry, you want to eat: *Let's eat soon – I'm hungry!*

hunt /hʌnt/ *verb* (**hunts, hunting, hunted**) to chase animals to catch or kill them: *Young lions have to learn to hunt.* **hunt for something** to try to find something: *I've hunted everywhere for my book but I can't find it.* ▶ **hunt** *noun*: *a hunt for my keys* ▶ **hunting** /ˈhʌntɪŋ/ *noun* (no plural) chasing and killing animals

hunter /ˈhʌntə(r)/ *noun* a person who chases and kills animals

hurdles

hurdles /ˈhɜːdlz/ *noun* (plural) a race in which you have to jump over a number of light fences called **hurdles**: *Do you know who won the 110m hurdles?*

hurl /hɜːl/ *verb* (**hurls, hurling, hurled** /hɜːld/) to throw something strongly: *She hurled the book across the room.*

hurrah, hurray = **hooray**

hurricane /ˈhʌrɪkən/ *noun* a storm with very strong winds

hurricane lamp /ˈhʌrɪkən læmp/ *noun* a lamp with glass sides to protect the flame from the wind

hurricane lamp

hurried /ˈhʌrid/ *adjective* done very quickly: *I had a hurried breakfast and ran to school.* ▶ **hurriedly** *adverb*: *I dressed hurriedly.*

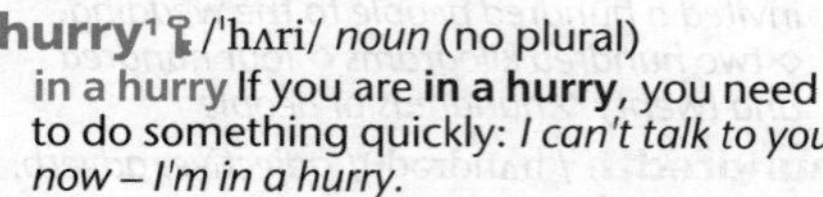

hurry¹ /ˈhʌri/ *noun* (no plural) **in a hurry** If you are **in a hurry**, you need to do something quickly: *I can't talk to you now – I'm in a hurry.*

hurry² /ˈhʌri/ *verb* (**hurries, hurrying, hurried** /ˈhʌrid/, **has hurried**) to move or do something quickly: *We hurried home after school.* **hurry up** to move or do something more quickly: *Hurry up or we'll be late!*

hurt /hɜːt/ *verb* (**hurts, hurting, hurt, has hurt**) **1** to make someone or something feel pain: *I fell and hurt my leg.* ◇ *Did you hurt yourself?* ◇ *You hurt her feelings* (= made her unhappy) *when you said she was stupid.* ◇ *These shoes hurt – they are too small.* **2** to feel pain: *My leg hurts.*

husband /ˈhʌzbənd/ *noun* the man that a woman is married to

husk /hʌsk/ *noun* the hard outside part of nuts and seeds: *coconut husks*

hut /hʌt/ *noun* a small building with one room. **Huts** can be made of mud, bricks, wood or metal.

hydroelectric /ˌhaɪdrəʊɪˈlektrɪk/ *adjective* **1** using the power of water to produce electricity: *a hydroelectric dam* **2** power produced by moving water

hydrogen /ˈhaɪdrədʒən/ *noun* (no plural) a light gas that you cannot see or smell: *Water is made of hydrogen and oxygen.*

hyena /haɪˈiːnə/ *noun* (*plural* **hyenas** *or* **hyena**) a wild dog that has short back legs and longer front legs

hygiene /ˈhaɪdʒiːn/ *noun* (no plural) keeping yourself and things around you clean: *Good hygiene is very important when you are preparing food.* ▶ **hygienic** /haɪˈdʒiːnɪk/ *adjective* clean OPPOSITE **unhygienic**

hymn /hɪm/ *noun* a song that Christians sing in church

hyphen /ˈhaɪfn/ *noun* a mark (-) that you use in writing. It joins words together (for example **left-handed**) or shows that a word continues on the next line. ➲ Look at page A17.

Ii

I, i /aɪ/ *noun* (*plural* **I's, i's** /aɪz/) the ninth letter of the English alphabet: *'Island' begins with an 'I'.*

I /aɪ/ *pronoun* (*plural* **we**) the person who is speaking: *I am Tanzanian.* ◇ *I'll* (= I will) *see you tomorrow.* ◇ *I'm early, aren't I?*

ce /aɪs/ *noun* (no plural) water that has become hard because it is very cold: *Do you want ice in your drink?*

> ❖ **WORD FAMILY**
> **ice iced icy**

ceberg /ˈaɪsbɜːɡ/ *noun* a very big piece of ice in the sea

ce cream /ˌaɪs ˈkriːm/ *noun* very cold sweet food made from milk: *Do you like ice cream? ◇ Two chocolate ice creams, please.* ➲ Picture at **cone**.

ce cube /ˈaɪs kjuːb/ *noun* a small piece of ice that you put in a drink to make it cold

ced /aɪst/ *adjective* **1** very cold: *iced water* **2** covered with **icing**: *iced cakes*

ce lolly /ˌaɪs ˈlɒli/ *noun* (*plural* **ice lollies**) a piece of sweet ice on a stick

cing /ˈaɪsɪŋ/ *noun* (no plural) sweet stuff that you use for covering cakes: *a cake with pink icing*

con /ˈaɪkɒn/ *noun* a small picture on a computer screen: *Click on the icon to start the program.*

ICT /ˌaɪ siː ˈtiː/ *noun* (no plural) the study of how to use computers, the Internet and other technology ℹ **ICT** is short for 'information and communications technology'.

ICU ➲ Look at **intensive care**.

icy /ˈaɪsi/ *adjective* (**icier**, **iciest**) **1** covered with ice: *icy roads* **2** very cold: *an icy wind*

I'd /aɪd/ **1** = I had **2** = I would

ID /ˌaɪ ˈdiː/ *short for* IDENTIFICATION

idea /aɪˈdɪə/ *noun* **1** a plan or new thought: *It was a good idea to bring some water with us. ◇ I've got an idea. Let's go swimming!* **2** a picture in your mind: *The pictures give you a good idea of what Algeria is like. ◇ I've got no idea* (= I do not know) *where she is.* **3** what you believe: *My parents have very strict ideas about who I can play with.*

ideal /aɪˈdiːəl/ *adjective* the best or exactly right: *This is an ideal place for a fire.*

identical /aɪˈdentɪkl/ *adjective* exactly the same: *These two cameras are identical. ◇ identical twins*

identification /aɪˌdentɪfɪˈkeɪʃn/ *noun* (no plural) **1** identifying someone or something: *The identification of bodies after the accident was difficult.* **2** something that shows who you are, for example a passport: *Do you have any identification?* ℹ The short form is **ID**.

identify /aɪˈdentɪfaɪ/ *verb* (**identifies**, **identifying**, **identified** /aɪˈdentɪfaɪd/, **has identified**) to say or know who someone is or what something is: *The police have not identified the dead man yet.*

> ❖ **WORD FAMILY**
> **identify identification identity**

identity /aɪˈdentəti/ *noun* (*plural* **identities**) who or what a person or thing is: *The identity of the killer is not known.*

identity card /aɪˈdentəti kɑːd/ *noun* a card that shows who you are

idiom /ˈɪdiəm/ *noun* a group of words with a special meaning: *The idiom 'break someone's heart' means 'make someone very unhappy'.*

idiomatic /ˌɪdiəˈmætɪk/ *adjective* using language with natural expressions: *She speaks fluent and idiomatic English.*

idiot /ˈɪdiət/ *noun* a person who is stupid or does something silly: *I was an idiot to forget my key.*

idle /ˈaɪdl/ *adjective* A person who is **idle** does not want to work. SAME MEANING **lazy**

idol /ˈaɪdl/ *noun* **1** something that people treat as a god **2** a famous person that people love: *Messi is the idol of millions of football fans.*

i.e. /ˌaɪ ˈiː/ this is what I mean: *You can buy hot drinks, i.e. tea and coffee, in town.* ℹ **i.e.** is usually used in writing.

if /ɪf/ *conjunction* **1** a word that you use to say what is possible or true when another thing happens or is true: *If you press this button, the machine starts. ◇ If you see him, give him this letter. ◇ If your feet were smaller, you could wear my shoes. ◇ If I won the prize, I'd be very proud. ◇ I may see you tomorrow. If not, I'll see you next week.* ➲ Note at **case**. **2** a word that shows a question; whether: *Do you know if Wasike is at home? ◇ She asked me if I wanted to go to the park.* **3** every time; whenever: *If visitors come to our class we sing to them.*
as if in a way that makes you think something: *She looks as if she has been on holiday.*
if only words that show that you want something very much: *If only I could drive!*

ignorance /ˈɪɡnərəns/ *noun* (no plural) not knowing about something: *Her ignorance surprised me.*

ignorant /ˈɪɡnərənt/ *adjective* If you are **ignorant**, you do not know about something: *I'm very ignorant about computers.*

ignore 🔑 /ɪɡˈnɔː(r)/ *verb* (**ignores, ignoring, ignored** /ɪɡˈnɔːd/) to know about someone or something, but to not do anything about it: *He ignored the warning and swam a long way from the shore.* ◇ *I said hello to her, but she just ignored me!*

il- /ɪl/ *prefix* You can add **il-** to the beginning of some words to give them the opposite meaning: *illegal* (= not legal)

I'll /aɪl/ **1** = I shall **2** = I will

ill 🔑 /ɪl/ *adjective* **1** not well; not in good health: *Kamal is in bed because he is ill.* ◇ *I feel too ill to go to school.* ℹ The noun is **illness**. **2** bad: *ill health*

be taken ill become ill: *Chebet was taken ill at school.*

illegal 🔑 /ɪˈliːɡl/ *adjective* not allowed by the law; not legal: *It is illegal to carry a gun.* ℹ **Against the law** means the same.
▸ **illegally** /ɪˈliːɡəli/ *adverb*: *She came into the country illegally.*

illiterate /ɪˈlɪtərət/ *adjective* not able to read or write OPPOSITE **literate**
▸ **illiteracy** /ɪˈlɪtərəsi/ *noun* (no plural) OPPOSITE **literacy**: *The illiteracy rate is still too high in many parts of the world.*

illness 🔑 /ˈɪlnəs/ *noun* (*plural* **illnesses**) being ill: *Cancer is a serious illness.* ◇ *He could not come to the meeting because of illness.*

ill-treat /ˌɪl ˈtriːt/ *verb* (**ill-treats, ill-treating, ill-treated**) to do unkind things to a person or an animal: *This dog has been ill-treated.*

illustrate /ˈɪləstreɪt/ *verb* (**illustrates, illustrating, illustrated**) to add pictures to show something more clearly: *The book is illustrated with colour photographs.*

illustration /ˌɪləˈstreɪʃn/ *noun* a picture: *This dictionary has a lot of illustrations.*

I'm /aɪm/ = I am

im- /ɪm/ *prefix* You can add **im-** to the beginning of some words to give them the opposite meaning: *impatient* (= not patient)

image 🔑 /ˈɪmɪdʒ/ *noun* **1** a picture in people's minds of someone or something: *A lot of people have an image of London as cold and rainy.* **2** a picture on paper or in a mirror: *images of war*

imaginary /ɪˈmædʒɪnəri/ *adjective* not real; only in your mind: *The film is about an imaginary country.*

imagination 🔑 /ɪˌmædʒɪˈneɪʃn/ *noun* (no plural) being able to think of new ideas or make pictures in your mind: *You need a lot of imagination to write stories for children.* ◇ *You didn't really see a ghost – it was just your imagination.*

imagine 🔑 /ɪˈmædʒɪn/ *verb* (**imagines, imagining, imagined** /ɪˈmædʒɪnd/) **1** to make a picture of something in your mind: *Can you imagine what the world was like one million years ago.* ◇ *I closed my eyes and imagined I was lying on a beach.* **2** to think that something will happen or that something is true: *I imagine Boke will come by car.*

imam /ɪˈmɑːm/ *noun* a Muslim religious leader

imitate /ˈɪmɪteɪt/ *verb* (**imitates, imitating, imitated**) to try to do the same as someone or something; to copy someone or something: *He imitated his teacher's voice.*

imitation /ˌɪmɪˈteɪʃn/ *noun* something that you make to look like another thing; a copy: *It's not a diamond, it's only a glass imitation.* ◇ *imitation leather*

immature /ˌɪməˈtjʊə(r)/ *adjective* not like an adult; not fully grown OPPOSITE **mature**

immediate 🔑 /ɪˈmiːdiət/ *adjective* happening at once: *I can't wait – I need an immediate answer.*

immediately 🔑 /ɪˈmiːdiətli/ *adverb* now; at once: *Come here immediately!*

> ❖ **SPELLING**
> Remember! You spell **immediately** with **mm**.

immense /ɪˈmens/ *adjective* very big: *immense problems*

immensely /ɪˈmensli/ *adverb* very or very much: *We enjoyed the match immensely.*

immigrant /ˈɪmɪɡrənt/ *noun* a person who comes to another country to live there: *Many immigrants to East Africa have come from Asia.*

immigration /ˌɪmɪˈɡreɪʃn/ *noun* (no plural) coming to another country to live there

immune /ɪˈmjuːn/ *adjective* safe, so that you cannot get a disease: *You're immune to measles if you've had it before.*
▸ **immunity** /ɪˈmjuːnəti/ *noun* (no plural): *a lack of immunity to malaria*

immunize /ˈɪmjunaɪz/ *verb* (**immunizes, immunizing, immunized** /ˈɪmjunaɪzd/) to make someone safe from a disease: *The children have been immunized against measles.* ➲ Look at **vaccinate**. ▸ **immunization** /ˌɪmjunaɪˈzeɪʃn/ *noun*: *a programme of immunization*

impala /ɪmˈpɑːlə/ *noun* a kind of **antelope** with curly horns

impatience /ɪmˈpeɪʃns/ *noun* (no plural) not being calm when you are waiting: *He showed his impatience by looking at his watch five or six times.* OPPOSITE **patience**

impatient /ɪmˈpeɪʃnt/ *adjective* If you are impatient, you do not want to wait for something: *Don't be so impatient! The bus will be here soon.* OPPOSITE **patient** ▸ **impatiently** *adverb*: *'Hurry up!' she said impatiently.*

imply /ɪmˈplaɪ/ *verb* (**implies, implying, implied** /ɪmˈplaɪd/, **has implied**) to mean something without saying it: *He asked if I had any work to do. He was implying that I was lazy.*

impolite /ˌɪmpəˈlaɪt/ *adjective* rude; not polite OPPOSITE **polite**

import /ɪmˈpɔːt/ *verb* (**imports, importing, imported**) to buy things from another country and bring them into your country: *Britain imports coffee from Kenya.* OPPOSITE **export** ▸ **import** /ˈɪmpɔːt/ *noun* a thing that is imported OPPOSITE **export** ▸ **importer** /ɪmˈpɔːtə(r)/ *noun* a person, company or country that imports things OPPOSITE **exporter**

importance /ɪmˈpɔːtns/ *noun* (no plural) being important; value: *Oil is of great importance to industry.*

important /ɪmˈpɔːtnt/ *adjective* **1** If something is important, you must do, have or think about it: *It is important to sleep well the night before an exam.* ◇ *I think that happiness is more important than money.* **2** powerful or special: *The president is a very important person.* OPPOSITE **unimportant**

impossible /ɪmˈpɒsəbl/ *adjective* If something is impossible, you cannot do it, or it cannot happen: *It is impossible to finish this work by five o'clock.* ◇ *The house was impossible to find.* OPPOSITE **possible** ▸ **impossibility** /ɪmˌpɒsəˈbɪləti/ *noun* (*plural* **impossibilities**): *I can't lend you 100 000 shillings. It's an impossibility!*

impress /ɪmˈpres/ *verb* (**impresses, impressing, impressed** /ɪmˈprest/) to make someone have good feelings or thoughts about you or about something that is yours: *He was so impressed by our performance that he asked us to sing on the radio.*

impression /ɪmˈpreʃn/ *noun* feelings or thoughts you have about someone or something: *My first impressions of the city were not very good.* ◇ *What's your impression of the new teacher?*
make an impression to give someone a certain idea of yourself: *He made a good impression on his first day at school.*

impressive /ɪmˈpresɪv/ *adjective* If something is impressive, people admire it, for example because it is very good or very big: *an impressive building* ◇ *Your work is very impressive.*

imprison /ɪmˈprɪzn/ *verb* (**imprisons, imprisoning, imprisoned** /ɪmˈprɪznd/) to put someone in prison: *He was imprisoned for armed robbery.* ▸ **imprisonment** /ɪmˈprɪznmənt/ *noun* (no plural) being in prison: *two years' imprisonment*

improbable /ɪmˈprɒbəbl/ *adjective* not likely to happen or to be true: *Her story seems very improbable.* OPPOSITE **probable**

improve /ɪmˈpruːv/ *verb* (**improves, improving, improved** /ɪmˈpruːvd/) to become better or make something better: *Your writing has improved a lot this year.* ◇ *You must improve your spelling.*

improvement /ɪmˈpruːvmənt/ *noun* a change that makes something better than it was before: *There has been a big improvement in Boke's work.*

impulse /ˈɪmpʌls/ *noun* a sudden strong wish to do something: *She felt an impulse to run away.*

in[1] /ɪn/ *adverb* **1** to a place, from outside: *I opened the door and went in.* **2** at home or at work: *'Can I speak to Nafula, please?' 'I'm sorry – she's not in.'* OPPOSITE **out**

in[2] /ɪn/ *preposition* **1** a word that shows where: *Entebbe is in Uganda.* ◇ *He put his hand in the water.* ◇ *Njoki is in bed.* **2** a word that shows when: *My birthday is in May.* ◇ *He started school in 2012.* ➲ Look at page A11. **3** a word that shows how long;

after: *I'll be ready in ten minutes.* **4** a word that shows how someone or something is: *This room is in a mess.* ◇ *Tanei was in tears* (= she was crying). **5** a word that shows what clothes someone is wearing: *He was dressed in a suit.* **6** a word that shows what way, what language, etc: *Write your name in capital letters.* ◇ *They were speaking in French.* **7** a word that shows someone's job: *He's in the army.* **8** making something: *There are 100 centimetres in a metre.* ◇ *Sit in a circle.*

in- /ɪn/ *prefix* You can add **in-** to the beginning of some words to give them the opposite meaning: *incomplete* (= not complete)

inability /ˌɪnəˈbɪləti/ *noun* (no plural) not being able to do something: *He has an inability to talk about his problems.*

inaccurate /ɪnˈækjərət/ *adjective* not correct; with mistakes in it: *The report in the newspaper was inaccurate.* OPPOSITE **accurate**

inadequate /ɪnˈædɪkwət/ *adjective* not as much as you need, or not good enough: *These tyres are inadequate for this road.* ◇ *inadequate food* OPPOSITE **adequate**

inappropriate /ˌɪnəˈprəupriət/ *adjective* not suitable: *That shirt is rather inappropriate for the occasion.* OPPOSITE **appropriate**

inbox /ˈɪnbɒks/ *noun* (*plural* **inboxes** /ˈɪnbɒksɪz/) the place on a computer where you can see new email messages

incapable /ɪnˈkeɪpəbl/ *adjective* not able to do something: *He's incapable of lying.* OPPOSITE **capable**

inch /ɪntʃ/ *noun* (*plural* **inches**) a measure of length (= 2.54 centimetres). There are twelve inches in a **foot**: *I am five foot six inches tall.* ◇ *a twelve-inch ruler* ➲ Look at **foot**.

incident /ˈɪnsɪdənt/ *noun* something that happens: *Nduku told us about a funny incident at school, when her teacher fell off the chair!*

incidentally /ɪnsɪˈdentəli/ *adverb* a word that you say when you are going to talk about something different: *Juma helped us to move the table. Incidentally, he has a new car.*

inclined /ɪnˈklaɪnd/ *adjective*
be inclined to **1** to be likely to do something: *I don't want to tell Robi about this – she's inclined to get angry.* **2** to want to do something: *I'm inclined to agree with you.*

include ⚷ /ɪnˈkluːd/ *verb* (**includes, including, included**) **1** to have someone or something as one part of the whole: *The price of the room includes breakfast.* **2** to make someone or something part of a group: *Have you included tea on the list of things to buy?* ➲ Look at **exclude**.

including ⚷ /ɪnˈkluːdɪŋ/ *preposition* with; if you count: *There were five people in the car, including the driver.* ➲ Look at **excluding**.

inclusive /ɪnˈkluːsɪv/ *adjective* including everything; including particular things: *The price is inclusive of tax.*

income /ˈɪnkʌm/ *noun* all the money that someone receives for their work, business, etc: *What was your income last year?*

income tax /ˈɪnkʌm tæks/ *noun* (no plural) the money that a person pays to the government from the money that they earn

incompetent /ɪnˈkɒmpɪtənt/ *adjective* not good at something: *He's completely incompetent at cookery.* OPPOSITE **competent** ▸ **incompetence** /ɪnˈkɒmpɪtəns/ *noun* (no plural)

incomplete /ˌɪnkəmˈpliːt/ *adjective* not finished; with parts missing: *This list is incomplete.* OPPOSITE **complete**

inconsiderate /ˌɪnkənˈsɪdərət/ *adjective* A person who is **inconsiderate** does not think or care about other people and their feelings: *It's inconsiderate of you to make so much noise when people are asleep.* OPPOSITE **considerate**

inconsistent /ˌɪnkənˈsɪstənt/ *adjective* not always the same: *She's very inconsistent – sometimes her work is good and sometimes it's poor.* OPPOSITE **consistent**

inconvenience /ˌɪnkənˈviːniəns/ *noun* (no plural) problems or difficulty: *The repairs to the road caused a lot of inconvenience to drivers.* ◇ *We apologize for any inconvenience.*

inconvenient /ˌɪnkənˈviːniənt/ *adjective* If something is **inconvenient**, it gives you problems or difficulty: *She came at an inconvenient time – I was just going out.* OPPOSITE **convenient**

incorrect /ˌɪnkəˈrekt/ *adjective* not correct; not right or true: *It is incorrect to say that two plus two equals five.* ▸ **incorrectly** *adverb*: *The name was spelt incorrectly.*

increase ⚷ /ɪnˈkriːs/ *verb* (**increases, increasing, increased** /ɪnˈkriːst/) to become bigger or more; to make something bigger or more: *The number of women who go to work has increased.* OPPOSITE **decrease** ▸ **increase** /ˈɪnkriːs/ *noun*: *There has been an increase in road accidents.* ◇ *a price increase* OPPOSITE **decrease** ▸ **increasingly** /ɪnˈkriːsɪŋli/ *adverb* more and more

incredible /ɪnˈkredəbl/ *adjective* **1** surprising and very difficult to believe: *Juma told us an incredible story about his grandmother catching a thief.* **2** very great: *She earns an incredible amount of money.* ▸ **incredibly** /ɪnˈkredəbli/ *adverb* extremely: *He's incredibly clever.*

indeed 🔑 /ɪnˈdiːd/ *adverb* **1** a word that makes 'very' stronger: *Thank you very much indeed.* ◇ *She's very happy indeed.* **2** really; certainly: *'Did you have a good holiday?' 'I did indeed.'*

indefinite /ɪnˈdefɪnət/ *adjective* not definite; not clear or certain: *They are staying for an indefinite length of time.*

indefinitely /ɪnˈdefɪnətli/ *adverb* for a long time, perhaps for ever: *I can't wait indefinitely.*

independence /ˌɪndɪˈpendəns/ *noun* (no plural) being free from another person, thing or country: *Kenya gained full independence in 1963.*

independent 🔑 /ˌɪndɪˈpendənt/ *adjective* **1** not controlled by another person, thing or country: *Zimbabwe has been independent since 1980.* **2** A person who is independent does not need help: *She lives alone now and she is very independent.*

> ❖ **SPELLING**
>
> Remember! You spell **independent** with three **e**s.

index /ˈɪndeks/ *noun* (*plural* **indexes**) a list of words from A to Z at the end of a book. It tells you what things are in the book and where you can find them.

indicate /ˈɪndɪkeɪt/ *verb* (**indicates, indicating, indicated**) **1** to show something, usually by pointing with your finger: *Can you indicate your school on this map?* **2** to give a sign about something: *Black clouds indicate that it's going to rain.* **3** to show that your car is going to turn by using a light: *You should indicate left now.*

indication /ˌɪndɪˈkeɪʃn/ *noun* something that shows something: *He gave no indication that he was angry.* SAME MEANING **sign**

indicator /ˈɪndɪkeɪtə(r)/ *noun* a light on a car that shows that it is going to turn left or right

indignant /ɪnˈdɪɡnənt/ *adjective* angry because someone has done or said something that you do not like or agree with: *She was indignant when I said she was lazy.* ▸ **indignantly** *adverb*: *'I'm not late,' he said indignantly.* ▸ **indignation** /ˌɪndɪɡˈneɪʃn/ *noun* (no plural) a feeling of anger and surprise

indirect /ˌɪndəˈrekt/ *adjective* not straight or direct: *We came an indirect way to avoid the city centre.* ▸ **indirectly** *adverb*: *The new rules affect us all, directly or indirectly.*

indirect speech = **reported speech**

indiscipline /ɪnˈdɪsɪplɪn/ *noun* (no plural) bad behaviour in a group of people: *Parents complained of indiscipline in schools.*

individual[1] 🔑 /ˌɪndɪˈvɪdʒuəl/ *adjective* **1** for only one person or thing: *He had individual lessons to help him learn to read.* **2** single and different: *Each individual country has its own flag.* ▸ **individually** /ˌɪndɪˈvɪdʒuəli/ *adverb* separately; alone; not together: *The teacher spoke to each pupil individually.*

individual[2] /ˌɪndɪˈvɪdʒuəl/ *noun* one person: *Teachers must treat each child as an individual.*

indoor /ˈɪndɔː(r)/ *adjective* done or used inside a building: *an indoor swimming pool* ◇ *indoor games* OPPOSITE **outdoor**

indoors /ˌɪnˈdɔːz/ *adverb* in or into a building: *Let's go indoors.* OPPOSITE **outdoors**

industrial /ɪnˈdʌstriəl/ *adjective* **1** of or about making things in factories: *industrial machines* **2** with a lot of factories: *This is an important industrial centre.*

industry 🔑 /ˈɪndəstri/ *noun* **1** (no plural) the work of making things in factories: *Is there much industry in your country?* **2** (*plural* **industries**) all the companies that make the same thing: *the textile industry*

inefficient /ˌɪnɪˈfɪʃnt/ *adjective* A person or thing that is **inefficient** does not work well or in the best way: *This machine is very old and inefficient.* OPPOSITE **efficient**

inevitable /ɪnˈevɪtəbl/ *adjective* If something is **inevitable**, it will certainly happen: *The accident was inevitable – he was running too fast.*

▶ **inevitably** /ɪnˈevɪtəbli/ *adverb*: *New buildings inevitably cost a lot of money.*

inexpensive /ˌɪnɪksˈpensɪv/ *adjective* Something that is **inexpensive** does not cost a lot of money: *an inexpensive watch* SAME MEANING **cheap** OPPOSITE **expensive**

inexperienced /ˌɪnɪkˈspɪəriənst/ *adjective* If you are **inexperienced**, you do not know about something because you have not done it many times before: *a young inexperienced cyclist* OPPOSITE **experienced**

infect /ɪnˈfekt/ *verb* (**infects, infecting, infected**) **1** to give a disease to someone: *He infected the other children in the class with his cold.* **2** to make a **virus** (= a problem with a computer that stops it working) spread to another computer: *My computer has been infected with a virus.*

infected /ɪnˈfektɪd/ *adjective* full of small living things (called **germs**) that can make you ill: *Clean that cut or it could become infected.*

infection 🔑 /ɪnˈfekʃn/ *noun* a disease: *Kirezi has an ear infection.*

infectious /ɪnˈfekʃəs/ *adjective* An **infectious** disease goes easily from one person to another. ➲ Look at **contagious**.

inferior /ɪnˈfɪəriə(r)/ *adjective* not as good or important as another person or thing: *Soila's work is so good that she makes the other students feel inferior.* OPPOSITE **superior**

infertile /ɪnˈfɜːtaɪl/ *adjective* where plants do not grow well: *infertile soil* OPPOSITE **fertile**

infinite /ˈɪnfɪnət/ *adjective* with no end; too much or too many to count or measure: *There is an infinite number of stars in the sky.*

infinitive /ɪnˈfɪnətɪv/ *noun* the simple form of a verb: *'Eat', 'go' and 'play' are all infinitives.*

inflate /ɪnˈfleɪt/ *verb* (**inflates, inflating, inflated**) to fill something with air or gas to make it bigger: *He inflated the tyre.*

> ❖ **SPEAKING**
>
> It is more usual to say **blow up** or **pump up**.

inflation /ɪnˈfleɪʃn/ *noun* (no plural) a general rise in prices in a country: *The government is trying to control inflation.*

influence¹ 🔑 /ˈɪnfluəns/ *noun* **1** (no plural) the power to change what someone believes or does: *Television has a strong influence on people.* **2** (*plural* **influences**) a person or thing that can change someone or something: *Deng's new friend is a good influence on him.*

influence² /ˈɪnfluəns/ *verb* (**influences, influencing, influenced** /ˈɪnfluənst/) to change someone or something; to make someone do what you want: *She is easily influenced by her friends.*

inform 🔑 /ɪnˈfɔːm/ *verb* (**informs, informing, informed** /ɪnˈfɔːmd/) to tell something to someone: *You should inform the police of the accident.* ❶ The noun is **information**.

informal 🔑 /ɪnˈfɔːml/ *adjective* You use informal language or behave in an informal way in situations that are friendly and easy, not serious or important, and with people that you know well. You do not usually use informal words when you write (except in letters to people that you know well): *I wear uniform when I'm at school, but more informal clothes at weekends.* ◇ *an informal letter* OPPOSITE **formal** ▶ **informally** /ɪnˈfɔːməli/ *adverb*: *The students talked informally to each other.*

information 🔑 /ˌɪnfəˈmeɪʃn/ *noun* (no plural) what you tell someone; facts: *Can you give me some information about buses to Meru?* ➲ Look at the verb **inform**.

> ❖ **GRAMMAR**
>
> Be careful! You cannot say 'an information'. You can say 'some information' or 'a piece of information': *She gave me an interesting piece of information.*

infrequent /ɪnˈfriːkwənt/ *adjective* not happening often: *We only make infrequent visits to the city as it is so far away.* ▶ **infrequently** /ɪnˈfriːkwəntli/ *adverb*: *I see them very infrequently.*

infusion /ɪnˈfjuːʒn/ *noun* **1** putting a substance into a person's body because they are ill **2** a drink or medicine that you make by leaving **herbs** (= types of plant), etc. in hot water

ingredient /ɪnˈgriːdiənt/ *noun* one of the things that you put in when you make something to eat: *The ingredients for this cake are flour, butter, sugar and eggs.*

inhabitant /ɪnˈhæbɪtənt/ *noun* a person or an animal that lives in a place: *The town has 30 000 inhabitants.*

inhabited /ɪn'hæbɪtɪd/ *adjective* **be inhabited** to have people or animals living there: *The South Pole is inhabited by penguins.*

inhale /ɪn'heɪl/ *verb* (**inhales, inhaling, inhaled** /ɪn'heɪld/) to breathe in air, smoke, etc: *She closed her eyes and inhaled the morning air.*

inherit /ɪn'herɪt/ *verb* (**inherits, inheriting, inherited**) to receive something from someone who has died: *Moraa inherited some money from her grandmother.* ▸ **inheritance** /ɪn'herɪtəns/ *noun* something that you inherit

initial /ɪ'nɪʃl/ *adjective* first: *Our initial idea was to walk, but then we decided to go by bus.* ▸ **initially** /ɪ'nɪʃəli/ *adverb* in the beginning; at first: *Initially I hated maths, but now I love it!*

initials /ɪ'nɪʃlz/ *noun* (plural) the first letters of your names: *Juma Mwangola's initials are J. M.*

initiate /ɪ'nɪʃieɪt/ *verb* (**initiates, initiating, initiated**) to make something begin or someone begin something for the first time: *to initiate peace talks* ◇ *His uncle initiated him into the pleasures of sailing.*

inject /ɪn'dʒekt/ *verb* (**injects, injecting, injected**) to use a special needle to put a drug into a person's body ▸ **injection** /ɪn'dʒekʃn/ *noun*: *The doctor gave the baby an injection.*

injure /'ɪndʒə(r)/ *verb* (**injures, injuring, injured** /'ɪndʒəd/) to hurt someone or something: *She injured her arm when she was climbing a tree.* ◇ *Pembe was injured in a car accident.* ▸ **injured** /'ɪndʒəd/ *adjective*: *The injured woman was taken to hospital.*

injury 🔑 /'ɪndʒəri/ *noun* (*plural* **injuries**) damage to the body of a person or an animal: *He had serious head injuries.*

injury time /'ɪndʒəri taɪm/ *noun* (no plural) time added at the end of a game of football, etc. when there has been time lost because of injuries to players

injustice /ɪn'dʒʌstɪs/ *noun* (no plural) not being fair or right: *People are angry about the injustice of the new tax.* OPPOSITE **justice**

ink /ɪŋk/ *noun* a coloured liquid for writing and printing: *The words on this page are printed in black and blue ink.*

inland /'ɪnlənd/ *adjective* in the middle of a country, not near the sea: *an inland lake* ▸ **inland** /ˌɪn'lænd/ *adverb* in or towards the middle of a country

inner /'ɪnə(r)/ *adjective* of the inside; in the centre: *the inner city* OPPOSITE **outer**

innocent /'ɪnəsnt/ *adjective* If you are **innocent**, you have not done wrong: *The police say Juma stole the money, but I think he's innocent.* OPPOSITE **guilty** ▸ **innocence** /'ɪnəsns/ *noun* (no plural): *The prisoner's family are sure of her innocence.* OPPOSITE **guilt**

inoculate /ɪ'nɒkjuleɪt/ *verb* (**inoculates, inoculating, inoculated**) to protect someone from a disease by giving them an **injection** (= putting a substance under their skin with a needle): *The children were inoculated against measles.* ▸ **inoculation** /ɪˌnɒkju'leɪʃn/ *noun*: *a course of inoculations*

inpatient /'ɪnpeɪʃnt/ *noun* a person who stays in a hospital for treatment: *Moraa was an inpatient at Webuye Hospital for two weeks.*

inquire, inquiry = **enquire, enquiry**

insane /ɪn'seɪn/ *adjective* mad OPPOSITE **sane**

insects

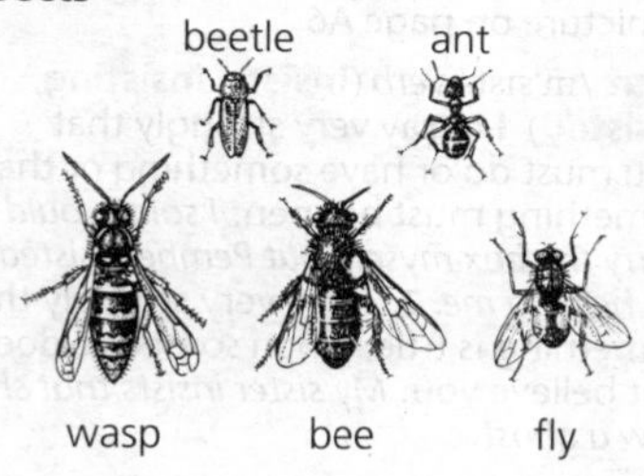

insect 🔑 /'ɪnsekt/ *noun* a very small animal that has six legs: *Ants, flies, butterflies and beetles are all insects.*

insecticide /ɪn'sektɪsaɪd/ *noun* a substance that is used to kill insects on crops

insecure /ˌɪnsɪ'kjʊə(r)/ *adjective* **1** not safe or firm: *An actor's job is very insecure.* **2** worried and not sure about yourself: *Since their father left, the children have felt very insecure.* ▸ **insecurity** /ˌɪnsɪ'kjʊərəti/ *noun* (no plural): *She had feelings of insecurity.*

insensitive /ɪn'sensətɪv/ *adjective* **1** not knowing or caring how other people feel: *That was a very insensitive remark.*

2 not feeling something; not easy to hurt or damage: *He seems insensitive to pain.* OPPOSITE **sensitive**

insert /ɪnˈsɜːt/ *verb* (**inserts, inserting, inserted**) to put something into something or between two things: *Insert the key into the lock.*

inside[1] /ɪnˈsaɪd/ *noun* the part near the middle of something: *The inside of a coconut is white and the outside is brown.* ◇ *He did not see the inside of the house before he bought it.* OPPOSITE **outside**

inside out with the wrong side on the outside: *Your jumper is inside out!*

inside out

inside[2] /ˈɪnsaɪd/ *adjective* in or near the middle: *the inside pages of a newspaper* OPPOSITE **outside**

inside[3] /ɪnˈsaɪd/ *preposition, adverb* in or to the inside of something: *What's inside the box?* ◇ *It's too hot – let's go inside* (= into the building). OPPOSITE **outside**
➲ picture on page A6

insist /ɪnˈsɪst/ *verb* (**insists, insisting, insisted**) **1** to say very strongly that you must do or have something or that something must happen: *I said I could carry the box myself, but Pembe insisted on helping me.* **2** to say very strongly that something is true, when someone does not believe you: *My sister insists that she saw a ghost.*

inspect /ɪnˈspekt/ *verb* (**inspects, inspecting, inspected**) **1** to look at something carefully: *He inspected the car before he bought it.* **2** to visit a place or a group of people to see that work is done well: *The kitchens are inspected every week.* ▶ **inspection** /ɪnˈspekʃn/ *noun*: *The police made an inspection of the house.*

inspector /ɪnˈspektə(r)/ *noun* **1** a person whose job is to see that things are done correctly: *On the bus, the inspector asked to see my ticket.* ◇ *a factory inspector* **2** a police officer

inspiration /ˌɪnspəˈreɪʃn/ *noun* a person or thing that gives you ideas which help you do something good, for example write or paint: *The beauty of the mountains is an inspiration to many artists.*

inspire /ɪnˈspaɪə(r)/ *verb* (**inspires, inspiring, inspired** /ɪnˈspaɪəd/) **1** to give someone ideas that help them do something good, for example write or paint: *His wife inspired him to write this poem.* **2** to make someone feel or think something: *Her words inspired us all with hope.*

install /ɪnˈstɔːl/ *verb* (**installs, installing, installed** /ɪnˈstɔːld/) to put a new thing in its place so it is ready to use: *They installed a water tank in the school.*

instalment /ɪnˈstɔːlmənt/ *noun* **1** one part of a long story on radio or television, or in a magazine: *Did you read the last instalment?* **2** a part of the cost of something that you pay each week, month, etc: *She's paying for her new car in twelve monthly instalments.*

instance /ˈɪnstəns/ *noun* an example: *There have been many instances of forest fires this year.*

for instance as an example: *There are many things to see in Kenya – for instance Mount Kenya and Amboseli National Park.*

instant[1] /ˈɪnstənt/ *adjective* **1** that happens very quickly; immediate: *The film was an instant success.* **2** quick and easy to prepare: *an instant meal* ▶ **instantly** *adverb* immediately; at once: *I asked him a question and he replied instantly.*

instant[2] /ˈɪnstənt/ *noun* a very short time; a moment: *She thought for an instant before she answered.*

instant coffee /ˌɪnstənt ˈkɒfi/ *noun* (no plural) coffee that you make quickly with coffee powder and hot water

instead /ɪnˈsted/ *adverb* in the place of someone or something: *We haven't got any coffee. Would you like tea instead?* ◇ *Teta can't go to the meeting so I will go instead.* ▶ **instead of** /ɪnˈsted əv/ *preposition* in the place of: *He's been playing football all afternoon instead of studying.* ◇ *Can you come at 7.30 instead of 8.00?*

instinct /ˈɪnstɪŋkt/ *noun* something that makes people and animals do certain things without thinking or learning about them: *Birds build their nests by instinct.* ▶ **instinctive** /ɪnˈstɪŋktɪv/ *adjective*: *Animals have an instinctive fear of fire.*

institute /ˈɪnstɪtjuːt/ *noun* a group of people who meet to study or talk about a special thing; the building where they meet: *the Institute of Science*

nstitution /ˌɪnstɪˈtjuːʃn/ *noun* a big building like a bank, hospital, prison or school, and all the people in it: *Makerere University is one of the largest institutions in East Africa.*

nstruct /ɪnˈstrʌkt/ *verb* (**instructs**, **instructing**, **instructed**) **1** to tell someone what they must do: *He instructed the driver to take him to the airport.* **2** to teach someone: *She instructed me in how to use the computer.*

nstruction /ɪnˈstrʌkʃn/ *noun* **1** (*plural* **instructions**) words that tell you what you must do or how to do something: *Read the instructions on the box before you make the cake.* **2** (no plural) teaching or being taught something: *driving instruction*

nstructor /ɪnˈstrʌktə(r)/ *noun* a person who teaches you how to do something: *a driving instructor*

instrument /ˈɪnstrəmənt/ *noun* **1** a thing that you use for doing a special job: *A telescope is an instrument used for looking at things that are a long way away.* ◇ *medical instruments* (= used by doctors) **2** a thing that you use for playing music: *Guitars and drums are musical instruments.* ◇ *What instrument do you play?*

insufficient /ˌɪnsəˈfɪʃnt/ *adjective* not enough: *We had insufficient time for the test.* OPPOSITE **sufficient** ❶ We usually use **not enough**: *We didn't have enough time for the test.*

insult /ɪnˈsʌlt/ *verb* (**insults**, **insulting**, **insulted**) to be rude to someone: *She insulted my brother by saying he was ugly.* ▶ **insult** /ˈɪnsʌlt/ *noun* something rude that you say or do to someone: *The boys shouted insults at each other.*

insurance /ɪnˈʃɔːrəns/ *noun* (no plural) an agreement where you pay money to a company so that it will give you a lot of money if something bad happens: *When I crashed my car, the insurance paid for the repairs.*

insure /ɪnˈʃɔː(r)/ *verb* (**insures**, **insuring**, **insured** /ɪnˈʃɔːd/) to pay money to a company, so that it will give you money if something bad happens: *Have you insured your house against fire?* ◇ *My car isn't insured.*

intelligence /ɪnˈtelɪdʒəns/ *noun* (no plural) being able to think, learn and understand quickly and well: *He is a man of great intelligence.* ◇ *an intelligence test*

intelligent /ɪnˈtelɪdʒənt/ *adjective* able to think, learn and understand quickly and well: *Their daughter is very intelligent.*

intend /ɪnˈtend/ *verb* (**intends**, **intending**, **intended**) to plan to do something: *When do you intend to go to Addis Ababa?*
be intended for someone or **something** to be for someone or something: *This dictionary is intended for elementary learners of English.*

> ❖ **WORD FAMILY**
> **intend intention**
> **intentional**: OPPOSITE **unintentional**

intense /ɪnˈtens/ *adjective* very great or strong: *intense pain* ◇ *The heat from the fire was intense.*

intensive care /ɪnˌtensɪv ˈkeə(r)/ *noun* (no plural) **1** special care for people in hospital who are very ill: *She needed intensive care for several days.*
2 (also **intensive care unit**) (also **ICU** /ˌaɪ siː ˈjuː/) the part of a hospital that provides **intensive care**

intention /ɪnˈtenʃn/ *noun* what you plan to do: *They have no intention of getting married.*

intentional /ɪnˈtenʃənl/ *adjective* that you want and plan to do, and do not do by mistake: *I'm sorry I upset you – it wasn't intentional!* ▶ **intentionally** /ɪnˈtenʃənəli/ *adverb*: *They broke the window intentionally – it wasn't an accident.*

inter- /ˈɪntə(r)/ *prefix* between: *an inter-school football competition* ◇ *an international festival*

interactive /ˌɪntərˈæktɪv/ *adjective* If something is **interactive**, it allows information to be passed in both directions between a computer and the person who uses it: *The new classrooms have interactive whiteboards.*

interest[1] /ˈɪntrəst/ *noun* **1** (no plural) wanting to know or learn about someone or something: *He read the story with interest.* **2** (*plural* **interests**) something that you like doing or learning about: *His interests are computers and rock music.*
3 (no plural) the extra money that you pay back if you borrow money or that you receive if you put money in a bank: *Interest rates have risen by 1%.*
take an interest in someone or **something** want to know about someone or something: *He takes no interest in politics.*

interest² 🔑 /ˈɪntrəst/ *verb* (**interests, interesting, interested**) to make someone want to know more: *Fashion doesn't interest her.*

interested 🔑 /ˈɪntrəstɪd/ *adjective* If you are interested in someone or something, you want to know more about them: *Are you interested in cars?* OPPOSITE **uninterested**

> ❖ **interested** or **interesting**?
>
> If you enjoy something or want to know more about it, you are **interested**: *He's very interested in music.*
>
> The person or thing that makes you feel like this is **interesting**: *I'm reading such an interesting book.*

interesting 🔑 /ˈɪntrəstɪŋ/ *adjective* A person or thing that is interesting makes you want to know more about them or it: *This book is very interesting.* ◇ *That's an interesting idea!* OPPOSITE **boring**

interfere /ˌɪntəˈfɪə(r)/ *verb* (**interferes, interfering, interfered** /ˌɪntəˈfɪəd/) **1** to try to do something with or for someone, when they do not want your help: *Don't interfere! Let Pembe decide what he wants to do.* **2** to stop something from being done well: *His interest in football often interferes with his studies.* **3** to change or touch something without asking if you can: *Who's been interfering with the clock? It's stopped.* ▶ **interference** /ˌɪntəˈfɪərəns/ *noun*: *Go away! I don't want any interference when I'm working!*

interior /ɪnˈtɪəriə(r)/ *noun* the inside part: *We painted the interior of the house white.* ▶ **interior** *adjective*: *interior walls* OPPOSITE **exterior**

interjection /ˌɪntəˈdʒekʃn/ *noun* a word or phrase that you use because you are surprised, angry, etc: *'Oh!' and 'Hurray!' are interjections.* SAME MEANING **exclamation**

intermediate /ˌɪntəˈmiːdiət/ *adjective* that comes between two people or things; in the middle: *She's in an intermediate class.*

internal /ɪnˈtɜːnl/ *adjective* of or on the inside: *He has internal injuries* (= inside his body). OPPOSITE **external** ▶ **internally** /ɪnˈtɜːnəli/ *adverb* on the inside

international 🔑 /ˌɪntəˈnæʃnəl/ *adjective* between different countries: *an international football match* ◇ *an international flight*

the Internet 🔑 /ði ˈɪntənet/ (also **the Net**) *noun* (no plural) the international system of computers that makes it possible for you to see information from all around the world on your computer and to send information to other computers: *You can find out almost anything on the Internet.* ◇ *Do you have Internet access?*

interpret /ɪnˈtɜːprɪt/ *verb* (**interprets, interpreting, interpreted**) to say in one language what someone has said in another language: *I can't speak Arabic – can you interpret for me?*

interpreter /ɪnˈtɜːprɪtə(r)/ *noun* a person whose job is to say in one language what someone has said in another language: *The President had an interpreter when he went to China.*

interrupt 🔑 /ˌɪntəˈrʌpt/ *verb* (**interrupts, interrupting, interrupted**) **1** to stop someone speaking or doing something by saying or doing something yourself: *Please don't interrupt me when I'm speaking.* **2** to stop something for a time: *The war interrupted travel between the two countries.* ▶ **interruption** /ˌɪntəˈrʌpʃn/ *noun*: *I can't do my homework here. There are too many interruptions.*

interval /ˈɪntəvl/ *noun* a short time between two parts of a play or concert: *We bought drinks in the interval.*

interview¹ 🔑 /ˈɪntəvjuː/ *noun* **1** a meeting when someone asks you questions to see if you are suitable for a job, a course of study at college, etc: *She's got an interview for a new job tomorrow.* **2** a meeting when someone answers questions for a newspaper or for a television or radio programme: *There was an interview with the president on TV last night.*

interview² /ˈɪntəvjuː/ *verb* (**interviews, interviewing, interviewed** /ˈɪntəvjuːd/) to ask someone questions in an interview: *They interviewed six people for the job.* ▶ **interviewer**: *The interviewer asked the actor about his new film.*

into 🔑 /ˈɪntə; ˈɪntu; ˈɪntuː/ *preposition* **1** to the middle or the inside of something: *Come into the house.* ◇ *I went into town.* ◇ *He fell into the river.* OPPOSITE **out of** ➲ picture on page A7 **2** a word that shows how someone or something changes: *When it is very cold, water changes into ice.* ◇ *They made the room into a bedroom.* **3** against something: *The car crashed into a tree.* **4** a word that you use when you

divide a number: *4 into 12 is 3.*
be into something to like something; to be interested in something: *What sort of music are you into?*

intolerant /ɪnˈtɒlərənt/ *adjective* If you are **intolerant**, you are not able to let people do things that you may not like or understand: *She is very intolerant of young children.* OPPOSITE **tolerant** ▸ **intolerance** /ɪnˈtɒlərəns/ *noun* (no plural): *religious intolerance* OPPOSITE **tolerance**

intravenous /ˌɪntrəˈviːnəs/ *adjective* medicine going into someone's **vein** (= one of the small tubes in the body) because they are ill: *intravenous fluids*
ℹ The short form is **IV**.

introduce 🔑 /ˌɪntrəˈdjuːs/ *verb* (**introduces, introducing, introduced** /ˌɪntrəˈdjuːst/) **1** to bring people together for the first time and tell each of them the name of the other: *She introduced me to her brother.* **2** to bring in something new: *This law was introduced in 2013.*
introduce yourself to tell someone your name: *He introduced himself to me.*

introduction 🔑 /ˌɪntrəˈdʌkʃn/ *noun* **1** (no plural) bringing in something new: *the introduction of computers into schools* **2** (*plural* **introductions**) bringing people together to meet each other: *Introductions were made and the talks began.* **3** (*plural* **introductions**) a piece of writing at the beginning of a book that tells you about the book: *Have you read the introduction?*

invade /ɪnˈveɪd/ *verb* (**invades, invading, invaded**) to go into another country to attack it: *They invaded the country with tanks and guns.* ▸ **invader** /ɪnˈveɪdə(r)/ *noun* a person who **invades**

invalid /ˈɪnvəlɪd/ *noun* a person who is very ill and needs another person to look after them: *She has been an invalid since the accident.*

invaluable /ɪnˈvæljuəbl/ *adjective* very useful: *Your help was invaluable.*

invariably /ɪnˈveəriəbli/ *adverb* almost always: *He invariably arrives late.*

invasion /ɪnˈveɪʒn/ *noun* a time when an army from one country goes into another country to attack it: *the invasion of Lebanon*

invent 🔑 /ɪnˈvent/ *verb* (**invents, inventing, invented**) **1** to make or think of something for the first time: *Who invented the bicycle?* **2** to tell something that is not true: *She invented a story about where she was last night.* ▸ **inventor** /ɪnˈventə(r)/ *noun* a person who makes or thinks of something new

invention /ɪnˈvenʃn/ *noun* **1** (*plural* **inventions**) a thing that someone has made for the first time **2** (no plural) inventing something: *The invention of the telephone changed the world.*

inverted commas /ɪnˌvɜːtɪd ˈkɒməz/ = **quotation marks**

invest /ɪnˈvest/ *verb* (**invests, investing, invested**) to give money to a business or bank so that you will get more money back: *He invested all his money in the company.* ▸ **investment** /ɪnˈvestmənt/ *noun* **investing** money; money that you **invest**: *an investment of one million shillings*

investigate 🔑 /ɪnˈvestɪgeɪt/ *verb* (**investigates, investigating, investigated**) to try to find out about something: *The police are investigating the murder.* ▸ **investigation** /ɪnˌvestɪˈgeɪʃn/ *noun*: *The police are holding an investigation into the fire.*

invigilate /ɪnˈvɪdʒɪleɪt/ *verb* (**invigilates, invigilating, invigilated**) to watch the people taking an exam or test ▸ **invigilator** /ɪnˈvɪdʒɪleɪtə(r)/ *noun*

invisible /ɪnˈvɪzəbl/ *adjective* If something is **invisible**, you cannot see it: *Wind is invisible.* OPPOSITE **visible**

invitation 🔑 /ˌɪnvɪˈteɪʃn/ *noun* If you have an invitation to go somewhere, someone has spoken or written to you and asked you to go: *Shema sent us an invitation to his wedding.*

invite 🔑 /ɪnˈvaɪt/ *verb* (**invites, inviting, invited**) to ask someone to come to a party, meeting, etc: *Kirezi invited us to her house.* ◇ *Let's invite them for dinner.*

invoice /ˈɪnvɔɪs/ *noun* a list that shows how much you must pay for things that someone has sold you, or for work that someone has done for you

involve 🔑 /ɪnˈvɒlv/ *verb* (**involves, involving, involved** /ɪnˈvɒlvd/) **1** to have something as a part: *The game involves working in teams.* **2** to make someone take part in something: *A lot of people were involved in planning the event.*

inward /ˈɪnwəd/ (also **inwards** /ˈɪnwədz/) *adverb* towards the inside or centre: *The doors open inwards.* OPPOSITE **outward**

ir- /ɪr/ *prefix* You can add **ir-** to the

beginning of some words to give them the opposite meaning: *irregular* (= not regular)

irio *noun* (no plural) (East African English) food made from a mixture of potatoes, green vegetables, **peas** and **maize**

iron¹ 🔑 /ˈaɪən/ *noun*

> ❖ **PRONUNCIATION**
> **Iron** sounds like **lion**, because we do not say the 'r'.

1 (no plural) a strong hard metal: *The gates are made of iron.* ◇ *an iron bar* **2** (*plural* **irons**) an electrical thing that gets hot and that you use for making clothes smooth: *She has a steam iron.*

iron² 🔑 /ˈaɪən/ *verb* (**irons**, **ironing**, **ironed** /ˈaɪənd/) to make clothes smooth with an iron: *Can you iron this shirt for me?*

> ❖ **SPEAKING**
> When we talk about ironing a lot of clothes, we often say **do the ironing**: *I've done the ironing.*

ironing /ˈaɪənɪŋ/ *noun* (no plural) clothes that you must iron: *There's a pile of ironing on the chair.*

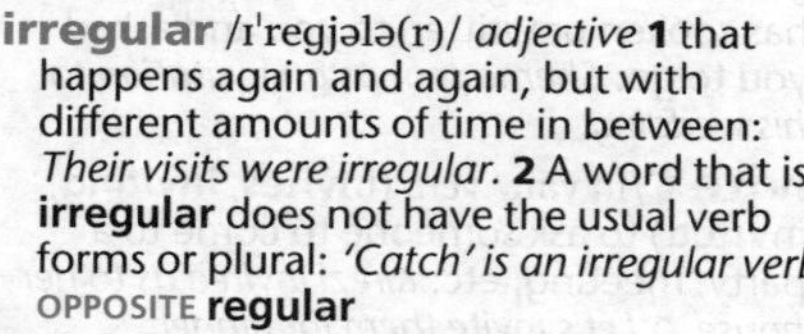

ironing board /ˈaɪənɪŋ bɔːd/ *noun* a special long table where you iron clothes

irregular /ɪˈregjələ(r)/ *adjective* **1** that happens again and again, but with different amounts of time in between: *Their visits were irregular.* **2** A word that is **irregular** does not have the usual verb forms or plural: *'Catch' is an irregular verb.* OPPOSITE **regular**

irrelevant /ɪˈreləvənt/ *adjective* not connected with something and not important: *We are good friends. She is older than me, but that is irrelevant.*

irresponsible /ˌɪrɪˈspɒnsəbl/ *adjective* An **irresponsible** person is someone that you cannot trust. OPPOSITE **responsible**

irrigate /ˈɪrɪgeɪt/ *verb* (**irrigates**, **irrigating**, **irrigated**) to make water go to land where crops grow: *Water from the lake is used to irrigate the crops.* ▸ **irrigation** /ˌɪrɪˈgeɪʃn/ *noun* (no plural)

irritate /ˈɪrɪteɪt/ *verb* (**irritates**, **irritating**, **irritated**) **1** to make someone quite angry: *He irritates me when he asks so many questions.* **2** to make a part of your body hurt a little: *That soap irritates my skin.* ▸ **irritation** /ˌɪrɪˈteɪʃn/ *noun*: *This plant causes irritation to your skin.*

is *form of* BE

isikuti = **esikuti**

Islam /ˈɪzlɑːm/ *noun* (no plural) the religion of Muslim people. Islam teaches that there is only one God and that Muhammad is th person God has chosen to give his messag to people (his **Prophet**). ▸ **Islamic** /ɪzˈlæmɪk/ *adjective*: *Islamic law*

island 🔑 /ˈaɪlənd/ *noun*

> ❖ **PRONUNCIATION**
> **Island** sounds like **highland** because we do not say the 's'.

a piece of land with water all around it: *Zanzibar is an island.*

isle /aɪl/ *noun* an island: *the British Isles*
ℹ **Isle** is usually used in names of islands.

isn't /ˈɪznt/ = **is not**

isolated /ˈaɪsəleɪtɪd/ *adjective* far from othe people or things: *an isolated house in the mountains*

isolation /ˌaɪsəˈleɪʃn/ *noun* (no plural) being away from other people or things: *He was kept in isolation in hospital.*

issue¹ 🔑 /ˈɪʃuː/ *noun* **1** an important problem that people talk about: *Pollution is a serious issue.* **2** a magazine or newspaper of a particular day, week or month: *Have you read this week's issue of the magazine?*

issue² /ˈɪʃuː/ *verb* (**issues**, **issuing**, **issued** /ˈɪʃuːd/) to give something to people: *The soldiers were issued with uniforms.*

it 🔑 /ɪt/ *pronoun* (*plural* **they**, **them**) **1** a word that shows a thing or an animal: *I've got a new shirt. It's* (= it is) *blue.* ◇ *Where is the coffee? I can't find it.* ◇ *I could hear a bird but I couldn't see it.* **2** a word that points to an idea that follows: *It is difficult to learn Arabic.* **3** a word that shows who someone is: *'Who's on the phone?' 'It's Ali.'* **4** a word at the beginning of a sentence about time, the weather, distance, etc: *It's six o'clock.* ◇ *It's hot today.* ◇ *It's 100 kilometres to Moyale.*

italics /ɪˈtælɪks/ *noun* (plural) letters that lean to the side: *This sentence is in italics.*

itch /ɪtʃ/ *verb* (**itches**, **itching**, **itched** /ɪtʃt/) to have a feeling on your skin that makes you want to rub or scratch it: *My nose is itching.* ◇ *This shirt makes me itch.* ▸ **itch** *noun* (*plural* **itches**): *I've got an itch.* ▸ **itchy** *adjective* If something is **itchy**, it **itches** or it makes you **itch**: *itchy skin*

t'd /ˈɪtəd/ **1 = it had 2 = it would**

tem /ˈaɪtəm/ *noun* **1** one thing in a list or group of things: *She had the most expensive item on the menu.* ◇ *an item of clothing* **2** a piece of news: *There was an interesting item on TV about South Africa.*

t'll /ˈɪtl/ = **it will**

t's /ɪts/ **1 = it is 2 = it has**

ts /ɪts/ *adjective* of the thing or animal that you have just talked about: *The dog has hurt its leg.* ◇ *The company has its factory in Nakuru.*

> ❖ **its or it's?**
> Be careful. **Its** and **it's** are not the same: *The bird has broken its wing* (= the wing belongs to the bird). ◇ *It's* (= it is) *Monday today.*

tself /ɪtˈself/ *pronoun* (*plural* **themselves** /ðəmˈselvz/) **1** a word that shows the same thing or animal that you have just talked about: *The cat was washing itself.* **2** a word that makes 'it' stronger: *The hotel itself was nice but I didn't like the town.*
by itself 1 alone: *The house stands by itself in the forest.* **2** without being controlled by a person: *The machine will start by itself.*

V /ˌaɪ ˈviː/ = **intravenous**

've /aɪv/ = **I have**

ivory /ˈaɪvəri/ *noun* (no plural) the hard white stuff that the **tusks** (= long teeth) of an **elephant** are made of

J, j /dʒeɪ/ *noun* (*plural* **J's, j's** /dʒeɪz/) the tenth letter of the English alphabet: *'Jam' begins with a 'J'.*

jackal /ˈdʒækl/ *noun* a wild dog with long legs and pointed ears. **Jackals** hunt in groups or look for dead animals to eat.

jackal

jacket /ˈdʒækɪt/ *noun* a short coat with sleeves: *He was wearing a leather jacket.* ➲ Picture at **suit**[1].

jagged /ˈdʒægɪd/ *adjective* rough, with a lot of sharp points: *jagged rocks*

jaguar

jaguar /ˈdʒægjuə(r)/ *noun* a wild animal like a big cat. It has yellow fur with black spots.

jail (also **gaol**) /dʒeɪl/ *noun* a prison: *He was sent to jail for two years.* ◇ *He faces a maximum jail term of 25 years.* ▸ **jail** *verb* (**jails**, **jailing**, **jailed** /dʒeɪld/) to put someone in prison: *She was jailed for stealing from her employer.*

jam[1] /dʒæm/ *noun* **1** (no plural) food made from fruit and sugar. You eat jam on bread: *a jar of apricot jam* **2** (*plural* **jams**) a lot of people or things in a place, so that it is difficult to move: *a traffic jam*

jam[2] /dʒæm/ *verb* (**jams**, **jamming**, **jammed** /dʒæmd/) **1** to push something into a place where there is not much space: *She jammed all her clothes into a suitcase.* **2** to fix something or become fixed so that you cannot move it: *I can't open the window. It's jammed.*

January /ˈdʒænjuəri/ *noun* the first month of the year

jar /dʒɑː(r)/ *noun* a glass container for food: *a jar of coffee* ➲ Picture at **container**.

jargon /ˈdʒɑːgən/ *noun* (no plural) special or technical words that are used by people who work in a particular job and that other people do not understand: *The doctor confused us with so much medical jargon.*

javelin /ˈdʒævəlɪn/ *noun* a long pointed stick that people throw as a sport

jaw /dʒɔː/ *noun* one of the two bones in the head of a person or an animal that hold the teeth ➲ picture on page A13

jazz /dʒæz/ *noun* (no plural) a kind of music with a strong beat

jealous /ˈdʒeləs/ *adjective* **1** angry or sad because you want what another person has: *Kamal was jealous of his brother's new shoes.* **2** angry or sad because you are afraid of losing someone's love: *Her husband gets jealous if she speaks to other* men. ▶ **jealousy** /ˈdʒeləsi/ *noun* (no plural) being **jealous**

jeans ⚷ /dʒiːnz/ *noun* (plural) trousers made of strong cotton material (called **denim**). Jeans are usually blue: *a pair of jeans* ◇ *She wore jeans and a T-shirt.*

Jeep™

Jeep™ /dʒiːp/ *noun* a strong car that can go well over rough land ℹ **Jeep** is a trademark.

jelly /ˈdʒeli/ *noun* (*plural* **jellies**) a soft food made from fruit juice and sugar, that shakes when you move it

jellyfish /ˈdʒelifɪʃ/ *noun* (*plural* **jellyfish** *or* **jellyfishes**) a soft, round sea animal, that you can see through

jellyfish

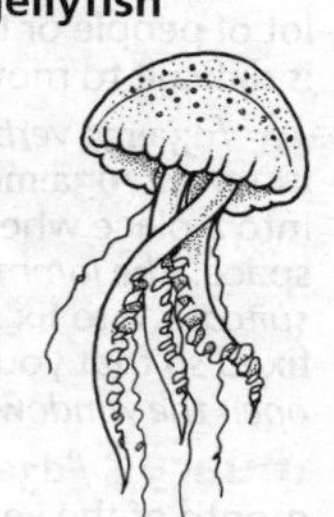

jembe *noun* (East African English) a farming tool used for turning and breaking up soil

jembe

jerk /dʒɜːk/ *noun* a sudden pull or other movement: *The bus started with a jerk.* ▶ **jerk** *verb* (**jerks, jerking, jerked** /dʒɜːkt/): *The car jerked forward.* ◇ *She jerked the door open.*

jet /dʒet/ *noun* **1** a plane that flies when its engines push out hot gas: *They flew to Australia on a jumbo jet* (= a very large plane). **2** liquid or gas that is coming very fast out of a small hole: *jets of water* ◇ *a jet of gas*

jet lag /ˈdʒet læg/ *noun* (no plural) a very tired feeling that you may have after a long journey by plane

jetty /ˈdʒeti/ *noun* (*plural* **jetties**) a wall or platform where boats can be tied so that people can get on and off

jetty

Jew /dʒuː/ *noun* a person who follows the old religion of Israel (called **Judaism**) ▶ **Jewish** /ˈdʒuːɪʃ/ *adjective*: *They are Jewish.*

jewel /ˈdʒuːəl/ *noun* a beautiful stone, for example a diamond, that is very valuable SAME MEANING **gem**

jeweller /ˈdʒuːələ(r)/ *noun* a person who sells, makes or repairs jewellery and watches

❖ **WORD BUILDING**

A shop that sells jewellery and watches is called a **jeweller's**.

jewellery ⚷ /ˈdʒuːəlri/ *noun* (no plural) things that people wear to decorate their fingers, ears, arms, etc: *She wears a lot of jewellery.*

❖ **GRAMMAR**

Be careful! You cannot say 'a jewellery' or 'jewelleries'. You can say 'some jewellery' or 'a piece of jewellery'.

jigger /ˈdʒɪgə(r)/ *noun* a very small insect that lays its eggs under your skin

jigsaw

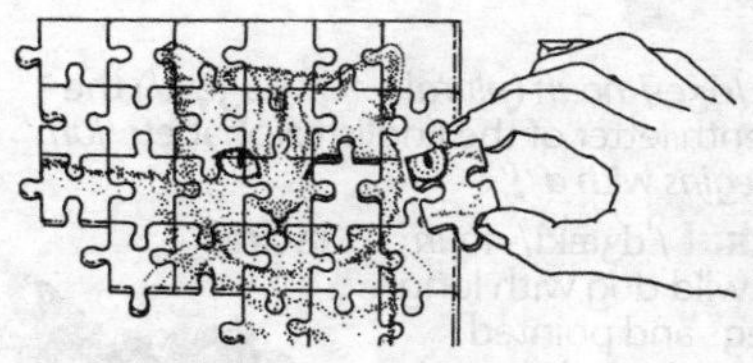

jigsaw /ˈdʒɪgsɔː/ (also **jigsaw puzzle** /ˈdʒɪgsɔː pʌzl/) *noun* a picture in many pieces that you must put together

jiko *noun* (East African English) a container used for burning **charcoal** or small pieces of wood. It is used for cooking or to give heat.

job 🔑 /dʒɒb/ *noun* **1** the work that a person does for money: *He has left school but he hasn't got a job.* ◇ *She's looking for a new job.* ◇ *Kisoso's just lost his job.* **2** a piece of work that you must do: *I have a lot of jobs to do in the house.*
a good job a good or lucky thing: *It's a good job that I was at home when you phoned.*
make a good job of something to do something well: *You made a good job of the painting.*
out of a job If someone is **out of a job**, they do not have work that they are paid to do.

jockey /ˈdʒɒki/ *noun* (*plural* **jockeys**) a person who rides horses in races

jog /dʒɒg/ *verb* (**jogs, jogging, jogged** /dʒɒgd/) **1** to run slowly for exercise: *I jogged round the park.* ❶ We often say **go jogging**: *I go jogging every morning.* **2** to push or touch something a little, so that it moves: *She jogged my arm and I spilled my drink.* ▶ **jog** *noun* (no plural) a slow run for exercise: *I went for a jog.* ▶ **jogging** /ˈdʒɒgɪŋ/ *noun* (no plural) running slowly for exercise

jogger /ˈdʒɒgə(r)/ *noun* a person who runs slowly for exercise

join 🔑 /dʒɔɪn/ *verb* (**joins, joining, joined** /dʒɔɪnd/) **1** to bring or fix one thing to another thing: *The new road joins the two villages.* ◇ *Join the two pieces of wood together.* **2** to come together with someone or something: *This road joins the highway soon.* ◇ *I was invited to join them for the day.* **3** to become a member of a group: *He joined the army.*
join in to do something with other people: *We're playing football. Do you want to join in?*

joint[1] /dʒɔɪnt/ *noun* **1** a part of the body where two bones come together. Elbows and knees are joints. **2** a place where two parts of something join together: *the joints of a pipe* **3** a big piece of meat that you cook: *a joint of beef*

joint[2] /dʒɔɪnt/ *adjective* that people do or have together: *Nigeria won, and Spain and Denmark finished joint second.*

joke[1] 🔑 /dʒəʊk/ *noun* something that you say or do to make people laugh: *She told us a joke.*
play a joke on someone to do something to someone to make other people laugh; to trick someone: *They played a joke on Ali – they hid his coat.*

joke[2] 🔑 /dʒəʊk/ *verb* (**jokes, joking, joked** /dʒəʊkt/) to say things that are not serious; to say funny things: *I didn't really mean what I said – I was only joking.*

jolly /ˈdʒɒli/ *adjective* (**jollier, jolliest**) happy and full of fun

jolt /dʒəʊlt/ *noun* a sudden movement: *The train stopped with a jolt.* ▶ **jolt** *verb* (**jolts, jolting, jolted**) to make something or someone move suddenly: *The car stopped suddenly and the passengers were jolted forwards.*

jot /dʒɒt/ *verb* (**jots, jotting, jotted**)
jot down to write something quickly: *I jotted down his phone number.*

journal /ˈdʒɜːnl/ *noun* a magazine about one special thing: *a medical journal*

journalism /ˈdʒɜːnəlɪzəm/ *noun* (no plural) the work of writing about the news for newspapers, magazines, television or radio

journalist 🔑 /ˈdʒɜːnəlɪst/ *noun* a person whose job is to write about the news for newspapers, magazines, television or radio: *He's a journalist with a French newspaper.*

journey 🔑 /ˈdʒɜːni/ *noun* (*plural* **journeys**) going from one place to another: *Did you have a good journey?* ◇ *The bus journey took about 12 hours.*

joy /dʒɔɪ/ *noun* (no plural) a very happy feeling: *Their children always give them so much joy.*

joyful /ˈdʒɔɪfl/ *adjective* very happy: *This is a joyful occasion for the school.*

joystick /ˈdʒɔɪstɪk/ *noun* a handle that you move to control something, for example a computer or a plane

juakali *noun* (no plural) a Kiswahili word meaning 'hot sun'. ❶ We use 'juakali' for talking about informal jobs that people do to earn a living, especially making useful things to sell from metal and wood: *the juakali industry* ◇ *a juakali mechanic*

Judaism /ˈdʒuːdeɪɪzəm/ *noun* (no plural) the religion of the Jewish people

judge[1] 🔑 /dʒʌdʒ/ *noun* **1** the person in a court of law who decides how to punish someone: *The judge sent the man to prison for 20 years.* **2** a person who chooses the winner of a competition: *The judges have made their decision.*

judge[2] 🔑 /dʒʌdʒ/ *verb* (**judges, judging, judged** /dʒʌdʒd/) **1** to decide if something is good or bad, right or wrong, etc: *Schools should not be judged only on exam results.* **2** to decide who or what wins a competition: *The head teacher judged the painting competition.*

judgement ⚷ /ˈdʒʌdʒmənt/ *noun* **1** what you think about someone or something: *In my judgement, she will make an excellent team leader.* **2** what a judge in a court of law decides: *The judgement will be given tomorrow.*

judiciary /dʒuˈdɪʃəri/ *noun* (*plural* **judiciaries**) the judges of a country or a state: *The country has a hard-working judiciary.*

judo /ˈdʒuːdəʊ/ *noun* (no plural) a sport where two people fight and try to throw each other onto the floor

jug /dʒʌg/ *noun* a container with a handle that you use for holding or pouring water, milk, etc.

jug

juggle /ˈdʒʌgl/ *verb* (**juggles, juggling, juggled** /ˈdʒʌgld/) to keep two or more things in the air by throwing and catching them quickly: *The clown juggled three oranges.* ▶ **juggler** /ˈdʒʌglə(r)/ *noun* a person who juggles

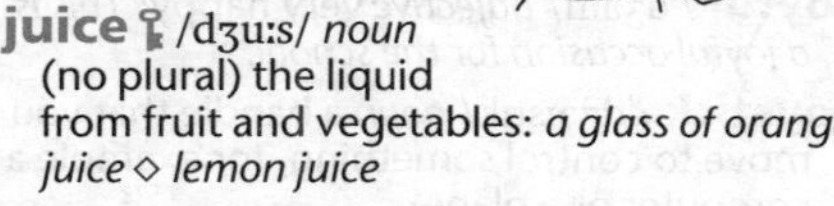

juice ⚷ /dʒuːs/ *noun* (no plural) the liquid from fruit and vegetables: *a glass of orange juice* ◇ *lemon juice*

juicy /ˈdʒuːsi/ *adjective* (**juicier, juiciest**) with a lot of juice: *big juicy tomatoes*

jukebox /ˈdʒuːkbɒks/ *noun* (*plural* **jukeboxes**) a machine in a cafe or bar that plays music when you put money in it

July ⚷ /dʒuˈlaɪ/ *noun* the seventh month of the year

jumble[1] /ˈdʒʌmbl/ *verb* (**jumbles, jumbling, jumbled** /ˈdʒʌmbld/)
jumble up to mix things so that they are untidy or in the wrong place: *I can't find the photo I was looking for – they are all jumbled up in this box.*

jumble[2] /ˈdʒʌmbl/ *noun* (no plural) a lot of things that are mixed together in an untidy way: *a jumble of old clothes and books*

jumble sale /ˈdʒʌmbl seɪl/ *noun* a sale of things that people do not want any more. Clubs, churches and schools often have **jumble sales** to get money.

jump ⚷ /dʒʌmp/ *verb* (**jumps, jumping, jumped** /dʒʌmpt/) **1** to move quickly off the ground, using your legs to push you up: *The cat jumped onto the table.* ◇ *The horse jumped over the wall.* **2** to move quickly: *He jumped into the car and drove away.* **3** to move suddenly because you are surprised or frightened: *A loud noise made me jump.* ▶ **jump** *noun*: *With one jump, the horse was over the fence.*

jumper /ˈdʒʌmpə(r)/ *noun* a warm piece of clothing with sleeves, that you wear on the top part of your body. **Jumpers** are often made of wool.

junction /ˈdʒʌŋkʃn/ *noun* a place where roads or railway lines meet: *Turn right at the next junction.*

June ⚷ /dʒuːn/ *noun* the sixth month of the year

jungle /ˈdʒʌŋgl/ *noun* a thick forest in a hot part of the world: *There are jungles in the Congo River basin.* ➲ Note at **forest**.

junior /ˈdʒuːniə(r)/ *adjective* **1** less important: *He's a junior officer in the army.* **2** younger: *a junior pupil* OPPOSITE **senior**

junk /dʒʌŋk/ *noun* (no plural) things that are old or useless: *The cupboard is full of junk.*

junk food /ˈdʒʌŋk fuːd/ *noun* (no plural) food that is not very good for you, but that is easy to prepare or ready to eat

junk mail /ˈdʒʌŋk meɪl/ *noun* (no plural) advertisements that companies send by post to people who have not asked for them

jury /ˈdʒʊəri/ *noun* (*plural* **juries**) a group of people in a court of law who decide if someone has done something wrong or not: *The jury decided that the woman was guilty of stealing the car.*

just[1] ⚷ /dʒʌst/ *adverb* **1** a very short time before: *Opiyo isn't here – he's just gone out.* **2** at this or that moment; now or very soon: *I'm just going to make some coffee.* ◇ *She phoned just as I was going to bed.* **3** only: *It's just a small present.* **4** almost not: *I ran fast and I just caught the bus.* **5** a word that makes what you say stronger: *Just look at that funny little dog!*

just a minute; **just a moment** wait for a short time: *Just a minute – there's someone at the door.*

just now 1 at this time; now: *I can't talk to you just now. I'm busy.* **2** a short time before: *Where's Nduku? She was here just now.*

just then at that exact moment: *I decided to walk home, but just then the bus arrived.*

just[2] /dʒʌst/ *adjective* fair and right: *a just punishment* OPPOSITE **unjust**

justice /ˈdʒʌstɪs/ *noun* (no plural) **1** being fair and right: *Justice for all!* OPPOSITE **injustice 2** the law: *British justice*

justify /ˈdʒʌstɪfaɪ/ *verb* (**justifies, justifying, justified** /ˈdʒʌstɪfaɪd/, **has justified**) to be or give a good reason for something: *Can you justify what you did?*

Kk

K, k /keɪ/ *noun* (*plural* **K's, k's** /keɪz/) the eleventh letter of the English alphabet: *'King' begins with a 'K'.*

kachumbari *noun* (no plural) (East African English) food made from a mixture of vegetables such as tomatoes, onions and **cabbage**, cut very small

kale /keɪl/ *noun* (no plural) a vegetable with dark green leaves that we cook

kanga (also **leso**) *noun* (East African English) a piece of loose clothing for a woman or girl that she ties round her body

kangaroo /ˌkæŋgəˈruː/ *noun* (*plural* **kangaroos**) an animal in Australia that jumps on its strong back legs

kangaroo

kanzu *noun* (East African English) a long white loose piece of clothing for men

karate /kəˈrɑːti/ *noun* (no plural) a Japanese sport where people fight with their hands and feet

kayamba *noun* (East African English) a musical instrument that you shake to make a noise

kebab /kɪˈbæb/ *noun* small pieces of meat, vegetables, etc. cooked on a stick

keel /kiːl/ *noun* the long piece of wood or metal on the bottom of a boat that stops it falling over in the water

keen /kiːn/ *adjective* (**keener, keenest**) **1** If you are **keen**, you want to do something and are interested in it: *Achal was keen to go out but I wanted to stay at home.* ◇ *Odoi is a keen swimmer.* **2** very good or strong: *keen eyesight*

be keen on someone or **something** like someone or something very much: *My brother is keen on football.*

keep 🔑 /kiːp/ *verb* (**keeps, keeping, kept** /kept/, **has kept**) **1** to have something and not give it to another person: *You can keep that book – I don't need it.* **2** to continue in the same way and not change: *Keep still – I want to take your photograph.* **3** to make someone or something stay the same and not change: *Keep this door closed.* ◇ *You must keep the baby warm.* **4** to have something in a special place: *Where do you keep the coffee?* **5** to not stop doing something; to do something many times: *Keep walking until you see the school, then turn left.* ◇ *She keeps forgetting my name.* **6** to save something for someone: *Please keep a seat for me.* ◇ *Please keep me a seat.* **7** to look after and buy food and other things for a person or an animal: *It costs a lot to keep a family of four.* ◇ *They keep sheep and goats on their farm.* **8** to stay fresh: *Will this fish keep until tomorrow?*

keep away from someone or **something** to not go near someone or something: *Keep away from the river please, children.*

keep someone from to stop someone from doing something: *You can't keep me from going out!*

keep going to continue; to not stop: *I was tired but I kept going to the end of the race.*

keep off something to not go on something: *Keep off the grass!*

keep on to not stop doing something; to do something many times: *We kept on studying all night!* ◇ *That man keeps on looking at me.*

keep out to stay outside: *The sign on the door said 'Danger. Keep out!'*

keep someone or **something out** to stop someone or something from going in: *We put a fence round the garden to keep the goats out.*

keep up with someone or **something** to go as fast as another person or thing so that you are together: *Don't walk so quickly – I can't keep up with you.*

keeper /ˈkiːpə(r)/ *noun* a person who looks after something: *He's a keeper at the game reserve – he looks after the lions.* ➲ Look at **goalkeeper**.

kennel /ˈkenl/ *noun* a small house where a dog sleeps

kept *form of* KEEP

kerb /kɜːb/ *noun* the edge of a path next to a road: *They stood on the kerb waiting to cross the road.*

kerosene /ˈkerəsiːn/ *noun* (no plural) a type of oil that we use in cookers, lamps, etc. SAME MEANING **paraffin**

ketchup /ˈketʃəp/ *noun* (no plural) a cold sauce made from tomatoes: *Do you want ketchup on your chips?*

kettle /ˈketl/ *noun* a metal or plastic pot that you use for making water hot: *Put the kettle on* (= fill it with water and make it start to get hot).

kettles

key¹ 🔑 /kiː/ *noun* (*plural* **keys**) **1** a piece of metal that opens or closes a lock: *He turned the key and opened the door.* **2** one of the parts of a computer, piano, etc. that you press with your fingers: *Pianos have black and white keys.* **3** answers to questions: *Check your answers with the key at the back of the book.*

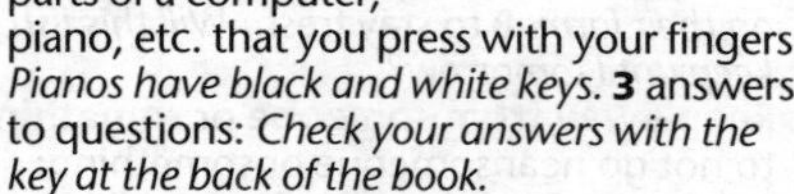

key

key² /kiː/ *verb* (**keys**, **keying**, **keyed** /kiːd/)

key in to put words or numbers into a computer by pressing the keys: *Key in your name.*

keyboard /ˈkiːbɔːd/ *noun* **1** all the keys on a computer, piano, etc. ➲ Picture at **computer**. **2** a musical instrument like a small electrical piano: *a keyboard player*

keyhole /ˈkiːhəʊl/ *noun* a hole in a lock where you put a key

keypad /ˈkiːpæd/ *noun* a small set of buttons with numbers on that you press when you use a thing like a telephone or a computer

kg *short for* KILOGRAM

khat /kɑːt/ (also **miraa**) *noun* (no plural) the leaves of a plant that people use as a drug

kick¹ 🔑 /kɪk/ *verb* (**kicks**, **kicking**, **kicked** /kɪkt/) **1** to hit someone or something with your foot: *I kicked the ball to Katee.* **2** to move your foot or feet up quickly: *The child was kicking and screaming.*

kick off to start a game of football

kick someone out to make someone leave a place: *The boys were kicked out of the cinema because they were noisy*

kick

He was **kicking** a ball about outside.

kick² 🔑 /kɪk/ *noun* **1** hitting something or someone with your foot, or moving your foot or feet up quickly: *Kamau gave the ball a kick.* **2** a feeling of excitement: *He gets a kick out of running really fast.*

kick-off /ˈkɪk ɒf/ *noun* the start of a game of football: *The kick-off is at 2.30.*

kid /kɪd/ *noun* **1** a child: *How old are your kids?* ❶ This is an informal word. **2** a young goat

kidnap /ˈkɪdnæp/ *verb* (**kidnaps**, **kidnapping**, **kidnapped** /ˈkɪdnæpt/) to take someone away and hide them, so that their family or friends will pay you money to free them: *The son of a rich man was kidnapped today.* ▸ **kidnapper** /ˈkɪdnæpə(r)/ *noun* a person who **kidnaps** someone

kidney /ˈkɪdni/ *noun* (*plural* **kidneys**) one of two parts inside your body that take waste liquid from your blood

kikoi *noun* (East African English) a piece of coloured cotton cloth with lines on it that people wear

kikoi

kill 🔑 /kɪl/ *verb* (**kills**, **killing**, **killed** /kɪld/) to make someone or something die: *The police do not know who killed the old man.* ◇ *Three people were killed in the accident.* ▸ **killer** /ˈkɪlə(r)/ *noun* a person, animal or thing that kills

kilo /ˈkiːləʊ/ *noun* (*plural* **kilos**) *short for* KILOGRAM

kilogram 🔑 (also **kilogramme**) /ˈkɪləgræm/ (also **kilo**) *noun* a measure of weight. There are 1 000 grams in a kilogram: *I bought two kilos of potatoes.* ❶ The short way of writing 'kilogram' is **kg**: *1 kg of bananas*

kilometre /ˈkɪləmiːtə(r); kɪˈlɒmɪtə(r)/ *noun* a measure of length. There are 1 000 metres in a kilometre. ❶ The short way of writing 'kilometre' is **km**: *They live 100 km from Lodwar.*

kilt /kɪlt/ *noun* a skirt that men in Scotland sometimes wear

kind¹ /kaɪnd/ *adjective* (**kinder**, **kindest**) friendly and good to other people: *'Can I carry your bag?' 'Thanks. That's very kind of you.'* ◇ *Be kind to animals.*

> ❖ **WORD FAMILY**
> **kind**: OPPOSITE **unkind**
> **kindly** **kindness**

kind² /kaɪnd/ *noun* a group of things or people that are the same in some way; a sort or type: *What kind of car do you have?* ◇ *There are three different kinds of mosquito.*
kind of words that you use when you are not sure about something: *He looks kind of tired.*

kind-hearted /ˌkaɪnd ˈhɑːtɪd/ *adjective* A person who is **kind-hearted** is kind and gentle to other people.

kindly¹ /ˈkaɪndli/ *adverb* in a kind way: *She kindly helped me cook the dinner.*

kindly² /ˈkaɪndli/ *adjective* (**kindlier**, **kindliest**) kind and friendly: *a kindly old man*

kindness /ˈkaɪndnəs/ *noun* (no plural) being kind: *Thank you for your kindness.*

king /kɪŋ/ *noun* a man who rules a country and who is from a royal family: *King Hussein of Jordan* ➲ Look at **queen**.

kingdom /ˈkɪŋdəm/ *noun* a country where a king or queen rules: *the United Kingdom*

kingfisher /ˈkɪŋfɪʃə(r)/ *noun* a small bright bird that catches fish in rivers

kiondo *noun* (East African English) a bag with long handles, made from the leaves of a large plant (called **sisal**)

kiosk /ˈkiːɒsk/ *noun* a small shop in a street where you can buy things like sweets and newspapers through an open window

kiss /kɪs/ *verb* (**kisses**, **kissing**, **kissed** /kɪst/) to touch someone with your lips to show love or to say hello or goodbye: *She kissed me on the cheek.* ▶ **kiss** *noun* (*plural* **kisses**): *Give me a kiss!*

Kiswahili (also **Swahili**) *noun* (no plural) a language that many of the people of East Africa speak: *Do you speak Kiswahili at home?*

kit /kɪt/ *noun* **1** all the clothes or other things that you need to do something or to play a sport: *Where is my football kit?* ◇ *a tool kit* **2** a set of small pieces that you put together to make something: *a kit for making a model plane*

kitchen /ˈkɪtʃɪn/ *noun* a room where you cook food: *I need some help in the kitchen.*

kite /kaɪt/ *noun* a light toy made of paper or cloth on a long string. You can make a **kite** fly in the wind: *The children were flying kites on the hill.*

kitenge *noun* (East African English) a large piece of coloured cloth with patterns on it, that women wear

kitten /ˈkɪtn/ *noun* a young cat ➲ Picture at **cat**.

km *short for* KILOMETRE

knee /niː/ *noun* the part in the middle of your leg where it bends: *I fell and cut my knee.* ➲ picture on page A13

> ❖ **PRONUNCIATION**
> Be careful. We do not say the **k** in words beginning with **kn**, so **knot** sounds the same as **not**, **know** sounds the same as **no**, etc.

kneel /niːl/ *verb* (**kneels**, **kneeling**, **knelt** /nelt/ *or* **kneeled** /niːld/, **has knelt** *or* **has kneeled**) to go down or stay with your knees on the ground: *He knelt down to pray.* ◇ *The girl was kneeling on the floor.*

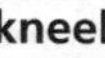

knew *form of* KNOW

knickers /ˈnɪkəz/ = **panties**

knife /naɪf/ *noun* (*plural* **knives** /naɪvz/) a sharp metal thing with a handle, that you use to cut things or to fight: *Use a sharp knife to chop the onions.*

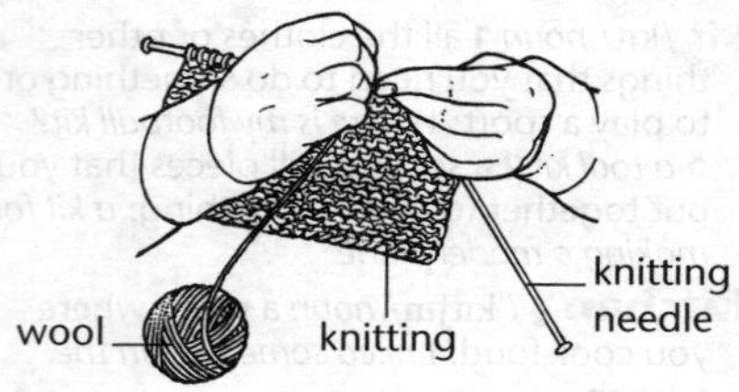

knit /nɪt/ *verb* (**knits, knitting, knitted**) to use long sticks (called **knitting needles**) to make clothes from wool: *My grandmother knitted this hat for me.*

knitting /ˈnɪtɪŋ/ *noun* (no plural) **1** making clothes from wool: *Her hobbies are knitting and football.* **2** something that you are **knitting**: *Put your knitting away.*

knitting needle /ˈnɪtɪŋ niːdl/ *noun* one of two long metal or plastic sticks that you use for making clothes from wool

knives *plural of* KNIFE

knob /nɒb/ *noun* **1** a round handle on a door or drawer: *a wooden doorknob* **2** a round thing that you turn to control part of a machine

knock[1] /nɒk/ *verb* (**knocks, knocking, knocked** /nɒkt/) **1** to hit something to make a noise: *I knocked on the door, but nobody answered.* **2** to hit something hard: *I knocked my head on the door.* ◇ *She knocked a glass off the table.*
knock someone down; knock someone over to hit someone so that they fall onto the ground: *The little boy was knocked down by a car.*
knock something down to break a building so that it falls down: *They knocked down the old houses and built a school in their place.*
knock someone out to hit someone hard so that they cannot get up again for a while
knock something over to hit something so that it falls: *I knocked over a jug and broke it.*

knock[2] /nɒk/ *noun* hitting something hard or the sound that this makes: *I heard a knock at the door.*

knot[1] /nɒt/ *noun* a place where you have tied two ends of rope, string, etc. tightly together: *I tied a knot in the rope.* ◇ *Can you undo this knot* (= make it loose)*?*

knot (illustration label)

knot[2] /nɒt/ *verb* (**knots, knotting, knotted**) to tie a knot in something: *He knotted the ends of the rope together.*

know /nəʊ/ *verb* (**knows, knowing, knew** /njuː/, **has known** /nəʊn/) **1** to have something in your head, because you have learnt it: *I don't know her name.* ◇ *He knows a lot about cars.* ◇ *Do you know how to use this machine?* ◇ *'You're late!' 'Yes, I know.'* **2** to have met or seen someone or something before, perhaps many times: *I have known Mwita for six years.* ◇ *I know that part of the country quite well.*
get to know someone to start to know someone well: *I liked him when I got to know him.*
let someone know to tell someone: *Let me know if you need any help.*
you know words that you use when you are thinking about what to say next

knowledge /ˈnɒlɪdʒ/ *noun* (no plural) what you know and understand about something: *He has a good knowledge of African history.*

knuckle /ˈnʌkl/ *noun* the bones where your fingers join your hand and where your hands bend

kph a way of measuring how fast something is moving. **Kph** is short for 'kilometres per hour'.

kudu /ˈkuːduː/ *noun* (*plural* **kudu** *or* **kudus** /ˈkuːduːz/) a large **antelope** with white stripes on its sides and twisted horns

kwacha /ˈkwɑːtʃə/ *noun* (*plural* **kwacha**) the money that people use in Zambia and Malawi

kwashiorkor /ˌkwæʃɪˈɔːkə(r)/ *noun* (no plural) a serious illness that very young children can get if they do not eat enough **protein** (= a substance in foods such as milk, meat and fish)

L, l /el/ *noun* (*plural* **L's, l's** /elz/) **1** the twelfth letter of the English alphabet: *'Lake' begins with an 'L'.* **2** *short for* LITRE

lab /læb/ *short for* LABORATORY: *a lab coat* (= a white coat that scientists wear) ◇ *a lab result*

label¹ /ˈleɪbl/ *noun* a piece of paper or plastic on something that tells you about it: *The label on the bottle says 'Made in Kenya'.*

label² /ˈleɪbl/ *verb* (**labels**, **labelling**, **labelled** /ˈleɪbld/) to put a **label** on something: *I labelled all the boxes with my name and address.*

laboratory /ləˈbɒrətri/ *noun* (*plural* **laboratories**) a special room where scientists work: *laboratory tests*
ℹ The short form is **lab**.

labour /ˈleɪbə(r)/ *noun* (no plural) hard work that you do with your hands and body: *The use of child labour was condemned by the minister.*

labourer /ˈleɪbərə(r)/ *noun* a person who does hard work with their hands and body: *a farm labourer*

lace /leɪs/ *noun* (*plural* **laces**) a string that you tie to close a shoe

laces

lace

lack¹ 🔑 /læk/ *noun* (no plural) not having something or not having enough of something: *There is a lack of good teachers.*

lack² /læk/ *verb* (**lacks**, **lacking**, **lacked** /lækt/) to not have something, or not have enough of something: *The children lacked the food they needed.*
be lacking to be needed: *Money is lacking for a new school.*

lad /læd/ *noun* a boy or young man

ladder /ˈlædə(r)/ *noun* two tall pieces of metal or wood with shorter pieces (called **rungs**) between them. You use a **ladder** for climbing up something.

ladder

rung

lady 🔑 /ˈleɪdi/ *noun* (*plural* **ladies**) a polite way of saying 'woman': *an old lady* ➲ Look at **gentleman**.

laid *form of* LAY¹

lain *form of* LIE¹

lake 🔑 /leɪk/ *noun* a big area of water with land all around it: *Lake Victoria* ◇ *We went swimming in the lake.*

lamb /læm/ *noun*

> ❖ **PRONUNCIATION**
> **Lamb** sounds like **ham** because we do not say the 'b'.

1 (*plural* **lambs**) a young sheep **2** (no plural) meat from a lamb ➲ Look at **sheep**.

lame /leɪm/ *adjective* If an animal is **lame**, it cannot walk well because it has hurt its leg or foot: *The ox went lame and couldn't work.*

lamp 🔑 /læmp/ *noun* a thing that gives light: *It was dark, so I switched on the lamp.*

lamp

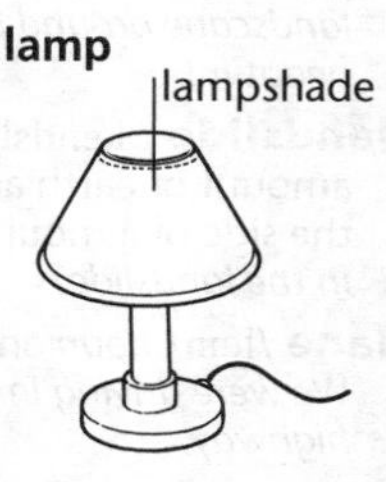

lamp post /ˈlæmp pəʊst/ *noun* a tall thing in the street with a light on the top

lampshade /ˈlæmpʃeɪd/ *noun* a cover for a lamp

land¹ 🔑 /lænd/ *noun* **1** (no plural) the part of the earth that is not the sea: *After two weeks in a boat, we were happy to see land.* **2** (no plural) a piece of ground: *They have bought some land and they are* *going to build a house on it.* ◇ *farming land* **3** (*plural* **lands**) a country: *She returned to the land where she was born.* ℹ In this meaning, **country** is the word that we usually use.

land² /lænd/ *verb* (**lands, landing, landed**) **1** to come onto the ground from the air or from the sea: *The plane landed at Wilson Airport.* ◇ *The boat has landed.* ➲ Look at **take off**. **2** to bring an aircraft down onto the ground: *The pilot landed the plane safely.*

landing /ˈlændɪŋ/ *noun* **1** coming down onto the ground: *The plane made a safe landing in a field.* OPPOSITE **take-off** **2** a flat place at the top of stairs in a building: *There's a telephone on the landing.*

landlady /ˈlændleɪdi/ *noun* (*plural* **landladies**) **1** a woman who has a house and lets you live there if you pay her money **2** a woman who has a small hotel

landlord /ˈlændlɔːd/ *noun* **1** a man who has a house and lets you live there if you pay him money **2** a man who has a small hotel

landmark /ˈlændmɑːk/ *noun* a big building or another thing that you can see easily from far away: *Mount Kilimanjaro is Tanzania's most famous landmark.*

landmine /ˈlændmaɪn/ *noun* a bomb that is hidden under the ground, which explodes when vehicles or people move over it

landscape /ˈlændskeɪp/ *noun* everything you can see in an area of land: *The landscape around Lake Victoria is very beautiful.*

landslide /ˈlændslaɪd/ *noun* a large amount of earth and rock that falls down the side of a mountain: *Was anyone killed in the landslide?*

lane /leɪn/ *noun* one part of a wide road: *We were driving in the middle lane of the highway.*

language /ˈlæŋgwɪdʒ/ *noun* **1** (no plural) words that people say or write **2** (*plural* **languages**) words that a certain group of people say and write: *'Do you speak any foreign languages?' 'Yes, I speak French and German.'*

lantern /ˈlæntən/ *noun* a lamp that you can carry outside

lap /læp/ *noun* **1** the flat part at the top of your legs when you are sitting: *The child sat on his mother's lap.* **2** going once round the track in a race: *The runner fell on the last lap.*

large /lɑːdʒ/ *adjective* (**larger, largest**) big: *They live in a large house.* ◇ *She has a large family.* ◇ *Have you got this shirt in a larger size?* OPPOSITE **small** ➲ picture on page A5

largely /ˈlɑːdʒli/ *adverb* mostly; mainly: *The room is largely used for meetings.*

larva /ˈlɑːvə/ *noun* (*plural* **larvae** /ˈlɑːviː/) an insect that has come out of an egg and looks like a short fat **worm**

laser /ˈleɪzə(r)/ *noun* an instrument that makes a very strong line of light (called a **laser beam**). Some **lasers** are used to cut metal and others are used by doctors in operations.

last¹ /lɑːst/ *adjective* **1** after all the others: *December is the last month of the year.* OPPOSITE **first** **2** just before now: *It's June now, so last month was May.* ◇ *I was at school last week, but this week I'm on holiday.* **3** only one left: *Can the last person in the room switch off the light, please?*

last night yesterday in the evening or in the night: *Did you go out last night?*

▶ **lastly** *adverb* finally, as the last thing: *Lastly, I want to thank my parents for all their help.*

last² /lɑːst/ *adverb* **1** after all the others: *He finished last in the race.* **2** at a time that is nearest to now: *I last saw Karimi in 2013.* OPPOSITE **first**

last³ /lɑːst/ *noun* (no plural) a person or thing that comes after all the others; what comes at the end: *I was the last to arrive at the party.* OPPOSITE **first**

at last in the end; after some time: *She waited all week, and at last the letter arrived.*

last⁴ /lɑːst/ *verb* (**lasts, lasting, lasted**) **1** to continue for a time: *The film lasted for three hours.* ◇ *I hope the good weather will last until the weekend.* **2** to be enough for a certain time: *We have enough food to last us till next week.*

last-born /ˈlɑːst bɔːn/ *noun* (no plural) a person's youngest child: *Rono was the last-born of six children in the family.*

late 🔑 /leɪt/ *adjective, adverb* (**later, latest**) **1** after the usual or right time: *I went to bed late last night.* ◇ *I was late for school today* (= I arrived late). ◇ *My bus was late.* OPPOSITE **early** **2** near the end of a time: *They arrived in the late afternoon.* ◇ *She's in her late twenties* (= between the ages of about 25 and 29). OPPOSITE **early** **3** no longer alive; dead: *Her late husband was a doctor.*
a late night an evening when you go to bed later than usual
at the latest not later than: *Please be here by twelve o'clock at the latest.*

lately /ˈleɪtli/ *adverb* not long ago; recently: *Have you seen Robi lately?* ◇ *The weather has been very bad lately.*

later¹ 🔑 /ˈleɪtə(r)/ *adverb* at a time in the future; after the time you are talking about: *See you later.* OPPOSITE **earlier**
later on at a time in the future; after the time you are talking about: *I'm going out later on.*

later² 🔑 /ˈleɪtə(r)/ *adjective* **1** coming after something else or at a time in the future: *The match will be played at a later date.* **2** near the end of a period of time: *the later part of the twentieth century* OPPOSITE **earlier**

latest /ˈleɪtɪst/ *adjective* newest: *the latest fashions*

latrine /ləˈtriːn/ *noun* a hole in the ground that is used as a toilet

latter¹ /ˈlætə(r)/ *adjective* last: *She couldn't walk very well in the latter part of her life.*

the latter² /ðə ˈlætə(r)/ *noun* (no plural) the second of two things or people: *If I had to choose between football and swimming, I would choose the latter.* ➲ Look at **former²**.

laugh¹ 🔑 /lɑːf/ *verb* (**laughs, laughing, laughed** /lɑːft/)

> ❖ **PRONUNCIATION**
> **gh** in **laugh** and **laughter** sounds like 'f'.

to make sounds that show you are happy or that you think something is funny: *His jokes always make me laugh.*
laugh at someone or **something** to laugh to show that you think someone or something is funny or silly: *The children laughed at the clown.* ◇ *They all laughed at me when I said I was frightened of dogs.*

laugh² 🔑 /lɑːf/ *noun* the sound you make when you are happy or when you think something is funny: *My brother has a loud laugh.* ◇ *She told us a joke and we all had a good laugh.*
for a laugh as a joke; for fun: *The boys put a spider in her bed for a laugh.*

laughter /ˈlɑːftə(r)/ *noun* (no plural) the sound of people laughing: *I could hear laughter in the next room.*

launch /lɔːntʃ/ *verb* (**launches, launching, launched** /lɔːntʃt/) **1** to put a ship into the water or a **spacecraft** (= a vehicle that travels into space) into the sky: *This ship was launched in 1967.* **2** to start something new: *The magazine was launched last year.* ▶ **launch** *noun* (*plural* **launches**): *There was huge excitement at the launch of a new phone.*

laundry /ˈlɔːndri/ *noun* **1** (no plural) clothes that you must wash or that you have washed: *a laundry basket* **2** (*plural* **laundries**) a place where you send things like sheets and clothes so that someone can wash them for you

lava /ˈlɑːvə/ *noun* (no plural) hot liquid rock that comes out of a **volcano** (= a mountain with a hole in the top)

lavatory /ˈlævətri/ *noun* (*plural* **lavatories**) a large bowl with a seat that you use when you need to empty waste from your body. The room that it is in is also called a **lavatory**: *Where's the lavatory, please?* ℹ **Toilet** is the word that we usually use.

law 🔑 /lɔː/ *noun*

> ❖ **PRONUNCIATION**
> **Law** sounds like **more**.

1 a rule of a country that says what people may and may not do: *There is a law against stealing.* ➲ Look at **legal**. **2 the law** (no plural) all the laws of a country ➲ Look at **lawyer**.
against the law not allowed by the rules of a country: *Murder is against the law.*
break the law to do something that the laws of a country say you must not do: *I have never broken the law.*

law court /ˈlɔː kɔːt/ *noun* a place where people (a **judge** or **jury**) decide if someone has done something wrong, and what the punishment will be

lawn /lɔ:n/ *noun* a piece of short grass in a garden or park: *They were sitting on the lawn.*

lawnmower /ˈlɔ:nməʊə(r)/ (also **mower**) *noun* a machine that cuts grass

lawnmower

lawyer /ˈlɔ:jə(r)/ *noun* a person who has studied the law and who helps people or talks for them in a court of law

lay[1] /leɪ/ *verb* (**lays, laying, laid** /leɪd/, **has laid**) **1** to put something carefully on another thing: *I laid the papers on the desk.* **2** to make an egg: *Birds and insects lay eggs.* ➲ Look at **table**.

lay[2] *form of* LIE[1]

layer /ˈleɪə(r)/ *noun* something flat that lies on another thing or that is between other things: *The table was covered with a thin layer of dust.* ◇ *It was so cold at night we had to wear four layers of clothing.*

lazy /ˈleɪzi/ *adjective* (**lazier, laziest**) A person who is lazy does not want to work: *Don't be so lazy – come and help me!* ◇ *My teacher said I was lazy.* ▸ **lazily** /ˈleɪzili/ *adverb* in a slow, lazy way: *She walked lazily across the room.* ▸ **laziness** /ˈleɪzinəs/ *noun* (no plural) being lazy

lb *short for* POUND[1]

lead[1] /li:d/ *verb* (**leads, leading, led** /led/, **has led**)

> ❖ **PRONUNCIATION**
>
> **Lead** (verb) sounds like **need**.

1 to take a person or an animal somewhere by going in front: *He led me to my room.* **2** to be the first or the best, for example in a race or game: *Who's leading in the race?* **3** to go to a place: *This path leads to the river.* **4** to control a group of people: *The team was led by Kamau Muben.*

lead to something to make something happen: *Eating too much sugar can lead to health problems.*

> ❖ **WORD FAMILY**
>
> **lead leader leadership leading**

lead[2] /li:d/ *noun*

> ❖ **PRONUNCIATION**
>
> In these meanings, **lead** sounds like **need.**

1 (no plural) going in front or doing something first **2** (*plural* **leads**) a long piece of leather or a chain that you tie to a dog's neck so that it walks with you **3** (*plural* **leads**) a long piece of wire that brings electricity to things like lamps and machines

be in the lead to be in front: *Wasike was in the lead right from the start of the race.*

lead[3] /led/ *noun*

> ❖ **PRONUNCIATION**
>
> In these meanings, **lead** sounds like **red**.

1 (no plural) a soft grey metal that is very heavy. **Lead** is used to make things like water pipes. **2** (*plural* **leads**) the grey part inside a pencil

leader /ˈli:də(r)/ *noun* **1** a person who controls a group of people: *They chose a new leader.* **2** a person or group that is the first or the best: *The leader is ten metres in front of the other runners.*

leadership /ˈli:dəʃɪp/ *noun* (no plural) controlling a group of people: *The country is under new leadership* (= has new leaders).

leading /ˈli:dɪŋ/ *adjective* best or very important: *a leading writer*

leaf /li:f/ *noun* (*plural* **leaves** /li:vz/) one of the flat green parts that grow on a plant or tree: *The leaves turn red in autumn.* ➲ pictures at **plant** and **tree** ➲ Picture at **plant**[1], **tree**.

leaflet /ˈli:flət/ *noun* a piece of paper with writing on it that tells you about something: *A young boy was handing out leaflets in the street.*

league /li:g/ *noun* **1** a group of teams that play against each other in a sport: *the football league* **2** a group of people or countries that work together to do something: *the Arab League*

leak[1] /li:k/ *verb* (**leaks, leaking, leaked** /li:kt/) **1** to have a hole that liquid or gas can go through: *The roof of our house leaks when it rains.* ◇ *The boat is leaking.* **2** to go out through a hole: *Water is leaking from the pipe.*

eak² /liːk/ *noun* a small hole that liquid or gas can go through: *There's a leak in the roof.*

ean¹ /liːn/ *verb* (**leans, leaning, leant** /lent/ *or* **leaned** /liːnd/, **has leant** *or* **has leaned**) **1** to not be straight; to bend forwards, backwards or to the side **2** to put your body or a thing against another thing: *Lean your bike against the wall.*

ean² /liːn/ *adjective* (**leaner, leanest**) **1** thin but strong: *He is tall and lean.* **2 Lean** meat does not have very much fat.

eap /liːp/ *verb* (**leaps, leaping, leapt** /lept/ *or* **leaped** /liːpt/, **has leapt** *or* **has leaped**) to make a big jump: *The cat leapt onto the table.* ▸ **leap** *noun* a big jump: *With one leap, he was over the wall.*

eap year /ˈliːp jɪə(r)/ *noun* a year when February has 29 days. **Leap years** happen every four years.

earn /lɜːn/ *verb* (**learns, learning, learnt** /lɜːnt/ *or* **learned** /lɜːnd/, **has learnt** *or* **has learned**) **1** to find out something, or how to do something, by studying or by doing it often: *Ali is learning to swim.* ◇ *I learnt English at school.* ◇ *Learn this list of words for homework* (= so you can remember them). ➲ Look at **teach**. **2** to hear about something: *I was sorry to learn of your father's death.*

earner /ˈlɜːnə(r)/ *noun* a person who is learning: *This dictionary is for learners of English.*

least¹ /liːst/ *adjective, pronoun* the smallest amount of something: *Shayo earns a lot of money, Juma earns less, and Wasike earns the least.* OPPOSITE **most** ➲ Look at **less¹**.

least² /liːst/ *adverb* less than all others: *This is the least expensive camera in the shop.* OPPOSITE **most** ➲ Look at **less²**.
at least 1 not less than: *It will cost at least 1 500 shillings.* **2** although other things are bad: *We're not rich, but at least we're happy.*
not in the least not at all: *'Are you angry?' 'Not in the least!'*

leather /ˈleðə(r)/ *noun* (no plural) the skin of an animal that is used to make things like shoes, jackets or bags: *a leather jacket*

leave¹ /liːv/ *verb* (**leaves, leaving, left** /left/, **has left**) **1** to go away from someone or something: *The bus leaves at 8.40.* ◇ *He left school last year.* **2** to let someone or something stay in the same place or in the same way: *Ereng left the door open.* **3** to not bring something with you: *I left my books at home.* ➲ Note at **forget**. **4** to make something stay; to not use something: *Leave some food for me!*
leave someone alone to not speak to or touch someone: *Leave me alone – I'm busy!*
leave something alone to not touch or take something: *Leave that bag alone – it's mine!*
leave someone or **something behind** to not take someone or something with you: *She went shopping and left the children behind.*
leave for to start a journey to a place: *Mrs Omenya is leaving for Cairo tomorrow.*
leave someone or something out to not include someone or something; to not put in or do something: *The other children left him out of the game.* ◇ *I left out question 3 in the exam because it was too difficult.*
leave something to someone 1 to let someone do a job for you: *I left the cooking to my sister.* **2** to give something to someone when you die: *She left all her money to her sons.*

leave² /liːv/ *noun* (no plural) a time when someone does not go to work: *He has 25 days' leave each year.*
on leave having a holiday from one's job: *He's on leave from the army.*

leaves *plural of* LEAF

lecture /ˈlektʃə(r)/ *noun* a talk to a group of people to teach them about something: *She gave an interesting lecture on African history.* ▸ **lecture** *verb* (**lectures, lecturing, lectured** /ˈlektʃəd/): *Professor Okelo lectures on history.*

lecturer /ˈlektʃərə(r)/ *noun* a person who gives talks to people to teach them about a subject: *He is a university lecturer.*

led *form of* LEAD¹

ledge /ledʒ/ *noun* a long narrow flat place, for example under a window or on the side of a mountain: *a window ledge*

ledger /ˈledʒə(r)/ *noun* a book in which a business records the money it has paid and received

left[1] 🔑 /left/ *adjective, adverb* opposite of right: *Turn left at the church.* ◇ *My left leg hurts.*

left[2] 🔑 /left/ *noun* (no plural) the left side or direction: *The house is on your left.* ◇ *In Kenya we drive on the left.* OPPOSITE **right**

left[3] *form of* LEAVE[1]

be left be there after the rest has gone: *There is not much food left.*

left-click /ˌleft ˈklɪk/ *verb* (**left-clicks, left-clicking, left-clicked** /ˌleft ˈklɪkt/) to press the button on the left on a computer mouse: *Now left-click on 'Save'.*

left-hand /ˈleft hænd/ *adjective* of or on the left: *Your heart is on the left-hand side of your body.*

left-handed /ˌleft ˈhændɪd/ *adjective* If you are **left-handed**, you use your left hand more easily than your right hand, for example when you write.

left-luggage office /ˌleft ˈlʌgɪdʒ ɒfɪs/ (also **left luggage**) *noun* a place where you can leave your luggage for a short time

leftovers /ˈleftəʊvəz/ *noun* (plural) food that has not been eaten when you have finished a meal

leg 🔑 /leg/ *noun* **1** one of the long parts of the body of a person or an animal that is used for walking and standing: *A dog has four legs.* ➲ picture on page A13 **2** one of the parts of a pair of trousers that covers your leg: *These jeans are too long in the leg.* **3** one of the long parts that a table or chair stands on: *a table leg*

pull someone's leg to try to make someone believe something that is not true, for fun: *I didn't really see a ghost – I was only pulling your leg!*

legal 🔑 /ˈliːgl/ *adjective* **1** allowed by the law: *In many parts of America, it is legal to carry a gun.* OPPOSITE **illegal** **2** of or about the law: *legal advice* ▶ **legally** /ˈliːgəli/ *adverb*: *They are not legally married.*

legend /ˈledʒənd/ *noun* **1** an old story that is perhaps not true: *the legend of Bimwili and the Zimwi* **2** a famous person or event: *marathon legend Paul Tergat*

▶ **legendary** /ˈledʒəndri/ *adjective*: *the legendary athlete Doctor Kipchoge Keino* ◇ *The snows of Kilimanjaro are legendary.*

leggings /ˈlegɪŋz/ *noun* (plural) a piece of clothing for a woman or girl that fits tightly over both legs, like a very thin pair of trousers

legislature /ˈledʒɪsleɪtʃə(r)/ *noun* a group of people who have the power to make and change laws: *the national/state legislature*

leisure /ˈleʒə(r)/ *noun* (no plural) the time when you are not working and can do what you want: *What do you do in your leisure time?*

lemon 🔑 /ˈlemən/ *noun* a yellow fruit with juice that tastes sharp (**sour**)

lemon

lemonade /ˌleməˈneɪd/ *noun* **1** (no plural) a sweet clear drink with bubbles in it **2** (*plural* **lemonades**) a glass of this drink

lend 🔑 /lend/ *verb* (**lends, lending, lent** /lent/, **has lent**) to give something to someone for a short time: *Wasike lent me his bike.* ➲ Picture at **borrow**.

lend a hand to help someone: *Can you lend me a hand with these books?*

length 🔑 /leŋθ/ *noun* (no plural) how long something is: *The table is two metres in length.* ◇ *We measured the length of the room.* ➲ picture on page A12

lengthen /ˈleŋθən/ *verb* (**lengthens, lengthening, lengthened** /ˈleŋθənd/) to become longer or make something longer

lengthy /ˈleŋθi/ *adjective* (**lengthier, lengthiest**) long: *a lengthy meeting*

lens /lenz/ *noun* (*plural* **lenses**) a special piece of glass in things like cameras or glasses ➲ Look at **contact lens**.

lent *form of* LEND

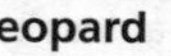

lentil /ˈlentl/ *noun* a small round dried seed. You cook **lentils** in water before you eat them: *lentil soup*

leopard /ˈlepəd/ *noun* a wild animal like a big cat with yellow fur and dark spots

leper /ˈlepə(r)/ *noun* a person who has **leprosy** (= a serious disease that affects the skin and can make parts of the body fall off)

leso = **kanga**

less[1] /les/ *adjective, pronoun* a smaller amount of something; not so much: *A poor person has less money than a rich person.* ◇ *I'm too fat – I should eat less.* OPPOSITE **more** ➲ Look at **least**[1].

less[2] /les/ *adverb* not so much: *It rains less in January.* ◇ *He's less intelligent than his sister.* OPPOSITE **more** ➲ Look at **least**[2].

-less /ləs/ *suffix* without: *lifeless* ◇ *a toothless old man* ◇ *worthless coins* ◇ *merciless* (= without mercy)

lesson /ˈlesn/ *noun* a time when you learn something with a teacher: *I was late for school and missed the first lesson.*

let /let/ *verb* (**lets, letting, let, has let**) **1** to allow someone or something to do something: *Her parents won't let her go out with her friends.* ◇ *Let me carry your bag.* ◇ *Let the dog in* (= let it come in). **2** to allow someone to use your house or land if they pay you: *Have you got any rooms to let?*

let's You use 'let's' to ask someone to do something with you: *Let's go to the cinema tomorrow.*

let someone down to not do something that you promised to do for someone: *Robi let me down. We agreed to meet at six o'clock but she didn't come.*

let go of someone or **something**; **let someone** or **something go** to stop holding someone or something: *Let go of my hand!* ◇ *Let me go. You're hurting me!*

let someone off to not punish someone: *He wasn't sent to prison – the judge let him off.*

letter /ˈletə(r)/ *noun* **1** a piece of writing that one person sends to another person: *Did you post my letter?* ◇ *She wrote a letter to her mother.* **2** a sign in writing: *Z is the last letter in the English alphabet.*

> ❖ **WORD BUILDING**
>
> A, B and C are **capital** letters, and a, b and c are **small** letters.

letter box /ˈletə bɒks/ *noun* (*plural* **letter boxes**) **1** a small box outside a house or a building, or a hole in a door, for putting letters through **2** a box in the street where you put letters that you want to send

lettuce /ˈletɪs/ *noun* a plant with big leaves that you eat without cooking, in salads

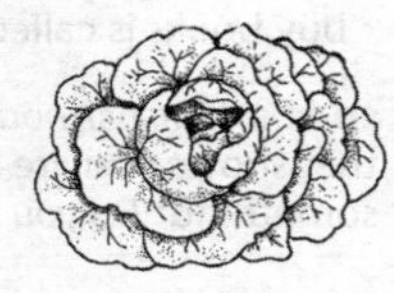

level[1] /ˈlevl/ *adjective* **1** with no part higher than another part; flat: *We need level ground to play football on.* ◇ *This shelf isn't level.* **2** with the same heights, points, positions, etc: *The two teams are level with 40 points each.* ◇ *His head is level with his mother's shoulder.*

level[2] /ˈlevl/ *noun* how high something is: *The town is 500 metres above sea level.* ◇ *an elementary-level French class*

level crossing /ˌlevl ˈkrɒsɪŋ/ *noun* a place where a railway line goes over a road

lever /ˈliːvə(r)/ *noun* **1** a bar for lifting something heavy or opening something. You put one end under the thing you want to lift or open, and push the other end. **2** a thing that you pull or push to make a machine work: *Pull this lever.*

liable /ˈlaɪəbl/ *adjective* If you are **liable** to do something, you usually do it or you will probably do it: *He's liable to get angry if you don't do what he says.*

liar /ˈlaɪə(r)/ *noun* a person who says or writes things that are not true: *I don't believe her – she's a liar.* ❶ The verb is **lie**.

liberal /ˈlɪbərəl/ *adjective* A person who is **liberal** lets other people do and think what they want: *Adisa's parents are very liberal, but mine are quite strict.*

liberate /ˈlɪbəreɪt/ *verb* (**liberates, liberating, liberated**) to make someone or something free: *France was liberated in 1945.*

liberty /ˈlɪbəti/ *noun* (no plural) being free to go where you want and do what you want

librarian /laɪˈbreəriən/ *noun* a person who works in a library

library /ˈlaɪbrəri/ *noun* (*plural* **libraries**) a room or building where you go to borrow or read books

> ❖ **library** or **bookshop**?
>
> Be careful! You cannot buy books from a **library**. The place where you buy books is called a **bookshop**.

licence /ˈlaɪsns/ *noun* a piece of paper that shows you are allowed to do or have something: *Do you have a driving licence?*

> ❖ **SPELLING**
>
> Be careful! **Licence** with a **c** is a noun, but **license** with an **s** is a verb.

license /ˈlaɪsns/ *verb* (**licenses**, **licensing**, **licensed** /ˈlaɪsnst/) to give someone a **licence**: *This shop is licensed to sell pets.*

lick /lɪk/ *verb* (**licks**, **licking**, **licked** /lɪkt/) to move your tongue over something: *The cat was licking its paws.*

lids

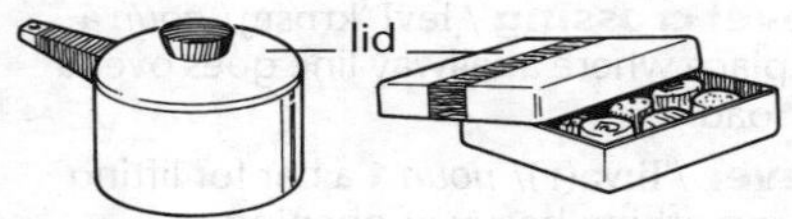

lid /lɪd/ *noun* the top part of a box, pot or other container that covers it and that you can take off: *I can't get the lid of this jar.* ➲ Look at **eyelid**. ➲ Picture at **container**.

lie[1] /laɪ/ *verb* (**lies**, **lying**, **lay** /leɪ/, **has lain** /leɪn/) **1** to put your body flat on something so that you are not sitting or standing: *He lay on the bed.* **2** to have your body flat on something: *The baby was lying on its back.* **3** to be or stay on something: *His clothes lay on the floor where he had left them.*
lie down to put or have your body flat on something: *She lay down on the bed*

lie[2] /laɪ/ *verb* (**lies**, **lying**, **lied** /laɪd/, **has lied**) to say something that you know is not true: *He lied about his age. He said he was 16 but really he's 14.* ⓘ A person who lies is a **liar**.

lie[3] /laɪ/ *noun* something you say that you know is not true: *She told me a lie.*

lieutenant /lefˈtenənt/ *noun* an officer in the army or navy

life /laɪf/ *noun* **1** (no plural) People, animals and plants have life, but things like stone, metal and water do not: *Do you believe there is life after death?* ◇ *Is there life on the moon?* **2** (*plural* **lives** /laɪvz/) being alive: *Many people lost their lives* (= died) *in the fire.* ◇ *The doctor saved her life* (= stopped her dying). **3** (*plural* **lives**) the time that you have been alive: *He has lived here all his life.* **4** (no plural) the way that you live: *an unhappy life* **5** (no plural) energy; being busy and interested: *Young children are full of life.*
lead a life to live in a certain way: *She leads a busy life.*

lifebelt /ˈlaɪfbelt/ *noun* a big ring that you hold or wear if you fall into water to stop you from dying in the water (**drowning**)

lifeboat /ˈlaɪfbəʊt/ *noun* a boat that goes to help people who are in danger at sea

life jacket

life jacket /ˈlaɪf dʒækɪt/ *noun* a special jacket that you wear in a boat to help you float if you fall in the water

lifesaver /ˈlaɪfseɪvə(r)/ *noun* something that helps someone in a difficult situation: *Safety belts are a lifesaver and should be worn on all car journeys.*

life skills /ˈlaɪf skɪlz/ *noun* (plural) useful skills that you need for everyday life: *Sharing with a brother or sister can help children learn important life skills.*

lifestyle /ˈlaɪfstaɪl/ *noun* the way that you live: *They have a healthy lifestyle.*

lifetime /ˈlaɪftaɪm/ *noun* all the time that you are alive: *There have been a lot of changes in my grandmother's lifetime.*

lift

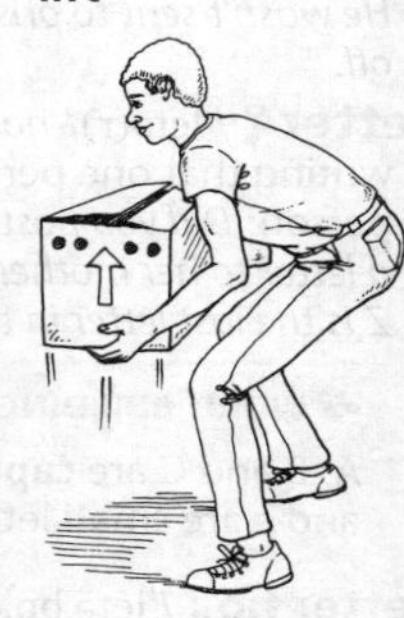

lift[1] /lɪft/ *verb* (**lifts**, **lifting**, **lifted**) to move someone or something up: *I can't lift this box. It's too heavy.* ◇ *Lift your arm.*

lift[2] /lɪft/ *noun* **1** a machine that takes people and things up and down in a high building: *Shall we use the stairs or take the lift?* **2** a free journey in another person's car: *Can you give me a lift to Namanga?*

light[1] 🔑 /laɪt/ *noun* **1** (no plural) Light comes from the sun, fire and lamps. It makes us able to see things: *The sunlight was very bright.* ◇ *The light was not very good so it was difficult to read.* **2** (*plural* **lights**) a thing that gives light, for example an electric lamp: *Put the lights on.* ➲ Look at **traffic lights**.

> ❖ **WORD BUILDING**
>
> A light can be **on** or **off**. You can **put**, **turn** or **switch** a light **on**, **off** or **out**: *Turn the lights off before you go to bed.* ◇ *It's getting dark. Shall I switch the light on?*

3 (no plural) something, for example a match, that you use to start a cigarette burning: *Have you got a light?*
set light to something to make something start to burn

light[2] 🔑 /laɪt/ *adjective* (**lighter**, **lightest**) **1** with a lot of light: *It was a light and sunny day.* ◇ *The room has a lot of windows so it's very light.* OPPOSITE **dark** **2** with a pale colour: *a light blue shirt* OPPOSITE **dark** **3** easy to lift or move; not heavy: *Will you carry this bag for me? It's very light.* OPPOSITE **heavy** ➲ Picture at **heavy**. **4** not very much or not very strong: *light rain* ◇ *I had a light breakfast.*
▶ **lightly** *adverb*: *She touched me lightly on the arm.*

light[3] 🔑 /laɪt/ *verb* (**lights**, **lighting**, **lit** /lɪt/ *or* **lighted**, **has lit** *or* **has lighted**) **1** to make something start to burn: *Will you light the fire?* **2** to give light to something: *The room is lit by two big lamps.*

light bulb /ˈlaɪt bʌlb/ *noun* the glass part of an electric lamp that gives light

lighter /ˈlaɪtə(r)/ *noun* a thing for lighting cigarettes

lighthouse /ˈlaɪthaʊs/ *noun* (*plural* **lighthouses** /ˈlaɪthaʊzɪz/) a tall building by or in the sea, with a strong light to show ships that there are rocks

lighting /ˈlaɪtɪŋ/ *noun* (no plural) the kind of lights that a place has: *street lighting*

lightning /ˈlaɪtnɪŋ/ *noun* (no plural) a sudden bright light in the sky when there is a storm: *He was struck* (= hit) *by lightning.* ➲ Look at **thunder**[1].

like[1] 🔑 /laɪk/ *verb* (**likes**, **liking**, **liked** /laɪkt/) to feel that someone or something is good or nice; to enjoy something: *Do you like your new teacher?* ◇ *I don't like carrots.* ◇ *I like playing tennis.* ◇ *I don't like you staying out so late.*
OPPOSITE **dislike**
if you like if you want: *'Shall we go out?' 'Yes, if you like.'*

> ❖ **GRAMMAR**
>
> **Would like** is a more polite way of saying **want**: *Would you like some coffee?* ◇ *I'd like to speak to the manager.*
>
> It is not the same as **Do you like?**: *Do you like tea?* ◇ *Do you like listening to music?*

like[2] 🔑 /laɪk/ *preposition, conjunction* **1** the same as someone or something: *She is wearing a dress like mine.* ◇ *Wasike looks like his father.* ➲ Look at **unlike**. **2** in the same way as someone or something: *She acted like a child.* **3** for example: *I bought a lot of things, like books and clothes.*
what is … like? words that you say when you want to know more about someone or something: *'What's that book like?' 'It's very interesting.'*

likely 🔑 /ˈlaɪkli/ *adjective* (**likelier**, **likeliest**) If something is likely, it will probably happen: *It's likely that she will agree.* ◇ *They are likely to be late.* OPPOSITE **unlikely** ▶ **likelihood** /ˈlaɪklihʊd/ *noun* (no plural): *There's very little likelihood of that happening.*

likeness /ˈlaɪknəs/ *noun* (no plural) being or looking the same: *There's a strong likeness between Karimi and his brother.*

likewise /ˈlaɪkwaɪz/ *adverb* the same: *I sat down and Sarika did likewise.*

lily /ˈlɪli/ *noun* (*plural* **lilies**) a plant with big flowers

limb /lɪm/ *noun*

> ❖ **PRONUNCIATION**
>
> **Limb** sounds like **him** because we do not say the 'b'.

an arm or a leg

lime /laɪm/ *noun* a small green fruit like a lemon

limestone /ˈlaɪmstəʊn/ *noun* (no plural) a kind of rock, used for building and for making **cement**

limit¹ 🔑 /ˈlɪmɪt/ *noun* the most that is possible or allowed: *What is the speed limit?* (= how fast are you allowed to go?)

limit² 🔑 /ˈlɪmɪt/ *verb* (**limits, limiting, limited**) to do or have no more than a certain amount or number: *There's only room for 100 people, so we must limit the number of tickets we sell.*

limp /lɪmp/ *verb* (**limps, limping, limped** /lɪmpt/) to walk with difficulty because you have hurt your foot or leg ▶ **limp** *noun* (no plural): *She walks with a limp.*

line¹ 🔑 /laɪn/ *noun* **1** a long thin mark like this _: *Draw a straight line.* ◇ *The ball crossed the line, so it was a goal.* **2** people or things beside each other or one after the other: *Stand in a line.* **3** all the words that are beside each other on a page: *How many lines are there on this page?* ◇ *I don't know the next line of the poem.* **4** what a train moves along: *They are doing repairs to the line.* **5** a very long wire for telephones or electricity: *I tried to phone him but the line was busy.*

line² /laɪn/ *verb* (**lines, lining, lined** /laɪnd/) **1** to stand or be in lines along something: *People lined the street to watch the race.* **2** to cover the inside of something with a different material: *The jiko is made of metal lined with clay.*
line up to stand in a line or make a line

linen /ˈlɪnɪn/ *noun* (no plural) **1** a kind of strong cloth: *a white linen jacket* **2** sheets and other things made of cloth that we use in the home

liner /ˈlaɪnə(r)/ *noun* **1** a big ship that carries people a long way **2** a bag that you put inside something to keep it clean: *a dustbin liner*

linesman /ˈlaɪnzmən/ *noun* (*plural* **linesmen** /ˈlaɪnzmən/) a person who helps the **referee** (= the person who controls the game) in football, tennis, etc.

linger /ˈlɪŋgə(r)/ *verb* (**lingers, lingering, lingered** /ˈlɪŋgəd/) to stay somewhere for a long time: *They lingered in the park after the end of the concert.*

lining /ˈlaɪnɪŋ/ *noun* material that covers the inside of something: *My coat has a thick lining so it's very warm.*

link¹ /lɪŋk/ *noun* **1** something that joins things or people together: *There's a link between diet and good health.* **2** one of the round parts in a chain **3** a place on the Internet that is joined to another place: *To visit our website, click on this link.*

link² /lɪŋk/ *verb* (**links, linking, linked** /lɪŋkt/) to join two people or things: *A new railway line links the two cities.*

lions

lion /ˈlaɪən/ *noun* a wild animal like a big cat with yellow fur. **Lions** live in Africa and parts of Asia.

> ❖ **WORD BUILDING**
> A female lion is called a **lioness** and a young lion is called a **cub**.

lip 🔑 /lɪp/ *noun* one of the two soft red parts above and below your mouth: *She licked her lips.* ➲ picture on page A13

lipstick /ˈlɪpstɪk/ *noun* colour that some women put on their lips: *Mother put on some lipstick.*

liquid 🔑 /ˈlɪkwɪd/ *noun* anything that is not a solid or a gas. Water, oil and milk are liquids: *She poured the liquid into a bottle.* ▶ **liquid** *adjective*: *liquid gold*

> ❖ **WORD BUILDING**
> There are many different types of liquids. Here are some of them: **milk, paraffin, petrol** and **water**. Can you think of any others?

list¹ 🔑 /lɪst/ *noun* a lot of names or other things that you write, one after another: *a shopping list* (= of things that you must buy)

list² 🔑 /lɪst/ *verb* (**lists, listing, listed**) to write or say a list: *The teacher listed all our names.*

listen /ˈlɪsn/ *verb* (**listens, listening, listened** /ˈlɪsnd/)

> ❖ **PRONUNCIATION**
> We do not say the 't' in **listen**.

to hear something when you are trying to hear it: *I was listening to the radio.* ◇ *Listen! I want to tell you something.* ➲ Note at **hear**.

lit *form of* LIGHT[3]

literacy /ˈlɪtərəsi/ *noun* (no plural) the ability to read and write: *basic literacy skills*

literate /ˈlɪtərət/ *adjective* able to read or write OPPOSITE **illiterate** ▶ **literacy** /ˈlɪtərəsi/ *noun* (no plural) the ability to read and write OPPOSITE **illiteracy**

literature /ˈlɪtrətʃə(r)/ *noun* (no plural) books, plays and poetry: *He is studying African literature.*

litigation /ˌlɪtɪˈgeɪʃn/ *noun* (no plural) the process of taking legal action in a court of law: *The cost of litigation is too high for many people.*

litre /ˈliːtə(r)/ *noun* a measure of liquid. There are 100 **centilitres** in a litre: *ten litres of petrol* ⓘ The short way of writing 'litre' is **l**: *20 l*

litter[1] /ˈlɪtə(r)/ *noun* **1** (no plural) pieces of paper and other things that people leave on the ground: *The park was full of litter after the concert.* **2** (*plural* **litters**) all the baby animals that are born to the same mother at the same time: *The dog had a litter of six puppies.*

litter[2] /ˈlɪtə(r)/ *verb* (**litters, littering, littered** /ˈlɪtəd/) to be or make something untidy with **litter**: *My desk was littered with papers.*

little[1] /ˈlɪtl/ *adjective* **1** not big; small: *a little village* ➲ picture on page A5 **2** young: *a little girl* **3** not much: *We have very little money.*

little[2] /ˈlɪtl/ *adverb* not much: *I'm tired – I slept very little last night.*
a little quite; rather: *This skirt is a little too short for me.* ➲ Note at **very[1]**.

little[3] /ˈlɪtl/ *pronoun* a small amount; not much: *There wasn't much food so we all just had a little.* ◇ *I did very little today.*
a little some but not much: *I speak a little French.*
little by little slowly: *Little by little she started to feel better.*

> ❖ **little** or **a little**?
> Be careful! **Little** and **a little** are not the same. Look at these examples: *There is little* (= not much) *sugar left in the jar.* ◇ *There is a little* (= some) *sugar left in the jar.*
> Look also at **few**.

live[1] /lɪv/ *verb* (**lives, living, lived** /lɪvd/) **1** to be or stay alive: *You can't live without water.* ◇ *He lived to the age of 93.* **2** to have your home somewhere: *Where do you live?* **3** to spend your life in a certain way: *They live a quiet life in the village.*
live on something 1 to eat or drink only one thing: *Cows live on grass.* **2** to have a certain amount of money: *They live on less than 2 000 shillings a week.*
live up to something to be as good as you expect: *The school lives up to its reputation.*

live[2] /laɪv/ *adjective* **1** not dead: *The snake ate a live mouse.* **2** If a radio or television programme is **live**, you see or hear it at the same time as it happens: *a live football match* **3** with electricity passing through it: *Don't touch that wire – it's live!*

lively /ˈlaɪvli/ *adjective* (**livelier, liveliest**) full of life; always moving or doing things: *The children are very lively.*

liver /ˈlɪvə(r)/ *noun* the part inside the body of a person or an animal that cleans the blood ➲ picture on page A13

lives *plural of* LIFE

livestock /ˈlaɪvstɒk/ *noun* (no plural) animals that people keep on farms

living[1] /ˈlɪvɪŋ/ *adjective* alive; not dead: *They say he is the greatest living writer.*

living[2] /ˈlɪvɪŋ/ *noun* (no plural) **1** the way that you get money: *What do you do for a living?* **2** the way that you live

living room /ˈlɪvɪŋ ruːm/ (*also* **sitting room** /ˈsɪtɪŋ ruːm/) *noun* a room in a house where people sit and watch television, talk, etc.

lizard /ˈlɪzəd/ *noun* a small animal that has four legs, a long tail and rough skin

lizard

load[1] /ləʊd/ *noun* **1** something that is carried: *The lorry* *brought another load of wood.* **2 loads** (plural) a lot: *We've got loads of time.*

load² 🔑 /ləʊd/ *verb* (**loads, loading, loaded**) **1** to put things in or on something, for example a car or ship, that will carry them: *Two men loaded the furniture into the van.* ◇ *They're loading the plane now.* OPPOSITE **unload** **2** to put bullets in a gun or film in a camera: *Is that gun loaded?*

loaf /ləʊf/ *noun* (*plural* **loaves** /ləʊvz/) a big piece of bread: *a loaf of bread*

loan¹ 🔑 /ləʊn/ *noun* money that someone lends you: *The bank gave her a loan of 250 000 shillings to buy a car.*

loan² /ləʊn/ *verb* (**loans, loaning, loaned** /ləʊnd/) to lend something: *This book is loaned from the library.*

lobster /ˈlɒbstə(r)/ *noun* a sea animal with a hard shell, eight legs and a long tail

lobster

local 🔑 /ˈləʊkl/ *adjective* of a place near you: *Her children go to the local school.* ◇ *a local newspaper* ◇ *local government* ▸ **locally** /ˈləʊkəli/ *adverb*: *Do you work locally?*

located /ləʊˈkeɪtɪd/ *adjective* in a place: *The factory is located just outside Mombasa.*

location /ləʊˈkeɪʃn/ *noun* a place: *The house is in a quiet location on a hill.*

lock¹ 🔑 /lɒk/ *noun* a metal thing that keeps a door, gate, box, etc. closed so that you cannot open it without a key: *I heard the key turn in the lock.*

lock

key

lock² 🔑 /lɒk/ *verb* (**locks, locking, locked** /lɒkt/) to close something with a key: *Don't forget to lock the door when you leave.* OPPOSITE **unlock**

lock something away to put something in a place that you close with a key: *The paintings are locked away at night.*

lock someone in to lock a door so that someone cannot go out: *The prisoners were locked in every night.*

lock someone out to lock a door so that someone cannot get in

lock up to lock all the doors and windows of a building

locker /ˈlɒkə(r)/ *noun* a small cupboard, with a lock, for keeping things in, for example in a school or at station

locust /ˈləʊkəst/ *noun* an insect that flies in very large groups and destroys crops

locust

lodge /lɒdʒ/ *verb* (**lodges, lodging, lodged** /lɒdʒd/) to pay to live in another person's house: *I lodged with a family when I was studying in Jinja.* ▸ **lodger** /ˈlɒdʒə(r)/ *noun*: *We have two lodgers.*

loft /lɒft/ *noun* the room or space under the roof of a house: *My old books are in a box in the loft.*

log¹ /lɒg/ *noun* a thick round piece of wood from a tree: *Put a log on the fire.*

log

log² /lɒg/ *verb* (**logs, logging, logged** /lɒgd/) to cut down trees in a forest for their wood

log in; log on to start using a computer

log off; log out to stop using a computer

logging /ˈlɒgɪŋ/ *noun* (no plural) the work of cutting down trees for their wood

lonely 🔑 /ˈləʊnli/ *adjective* (**lonelier, loneliest**) **1** unhappy because you are not with other people: *I was very lonely when I first came to this town.* **2** far from other places: *a lonely house in the hills* ▸ **loneliness** /ˈləʊnlinəs/ *noun* (no plural) being lonely

long¹ 🔑 /lɒŋ/ *adjective* (**longer** /ˈlɒŋgə(r)/, **longest** /ˈlɒŋgɪst/) **1** far from one end to the other: *This is the longest road in Uganda.* ◇ *She has long black hair.* OPPOSITE **short** ➲ picture on page A5 **2** You use 'long' to say or ask how far something is from one end to the other: *How long is the table?* ◇ *The wall is 5 metres long.* ➲ picture on page A12

3 that continues for a lot of time: *a long film* OPPOSITE **short** **4** You use 'long' to say or ask about the time from the beginning to the end of something: *How long is the lesson?*

ong² /lɒŋ/ *adverb* for a lot of time: *I can't stay long.*
as long as; so long as if: *You can borrow the book as long as you promise not to lose it.*
for long for a lot of time: *I won't be out for long.*
long after at a time much after
long ago many years in the past: *Long ago there were no cars.*
long before at a time much before: *My grandfather died long before I was born.*
no longer; not any longer not now; not as before: *She doesn't live here any longer.*

ong³ /lɒŋ/ *verb* (**longs, longing, longed** /lɒŋd/) to want something very much: *I long to see my family again.* ◇ *She's longing for a letter from her parents.*

ong-distance /ˌlɒŋ ˈdɪstəns/ *adjective* travelling between places that are far apart: *long-distance flights* ◇ *a long-distance runner* (= one who takes part in a long-distance race)

longing /ˈlɒŋɪŋ/ *noun* a strong feeling of wanting something

the long jump /ðə ˈlɒŋ dʒʌmp/ *noun* (no plural) a sport where you try to jump as far as you can

long-sighted /ˌlɒŋ ˈsaɪtɪd/ *adjective* not able to see things clearly if they are close to you OPPOSITE **short-sighted**

long-term /ˌlɒŋ ˈtɜːm/ *adjective* lasting for a long period of time: *What are her long-term plans?*

look¹ /lʊk/ *verb* (**looks, looking, looked** /lʊkt/) **1** to turn your eyes towards someone or something and try to see them: *Look at this picture.* ◇ *You should look both ways before you cross the road.* ➲ Note at **see**. **2** to seem to be; to appear: *You look tired!* **3** You say 'look' to make someone listen to you: *Look, I need some money.*
look after someone or **something** to take care of someone or something: *Can you look after my children for a few hours?*
look as if; look as though to seem or appear: *It looks as if it's going to rain.*
look down on someone to think that you are better than someone: *Don't look down on people who have less money than you.*
look for someone or **something** to try to find someone or something: *I'm looking for my keys.*
look forward to something to wait for something with pleasure: *I'm looking forward to seeing you again.*
look into something to study something carefully: *We will look into the problem.*
look like someone or **something** **1** to seem to be something: *That looks like a good book.* **2** words that you use to ask about someone's appearance: *'What does he look like?' 'He's tall and very good-looking.'* **3** to have the same appearance as someone or something: *She looks like her mother.*
look out! to be careful!: *Look out! There's a car coming!*
look out for someone or **something** to pay attention and try to see someone or something: *Look out for thieves!*
look round to visit a place: *We looked round the museum.*
look something up to try to find information about something in a book or on a computer: *How many words did you look up in the dictionary?*
look up to someone to think that someone is very good or clever; to respect someone: *She loved and looked up to her parents.* SAME MEANING **admire**

look² /lʊk/ *noun* **1** turning your eyes towards someone or something; looking: *Hawa gave me an angry look!* **2** the way something seems: *I don't like the look of that dog. I think it wants to attack us.* **3 looks** (plural) how a person's face and body is: *She was blessed with good looks.*
have a look **1** to see something: *Can I have a look at your photos?* **2** to try to find something: *I've had a look for your pen, but I can't find it.*
have a look round to see many parts of a place: *We had a look round the museum.*

loop /luːp/ *noun* a round shape made by something like string or rope

loop

loose /luːs/ *adjective* (**looser, loosest**) **1** not tied or fixed: *The dog broke* *its chain and got loose.* ◇ *One of his teeth is loose.* **2** not tight: *a loose white dress* ▶ **loosely** *adverb* not tightly or firmly: *The rope was tied loosely round a tree.*

> ❖ **SPELLING**
>
> Be careful! **Loose** is an adjective but **lose** with one **o** is a verb.

loosen /ˈluːsn/ *verb* (**loosens, loosening, loosened** /ˈluːsnd/) to become looser or make something looser: *Can you loosen this knot? It's too tight.* OPPOSITE **tighten**

loquat /ˈləʊkwɒt/ *noun* a small yellow fruit like an egg

Lord /lɔːd/ *noun* **the Lord** (no plural) God or Jesus Christ

lorry ⚷ /ˈlɒri/ *noun* (*plural* **lorries**) a big vehicle for carrying heavy things

lorry

lose ⚷ /luːz/ *verb* (**loses, losing, lost** /lɒst/, **has lost**) **1** to be unable to find something or someone: *I can't open the door because I've lost my key.* **2** to not have someone or something that you had before: *He lost his job when the factory closed.* **3** to not win: *Our team lost the match.*

> ❖ **WORD FAMILY**
>
> lose loser losing loss lost

loser /ˈluːzə(r)/ *noun* a person who does not win a game, race or competition OPPOSITE **winner**

losing /ˈluːzɪŋ/ *adjective* that loses a game, race or competition: *the losing team*

loss ⚷ /lɒs/ *noun* (*plural* **losses**) **1** losing something: *She hasn't recovered from the loss* (= death) *of her brother.* ◇ *job losses* **2** how much money a business loses: *The company made a huge loss last year.* OPPOSITE **profit**
at a loss If you are **at a loss**, you do not know what to do or say.

lost[1] ⚷ /lɒst/ *adjective* **1** If you are lost, you do not know where you are: *I took the wrong road and now I'm lost.* ◇ *Take this map so that you don't get lost!* **2** If something is lost, you cannot find it: *I'm still looking for that lost file.*

lost[2] *form of* LOSE

lost property /ˌlɒst ˈprɒpəti/ *noun* (no plural) things that people have lost: *I left my bag on the bus, so I went to the lost property office at the station.*

lot[1] /lɒt/ *noun*
a lot very much; a big amount or number: *We ate a lot.*
a lot of; lots of a big number or amount of something: *She's got a lot of friends.* ◇ *Lots of love from Kendi* (= words at the end of a letter).

lot[2] ⚷ /lɒt/ *adverb*
a lot very much or often: *Your flat is a lot bigger than mine.* ◇ *I go to the park a lot.*

lotion /ˈləʊʃn/ *noun* liquid that you put on your skin: *body lotion*

loud ⚷ /laʊd/ *adjective, adverb* (**louder, loudest**) that makes a lot of noise; not quiet: *I couldn't hear what he said because the music was too loud.* ◇ *loud voices* ◇ *Please speak a bit louder – I can't hear you.* OPPOSITE **quiet**
out loud so that other people can hear it: *I read the story out loud.* ▶ **loudly** *adverb*: *She laughed loudly.*

loudspeaker /ˌlaʊdˈspiːkə(r)/ *noun* an instrument for making sounds louder: *Music was coming from the loudspeakers.*

lounge /laʊndʒ/ *noun* a room in a house or hotel where you can sit in comfortable chairs

love[1] ⚷ /lʌv/ *verb* (**loves, loving, loved** /lʌvd/) **1** to have a strong warm feeling for someone: *I love him very much.* ◇ *She loves her parents.* **2** to like something very much: *I love swimming.* ◇ *I would love to go to America.* OPPOSITE **hate**

love[2] ⚷ /lʌv/ *noun* **1** (no plural) a strong warm feeling of liking someone or something: *Their love for each other was very strong.* ◇ *a love of football* ➲ Look at **hate**[2]. **2** (*plural* **loves**) a person that you love: *Yes, my love.* **3** (no plural) (also **love from**) a way of ending a letter to someone that you know well: *Lots of love from Nafula.* **4** (no plural) a word in the game of **tennis** that means zero: *The score is 15-love.*
be in love with someone to love someone: *He says he is in love with her and they are going to get married.*
fall in love with someone to begin to love someone: *He fell in love with Sarika the first time they met.*

lovely /ˈlʌvli/ *adjective* (**lovelier, loveliest**) beautiful or very nice: *That's a lovely dress.* ◇ *The evening sky looks lovely.* ◇ *It's lovely to see you again.*

loving /ˈlʌvɪŋ/ *adjective* feeling or showing love: *loving parents*

low 🔑 /ləʊ/ *adjective* (**lower, lowest**) **1** near the ground: *There was a low wall round the garden.* ◇ *a low bridge* OPPOSITE **high** **2** less than usual: *low temperatures* ◇ *low pay* OPPOSITE **high** **3** soft and quiet: *I heard low voices in the next room.* **4** deep; not high: *a low sound* ▶ **low** *adverb* near the ground: *The plane flew low over the fields.*

lower[1] /ˈləʊə(r)/ *verb* (**lowers, lowering, lowered** /ˈləʊəd/) **1** to move someone or something down: *They lowered the flag.* **2** to make something less: *Please lower your voice* (= speak more quietly). OPPOSITE **raise**

lower[2] /ˈləʊə(r)/ *adjective* that is under another; bottom: *the lower lip* OPPOSITE **upper**

lowland /ˈləʊlənd/ *noun* an area of land that is not very high: *the lowlands of Kenya*

loyal /ˈlɔɪəl/ *adjective* A person who is **loyal** does not change their friends or beliefs: *a loyal friend* ◇ *He is loyal to the team.* OPPOSITE **disloyal** ▶ **loyalty** /ˈlɔɪəlti/ *noun* (no plural) being **loyal**: *Loyalty to your friends is very important.*

luck 🔑 /lʌk/ *noun* (no plural) **1** good things that happen to you that you cannot control: *Wish me luck for my exams!* **2** things that happen to you that you cannot control; chance: *Losing my purse was pure bad luck.*
bad luck; hard luck words that you say to someone when you are sorry that they did not have good luck
be in luck to have good things happen to you: *I was in luck – the shop had the book I wanted.*
good luck words that you say to someone when you hope that they will do well: *Good luck! I'm sure you'll win.*

lucky 🔑 /ˈlʌki/ *adjective* (**luckier, luckiest**) **1** If you are lucky, you have good luck: *She had a bad accident and she is lucky to be alive.* **2** Something that is lucky brings good luck: *My lucky number is 3.* OPPOSITE **unlucky** ▶ **luckily** /ˈlʌkɪli/ *adverb* it is lucky that: *I was late, but luckily they waited for me.*

luggage 🔑 /ˈlʌgɪdʒ/ *noun* (no plural) bags and suitcases that you take with you when you travel: *'How much luggage have you got?' 'Only one suitcase.'*

> ❖ **GRAMMAR**
> Be careful! You cannot say 'a luggage' or 'luggages'. You can say 'some luggage' or 'a piece of luggage'. You can also use **a bag** or **a suitcase** instead.

lump 🔑 /lʌmp/ *noun* **1** a hard piece of something: *two lumps of sugar* ◇ *a lump of coal* ➲ picture on page A4 **2** a part in or on your body which has become hard and bigger: *I've got a lump on my head where I hit it.*

lunch 🔑 /lʌntʃ/ *noun* (*plural* **lunches**) a meal that you eat in the middle of the day: *What would you like for lunch?* ◇ *What time do you usually have lunch?* ➲ Note at **meal**.

lunchtime /ˈlʌntʃtaɪm/ *noun* the time when you eat lunch: *I'll meet you at lunchtime.*

lung /lʌŋ/ *noun* one of the two parts inside your body that you use for breathing ➲ picture on page A13

luxurious /lʌgˈʒʊəriəs/ *adjective* very comfortable and expensive: *a luxurious hotel*

luxury /ˈlʌkʃəri/ *noun* **1** (no plural) a way of living when you have all the expensive and beautiful things that you want: *They live in luxury in a beautiful house in Kololo.* ◇ *a luxury hotel* **2** (*plural* **luxuries**) something that is very nice and expensive that you do not really need: *Eating in a restaurant is a luxury for most people.*

lying *form of* LIE[1]

Mm

M, m /em/ *noun* (*plural* **M's, m's** /emz/) **1** the thirteenth letter of the English alphabet: *'Milk' begins with an 'M'.* **2** m short for METRE

machine ⚷ /mə'ʃi:n/ *noun* a thing with parts that move to do work or to make something. Machines often use electricity: *a washing machine* ◊ *This machine does not work.* ➲ Look at **machinery**.

machine gun /mə'ʃi:n gʌn/ *noun* a gun that can send out a lot of bullets very quickly

machinery /mə'ʃi:nəri/ *noun* (no plural) **1** the parts of a machine: *the machinery inside a clock* **2** a group of machines: *The factory has bought some new machinery.*

mad ⚷ /mæd/ *adjective* (**madder, maddest**) **1** ill in your mind **2** very stupid; crazy: *I think you're mad to go out in this storm!* **3** very angry: *He was mad at me for losing his watch.*
be mad about someone or **something** to like someone or something very much: *Ali is mad about football.*
drive someone mad to make someone very angry: *This noise is driving me mad!*
go mad 1 to become ill in your mind: *He went mad.* **2** to become very angry: *Your mother will go mad when she finds out what you did at school.*

madam /'mædəm/ *noun* (no plural) **1** a polite way of speaking to a woman, instead of using her name: *'Can I help you, madam?' asked the shop assistant.* **2 Madam** a word that you use at the beginning of a business letter to a woman: *Dear Madam …* ➲ Look at **sir**.

made *form of* MAKE¹
made of something from this material: *This shirt is made of cotton.*

madness /'mædnəs/ *noun* (no plural) stupid behaviour that could be dangerous: *It would be madness to take a boat out in this terrible weather.*

magazine ⚷ /ˌmægə'zi:n/ *noun* a kind of thin book with a paper cover that you can buy every week or every month. It has a lot of different stories and pictures inside: *She writes for a magazine.*

magic ⚷ /'mædʒɪk/ *noun* (no plural) **1** a special power that can make strange or impossible things happen: *The witch changed the prince into a frog by magic.* **2** clever tricks that someone can do to surprise people: *We went to a magic show.*
▸ **magic** *adjective*: *magic tricks*

magical /'mædʒɪkl/ *adjective* **1** having special powers: *The witch had magical powers.* **2** wonderful and exciting: *We spent a magical day on the island.*

magician /mə'dʒɪʃn/ *noun* **1** a person who does clever tricks to surprise people **2** a man in stories who has strange, unusual powers: *The magician turned the boy into a dog.*

magistrate /'mædʒɪstreɪt/ *noun* a judge in a court of law who decides how to punish people for small crimes

magnet

magnet /'mægnət/ *noun* a piece of metal that can make other metal things move towards it

magnetic /mæg'netɪk/ *adjective* able to make other metal things move towards it: *Is this metal magnetic?*

magnificent /mæg'nɪfɪsnt/ *adjective* very good or beautiful: *What a magnificent view!*

magnify /'mægnɪfaɪ/ *verb* (**magnifies, magnifying, magnified** /'mægnɪfaɪd/, **has magnified**) to make something look bigger than it really is: *We magnified the insect under a microscope.*

magnifying glass

magnifying glass /'mægnɪfaɪɪŋ glɑ:s/ *noun* (*plural* **magnifying glasses**) a special piece of glass that you hold in your hand. It makes things look bigger than they really are.

mahogany /mə'hɒgəni/ *noun* (no plural) very dark wood that is used for making furniture

maid /meɪd/ *noun* a woman who does work like cleaning in a hotel or large house

mail 🔑 /meɪl/ *noun* (no plural) **1** the way of sending and receiving letters, parcels, etc; post: *a mail service* ➲ Look at **airmail**. **2** letters and parcels that you send or receive; post: *Is there any mail for me?* ▶ **mail** *verb* (**mails**, **mailing**, **mailed** /meɪld/) to send something in the mail: *I'll mail the money to you.* ➲ Look at **email**.

maim /meɪm/ *verb* (**maims**, **maiming**, **maimed** /meɪmd/) to hurt someone very badly

main 🔑 /meɪn/ *adjective* most important: *My main reason for joining a club is to make friends.*

the mainland /ðə ˈmeɪnlænd/ *noun* (no plural) the main part of a country, not including any islands: *mainland Tanzania*

mainly 🔑 /ˈmeɪnli/ *adverb* mostly: *The students here are mainly between 19 and 23 years old.* ◇ *She eats mainly vegetables.*

main road /ˌmeɪn ˈrəʊd/ *noun* a big important road between towns

maintain /meɪnˈteɪn/ *verb* (**maintains**, **maintaining**, **maintained** /meɪnˈteɪnd/) **1** to continue with something: *If he can maintain this speed, he'll win the race.* **2** to keep something working well: *The roads are well maintained.*

maintenance /ˈmeɪntənəns/ *noun* (no plural) things that you do to keep something working well: *maintenance of a machine*

maize

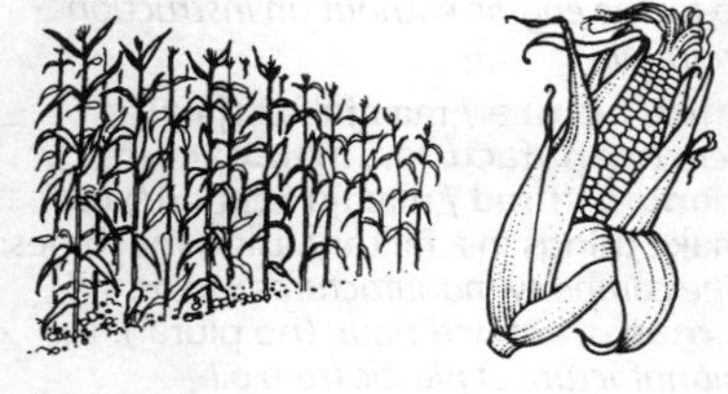

maize /meɪz/ *noun* (no plural) a tall plant with big yellow seeds (called **grain**) that you can eat or use to make flour

Majesty /ˈmædʒəsti/ *noun* (*plural* **Majesties**) a word that you use to talk to or about a king or queen: *Her Majesty Queen Elizabeth II*

majimbo *noun* (East African English) a system of government in a country with several smaller states, each of which has some power

major¹ /ˈmeɪdʒə(r)/ *adjective* very large, important or serious: *There are airports in all the major cities.* ◇ *major problems* OPPOSITE **minor**

major² /ˈmeɪdʒə(r)/ *noun* an officer in the army

majority /məˈdʒɒrəti/ *noun* (no plural) most things or people in a group: *The majority of Africans can speak more than one language.* OPPOSITE **minority**

make¹ 🔑 /meɪk/ *verb* (**makes**, **making**, **made** /meɪd/, **has made**) **1** to put things together so that you have a new thing: *They make cars in that factory.* ◇ *He made a box out of some pieces of wood.* **2** to cause something to be or to happen; to produce something: *The plane made a loud noise when it landed.* ◇ *Running makes you tired.* ◇ *That film made me cry.* ◇ *I made a mistake.* **3** to force someone to do something: *My father made me stay at home.* **4** a word that you use with money, numbers and time: *She makes* (= earns) *a lot of money.* ◇ *Five and seven make twelve.* ◇ *'What's the time?' 'I make it* (= my watch says it is) *six o'clock.'* **5** to give someone a job: *They made him President.* **6** to be able to go somewhere: *I'm sorry, but I can't make the team practice on Friday.*

make do with something to use something that is not very good, because there is nothing better: *We didn't have a table, but we made do with some boxes.*

make something into something to change something so that it becomes a different thing: *They made the office into a classroom.*

make something out to be able to see or understand something that is not clear: *It was dark and I couldn't make out the words on the sign.*

make something up to tell something that is not true: *Nobody believes that story – he made it up!*

make up to end an argument with someone: *Katee and Mwita had a quarrel last week, but they've made up now.*

make² 🔑 /meɪk/ *noun* the name of the company that made something: *'What make is that car?' 'It's a Ford.'*

maker /ˈmeɪkə(r)/ *noun* a person or company that makes something: *a film maker*

make-up /ˈmeɪk ʌp/ *noun* (no plural) special powders and creams that people put on their faces to make themselves more attractive. Actors also wear

make-up to make themselves look different: *She put on her make-up.*

makuti *noun* (no plural) (East African English) the leaves of a palm tree. **Makuti** can be used to make fences and **baskets** (= containers for carrying things) or as a roof covering

malaria /məˈleəriə/ *noun* (no plural) a dangerous illness that you get from the bite of a small flying insect (called a **mosquito**)

male 🔑 /meɪl/ *adjective* A male animal or person belongs to the sex that cannot have babies: *A cock is a male chicken.* ▸ **male** *noun*: *If you look at these fish you can see that the males are bigger than the females.* ➲ Look at **female**.

malnutrition /ˌmælnjuːˈtrɪʃn/ *noun* (no plural) an illness that you get when you do not eat enough food

mamba /ˈmæmbə/ *noun* a dangerous black or green snake

mammal /ˈmæml/ *noun* any animal that drinks milk from its mother's body when it is young: *Dogs, horses, whales and people are all mammals.*

man 🔑 /mæn/ *noun* **1** (*plural* **men** /men/) an adult male person: *I saw a tall man with a beard.* **2** (*plural* **men**) any person: *All men must have water to live.* **3** (no plural) all humans; people: *How long has man lived on the earth?*

manage 🔑 /ˈmænɪdʒ/ *verb* (**manages, managing, managed** /ˈmænɪdʒd/) **1** to be able to do something that is difficult: *The box was heavy but she managed to carry it.* **2** to control someone or something: *She manages a team of ten people.*

❖ **WORD FAMILY**
manage **management** **manager**

management /ˈmænɪdʒmənt/ *noun* (no plural) **1** control of something, for example a business, and the people who work in it: *good management* **2** all the people who control a business: *The factory is under new management.*

manager 🔑 /ˈmænɪdʒə(r)/ *noun* a person who controls a business, bank, hotel, etc: *Ereng is the manager of a shop.* ◇ *a bank manager*

manageress /ˌmænɪdʒəˈres/ *noun* (*plural* **manageresses**) a woman who controls a shop or restaurant

managing director /ˌmænɪdʒɪŋ dəˈrektə(r)/ *noun* the person who controls a big business

mandazi *noun* (plural) (East African English) small cakes made of flour, milk or water, and sugar, mixed together and fried

mane /meɪn/ *noun* the long hair on the neck of a horse or lion ➲ Picture at **lion**.

mango /ˈmæŋɡəʊ/ *noun* (*plural* **mangoes** *or* **mangos**) a fruit that is yellow or red on the outside and yellow on the inside and has a large seed

mangrove /ˈmæŋɡrəʊv/ *noun* a tree that grows in salt water and has its roots above the ground: *mangrove swamps*

mankind /mænˈkaɪnd/ *noun* (no plural) all the people in the world

man-made /ˌmæn ˈmeɪd/ *adjective* made by people; not natural: *man-made materials*

manner /ˈmænə(r)/ *noun* **1** (no plural) the way that you do something or the way that something happens: *Don't get angry. Let's try to talk about this in a calm manner.* **2 manners** (plural) the way you behave when you are with other people: *My parents taught us good manners.* ◇ *It's bad manners to talk with your mouth full.*

manual[1] /ˈmænjuəl/ *adjective* that you do with your hands: *Do you prefer manual work or office work?* ▸ **manually** /ˈmænjuəli/ *adverb* using your hands: *This machine is operated manually.*

manual[2] /ˈmænjuəl/ *noun* a book that tells you how to do something: *It'll be difficult to fix the engine without an instruction manual.*

manufacture /ˌmænjuˈfæktʃə(r)/ *verb* (**manufactures, manufacturing, manufactured** /ˌmænjuˈfæktʃəd/) to make things in a factory using machines: *The company manufactures radios.* ▸ **manufacture** *noun* (no plural): *the manufacture of plastic from oil*

manufacturer /ˌmænjuˈfæktʃərə(r)/ *noun* a person or company that makes something: *If it doesn't work, send it back to the manufacturer.*

manure /məˈnjʊə(r)/ *noun* (no plural) the waste matter from animals that is put on the ground to help plants and crops grow

many 🔑 /ˈmeni/ *adjective* (**more, most**) *pronoun* a large number of people or things: *Many people in this country are very poor.* ◇ *There aren't many students in* *my class.* ◇ *Many of these books are very old.* ◇ *There are too many mistakes in your homework.*

❖ **GRAMMAR**

We use **many** with countable nouns (= things you can count). We usually use it in negative sentences, in questions, and after 'too', 'so', 'as' and 'how'. In other sentences we use **a lot (of)**: *She's got a lot of books.* ➲ Look at **much**[1].

as many as the same number that: *Take as many cakes as you want.*

how many ...? words that you use to ask about the number of people or things: *How many brothers and sisters have you got?*

manyatta *noun* (East African English) a group of small houses with a fence around them, especially where Maasai people live

map /mæp/ *noun* a drawing of a town, a country or the world. It shows things like mountains, rivers and roads: *Can you find Japan on the map?* ◇ *a street map of Dar es Salaam* ◇ *a road map* (= one especially for someone who is driving a car)

❖ **WORD BUILDING**

A book of maps is called an **atlas**.

marabou stork /ˌmærəbuː ˈstɔːk/ *noun* a type of large bird with long legs that eats fish, insects, etc. and dead animals

marabou stork

marathon /ˈmærəθən/ *noun* a very long race when people run about 42 kilometres

marble /ˈmɑːbl/ *noun* **1** (no plural) very hard stone that is used to make buildings and models of people (**statues**): *Marble is always cold when you touch it.* **2** (*plural* **marbles**) a small glass ball that you use in a children's game: *They are playing marbles.*

March /mɑːtʃ/ *noun* the third month of the year

march[1] /mɑːtʃ/ *verb* (**marches, marching, marched** /mɑːtʃt/) **1** to walk like a soldier: *The soldiers marched along the road.* **2** to walk with a large group of people to show that you have strong feelings about something: *They marched through the town shouting 'Stop the war!'*

march[2] /mɑːtʃ/ *noun* (*plural* **marches**) **1** a journey made by soldiers walking together: *The soldiers were tired after the long march.* **2** a long walk by a large group of people to show that they have strong feelings about something: *a peace march*

margarine /ˌmɑːdʒəˈriːn/ *noun* (no plural) soft yellow food that looks like butter, but is not made of milk. You put it on bread or use it in cooking.

margin /ˈmɑːdʒɪn/ *noun* the space at the side of a page that has no writing or pictures in it

marine /məˈriːn/ *adjective* connected with the sea: *Marine life includes many plants, as well as fish and other creatures.*

marital status /ˌmærɪtl ˈsteɪtəs/ *noun* (no plural) if a person is married or single, etc.

maritime /ˈmærɪtaɪm/ *adjective* connected with the sea or ships: *the country's maritime history*

mark[1] /mɑːk/ *noun* **1** a spot or line that makes something less good than it was before: *There's a dirty mark on the front of your shirt.* **2** a shape or special sign on something: *The marks on her face show that she's married.* **3** a number or letter that a teacher gives for your work to show how good it is: *She got very good marks in the exam.*

mark[2] /mɑːk/ *verb* (**marks, marking, marked** /mɑːkt/) **1** to put a sign on something by writing or drawing on it: *The price is marked on the bottom of the box.* **2** to put a tick (✓) or cross (X) on school work to show if it is right or wrong, or to write a number or letter to show how good it is: *The teacher marked all my answers wrong.* **3** to show where something is: *This cross marks the place where he died.*

market[1] /ˈmɑːkɪt/ *noun* **1** a place where people go to buy and sell things, usually outside: *There is a fruit and vegetable market in the town.* **2** the people who want to buy something: *Britain is an important market for Kenyan coffee.*

market[2] /ˈmɑːkɪt/ *verb* (**markets, marketing, marketed**) to sell something using advertisements: *Companies spend millions marketing their products.*

marketing /ˈmɑːkɪtɪŋ/ *noun* (no plural) using advertisements to help a company sell its products: *She works in the marketing department.*

marooned /məˈruːn/ *adjective* in a place that you cannot leave: *The sailors were marooned on a desert island.*

marriage /ˈmærɪdʒ/ *noun* **1** the time when two people are together as husband and wife: *They had a long and happy marriage.* **2** the time when a man and woman become husband and wife: *The marriage will take place in church.* SAME MEANING **wedding**

married /ˈmærid/ *adjective* having a husband or wife: *How long have they been married?* ◇ *Odoi is married to Nakato.* OPPOSITE **single, unmarried**

get married become the husband or wife of someone: *Shema and Kirezi got married last year.*

marry /ˈmæri/ *verb* (**marries, marrying, married** /ˈmærid/, **has married**) to become someone's husband or wife: *Will you marry me?* ◇ *They married when they were very young.*

> ❖ **SPEAKING**
> It is more usual to say **get married**.

Mars /mɑːz/ *noun* (no plural) the planet that is fourth in order of distance from the sun

marsh /mɑːʃ/ *noun* (*plural* **marshes**) soft wet ground

marshal /ˈmɑːʃl/ *noun* a person who helps to organize or control a public event: *Marshals are directing traffic in the car park.*

marvellous /ˈmɑːvələs/ *adjective* very good; wonderful: *I had a marvellous holiday.*

masculine /ˈmæskjəlɪn/ *adjective* of or like a man; right for a man: *a masculine voice* ➲ Look at **feminine**.

mash /mæʃ/ *verb* (**mashes, mashing, mashed** /mæʃt/) to press and mix food to make it soft: *mashed potatoes*

mask /mɑːsk/ *noun* a thing that you wear over your face to hide or protect it: *The thieves were wearing masks.* ◇ *The doctors and nurses all wore masks.*

Mass /mæs/ *noun* (*plural* **Masses**) a service in the Roman Catholic church

mass /mæs/ *noun* (*plural* **masses**) a large amount or number of something: *a mass of rock* ◇ *masses of people*

massacre /ˈmæsəkə(r)/ *noun* the cruel killing of a lot of people ▶ **massacre** *verb* (**massacres, massacring, massacred** /ˈmæsəkəd/): *Hundreds of innocent people were massacred in the attack.*

massive /ˈmæsɪv/ *adjective* very big: *The house is massive – it has six bedrooms!*

mast /mɑːst/ *noun* **1** a tall piece of wood or metal that holds the sails on a boat **2** a very tall metal thing that sends out sounds or pictures for radio, television or phones

master[1] /ˈmɑːstə(r)/ *noun* **1** a man who has people or animals in his control: *The dog ran to its master.* **2** a male teacher: *The games master blew his whistle.*

master[2] /ˈmɑːstə(r)/ *verb* (**masters, mastering, mastered** /ˈmɑːstəd/) to learn how to do something well: *It takes a long time to master a foreign language.*

master of ceremonies /ˌmɑːstər əv ˈserəməniz/ *noun* a person who introduces guests at a formal occasion ❶ The short form is **MC**.

masterpiece /ˈmɑːstəpiːs/ *noun* a very good painting, book, film, etc: *His new book is a masterpiece.*

mat /mæt/ *noun* **1** a small thing that covers a part of the floor: *Wipe your feet on the mat before you go in.* **2** a small thing that you put on a table under a hot dish or cup or a glass: *a table mat*

matatu *noun* (East African English) a small bus used for public transport

match[1] /mætʃ/ *noun* **1** (*plural* **matches**) a special short thin piece of wood that makes fire when you rub it on something rough: *He struck a match and lit the fire.* ◇ *a box of matches* **2** (*plural* **matches**) a game between two people or teams: *a football match* ◇ *a boxing match* **3** (no plural) something that looks good with something else, for example because it has the same colour, shape or pattern: *Your shoes and dress are a good match.*

matches

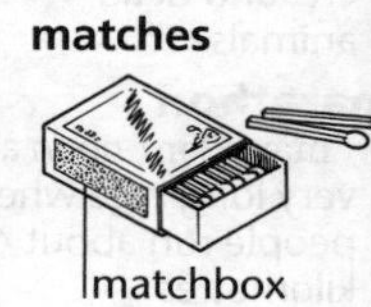

match[2] /mætʃ/ *verb* (**matches, matching, matched** /mætʃt/) **1** to have the same colour, shape or pattern as something else, or to look good with something else: *Her socks match her* *dress.* **2** to find something that is like another thing or that you can put with it: *Match the word with the right picture.* ▸ **matching** /ˈmætʃɪŋ/ *adjective*: *She was wearing a blue skirt and matching jacket.*

matchbox /ˈmætʃbɒks/ *noun* (*plural* **matchboxes**) a small box for matches

mate[1] /meɪt/ *noun* **1** a friend: *He went to the match with his mates.* ❶ This is an informal word. **2** a person who lives, works or studies with you: *Ali is one of my classmates.* ◇ *a flatmate* **3** one of two animals that come together to make young animals: *The bird is looking for a mate.*

mate[2] /meɪt/ *verb* (**mates, mating, mated**) When animals **mate**, they come together to make young animals.

material ⚷ /məˈtɪəriəl/ *noun* **1** what you use for making or doing something: *Wood and stone are building materials.* ◇ *writing materials* (= pens, pencils and paper, etc.) **2** stuff that is made of wool, cotton, etc. and that you use for making clothes and other things; cloth: *I don't have enough material to make a dress.*

mathematics ⚷ /ˌmæθəˈmætɪks/ (also **maths** /mæθs/) *noun* (no plural) the study of numbers, measurements and shapes: *Maths is my favourite subject.* ▸ **mathematical** /ˌmæθəˈmætɪkl/ *adjective*: *a mathematical problem*

matoke *noun* (no plural) (East African English) a kind of food that we make from boiled bananas

matter[1] ⚷ /ˈmætə(r)/ *noun* something that you must talk about or do: *There is a matter I would like to discuss with you.*
as a matter of fact words that you use when you say something true, important or interesting: *I'm going home early today. As a matter of fact, it's my birthday.*
be the matter with someone or **something** to be the reason for problems or unhappiness: *Nakato is crying. What's the matter with her?* ◇ *There is something the matter with my eye.*
no matter how, what, when, who, etc. however, whatever, whenever, whoever, etc: *No matter how hard I try, I can't open the door.*

matter[2] ⚷ /ˈmætə(r)/ *verb* (**matters, mattering, mattered** /ˈmætəd/) to be important: *It doesn't matter if you're late – we'll wait for you.*

mattress /ˈmætrəs/ *noun* (*plural* **mattresses**) the thick soft part of a bed

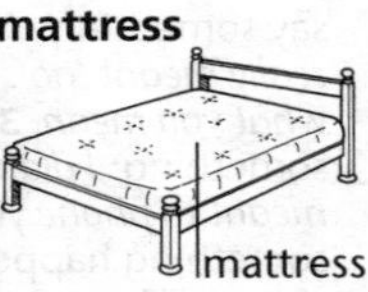

mature /məˈtjʊə(r)/ *adjective* like an adult; fully grown OPPOSITE **immature**

mauve /məʊv/ *adjective* purple: *a mauve hat*

maximum /ˈmæksɪməm/ *noun* (no plural) the most; the biggest possible size, amount or number: *This plane can carry a maximum of 150 people.* ▸ **maximum** *adjective*: *The car's maximum speed is 110 kilometres per hour.* OPPOSITE **minimum**

May ⚷ /meɪ/ *noun* the fifth month of the year

may ⚷ /meɪ/ *modal verb* **1** a word that shows what will perhaps happen or what is possible: *I may go to Mombasa on Saturday.* ◇ *He may not be here.* **2** to be allowed to do something: *May I open the window?* ◇ *You may stay here tonight.* **3** to hope something will happen: *May you be happy in your new house.* ➲ Note at **modal verb**.

maybe ⚷ /ˈmeɪbi/ *adverb* perhaps; possibly: *'Are you going out tonight?' 'Maybe.'* ◇ *Maybe you should phone him.*

mayor /meə(r)/ *noun* the leader of a **council** (= a group of people who control a town or city)

MB *short for* MEGABYTE

MC /ˌem ˈsiː/ *short for* MASTER OF CEREMONIES

me ⚷ /miː/ *pronoun* (*plural* **us**) the person who is speaking: *When he saw me he told me about the accident.* ◇ *'Who broke the window?' 'It was me.'*

meadow /ˈmedəʊ/ *noun* a field of grass

meal ⚷ /miːl/ *noun* food that you eat at a certain time of the day: *Breakfast is the first meal of the day.*

> ❖ **WORD BUILDING**
>
> **Breakfast**, **lunch** and **dinner** (and sometimes **tea** and **supper**) are the usual meals of the day.

mean[1] ⚷ /miːn/ *verb* (**means, meaning, meant** /ment/, **has meant**) **1** to say or show something in a different way; to have as a meaning: *What does 'medicine' mean?* ◇ *The red light means that you*

have to stop here. **2** to plan or want to say something: *She said 'yes' but she really meant 'no'.* ◇ *I don't understand what you mean.* **3** to plan or want to do something: *I didn't mean to hurt you.* ◇ *I meant to phone you, but I forgot.* **4** to make something happen: *This storm means there will be no sport today.*
be meant to **1** If you are **meant to** do something, you should do it: *You're not meant to walk on the grass.* **2** If something is **meant to** be true, people say it is true: *This is meant to be a good film.*
mean something to someone to be important to someone: *My family means a lot to me.*

mean² /miːn/ *adjective* (**meaner, meanest**) **1** A person who is **mean** does not like to give things or to spend money: *Egesa is very mean – he hates spending his money on other people.* OPPOSITE **generous** **2** unkind: *It was mean of you to say that Teta was ugly.*

meaning /ˈmiːnɪŋ/ *noun* what something means or shows: *This word has two different meanings.*

means /miːnz/ *noun* (*plural* **means**) a way of doing something; a way of going somewhere: *I don't have a car and there are no buses, so I haven't got any means of getting to Arusha.*
by means of something by using something: *They chose the best student by means of a written test and interview.*
by no means not at all: *I am by no means certain that I can come.*

meant *form of* MEAN¹

meantime /ˈmiːntaɪm/ *noun* (no plural)
in the meantime in the time between two things happening: *The police will be here soon; in the meantime you should stay calm.*

meanwhile /ˈmiːnwaɪl/ *adverb* **1** at the same time as another thing is happening: *My mother cooked the dinner and meanwhile I cleaned the house.* **2** in the time between two things happening: *I'm going to buy a bed next week, but meanwhile I'm sleeping on the floor.*

measles /ˈmiːzlz/ *noun* (no plural) an illness that makes small red spots come on your skin: *My little brother has got measles.*

measure¹ /ˈmeʒə(r)/ *verb* (**measures, measuring, measured** /ˈmeʒəd/) **1** to find the size, weight or amount of someone or something: *I measured the box with a ruler.* **2** to be a certain size or amount: *This room measures six metres across.*

measure² /ˈmeʒə(r)/ *noun* a way of showing the size or amount of somethin[g]: *A metre is a measure of length.*

measurement /ˈmeʒəmənt/ *noun* how long, wide, high, etc. something is: *What are the measurements of the kitche[n]*

meat /miːt/ *noun* (no plural) the parts [of] an animal's body that you can eat: *You c[an] buy meat at a butcher's.*

mechanic /məˈkænɪk/ *noun* a person whose job is to repair or work with machines: *a car mechanic*

mechanical /məˈkænɪkl/ *adjective* move[d,] done or made by a machine: *They used a mechanical drill to break up the road.*

mechanics /məˈkænɪks/ *noun* (no plural) the study of how machines work

medal /ˈmedl/ *noun* a piece of metal with words and pictures on it that is given to someone who has done something very good: *She won a gold medal in the Olymp[ic] Games.*

media /ˈmiːdiə/ *noun* (plural) **the media** television, radio and newspapers: *The media are always interested in the lives of film stars.*

medical /ˈmedɪkl/ *adjective* of or abou[t] medicine, hospitals or doctors: *a medical student* ◇ *medical treatment*

medicinal /məˈdɪsɪnl/ *adjective* useful for making you better when you are ill: *medicinal herbs and plants* ◇ *medicinal drugs*

medicine /ˈmedsn; ˈmedɪsn/ *noun* **1** (no plural) the science of understandin[g] illnesses and making sick people well again: *He studied medicine for five years before becoming a doctor.* **2** (*plural* **medicines**) pills or special drinks that hel[p] you to get better when you are ill: *Take this medicine every morning.* ➲ Note at **chemist**.

medium /ˈmiːdiəm/ *adjective* not big and not small; middle: *What size shirt do you need – small, medium or large?* ◇ *He is of medium height.*

meet /miːt/ *verb* (**meets, meeting, me[t]** /met/, **has met**) **1** to come together at a certain time and place when you have planned it: *Let's meet outside the Town Ha[ll] at eight o'clock.* **2** to see and say hello to someone: *I met Hawa in the library today.* **3** to see and speak to someone for the firs[t] time: *Have you met Shayo?* **4** to go to a place and wait for someone to arrive: *Can you meet me outside school at five?* **5** to join together with something: *The two paths meet on the other side of the hill.*

meeting 🔑 /ˈmiːtɪŋ/ *noun* **1** a time when a group of people come together for a special reason: *We had a meeting to talk about the plans for the school trip.* **2** two or more people coming together: *Dad, do you remember your first meeting with Mum?*

megabyte /ˈmegəbaɪt/ *noun* a measure of computer memory or information. There are about a million **bytes** in a **megabyte**. ℹ The short way of writing 'megabyte' is **MB**.

melody /ˈmelədi/ *noun* (*plural* **melodies**) a group of musical notes that make a nice sound when you play or sing them together; a tune: *This song has a lovely melody.*

melon /ˈmelən/ *noun* a big round yellow or green fruit with a lot of seeds inside

melon

melt 🔑 /melt/ *verb* (**melts, melting, melted**) to warm something so that it becomes liquid; to get warmer so that it becomes liquid: *Melt the butter in a saucepan.* ◇ *The ice melted in his drink.*

member 🔑 /ˈmembə(r)/ *noun* a person who is in a group: *I'm a member of the school football team.*

Member of Parliament /ˌmembər əv ˈpɑːləmənt/ *noun* a person that the people of a town or city choose to speak for them in politics ℹ The short form is **MP**.

membership /ˈmembəʃɪp/ *noun* (no plural) being in a group: *Membership of the club depends on age and ability.* ◇ *an annual membership fee*

memo /ˈmeməʊ/ (*plural* **memos**) *noun* a note that someone writes to a person they work with: *I sent you a memo about the meeting on Friday.*

memorable /ˈmemərəbl/ *adjective* easy to remember because it is special in some way: *Their wedding was a very memorable day.*

memorandum /ˌmeməˈrændəm/ *noun* (*plural* **memoranda** /ˌmeməˈrændə/) = **memo**

memorial /məˈmɔːriəl/ *noun* something that people build or do to help us remember someone, or something that happened: *The statue is a memorial to all the soldiers who died in the war.*

memorize /ˈmeməraɪz/ *verb* (**memorizes, memorizing, memorized** /ˈmeməraɪzd/) to learn something so that you can remember it exactly: *We have to memorize a poem for homework.*

memory 🔑 /ˈmeməri/ *noun* (*plural* **memories**) **1** the power to remember things: *She's got a very good memory – she never forgets people's names.* **2** something that you remember: *I have very happy memories of my childhood.* **3** the part of a computer that holds information: *I don't have enough memory to download the information.*

> ❖ **WORD FAMILY**
>
> **memory memorable memorize**

memory stick /ˈmeməri stɪk/ (also **flash drive** /ˈflæʃ draɪv/) *noun* a small piece of equipment that you can carry around with you and use to store information from a computer

men *plural of* MAN

mend /mend/ *verb* (**mends, mending, mended**) to make something good again when it was broken: *Can you mend this chair?* SAME MEANING **repair**
mend your ways to stop behaving badly

-ment /mənt/ *suffix* a way of making a noun from a verb: *enjoyment* ◇ *payment* ◇ *government*

mental 🔑 /ˈmentl/ *adjective* of or in your mind: *mental illness* ▸ **mentally** /ˈmentəli/ *adverb*: *He is mentally ill.*

mention 🔑 /ˈmenʃn/ *verb* (**mentions, mentioning, mentioned** /ˈmenʃnd/) to speak or write a little about something: *When I spoke to Nafula, she mentioned that her son had started school.* ◇ *He didn't mention Njoki in his letter.*
don't mention it polite words that you say when someone says 'thank you': *'Thanks very much.' 'Don't mention it.'*
▸ **mention** *noun*: *There was no mention of the accident in the newspaper.*

menu /ˈmenjuː/ *noun* (*plural* **menus**) **1** a list of the food that you can choose in a restaurant: *What's on the menu?* ◇ *Can I have the menu, please?* **2** a list on the screen of a computer that shows what you can do

merchant /ˈmɜːtʃənt/ *noun* a person who buys and sells things, especially from and to other countries

mercy /ˈmɜːsi/ *noun* (no plural) being kind and not hurting someone who has done wrong: *The prisoners asked the president for mercy.*
be at the mercy of someone or **something** to have no power against someone or something: *Farmers are at the mercy of the weather.*

mere /mɪə(r)/ *adjective* only; not more than: *She was a mere child when her parents died.*

merely /ˈmɪəli/ *adverb* only: *I don't want to buy the book – I am merely asking how much it costs.*

merge /mɜːdʒ/ *verb* (**merges**, **merging**, **merged** /mɜːdʒd/) to join together with something else: *The two small companies merged into one large one.*

merit /ˈmerɪt/ *noun* what is good about someone or something: *What are the merits of this plan?*

mermaid /ˈmɜːmeɪd/ *noun* a woman in stories who has a fish's tail and lives in the sea

merry /ˈmeri/ *adjective* (**merrier**, **merriest**) happy and full of fun: *Merry Christmas!*

mesh /meʃ/ *noun* (no plural) a material like a strong net that is made of wire, plastic or thread: *We made a fence from wire mesh.*

mess[1] /mes/ *noun* (no plural) **1** a lot of untidy or dirty things all in the wrong place: *There was a terrible mess after the party.* **2** a person or thing that is untidy or dirty: *My hair is a mess!*
be in a mess 1 to be untidy: *This classroom is in a mess.* **2** to have problems: *She's in a mess – she's got no money and nowhere to live.*

mess[2] /mes/ *verb* (**messes**, **messing**, **messed** /mest/)
mess about; **mess around** to do something in a silly way; to play when you should be working: *Stop messing around and finish your work!*
mess something up 1 to do something badly or make something go wrong: *The bad weather messed up our plans for the weekend.* **2** to make something untidy or dirty

message 🔑 /ˈmesɪdʒ/ *noun* words that one person sends to another: *Could you give a message to Moraa, please? Please tell her I will be late.* ◇ *Mr Baucha is not here at the moment. Can I take a message?*

messenger /ˈmesɪndʒə(r)/ *noun* a perso who brings a message

messy /ˈmesi/ *adjective* (**messier**, **messiest**) **1** untidy or dirty: *a messy kitchen* **2** that makes you untidy or dirty: *Painting is a messy job.*

met *form of* MEET

metal 🔑 /ˈmetl/ *noun* Iron, lead, tin and gold are all metals: *This chair is made of metal.* ◇ *a metal box*

> ❖ **WORD BUILDING**
> There are many different types of metals. Here are some of them: **aluminium, brass, gold, iron, steel** and **tin**. Do you know any others?

metallic /məˈtælɪk/ *adjective* **1** looking like metal; making a noise like metal **2** made of metal

meter /ˈmiːtə(r)/ *noun* a machine that measures or counts something: *An electricity meter shows how much electrici you have used.*

method 🔑 /ˈmeθəd/ *noun* a way of doin something: *What is the best method of cooking fish?*

metre 🔑 /ˈmiːtə(r)/ *noun* a measure of length. There are 100 **centimetres** in a metre: *The wall is eight metres long.*
ℹ The short way of writing 'metre' is **m**: *2 m*

metric /ˈmetrɪk/ *adjective* using metres, grams, litres, etc. to measure things

miaow /miˈaʊ/ *noun* a sound that a cat makes ► **miaow** *verb* (**miaows**, **miaowing**, **miaowed** /miˈaʊd/): *Why is the cat miaowing?*

mice *plural of* MOUSE

microblogging /ˈmaɪkrəʊblɒgɪŋ/ *noun* (no plural) the activity of sending short messages over the Internet to lots of people at the same time

microchip /ˈmaɪkrəʊtʃɪp/ (also **chip**) *noun* a very small thing inside a computer, etc. that makes it work

microcomputer /ˈmaɪkrəʊkəmpjuːtə(r *noun* a small computer

microphone

microphone /ˈmaɪkrəfəʊn/ *noun* an electrical thing that makes sounds louder or records them so you can listen to them later

microscope

microscope /ˈmaɪkrəskəʊp/ *noun* an instrument with special glass in it, that makes very small things look much bigger: *The scientist looked at the hair under the microscope.*

microwave /ˈmaɪkrəweɪv/ (also **microwave oven** /ˌmaɪkrəweɪv ˈʌvn/) *noun* a special oven that cooks food very quickly

mid (also **mid-**) /mɪd/ *adjective* (in) the middle of: *I'm going on holiday in mid July.* ◇ *mid-morning tea*

midday /ˌmɪdˈdeɪ/ *noun* (no plural) twelve o'clock in the day: *We met at midday.*

middle /ˈmɪdl/ *noun* **1** the part that is the same distance from the sides, edges or ends of something: *A mango has a stone in the middle.* **2** the time after the beginning and before the end: *The storm started in the middle of the night.*
be in the middle of to be busy doing something: *I can't speak to you now – I'm in the middle of cooking dinner.* ▶ **middle** *adjective*: *There are three houses and ours is the middle one.*

middle-aged /ˌmɪdl ˈeɪdʒd/ *adjective* not old and not young; between the ages of about 40 and 60: *a middle-aged man*

midnight /ˈmɪdnaɪt/ *noun* (no plural) twelve o'clock at night: *The flight left at midnight.*

midway /ˌmɪdˈweɪ/ *adverb* in the middle: *The village is midway between Tabora and Dodoma.*

midwife /ˈmɪdwaɪf/ *noun* (*plural* **midwives** /ˈmɪdwaɪvz/) a person who helps women have their babies

might /maɪt/ *modal verb* **1** a word for 'may' in the past: *He said he might be late, but he was early.* **2** a word that shows what will perhaps happen or what is possible: *Don't run because you might fall.* ◇ *'Where's Hawa?' 'I don't know – she might be in the kitchen.'* ➲ Note at **modal verb**.

mighty /ˈmaɪti/ *adjective* (**mightier**, **mightiest**) very great, strong or powerful: *a mighty ocean*

migrate /maɪˈgreɪt/ *verb* (**migrates**, **migrating**, **migrated**) **1** If animals or birds **migrate**, they move from one part of the world to another every year. **2** When people **migrate**, they go to live and work in another place: *Many people migrate from the villages to the towns and cities.* ▶ **migration** /maɪˈgreɪʃn/ *noun*: *the annual migration of the wildebeest*

mild /maɪld/ *adjective* (**milder**, **mildest**) gentle; not strong or extreme: *This curry has a mild taste.* ◇ *The temperature in this region ranges from very hot to mild.*

mile /maɪl/ *noun* a measure of length that is used in some countries (= 1.6 kilometres): *We live three miles from the sea.*

military /ˈmɪlətri/ *adjective* of or for soldiers or the army: *a military camp* ◇ *military action*

milk[1] /mɪlk/ *noun* (no plural) the white liquid that a mother makes in her body to give to her baby. People drink the milk that cows and some other animals make: *Do you want milk in your tea?*

milk[2] /mɪlk/ *verb* (**milks**, **milking**, **milked** /mɪlkt/) to take milk from a cow or another animal

milky /ˈmɪlki/ *adjective* with a lot of milk in it: *milky tea*

mill /mɪl/ *noun* **1** a building where a machine makes grain into flour **2** a factory for making things like cloth or paper: *a paper mill*

millet /ˈmɪlɪt/ *noun* (no plural) a kind of grass with very small seeds that you can eat or use to make flour

millimetre /ˈmɪlimiːtə(r)/ *noun* a measure of length. There are ten **millimetres** in a **centimetre**. ℹ The short way of writing 'millimetre' is **mm**: *60 mm*

million /ˈmɪljən/ *number* 1 000 000; one thousand thousand: *About 29 million people live in this country.* ◇ *millions of dollars* ◇ *six million shillings*

millionaire /ˌmɪljəˈneə(r)/ *noun* a very rich person who has more than a million pounds, dollars, etc.

millionth /ˈmɪljənθ/ *adjective, adverb, noun* 1 000 000th; each of one million equal parts of something

millipede /ˈmɪlipiːd/ *noun* a small creature like an insect, with a long thin body divided into many sections, each with two pairs of legs

millipede

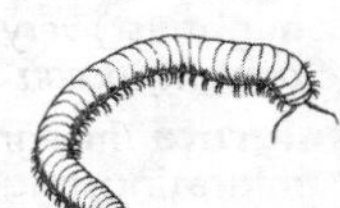

mime /maɪm/ *verb* (**mimes, miming, mimed** /maɪmd/) to tell something by your actions, not by speaking

mince /mɪns/ *verb* (**minces, mincing, minced** /mɪnst/) to cut meat into very small pieces, using a special machine: *minced meat* ▶ **mince** *noun* (no plural) meat in very small pieces

mind¹ /maɪnd/ *noun* the part of you that thinks and remembers: *He has a very quick mind.*
change your mind to have an idea, then decide to do something different: *I planned to study last night but then changed my mind and read a book.*
have something on your mind to be worried about something: *I've got a lot on my mind at the moment.*
make up your mind to decide something: *Shall I buy the blue shirt or the red one? I can't make up my mind.*

mind² /maɪnd/ *verb* (**minds, minding, minded**) **1** to feel unhappy or angry about something: *'Do you mind if I sit here?' 'No, I don't mind.'* (= you may sit here) **2** to be careful of someone or something: *Mind the step!* ◇ *Mind out! There's a dog in the road.*
do you mind ...?; would you mind ...? please could you?: *It's cold – would you mind closing the window?*
I don't mind it is not important to me which thing: *'Do you want tea or coffee?' 'I don't mind.'*
never mind don't worry; there is no problem; it doesn't matter: *'I forgot your book.' 'Never mind, I don't need it today.'*

mindful /ˈmaɪndfl/ *adjective* remembering something: *Drivers were warned to be mindful of other road users.*

mine¹ /maɪn/ *noun* a very big hole in the ground where people work to get things like coal, gold or diamonds: *a coal mine*
▶ **mine** *verb* (**mines, mining, mined** /maɪnd/) to dig in the ground for things like coal or gold

mine² /maɪn/ *pronoun* something that belongs to me: *That bike is mine.* ◇ *Are those books mine or yours?*

miner /ˈmaɪnə(r)/ *noun* a person who works in a mine

mineral /ˈmɪnərəl/ *noun* **Minerals** are things like coal, gold, salt or oil that come from the ground and that people use. Some **minerals** are also in food and drink and we need them to keep us healthy.

mini- /ˈmɪni/ *prefix* very small: *They played a short game of minigolf.*

miniature /ˈmɪnətʃə(r)/ *adjective* very small; much smaller than usual: *The children made a miniature village.*

minibus /ˈmɪnibʌs/ *noun* (*plural* **minibuses**) a small bus, usually for about 12 people

minimum /ˈmɪnɪməm/ *noun* (no plural) the smallest size, amount or number that is possible: *We need a minimum of six people to play this game.* ▶ **minimum** *adjective*: *What is the minimum age for leaving school in your country?*
OPPOSITE **maximum**

minister /ˈmɪnɪstə(r)/ *noun* **1** one of the most important people in a government: *the Minister of Education* **2** a priest in some Christian churches

ministry /ˈmɪnɪstri/ *noun* (*plural* **ministries**) a part of the government that controls one special thing: *the Ministry of Defence*

minor /ˈmaɪnə(r)/ *adjective* not very big or important: *Don't worry – it's only a minor problem.* ◇ *a minor road* OPPOSITE **major**

minority /maɪˈnɒrəti/ *noun* (no plural) the smaller part of a group: *Only a minority of the people in that country speak English.*
OPPOSITE **majority**

mint /mɪnt/ *noun* **1** (no plural) a small plant with a strong fresh taste and smell, that you put in food and drinks: *mint tea* **2** (*plural* **mints**) a sweet with this taste

minus /ˈmaɪnəs/ *preposition* **1** less; when you take away: *Six minus two is four* (6–2=4). ➲ Look at **plus**. **2** below zero: *The temperature fell to minus ten degrees.*

minute¹ /ˈmɪnɪt/ *noun* a measure of time. There are 60 **seconds** in a minute and 60 minutes in an **hour**: *It's nine*

minutes past six. ◇ *The bus leaves in ten minutes.*
in a minute very soon: *I'll be ready in a minute.*
the minute as soon as: *Phone me the minute you arrive.*

minute[2] /maɪˈnjuːt/ *adjective* very small: *I can't read his writing – it's minute.*

the minutes /ðə ˈmɪnɪts/ *noun* (plural) a record of what people say or decide at a formal meeting: *Achal will take* (= write down) *the minutes.*

miraa = **khat**

miracle /ˈmɪrəkl/ *noun* a wonderful and surprising thing that happens and that you cannot explain: *It's a miracle that he wasn't killed when he fell from the window.*

miraculous /mɪˈrækjələs/ *adjective* wonderful and surprising: *a miraculous escape*

mirror

mirror 🔑 /ˈmɪrə(r)/ *noun* a piece of special glass where you can see yourself: *Look in the mirror.*

mis- /mɪs/ *prefix* You can add **mis-** to the beginning of some words to show that something is done wrong or badly: *misbehave* (= behave badly) ◇ *misunderstand* (= not understand correctly)

miserable /ˈmɪzrəbl/ *adjective* **1** If you are **miserable**, you are very sad: *I waited in the rain for an hour, feeling wet and miserable.* **2** If something is **miserable**, it makes you very sad: *That's miserable news.*

misery /ˈmɪzəri/ *noun* (no plural) great unhappiness

misfortune /ˌmɪsˈfɔːtʃuːn/ *noun* something bad that happens; bad luck: *We had the misfortune to miss the bus and get caught in the rain.*

mislead /ˌmɪsˈliːd/ *verb* (**misleads**, **misleading**, **misled** /ˌmɪsˈled/, **has misled**) to make someone believe something that is not true: *You misled me when you said you didn't know him.*
▶ **misleading** /ˌmɪsˈliːdɪŋ/ *adjective*: *The advertisement is very misleading.*

misprint /ˈmɪsprɪnt/ *noun* a mistake in printing or typing

Miss 🔑 /mɪs/ a word that you use before the name of a girl or woman who is not married: *Dear Miss Buke, …* ➲ Look at **Mr**, **Mrs**.

miss 🔑 /mɪs/ *verb* (**misses**, **missing**, **missed** /mɪst/) **1** to not hit or catch something: *I tried to hit the ball but I missed.* **2** to feel sad about someone or something that has gone: *I'll miss you when you go away.* **3** to be too late for a bus, plane, train or boat: *I just missed my bus.* OPPOSITE **catch** **4** to not see, hear, etc. something: *You missed a good football match on TV last night.*
miss something out to not put in or do something; to not include something: *I didn't finish the exam – I missed out two questions.*

missile /ˈmɪsaɪl/ *noun* a thing that you throw or send through the air to hurt someone: *The boys were throwing stones, bottles and other missiles.* ◇ *nuclear missiles*

missing 🔑 /ˈmɪsɪŋ/ *adjective* lost, or not in the usual place: *The police are looking for the missing child.* ◇ *My purse is missing. Have you seen it?*

mission /ˈmɪʃn/ *noun* a journey to do a special job: *They were sent on a mission to the moon.*

missionary /ˈmɪʃənri/ *noun* (*plural* **missionaries**) a person who goes to another country to teach people about a religion

misspell /ˌmɪsˈspel/ *verb* (**misspells**, **misspelling**, **misspelt** /ˌmɪsˈspelt/ *or* **misspelled** /ˌmɪsˈspeld/) to make a mistake in spelling a word: *You've misspelt my name – it should have two t's.*

mist /mɪst/ *noun* thin cloud near the ground, that is difficult to see through: *Early in the morning, the lake was covered in mist.* ▶ **misty** *adjective* (**mistier**, **mistiest**): *a misty morning*

mistake[1] 🔑 /mɪˈsteɪk/ *noun* something that you think or do that is wrong: *You have made a lot of spelling mistakes in this letter.* ◇ *It was a mistake to go by bus – the journey took many hours!*
by mistake when you did not plan to do

it: *I took your book by mistake – I thought it was mine.*

mistake² /mɪˈsteɪk/ *verb* (**mistakes, mistaking, mistook** /mɪˈstʊk/, **has mistaken** /mɪˈsteɪkən/) to think that someone or something is a different person or thing: *I'm sorry – I mistook you for someone else.*

mistaken /mɪˈsteɪkən/ *adjective* wrong: *I said she was Algerian but I was mistaken – she's from Morocco.*

mistress /ˈmɪstrəs/ *noun* (*plural* **mistresses**) a female teacher: *The games mistress ran across the field.*

misunderstand /ˌmɪsʌndəˈstænd/ *verb* (**misunderstands, misunderstanding, misunderstood** /ˌmɪsʌndəˈstʊd/, **has misunderstood**) to not understand something correctly: *I'm sorry, I misunderstood what you said.*

misunderstanding /ˌmɪsʌndəˈstændɪŋ/ *noun* not understanding something correctly: *I think there's been a misunderstanding. I ordered two tickets, not four.*

misuse /ˌmɪsˈjuːz/ *verb* (**misuses, misusing, misused** /ˌmɪsˈjuːzd/) to use something in the wrong way ▶ **misuse** /ˌmɪsˈjuːs/ *noun*: *alcohol/drug misuse*

❖ **PRONUNCIATION**

Be careful! The verb **misuse** sounds like **news**, but the noun **misuse** sounds like **juice**.

mix /mɪks/ *verb* (**mixes, mixing, mixed** /mɪkst/) **1** to put different things together to make something new: *Mix yellow and blue paint together to make green.* **2** to join together to make something new: *Oil and water don't mix.* **3** to be with and talk to other people: *She is very shy and doesn't mix well.*

mix up 1 to think that one person or thing is a different person or thing: *People often mix Katee up with his brother.* **2** to make things untidy: *Don't mix up my papers!*

mixed /mɪkst/ *adjective* of different kinds: *He is African and his wife is Chinese, so their children are of mixed race.* ◇ *a mixed class* (= of boys and girls together)

mixer /ˈmɪksə(r)/ *noun* a machine that mixes things: *a cement mixer*

mixture /ˈmɪkstʃə(r)/ *noun* something that you make by mixing different things together: *Air is a mixture of gases.*

mm *short for* MILLIMETRE

moan /məʊn/ *verb* (**moans, moaning, moaned** /məʊnd/) **1** to make a long sad sound when you are hurt or very unhappy: *He was moaning with pain.* **2** to talk a lot about something that you do not like: *He's always moaning about his coach.* ▶ **moan** *noun*: *I heard a loud moan.*

mob /mɒb/ *noun* a big noisy group of people who are shouting or fighting

mobile /ˈməʊbaɪl/ *adjective* able to move easily from place to place: *A mobile clinic visits the village every few months.*

mobile phone /ˌməʊbaɪl ˈfəʊn/ (*also* **cell phone, mobile**) *noun* a telephone that you can carry around with you: *I'll ring you on your mobile tonight.*

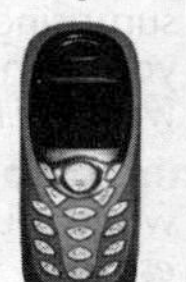
mobile phone

modal verb /ˌməʊdl ˈvɜːb/ *noun* a verb, for example 'might', 'can' or 'must', that you use with another verb

❖ **GRAMMAR**

Can, could, may, might, should, must, will, shall, would and **ought to** are modal verbs.

Modal verbs do not have an 's' in the 'he/she' form: *She **can** drive.*

After modal verbs (except **ought to**), you use the infinitive without 'to': *I **must go** now.* ◇ *You **ought to go** home now.*

You make questions and negative sentences without 'do' or 'did': ***Will** you come with me?* ◇ *They **might not** know.*

model¹ /ˈmɒdl/ *noun* **1** a small copy of something: *a model plane* **2** a person who wears clothes at a special show or for photographs, so that people will see them and buy them: *She works as a fashion model.* **3** one of the cars, machines, etc. that a certain company makes: *This pickup is the very latest model.* **4** a person who sits or stands so that an artist can draw, paint or photograph them

model² /ˈmɒdl/ *verb* (**models, modelling, modelled** /ˈmɒdld/) to wear and show clothes as a model: *The company asked Awino to model their clothes.*

moderate /ˈmɒdərət/ *adjective* in the middle; not too much and not too little;

not too big and not too small: *The team enjoyed only moderate success last season.*

modern 🔑 /ˈmɒdn/ *adjective* of the present time; of the kind that is usual now: *modern methods of farming* ◇ *The airport is very modern.*

modest /ˈmɒdɪst/ *adjective* A person who is **modest** does not talk much about good things that they have done or about things that they can do well: *You didn't tell me you could sing so well – you're very modest!* ▶ **modestly** *adverb*: *He spoke quietly and modestly about his success.* ▶ **modesty** /ˈmɒdəsti/ *noun* (no plural) being **modest**

moist /mɔɪst/ *adjective* a little wet: *Keep the earth moist or the plant will die.*

moisture /ˈmɔɪstʃə(r)/ *noun* (no plural) small drops of water on something or in the air

mole /məʊl/ *noun* a small dark spot on a person's skin

molecule /ˈmɒlɪkjuːl/ *noun* the smallest part that something can be divided into without changing its chemical nature ➲ Look at **atom**.

moment 🔑 /ˈməʊmənt/ *noun* a very short time: *He thought for a moment before he answered.* ◇ *Can you wait a moment?*
at the moment now: *She's away at the moment, but she'll be back next week.*
in a moment very soon: *He'll be here in a moment.*
the moment as soon as: *Tell Juma to phone me the moment he arrives.*

monarch /ˈmɒnək/ *noun* a king or queen

monarchy /ˈmɒnəki/ *noun* (*plural* **monarchies**) a country that has a king or queen

monastery /ˈmɒnəstri/ *noun* (*plural* **monasteries**) a place where religious men (called **monks**) live, work and **pray** (= speak to God)

Monday 🔑 /ˈmʌndeɪ/ *noun* the second day of the week, next after Sunday

money 🔑 /ˈmʌni/ *noun* (no plural)

> ❖ **PRONUNCIATION**
> **Money** sounds like **funny**.

small round metal things (called **coins**) and pieces of paper (called **notes**) that you use when you buy or sell something: *How much money did you spend?* ◇ *This jacket cost a lot of money.*
make money to get or earn money

money order /ˈmʌni ɔːdə(r)/ (also **postal order**) *noun* a piece of paper that you can buy at a bank or post office and send to someone instead of money

mongoose

mongoose /ˈmɒŋguːs/ *noun* a small animal with fur, that eats snakes, etc.

monitor /ˈmɒnɪtə(r)/ *noun* the part of a computer like a television that shows pictures or information ➲ Picture at **computer**. ➲ Look at **screen**.

monk /mʌŋk/ *noun* a religious man who lives with other religious men in a **monastery**

monkey

monkey /ˈmʌŋki/ *noun* (*plural* **monkeys**) an animal with a long tail, that can climb trees

monster /ˈmɒnstə(r)/ *noun* an animal in stories that is big, ugly and frightening: *A dragon is a kind of monster.*

month 🔑 /mʌnθ/ *noun* **1** one of the twelve parts of a year: *December is the last month of the year.* ◇ *We went on holiday last month.* ◇ *My exams start at the end of the month.* **2** about four weeks: *She was in hospital for a month.*

monthly /ˈmʌnθli/ *adjective, adverb* that happens or comes every month or once a month: *a monthly magazine* ◇ *He is paid monthly.*

monument /ˈmɒnjumənt/ *noun* a thing that is built to help people remember a person or something that happened: *This is a monument to Nelson Mandela.*

moo /muː/ *noun* (*plural* **moos**) the sound that a cow makes ▶ **moo** *verb* (**moos**,

mooing, mooed /mu:d/): *Cows were mooing in the barn.*

mood /mu:d/ *noun* how you feel: *The teacher is in a bad mood because he's lost his glasses.* ◇ *Our teacher was in a very good mood today.*
be in the mood for something to feel that you want something: *I'm not in the mood for studying.*

moon /mu:n/ *noun* **the moon** (no plural) the big thing that shines in the sky at night

moonlight /ˈmu:nlaɪt/ *noun* (no plural) the light from the moon

moor /mɔ:(r)/ *verb* (**moors, mooring, moored** /mɔ:d/) to tie a boat or ship to something so that it will stay in one place

mop

mop /mɒp/ *noun* a thing with a long handle that you use for washing floors
▶ **mop** *verb* (**mops, mopping, mopped** /mɒpt/) to clean something with a cloth or mop: *I mopped the floor.*

moral[1] /ˈmɒrəl/ *adjective* about what you think is right or wrong: *Some people do not eat meat for moral reasons.* ◇ *a moral problem*
▶ **morally** /ˈmɒrəli/ *adverb*: *It's morally wrong to tell lies.* ▶ **morality** /məˈræləti/ *noun* (no plural): *Standards of morality are dropping.*

moral[2] /ˈmɒrəl/ *noun* a lesson about what is right and wrong, that you can learn from a story or from something that happens: *The moral of the story is that we should be kind to animals.*

more[1] /mɔ:(r)/ *adjective, pronoun* a bigger amount or number of something: *You've got more money than I have.* ◇ *Can I have some more bread?* ◇ *We need two more chairs.* ◇ *There aren't any more pens.*
OPPOSITE **less** ➲ Look at **most[1]**.

more[2] /mɔ:(r)/ *adverb* **1** a word that makes an adjective or adverb stronger: *Your book was more expensive than mine.* ◇ *Please speak more slowly.* **2** a bigger amount or number: *I like Sarika more than her brother.* OPPOSITE **less** ➲ Look at **most[2]**.
more or less almost, but not exactly: *We are more or less the same age.*
not any more not as before; not any longer: *They don't live here any more.*
once more again: *Let's practise the song once more.*

morning /ˈmɔ:nɪŋ/ *noun* the first part of the day, between the time when the sun comes up and midday: *I went swimming this morning.* ◇ *I'm going to Zanzibar tomorrow morning.* ◇ *The letter arrived on Tuesday morning.* ◇ *I felt ill all morning.*
in the morning 1 not in the afternoon or evening: *I start work at nine o'clock in the morning.* **2** tomorrow during the morning: *I'll see you in the morning.*

mortality /mɔ:ˈtæləti/ *noun* (no plural) **1** the fact that you will die **2** the number of deaths at one time or place: *Infant mortality is high in the region.*

mortar /ˈmɔ:tə(r)/ *noun* **1** (no plural) a mixture of **cement**, sand and water that you put between bricks when you are building something **2** a strong bowl in which we hit things with a **pestle** (= a small heavy tool)

mortgage /ˈmɔ:gɪdʒ/ *noun* money that someone borrows to buy a house

mortuary /ˈmɔ:tʃəri/ *noun* (*plural* **mortuaries**) a place where dead bodies are kept before they are buried

mosque /mɒsk/ *noun* a building where Muslims go to speak to God (to **pray**)

mosquito

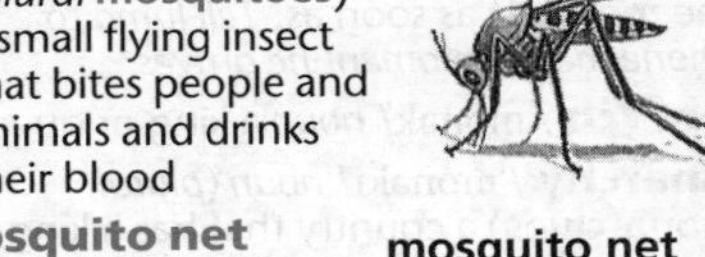

mosquito /məˈski:təʊ/ *noun* (*plural* **mosquitoes**) a small flying insect that bites people and animals and drinks their blood

mosquito net

mosquito net /məˈski:təʊ net/ (also **bed net**) *noun* light material that you hang over a bed to keep **mosquitoes** away from you

moss /mɒs/ *noun* (no plural) a soft green plant that grows like a carpet on things like trees and stones

most[1] /məʊst/ *adjective, pronoun* the biggest amount or number of something: *Ali did a lot of work, but I did the most.* ◇ *He was ill for most of last week.* OPPOSITE **least**
➲ Look at **more[1]**.
at most; at the most not more than; but not more: *We can stay two days at the mos*

make the most of something to use something in the best way: *We only have one free day, so let's make the most of it.*

most² 🔑 /məʊst/ *adverb* more than all others: *She's the most beautiful girl I have ever seen.* ◇ *Which film did you most enjoy?* OPPOSITE **least**

mostly 🔑 /ˈməʊstli/ *adverb* almost all: *The pupils in my class are mostly 13 years old.*

motel /məʊˈtel/ *noun* a hotel for people who are travelling by car

moth /mɒθ/ *noun* an insect with big wings that flies at night

moth

mother 🔑 /ˈmʌðə(r)/ *noun* a woman who has a child: *My mother was 20 when I was born.* ➲ Look at **mum**.

motherhood /ˈmʌðəhʊd/ *noun* (no plural) being a mother

mother-in-law /ˈmʌðər ɪn lɔː/ *noun* (*plural* **mothers-in-law**) the mother of someone's husband or wife

mother tongue /ˈmʌðə tʌŋ/ *noun* the first language that you learn to speak

motion /ˈməʊʃn/ *noun* **1** (no plural) movement **2** (*plural* **motions**) something that you discuss and vote on: *The motion for our debate is 'Watching television is harmful for children'.*
in motion moving: *Don't put your head out of the window while the bus is in motion.*

motive /ˈməʊtɪv/ *noun* a reason for doing something: *Was there a motive for the murder?*

motor /ˈməʊtə(r)/ *noun* the part inside a machine that makes it move or work: *an electric motor*

motorbike

motorbike 🔑 /ˈməʊtəbaɪk/ (also **motorcycle**) *noun* a vehicle with two wheels and an engine

motorboat /ˈməʊtəbəʊt/ *noun* a small fast boat that has an engine

motorcycle /ˈməʊtəsaɪkl/ = **motorbike**

motorcyclist /ˈməʊtəsaɪklɪst/ *noun* a person who rides a motorbike

motorist /ˈməʊtərɪst/ *noun* a person who drives a car

mould¹ /məʊld/ *noun* **1** (*plural* **moulds**) an empty container for making things into a certain shape: *He poured the hot metal into the mould to make the statue.* **2** (no plural) soft green, grey or blue stuff that grows on food that is too old ▸ **mouldy** *adjective* covered with mould: *mouldy bread*

mould² /məʊld/ *verb* (**moulds, moulding, moulded**) to make something soft into a certain shape: *The children moulded the animals out of clay.*

mound /maʊnd/ *noun* **1** a small hill **2** a pile of things: *a mound of old books and newspapers*

Mount /maʊnt/ *noun* You use 'Mount' before the name of a mountain: *Mount Kenya* ❶ The short way of writing 'Mount' is **Mt**: *Mt Kilimanjaro*

mountain 🔑 /ˈmaʊntən/ *noun* a very high hill: *Everest is the highest mountain in the world.* ◇ *We climbed the mountain.*

mountain bike /ˈmaʊntən baɪk/ *noun* a bicycle with a strong frame and wide tyres that you can use to ride over rough ground

mountaineer /ˌmaʊntəˈnɪə(r)/ *noun* a person who climbs mountains
▸ **mountaineering** /ˌmaʊntəˈnɪərɪŋ/ *noun* (no plural) the sport of climbing mountains

mourn /mɔːn/ *verb* (**mourns, mourning, mourned** /mɔːnd/) to feel very sad, usually because someone has died: *She is still mourning her father.* ▸ **mourner** /ˈmɔːnə(r)/ *noun*: *Mourners filled the church for his funeral.*

mourning /ˈmɔːnɪŋ/ *noun* (no plural) a time when people are very sad because someone has died: *They are in mourning for their son.*

mouse 🔑 /maʊs/ *noun* **1** (*plural* **mice** /maɪs/) a small animal with a long tail: *Our cat caught a mouse.* **2** (*plural* **mice, mouses**) a thing that you move with your hand to tell a computer what to do

mouse

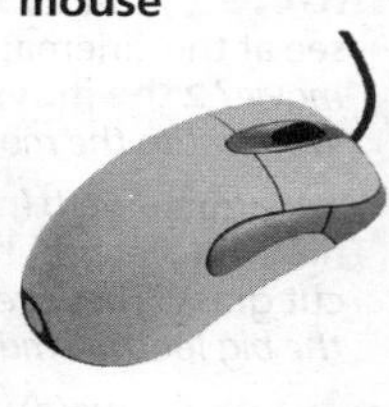

mouse mat /ˈmaʊs mæt/ (also **mouse pad** /ˈmaʊs pæd/) *noun* a piece of soft material that you put a computer mouse on to help it to move more easily

moustache /məˈstɑːʃ/ *noun* the hair above a man's mouth, below his nose: *He has got a moustache.*

mouth 🔑 /maʊθ/ *noun* (*plural* **mouths** /maʊðz/) **1** the part of your face below your nose that you use for eating and speaking: *Open your mouth, please!* ➲ picture on page A13 **2** the place where a river goes into the sea: *a town at the mouth of the river*

mouthful /ˈmaʊθfʊl/ *noun* the amount of food or drink that you can put in your mouth at one time: *a mouthful of food*

move[1] 🔑 /muːv/ *verb* (**moves**, **moving**, **moved** /muːvd/) **1** to go from one place to another; to change the way you are standing or sitting: *Don't get off the bus while it's moving.* ◇ *She moved closer to the fire because she was cold.* **2** to put something in another place or another way: *Can you move your chair, please?* **3** to go to live in another place: *His family moved from Kilgoris to Ukunda last year.* ◇ *We are moving house soon.*

move in to go to live in a house or flat: *He's got a new flat – he's moving in next week.*

move out to leave a house or flat where you were living

move[2] 🔑 /muːv/ *noun* **1** going from one place to another; changing the way you are standing or sitting: *The police are watching every move she makes.* **2** going to live in a new place: *We need a big van for the move.*

get a move on to hurry: *Get a move on or you'll be late for school!*

movement 🔑 /ˈmuːvmənt/ *noun* **1** moving or being moved: *The old man's movements were slow and painful.* **2** a group of people who have the same ideas or beliefs: *a political movement*

movie 🔑 /ˈmuːvi/ *noun* **1** a film that you see at the cinema: *Would you like to see a movie?* **2 the movies** (plural) the cinema: *We went to the movies last week.*

mow /məʊ/ *verb* (**mows**, **mowing**, **mowed** /məʊd/, **has mown** /məʊn/) to cut grass: *They are mowing the grass before the big football match.*

mower /ˈməʊə(r)/ = **lawnmower**

MP /ˌem ˈpiː/ *short for* **MEMBER OF PARLIAMENT**

MP3 player /ˌem piː ˈθriː pleɪə(r)/ *noun* a small piece of computer equipment that you use to listen to music from the Internet

mph a way of measuring how fast something is moving: *The bus was travelling at 50 mph.* ℹ **Mph** is short for 'miles per hour'.

Mr 🔑 /ˈmɪstə(r)/ a word that you use before the name of a man: *Mr Mwita Otieno* ◇ *Mr Chepkwony*

Mrs 🔑 /ˈmɪsɪz/ a word that you use before the name of a woman who is married: *Mrs Awino Njehu* ◇ *Mrs Karomo* ➲ Look at **Miss**, **Ms**.

Ms /məz; mɪz/ a word that you use before the name of any woman, instead of **Mrs** or **Miss**: *Ms Awino Kamau*

Mt *short for* **MOUNT**

much[1] 🔑 /mʌtʃ/ *adjective* (**much**, **more**, **most**) *pronoun* a big amount of something; a lot of something: *I haven't got much money.* ◇ *There was so much food that we couldn't eat it all.* ◇ *'Do you like it?' 'No, not much.'*

> ❖ **GRAMMAR**
>
> We use **much** with uncountable nouns (= things you cannot count). We usually use it only in negative sentences, in questions, and after 'too', 'so', 'as' and 'how'. In other sentences we use **a lot (of)**: *She's got a lot of money.* ➲ Look at **many**.

as much as the same amount that: *Take as much paper as you need.*

how much ...? **1** what amount?: *How much meat do you want?* **2** what price?: *How much is this shirt?*

much[2] 🔑 /mʌtʃ/ *adverb* a lot: *I don't like him very much.* ◇ *I am much older than him.*

mud 🔑 /mʌd/ *noun* (no plural) soft wet earth: *Kisoso came home from the football match covered in mud.*

muddle /ˈmʌdl/ *verb* (**muddles**, **muddling**, **muddled** /ˈmʌdld/)

muddle someone (up) to mix someone's ideas so that they cannot understand or think clearly: *Don't ask so many questions you're muddling me up.*

muddle someone or **something up** to think that one person or thing is a

different person or thing: *I always muddle Teta up with her sister.*
muddle something up to make something untidy: *You've muddled all my papers up!* ▸ **muddle** *noun*: *Your room is in a terrible muddle.* ◇ *I was in such a muddle that I couldn't find anything.*

muddy /ˈmʌdi/ *adjective* (**muddier, muddiest**) covered with mud: *When it rains, the roads get very muddy.*

mudguard /ˈmʌdɡɑːd/ *noun* a curved cover over a wheel of a bicycle

mug¹ /mʌɡ/ *noun* a big cup with straight sides: *a mug of tea*

mug² /mʌɡ/ *verb* (**mugs, mugging, mugged** /mʌɡd/) to attack someone in the street and take their money ▸ **mugger** /ˈmʌɡə(r)/ *noun* a person who **mugs** someone ▸ **mugging** /ˈmʌɡɪŋ/ *noun* (no plural) the crime of attacking someone in the street and taking their money

mule /mjuːl/ *noun* an animal whose parents were a horse and a **donkey**

multicoloured /ˌmʌltiˈkʌləd/ *adjective* with many colours: *multicoloured birds*

multiply /ˈmʌltɪplaɪ/ *verb* (**multiplies, multiplying, multiplied** /ˈmʌltɪplaɪd/, **has multiplied**) to make a number bigger by a certain number of times: *Two multiplied by three is six* (2 x 3 = 6). ◇ *Multiply three and seven together.* ▸ **multiplication** /ˌmʌltɪplɪˈkeɪʃn/ *noun* (no plural) multiplying a number

multi-storey car park /ˌmʌlti stɔːri ˈkɑː pɑːk/ *noun* a large building with several floors for parking cars in

mum /mʌm/ *noun* mother: *This is my mum.* ◇ *Can I have an apple, Mum?* ❶ Children sometimes use the word **mummy** /ˈmʌmi/.

mumble /ˈmʌmbl/ *verb* (**mumbles, mumbling, mumbled** /ˈmʌmbld/) to speak quietly in a way that is not clear, so that people cannot hear you well: *She mumbled something about a visitor, but I didn't hear what she said.*

municipal /mjuːˈnɪsɪpl/ *adjective* connected with a town or city that has its own local government: *municipal elections/councils*

murder¹ /ˈmɜːdə(r)/ *verb* (**murders, murdering, murdered** /ˈmɜːdəd/) to kill someone when you have decided to do it: *Police believe the dead man was murdered.* ▸ **murderer** /ˈmɜːdərə(r)/ *noun* a person who has murdered someone: *The police have caught the murderer.*

murder² /ˈmɜːdə(r)/ *noun* murdering someone: *He was sent to prison for the murder of a police officer.*

murmur /ˈmɜːmə(r)/ *verb* (**murmurs, murmuring, murmured** /ˈmɜːməd/) to speak in a low quiet voice or make a low sound that is not very clear: *He murmured something in his sleep.* ▸ **murmur** *noun*: *I heard the murmur of voices from the next room.* ◇ *the murmur of the wind in the trees*

murram /ˈmʌrəm/ *noun* (no plural) a type of hard soil that is full of small stones. We use **murram** to make small roads.

muscle /ˈmʌsl/ *noun* one of the parts inside your body that become tight or loose to help you move: *Her muscles ached after all that exercise.*

museum /mjuˈziːəm/ *noun* a building where people can look at old or interesting things: *Have you ever been to the National Museum?*

mushroom /ˈmʌʃrʊm/ *noun* a plant that you can eat, with a flat top and no leaves

mushroom

music /ˈmjuːzɪk/ *noun* (no plural) **1** the sounds that you make by singing, or by playing instruments: *What sort of music do you like?* **2** signs on paper to show people what to sing or play: *Can you read music?*

> ❖ **WORD BUILDING**
>
> Some types of music are **pop, rock, jazz, soul, reggae, rap** and **classical**.

musical /ˈmjuːzɪkl/ *adjective* **1** of music: *Can you play a musical instrument* (= the guitar, the trumpet, etc.)? **2** good at making music: *She's a very musical child – she's always singing and dancing.*

musician /mjuˈzɪʃn/ *noun* a person who writes music or plays a musical instrument

Muslim /ˈmʊzlɪm/ *noun* a person who follows the religion of **Islam** ▸ **Muslim** *adjective*: *the Muslim way of life*

must 🔑 /məst; mʌst/ *modal verb* **1** a word that you use to tell someone what to do or what is necessary: *You must look before you cross the road.*

❖ **GRAMMAR**

You use **must not** or the short form **mustn't** /ˈmʌsnt/ to tell people **not** to do something: *You mustn't be late.*

When you want to say that someone can do something if they want, but that it is not necessary, you use **don't have to**: *You don't have to do your homework today* (= you can do it today if you want, but it is not necessary).

2 a word that shows that you are sure something is true: *You must be tired after your long journey.* ◇ *I can't find my keys. I must have left them at home.* ➲ Note at **modal verb.**

mustard /ˈmʌstəd/ *noun* (no plural) a thick yellow sauce with a very strong taste, that you eat with meat

mustn't /ˈmʌsnt/ = **must not**

mutter /ˈmʌtə(r)/ *verb* (**mutters, muttering, muttered** /ˈmʌtəd/) to speak in a low quiet voice that is difficult to hear: *He muttered something about going home, and left the room.*

mutton /ˈmʌtən/ *noun* (no plural) meat from a sheep

Mwalimu *noun* (East African English) a word that you use before the name of someone who is respected as a teacher: *Mwalimu Nyerere*

mwananchi *noun* (*plural* **wananchi**) (East African English) an ordinary person; a member of the public

my 🔑 /maɪ/ *adjective* of me: *Where is my watch?* ◇ *These are my books, not yours.* ◇ *I've hurt my arm.*

myself 🔑 /maɪˈself/ *pronoun* (*plural* **ourselves**) **1** a word that shows the same person as the one who is speaking: *I hurt myself.* ◇ *I bought myself a new shirt.* **2** a word that makes 'I' stronger: *'Did you buy this bread?' 'No, I made it myself.'*

by myself 1 alone; without other people: *I live by myself.* **2** without help: *When I was eight years old my mother let me cook by myself.* ➲ Look at **herself, himself, itself, yourself**.

mysterious 🔑 /mɪˈstɪəriəs/ *adjective* Something that is mysterious is strange and you do not know about it or understand it: *We saw some mysterious lights in the sky.* ▸ **mysteriously** *adverb*: *The plane disappeared mysteriously.*

mystery /ˈmɪstri/ *noun* (*plural* **mysteries**) something strange that you cannot understand or explain: *The police say that the man's death is still a mystery.*

myth /mɪθ/ *noun* **1** a very old story **2** a story or belief that is not true

Mzee *noun* (East African English) a word that you use before the name of a person who is respected because of their age, knowledge or power: *Mzee Kenyatta*

mzungu *noun* (*plural* **wazungu**) (East African English) a white person from Europe: *Fichtner was the only mzungu in the group.*

Nn

N, n /en/ *noun* (*plural* **N's, n's** /enz/) the fourteenth letter of the English alphabet: *'Nice' begins with an 'N'.*

nagana /nəˈɡɑːnə/ *noun* (no plural) a serious illness that cattle get from a type of fly (a **tsetse** fly)

nail 🔑 /neɪl/ *noun* **1** the hard part at the end of a finger or toe: *toenails* ◇ *fingernails* ➲ picture on page A4 **2** a small thin piece of metal with one sharp end which you hit into wood (with a **hammer**) to fix things together ➲ Picture at **hammer**[1]. ▸ **nail** *verb* (**nails, nailing, nailed** /neɪld/) to fix something to another thing with a nail: *I nailed the pieces of wood together.*

naked /ˈneɪkɪd/ *adjective* If you are **naked**, you are not wearing any clothes.

name[1] 🔑 /neɪm/ *noun* a word or words that you use to call or talk about a person or thing: *My name is Njoki Mutungi.* ◇ *What's your name?* ◇ *Do you know the name of this flower?*

call someone names to say bad, unkind words about someone: *Bigogo cried because the other children were calling him names.*

> ❖ **WORD BUILDING**
> Your **first name** is the name that your parents give you when you are born. In Christian countries this is also called your **Christian name**. Some people also have a second name called a **middle name**. Your **surname** is the name that everybody in your family has. A **nickname** is a name that your friends or family sometimes call you instead of your real name.

name² 🔑 /neɪm/ *verb* (**names**, **naming**, **named** /neɪmd/) **1** to give a name to someone or something: *They named their baby Ngenzi.* ◇ *They named him Karimi after his grandfather* (= gave him the same name as his grandfather). **2** to know and say the name of someone or something: *The head teacher could name every one of his 600 pupils.*

namely /ˈneɪmli/ *adverb* You use 'namely' when you are going to name a person or thing that you have just said something about: *Only two pupils were late, namely Moraa and Wasike.*

name tag /ˈneɪm tæg/ *noun* a small piece of plastic, etc. that you wear, with your name on it

nap /næp/ *noun* a short sleep that you have during the day: *I had a nap after lunch.*

napkin /ˈnæpkɪn/ *noun* a piece of cloth or paper that you use when you are eating to clean your mouth and hands and to keep your clothes clean SAME MEANING **serviette**

nappy /ˈnæpi/ *noun* (*plural* **nappies**) a piece of cloth or strong paper that a baby wears around its bottom and between its legs

narrow 🔑 /ˈnærəʊ/ *adjective* (**narrower**, **narrowest**) not far from one side to the other: *The road was too narrow for two cars to pass.* OPPOSITE **wide**, **broad**
have a narrow escape If you **have a narrow escape**, something bad almost happens to you: *You had a very narrow escape – your car nearly hit a tree.*

narrowly /ˈnærəʊli/ *adverb* only just: *The car narrowly missed hitting me.*

nasty /ˈnɑːsti/ *adjective* (**nastier**, **nastiest**) bad; not nice: *There's a nasty smell in this room.* ◇ *Don't be so nasty!*

nation /ˈneɪʃn/ *noun* a country and all the people who live in it

national 🔑 /ˈnæʃnəl/ *adjective* of or for all of a country: *the national athletics championship* ◇ *national newspapers*

national anthem /ˌnæʃnəl ˈænθəm/ *noun* the song of a country

nationality /ˌnæʃəˈnæləti/ *noun* (*plural* **nationalities**) belonging to a certain country: *'What nationality are you?' 'I'm Ugandan.'*

national park /ˌnæʃnəl ˈpɑːk/ *noun* a large area of beautiful land that the government looks after

native¹ /ˈneɪtɪv/ *adjective* connected with the place where you were born: *I returned to my native country.*

native² /ˈneɪtɪv/ *noun* a person who was born in a place: *He lives in Naivasha but he's a native of Kwale.*

natural 🔑 /ˈnætʃrəl/ *adjective* **1** made by nature, not by people: *This part of the country is an area of great natural beauty.* ◇ *Earthquakes and floods are natural disasters.* **2** normal or usual: *It's natural for parents to feel sad when their children leave home.*

naturally /ˈnætʃrəli/ *adverb* **1** in a way that is not made or caused by people: *Is your hair naturally straight?* **2** of course: *You didn't answer the telephone, so I naturally thought you were out.* **3** in a normal way: *Try to stand naturally while I take a photo.*

nature 🔑 /ˈneɪtʃə(r)/ *noun* **1** (no plural) everything in the world that was not made by people: *the beauty of nature* **2** (*plural* **natures**) the way a person or thing is: *Our cat has a very friendly nature.*

> ❖ **WORD FAMILY**
> **nature**
> **natural**: OPPOSITE **unnatural**
> **naturally**

naughty /ˈnɔːti/ *adjective* (**naughtier**, **naughtiest**) You say that a child is **naughty** when they do bad things or do not do what you ask them to do: *She's the naughtiest child in the class.*

nausea /ˈnɔːziə/ *noun* (no plural) the feeling that food is going to come up from your stomach and out of your mouth

naval /ˈneɪvl/ *adjective* of a navy: *a naval officer*

navigate /ˈnævɪgeɪt/ *verb* (**navigates**, **navigating**, **navigated**) to use a map, etc. to find which way a ship, a plane or a car should go: *Long ago, sailors used the stars to navigate.* ▶ **navigator** /ˈnævɪgeɪtə(r)/ *noun* a person who **navigates**

navy 🔑 /ˈneɪvi/ *noun* (*plural* **navies**) the ships that a country uses when there is a war, and the people who work on them: *Ereng is in the navy.*

navy blue /ˌneɪvi ˈbluː/ *adjective* dark blue

ndugu *noun* (East African English) a word used in Tanzania to show respect for someone: *Ndugu Sumaye*

near[1] 🔑 /nɪə(r)/ *adjective, adverb* (**nearer, nearest**) not far; close: *Let's walk to my house. It's quite near.* ◇ *Where's the nearest hospital?* ➲ picture on page A6

near[2] 🔑 /nɪə(r)/ *preposition* close to someone or something: *I live very near my school – just five minutes' walk.*

nearby 🔑 /ˈnɪəbaɪ/ *adjective* not far away; close: *We took her to a nearby hospital.* ▶ **nearby** /nɪəˈbaɪ/ *adverb*: *After school I went to see my aunt, who lives nearby.*

nearly 🔑 /ˈnɪəli/ *adverb* almost; not quite: *I'm nearly 12 – it's my birthday next week.* ◇ *She was so ill that she nearly died.*
not nearly not at all: *The test today wasn't nearly as difficult as I thought it would be.*

neat /niːt/ *adjective* (**neater, neatest**) with everything in the right place; tidy: *Keep your room neat and tidy.* ▶ **neatly** *adverb*: *Write your name neatly.*

necessarily /ˌnesəˈserəli/ *adverb*
not necessarily not always: *Big men aren't necessarily strong.*

necessary 🔑 /ˈnesəsəri/ *adjective* If something is necessary, you must have or do it: *Warm clothes are necessary for camping.*

> ❖ **WORD FAMILY**
> **necessary**: OPPOSITE **unnecessary**
> **necessarily** **necessity**

necessity /nəˈsesəti/ *noun* (*plural* **necessities**) something that you must have: *Food and clothes are necessities of life.*

neck 🔑 /nek/ *noun* **1** the part of your body between your shoulders and your head: *Malika usually wears a chain round her neck.* ➲ picture on page A13 **2** the part of a piece of clothing that goes round your neck: *He wore a sweater with a round neck.* **3** the thin part at the top of a bottle

necklace /ˈnekləs/ *noun* a pretty thing that you wear round your neck: *a gold necklace*

necktie /ˈnektaɪ/ = **tie**[2]

nectar /ˈnektə(r)/ *noun* (no plural) a sweet liquid in flowers that bees use to make **honey** (= the sweet food that we eat)

need[1] 🔑 /niːd/ *verb* (**needs, needing, needed**) **1** If you need something, you must have it: *All plants and animals need water.* ◇ *You don't need to bring money – I'll pay.* **2** If you need to do something, you must do it: *Odoi is very ill. He needs to go to hospital.* ◇ *'Do we need to pay now, or can we pay next week?' 'You needn't pay now.'/'You don't need to pay now.'*

need[2] 🔑 /niːd/ *noun*
be in need of something to want something important and necessary that is not there: *She's in need of a rest.*

needle 🔑 /ˈniːdl/ *noun* **1** a small thin piece of metal with a hole at one end and a sharp point at the other. You use a needle for sewing: *If you give me a needle and thread, I'll sew the button on your shirt.* ➲ Picture at **sew**. ➲ Look at **knitting needle**. **2** something that is like a needle: *the needle of a compass* **3** a very thin pointed leaf: *Pine trees and fir trees have needles.*

needn't /ˈniːdnt/ = **need not**

negative[1] 🔑 /ˈnegətɪv/ *adjective* using words like 'no', 'not' and 'never': *'I don't like tea' is a negative sentence.*

negative[2] /ˈnegətɪv/ *noun* a piece of film that you use to make a photograph. On a **negative**, dark things are light and light things are dark.

neglect /nɪˈglekt/ *verb* (**neglects, neglecting, neglected**) to not take care of someone or something: *The dog was dirty and thin because its owner had neglected it.* ▶ **neglect** *noun* (no plural): *The house was in a state of neglect.* ▶ **neglected** /nɪˈglektɪd/ *adjective*: *neglected children*

negligence /ˈneglɪdʒəns/ *noun* (no plural) not being careful: *His negligence caused the accident.* ▶ **negligent** /ˈneglɪdʒənt/ *adjective*: *The school had been negligent in not informing parents about the incident.*

neigh /neɪ/ *noun* the sound that a horse makes ▶ **neigh** *verb* (**neighs, neighing, neighed** /neɪd/): *The horse neighed and galloped off.*

neighbour[1] /ˈneɪbə(r)/ *noun* a person who lives near you: *Don't make so much noise or you'll wake the neighbours.*

❖ **WORD BUILDING**

Your **next-door neighbour** is the person who lives in the house nearest to your house.

neighbour[2] /ˈneɪbə(r)/ *verb* To neighbour something is to be next to or near it: *The tea farm neighbours our school.*

neighbourhood /ˈneɪbəhʊd/ *noun* a part of a town: *They live in a friendly neighbourhood.*

neighbouring /ˈneɪbərɪŋ/ *adjective* that is near: *We played football against a team from the neighbouring village.*

neither[1] /ˈnaɪðə(r); ˈniːðə(r)/ *adjective, pronoun* not one and not the other of two things or people: *Neither book was very interesting.* ◇ *Neither of the boys can swim.*

neither[2] /ˈnaɪðə(r); ˈniːðə(r)/ *adverb* (used in sentences with 'not') also not: *Ngenzi can't run very fast and neither can I.* ◇ *'I don't like football.' 'Neither do I.'*
neither ... nor not ... and not: *Neither Njoki nor I went on the trip.*

nephew /ˈnefjuː/ *noun* the son of someone's brother or sister; the son of someone's wife's or husband's brother or sister

nerve /nɜːv/ *noun* **1** (*plural* **nerves**) one of the long thin things inside your body that carry feelings and messages to and from your brain: *The pain was caused by a trapped nerve.* **2 nerves** (plural) being worried or afraid: *Kamal breathed deeply to calm his nerves.* **3** (no plural) being brave or calm when there is danger: *You need a lot of nerve to catch a snake.*
get on someone's nerves to annoy someone: *Stop making that noise – you're getting on my nerves!*

nervous /ˈnɜːvəs/ *adjective* **1** worried or afraid: *I'm quite nervous about starting my new school.* **2** of the nerves in your body: *the nervous system* ▶ **nervously** *adverb*: *He laughed nervously because he didn't know what to say.* ▶ **nervousness** /ˈnɜːvəsnəs/ *noun* (no plural) being nervous

-ness /-nəs/ *suffix* a way of making a noun from an adjective: *blindness* ◇ *happiness*

nest[1] /nest/ *noun* a place where a bird, a snake, an insect, etc. lives and lays its eggs or keeps its babies: *a bird's nest*

nest[2] /nest/ *verb* (**nests, nesting, nested**) to make and live in a **nest**: *The ducks are nesting by the river.*

nets

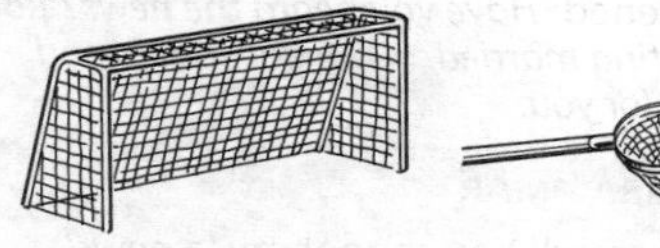

net /net/ *noun* material that is made of long pieces of string, etc. with holes between them: *a fishing net* ◇ *a tennis net*

the Net /ðə ˈnet/ = **Internet**

netball /ˈnetbɔːl/ *noun* (no plural) a game where two teams of seven players try to throw a ball through a high round net

netball

She is playing **netball**.

network /ˈnetwɜːk/ *noun* a large group of things that are connected to one another across a country, etc: *the railway network*

never /ˈnevə(r)/ *adverb* not at any time; not ever: *She never works on Saturdays.* ◇ *I've never been to Mwanza.* ◇ *I will never forget you.*

nevertheless /ˌnevəðəˈles/ *adverb* but; however; although that is true: *They played very well. Nevertheless, they didn't win.*

new /njuː/ *adjective* (**newer, newest**) **1** Something that is new has just been made or bought: *I bought a new pair of shoes yesterday.* ◇ *Do you like my new hairstyle?* **2** that you have not seen, had, learnt, etc. before: *Our new flat is much bigger than our old one.* ◇ *The teacher usually explains the new words to us.*
OPPOSITE **old**
new to something If you are **new to something**, you are at a place or doing something for the first time: *They are new to the town and they don't have any friends there.*

newcomer /ˈnjuːkʌmə(r)/ *noun* a person who has just come to a place

newly /ˈnjuːli/ *adverb* not long ago; recently: *Our school is newly built.*

new moon /ˌnjuː ˈmuːn/ *noun* the time when you can see only the first thin part of the moon

news 🔑 /njuːz/ *noun* (no plural) **1** words that tell people about things that have just happened: *Have you heard the news? Robi is getting married.* ◇ *I've got some good news for you.*

> ❖ **GRAMMAR**
>
> Be careful! You cannot say 'a news'. You can say 'some news' or 'a piece of news': *Kamau told us an interesting piece of news.*

2 the news a programme on television or radio that tells people about important things that have just happened: *We heard about the plane crash on the news.*
break the news to tell someone about something important that has happened: *Have you broken the news to your mother?*

newscaster /ˈnjuːzkɑːstə(r)/ = **newsreader**

newsman /ˈnjuːzmæn/ *noun (plural* **newsmen** /ˈnjuːzmen/) a person who collects and writes stories for newspapers, TV or radio: *a crowd of reporters and TV newsmen*

newspaper 🔑 /ˈnjuːzpeɪpə(r)/ *noun* **1** (*plural* **newspapers**) large pieces of paper with news, advertisements and other things printed on them, that you can buy every day or every week: *My father reads the newspaper every day.* **2** (no plural) paper taken from old newspapers: *Cover the floor with newspaper.*

newsreader /ˈnjuːzriːdə(r)/ (also **newscaster**) *noun* a person who reads the news on the radio or TV

newt /njuːt/ *noun* a small animal with short legs and a tail that can live on land or in water

newt

new year /ˌnjuː ˈjɪə(r)/ *noun* (no plural) the beginning of the year; the time around 1 January: *Happy New Year!*

> ❖ **WORD BUILDING**
>
> 1 January is called **New Year's Day** and 31 December is called **New Year's Eve**.

next[1] 🔑 /nekst/ *adjective* **1** that comes after this one: *I'm starting at my new school next week.* ◇ *Go straight on, then take the next road on the right.* **2** nearest to this one: *I live in the next village.*
next to at the side of someone or something; beside: *The bank is next to the post office.* ➲ picture on page A6

next[2] 🔑 /nekst/ *adverb* after this; then: *I've finished this work. What shall I do next?*

next[3] 🔑 /nekst/ *noun* (no plural) the person or thing that comes after this one: *Fatma came first and Robi was the next to arrive.*

next door /ˌnekst ˈdɔː(r)/ *adjective, adverb* in or to the nearest house: *Who lives next door?* ◇ *next-door neighbours*

ngoma *noun* (East African English) a drum

ngoma

nibble /ˈnɪbl/ *verb* (**nibbles, nibbling, nibbled** /ˈnɪbld/) to eat something in very small bites: *The rabbit was nibbling some leaves.*

nice 🔑 /naɪs/ *adjective* (**nicer, nicest**) pleasant, good or kind: *Did you have a nice trip?* ◇ *All our teachers are very nice.* ◇ *It's nice to see you.*
nice and ... words that show that you like something: *It's nice and warm by the fire.*
▶ **nicely** /ˈnaɪsli/ *adverb*: *You can have a cake if you ask nicely* (= politely).

nickname /ˈnɪkneɪm/ *noun* a name that your friends or family sometimes call you instead of your real name ➲ Note at **name**[1]

niece /niːs/ *noun* the daughter of someone's brother or sister; the daughter of someone's wife's or husband's brother or sister

night 🔑 /naɪt/ *noun* **1** the time when it is dark because there is no light from the sun: *She stayed at my house last night.* ◇ *The baby cried all night.* **2** the part of the day between the afternoon and when you go to bed: *I went to bed early on Monday night.* ℹ **Tonight** means the night or evening of today.

nightdress /ˈnaɪtdres/ (*plural* **nightdresses**) *noun* (also **nightie** /ˈnaɪti/) *noun* a loose dress that a woman or girl wears in bed

nightly /ˈnaɪtli/ *adjective, adverb* that happens or comes every night: *a nightly TV show* ◇ *The programme is broadcast nightly.*

nightmare /ˈnaɪtmeə(r)/ *noun* **1** a dream that frightens you: *I had a nightmare last night.* **2** something that is very bad or frightening: *Crossing the river in the dark was a nightmare.*

night-time /ˈnaɪt taɪm/ *noun* (no plural) the time when it is dark: *She is afraid to go out at night-time.* OPPOSITE **daytime**

nil /nɪl/ *noun* (no plural) nothing: *Our team won the match by two goals to nil.*

nine ⚷ /naɪn/ *number* 9

nineteen ⚷ /ˌnaɪnˈtiːn/ *number* 19

nineteenth /ˌnaɪnˈtiːnθ/ *adjective, adverb, noun* 19th

ninetieth /ˈnaɪntiəθ/ *adjective, adverb, noun* 90th

ninety ⚷ /ˈnaɪnti/ *number* **1** 90 **2 the nineties** (plural) the numbers, years or temperature between 90 and 99
in your nineties between the ages of 90 and 99

ninth /naɪnθ/ *adjective, adverb, noun* **1** 9th **2** one of nine equal parts of something; ⅑

nitrogen /ˈnaɪtrədʒən/ *noun* (no plural) a gas in the air

no[1] (also **No**) *short for* NUMBER[1]

no[2] ⚷ /nəʊ/ *adjective* **1** not one; not any: *I have no money – my purse is empty.* **2** a word that shows you are not allowed to do something: *The sign said 'No swimming'.* ➲ Note at **none**.

no[3] /nəʊ/ a word that you use to show that something is not right or true, or that you do not want something; not yes: *'Do you want a drink?' 'No, thank you.'* ◇ *'He's from Zimbabwe.' 'No he isn't. He's South African.'* OPPOSITE **yes**
oh no! words that you say when something bad happens: *Oh no! I've broken my watch!*

no[4] /nəʊ/ *adverb* not any: *I'm a good swimmer but I'm no better than you.*

Nobel Peace Prize /nəʊˌbel ˈpiːs praɪz/ *noun* a prize that is given each year to someone in the world who works hard for peace

noble /ˈnəʊbl/ *adjective* (**nobler**, **noblest**) good, honest and caring about other people: *a noble leader*

nobody ⚷ /ˈnəʊbədi/ *pronoun* no person; not anyone: *Nobody in our class speaks French.* ◇ *There was nobody at home.* SAME MEANING **no one**

nod /nɒd/ *verb* (**nods**, **nodding**, **nodded**) to move your head down and up again quickly as a way of saying 'yes' or 'hello' to someone: *'Do you understand?' asked the teacher, and everybody nodded.* ➲ note at **head** ► **nod** *noun*: *I'll give you a nod when it's time to start the show.*

noise ⚷ /nɔɪz/ *noun* **1** something that you hear; a sound: *I heard a noise upstairs.* **2** a loud sound that you do not like: *What a terrible noise!* ◇ *Don't make so much noise!*

noisy ⚷ /ˈnɔɪzi/ *adjective* (**noisier**, **noisiest**) **1** full of loud noise: *The restaurant was too noisy.* **2** If a person or thing is noisy, they make a lot of noise: *The children are very noisy.* OPPOSITE **quiet** ► **noisily** /ˈnɔɪzɪli/ *adverb*: *He ate his dinner noisily.*

nomad /ˈnəʊmæd/ *noun* a member of a group of people who move from place to place with their animals to find water and grass ► **nomadic** /nəʊˈmædɪk/ *adjective*: *Many shepherds have changed from a nomadic to a settled life.*

non- /nɒn/ *prefix* You can add **non-** to the beginning of some words to give them the opposite meaning: *a non-contact sport* (= a sport in which you do not touch anyone else) ◇ *This bus is non-stop* (= it does not stop before the end of the journey).

none ⚷ /nʌn/ *pronoun* not any; not one: *She has eaten all the bananas – there are none in the box.* ◇ *I went to every bookshop, but none of them had the book I wanted.*

> ❖ **none** and **no**
>
> **No** must go in front of a noun, but **none** is used instead of a noun: *There is no milk left.* ◇ *'How much milk is left?' 'None.'*
>
> You can also use **not any**. Look at these sentences: *We have no milk.* = *We haven't any milk.* ◇ *There is none left.* = *There isn't any left.*

nonsense ⚷ /ˈnɒnsns/ *noun* (no plural) words or ideas that have no meaning or that are not true: *It's nonsense to say that Achal is lazy.*

noon /nuːn/ *noun* (no plural) twelve o'clock in the middle of the day: *I met Bigogo at noon.*

no one ⚷ /ˈnəʊ wʌn/ *pronoun* no person; not anyone: *There was no one in the classroom.* ◇ *No one saw me go into the house.* SAME MEANING **nobody**

nor ⚷ /nɔː(r)/ *conjunction* (used after

'neither' and 'not') also not: *If Shayo doesn't go, nor will Adisa.* ◇ *'I don't like eggs.' 'Nor do I.'* ◇ *Neither Ajuma nor I eat meat.*

normal 🔑 /'nɔːml/ *adjective* usual and ordinary; not different or special: *I will be home at the normal time.*

normally 🔑 /'nɔːməli/ *adverb* **1** usually: *I normally go to bed at about eleven o'clock.* **2** in a normal way: *He isn't behaving normally.*

north 🔑 /nɔːθ/ *noun* (no plural) the direction that is on your left when you watch the sun come up in the morning: *the north of Tanzania* ▶ **north** *adjective, adverb*: *North Africa* ◇ *a north wind* (= that comes from the north) ◇ *We travelled north from Nairobi to Nanyuki.*

northern 🔑 /'nɔːðən/ *adjective* in or of the north part of a place: *Mwanza is in northern Tanzania.*

nose 🔑 /nəʊz/ *noun* **1** the part of your face, above your mouth, that you use for breathing and smelling: *Breathe in through your nose and out through your mouth.* ➲ picture on page A13 **2** the front part of a plane

blow your nose to blow air through your nose to clear it, into a piece of cloth or paper (a **handkerchief** or a **tissue**)

nostril /'nɒstrəl/ *noun* one of the two holes in your nose ➲ picture on page A13

nosy /'nəʊzi/ *adjective* (**nosier**, **nosiest**) too interested in other people's lives and in things that you should not be interested in: *'Where are you going?' 'Don't be so nosy!'*

not 🔑 /nɒt/ *adverb* a word that gives the opposite meaning to another word or a sentence: *I'm not hungry.* ◇ *They did not arrive.* ◇ *I can come tomorrow, but not on Tuesday.* ◇ *'Are you angry with me?' 'No, I'm not.'*

> ❖ **GRAMMAR**
>
> We often say and write **n't**: *Deng isn't* (= is not) *here.* ◇ *I haven't* (= have not) *got any sisters.*

not at all 1 no; not a little bit: *'Are you tired?' 'Not at all.'* **2** polite words that you say when someone has said 'thank you': *'Thanks for your help.' 'Oh, not at all.'*

note[1] 🔑 /nəʊt/ *noun* **1** some words that you write quickly to help you remember something: *I made a note of her address.* **2** a short letter: *Moraa sent me a note to thank me for the present.* **3** a piece of paper money: *a 500-shilling note* **4** a short piece of extra information about something in a book: *Look at the note on page 39.* **5** one sound in music, or a mark on paper that shows a sound in music: *I can play a few notes of this song.*

take notes to write when someone is speaking so that you can remember their words later: *The teacher asked us to take notes in the lesson.*

note[2] 🔑 /nəʊt/ *verb* (**notes**, **noting**, **noted**) to notice and remember something: *Please note that all the shops are closed on Sundays.*

note down to write something so that you can remember it: *The police officer noted down my name and address.*

notebook /'nəʊtbʊk/ *noun* a small book where you write things that you want to remember

notepad /'nəʊtpæd/ *noun* some pieces of paper that are joined together at one edge, where you write things that you want to remember

notepaper /'nəʊtpeɪpə(r)/ *noun* (no plural) paper that you write letters on

nothing 🔑 /'nʌθɪŋ/ *pronoun* not anything; no thing: *There's nothing in this bottle – it's empty.* ◇ *I've finished all my work and I've got nothing to do.*

for nothing 1 for no money; free: *You can have these books for nothing. I don't want them.* **2** without a good result: *I went to the station for nothing – she wasn't on the bus.*

have nothing on If you **have nothing on**, you are not wearing any clothes.

nothing but only: *He talks about nothing but football.*

nothing like not the same as someone or something in any way: *He's nothing like his brother.*

notice[1] 🔑 /'nəʊtɪs/ *noun* **1** (*plural* **notices**) a piece of writing that tells people something: *The notice on the wall says 'NO ENTRY'.* **2** (no plural) a warning that something is going to happen: *Our teacher gave us two weeks' notice of the science exam.*

at short notice with not much time to get ready: *I was asked to play at short notice and I didn't have time to get my football boots.*

give in or **hand in your notice** to tell the person you work for that you are going to leave your job

take no notice of someone or **something** to not listen to or look at someone or something; to not pay attention to someone or something: *Take no notice of what she said – she's not feeling well.*

notice² 🔑 /ˈnəʊtɪs/ *verb* (**notices, noticing, noticed** /ˈnəʊtɪst/) to see someone or something: *Did you notice what she was wearing?* ◇ *I noticed that he was using a new pen.* ◇ *I noticed him getting on the bus.*

noticeable /ˈnəʊtɪsəbl/ *adjective* easy to see: *I've got a mark on my shirt. Is it noticeable?*

noticeboard /ˈnəʊtɪsbɔːd/ *noun* a flat piece of wood on a wall. You put information on a **noticeboard** so everyone can read it: *The teacher put the exam results on the noticeboard.*

nought /nɔːt/ *noun* the number 0

noun /naʊn/ *noun* a word that is the name of a person, place, thing or idea: *'Ali', 'Asia, 'cat' and 'luck' are all nouns.*

nourish /ˈnʌrɪʃ/ *verb* (**nourishes, nourishing, nourished** /ˈnʌrɪʃt/) to give someone the right kind of food so that they can grow and be healthy ▶ **nourishing** /ˈnʌrɪʃɪŋ/ *adjective*: *a nourishing meal*

novel 🔑 /ˈnɒvl/ *noun* a book that tells a story about people and things that are not real: *'A Grain of Wheat' is a novel by Ngugi wa Thiong'o.*

novelist /ˈnɒvəlɪst/ *noun* a person who writes novels

November 🔑 /nəʊˈvembə(r)/ *noun* the eleventh month of the year

now¹ 🔑 /naʊ/ *adverb* **1** at this time: *I can't see you now – can you come back later?* ◇ *She was in Dar es Salaam but she's living in Arusha now.* ◇ *Don't wait – do it now!* **2** a word that you use when you start to talk about something new, or to make people listen to you: *I've finished writing this letter. Now, what shall we have for dinner?* ◇ *Be quiet now!*

from now on after this time; in the future: *From now on your teacher will be Mr Rashidi.*

now and again; now and then sometimes, but not often: *We go to the cinema now and again.*

now² /naʊ/ *conjunction* because something has happened: *Now that Deng has arrived, we can start dinner.*

nowadays /ˈnaʊədeɪz/ *adverb* at this time: *A lot of people work with computers nowadays.*

nowhere 🔑 /ˈnəʊweə(r)/ *adverb* not anywhere; at, in or to no place: *There's nowhere to stay in this village.*

nowhere near not at all: *I'm nowhere near as tall as my brother.*

nshima (also **nsima**) *noun* (no plural) (East African English) soft food that we make from **maize** flour and hot water

nuclear 🔑 /ˈnjuːkliə(r)/ *adjective* **1** connected with the centre of **atoms** (the very small things that everything is made of): *nuclear physics* **2** using the great power that is made by breaking the central parts of **atoms**: *nuclear energy*

nudge /nʌdʒ/ *verb* (**nudges, nudging, nudged** /nʌdʒd/) to touch or push someone or something with your elbow: *Nudge me if I fall asleep in class.* ▶ **nudge** *noun*: *Njoki gave me a nudge.*

nuisance /ˈnjuːsns/ *noun* a person or thing that causes you trouble: *I've lost my keys. What a nuisance!*

numb /nʌm/ *adjective*

> ❖ **PRONUNCIATION**
>
> **Numb** sounds like **come** because we do not say the 'b'.

not able to feel anything: *My fingers were numb with cold.*

number¹ 🔑 /ˈnʌmbə(r)/ *noun* **1** a word like 'two' or 'fifteen', or a symbol or group of symbols like 7 or 130: *Choose a number between ten and one hundred.* ◇ *Our telephone number is 453653.* ❶ We sometimes write **No.** or **no.**: *I live at house no.47.* **2** a group of more than one person or thing: *A large number of people were waiting for the bus.* ◇ *There are a number of ways you can cook an egg.*

number² /ˈnʌmbə(r)/ *verb* (**numbers, numbering, numbered** /ˈnʌmbəd/) to give a number to something: *Number the pages from one to ten.*

number plate /ˈnʌmbə pleɪt/ *noun* the flat piece of metal on the front and back of a car that has numbers and letters on it (its **registration number**) ➲ Picture at **car**.

numerous /ˈnjuːmərəs/ *adjective* very many: *He writes a lot of letters because he has numerous friends.*

nun /nʌn/ *noun* a religious woman who lives with other religious women in a **convent**

nurse[1] 🔑 /nɜːs/ *noun* a person whose job is to look after people who are sick or hurt: *My sister works as a nurse in a hospital.* ➲ Look at **nursing**.

nurse[2] /nɜːs/ *verb* (**nurses**, **nursing**, **nursed** /nɜːst/) to look after someone who is sick or hurt: *I nursed my father when he was ill.*

nursery /ˈnɜːsəri/ *noun* (*plural* **nurseries**) **1** a place where young children can stay when their parents are at work **2** a place where people grow and sell plants

nursery school /ˈnɜːsəri skuːl/ *noun* a school for very young children

nursing /ˈnɜːsɪŋ/ *noun* (no plural) the job of being a nurse: *He has decided to go into nursing when he leaves school.*

nut 🔑 /nʌt/ *noun* **1** the hard fruit of a tree, plant or bush: *coconuts, groundnuts and cashew nuts* **2** a small piece of metal with a hole in the middle that you put on the end of a long piece of metal (called a **bolt**). You use nuts and bolts for fixing things together.

nutrition /njuˈtrɪʃn/ *noun* (no plural) the food that we eat and how it makes us healthy or not: *Good nutrition is important for children.*

nutritious /njuˈtrɪʃəs/ *adjective* **Nutritious** food is good for you.

nyama choma *noun* (no plural) (East African English) meat that is cooked over a fire

nyatiti *noun* (East African English) a musical instrument with eight strings that you play with your fingers

nylon /ˈnaɪlɒn/ *noun* (no plural) very strong material made by machines. **Nylon** is used for making clothes and other things: *nylon thread*

Oo

O, o /əʊ/ *noun* (*plural* **O's, o's** /əʊz/) **1** the fifteenth letter of the English alphabet: *'Orange' begins with an 'O'.* **2** a way of saying the number '0'

O /əʊ/ = **oh**

oak /əʊk/ *noun* **1** (*plural* **oaks**) a kind of large tree **2** (no plural) the wood of an oak tree: *an oak table*

oar /ɔː(r)/ *noun* a long piece of wood with one flat end. You use **oars** to move a small boat through water (to **row**). ➲ Picture at **rowing boat**. ➲ Look at **paddle**[1].

oasis /əʊˈeɪsɪs/ *noun* (*plural* **oases** /əʊˈeɪsiːz/) a place in a desert that has trees and water

oath /əʊθ/ *noun* a serious promise: *He took an oath in front of a lawyer.*

oats /əʊts/ *noun* (plural) a plant with seeds that we use as food for people and animals: *We make porridge from oats.*

obedient /əˈbiːdiənt/ *adjective* An **obedient** person does what someone tells them to do: *He was an obedient child.* ▶ **obedience** /əˈbiːdiəns/ *noun* (no plural) being **obedient** OPPOSITE **disobedience** ▶ **obediently** *adverb*: *I called the dog and it followed me obediently.*

obey /əˈbeɪ/ *verb* (**obeys**, **obeying**, **obeyed** /əˈbeɪd/) to do what someone or something tells you to do: *You must obey the law.*

> ❖ **WORD FAMILY**
> **obey**: OPPOSITE **disobey**
> **obedient**: OPPOSITE **disobedient**
> **obedience**: OPPOSITE **disobedience**

object[1] 🔑 /ˈɒbdʒɪkt/ *noun* **1** a thing that you can see and touch: *There was a small round object on the table.* **2** what you plan to do: *His object in life is to become as rich as possible.* **3** In the sentence 'Saisa painted the door', the object of the sentence is 'the door'. ➲ Look at **subject**.

object[2] /əbˈdʒekt/ *verb* (**objects**, **objecting**, **objected**) to not like something or not agree with something: *I object to the plan.*

objection /əb'dʒekʃn/ *noun* saying or feeling that you do not like something or that you do not agree with something: *I have no objections to the plan.*

obligation /ˌɒblɪ'geɪʃn/ *noun* something that you must do: *We have an obligation to help.*

oblige /ə'blaɪdʒ/ *noun* (**obliges, obliging, obliged** /ə'blaɪdʒd/)
be obliged to If you are **obliged to** do something, you must do it: *You are not obliged to come if you do not want to.*

oblong /'ɒblɒŋ/ *adjective, noun* = **rectangle**

observation /ˌɒbzə'veɪʃn/ *noun* (no plural) watching or being watched carefully
be under observation to be watched carefully: *The police kept the house under observation.*

observe /ə'bzɜːv/ *verb* (**observes, observing, observed** /ə'bzɜːvd/) to watch someone or something carefully; to see someone or something: *The police observed a man leaving the house.*

obsess /əb'ses/ *verb* (**obsesses, obsessing, obsessed** /əb'sest/)
be obsessed with someone or **something** to think about someone or something all the time: *Kamau is obsessed with football.*

obsession /əb'seʃn/ *noun* a person or thing that you think about all the time: *Cars are his obsession.*

obstacle /'ɒbstəkl/ *noun* **1** something that is in front of you, that you must go over or round before you can go on: *The horse jumped over the obstacle.* **2** a problem that stops you doing something or makes it difficult

obstinate /'ɒbstɪnət/ *adjective* An **obstinate** person does not change their ideas or do what other people want them to do: *He's too obstinate to say he's sorry.*

obstruct /əb'strʌkt/ *verb* (**obstructs, obstructing, obstructed**) to be in the way so that someone or something cannot go past: *Please move your car – you're obstructing the traffic.* ▶ **obstruction** /əb'strʌkʃn/ *noun* a thing that stops someone or something from going past: *The train had to stop because there was an obstruction on the line.*

obtain ⚷ /əb'teɪn/ *verb* (**obtains, obtaining, obtained** /əb'teɪnd/) to get something: *Where can I obtain a visa for Egypt?* ℹ **Get** is the word that we usually use.

obvious ⚷ /'ɒbviəs/ *adjective* very clear and easy to see or understand: *It's obvious that she's not happy.* ▶ **obviously** *adverb* it is easy to see or understand that; clearly: *He obviously trains very hard – he's so much better than the other runners.*

occasion ⚷ /ə'keɪʒn/ *noun* **1** a time when something happens: *I've been to Kampala on three or four occasions.* **2** a special time: *A wedding is a big family occasion.*

occasional /ə'keɪʒənl/ *adjective* that happens sometimes, but not very often: *We get the occasional storm at this time of year.*

occasionally /ə'keɪʒənəli/ *adverb* sometimes, but not often: *I go to Nakuru occasionally.*

occupation /ˌɒkju'peɪʃn/ *noun* **1** (*plural* **occupations**) a job: *What is your father's occupation?* ℹ **Job** is the word that we usually use. **2** (*plural* **occupations**) something that you do in your free time: *Fishing is his favourite occupation.* **3** (no plural) living in a house, room, etc: *The new house is now ready for occupation.* **4** (no plural) taking and keeping a town or country in war

occupy /'ɒkjupaɪ/ *verb* (**occupies, occupying, occupied** /'ɒkjupaɪd/) **1** to live or be in a place: *That building is occupied by students.* **2** to make someone busy; to take someone's time: *The children occupy most of her free time.* **3** to take and keep control of a country, town, etc. in a war: *The Americans occupied Japan from 1945 to 1952.* ▶ **occupied** /'ɒkjupaɪd/ *adjective* **1** busy: *This work will keep me occupied all week.* **2** being used: *Excuse me – is this seat occupied?*

occur ⚷ /ə'kɜː(r)/ *verb* (**occurs, occurring, occurred** /ə'kɜːd/) to happen: *The accident occurred this morning.*
occur to someone to come into someone's mind: *It occurred to me that she didn't know our new address.*

ocean ⚷ /'əʊʃn/ *noun* a very big sea: *the Indian Ocean*

ochre /'əʊkə(r)/ *noun* (no plural) a yellow, brown or red colour that is made from earth: *traditional cloth dyed with ochre*

o'clock ⚷ /ə'klɒk/ *adverb* a word that you use after the numbers one to twelve for saying what time it is: *I left home at four* *o'clock and arrived in Mombasa at half past five.* ➲ Look at page A10.

> ❖ **GRAMMAR**
> Be careful! The word 'o'clock' is only used with full hours. You cannot say: *I arrived at half past five o'clock.*

October 🔑 /ɒkˈtəʊbə(r)/ *noun* the tenth month of the year

octopus /ˈɒktəpəs/ *noun* (*plural* **octopuses**) a sea animal with eight arms

octopus

odd 🔑 /ɒd/ *adjective* **1** (**odder, oddest**) strange or unusual: *It's odd that he left without telling anyone.* **2** Odd numbers cannot be divided exactly by two: *1, 3, 5 and 7 are all odd numbers.* OPPOSITE **even** **3** part of a pair when the other one is not there: *You're wearing odd socks! One is black and the other is green!*
the odd one out one that is different from all the others: *'Apple', 'orange', 'cabbage' – which is the odd one out?*

oddly /ˈɒdli/ *adverb* in a strange way: *She behaved very oddly.*

odds and ends /ˌɒdz ən ˈendz/ *noun* (plural) different small things that are not important: *Kendi went out to buy a few odds and ends that she needed.*

of 🔑 /əv; ɒv/ *preposition* **1** a word that shows who or what has or owns something: *the back of the chair* ◇ *What's the name of this mountain?* ◇ *the plays of Shakespeare* **2** a word that you use after an amount, etc: *a litre of water* ◇ *the fourth of July* **3** a word that shows what something is or what is in something: *a piece of wood* ◇ *a cup of tea* ◇ *Is this shirt made of cotton?* **4** a word that shows who: *That's very kind of you.* **5** a word that shows that someone or something is part of a group: *One of her friends is a doctor.* **6** a word that you use with some adjectives and verbs: *I'm proud of you.* ◇ *This perfume smells of roses.*

off[1] 🔑 /ɒf/ *preposition, adverb* **1** down or away from something: *He fell off the roof.* ◇ *We got off the bus.* ◇ *The thief ran off.* **2** used for talking about removing something: *If you're hot, take your coat off.* ◇ *Clean that mud off your face.* OPPOSITE **on** **3** not working; not being used: *All the lights are off.* OPPOSITE **on** **4** away: *My birthday is not far off.* **5** not at work or school: *I had the day off yesterday.* **6** joined to something: *The village is just off the highway.*

off[2] /ɒf/ *adjective* not fresh: *This milk is off. It smells horrible!*

offence 🔑 /əˈfens/ *noun* something you do that is against the law: *It is an offence to drive at night without lights.* ◇ *a capital offence* (= one for which the punishment is death)
take offence to become angry or unhappy: *He took offence because I said hi[s] spelling was bad.*

offend /əˈfend/ *verb* (**offends, offending, offended**) to make someone feel angry or unhappy; to hurt someone's feelings: *She was offended when you said she was silly.*

offer[1] 🔑 /ˈɒfə(r)/ *verb* (**offers, offering, offered** /ˈɒfəd/) to say or show that you will do or give something if another person wants it: *She offered me a cake.* ◇ *I offered to help her.*

offer[2] 🔑 /ˈɒfə(r)/ *noun* when you say you will do or give something if another person wants it: *Thanks for the offer, but I don't need any help.*

office 🔑 /ˈɒfɪs/ *noun* **1** a room or building with desks and telephones, where people work: *I work in an office.* **2** a room or building where you can buy something or get information: *The ticket office is at the front of the station.* ◇ *the post office* **3** one part of the government: *the Foreign Office*

officer 🔑 /ˈɒfɪsə(r)/ *noun* **1** a person in the army, navy or air force who gives orders to other people: *a naval officer* **2** a person who does important work, especially for the government: *a prison officer* ◇ *police officers*

official[1] 🔑 /əˈfɪʃl/ *adjective* of or from the government or someone who is important: *an official report* OPPOSITE **unofficial** ▸ **officially** /əˈfɪʃəli/ *adverb*: *He thinks he's got the job, but they will tell him officially on Friday.*

official[2] /əˈfɪʃl/ *noun* a person who does important work, especially for the government: *government officials*

officiate /əˈfɪʃieɪt/ *verb* (**officiates, officiating, officiated**) to do official duties: *He baptized children and officiated at weddings.*

often 🔑 /ˈɒfn/ *adverb* many times: *We often play football on Sundays.* ◇ *I've often seen her at the market.* ◇ *I don't write to*

him very often. ◇ *How often do you visit her?*
every so often sometimes, but not often: *Every so often she phones me.*

> **❖ WORD BUILDING**
> These words tell us how often something happens: **always, usually, often, frequently, sometimes, occasionally, rarely, hardly ever** and **never.**

ogre /ˈəʊgə(r)/ *noun* a very big person in stories who eats people

oh /əʊ/ *exclamation* **1** a word that shows a strong feeling, like surprise or fear: *Oh no! I've lost my phone!* **2** a word that you say before other words: *'What time is it?' 'Oh, about two o'clock.'*
Oh dear words that show you are surprised or unhappy: *Oh dear – have you hurt yourself?*
Oh well words that you use when you are not happy about something, but you cannot change it: *'I'm too busy to play football now.' 'Oh well, I'll see you later then.'*

oil 🔑 /ɔɪl/ *noun* (no plural) **1** a thick liquid that comes from plants or animals and that you use in cooking: *Fry the onions in oil.* **2** a thick liquid that comes from under the ground or the sea. We burn oil or use it in machines: *He put some oil in the car.*

oil painting /ˈɔɪl peɪntɪŋ/ *noun* a picture that has been done with paint made from oil

oily /ˈɔɪli/ *adjective* (**oilier**, **oiliest**) like oil or covered with oil: *This fish is very oily.* ◇ *an oily liquid*

OK[1] 🔑 (also **okay**) /ˌəʊˈkeɪ/ *exclamation* yes; all right: *'Do you want to go out to play?' 'OK.'*

OK[2] 🔑 (also **okay**) /ˌəʊˈkeɪ/ *adjective, adverb* all right; good or well enough: *Is it okay to sit here?*

okra /ˈɒkrə/ *noun* (no plural) a small, thin, green vegetable with seeds inside

old 🔑 /əʊld/ *adjective* (**older**, **oldest**) **1** If you are old, you have lived for a long time: *My grandfather is very old.* ◇ *My sister is older than me.* OPPOSITE **young** ➲ picture on page A5 **2** made or bought a long time ago: *an old house* OPPOSITE **new** **3** You use 'old' to show the age of someone or something: *He's nine years old.* ◇ *How old are you?* ◇ *a six-year-old boy* **4** that you did or had before now: *Our old house was much smaller than this one.* OPPOSITE **new** **5** that you have known for a long time: *Chebet is an old friend – we live in the same village.* ▶ **the old** *noun* (plural) old people

old age /ˌəʊld ˈeɪdʒ/ *noun* (no plural) the part of your life when you are old OPPOSITE **youth**

old-fashioned 🔑 /ˌəʊld ˈfæʃnd/ *adjective* not modern; that people do not often use or wear now: *She prefers to use her old-fashioned typewriter rather than a computer.* ➲ Look at **fashionable**.

olive /ˈɒlɪv/ *noun* a small green or black fruit, that people eat or make into oil

the Olympic Games /ði əˌlɪmpɪk ˈgeɪmz/ (also **the Olympics** /ði əˈlɪmpɪks/) *noun* (plural) an international sports competition that is organized every four years in a different country

omelette /ˈɒmlət/ *noun* eggs that you mix together and cook in oil

omena *noun* (*plural* **omena**) (East African English) very small fish that are dried and used to make a dish with tomatoes and milk: *I ate ugali and omena for supper.*

omit /əˈmɪt/ *verb* (**omits**, **omitting**, **omitted**) to not include something; to leave something out: *Omit question 2 and do question 3.* ℹ It is more usual to say **leave out**.

omnivore /ˈɒmnɪvɔː(r)/ *noun* any animal that eats plants and meat

on 🔑 /ɒn/ *preposition, adverb* **1** a word that shows where something is: *Your book is on the table.* ◇ *The number is on the door.* ◇ *We watched the race on television.* ◇ *I've got a cut on my hand.* ➲ picture on page A6 **2** a word that shows when: *My birthday is on 6 May.* ◇ *I'll see you on Monday.* ➲ Look at page A11. **3** a word that shows that someone or something continues: *You can't stop here – drive on.* **4** about: *I read a book on cars.* **5** working; being used: *Is the light on or off?* OPPOSITE **off** **6** using something: *I spoke to Deng on the telephone.* ◇ *I came here on foot* (= walking). **7** covering your body: *Put your coat on.* OPPOSITE **off** **8** happening: *What's on at the cinema?* **9** when something happens: *On her return from holiday, she found a*

letter waiting for her.
on and on without stopping: *He went* (= talked) *on and on about his favourite band.*

once[1] /wʌns/ *adverb* **1** one time: *I've only been to Kampala once.* ◇ *He phones us once a week* (= once every week). **2** at some time in the past: *This house was once a school.*
at once 1 immediately; now: *Come here at once!* **2** at the same time: *I can't do two things at once!*
for once this time only: *For once I agree with you.*
once again; **once more** again, as before: *Can you explain it to me once more?*
once or twice a few times; not often: *I've only met them once or twice.*

once[2] /wʌns/ *conjunction* as soon as: *Once you've finished your homework you can go out.*

one[1] /wʌn/ *number, adjective* **1** the number 1: *One and one make two* (1 + 1 = 2). ◇ *Only one person spoke.* ◇ *One of my friends went to Egypt.* **2** a: *I saw her one day last week.* **3** only: *You are the one person I can trust.* **4** the same: *All the birds flew in one direction.*
one by one first one, then the next, etc; one at a time: *Please come in one by one.*

one[2] /wʌn/ *pronoun* **1** a word that you say instead of the name of a person or thing: *I've got some bananas. Do you want one?* ◇ *'Which shirt do you prefer?' 'This one.'* ◇ *Here are some books – take the ones you want.* **2** any person; a person: *One can get to Nairobi in three hours.*

> ❖ **SPEAKING**
> It is formal to use 'one' in this way. We usually use **you**.

one another /ˌwʌn əˈnʌðə(r)/ *pronoun* words that show that someone does the same thing as another person: *Teta and Kendi looked at one another* (= Teta looked at Kendi and Kendi looked at Teta).

oneself /wʌnˈself/ *pronoun* **1** a word that shows the same person as 'one' in a sentence: *One should be careful not to hurt oneself.* **2** a word that makes 'one' stronger: *One can do it oneself.*
by oneself 1 alone; without other people **2** without help

one-way /ˌwʌn ˈweɪ/ *adjective* **1** A **one-way** street is a street where someone can drive in one direction only. **2** A **one-way** ticket is a ticket to travel to a place, but not back again. ➲ Look at **return**[2].

onion /ˈʌnjən/ *noun* a round vegetable with a strong taste and smell: *Cutting onions can make you cry.*

onion

online /ˌɒnˈlaɪn/ *adjective, adverb* using a computer or the Internet: *Online shopping is both cheap and convenient.*

only[1] /ˈəʊnli/ *adjective* with no others: *She's the only girl in her class – all the other pupils are boys.*
an only child a child who has no brothers or sisters

only[2] /ˈəʊnli/ *adverb* and nobody or nothing else; no more than: *She has six sons and only one daughter.* ◇ *We can't have dinner now. It's only four o'clock!* ◇ *We only waited five minutes.*
only just 1 a short time before: *We've only just arrived.* **2** almost not: *We only just had enough money to pay for the bus.*

only[3] /ˈəʊnli/ *conjunction* but: *I'd like to come with you, only I don't have time.*

onto (also **on to**) /ˈɒntə; ˈɒntu; ˈɒntuː/ *preposition* to a place on someone or something: *The cat jumped on to the table* ◇ *The bottle fell onto the floor.*

onwards /ˈɒnwədz/ (also **onward** /ˈɒnwəd/) *adverb* **1** and after: *I shall be at home from eight o'clock onwards.* **2** forward; further: *The soldiers marched onwards until they came to a bridge.*

open[1] /ˈəʊpən/ *adjective* **1** not closed, so that people or things can go in or out: *Leave the windows open.* **2** not closed or covered, so that you can see inside: *The book lay open on the table.* ◇ *an open box* **3** ready for people to go in: *The bank is open from 9 a.m. to 4.30 p.m.* **4** that anyon can do, visit, etc: *The competition is open to all children under the age of 14.* **5** with not many buildings, trees, etc: *open fields*

> ❖ **WORD FAMILY**
> **open** *adjective*, **open** *verb*, **open** *noun*
> **opener** **opening** **openly**

open[2] /ˈəʊpən/ *verb* (**opens**, **opening**, **opened** /ˈəʊpənd/) **1** to move so that people or things can go in, out or through: *It was hot, so I opened a window.* ◇ *The door opened and a man came in.*

2 to move so that something is not closed or covered: *Open your eyes!* **3** to fold something out or back, to show what is inside: *Open your books.* **4** to be ready for people to use; to start: *Banks don't open on Sundays.* **5** to say that something can start or is ready: *The President opened the new hospital.* OPPOSITE **close, shut**

open³ /ˈəʊpən/ *noun* (no plural)
in the open outside: *I like sleeping out in the open.*

open-air /ˌəʊpən ˈeə(r)/ *adjective* outside: *an open-air concert*

opener /ˈəʊpnə(r)/ *noun* a thing that you use for opening tins or bottles: *a bottle opener*

opening /ˈəʊpnɪŋ/ *noun* **1** a hole or space in something where people or things can go in and out: *The sheep got out of the field through an opening in the fence.* **2** when something is opened: *the opening of the new theatre*

openly /ˈəʊpənli/ *adverb* not secretly; without trying to hide anything: *She told me openly that she didn't agree.*

opera /ˈɒprə/ *noun* a play where the actors sing most of the words

operate 🔑 /ˈɒpəreɪt/ *verb* (**operates, operating, operated**) **1** to work or make something work: *I don't know how this machine operates.* ◇ *How do you operate this machine?* **2** to cut a person's body to take out or repair a part inside: *The doctor will operate on her leg tomorrow.*

> ❖ **WORD BUILDING**
>
> A doctor who operates is called a **surgeon**. A surgeon's work is called **surgery**.

operation 🔑 /ˌɒpəˈreɪʃn/ *noun* **1** cutting a person's body to take out or repair a part inside: *He had an operation on his eye.* **2** something that happens, that needs a lot of people or careful planning: *a military operation*

operator /ˈɒpəreɪtə(r)/ *noun* **1** a person who makes a machine work: *She's a computer operator.* **2** a person who works for a telephone company and helps people to make calls: *The operator put me through to the number I wanted.*

opinion 🔑 /əˈpɪniən/ *noun* what you think about something: *What's your opinion of his work?* ◇ *In my opinion,* (= I think that) *she's wrong.*

opponent /əˈpəʊnənt/ *noun* a person against you in a fight or a game: *The team beat their opponents easily.*

opportunity 🔑 /ˌɒpəˈtjuːnəti/ *noun* (*plural* **opportunities**) a time when you can do something that you want to do; a chance: *I've seen her many times but I've never had the opportunity to talk to her.*

oppose /əˈpəʊz/ *verb* (**opposes, opposing, opposed** /əˈpəʊzd/) to try to stop or change something because you do not like it: *A lot of people opposed the new law.*
as opposed to something words that you use to show that you are talking about one thing, not something different: *She teaches at the college, as opposed to the university.*
be opposed to something to disagree strongly with something: *I am opposed to the plan.*

> ❖ **WORD FAMILY**
>
> **oppose opposite opposition opponent**

opposer /əˈpəʊzə(r)/ *noun* a person who speaks against the subject you are discussing: *The opposers in our debate can speak for three minutes.*

opposite¹ 🔑 /ˈɒpəzɪt/ *adjective, adverb, preposition* **1** across from where someone or something is; on the other side: *The church is on the opposite side of the road from the school.* ◇ *You sit here, and I'll sit opposite.* ◇ *The bank is opposite the supermarket.* ➲ picture on page A6 **2** as different as possible: *North is the opposite direction to south.*

> ❖ **SPELLING**
>
> Remember! You spell **opposite** with **pp**.

opposite² 🔑 /ˈɒpəzɪt/ *noun* a word or thing that is as different as possible from another word or thing: *'Hot' is the opposite of 'cold'.*

opposition /ˌɒpəˈzɪʃn/ *noun* (no plural) disagreeing with something and trying to stop it: *There was a lot of opposition to the plan.*

optician /ɒpˈtɪʃn/ *noun* a person who finds out how well you can see and sells you glasses

> ❖ **WORD BUILDING**
>
> The place where an optician works is called an **optician's**.

optimism /ˈɒptɪmɪzəm/ *noun* (no plural) thinking that good things will happen OPPOSITE **pessimism**

optimist /ˈɒptɪmɪst/ *noun* a person who thinks that good things will happen OPPOSITE **pessimist**

optimistic /ˌɒptɪˈmɪstɪk/ *adjective* If you are **optimistic**, you think that good things will happen: *I'm optimistic about winning.* OPPOSITE **pessimistic**

option /ˈɒpʃn/ *noun* a thing that you can choose: *If you're going to Kisumu, there are two options – you can go by bus or by plane.*

optional /ˈɒpʃənl/ *adjective* that you can choose or not choose: *All students must learn English, but French is optional.* OPPOSITE **compulsory**

or 🔑 /ɔː(r)/ *conjunction* **1** a word that joins the words for different things that you can choose: *Is it blue or green?* ◇ *Are you coming or not?* ◇ *We can buy meat, chicken or fish.* **2** if not, then: *Go now, or you'll be late.*

oral /ˈɔːrəl/ *adjective* spoken, not written: *an oral test in English*

orange[1] 🔑 /ˈɒrɪndʒ/ *noun* **1** a round fruit with a colour between red and yellow, and a thick skin: *Have some orange juice.* **2** a colour between red and yellow: *Orange is my favourite colour.*

orange

orange[2] 🔑 /ˈɒrɪndʒ/ *adjective* with a colour that is between red and yellow: *orange paint*

orbit /ˈɔːbɪt/ *noun* the path of one thing that is moving round another thing in space ▸ **orbit** *verb* (**orbits**, **orbiting**, **orbited**) to move round something in space: *The spacecraft is orbiting the moon.*

orchard /ˈɔːtʃəd/ *noun* a place where a lot of fruit trees grow

orchestra /ˈɔːkɪstrə/ *noun* a big group of people who play different musical instruments together

orchid /ˈɔːkɪd/ *noun* a beautiful plant that has unusual flowers with bright colours

ordeal /ɔːˈdiːl/ *noun* a very bad or painful thing that happens to someone: *He was lost in the mountains for a week without food or water – it was a terrible ordeal.*

order[1] 🔑 /ˈɔːdə(r)/ *noun* **1** (no plural) the way that you place people or things together: *The names are in alphabetical order* (= with the names that begin with A first, then B, then C, etc.) **2** (no plural) when everything is in the right place or everybody is doing the right thing: *Our teacher likes order in the classroom.* **3** (*plural* **orders**) words that tell someone to do something: *Soldiers must always obey orders.* **4** (*plural* **orders**) asking someone to make, send or bring you something: *The waiter came and took our order* (= we told him what we wanted to eat).
in order with everything in the right place: *Are these papers in order?*
in order to so that you can do something: *We arrived early in order to buy our tickets.*
out of order not working: *I couldn't ring you – the phone was out of order.*

order[2] 🔑 /ˈɔːdə(r)/ *verb* (**orders**, **ordering**, **ordered** /ˈɔːdəd/) **1** to tell someone that they must do something: *The doctor ordered me to stay in bed.* **2** to say that you want something to be made, sent, brought, etc: *The shop didn't have the book I wanted, so I ordered it.* ◇ *When the waiter came I ordered an omelette.*

orderly /ˈɔːdəli/ *adjective* **1** tidy: *Her room is very orderly.* **2** calm: *We walked into school in an orderly way.* OPPOSITE **disorderly**

ordinary 🔑 /ˈɔːdnri/ *adjective* normal; not special or unusual: *Deng was wearing a suit, but I was in my ordinary clothes.*
out of the ordinary unusual; strange: *Did you see anything out of the ordinary?*

ore /ɔː(r)/ *noun* rock or earth from which you get metal: *iron ore*

organ /ˈɔːgən/ *noun* **1** a part of the body that has a special purpose, for example the heart or the liver **2** a big musical instrument like a piano, with pipes that air goes through to make sounds

organic /ɔːˈgænɪk/ *adjective* **1** of living things: *organic chemistry* **2** grown in a natural way, without using chemicals: *organic vegetables*

organization 🔑 /ˌɔːgənaɪˈzeɪʃn/ *noun* **1** (*plural* **organizations**) a group of people who work together for a special purpose: *He works for an organization that helps old people.* **2** (no plural) planning or arranging something: *She's busy with the organization of her daughter's wedding.*

organize 🔑 /ˈɔːgənaɪz/ *verb* (**organizes**, **organizing**, **organized** /ˈɔːgənaɪzd/) to plan or arrange something: *Our teacher has organized a visit to the museum.*

organized 🔑 /ˈɔːɡənaɪzd/ *adjective* with everything planned or arranged: *She is very organized - she never forgets anything.*

oriental /ˌɔːriˈentl/ *adjective* of or from eastern countries, for example China or Japan: *oriental art*

origin /ˈɒrɪdʒɪn/ *noun* the beginning; the start of something: *What do we know about the origins of life on earth?*

original 🔑 /əˈrɪdʒənl/ *adjective* **1** first; earliest: *Show me your original plan.* **2** new and different: *His poems are very original.* **3** real, not copied: *original paintings* ▶ **original** *noun*: *This is a copy of the letter – the original is in the museum.*

originally /əˈrɪdʒənəli/ *adverb* in the beginning; at first: *This building was originally the home of a rich family, but now it's a hotel.*

ornament /ˈɔːnəmənt/ *noun* a thing that we have because it is beautiful, not because it is useful ▶ **ornamental** /ˌɔːnəˈmentl/ *adjective*: *an ornamental fountain*

orphan /ˈɔːfn/ *noun* a child whose mother and father are dead

orphanage /ˈɔːfənɪdʒ/ *noun* a home for children whose mother and father are dead

ostrich /ˈɒstrɪtʃ/ *noun* (*plural* **ostriches**) a very big African bird. **Ostriches** have very long legs and can run fast, but they cannot fly.

ostrich

other 🔑 /ˈʌðə(r)/ *adjective, pronoun* as well as or different from the one or ones I have said: *The goalkeeper is from Ethiopia, but the other players are all Kenyan.* ◇ *I can only find one shoe. Have you seen the other one?* ◇ *I saw her on the other side of the road.* ◇ *Ajuma and Adisa arrived at nine o'clock, but the others* (= the other people) *were late.*

other than except; apart from: *I haven't told anybody other than you.*

some ... or other words that show you are not sure: *I can't find my pen. I know I put it somewhere or other.*

the other day not many days ago: *I saw your brother the other day.*

otherwise[1] 🔑 /ˈʌðəwaɪz/ *adverb* **1** in all other ways: *The house is a bit small, but otherwise it's perfect.* **2** in a different way: *Most people agreed, but Moraa thought otherwise.*

otherwise[2] /ˈʌðəwaɪz/ *conjunction* if not: *Hurry up, otherwise you'll be late.*

ouch /aʊtʃ/ *exclamation* You say 'ouch' when you suddenly feel pain: *Ouch! That hurts!*

ought to 🔑 /ˈɔːt tə; ˈɔːt tu; ˈɔːt tuː/ *modal verb*

> ❖ **PRONUNCIATION**
>
> **Ought** sounds like **sport**.

1 words that you use to tell or ask someone what is the right thing to do: *It's late – you ought to go home.* ◇ *Ought I to ring her?* **2** words that you use to say what you think will happen or what you think is true: *Juma has worked very hard, so he ought to pass the exam.* ◇ *These shoes ought to be comfortable, because they were very expensive.* ➲ Note at **modal verb**.

ounce /aʊns/ *noun* a measure of weight (= 28.35 grams). There are 16 ounces in a **pound**: *four ounces of flour* ℹ The short way of writing 'ounce' is **oz**: *6 oz butter* ➲ Look at **pound**[1].

our 🔑 /ɑː(r); ˈaʊə(r)/ *adjective* of us: *This is our house.*

ours 🔑 /ɑːz; ˈaʊəz/ *pronoun* something that belongs to us: *Your house is bigger than ours.*

ourselves 🔑 /ɑːˈselvz; aʊəˈselvz/ *pronoun* (plural) **1** a word that shows the same people that you have just talked about: *We made ourselves some coffee.* **2** a word that makes 'we' stronger: *We built the house ourselves.*

by ourselves 1 alone; without other people: *We sat by ourselves while everyone else was dancing.* **2** without help

out 🔑 /aʊt/ *adverb* **1** away from a place; from inside: *When you go out, please close the door.* ◇ *She opened the box and took out a dress.* OPPOSITE **in 2** not at home: *I phoned Kamau but he was out.* ◇ *I can't go out tonight because I have to study.* OPPOSITE **in 3** not burning or shining: *The fire went out.* **4** not hidden; that you can see: *Look! The sun is out!* ◇ *All the flowers are out* (= open). **5** in a loud voice: *She cried out in pain.*

outbox /ˈaʊtbɒks/ *noun* (*plural* **outboxes**) the place on a computer where new email messages that you write are stored before you send them

outbreak /ˈaʊtbreɪk/ *noun* the sudden start of something: *There have been outbreaks of fighting in the city.*

outcome /ˈaʊtkʌm/ *noun* a result: *Have you heard the outcome of your application yet?*

outdoor /ˈaʊtdɔː(r)/ *adjective* done or used outside a building: *Football and cricket are outdoor games.* OPPOSITE **indoor**

outdoors 🔑 /ˌaʊtˈdɔːz/ *adverb* outside a building: *In summer we sometimes eat outdoors.* OPPOSITE **indoors**

outer /ˈaʊtə(r)/ *adjective* on the outside; far from the centre: *Remove the outer leaves from the cabbage.* OPPOSITE **inner**

outfit /ˈaʊtfɪt/ *noun* a set of clothes that you wear together: *I like your outfit.*

outing /ˈaʊtɪŋ/ *noun* a short journey to enjoy yourself or to learn about a place: *We went on a school outing to a factory last week.*

outline /ˈaʊtlaɪn/ *noun* a line that shows the shape or edge of something: *It was dark, but we could see the outline of the trees on the hill.*

outlook /ˈaʊtlʊk/ *noun* what will probably happen: *With all these talented young runners, the outlook is good for Kenyan athletics.*

out of 🔑 /ˈaʊt əv/ *preposition* **1** words that show where from: *She took a key out of her pocket.* ◇ *She got out of bed.* OPPOSITE **into** ➲ picture on page A7 **2** not in: *Fish can't live out of water.* **3** by using something; from: *He made a table out of some old pieces of wood.* **4** from that number: *Nine out of ten people are scared of snakes.* **5** because of: *Malika helped us out of kindness.* **6** without something that you had or that you need: *We're out of tea.* ◇ *She's been out of work for six months.*

outpatient /ˈaʊtpeɪʃnt/ *noun* a person who goes to a hospital for treatment but does not stay there during the night: *an outpatient clinic* ➲ Look at **inpatient**.

output /ˈaʊtpʊt/ *noun* (no plural) the amount of things that someone or something has made or done: *What was the factory's output last year?*

outside[1] 🔑 /ˌaʊtˈsaɪd/ *noun* the part of something that is away from the middle: *The outside of a coconut is brown and the inside is white.* OPPOSITE **inside**

outside[2] 🔑 /ˈaʊtsaɪd/ *adjective* away from the middle of something: *The outside walls of the house were painted white.* OPPOSITE **inside**

outside[3] 🔑 /ˌaʊtˈsaɪd/ *preposition, adverb* not in; in or to a place that is not inside a building: *I left my bicycle outside the shop.* ◇ *Come outside and see our animals!* OPPOSITE **inside**

outskirts /ˈaʊtskɜːts/ *noun* (plural) the parts of a town or city that are far from the centre: *The airport is on the outskirts of the city.*

outstanding /ˌaʊtˈstændɪŋ/ *adjective* very good; much better than others: *Her work is outstanding.*

outstretched /ˌaʊtˈstretʃt/ *adjective* reaching as far as possible: *She ran into her mother's outstretched arms.*

outward /ˈaʊtwəd/ (also **outwards** /ˈaʊtwədz/) *adverb* towards the outside: *The windows open outwards.* OPPOSITE **inward**

oval /ˈəʊvl/ *noun* a shape like an egg ➲ picture on page A12 ▶ **oval** *adjective* with a shape like an egg: *an oval mirror*

oven 🔑 /ˈʌvn/ *noun* the part of a cooker that has a door. You put food inside an oven to cook it: *Take the cake out of the oven.*

over[1] 🔑 /ˈəʊvə(r)/ *adverb, preposition* **1** above something; higher than something: *A plane flew over our heads.* ◇ *There is a sign over the door.* **2** on someone or something so that it covers them or it: *She put a blanket over the sleeping child.* **3** down: *I fell over in the street.* **4** across; to the other side of something: *The dog jumped over the wall.* ◇ *a bridge over a river* ➲ picture on page A7 **5** so that the other side is on top: *Turn the paper over.* **6** more than a number, price, etc: *She lived in Egypt for over 20 years.* ◇ *This game is for children of ten and over.* **7** not used: *After shopping at the market, I still had a few shillings left over.* **8** from one place to another: *Come over and see us on Saturday.* **9** a word that shows that you repeat something: *He said the same thing over and over again* (= many times). ◇ *The audience liked the song so much that she sang it all over again* (= again, from the beginning).

all over in every part: *She travels all over the world.*

over here here: *Come over here!*
over there there: *Go over there and see if you can help.*

over² /ˈəʊvə(r)/ *adjective* finished: *My exams are over.*

over- /ˈəʊvə(r)/ *prefix* You can add **over-** to the beginning of a lot of words to give them the meaning 'too much': *overeat* (= eat too much) ◇ *Don't oversleep tomorrow* (= sleep too long).

overall¹ /ˌəʊvərˈɔːl/ *adjective* of everything; total: *The overall cost of the repairs will be about 5 000 shillings.* ▸ **overall** *adverb*: *How much will it cost overall?*

overall² /ˈəʊvərɔːl/ *noun* a kind of coat that you wear over your clothes to keep them clean when you are working

overalls /ˈəʊvərɔːlz/ *noun* (plural) a piece of clothing that covers your legs, body and arms. You wear it over your other clothes to keep them clean when you are working.

overboard /ˈəʊvəbɔːd/ *adverb* over the side of a boat and into the water: *She fell overboard.*

overcoat /ˈəʊvəkəʊt/ *noun* **1** a long warm coat that you wear in cold weather **2** a long coat that you wear to protect your clothes at work

overcome /ˌəʊvəˈkʌm/ *verb* (**overcomes, overcoming, overcame** /ˌəʊvəˈkeɪm/, **has overcome**) to find an answer to a difficult thing in your life; to control something: *He overcame his fear of water.*

overcrowded /ˌəʊvəˈkraʊdɪd/ *adjective* too full of people: *The buses are overcrowded at this time of day.*

overdose /ˈəʊvədəʊs/ *noun* an amount of a drug or medicine that is too large and so is not safe: *to take an overdose*

overdraft /ˈəʊvədrɑːft/ *noun* when you spend more money than you have in the bank

overdue /ˌəʊvəˈdjuː/ *adjective* late: *Our landlady is angry because the rent is overdue.*

overflow /ˌəʊvəˈfləʊ/ *verb* (**overflows, overflowing, overflowed** /ˌəʊvəˈfləʊd/) to come over the edge of something because there is too much in it: *After the rain, the river overflowed its banks.*

overgrown /ˌəʊvəˈgrəʊn/ *adjective* covered with plants that have grown too big: *The house was empty and the garden was overgrown.*

overhead /ˈəʊvəhed/ *adjective* above your head: *an overhead light* ▸ **overhead** /ˌəʊvəˈhed/ *adverb*: *A plane flew overhead.*

overhear /ˌəʊvəˈhɪə(r)/ *verb* (**overhears, overhearing, overheard** /ˌəʊvəˈhɜːd/, **has overheard**) to hear what someone is saying when they are speaking to another person, not to you: *I overheard Boke saying that she was unhappy.*

overlap /ˌəʊvəˈlæp/ *verb* (**overlaps, overlapping, overlapped** /ˌəʊvəˈlæpt/) When two things **overlap**, part of one thing covers part of the other thing: *The tiles on the roof overlap.*

overload /ˌəʊvəˈləʊd/ *verb* (**overloads, overloading, overloaded**) to put too many people or things into something: *The little boat was overloaded.*

overlook /ˌəʊvəˈlʊk/ *verb* (**overlooks, overlooking, overlooked** /ˌəʊvəˈlʊkt/) **1** to look down on something from above: *My room overlooks the river.* **2** to not see or notice something: *He overlooked a spelling mistake.*

overnight /ˌəʊvəˈnaɪt/ *adjective, adverb* for or during the night: *an overnight journey* ◇ *They stayed at our house overnight.*

overpopulated /ˌəʊvəˈpɒpjuleɪtɪd/ *adjective* If a country or a city is **overpopulated**, it has too many people living in it. ▸ **overpopulation** /ˌəʊvəˌpɒpjuˈleɪʃn/ *noun* (no plural)

oversleep /ˌəʊvəˈsliːp/ *verb* (**oversleeps, oversleeping, overslept** /ˌəʊvəˈslept/, **has overslept**) to sleep too long and not wake up at the right time: *I overslept and was late for school.*

overtake /ˌəʊvəˈteɪk/ *verb* (**overtakes, overtaking, overtook** /ˌəʊvəˈtʊk/, **has overtaken** /ˌəʊvəˈteɪkən/) to go past someone or something that is going more slowly: *The car overtook a bus and a truck.*

overtime /ˈəʊvətaɪm/ *noun* (no plural) extra time that a person spends at work: *She has done a lot of overtime this week.*

overweight /ˌəʊvəˈweɪt/ *adjective* too heavy or fat: *The doctor said I was overweight and that I should eat less.*

overwhelming /ˌəʊvəˈwelmɪŋ/ *adjective* very great or strong: *an overwhelming feeling of loneliness*

ow /aʊ/ *exclamation* You say 'ow' when you suddenly feel pain: *Ow! You're standing on my foot.*

owe 🔑 /əʊ/ *verb* (**owes, owing, owed** /əʊd/) **1** to have to pay money to someone because they have given you something: *I lent you 50 shillings last week and 50 shillings the week before, so you owe me 100 shillings.* **2** to feel that you have something because of what another person has done: *She owes her life to the man who pulled her out of the river.*

owing to /ˈəʊɪŋ tu/ *preposition* because of: *The bus was late owing to an accident earlier in the day.*

owl /aʊl/ *noun* a bird that flies at night and eats small animals

owl

own¹ 🔑 /əʊn/ *adjective, pronoun* You use 'own' to say that something belongs to a person or thing: *Is that your own camera or did you borrow it?* ◇ *I would like to have my own room* (= for me and nobody else).

> ❖ **GRAMMAR**
>
> Be careful! You cannot use **own** after 'a' or 'the'. You cannot say ~~*I would like an own room.*~~ You say: *I would like my own room* or: *I would like a room of my own.*

get your own back on someone to do something bad to someone who has done something bad to you: *He said he would get his own back on me for breaking his watch.*

of your own that belongs to you and not to anyone else: *I want a home of my own.*

on your own 1 alone: *She lives on her own.* **2** without help: *I can't move this box on my own – can you help me?*

own² 🔑 /əʊn/ *verb* (**owns, owning, owned** /əʊnd/) to have something that is yours: *We don't own our flat – we rent it.*

own up to say that you have done something wrong: *Nobody owned up to breaking the window.*

owner 🔑 /ˈəʊnə(r)/ *noun* a person who has something: *Who is the owner of this pen?*

own goal /ˌəʊn ˈgəʊl/ *noun* If you score an **own goal** in football, you put the ball by mistake into your team's goal.

ox /ɒks/ *noun* (*plural* **oxen** /ˈɒksn/) a mal cow. **Oxen** are sometimes used to pull heavy things on farms.

oxygen /ˈɒksɪdʒən/ *noun* (no plural) a gas in the air. Plants and animals need **oxygen** to live.

oz *short for* OUNCE

ozone /ˈəʊzəʊn/ *noun* (no plural) a gas ir the air

Pp

P, p /piː/ *noun* (*plural* **P's, p's** /piːz/) **1** the sixteenth letter of the English alphabet: *'Pencil' begins with a 'P'.* **2 p** *short for* PA

p.a. *short for* PER ANNUM

pace /peɪs/ *noun* **1** a step: *Take two paces forward.* **2** how fast you do something o how fast something happens: *The race began at a fast pace.*

keep pace with someone or **somethir** to go as fast as someone or something: *She couldn't keep pace with the other runners.*

pack¹ 🔑 /pæk/ *noun* **1** a group of things that you buy together: *I bought a pack o five exercise books.* **2** a group of animals that hunt together: *a pack of hyenas* **3 a** set of 52 cards that are used for playing games: *Have you got a pack of cards?*

pack² 🔑 /pæk/ *verb* (**packs, packing, packed** /pækt/) **1** to put things into a bag or suitcase before you go somewhere: *Have you packed your suitcase?* ◇ *Don't forget to pack your toothbrush.* **2** to put things into a box, bag, etc: *Pack all these books into boxes.* OPPOSITE **unpack**

pack up 1 to stop doing something: *At two o'clock we packed up and went home.* **2** If a machine **packs up**, it stops working.

package 🔑 /ˈpækɪdʒ/ *noun* something that is wrapped in paper SAME MEANING **parcel**

packaging /ˈpækɪdʒɪŋ/ *noun* (no plural material like paper, cardboard or plasti that is used to wrap things that you bu or that you send

packed /pækt/ *adjective* full: *The bus was packed.*

packet /ˈpækɪt/ *noun* a small box or bag that you buy things in: *an empty crisp packet* ◇ *a packet of biscuits* ➲ Picture at **container**.

pact /pækt/ *noun* an important agreement to do something: *They made a pact not to tell anyone their secret.*

pad /pæd/ *noun* **1** some pieces of paper that are joined together at one end: *a writing pad* **2** a thick flat piece of soft material: *Footballers wear pads on their legs to protect them.* ◇ *Use a pad of cotton wool to clean the cut.* ➲ Picture at **cricket**.

paddle[1] /ˈpædl/ *noun* a short piece of wood with a flat end, that you use for moving a boat through water ➲ Look at **oar**.

paddle[2] /ˈpædl/ *verb* (**paddles, paddling, paddled** /ˈpædld/) **1** to move a small boat through water with a **paddle**: *We paddled up the river.* **2** to walk in water that is not deep, with no shoes on your feet: *The children were paddling in the sea.*

padlock /ˈpædlɒk/ *noun* a lock that you use on things like gates and bicycles

padlock

page /peɪdʒ/ *noun* a piece of paper in a book, magazine or newspaper: *Please turn to page 120.* ◇ *What page is the story on?* ℹ The short way of writing 'page' is **p**.

paid *form of* PAY[1]

pain /peɪn/ *noun* **1** (*plural* **pains**) the feeling that you have in your body when you are hurt or ill: *I've got a pain in my leg.* ◇ *He's in pain.* **2** (no plural) unhappiness: *Her eyes were full of pain.*

painful /ˈpeɪnfl/ *adjective* Something that is painful gives pain: *I've cut my leg – it's very painful.* OPPOSITE **painless**

painkiller /ˈpeɪnkɪlə(r)/ *noun* a drug that makes pain less strong

painless /ˈpeɪnləs/ *adjective* Something that is **painless** does not give any pain: *a painless injection* OPPOSITE **painful**

paint[1] /peɪnt/ *noun* a coloured liquid that you put on things with a brush, to change the colour or to make a picture: *red paint* ◇ *Is the paint dry yet?*

paint

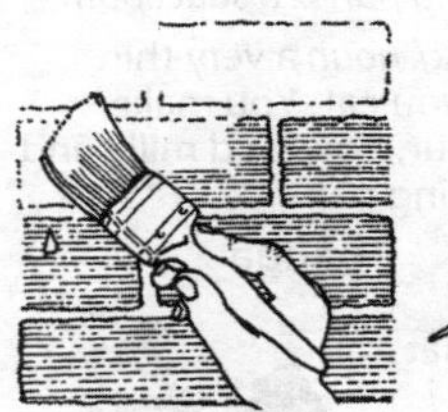

paint[2] /peɪnt/ *verb* (**paints, painting, painted**) **1** to put paint on something to change the colour: *We painted the walls grey.* **2** to make a picture of someone or something with paints: *I'm painting some flowers.* ◇ *My sister paints very well.*

paintbrush /ˈpeɪntbrʌʃ/ *noun* (*plural* **paintbrushes**) a brush that you use for painting

painter /ˈpeɪntə(r)/ *noun* **1** a person whose job is to paint things like walls or houses **2** a person who paints pictures: *Fatma is a talented painter.*

painting /ˈpeɪntɪŋ/ *noun* a picture that someone makes with paint: *The teacher put our paintings up on the wall.*

pair /peə(r)/ *noun* **1** two things of the same kind that you use together: *a pair of shoes* ◇ *a pair of earrings* ➲ picture on page A4 **2** a thing with two parts that are joined together: *a pair of glasses* ◇ *a pair of scissors* ◇ *I bought two pairs of trousers.* **3** two people or animals together: *a pair of ducks*

in pairs with two things or people together: *Shoes are only sold in pairs.*

palace /ˈpæləs/ *noun* a very large house where a king, queen or another important person lives: *The Queen lives at Buckingham Palace.*

pale /peɪl/ *adjective* (**paler, palest**) with a light colour; not strong or dark: *a pale blue dress* OPPOSITE **dark, deep**

palette /ˈpælət/ *noun* a thin board that an artist uses to mix colours on

palette

palm /pɑːm/ *noun* **1** the flat part of the front of your hand ➲ picture on page A13 **2** (also **palm tree**) a tree that has no branches and a lot of big leaves at the top: *a coconut palm*

pan /pæn/ *noun* a metal pot that you use for cooking: *a frying pan* ◇ *a saucepan*

pancake /ˈpænkeɪk/ *noun* a very thin round thing that you eat. You make **pancakes** with flour, eggs and milk, and cook them in a frying pan.

panda

panda /ˈpændə/ *noun* a large black and white bear, that lives in China

pane /peɪn/ *noun* a piece of glass in a window

panel /ˈpænl/ *noun* **1** a flat piece of wood, metal or glass that is part of a door, wall or ceiling **2** a flat part on a machine, where there are things to help you control it: *the control panel of an aircraft*

panga *noun* (East African English) a large, heavy knife

panic /ˈpænɪk/ *noun* a sudden feeling of fear that you cannot control and that makes you do things without thinking carefully: *There was panic in the shop when the fire started.* ▶ **panic** *verb* (**panics, panicking, panicked** /ˈpænɪkt/): *Don't panic!*

pant /pænt/ *verb* (**pants, panting, panted**) to take in and let out air quickly through your mouth, for example after running or because you are very hot: *The dog was panting.*

panther

panther /ˈpænθə(r)/ *noun* a wild animal like a big cat. **Panthers** are usually black.

panties /ˈpæntiz/ (also **knickers**) *noun* (plural) a small piece of clothing that a woman or girl wears under her other clothes, between the middle of her body and the top of her legs: *a pair of panties*

pants /pænts/ *noun* (plural) a small piece of clothing that you wear under your other clothes, between the middle of your body and the top of your legs: *a pair of pants*

papaya /pəˈpaɪə/ = **pawpaw**

paper /ˈpeɪpə(r)/ *noun* **1** (no plural) thin material for writing or drawing on or for wrapping things in: *The pages of this book are made of paper.* ◇ *a sheet of paper* ◇ *a paper bag* **2** (*plural* **papers**) a newspaper: *Have you seen today's paper?* **3 papers** (plural) important pieces of paper with writing on them: *The police officer asked to see my papers* (= for example, a passport or an identity card). **4** (*plural* **papers**) a group of questions in an examination: *The English paper was easy.*

paperback /ˈpeɪpəbæk/ *noun* a book with a paper cover ➲ Look at **hardback**.

paper clip

paper clip /ˈpeɪpə klɪp/ *noun* a small metal thing that you use for holding pieces of paper together

papyrus /pəˈpaɪrəs/ *noun* paper made from **papyrus** (= a type of plant) that was used in ancient Egypt for writing and drawing on

parachutes

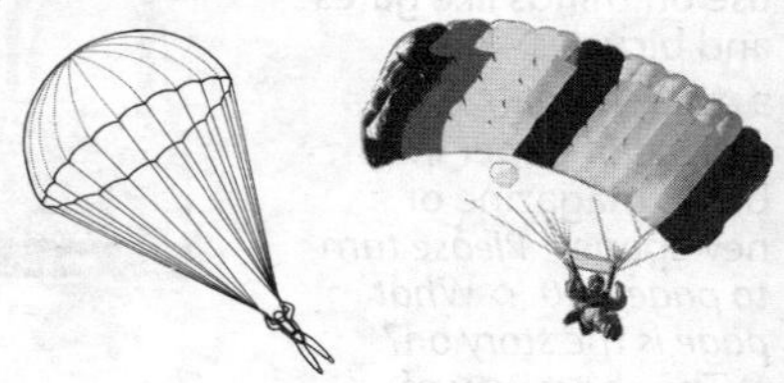

parachute /ˈpærəʃuːt/ *noun* a thing that you have on your back when you jump out of a plane and that opens, so that you will fall to the ground slowly

parade /pəˈreɪd/ *noun* a line of people who are walking together for a special reason, while other people watch them: *a military parade*

paradise /ˈpærədaɪs/ *noun* (no plural) **1** the place where some people think good people go after they die SAME MEANING **heaven** **2** a very beautiful place

paraffin /ˈpærəfɪn/ *noun* (no plural) a type of oil that we burn to make heat or light SAME MEANING **kerosene**

paragraph /ˈpærəgrɑːf/ *noun* a group of lines of writing. A **paragraph** always begins on a new line.

parallel /ˈpærəlel/ *adjective* **Parallel** lines are straight lines that are always the same distance from each other. ➲ picture at page A12

paralysed /ˈpærəlaɪzd/ *adjective* If you are **paralysed**, you cannot move your body or a part of it: *After the accident both her legs were paralysed.*

parcel /ˈpɑːsl/ *noun* something with paper around it, that you send or carry: *She sent a parcel of books to her aunt.* SAME MEANING **package**

parcel

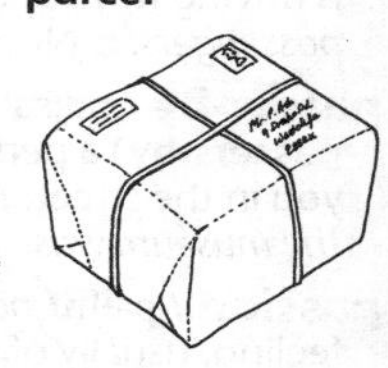

pardon /ˈpɑːdn/ *verb* (**pardons**, **pardoning**, **pardoned** /ˈpɑːdnd/) to forgive someone for something bad that they have done ℹ **Forgive** is the word that we usually use.
pardon? or **pardon me** **1** What did you say? **2** I am sorry.

parent 🔑 /ˈpeərənt/ *noun* a mother or father: *Both her parents are very nice.*

parish /ˈpærɪʃ/ *noun* (*plural* **parishes**) an area that has its own church and priest

park¹ 🔑 /pɑːk/ *noun* a large place with grass and trees, where anyone can go to walk, play games, etc: *We went for a walk in Uhuru Park.*

park² 🔑 /pɑːk/ *verb* (**parks**, **parking**, **parked** /pɑːkt/) to stop and leave a car, lorry, etc. somewhere for a time: *You can't park in this street.* ◇ *Our car is parked opposite the bank.* ▶ **parking** /ˈpɑːkɪŋ/ *noun* (no plural): *The sign says 'No Parking'.* ◇ *I can't find a parking space.*

parking meter /ˈpɑːkɪŋ miːtə(r)/ *noun* a machine that you put money into to pay for parking a car next to it

parliament /ˈpɑːləmənt/ *noun* the people who make the laws in a country: *the Kenyan parliament*

parrot /ˈpærət/ *noun* a bird with very bright feathers that can copy what people say

parrot

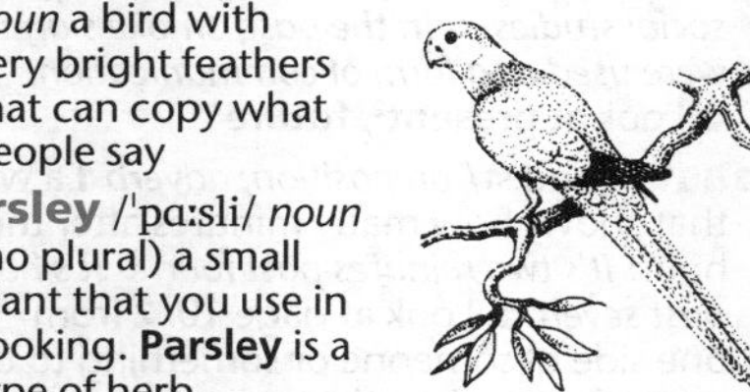

parsley /ˈpɑːsli/ *noun* (no plural) a small plant that you use in cooking. **Parsley** is a type of herb.

part¹ 🔑 /pɑːt/ *noun* **1** some, but not all of something; one of the pieces of something: *We spent part of the day on the beach.* ◇ *Which part of Tanzania do you come from?* **2** a piece of a machine: *Is there a shop near here that sells bicycle parts?* **3** the person you are in a play or film: *She played the part of the old woman.*
take part in something to do something together with other people: *All the children took part in the concert.*

part² /pɑːt/ *verb* (**parts**, **parting**, **parted**) to go away from each other: *We parted at the corner. Achal got on the bus and I went home.*

participant /pɑːˈtɪsɪpənt/ *noun* a person who does something together with other people: *All participants will receive a certificate at the end of the course.*

participate /pɑːˈtɪsɪpeɪt/ *verb* (**participates**, **participating**, **participated**) to do something together with other people: *Ten countries participated in the discussions.* ▶ **participation** /pɑːˌtɪsɪˈpeɪʃn/ *noun* (no plural) doing something together with other people

participle /pɑːˈtɪsɪpl/ *noun* a form of a verb: *The present participle of 'eat' is 'eating' and the past participle is 'eaten'.*

particle /ˈpɑːtɪkl/ *noun* **1** a small word that is not as important as a noun, verb or adjective: *In the verb 'look up', 'up' is a particle.* **2** a very small piece: *particles of dust*

particular 🔑 /pəˈtɪkjələ(r)/ *adjective* **1** one only, and not any other: *You need a particular kind of flour to make bread.* **2** special or more than usual: *The road is very muddy, so take particular care when you are driving.* **3** If you are particular, you want something to be exactly right: *He's very particular about his food.*
in particular more than others: *Is there anything in particular you want to do this weekend?*

particularly 🔑 /pəˈtɪkjələli/ *adverb* more than others; especially: *I'm particularly tired today.* ◇ *I don't particularly like fish.*

parties *plural of* PARTY

parting /ˈpɑːtɪŋ/ *noun* **1** a line that you make on your head by combing your hair in different directions **2** when people leave each other: *It was a sad parting for Shayo and Malika.*

partly 🔑 /ˈpɑːtli/ *adverb* not completely but in some way: *The window was partly open.* ◇ *The accident was partly my fault and partly the other boy's.*

partner ⚿ /ˈpɑːtnə(r)/ *noun* **1** a person's husband, wife, boyfriend or girlfriend: *Bring your partner.* **2** a person you are dancing with, or playing a game with: *She's my tennis partner.* **3** one of the people who owns a business: *He is a partner in a law firm.*

partnership /ˈpɑːtnəʃɪp/ *noun* being partners: *The two sisters went into partnership and opened a shop.*

part of speech /ˌpɑːt əv ˈspiːtʃ/ *noun* 'Noun', 'verb', 'adjective' and 'adverb' are parts of speech.

part-time /ˌpɑːt ˈtaɪm/ *adjective, adverb* for only a part of the day or week: *She's got a part-time job in a cafe.* ◇ *Ajuma works part-time.* ➲ Look at **full-time**.

party ⚿ /ˈpɑːti/ *noun* (*plural* **parties**) **1** a meeting of friends, often in someone's house, to eat, drink and perhaps dance: *We're having a party this Saturday. Can you come?* ◇ *a birthday party* **2** a group of people who have the same ideas about politics: *a member of the Democratic Party* **3** a group of people who are travelling or working together: *a party of tourists*

pass[1] /pɑːs/ *noun* (*plural* **passes**) **1** doing well enough in an examination: *How many passes did you get in your exams?* **2** a special piece of paper or card that says you can go somewhere or do something: *You need a pass to get into the factory.* **3** kicking, throwing or hitting a ball to someone in a game **4** a road or way through mountains

pass[2] ⚿ /pɑːs/ *verb* (**passes, passing, passed** /pɑːst/) **1** to go by someone or something: *She passed me in the street.* ◇ *Do you pass any shops on your way to the station?* **2** to give something to someone: *Could you pass me the salt, please?* **3** to go by: *A week passed before his letter arrived.* **4** to do well enough in an examination or test: *Did you pass your maths test?* OPPOSITE **fail** **5** to spend time: *How did you pass the time in hospital?*

pass away to die: *He passed away in his sleep.*

pass on 1 to give or tell something to another person: *Will you pass on a message to Deng for me?* **2** to die

pass through to go through a place: *The bus passes through Nakuru on its way to Nairobi.*

passage ⚿ /ˈpæsɪdʒ/ *noun* **1** a short part of a book or speech: *We studied a passage from the story for homework.* **2** a narrow way, for example between two buildings

passbook /ˈpɑːsbʊk/ *noun* a small book that contains a record of the money you put into and take out of a bank account

passenger ⚿ /ˈpæsɪndʒə(r)/ *noun* a person who is travelling in a car, bus, train, plane, etc, but not the person who is driving it: *The plane was carrying 200 passengers.* ➲ Note at **train**[1].

passer-by /ˌpɑːsə ˈbaɪ/ *noun* (*plural* **passers-by**) a person who is walking past you in the street: *I asked a passer-by where the museum was.*

passion /ˈpæʃn/ *noun* a very strong feeling, usually of love, but sometimes of anger or hate

passionate /ˈpæʃənət/ *adjective* with very strong feelings: *He's passionate about athletics.*

passion fruit /ˈpæʃn fruːt/ *noun* a sweet, round fruit that has a purple skin and many seeds inside

passive /ˈpæsɪv/ *noun* (no plural) the form of a verb that shows that the action is done by a person or thing to another person or thing: *In the sentence 'The car was stolen', the verb is in the passive.* OPPOSITE **active**

passport ⚿ /ˈpɑːspɔːt/ *noun* a small book with your name and photograph in it. You must take it with you when you travel to other countries.

password /ˈpɑːswɜːd/ *noun* a secret word that you use to enter a place or start using a computer

past[1] ⚿ /pɑːst/ *adjective* **1** of the time that has gone: *We will forget your past mistakes.* **2** last; just before now: *He has been ill for the past week.*

past[2] ⚿ /pɑːst/ *noun* (no plural) the time before now, and the things that happened then: *We learn about the past in social studies.* ◇ *In the past, smoke signals were used as a form of communication.* ➲ Look at **present**[2], **future**[1].

past[3] ⚿ /pɑːst/ *preposition, adverb* **1** a word that shows how many minutes after the hour: *It's two minutes past four.* ◇ *It's half past seven.* ➲ Look at page 10. **2** from one side of someone or something to the other; by; on the other side of someone or something: *Go past the park, then turn left.* ◇ *The bus went past without stopping.*

paste[1] /peɪst/ *noun* (no plural) soft wet stuff, sometimes used for sticking paper to things: *Mix the powder with water to make a paste.*

paste[2] /peɪst/ *verb* (**pastes**, **pasting**, **pasted**) **1** to stick something to something else with **paste**: *Paste the picture into your books.* **2** on a computer, to copy and move writing or pictures from one place to another: *You can cut and paste the figures into your essay.*

pastime /ˈpɑːstaɪm/ *noun* something that you like doing when you are not at school: *Painting is her favourite pastime.*

pastor /ˈpɑːstə(r)/ *noun* a minister in charge of a Christian church or group

pastoral /ˈpɑːstərəl/ *adjective* **1** of or about farming or keeping animals: *pastoral regions* ◇ *pastoral communities* **2** of or about the work of a priest or teacher, giving help about personal matters: *pastoral care*

pastoralism /ˈpɑːstərəlɪzəm/ *noun* (no plural) moving animals from place to place to find water and grass

pastoralist /ˈpɑːstərəlɪst/ *noun* a member of a group of people who move with their animals to find water and grass

pastry /ˈpeɪstri/ *noun* (no plural) a mixture of flour, fat and water that is used for making **pies** ➲ Picture at **pie**.

the past tense /ðə ˌpɑːst ˈtens/ (also **the past**) *noun* the form of a verb that you use to talk about the time before now: *The past tense of 'bring' is 'brought'.* ➲ Look at **present tense**, **future tense**.

pasture /ˈpæstʃə(r)/ *noun* land that is covered with grass that animals can eat: *During the hot dry season these nomads move their cattle to better pastures.*

pat /pæt/ *verb* (**pats**, **patting**, **patted**) to touch someone or something lightly with your hand flat: *She patted the dog on the head.* ▸ **pat** *noun*: *He gave me a pat on the shoulder.*

patch /pætʃ/ *noun* (*plural* **patches**) **1** a piece of cloth that you use to cover a hole in things like clothes: *I sewed a patch on my jeans.* **2** a small piece of something that is not the same as the other parts: *a black cat with a white patch on its back*

path 🔑 /pɑːθ/ *noun* (*plural* **paths** /pɑːðz/) a way across a piece of land, where people can walk: *a path through the trees*

patience /ˈpeɪʃns/ *noun* (no plural) staying calm and not getting angry when you are waiting for something, or when you have problems: *Growing tea takes hard work and patience.* OPPOSITE **impatience**
lose patience with someone to become angry with someone: *She was walking so slowly that her sister finally lost patience with her.*

patient[1] 🔑 /ˈpeɪʃnt/ *adjective* able to stay calm and not get angry when you are waiting for something or when you have problems: *Just sit there and be patient. Your mum will be here soon.* OPPOSITE **impatient**
▸ **patiently** *adverb*: *She waited patiently for the bus.*

patient[2] 🔑 /ˈpeɪʃnt/ *noun* a sick person that a doctor is looking after

patrol /pəˈtrəʊl/ *noun* a group of people, ships, aircraft, etc. that go round a place to see that everything is all right: *an army patrol*
on patrol going round a place to see that everything is all right: *There are usually police on patrol in the town at night.* ▸ **patrol** *verb* (**patrols**, **patrolling**, **patrolled** /pəˈtrəʊld/): *A guard patrols the grounds at night.*

patron /ˈpeɪtrən/ *noun* **1** a person who gives support to an organization such as a charity **2** (in Eastern Africa) a teacher who is in charge of a club at school: *Mr Rono is the patron of the Music Club.*

patter /ˈpætə(r)/ *verb* (**patters**, **pattering**, **pattered** /ˈpætəd/) to make quick light sounds: *Rain pattered against the window.*
▸ **patter** *noun* (no plural): *the patter of children's feet on the stairs*

pattern 🔑 /ˈpætn/ *noun* **1** shapes and colours on something: *My favourite dress has a yellow flower pattern on a blue background.* **2** a thing that you copy when you make something: *I bought some material and a pattern to make a new skirt.*

patterned /ˈpætnd/ *adjective* with shapes and colours on it: *a patterned shirt*

pause /pɔːz/ *noun* a short stop: *She played for 30 minutes without a pause.* ▸ **pause** *verb* (**pauses**, **pausing**, **paused** /pɔːzd/) to stop for a short time: *He paused before answering my question.*

pavement /ˈpeɪvmənt/ (also **sidewalk**) *noun* the part at the side of a road where people can walk

paw /pɔː/ *noun* the foot of an animal, for example a dog, cat or lion ➲ Picture at **cat**, **lion**.

pawpaw /ˈpɔːpɔː/ (also **papaya** /pəˈpaɪə/) *noun* a large fruit that has a green skin and is orange on the inside with small black seeds

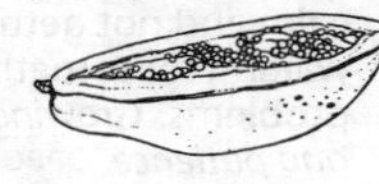
pawpaw

pay¹ 🔑 /peɪ/ *verb* (**pays, paying, paid** /peɪd/, **has paid**) **1** to give money to get something: *He paid 1000 shillings for the shirt.* ◇ *Are you paying in cash?* **2** to give money for work that someone does: *He paid the builder for mending the roof.*
pay back to give back the money that someone has lent to you: *Can you lend me 500 shillings? I'll pay you back soon.*
pay someone back to hurt someone who has hurt you: *One day I'll pay her back for lying to me!*

pay² 🔑 /peɪ/ *noun* (no plural) the money that a person gets for work: *Her job is hard work, but the pay is good.*

payment 🔑 /ˈpeɪmənt/ *noun* **1** (no plural) paying or being paid: *This cheque is in payment for the work you have done.* **2** (*plural* **payments**) an amount of money that you pay: *She makes monthly payments of 1000 shillings.*

payphone /ˈpeɪfəʊn/ *noun* a telephone that you put money in to make a call

PC /ˌpiː ˈsiː/ *noun* a small computer ℹ **PC** is short for 'personal computer'.

PE /ˌpiː ˈiː/ *short for* PHYSICAL EDUCATION

pea /piː/ *noun* a very small round green vegetable. **Peas** grow in **pods**.

peace 🔑 /piːs/ *noun* (no plural) **1** a time when there is no war, fighting or trouble between people or countries: *The countries have been at peace for more than ten years.* **2** being quiet and calm: *the peace of the countryside at night*
make peace to agree to end a war or fight: *The two countries made peace.*

peaceful 🔑 /ˈpiːsfl/ *adjective* **1** with no fighting: *a peaceful demonstration* **2** quiet and calm: *a peaceful evening* ▸ **peacefully** /ˈpiːsfəli/ *adverb*: *She's sleeping peacefully.*

peach /piːtʃ/ *noun* (*plural* **peaches**) a soft round fruit with a yellow and red skin and a large stone in the centre

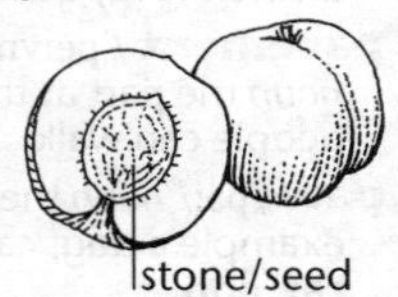

peach

peacock

peacock /ˈpiːkɒk/ *noun* a large bird with beautiful long blue and green feathers in its tail ℹ A female **peacock** is called a **peahen**.

peak /piːk/ *noun* **1** the pointed top of a mountain **2** the time when something is highest, biggest, etc: *The traffic is at its peak between five and six in the evening.* **3** the pointed front part of a hat that is above your eyes

peanut /ˈpiːnʌt/ = **groundnut**

pear /peə(r)/ *noun*

> ❖ **PRONUNCIATION**
> **Pear** and **pair** sound the same.

a fruit that is green or yellow on the outside and white on the inside

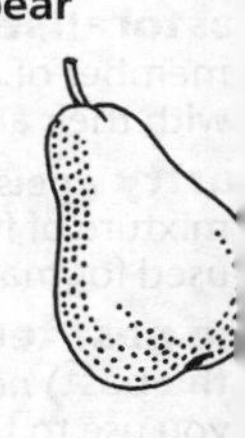
pear

pearl /pɜːl/ *noun* a small round white thing that grows inside the shell of an **oyster** (= a kind of sea animal). **Pearls** are used to make jewellery: *a pearl necklace*

pebble /ˈpebl/ *noun* a small round stone

peck /pek/ *verb* (**pecks, pecking, pecked** /pekt/) When a bird **pecks** something, it eats or bites it quickly: *The hens were pecking at the corn.*

peculiar /pɪˈkjuːliə(r)/ *adjective* strange; not usual: *What's that peculiar smell?*

pedal /ˈpedl/ *noun* a part of a bicycle or other machine that you move with your feet ➲ Picture at **bicycle**. ▸ **pedal** *verb* (**pedals, pedalling, pedalled** /ˈpedld/): *I jumped on my bike and pedalled down the road.*

pedestrian /pəˈdestriən/ *noun* a person who is walking in the street

pedestrian crossing /pəˌdestriən ˈkrɒsɪŋ/ *noun* a place where cars must stop so that people can cross the road

peel¹ /piːl/ *noun* (no plural) the outside

part of some fruit and vegetables: *orange peel*

peel[2] /pi:l/ *verb* (**peels, peeling, peeled** /pi:ld/) **1** to take the outside part off a fruit or vegetable: *Can you peel the potatoes?* **2** to come off in thin pieces: *The paint is peeling off the walls.*

peep /pi:p/ *verb* (**peeps, peeping, peeped** /pi:pt/) **1** to look at something quickly or secretly: *I peeped through the window and saw her.* **2** to come out for a short time: *The moon peeped out from behind the clouds.*

peer[1] /pɪə(r)/ *verb* (**peers, peering, peered** /pɪəd/) to look closely at something because you cannot see well: *I peered outside but I couldn't see anything because it was dark.*

peer[2] /pɪə(r)/ *noun* a person who is the same age as you: *She is popular with her peers.*

peg /peg/ *noun* **1** a small thing on a wall or door where you can hang clothes: *Your coat is on the peg.* **2** a small wooden or plastic thing that holds wet clothes on a line when they are drying: *a clothes peg*

pelican /ˈpelɪkən/ *noun* a type of bird with a very large **beak** (= the hard part of its mouth) that it uses for catching and holding fish

pelican

pen 🔑 /pen/ *noun* **1** a thing that you use for writing with a coloured liquid (called **ink**): *She marked our work in red pen.* **2** a small place with a fence around it for keeping animals in: *The sheep are kept in a pen at night.*

pens

penalty /ˈpenəlti/ *noun* (*plural* **penalties**) a punishment: *The penalty for returning your books late is 100 Tanzanian shillings per day* (= you must pay 100 shillings each day). ◇ *The referee gave a penalty kick to the home team.*

the penalty area /ðə ˈpenəlti eəriə/ *noun* the marked area in front of the goal in football

pencil 🔑 /ˈpensl/ *noun* a thin piece of wood with grey or coloured stuff inside it. Pencils are used for writing or drawing.

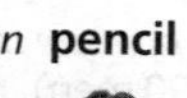
pencil

penfriend /ˈpenfrend/ (also **pen pal**) *noun* a person that you write to but have probably never met

penguin

penguin /ˈpeŋgwɪn/ *noun* a black and white bird that lives in very cold places. **Penguins** can swim but they cannot fly.

penknife /ˈpen naɪf/ *noun* (*plural* **penknives** /ˈpen naɪvz/) a small knife that you can carry in your pocket

penknife

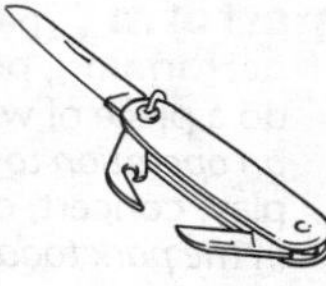

pen pal /ˈpen pæl/ = **penfriend**

pension /ˈpenʃn/ *noun* money that someone gets from a government or a company when they are old and do not work any more (when they are **retired**) ▸ **pensioner** /ˈpenʃənə(r)/ *noun* a person who has a **pension**

people 🔑 /ˈpi:pl/ *noun* (plural) more than one person: *How many people came to the meeting?* ◇ *People in this region are famous for being friendly.*

pepper /ˈpepə(r)/ *noun* **1** (no plural) powder with a hot taste that you put on food: *salt and pepper* **2** (*plural* **peppers**) a red, green or yellow vegetable with a lot of white seeds inside

peppermint /ˈpepəmɪnt/ *noun* **1** (no plural) a plant with a strong fresh taste and smell. It is used to make things like sweets and medicines. **2** (*plural* **peppermints**) a sweet with this taste

per /pə(r)/ *preposition* for each; in each: *They pay him 750 shillings per day.* ◇ *He was driving at 60 kilometres per hour.*

per annum /pər ˈænəm/ *adverb* each year: *The bank pays interest at 5% per annum.* ℹ The short way of writing 'per annum' is **p.a.**

per cent /pə ˈsent/ *noun* (no plural) %; in each hundred: *90 per cent of the people* *who work here are men* (= in 100 people there are 90 men). ▶ **percentage** /pəˈsentɪdʒ/ *noun*: *'What percentage of pupils passed the exam?' 'Oh, about 80 per cent.'*

perch[1] /pɜːtʃ/ *noun* (*plural* **perches**) a place where a bird sits

perch[2] /pɜːtʃ/ *verb* (**perches**, **perching**, **perched** /pɜːtʃt/) to sit on something narrow: *The bird perched on a branch.* ◇ *We perched on high stools.*

perfect 🔑 /ˈpɜːfɪkt/ *adjective* **1** so good that it cannot be better; with nothing wrong: *Her English is perfect.* ◇ *This soil is perfect for growing maize.* **2** made from 'has', 'have' or 'had' and the past **participle** of a verb: *perfect tenses*

perfectly /ˈpɜːfɪktli/ *adverb* **1** completely; very: *I'm perfectly all right.* **2** in a perfect way: *She played the piece of music perfectly.*

perform 🔑 /pəˈfɔːm/ *verb* (**performs**, **performing**, **performed** /pəˈfɔːmd/) **1** to do a piece of work: *The doctor performed an operation to save her life.* **2** to be in a play, concert, etc: *The band is performing in the park today.*

performance 🔑 /pəˈfɔːməns/ *noun* **1** (*plural* **performances**) a time when a play, etc. is shown, or music is played in front of a lot of people: *We went to the afternoon performance of the play.* **2** (no plural) how well you do something: *My parents were pleased with my performance in the exam.*

performer /pəˈfɔːmə(r)/ *noun* a person who is in a play, concert, etc.

perfume /ˈpɜːfjuːm/ *noun* **1** a liquid with a nice smell that you put on your body: *a bottle of perfume* **2** a nice smell

perhaps 🔑 /pəˈhæps/ *adverb* a word that you use when you are not sure about something: *I don't know where she is – perhaps she's still at work.* ◇ *There were three men, or perhaps four.*

perimeter /pəˈrɪmɪtə(r)/ *noun* the outside edge of a shape or a piece of land

period 🔑 /ˈpɪəriəd/ *noun* **1** an amount of time: *He was ill four times in a period of six months.* **2** a certain time in the life of a person or the history of a country: *What period of history are you studying?* **3** a lesson: *We have seven periods of English a week.* **4** the time when a woman loses blood from her body each month

periodical /ˌpɪəriˈɒdɪkl/ *noun* a magazine about a serious subject

perish /ˈperɪʃ/ *verb* (**perishes**, **perishing**, **perished** /ˈperɪʃt/) to die ℹ **Die** is the word that we usually use.

permanent 🔑 /ˈpɜːmənənt/ *adjective* Something that is permanent continues for ever or for a very long time and does not change: *She is looking for a permanent job.* OPPOSITE **temporary** ▶ **permanently** *adverb*: *Has he left permanently or is he coming back?* OPPOSITE **temporarily**

permission 🔑 /pəˈmɪʃn/ *noun* (no plural) allowing someone to do something: *She gave me permission to leave early.*

permit[1] /pəˈmɪt/ *verb* (**permits**, **permitting**, **permitted**) to allow someone to do something: *You are not permitted to use mobile phones here.* ℹ **Allow** is the word that we usually use.

permit[2] /ˈpɜːmɪt/ *noun* a piece of paper that says you can do something or go somewhere: *Has she got a work permit?*

perpendicular /ˌpɜːpənˈdɪkjələ(r)/ *adjective* at an angle of 90 degrees to something: *The line CD is perpendicular to the line AB.* ➲ Look at **horizontal**, **vertical**

persist /pəˈsɪst/ *verb* (**persists**, **persisting**, **persisted**) **1** to continue to do something even if it is difficult or other people say you are wrong: *Why do you persist in blaming yourself for what happened?* **2** to continue to exist: *If the symptoms persist, consult your doctor.* ▶ **persistence** /pəˈsɪstəns/ *noun* (no plural): *Finally her persistence was rewarded and she got what she wanted.*

person 🔑 /ˈpɜːsn/ *noun* (*plural* **people** /ˈpiːpl/) a man or woman: *I think she's the best person for the job.*

in person seeing someone, not just speaking on the telephone or writing a letter: *I want to speak to her in person.*

personal 🔑 /ˈpɜːsənl/ *adjective* of or for one person; private: *This letter is personal – you can't read it.*

personal computer /ˌpɜːsənl kəmˈpjuːtə(r)/ = **PC**

personality /ˌpɜːsəˈnæləti/ *noun* (*plural* **personalities**) **1** what sort of person you are; your character: *Fatma has a great personality.* **2** a famous person: *a television personality*

personally /ˈpɜːsənəli/ *adverb* You say 'personally' when you are saying what you think about something: *Personally, I like her, but a lot of people don't.*

persuade 🔑 /pə'sweɪd/ *verb* (**persuades, persuading, persuaded**) to make someone think or do something by talking to them: *They tried to persuade me to join their club.*

persuasion /pə'sweɪʒn/ *noun* (no plural) making someone think or do something: *After a lot of persuasion she agreed to come.*

pessimism /'pesɪmɪzəm/ *noun* (no plural) thinking that bad things will happen OPPOSITE **optimism**

pessimist /'pesɪmɪst/ *noun* a person who thinks that bad things will happen OPPOSITE **optimist**

pessimistic /ˌpesɪ'mɪstɪk/ *adjective* If you are pessimistic, you think that bad things will happen: *Don't be so pessimistic!* OPPOSITE **optimistic**

pest /pest/ *noun* **1** an insect or animal that damages plants or food **2** a person or thing that annoys you: *My sister is being a real pest!*

pesticide /'pestɪsaɪd/ *noun* a chemical that is used for killing **pests**, especially insects that eat food crops: *crops sprayed with pesticide*

pestle /'pesl/ *noun* a tool that we use to crush things in a strong bowl (a **mortar**)

pet 🔑 /pet/ *noun* **1** an animal that you keep in your home: *I've got two pets – a cat and a dog.* **2** a child that a teacher or a parent likes best: *She's the teacher's pet.*

petal /'petl/ *noun* one of the coloured parts of a flower ➲ Picture at **plant**[1].

petition /pə'tɪʃn/ *noun* a special letter, from a group of people, that asks for something: *Thousands of people signed the petition for a new clinic.*

petrol 🔑 /'petrəl/ (also **gasoline**) *noun* (no plural) a liquid that you put in a car to make the engine work

petrol station /'petrəl steɪʃn/ *noun* a place where you can buy petrol

petty /'peti/ *adjective* small and not very serious: *Petty crime, such as shoplifting, is a problem.*

phantom /'fæntəm/ *noun* a spirit of a dead person that people think they see

> ❖ **SPEAKING**
>
> **Ghost** is the word that we usually use.

pharmacist /'fɑːməsɪst/ = **chemist**

phase /feɪz/ *noun* a time when something is changing or growing: *Many farmers watch the phases of the moon carefully.*

philosopher /fɪ'lɒsəfə(r)/ *noun* a person who studies ideas about the meaning of life

philosophy /fɪ'lɒsəfi/ *noun* **1** (no plural) the study of ideas about the meaning of life **2** (*plural* **philosophies**) what one person thinks about life: *Enjoy yourself today and don't worry about tomorrow – that's my philosophy!*

phone[1] 🔑 /fəʊn/ *noun* a telephone; an instrument that you use for talking to someone who is in another place: *The phone's ringing – can you answer it?* ◇ *I need to make a phone call.*
on the phone using a telephone to speak to someone: *Hawa was on the phone for an hour.*

phone[2] 🔑 /fəʊn/ *verb* (**phones, phoning, phoned** /fəʊnd/) to use a telephone: *I phoned my grandmother last night.*

phone book /'fəʊn bʊk/ *noun* a book of people's names, addresses and telephone numbers

phone box /'fəʊn bɒks/ = **telephone box**

phone call /'fəʊn kɔːl/ *noun* when you use the phone to talk to someone

phone number /'fəʊn nʌmbə(r)/ *noun* the number of a particular phone that you use when you want to make a call to it: *What's your phone number?*

phonetic /fə'netɪk/ *adjective* using special signs to show how to say words: *The phonetic alphabet is used to show pronunciation.*

phonetics /fə'netɪks/ *noun* (no plural) the study of the sounds that people make when they speak

photo 🔑 /'fəʊtəʊ/ *noun* (*plural* **photos**) *short for* PHOTOGRAPH

photocopy /'fəʊtəʊkɒpi/ *noun* (*plural* **photocopies**) a copy of something on paper that you make with a special machine (called a **photocopier**)
▶ **photocopy** *verb* (**photocopies, photocopying, photocopied** /'fəʊtəʊkɒpid/): *Can you photocopy this letter?*

photograph 🔑 /'fəʊtəgrɑːf/ (also **photo**) *noun* a picture that you take with a camera: *I took a photo of Mount Kilimanjaro.*
▶ **photograph** *verb* (**photographs, photographing, photographed** /'fəʊtəgrɑːft/) to take a photograph of

someone or something: *The winner was photographed holding his prize.*

❖ **WORD FAMILY**
photo photograph photographer photography photographic

photographer 🔑 /fəˈtɒɡrəfə(r)/ *noun* a person who takes photographs: *He works as a fashion photographer.*

photographic /ˌfəʊtəˈɡræfɪk/ *adjective* about photographs or photography: *photographic equipment*

photography /fəˈtɒɡrəfi/ *noun* (no plural) taking photographs

photoshop (also **Photoshop**) /ˈfəʊtəʊʃɒp/ *verb* (**photoshops**, **photoshopping**, **photoshopped** /ˈfəʊtəʊʃɒpt/) to change a picture or photograph using a computer program: *I'm sure this picture has been photoshopped.*

photosynthesis /ˌfəʊtəʊˈsɪnθəsɪs/ *noun* (no plural) the process by which green plants turn **carbon dioxide** (= a gas) and water into food using energy obtained from light from the sun

phrase 🔑 /freɪz/ *noun*

❖ **PRONUNCIATION**
Phrase sounds like **days**.

a group of words that you use together as part of a sentence: *'First of all' and 'a piece of paper' are phrases.*

physical 🔑 /ˈfɪzɪkl/ *adjective* You use 'physical' about things that you feel or do with your body: *physical exercise* ▸ **physically** /ˈfɪzɪkli/ *adverb*: *I'm not physically fit.*

physical education /ˌfɪzɪkl edʒuˈkeɪʃn/ *noun* (no plural) sports that you do at school ℹ The short form is **PE**.

physicist /ˈfɪzɪsɪst/ *noun* a person who studies or knows a lot about **physics**

physics /ˈfɪzɪks/ *noun* (no plural) the study of things like heat, light and sound

pianist /ˈpiːənɪst/ *noun* a person who plays the piano

piano 🔑 /piˈænəʊ/ *noun* (*plural* **pianos**) a big musical instrument that you play by pressing black and white bars (called **keys**)

piano

pick¹ 🔑 /pɪk/ *verb* (**picks**, **picking**, **picked** /pɪkt/) **1** to take the person or thing you like best; to choose: *They picked Ngenzi as their captain.* **2** to take a flower, fruit or vegetable from the place where it grows: *Picking tea is very hard work.*
pick out to be able to see someone or something among a lot of others: *Can you pick out my father in this photo?*
pick up 1 to take and lift someone or something: *She picked up the bags and put them on the table.* ◇ *The phone stopped ringing just as I picked it up.* **2** to come to take someone or something away: *I picked up my post from the post office.* **3** to learn something without really studying it: *Did you pick up any French while you were in West Africa?*

pick² /pɪk/ *noun* (no plural) what you choose; your choice
take your pick to choose what you like: *We've got red, green and blue shirts. Take your pick.*

picket /ˈpɪkɪt/ *verb* (**pickets**, **picketing**, **picketed**) to stand outside the place where you work when there is a **strike** (= a time when people are refusing to work), and try to stop other people going to work ▸ **picket** *noun* a person or group of people who **picket**: *There was a picket outside the hospital.*

pickpocket /ˈpɪkpɒkɪt/ *noun* a person who steals things from people's pockets

pickup /ˈpɪkʌp/ *noun* a small lorry with no roof on the back

pickup

picture 🔑 /ˈpɪktʃə(r)/ *noun* **1** a drawing, painting or photograph: *Ajuma drew a picture of her dog.* ◇ *They showed us some pictures of their wedding.* **2 the pictures** (plural) the cinema: *We're going to the pictures this evening.*
take a picture to photograph something: *I took a picture of the house.*

pie /paɪ/ *noun* meat, fruit, vegetables, etc. with **pastry** (= a mixture of flour, butter and water): *an apple pie*

pie

pastry

piece 🔑 /piːs/ *noun* **1** a part of something: *We covered the hole with a piece of wood.* ◇ *a piece of broken glass* ➲ picture on page A1

2 one single thing: *Have you got a piece of paper?* ◇ *That's an interesting piece of news.*
fall to pieces to break into pieces: *The chair fell to pieces when I sat on it.*
in pieces broken: *The teapot lay in pieces on the floor.*
a piece of cake a thing that is very easy to do: *Can I ride a bike? It's a piece of cake!*
take something to pieces to divide something into its parts: *He took the bed to pieces to get it through the door.*

piecework /ˈpiːswɜːk/ *noun* (no plural) If someone does **piecework**, they are paid for the amount they do, not for the hours they work.

pie chart /ˈpaɪ tʃɑːt/ (also **circle graph**) *noun* a circle with parts that show how much of different things there is

pie chart

oranges
pears
bananas
plums

the types of fruit in the shop

pier /pɪə(r)/ *noun* a long thing that is built from the land into the sea, where people can walk or get on and off boats

pierce /pɪəs/ *verb* (**pierces**, **piercing**, **pierced** /pɪəst/) to make a hole in something with a sharp point: *The nail pierced her skin.* ◇ *When did you have your ears pierced?*

piercing /ˈpɪəsɪŋ/ *adjective* A **piercing** sound is very loud and sharp: *We heard a piercing cry.*

pig /pɪɡ/ *noun* a fat animal that people keep on farms for its meat

❖ **WORD BUILDING**
A young pig is called a **piglet**. Meat from a pig is called **pork**, **bacon** or **ham**.

pigeon /ˈpɪdʒɪn/ *noun* a grey bird that you often see in towns

piglet /ˈpɪɡlət/ *noun* a young pig

pigsty /ˈpɪɡstaɪ/ *noun* (*plural* **pigsties**) a small building where pigs live

pilaf /ˈpiːlæf/ (also **pilau** /ˈpiːlaʊ/) *noun* (no plural) rice that is cooked with spices and meat or vegetables

pile¹ /paɪl/ *noun* a lot of things on top of one another; a large amount of something: *There's a pile of clothes on the floor.* ◇ *a pile of earth* ➲ picture on page A4

pile² /paɪl/ *verb* (**piles**, **piling**, **piled** /paɪld/) to put a lot of things on top of one another: *She piled the boxes on the table.*

pilgrim /ˈpɪlɡrɪm/ *noun* a person who travels a long way to a place because it has a special religious meaning

pilgrimage /ˈpɪlɡrɪmɪdʒ/ *noun* a journey that a **pilgrim** makes

pill /pɪl/ *noun* a small round hard piece of medicine that you swallow: *Take one of these pills before every meal.*

pillar /ˈpɪlə(r)/ *noun* a tall strong piece of stone, wood or metal that holds up a building

pillow

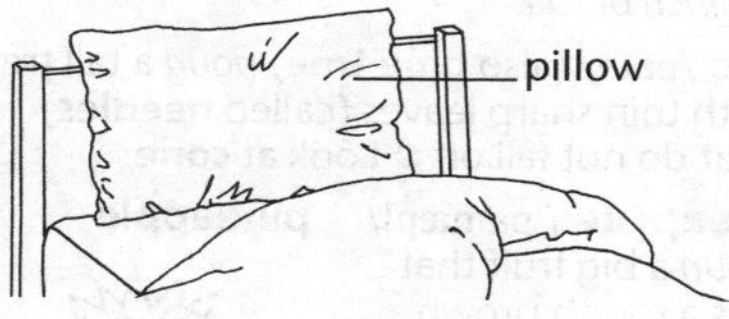

pillow /ˈpɪləʊ/ *noun* a soft thing that you put under your head when you are in bed

pillowcase /ˈpɪləʊkeɪs/ *noun* a cover for a **pillow**

pilot /ˈpaɪlət/ *noun* **1** a person who flies an aircraft: *He wants to be an airline pilot.* **2** a person who guides a ship along a river, into a **harbour** (= a place where ships can stay safely), etc.

PIN /pɪn/ (also **PIN number** /ˈpɪn nʌmbə(r)/) *noun* a number that a bank gives someone so that they can use a plastic card to take money out of a machine at a bank (called a **cash machine**)

pins

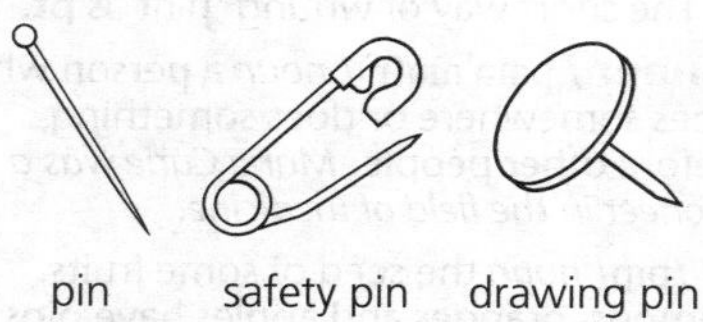

pin¹ /pɪn/ *noun* a small thin piece of metal with a flat part at one end and a sharp point at the other. You use a pin for holding pieces of cloth or paper together.

pin² /pɪn/ *verb* (**pins**, **pinning**, **pinned** /pɪnd/) **1** to fix things together with a pin or pins: *Pin the pieces of material together before you sew them.* ◇ *Could you pin this notice to the board?* **2** to hold someone or something so that they cannot move: *He tried to get away, but they pinned him against the wall.*

pinch[1] /pɪntʃ/ *verb* (**pinches, pinching, pinched** /pɪntʃt/) **1** to press someone's skin tightly between your thumb and finger: *Don't pinch me – it hurts!* **2** to steal something: *Who's pinched my pen?*
ℹ This is an informal use.

pinch[2] /pɪntʃ/ *noun* (*plural* **pinches**) **1** pressing someone's skin tightly between your thumb and finger: *He gave my leg a pinch.* **2** how much of something you can hold between your thumb and finger: *Add a pinch of salt.*

pine /paɪn/ (also **pine tree**) *noun* a tall tree with thin sharp leaves (called **needles**) that do not fall off ➲ Look at **cone**.

pineapple /ˈpaɪnæpl/ *noun* a big fruit that has a rough brown skin and is yellow inside

pineapple

pine tree /ˈpaɪn triː/ = **pine**

pink 🔑 /pɪŋk/ *adjective* with a light red colour: *a pink jumper*
▶ **pink** *noun*: *She was dressed in pink.*

pins and needles /ˌpɪnz ən ˈniːdlz/ *noun* (plural) the strange feeling that you sometimes get in a part of your body when you have not moved it for a long time

pint /paɪnt/ *noun* a measure of liquid (= 0.57 litres). There are eight pints in a **gallon**: *a pint of beer* ◇ *two pints of milk*
ℹ The short way of writing 'pint' is **pt**.

pioneer /ˌpaɪəˈnɪə(r)/ *noun* a person who goes somewhere or does something before other people: *Marie Curie was a pioneer in the field of medicine.*

pip /pɪp/ *noun* the seed of some fruits. Lemons, oranges and apples have pips.
➲ Picture at **apple**.

pipe 🔑 /paɪp/ *noun* **1** a long tube that takes water, oil, gas, etc. from one place to another: *a leaking water pipe* **2** a thing that a person puts **tobacco** (= dried leaves of a plant) in to smoke it: *My uncle smokes a pipe.* **3** a musical instrument that you blow

pipeline /ˈpaɪplaɪn/ *noun* a big pipe that carries oil or gas a long way

pirate /ˈpaɪrət/ *noun* a person on a ship who robs other ships

pistol /ˈpɪstl/ *noun* a small gun

pit /pɪt/ *noun* **1** a deep hole in the ground **2** a deep hole that people make in the ground to take out coal

pitch[1] /pɪtʃ/ *noun* (*plural* **pitches**) **1** a piece of ground where you play games like football or **cricket** **2** how high or low a sound is

pitch[2] /pɪtʃ/ *verb* (**pitches, pitching, pitched** /pɪtʃt/) to put up a tent: *We pitched our tent under a big tree.*

pity[1] 🔑 /ˈpɪti/ *noun* (no plural) sadness for a person or an animal who is in pain or who has problems: *I felt pity for the old man so I gave him some food.*
it's a pity; what a pity it is sad: *It's a pity you can't come to the play.*
take pity on someone to help someone because you feel sad for them: *I took pity on her and gave her some money.*

pity[2] /ˈpɪti/ *verb* (**pities, pitying, pitied** /ˈpɪtid/) to feel sad for someone who is in pain or who has problems: *I really pity people who haven't got anywhere to live.*

pizza /ˈpiːtsə/ *noun* (*plural* **pizzas**) a round piece of flat bread with tomatoes, cheese and other things on top, that is cooked in an oven

place[1] 🔑 /pleɪs/ *noun* **1** where someone or something is: *Put the book back in the right place.* **2** a building, town, country, etc: *Zanzibar is a very interesting place.* ◇ *Do you know a good place to fish?* **3** a seat or space for one person: *An old man was sitting in my place.* **4** where you are in a race, test, etc: *Tanei finished in second place.*
in place where it should be; in the right place: *The glue held the paper in place.*
in place of someone or **something** instead of someone or something: *Rono became goalkeeper in place of Ereng, who had broken his leg.*
take place to happen: *The concert will take place on 22 May.*

place[2] 🔑 /pleɪs/ *verb* (**places, placing, placed** /pleɪst/) to put something somewhere: *I placed the eggs carefully on the table.*

plain[1] 🔑 /pleɪn/ *adjective* (**plainer, plainest**) **1** with no pattern; all one colour: *She wore a plain blue dress.*

2 simple and ordinary: *plain food* **3** easy to see, hear or understand; clear: *It's plain that he's unhappy.* **4** not pretty: *She was a plain child.*

plain² /pleɪn/ *noun* a large piece of flat land

plainly /ˈpleɪnli/ *adverb* clearly: *They were plainly very angry.*

plaintiff /ˈpleɪntɪf/ (also **complainant**) *noun* a person who makes a formal complaint (called a **plaint**) against someone in court of law

plait /plæt/ *verb* (**plaits**, **plaiting**, **plaited**)

> ❖ **PRONUNCIATION**
>
> **Plait** sounds like **flat**.

to put long pieces of hair, rope, etc. over and under each other to make one thick piece: *Her hair is plaited.* ▶ **plait** *noun* a long piece of hair that someone has **plaited**: *She wears her hair in plaits.*

plan¹ ⚷ /plæn/ *noun* **1** something that you have decided to do, and how to do it: *What are your plans for next year?* ◇ *They have plans to build a new school.* **2** a map: *a street plan of Nairobi* **3** a drawing for a new building, machine, etc: *Have you seen the plans for the new shopping centre?*

plan² ⚷ /plæn/ *verb* (**plans**, **planning**, **planned** /plænd/) to decide what you are going to do and how you are going to do it: *They're planning a harambee in the school next week.* ◇ *I'm planning to go to university.*

plane

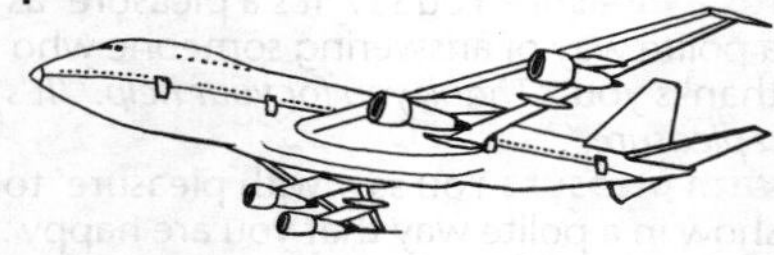

plane ⚷ /pleɪn/ *noun* a vehicle with wings that can fly through the air: *She went to Mbarara by plane.*

> ❖ **WORD BUILDING**
>
> A plane **lands** and **takes off** at an **airport**.

planet ⚷ /ˈplænɪt/ *noun* a large round thing in space that moves around the sun: *Earth, Mars and Venus are planets.*

plank /plæŋk/ *noun* a long flat piece of wood

plant¹ ⚷ /plɑːnt/ *noun* anything that grows from the ground: *Don't forget to water the plants.* ◇ *These plants will grow in any conditions.*

plant

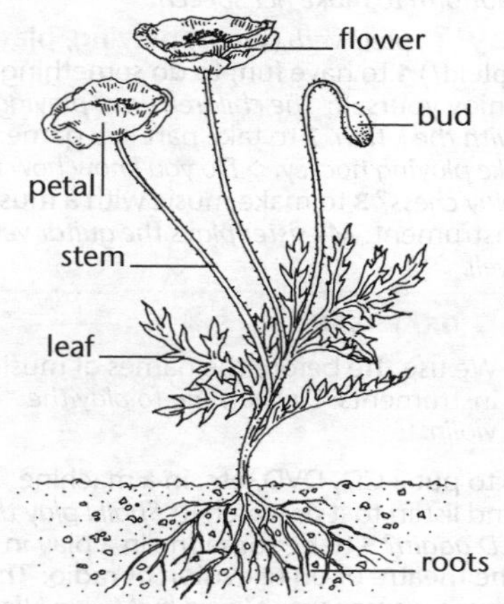

plant² ⚷ /plɑːnt/ *verb* (**plants**, **planting**, **planted**) to put plants or seeds in the ground to grow: *We planted some potatoes.*

plantation /plɑːnˈteɪʃn/ *noun* a piece of land where things like tea, cotton or rubber grow: *a sugar plantation*

plaster /ˈplɑːstə(r)/ *noun* **1** (*plural* **plasters**) a small piece of sticky material that you put over a cut on your body to keep it clean **2** (no plural) white stuff that you put round a broken arm or leg. It becomes hard and keeps the arm or leg safe until it is better: *When I broke my leg it was in plaster for two months.* **3** (no plural) soft stuff that becomes hard and smooth when it is dry. **Plaster** is used for covering walls.

plastic ⚷ /ˈplæstɪk/ *noun* (no plural) a strong light material that is made in factories. Plastic is used for making a lot of different things: *This ball is made of plastic.*

plate

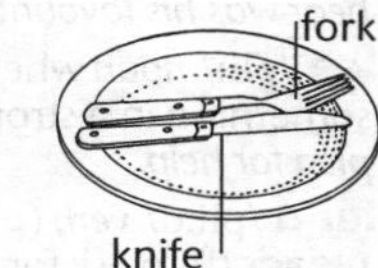

plate ⚷ /pleɪt/ *noun* a round flat thing that you put food on ➲ Look at **number plate**.

platform ⚷ /ˈplætfɔːm/ *noun* **1** the part of a railway station where you stand to wait for a train: *Which platform* *does the Mombasa train stop at?* **2** a place that is higher than the floor, where people stand so that other people can see and hear them: *The head teacher went up to the platform to make her speech.*

play[1] 🔑 /pleɪ/ *verb* (**plays, playing, played** /pleɪd/) **1** to have fun; to do something to enjoy yourself: *The children were playing with the kitten.* **2** to take part in a game: *I like playing hockey.* ◇ *Do you know how to play chess?* **3** to make music with a musical instrument: *My sister plays the guitar very well.*

> ❖ **GRAMMAR**
>
> We use **the** before the names of musical instruments: *I'm learning to play the violin.*

4 to put a CD, DVD, etc. in a machine and listen to it or watch it: *Shall I play the CD again?* **5** to be someone in a play in the theatre or on television or radio: *The young woman was played by Moraa Njehu.*

play[2] 🔑 /pleɪ/ *noun* **1** (*plural* **plays**) a story that you watch in the theatre or on television, or listen to on the radio: *We went to see a play at the National Theatre.* **2** (no plural) games; what children do for fun: *work and play*

> ❖ **GRAMMAR**
>
> Be careful! We **play** football, cards, etc. or we **have a game of** football, cards, etc. (not **a play**).

player 🔑 /ˈpleɪə(r)/ *noun* **1** a person who plays a game: *hockey players* **2** a person who plays a musical instrument: *a trumpet player*

playful /ˈpleɪfl/ *adjective* full of fun; not serious

playground /ˈpleɪgraʊnd/ *noun* a piece of land where children can play

playing card /ˈpleɪɪŋ kɑːd/ = **card**

playing field /ˈpleɪɪŋ fiːld/ *noun* a field for sports like football and **cricket**

plaything /ˈpleɪθɪŋ/ *noun* a toy: *The teddy bear was his favourite plaything.*

plea /pliː/ *noun* when you ask for something in a strong way: *He made a plea for help.*

plead /pliːd/ *verb* (**pleads, pleading, pleaded**) to ask for something in a very strong way: *He pleaded with his parents to buy him a guitar.*
plead guilty to say in a court of law that you did something wrong: *She pleaded guilty to murder.*
plead not guilty to say in a court of law that you did not do something wrong

pleasant 🔑 /ˈpleznt/ *adjective* nice, enjoyable or friendly: *It's very pleasant to sit and relax with a cold drink.* ◇ *He's a very pleasant person.* ▶ **pleasantly** *adverb*: *She smiled pleasantly.*

please[1] 🔑 /pliːz/ a word that you use when you ask politely: *What's the time, please?* ◇ *Two cups of coffee, please.*

> ❖ **WORD BUILDING**
>
> You use **yes, please** to say that you will have something: *'Would you like a drink?' 'Yes, please.'*

please[2] 🔑 /pliːz/ *verb* (**pleases, pleasing, pleased** /pliːzd/) to make someone happy: *I wore my best clothes to please my mother.*

> ❖ **WORD FAMILY**
>
> **please pleased pleasure**
> **pleasant**: OPPOSITE **unpleasant**

pleased 🔑 /pliːzd/ *adjective* happy: *He wasn't very pleased to see me.* ◇ *Are you pleased with your new shoes?*

pleasure 🔑 /ˈpleʒə(r)/ *noun* **1** (no plural) the feeling of being happy or enjoying something: *I go fishing for pleasure, not for money.* **2** (*plural* **pleasures**) something that makes you happy: *It was a pleasure to meet you.*
it's a pleasure You say 'it's a pleasure' as a polite way of answering someone who thanks you: *'Thank you for your help.' 'It's a pleasure.'*
with pleasure You say 'with pleasure' to show in a polite way that you are happy to do something: *'Can you help me move these boxes?' 'Yes, with pleasure.'*

pleat /pliːt/ *noun* a fold in a piece of cloth

plenty 🔑 /ˈplenti/ *pronoun* as much or as many as you need; a lot: *Do you want to stay for dinner? There's plenty of food.*

pliers /ˈplaɪəz/ *noun* (plural) a tool for holding things tightly or for cutting wire: *Have you got a pair of pliers?*

pliers

plod /plɒd/ *verb* (**plods, plodding, plodded**) to walk slowly in a heavy tired way: *We plodded up the hill in the rain.*

plot[1] /plɒt/ *noun* **1** a secret plan to do something that is wrong: *a plot to kill the president* **2** what happens in a story, play or film: *This book has a very exciting plot.*

plot[2] /plɒt/ *verb* (**plots**, **plotting**, **plotted**) to make a secret plan to do something that is wrong: *They plotted to rob the bank.*

plough /plaʊ/ *noun*

> ❖ **PRONUNCIATION**
>
> **Plough** sounds like **now**.

a machine used on farms for digging and turning over the soil: *Ploughs are pulled by animals or tractors.* ▶ **plough** *verb* (**ploughs**, **ploughing**, **ploughed** /plaʊd/) to use a **plough** to dig and turn over the soil: *The farmer ploughed his fields.*

plugs

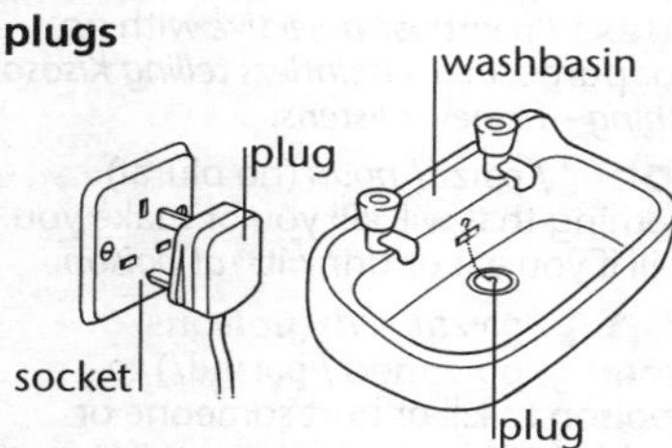

plug[1] /plʌg/ *noun* **1** a thing that joins a lamp, machine, etc. to a place in the wall (called a **socket**) where there is electricity **2** a round thing that you put in the hole in a bath, etc. to stop the water going out

plug[2] /plʌg/ *verb* (**plugs**, **plugging**, **plugged** /plʌgd/) to fill a hole with something: *I plugged the hole in the pipe with plastic.*

plug in to put an electric **plug** into a place in the wall where there is electricity: *Can you plug the radio in, please?* ◇ *The lamp isn't plugged in.* OPPOSITE **unplug**

plum /plʌm/ *noun* a soft round fruit with a stone in the middle

plumber /ˈplʌmə(r)/ *noun*

> ❖ **PRONUNCIATION**
>
> **Plumber** and **plumbing** sound like **drummer** and **drumming**, because you do not say the 'b'.

a person whose job is to put in and repair things like water pipes

plumbing /ˈplʌmɪŋ/ *noun* (no plural) **1** the pipes that carry water into and around a building: *The builders are putting in the plumbing.* **2** the work of putting in and repairing things like water pipes

plump /plʌmp/ *adjective* (**plumper**, **plumpest**) quite fat, in a nice way: *a plump baby*

plunge /plʌndʒ/ *verb* (**plunges**, **plunging**, **plunged** /plʌndʒd/) **1** to jump or fall suddenly into something: *She plunged into the pool.* **2** to push something suddenly and strongly into something else: *I plunged my hand into the water.*

plural 🔑 /ˈplʊərəl/ *noun* the form of a word that shows there is more than one: *The plural of 'child' is 'children'.* ▶ **plural** *adjective*: *Most plural nouns in English end in 's'.* ➲ Look at **singular**.

plus /plʌs/ *preposition* added to; and: *Two plus three is five* (2 + 3 = 5). ◇ *The bus can carry 52 passengers plus the driver.* ➲ Look at **minus**.

ply /plaɪ/ *verb* (**plies**, **plying**, **plied** /plaɪd/) to travel regularly between two particular places: *These matatus ply the route between Meru and Nanyuki daily.*

p.m. /ˌpiː ˈem/ You use **p.m.** after a time to show that it is between midday and midnight. **p.m.** is from the Latin 'post meridiem': *The bus leaves at 3 p.m.*

> ❖ **WORD BUILDING**
>
> We use **a.m.** for times between midnight and midday.

pneumonia /njuːˈməʊniə/ *noun* (no plural)

> ❖ **PRONUNCIATION**
>
> We do not say the 'p' at the beginning of **pneumonia**.

a serious illness of the **lungs** (= the parts inside your body that you use for breathing)

poach /pəʊtʃ/ *verb* (**poaches**, **poaching**, **poached** /pəʊtʃt/) **1** to cook food gently in or over water or milk: *a poached egg* **2** to kill and steal animals, birds or fish from another person's land ▶ **poacher** /ˈpəʊtʃə(r)/ *noun* a person who kills or steals animals, birds or fish from another person's land

PO box /ˌpiː ˈəʊ bɒks/ *noun* (*plural* **PO boxes**) a box in a post office for keeping the letters of a person or an office: *The address is PO box 40911 - 00200, Nairobi.*

pocket

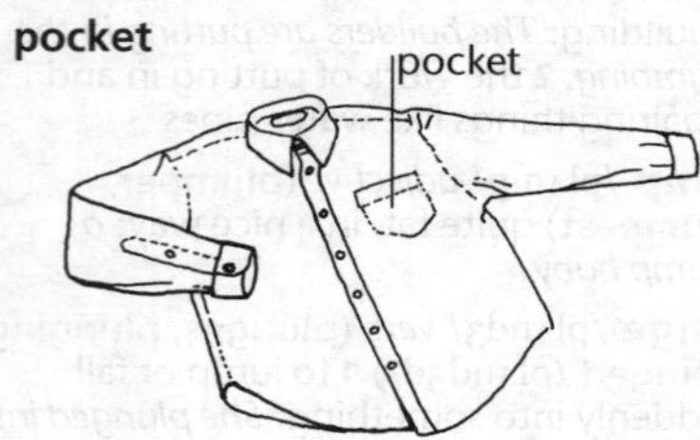

pocket /ˈpɒkɪt/ *noun* a small bag in your clothes for carrying things: *I put the key in my pocket.*
pick someone's pocket to steal money from someone's pocket or bag

pocket money /ˈpɒkɪt mʌni/ *noun* (no plural) money that parents give to a child each week to buy things: *How much pocket money do you get?*

pod /pɒd/ *noun* the long green part of some plants, that has seeds inside it: *Peas grow in pods.*

poem /ˈpəʊɪm/ *noun* a piece of writing, usually with short lines that may have repeated sounds at the ends. Poems try to show feelings or ideas: *I have written a poem.*

❖ **WORD FAMILY**

poem poet poetic poetry

poet /ˈpəʊɪt/ *noun* a person who writes poems: *Ken Saro-Wiwa was a famous Nigerian poet.*

poetic /pəʊˈetɪk/ *adjective* of or like **poets** or poetry: *poetic language*

poetry /ˈpəʊətri/ *noun* (no plural) poems: *Okot p'Bitek wrote beautiful poetry.*

point¹ /pɔɪnt/ *noun* **1** a small round mark that shows part of a number: *2.5* (= two point five) **2** a certain time or place: *The other team scored a second goal and at that point I knew we couldn't win the match.* **3** the most important idea; the purpose or reason: *The point of going to school is to learn.* ◇ *What's the point of phoning her? She never answers.* **4** the sharp end of something: *the point of a needle* **5** a mark that you win in a game or sport: *Our team scored six points.*
be on the point of If you are **on the point of** doing something, you are going to do it very soon: *I was on the point of going out when there was a knock at the door.*
point of view your way of thinking about something: *I understand your point of view.*
there's no point in there is no good reason to do something: *There's no point in waiting for Nduku – she isn't coming.*

point² /pɔɪnt/ *verb* (**points, pointing, pointed**) to show where something is using your finger, a stick, etc: *I asked him where the bank was and he pointed across the road.* ◇ *There was a sign pointing towards the beach.*
point something at someone or **something** to hold something towards someone or something: *She pointed her camera at him.*
point out to tell or show something: *Hawa pointed out that my bag was open.*

pointed /ˈpɔɪntɪd/ *adjective* with a sharp end: *He was making holes in the ground with a pointed stick.*

pointless /ˈpɔɪntləs/ *adjective* with no use or purpose: *It's pointless telling Kisoso anything – he never listens.*

poison¹ /ˈpɔɪzn/ *noun* (no plural) something that will kill you or make you very ill if you eat or drink it: *rat poison*

poison² /ˈpɔɪzn/ *verb* (**poisons, poisoning, poisoned** /ˈpɔɪznd/) to use poison to kill or hurt someone or something: *Someone had poisoned his food.*

poisonous /ˈpɔɪzənəs/ *adjective* Something that is poisonous will kill you or make you very ill if you eat or drink it: *Some berries are poisonous.*

poke /pəʊk/ *verb* (**pokes, poking, poked** /pəʊkt/) **1** to push someone or something hard with your finger or another long thin thing: *She poked me in the eye with a pencil.* **2** to push something quickly somewhere: *Kisoso poked his head out of the window.* ▸ **poke** *noun*: *I gave her a poke to wake her up.*

polar /ˈpəʊlə(r)/ *adjective* of the North or South Pole

pole /pəʊl/ *noun* **1** a long thin piece of wood or metal. Poles are often used to hold something up: *tent poles* ◇ *a flagpole* **2** one of two places at the top and bottom of the earth: *the North Pole* ◇ *the South Pole*

police /pəˈliːs/ *noun* (plural) a group of people whose job is to make sure that people do not break the laws of a country: *Have the police found the murderer?* ◇ *a police car*

police force /pəˈliːs fɔːs/ *noun* all the police officers in a country or part of a country

policeman /pəˈliːsmən/ *noun* (*plural* **policemen** /pəˈliːsmən/) a man who works in the police

police officer /pəˈliːs ɒfɪsə(r)/ *noun* a policeman or policewoman

police station /pəˈliːs steɪʃn/ *noun* an office where police officers work

policewoman /pəˈliːswʊmən/ *noun* (*plural* **policewomen** /pəˈliːswɪmɪn/) a woman who works in the police

policy /ˈpɒləsi/ *noun* (*plural* **policies**) the plans of a group of people: *What is the government's policy on education?*

polish[1] /ˈpɒlɪʃ/ *verb* (**polishes**, **polishing**, **polished** /ˈpɒlɪʃt/) to rub something so that it shines: *Have you polished your shoes?*

polish[2] /ˈpɒlɪʃ/ *noun* (no plural) stuff that you put on something to make it shine: *furniture polish*

polite 🔑 /pəˈlaɪt/ *adjective* If you are polite, you are helpful and kind to other people and you do not do or say things that make people sad or angry: *It is polite to say 'please' when you ask for something.* OPPOSITE **impolite**, **rude** ▸ **politely** *adverb*: *He asked politely for a glass of water.* ▸ **politeness** /pəˈlaɪtnəs/ *noun* (no plural) being polite

political 🔑 /pəˈlɪtɪkl/ *adjective* of or about the work of government: *Which political party is in power in your country?* ◇ *political beliefs* ▸ **politically** /pəˈlɪtɪkli/ *adverb*: *a politically powerful country*

politician 🔑 /ˌpɒləˈtɪʃn/ *noun* a person who works in the government or who wants to work in the government: *Members of Parliament are politicians.*

politics 🔑 /ˈpɒlətɪks/ *noun* (no plural) **1** the work of government: *Are you interested in politics?* **2** the study of government: *She studied Politics at university.*

pollen /ˈpɒlən/ *noun* (no plural) the yellow powder in flowers

pollinate /ˈpɒlineɪt/ *verb* (**pollinates**, **pollinating**, **pollinated**) to carry the yellow powder (**pollen**) of a flower to another flower of the same type so that it can produce seeds. Insects, birds and the wind **pollinate** flowers.

▸ **pollination** /ˌpɒləˈneɪʃn/ *noun* (no plural): *Natural pollination may occur by wind.*

pollute /pəˈluːt/ *verb* (**pollutes**, **polluting**, **polluted**) to make air, rivers, etc. dirty and dangerous: *Many rivers are polluted with chemicals from factories.*

pollution /pəˈluːʃn/ *noun* (no plural) **1** making air, rivers, etc. dirty and dangerous: *As the amount of traffic in the city grows, the pollution gets worse.* **2** dirty and dangerous stuff from cars, factories, etc.

polytechnic /ˌpɒliˈteknɪk/ *noun* a place where you can go after you have finished school to learn technical, scientific and other subjects

pond /pɒnd/ *noun* a small area of water: *There is a fish pond in the park.*

pool 🔑 /puːl/ *noun* **1** a little liquid or light on the ground: *After the rain there were pools of water on the road.* ◇ *She was lying in a pool of blood.* **2** a place for swimming: *Chebet dived into the pool.*

poor 🔑 /pɔː(r)/ *adjective* (**poorer**, **poorest**) **1** with very little money ℹ The noun is **poverty**. OPPOSITE **rich** **2** a word that you use when you feel sad because someone has problems: *Poor Nakato! She's feeling ill.* **3** not good: *My grandfather is in very poor health.*

poorly /ˈpɔːli/ *adverb* not well; badly: *The street is poorly lit.*

pop[1] /pɒp/ *noun* (no plural) **1** modern music that a lot of young people like: *What's your favourite pop group?* ◇ *pop music* ◇ *a pop singer* **2** a short sharp sound: *The cork came out of the bottle with a loud pop.*

pop[2] /pɒp/ *verb* (**pops**, **popping**, **popped** /pɒpt/) to make a short sharp sound; to make something make a short sharp sound: *The balloon will pop if you put a pin in it.* ◇ *He popped the balloon.*

popcorn /ˈpɒpkɔːn/ *noun* (no plural) light white balls of cooked grain, which are covered in salt or sugar

pope /pəʊp/ *noun* the most important person in the Roman Catholic Church: *Pope Francis*

popular 🔑 /ˈpɒpjələ(r)/ *adjective* liked by a lot of people: *Football is a popular sport all over the world.* OPPOSITE **unpopular**

popularity /ˌpɒpjuˈlærəti/ *noun* (no plural) being liked by a lot of people

populate /ˈpɒpjuleɪt/ *verb* (**populates, populating, populated**) to fill a place with people: *Rwanda is a densely populated country.*

population /ˌpɒpjuˈleɪʃn/ *noun* the number of people who live in a place: *What is the population of your country?*

porcupine /ˈpɔːkjupaɪn/ *noun* a small animal that is covered with long stiff parts like needles (called **quills**)

pork /pɔːk/ *noun* (no plural) meat from a pig ➲ Note at **pig**.

porridge /ˈpɒrɪdʒ/ *noun* (no plural) soft food that we make by boiling grain with liquid: *porridge oats*

port 🔑 /pɔːt/ *noun* a town or city by the sea, where ships arrive and leave: *Mombasa is the largest port in East Africa.*

portable /ˈpɔːtəbl/ *adjective* that you can move or carry easily: *a portable television*

porter /ˈpɔːtə(r)/ *noun* **1** a person whose job is to carry people's bags in places like hotels **2** a person whose job is to look after the entrance of a hotel or other large building

portion /ˈpɔːʃn/ *noun* a part of something that one person gets: *He gave a portion of the money to each of his children.* ◇ *a large portion of chips*

portrait /ˈpɔːtreɪt/ *noun* a painting or picture of a person

position 🔑 /pəˈzɪʃn/ *noun* **1** the place where someone or something is: *Can you show me the position of your village on the map?* **2** the way a person is sitting or lying, or the way a thing is standing: *She was still sitting in the same position when I came back.* **3** how things are at a certain time: *He's in a difficult position – he hasn't got enough money to finish his studies.*
in position in the right place: *The dancers were in position, waiting for the music to start.*

positive 🔑 /ˈpɒzətɪv/ *adjective* **1** completely certain: *Are you positive that you closed the door?* **2** that helps you or gives you hope: *The teacher was very positive about my work.*

positively /ˈpɒzətɪvli/ *adverb* really; certainly: *The idea is positively stupid.*

possess /pəˈzes/ *verb* (**possesses, possessing, possessed** /pəˈzest/) to have or own something: *He lost everything that he possessed in the fire.*

> ❖ **SPEAKING**
>
> **Have** and **own** are the words that we usually use.

possession /pəˈzeʃn/ *noun* **1** (no plural) having or owning something: *The possession of drugs is a crime.*
2 possessions (plural) the things that you have or own

> ❖ **SPELLING**
>
> Remember! You spell **possession** with **ss** and **ss**.

possibility 🔑 /ˌpɒsəˈbɪləti/ *noun* (*plural* **possibilities**) something that might happen: *There's a possibility that we'll have to wait a long time, so take a book.*

possible 🔑 /ˈpɒsəbl/ *adjective* If something is possible, it can happen or you can do it: *Is it possible to get to Egypt by train?* ◇ *I'll phone you as soon as possible.*

> ❖ **WORD FAMILY**
>
> **possible**: OPPOSITE **impossible**
> **possibility**: OPPOSITE **impossibility**
> **possibly**

possibly 🔑 /ˈpɒsəbli/ *adverb* **1** perhaps: *'Will you be free tomorrow?' 'Possibly.'* **2** in a way that can be done: *I'll come as soon as I possibly can.*

post[1] 🔑 /pəʊst/ *noun* **1** (no plural) the way of sending and receiving letters, parcels, etc: *I sent your present by post.* **2** (no plural) letters and parcels that you send or receive: *Did you get any post this morning?* **3** (*plural* **posts**) a tall piece of wood or metal that stands in the ground to hold something or to show where something is: *The sign had fallen off the post.* ◇ *a lamp post* **4** (*plural* **posts**) a message that you send as part of a discussion on the Internet, or a piece of writing that you put on a website: *I love reading her posts because I learn so much.*

post[2] 🔑 /pəʊst/ *verb* (**posts, posting, posted**) **1** to send a letter or parcel: *Could you post this letter for me?* **2** to send someone to a place to do a job: *Robi's company have posted her to Japan for two* *years.* **3** to put information or pictures on a website: *He posted the news on Twitter.*

postage /ˈpəʊstɪdʒ/ *noun* (no plural) money that you must pay when you send a letter or parcel

postal /ˈpəʊstl/ *adjective* connected with sending and receiving letters, packages, etc: *postal collections*

postal order /ˈpəʊstl ɔːdə(r)/ = **money order**

postbox /ˈpəʊstbɒks/ *noun* (*plural* **postboxes**) a box in the street where you put letters that you want to send

postcard /ˈpəʊstkɑːd/ *noun* a card with a picture on one side, that you write on and send by post

postcard

poster /ˈpəʊstə(r)/ *noun* a big piece of paper on a wall, with a picture or words on it

postman /ˈpəʊstmən/ *noun* (*plural* **postmen** /ˈpəʊstmən/) (in some countries) a person who takes (**delivers**) letters and parcels to people

post office 🔑 /ˈpəʊst ɒfɪs/ *noun* a building where you go to send letters and packages and to buy stamps

postpone /pəˈspəʊn/ *verb* (**postpones, postponing, postponed** /pəˈspəʊnd/) to say that something will happen at a later time, not now: *Juma is not here, so we will postpone the meeting until tomorrow.*

posture /ˈpɒstʃə(r)/ *noun* (no plural) the way that a person sits, stands, walks, etc: *She has very good posture.*

pot 🔑 /pɒt/ *noun* **1** a deep round container for cooking: *a big pot of soup* **2** a container that you use for a special thing: *a pot of paint* ◇ *a plant pot*

potato 🔑 /pəˈteɪtəʊ/ *noun* (*plural* **potatoes**) a round vegetable that grows under the ground, that is white on the inside and brown or yellow on the outside. You cook it before you eat it: *a baked potato* ➲ Look at **sweet potato**.

pothole /ˈpɒthəʊl/ *noun* a hole in a road

pottery /ˈpɒtəri/ *noun* (no plural) **1** cups, plates and other things made from **clay** (= heavy earth that becomes hard when it dries): *They make pottery in this factory.* **2** making cups, plates and other things from **clay**: *He makes his living from pottery.*

poultry /ˈpəʊltri/ *noun* (plural) birds that people keep on farms for their eggs or their meat. Chickens are **poultry**.

pounce /paʊns/ *verb* (**pounces, pouncing, pounced** /paʊnst/) to jump on someone or something suddenly: *The cat pounced on the bird.*

pound[1] 🔑 /paʊnd/ *noun* **1** a measure of weight (= 0.454 kilograms). There are 16 **ounces** in a pound: *two pounds of sugar* ◇ *a hundred-pound sack of potatoes* ℹ The short way of writing 'pound' is **lb**. **2** money that people use in Britain. There are 100 pence in a pound. ℹ The sign is **£**.

pound[2] /paʊnd/ *verb* (**pounds, pounding, pounded**) to make something into very small pieces or powder by hitting it many times. ℹ You pound things with a **pestle** (= a special tool) in a **mortar** (= a strong bowl).

pour 🔑 /pɔː(r)/ *verb* (**pours, pouring, poured** /pɔːd/) **1** to make liquid flow out of or into something: *She poured water from the jug into a cup.* **2** to flow quickly: *Oil poured out of the damaged ship.* **it's pouring** it is raining very hard

pour

poverty /ˈpɒvəti/ *noun* (no plural) being poor: *There are many people living in poverty in this city.*

powder 🔑 /ˈpaʊdə(r)/ *noun* dry stuff that is made of a lot of very small pieces: *washing powder* (= for washing clothes)

power 🔑 /ˈpaʊə(r)/ *noun* **1** (no plural) being strong; being able to do something: *the power of the storm* ◇ *I did everything in my power* (= everything I could do) *to help her.* **2** (no plural) being able to make people do what you want: *The president has a lot of power.* **3** (no plural) what makes things work; energy: *Press the power button to start your computer.* ◇ *nuclear power* **4** (*plural* **powers**) the right to do something: *Police officers have the power to arrest people.* **5** (*plural* **powers**) a strong person or country: *There is a meeting of world powers in Rome next week.*

powerful 🔑 /ˈpaʊəfl/ *adjective* **1** very strong; with a lot of power: *The car has a very powerful engine.* ◇ *The president is very powerful.* OPPOSITE **powerless** **2** that you can smell or hear clearly, or feel strongly: *a powerful drug*

powerless /ˈpaʊələs/ *adjective* not having any power; not able to do anything: *I was powerless to help.* OPPOSITE **powerful**

power point /ˈpaʊə pɔɪnt/ *noun* a place in a wall where you can connect a lamp, a machine etc. to the electricity SAME MEANING **socket**

power station /ˈpaʊə steɪʃn/ *noun* a place where electricity is made

practical 🔑 /ˈpræktɪkl/ *adjective* **1** that is about doing or making things, not just about ideas: *Have you got any practical experience of teaching?* **2** able to do useful things: *I'm not a very practical person.* **3** possible to do easily: *Your plan isn't practical.*

practically /ˈpræktɪkli/ *adverb* almost; nearly: *Don't go out – lunch is practically ready!* ◇ *You've been late for school practically every day this month!*

practice 🔑 /ˈpræktɪs/ *noun* (no plural) doing something many times so that you will do it well: *You need lots of practice to play the drums well.*
out of practice not good at something, because you have not done it for a long time

> ❖ **SPELLING**
> Remember! We spell the noun **practice** and the verb **practise**.

practise 🔑 /ˈpræktɪs/ *verb* (**practises**, **practising**, **practised** /ˈpræktɪst/) to do something many times so that you will do it well: *If you want to become a professional footballer, you must practise every day.*

praise /preɪz/ *verb* (**praises**, **praising**, **praised** /preɪzd/) to say that someone or something is good: *She was praised for her hard work.* ▶ **praise** *noun* (no plural): *The book has received a lot of praise.*

pram /præm/ *noun* a thing that a baby lies in to go out. It has wheels so that you can push it.

pram

prawn /prɔːn/ *noun* a small pink sea animal that you can eat

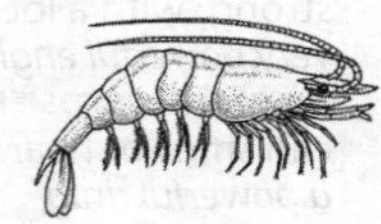
prawn

pray /preɪ/ *verb* (**prays**, **praying**, **prayed** /preɪd/) to speak to God or a god: *They prayed for help.*

prayer 🔑 /preə(r)/ *noun* words that you say when you speak to God or a god: *They said a prayer for peace.*

pre- /priː/ *prefix* You can add **pre-** to the beginning of some words to give them the meaning 'before': *pre-season football training* (= before the season starts) ◇ *Preheat the oven* (= heat it before you put the food in).

preach /priːtʃ/ *verb* (**preaches**, **preaching**, **preached** /priːtʃt/) to talk about God or a god to a group of people

precaution /prɪˈkɔːʃn/ *noun* something that you do so that bad things will not happen: *I took the precaution of closing all the windows when I went out.*

precious /ˈpreʃəs/ *adjective* **1** very valuable: *Diamonds are precious stones.* **2** that you love very much: *My family is very precious to me.*

precise /prɪˈsaɪs/ *adjective* exactly right: *I gave him precise instructions on how to get to my house.*

precisely /prɪˈsaɪsli/ *adverb* exactly: *They arrived at two o'clock precisely.*

predict /prɪˈdɪkt/ *verb* (**predicts**, **predicting**, **predicted**) to say what you think will happen: *She predicted that it would rain, and she was right.* ▶ **prediction** /prɪˈdɪkʃn/ *noun*: *His predictions were not correct.*

prefect /ˈpriːfekt/ *noun* a student in a school who is given special duties by the teacher

prefer 🔑 /prɪˈfɜː(r)/ *verb* (**prefers**, **preferring**, **preferred** /prɪˈfɜːd/) to like one thing or person better than another: *Would you prefer tea or coffee?* ◇ *Tanei wants to go for a walk but I would prefer to stay at home.* ◇ *He prefers going out to studying.*

preferable /ˈprefrəbl/ *adjective* better; that you like more: *I think living in a village is preferable to living in the city.* ▶ **preferably** /ˈprefrəbli/ *adverb*: *Come and see us any day, but preferably not next Wednesday.*

preference /ˈprefrəns/ *noun* liking one thing or person better than another: *We have mangoes and bananas – do you have a preference?*

prefix /ˈpriːfɪks/ *noun* (*plural* **prefixes**) a group of letters that you add to the beginning of a word to make another word: *The prefix 'im-' means 'not', so* *'impossible' means 'not possible'.* ➲ Look at **suffix**.

❖ **WORD BUILDING**

When we add a **prefix** to the beginning of a word, it changes the meaning of the word. **Dis-, il-, im-, in-, mis-, non-, re-** and **un-** are common **prefixes**: *I disagree* (= don't agree) *with you.* ◇ *I'll reheat the rice* (= heat it again).

pregnant 🔑 /ˈpregnənt/ *adjective* If a woman is pregnant, she has a baby growing in her body: *His wife is six months pregnant.*

prejudice /ˈpredʒədɪs/ *noun* a feeling of not liking someone or something, for a reason that is wrong or unfair: *She was a victim of racial prejudice.*

prejudiced /ˈpredʒədɪst/ *adjective* with strong and unfair ideas about someone or something, before you know much about them or it: *He is prejudiced against me because I'm a woman.*

premarital /ˌpriːˈmærɪtl/ *adjective* happening before marriage: *premarital sex*

preparation 🔑 /ˌprepəˈreɪʃn/ *noun* **1** (no plural) making something ready: *the preparation of food* **2 preparations** (plural) what you do to get ready for something: *wedding preparations*
in preparation for something to get ready for something: *I packed my bags in preparation for the journey.*

prepare 🔑 /prɪˈpeə(r)/ *verb* (**prepares, preparing, prepared** /prɪˈpeəd/) to make someone or something ready; to make yourself ready: *Nafula is in the kitchen preparing the dinner.* ◇ *I prepared well for the exam.*

prepared 🔑 /prɪˈpeəd/ *adjective* ready
prepared for something ready for something difficult or bad: *I wasn't prepared for all these problems.*
prepared to happy to do something: *I'm not prepared to give you any money.*

preposition /ˌprepəˈzɪʃn/ *noun* a word that you use before a noun or pronoun to show where, when, how, etc: *'In,' 'for,' 'after' and 'above' are all prepositions.* ◇ *In the sentence 'He travelled from Kisumu to Mombasa', 'from' and 'to' are prepositions.*

preschool /ˈpriːskuːl/ *adjective* before children are old enough to go to school: *the health of preschool children* ◇ *preschool education*

prescribe /prɪˈskraɪb/ *verb* (**prescribes, prescribing, prescribed** /prɪˈskraɪbd/) to say that someone must take a medicine: *The doctor prescribed some tablets for her illness.*

prescription /prɪˈskrɪpʃn/ *noun* a piece of paper where a doctor writes what medicine you need. You take it to a **chemist's** and get the medicine there.

presence /ˈprezns/ *noun* (no plural) being in a place: *She was so quiet that I didn't notice her presence.*
in the presence of someone with another person or other people there: *She signed the papers in the presence of a lawyer.*

present[1] 🔑 /ˈpreznt/ *adjective* **1** in a place: *There were 200 people present at the meeting.* OPPOSITE **absent 2** being or happening now: *What is your present address?*

present[2] 🔑 /ˈpreznt/ *noun* **1** (*plural* **presents**) something that you give to or get from someone: *a birthday present* **2** (no plural) the time now: *I can't help you at present – I'm too busy.* ➲ Look at **past**[2], **future**[2].

present[3] 🔑 /prɪˈzent/ *verb* (**presents, presenting, presented**) to give something to someone: *Who presented the prizes to the winners?*

presentation /ˌpreznˈteɪʃn/ *noun* **1** giving something to someone: *The presentation of the prizes will take place at 7.30.* **2** a meeting where someone shows or explains something to the people listening: *We each gave a short presentation on one of our hobbies.*

presently /ˈprezntli/ *adverb* **1** soon: *He will be here presently.* **2** now: *She's presently working in a hotel.*

the present tense /ðə ˌpreznt ˈtens/ (also **the present**) *noun* (no plural) the form of a verb that you use to talk about now ➲ Look at **past tense, future tense**.

preservation /ˌprezəˈveɪʃn/ *noun* (no plural) keeping something safe; making something stay the same: *the preservation of rare birds*

preserve /prɪˈzɜːv/ *verb* (**preserves, preserving, preserved** /prɪˈzɜːvd/) to keep something safe; to make something stay the same: *Parts of the town are new, but they have preserved many of the old buildings.*

president 🔑 /ˈprezɪdənt/ *noun* **1** the leader in many countries that do not have a king or queen: *the President of Tanzania* **2** the most important person in a big company, club, etc. ▶ **presidential** /ˌprezɪˈdenʃl/ *adjective* of a president or their work: *the presidential elections*

press¹ 🔑 /pres/ *verb* (**presses, pressing, pressed** /prest/) **1** to push something: *If you press this button, the door will open.* ◇ *She pressed her face against the window.* **2** to make clothes flat and smooth using an iron: *This suit needs pressing.*

press² 🔑 /pres/ *noun* **1** **the press** (no plural) newspapers and magazines and the people who write them: *She told her story to the press.* **2** (*plural* **presses**) pushing something: *Give the doorbell a press.* **3** (*plural* **presses**) a machine for printing things like books and newspapers

pressure 🔑 /ˈpreʃə(r)/ *noun* **1** the force that presses on something: *the air pressure in a car tyre* **2** a feeling of worry or unhappiness, for example because you have too many things to do: *the pressures of city life*

presume /prɪˈzjuːm/ *verb* (**presumes, presuming, presumed** /prɪˈzjuːmd/) to think that something is true but not be certain: *She's not home yet so I presume she's still at work.*

pretend 🔑 /prɪˈtend/ *verb* (**pretends, pretending, pretended**) to try to make someone believe something that is not true: *He didn't want to talk, so he pretended to be asleep.*

pretty¹ 🔑 /ˈprɪti/ *adjective* (**prettier, prettiest**) nice to look at: *a pretty little girl* ◇ *These flowers are very pretty.* ➲ Note at **beautiful**.

pretty² 🔑 /ˈprɪti/ *adverb* quite; fairly: *I feel pretty tired today.*

prevent 🔑 /prɪˈvent/ *verb* (**prevents, preventing, prevented**) to stop someone from doing something or to stop something happening: *Her parents want to prevent her from getting married.* ◇ *It is easier to prevent disease than to cure it.*

prevention /prɪˈvenʃn/ *noun* (no plural) stopping someone from doing something; stopping something from happening: *the prevention of crime*

previous 🔑 /ˈpriːviəs/ *adjective* that happened or came before or earlier: *Who was the previous owner of the car?* ▶ **previously** *adverb*: *The building had previously been used as a hotel.*

prey¹ /preɪ/ *noun* (no plural) an animal or bird that another animal or bird kills for food: *Zebra are prey for lions.*

prey² /preɪ/ *verb* (**preys, preying, preyed** /preɪd/)
prey on something If an animal or a bird **preys on** another animal or bird, it kills it for food.

price 🔑 /praɪs/ *noun* how much money you pay to buy something: *The price is 150 shillings.* ◇ *Prices in this country are very high.*

prick /prɪk/ *verb* (**pricks, pricking, pricked** /prɪkt/) to make a very small hole in something, or hurt someone, with a sharp point: *I pricked my finger on a needle.* ◇ *Prick the potatoes with a fork before you cook them.* ▶ **prick** *noun* a small sharp pain: *She felt the prick of a needle.*

prickle /ˈprɪkl/ *noun* a sharp point on a plant or an animal: *A cactus has prickles.*

prickly /ˈprɪkli/ *adjective* (**pricklier, prickliest**) covered with **prickles**: *a prickly bush*

pride /praɪd/ *noun* (no plural) **1** being pleased about something that you or others have done or about something that you have; being proud: *She showed us her painting with great pride.* **2** the feeling that you are better than other people

priest 🔑 /priːst/ *noun* a person who leads people in their religion: *a Buddhist priest*

primary /ˈpraɪməri/ *adjective* first; most important: *What is the primary cause of the illness?*

primary school /ˈpraɪməri skuːl/ *noun* a school for children between the ages of about six and fourteen

prime minister 🔑 /ˌpraɪm ˈmɪnɪstə(r)/ *noun* the leader of the government in some countries: *He had a meeting with the British prime minister.*

prince /prɪns/ *noun* **1** a man in a royal family, especially the son of a king or queen: *the Prince of Wales* **2** a man who is the ruler of a small country

princess /ˌprɪnˈses/ *noun* (*plural* **princesses**) a woman in a royal family, especially the daughter of a king or queen or the wife of a **prince**

principal¹ /ˈprɪnsəpl/ *adjective* most important: *His principal reason for going to Nairobi was to find a job.*

principal² /ˈprɪnsəpl/ *noun* a person who is in charge of a school or college

principally /ˈprɪnsəpli/ *adverb* mainly; mostly: *She sometimes travels to Europe, but she works principally in Africa.*

principle /ˈprɪnsəpl/ *noun* **1** a rule about how you should live: *He has very strong principles.* **2** a rule or fact about how something happens or works: *scientific principles*

print[1] 🔑 /prɪnt/ *verb* (**prints**, **printing**, **printed**) **1** to put words or pictures onto paper using a machine. Books, newspapers and magazines are printed: *They printed 8 000 copies of the book.* **2** to write with letters that are not joined together: *Please print your name and address clearly.* **3** to put a pattern onto cloth, paper, etc: *printed cotton*

print[2] /prɪnt/ *noun* **1** (no plural) letters that a machine makes on paper: *The print is too small to read.* **2** (*plural* **prints**) a mark where something has pressed: *footprints in the sand* **3** (*plural* **prints**) a copy on paper of a painting or photograph

printer /ˈprɪntə(r)/ *noun* **1** a person or company that prints things like books or newspapers **2** a machine that prints words from a computer ➲ Picture at **computer**.

priority 🔑 /praɪˈɒrəti/ *noun* (*plural* **priorities**) something that is more important than other things; something that should come first: *Education is a top priority.* ◇ *We give priority to families with small children.*

prison 🔑 /ˈprɪzn/ *noun* a place where people must stay when they have done something that is wrong: *He was sent to prison for robbing a bank.* ◇ *She was in prison for 15 years.* SAME MEANING **jail**

prisoner 🔑 /ˈprɪznə(r)/ *noun* a person who is in prison, or any person who is not free

private 🔑 /ˈpraɪvət/ *adjective* **1** for one person or a small group of people only, and not for anyone else: *The house has a private swimming pool* (= that only the people who live in the house can use). ◇ *You shouldn't read his letters – they're private.* **2** alone; without other people there: *She had a private meeting with the head teacher.* **3** not of your job: *She never talks about her private life with the people at work.* **4** not controlled by the government: *private schools* (= you must pay to go there)

in private alone; without other people there: *Can I speak to you in private?*

▶ **privately** *adverb*: *Let's go into my room – we can talk more privately there.*

privilege /ˈprɪvəlɪdʒ/ *noun* something special that only one person or a few people may do or have: *Pupils who behave well have special privileges.*

▶ **privileged** /ˈprɪvəlɪdʒd/ *adjective*: *I felt very privileged when I was invited to meet the President.*

prize 🔑 /praɪz/ *noun* something that you give to the person who wins a game, race, etc: *I won first prize in the painting competition.*

probable 🔑 /ˈprɒbəbl/ *adjective* If something is probable, it will almost certainly happen, or it is almost certainly true: *It is probable that he will be late.* OPPOSITE **improbable**

probably 🔑 /ˈprɒbəbli/ *adverb* almost certainly: *I will probably see you on Thursday.*

problem 🔑 /ˈprɒbləm/ *noun* **1** something that is difficult; something that makes you worry: *She has a lot of problems. Her mother is ill and her brother is in prison.* ◇ *I've got a problem with my knee – it hurts a lot.* **2** a question that you must answer by thinking about it: *I can't solve this problem.*

problem-solving /ˈprɒbləm sɒlvɪŋ/ *noun* (no plural) finding ways of dealing with difficult things

procedure /prəˈsiːdʒə(r)/ *noun* the usual or correct way for doing something: *What is the procedure for making a complaint?*

proceed /prəˈsiːd/ *verb* (**proceeds**, **proceeding**, **proceeded**) to continue; to go on: *If everyone is here, then we can proceed with the meeting.*

> ❖ **SPEAKING**
> **Continue** and **go on** are the words that we usually use.

proceedings /prəˈsiːdɪŋz/ *noun* (plural) the process of using a court of law to deal with a complaint or problem: *He began court proceedings against the newspaper.*

process[1] 🔑 /ˈprəʊses/ *noun* (*plural* **processes**) a number of actions, one after the other for doing or making something: *He explained the process of building a boat.* ◇ *Learning a language is usually a slow process.*

process[2] /ˈprəʊses/ *verb* (**processes**, **processing**, **processed** /ˈprəʊsest/)

to make something ready to use, sell, etc: *The tea is taken to the factory to be processed.*

procession /prəˈseʃn/ *noun* a line of people or cars that are moving slowly along: *There was a long procession of people at the funeral.*

produce[1] 🔑 /prəˈdjuːs/ *verb* (**produces, producing, produced** /prəˈdjuːst/) **1** to make or grow something: *This factory produces cars.* ◊ *What does the farm produce?* **2** to make something happen: *His hard work produced good results.* **3** to bring something out to show it: *She produced a ticket from her pocket.* **4** to organize something like a play or film: *The film was produced by Tosh Gitonga.*

> ❖ **WORD FAMILY**
> **produce** *verb*, **produce** *noun*
> **producer** **product** **production**

produce[2] /ˈprɒdjuːs/ *noun* (no plural) food that you grow on a farm or in a garden to sell: *fresh farm produce*

producer /prəˈdjuːsə(r)/ *noun* **1** a person who organizes something like a play or film: *a television producer* **2** a company or country that makes or grows something: *Kenya is an important producer of coffee.*

product 🔑 /ˈprɒdʌkt/ *noun* something that people make or grow to sell: *Coffee is one of Kenya's most important products.*

production 🔑 /prəˈdʌkʃn/ *noun* **1** (no plural) making or growing something: *the production of oil* **2** (*plural* **productions**) a play, film, etc: *He takes part in all the school productions.*

productive /prəˈdʌktɪv/ *adjective* doing or producing a lot

profession 🔑 /prəˈfeʃn/ *noun* a job that needs a lot of studying and special training: *She's a doctor by profession.*

professional 🔑 /prəˈfeʃənl/ *adjective* **1** of or about someone who has a profession: *I got professional advice from a lawyer.* **2** doing something for money as a job: *a professional footballer* ➲ Look at **amateur**.
▸ **professionally** /prəˈfeʃənəli/ *adverb*: *He plays football professionally.*

professor /prəˈfesə(r)/ *noun* a senior teacher at a university: *Professor Banjo*

profile /ˈprəʊfaɪl/ *noun* the shape of a person's face when you see it from the side

profit 🔑 /ˈprɒfɪt/ *noun* money that you get when you sell something for more than it cost to buy or make: *If you buy a bike for 800 shillings and sell it for 1000 shillings, you make a profit of 200 shillings.* OPPOSITE **loss**

profitable /ˈprɒfɪtəbl/ *adjective* If something is **profitable**, it brings you money: *a profitable business*

program[1] 🔑 /ˈprəʊɡræm/ *noun* a list of instructions that you give to a computer: *Load the program into the computer.*

program[2] /ˈprəʊɡræm/ *verb* (**programs, programming, programmed** /ˈprəʊɡræmd/) to give instructions to a computer

programme 🔑 /ˈprəʊɡræm/ *noun* **1** something on television or radio: *Did you watch that programme about lions on TV last night?* **2** a list of things that have been planned to happen: *The President will have a very full programme during his visit.* ◊ *What's your programme for tomorrow?*

programmer /ˈprəʊɡræmə(r)/ *noun* a person whose job is to write programs for a computer

progress[1] 🔑 /ˈprəʊɡres/ *noun* (no plural) moving forward or becoming better: *Mwita is making good progress in maths.* **in progress** happening: *Silence! Examination in progress.*

progress[2] 🔑 /prəˈɡres/ *verb* (**progresses, progressing, progressed** /prəˈɡrest/) to move forward or become better: *I felt more tired as the day progressed.*

prohibit /prəˈhɪbɪt/ *verb* (**prohibits, prohibiting, prohibited**) to say that people must not do something: *Running is prohibited in the school corridor.*

project 🔑 /ˈprɒdʒekt/ *noun* **1** a big plan to do something: *a project to build a new airport* **2** a piece of work that you do at school. You find out a lot about something and write about it: *We did a project on solar energy.*

projector /prəˈdʒektə(r)/ *noun* a machine that shows films, pictures or information on a wall or screen

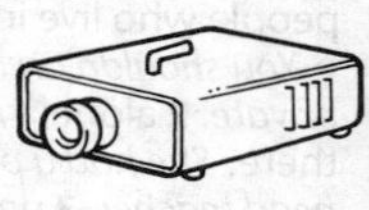
projector

prominent /ˈprɒmɪnənt/ *adjective* **1** easy to see, for example because it is bigger than usual: *prominent teeth* **2** important and famous: *a prominent writer*

promise[1] 🔑 /ˈprɒmɪs/ *verb* (**promises, promising, promised** /ˈprɒmɪst/) to say that you will certainly do or not do something: *She promised to give me the money today.* ◇ *I promise I'll come.* ◇ *Promise me that you won't be late!*

promise[2] 🔑 /ˈprɒmɪs/ *noun* saying that you will certainly do or not do something
break a promise to not do what you promised
keep a promise to do what you promised: *She kept her promise to visit regularly.*
make a promise to say that you will certainly do or not do something

promote /prəˈməʊt/ *verb* (**promotes, promoting, promoted**) to give someone a more important job: *She worked hard, and after a year she was promoted to manager.* ▸ **promotion** /prəˈməʊʃn/ *noun*: *The new job is a promotion for him.*

prompt /prɒmpt/ *adjective* quick: *She gave me a prompt answer.*

promptly /ˈprɒmptli/ *adverb* quickly; not late: *We arrived promptly at 2 p.m.*

pronoun /ˈprəʊnaʊn/ *noun* a word that you use in place of a noun: *'He', 'it', 'me' and 'them' are all pronouns.*

pronounce 🔑 /prəˈnaʊns/ *verb* (**pronounces, pronouncing, pronounced** /prəˈnaʊnst/) to make the sound of a letter or word: *How do you pronounce your name?* ◇ *You don't pronounce the 'b' at the end of 'comb'.*

pronunciation /prəˌnʌnsiˈeɪʃn/ *noun* how you say a word or words: *There are two different pronunciations for this word.* ◇ *His pronunciation is very good.*

proof 🔑 /pruːf/ *noun* (no plural) something that shows that an idea is true or that something happened: *There is no proof that Juma took the money.*
ℹ The verb is **prove**.

propel /prəˈpel/ *verb* (**propels, propelling, propelled** /prəˈpeld/) to move, drive or push something forward or in a particular direction: *a boat propelled only by oars*

propeller /prəˈpelə(r)/ *noun* a thing that is joined to the engine on a ship or a plane. It turns round fast to make the ship or plane move.

proper 🔑 /ˈprɒpə(r)/ *adjective* **1** right or correct: *I haven't got the proper tools to mend the car.* **2** real: *He hasn't got any proper friends.*

properly 🔑 /ˈprɒpəli/ *adverb* well or correctly: *Close the door properly.*

proper noun /ˌprɒpə ˈnaʊn/ *noun* a word which is the name of a person or a place: *'Ali' and 'Nairobi' are proper nouns.*
ℹ Proper nouns begin with a capital letter.

property 🔑 /ˈprɒpəti/ *noun* **1** (no plural) something that you have or own: *This book is the property of the school, so please be careful with it.* **2** (*plural* **properties**) a building and the land around it: *There are a lot of empty properties in the area.*

prophet /ˈprɒfɪt/ *noun* a person that God chooses to give his message to people

proportion /prəˈpɔːʃn/ *noun* **1** (*plural* **proportions**) a part of something: *A large proportion of people in Africa can speak two or more languages.* **2** (no plural) the amount or size of one thing compared to another thing: *What is the proportion of men to women in the factory?*

proposal /prəˈpəʊzl/ *noun* **1** a plan or idea about how to do something: *a proposal to build a new station* **2** asking someone to marry you

propose /prəˈpəʊz/ *verb* (**proposes, proposing, proposed** /prəˈpəʊzd/) **1** to say what you think should happen or be done: *I propose that we meet next week.* **2** to ask someone to marry you: *Juma proposed to Malika.*

proposer /prəˈpəʊzə(r)/ *noun* a person who speaks to support the subject you are discussing: *There are two proposers in our debate.*

prostitution /ˈprɒstɪtjuːt/ *noun* (no plural) earning money by having sex with people: *Many women were forced into prostitution.*

protect 🔑 /prəˈtekt/ *verb* (**protects, protecting, protected**) to keep someone or something safe: *Wear a hat to protect your head against the sun.* ◇ *Parents try to protect their children from danger.*
▸ **protective** /prəˈtektɪv/ *adjective*: *Wear protective clothing.*

protection 🔑 /prəˈtekʃn/ *noun* (no plural) keeping someone or something safe: *protection against disease*

protein /ˈprəʊtiːn/ *noun* a substance that is in food such as meat, fish and beans. It helps us to grow and be healthy.

protest[1] 🔑 /prəˈtest/ *verb* (**protests, protesting, protested**) to say or show strongly that you do not like something: *They protested against the government's plans.*

protest[2] 🔑 /ˈprəʊtest/ *noun* an action that shows publicly that you do not like something: *The riot began as a peaceful protest.*

Protestant /ˈprɒtɪstənt/ *noun* a person who believes in the Christian God and who is not a Roman Catholic

proud 🔑 /praʊd/ *adjective* (**prouder, proudest**) **1** If you feel proud, you are pleased about something that you or others have done or about something that you have: *They are very proud of their new house.* **2** A person who is proud thinks that they are better than other people: *She was too proud to say she was sorry.* ℹ The noun is **pride**. ▸ **proudly** *adverb*: *'I made this myself,' he said proudly.*

prove 🔑 /pruːv/ *verb* (**proves, proving, proved** /pruːvd/, **has proved** *or* **has proven** /ˈpruːvn/) to show that something is true: *The blood on his shirt proves that he is the murderer.* ℹ The noun is **proof**.

proverb /ˈprɒvɜːb/ *noun* a short sentence that people often say, that gives help or advice: *'Hurry hurry has no blessing' is an East African proverb.* ➲ Look at page A18.

provide 🔑 /prəˈvaɪd/ *verb* (**provides, providing, provided**) to give something to someone who needs it: *I'll provide the food for the party.* ◇ *School provides you with many of the skills you need in life.*

provided /prəˈvaɪdɪd/ (also **providing** /prəˈvaɪdɪŋ/) *conjunction* only if: *I'll go provided that the children can come with me.* ◇ *Phone me when you get home, providing it's not too late.*

province /ˈprɒvɪns/ *noun* a part of a country: *Rwanda has five provinces.* ▸ **provincial** /prəˈvɪnʃl/ *adjective* of a **province**: *the provincial government*

prune[1] /pruːn/ *noun* a dried **plum** (= a soft round fruit with a stone inside)

prune[2] /pruːn/ *verb* (**prunes, pruning, pruned** /pruːnd/) to cut away parts of trees or bushes

PS /ˌpiː ˈes/ You write 'PS' at the end of a letter, after your name, when you want to add something: *… Love from Katee. PS I'll see you next week.*

psychiatrist /saɪˈkaɪətrɪst/

> ❖ **PRONUNCIATION**
>
> We do not say the 'p' at the beginning of words starting with 'ps'.

noun a doctor who helps people who are ill in the mind

psychologist /saɪˈkɒlədʒɪst/ *noun* a person who studies or knows a lot about the mind and how it works

psychology /saɪˈkɒlədʒi/ *noun* (no plural) the study of the mind and how it works

pt *short for* PINT

PTO /ˌpiː tiː ˈəʊ/ please turn over; letters at the bottom of a page that tell you to turn to the next page

public[1] 🔑 /ˈpʌblɪk/ *adjective* of or for everybody: *a public telephone* ◇ *The President always has bodyguards when he walks in a public place.* ▸ **publicly** *adverb* to everybody; not secretly: *She spoke publicly about her friendship with the Prince.*

public[2] 🔑 /ˈpʌblɪk/ *noun* **the public** (no plural) all people: *The museum is open to the public between 10 a.m. and 4 p.m.*
in public when other people are there: *I don't want to talk about it in public.*

publication /ˌpʌblɪˈkeɪʃn/ *noun* **1** (no plural) making and selling a book, magazine, etc: *He became very rich after the publication of his first book.* **2** (*plural* **publications**) a book, magazine, etc.

public convenience /ˌpʌblɪk kənˈviːniəns/ *noun* a building or room with a toilet for anyone to use, for example in the street

publicity /pʌbˈlɪsəti/ *noun* (no plural) giving information about something so that people know about it: *There was a lot of publicity for the new film.*

public transport /ˌpʌblɪk ˈtrænspɔːt/ *noun* (no plural) buses and trains that everybody can use: *I usually travel by public transport.*

publish 🔑 /ˈpʌblɪʃ/ *verb* (**publishes, publishing, published** /ˈpʌblɪʃt/) to prepare and print a book, magazine or newspaper for selling: *This dictionary was published by Oxford University Press.* ▸ **publisher** /ˈpʌblɪʃə(r)/ *noun* a person or company that publishes books, magazines or newspapers

puddle /ˈpʌdl/ *noun* a little water on the ground

puff[1] /pʌf/ *verb* (**puffs**, **puffing**, **puffed** /pʌft/) **1** to come out in clouds: *Smoke was puffing out of the chimney.* **2** to breathe quickly: *She was puffing as she ran up the hill.* **3** to smoke a cigarette or pipe: *He sat puffing his cigarette.*

puff[2] /pʌf/ *noun* a small amount of air, wind, smoke, etc. that blows: *a puff of smoke*

pull

pull[1] 🔑 /pʊl/ *verb* (**pulls**, **pulling**, **pulled** /pʊld/) **1** to move someone or something strongly towards you: *She pulled the drawer open.* **2** to go forward, moving something behind you: *The cart was pulled by two oxen.* **3** to move something somewhere: *He pulled up his trousers.*
pull down to destroy a building: *The old school has been pulled down.*
pull in to drive a car to the side of the road and stop: *She pulled in to look at the map.*
pull yourself together to control your feelings after being upset: *Pull yourself together and stop crying.*
pull through to survive a difficult time or a bad illness
pull up to stop a car: *The driver pulled up at the traffic lights.*

pull[2] 🔑 /pʊl/ *noun* pulling something: *Give the rope a pull.*

pullover /ˈpʊləʊvə(r)/ *noun* a warm piece of clothing with sleeves, that you wear on the top part of your body. **Pullovers** are often made of wool.

pulse /pʌls/ *noun* the beating of your heart that you feel in different parts of your body, especially where your arm joins your hand (your **wrist**): *The nurse felt his pulse.*

pump[1] /pʌmp/ *noun* a machine that moves a liquid or gas into or out of something: *a bicycle pump* ◇ *a petrol pump*

pump[2] /pʌmp/ *verb* (**pumps**, **pumping**, **pumped** /pʌmpt/) to make a liquid or gas go somewhere: *Your heart pumps blood around your body.*
pump up to fill something with air, using a **pump**: *I pumped up my bicycle tyres.*

pumpkin /ˈpʌmpkɪn/ *noun* a very large round vegetable with a thick orange skin

pun /pʌn/ *noun* a funny use of a word that has two meanings, or that sounds the same as another word

> ❖ **SPEAKING**
>
> 'Have you ever seen an honest cheetah?' is a pun on the word **cheetah**, because the word for the animal sounds like a word for a person who cheats.

punch /pʌntʃ/ *verb* (**punches**, **punching**, **punched** /pʌntʃt/) **1** to hit someone or something hard with your closed hand (your **fist**): *She punched me in the stomach.* **2** to make a hole in something with a special tool: *The man at the entrance punched our tickets before we went in.*
▸ **punch** *noun* (*plural* **punches** /ˈpʌntʃɪz/) **1** a hard hit with your hand: *a punch on the chin* **2** a tool that you use for making holes in something: *a paper punch*

punctual /ˈpʌŋktʃuəl/ *adjective* If you are **punctual**, you come or do something at the right time: *Please try to be punctual for your classes.* ▸ **punctuality** /ˌpʌŋktʃuˈæləti/ *noun* (no plural): *Punctuality and hard work are very important.* ▸ **punctually** /ˈpʌŋktʃuəli/ *adverb*: *They arrived punctually at seven o'clock.*

punctuate /ˈpʌŋktʃueɪt/ *verb* (**punctuates**, **punctuating**, **punctuated**) to divide writing into sentences and phrases by adding **commas**, **full stops**, etc.

punctuation /ˌpʌŋktʃuˈeɪʃn/ *noun* (no plural) the marks that you use when you are writing: *Punctuation marks include full stops, commas and question marks.* ℹ Look at page A17

puncture /ˈpʌŋktʃə(r)/ *noun* a hole in a tyre, that lets the air go out: *My bike has got a puncture.* ▸ **puncture** *verb* (**punctures**, **puncturing**, **punctured** /ˈpʌŋktʃəd/) to make a **puncture** in something: *A nail punctured the tyre.*

punish 🔑 /ˈpʌnɪʃ/ *verb* (**punishes**, **punishing**, **punished** /ˈpʌnɪʃt/) to make someone suffer because they have done something wrong: *The children were punished for telling lies.*

punishment 🔑 /ˈpʌnɪʃmənt/ *noun* an act or way of punishing someone: *What is the* *punishment for murder in your country?* ◇ *The child was sent to bed as a punishment for being naughty.*

pupa /ˈpjuːpə/ *noun* (*plural* **pupae** /ˈpjuːpiː/) an insect at the time in its life when it is inside a hard case

pupil 🔑 /ˈpjuːpl/ *noun* a person who is learning at school: *There are forty pupils in the class.*

puppet /ˈpʌpɪt/ *noun* a small model of a person or an animal that you move by pulling strings or by putting your hand inside it and moving your fingers

puppy /ˈpʌpi/ *noun* (*plural* **puppies**) a young dog

purchase¹ /ˈpɜːtʃəs/ *verb* (**purchases, purchasing, purchased** /ˈpɜːtʃəst/) to buy something: *The company has purchased three new shops.* ℹ **Buy** is the word that we usually use.

purchase² /ˈpɜːtʃəs/ *noun* buying something; something that you have bought: *She made several purchases and then left.*

pure 🔑 /pjʊə(r)/ *adjective* (**purer, purest**) **1** not mixed with anything else; clean: *This shirt is pure cotton.* ◇ *pure mountain air* **2** complete or total: *What she said was pure nonsense.*

purely /ˈpjʊəli/ *adverb* completely or only: *I saw the letter purely by chance.*

purple 🔑 /ˈpɜːpl/ *adjective* with a colour between red and blue ▶ **purple** *noun*: *She often wears purple.*

purpose 🔑 /ˈpɜːpəs/ *noun* the reason for doing something: *What is the purpose of your visit?*
on purpose because you want to; not by accident: *'You've broken my pen!' 'I'm sorry, I didn't do it on purpose.'*

purr /pɜː(r)/ *verb* (**purrs, purring, purred** /pɜːd/) When a cat **purrs**, it makes a low sound that shows that it is happy.

purse /pɜːs/ *noun* a small bag that you keep money in

purse

pursue /pəˈsjuː/ *verb* (**pursues, pursuing, pursued** /pəˈsjuːd/) to follow someone or something because you want to catch them: *The police pursued the stolen car for several kilometres.* ℹ **Chase** is the word that we usually use.

pus /pʌs/ *noun* (no plural) a thick yellow or green liquid that may form in a part of your body that has been hurt

push

push 🔑 /pʊʃ/ *verb* (**pushes, pushing, pushed** /pʊʃt/) **1** to move someone or something strongly away from you: *The car broke down so we had to push it to a garage.* **2** to press something with your finger: *Push the button to ring the bell.* ▶ **push** *noun* (*plural* **pushes**): *She gave him a push and he fell.*

put 🔑 /pʊt/ *verb* (**puts, putting, put, has put**) to move something to a place: *She put the book on the table.* ◇ *He put his hand in his pocket.* ◇ *Put* (= write) *your name at the top of the page.*
put across to tell people your ideas and feelings clearly
put away to put something in its usual place: *She put the box away in the cupboard.*
put back 1 to return something to its place: *I don't mind if you borrow my books, but you must put them back afterwards.* **2** to move something to a later time: *The chairperson has put the meeting back until next week.*
put down to put something on another thing, for example on the floor or a table
put forward to suggest something: *She put forward a good idea.*
put someone off to make you feel that you do not like someone or something, or that you do not want to do something: *The accident put me off cycling.*
put something off to not do something until a later time: *He put off his holiday because the children were ill.*
put something on 1 to dress yourself in something: *Hurry up! Put your coat on.* OPPOSITE **take something off 2** to press or turn something to make an electrical thing start working: *I put on the TV.* ◇ *Put the lights on.* **3** to make a CD, DVD, etc. start to play: *Let's put a DVD on.*

put out to stop a fire or to stop a light shining: *She put out the fire with a bucket of water.*

put someone through to connect someone on the telephone to the person that they want to speak to: *Please put me through to the manager.*

put someone up to let someone sleep in your home: *Can you put me up for the night?*

put up with someone or **something** to suffer pain or problems without complaining: *We can't change the bad weather, so we have to put up with it.*

puzzle[1] /ˈpʌzl/ *noun* **1** something that is difficult to understand or explain: *Juma's reason for leaving the club is a puzzle to me.* **2** a game that is difficult and makes you think a lot ➲ Look at **crossword**, **jigsaw**.

puzzle[2] /ˈpʌzl/ *verb* (**puzzles**, **puzzling**, **puzzled** /ˈpʌzld/) to make you think a lot because you cannot understand or explain it: *Deng's illness puzzled the doctors.*

puzzled /ˈpʌzld/ *adjective* If you are **puzzled**, you cannot understand or explain something: *She was puzzled when he didn't answer her letter.* ◇ *He gave me a puzzled look.*

puzzling /ˈpʌzlɪŋ/ *adjective* If something is **puzzling**, you cannot understand or explain it.

pyjamas /pəˈdʒɑːməz/ *noun* (plural) a loose jacket and trousers that you wear in bed

pyramid /ˈpɪrəmɪd/ *noun* a shape with a flat bottom and three or four sides that come to a point at the top: *the pyramids of Egypt* ➲ picture on page A12

pyrethrum /paɪˈriːθrəm/ *noun* a kind of flower used for making stuff to kill insects

Qq

Q, q /kjuː/ *noun* (*plural* **Q's**, **q's** /kjuːz/) the seventeenth letter of the English alphabet: *'Queen' begins with a 'Q'.*

quack /kwæk/ *noun* the sound that a **duck** (= a kind of bird that lives on and near water) makes ▸ **quack** *verb* (**quacks**, **quacking**, **quacked** /kwækt/): *Ducks were quacking noisily on the pond.*

qualification /ˌkwɒlɪfɪˈkeɪʃn/ *noun* an examination that you have passed, or training or knowledge that you need to do a special job: *He left school with no qualifications.* ◇ *She has gained a qualification in teaching.*

qualified /ˈkwɒlɪfaɪd/ *adjective* having passed the exams or done the training necessary to do a special job: *She's a qualified nurse.*

qualify /ˈkwɒlɪfaɪ/ *verb* (**qualifies**, **qualifying**, **qualified** /ˈkwɒlɪfaɪd/) to get the right knowledge and training and pass exams so that you can do a certain job: *Kamal has qualified as a doctor.*

quality /ˈkwɒləti/ *noun* (no plural) how good or bad something is: *This furniture isn't very good quality.*

quantity /ˈkwɒntəti/ *noun* (*plural* **quantities**) how much of something there is; amount: *I only bought a small quantity of cheese.*

quarrel[1] /ˈkwɒrəl/ *verb* (**quarrels**, **quarrelling**, **quarrelled** /ˈkwɒrəld/) to talk angrily with someone because you do not agree: *They were quarrelling about money.*

quarrel[2] /ˈkwɒrəl/ *noun* a fight with words; an argument: *I had a quarrel with my brother.*

quarry /ˈkwɒri/ *noun* (*plural* **quarries**) a place where people cut stone out of the ground to make things like buildings or roads

quarter /ˈkwɔːtə(r)/ *noun* **1** one of four equal parts of something; ¼ : *a kilometre and a quarter* ◇ *You can walk there in three-quarters of an hour.* **2** three months: *You get a telephone bill every quarter.* **3** a part of a town: *the student quarter*

(a) quarter past 15 minutes after the hour: *It's quarter past two.* ◇ *I'll meet you at a quarter past.* ➲ Look at page A9.

(a) quarter to 15 minutes before the hour: *quarter to nine*

quarter-final /ˌkwɔːtə ˈfaɪnl/ *noun* In a competition, a **quarter-final** is one of the four games that are played to choose who will play in the **semi-finals**.

quay /kiː/ *noun* (*plural* **quays**) a place in a port where ships go so that people can move things on and off them: *A crowd was waiting on the quay.*

queen 🔑 /kwi:n/ *noun* **1** a woman who rules a country and who is from a royal family: *Queen Elizabeth II* (= the second), *the Queen of England* **2** the wife of a king **3** the largest and most important female in a group of insects: *the queen bee*

query¹ /ˈkwɪəri/ *noun* (*plural* **queries**) a question: *Phone me if you have any queries.*

query² /ˈkwɪəri/ *verb* (**queries**, **querying**, **queried** /ˈkwɪərid/) to ask a question about something that you think is wrong: *He queried the bill but the waitress said it was correct.*

question¹ 🔑 /ˈkwestʃən/ *noun* **1** something that you ask: *They asked me a lot of questions.* ◇ *She didn't answer my question.* ◇ *What is the answer to question 3?* **2** a problem that needs an answer: *We need more money. The question is, where are we going to get it from?*
in question that we are talking about: *On the day in question I was at my uncle's house.*
out of the question not possible: *No, I won't give you any more money. It's out of the question!*

question² 🔑 /ˈkwestʃən/ *verb* (**questions**, **questioning**, **questioned** /ˈkwestʃənd/) to ask someone questions about something: *The police questioned him about the stolen car.*

question mark /ˈkwestʃən mɑ:k/ *noun* the sign (?) that you write at the end of a question ➲ Look at page A17.

questionnaire /ˌkwestʃəˈneə(r)/ *noun* a list of questions for people to answer: *Please fill in* (= write the answers on) *the questionnaire.*

question tag /ˈkwestʃən tæg/ *noun* words that you put at the end of a sentence to make a question: *In the sentence 'You are from Uganda, aren't you?', 'aren't you' is a question tag.*

queue¹ /kju:/ *noun* a line of people who are waiting to do something: *There's a long queue in the bank.* ➲ picture on page A4

queue² /kju:/ (also **queue up**) *verb* (**queues**, **queuing**, **queued** /kju:d/) to stand in a **queue**: *We queued for a bus.*

quick 🔑 /kwɪk/ *adjective, adverb* (**quicker**, **quickest**) fast; that takes little time: *It's quicker to travel by plane than by train.* ◇ *Can I make a quick telephone call?* OPPOSITE **slow** ▶ **quickly** *adverb*: *Come quickly!*

quiet¹ 🔑 /ˈkwaɪət/ *adjective* (**quieter**, **quietest**) **1** with little sound or no sound: *Be quiet – the baby's asleep.* ◇ *a quiet voice* OPPOSITE **loud**, **noisy** **2** without many people or without many things happening: *The streets are very quiet at night.* ▶ **quietly** *adverb*: *Please close the door quietly.*

quiet² /ˈkwaɪət/ *noun* (no plural) when there is no noise: *I need quiet when I'm working.*

quilt /kwɪlt/ *noun* a soft thick cover for a bed. **Quilts** often have feathers inside.

quinine /ˈkwɪni:n/ *noun* (no plural) a medicine that is made from the outside of a special tree

quite 🔑 /kwaɪt/ *adverb* **1** not very; rather; fairly: *It's quite warm today, but it's not hot.* ◇ *He plays the guitar quite well.* ◇ *We waited quite a long time.* ➲ Note at **very¹**. **2** completely: *Dinner is not quite ready.*
quite a few or **quite a lot of** a lot of something: *There were quite a few people at the meeting.* ◇ *I study quite a lot in the evenings.*

quiz /kwɪz/ *noun* (*plural* **quizzes**) a game where you try to answer questions: *a quiz on television*

quotation /kwəʊˈteɪʃn/ (also **quote**) *noun* words that you say or write, that another person said or wrote before: *That's a quotation from a famous poem.*

quotation marks /kwəʊˈteɪʃn mɑ:ks/ (also **quotes**) *noun* (plural) the signs " " or ' ' that you use in writing before and after words that someone has said
ℹ Quotation marks are also known as 'inverted commas' or 'speech marks'. Look at page A17.

quote¹ /kwəʊt/ *verb* (**quotes**, **quoting**, **quoted**) to say or write something that another person said or wrote before: *She quoted from the Bible.*

quote² /kwəʊt/ = **quotation**

quotes /kwəʊts/ = **quotation marks**

Rr

R, r /ɑ:(r)/ *noun* (*plural* **R's, r's** /ɑ:z/) the eighteenth letter of the English alphabet: *'Rose' begins with an 'R'.*

rabbi /'ræbaɪ/ *noun* (*plural* **rabbis**) a teacher or leader of the Jewish religion

rabbit /'ræbɪt/ *noun* a small animal with long ears. **Rabbits** live in holes under the ground.

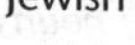

race¹ 🔑 /reɪs/ *noun* **1** a competition to see who can run, drive, ride, etc. fastest: *Who won the race?* ◇ *a horse race* **2 the races** (plural) a time when there are a lot of horse or dog races in one place **3** a group of people of the same kind, for example with the same colour of skin: *people of different races*

race² 🔑 /reɪs/ *verb* (**races, racing, raced** /reɪst/) to run, drive, ride, etc. in a competition to see who is the fastest: *The cars raced round the track.*

racecourse /'reɪskɔ:s/ (also **racetrack** /'reɪstræk/) *noun* a place where you go to see horse races

racial /'reɪʃl/ *adjective* connected with people's race: *racial differences*

racing /'reɪsɪŋ/ *noun* (no plural) a sport where horses, cars, etc. race against each other: *a racing car*

racism /'reɪsɪzəm/ *noun* (no plural) the belief that some groups (**races**) of people are better than others ▸ **racist** /'reɪsɪst/ *noun* a person who believes that some races of people are better than others ▸ **racist** *adjective*: *a racist comment*

rack /ræk/ *noun* a kind of shelf, made of bars, that you put things in or on: *Put your bag in the luggage rack* (= on a bus or train).

racket

racket (also **racquet**) /'rækɪt/ *noun* a thing that you use for hitting the ball in **tennis, badminton** and **squash**

radar /'reɪdɑ:(r)/ *noun* (no plural) a way of finding where a ship or an aircraft is and how fast it is travelling by using radio waves

radiation /ˌreɪdi'eɪʃn/ *noun* (no plural) dangerous energy that some substances send out

radiator /'reɪdieɪtə(r)/ *noun* **1** a part of a car that has water in it to keep the engine cold **2** a metal thing with hot water inside that you use to make a room warm

radio 🔑 /'reɪdiəʊ/ *noun* **1** (no plural) sending or receiving sounds that travel a long way through the air by special waves: *The captain of the ship sent a message by radio.* **2** (*plural* **radios**) a machine that brings voices or music from far away so that you can hear them: *We listened to an interesting programme on the radio.*

radius /'reɪdiəs/ *noun* (*plural* **radii** /'reɪdiaɪ/) the length of a straight line from the centre of a circle to the outside
➲ picture on page A12

raft /rɑ:ft/ *noun* a flat boat with no sides and no engine

rag /ræg/ *noun* **1** a small piece of old cloth that you use for cleaning **2 rags** (plural) clothes that are very old and torn: *She was dressed in rags.*

rage /reɪdʒ/ *noun* strong anger

raid /reɪd/ *noun* a sudden attack on a place: *a bank raid* ▸ **raid** *verb* (**raids, raiding, raided**): *Police raided the house looking for drugs.*

rail /reɪl/ *noun* **1** (*plural* **rails**) a long piece of wood or metal that is fixed to a wall or to something else: *She held on to the rail as she came down the steps.* **2 rails** (plural) the long pieces of metal that trains go on **3** (no plural) trains as a way of travelling: *I travelled by rail* (= in a train).

railings /'reɪlɪŋz/ *noun* (plural) a fence made of long pieces of metal: *I chained my bike to the railings.*

railway /ˈreɪlweɪ/ *noun* **1** (*also* **railway line**) the metal lines that trains go on from one place to another: *The railway was being repaired.* **2** a train service that carries people and things: *a railway timetable*

railway station /ˈreɪlweɪ steɪʃn/ *noun* a place where trains stop so that people can get on and off

rain[1] /reɪn/ *noun* **1** (no plural) the water that falls from the sky: *Light rain began to fall.* **2 the rains** (plural) in some countries, the only time of year when there is a lot of rain: *If the rains come late, the crops might fail.*

rain[2] /reɪn/ *verb* (**rains**, **raining**, **rained** /reɪnd/) When it rains, water falls from the sky: *It's raining.* ◇ *It rained all day.*

rainbow /ˈreɪnbəʊ/ *noun* a half circle of bright colours that you sometimes see in the sky when rain and sun come together

rainfall /ˈreɪnfɔːl/ *noun* (no plural) how much rain falls in one place during a month, year, etc: *The annual rainfall in Kampala is about 1200 millimetres.*

rainforest /ˈreɪnfɒrɪst/ *noun* a forest in a hot part of the world where there is a lot of rain

rainmaker /ˈreɪnmeɪkə(r)/ *noun* a person that people believe can make rain fall
▸ **rainmaking** /ˈreɪnmeɪkɪŋ/ *noun* (no plural) trying to make rain fall by using magic

rainy /ˈreɪni/ *adjective* (**rainier**, **rainiest**) with a lot of rain: *a rainy day* ◇ *the rainy season*

raise /reɪz/ *verb* (**raises**, **raising**, **raised** /reɪzd/) **1** to move something or someone up: *Raise your hand if you want to ask a question.* OPPOSITE **lower** **2** to make something bigger, higher, stronger, etc: *They've raised the price of petrol.* ◇ *She raised her voice* (= spoke louder). OPPOSITE **lower** **3** to get money from other people: *We raised 50 000 shillings for the hospital.* **4** to start to talk about something: *He raised an interesting question.*

rake

raisin /ˈreɪzn/ *noun* a dried **grape** (= a small green or purple fruit)

rake /reɪk/ *noun* a tool with a long handle that you use in a garden for collecting leaves or for making the soil flat

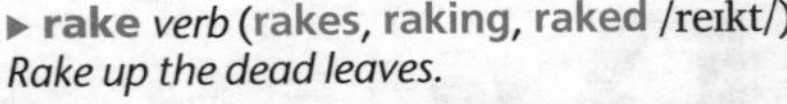
▸ **rake** *verb* (**rakes**, **raking**, **raked** /reɪkt/) *Rake up the dead leaves.*

rally /ˈræli/ *noun* (*plural* **rallies**) **1** a group of people walking or standing together to show that they feel strongly about something: *a peace rally* **2** a race for cars or motorbikes

ram[1] /ræm/ *verb* (**rams**, **ramming**, **rammed** /ræmd/) to crash into something or to push something with great force: *In the accident, a lorry rammed a car from behind.*

ram[2] /ræm/ *noun* a male sheep

ramp /ræmp/ *noun* a path that goes to a higher or lower place: *I pushed the wheelchair up the ramp.*

ran *form of* RUN[1]

random /ˈrændəm/ *adjective*
at random without any special plan: *She chose a few books at random.*

rang *form of* RING[2]

range[1] /reɪndʒ/ *noun* **1** different things of the same kind: *We study a range of subject at school.* **2** how far you can see, hear, travel, etc: *The radio has a range of 60 metres.* **3** the amount between the highes and the lowest: *The age range of the children is between eight and twelve.* **4** a lin of mountains or hills

range[2] /reɪndʒ/ *verb* (**ranges**, **ranging**, **ranged** /reɪndʒd/) to be at different point between two things: *The ages of the pupils in the class range from 12 to 14.*

ranger /ˈreɪndʒə(r)/ *noun* a person who takes care of a large area of land where wi animals live

rank /ræŋk/ *noun* how important someon is in a group of people, for example in an army: *'General' is one of the highest ranks i the army.*

ransom /ˈrænsəm/ *noun* money that you must pay so that a criminal will free a person that they have taken: *The kidnappers have demanded a ransom of a million shillings.*

rap[1] /ræp/ *noun* **1** a quick knock: *I heard a rap at the door.* **2** a kind of music in which singers speak the words of a song very quickly

rap[2] /ræp/ *verb* (**raps**, **rapping**, **rapped** /ræpt/) **1** to hit something quickly and lightly: *She rapped on the door.* **2** to speak the words of a song very quickly

rape /reɪp/ *verb* (**rapes**, **raping**, **raped** /reɪpt/) to make someone have sex when they do not want to ▸ **rape** *noun*: *He was sent to prison for rape.*

rapid /ˈræpɪd/ *adjective* quick; fast: *rapid changes* ▸ **rapidly** *adverb*: *Once she took the medicine she recovered rapidly.*

rare ⚷ /reə(r)/ *adjective* (**rarer**, **rarest**) **1** If something is rare, you do not find or see it often: *Gorillas are rare animals.* ◇ *It's rare to have rain in the dry season.* OPPOSITE **common** **2** Meat that is rare is only cooked a little: *He prefers his steak rare.*

rarely ⚷ /ˈreəli/ *adverb* not often: *I rarely go to bed very late.*

rash¹ /ræʃ/ *noun* (*plural* **rashes**) a lot of small red spots on your skin

rash² /ræʃ/ *adjective* (**rasher**, **rashest**) If you are **rash**, you do things too quickly, without thinking: *He made a rash decision to leave without telling anyone.*

raspberry /ˈrɑːzbəri/ *noun* (*plural* **raspberries**) a small soft red fruit: *raspberry jam*

rat /ræt/ *noun* an animal like a big mouse

rate /reɪt/ *noun* **1** the speed of something or how often something happens: *The crime rate was lower in 2014 than in 2013.* **2** the amount that something costs or that someone is paid: *His rate of pay is 500 shillings a day.*
at any rate anyway; whatever happens: *I hope to be back before ten o'clock – I won't be late at any rate.*

rather ⚷ /ˈrɑːðə(r)/ *adverb* more than a little but not very; quite: *We were rather tired after our long journey.* ◇ *It's rather a small room.*
rather than in the place of; instead of: *Can I have a banana rather than a mango?*
would rather would prefer to do something: *I would rather go swimming than play football.*

ratio /ˈreɪʃiəʊ/ *noun* (*plural* **ratios**) a way of showing the size or amount of something when you compare it to another: *There are thirty boys in this class and fifteen girls, so the ratio of boys to girls is two to one (2:1).*

ration /ˈræʃn/ *noun* a small amount of something that you are allowed to have when there is not enough for everybody to have what they want: *food rations*

rattle¹ /ˈrætl/ *verb* (**rattles**, **rattling**, **rattled** /ˈrætld/) **1** to make a lot of short sounds because it is shaking: *The windows were rattling all night in the wind.* **2** to shake something so that it makes a lot of small sounds: *She rattled the money in the tin.*

rattle² /ˈrætl/ *noun* **1** the noise of things hitting each other: *the rattle of empty bottles* **2** a toy that a baby can shake to make a noise

rattle

raw /rɔː/ *adjective* **1** not cooked: *raw meat* **2** natural; as it comes from the soil, from plants, etc: *raw sugar*

> ❖ **PRONUNCIATION**
> **Raw** sounds like **more**.

raw material /ˌrɑː məˈtɪəriəl/ *noun* a substance in its natural state before it is used to make something: *the cost of raw materials*

ray /reɪ/ *noun* (*plural* **rays**) a line of light or heat: *the rays of the sun*

razor /ˈreɪzə(r)/ *noun* a sharp thing that people use to cut hair off their bodies (to **shave**): *It took me a long time to shave because the razor wasn't very sharp.*

razor blade /ˈreɪzə bleɪd/ *noun* the thin metal part of a **razor** that cuts

Rd *short for* ROAD

re- /riː/ *prefix* You can add **re-** to the beginning of some words to give them the meaning 'again': *We rebuilt the fence after the storm* (= built it again). ◇ *Your homework is all wrong. Please redo it* (= do it again).

reach¹ ⚷ /riːtʃ/ *verb* (**reaches**, **reaching**, **reached** /riːtʃt/) **1** to arrive somewhere: *It was dark when we reached the town.* ◇ *Have you reached the end of the book yet?* **2** to put out your hand to do or get something; to be able to touch something: *I reached for the telephone.* ◇ *Can you get that book from the top shelf for me? I can't reach (it).*

reach² /riːtʃ/ *noun* (no plural)
beyond reach; **out of reach** too far away to touch: *Keep this medicine out of the reach of children.*
within reach near enough to touch or go to: *Do you live within reach of Kampala?*

react /riˈækt/ *verb* (**reacts**, **reacting**, **reacted**) to say or do something when another thing happens: *How did your mother react to the news?*

reaction ⚷ /riˈækʃn/ *noun* what you say or do because of something that has happened: *What was her reaction when you told her about the accident?*

read 🔑 /riːd/ *verb* (**reads**, **reading**, **read** /red/, **has read**) **1** to look at words and understand them: *Have you read this book? It's very interesting.* **2** to say words that you can see: *I read a story to the children.* ◇ *I like reading poems aloud.* **read out** to read something to other people: *The teacher read out the list of names.* ▸ **reading** /ˈriːdɪŋ/ *noun* (no plural): *My interests are reading and football.*

reader /ˈriːdə(r)/ *noun* **1** a person who reads something **2** a book for reading at school

ready 🔑 /ˈredi/ *adjective* **1** prepared so that you can do something: *I'll be ready to leave in five minutes.* **2** prepared so that you can use it: *Dinner will be ready soon.* **3** happy to do something: *He's always ready to help.* **get ready** to make yourself ready for something: *I'm getting ready to go out.*

ready-made /ˌredi ˈmeɪd/ *adjective* prepared and ready to use: *ready-made soup*

real 🔑 /rɪəl/ *adverb* **1** not just in the mind; that really exists: *The film is about something that happened in real life.* **2** true: *The name he gave to the police wasn't his real name.* **3** natural; not a copy: *This ring is real gold.* ➲ Look at **fake**[1]. **4** big or complete: *I've got a real problem.*

reality 🔑 /riˈæləti/ *noun* (no plural) the way that something really is: *The visit sounded like fun, but in reality it was hard work.*

realize 🔑 /ˈrɪəlaɪz/ *verb* (**realizes**, **realizing**, **realized** /ˈrɪəlaɪzd/) to understand or know something: *When I got home, I realized that I had lost my key.* ◇ *I didn't realize you were American.* ▸ **realization** /ˌrɪəlaɪˈzeɪʃn/ *noun* (no plural) understanding or knowing something

really 🔑 /ˈrɪəli/ *adverb* **1** in fact; actually: *Is Chebet really taller than you?* **2** very or very much: *I'm really hungry.* ◇ *'Do you like this music?' 'Not really.'* **3** a word that shows you are interested or surprised: *'I'm going to Egypt next year.' 'Really?'*

rear[1] /rɪə(r)/ *noun* (no plural) the back part: *The kitchen is at the rear of the house.* OPPOSITE **front**

rear[2] /rɪə(r)/ *adjective* at the back: *the rear window of a car*

rearrange /ˌriːəˈreɪndʒ/ *verb* (**rearranges**, **rearranging**, **rearranged** /ˌriːəˈreɪndʒd/) to change the position or order of things: *He has rearranged the furniture in his bedroom.*

reason 🔑 /ˈriːzn/ *noun* why you do something or why something happens: *The reason I didn't come to school was that I was ill.* ◇ *Is there any reason why you were late?*

reasonable 🔑 /ˈriːznəbl/ *adjective* **1** fair and willing to listen to what other people say: *Be reasonable! You can't ask one person to do all the work!* **2** fair or right: *I think 10 000 shillings is a reasonable price.* OPPOSITE **unreasonable**

reasonably /ˈriːznəbli/ *adverb* **1** quite, but not very: *The food was reasonably good.* **2** in a reasonable way: *Don't get angry – let's talk about this reasonably.*

reassure /ˌriːəˈʃɔː(r)/ *verb* (**reassures**, **reassuring**, **reassured** /ˌriːəˈʃɔːd/) to say or do something to make someone feel safer or happier: *The doctor reassured her that she was not seriously ill.* ▸ **reassurance** /ˌriːəˈʃɔːrəns/ *noun* (no plural) what you say to make someone feel safer or happier: *He needs reassurance that he is right.*

rebel[1] /ˈrebl/ *noun* a person who fights against the people in control

rebel[2] /rɪˈbel/ *verb* (**rebels**, **rebelling**, **rebelled** /rɪˈbeld/) to fight against the people in control: *She rebelled against her parents and went to live in the city.*

rebellion /rɪˈbeliən/ *noun* a time when a lot of people fight against the people in control in a country

rebuke /rɪˈbjuːk/ *verb* (**rebukes**, **rebuking**, **rebuked** /rɪˈbjuːkt/) to speak in an angry way to someone who has done something wrong: *The teacher rebuked Bigogo for being late.*

recall /rɪˈkɔːl/ *verb* (**recalls**, **recalling**, **recalled** /rɪˈkɔːld/) to remember something: *I can't recall the name of Sarika's brother.* ❶ **Remember** is the word that we usually use.

receipt /rɪˈsiːt/ *noun*

> ❖ **PRONUNCIATION**
>
> **Receipt** sounds like **seat**. We do not say the 'p'.

a piece of paper that shows you have paid for something: *Can I have a receipt?*

receive 🔑 /rɪˈsiːv/ *verb* (**receives**, **receiving**, **received** /rɪˈsiːvd/) to get something that someone has given or sent to you: *Did you receive my letter?* ❶ **Get** is the word that we usually use.

> ❖ **SPELLING**
>
> Remember! When the sound is /iː/, there is a spelling rule: **i before e, except after c**, so you spell **receive** with **ei** (not **ie**).

receiver /rɪˈsiːvə(r)/ *noun* the part of a telephone that you use for listening and speaking

recent 🔑 /ˈriːsnt/ *adjective* that happened a short time ago: *Is this a recent photo of your son?*

recently 🔑 /ˈriːsntli/ *adverb* not long ago: *I've been studying a lot recently – that's why I'm so tired.*

reception /rɪˈsepʃn/ *noun* **1** (no plural) the place where you go first when you arrive at a hotel, company, etc: *Leave your key at reception if you go out.* **2** (*plural* **receptions**) a big important party: *a wedding reception*

receptionist /rɪˈsepʃənɪst/ *noun* a person in a hotel, company, etc. who helps you when you arrive and who may also answer the telephone

recharge /ˌriːˈtʃɑːdʒ/ *verb* (**recharges, recharging, recharged** /ˌriːˈtʃɑːdʒd/) to put electricity into something again: *I need to recharge my phone.*

recipe /ˈresəpi/ *noun* a piece of writing that tells you how to cook something

recite /rɪˈsaɪt/ *verb* (**recites, reciting, recited**) to say something that you have learnt and remembered so that other people can hear it: *I am going to recite a poem at the school concert.*

reckless /ˈrekləs/ *adjective* A person who is **reckless** does dangerous things without thinking about what could happen: *reckless driving*

reckon /ˈrekən/ *verb* (**reckons, reckoning, reckoned** /ˈrekənd/) to believe something because you have thought about it: *I reckon it will take us about two hours to get there.*

recognition /ˌrekəgˈnɪʃn/ *noun* (no plural) knowing again someone or something that you have seen or heard before: *She looked at me with no sign of recognition* (= she didn't remember that she had seen me before). ❶ The verb is **recognize**.

recognize 🔑 /ˈrekəgnaɪz/ *verb* (**recognizes, recognizing, recognized** /ˈrekəgnaɪzd/) **1** to know again someone or something that you have seen or heard before: *I didn't recognize you without your glasses.* **2** to know that something is true: *They recognize that there is a problem.* ❶ The noun is **recognition**.

recommend 🔑 /ˌrekəˈmend/ *verb* (**recommends, recommending, recommended**) **1** to tell someone that a person or thing is good or useful: *Can you recommend a good book?* **2** to tell someone in a helpful way what you think they should do: *I recommend that you see a doctor.* ➲ Look at **advise**.

> ❖ **SPELLING**
>
> Remember! You spell **recommend** with one **c** and **mm**.

recommendation /ˌrekəmenˈdeɪʃn/ *noun* saying that something is good or useful: *I read this book on my brother's recommendation* (= because he said it was good).

record[1] 🔑 /ˈrekɔːd/ *noun* **1** notes about things that have happened: *Keep a record of all the money you spend.* **2** the best, fastest, highest, lowest, etc. that has been done in a sport: *She holds the world record for long jump.* ◇ *He ran the race in record time.*

break a record to do better than anyone has done before, for example in a sport

record[2] 🔑 /rɪˈkɔːd/ *verb* (**records, recording, recorded**) **1** to write notes about or make pictures of things that happen so you can remember them later: *In his diary he recorded everything that he did.* **2** to put music, a film, etc. onto a tape or disc so that you can listen to or watch it later: *Did you record that programme for me?*

recorder /rɪˈkɔːdə(r)/ *noun* a musical instrument that you blow. Children often play recorders. ➲ Look at **tape recorder, video**.

recording /rɪˈkɔːdɪŋ/ *noun* sounds or pictures on a tape, disc or film: *We listened to the recording of the concert.*

recover 🔑 /rɪˈkʌvə(r)/ *verb* (**recovers, recovering, recovered** /rɪˈkʌvəd/) **1** to become well or happy again after you have been ill or sad: *She is slowly recovering from her illness.* **2** to get back something that you have lost: *Police recovered the stolen car.*

recovery /rɪˈkʌvəri/ *noun* (no plural) when you feel well or happy again after you have been ill or sad: *He made a quick recovery after his illness.*

recreation /ˌrekriˈeɪʃn/ *noun* (no plural) relaxing and enjoying yourself when you are not working or at school: *Recreation activities such as dancing and playing cards are popular.*

rectangle /ˈrektæŋgl/ *noun* a shape with two long sides, two short sides and four angles of 90 degrees ➲ picture on page A12 SAME MEANING **oblong**
▶ **rectangular** /rekˈtæŋgjələ(r)/ *adjective* with the shape of a **rectangle**: *This page is rectangular.* SAME MEANING **oblong**

recycle /ˌriːˈsaɪkl/ *verb* (**recycles, recycling, recycled** /ˌriːˈsaɪkld/) to do something to materials like paper and glass so that they can be used again: *Old newspapers can be recycled.*

recycled /ˌriːˈsaɪkld/ *adjective* Something that is **recycled** has been used before: *recycled paper*

red ⚷ /red/ *adjective* (**redder, reddest**) **1** with the colour of blood: *She's wearing a bright red dress.* ◇ *red wine* **2** Red hair has a colour between red, orange and brown.
▶ **red** *noun*: *Tanei was dressed in red.*

reduce ⚷ /rɪˈdjuːs/ *verb* (**reduces, reducing, reduced** /rɪˈdjuːst/) to make something smaller or less: *I bought this shirt because the price was reduced from 900 shillings to 600.* ◇ *Reduce speed now* (= words on a road sign).

reduction /rɪˈdʌkʃn/ *noun* making something smaller or less: *price reductions* ◇ *There has been a reduction in unemployment.* SAME MEANING **decrease**

redundant /rɪˈdʌndənt/ *adjective* without a job because there is no more work available: *When the factory closed, 300 people were made redundant.*

reed /riːd/ *noun* a tall plant, like grass, that grows in or near water

reeds

reef /riːf/ *noun* a long line of rocks or plants just below or above the surface of the sea: *a coral reef*

reel /riːl/ *noun* a thing with round sides that holds wire, cotton for sewing, etc: *a reel of cotton*

reel
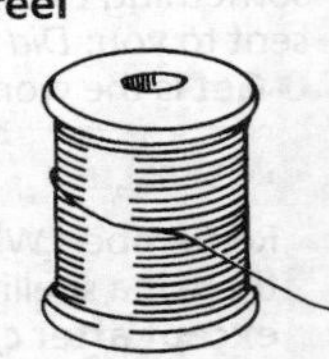
a **reel** of cotton

refer ⚷ /rɪˈfɜː(r)/ *verb* (**refers, referring, referred** /rɪˈfɜːd/)
refer to someone or **something** **1** to talk about someone or something: *When I said that some people are stupid, I wasn't referring to you!* **2** to be used to mean something: *The word 'child' refers here to anyone under the age of 16.* **3** to look in a book or ask someone for information: *If you don't understand a word, you may refer to your dictionaries.* ➲ Look at **reference**.

referee /ˌrefəˈriː/ *noun* **1** a person in a sport like football or **boxing** who controls the match **2** a person who writes about someone who is trying to get a job or a place at a college

reference /ˈrefrəns/ *noun* **1** what someone says or writes about something: *There are many references to my town in this book about Kenya.* **2** If someone gives you a **reference**, they write about you to someone who may give you a new job: *Did her boss give her a good reference?*

reference book /ˈrefrəns bʊk/ *noun* a book where you look for information: *A dictionary is a reference book.*

reflect /rɪˈflekt/ *verb* (**reflects, reflecting, reflected**) to send back light, heat or sound: *A mirror reflects a picture of you when you look in it.*

reflection /rɪˈflekʃn/ *noun* **1** (*plural* **reflections**) a picture that you see in a mirror or in water: *He looked into the pool and saw a reflection of himself.* **2** (no plural) sending back light, heat or sound

reform¹ /rɪˈfɔːm/ *verb* (**reforms, reforming, reformed** /rɪˈfɔːmd/) to change something to make it better: *The government wants to reform the education system in this country.*

reform² /rɪˈfɔːm/ *noun* a change to make something better: *political reform*

refresh /rɪˈfreʃ/ *verb* (**refreshes, refreshing, refreshed** /rɪˈfreʃt/) **1** to make someone feel cooler, stronger or less tired: *A sleep will refresh you after your long journey.* **2** to make the most recent information show on an Internet page: *Click here to refresh this document.*

refreshing /rɪˈfreʃɪŋ/ *adjective* making you feel cooler or less tired: *a cool, refreshing drink*

refreshments /rɪˈfreʃmənts/ *noun* (plural) food and drinks that you can buy in a place like a cinema or theatre: *Refreshments will be sold in the interval.*

refrigerator /rɪˈfrɪdʒəreɪtə(r)/ *noun* a big metal box for keeping food and drink cold and fresh ℹ **Fridge** is the word that we usually use.

refuge /ˈrefjuːdʒ/ *noun* a place where you are safe from someone or something **take refuge from something** to go to a safe place to get away from something bad or dangerous: *We took refuge from the hot sun under a tree.*

refugee /ˌrefjuˈdʒiː/ *noun* a person who must leave their country because of danger

refund /rɪˈfʌnd/ *verb* (**refunds**, **refunding**, **refunded**) to pay back money: *When the match was cancelled they refunded our money.* ▶ **refund** /ˈriːfʌnd/ *noun* money that is paid back to you: *The watch I bought was broken so I asked for a refund.*

refusal /rɪˈfjuːzl/ *noun* saying 'no' when someone asks you to do or have something: *a refusal to pay*

refuse[1] 🔑 /rɪˈfjuːz/ *verb* (**refuses**, **refusing**, **refused** /rɪˈfjuːzd/) to say 'no' when someone asks you to do or have something: *I asked Katee to help, but he refused.* ◇ *The shop assistant refused to give me my money back.* OPPOSITE **agree**

> ❖ **PRONUNCIATION**
>
> The verb **refuse** and the noun **refuse** do not sound the same. The stress comes on the second part of the verb, but on the first part of the noun.

refuse[2] /ˈrefjuːs/ *noun* (no plural) things that you throw away SAME MEANING **rubbish**

regard[1] /rɪˈɡɑːd/ *verb* (**regards**, **regarding**, **regarded**) to think of someone or something in a certain way: *I regard her as my best friend.*

regard[2] /rɪˈɡɑːd/ *noun* **1** (no plural) what you think about someone or something: *I have a high regard for his work* (= I think it is very good). **2** (no plural) care: *She shows no regard for other people's feelings.* **3 regards** (plural) kind wishes: *Please give my regards to your parents.*

reggae /ˈreɡeɪ/ *noun* (no plural) a type of West Indian music: *Bob Marley was a famous reggae singer.*

regiment /ˈredʒɪmənt/ *noun* a group of soldiers in an army

region 🔑 /ˈriːdʒən/ *noun* a part of a country or of the world: *There will be rain in northern regions today.*

regional /ˈriːdʒənl/ *adjective* of a certain region: *regional trade*

register[1] /ˈredʒɪstə(r)/ *noun* a list of names: *The teacher keeps a register of all the pupils in the class.*

register[2] /ˈredʒɪstə(r)/ *verb* (**registers**, **registering**, **registered** /ˈredʒɪstəd/) **1** to put a name on a list: *I would like to register for the drama course.* **2** to show a number or amount: *The thermometer registered 30 degrees Celsius.*

registration /ˌredʒɪˈstreɪʃn/ *noun* (no plural) putting a name on a list: *registration of births, marriages and deaths*

registration number /redʒɪˈstreɪʃn nʌmbə(r)/ *noun* the numbers and letters on the front and back of a car, etc.

regret[1] /rɪˈɡret/ *verb* (**regrets**, **regretting**, **regretted**) to feel sorry about something that you did: *He regrets selling his car.* ◇ *I don't regret what I said to her.*

regret[2] /rɪˈɡret/ *noun* a sad feeling about something that you did: *She had no regrets about moving to the city.*

regular 🔑 /ˈreɡjələ(r)/ *adjective* **1** that happens again and again with the same amount of space or time in between: *We have regular meetings every Monday morning.* ◇ *regular breathing* OPPOSITE **irregular** **2** who goes somewhere or does something often: *I've never seen him before – he's not one of my regular customers.* **3** usual: *Who is your regular doctor?* **4** A word that is regular has the usual verb forms or plural: *'Work' is a regular verb.* OPPOSITE **irregular** ▶ **regularly** *adverb*: *We meet regularly every Friday.*

regulation /ˌreɡjuˈleɪʃn/ *noun* something that controls what people do; a rule or law: *You can't leave bags here – it's against safety regulations.*

rehearsal /rɪˈhɜːsl/ *noun* a time when you **rehearse** a play or a piece of music:

There's a rehearsal for the play tonight.

rehearse /rɪˈhɜːs/ *verb* (**rehearses, rehearsing, rehearsed** /rɪˈhɜːst/) to do or say something again and again before you do it in front of other people: *We are rehearsing for the concert.*

reign[1] /reɪn/ *noun* a time when a king or queen rules a country: *The reign of Queen Elizabeth II began in 1952.*

❖ **PRONUNCIATION**

Reign sounds just like **rain**.

reign[2] /reɪn/ *verb* (**reigns, reigning, reigned** /reɪnd/) to be king or queen of a country: *The queen has reigned since 1952.*

reins /reɪnz/ *noun* long thin pieces of leather that a horse wears on its head so that the person riding it can control it

❖ **PRONUNCIATION**

Reins sounds just like **rains**.

reject /rɪˈdʒekt/ *verb* (**rejects, rejecting, rejected**) to say that you do not want someone or something: *He rejected my offer of help.*

rejoice /rɪˈdʒɔɪs/ *verb* (**rejoices, rejoicing, rejoiced** /rɪˈdʒɔɪst/) to feel or show great happiness: *Nafula rejoiced that her lost son was found.*

relate /rɪˈleɪt/ *verb* (**relates, relating, related**) to show or make a connection between two or more things
relate to someone or something to be connected to someone or something: *The last paragraph relates to the situation in our town.*

related /rɪˈleɪtɪd/ *adjective* in the same family; connected: *'Are those two boys related?' 'Yes, they're brothers.'*

relation 🔑 /rɪˈleɪʃn/ *noun* **1** a person in your family: *All their friends and relations came.* **2** a connection between two things: *There is no relation between the size of the countries and the number of people who live there.*

❖ **WORD BUILDING**

Your **relations** are your **mother** and **father, brothers, sisters, aunts, uncles, cousins, grandfather** and **grandmother**. How many do you have? Do you have a **brother-in-law** or a **sister-in-law**?

relationship 🔑 /rɪˈleɪʃnʃɪp/ *noun* how people, things or ideas are connected to each other; feelings between people: *I have a good relationship with my parents.* ◇ *The book is about the relationship between a boy and his grandfather.*

relative 🔑 /ˈrelətɪv/ *noun* a person in your family: *He is a distant relative of mine.* SAME MEANING **relation**

relatively /ˈrelətɪvli/ *adverb* quite: *This room is relatively small.*

relax 🔑 /rɪˈlæks/ *verb* (**relaxes, relaxing, relaxed** /rɪˈlækst/) **1** to rest and be calm; to become less worried or angry: *After a hard day at work I spent the evening relaxing in front of the television.* **2** to become less tight or make something become less tight: *Let your body relax.*

relaxation /ˌriːlækˈseɪʃn/ *noun* (no plural) time spent resting and being calm: *You need more rest and relaxation.*

relaxed 🔑 /rɪˈlækst/ *adjective* calm and not worried: *She felt relaxed after her holiday.* OPPOSITE **tense**

relay /ˈriːleɪ/ (also **relay race**) *noun* a race in which each member of a team runs or swims one part of the race: *She ran in the 4 x 100 metre relay.*

release[1] 🔑 /rɪˈliːs/ *verb* (**releases, releasing, released** /rɪˈliːst/) to let a person or an animal go free: *We opened the cage and released the bird.*

release[2] /rɪˈliːs/ *noun* when a person or an animal is allowed to go free: *the release of the prisoners*

relevant 🔑 /ˈreləvənt/ *adjective* connected with what you are talking or writing about; important: *Send me all the relevant information.* OPPOSITE **irrelevant**

reliable /rɪˈlaɪəbl/ *adjective* that you can trust: *She is reliable and hardworking.* ◇ *H… car is very reliable.* ⓘ The verb is **rely**.

relied *form of* RELY

relief 🔑 /rɪˈliːf/ *noun* (no plural) **1** what you feel when pain or worry stops: *It was a great relief to know she was safe.* **2** food or money for people who need it: *Many countries sent relief to the people who had lost their homes in the floods.*

relies *form of* RELY

relieved /rɪˈliːvd/ *adjective* pleased because a problem or danger has gone away: *I was relieved to hear that you weren't hurt in the accident.*

religion 🔑 /rɪˈlɪdʒən/ *noun* **1** (no plural) believing in a god **2** (*plural* **religions**) one of the ways of believing in a god, for example Christianity, Islam or Buddhism

religious 🔑 /rɪˈlɪdʒəs/ *adjective* **1** of religion: *a religious leader* **2** with a strong belief in a religion: *I'm not very religious.*

reluctance /rɪˈlʌktəns/ *noun* (no plural) not wanting to do something: *He agreed, but with great reluctance.*

reluctant /rɪˈlʌktənt/ *adjective* If you are **reluctant** to do something, you do not want to do it: *Rono was reluctant to give me the money.* ▶ **reluctantly** *adverb*: *Nakato reluctantly agreed to help with the housework.*

rely 🔑 /rɪˈlaɪ/ *verb* (**relies**, **relying**, **relied** /rɪˈlaɪd/, **has relied**)
rely on someone or **something** **1** to feel sure that someone or something will do what they should do: *You can rely on him to help you.* **2** to need someone or something: *Babies rely entirely on others for food.*

❖ **WORD FAMILY**
rely
reliable: OPPOSITE **unreliable**

remain 🔑 /rɪˈmeɪn/ *verb* (**remains**, **remaining**, **remained** /rɪˈmeɪnd/) **1** to stay after other people or things have gone: *After the fire, very little remained of the house.* **2** to stay the same way; to not change: *I asked her a question but she remained silent.*

remains /rɪˈmeɪnz/ *noun* (plural) what is left when most of something has gone: *the remains of an old house*

remark¹ /rɪˈmɑːk/ *verb* (**remarks**, **remarking**, **remarked** /rɪˈmɑːkt/) to say something: *'It's cold today,' he remarked.*

remark² 🔑 /rɪˈmɑːk/ *noun* something that you say: *He made a remark about the food.*

remarkable /rɪˈmɑːkəbl/ *adjective* unusual and surprising in a good way: *a remarkable discovery* ▶ **remarkably** /rɪˈmɑːkəbli/ *adverb*: *She speaks French remarkably well.*

remedy /ˈremədi/ *noun* (*plural* **remedies**) a way of making something better: *a remedy for toothache*

remember 🔑 /rɪˈmembə(r)/ *verb* (**remembers**, **remembering**, **remembered** /rɪˈmembəd/) to keep something in your mind or bring something back into your mind; to not forget something: *Can you remember his name?* ◇ *I remember posting the letter.* ◇ *Did you remember to go to the library?*

remind 🔑 /rɪˈmaɪnd/ *verb* (**reminds**, **reminding**, **reminded**) to make someone remember someone or something: *This song reminds me of when I was little.* ◇ *I reminded her to buy some bread.*

reminder /rɪˈmaɪndə(r)/ *noun* something that makes you remember

remote /rɪˈməʊt/ *adjective* (**remoter**, **remotest**) far from other places: *They live in a remote village in the mountains.*

remote control /rɪˌməʊt kənˈtrəʊl/ *noun* **1** (no plural) a way of controlling something from far away: *The doors can be opened by remote control.* **2** (*plural* **remote controls**) a piece of equipment that you use for controlling something from far away: *Where's the remote control for the TV?* ℹ We often just say **'the remote.'**

remote control

removal /rɪˈmuːvl/ *noun* when you take something off or away: *You may need permission for the removal of trees.*

remove 🔑 /rɪˈmuːv/ *verb* (**removes**, **removing**, **removed** /rɪˈmuːvd/) to take someone or something away or off: *The statue was removed from the museum.* ◇ *Please remove your shoes before entering the temple.*

❖ **SPEAKING**
It is more usual to use other words, for example **take away** or **take off**.

rename /ˌriːˈneɪm/ *verb* (**renames**, **renaming**, **renamed** /ˌriːˈneɪmd/) to give a new name to something or someone: *Our street has been renamed.* ◇ *Rename the file and save it.*

renew /rɪˈnjuː/ *verb* (**renews**, **renewing**, **renewed** /rɪˈnjuːd/) to get or give something new in the place of something old: *My passport expires soon so I'll have to go and renew it.*

rent¹ 🔑 /rent/ *verb* (**rents**, **renting**, **rented**) **1** to pay to live in a place or to use something that belongs to another person: *She rents a flat in the centre of* *town.* **2** to let someone live in a place or use something that belongs to you, if they pay you: *Mrs Kamau rents out rooms to students.*

rent² 🔑 /rent/ *noun* the money that you pay to live in a place or to use something that belongs to another person: *Our rent has gone up by 1000 shillings a month.*

repair¹ 🔑 /rɪˈpeə(r)/ *verb* (**repairs, repairing, repaired** /rɪˈpeəd/) to make something that is broken good again: *Can you repair my bike?* SAME MEANING **mend**

repair² /rɪˈpeə(r)/ *noun* something you do to make something that is broken good again: *The shop is closed for repairs to the roof.*

repay /rɪˈpeɪ/ *verb* (**repays, repaying, repaid** /rɪˈpeɪd/) **1** to pay back money to someone **2** to do something for someone to show your thanks: *How can I repay you for all your help?*

repayment /rɪˈpeɪmənt/ *noun* paying someone back: *monthly repayments*

repeat 🔑 /rɪˈpiːt/ *verb* (**repeats, repeating, repeated**) **1** to say or do something again: *He didn't hear my question, so I repeated it.* **2** to say what another person has said: *Repeat this sentence after me.* ▶ **repeat** *noun* something that is done again: *There are a lot of repeats of old programmes on TV.* ➲ Look at **repetition**.

repetition /ˌrepəˈtɪʃn/ *noun* (no plural) saying or doing something again: *This book is boring – it's full of repetition.* ℹ The verb is **repeat**.

replace 🔑 /rɪˈpleɪs/ *verb* (**replaces, replacing, replaced** /rɪˈpleɪst/) **1** to put something back in the right place: *Please replace the books on the shelf when you have finished with them.* **2** to take the place of someone or something: *When Kisoso was injured, Wasike replaced him as captain of the team.* **3** to put a new or different person or thing in the place of another: *The watch was broken so the shop replaced it with a new one.*

replacement /rɪˈpleɪsmənt/ *noun* **1** (*plural* **replacements**) a new or different person or thing that takes the place of another: *Opiyo is leaving the team so we need to find a replacement.* **2** (no plural) putting a new or different person or thing in the place of another

reply¹ 🔑 /rɪˈplaɪ/ *verb* (**replies, replying, replied** /rɪˈplaɪd/) to answer: *I have written to Juma but he hasn't replied.*

reply² 🔑 /rɪˈplaɪ/ *noun* (*plural* **replies**) an answer: *I had a reply to my letter.* **in reply** as an answer: *What did you say in reply to his question?*

report¹ 🔑 /rɪˈpɔːt/ *verb* (**reports, reporting, reported**) to tell or write about something that has happened: *We reported the accident to the police.*

report² 🔑 /rɪˈpɔːt/ *noun* **1** something that someone says or writes about something that has happened: *Did you read the newspaper reports about the earthquake?* **2** something that teachers write about a student's work: *I got a good report this term.*

reported speech /rɪˌpɔːtɪd ˈspiːtʃ/ (also **indirect speech** /ˌɪndərekt ˈspiːtʃ/) *noun* (no plural) saying what someone has said rather than repeating their exact words. In **reported speech**, 'I'll come later' becomes 'He said he'd (he would) come later'. ➲ Look at **direct speech**.

reporter /rɪˈpɔːtə(r)/ *noun* a person who writes in a newspaper or speaks on the radio or television about things that have happened

represent 🔑 /ˌreprɪˈzent/ *verb* (**represents, representing, represented**) **1** to be a sign for something: *The yellow lines on the map represent roads.* **2** to speak or do something for another person or other people: *Bekele represented Ethiopia at the Olympic Games.*

representative /ˌreprɪˈzentətɪv/ *noun* a person who speaks or does something for a group of people: *There were representatives from every country in Africa at the meeting.*

reproduce /ˌriːprəˈdjuːs/ *verb* (**reproduces, reproducing, reproduced** /ˌriːprəˈdjuːst/) When animals or plants **reproduce**, they have young ones.

reproduction /ˌriːprəˈdʌkʃn/ *noun* (no plural) producing babies or young animals or plants: *We are studying plant reproduction at school.*

reptile /ˈreptaɪl/ *noun* an animal with cold blood, that lays eggs. Snakes are **reptiles**.

> ❖ **WORD BUILDING**
>
> There are many different types of reptile. Here are some of them: **crocodile, lizard, snake, tortoise.** Do you know any others?

republic /rɪˈpʌblɪk/ *noun* a country where people choose the government and the leader (the **president**): *the Republic of South Africa*

reputation /ˌrepjuˈteɪʃn/ *noun* what people think or say about someone or something: *This school has a good reputation.*

request[1] /rɪˈkwest/ *verb* (**requests, requesting, requested**) to ask for something: *Passengers are requested not to bring hot drinks onto the bus.* ❶ It is more usual to say **ask (for)**.

request[2] /rɪˈkwest/ *noun* asking for something: *They made a request for money.*

require /rɪˈkwaɪə(r)/ *verb* (**requires, requiring, required** /rɪˈkwaɪəd/) to need something: *Do you require anything else?*

❖ **SPEAKING**

Need is the word that we usually use.

requirement /rɪˈkwaɪəmənt/ *noun* something that you need

requisition /ˌrekwɪˈzɪʃn/ *noun* an official written request for something: *a requisition form/order*

rescue[1] /ˈreskjuː/ *verb* (**rescues, rescuing, rescued**) to save someone or something from danger: *She rescued the child when he fell in the river.*

rescue[2] /ˈreskjuː/ *noun*
come or **go to someone's rescue** to try to help someone: *The police came to his rescue.*

research[1] /rɪˈsɜːtʃ/ *noun* (no plural) studying something carefully to find out more about it: *scientific research*

research[2] /rɪˈsɜːtʃ/ *verb* (**researches, researching, researched** /rɪˈsɜːtʃt/) to study something carefully to find out more about it: *Scientists are researching the causes of the disease.*

resemblance /rɪˈzembləns/ *noun* looking like someone or something: *There's no resemblance between my two brothers.*

resemble /rɪˈzembl/ *verb* (**resembles, resembling, resembled** /rɪˈzembld/) to look like someone or something: *Achal resembles her mother.* ❶ It is more usual to say **look like**.

resent /rɪˈzent/ *verb* (**resents, resenting, resented**) to feel angry about something because it is not fair: *Bigogo resented being treated like a baby.*

resentment /rɪˈzentmənt/ *noun* (no plural) a feeling of anger about something that is not fair

reservation /ˌrezəˈveɪʃn/ *noun* a room, seat or another thing that you have reserved: *He phoned the restaurant to make a reservation.*

reserve[1] /rɪˈzɜːv/ *verb* (**reserves, reserving, reserved** /rɪˈzɜːvd/) to ask someone to keep something for you to use at a later time: *I would like to reserve a single room for tomorrow night, please.*

reserve[2] /rɪˈzɜːv/ *noun* **1** something that you keep to use later: *reserves of food* **2** a person who will play in a game if another person cannot play **3** an area of land where the animals or plants are protected: *a game reserve*
in reserve for using later: *Don't spend all the money – keep some in reserve.*

reservoir /ˈrezəvwɑː(r)/ *noun* a big lake where a town or city keeps water to use later ➲ Picture at **dam**.

residence /ˈrezɪdəns/ *noun* **1** (no plural) living in a place: *Some birds have taken up residence in* (= started to live in) *our roof.* **2** (*plural* **residences**) the place where an important or famous person lives: *the Prime Minister's residence*

resident /ˈrezɪdənt/ *noun* a person who lives in a place

resign /rɪˈzaɪn/ *verb* (**resigns, resigning, resigned** /rɪˈzaɪnd/) to leave a job: *The director has resigned.*
resign yourself to something to accept something that you do not like: *There were a lot of people at the doctor's so Egesa resigned himself to a long wait.*

resignation /ˌrezɪɡˈneɪʃn/ *noun* saying that you want to leave your job
hand in your resignation to tell the person you work for that you are going to leave your job

resist /rɪˈzɪst/ *verb* (**resists, resisting, resisted**) **1** to fight against someone or something; to try to stop someone or something: *If he has a gun, don't try to resist.* **2** to refuse to do or have something that you want to do or have: *I can't resist sweets.*

resistance /rɪˈzɪstəns/ *noun* (no plural) when people try to stop something happening; fighting against someone or something: *There was a lot of resistance to the plan to build a new dam.*

resistant /rɪˈzɪstənt/ *adjective* **1** not harmed or affected by something: *We need plants that are resistant to disease.* **2** not wanting something and trying to stop it happening: *Older people can be resistant to change.*

resolution /ˌrezəˈluːʃn/ *noun* **1** (*plural* **resolutions**) something that you decide to do: *Tanei made a resolution to help her mother more often.* **2** (no plural) the act of solving a problem: *Leaders trained in conflict resolution worked to make peace between the groups.*

resort[1] /rɪˈzɔːt/ *noun* a place where a lot of people go on holiday: *Malindi is a popular tourist resort.*
last resort the only person or thing left that can help: *Nobody else will lend me the money; you are my last resort.*

resort[2] /rɪˈzɔːt/ *verb* (**resorts, resorting, resorted**)
resort to something to do the only thing you can to help you get what you want: *The workers finally resorted to a strike to get better pay.*

resources /rɪˈsɔːsɪz/ *noun* (plural) things that a person or a country has and can use: *Oil is one of our most important natural resources.*

respect[1] 🔑 /rɪˈspekt/ *noun* (no plural) **1** thinking that someone is very good or clever: *I have a lot of respect for your father.* **2** being polite to someone: *You should treat old people with respect.*

respect[2] 🔑 /rɪˈspekt/ *verb* (**respects, respecting, respected**) to think that someone is good or clever: *The students respect their teacher.*

respectable /rɪˈspektəbl/ *adjective* If a person or thing is **respectable**, people think they are good or correct: *She comes from a respectable family.*

respectful /rɪˈspektfl/ *adjective* If you are **respectful**, you are polite to other people: *They are always respectful to their teachers.*

respond /rɪˈspɒnd/ *verb* (**responds, responding, responded**) to do or say something to answer someone or something: *I said 'hello' and he responded by smiling.*

respondent /rɪˈspɒndənt/ (also **defendant**) *noun* (in a court of law) a person who is said to have done something wrong SAME MEANING **ACCUSED**

response /rɪˈspɒns/ *noun* an answer to someone or something: *I wrote to them but I've had no response.*

responsibility 🔑 /rɪˌspɒnsəˈbɪləti/ *noun* **1** (no plural) having to look after someone or something, so that it is your fault if something goes wrong: *She has responsibility for the whole team.* **2** (*plural* **responsibilities**) something that you must do; someone or something that you must look after: *Fixing the engine is my brother's responsibility.*

responsible 🔑 /rɪˈspɒnsəbl/ *adjective* **1** If you are responsible for someone or something, you must look after them: *The driver is responsible for the lives of the people on the bus.* **2** A responsible person is someone that you can trust: *They need a responsible person to look after their son.* OPPOSITE **irresponsible**
be responsible for something to be the person who made something bad happen: *Who was responsible for the accident?*

rest[1] 🔑 /rest/ *verb* (**rests, resting, rested**) **1** to sleep or be still and quiet: *We ran two miles and then rested for a while.* **2** to be on something; to put something on or against another thing: *His arms were resting on the table.*

rest[2] 🔑 /rest/ *noun* **1 the rest** (no plural) what is there when a part has gone: *If you don't want the rest, I'll eat it.* ◇ *I liked the beginning, but the rest of the film wasn't very good.* **2 the rest** (no plural) the other people or things: *My sisters prepared the food and the rest of us went for a walk.* **3** (*plural* **rests**) a time when you are sleeping or being still and quiet: *Let's stop here for a rest.*

restaurant 🔑 /ˈrestrɒnt/ *noun* a place where you buy a meal and eat it

rest house /ˈrest haʊs/ *noun* a house that you can pay to stay in when you are travelling

restless /ˈrestləs/ *adjective* not able to be still: *The children always get restless on long journeys.*

restore /rɪˈstɔː(r)/ *verb* (**restores, restoring, restored** /rɪˈstɔːd/) to make something as good as it was before: *The old church was restored.*

restrain /rɪˈstreɪn/ *verb* (**restrains, restraining, restrained** /rɪˈstreɪnd/)

to stop someone or something from doing something; to control someone or something: *I couldn't restrain my anger.*

restrict /rɪˈstrɪkt/ *verb* (**restricts, restricting, restricted**) to allow only a certain amount, size, sort, etc: *The government has restricted the number of immigrants entering the country.*

restriction /rɪˈstrɪkʃn/ *noun* a rule to control someone or something: *There are parking restrictions in the city centre.*

result[1] /rɪˈzʌlt/ *noun* **1** what happens because something else has happened: *The accident was a result of bad driving.* **2** the score or mark at the end of a game, competition or exam: *football results* ◇ *When will you know your exam results?*
as a result because of something: *I got up late, and as a result I missed the bus.*

result[2] /rɪˈzʌlt/ *verb* (**results, resulting, resulted**)
result in something to make something happen: *The accident resulted in the death of two drivers.*

the Resurrection /ðə ˌrezəˈrekʃn/ *noun* (no plural) (in the Christian religion) when Jesus Christ came back to life

retail /ˈriːteɪl/ *noun* (no plural) selling goods to people in shops: *He works in retail.* ➲ Look at **wholesale**. ▶ **retailer** *noun* a person who sells goods to people in shops

retire /rɪˈtaɪə(r)/ *verb* (**retires, retiring, retired** /rɪˈtaɪəd/) to stop working because you are a certain age: *My grandfather retired when he was 55.* ▶ **retired** /rɪˈtaɪəd/ *adjective*: *a retired teacher*

retirement /rɪˈtaɪəmənt/ *noun* (no plural) the time when a person stops working because they are a certain age: *What is the retirement age in your country?*

retreat /rɪˈtriːt/ *verb* (**retreats, retreating, retreated**) to move back or away from someone or something, for example because you have lost a fight: *The enemy is retreating.* ▶ **retreat** *noun*: *The army is now in retreat.*

return[1] /rɪˈtɜːn/ *verb* (**returns, returning, returned** /rɪˈtɜːnd/) **1** to come or go back to a place: *They returned from Kabale last week.* **2** to give, put, send or take something back: *Will you return this book to the library?*

return[2] /rɪˈtɜːn/ *noun* **1** (no plural) coming or going back to a place: *A big crowd welcomed the team at the airport on their return home.* **2** (no plural) giving, putting, sending or taking something back: *the return of the stolen money* **3** (*plural* **returns**) (also **return ticket** /rɪˌtɜːn ˈtɪkɪt/) a ticket to travel to a place and back again: *A return to Arusha, please.* ➲ Look at **single**[2].
in return If you do something in return for something else, you do it because someone has helped you or given you something: *We have bought you a present in return for all your help.*

returns /rɪˈtɜːnz/ *noun* (plural)
many happy returns words that you say on someone's birthday

reunion /ˌriːˈjuːniən/ *noun* a meeting of people who have not seen each other for a long time: *We had a family reunion on my grandfather's birthday.*

reuse /ˌriːˈjuːz/ *verb* (**reuses, reusing, reused** /ˌriːˈjuːzd/) to use something again: *Please reuse your envelopes.*

reveal /rɪˈviːl/ *verb* (**reveals, revealing, revealed** /rɪˈviːld/) to tell something that was a secret or show something that was hidden: *She refused to reveal any names to the police.*

revenge /rɪˈvendʒ/ *noun* (no plural)
get, have or **take revenge on someone** to do something bad to someone who has done something to you that makes you angry, unhappy, etc: *He plans to take revenge on the boy who hurt him.*

reverse[1] /rɪˈvɜːs/ *verb* (**reverses, reversing, reversed** /rɪˈvɜːst/) **1** to make a car, etc. go backwards: *He reversed the car into the garage.* **2** to turn something the other way round: *Writing is reversed in a mirror.*
reverse the charges to make a telephone call that the person you are calling will pay for

reverse[2] /rɪˈvɜːs/ *noun* (no plural) the opposite thing or way
in reverse in the opposite way; starting at the end and finishing at the beginning: *I wrote the story in reverse – I thought of the ending first and worked backwards.*

review[1] /rɪˈvjuː/ *noun* **1** a piece of writing in a newspaper or magazine that says what someone thinks about a book, film, play, etc: *The film got very good reviews.* **2** thinking again about something that happened before: *a review of all the main events of the year*

review² /rɪ'vjuː/ *verb* (**reviews**, **reviewing**, **reviewed** /rɪ'vjuːd/) **1** to write about a book, film, play, etc. and say what you think **2** to think again about something that happened before: *Let's review what we have learnt so far.*

revise /rɪ'vaɪz/ *verb* (**revises**, **revising**, **revised** /rɪ'vaɪzd/) **1** to study again something that you have learnt, especially before an exam: *I'm revising for the English test.* **2** to change something to make it better or more correct: *The book was revised.*

revision /rɪ'vɪʒn/ *noun* (no plural) studying again something that you have learnt, before an exam: *I haven't done any revision for the maths exam.*

revive /rɪ'vaɪv/ *verb* (**revives**, **reviving**, **revived** /rɪ'vaɪvd/) to become or make someone or something well or strong again: *They pulled the boy out of the river and tried to revive him, but he was dead.*

revolt /rɪ'vəʊlt/ *verb* (**revolts**, **revolting**, **revolted**) to fight against the people in control: *The army is revolting against the government.* ▶ **revolt** *noun* when people fight against the people in control ➲ Look at **revolution**.

revolting /rɪ'vəʊltɪŋ/ *adjective* very unpleasant; so bad that it makes you feel sick: *a revolting smell* SAME MEANING **horrible**, **disgusting**

revolution /ˌrevə'luːʃn/ *noun* **1** a fight by people against their government, to put a new government in its place: *The French Revolution was in 1789.* ⓘ The verb is **revolt**. **2** a big change in the way of doing things: *the Industrial Revolution*

reward¹ /rɪ'wɔːd/ *noun* a present or money that you give to someone because they have done something good or worked hard: *Our teacher is offering a small reward to anyone who finds her purse.*

reward² /rɪ'wɔːd/ *verb* (**rewards**, **rewarding**, **rewarded**) to give something to someone because they have done something good or worked hard: *Juma's parents bought him a bike to reward him for passing his exam.*

rewind /riː'waɪnd/ *verb* (**rewinds**, **rewinding**, **rewound** /riː'waʊnd/, **has rewound**) to make something such as a film or a tape (in a **tape recorder** or **video recorder**) go backwards: *Rewind the tape and play it again.*

rhinoceros /raɪ'nɒsərəs/ *noun* (*plural* **rhinoceros** *or* **rhinoceroses**)

> ❖ **PRONUNCIATION**
>
> We do not say the 'h' in words that begin with **rh**. For example, **rhyme** sounds like **time**.

a big wild animal with thick skin and a horn on its nose that lives in Africa and Asia ⓘ The short form is **rhino**. /'raɪnəʊ/

rhyme¹ /raɪm/ *noun* **1** when two words have the same sound, for example 'bell' and 'well': *Her poetry is written in rhyme.* **2** a short piece of writing where the lines end with the same sounds

rhyme² /raɪm/ *verb* (**rhymes**, **rhyming**, **rhymed** /raɪmd/) **1** to have the same sound as another word: *'Moon' rhymes with 'spoon' and 'chair' rhymes with 'bear'.* **2** to have lines that end with the same sounds: *This poem doesn't rhyme.*

rhythm /'rɪðəm/ *noun* a regular pattern of sounds that come again and again: *This music has a good rhythm.*

rib /rɪb/ *noun* one of the bones around your chest ➲ picture on page A13

ribbon /'rɪbən/ *noun* a long thin piece of pretty material for tying things: *She wore a pink ribbon in her hair.*

ribbon
bow
ribbon

rice ⚷ /raɪs/ *noun* (no plural) white or brown seeds from a plant that grows in hot countries, that we use as food: *Would you like rice or potatoes with your chicken?* ◇ *East Africa imports some rice from other countries.*

rich 🔑 /rɪtʃ/ *adjective* (**richer**, **richest**) **1** with a lot of money: *a rich family* OPPOSITE **poor** **2** with a lot of something: *Saudi Arabia is rich in oil.* **3** Food that is rich has a lot of fat or sugar in it: *a rich chocolate cake* ▶ **the rich** *noun* (plural) people who have a lot of money

rid 🔑 /rɪd/ *verb* **get rid of someone** or **something** to throw something away or become free of someone or something: *I got rid of my old coat and bought a new one.* ◇ *This dog is following me – I can't get rid of it.*

riddle /ˈrɪdl/ *noun* a question that has a clever or funny answer: *Here's a riddle: What has four legs but can't walk? The answer is a chair!*

ride[1] 🔑 /raɪd/ *verb* (**rides**, **riding**, **rode** /rəʊd/, **has ridden** /ˈrɪdn/) **1** to sit on a horse or bicycle and control it as it moves: *My brother taught me to ride a bike.* **2** to travel in a car, bus or train: *We rode in the back of the car.*

> ❖ **WORD BUILDING**
>
> When you control a car, bus or train, you **drive** it.

ride[2] 🔑 /raɪd/ *noun* a journey on a horse or bicycle, or in a car, bus or train: *We went for a ride on our bikes.* ◇ *a train ride*

rider /ˈraɪdə(r)/ *noun* a person who rides a horse or bicycle

ridge /rɪdʒ/ *noun* a long thin part of something that is higher than the rest, for example along the top of hills or mountains: *We walked along the ridge looking down at the valley below.*

ridiculous /rɪˈdɪkjələs/ *adjective* so silly that it makes people laugh: *You can't play football with a coconut – that's ridiculous!*

riding /ˈraɪdɪŋ/ *noun* (no plural) the sport of riding a horse

rifle /ˈraɪfl/ *noun* a long gun that you hold against your shoulder when you fire it

rift /rɪft/ *noun* a very large opening in the ground

rift valley /ˈrɪft væli/ *noun* a valley with steep sides formed when two breaks develop in the earth's surface and the land between them sinks: *Africa's Great Rift Valley is divided into three parts.*

right[1] 🔑 /raɪt/ *adjective* **1** correct or true: *That's not the right answer.* ◇ *'Are you Mr Kamotho?' 'Yes, that's right.'* OPPOSITE **wrong** **2** good; fair or what the law allows: *It's not right to leave young children alone in the house.* OPPOSITE **wrong** **3** best: *Is she the right person to ask for help?* OPPOSITE **wrong** **4** opposite of left: *Most people write with their right hand.*

right[2] 🔑 /raɪt/ *adverb* **1** correctly: *Have I spelt your name right?* OPPOSITE **wrong** ➲ Look at **rightly**. **2** exactly: *He was sitting right next to me.* **3** all the way: *Go right to the end of the road.* **4** immediately: *We left right after dinner.* **5** to the right side: *Turn right at the end of the street.* OPPOSITE **left** **right away** immediately; now: *Fetch the doctor right away!*

right[3] 🔑 /raɪt/ *noun* **1** (no plural) what is good or fair: *Young children have to learn the difference between right and wrong.* OPPOSITE **wrong** **2** (*plural* **rights**) what you are allowed to do, especially by law: *In Kenya, everyone has the right to vote at 18.* **3** (no plural) the right side or direction: *We live in the first house on the right.* OPPOSITE **left**

right[4] /raɪt/ **1** yes, I agree; yes, I will: *'I'll see you tomorrow.' 'Right.'* **2** You say 'right' to make someone listen to you: *Are you ready? Right, let's go.*

right angle /ˈraɪt æŋgl/ *noun* an angle of 90 degrees. A square has four **right angles**. ➲ Picture at **angle**.

right-click /ˌraɪt ˈklɪk/ *verb* (**right-clicks**, **right-clicking**, **right-clicked** /ˌraɪt ˈklɪkt/) to press the button on the right on a computer mouse: *You need to right-click on the 'My Computer' icon.*

right-hand /ˈraɪt hænd/ *adjective* of or on the right: *The shop is on the right-hand side of the road.*

right-handed /ˌraɪt ˈhændɪd/ *adjective* If you are **right-handed**, you use your right hand more easily than your left hand.

rightly /ˈraɪtli/ *adverb* correctly: *If I remember rightly, I arrived there in May.*

rigid /ˈrɪdʒɪd/ *adjective* **1** hard and not easy to bend or move **2** not able to be changed; strict: *My school has very rigid rules.*

rim /rɪm/ *noun* the edge of something round: *the rim of a cup*

rind /raɪnd/ *noun* the thick hard skin of some fruits, or of cheese or some types of meat: *lemon rind*

ring¹ 🔑 /rɪŋ/ *noun* **1** piece of jewellery that you wear on your finger: *a wedding ring* **2** a circle: *Please stand in a ring.* **3** a space with seats around it for a competition, performance, etc: *The boxers came into the ring.* **4** the sound that a bell makes: *There was a ring at the door.*

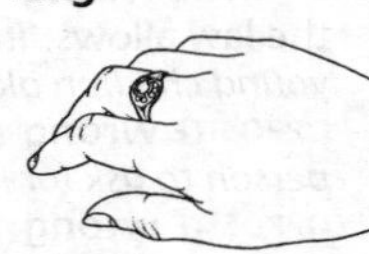
ring

give someone a ring to telephone someone: *I'll give you a ring later.*

ring² 🔑 /rɪŋ/ *verb* (**rings, ringing, rang** /ræŋ/, **has rung** /rʌŋ/) **1** to make a sound like a bell: *The telephone is ringing.* **2** to press or move a bell so that it makes a sound: *We rang the bell again but nobody answered.* **3** to telephone someone: *I'll ring you on Sunday.*

ring back to telephone someone again: *Achal isn't here now — can you ring back later?*

ring up to telephone someone: *Your brother rang up while you were out.*

rinse /rɪns/ *verb* (**rinses, rinsing, rinsed** /rɪnst/) to wash something with water to take away dirt or soap: *Wash your hair and rinse it well.*

riot /ˈraɪət/ *noun* when a group of people fight and make a lot of noise and trouble: *There were riots in the streets after the football match.* ▶ **riot** *verb* (**riots, rioting, rioted**): *The prisoners are rioting.*

rip /rɪp/ *verb* (**rips, ripping, ripped** /rɪpt/) to pull or tear in a rough, quick way: *I ripped my shirt on a nail.* ◇ *Ali ripped the letter open.*

rip up to tear something into small pieces: *She ripped the photo up.*

ripe /raɪp/ *adjective* (**riper, ripest**) Fruit that is **ripe** is ready to eat: *These melons aren't ripe – they're still hard.*

rise¹ 🔑 /raɪz/ *verb* (**rises, rising, rose** /rəʊz/, **has risen** /ˈrɪzn/) **1** to go up; to become higher or more: *Prices are rising.* OPPOSITE **fall** **2** If the sun or the moon rises, it moves up in the sky: *The sun rises in the east and sets* (= goes down) *in the west.* OPPOSITE **set**

rise² 🔑 /raɪz/ *noun* becoming higher or more: *a rise in the price of oil* ◇ *a pay rise*

risk¹ 🔑 /rɪsk/ *noun* the possibility that something bad may happen; danger: *Do you think there's any risk of a landslide?*

at risk in danger: *Children are at risk from this disease.*

take a risk or **risks** to do something when it is possible that something bad may happen because of it: *Don't take risks when you're riding a bicycle.*

risk² 🔑 /rɪsk/ *verb* (**risks, risking, risked** /rɪskt/) **1** to put someone or something in danger: *He risked his life to save the child from the burning house.* **2** to do something when there is a possibility that something bad may happen because of it: *If you don't work harder, you risk failing the exam.*

risky /ˈrɪski/ *adjective* (**riskier, riskiest**) dangerous

rival /ˈraɪvl/ *noun* a person who wants to do better than you or who is trying to take what you want: *Moraa and Awino are rivals for the prize.*

river 🔑 /ˈrɪvə(r)/ *noun* a long wide line of water that flows into the sea: *the River Nile*

riverbank /ˈrɪvəbæŋk/ *noun* the ground at the side of a river: *We stood on the riverbank, watching the boats.*

road 🔑 /rəʊd/ *noun* the way from one place to another, where cars can go: *Is this the road to Nakuru?* ◇ *The hotel is on Kamati Road.* ℹ The short way of writing 'Road' in addresses is **Rd**.

by road in a car, bus, etc: *It's a long journey by road – the train is faster.*

roadworks /ˈrəʊdwɜːks/ *noun* (plural) repairing or building roads

roam /rəʊm/ *verb* (**roams, roaming, roamed** /rəʊmd/) to walk or travel with no special plan: *Dogs were roaming the streets looking for food.*

roar¹ /rɔː(r)/ *verb* (**roars, roaring, roared** /rɔːd/) to make a loud deep sound: *The lion roared.* ◇ *Everybody roared with laughter.*

roar² /rɔː(r)/ *noun* a loud deep sound: *the roar of a plane's engines*

roast /rəʊst/ *verb* (**roasts, roasting, roasted**) to cook or be cooked in an oven or over a fire: *Roast the chicken in a hot oven.* ▶ **roast** *adjective*: *roast chicken*

rob 🔑 /rɒb/ *verb* (**robs, robbing, robbed** /rɒbd/) to take something that is not yours from a person or place: *They robbed a bank.* ➲ Note at **steal**.

robber /ˈrɒbə(r)/ *noun* a person who robs ➲ Note at **thief**.

robbery /ˈrɒbəri/ *noun* (*plural* **robberies**) taking something that is not yours from a bank, etc: *What time did the robbery take place?*

robot /ˈrəʊbɒt/ *noun* a machine that can work like a person: *This car was built by robots.*

rock¹ 🔑 /rɒk/ *noun* **1** (no plural) the very hard stuff that is in the ground and in mountains: *They drilled through the rock.* **2** (*plural* **rocks**) a big piece of this: *The ship hit the rocks.* **3** (also **rock music**) (no plural) a sort of modern music: *a rock concert*

rock² /rɒk/ *verb* (**rocks**, **rocking**, **rocked** /rɒkt/) to move slowly backwards and forwards or from side to side; to make someone or something do this: *The boat was rocking gently on the lake.* ◇ *I rocked the baby until she went to sleep.*

rocket /ˈrɒkɪt/ *noun* **1** an engine with long round sides that pushes up a vehicle that travels into space (a **spacecraft**) **2** a thing with long round sides that carries a bomb through the air **3** a **firework** that goes up into the air and then explodes

rock music /ˈrɒk mjuːzɪk/ = **rock¹**

rocky /ˈrɒki/ *adjective* (**rockier**, **rockiest**) with a lot of rocks: *a rocky path*

rod /rɒd/ *noun* a thin straight piece of wood or metal: *a fishing rod*

rode *form of* RIDE¹

role 🔑 /rəʊl/ *noun* **1** the person you are in a play or film: *The role of the king was played by Wasike Kamau.* **2** what a person does: *Your role is to tell other people what to do.*

roll¹ 🔑 /rəʊl/ *verb* (**rolls**, **rolling**, **rolled** /rəʊld/) **1** to move along, turning over and over; to make something go over and over: *The pencil rolled off the table on to the floor.* ◇ *We rolled the rock down the path.* **2** to move on wheels: *The car rolled down the hill.* **3** to make something flat by moving something heavy on top of it: *Roll the dough into a large circle.*

roll over to turn your body a different way when you are lying down: *She rolled over and went to sleep.*

roll up to make something into a long round shape or the shape of a ball: *Can you help me to roll up this carpet?*

roll² 🔑 /rəʊl/ *noun* something made into a long round shape by rolling it around itself many times: *a roll of material*

roll

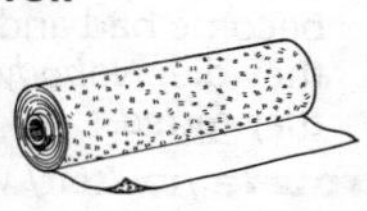

Rollerblade™ /ˈrəʊləbleɪd/ *noun* a boot with one row of narrow wheels on the bottom: *a pair of Rollerblades*

roller skate /ˈrəʊlə skeɪt/ *noun* a shoe with wheels on the bottom, for moving quickly on smooth ground ➲ Picture at **skate¹**. ▶ **roller skating** /ˈrəʊlə skeɪtɪŋ/ *noun* (no plural) moving on **roller skates**

Roman Catholic /ˌrəʊmən ˈkæθəlɪk/ (also **Catholic**) *noun* a member of the Christian Church that follows the Pope

romance /rəʊˈmæns/ *noun* **1** a time when two people are in love: *a romance between a doctor and a nurse* **2** a story about love: *She writes romances.*

romantic 🔑 /rəʊˈmæntɪk/ *adjective* about love; full of feelings of love: *a romantic film*

roof 🔑 /ruːf/ *noun* (*plural* **roofs**) the top of a building or car, that covers it

room 🔑 /ruːm/ *noun* **1** (*plural* **rooms**) one of the spaces with walls round it in a building: *How many rooms are there in the hotel?* ◇ *a classroom*

> ❖ **WORD BUILDING**
>
> A house or flat can have a **living room** (or **sitting room** or **lounge**), **bedrooms**, a **bathroom**, a **toilet**, a **kitchen**, and perhaps a **dining room**.

2 (no plural) space; enough space: *There's no room for you in the car.*

root 🔑 /ruːt/ *noun* the part of a plant that is under the ground: *the roots of a tree* ➲ Picture at **plant¹**.

rope 🔑 /rəʊp/ *noun* very thick strong string: *The rope broke and she fell.*

rope

rose¹ *form of* RISE¹

rose² /rəʊz/ *noun* a flower with a very sweet smell. It grows on a bush that has sharp points (called **thorns**) on it.

rosy /ˈrəʊzi/ *adjective* (**rosier**, **rosiest**) pink: *rosy cheeks*

rot /rɒt/ *verb* (**rots, rotting, rotted**) to become bad and soft, as things do when they die: *Nobody picked the mangoes so they rotted.*

rotate /rəʊˈteɪt/ *verb* (**rotates, rotating, rotated**) to move in circles: *The earth rotates around the sun.*

rotten /ˈrɒtn/ *adjective* old and not fresh; bad: *Rotten eggs smell horrible!*

rough 🔑 /rʌf/ *adjective* (**rougher, roughest**)

❖ **PRONUNCIATION**

Rough sounds like **stuff**.

1 not smooth or flat: *It was difficult to walk on the rough ground.* **2** not gentle or calm: *rough seas* **3** not exactly correct; made or done quickly: *Can you give me a rough idea how much it will cost?* ◇ *a rough drawing*

roughly /ˈrʌfli/ *adverb* **1** not gently: *He pushed me roughly away.* **2** about; not exactly: *The school will take roughly six months to build.*

round[1] 🔑 /raʊnd/ *adjective* **1** with the shape of a circle or a ball: *a round plate* **2** A **round** number is a whole number, especially one that ends in 0: *Forty is a round number.*

round[2] 🔑 /raʊnd/ *adverb, preposition* **1** on or to all sides of something, often in a circle: *The earth moves round the sun.* ◇ *We sat round the table.* ◇ *He tied a rope round the goat's neck.* **2** in the opposite direction or in another direction: *I turned round and went home again.* ◇ *Turn your chair round.* **3** in or to different parts of a place: *I'd like to travel round the whole of Africa one day.* **4** from one person to another: *Pass these papers round the class.* **5** to someone's house: *Come round* (= to my house) *at eight o'clock.* **6** to or on the other side of something: *There's a bank just round the corner.*

go round to be enough for everybody: *Are there enough plates to go round?*

round about nearly; not exactly: *It will cost round about 10 000 shillings.*

round and round round many times: *The bird flew round and round the room.*

round[3] /raʊnd/ *noun* **1** a lot of visits, one after another, for example as part of someone's job: *The doctor started his round early, visiting every patient in the hospital.* **2** one part of a game or competition: *the third round of the boxing match*

roundabout

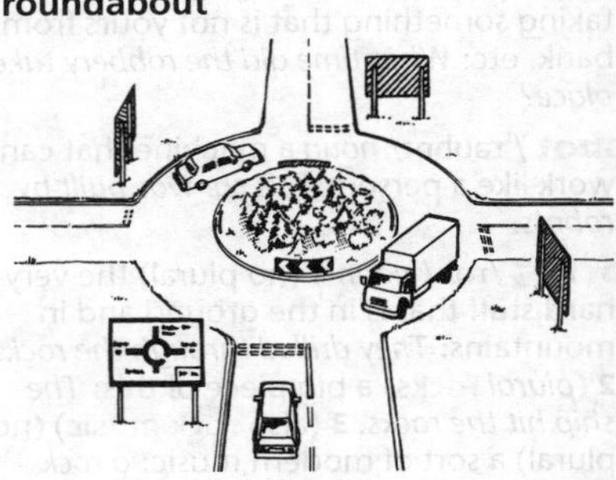

roundabout /ˈraʊndəbaʊt/ *noun* a place where roads meet, where cars must drive round a circle

round trip /ˌraʊnd ˈtrɪp/ *noun* a journey to a place and back again

roundworm /ˈraʊndwɜːm/ *noun* a kind of **worm** that lives inside the bodies of people and pigs

route 🔑 /ruːt/ *noun* a way from one place to another: *What is the quickest route from Kisumu to Kitale?*

routine /ruːˈtiːn/ *noun* your usual way of doing things: *My morning routine is to get up at seven, have breakfast, then go to school.*

row[1] 🔑 /rəʊ/ *noun*

❖ **PRONUNCIATION**

In this meaning, **row** sounds like **go**.

a line of people or things: *We sat in the front row of the class* (= the front line of seats). ◇ *a row of houses* ➲ picture on page A14

row[2] /rəʊ/ *verb* (**rows, rowing, rowed** /rəʊd/)

❖ **PRONUNCIATION**

In this meaning, **row** sounds like **go**.

to move a boat through water using long pieces of wood with flat ends (called **oars**): *We rowed across the lake.* ➲ Picture at **rowing boat**.

row[3] /raʊ/ *noun*

❖ **PRONUNCIATION**

In this meaning, **row** sounds like **now**.

1 (*plural* **rows**) a noisy argument between people who do not agree about something: *She had a row with her neighbour.* **2** (no plural) a loud noise: *The children were making a terrible row.*

rowing boat

rowing boat /ˈrəʊɪŋ bəʊt/ *noun* a small boat that you move through water using **oars** (= long pieces of wood with flat ends)

royal 🔑 /ˈrɔɪəl/ *adjective* of or about a king or queen: *the royal family*

royalty /ˈrɔɪəlti/ *noun* (no plural) kings, queens and their families

rub 🔑 /rʌb/ *verb* (**rubs**, **rubbing**, **rubbed** /rʌbd/) to move something backwards and forwards on another thing: *I rubbed my hands together to keep them warm.* ◇ *The cat rubbed its head against my leg.*
rub out to take writing or marks off something by using a rubber or a cloth: *I rubbed the word out and wrote it again.*
▸ **rub** *noun* (no plural): *Give your shoes a rub.*

rubber 🔑 /ˈrʌbə(r)/ *noun* **1** (no plural) material that we use to make things like car tyres: *They bounced a rubber ball.* **2** (*plural* **rubbers**) (also **eraser**) a small piece of rubber that you use for taking away marks that you have made with a pencil: *Use a rubber to rub out any mistakes.*

rubber band /ˌrʌbə ˈbænd/ *noun* a thin circle of rubber that you use for holding things together

rubbish 🔑 /ˈrʌbɪʃ/ *noun* (no plural) **1** things that you do not want any more: *old boxes, bottles and other rubbish* ◇ *Throw this rubbish in the bin.* **2** something that is bad, stupid or wrong: *You're talking rubbish!*

rucksack /ˈrʌksæk/ *noun* a bag that you carry on your back, for example when you are walking or climbing

rucksack

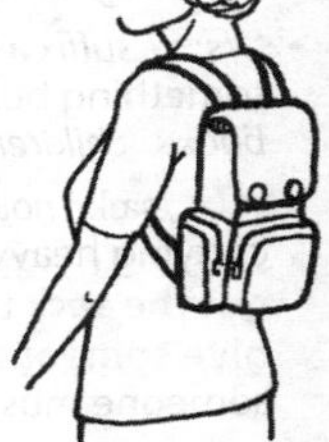

rudder /ˈrʌdə(r)/ *noun* a flat piece of wood or metal at the back of a boat or a plane. It moves to make the boat or plane go left or right.

rude 🔑 /ruːd/ *adjective* (**ruder**, **rudest**) **1** not polite: *It's rude to walk away when someone is talking to you.* **2** connected with sex, using the toilet, etc. in a way that might upset people: *rude words*
▸ **rudely** *adverb*: *'Shut up!' she said rudely.*

rug /rʌg/ *noun* **1** a small piece of thick material that you put on the floor **2** a thick piece of material that you put round your body to keep you warm

rug

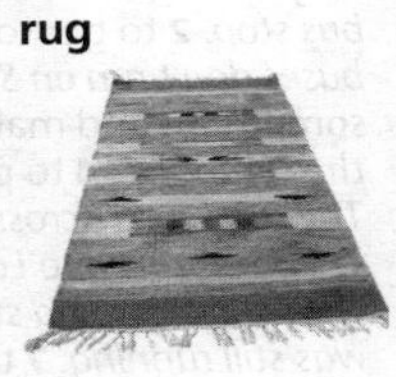

rugby /ˈrʌgbi/ *noun* (no plural) a game like football for two teams of 13 or 15 players. In **rugby**, you can kick and carry the ball.

ruin¹ 🔑 /ˈruːɪn/ *verb* (**ruins**, **ruining**, **ruined** /ˈruːɪnd/) to damage something badly so that it is no longer good; to destroy something completely: *I spilled coffee on my jacket and ruined it.* ◇ *The bad news ruined my day.*

ruin² /ˈruːɪn/ *noun* a building that has been badly damaged: *The old building is now a ruin.*
in ruins badly damaged or destroyed: *The city was in ruins after the war.*

rule¹ 🔑 /ruːl/ *noun* **1** (*plural* **rules**) something that tells you what you must or must not do: *It's against the rules to talk during an exam.* ◇ *break the rules* (= do something that you should not do) **2** (no plural) government: *India was once under British rule.*

rule² 🔑 /ruːl/ *verb* (**rules**, **ruling**, **ruled** /ruːld/) to control a country: *King John ruled England for 11 years.*

ruler /ˈruːlə(r)/ *noun* **1** a long piece of plastic, metal or wood that you use for drawing straight lines or for measuring things **2** a person who rules a country

ruler

ruling /ˈruːlɪŋ/ *noun* an official decision that an important person or group makes: *The judge will make a ruling on the case next week.*

rumble /ˈrʌmbl/ *verb* (**rumbles**, **rumbling**, **rumbled** /ˈrʌmbld/) to make a long deep sound: *I'm so hungry that my stomach is rumbling.* ▸ **rumble** *noun* (no plural): *the rumble of thunder*

rumour /ˈruːmə(r)/ *noun* something that a lot of people are talking about that is perhaps not true: *There's a rumour that our teacher is leaving.*

run¹ 🔑 /rʌn/ *verb* (**runs, running, ran** /ræn/, **has run**) **1** to move very quickly on your legs: *I was late, so I ran to the bus stop.* **2** to go; to make a journey: *The buses don't run on Sundays.* **3** to control something and make it work: *Who runs the company?* **4** to pass or go somewhere: *The road runs across the fields.* **5** to flow: *The river runs into Lake Victoria.* **6** to work: *The car had stopped but the engine was still running.* **7** to move something somewhere: *He ran a comb through his hair.*

run after someone or **something** to try to catch someone or something: *The children ran after the ball.*

run away to go quickly away from a place: *He ran away from home when he was 14.*

run out to come to an end: *My passport runs out next month.* SAME MEANING **expire**

run out of something to have no more of something: *We've run out of tea. Will you go and buy some?*

run over someone or **something** to drive over someone or something: *The dog was run over by a bus.*

> ❖ **WORD FAMILY**
>
> **run** *verb*, **run** *noun*
> **runner** **running**

run² 🔑 /rʌn/ *noun* moving very quickly on your legs: *I go for a run every morning.*

rung¹ *form of* RING²

rung² /rʌŋ/ *noun* one of the steps of a **ladder** (= a piece of equipment that helps you climb up something) ➲ Picture at **ladder**.

runner /ˈrʌnə(r)/ *noun* a person who runs

runner-up /ˌrʌnər ˈʌp/ *noun* (*plural* **runners-up** /ˌrʌnəz ˈʌp/) a person or team that comes second in a race or competition

running¹ /ˈrʌnɪŋ/ *noun* (no plural) the sport of running: *running shoes*

running² /ˈrʌnɪŋ/ *adjective* one after another: *We won the competition for three years running.*

runway /ˈrʌnweɪ/ *noun* (*plural* **runways**) a long hard piece of ground where planes take off and land

rural /ˈrʊərəl/ *adjective* of the country, not the town: *The book is about life in rural Kenya.*

rush¹ 🔑 /rʌʃ/ *verb* (**rushes, rushing, rushed** /rʌʃt/) **1** to go or come very quickly: *The children rushed out of school.* **2** to do something quickly or make someone do something quickly: *We rushed to finish the work on time.* **3** to take someone or something quickly to a place: *She was rushed to hospital.*

rush² 🔑 /rʌʃ/ *noun* (no plural) **1** a sudden quick movement: *At the end of the film there was a rush for the exits.* **2** a need to move or do something very quickly: *I can't stop now – I'm in a rush.*

rush hour /ˈrʌʃ aʊə(r)/ *noun* the time when a lot of people are going to or coming from work

rust /rʌst/ *noun* (no plural) red-brown stuff that you sometimes see on metal that has been wet ▶ **rust** *verb* (**rusts, rusting, rusted**) to become covered with **rust**: *My bike rusted because I left it out in the rain.*

rustle /ˈrʌsl/ *verb* (**rustles, rustling, rustled** /ˈrʌsld/) to make a sound like dry leaves moving together; to make something make this sound: *Stop rustling those papers– I can't hear the radio!* ▶ **rustle** *noun* (no plural): *the rustle of leaves*

rusty /ˈrʌsti/ *adjective* (**rustier, rustiest**) covered with **rust** (= red-brown stuff): *a rusty nail*

Ss

S, s /es/ *noun* (*plural* **S's, s's** /ˈesɪz/) the nineteenth letter of the English alphabet: *'Sun' begins with an 'S'.*

-'s /s; z/ *suffix* a way of showing that something belongs to someone: *Shema's book* ◇ *children's clothes*

sack¹ /sæk/ *noun* a big strong bag for carrying heavy things: *a sack of rice*

get the sack to lose your job

give someone the sack to say that someone must leave their job

sack² /sæk/ *verb* (**sacks**, **sacking**, **sacked** /sækt/) to say that someone must leave their job: *The manager sacked her because she was always late.*

sacred /ˈseɪkrɪd/ *adjective* with a special religious meaning

sacrifice /ˈsækrɪfaɪs/ *verb* (**sacrifices**, **sacrificing**, **sacrificed** /ˈsækrɪfaɪst/) **1** to kill an animal as a present to a god: *They sacrificed a lamb.* **2** to stop doing or having something important so that you can help someone or to get something else: *She sacrificed everything for her children.* ▶ **sacrifice** *noun*: *They made a lot of sacrifices to pay for their son to go to university.*

sad 🔑 /sæd/ *adjective* (**sadder**, **saddest**) **1** unhappy: *The children were very sad when their dog died.* **2** that makes you feel unhappy: *a sad story*
OPPOSITE **happy** ▶ **sadly** *adverb*: *She looked sadly at the empty house.*
▶ **sadness** /ˈsædnəs/ *noun* (no plural) the feeling of being sad

saddle /ˈsædl/ *noun* a seat on a horse or bicycle ➲ Picture at **bicycle**.

safari /səˈfɑːri/ *noun* (*plural* **safaris**) **1** a journey to look at wild animals, usually in Africa **2** a journey, especially a long one

the Safari Rally /ðə səˈfɑːri ræli/ *noun* (in Kenya) a race for cars that takes place every year

safe¹ 🔑 /seɪf/ *adjective* (**safer**, **safest**) **1** not in danger; not hurt: *Don't go out alone at night – you won't be safe.* **2** not dangerous: *Is it safe to swim in this river?* ◇ *Always keep medicines in a safe place.*
safe and sound not hurt or broken: *The child was found safe and sound.* ▶ **safely** *adverb*: *Phone your parents to tell them you have arrived safely.*

safe² /seɪf/ *noun* a strong metal box with a lock where you keep money or things like jewellery

safety 🔑 /ˈseɪfti/ *noun* (no plural) being safe: *New safety measures have been introduced .* ◇ *We want to improve road safety* (= prevent accidents) *near the school.*

safety belt /ˈseɪfti belt/ *noun* a long thin piece of material that you put round your body in a car or a plane to keep you safe in an accident SAME MEANING **seat belt**

safety pin /ˈseɪfti pɪn/ *noun* a pin that you use for joining things together. It has a cover over the point so that it is not dangerous. ➲ Picture at **pin¹**.

sag /sæg/ *verb* (**sags**, **sagging**, **sagged** /sægd/) to bend or hang down: *The bed is very old and it sags in the middle.*

said *form of* SAY¹

sail

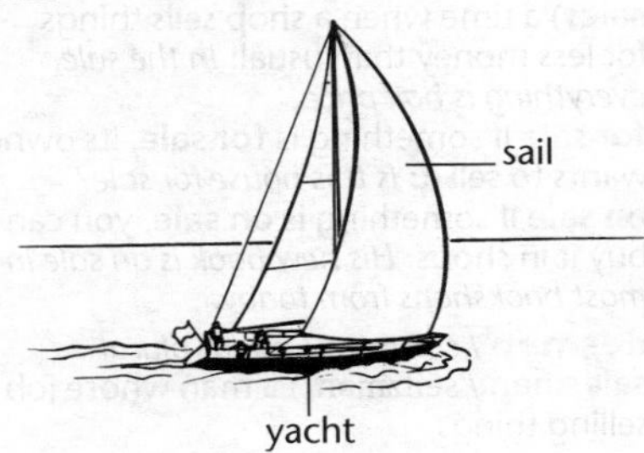

sail¹ 🔑 /seɪl/ *noun*

> ❖ **PRONUNCIATION**
> **Sail** and **sale** sound the same.

a big piece of cloth on a boat. The wind blows against the sail and moves the boat along.

sail² 🔑 /seɪl/ *verb* (**sails**, **sailing**, **sailed** /seɪld/) **1** to travel on water: *The ship sailed along the coast.* **2** to control a boat with sails: *The crew sailed the boat from Zanzibar to India.* ▶ **sailing** /ˈseɪlɪŋ/ *noun* (no plural) the sport of controlling a boat with sails

sailor 🔑 /ˈseɪlə(r)/ *noun* a person who works on a ship: *The boat sank with six sailors on board.*

saint /seɪnt/ *noun* a very good and holy person: *Saint Nicholas*

> ❖ **PRONUNCIATION**
> You usually say /snt/ before names. The short way of writing 'Saint' before names is **St**: *St George's church*

sake /seɪk/ *noun*
for goodness' sake; for Heaven's sake something that you say to show that you are angry: *For goodness' sake, be quiet!*
for the sake of someone or **something; for someone's** or **something's sake** to help someone or something; because of someone or something: *They stayed together for the sake of their children.*

salad /ˈsæləd/ *noun* a dish of cold vegetables that are usually not cooked: *grilled fish with salad*

salary /ˈsæləri/ *noun* (*plural* **salaries**) money that a person receives every month for the work that they do

sale /seɪl/ *noun* **1** (no plural) selling something: *a sale of used toys* **2** (*plural* **sales**) a time when a shop sells things for less money than usual: *In the sale, everything is half price.*
for sale If something is **for sale**, its owner wants to sell it: *Is this house for sale?*
on sale If something is **on sale**, you can buy it in shops: *His new book is on sale in most bookshops from today.*

salesman /ˈseɪlzmən/ *noun* (*plural* **salesmen** /ˈseɪlzmən/) a man whose job is selling things

salesperson /ˈseɪlzpɜːsn/ *noun* (*plural* **salespeople** /ˈseɪlzpiːpl/) a man or woman whose job is selling things

saleswoman /ˈseɪlzwʊmən/ *noun* (*plural* **saleswomen** /ˈseɪlzwɪmɪn/) a woman whose job is selling things

saliva /səˈlaɪvə/ *noun* (no plural) the liquid in your mouth that helps you to swallow food

salon /ˈsælɒn/ *noun* a shop where you can have beauty or hair treatment: *a beauty salon*

salt /sɔːlt/ *noun* (no plural) white stuff that comes from sea water and from the earth. We put it on food to make it taste better: *Add a little salt and pepper.* ▶ **salty** *adjective* (**saltier**, **saltiest**) with salt in it: *Sea water is salty.*

salute /səˈluːt/ *verb* (**salutes**, **saluting**, **saluted**) to make the special sign that soldiers make, by lifting your hand to your head: *The soldiers saluted as the President walked past.* ▶ **salute** *noun*: *The soldier gave a salute.*

sambaza *verb* (East African English) to share good or useful things with other people: *You can pay bills here and sambaza money to your family.*

same[1] /seɪm/ *adjective*
the same not different; not another: *My sister and I like the same kind of music.* ◇ *I've lived in the same town all my life.* ◇ *He went to the same school as my brother.*

same[2] /seɪm/ *pronoun*
all or **just the same** anyway: *I understand why you're angry. All the same, I think you should say sorry.*
same to you words that you use for saying to someone what they have said to you: *'Good luck in the exam.' 'Same to you.'*
the same not a different person or thing: *Do these two words mean the same?* ◇ *Your shoes are the same as mine.*

samosa /səˈməʊsə/ *noun* a thin pie in the shape of a triangle, that is filled with meat or vegetables and fried

sample /ˈsɑːmpl/ *noun* a small amount of something that shows what the rest is like: *The shop was giving away free samples of shampoo.* ◇ *The doctor took a blood sample.*

sand /sænd/ *noun* (no plural) powder made of very small pieces of rock, that you find next to the sea and in deserts

sandal /ˈsændl/ *noun* a light open shoe

sandals

a pair of **sandals**

sand dune /ˈsænd djuːn/ *noun* a small hill of sand

sandy /ˈsændi/ *adjective* (**sandier**, **sandiest**) with sand: *a sandy beach*

sane /seɪn/ *adjective* (**saner**, **sanest**) with a normal healthy mind; not mad OPPOSITE **insane**

sang *form of* SING

sanitary /ˈsænətri/ *adjective* **1** about keeping people healthy: *We pay tax on sanitary services.* **2** clean; not having dirt that could bring disease: *The new houses were more sanitary than the old ones.*

sanitation /ˌsænɪˈteɪʃn/ *noun* (no plural) ways of keeping places clean and people healthy, for example by removing rubbish and dirty water

sank *form of* SINK[1]

sarcastic /sɑːˈkæstɪk/ *adjective* If you are **sarcastic**, you say the opposite of what you mean, in an unkind way.

sardine /sɑːˈdiːn/ *noun* a very small fish that you can eat

sari /ˈsɑːri/ *noun* (*plural* **saris**) a long piece of material that Indian women wear around their bodies as a dress

sat *form of* SIT

satchel /ˈsætʃəl/ *noun* a bag that children use for carrying books to and from school

satellite /ˈsætəlaɪt/ *noun* **1** a thing in space that moves round a planet: *The moon is a satellite of the earth.* **2** a thing that people have sent into space. **Satellites** travel round the earth and send back pictures or television and radio signals: *satellite television*

satin /ˈsætɪn/ *noun* (no plural) very shiny smooth cloth

satisfaction /ˌsætɪsˈfækʃn/ *noun* (no plural) being pleased with what you or other people have done: *She looked at her painting with satisfaction.*

satisfactory /ˌsætɪsˈfæktəri/ *adjective* good enough, but not very good: *Her work is satisfactory.*

satisfied /ˈsætɪsfaɪd/ *adjective* pleased because you have had or done what you wanted: *a satisfied customer*

satisfy /ˈsætɪsfaɪ/ *verb* (**satisfies, satisfying, satisfied** /ˈsætɪsfaɪd/) to give someone what they want or need; to be good enough to make someone pleased: *Nothing he does satisfies his father.*

❖ **WORD FAMILY**

satisfy satisfied satisfying
satisfactory: OPPOSITE **unsatisfactory**
satisfaction

satisfying /ˈsætɪsfaɪɪŋ/ *adjective* Something that is **satisfying** makes you pleased because it is what you want: *a satisfying result*

Saturday /ˈsætədeɪ/ *noun* the seventh day of the week, next after Friday

sauce /sɔːs/ *noun* a thick liquid that you eat on or with other food: *tomato sauce*

saucepan /ˈsɔːspən/ *noun* a round metal container for cooking

saucepan

saucer /ˈsɔːsə(r)/ *noun* a small round plate that you put under a cup ➲ Picture at **cup**.

sausages

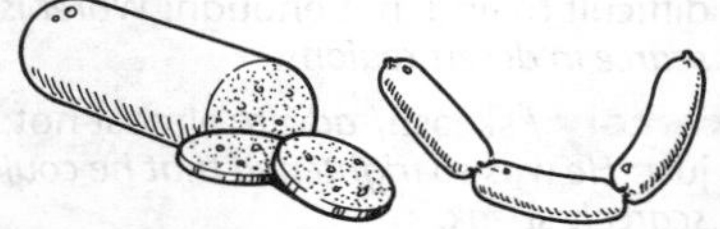

sausage /ˈsɒsɪdʒ/ *noun* meat that is cut into very small pieces and put inside a long, thin skin

savage /ˈsævɪdʒ/ *adjective* wild or fierce: *a savage attack by a large dog*

savannah (also **savanna**) /səˈvænə/ *noun* (no plural) dry land with a little grass and a few or no trees: *Mount Kilimanjaro rises straight up out of the African savannah.*

save /seɪv/ *verb* (**saves, saving, saved** /seɪvd/) **1** to take someone or something away from danger: *He saved me from the fire.* ◇ *The doctor saved her life.* **2** to keep something, especially money, to use later: *I've saved enough money to buy a new bag.* ◇ *Save some of the meat for tomorrow.* **3** to keep something for someone: *Can you save me a seat?* **4** to use less of something: *She saves money by making her own clothes.* **5** to stop someone from scoring a goal, for example in football **6** to store information in a computer: *Don't forget to save the file before you close it.*

save up for something to keep money to buy something later: *I'm saving up for a new bike.*

savings /ˈseɪvɪŋz/ *noun* (plural) money that you are keeping to use later: *I opened a savings account at my local bank.*

saviour /ˈseɪvjə(r)/ *noun* a person who rescues or saves someone from danger

saw¹ *form of* SEE

saw² /sɔː/ *noun* a metal tool for cutting wood

saw

▶ **saw** *verb* (**saws, sawing, sawed** /sɔːd/, **has sawn** /sɔːn/): *She sawed a branch off the tree.*

sawdust /ˈsɔːdʌst/ *noun* (no plural) powder that falls when someone saws wood

saxophone /ˈsæksəfəʊn/ *noun* a musical instrument made of metal that you play by blowing into it

ℹ We sometimes use the short form **sax**: *He plays the sax.*

saxophone

say¹ 🔑 /seɪ/ *verb* (**says** /sez/, **saying**, **said** /sed/, **has said**) **1** to make words with your mouth: *You say 'please' when you ask for something.* ◇ *'This is my room,' he said.* ◇ *She said that she was cold.*

❖ **say** or **tell**?

Say and **tell** are not used in the same way. Look at these sentences: *Robi said 'I'm ready.'* ◇ *Robi said that she was ready.* ◇ *Robi said to me that she was ready.* ◇ *Robi told me that she was ready.* ◇ *Robi told me to close the door.*

2 to give information: *The notice on the door said 'Private'.* ◇ *The clock says half past three.*
that is to say what I mean is ...: *I'll see you in a week, that's to say next Monday.*

say² /seɪ/ *noun* (no plural)
have a say to have the right to help decide something: *I would like to have a say in what we do with the money.*

saying /ˈseɪɪŋ/ *noun* a sentence that people often say, that gives advice about something: *'Look before you leap' is an old saying.*

scab /skæb/ *noun* a hard covering that grows over your skin where it is cut or broken

scaffolding

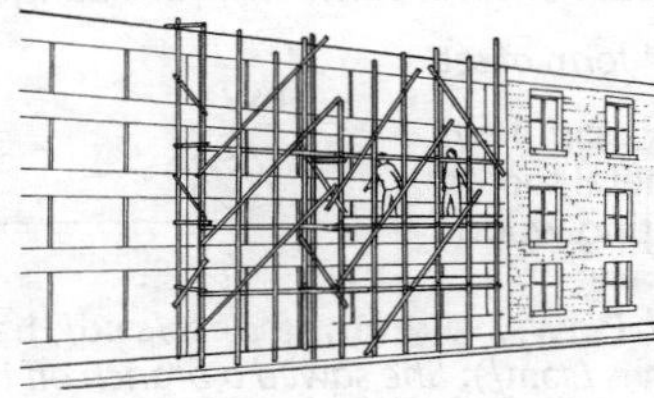

scaffolding /ˈskæfəldɪŋ/ *noun* (no plural) metal bars and pieces of wood joined together, where people like painters can stand when they are working on high parts of a building

scald /skɔːld/ *verb* (**scalds**, **scalding**, **scalded**) to burn someone or something with very hot liquid

scale 🔑 /skeɪl/ *noun* **1** a set of marks on something for measuring: *This ruler has one scale in centimetres and one scale in inches.* **2** how distances are shown on a map: *This map has a scale of one centimetre to ten kilometres.* **3** one of the flat hard things that cover the body of animals like fish and snakes ➲ Picture at **fish¹**.

scales

scales /skeɪlz/ *noun* (plural) a machine for showing how heavy people or things are

scalp /skælp/ *noun* the skin on the top of your head, under your hair

scamper /ˈskæmpə(r)/ *verb* (**scampers**, **scampering**, **scampered** /ˈskæmpəd/) to run quickly, like small animals or children

scan /skæn/ *verb* (**scans**, **scanning**, **scanned** /skænd/) **1** to look carefully because you are trying to find something: *They scanned the sea, looking for a boat.* **2** to read something quickly: *Hawa scanned the list until she found her name.* **3** to use a machine (called a **scanner**) to pass light over words or pictures on paper to copy them into a computer **4** to use a machine to see what is inside someone's body or inside an object such as a suitcase ▸ **scan** *noun*: *a brain scan*

scandal /ˈskændl/ *noun* **1** (*plural* **scandals**) something that makes a lot of people talk about it, perhaps in an angry way: *There was a big scandal when the referee admitted accepting money from the team.* **2** (no plural) unkind talk about someone that gives you a bad idea of them

scanner /ˈskænə(r)/ *noun* **1** a machine that gives a picture of the inside of something. Doctors use one kind of **scanner** to look inside people's bodies. **2** a piece of equipment that copies words and pictures from paper into a computer

scar /skɑː(r)/ *noun* a mark on your skin, that an old cut has left ▸ **scar** *verb* (**scars**, **scarring**, **scarred** /skɑːd/) to make a **scar** on skin: *His face was badly scarred by the accident.*

scarce /skeəs/ *adjective* (**scarcer**, **scarcest**) difficult to find; not enough: *Water is scarce in desert regions.*

scarcely /ˈskeəsli/ *adverb* almost not; only just: *He was so frightened that he could scarcely speak.*

scare¹ /skeə(r)/ *verb* (**scares**, **scaring**, **scared** /skeəd/) to make someone frightened: *That noise scared me!*

scare² /skeə(r)/ *noun* a feeling of being frightened: *You gave me a scare!*

scared /skeəd/ *adjective* frightened: *Moraa is scared of the dark.*

scarf /skɑːf/ *noun* (*plural* **scarves** /skɑːvz/) a piece of material that you wear around your neck or head

scarlet /ˈskɑːlət/ *adjective* with a bright red colour

scatter /ˈskætə(r)/ *verb* (**scatters, scattering, scattered** /ˈskætəd/) **1** to move quickly in different directions: *The crowd scattered when the lorry came towards them.* **2** to throw things so that they fall in a lot of different places: *She scattered the seeds on the soil.*

scene 🔑 /siːn/ *noun*

> ❖ **PRONUNCIATION**
>
> **Scene** sounds the same as **seen** because we do not say the 'c'.

1 a place where something happened: *The police arrived at the scene of the crime.* **2** what you see in a place; a view: *He painted scenes of life in the countryside.* **3** part of a play or film: *Act 1, Scene 2 of Shakespeare's 'Hamlet'* ▸ **scenic** /ˈsiːnɪk/ *adjective*: *Tsavo East is an area of great scenic beauty.*

scenery /ˈsiːnəri/ *noun* (no plural) **1** the things like mountains, rivers and forests that you see around you in the countryside: *What beautiful scenery!* **2** things on the stage of a theatre that make it look like a real place

scent /sent/ *noun* **1** (*plural* **scents**) a smell: *This flower has no scent.* **2** (no plural) a liquid with a nice smell, that you put on your body: *a bottle of scent* ▸ **scented** /ˈsentɪd/ *adjective* with a nice smell: *scented soap*

schedule /ˈʃedjuːl/ *noun* a plan or list of times when things will happen or be done: *I've got a busy schedule next week.*
behind schedule late: *We're behind schedule with the work.*
on schedule with everything happening at the right time: *We are on schedule to finish the work in May.*

scheme /skiːm/ *noun* a plan: *a scheme to build more houses*

scholar /ˈskɒlə(r)/ *noun* a person who has learnt a lot about something: *a famous history scholar*

scholarship /ˈskɒləʃɪp/ *noun* money that is given to a good student to help them to continue studying: *Kisoso won a scholarship to Nairobi University.*

school 🔑 /skuːl/ *noun* **1** (*plural* **schools**) a place where children go to learn: *Chebet is at school.* ◇ *Which school do you go to?* **2** (no plural) being at school: *I love school!* ◇ *He left school when he was 16.* ◇ *School starts at eight o'clock.* **3** (*plural* **schools**) a place where you go to learn a special thing: *a law school*

schoolboy /ˈskuːlbɔɪ/ *noun* a boy who goes to school

schoolchild /ˈskuːltʃaɪld/ *noun* (*plural* **schoolchildren** /ˈskuːltʃɪldrən/) a boy or girl who goes to school

schooldays /ˈskuːldeɪz/ *noun* (plural) the time in your life when you are at school

schoolgirl /ˈskuːlgɜːl/ *noun* a girl who goes to school

science 🔑 /ˈsaɪəns/ *noun* the study of natural things: *I'm interested in science.* ◇ *Biology, chemistry and physics are all sciences.*

> ❖ **WORD FAMILY**
>
> **science** **scientist** **scientific**

science fiction /ˌsaɪəns ˈfɪkʃn/ *noun* (no plural) stories about things like travel in space, life on other planets or life in the future

scientific 🔑 /ˌsaɪənˈtɪfɪk/ *adjective* of or about science: *a scientific experiment*

scientist 🔑 /ˈsaɪəntɪst/ *noun* a person who studies science or works with science: *She is a research scientist.*

scissors 🔑 /ˈsɪzəz/ *noun* (plural) a tool for cutting that has two sharp parts that are joined together: *These scissors aren't very sharp.*

scissors

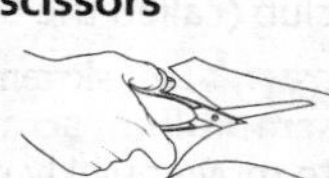

a pair of **scissors**

> ❖ **GRAMMAR**
>
> Be careful! You cannot say 'a scissors'. You can say a **pair of scissors**: *I need a pair of scissors.* (or: *I need some scissors.*)

scoop /skuːp/ *verb* (**scoops, scooping, scooped** /skuːpt/) to use a container or your hands to take something up or out: *I scooped some water out of the river with a bucket.*

scooter /ˈskuːtə(r)/ *noun* a light motorbike with a small engine

score¹ 🔑 /skɔː(r)/ *noun* the number of points, goals, etc. that you win in a game or competition: *The winner got a score of 320.*

score² 🔑 /skɔː(r)/ *verb* (**scores, scoring, scored** /skɔːd/) to win a point in a game or competition: *Mariga scored four goals against Namibia.*

scoreboard /ˈskɔːbɔːd/ *noun* a large board that shows the score during a game or competition

scorer /ˈskɔːrə(r)/ *noun* **1** a player who scores points, goals, etc: *He is the team's top scorer.* **2** a person who keeps a record of the points, goals, etc. scored in a game or competition

scorn /skɔːn/ *noun* (no plural) the strong feeling you have when you think that someone or something is not good enough: *He was full of scorn for my idea.*

scorpion /ˈskɔːpiən/ *noun* an animal that has eight legs and lives in hot, dry places. A **scorpion** has a long tail with a sharp part that can hurt you (a **sting**).

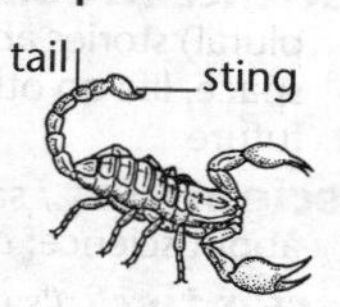

scout /skaʊt/ *noun* a member of a special club (called the **Scouts**) for boys and girls

scramble /ˈskræmbl/ *verb* (**scrambles, scrambling, scrambled** /ˈskræmbld/) to move quickly up or over something, using your hands to help you: *They scrambled over the wall.*

scrambled eggs /ˌskræmbld ˈegz/ *noun* (plural) eggs that you mix together with milk and cook in a pan with butter

scrap /skræp/ *noun* **1** (*plural* **scraps**) a small piece of something: *a scrap of paper* **2** (no plural) something you do not want any more but that is made of material that can be used again: *scrap paper* ◇ *scrap metal*

scrape /skreɪp/ *verb* (**scrapes, scraping, scraped** /skreɪpt/) **1** to move a rough or sharp thing across something: *I scraped the mud off my shoes with a knife.* **2** to hurt or damage something by moving it against a rough or sharp thing: *I fell and scraped my knee on the wall.*

scratch¹ 🔑 /skrætʃ/ *verb* (**scratches, scratching, scratched** /skrætʃt/) **1** to cut or make a mark on something with a sharp thing: *The cat scratched me!* **2** to move your nails across your skin: *She scratched her head.*

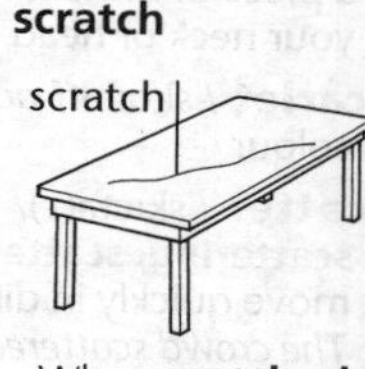

Who **scratched** the table?

scratch² /skrætʃ/ *noun* (*plural* **scratches**) a cut or mark that a sharp thing makes: *Her hands were covered in scratches from the bush.*
from scratch from the beginning: *I threw away the letter I was writing and started again from scratch.*

scratch card /ˈskrætʃ kɑːd/ *noun* **1** a card you can buy that has an area which you scratch off to see if you have won a prize **2** a card you can buy for a mobile phone, so that you can make calls

scream¹ /skriːm/ *verb* (**screams, screaming, screamed** /skriːmd/) to make a loud high cry that shows you are afraid or hurt: *She saw the snake and screamed.* ◇ *He screamed for help.*

scream² /skriːm/ *noun* a loud high cry: *a scream of pain*

screech /skriːtʃ/ *verb* (**screeches, screeching, screeched** /skriːtʃt/) to make a loud high sound: *The car's brakes screeched as it stopped suddenly.*

screen 🔑 /skriːn/ *noun* **1** the flat part of a television or computer where you see pictures or words ➲ Picture at **computer**. **2** the flat thing on the wall of a cinema, where you see films: *They sat close to the screen.* **3** a kind of thin wall that you can move around. Screens are used to keep away cold, light, etc. or to stop people from seeing something: *The nurse put a screen around the bed.*

screw¹ /skruː/ *noun* a small metal thing with a sharp end, that you use for fixing things together. You push it into something by turning it with a **screwdriver**.

screw

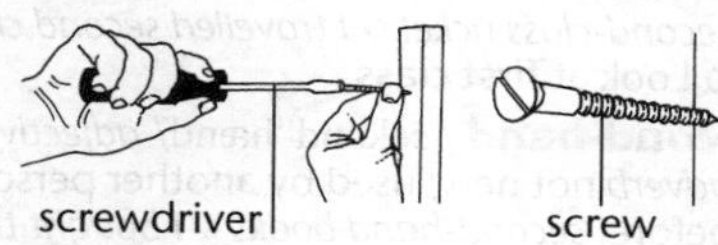

screw² /skruː/ *verb* (**screws, screwing, screwed** /skruːd/) **1** to fix something to another thing using a **screw 2** to turn something to fix it to another thing: *Screw the lid on the jar.* OPPOSITE **unscrew**
screw up to make paper or material into a ball with your hand: *He screwed up the letter and threw it in the bin.*

screwdriver /ˈskruːdraɪvə(r)/ *noun* a tool for turning **screws** ➲ Picture at **screw¹**.

scribble /ˈskrɪbl/ *verb* (**scribbles, scribbling, scribbled** /ˈskrɪbld/) to write something or make marks on paper quickly and without care: *The children scribbled in my book.*

script /skrɪpt/ *noun* the written words that actors speak in a play or film

scrub¹ /skrʌb/ *verb* (**scrubs, scrubbing, scrubbed** /skrʌbd/) to rub something hard to clean it, usually with a brush and soap and water: *He scrubbed the floor.*

scrub² /skrʌb/ *noun* (no plural) small trees and plants that grow in hot dry places

scruffy /ˈskrʌfi/ *adjective* (**scruffier, scruffiest**) untidy and perhaps dirty: *She was wearing scruffy clothes.*

sculptor /ˈskʌlptə(r)/ *noun* a person who makes shapes from things like stone or wood

sculpture /ˈskʌlptʃə(r)/ *noun* **1** (no plural) making shapes from things like stone or wood **2** (*plural* **sculptures**) a shape made from things like stone or wood

sea 🔑 /siː/ *noun*

> ❖ **PRONUNCIATION**
> **Sea** sounds just like **see**.

1 (no plural) the salt water that covers large parts of the earth: *We went for a swim in the sea.* ◇ *The sea is very rough today.* **2** (*plural* **seas**) a big area of salt water: *the Black Sea*
at sea travelling on the sea: *We spent three weeks at sea.*

the seabed /ðə ˈsiːbed/ *noun* (no plural) the floor of the sea

seafarer /ˈsiːfeərə(r)/ *noun* a sailor

seafood /ˈsiːfuːd/ *noun* (no plural) fish and small animals from the sea that you can eat

seagull /ˈsiːgʌl/ (also **gull**) *noun* a big grey or white bird with a loud cry, that lives near the sea

seal¹ /siːl/ *noun* an animal with short fur that lives in and near the sea, and that eats fish

seal

seal² /siːl/ *verb* (**seals, sealing, sealed** /siːld/) to close something tightly by sticking two parts together: *She sealed the envelope.*

seam /siːm/ *noun* a line where two pieces of cloth are joined together

seaman /ˈsiːmən/ *noun* (*plural* **seamen** /ˈsiːmən/) a member of the navy or a sailor on a ship: *Seaman Hamisi* ◇ *a merchant seaman*

search¹ 🔑 /sɜːtʃ/ *verb* (**searches, searching, searched** /sɜːtʃt/) to look carefully because you are trying to find someone or something: *I searched everywhere for my pen.*

search² 🔑 /sɜːtʃ/ *noun* (*plural* **searches**) **1** when you try to find someone or something: *I found my key after a long search.* **2** when you use a computer to look for information: *I'll do a search on the Internet.*
in search of someone or **something** looking for someone or something: *We drove round the town in search of a cheap hotel.*

seashell /ˈsiːʃel/ *noun* the hard outside part of a small animal that lives in the sea

seashells

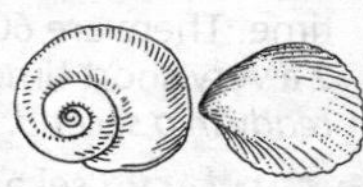

seashore /ˈsiːʃɔː(r)/ *noun* (no plural) the land next to the sea; the beach

seasick /ˈsiːsɪk/ *adjective* If you are **seasick**, you feel ill in your stomach because the boat you are on is moving a lot. ▸ **seasickness** /ˈsiːsɪknəs/ *noun* (no plural): *Do you suffer from seasickness?*

seasons

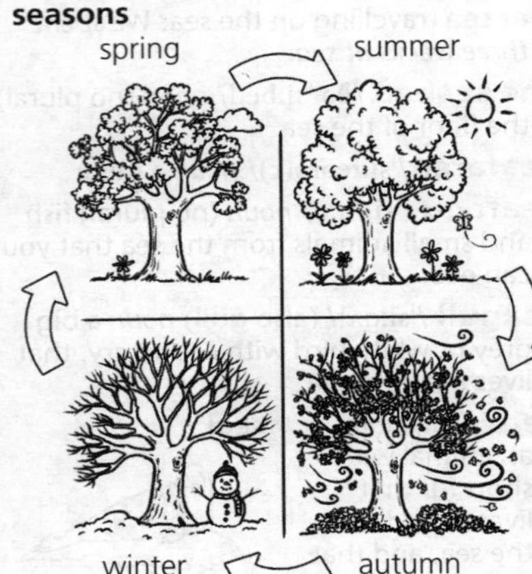

season /ˈsiːzn/ *noun* **1** one of the four parts of the year in cool countries. The four seasons are **spring, summer, autumn** and **winter**. **2** a special time of the year for something: *The football season starts soon.*

seat /siːt/ *noun* something that you sit on: *the back seat of a car* ◇ *We had seats at the front of the theatre.*
take a seat to sit down: *Please take a seat.*

seat belt /ˈsiːt belt/ *noun* a long thin piece of material that you put round your body in a car or a plane to keep you safe in an accident SAME MEANING **safety belt**

seaweed /ˈsiːwiːd/ *noun* (no plural) a plant that grows in the sea

second[1] /ˈsekənd/ *adjective, adverb* next after first: *February is the second month of the year.*

second[2] /ˈsekənd/ *noun* (no plural) a person or thing that comes next after the first: *Today is the second of April (April 2nd).* ◇ *I was the first to arrive, and Nafula was the second.*

second[3] /ˈsekənd/ *noun* **1** a measure of time. There are 60 seconds in a **minute**. **2** a very short time: *Wait a second!* ◇ *I'll be ready in a second.*

secondary /ˈsekəndri/ *adjective* **1** not as important as something else: *Speed is what matters in this race – age is secondary.* **2** caused by or developing from something

secondary school /ˈsekəndri skuːl/ *noun* a school for pupils between the ages of about 13 and 18

second class /ˌsekənd ˈklɑːs/ *noun* (no plural) the part of a train, plane, etc. that it is cheaper to travel in: *We sat in second class.* ► **second class** *adjective, adverb*: *a second-class ticket* ◇ *I travelled second class.* ➲ Look at **first class**.

second-hand /ˌsekənd ˈhænd/ *adjective, adverb* not new; used by another person before: *second-hand books* ◇ *I bought this bag second-hand.*

secondly /ˈsekəndli/ *adverb* a word that you use when you are giving the second thing in a list: *Firstly, it's too expensive and secondly, we don't really need it.*

secrecy /ˈsiːkrəsi/ *noun* (no plural) not telling other people: *They worked in secrecy.*

secret[1] /ˈsiːkrət/ *adjective* If something is secret, other people do not or must not know about it: *They kept their plans secret* (= they did not tell anyone about them). ◇ *a secret meeting*

❖ **WORD FAMILY**
secret *adjective*, **secret** *noun*
secretly **secretive**

secret[2] /ˈsiːkrət/ *noun* something that you do not or must not tell other people: *I can't tell you where I'm going – it's a secret.* ◇ *Can you keep a secret?*
in secret without other people knowing: *They met in secret.*

secretarial /ˌsekrəˈteəriəl/ *adjective* connected with the work of a secretary: *a secretarial college*

secretary /ˈsekrətri/ *noun* (*plural* **secretaries**) **1** a person who types letters, answers the telephone and does other things in an office **2** an important person in the government: *the Cabinet Secretary for Education*

secretary bird /ˈsekrətri bɜːd/ *noun* a large bird with long legs that eats snakes

secretive /ˈsiːkrətɪv/ *adjective* If you are **secretive**, you do not like to tell other people about yourself or your plans: *Mwita is very secretive about his family.*

secretly /ˈsiːkrətli/ *adverb* without other people knowing: *We are secretly planning a big party for her.*

sect /sekt/ *noun* a group of people who believe something a little different from other people in a religion

section 🔑 /ˈsekʃn/ *noun* one of the parts of something: *This section of the road is closed.*

secure /sɪˈkjʊə(r)/ *adjective* **1** If you are **secure**, you feel safe and you are not worried: *The children felt very secure in their new school.* **2** safe: *Don't climb that ladder – it's not very secure* (= it may fall). **3** well locked or protected so that nobody can go in or out: *This gate isn't very secure.*
▶ **securely** *adverb*: *Are all the windows securely closed?*

> ❖ **WORD FAMILY**
> **secure**: OPPOSITE **insecure**
> **security**: OPPOSITE **insecurity**

security /sɪˈkjʊərəti/ *noun* (no plural) **1** the feeling of being safe: *Children need love and security.* **2** things that you do to keep a place safe: *We need better security at airports.*

see 🔑 /siː/ *verb* (**sees**, **seeing**, **saw** /sɔː/, **has seen** /siːn/) **1** to know something using your eyes: *It was so dark that I couldn't see anything.* ◇ *Can you see that plane?* ◇ *I saw my friends walking along the road.*

> ❖ **see**, **look** or **watch**?
> When you **see** something, you know about it with your eyes, without trying: *Suddenly I saw a bird fly past the window.*
> When you **look at** something, you turn your eyes towards it because you want to see it: *Look at this picture carefully.*
> When you **watch** something, you look at it for some time: *They watched the Safari Rally.*

2 to visit or meet someone: *I'll see you outside the station at ten o'clock.* **3** to understand something: *'You have to turn the key this way.' 'I see.'* **4** to find out about something: *Look in the newspaper to see what time the film starts.* **5** to make certain about something: *Please see that everybody is here.*
I'll see; we'll see I will think about what you have said and tell you what I have decided later: *'Will you lend me the money?' 'I'll see.'*
let's see; let me see words that you use when you are thinking or trying to remember something: *Let's see, where did I put my book?*
seeing that; seeing as because: *Seeing that you've got nothing to do, you can help me!*
see you; see you later goodbye
see someone off to go to an airport or a station to say goodbye to someone who is leaving
see to someone or **something** to do what you need to do for someone or something: *Sit down – I'll see to the dinner.*

seed 🔑 /siːd/ *noun* the small hard part of a plant from which a new plant grows ➲ Picture at **avocado**, **peach**, **watermelon**.

seedbed /ˈsiːdbed/ *noun* an area of soil for planting seeds in

seedling /ˈsiːdlɪŋ/ *noun* a young plant that has grown from a seed: *tomato seedlings*

seek /siːk/ *verb* (**seeks**, **seeking**, **sought** /sɔːt/, **has sought**) to try to find or get something: *You should seek help.*

seem 🔑 /siːm/ *verb* (**seems**, **seeming**, **seemed** /siːmd/) to make you think that something is true: *She seems tired.* ◇ *My mother seems to like you.* ◇ *Ajuma seems like* (= seems to be) *a nice girl.*

seen *form of* SEE

see-saw /ˈsiː sɔː/ *noun* a special piece of wood that can move up and down when a child sits on each end ➲ Picture at **balance**[2].

seize /siːz/ *verb* (**seizes**, **seizing**, **seized** /siːzd/) to take something quickly and strongly: *The thief seized my bag and ran away.*

seldom /ˈseldəm/ *adverb* not often: *It seldom rains in the desert.*

select /sɪˈlekt/ *verb* (**selects**, **selecting**, **selected**) to take the person or thing that you like best; to choose: *The manager has selected two new players for the team.* ❶ **Choose** is the word that we usually use.

selection /sɪˈlekʃn/ *noun* **1** (no plural) taking the person or thing you like best: *the selection of a new president* **2** (*plural* **selections**) a group of people or things that someone has chosen, or a group of things that you can choose from: *This shop has a good selection of books.*

self- /self/ *prefix* by yourself; for yourself: *He is self-taught – he never went to university.*

self-confident /ˌself ˈkɒnfɪdənt/ *adjective* sure about yourself and what you can do

self-conscious /ˌself ˈkɒnʃəs/ *adjective* worried about what other people think of you: *She walked into the classroom feeling very self-conscious.*

self-control /ˌself kənˈtrəʊl/ *noun* (no plural) the ability to control yourself and your emotions: *Ngenzi lost his self-control and started shouting angrily.*

self-employed /ˌself ɪmˈplɔɪd/ *adjective* A person who is **self-employed** works for herself or himself, not for someone else's company: *He's a self-employed electrician.*

self-esteem /ˌself ɪˈstiːm/ *noun* (no plural) being happy with yourself and what you can do

selfish /ˈselfɪʃ/ *adjective* If you are **selfish**, you think too much about what you want and not about what other people want: *It was selfish of you to go out when your mother was ill.* OPPOSITE **unselfish**
▶ **selfishly** *adverb*: *He behaved very selfishly.* ▶ **selfishness** /ˈselfɪʃnəs/ *noun* (no plural): *Her selfishness made me very angry.*

selfless /ˈselfləs/ *adjective* thinking more about what other people want than what you want SAME MEANING **unselfish** OPPOSITE **selfish**

self-pity /ˌself ˈpɪti/ *noun* (no plural) when you think too much about your own problems and feel sorry for yourself

self-respect /ˌself rɪˈspekt/ *noun* (no plural) when you feel proud that what you do or say is right and good

self-service /ˌself ˈsɜːvɪs/ *adjective* In a **self-service** shop or restaurant you take what you want and then pay for it.

sell 🔑 /sel/ *verb* (**sells, selling, sold** /səʊld/, **has sold**) to give something to someone who pays you money for it: *I sold my guitar for 4 000 shillings.* ◇ *He sold me a ticket.* ◇ *Does that shop sell pencils?*
➲ Look at **buy**.
sell out to be sold completely so that there are no more left: *I went to the shop to buy a cake, but they had all sold out.*
sell out of something to sell all that you have of something: *We have oranges, but we have sold out of bananas.*

semen /ˈsiːmən/ *noun* (no plural) the white liquid that is produced by male sex organs

semi- /ˈsemi/ *prefix* half: *A semicircle is a half circle.*

semi-arid /ˌsemi ˈærɪd/ *adjective* dry; with not much rain: *the semi-arid lands of Eastern Africa*

semicolon /ˌsemiˈkəʊlən/ *noun* a mark (;) that you use in writing to separate parts of a sentence ➲ Look at page A17.

semi-final /ˌsemi ˈfaɪnl/ *noun* In a competition, a **semi-final** is one of the two games that are played to find out who will play in the **final**.

senate /ˈsenət/ *noun* one of the parts of the government in some countries

senator /ˈsenətə(r)/ *noun* a member of a **senate**

send 🔑 /send/ *verb* (**sends, sending, sent** /sent/, **has sent**) **1** to make something go somewhere: *I sent a letter to Nakato.* ◇ *Have you sent your parents a letter?* **2** to make someone go somewhere: *My company is sending me to Nairobi.* ◇ *He was sent to prison for ten years.*
send for someone or **something** to ask for someone or something to come to you: *Send for a doctor!*
send off 1 to post something: *I'll send the letter off today.* **2** to order someone to leave the field in a sports game: *Oliech was sent off for a foul.*

senior 🔑 /ˈsiːniə(r)/ *adjective* **1** more important: *a senior officer in the army* **2** older: *a senior pupil* OPPOSITE **junior**

sensation /senˈseɪʃn/ *noun* **1** a feeling: *I felt a burning sensation on my skin.* **2** great excitement or interest; something that makes people very excited: *The new film caused a sensation.*

sensational /senˈseɪʃənl/ *adjective* very exciting or interesting: *sensational news*

sense[1] 🔑 /sens/ *noun* **1** (*plural* **senses**) the power to see, hear, smell, taste or touch: *Dogs have a good sense of smell.* **2** (no plural) the ability to feel or understand something: *The boy had no sense of right and wrong.* **3** (no plural) the ability to think carefully about something and to do the right thing: *She had the sense to call the police.* **4** (*plural* **senses**) a meaning: *This word has four senses.*
make sense to be possible to understand: *What does this sentence mean? It doesn't make sense to me.*

sense² /sens/ *verb* (**senses, sensing, sensed** /senst/) to understand or feel something: *I sensed that he was worried.*

sensible 🔑 /ˈsensəbl/ *adjective* able to think carefully about something and to do the right thing: *It was very sensible of you to call the police when you saw the accident.* ▶ **sensibly** /ˈsensəbli/ *adverb*: *This road is dangerous so please drive sensibly.*

sensitive 🔑 /ˈsensətɪv/ *adjective* **1** A person who is sensitive understands and is careful about other people's feelings: *He's a very sensitive man.* OPPOSITE **insensitive** **2** If you are sensitive about something, you easily become worried or unhappy about it: *Don't say anything bad about her work – she's very sensitive about it.* **3** If something is sensitive, it is easy to hurt or damage it: *sensitive skin* OPPOSITE **insensitive**

sent *form of* SEND

sentence¹ 🔑 /ˈsentəns/ *noun* **1** a group of words that tells you something or asks a question. When a sentence is written, it always begins with a capital letter and usually ends with a full stop: *Remember to write in full sentences.* **2** the punishment that a judge gives to someone in a court of law: *20 years in prison was a harsh sentence.*

sentence² /ˈsentəns/ *verb* (**sentences, sentencing, sentenced** /ˈsentənst/) to tell someone in a court of law what their punishment will be: *The judge sentenced the man to two years in prison.*

separate¹ 🔑 /ˈseprət/ *adjective* **1** away from something; not together or not joined: *Cut the dough into eight separate pieces.* ◇ *In my school, the older children are separate from the younger ones.* **2** different; not the same: *We stayed in separate rooms in the same hotel.* ▶ **separately** *adverb*: *Shall we pay separately or together?*

separate² 🔑 /ˈsepəreɪt/ *verb* (**separates, separating, separated**) **1** to stop being together: *My parents separated when I was a baby.* **2** to divide people or things; to keep people or things away from each other: *The teacher separated the class into two groups.* **3** to be between two things: *The Mediterranean separates Europe and Africa.* ▶ **separation** /ˌsepəˈreɪʃn/ *noun*: *The separation from my family and friends made me very unhappy.*

September 🔑 /sepˈtembə(r)/ *noun* the ninth month of the year

sergeant /ˈsɑːdʒənt/ *noun* an officer in the army or the police

sergeant-at-arms /ˌsɑːdʒənt ət ˈɑːmz/ *noun* (*plural* **sergeants-at-arms**) a person whose job is to keep order during meetings of a **parliament**

serial /ˈsɪəriəl/ *noun* a story that is told in parts on television or radio, or in a magazine

series 🔑 /ˈsɪəriːz/ *noun* (*plural* **series**) **1** a number of things of the same kind that come one after another: *I heard a series of shots and then silence.* **2** a number of television or radio programmes, often on the same subject, that come one after another: *a TV series on dinosaurs*

serious 🔑 /ˈsɪəriəs/ *adjective* **1** very bad: *That was a serious mistake.* ◇ *They had a serious accident.* **2** important: *a serious decision* **3** not funny: *a serious film* **4** If you are serious, you are not joking or playing: *Are you serious about going to live with your grandmother?* ◇ *You look very serious. Is something wrong?* ▶ **seriousness** /ˈsɪəriəsnəs/ *noun* (no plural): *The boy didn't understand the seriousness of his crime.*

seriously 🔑 /ˈsɪəriəsli/ *adverb* in a serious way: *She's seriously ill.*
take someone or **something seriously** to show that you know someone or something is important: *Don't take what he says too seriously – he is always joking.*

sermon /ˈsɜːmən/ *noun* a talk that a priest gives in church

serum /ˈsɪərəm/ *noun* (no plural) a thin liquid that comes from blood

servant /ˈsɜːvənt/ *noun* a person who works in another person's house, doing work like cooking and cleaning

serve 🔑 /sɜːv/ *verb* (**serves, serving, served** /sɜːvd/) **1** to do work for other people: *During the war he served in the army.* **2** to give food or drink to someone: *Breakfast is served from 7.30 to 9.00 a.m.* **3** to help someone in a shop to buy things: *Which assistant served you when you bought the shoes?*
it serves you right it is right that this bad thing has happened to you: *'I feel ill.' 'It serves you right for eating so much!'*

service 🔑 /ˈsɜːvɪs/ *noun* **1** (*plural* **services**) a business that does useful work for all the people in a country or an area: *This town has a good bus service.* ◇ *the postal service* **2** (no plural) help or work that you do for someone: *She left the company after ten years of service.* **3** (no plural) the work that someone does for customers in a shop, restaurant or hotel: *The food was good but the service was very slow.* **4** (*plural* **services**) a meeting in a church with prayers and singing: *We went to the evening service.* **5** (*plural* **services**) the time when someone looks at a car or machine to see that it is working well: *The car needs a service.*

serviette /ˌsɜːviˈet/ *noun* a piece of cloth or paper that you use when you are eating to clean your mouth and hands and to keep your clothes clean SAME MEANING **napkin**

serving dish /ˈsɜːvɪŋ dɪʃ/ *noun* a large plate to put food on when it is ready to eat

sesame /ˈsesəmi/ = **SIMSIM**

session /ˈseʃn/ *noun* a time when people meet to do something: *The first training session is at nine o'clock.*

set[1] ⚷ /set/ *noun* a group of things of the same kind, or a group of things that you use together: *a set of six glasses* ◇ *My grandfather still has a full set of teeth.*

set[2] ⚷ /set/ *verb* (**sets, setting, set, has set**) **1** to put something somewhere: *Dad set the plate in front of me.* **2** to make something ready to use or to start working: *I set my alarm clock for seven o'clock.* ◇ *I set the table* (= put knives, forks, spoons, etc. on it). **3** to make something happen: *They set the rubbish on fire* (= made it start to burn). **4** When the sun sets, it goes down from the sky: *We watched the sun setting.* OPPOSITE **rise** **5** to decide what something will be; to fix something: *Let's set a date for the meeting.* **6** to give someone work to do: *Our teacher set us a lot of homework.* **7** to become hard or solid: *Wait for the cement to set.*
set off; set out to start a journey: *We set off for Kisumu at two o'clock.*
set something out to arrange things: *Try to set out your answers clearly.*
set sail to start a journey on a ship: *We set sail for Malindi at high tide.*
set up to start something: *The company was set up in 1981.*

settee /seˈtiː/ *noun* a long soft seat for more than one person SAME MEANING **SOFA**

setting /ˈsetɪŋ/ *noun* the place where something is or where something happens: *The house is in a beautiful setting on top of a hill.*

settle ⚷ /ˈsetl/ *verb* (**settles, settling, settled** /ˈsetld/) **1** to go to live in a new place and stay there: *Adisa left Nairobi and went to settle in the north of Kenya.* **2** to decide something after talking with someone; to end a discussion or an argument: *Have you settled your argument with Tanei?* **3** to come down and rest somewhere: *The bird settled on a branch.* **4** to pay something: *Have you settled your bill?*
settle down 1 to sit down or lie down so that you are comfortable: *I settled down in front of the television.* **2** to become calm and quiet: *The children settled down and went to sleep.* **3** to begin to have a calm life in one place: *When is she going to get married and settle down?*
settle in to start to feel happy in a new place: *We only moved to this flat last week and we haven't settled in yet.*

settlement /ˈsetlmənt/ *noun* **1** an agreement about something after talking or arguing: *After long talks about pay, the workers and their boss reached a settlement.* **2** a group of homes in a place where no people have lived before: *a settlement in the mountains*

seven ⚷ /ˈsevn/ *number* 7

seventeen ⚷ /ˌsevnˈtiːn/ *number* 17

seventeenth ⚷ /ˌsevnˈtiːnθ/ *adjective, adverb, noun* 17th

seventh ⚷ /ˈsevnθ/ *adjective, adverb, noun* **1** 7th **2** one of seven equal parts of something; $\frac{1}{7}$

seventieth ⚷ /ˈsevntiəθ/ *adjective, adverb, noun* 70th

seventy ⚷ /ˈsevnti/ *number* **1** 70 **2 the seventies** (plural) the numbers, years or temperature between 70 and 79
in your seventies between the ages of 70 and 79

several ⚷ /ˈsevrəl/ *adjective, pronoun* more than two but not many: *I've read this book several times.* ◇ *Several letters arrived this morning.* ◇ *If you need a pen, there are several on the table.*

severe /sɪˈvɪə(r)/ *adjective* (**severer, severest**) **1** not kind or gentle: *severe punishment* **2** very bad: *a severe headache* ◇ *a severe injury* ▸ **severely** *adverb*: *They* *punished him severely.* ◇ *She was severely injured in the accident.*

sew 🔑 /səʊ/ *verb* (**sews**, **sewing**, **sewed** /səʊd/, **has sewed** *or* **has sewn** /səʊn/)

❖ **PRONUNCIATION**

Sew sounds like **so**.

to use a needle and cotton to join pieces of material together or to join something to material: *He sewed a button on his shirt.* ◇ *Can you sew?*

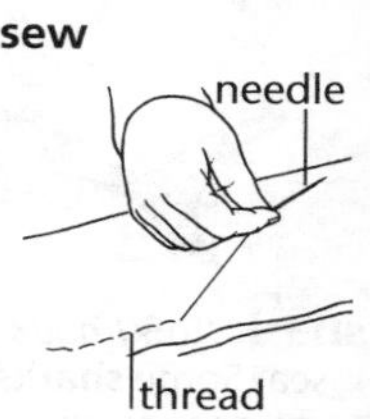

sewer /ˈsuːə(r)/ *noun* a pipe under the ground that carries human waste away from houses, factories and other buildings

sewing 🔑 /ˈsəʊɪŋ/ *noun* (no plural) something that you sew: *I enjoy both knitting and sewing.*

sewing machine /ˈsəʊɪŋ məʃiːn/ *noun* a machine that you use for sewing

sex 🔑 /seks/ *noun* **1** (*plural* **sexes**) being a male or a female: *What sex is your dog?* ◇ *the male sex* **2** (no plural) when two people put their bodies together, sometimes to make a baby: *She had sex with him.*

sextant /ˈsekstənt/ *noun* an instrument that you use to find the exact position of a ship or a plane

sexual 🔑 /ˈsekʃuəl/ *adjective* connected with sex: *the sexual organs*

sh /ʃ/ *exclamation* be quiet!: *Sh! You'll wake the baby up!*

shabby /ˈʃæbi/ *adjective* (**shabbier**, **shabbiest**) old and untidy or dirty because you have used it a lot: *a shabby coat* ▸ **shabbily** /ˈʃæbɪli/ *adverb*: *She was shabbily dressed.*

shade[1] 🔑 /ʃeɪd/ *noun* **1** (no plural) a place where it is dark and cool because the sun doesn't shine there: *We sat in the shade of a big tree.* **2** (*plural* **shades**) a thing that keeps strong light from your eyes: *I bought a new shade for the lamp.* **3** (*plural* **shades**) how light or dark a colour is: *I'm looking for a shirt in a darker shade of green.*

shade[2] /ʃeɪd/ *verb* (**shades**, **shading**, **shaded**) to stop light from shining on something: *He shaded his eyes with his hand.*

shadow 🔑 /ˈʃædəʊ/ *noun* a dark shape that you see near someone or something that is in front of the light: *Their shadows lengthened as the sun went down.*

shady /ˈʃeɪdi/ *adjective* (**shadier**, **shadiest**) not in bright sun: *We sat in a shady area under the trees.*

shake 🔑 /ʃeɪk/ *verb* (**shakes**, **shaking**, **shook** /ʃʊk/, **has shaken** /ˈʃeɪkən/) **1** to move quickly from side to side or up and down: *The house shakes when trains go past.* ◇ *He was shaking with fear.* **2** to make something move quickly from side to side or up and down: *Shake the bottle before opening it.* ◇ *An explosion shook the windows.*

shake hands to hold someone's hand and move it up and down when you meet them

shake your head to move your head from side to side to mean 'no' ➲ Note at **head**[1].

shaky /ˈʃeɪki/ *adjective* (**shakier**, **shakiest**) **1** shaking because you are ill or frightened: *You've got shaky hands.* **2** not firm; not strong: *Don't sit in that chair – it's a bit shaky.*

shall 🔑 /ʃəl; ʃæl/ *modal verb*

❖ **GRAMMAR**

The negative form of **shall** is **shall not** or the short form **shan't** /ʃɑːnt/: *I shan't be there.*

The short form of **shall** is **'ll**. We often use this: *I'll* (= I shall) *see you tomorrow.*

1 a word that you use instead of 'will' with 'I' and 'we' to show the future: *I shall see you tomorrow.* **2** a word that you use when you ask what is the right thing to do: *Shall I close the window?* ◇ *What shall we do tomorrow?* ➲ Look at **modal verb**.

shallow /ˈʃæləʊ/ *adjective* (**shallower**, **shallowest**) not deep; with not much water: *This part of the river is shallow – we can walk across.* ➲ picture on page A5

shamba *noun* (East African English) a small farm or a field that is used for growing crops

shame ⚷ /ʃeɪm/ *noun* (no plural) the unhappy feeling that you have when you have done something wrong or stupid: *I was filled with* (= felt a lot of) *shame after I lied to my parents.* ℹ The adjective is **ashamed**.

it's a shame; what a shame it is sad; I am sorry: *It's a shame that you have to leave now.*

shameful /ˈʃeɪmfl/ *adjective* wrong; that you should feel bad about: *What he did was shameful.*

shameless /ˈʃeɪmləs/ *adjective* doing bad things without caring what other people think: *shameless greed*

shampoo /ʃæmˈpuː/ *noun* (*plural* **shampoos**) a special liquid for washing your hair: *a bottle of shampoo*
▸ **shampoo** *verb* (**shampoos**, **shampooing**, **shampooed** /ʃæmˈpuːd/): *How often do you shampoo your hair?*

shan't /ʃɑːnt/ = **shall not**

shape¹ ⚷ /ʃeɪp/ *noun* **1** (*plural* **shapes**) what you see if you draw a line round something; the form of something: *What shape is the table – round or square?* ◇ *I made a bowl in the shape of a fish.* ◇ *Circles, squares and triangles are all different shapes.* **2** (no plural) how good or bad something is; how healthy someone is: *He was in bad shape after the accident.*

out of shape not in the right shape: *That jumper's gone out of shape.*

shape² ⚷ /ʃeɪp/ *verb* (**shapes**, **shaping**, **shaped** /ʃeɪpt/) to give a certain shape to something: *She shaped the clay into a pot.*

shaped ⚷ /ʃeɪpt/ *adjective* with a certain shape: *That rock is shaped like a cat.* ◇ *an L-shaped room*

share¹ ⚷ /ʃeə(r)/ *verb* (**shares**, **sharing**, **shared** /ʃeəd/) **1** to give parts of something to different people: *Share these sweets with your friends.* ◇ *We shared the stew between three of us.* **2** to have or use something with another person: *I share a bedroom with my sister.*

share² ⚷ /ʃeə(r)/ *noun* a part of something bigger that each person has: *Here is your share of the cake.* ◇ *I did my share of the work.*

shark

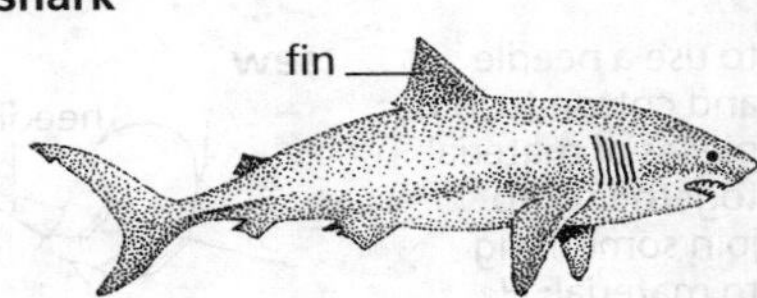

shark /ʃɑːk/ *noun* a big fish that lives in the sea. Some **sharks** have sharp teeth and are dangerous.

sharp¹ ⚷ /ʃɑːp/ *adjective* (**sharper**, **sharpest**) **1** with an edge or point that cuts or makes holes easily: *a sharp knife* ◇ *a sharp needle* OPPOSITE **blunt** **2** strong and sudden: *a sharp bend in the road* ◇ *I felt a sharp pain in my leg.* **3** clear and easy to see: *We could see the sharp outline of the mountains against the sky.* **4** able to see, hear or learn well: *She's got a very sharp mind.* ◇ *sharp eyes* **5** sudden and angry: *sharp words* **6** with a taste like lemons: *If your drink tastes too sharp, add some sugar.* ▸ **sharply** *adverb*: *The road bends sharply to the left.* ◇ *'Please go away!' he said sharply.*

> ❖ **WORD FAMILY**
> **sharp** *adjective*, **sharp** *adverb*
> **sharpen** **sharpener**

sharp² /ʃɑːp/ *adverb* **1** exactly: *Be here at six o'clock sharp.* **2** with a big change of direction: *Turn sharp right at the next corner.*

sharpen /ˈʃɑːpən/ *verb* (**sharpens**, **sharpening**, **sharpened** /ˈʃɑːpənd/) to make something sharp or sharper: *sharpen a knife*

sharpener /ˈʃɑːpnə(r)/ *noun* a thing that you use for making something sharp: *a pencil sharpener* ➲ Picture at **pencil**.

shatter /ˈʃætə(r)/ *verb* (**shatters**, **shattering**, **shattered** /ˈʃætəd/) to break into very small pieces; to break something into very small pieces: *The glass hit the floor and shattered.* ◇ *The explosion shattered the windows.*

shave /ʃeɪv/ *verb* (**shaves**, **shaving**, **shaved** /ʃeɪvd/) to cut hair off your face o body by cutting it very close with a **razor**: *He shaves every morning.* ▶ **shave** *noun*: *I haven't had a shave today.*

shaver /ˈʃeɪvə(r)/ *noun* an electric tool that you use for **shaving** ➲ Look at **razor**.

shawl /ʃɔːl/ *noun* a big piece of cloth that a woman wears round her shoulders, or that you put round a baby

she 🔑 /ʃiː/ *pronoun* a woman or girl who the sentence is about: *'Where's your sister?' 'She's* (= she is) *at work.'*

shed[1] /ʃed/ *noun* a small building where you keep things or animals: *We keep our tools in a small shed.*

shed[2] /ʃed/ *verb* (**sheds**, **shedding**, **shed**, **has shed**) to let something fall off: *The snake shed its skin.*

she'd /ʃiːd/ **1** = **she had** **2** = **she would**

sheep

sheep 🔑 /ʃiːp/ *noun* (*plural* **sheep**) an animal that people keep on farms for its meat and its wool

> ❖ **WORD BUILDING**
>
> A young sheep is called a **lamb**. Meat from a young sheep is also called **lamb**.
>
> A female sheep is called a **ewe**. A male sheep is called a **ram**.

sheer /ʃɪə(r)/ *adjective* **1** complete: *sheer nonsense* **2** very steep: *a sheer drop to the sea*

sheet 🔑 /ʃiːt/ *noun* **1** a big piece of thin material for a bed: *I put some clean sheets on the bed.* **2** a thin flat piece of something like paper, glass or metal: *a sheet of writing paper*

shelf 🔑 /ʃelf/ *noun* (*plural* **shelves** /ʃelvz/) a long flat piece of wood on a wall or in a cupboard, where things can stand: *Put the plates on the shelf.* ➲ Look at **bookshelf**.

shell 🔑 /ʃel/ *noun* the hard outside part of birds' eggs and nuts, and of some animals ➲ Picture at **coconut, crab, egg, groundnut, snail, tortoise.** ➲ Look at **seashell**.

she'll /ʃiːl/ = **she will**

shellfish /ˈʃelfɪʃ/ *noun* (*plural* **shellfish**) a kind of animal that lives in water and that has a shell

shelter[1] /ˈʃeltə(r)/ *noun* **1** (no plural) being safe from bad weather or danger: *We took shelter from the rain under a tree.* ◇ *People ran for shelter when the bombs started to fall.* **2** (*plural* **shelters**) a place where you are safe from bad weather or danger: *a bus shelter* (= for people who are waiting at a bus stop)

shelter[2] /ˈʃeltə(r)/ *verb* (**shelters**, **sheltering**, **sheltered** /ˈʃeltəd/) **1** to make someone or something safe from bad weather or danger: *The trees shelter the house from the wind.* **2** to go to a place where you will be safe from bad weather or danger: *Let's shelter from the rain under that tree.*

shelves

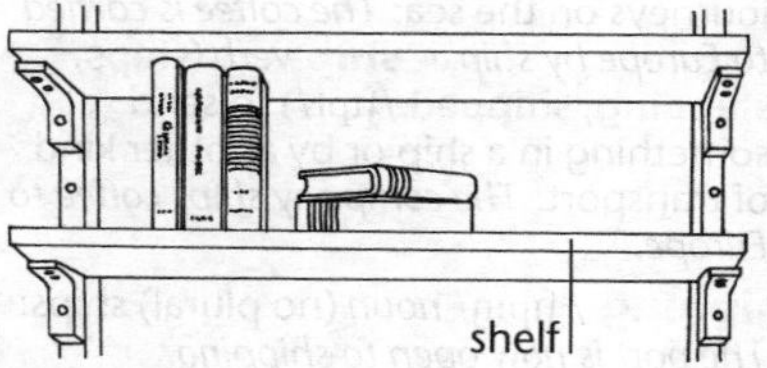

shelves *plural of* **SHELF**

Sheng *noun* (no plural) (East African English) a simple language that young people in cities in Kenya use, that includes words from English, Kiswahili and other African languages

shepherd /ˈʃepəd/ *noun* a person who looks after sheep

she's /ʃiːz/ **1** = **she is** **2** = **she has**

shield[1] /ʃiːld/ *noun* a big piece of metal, wood or leather that soldiers carried in front of their bodies when they were fighting in wars long ago. Some police officers carry **shields** now.

shield[2] /ʃiːld/ *verb* (**shields**, **shielding**, **shielded**) to keep someone or something safe from danger or from being hurt: *She shielded her eyes from the sun with her hand.*

shift[1] /ʃɪft/ *verb* (**shifts**, **shifting**, **shifted**) to move something to another place: *Can you help me to shift the bed?*

shift[2] /ʃɪft/ *noun* a group of workers who begin work when another group finishes: *Each shift in the factory works for eight hours.* ◇ *the night shift*

shifting cultivation /ˌʃɪftɪŋ ˌkʌltɪˈveɪʃn/ *noun* (no plural) a way of farming in which a farmer grows crops on a piece of land for a long time until they do not grow well there any more, then the farmer uses a new piece of land

shilling /ˈʃɪlɪŋ/ *noun* money that people use in several East African countries: *A hundred cents make one shilling.* ◇ *The car cost 500 000 shillings.*

shine 🔑 /ʃaɪn/ *verb* (**shines, shining, shone** /ʃɒn/, **has shone**) **1** to give out light: *The sun is shining.* **2** to be bright: *I polished my shoes until they shone.* ▶ **shine** *noun* (no plural) a bright appearance: *This shampoo gives your hair a lovely shine.*

shiny 🔑 /ˈʃaɪni/ *adjective* (**shinier, shiniest**) causing a bright effect when in the sun or in light: *a shiny new car*

ship 🔑 /ʃɪp/ *noun* a big boat for long journeys on the sea: *The coffee is carried to Europe by ship.* ▶ **ship** *verb* (**ships, shipping, shipped** /ʃɪpt/) to send something in a ship or by another kind of transport: *The company ships coffee to Europe.*

shipping /ˈʃɪpɪŋ/ *noun* (no plural) ships: *The port is now open to shipping.*

shipwreck /ˈʃɪprek/ *noun* an accident at sea when a ship breaks in bad weather or on rocks
be shipwrecked to be on a ship when it is in a **shipwreck**: *They were shipwrecked off the coast of Tanzania.*

shirt 🔑 /ʃɜːt/ *noun* a thin piece of clothing that you wear on the top part of your body: *He wore a shirt and tie.*

shirt

shiver /ˈʃɪvə(r)/ *verb* (**shivers, shivering, shivered** /ˈʃɪvəd/) to shake because you are cold, frightened or ill: *We were shivering with cold.*

shock[1] 🔑 /ʃɒk/ *noun* **1** a very bad surprise: *The news of his death was a shock to all of us.* **2** a sudden pain when electricity goes through your body: *Don't touch that wire – you'll get an electric shock.*

shock[2] 🔑 /ʃɒk/ *verb* (**shocks, shocking, shocked** /ʃɒkt/) to give someone a very bad surprise; to upset someone: *She was shocked by his death.*

shocking 🔑 /ˈʃɒkɪŋ/ *adjective* If something is shocking, it makes you feel upset, angry, or surprised in a very bad way: *a shocking crime*

shoes

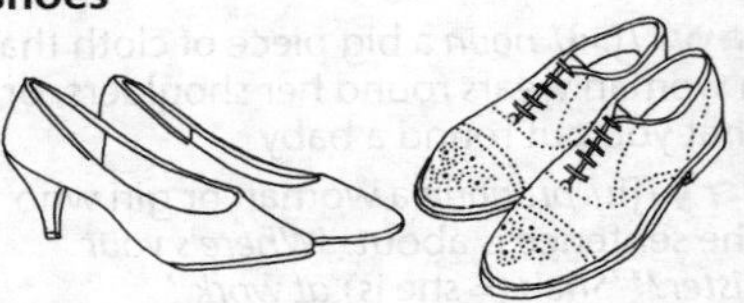

two pairs of **shoes**

shoe 🔑 /ʃuː/ *noun* a covering made of leather or plastic that you wear on your foot: *a pair of shoes* ◇ *What size are these shoes?* ◇ *What size shoes do you take?* ◇ *a shoe shop*

shoelace /ˈʃuːleɪs/ *noun* a string that you tie to close a shoe: *Tie your shoelaces.*

shoemaker /ˈʃuːmeɪkə(r)/ *noun* a person whose job is making shoes and boots

shoeshine /ˈʃuːʃaɪn/ *noun* (no plural) the job of cleaning people's shoes for money

shone *form of* SHINE

shook *form of* SHAKE

shoot[1] 🔑 /ʃuːt/ *verb* (**shoots, shooting, shot** /ʃɒt/, **has shot**) **1** to send a bullet from a gun or an arrow from a **bow**; to hurt or kill a person or an animal with a gun: *She shot an arrow at the target.* ◇ *The police officer was shot in the arm.* **2** to move quickly or suddenly: *The car shot past us.* **3** to make a film: *They are shooting a film about the war.* **4** to try to kick or hit the ball into the goal in a sport like football: *You've got the ball. Shoot!* ➲ Look at **shot**[2].

shoot[2] /ʃuːt/ *noun* a new part of a plant: *The first shoots appear after the rains.*

shop[1] 🔑 /ʃɒp/ *noun* a building where you buy things: *a bookshop* ◇ *a clothes shop*

shop[2] 🔑 /ʃɒp/ *verb* (**shops, shopping, shopped** /ʃɒpt/) to go to buy things from shops: *I'm shopping for some new clothes.*
ℹ It is more usual to say **go shopping**.
▶ **shopper** /ˈʃɒpə(r)/ *noun* a person who is buying things: *The streets were full of shoppers.*

shop assistant /ˈʃɒp əsɪstənt/ (also **shop attendant** /ˈʃɒp ətendənt/) *noun* a person who works in a shop

shopkeeper /ˈʃɒpkiːpə(r)/ *noun* a person who owns a small shop

shoplifting /ˈʃɒplɪftɪŋ/ *noun* (no plural) stealing things from shops ▸ **shoplifter** /ˈʃɒplɪftə(r)/ *noun* a person who steals things from shops

shopping 🔑 /ˈʃɒpɪŋ/ *noun* (no plural) **1** buying things from shops: *She does her shopping after work.* **2** the things that you have bought in a shop: *Will you carry my shopping for me?*
go shopping to go to buy things from shops

shopping centre /ˈʃɒpɪŋ sentə(r)/ *noun* a place where there are a lot of shops together

shopping mall /ˈʃɒpɪŋ mɔːl/ *noun* a big building where there are a lot of shops together

shore /ʃɔː(r)/ *noun* the land next to the sea or a lake

short 🔑 /ʃɔːt/ *adjective* (**shorter**, **shortest**) **1** very little from one end to the other: *Her hair is very short.* ◇ *We live a short distance from the beach.* OPPOSITE **long** ➲ picture on page A5 **2** very little from the bottom to the top: *I'm too short to reach the top shelf.* ◇ *a short fat man* OPPOSITE **tall** **3** that only lasts for a little time: *The prayer was very short.* ◇ *a short rest* OPPOSITE **long** ℹ The verb is **shorten**.
be short of something to not have enough of something: *I'm short of money this month.*
for short as a short way of saying or writing something: *My brother's name is Kiptanui, but we call him 'Kip' for short.*
short for something a short way of saying or writing something: *'Kim' is short for 'Kimani'.*

shortage /ˈʃɔːtɪdʒ/ *noun* when there is not enough of something: *a water shortage* ◇ *There is a shortage of teachers.*

short-change /ˌʃɔːt ˈtʃeɪndʒ/ *verb* (**short-changes**, **short-changing**, **short-changed** /ˌʃɔːt ˈtʃeɪndʒd/) to not give enough money back to someone who has paid for something: *I think I was short-changed in that shop this morning.*

shortcut /ˈʃɔːtkʌt/ *noun* a shorter way to get somewhere: *We took a shortcut to school across the field.*

shorten /ˈʃɔːtn/ *verb* (**shortens**, **shortening**, **shortened** /ˈʃɔːtnd/) to become shorter or to make something shorter: *The trousers were too long, so I shortened them.*

shortly /ˈʃɔːtli/ *adverb* soon: *The doctor will see you shortly, Mr Githinji.* ◇ *We left shortly after six o'clock.*

shorts

shorts /ʃɔːts/ *noun* (plural) short trousers that end above your knees: *a new pair of shorts*

a pair of **shorts**

short-sighted /ˌʃɔːt ˈsaɪtɪd/ *adjective* able to see things clearly only if they are very close to you OPPOSITE **long-sighted**

short-term /ˌʃɔːt ˈtɜːm/ *adjective* lasting for a short period of time: *short-term plans*

shot[1] 🔑 /ʃɒt/ *noun* **1** firing a gun, or the noise that this makes: *He fired a shot.* **2** a photograph: *This is a good shot of you.* **3** kicking or hitting a ball in a sport like football: *Good shot!*

shot[2] *form of* SHOOT[1]

shot-put

the shot-put /ðə ˈʃɒt pʊt/ *noun* (no plural) the sport of throwing a heavy metal ball (called a **shot**) as far as possible

should 🔑 /ʃʊd/ *modal verb*

❖ **PRONUNCIATION**
Should sounds like **good**.

1 a word that you use to tell or ask someone what is the right thing to do: *If you feel ill, you should stay in bed.* ◇ *Should I apologize to her for being so rude?* ◇ *You shouldn't eat so many sweets.* **2** a word that you use to say what you think will happen or what you think is true: *They should arrive soon.* **3** the word for 'shall' in the past: *We asked if we should help her.*
➲ Look at **modal verb**.

❖ **GRAMMAR**
The negative form of 'should' is **should not** or the short form **shouldn't** /ˈʃʊdnt/ and is used to tell someone what you think is wrong or bad: *You shouldn't eat so fast.*

shoulder 🔑 /ˈʃəʊldə(r)/ *noun*

> ❖ **PRONUNCIATION**
> **Shoulder** sounds like **older**.

the part of your body between your neck and your arm ➲ picture on page A13

shouldn't /ˈʃʊdnt/ = **should not**

shout 🔑 /ʃaʊt/ *verb* (**shouts, shouting, shouted**) to speak very loudly: *Don't shout at me!* ◇ *'Go back!' she shouted.* ▶ **shout** *noun*: *We heard a shout for help.*

shove /ʃʌv/ *verb* (**shoves, shoving, shoved** /ʃʌvd/) to push someone or something in a rough way: *They shoved him through the door.*

shovel[1] /ˈʃʌvl/ *noun* a tool like a **spade** with a short handle, that you use for moving earth, sand, etc.

shovel[2] /ˈʃʌvl/ *verb* (**shovels, shovelling, shovelled** /ˈʃʌvld/) to move something with a **shovel**: *We shovelled the sand onto the lorry.*

show[1] 🔑 /ʃəʊ/ *verb* (**shows, showing, showed** /ʃəʊd/, **has shown** /ʃəʊn/, *or* **has showed**) **1** to let someone see something: *She showed me her new bag.* ◇ *You have to show your ticket on the train.* **2** to make something clear; to explain something to someone: *Can you show me how to use the computer?* **3** to appear or be seen: *The anger showed in his face.*
show off to talk loudly or do something silly to make people notice you: *Chebet is always talking about how much money she has, just to show off.*
show something off to let people see something that is new or beautiful: *Egesa wanted to show off his new jacket.*
show someone round to go with someone and show them everything in a building: *Moraa showed me round the school.*
show up to arrive: *What time did they show up yesterday evening?*

show[2] 🔑 /ʃəʊ/ *noun* **1** something that you watch at the theatre or on television: *a comedy show* ◇ *Did you enjoy the show?* **2** a group of things in one place that people go to see: *a flower show*
on show in a place where people can see it: *The paintings are on show at the National Gallery until 15 May.*

shower 🔑 /ˈʃaʊə(r)/ *noun* **1** a place where you can wash by standing under water that falls from above you: *There's a shower in the bathroom.* **2** washing yourself in a shower: *I had a shower after work.* **3** rain that falls for a short time: *Tomorrow there will be sunshine and showers.*

shown *form of* SHOW[1]

show-off /ˈʃəʊ ɒf/ *noun* a person who tries to show how clever they are so that other people will notice them

shrank *form of* SHRINK

shred /ʃred/ *noun* a small thin piece torn or cut off something: *shreds of paper*

shriek /ʃriːk/ *verb* (**shrieks, shrieking, shrieked** /ʃriːkt/) to make a loud high cry: *She shrieked in fear* (= because she was afraid). ▶ **shriek** *noun*: *He gave a shriek of pain.*

shrill /ʃrɪl/ *adjective* (**shriller, shrillest**) A **shrill** sound is high and loud: *a shrill whistle*

shrimp /ʃrɪmp/ *noun* a small sea animal that you can eat

shrine /ʃraɪn/ *noun* a special holy place

shrink /ʃrɪŋk/ *verb* (**shrinks, shrinking, shrank** /ʃræŋk/ *or* **shrunk** /ʃrʌŋk/, **has shrunk**) to become smaller or make something smaller: *My trousers shrank when I washed them.*

shrub /ʃrʌb/ *noun* a plant like a small low tree

shrug /ʃrʌg/ *verb* (**shrugs, shrugging, shrugged** /ʃrʌgd/) to move your shoulders to show that you do not know or do not care about something: *I asked her where Ali was but she just shrugged.* ▶ **shrug** *noun* (no plural): *He answered my question with a shrug.*

shrug

He **shrugged** his shoulders.

shrunk *form of* SHRINK

shudder /ˈʃʌdə(r)/ *verb* (**shudders, shuddering, shuddered** /ˈʃʌdəd/) to shake, for example because you are afraid: *He shuddered when he saw the snake.* ▶ **shudder** *noun*: *She felt a shudder of fear.*

shuffle /ˈʃʌfl/ *verb* (**shuffles, shuffling, shuffled** /ˈʃʌfld/) **1** to walk slowly, without taking your feet off the ground: *The old man shuffled along the road.* **2** to mix a set of cards before a game

shuka *noun* (East African English) a red **blanket** (a thick piece of cloth) with a pattern of squares on it, that Maasai people wear

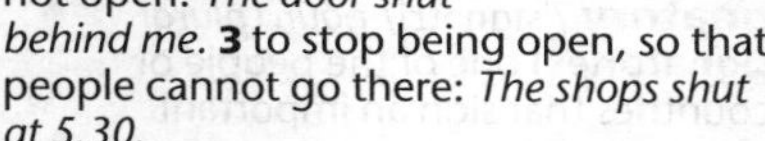
shuka

shut[1] ⚷ /ʃʌt/ *verb* (**shuts**, **shutting**, **shut**, **has shut**) **1** to move something so that it is not open: *Could you shut the door, please?* **2** to move so that it is not open: *The door shut behind me.* **3** to stop being open, so that people cannot go there: *The shops shut at 5.30.*

shut down to close and stop working; to make something close and stop working: *The factory shut down last year.*

shut up to stop talking: *Shut up and listen!* ❶ This expression is quite rude.

shut[2] ⚷ /ʃʌt/ *adjective* closed; not open: *The school is shut today.* ◇ *Is the door shut?*

shutter /ˈʃʌtə(r)/ *noun* a wooden or metal thing that covers the outside of a window: *Close the shutters.*

shutters

shuttle /ˈʃʌtl/ *noun* **1** a plane or a bus that goes to a place and then back again and again **2** = **space shuttle**

shy ⚷ /ʃaɪ/ *adjective* (**shyer**, **shyest**) not able to talk easily to people you do not know: *He was too shy to speak to her.*
▸ **shyness** /ˈʃaɪnəs/ *noun* (no plural) being shy

sick ⚷ /sɪk/ *adjective* (**sicker**, **sickest**) not well; ill: *She's looking after her sick mother.* ➲ Look at **sickness**.

be sick When you are **sick**, food comes up from your stomach and out of your mouth.

be sick of something to have had or done too much of something, so that you do not want it any longer: *I'm sick of being inside – let's go for a walk.*

feel sick to feel that food is going to come up from your stomach

sickle /ˈsɪkl/ *noun* a tool for cutting grass, grain, etc. that has a handle and a long curved **blade** (= sharp part)

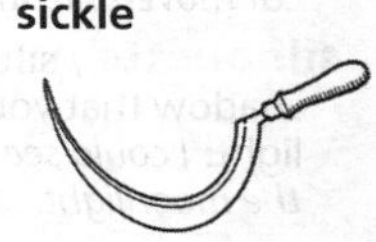
sickle

sickness /ˈsɪknəs/ *noun* (no plural) being ill: *He could not work for a long time because of sickness.*

side ⚷ /saɪd/ *noun* **1** one of the flat outside parts of something: *A box has six sides.* ◇ *A piece of paper has two sides.* **2** the part of something that is not the front, back, top or bottom: *There is a door at the side of the house.* ➲ Picture at **back**[1]. **3** the edge of something; the part that is away from the middle: *I stood at the side of the road.* **4** the right or left part of something: *He lay on his side.* ◇ *We drive on the left side of the road in Kenya.* **5** one of two groups of people who fight or play a game against each other: *Which side won?*

be on someone's side to agree with or help someone in a fight or an argument: *Robi said I was wrong, but Nduku was on my side.*

side by side next to each other: *They walked side by side.*

take sides to show that you agree with one person, and not the other, in a fight or an argument

sidewalk /ˈsaɪdwɔːk/ *noun* = **pavement**

sideways /ˈsaɪdweɪz/ *adjective*, *adverb* **1** to or from the side: *She looked sideways at the girl next to her.* **2** with one of the sides first: *We carried the table sideways through the door.*

siege /siːdʒ/ *noun* **1** when an army stays outside a town for a long time so that people and things cannot get in or out **2** when police stay outside a building for a long time to try to make a criminal come out

sieve /sɪv/ *noun* a tool with a metal or plastic net, that we use to separate solid things from liquid things, etc.
▸ **sieve** *verb* (**sieves**, **sieving**, **sieved** /sɪvd/): *Sieve the sand to remove any stones.*

sieve

sigh /saɪ/ *verb* (**sighs**, **sighing**, **sighed** /saɪd/)

> ❖ **PRONUNCIATION**
> **Sigh** sounds like **my**.

to breathe once very deeply when you are sad, tired, pleased, etc. ▸ **sigh** *noun*: *'I wish I had more money,' he said with a sigh.*

sight ⚷ /saɪt/ *noun*

❖ **PRONUNCIATION**

Sight and **site** sound the same.

1 (no plural) the power to see: *She has poor sight* (= she cannot see well). SAME MEANING **eyesight** **2** (no plural) seeing someone or something: *When we reached the top of the hill we had our first sight of the city.* **3** (*plural* **sights**) something that you see: *The mountains were a beautiful sight.* **4** (*plural* **sights**) the interesting places to visit: *What are the main sights of Kenya?*
at first sight when you see someone or something for the first time: *He fell in love with her at first sight.*
catch sight of someone or **something** to see someone or something suddenly: *I caught sight of Egesa in the crowd.*
come into sight to come where you can see it: *The bus came into sight.*
in sight where you can see it: *Is the land in sight yet?*
lose sight of someone or **something** to no longer be able to see someone or something: *After an hour at sea we lost sight of land.*
out of sight where you cannot see it: *We watched until the car was out of sight.*

sightseeing /ˈsaɪtsiːɪŋ/ *noun* (no plural) visiting interesting places: *We did some sightseeing in Kampala.*

sightseer /ˈsaɪtsiːə(r)/ *noun* a person who is visiting interesting places: *The town was full of sightseers.*

signs

sign[1] ⚷ /saɪn/ *noun*

❖ **PRONUNCIATION**

Sign sounds like **nine**.

1 a mark, shape or movement that has a special meaning: *+ and – are signs that mean 'plus' and 'minus'.* ◇ *I put up my hand as a sign for him to stop.* **2** a thing with writing or a picture on it that tells you something: *The sign said 'No Entry'.* ◇ *a road sign* **3** something that tells you about another thing: *Dark clouds are a sign of rain.*

sign[2] ⚷ /saɪn/ *verb* (**signs**, **signing**, **signed** /saɪnd/) to write your name in your own way on something: *Sign here, please.* ◇ *I signed the letter.* ℹ The noun is **signature**.

signal ⚷ /ˈsɪgnəl/ *noun* a light, sound or movement that tells you something without words: *A red light is a signal for cars to stop.* ▶ **signal** *verb* (**signals**, **signalling**, **signalled** /ˈsɪgnəld/) to make a signal: *The police officer signalled to the children to cross the road.*

signatory /ˈsɪgnətri/ *noun* (*plural* **signatories**) one of the people or countries that sign an important agreement.

signature /ˈsɪgnətʃə(r)/ *noun* your name that you have written in your own way ℹ The verb is **sign**. ➲ Picture at **cheque**.

significance /sɪgˈnɪfɪkəns/ *noun* (no plural) the importance or meaning of something: *What is the significance of this discovery?*

significant /sɪgˈnɪfɪkənt/ *adjective* important; with a special meaning: *The police say that the time of the robbery was very significant.*

signpost /ˈsaɪnpəʊst/ *noun* a sign beside a road, that shows the way to a place and how far it is

Sikh /siːk/ *noun* a person who follows **Sikhism** (= one of the religions of India)

silence ⚷ /ˈsaɪləns/ *noun* **1** (no plural) When there is silence, there is no sound: *I can only work in complete silence.* **2** (*plural* **silences**) a time when nobody speaks or makes a noise: *There was a long silence before she answered the question.*
in silence without speaking or making a noise: *We ate our dinner in silence.*

silencer /ˈsaɪlənsə(r)/ *noun* a thing that you fix to a machine to reduce the noise it makes

silent /ˈsaɪlənt/ *adjective* **1** with no sound; completely quiet: *Everyone was asleep, and the house was silent.* **2** If you are **silent**, you are not speaking: *I asked him a question and he was silent for a moment before he answered.* ▶ **silently** *adverb*: *The cat moved silently towards the bird.*

silhouette /ˌsɪluˈet/ *noun* a dark shape or shadow that you see against something light: *I could see the silhouette of a boy in the moonlight.*

silk /sɪlk/ *noun* (no plural) thin smooth cloth that is made from the threads that an insect (called a **silkworm**) makes: *a silk shirt*

silly 🔑 /ˈsɪli/ *adjective* (**sillier**, **silliest**) stupid; not clever: *Don't be so silly!* ◇ *It was silly of you to leave the door open when you went out.*

silver[1] 🔑 /ˈsɪlvə(r)/ *noun* (no plural) **1** a shiny grey metal that is very valuable: *a silver necklace* **2** things that are made of silver, for example knives, forks and plates

silver[2] /ˈsɪlvə(r)/ *adjective* with the colour of silver: *silver paper*

SIM card /ˈsɪm kɑːd/ *noun* a plastic card inside a mobile phone that stores information about the phone and the person using it

similar 🔑 /ˈsɪmələ(r)/ *adjective* the same in some ways but not completely the same: *Rats are similar to mice, but they are bigger.* ◇ *Hawa and her sister look very similar.*

similarity /ˌsɪməˈlærəti/ *noun* (*plural* **similarities**) a way that people or things are the same: *There are a lot of similarities between the two countries.* OPPOSITE **difference**

simple 🔑 /ˈsɪmpl/ *adjective* (**simpler**, **simplest**) **1** easy to do or understand: *This dictionary is written in simple English.* ◇ *'How do you open this?' 'I'll show you – it's simple.'* OPPOSITE **difficult** **2** without a lot of different parts or extra things; plain: *She wore a simple black dress.* ◇ *a simple meal* ➲ Look at **complex**[1], **complicated**.

> ❖ **WORD FAMILY**
>
> **simple** **simply** **simplicity** **simplify**

simplicity /sɪmˈplɪsəti/ *noun* (no plural) being simple: *I like the simplicity of these paintings.*

simplify /ˈsɪmplɪfaɪ/ *verb* (**simplifies**, **simplifying**, **simplified** /ˈsɪmplɪfaɪd/) to make something easier to do or understand: *The story has been simplified so that the children can understand it.*

simply /ˈsɪmpli/ *adverb* **1** in a simple way: *Please explain it more simply.* **2** only: *Don't get angry – I'm simply asking you to help.* **3** really: *Her work is simply excellent!*

simsim (also **sesame**) *noun* (no plural) (East African English) a plant with small seeds. You can use **simsim** oil and seeds in cooking.

sin /sɪn/ *noun* something that your religion says you should not do, because it is very bad: *Stealing is a sin.* ► **sin** *verb* (**sins**, **sinning**, **sinned** /sɪnd/) to do something that your religion says is very bad

since[1] 🔑 /sɪns/ *preposition* in all the time after: *I haven't seen him since 2012.* ◇ *She has been ill since Sunday.*

> ❖ **for** or **since**?
>
> We use **for** to say how long something has continued, for example in **hours**, **days** or **years**: *She has been ill for three days.* ◇ *I've lived here for three years.*
>
> We use **since** with points of time in the past, for example a **time** on the clock, a **date** or an **event**: *He's been working since 6 o'clock.* ◇ *I have lived here since I was a child.*

since[2] 🔑 /sɪns/ *conjunction* **1** from the time when: *She has lived here since she was a child.* ◇ *Nduku hasn't written since she went to university.* **2** because: *Since it's your birthday, I'll buy you a drink.* SAME MEANING **as**

since[3] 🔑 /sɪns/ *adverb* from then until now: *Deng left three years ago and we haven't seen him since.*
ever since in all the time from then until now: *Odoi went to Bungoma in 2012 and he has lived there ever since.*

sincere /sɪnˈsɪə(r)/ *adjective* If you are **sincere**, you are honest and you mean what you say: *I was being sincere when I said I wanted to help.*

sincerely /sɪnˈsɪəli/ *adverb* in a **sincere** way: *I sincerely believe that this is the right decision.*
Yours sincerely words that you write at the end of a letter, before your name

sing 🔑 /sɪŋ/ *verb* (**sings**, **singing**, **sang** /sæŋ/, **has sung** /sʌŋ/) to make music with your voice: *She sang a song.* ◇ *The birds were singing.*

singer 🔑 /ˈsɪŋə(r)/ *noun* a person who sings

single[1] 🔑 /ˈsɪŋgl/ *adjective* **1** only one: *There wasn't a single cloud in the sky.* **2** not married: *Is she married or single?* **3** for one person: *I would like to book a single room, please.* ◇ *a single bed* ➲ Look at **double**[1]. **4** for a journey to a place, but not back again: *How much is a single ticket to Musoma, please?* OPPOSITE **return**
every single each: *You answered every single question correctly.*

single[2] /ˈsɪŋgl/ *noun* **1** a ticket for a journey to a place, but not back again: *A single to Kampala, please.* ➲ Look at **return**[2]. **2** a piece of recorded music that consists of one song; a CD that a single is recorded on: *Have you heard Amani's new single?* ➲ Look at **album**.

singular /ˈsɪŋgjələ(r)/ *noun* (no plural) the form of a word that you use for one person or thing: *The singular of 'men' is 'man'.* ▶ **singular** *adjective*: *'Table' is a singular noun.* ➲ Look at **plural**.

sink[1] ⚷ /sɪŋk/ *verb* (**sinks**, **sinking**, **sank** /sæŋk/, **has sunk** /sʌŋk/) **1** to go down under water: *If you throw a stone into water, it sinks.* ◇ *The fishing boat sank to the bottom of the sea.* ➲ Look at **float**. **2** to make a ship go down under water: *The ship was sunk by a bomb.* **3** to go down: *The sun sank behind the hills.*

sink[2] /sɪŋk/ *noun* the place in a kitchen where you wash dishes

sip /sɪp/ *verb* (**sips**, **sipping**, **sipped** /sɪpt/) to drink something slowly, taking only a little each time: *She sipped her coffee.* ▶ **sip** *noun*: *Can I have a sip of your drink?*

sir ⚷ /sɜː(r)/ *noun* **1** (no plural) a polite way of speaking to a man, instead of using his name: *'Can I help you, sir?' asked the shop assistant.* **2 Sir** (no plural) a word that you use at the beginning of a business letter to a man: *Dear Sir …* ➲ Look at **madam**.

siren /ˈsaɪrən/ *noun* a machine that makes a long loud sound to warn people about something. Police cars and fire engines have **sirens**.

sisal /ˈsaɪsl/ *noun* (no plural) a plant with long leaves that we use to make rope, floor covering, etc.

sister ⚷ /ˈsɪstə(r)/ *noun* **1** Your sister is a girl or woman who has the same parents as you: *I've got two sisters and one brother.* ◇ *Robi and Hawa are sisters.* **2** a nurse in a hospital

sister-in-law /ˈsɪstər ɪn lɔː/ *noun* (*plural* **sisters-in-law**) **1** the sister of someone's wife or husband **2** the wife of someone's brother

sit ⚷ /sɪt/ *verb* (**sits**, **sitting**, **sat** /sæt/, **has sat**) **1** to rest on your bottom: *We sat in the garden all afternoon.* ◇ *She was sitting on a bench.* **2** (also **sit down**) to put yourself down on your bottom: *Come and sit next to me.* ◇ *She came into the room and sat down.* **3** to do an examination: *The students will sit their exams in June.*
sit up to sit when you have been lying: *He sat up in bed and looked at the clock.*

site /saɪt/ *noun* a place where something is, was, or will be: *The station was built on the site of an old farm.* ◇ *a campsite*

sitting room = **living room**

situated /ˈsɪtʃueɪtɪd/ *adjective* in a place: *The hotel is situated close to the beach.*

situation ⚷ /ˌsɪtʃuˈeɪʃn/ *noun* the things that are happening in a certain place or at a certain time: *Boke is in a difficult situation – she can't decide what to do.*

six ⚷ /sɪks/ *number* (*plural* **sixes**) 6

sixteen ⚷ /ˌsɪksˈtiːn/ *number* 16

sixteenth /ˌsɪksˈtiːnθ/ *adjective, adverb, noun* 16th

sixth /sɪksθ/ *adjective, adverb, noun* **1** 6th **2** one of six equal parts of something; ⅙

sixtieth /ˈsɪkstiəθ/ *adjective, adverb, noun* 60th

sixty ⚷ /ˈsɪksti/ *number* **1** 60 **2 the sixties** (plural) the numbers, years or temperature between 60 and 69
in your sixties between the ages of 60 and 69

size ⚷ /saɪz/ *noun* **1** (no plural) how big or small something is: *My bedroom is the same size as yours.* **2** (*plural* **sizes**) an exact measurement: *Have you got these shoes in a bigger size?*

skates

roller skates ice skates

skate[1] /skeɪt/ *noun* a boot with wheels or a long sharp piece of metal under it, that you wear for moving on smooth ground or on ice: *a pair of roller skates* ◇ *ice skates*

skate[2] /skeɪt/ *verb* (**skates**, **skating**, **skated**) to move on **skates**: *Can you skate?*

skateboard /ˈskeɪtbɔːd/ *noun* a long piece of wood or plastic on wheels. You stand on it as it moves over the ground.

skateboard

▶ **skateboarder** /ˈskeɪtbɔːdə(r)/ *noun*: *There is a special area for skateboarders in the park.*

skeleton /ˈskelɪtn/ *noun* the bones of a whole animal or person

skeleton

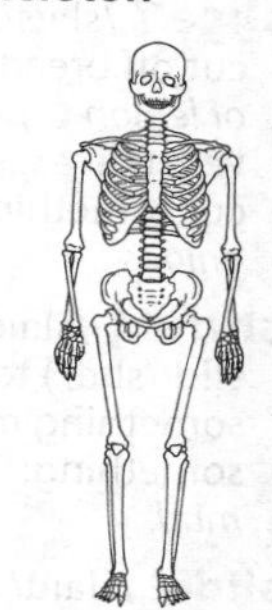

sketch /sketʃ/ *verb* (**sketches**, **sketching**, **sketched** /sketʃt/) to draw something quickly: *I sketched the house.* ▶ **sketch** *noun* (*plural* **sketches**) a picture that you draw quickly

skid /skɪd/ *verb* (**skids**, **skidding**, **skidded**) If a car, lorry, etc. **skids**, it moves suddenly and in a dangerous way to the side, for example because the road is wet: *The lorry skidded on the wet road.*

skies *plural of* SKY

skilful /ˈskɪlfl/ *adjective* very good at doing something: *a skilful tennis player* ▶ **skilfully** /ˈskɪlfəli/ *adverb*: *The food was skilfully prepared.*

skill ⚷ /skɪl/ *noun* **1** (no plural) being able to do something well: *You need great skill to fly a plane.* **2** (*plural* **skills**) a thing that you can do well: *What skills do you need for this job?*

❖ **WORD FAMILY**

skill skilful skilfully
skilled: OPPOSITE **unskilled**

skilled /skɪld/ *adjective* good at something because you have learnt about or done it for a long time: *skilled workers*

skin ⚷ /skɪn/ *noun* **1** (no plural) what covers the outside of a person or an animal's body: *She has dark skin.* **2** (*plural* **skins**) the outside part of some fruits and vegetables: *a banana skin* ➲ Picture at **banana**.

skinny /ˈskɪni/ *adjective* (**skinnier**, **skinniest**) too thin: *He's very skinny – he doesn't eat enough.*

skip /skɪp/ *verb* (**skips**, **skipping**, **skipped** /skɪpt/) **1** to move along quickly with little jumps from one foot to the other foot: *The child skipped along the road.* **2** to jump many times over a rope that is turning **3** to not do or have something that you should do or have: *I skipped my class today and went swimming.* ▶ **skip** *noun* a little jump

skipping rope /ˈskɪpɪŋ rəʊp/ *noun* a rope that you use for **skipping**

skirt ⚷ /skɜːt/ *noun* a piece of clothing for a woman or girl that hangs from the middle of the body: *She was wearing a long blue skirt.*

skull /skʌl/ *noun* the bones in the head of a person or an animal

sky ⚷ /skaɪ/ *noun* (*plural* **skies**) the space above the earth where you can see the sun, moon and stars: *a beautiful blue sky* ◇ *There are no clouds in the sky.*

skyscraper /ˈskaɪskreɪpə(r)/ *noun* a very tall building: *He works on the 49th floor of a skyscraper.*

slab /slæb/ *noun* a thick flat piece of something: *slabs of stone* ◇ *a big slab of meat*

slam /slæm/ *verb* (**slams**, **slamming**, **slammed** /slæmd/) to close something or put something down with a loud noise: *She slammed the door angrily.* ◇ *He slammed the book on the table and went out.*

slang /slæŋ/ *noun* (no plural) words that a certain group of people use when they are talking: *'Dude' is slang for 'man'.* ❶ You do not use **slang** when you need to be polite, and you do not usually use it in writing.

slant /slɑːnt/ *verb* (**slants**, **slanting**, **slanted**) Something that **slants** has one side higher than the other or does not stand straight up: *My handwriting slants to the left.*

slap /slæp/ *verb* (**slaps**, **slapping**, **slapped** /slæpt/) to hit someone with the flat inside part of your hand: *He slapped me in the face.* ▶ **slap** *noun*: *She gave me a slap across the face.*

slash /slæʃ/ *verb* (**slashes**, **slashing**, **slashed** /slæʃt/) to make a long cut with a sharp object: *We slashed our way through the undergrowth with sticks.*

slaughter /ˈslɔːtə(r)/ *verb* (**slaughters**, **slaughtering**, **slaughtered** /ˈslɔːtəd/) **1** to kill an animal for food **2** to kill a lot of people in a cruel way ▶ **slaughter** *noun* (no plural) killing animals or people

slave /sleɪv/ *noun* a person who belongs to another person and must work for that person for no money

slavery /ˈsleɪvəri/ *noun* (no plural) **1** being a **slave**: *They lived in slavery.* **2** having **slaves**: *When did slavery end in America?*

sleep[1] /sliːp/ *verb* (**sleeps, sleeping, slept** /slept/, **has slept**) to rest with your eyes closed, as you do at night: *I sleep for eight hours a night.* ◇ *Did you sleep well?*
not sleep a wink to not be able to sleep: *I didn't sleep a wink last night.*

❖ **SPEAKING**

Be careful! We usually say **be asleep** not **be sleeping**: *I was asleep when you phoned.*

We use **go to sleep** or **fall asleep** to talk about starting to sleep: *She got into bed and went to sleep.*

sleep[2] /sliːp/ *noun* (no plural) a time when you rest with your eyes closed, as you do at night: *I didn't get any sleep last night.*
go to sleep to start to sleep: *I got into bed and soon went to sleep.*

❖ **WORD FAMILY**

sleep *noun*, **sleep** *verb*
sleepy **sleepless**

sleeping sickness /ˈsliːpɪŋ ˌsɪknəs/ *noun* (no plural) a serious illness that makes you want to sleep. You get **sleeping sickness** from **tsetse flies**.

sleepless /ˈsliːpləs/ *adjective* without sleep: *He had a sleepless night worrying about exams.*

sleepy /ˈsliːpi/ *adjective* (**sleepier, sleepiest**) **1** tired and ready to sleep: *I felt sleepy after that big meal.* **2** quiet, with not many things happening: *a sleepy little village*

sleet /sliːt/ *noun* (no plural) snow and rain together

sleeve

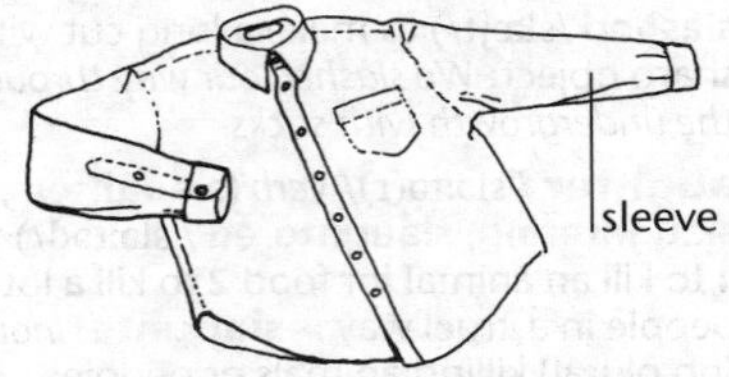

sleeve /sliːv/ *noun* the part of a coat, dress, shirt, etc. that covers your arm: *a shirt with short sleeves* ➲ Picture at **shirt**.

slender /ˈslendə(r)/ *adjective* thin, in a nice way: *She has long, slender legs.*

slept *form of* SLEEP[1]

slice /slaɪs/ *noun* a thin piece that you cut off bread, meat or other food: *a slice of lemon* ➲ picture on page A4 ▶ **slice** *verb* (**slices, slicing, sliced** /slaɪst/) to cut something into slices: *Slice the onions.*

slide[1] /slaɪd/ *verb* (**slides, sliding, slid** /slɪd/) to move smoothly or make something move smoothly across something: *The children were sliding in the mud.*

slide[2] /slaɪd/ *noun* **1** a long metal thing that children play on. They climb up steps, sit down, and then slide down the other side. **2** a small image that you show on a **screen**, using a special machine (called a **projector**)

slide

slight /slaɪt/ *adjective* (**slighter, slightest**) small; not important or serious: *I've got a slight problem.* ◇ *a slight headache*

slightly /ˈslaɪtli/ *adverb* a little: *I'm feeling slightly better today.* ➲ Note at **very**[1].

slim /slɪm/ *adjective* (**slimmer, slimmest**) thin, but not too thin: *a tall slim man*

sling[1] /slɪŋ/ *noun* a piece of cloth that you wear to hold up an arm that is hurt: *She's got her arm in a sling.*

sling[2] /slɪŋ/ *verb* (**slings, slinging, slung** /slʌŋ/, **has slung**) to throw something without care: *He slung his clothes on the floor.*

slip[1] /slɪp/ *verb* (**slips, slipping, slipped** /slɪpt/) **1** to move smoothly over something by mistake and fall or almost fall: *He slipped in the mud and broke his leg.* ➲ Look at **slippery**. **2** to go quickly and quietly so that nobody sees you: *Adisa slipped out of the room when the children were asleep.* **3** to put something in a place quickly and quietly: *He slipped the money into his pocket.*

slip[2] /slɪp/ *noun* **1** a small piece of paper: *Write your address on this slip of paper.* **2** a small mistake: *I made a slip.*

slipper /ˈslɪpə(r)/ (also **flip-flop**) *noun* a light open shoe that has a piece of leather, plastic, etc. that goes between your big toe and the one next to it: *a pair of beaded slippers*

slippers

slippery /ˈslɪpəri/ *adjective* so smooth or wet that you cannot move on it or hold it easily: *The road was wet and slippery.* ◇ *The skin of a fish is slippery.*

slit /slɪt/ *noun* a long thin hole or cut ▶ **slit** *verb* (**slits**, **slitting**, **slit**, **has slit**) to make a long thin cut in something: *I slit the envelope open with a knife.*

slither /ˈslɪðə(r)/ *verb* (**slithers**, **slithering**, **slithered** /ˈslɪðəd/) to move along like a snake: *The snake slithered across the floor.*

slogan /ˈsləʊgən/ *noun* a short sentence or group of words that is easy to remember. **Slogans** are used to make people believe something or buy something: *'Faster than light' is the slogan for the new car.*

slope[1] /sləʊp/ *noun* a piece of ground that is higher at one end than at the other, like the side of a hill: *We walked down the mountain slope.*

slope[2] /sləʊp/ *verb* (**slopes**, **sloping**, **sloped** /sləʊpt/) to be higher at one end than the other: *The field slopes down to the river.* ◇ *a sloping roof*

slot /slɒt/ *noun* a long thin hole that you push something through: *Put a coin in the slot and take your ticket.*

slot machine /ˈslɒt məʃiːn/ *noun* a machine that gives you things like drinks or sweets when you put money in a small hole

slow[1] ⚷ /sləʊ/ *adjective* (**slower**, **slowest**) **1** A person or thing that is slow does not move or do something quickly: *a slow train* ◇ *She hasn't finished her work yet – she's very slow.* **2** If a clock or watch is slow, it shows a time that is earlier than the real time: *My watch is five minutes slow.* ➲ Look at **quick**, **fast**[1]. ➲ Note at **clock**. ▶ **slowly** *adverb*: *The old lady walked slowly up the hill.* ➲ Look at **quickly**, **fast**[2].

slow[2] /sləʊ/ *adverb* (**slower**, **slowest**) slowly: *Please drive slower.*

slow[3] /sləʊ/ *verb* (**slows**, **slowing**, **slowed** /sləʊd/)

slow down to start to go more slowly; to make someone or something start to go more slowly: *The train slowed down as it came into the station.* ◇ *Don't talk to me when I'm working – it slows me down.*

slug /slʌg/ *noun* a small soft animal that moves slowly and eats plants

slug

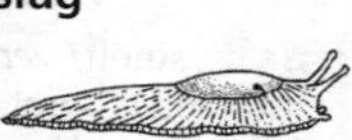

slum /slʌm/ *noun* a poor part of a city where people live in old dirty buildings

slung *form of* SLING[2]

sly /slaɪ/ *adjective* A person who is **sly** tricks people or does things secretly.

smack /smæk/ *verb* (**smacks**, **smacking**, **smacked** /smækt/) to hit someone with the inside part of your hand: *They never smack their children.* ▶ **smack** *noun*: *She gave her son a smack.*

small ⚷ /smɔːl/ *adjective* (**smaller**, **smallest**) **1** not big; little: *This dress is too small for me.* ◇ *My house is smaller than yours.* **2** young: *They have two small children.* ➲ picture on page A5

smart /smɑːt/ *adjective* (**smarter**, **smartest**) **1** right for a special or important time; clean and tidy: *She wore smart clothes for the concert.* ◇ *He looks very smart in his new jacket.* **2** clever: *She's smarter than her sister.* ▶ **smartly** *adverb*: *She was very smartly dressed.*

smartphone /ˈsmɑːtfəʊn/ *noun* a mobile phone that can also do some of the things that a computer can do

smash /smæʃ/ *verb* (**smashes**, **smashing**, **smashed** /smæʃt/) **1** to break something into many pieces: *The boys smashed the window.* **2** to break into many pieces: *I dropped the plate but it didn't smash.* ▶ **smash** *noun* (no plural) the loud noise when something breaks into pieces: *The glass hit the floor with a smash.*

smear /smɪə(r)/ *verb* (**smears**, **smearing**, **smeared** /smɪəd/) to spread soft stuff on something, making it dirty: *The child smeared porridge over his clothes.* ▶ **smear** *noun* a dirty mark: *She had smears of paint on her dress.*

smell ⚷ /smel/ *verb* (**smells**, **smelling**, **smelt** /smelt/ *or* **smelled** /smeld/, **has smelt** *or* **has smelled**) **1** to notice something with your nose: *Can you smell smoke?* ◇ *I can smell something burning!* **2** If something smells, you notice it with your nose: *This fish smells bad.* ◇ *The perfume smells of roses.* **3** to have a bad smell: *Your feet smell!* ▸ **smell** *noun* something that you notice with your nose: *There's a smell of gas in this room.*

smelly /ˈsmeli/ *adjective* (**smellier**, **smelliest**) with a bad smell: *smelly socks*

smelt /smelt/ *verb* (**smelts**, **smelting**, **smelted**) to get metal from rock or earth (**ore**) by making it very hot

smile 🔑 /smaɪl/ *verb* (**smiles**, **smiling**, **smiled** /smaɪld/) to move your mouth to show that you are happy or that you think something is funny: *He smiled at me.* ▸ **smile** *noun*: *She had a big smile on her face.*

smiley /ˈsmaɪli/ *noun* (*plural* **smileys**) the symbol :-) representing a smiling face. You can use it in emails or text messages to show that you are happy or joking.

smoke[1] 🔑 /sməʊk/ *noun* (no plural) the grey or black gas that you see in the air when something is burning: *The room was full of smoke.* ◇ *cigarette smoke*

smoke[2] 🔑 /sməʊk/ *verb* (**smokes**, **smoking**, **smoked** /sməʊkt/) to breathe in smoke through a cigarette, etc. and let it out again: *He was smoking a cigarette.* ◇ *Does she smoke?* ▸ **smoking** /ˈsməʊkɪŋ/ *noun* (no plural): *No smoking in the theatre.*

❖ **WORD FAMILY**

smoke *noun*, **smoke** *verb*
smoker **smoked** **smoky**

smoked /sməʊkt/ *adjective* prepared by putting it over a wood fire so that you can keep it for a long time: *smoked fish*

smoker /ˈsməʊkə(r)/ *noun* **1** a person who smokes **2** a tool that you use to blow smoke into a home for bees (**beehive**), so that you can collect the sweet food that we eat (**honey**)

smoky /ˈsməʊki/ *adjective* (**smokier**, **smokiest**) full of smoke: *a smoky room*

smooth 🔑 /smuːð/ *adjective* (**smoother**, **smoothest**) **1** flat; not rough: *Babies have smooth skin.* **2** moving gently: *The weather was good so we had a very smooth flight.* OPPOSITE **bumpy** ▸ **smoothly** *adverb*: *The plane landed smoothly.*

smoothie /ˈsmuːði/ *noun* a drink made of fruit mixed with milk or ice cream: *a banana smoothie*

smother /ˈsmʌðə(r)/ *verb* (**smothers**, **smothering**, **smothered** /ˈsmʌðəd/) **1** to kill someone by covering their face so that they cannot breathe **2** to cover a thing with too much of something: *He smothered his food with salt.*

SMS /ˌes em ˈes/ *noun* (no plural) a system for sending short written messages from one mobile phone to another ➲ Look at **text message**.

smuggle /ˈsmʌɡl/ *verb* (**smuggles**, **smuggling**, **smuggled** /ˈsmʌɡld/) to take things secretly into or out of a country: *They were trying to smuggle drugs into the country.* ▸ **smuggler** /ˈsmʌɡlə(r)/ *noun*: *drug smugglers*

snack /snæk/ *noun* a small quick meal: *We had a snack on the way.*

snack bar /ˈsnæk bɑː(r)/ *noun* a place where you can buy and eat **snacks**

snag /snæɡ/ *noun* a small problem: *The work will be finished tomorrow if there are no snags.*

snail /sneɪl/ *noun* a small soft animal with a hard shell on its back. **Snails** move very slowly.

snail
shell

snake 🔑 /sneɪk/ *noun* an animal with a long thin body and no legs: *Do these snakes bite?*

snake

snap[1] /snæp/ *verb* (**snaps**, **snapping**, **snapped** /snæpt/) **1** to break suddenly with a sharp noise: *He snapped the pencil in two.* **2** to say something in a quick angry way: *'Go away – I'm busy!' she snapped.* **3** to try to bite someone or something: *The dog snapped at my leg.*

snap[2] /snæp/ (also **snapshot** /ˈsnæpʃɒt/) *noun* a photograph: *She showed us her family snaps.*

snarl /snɑːl/ *verb* (**snarls**, **snarling**, **snarled** /snɑːld/) When an animal **snarls**, it shows its teeth and makes a low angry sound: *A dog snarled at her.*

snatch /snætʃ/ *verb* (**snatches**, **snatching**, **snatched** /snætʃt/) to take something in a rough and sudden way: *He snatched her money and ran away.*

sneak /sni:k/ *verb* (**sneaks**, **sneaking**, **sneaked** /sni:kt/) to go somewhere very quietly so that nobody sees or hears you: *She sneaked out of the classroom while the teacher wasn't looking.*

sneer /snɪə(r)/ *verb* (**sneers**, **sneering**, **sneered** /snɪəd/) to speak or smile in an unkind way to show that you do not like someone or something or that you think they are not good enough: *I told her about my idea, but she just sneered at it.* ▶ **sneer** *noun* an unkind smile

sneeze /sni:z/ *verb* (**sneezes**, **sneezing**, **sneezed** /sni:zd/) to send air out of your nose and mouth with a sudden loud noise, for example because you have a cold: *Pepper makes you sneeze.* ▶ **sneeze** *noun*: *She gave a loud sneeze.*

sneeze

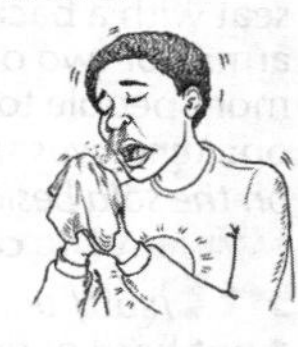

sniff /snɪf/ *verb* (**sniffs**, **sniffing**, **sniffed** /snɪft/) **1** to make a noise by suddenly taking in air through your nose. People sometimes sniff when they have a cold or when they are crying. **2** to smell something: *The dog was sniffing the meat.* ▶ **sniff** *noun*: *I heard a loud sniff.*

snooze /snu:z/ *verb* (**snoozes**, **snoozing**, **snoozed** /snu:zd/) to sleep for a short time ▶ **snooze** *noun*: *I had a snooze after lunch.*

snore /snɔ:(r)/ *verb* (**snores**, **snoring**, **snored** /snɔ:d/) to make a noise in your nose and throat when you are asleep: *He was snoring loudly.*

snort /snɔ:t/ *verb* (**snorts**, **snorting**, **snorted**) to make a noise by blowing air through the nose: *The horse snorted.*

snow ⚷ /snəʊ/ *noun* (no plural) soft white stuff that falls from the sky in cool countries when it is very cold: *Snow lay thick on the ground.* ▶ **snow** *verb* (**snows**, **snowing**, **snowed** /snəʊd/) When it snows, snow falls from the sky: *It often snows in the mountains.*

snowy /ˈsnəʊi/ *adjective* (**snowier**, **snowiest**) with a lot of snow: *snowy weather*

so[1] ⚷ /səʊ/ *adverb* **1** a word that you use when you say how much, how big, etc. something is: *This bag is so heavy that I can't carry it.* ◇ *I'm so tired I can't keep my eyes open.*

> ❖ **so** or **such**?
>
> You use **so** before an adjective that is used without a noun: *It was so cold that we stayed at home.* ◇ *This book is so exciting.*
>
> You use **such** before a noun that has an adjective in front of it: *It was such a cold night that we stayed at home.* ◇ *This is such an exciting book.*

2 a word that makes another word stronger: *Why are you so late?* **3** also: *Nduku is a teacher and so is her husband.* ◇ *'I like this music.' 'So do I.'*

> ❖ **GRAMMAR**
>
> In negative sentences, we use **neither** or **nor**: *'I don't like this music.' 'Neither do I.'* ◇ *If Rono doesn't go, nor will Ali.*

4 You use 'so' instead of saying words again: *'Is Ngenzi coming?' 'I think so.'* (= I think that he is coming)

and so on and other things like that: *The shop sells pens, paper and so on.*

not so ... as words that show how two people or things are different: *He's not so tall as his brother.*

or so words that you use to show that a number is not exactly right: *Forty or so people came to the party.*

so[2] ⚷ /səʊ/ *conjunction* **1** because of this or that: *The shop is closed so I can't buy any bread.* **2** (also **so that**) in order that: *Speak louder so that everybody can hear you.* ◇ *I'll draw you a map so you can find my house.*

so what? why is that important or interesting?: *'It's late.' 'So what? There's no school tomorrow.'*

soak /səʊk/ *verb* (**soaks**, **soaking**, **soaked** /səʊkt/) **1** to make someone or something very wet: *It was raining when I went out. I got soaked!* **2** to be in a liquid; to let something stay in a liquid: *He left his dirty shirts to soak in soapy water.*

soak up to take in a liquid: *The cloth soaked up all the water.*

soaking /ˈsəʊkɪŋ/ *adjective* very wet: *This towel is soaking.*

soap ⚷ /səʊp/ *noun* (no plural) stuff that you use with water for washing and cleaning: *a bar of soap* ▶ **soapy** *adjective* with soap in it: *soapy water*

soap opera /ˈsəʊp ɒprə/ *noun* a story about the lives of a group of people, that is on the TV or radio every day or several times each week

soap powder /ˈsəʊp paʊdə(r)/ *noun* (no plural) powder that you use for washing clothes

soapstone /ˈsəʊpstəʊn/ *noun* (no plural) a kind of soft stone that feels like soap: *soapstone carvings*

soar /sɔː(r)/ *verb* (**soars**, **soaring**, **soared** /sɔːd/) **1** to fly high in the sky **2** to go up very fast: *Prices are soaring.*

sob /sɒb/ *verb* (**sobs**, **sobbing**, **sobbed** /sɒbd/) to cry loudly, making short sounds ▸ **sob** *noun*: *'I don't want to go!' he said with a sob.*

sober /ˈsəʊbə(r)/ *adjective* not drunk

so-called /ˌsəʊ ˈkɔːld/ *adjective* a word that you use to show that you do not think another word is correct: *Her so-called friends did not help her* (= they are not really her friends).

soccer /ˈsɒkə(r)/ *noun* (no plural) football

social 🔑 /ˈsəʊʃl/ *adjective* of people together; of being with other people: *the social problems of big cities* ◇ *Teta has a busy social life* (= she goes out with friends a lot).

social media /ˌsəʊʃl ˈmiːdiə/ *noun* (no plural) websites and computer programs used for **social networking**: *Social media is changing the way people communicate, work and shop.*

social networking /ˌsəʊʃl ˈnetwɜːkɪŋ/ *noun* (no plural) communicating with your friends or people who share your interests using a website or other service on the Internet: *a social networking website*

social security /ˌsəʊʃl sɪˈkjʊərəti/ *noun* (no plural) money that a government pays to someone who is poor, for example because they have no job

social studies /ˌsəʊʃl ˈstʌdiz/ *noun* (plural) the study of people and how they live, behave, etc.

social worker /ˈsəʊʃl wɜːkə(r)/ *noun* a person whose job is to help people who have problems, for example because they are poor or ill

society 🔑 /səˈsaɪəti/ *noun* **1** (no plural) a group of people living together, with the same ideas about how to live **2** (*plural* **societies**) a group of people who are interested in the same thing: *a music society*

sock 🔑 /sɒk/ *noun* a thing that you wear on your foot, inside your shoe

socks

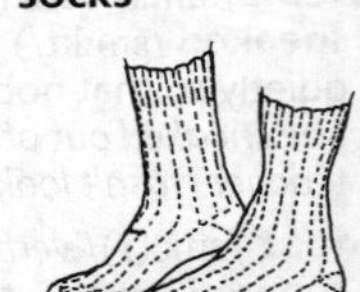

a pair of **socks**

socket /ˈsɒkɪt/ *noun* a place in a wall where you can connect a lamp, a machine, etc. to the electricity ➲ Picture at **plug**[1].

sofa /ˈsəʊfə/ *noun* a long comfortable seat with a back and arms, for two or more people to sit on: *Kendi was sitting on the sofa beside me.* SAME MEANING **couch**

sofa

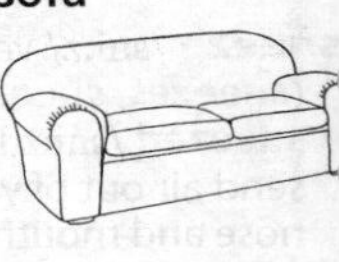

soft 🔑 /sɒft/ *adjective* (**softer**, **softest**) **1** not hard or firm; that moves when you press it: *The ground is soft here.* ◇ *a soft bed* **2** smooth and nice to touch; not rough: *soft skin* ◇ *My cat's fur is very soft.* **3** quiet or gentle; not loud: *soft music* ◇ *He has a very soft voice.* **4** not bright or strong: *the soft light of a candle* **5** kind and gentle; not strict: *She's too soft with her class and they don't do any work.* OPPOSITE **tough**

soft drink /ˌsɒft ˈdrɪŋk/ *noun* a cold drink with no alcohol in it, for example orange juice

softly /ˈsɒftli/ *adverb* gently or quietly: *She spoke very softly.*

software /ˈsɒftweə(r)/ *noun* (no plural) programs for a computer

softwood /ˈsɒftwʊd/ *noun* wood from trees that are easy to grow and to cut down

soggy /ˈsɒgi/ *adjective* (**soggier**, **soggiest**) very wet, soft and unpleasant

soil 🔑 /sɔɪl/ *noun* (no plural) what plants and trees grow in; earth: *Crops need fertile soil.*

solar /ˈsəʊlə(r)/ *adjective* of or using the sun: *solar energy*

the solar system /ðə ˈsəʊlə sɪstəm/ *noun* (no plural) the sun and the planets that move around it

sold *form of* SELL

be sold out When things are **sold out**, there are no more to sell: *I'm sorry – the bananas are sold out.*

soldier 🔑 /ˈsəʊldʒə(r)/ *noun* a person in an army: *All the soldiers were in uniform.*

sole[1] /səʊl/ *noun* the bottom part of your foot or of a shoe: *These boots have rubber soles.*

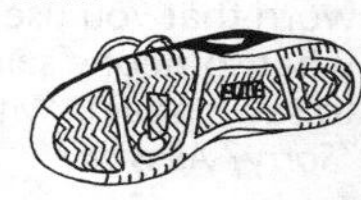

sole[2] /səʊl/ *adjective* only: *His sole interest is football.*

solemn /ˈsɒləm/ *adjective* serious: *slow, solemn music* ▶ **solemnly** *adverb*: *'I've got some bad news for you,' he said solemnly.*

solid[1] 🔑 /ˈsɒlɪd/ *adjective* **1** hard, not like a liquid or a gas: *Water becomes solid when it freezes.* **2** with no empty space inside; made of the same material inside and outside: *a solid rubber ball* ◇ *This ring is solid gold.*

solid[2] 🔑 /ˈsɒlɪd/ *noun* a substance that is not a liquid or gas: *Milk is a liquid and bread is a solid.*

solitary /ˈsɒlətri/ *adjective* without others; alone: *She went for a long solitary walk.*

solo[1] /ˈsəʊləʊ/ *noun* (*plural* **solos**) a piece of music for one person to sing or play: *a piano solo*

solo[2] /ˈsəʊləʊ/ *adjective, adverb* alone; without other people: *She flew solo across the Atlantic.*

solution 🔑 /səˈluːʃn/ *noun* the answer to a question or problem: *I can't find a solution to this puzzle.* ℹ The verb is **solve**.

solve 🔑 /sɒlv/ *verb* (**solves, solving, solved** /sɒlvd/) to find the answer to a question, problem or puzzle: *The police are still trying to solve the crime.* ℹ The noun is **solution**.

some 🔑 /sʌm/ *adjective, pronoun*

> ❖ **PRONUNCIATION**
>
> **Some** and **sum** sound the same.

1 a number or an amount of something: *I bought some tomatoes and some butter.* ◇ *I've made some coffee. Do you want some?* **2** part of a number or amount of something: *Some of the children can swim, but the others can't.* **3** I do not know which: *There's some man at the door who wants to see you.*

some more a little more or a few more: *Have some more coffee.* ◇ *Some more people arrived.*

some time quite a long time: *We waited for some time but she did not come.*

> ❖ **GRAMMAR**
>
> In questions and after 'not' and 'if', we usually use **any**: *Did you buy any apples?* ◇ *I didn't buy any meat.* ◇ *If you have any questions, ask me now.*
>
> If you think the answer to the question will be 'yes', use **some**: *Would you like some cake?*

somebody 🔑 /ˈsʌmbədi/ = **someone**

somehow 🔑 /ˈsʌmhaʊ/ *adverb* in some way that you do not know: *We must find her somehow.*

someone 🔑 /ˈsʌmwʌn/ (also **somebody**) *pronoun* a person; a person that you do not know: *There's someone at the door.* ◇ *Somebody has broken the window.* ◇ *Ask someone else* (= another person) *to help you.*

> ❖ **GRAMMAR**
>
> In questions and after 'not' and 'if', we usually use **anybody** or **anyone**: *Did anybody call while I was out?* ◇ *She doesn't know anyone in the team.*
>
> If you think the answer to the question will be 'yes', use **someone**: *Has someone borrowed my book?*

somersault /ˈsʌməsɔːlt/ *noun* a movement when you turn your body with your feet going over your head: *The children were doing somersaults.*

something 🔑 /ˈsʌmθɪŋ/ *pronoun* a thing; a thing you cannot name: *There's something under the table. What is it?* ◇ *I want to tell you something.* ◇ *Would you like something else* (= another thing) *to eat?*

something like the same as someone or something, but not in every way: *A rat is something like a mouse, but bigger.*

sometime /ˈsʌmtaɪm/ *adverb* at a time that you do not know exactly: *I'll arrive sometime tomorrow.*

sometimes 🔑 /ˈsʌmtaɪmz/ *adverb* not very often; not all the time: *He sometimes writes to me.* ◇ *Sometimes I walk to school and sometimes I go by bus.*

somewhere 🔑 /ˈsʌmweə(r)/ *adverb* at, in or to a place that you do not know exactly: *They live somewhere near here.*

◇ *'Did she go to Nyali?' 'No, I think she went somewhere else* (= to another place) *on the coast.'*

son /sʌn/ *noun*

❖ PRONUNCIATION

Son and **sun** sound the same.

a boy or man who is someone's child: *They have a son and two daughters.*

song /sɒŋ/ *noun* **1** (*plural* **songs**) a piece of music with words that you sing: *a pop song* **2** (no plural) singing; music that a person or bird makes

son-in-law /ˈsʌn ɪn lɔː/ *noun* (*plural* **sons-in-law**) the husband of someone's daughter

soon /suːn/ *adverb* not long after now, or not long after a certain time: *Awino will be home soon.* ◇ *She arrived soon after two o'clock.* ◇ *Goodbye! See you soon!*
as soon as at the same time that; when: *Phone me as soon as you get home.*
sooner or later at some time in the future: *Don't worry – I'm sure he will write to you sooner or later.*

soot /sʊt/ *noun* (no plural) black powder that comes from smoke

soothe /suːð/ *verb* (**soothes, soothing, soothed** /suːðd/) to make someone feel calmer and less unhappy: *The baby was crying, so I tried to soothe her by singing to her.* ▶ **soothing** /ˈsuːðɪŋ/ *adjective*: *soothing music*

soprano /səˈprɑːnəʊ/ *noun* (*plural* **sopranos**) the highest singing voice; a girl, boy or woman with this voice: *Most of the girls in the choir sing soprano.*

sore[1] /sɔː(r)/ *adjective* If a part of your body is sore, it gives you pain: *My feet were sore after the long walk.* ◇ *I've got a sore throat.*

sore[2] /sɔː(r)/ *noun* a place on your skin that is painful and red because there is something wrong: *His legs were covered in sores.*

sorghum /ˈsɔːgəm/ *noun* (no plural) a kind of grass with a lot of very small seeds that we can make into flour

sorrow /ˈsɒrəʊ/ *noun* (no plural) sadness

sorry /ˈsɒri/ *adjective* **1** a word that you use when you feel bad about something you have done: *I'm sorry I didn't phone you.* ◇ *Sorry I'm late!* ◇ *I'm sorry for losing your pen.* **2** sad: *I'm sorry you can't come with us.* **3** a word that you use to say 'no' politely: *I'm sorry – I can't help you.* **4** a word that you use when you did not hear what someone said and you want them to say it again: *'My name is Ali Kiptoon.' 'Sorry? Ali who?'*
feel sorry for someone to feel sad because someone has problems: *I felt sorry for her when her mother was ill.*

sort[1] /sɔːt/ *noun* a group of things or people that are the same in some way; a type or kind: *What sort of food do you like best?* ◇ *We found all sorts of shells on the beach.*
sort of words that you use when you are not sure about something: *It's sort of long and thin, a bit like a sausage.*

sort[2] /sɔːt/ *verb* (**sorts, sorting, sorted**) to put things into groups: *The machine sorts the rocks into large ones and small ones.*
sort out 1 to make something tidy: *I sorted out the kitchen.* **2** to find an answer to a problem

SOS /ˌes əʊ ˈes/ *noun* a call for help from a ship or a plane that is in danger

so that /ˈsəʊ ðət; ˈsoʊ ðæt/ = **so**[2]

sought *form of* SEEK

soul /səʊl/ *noun* **1** (*plural* **souls**) the part of a person that some people believe does not die when the body dies **2** (also **soul music**) (no plural) a kind of African American music: *a soul singer*
not a soul not one person: *I looked everywhere, but there wasn't a soul in the building.*

sound[1] /saʊnd/ *noun* something that you hear: *I heard the sound of a baby crying.* ◇ *Light travels faster than sound.*

sound[2] /saʊnd/ *verb* (**sounds, sounding, sounded**) to seem a certain way when you hear it: *He sounded angry when I spoke to him on the phone.* ◇ *That sounds like a good idea.* ◇ *She told me about the book – it sounds interesting.*

sound[3] /saʊnd/ *adjective* **1** healthy or strong: *sound teeth* **2** right and good: *sound advice*

sound[4] /saʊnd/ *adverb*
sound asleep sleeping very well: *The children are sound asleep.*

soup /suːp/ *noun* (no plural) liquid food that you make by cooking things like vegetables or meat in water: *chicken soup*

sour /ˈsaʊə(r)/ *adjective* **1** with a taste like lemons: *If it's too sour, put some sugar in it.* **2 Sour** milk tastes bad because it is not fresh: *This milk has gone sour.*

source /sɔːs/ *noun* a place where something comes from: *Our information comes from many sources.*

south 🔑 /saʊθ/ *noun* (no plural) the direction that is on your right when you watch the sun come up in the morning ➲ Picture at **compass**. ▶ **south** *adjective, adverb*: *Brazil is in South America.* ◇ *Birds fly south in the winter.*

southern 🔑 /ˈsʌðən/ *adjective* connected with, in or from the south part of a place: *Nairobi is in southern Kenya.*

souvenir /ˌsuːvəˈnɪə(r)/ *noun* something that you keep to remember a place or something that happened: *I brought back this straw hat as a souvenir of Spain.*

sow /səʊ/ *verb* (**sows**, **sowing**, **sowed** /səʊd/, **has sown** /səʊn/, *or* **has sowed**) to put seeds in the ground: *The farmer sowed the field with corn.*

soya /ˈsɔɪə/ *noun* (no plural) the plant that **soya beans** grow on; the food that is made from **soya beans**: *soya flour*

soya bean /ˈsɔɪə biːn/ *noun* a type of **bean** (= a seed from a plant) that we can cook and eat, or that is made into flour, oil or milk

space 🔑 /speɪs/ *noun* **1** (no plural) a place that is big enough for someone or something to go into it or onto it: *Is there space for me in your car?* **2** (*plural* **spaces**) an empty place between other things: *There is a space here for you to write your name.* **3** (no plural) the place far away outside the earth, where all the planets and stars are: *space travel*

spacecraft /ˈspeɪskrɑːft/ *noun* (*plural* **spacecraft**) a vehicle that travels in space

spaceship /ˈspeɪsʃɪp/ *noun* a vehicle that travels in space, carrying people

space shuttle /ˈspeɪs ʃʌtl/ (also **shuttle**) *noun* a vehicle that can travel into space and land like a plane when it comes back to earth

spacious /ˈspeɪʃəs/ *adjective* with a lot of space inside: *a spacious house*

spade /speɪd/ *noun* **1** a tool that you use for moving sand, soil, etc. **2** (**spades**) (plural) the playing cards (= the set of cards used for playing games) that have the shape ♠ on them: *the queen of spades*

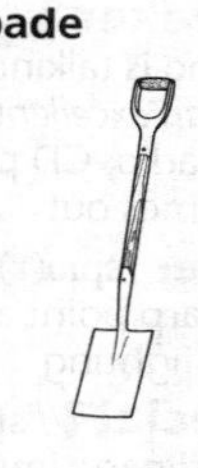
spade

spaghetti /spəˈgeti/ *noun* (no plural) a kind of food made from flour and water, that looks like long pieces of string

spanner /ˈspænə(r)/ *noun* a tool that you use for turning **nuts** and **bolts**

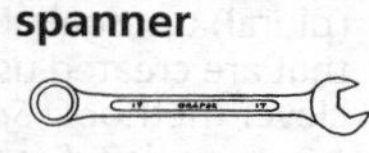
spanner

spare¹ /speə(r)/ *adjective* **1** extra; that you do not need now: *Have you got a spare pen that I can borrow?* **2 Spare** time is time when you are not studying or working: *What do you do in your spare time?*

spare² /speə(r)/ *verb* (**spares**, **sparing**, **spared** /speəd/) to be able to give something to someone: *I can't spare the time to help you today.* ◇ *Can you spare any money?*

spark /spɑːk/ *noun* a very small piece of fire

sparkle /ˈspɑːkl/ *verb* (**sparkles**, **sparkling**, **sparkled** /ˈspɑːkld/) to shine with a lot of very small points of light: *The sea sparkled in the sunlight.* ◇ *Her eyes sparkled with excitement.* ▶ **sparkle** *noun* (no plural): *the sparkle of diamonds*

sparkling /ˈspɑːklɪŋ/ *adjective* **1** shining with a lot of very small points of light: *She has sparkling eyes.* **2** used about a drink that has bubbles or gas in it, especially water SAME MEANING **fizzy** ➲ Look at **still²**.

sparrow /ˈspærəʊ/ *noun* a small brown bird

spat *form of* SPIT

speak 🔑 /spiːk/ *verb* (**speaks**, **speaking**, **spoke** /spəʊk/, **has spoken** /ˈspəʊkən/) **1** to say words; to talk to someone: *Please speak more slowly.* ◇ *Can I speak to Juma Kamotho, please?* (= words that you say on the telephone) **2** to know and use a language: *Can you speak French?* **3** to talk to a group of people: *He spoke to the class about his life as an artist.* ➲ Look at **speech**.

speak up to talk louder: *Can you speak up? I can't hear you!*

speaker 🔑 /ˈspiːkə(r)/ *noun* **1** a person who is talking to a group of people: *She is an excellent public speaker.* **2** the part of a radio, CD player, etc. where the sound comes out

spear /spɪə(r)/ *noun* a long stick with a sharp point at one end, used for hunting or fighting

special 🔑 /ˈspeʃl/ *adjective* **1** not usual or ordinary; important for a reason: *It's my birthday today so we are having a special dinner.* **2** for a particular person or thing: *He goes to a special school for deaf children.*

special effects /ˌspeʃl ɪˈfekts/ *noun* (plural) unusual pieces of action in a film that are created using computers or other clever methods: *Science fiction films often have wonderful special effects.*

specialist /ˈspeʃəlɪst/ *noun* a person who knows a lot about something: *She's a specialist in East African art.*

specialize /ˈspeʃəlaɪz/ *verb* (**specializes, specializing, specialized** /ˈspeʃəlaɪzd/)
specialize in something to study or know a lot about one special thing: *This doctor specializes in natural medicine.*

specially /ˈspeʃəli/ *adverb* **1** for a particular person or thing: *I made this cake specially for you.* **2** very; more than usual or more than others: *The food was not specially good.*

special needs /ˌspeʃl ˈniːdz/ *noun* (plural) needs that a person has because of mental and physical problems: *She teaches children with special needs.*

species /ˈspiːʃiːz/ *noun* (*plural* **species**) a group of animals or plants that are the same in some way: *a rare species of plant*

specific /spəˈsɪfɪk/ *adjective* **1** particular: *Is there anything specific that you want to talk about?* **2** exact and clear: *He gave us specific instructions on how to get there.* ▶ **specifically** /spəˈsɪfɪkli/ *adverb*: *I specifically asked you to write in pencil, not pen.*

specimen /ˈspesɪmən/ *noun* a small amount or part of something that shows what the rest is like; one example of a group of things: *a specimen of rock* ◇ *The doctor took a specimen of blood for testing.*

speck /spek/ *noun* a very small bit of something: *specks of dust*

spectacles /ˈspektəklz/ *noun* (plural) pieces of special glass that you wear over your eyes to help you see better: *a pair of spectacles* ❶ It is more usual to say **glasses**.

spectacular /spekˈtækjələ(r)/ *adjective* wonderful to see: *There was a spectacular view from the top of the mountain.*

spectator /spekˈteɪtə(r)/ *noun* a person who watches something that is happening: *There were 2 000 spectators at the football match.*

sped *form of* SPEED[2]

speech 🔑 /spiːtʃ/ *noun* **1** (*plural* **speeches**) a talk that you give to a group of people: *The President made a speech.* **2** (no plural) the power to speak, or the way that you speak: *The illness affected her speech.*

speed[1] 🔑 /spiːd/ *noun* how fast something goes: *The car was travelling at a speed of 50 kilometres an hour.* ◇ *a high-speed train* (= one that goes very fast)

speed[2] /spiːd/ *verb* (**speeds, speeding, sped** /sped/ *or* **speeded, has sped** *or* **has speeded**) **1** to go or move very quickly: *He sped past me on his bike.* **2** to drive too fast: *The police stopped her because she was speeding.*
speed up to go faster; to make something go faster

speed limit /ˈspiːd lɪmɪt/ *noun* the fastest that people are allowed to drive along a road: *What's the speed limit in towns?*

speedometer /spiːˈdɒmɪtə(r)/ *noun* a piece of equipment in a vehicle that shows you how fast you are travelling

spell[1] /spel/ *verb* (**spells, spelling, spelt** /spelt/ *or* **spelled** /speld/, **has spelt** *or* **has spelled**) to use the right letters to make a word: *'How do you spell your name?' 'A-Z-I-Z.'* ◇ *You have spelt this word wrong.*

spell[2] /spel/ *noun* magic words
put a spell on someone to say magic words to someone to change them or to make them do what you want: *The witch put a spell on the prince.*

spellcheck /ˈspeltʃek/ *verb* (**spellchecks, spellchecking, spellchecked** /ˈspeltʃekt/) to use a computer program to check that you have written words correctly: *I just need to spellcheck my essay.* ▶ **spellcheck** *noun*: *Have you done a spellcheck?*

spellchecker /ˈspeltʃekə(r)/ *noun* a computer program that checks that you have written words correctly

spelling /ˈspelɪŋ/ *noun* the right way of writing a word: *Look in your dictionary to find the right spelling.*

spend 🔑 /spend/ *verb* (**spends, spending, spent** /spent/, **has spent**) **1** to pay money for something: *Ajuma spends a lot of money on clothes.* **2** to use time for something: *I spent two weeks in hospital.* ◇ *He spends a lot of time sleeping.*

sphere /sfɪə(r)/ *noun* any round thing that is like a ball: *The Earth is a sphere.* ➲ picture on page A12

spice 🔑 /spaɪs/ *noun* a powder or the seeds from a plant that you can put in food to give it a stronger taste: *They use a lot of spices, especially ginger and pepper.* ▶ **spicy** /ˈspaɪsi/ *adjective* (**spicier, spiciest**) with spices in it: *Indian food is usually spicy.*

spider 🔑 /ˈspaɪdə(r)/ *noun* a small animal with eight legs, that catches and eats insects: *Spiders spin webs to catch flies.*

spider

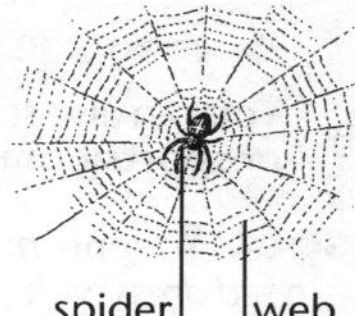

spied *form of* SPY²

spies 1 *plural of* SPY¹ **2** *form of* SPY²

spike /spaɪk/ *noun* a piece of metal with a sharp point: *The fence has spikes along the top.*

spill /spɪl/ *verb* (**spills, spilling, spilt** /spɪlt/ *or* **spilled** /spɪld/, **has spilt** *or* **has spilled**) If you **spill** a liquid, it flows out of something by accident: *I've spilt my tea!* ◇ *Don't spill the water.*

spill

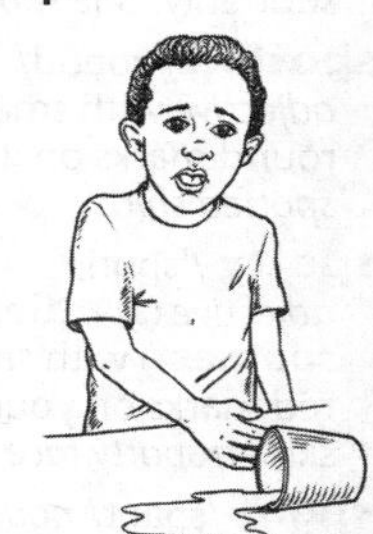

He **spilt** his drink

spin /spɪn/ *verb* (**spins, spinning, spun** /spʌn/, **has spun**) **1** to turn round quickly; to turn something round quickly: *She spun a coin on the table.* **2** to make thread from wool or cotton **3** to make a **web** (= a thin net): *The spider spun a web.*

spinach /ˈspɪnɪtʃ/ *noun* (no plural) a vegetable with big green leaves

spinach

spine /spaɪn/ *noun* the line of bones in your back ➲ picture on page A13

spiral /ˈspaɪrəl/ *noun* a long shape that goes round and round as it goes up: *A spring is a spiral.* ▶ **spiral** *adjective*: *a spiral staircase*

spiral

spirit 🔑 /ˈspɪrɪt/ *noun* **1** the part of a person that is not the body. Some people think that your spirit does not die when your body dies. **2 spirits** (plural) alcoholic drinks. Whisky and brandy are spirits. **3 spirits** (plural) how you feel: *She's in high spirits* (= happy) *today.*

spit /spɪt/ *verb* (**spits, spitting, spat** /spæt/, **has spat**) to send liquid or food out from your mouth: *He spat on the ground.* ◇ *The baby spat her food out.*

spite 🔑 /spaɪt/ *noun* (no plural) wanting to hurt or upset someone: *She broke my watch out of spite* (= because she wanted to upset me).
in spite of something although something is true; not noticing or not caring about something: *I slept well in spite of the noise.* ◇ *In spite of the bad weather, we went out.*

> ❖ **although** and **in spite of**
>
> Look at how we use these: *Although she was ill, she went to school* ◇ *In spite of her illness, she went to school.*

splash¹ /splæʃ/ *verb* (**splashes, splashing, splashed** /splæʃt/) **1** to throw drops of liquid over someone or something and make them or it wet: *The car splashed us as it drove past.* **2** to move through water so that drops of it fly in the air: *The children were splashing around in the pool.*

splash² /splæʃ/ *noun* (*plural* **splashes**) **1** the sound that a person or thing makes when they fall into water: *Ali jumped into the river with a big splash.* **2** a place where liquid has fallen: *There were splashes of paint on the floor.*

splendid /ˈsplendɪd/ *adjective* very beautiful or very good: *a splendid view* ◇ *What a splendid idea!*

splinter /ˈsplɪntə(r)/ *noun* a thin sharp piece of wood or glass that has broken off a bigger piece: *I've got a splinter in my finger.*

split¹ /splɪt/ *verb* (**splits, splitting, split, has split**) **1** to break something into two parts: *I split the wood with an axe.* **2** to break open: *His jeans split when he sat down.* **3** to share something; to give a part to each person: *We split the money between us.*

split up to stop being together: *He has split up with his wife.*

split² /splɪt/ *noun* a long cut or hole in something

spoil /spɔɪl/ *verb* (**spoils, spoiling, spoilt** /spɔɪlt/ *or* **spoiled** /spɔɪld/, **has spoilt** *or* **has spoiled**) **1** to make something less good than before: *The mud spoiled my shoes.* ◇ *The bad news spoilt my day.* **2** to give a child too much so that they think they can always have what they want: *She spoils her grandchildren.* ◇ *a spoilt child*

spoke¹ *form of* SPEAK

spoke² /spəʊk/ *noun* one of the thin pieces of wire that join the middle of a wheel to the outside, for example on a bicycle ➲ Picture at **bicycle**.

spoken *form of* SPEAK

spokesperson /ˈspəʊkspɜːsn/ *noun* a person who tells someone what a group of people has decided

> ❖ **WORD BUILDING**
>
> You can also say **spokesman**, /ˈspəʊksmən/ or **spokeswoman** /ˈspəʊkswʊmən/.

sponge /spʌndʒ/ *noun* **1** a soft thing with a lot of small holes in it, that you use for washing yourself or cleaning things **2** a soft light cake

sponsor /ˈspɒnsə(r)/ *noun* **1** a person or company that gives money so that an event can happen **2** a person who pays money to charity if someone else completes a particular activity: *I'm collecting sponsors for next week's charity walk.* ► **sponsor** *verb* (**sponsors, sponsoring, sponsored** /ˈspɒnsəd/): *The match was sponsored by a local firm.*

spoon /spuːn/ *noun* a thing with a round end that you use for putting food in your mouth or for mixing: *a wooden spoon* ◇ *a teaspoon*

spoon

spoonful /ˈspuːnfʊl/ *noun* the amount that you can put in one spoon: *Two spoonfuls of sugar in my tea, please.*

sport /spɔːt/ *noun* a game that you do to keep your body strong and well and because you enjoy it: *Hawa does a lot of sport.* ◇ *Football, swimming and athletics are all sports.*

> ❖ **WORD BUILDING**
>
> There are many different types of sport. Here are some of them: **basketball, cricket, football, running, tennis** and **volleyball**.

sports car /ˈspɔːts kɑː(r)/ *noun* a fast car, often with a roof that you can open

sportsperson /ˈspɔːtspɜːsn/ *noun* (*plural* **sportspersons** /ˈspɔːtspɜːsnz/ *or* **sportspeople** /ˈspɔːtspiːpl/) a person who plays sport

> ❖ **WORD BUILDING**
>
> You can also say **sportsman** /ˈspɔːtsmən/ or **sportswoman** /ˈspɔːtswʊmən/

spot¹ /spɒt/ *noun* **1** a small round mark: *a red dress with white spots* ➲ Picture at **spotted**. **2** a small red mark on your skin: *A lot of teenagers get spots on their face.* **3** a place: *This is a good spot for camping.*

spot² /spɒt/ *verb* (**spots, spotting, spotted**) to see someone or something suddenly: *She spotted him in the crowd.*

spotted /ˈspɒtɪd/ *adjective* with small round marks on it: *a spotted shirt*

spotted

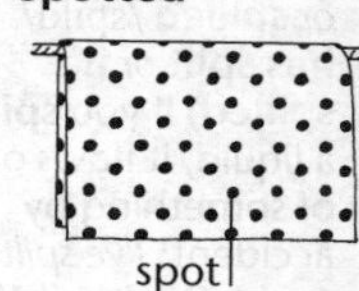

spotty /ˈspɒti/ *adjective* (**spottier, spottiest**) with small red marks on your skin: *a spotty face*

spout /spaʊt/ *noun* the part of a container that is like a short tube, where liquid comes out: *I broke the spout of my teapot.*

sprain /spreɪn/ *verb* (**sprains, spraining, sprained** /spreɪnd/) to hurt part of your body by turning it suddenly: *Bigogo fell and sprained his ankle.*

sprang *form of* SPRING²

spray¹ /spreɪ/ *noun* **1** (no plural) liquid in very small drops that flies through the air: *spray from the sea* **2** (*plural* **sprays**) liquid in a can that comes out in very

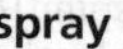
spray

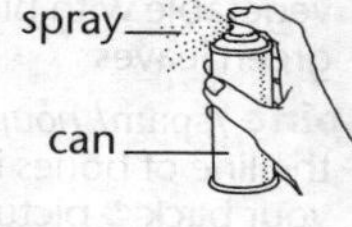

small drops when you press a button: *body spray*

spray[2] /spreɪ/ *verb* (**sprays, spraying, sprayed** /spreɪd/) to make very small drops of liquid fall on something: *someone has sprayed paint on the wall.*

spread 🔑 /spred/ *verb* (**spreads, spreading, spread, has spread**) **1** to open something so that you can see all of it: *The bird spread its wings and flew away.* ◇ *Spread out the map on the table.* **2** to put soft stuff all over something: *I spread butter on the bread.* **3** to move to other places or to other people; to make something do this: *Fire quickly spread to other parts of the building.* ◇ *Rats spread disease.* ▶ **spread** *noun* (no plural): *Doctors are trying to stop the spread of the disease.*

spreadsheet /ˈspredʃiːt/ *noun* a computer program for working with rows of numbers

spring

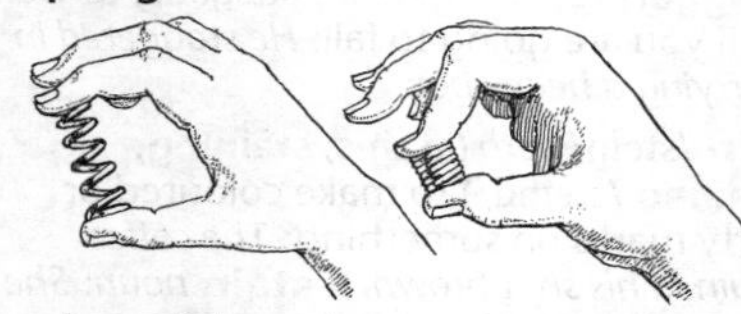

spring[1] 🔑 /sprɪŋ/ *noun* **1** in cool countries, the part of the year after winter, when plants start to grow **2** a thin piece of metal that is bent round and round. A spring will go back to the same size and shape after you push or pull it. **3** a place where water comes out of the ground: *Hot springs were popular with tourists, who came to enjoy the natural warm waters.*

spring[2] /sprɪŋ/ *verb* (**springs, springing, sprang** /spræŋ/, **has sprung** /sprʌŋ/) to jump or move suddenly: *The cat sprang on the mouse.*

sprinkle /ˈsprɪŋkl/ *verb* (**sprinkles, sprinkling, sprinkled** /ˈsprɪŋkld/) to throw drops or small pieces of something on another thing: *Sprinkle some sugar on the fruit.*

sprint /sprɪnt/ *verb* (**sprints, sprinting, sprinted**) to run a short distance very fast

sprout[1] /spraʊt/ (also **Brussels sprout**) *noun* a very small round green vegetable in the form of a tight ball of leaves

sprout[2] /spraʊt/ *verb* (**sprouts, sprouting, sprouted**) to start to grow: *New leaves are sprouting on the trees.*

sprung *form of* SPRING[2]

spun *form of* SPIN

sputum /ˈspjuːtəm/ *noun* (no plural) liquid that you cough up when you are ill: *blood in the sputum*

spy[1] /spaɪ/ *noun* (*plural* **spies**) a person who tries to learn secret things about another country, person or company

spy[2] /spaɪ/ *verb* (**spies, spying, spied** /spaɪd/) to try to learn secret things about someone or something

spy on someone to watch someone or something secretly

squad /skwɒd/ *noun* a small group of people who work together: *Uganda's football squad* ◇ *a squad of police officers*

square[1] 🔑 /skweə(r)/ *noun* **1** a shape with four straight sides that are the same length ➲ picture on page A12: *Break the chocolate into squares.* **2** an open space in a town with buildings around it: *the market square* ◇ *City Square*

square[2] 🔑 /skweə(r)/ *adjective* with four straight sides that are the same length, and four right angles: *a square table*

❖ **WORD BUILDING**

A **square metre** is an area that is one metre long on each side.

squash[1] /skwɒʃ/ *verb* (**squashes, squashing, squashed** /skwɒʃt/) **1** to press something hard and make it flat: *She sat on my hat and squashed it.* **2** to push a lot of people or things into a small space: *We squashed five bags into the cupboard.*

squash[2] /skwɒʃ/ *noun* **1** (no plural) a game where two players hit a small ball against a wall in a special room (called a **court**): *Have you ever played squash?* **2** (*plural* **squash** or **squashes**) a type of vegetable that grows on the ground, often with yellow or green skin **3** (no plural) a drink made from fruit juice and sugar. You add water before you drink it: *a glass of orange squash*

squat /skwɒt/ *verb* (**squats, squatting, squatted**) **1** to sit with your feet on the ground, your legs bent and your bottom just above the ground: *I squatted down to light the fire.* **2** to live in an empty building that is not yours and that you do not pay for

squatter /ˈskwɒtə(r)/ *noun* a person who lives in an empty building without the owner's permission

squeak /skwiːk/ *verb* (**squeaks, squeaking, squeaked** /skwiːkt/) to make a short high sound like a mouse: *The door was squeaking, so I put some oil on it.* ▶ **squeak** noun: *the squeak of a mouse* ▶ **squeaky** (**squeakier, squeakiest**) adjective: *He's got a squeaky voice.*

squeal /skwi:l/ verb (**squeals, squealing, squealed** /skwi:ld/) to make a loud high sound like a pig: *The children squealed with excitement.* ▶ **squeal** noun: *the squeal of a pig*

squeegee /'skwi:dʒi:/ noun a tool with a rubber edge that you use to move liquid across a surface: *Use a squeegee to make the windows really clean.*

squeeze /skwi:z/ verb (**squeezes, squeezing, squeezed** /skwi:zd/) **1** to press something hard: *I squeezed an orange* (= to make the juice come out). **2** to go into a small space; to push too much into a small space: *Fifty people squeezed into the small room.* ◇ *Can you squeeze another person onto that bench?* ▶ **squeeze** noun: *She gave my arm a squeeze.*

squeeze

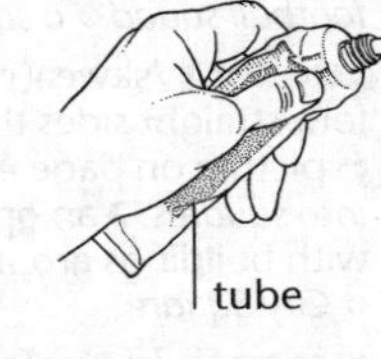

squirrel /'skwɪrəl/ noun a small grey or brown animal with a big thick tail. **Squirrels** live in trees and eat nuts.

squirrel

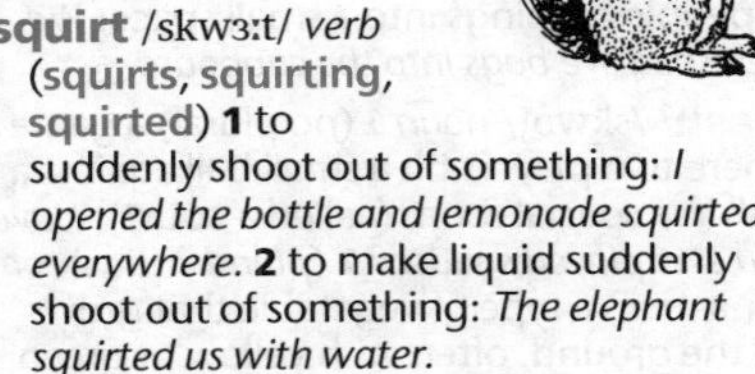

squirt /skwɜ:t/ verb (**squirts, squirting, squirted**) **1** to suddenly shoot out of something: *I opened the bottle and lemonade squirted everywhere.* **2** to make liquid suddenly shoot out of something: *The elephant squirted us with water.*

St **1** *short for* SAINT **2** St. *short for* STREET

stab /stæb/ verb (**stabs, stabbing, stabbed** /stæbd/) to push a knife or another sharp thing into someone or something: *He was stabbed in the back.*

stable¹ /'steɪbl/ adjective Something that is stable will not move, fall or change: *Don't stand on that table – it's not very stable.* OPPOSITE **unstable**

stable² /'steɪbl/ noun a building where you keep horses

stack¹ /stæk/ noun a lot of things on top of one another: *a stack of books*

stack² /stæk/ verb (**stacks, stacking, stacked** /stækt/) to put things on top of one another: *I stacked the chairs after the concert.*

stadium /'steɪdiəm/ noun a place with seats around it where you can watch sports matches: *a football stadium*

staff /stɑ:f/ noun (plural) the group of people who work in a place: *The hotel staff were very friendly.* ◇ *Three members of staff are sick today.*

staffroom /stɑ:fru:m/ noun a room in a school where teachers can work and rest

stage 🔑 /steɪdʒ/ noun **1** the part of a theatre where actors, dancers, etc. stand and move: *The audience cheered when he came on stage.* **2** a certain time in a longer set of things that happen: *The first stage of the course lasts for two weeks.*
at this stage now: *At this stage I don't know what I'll do when I leave school.*

stagger /'stægə(r)/ verb (**staggers, staggering, staggered** /'stægəd/) to walk as if you are going to fall: *He staggered in carrying a heavy box.*

stain /steɪn/ verb (**stains, staining, stained** /steɪnd/) to make coloured or dirty marks on something: *The coffee stained his shirt brown.* ▶ **stain** noun: *She had blood stains on her dress.*

stair 🔑 /steə(r)/ noun one of a number of steps that lead up and down inside a building: *I ran up the stairs.* ➲ Look at **downstairs, upstairs**.

staircase /'steəkeɪs/ (also **stairway** /'steəweɪ/) noun a long set of stairs

stale /steɪl/ adjective (**staler, stalest**) not fresh: *stale bread* ◇ *stale air*

stalk /stɔ:k/ noun one of the long thin parts of a plant that the flowers, leaves or fruit grow on

stall

stall /stɔ:l/ noun a big table with things on it that someone wants to sell, for example in a street or market: *a fruit stall*

stammer /ˈstæmə(r)/ *verb* (**stammers**, **stammering**, **stammered** /ˈstæməd/) to say the same sound many times when you are trying to say a word: *'B-b-b-but wait for me,' she stammered.*

stamp[1] 🔑 /stæmp/ *noun* **1** a small piece of paper that you put on a letter to show that you have paid to send it ➲ picture on page A15: *I stuck a stamp on the letter and posted it.* **2** a small piece of wood or metal that you press on paper to make marks or words: *a date stamp*

stamp[2] /stæmp/ *verb* (**stamps**, **stamping**, **stamped** /stæmpt/) **1** to put your foot down quickly and hard: *She stamped on the spider and killed it.* **2** to walk by putting your feet down hard and loudly: *Ajuma stamped angrily out of the room.* **3** to press a small piece of wood or metal on paper to make marks or words: *They stamped my passport at the airport.*

stand[1] 🔑 /stænd/ *verb* (**stands**, **standing**, **stood** /stʊd/, **has stood**) **1** to be on your feet: *She was standing by the door.* **2** (also **stand up**) to get up on your feet: *The teacher asked us all to stand up.* **3** to be in a place: *The village stands on a hill.* **4** to put something somewhere: *I stood the ladder against the wall.*

can't stand someone or **something** to hate someone or something: *I can't stand this music.*

stand by 1 to watch but not do anything: *How can you stand by while those boys kick the cat?* **2** to be ready to do something: *Stand by until I call you!*

stand by someone to help someone when they need it: *Kendi's parents stood by her when she was in trouble.*

stand for something to be a short way of saying or writing something: *USA stands for 'United States of America'.*

stand out to be easy to see: *Pembe stands out in a crowd because he is so tall.*

stand still to not move: *Stand still while I take your photograph.*

stand up for someone or **something** to say that someone or something is right; to support someone or something: *Everyone else said I was wrong, but my sister stood up for me.*

stand up to someone to show that you are not afraid of someone

stand[2] 🔑 /stænd/ *noun* **1** a table or small shop where you can buy things or get information: *a news stand* (= where you can buy newspapers and magazines) **2** a piece of furniture that you can put things on: *a coat stand*

standard[1] 🔑 /ˈstændəd/ *noun* how good someone or something is: *Her work is of a very high standard* (= very good).

standard[2] /ˈstændəd/ *adjective* normal; not special: *Clothes are sold in standard sizes.*

standard of living /ˌstændəd əv ˈlɪvɪŋ/ *noun* (*plural* **standards of living**) how rich or poor you are: *They have a low standard of living* (= they are poor).

stank *form of* STINK

staple /ˈsteɪpl/ *noun* a small, very thin piece of metal that you push through pieces of paper to join them together, using a special tool (called a **stapler**)
▶ **staple** *verb* (**staples**, **stapling**, **stapled** /ˈsteɪpld/): *Staple the pieces of paper together.*

star[1] 🔑 /stɑː(r)/ *noun* **1** one of the small bright lights that you see in the sky at night: *We looked up at the stars.* **2** a shape with points: *We put a star on top of the Christmas tree.* ➲ picture on page A12 **3** a famous person, for example an actor or a singer: *a film star*

star[2] 🔑 /stɑː(r)/ *verb* (**stars**, **starring**, **starred** /stɑːd/) **1** to be an important actor in a play or film: *He has starred in many films.* **2** to have someone as a star: *The film stars Lupita Nyong'o.*

starch /stɑːtʃ/ *noun* (no plural) **1** a white substance that is found in food such as potatoes, rice and bread: *There's too much starch in your diet.* **2** a substance that you use for making cloth stiff

stare 🔑 /steə(r)/ *verb* (**stares**, **staring**, **stared** /steəd/) to look at someone or something for a long time: *Everybody stared at her hat.* ◇ *He was staring out of the window.*

start[1] 🔑 /stɑːt/ *verb* (**starts**, **starting**, **started**) **1** to begin to do something: *I start school at eight o'clock.* ◇ *It started raining.* ◇ *She started to cry.* **2** to begin to happen; to make something begin to happen: *The film starts at 7.30.* ◇ *The police do not know who started the fire.* **3** to begin to work or move; to make something begin to work or move: *The engine won't start.* ◇ *I can't start the car.*

start off to begin: *The teacher started off by asking us our names.*

start² 🔑 /stɑːt/ *noun* **1** the beginning or first part of something: *She arrived after the start of the meeting.* OPPOSITE **finish** **2** starting something: *We have got a lot to do, so let's make a start.*
for a start words that you use when you give your first reason for something: *'Why can't I go to school?' 'Well, for a start, you're not old enough yet.'*

starter /ˈstɑːtə(r)/ *noun* a small amount of food that you eat as the first part of a meal: *I chose soup for my starter.*

startle /ˈstɑːtl/ *verb* (**startles, startling, startled** /ˈstɑːtld/) to make someone suddenly surprised or frightened: *You startled me when you knocked on the window.*

starvation /stɑːˈveɪʃn/ *noun* (no plural) when people are ill or die because they do not have enough food: *The child died of starvation.*

starve /stɑːv/ *verb* (**starves, starving, starved** /stɑːvd/) to die because you do not have enough to eat: *People are starving in some parts of the world.*
be starving to be very hungry: *When will dinner be ready? I'm starving!*

state¹ 🔑 /steɪt/ *noun* **1** (no plural) how someone or something is: *The room is in a terrible state* (= untidy or dirty)! **2** (*plural* **states**) a country and its government: *Many schools are owned by the state.* **3** (*plural* **states**) a part of a country: *Texas is a state in the United States of America.*
state of mind how you feel: *What state of mind is he in?*

state² 🔑 /steɪt/ *verb* (**states, stating, stated**) to say or write something: *I stated in my letter that I was sorry for what I did.*

statement 🔑 /ˈsteɪtmənt/ *noun* something that you say or write: *The driver made a statement to the police about the accident.* ➲ Look at **bank statement**.

station 🔑 /ˈsteɪʃn/ *noun* **1** a railway station; a place where trains stop so that people can get on and off: *I get off at the next station.* **2** a place where buses start and end their journeys: *a bus station* **3** a building for some special work: *a police station* **4** a television or radio company: *He tuned to a different station.*

stationery /ˈsteɪʃənri/ *noun* (no plural) paper, pens and other things that you use for writing

station wagon /ˈsteɪʃn wægən/ *noun* a long car with a door at the back and space behind the back seat for carrying things

statistics /stəˈtɪstɪks/ *noun* (plural) numbers that give information about something: *Statistics show that women live longer than men.*

statue /ˈstætʃuː/ *noun* the shape of a person or an animal that is made of stone or metal: *They erected a statue of Nelson Mandela in the square.*

stay¹ 🔑 /steɪ/ *verb* (**stays, staying, stayed** /steɪd/) **1** to be in the same place and not go away: *Stay here until I come back.* ◇ *I stayed in the house all morning.* **2** to continue in the same way and not change: *I tried to stay awake.* **3** to live somewhere for a short time: *I stayed with my friend in Kisumu.* ◇ *Which hotel are you staying at?*
stay behind to be somewhere after other people have gone: *The teacher asked me to stay behind after the lesson.*
stay in to be at home and not go out: *I'm staying in this evening because I'm tired.*
stay up to not go to bed: *We stayed up until after midnight.*

stay² 🔑 /steɪ/ *noun* (*plural* **stays**) a short time when you live somewhere: *Did you enjoy your stay in London?*

STD /ˌes tiː ˈdiː/ short for 'sexually transmitted disease'. **STD** is a disease that is spread through having sex.

steady 🔑 /ˈstedi/ *adjective* (**steadier, steadiest**) **1** If something is steady, it does not move or shake: *Hold the ladder steady while I stand on it.* OPPOSITE **unsteady** **2** If something is steady, it stays the same: *We drove at a steady speed.* ◇ *steady rain*
▶ **steadily** /ˈstedɪli/ *adverb*: *Prices are falling steadily.*

steak /steɪk/ *noun* a thick flat piece of meat or fish

steal 🔑 /stiːl/ *verb* (**steals, stealing, stole** /stəʊl/, **has stolen** /ˈstəʊlən/) to secretly take something that is not yours: *Her money has been stolen.*

> ❖ **WORD BUILDING**
>
> A person who steals is called a **thief**.
>
> A thief **steals** things, but **robs** people and places: *They stole my camera.* ◇ *I've been robbed.* ◇ *They robbed a bank.*

steam[1] 🔑 /stiːm/ *noun* (no plural) the gas that water becomes when it gets very hot: *There was steam coming from my cup of coffee.*

steam[2] /stiːm/ *verb* (**steams**, **steaming**, **steamed** /stiːmd/) **1** to send out steam: *a steaming bowl of soup* **2** to cook something in steam: *steamed vegetables*

steamer /ˈstiːmə(r)/ (also **steamship** /ˈstiːmʃɪp/) *noun* a ship that is driven by the power of steam

steel /stiːl/ *noun* (no plural) very strong metal that is used for making things like knives, tools or machines

steep /stiːp/ *adjective* (**steeper**, **steepest**) A **steep** hill, mountain or road goes up quickly from a low place to a high place: *I can't cycle up the hill – it's too steep.* ▸ **steeply** *adverb*: *The path climbed steeply up the side of the mountain.*

steeplechase /ˈstiːpltʃeɪs/ *noun* a long race around a special path (a **track**) in which people or horses jump over gates, water, etc.

steer /stɪə(r)/ *verb* (**steers**, **steering**, **steered** /stɪəd/) to make a car, boat, bicycle, etc. go the way that you want by turning a wheel or handle

steering wheel /ˈstɪərɪŋ wiːl/ *noun* the wheel that a person turns to make a car go left or right ➲ Picture at **car**.

stem /stem/ *noun* the long thin part of a plant that the flowers and leaves grow on ➲ Picture at **plant**[1].

step[1] 🔑 /step/ *noun* **1** a movement when you move your foot up and then put it down in another place to walk, run or dance: *She took a step forward and then stopped.* **2** a place to put your foot when you go up or down: *These steps go down to the garden.* **3** one thing in a list of things that you must do: *What is the first step in learning to paint?*
step by step doing one thing after another; slowly: *This book shows you how to play the guitar, step by step.*

step[2] 🔑 /step/ *verb* (**steps**, **stepping**, **stepped** /stept/) to move your foot up and put it down in another place when you walk: *You stepped on my foot!*

stepfather /ˈstepfɑːðə(r)/ *noun* a man who has married your mother but who is not your father ➲ Note at **stepmother**.

stepladder /ˈsteplædə(r)/ *noun* a short **ladder** (= a piece of equipment that helps you climb up something)

stepmother /ˈstepmʌðə(r)/ *noun* a woman who has married your father but who is not your mother

> ❖ **WORD BUILDING**
>
> The child of your stepmother or stepfather is your **stepbrother** or **stepsister**.

stereo /ˈsteriəʊ/ *noun* (*plural* **stereos**) a machine for playing CDs or tapes, with two parts (called **speakers**) that the sound comes from: *a stereo system* ▸ **stereo** *adjective* with the sound coming from two speakers: *a stereo CD player*

stereo

sterile /ˈsteraɪl/ *adjective* completely clean: *Hospitals have sterile needles for stitching cuts and wounds.*

stern[1] /stɜːn/ *adjective* (**sterner**, **sternest**) serious and strict with people; not smiling: *Our teacher is very stern.*

stern[2] /stɜːn/ *noun* the back end of a boat OPPOSITE **bow**

stethoscope /ˈsteθəskəʊp/ *noun* the thing that a doctor uses to listen to your heart and to how you breathe

stew /stjuː/ *noun* food that you make by cooking meat or vegetables in liquid for a long time: *beef stew* ▸ **stew** *verb* (**stews**, **stewing**, **stewed** /stjuːd/) to cook something slowly in liquid: *stewed fruit*

steward /ˈstjuːəd/ *noun* a man whose job is to look after people on a plane or a ship ➲ Look at **flight attendant**.

stewardess /ˌstjuːəˈdes/ *noun* (*plural* **stewardesses**) a woman whose job is to look after people on a plane or a ship ➲ Look at **flight attendant**.

stick[1] 🔑 /stɪk/ *noun* **1** a long thin piece of wood: *We found some sticks and made a fire.* ◇ *The old man walked with a stick.* **2** a long thin thing that is used in some sports to control the ball: *a hockey stick* **3** a long thin piece of something: *a stick of chalk*

stick[2] 🔑 /stɪk/ *verb* (**sticks**, **sticking**, **stuck** /stʌk/, **has stuck**) **1** to push a pointed thing into something: *Stick a fork into the meat to see if it's cooked.* **2** to join

something to another thing with a sticky substance; to become joined in this way: *I stuck a stamp on the envelope.* **3** to be fixed in one place so that it cannot move: *This door always sticks* (= it won't open). **4** to put something somewhere: *Stick that box on the floor.* ℹ This is an informal use.
stick out to come out of the side or top of something so you can see it easily: *The boy's head was sticking out of the window.*
stick something out to push something out: *Don't stick your tongue out!*
stick to something to continue with something and not change it: *We're sticking to Robi's plan.*
stick up for someone or **something** to say that someone or something is right: *Everyone else said I was wrong, but Chebet stuck up for me.*

sticker /ˈstɪkə(r)/ *noun* a small piece of paper with a picture or words on it, that you can stick onto things: *She has a sticker on the window of her car.*

sticky 🔑 /ˈstɪki/ *adjective* (**stickier**, **stickiest**) Something that is sticky can stick to things or is covered with something that can stick to things: *Glue is sticky.* ◇ *sticky fingers*

stiff /stɪf/ *adjective* (**stiffer**, **stiffest**) hard and not easy to bend or move: *stiff cardboard*

still[1] 🔑 /stɪl/ *adverb* **1** a word that you use to show that something has not changed: *Do you still live in Nakuru?* ◇ *Is it still raining?* **2** although that is true: *She felt ill, but she still went to the party.* **3** a word that you use to make another word stronger: *It was cold yesterday, but today it's colder still.*

still[2] 🔑 /stɪl/ *adjective* **1** without moving: *Please stand still while I take a photo.* ◇ *The water was very still.* **2** used about a drink that does not have any bubbles or gas in it OPPOSITE **fizzy**, **sparkling** ▶ **stillness** /ˈstɪlnəs/ *noun* (no plural): *the stillness of the night*

sting[1] /stɪŋ/ *verb* (**stings**, **stinging**, **stung** /stʌŋ/, **has stung**) **1** If an insect or a plant **stings** you, it hurts you by pushing a small sharp part into your skin: *I've been stung by a bee!* **2** to feel a sudden sharp pain: *The smoke made my eyes sting.*

sting[2] /stɪŋ/ *noun* **1** the sharp part of some insects that can hurt you: *A wasp's sting is in its tail.* ➲ Picture at **scorpion**. **2** a place on your skin where an insect or a plant has **stung** you: *a bee sting*

stink /stɪŋk/ *verb* (**stinks**, **stinking**, **stank** /stæŋk/, **has stunk** /stʌŋk/) to have a very bad smell: *That fish stinks!* ▶ **stink** *noun* (no plural): *What a horrible stink!*

stir /stɜː(r)/ *verb* (**stirs**, **stirring**, **stirred** /stɜːd/) **1** to move a spoon or another thing round and round to mix something: *He put sugar in his coffee and stirred it.* **2** to move a little or make something move a little: *The wind stirred the leaves.*

stitch[1] /stɪtʃ/ *noun* (*plural* **stitches**) **1** one movement in and out of a piece of material with a needle and thread when you are sewing **2** one of the small circles of wool that you put round a needle when you are knitting

stitch[2] /stɪtʃ/ *verb* (**stitches**, **stitching**, **stitched** /stɪtʃt/) to make **stitches** in something; to sew something: *I stitched a button on my skirt.*

stock[1] /stɒk/ *noun* things that a shop keeps ready to sell: *That bookshop has a big stock of dictionaries.*
in stock ready to sell: *We have your size in stock.*
out of stock not there to sell: *I'm sorry, that book is out of stock at the moment.*

stock[2] /stɒk/ *verb* (**stocks**, **stocking**, **stocked** /stɒkt/) to keep something ready to sell: *We don't stock umbrellas.*

stocking /ˈstɒkɪŋ/ *noun* a long thin thing that a woman wears over her leg and foot: *a pair of stockings*

stole, **stolen** *forms of* STEAL

stomach 🔑 /ˈstʌmək/ *noun* **1** the part inside your body where food goes after you eat it: *You shouldn't exercise on a full stomach.* **2** the front part of your body below your chest and above your legs ➲ picture on page A13

stomach ache /ˈstʌmək eɪk/ *noun* (no plural) a pain in your stomach: *I've got stomach ache.*

stone 🔑 /stəʊn/ *noun* **1** (no plural) the very hard stuff that is in the ground. Stone is sometimes used for building: *a stone wall* **2** (*plural* **stones**) a small piece of stone: *The children were throwing stones into the river.* **3** (*plural* **stones**) the hard part in the middle of some fruits: *Avocados have a large stone.*

stone

stone | peach

4 (*plural* **stones**) a small piece of beautiful rock that is very valuable: *A diamond is a precious stone.* **5** (*plural* **stone**) a measure of weight (=6.3 kilograms). There are 14 **pounds** in a stone: *I weigh eight stone.*

stony /ˈstəʊni/ *adjective* (**stonier**, **stoniest**) with a lot of stones in or on it: *stony ground*

stood *form of* STAND[1]

stool /stuːl/ *noun* a small seat with no back

stool

stoop /stuːp/ *verb* (**stoops**, **stooping**, **stooped** /stuːpt/) If you **stoop**, you bend your body forward and down: *She stooped to pick up the baby.*

stop[1] /stɒp/ *verb* (**stops**, **stopping**, **stopped** /stɒpt/) **1** to finish moving or working; to become still: *The train stopped at every station.* ◇ *The clock has stopped.* ◇ *I stopped to post a letter.* **2** to not do something any more; to finish: *Stop making that noise!* **3** to make someone or something finish moving or doing something: *Squeeze both brakes to stop the bike.*

stop someone (from) doing something to not let someone do something: *My dad stopped me from going out.*

stop[2] /stɒp/ *noun* **1** the moment when someone or something finishes moving: *The lorry came to a stop.* **2** a place where buses or trains stop so that people can get on and off: *I'm getting off at the next stop.*

put a stop to something to make something finish: *A teacher put a stop to the fight.*

stoppage time /ˈstɒpɪdʒ taɪm/ *noun* (no plural) extra time at the end of a game of football, etc. if the game has stopped in the middle for any reason

store[1] /stɔː(r)/ *noun* **1** a big shop **2** things that you are keeping to use later: *a store of food*

store[2] /stɔː(r)/ *verb* (**stores**, **storing**, **stored** /stɔːd/) to keep something to use later: *The information is stored on a computer.*

storey /ˈstɔːri/ *noun* (*plural* **storeys**) one level in a building: *The building has four storeys.*

storm[1] /stɔːm/ *noun* very bad weather with strong winds and rain: *Look at those black clouds. I think there's going to be a storm.* ◇ *a terrible thunderstorm* (= a storm with thunder and lightning)

storm[2] /stɔːm/ *verb* (**storms**, **storming**, **stormed** /stɔːmd/) to move in a way that shows you are angry: *He stormed out of the room.*

stormy /ˈstɔːmi/ *adjective* (**stormier**, **stormiest**) If the weather is stormy, there is strong wind and rain: *a stormy night*

story /ˈstɔːri/ *noun* (*plural* **stories**) **1** words that tell you about people and things that are not real: *I write stories for children as a hobby.* ◇ *a ghost story* **2** words that tell you about things that really happened: *My grandmother told me stories about when she was a child.*

stove /stəʊv/ *noun* **1** a cooker **2** a closed metal box in which you burn wood or coal to heat a room

stowaway /ˈstəʊəweɪ/ *noun* a person who hides in a ship or plane so that they can travel without paying

straight

straight

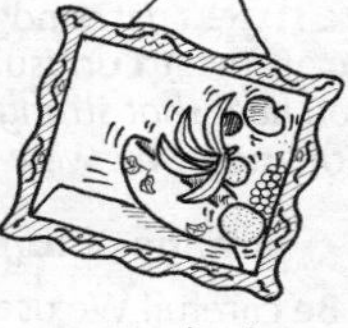

crooked

straight[1] /streɪt/ *adjective* (**straighter**, **straightest**) **1** with no curve or bend: *Use a ruler to draw a straight line.* ➲ Picture at **wavy**. **2** with one side as high as the other: *This picture isn't straight.*
OPPOSITE **crooked**

get something straight make sure that you understand something completely: *Let's get this straight. Are you sure you left your bike at school?*

straight[2] /streɪt/ *adverb* **1** in a straight line: *Look straight in front of you.* **2** without stopping or doing anything else; directly: *Come straight home.* ◇ *She walked straight past me.*

straight away immediately; now: *I'll do it straight away.*

straight on without turning: *Go straight on until you come to the bank, then turn left.*

straighten /ˈstreɪtn/ *verb* (**straightens, straightening, straightened** /ˈstreɪtnd/) to become or make something straight

straightforward /ˌstreɪtˈfɔːwəd/ *adjective* easy to understand or do: *The question was straightforward.*

strain¹ /streɪn/ *verb* (**strains, straining, strained** /streɪnd/) **1** to pour a liquid through something with small holes in it, to take away any other things in the liquid: *You haven't strained the tea – there are tea leaves in it.* **2** to try very hard: *Her voice was so quiet that I had to strain to hear her.* **3** to hurt a part of your body by making it work too hard: *Don't read in the dark. You'll strain your eyes.*

strain² /streɪn/ *noun* **1** being pulled or made to work too hard: *The rope broke under* (= because of) *the strain.* **2** hurting a part of your body by making it work too hard: *back strain*

strand /strænd/ *noun* one piece of thread or hair

stranded /ˈstrændɪd/ *adjective* left in a place that you cannot get away from: *The car broke down and I was stranded on a lonely road.*

strange ⚿ /streɪndʒ/ *adjective* (**stranger, strangest**) **1** unusual or surprising: *Did you hear that strange noise?* **2** that you do not know: *We were lost in a strange town.*

> ❖ **strange** or **foreign**?
>
> Be careful! We use **foreign**, not **strange**, to talk about a person or thing that comes from another country.

strangely /ˈstreɪndʒli/ *adverb* in a surprising or unusual way: *She usually talks a lot, but today she was strangely quiet.*

stranger /ˈstreɪndʒə(r)/ *noun* **1** a person who you do not know **2** a person who is in a place that he/she does not know: *I'm a stranger to this city.*

> ❖ **stranger** or **foreigner**?
>
> Be careful! We use the word **foreigner** for a person who comes from another country.

strangle /ˈstræŋgl/ *verb* (**strangles, strangling, strangled** /ˈstræŋgld/) to kill someone by pressing their neck very tightly

strap¹ /stræp/ *noun* a long flat piece of material that you use for carrying something or for keeping something in place: *a leather watch strap*

straps

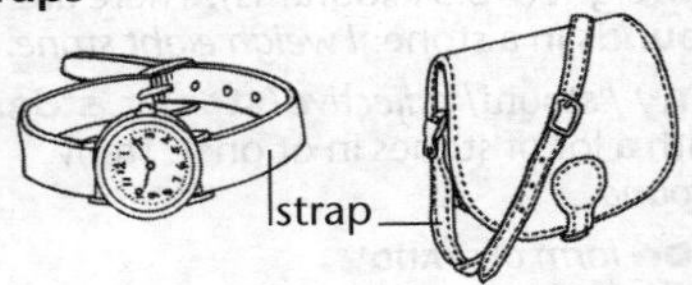

strap² /stræp/ *verb* (**straps, strapping, strapped** /stræpt/) to hold something in place with a **strap**: *I strapped the bag onto the back of my bike.*

straw /strɔː/ *noun* **1** (no plural) dried plants like **wheat**: *The cows sleep on a bed of straw.* ◇ *a straw hat* **2** (*plural* **straws**) a thin paper or plastic tube that you can drink through

the last straw the last of many bad things that happen, that finally makes you lose hope

stray /streɪ/ *adjective* lost and away from home: *a stray dog* ▸ **stray** *noun* (*plural* **strays**) an animal that has no home

streak /striːk/ *noun* a long thin line: *She's got streaks of grey in her hair.* ◇ *a streak of lightning*

stream¹ /striːm/ *noun* **1** a small river **2** moving liquid, or moving things or people: *a stream of blood* ◇ *a stream of cars*

stream² /striːm/ *verb* (**streams, streaming, streamed** /striːmd/) to move like water: *Tears were streaming down his face.*

streamline /ˈstriːmlaɪn/ *verb* (**streamlines, streamlining, streamlined** /ˈstriːmlaɪnd/) to give something like a car or boat a long smooth shape so that it can go fast through air or water

street ⚿ /striːt/ *noun* a road in a city or town with buildings along the sides: *I saw Kendi walking down the street.* ◇ *The shop is on Biashara Street.* ℹ The short way of writing 'Street' in addresses is **St.**: *17 Mfangano St.*

strength ⚿ /streŋθ/ *noun* (no plural) being strong: *I don't have the strength to lift this box – it's too heavy.* OPPOSITE **weakness**

strengthen /ˈstreŋθn/ *verb* (**strengthens, strengthening, strengthened** /ˈstreŋθnd/) to make something stronger OPPOSITE **weaken**

stress[1] /stres/ *noun* **1** (*plural* **stresses**) saying one word or part of a word more strongly than another: *In the word 'dictionary', the stress is on the first part of the word.* **2** (no plural) a feeling of worry because of problems in your life: *She's suffering from stress because she's got too much work to do.*

stress[2] /stres/ *verb* (**stresses**, **stressing**, **stressed** /strest/) **1** to say something strongly to show that it is important: *I must stress how important this meeting is.* **2** to say one word or part of a word more strongly than another: *You should stress the first part of the word 'happy'.*

stressful /ˈstresfl/ *adjective* causing a lot of worry: *a stressful day*

stretch[1] 🔑 /stretʃ/ *verb* (**stretches**, **stretching**, **stretched** /stretʃt/) **1** to pull something to make it longer or wider; to become longer or wider: *This sweater has stretched.* **2** to push your arms and legs out as far as you can: *Ali got out of bed and stretched.* **3** to cover a large area: *The beach stretches for kilometres.*
stretch out to lie down with all your body flat: *The cat stretched out and went to sleep.*

stretch[2] /stretʃ/ *noun* (*plural* **stretches**) a piece of land or water: *This is a dangerous stretch of road.*

stretcher /ˈstretʃə(r)/ *noun* a kind of bed for carrying someone who is ill or hurt: *They carried him to the ambulance on a stretcher.*

strict 🔑 /strɪkt/ *adjective* (**stricter**, **strictest**) If you are strict, you make people do what you want and do not allow them to behave badly: *Her parents are very strict – she always has to be home before ten o'clock.* ◇ *The school has strict rules.*

strictly /ˈstrɪktli/ *adverb* **1** definitely; in a strict way: *Talking is strictly forbidden.* **2** exactly: *That is not strictly true.*

stride /straɪd/ *verb* (**strides**, **striding**, **strode** /strəʊd/) to walk with long steps: *The police officer strode across the road.*
▸ **stride** *noun* a long step

strike[1] /straɪk/ *noun* a time when people are not working because they want more money or are angry about something: *There are no buses today because the drivers are on strike.*

strike[2] /straɪk/ *verb* (**strikes**, **striking**, **struck** /strʌk/, **has struck**) **1** to hit someone or something: *A stone struck me on the back of the head.*

> ❖ **SPEAKING**
>
> **Hit** is the more usual word, but when you talk about **lightning**, you always use **strike**: *The tree was struck by lightning.*

2 to stop working as a protest: *The nurses are going to strike for better pay.* **3** to ring a bell so that people know what time it is: *The clock struck nine.* **4** to come suddenly into your mind: *It suddenly struck me that she looked like my sister.*
strike a match to make fire with a match

striker /ˈstraɪkə(r)/ *noun* in football, the player whose job is to score goals

striking /ˈstraɪkɪŋ/ *adjective* If something is **striking**, you notice it because it is very unusual or interesting: *That's a very striking hat.*

string 🔑 /strɪŋ/ *noun* **1** very thin rope that you use for tying things: *I tied up the parcel with string.* ◇ *The little boy held a balloon on the end of a string.* **2** a line of things on a piece of thread: *She was wearing a string of blue beads.* ➲ picture on page A4 **3** a piece of thin wire, etc. on a musical instrument: *guitar strings* ➲ Picture at **zeze**.

strip[1] /strɪp/ *noun* a long thin piece of something: *a strip of paper*

strip[2] /strɪp/ *verb* (**strips**, **stripping**, **stripped** /strɪpt/) **1** to take off what is covering something: *I stripped the paint off the walls.* **2** (also **strip off**) to take off your clothes: *She stripped off and ran into the sea.*

stripe /straɪp/ *noun* a long thin line of colour: *Zebras have black and white stripes.*
▸ **striped** /straɪpt/ *adjective* with stripes: *He wore a blue and white striped shirt.*

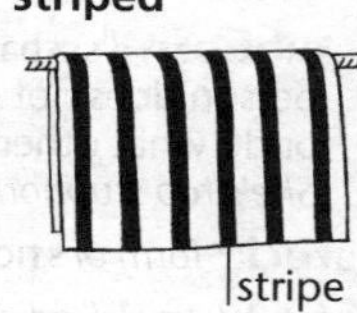

> ❖ **SPELLING**
>
> Be careful! There is one **p** in **striped**, but there are two **p**s in **stripped**.

strode *form of* STRIDE

stroke[1] /strəʊk/ *verb* (**strokes**, **stroking**, **stroked** /strəʊkt/) to move your hand gently over someone or something to show love: *She stroked his hair.*

stroke[2] /strəʊk/ *noun* **1** a movement that you make with your arms when you are swimming, playing sports such as **tennis**, etc. **2** a sudden serious illness when the brain stops working properly: *He had a stroke.*

stroll /strəʊl/ *verb* (**strolls, strolling, strolled** /strəʊld/) to walk slowly: *We strolled along the beach.* ▸ **stroll** *noun*: *We went for a stroll by the river.*

strong ⚷ /strɒŋ/ *adjective* (**stronger** /ˈstrɒŋgə(r)/, **strongest** /ˈstrɒŋgɪst/) **1** with a powerful body, so that you can carry heavy things: *I need someone strong to help me move this desk.* ➲ picture on page A5 **2** that you cannot break easily: *Don't stand on that chair – it's not very strong.* ◇ *a strong belief* **3** that you can see, taste, smell, hear or feel very clearly: *a cup of strong coffee* ◇ *a strong smell of oranges* ◇ *strong winds* ❶ The noun is **strength**. OPPOSITE **weak** ▸ **strongly** *adverb*: *I strongly believe that he is wrong.*

struck *form of* STRIKE[2]

structure ⚷ /ˈstrʌktʃə(r)/ *noun* **1** the way that something is made: *We are studying the structure of a bird's wing.* **2** a building or another thing that people have made with many parts: *The new hotel is a tall glass and brick structure.*

struggle /ˈstrʌgl/ *verb* (**struggles, struggling, struggled** /ˈstrʌgld/) **1** to try very hard to do something that is not easy: *We struggled to lift the heavy box.* **2** to move your arms and legs a lot when you are fighting or trying to get free: *She struggled to get away from her attacker.* ▸ **struggle** *noun*: *In 1862 the American slaves won their struggle for freedom.*

stubborn /ˈstʌbən/ *adjective* A **stubborn** person does not change their ideas easily or do what other people want them to do: *She's too stubborn to say sorry.*

stuck[1] *form of* STICK[2]

stuck[2] /stʌk/ *adjective* **1** not able to move: *This drawer is stuck – I can't open it.* ◇ *I was stuck far from home with no money.* **2** not able to do something because it is difficult: *If you get stuck, ask your teacher for help.*

student ⚷ /ˈstjuːdnt/ *noun* a person who is studying at school, university or college: *Ali is a history student.*

studio /ˈstjuːdiəʊ/ *noun* (*plural* **studios**) **1** a room where an artist works **2** a room where people make films, radio and television programmes, or records: *a television studio*

study[1] ⚷ /ˈstʌdi/ *verb* (**studies, studying, studied** /ˈstʌdid/) **1** to spend time learning about something: *He studied Physics at university.* **2** to look at something carefully: *We studied the map before we left.*

study[2] ⚷ /ˈstʌdi/ *noun* (*plural* **studies**) **1** learning about something: *Geography is the study of the earth.* **2** a room in a house where you go to study, read or write

stuff[1] ⚷ /stʌf/ *noun* (no plural) any material, substance or group of things: *What's this blue stuff on the wall?* ◇ *Put you stuff in this bag.*

stuff[2] /stʌf/ *verb* (**stuffs, stuffing, stuffed** /stʌft/) **1** to fill something with something: *The pillow was stuffed with feathers.* **2** to push something quickly into another thing: *He took the money quickly and stuffed it into his pocket.*

stuffy /ˈstʌfi/ *adjective* (**stuffier, stuffiest**) If a room is **stuffy**, it has no fresh air in it: *Open the window – it's very stuffy in here.*

stumble /ˈstʌmbl/ *verb* (**stumbles, stumbling, stumbled** /ˈstʌmbld/) to hit your foot against something when you are walking or running, and almost fall: *The old lady stumbled and fell as she was going upstairs.*

stump /stʌmp/ *noun* the small part that is left when something is cut off or broken: *a tree stump*

stun /stʌn/ *verb* (**stuns, stunning, stunned** /stʌnd/) **1** to hit a person or an animal on the head so hard that they cannot see, think or make a sound for a short time **2** to make someone very surprised: *His sudden death stunned his family and friends.*

stung *form of* STING[1]

stunk *form of* STINK

stunning /ˈstʌnɪŋ/ *adjective* very beautiful, wonderful: *a stunning dress*

stunt /stʌnt/ *noun* something dangerous or difficult that you do to make people look at you: *Action films have a lot of exciting stunts.*

stupid ⚷ /ˈstjuːpɪd/ *adjective* not intelligent; silly: *Don't be so stupid!* ◇ *What a stupid question!* ▸ **stupidity** /stjuːˈpɪdəti/ *noun* (no plural) being stup

▸ **stupidly** *adverb*: *I stupidly forgot to close the door.*

stutter /ˈstʌtə(r)/ *verb* (**stutters, stuttering, stuttered** /ˈstʌtəd/) to say the same sound many times when you are trying to say a word: *'I d-d-don't understand,' he stuttered.*

style /staɪl/ *noun* **1** a way of doing, making or saying something: *I don't like his style of writing.* **2** the shape or kind of something: *This shop sells shirts in lots of different colours and styles.* ◇ *a hairstyle*

subject /ˈsʌbdʒɪkt/ *noun* **1** the person or thing that you are talking or writing about: *What is the subject of the talk?* **2** something you study at school, university or college: *What's your favourite subject?* **3** the word in a sentence that does the action of the verb: *In the sentence 'Hawa ate the bread', 'Hawa' is the subject.* ➲ Look at **object**[1]. **4** a person who belongs to a certain country: *Kenyan subjects*

submarine /ˌsʌbməˈriːn/ *noun* a boat that can travel under the sea

submarine

sub-Saharan /ˌsʌb səˈhɑːrən/ *adjective* about places in Africa that are south of the Sahara Desert: *sub-Saharan Africa*

subscription /səbˈskrɪpʃn/ *noun* money that you pay, for example to get the same magazine each month or to join a club: *I've got a subscription to 'Modern Music' magazine.*

subside /səbˈsaɪd/ *verb* (**subsides, subsiding, subsided**) to become calmer or quieter: *The storm has subsided now.*

subsistence /sʌbˈsɪstəns/ *noun* producing only enough food to use, not enough to sell: *a subsistence crop* ◇ *subsistence farming*

substance /ˈsʌbstəns/ *noun* anything that you can see, touch or use for making things; a material: *Stone is a hard substance.* ◇ *chemical substances*

substitute /ˈsʌbstɪtjuːt/ *noun* a person or thing that you put in the place of another: *Our goalkeeper was ill, so we found a substitute.* ▸ **substitute** *verb* (**substitutes, substituting, substituted**) to put someone or something in the place of another: *You can substitute butter for oil if you prefer.*

subtitles /ˈsʌbtaɪtlz/ *noun* (plural) words at the bottom of a film that help you to understand it: *It was a French film with English subtitles.*

subtract /səbˈtrækt/ *verb* (**subtracts, subtracting, subtracted**) to take a number away from another number: *If you subtract 6 from 9, you get 3.* OPPOSITE **add** ▸ **subtraction** /səbˈtrækʃn/ *noun* (no plural) taking a number away from another number ➲ Look at **addition**.

suburb /ˈsʌbɜːb/ *noun* one of the parts of a town or city outside the centre: *We live in the suburbs of Nairobi.*

subway /ˈsʌbweɪ/ *noun* (*plural* **subways**) a path that goes under a busy road, so that people can cross safely

succeed /səkˈsiːd/ *verb* (**succeeds, succeeding, succeeded**) to do or get what you wanted to do or get: *She finally succeeded in passing the exam* ◇ *I tried to get a ticket for the match, but I didn't succeed.* OPPOSITE **fail**

> ❖ **WORD FAMILY**
> **succeed** **success**
> **successful**: OPPOSITE **unsuccessful**

success /səkˈses/ *noun* **1** (no plural) doing or getting what you wanted; doing well: *I wish you success with your studies.* **2** (*plural* **successes**) someone or something that does well or that people like a lot: *The film 'Titanic' was a great success.* OPPOSITE **failure**

> ❖ **SPELLING**
> Remember! You spell **success** with **cc** and **ss**.

successful /səkˈsesfl/ *adjective* If you are successful, you have got or done what you wanted, or you have become popular, rich, etc: *a successful actor* ◇ *The party was very successful.* ▸ **successfully** /səkˈsesfəli/ *adverb*: *He completed his studies successfully.*

such /sʌtʃ/ *adjective* **1** a word that you use when you say how much, how big, etc. something is: *It was such a nice day that we decided to go to the beach.* ➲ Note at **so**[1]. **2** a word that makes another word stronger: *He wears such strange clothes.* **3** like this or that: *'Can I speak to Mrs Mwangi?' 'I'm sorry. There's no such person here.'*

such as like something; for example: *You*

can see animals such as lions, elephants and crocodiles.

suck /sʌk/ *verb* (**sucks**, **sucking**, **sucked** /sʌkt/) **1** to pull something into your mouth, using your lips: *The baby sucked milk from its bottle.* **2** to hold something in your mouth and touch it a lot with your tongue: *She was sucking a sweet.*

sudden /ˈsʌdn/ *adjective* If something is sudden, it happens quickly when you do not expect it: *His death was very sudden.* **all of a sudden** suddenly: *We were sleeping when all of a sudden the door opened.*

suddenly /ˈsʌdnli/ *adverb* quickly and unexpectedly: *He left very suddenly.* ◇ *Suddenly there was a loud noise.*

sudoku /ˌsuˈdəʊkuː/ *noun* a number game where you have to write the numbers 1 to 9 in square spaces in a particular pattern

sue /suː/ *verb* (**sues**, **suing**, **sued** /suːd/) (in law) to ask for money from someone because they have done something bad to you: *He sued the restaurant after getting food poisoning.*

suffer /ˈsʌfə(r)/ *verb* (**suffers**, **suffering**, **suffered** /ˈsʌfəd/) to feel pain, sadness or something else that is not pleasant: *I'm suffering from toothache.*

sufficient /səˈfɪʃnt/ *adjective* as much or as many as you need or want; enough: *There was sufficient food to last two weeks.* OPPOSITE **insufficient** ❶ **Enough** is the word that we usually use.

suffix /ˈsʌfɪks/ *noun* (*plural* **suffixes**) letters that you add to the end of a word to make another word: *If you add the suffix '-ly' to the adjective 'quick', you make the adverb 'quickly'.* ➲ Look at **prefix**.

> ❖ **GRAMMAR**
>
> **-ly**, **-ness**, **-ful** and **-ment** are common suffixes: *happy – happily – happiness* ◇ *beauty – beautiful* ◇ *entertain – entertainment*

suffocate /ˈsʌfəkeɪt/ *verb* (**suffocates**, **suffocating**, **suffocated**) to die or make someone die because there is no air to breathe

sufuria

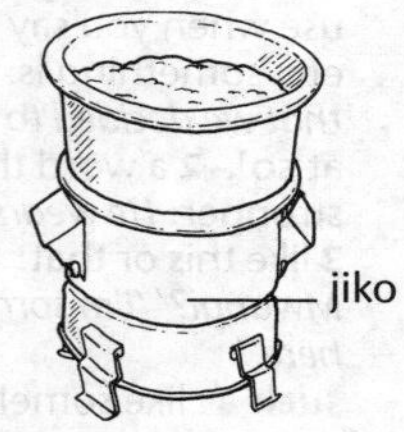

sufuria *noun* (East African English) a metal cooking pot

sugar /ˈʃʊgə(r)/ *noun* **1** (no plural) sweet stuff that comes from some sorts of plant: *Do you take sugar in your coffee?* **2** (*plural* **sugars**) the amount of sugar that a small spoon holds: *Two sugars, please.*

sugar cane /ˈʃʊgə keɪn/ *noun* (no plural) very tall, thick grass that sugar is made from

suggest /səˈdʒest/ *verb* (**suggests**, **suggesting**, **suggested**) to say what you think someone should do or what should happen: *I suggest that you stay here tonight.* ◇ *Awino suggested going for a walk.* ◇ *What do you suggest I say to Rono?*

suggestion /səˈdʒestʃən/ *noun* a plan or an idea that someone thinks of for someone else to discuss and consider: *I don't know what to give her for her birthday. Have you got any suggestions?* ◇ *I would like to make a suggestion.*

suicide /ˈsuːɪsaɪd/ *noun* killing yourself **commit suicide** to kill yourself

suit

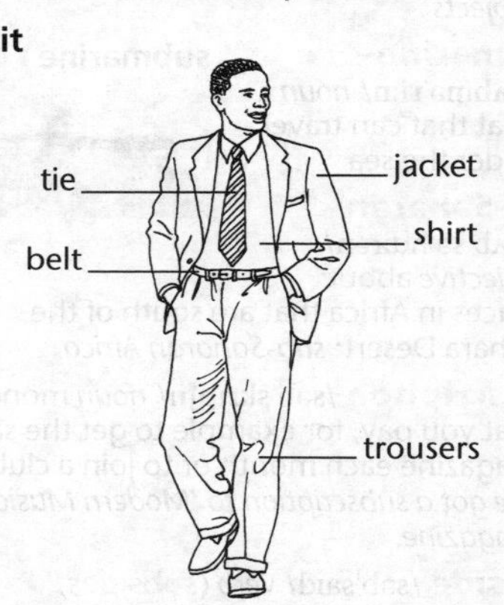

suit¹ /suːt/ *noun*

> ❖ **PRONUNCIATION**
>
> **Suit** sounds like **boot**.

a jacket and trousers, or a jacket and skirt, that you wear together and that are made from the same material

suit² /suːt/ *verb* (**suits**, **suiting**, **suited**) **1** If something suits you, it looks good on you: *Does this hat suit me?* **2** to be right for you; to be what you want or need: *Would it suit you if I came at five o'clock?*

suitable /ˈsuːtəbl/ *adjective* right for someone or something: *This film isn't suitable for children.* OPPOSITE **unsuitable**

▶ **suitably** /ˈsuːtəbli/ *adverb*: *Boke wasn't suitably dressed for a long walk in the sun.*

suitcase /ˈsuːtkeɪs/ *noun* a large bag with flat sides that you carry your clothes in when you travel: *Have you packed your suitcase?*

suitcase

sukumawiki *noun* (no plural) (East African English) a vegetable with dark green leaves that we cook SAME MEANING **kale**

sulk /sʌlk/ *verb* (**sulks**, **sulking**, **sulked** /sʌlkt/) to not speak because you are angry about something: *She's sulking because the teacher told her off.*

sum /sʌm/ *noun* **1** a simple piece of work with numbers, for example adding or dividing: *Children learn how to do sums.* **2** an amount of money: *The club paid a large sum of money for the player.* **3** the answer that you have when you add numbers together: *The sum of two and five is seven.*

summary /ˈsʌməri/ *noun* (*plural* **summaries**) a short way of telling something by giving only the most important facts: *Here is a summary of the news …* ▶ **summarize** *verb* (**summarizes**, **summarizing**, **summarized** /ˈsʌməraɪzd/) to make a **summary** of something: *Could you summarize the story so far?*

summer /ˈsʌmə(r)/ *noun* in cool countries, the warmest time of the year: *Many people in Europe go on their summer holidays in August.*

summit /ˈsʌmɪt/ *noun* the top of a mountain

sun /sʌn/ *noun* (no plural) **1 the sun** the big round thing in the sky that gives us light in the day, and heat: *The sun is shining.* **2** light and heat from the sun: *We sat in the sun all morning.* ➲ Look at **sunny**.

sunbathe /ˈsʌnbeɪð/ *verb* (**sunbathes**, **sunbathing**, **sunbathed** /ˈsʌnbeɪðd/) to lie in the sun: *We sunbathed on the beach.*

sunblock /ˈsʌnblɒk/ *noun* (no plural) cream that you put on your skin to protect it completely from the sun

sunburn /ˈsʌnbɜːn/ *noun* (no plural) red painful skin that you get when you have been in the hot sun for too long ▶ **sunburned** /ˈsʌnbɜːnd/ (also **sunburnt** /ˈsʌnbɜːnt/) *adjective*: *sunburned shoulders*

suncream /ˈsʌnkriːm/ *noun* (no plural) cream that you put on your skin to protect it from the sun

Sunday /ˈsʌndeɪ/ *noun* the first day of the week; the day before Monday

sunflower /ˈsʌnflaʊə(r)/ *noun* a tall plant with big yellow flowers and brown seeds. We use **sunflower** seeds for food and oil.

sung *form of* SING

sunglasses /ˈsʌŋɡlɑːsɪz/ *noun* (plural) glasses with dark glass in them that you wear in strong light: *a pair of sunglasses*

sunk *form of* SINK[1]

sunlight /ˈsʌnlaɪt/ *noun* (no plural) the light from the sun

sunny /ˈsʌni/ *adjective* (**sunnier**, **sunniest**) bright with light from the sun: *a sunny day*

sunrise /ˈsʌnraɪz/ *noun* (no plural) the time in the morning when the sun comes up

sunset /ˈsʌnset/ *noun* the time in the evening when the sun goes down: *The park closes at sunset.*

sunshine /ˈsʌnʃaɪn/ *noun* (no plural) the light and heat from the sun: *We sat outside in the sunshine.*

super /ˈsuːpə(r)/ *adjective* very good; wonderful: *That was a super meal.* ◇ *His new car is super.*

superb /suːˈpɜːb/ *adjective* very good or beautiful: *a superb holiday* ◇ *The view from the window is superb.*

superhero /ˈsuːpəhɪərəʊ/ *noun* (*plural* **superheroes**) a person, especially someone in a play, film or book, who has great strength or power and uses it to help people

superior /suːˈpɪəriə(r)/ *adjective* better or more important than another person or thing: *This brand of coffee is superior to cheaper brands.* OPPOSITE **inferior**

superlative /suːˈpɜːlətɪv/ *noun* the form of an adjective or adverb that shows the most of something: *'Most intelligent', 'best' and 'fastest' are all superlatives.* ▶ **superlative** *adjective*: *'Youngest' is the superlative form of 'young'.*

supermarket /ˈsuːpəmɑːkɪt/ *noun* a big shop where you can buy food and other things. You choose what you want to buy, and then pay for everything when you leave.

supermodel /ˈsuːpəmɒdl/ *noun* a very famous and successful **model** (= a person who wears clothes at fashion shows or for photographs in magazines)

supersonic /ˌsuːpəˈsɒnɪk/ *adjective* faster than the speed of sound: *a supersonic plane*

superstition /ˌsuːpəˈstɪʃn/ *noun* a belief in good and bad luck and other things that cannot be explained: *People say that walking under a ladder brings bad luck, but it's just a superstition.* ▶ **superstitious** /ˌsuːpəˈstɪʃəs/ *adjective* If you are **superstitious**, you believe in good and bad luck and other things that cannot be explained.

supervise /ˈsuːpəvaɪz/ *verb* (**supervises, supervising, supervised** /ˈsuːpəvaɪzd/) to watch to see that people are working correctly: *I supervised the builders.* ▶ **supervision** /ˌsuːpəˈvɪʒn/ *noun* (no plural) **supervising** or being **supervised**: *Children must not play here without supervision.* ▶ **supervisor** /ˈsuːpəvaɪzə(r)/ *noun* a person who **supervises**

supper /ˈsʌpə(r)/ *noun* the last meal of the day: *We had supper and then went to bed.* ➲ Note at **meal**.

supply[1] ⚷ /səˈplaɪ/ *noun* (*plural* **supplies**) an amount of something that you need: *supplies of food*

supply[2] /səˈplaɪ/ *verb* (**supplies, supplying, supplied** /səˈplaɪd/) to give or sell something that someone needs: *The school supplies us with books.* ◇ *The lake supplies water to thousands of people.*

support[1] ⚷ /səˈpɔːt/ *verb* (**supports, supporting, supported**) **1** to hold someone or something up, so that they do not fall: *The bridge isn't strong enough to support heavy lorries.* **2** to help someone to live by giving things like money, a home or food: *She has three children to support.* **3** to say that you think that someone or something is right or the best: *Everybody else said I was wrong but Kendi supported me.* ◇ *Which football team do you support?*

support[2] /səˈpɔːt/ *noun* **1** (no plural) help: *Thank you for all your support.* **2** (*plural* **supports**) something that holds up another thing: *a roof support*

supporter /səˈpɔːtə(r)/ *noun* a person who helps someone or something by giving money, by showing interest, etc: *football supporters*

suppose ⚷ /səˈpəʊz/ *verb* (**supposes, supposing, supposed** /səˈpəʊzd/)
1 to think that something is true or will happen but not be sure: *'Where's Moraa?' 'I don't know – I suppose she's still at work.'*
2 a word that you use when you agree with something but are not happy about it: *'Can I borrow your pen?' 'Yes, I suppose so – but don't lose it.'*
be supposed to 1 If you are supposed to do something, you should do it: *They were supposed to meet us here.* ◇ *You're not supposed to play in this room.* **2** If something is supposed to be true, people say it is true: *This is supposed to be a good restaurant.*

supposing /səˈpəʊzɪŋ/ *conjunction* if: *Supposing we miss the bus, how will we get to school on time?*

supreme /suːˈpriːm/ *adjective* highest or most important: *the Supreme Court*

sure ⚷ /ʃɔː(r)/ *adjective* (**surer, surest**) *adverb* If you are **sure**, you know that something is true or right: *I'm sure I've seen that man before.* ◇ *If you're not sure how to do it, ask your teacher.*
be sure to If you are sure to do something, you will certainly do it: *If you work hard, you're sure to pass the exam.*
for sure without any doubt: *I think he's coming to the meeting but I don't know for sure.*
make sure to check something so that you are certain about it: *I think they are arriving about eight, but I'll phone to make sure.* ◇ *Make sure you don't leave your bag on the bus.*
sure enough as I thought: *I said they would be late, and sure enough they were.*

surely /ˈʃɔːli/ *adverb* a word that you use when you think that something must be true, or when you are surprised: *Surely you know where your brother works!*

surf[1] /sɜːf/ *noun* (no plural) the white part on the top of waves in the sea

surf[2] /sɜːf/ *verb* (**surfs, surfing, surfed** /sɜːft/) to stand on a long piece of wood or plastic (called a **surfboard**) and ride on a wave
surf the Net; surf the Internet to use the Internet

▶ **surfer** /ˈsɜːfə(r)/ *noun*: *The beach is popular with surfers.* ◇ *Internet surfers*

surface 🔑 /ˈsɜːfɪs/ *noun* **1** the outside part of something: *A tomato has a shiny red surface.* **2** the top of water: *She dived below the surface.*

surfing

surfing /ˈsɜːfɪŋ/ *noun* (no plural) the sport of riding over waves on a long piece of wood or plastic (called a **surfboard**) ℹ You can say **go surfing**: *We went surfing.*

surgeon /ˈsɜːdʒən/ *noun* a doctor who cuts your body to take out or repair a part inside. This is called an **operation**: *a brain surgeon*

surgery /ˈsɜːdʒəri/ *noun* **1** (no plural) cutting someone's body to take out or repair a part inside: *He needed surgery after the accident.* **2** (*plural* **surgeries**) a place where you go to see a doctor or dentist

surname /ˈsɜːneɪm/ *noun* the name that a family has. Your surname is usually your last name: *Her name is Chebet Ondieki. Ondieki is her surname.* ➲ Note at **name**[1].

surprise[1] 🔑 /səˈpraɪz/ *noun* **1** (no plural) the feeling that you have when something happens suddenly that you did not expect: *She looked at me in surprise when I told her the news.* **2** (*plural* **surprises**) something that happens when you do not expect it: *Don't tell him about the birthday party – it's a surprise!*
take someone by surprise to happen when someone does not expect it: *Your phone call took me by surprise – I thought you were on holiday.*
to my surprise I was surprised that: *I thought she would be angry but, to my surprise, she smiled.*

surprise[2] 🔑 /səˈpraɪz/ *verb* (**surprises, surprising, surprised** /səˈpraɪzd/) to do something that someone does not expect: *I arrived early to surprise her.*

surprised 🔑 /səˈpraɪzd/ *adjective* If you are surprised, you feel or show surprise: *I was surprised to see Kamal yesterday – I thought he was in hospital.*

surprising 🔑 /səˈpraɪzɪŋ/ *adjective* If something is surprising, it makes you feel surprise: *The news was surprising.*
▶ **surprisingly** *adverb*: *The exam was surprisingly easy.*

surrender /səˈrendə(r)/ *verb* (**surrenders, surrendering, surrendered** /səˈrendəd/) to stop fighting because you cannot win: *After six hours on the roof, the man surrendered to the police.*

surround 🔑 /səˈraʊnd/ *verb* (**surrounds, surrounding, surrounded**) to be or go all around something: *The lake is surrounded by trees.*

surroundings /səˈraʊndɪŋz/ *noun* (plural) everything around you, or the place where you live: *The farm is in beautiful surroundings.* ◇ *I don't like seeing animals in cages – I prefer to see them in their natural surroundings.*

survey /ˈsɜːveɪ/ *noun* (*plural* **surveys**) asking questions about what people think or do, or what is happening: *We did a survey of people's favourite TV programmes.*

survive 🔑 /səˈvaɪv/ *verb* (**survives, surviving, survived** /səˈvaɪvd/) to continue to live after a difficult or dangerous time: *Camels can survive for many days without water.* ◇ *Only one person survived the plane crash.*
▶ **survival** /səˈvaɪvl/ *noun* (no plural) surviving: *Food and water are necessary for survival.* ▶ **survivor** /səˈvaɪvə(r)/ *noun*: *The government sent help to the survivors of the earthquake.*

suspect[1] /səˈspekt/ *verb* (**suspects, suspecting, suspected**) **1** to think that something is true, but not be certain: *Karimi wasn't at school today – I suspect that he's ill.* **2** to think that someone has done something wrong but not be certain: *They suspect Shema of stealing the money.*

suspect[2] /ˈsʌspekt/ *noun* a person who someone thinks has done something wrong: *The police have arrested two suspects.*

suspicion /səˈspɪʃn/ *noun* **1** (*plural* **suspicions**) an idea that is not totally certain: *We have a suspicion that he is unhappy.* **2** (no plural) a feeling that someone has done something wrong:

When she saw all the money in his wallet she was filled with suspicion.

suspicious /sə'spɪʃəs/ *adjective* **1** If you are **suspicious**, you do not believe someone or something, or you feel that something is wrong: *The police are suspicious of her story.* **2** A person or thing that is **suspicious** makes you feel that something is wrong: *There was a man waiting outside the school. He looked very suspicious.* ▶ **suspiciously** *adverb*: *'What are you doing here?' the woman asked suspiciously.*

sustain /sə'steɪn/ *verb* **1** to make something continue for some time: *The teacher managed to sustain everyone's interest until the end of the lesson.* **2** (in law) to decide that a claim is correct: *Objection sustained!* (= said by a judge to show that they agree when a lawyer says something is wrong)

Swahili = **Kiswahili**

swallow[1] /'swɒləʊ/ *verb* (**swallows, swallowing, swallowed** /'swɒləʊd/) to make food or drink move down your throat from your mouth: *I can't swallow these tablets without water.*

swallow[2] /'swɒləʊ/ *noun* a small bird

swallow

swam *form of* SWIM

swamp /swɒmp/ *noun* soft wet ground

swap (also **swop**) /swɒp/ *verb* (**swaps, swapping, swapped** /swɒpt/) to change one thing for another thing; to give one thing and get another thing for it: *Do you want to swap chairs with me?* (= you have my chair and I'll have yours) ◇ *I swapped my T-shirt for Juma's belt.*

swarm[1] /swɔ:m/ *noun* a big group of flying insects: *a swarm of bees*

swarm[2] /swɔ:m/ *verb* (**swarms, swarming, swarmed** /swɔ:md/) to fly or move quickly in a big group: *The fans swarmed into the stadium.*

sway /sweɪ/ *verb* (**sways, swaying, swayed** /sweɪd/) to move slowly from side to side: *The trees were swaying in the wind.*

swear /sweə(r)/ *verb* (**swears, swearing, swore** /swɔ:(r)/, **has sworn** /swɔ:n/) **1** to say bad words: *Don't swear at your mother!* **2** to make a serious promise: *He swears that he is telling the truth.*

swear word /'sweə wɜ:d/ *noun* a bad word

sweat /swet/ *noun* (no plural) water that comes out of your skin when you are hot or afraid: *He wiped the sweat from his face.* ▶ **sweat** *verb* (**sweats, sweating, sweated**) to have sweat coming out of your skin: *The room was so hot that everyone was sweating.*

sweater /'swetə(r)/ *noun* a warm piece of clothing with sleeves, that you wear on the top part of your body. **Sweaters** are often made of wool.

sweatshirt /'swetʃɜ:t/ *noun* a piece of clothing with long sleeves, made of thick cotton, that you wear on the top part of your body

sweaty /'sweti/ *adjective* (**sweatier, sweatiest**) covered with sweat: *sweaty socks*

sweep /swi:p/ *verb* (**sweeps, sweeping, swept** /swept/, **has swept**) **1** to clean something by moving dirt or other things away with a brush on a long handle (called a **broom**): *I swept the floor.* **2** to push something along or away quickly and strongly: *The bridge was swept away by the floods.*

sweep up to move something away with a brush: *I swept up the broken glass.*

sweet[1] /swi:t/ *adjective* (**sweeter, sweetest**) **1** with the taste of sugar: *Honey is sweet.* **2** pretty: *What a sweet little girl!* **3** kind and gentle: *It was sweet of you to help me.* **4** with a good smell: *the sweet smell of roses*

sweet[2] /swi:t/ *noun* **1** a small piece of sweet food, made of boiled sugar, chocolate, etc: *He bought a packet of sweets for the children.* **2** sweet food that you eat at the end of a meal: *Do you want a sweet?*

sweetly /'swi:tli/ *adverb* in a pretty, kind or nice way: *She smiled sweetly.*

sweet potato /ˌswi:t pə'teɪtəʊ/ *noun* (*plural* **sweet potatoes**) a sweet vegetable that looks like a red potato but is yellow inside

swell /swel/ *verb* (**swells, swelling, swelled** /sweld/, **has swollen** /'swəʊlən/ or **has swelled**)

swell up to become bigger or thicker

than it usually is: *After he hurt his ankle it began to swell up.* ➲ Look at **swollen²**.

swelling /ˈswelɪŋ/ *noun* a place on the body that is bigger or fatter than it usually is: *She has got a swelling on her head where she fell and hit it.*

swept *form of* SWEEP

swerve /swɜːv/ *verb* (**swerves**, **swerving**, **swerved** /swɜːvd/) to turn suddenly so that you do not hit someone or something: *The driver swerved when she saw the child in the road.*

swift /swɪft/ *adjective* (**swifter**, **swiftest**) quick or fast: *We made a swift decision.*
▶ **swiftly** *adverb*: *She ran swiftly up the stairs.*

swim /swɪm/ *verb* (**swims**, **swimming**, **swam** /swæm/, **has swum** /swʌm/) to move your body through water: *Can you swim?* ◇ *I swam across the lake.*
▶ **swim** *noun* (no plural): *Let's go for a swim.* ▶ **swimmer** /ˈswɪmə(r)/ *noun* a person who swims: *He's a good swimmer.*
▶ **swimming** /ˈswɪmɪŋ/ *noun* (no plural): *Swimming is my favourite sport.*

❖ **GRAMMAR**

When you talk about spending time swimming as a sport, you usually say **go swimming**: *I go swimming every day.*

swimming costume /ˈswɪmɪŋ kɒstjuːm/ (also **swimsuit**) *noun* a piece of clothing that a woman or girl wears for swimming

swimming pool /ˈswɪmɪŋ puːl/ *noun* a special place where you can swim: *There's an outdoor swimming pool.*

swimming trunks /ˈswɪmɪŋ trʌŋks/ *noun* (plural) short trousers that a man or boy wears for swimming

swimsuit /ˈswɪmsuːt/ = **swimming costume**

swing¹ /swɪŋ/ *verb* (**swings**, **swinging**, **swung** /swʌŋ/, **has swung**) **1** to hang from something and move backwards and forwards or from side to side through the air: *The monkey was swinging from a tree.* **2** to make someone or something move in this way: *He swung his arms as he walked.* **3** to move in a curve: *The door swung open.*

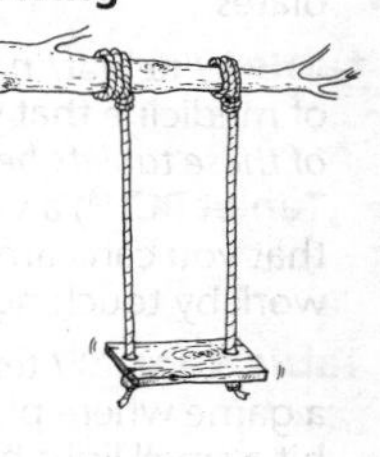

swing² /swɪŋ/ *noun* a seat that hangs down. Children sit on it to move backwards and forwards through the air.

switch¹ /swɪtʃ/ *noun* (*plural* **switches**) a small thing that you press to stop or start electricity: *Where is the light switch?*

switch

switch² /swɪtʃ/ *verb* (**switches**, **switching**, **switched** /swɪtʃt/) to change to something different: *I switched to another seat because I couldn't see the film.*
switch off to press something to stop electricity: *I switched the TV off.* ◇ *Don't forget to switch off the lights!*
switch on to press something to start electricity: *Switch the radio on.*

switchboard /ˈswɪtʃbɔːd/ *noun* the place in a large office where someone answers telephone calls and sends them to the right people

swollen¹ *form of* SWELL

swollen² /ˈswəʊlən/ *adjective* thicker or fatter than it usually is: *a swollen ankle* ➲ Look at **swell**.

swoop /swuːp/ *verb* (**swoops**, **swooping**, **swooped** /swuːpt/) to fly down quickly: *The bird swooped down to catch a fish.*

swop = **swap**

sword /sɔːd/ *noun*

❖ **PRONUNCIATION**

We do not say the 'w' in this word, so it sounds like **cord**.

a long sharp knife for fighting

swore, **sworn** *forms of* SWEAR

swot¹ /swɒt/ *verb* (**swots**, **swotting**, **swotted**) to study hard before an exam: *Boke is swotting for her test next week.*

swot² /swɒt/ *noun* a person who spends too much time studying ❶ This is an informal word.

swum *form of* SWIM

swung *form of* SWING¹

syllable /ˈsɪləbl/ *noun* a part of a word that has one **vowel** sound when you say it. 'Swim' has one **syllable** and 'system' has two **syllables**.

syllabus /ˈsɪləbəs/ *noun* (*plural* **syllabuses**) a list of all the things that you must study on a course

symbol ⚷ /ˈsɪmbl/ *noun* a mark, sign or picture that shows something: *+ and – are symbols for plus and minus in mathematics.* ◇ *A dove is the symbol of peace.*

sympathetic /ˌsɪmpəˈθetɪk/ *adjective* If you are **sympathetic**, you show that you understand other people's feelings when they have problems: *Everyone was very sympathetic when I was ill.*
▸ **sympathetically** /ˌsɪmpəˈθetɪkli/ *adverb*: *He smiled sympathetically.*

sympathize /ˈsɪmpəθaɪz/ *verb* (**sympathizes, sympathizing, sympathized** /ˈsɪmpəθaɪzd/)
sympathize with someone to show that you understand someone's feelings when they have problems: *I sympathize with you – I've got a lot of work too.*

sympathy /ˈsɪmpəθi/ *noun* (no plural) understanding another person's feelings and problems: *She wrote me a letter of sympathy when my father died.*

❖ **WORD FAMILY**
sympathy **sympathize**
sympathetic: OPPOSITE **unsympathetic**

symphony /ˈsɪmfəni/ *noun* (*plural* **symphonies**) a long piece of music for a lot of musicians playing together: *Beethoven's fifth symphony*

symptom /ˈsɪmptəm/ *noun* something that shows that you have an illness: *The main symptom of malaria is a high fever.*

synagogue /ˈsɪnəgɒg/ *noun* a building where Jewish people go to speak to God (to **pray**)

syndrome /ˈsɪndrəʊm/ *noun* a group of signs or changes in the body that are typical of an illness: *This syndrome is associated with frequent coughing.*

synthetic /sɪnˈθetɪk/ *adjective* made by people; not natural: *Nylon is a synthetic material, but wool is natural.*

syringe /sɪˈrɪndʒ/ *noun* a plastic or glass tube with a needle that is used for taking blood out of the body or putting drugs into the body

syringe

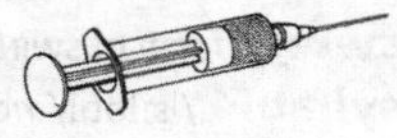

syrup /ˈsɪrəp/ *noun* (no plural) thick sweet liquid made with sugar and water or fruit juice: *ginger in syrup*

system ⚷ /ˈsɪstəm/ *noun* **1** a group of things or parts that work together: *the railway system* ◇ *We have a new computer system at school.* **2** a group of ideas or ways of doing something: *What system of government do you have in your country?*

Tt

T, t /tiː/ *noun* (*plural* **T's, t's** /tiːz/) the twentieth letter of the English alphabet: *'Table' begins with a 'T'.*

taarab /ˈtɑːrʌb/ *noun* (no plural) a type of music that people in East Africa play, especially along the coast

table ⚷ /ˈteɪbl/ *noun* **1** a piece of furniture with a flat top on legs **2** a list of facts or numbers: *There is a table of irregular verbs at the back of this dictionary.*
set or **lay the table** to put spoons, knives, forks, plates, etc. on the table before you eat

table

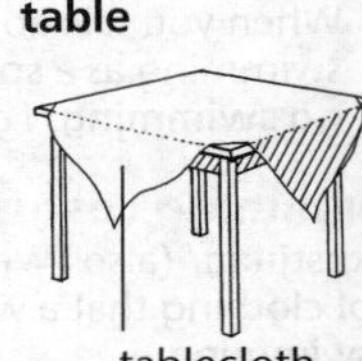

tablecloth /ˈteɪblklɒθ/ *noun* a cloth that you put over a table, especially when you have a meal ➲ Picture at **table**.

tablespoon /ˈteɪblspuːn/ *noun* a big spoon that you use for putting food on plates

tablet /ˈtæblət/ *noun* **1** a small hard piece of medicine that you swallow: *Take two of these tablets before every meal.* **2** (also **Tablet PC™**) a very small, flat computer that you can carry with you and that you work by touching the screen

table tennis /ˈteɪbl tenɪs/ *noun* (no plural) a game where players use a round **bat** to hit a small light ball over a net on a big table

taboo /təˈbuː/ *noun* (*plural* **taboos** /təˈbuːz/) something that you must not say or do because it might make someone feel angry or unhappy

tackle /ˈtækl/ *verb* (**tackles, tackling, tackled** /ˈtækld/) **1** to start to do a difficult job: *I'm going to tackle my homework now.* ◇ *How shall we tackle this problem?* **2** to try to take the ball from someone in a game like football **3** to try to catch and hold someone: *I tackled the thief but he ran away.*

tact /tækt/ *noun* (no plural) knowing how and when to say things so that you do not upset people: *She told him the meal was horrible – she's got no tact.*

tactful /ˈtæktfl/ *adjective* careful not to say or do things that may make people unhappy or angry: *Try to be tactful about her new haircut.* ▶ **tactfully** /ˈtæktfəli/ *adverb* in a **tactful** way

tactics /ˈtæktɪks/ *noun* (plural) the methods that you use to do or win something: *The coach discussed tactics with his team.*

tactless /ˈtæktləs/ *adjective* saying or doing things that may make people unhappy or angry: *It was tactless of you to ask how old she was.*

tag /tæg/ *noun* a small piece of paper or material fixed to something, that tells you about it: *I looked at the price tag to see how much the dress cost.* SAME MEANING **label**

tail 🔑 /teɪl/ *noun* **1** the long thin part at the end of an animal's body: *The dog wagged its tail.* ➲ Picture at **cat, fish**[1], **horse, scorpion, lion**. **2** the part at the back of something: *the tail of a plane* **3** **tails** (plural) the side of a coin that does not have the head of a person on it ➲ Note at **head**[1].

tailor /ˈteɪlə(r)/ *noun* a person whose job is to make clothes, especially for men

take 🔑 /teɪk/ *verb* (**takes, taking, took** /tʊk/, **has taken** /ˈteɪkn/) **1** to move something or go with someone to another place: *Take your coat with you – it's cold.* ◇ *She took her son to the hospital.* ➲ Look at **bring**. **2** to put your hand round something and hold it: *She took the baby in her arms.* ◇ *Take this money – it's yours.* **3** to steal something: *Someone has taken my bike.* **4** to need an amount of time: *The journey took four hours.* **5** to travel in a bus, train, etc: *I took a taxi to the hospital.* **6** to eat or drink something: *I took the medicine.* **7** to agree to have something: *We'll have to pay cash because they don't take cheques.* ➲ Note at **exam, tooth**.

it takes you need something: *It takes a long time to learn a language.*

take after someone to be or look like someone in your family: *She takes after her mother.*

take away to remove something: *He took the knife away from the child.*

take down to write something that someone says: *He took down my address.*

take off When a plane **takes off**, it leaves the ground. OPPOSITE **land**

take something off **1** to remove clothes: *Take your shoes off.* OPPOSITE **put something on** **2** to have time as a holiday, not working: *She is taking a week off in June.*

take over to look after a business, etc. when another person stops: *Rono took over the farm when his father died.*

take up to use or fill time or space: *The bed takes up half the room.* ◇ *The new baby takes up all her time.*

takeaway /ˈteɪkəweɪ/ *noun* (*plural* **takeaways**) **1** a restaurant that sells hot food that you take out to eat somewhere else: *a Chinese takeaway* **2** the food that you buy there: *Let's have a takeaway.*

take-off /ˈteɪk ɒf/ *noun* the time when a plane leaves the ground: *The plane was ready for take-off.* OPPOSITE **landing**

talcum powder /ˈtælkəm paʊdə(r)/ *noun* (no plural) a soft powder that is used to make the body smell good

tale /teɪl/ *noun* a story: *My mother used to tell us tales about giants and ogres.*

talent /ˈtælənt/ *noun* the natural ability to do something very well: *Adisa has a talent for drawing.*

talented /ˈtæləntɪd/ *adjective* having a natural ability to do something very well: *a talented musician*

talk[1] 🔑 /tɔːk/ *verb* (**talks, talking, talked** /tɔːkt/) to speak to someone; to say words: *She is talking to her friend on the phone.* ◇ *We talked about our holiday.*

talk[2] 🔑 /tɔːk/ *noun* **1** when two or more people talk about something: *Sarika and I had a long talk about the problem.* ◇ *The two countries are holding talks to try and end the war.* **2** when a person speaks to a group of people: *Professor Olumbe gave an interesting talk on Chinese art.*

talkative /ˈtɔːkətɪv/ *adjective* A person who is **talkative** talks a lot.

tall /tɔːl/ *adjective* (**taller, tallest**) **1** A person or thing that is tall goes up a long way: *a tall tree* ◇ *Juma is taller than his brother.* OPPOSITE **short** **2** You use 'tall' to say or ask how far it is from the bottom to the top of someone or something: *How tall are you?* ◇ *She's 1.62 metres tall.* ➲ Note at **high**[1].

tamarind /ˈtæmərɪnd/ *noun* the fruit of a **tamarind** tree. The inside of the fruit is brown and is used in cooking.

tame[1] /teɪm/ *adjective* (**tamer, tamest**) A **tame** animal is not wild and is not afraid of people: *a tame parrot*

tame[2] /teɪm/ *verb* (**tames, taming, tamed** /teɪmd/) to make a wild animal easy to control

tamper /ˈtæmpə(r)/ *verb* (**tampers, tampering, tampered** /ˈtæmpəd/) **tamper with something** to make changes to something without asking if you can: *Don't tamper with the computer when I'm not there – you might damage it.*

tangerine /ˌtændʒəˈriːn/ *noun* a fruit like a small sweet orange, with a skin that is easy to take off

tangle /ˈtæŋgl/ *verb* (**tangles, tangling, tangled** /ˈtæŋgld/) to mix or twist something like string or hair so that it is difficult to separate OPPOSITE **untangle** ▶ **tangle** *noun*: *This string is in a tangle.*

tangled /ˈtæŋgld/ *adjective* twisted together in an untidy way: *If you don't comb your hair it will get all tangled.*

tank /tæŋk/ *noun* **1** a container for liquids or gas: *a petrol tank* (in a car) ◇ *a water tank* **2** a strong heavy vehicle with big guns. **Tanks** are used by armies in wars.

tank

tanker /ˈtæŋkə(r)/ *noun* a lorry or ship that carries petrol or oil: *an oil tanker*

tanning /ˈtænɪŋ/ *noun* (no plural) making leather from animal skins

tap[1] /tæp/ *noun* **1** a thing that you turn to make water come out of a pipe: *Turn the tap off.* **2** a light hit with your hand or fingers: *They heard a tap at the door.*

tap[2] /tæp/ *verb* (**taps, tapping, tapped** /tæpt/) to hit or touch someone or something quickly and lightly: *She tapped me on the shoulder.* ◇ *I tapped on the window.*

tape[1] /teɪp/ *noun* **1** a long thin piece of special plastic in a plastic box that is used to record sound, music or moving pictures so that you can listen to or watch it later: *They recorded the interview on tape.* **2** a long thin piece of material or paper: *She repaired the page with sticky tape.*

tape[2] /teɪp/ *verb* (**tapes, taping, taped** /teɪpt/) to record sound, music or moving pictures on tape so that you can listen to or watch it later: *They taped the match and watched it the next day.*

tape measure /ˈteɪp meʒə(r)/ *noun* a long thin piece of metal, plastic or cloth for measuring things

tape recorder /ˈteɪp rɪkɔːdə(r)/ *noun* a machine that can record sound or music on tape and play it again later

tapestry /ˈtæpəstri/ *noun* (*plural* **tapestries**) a piece of cloth with pictures on it made from coloured thread

tar /tɑː(r)/ *noun* (no plural) black stuff that is thick and sticky when it is hot, and hard when it is cold. **Tar** is used for making roads.

target /ˈtɑːgɪt/ *noun* **1** a thing that you try to hit with a bullet, an arrow, etc: *The bomb hit its target.* **2** something that you are trying to do or finish: *Our target is to finish the book by the end of term.*

task /tɑːsk/ *noun* a piece of work that you must do; a job: *I had the task of cleaning the floors.*

taste[1] /teɪst/ *noun* **1** (no plural) the power to know about food and drink with your mouth: *Kamal has a good sense of taste.* **2** (*plural* **tastes**) the feeling that a certain food or drink gives in your mouth: *Sugar has a sweet taste and lemons have a sour taste.* ◇ *I don't like the taste of this fru*[it.] **3** (*plural* **tastes**) a little bit of food or drin[k:] *Have a taste of the stew to see if you like it.* **4** (no plural) being able to choose nice things: *She has good taste in clothes.*

taste[2] /teɪst/ *verb* (**tastes, tasting, tasted**) **1** to feel or know a certain food or drink in your mouth: *Can you taste onion in this stew?* **2** to eat or drink a little of something: *Taste this meat to see if you like it.* **3** to give a certain feeling when yo[u] put it in your mouth: *Honey tastes very sweet.*

tasteless /ˈteɪstləs/ *adjective* with little or no flavour: *These vegetables are tasteless.* OPPOSITE **tasty**

tasty /ˈteɪsti/ *adjective* (**tastier**, **tastiest**) good to eat: *The soup was very tasty.* OPPOSITE **tasteless**

tattoo /təˈtuː/ *noun* (*plural* **tattoos**) a picture on someone's skin, made with a needle and coloured liquid: *He had a tattoo of a snake on his arm.*

taught *form of* TEACH

tax[1] 🔑 /tæks/ *noun* (*plural* **taxes**) money that people have to pay to the government. People pay tax from the money they earn or when they buy things: *There is a tax on petrol in this country.*

tax[2] /tæks/ *verb* (**taxes**, **taxing**, **taxed** /tækst/) to make someone pay tax

taxi 🔑 /ˈtæksi/ *noun* (*plural* **taxis**) (*also* **cab**) a car with a driver that you pay to take you somewhere: *I took a taxi to the airport.* ◇ *I came by taxi.*

TB /ˌtiː ˈbiː/ *short for* TUBERCULOSIS

tea 🔑 /tiː/ *noun* **1** (no plural) a brown drink that you make with hot water and the dry leaves of a special plant: *Would you like a cup of tea?* **2** (*plural* **teas**) a cup of this drink: *Two teas, please.* **3** (no plural) the dry leaves that you use to make tea: *We've run out of tea.* **4** a small meal that you eat in the afternoon or early evening: *They had egg salad for tea.* ➲ Note at **meal**.

teabag /ˈtiːbæg/ *noun* a small paper bag with tea leaves inside. You use it to make tea.

teach 🔑 /tiːtʃ/ *verb* (**teaches**, **teaching**, **taught** /tɔːt/, **has taught**) to give someone lessons; to tell or show someone how to do something: *Mr Nassir taught us some French.* ◇ *My mother taught me to knit.* ➲ Look at **learn**. ▸ **teaching** /ˈtiːtʃɪŋ/ *noun* (no plural) the job of a teacher

teacher 🔑 /ˈtiːtʃə(r)/ *noun* a person whose job is to teach: *He's my English teacher.* ◇ *a duty/class teacher*

teacup /ˈtiːkʌp/ *noun* a cup that we drink tea from

team 🔑 /tiːm/ *noun* **1** a group of people who play a sport or a game together against another group: *Which team do you play for?* ◇ *a football team* **2** a group of people who work together: *a team of doctors*

teammate /ˈtiːmmeɪt/ *noun* a person in the same team or group as you

teamwork /ˈtiːmwɜːk/ *noun* (no plural) when people work well together

teapot

teapot /ˈtiːpɒt/ *noun* a special pot for making and pouring tea

tear[1] 🔑 /tɪə(r)/ *noun*

> ❖ **PRONUNCIATION**
> **Tear** with this meaning sounds like **near** or **cheer**.

a drop of water that comes from your eye when you cry: *I had tears in my eyes.*
be in tears to be crying: *I was in tears at the end of the film.*
burst into tears to suddenly start to cry: *He read the letter and burst into tears.*

tear

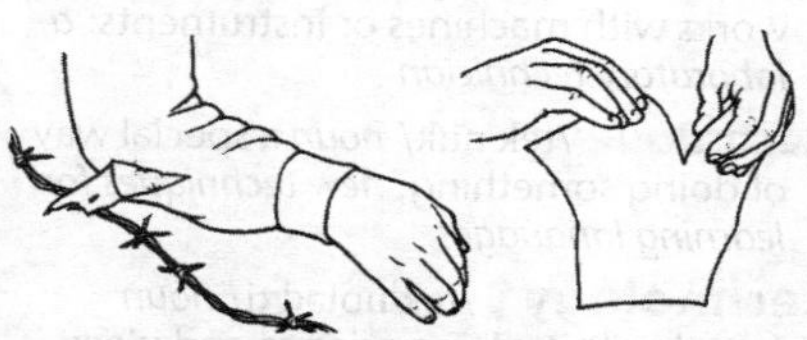

"Oh no! I've **torn** my shirt!" She **tore** the letter in half.

tear[2] 🔑 /teə(r)/ *verb* (**tears**, **tearing**, **tore** /tɔː(r)/, **has torn** /tɔːn/)

> ❖ **PRONUNCIATION**
> **Tear** with this meaning sounds like **hair** or **care**.

1 to pull something apart or make an untidy hole in something: *She tore her dress on a nail.* ◇ *I tore the piece of paper in half.* ◇ *I can't use this bag – it's torn.* **2** to pull something away from someone or something in a rough and sudden way: *I tore a page out of the book.* **3** to come apart; to break: *Paper tears easily.* **4** to move very fast: *He tore down the street.*
tear up to pull something into small pieces: *I tore the letter up and threw it away.*

tear[3] /teə(r)/ *noun*

❖ **PRONUNCIATION**

Tear with this meaning sounds like **hair** or **care**.

an untidy hole in something like paper or material: *You've got a tear in your shirt.*

tearful /ˈtɪəfl/ *adjective* crying, or about to cry

tease /tiːz/ *verb* (**teases, teasing, teased** /tiːzd/) to say unkind things to someone because you think it is funny: *People often tease me because I'm short.*

teaspoon /ˈtiːspuːn/ *noun* a small spoon that you use for putting sugar into tea or coffee

tea towel /ˈtiː taʊəl/ *noun* a small cloth that you use for drying things like plates and cups after you wash them

technical /ˈteknɪkl/ *adjective* of or about the machines and materials used in science and in making things: *He has great technical knowledge.*

technician /tekˈnɪʃn/ *noun* a person who works with machines or instruments: *a laboratory technician*

technique /tekˈniːk/ *noun* a special way of doing something: *new techniques for learning languages*

technology /tekˈnɒlədʒi/ *noun* (no plural) studying science and ideas about how things work, and using this to build and make things: *Technology is very important for the future.* ◇ *computer technology*

teddy bear /ˈtedi beə(r)/ (also **teddy** *plural* **teddies**) *noun* a toy for children that looks like a bear

teddy bear

tedious /ˈtiːdiəs/ *adjective* very long and not interesting: *a tedious journey*

teenager /ˈtiːneɪdʒə(r)/ *noun* a person who is between the ages of 13 and 19
▸ **teenage** /ˈtiːneɪdʒ/ *adjective*: *a teenage boy*

teens /tiːnz/ *noun* (plural) the time when you are between the ages of 13 and 19: *She is in her teens.*

teeth *plural of* TOOTH

telegram /ˈtelɪɡræm/ *noun* a message that you send very quickly by radio or by electric wires

telephone[1] /ˈtelɪfəʊn/ *noun* an instrument that you use for talking to someone who is in another place: *What's your telephone number?* **Phone** is the more usual word.

telephone[2] /ˈtelɪfəʊn/ *verb* (**telephones, telephoning, telephoned** /ˈtelɪfəʊnd/) to use a telephone to speak to someone: *I must telephone my aunt.* **Phone** or **call** are the more usual words.

telephone booth /ˈtelɪfəʊn buːð/ (also **phone booth**) *noun* a small place in a hotel, restaurant or in the street that contains a telephone for public use

telephone box /ˈtelɪfəʊn bɒks/ *noun* (*plural* **telephone boxes**) (also **phone box**) a kind of small building in the street or in a public place that has a telephone in it

telephone directory /ˈtelɪfəʊn dɪrektəri/ *noun* (*plural* **telephone directories**) a book of people's names, addresses and telephone numbers
SAME MEANING **phone book**

telescope /ˈtelɪskəʊp/ *noun* a long round instrument with special glass inside it. You use it to look at things that are a long way from you.

television /ˈtelɪvɪʒn/ *noun* **1** (*plural* **televisions**) (also **television set**) a machine like a box with a screen, that shows moving pictures with sound: *Please turn the television off.* **2** (no plural) things that you watch on a television: *I watched television last night.* ◇ *What's on television?* ◇ *a television programme* **3** a way of sending pictures and sounds so that people can watch them on television: *satellite television* The short forms are **telly** and **TV**.

tell /tel/ *verb* (**tells, telling, told** /təʊld/, **has told**) **1** to give information to someone by speaking or writing: *I told her my new address.* ◇ *This book tells you how to make bread.* ◇ *He told me that he was tired.* **2** to say what someone must do: *Our teacher told us to read this book.* ➲ Note at **say**[1].

can tell to know, guess or understand something: *I can tell that he's been crying because his eyes are red.* ◇ *I can't tell the*

difference between Kamal and his brother. They look exactly the same!
tell someone off to speak to someone in an angry way because they have done something wrong: *I told the children off for making so much noise.*

telly /ˈteli/ *short for* TELEVISION

temper /ˈtempə(r)/ *noun* how you feel: *She's in a bad temper this morning.*
have a temper If you **have a temper**, you often get angry and cannot control what you do or say: *He has a terrible temper.*
in a temper angry: *She's in a temper because she's tired.*
lose your temper to suddenly become angry

temperate /ˈtempərət/ *adjective* not very hot and not very cold: *The Nairobi area has a temperate climate.*

temperature 🔑 /ˈtemprətʃə(r)/ *noun* how hot or cold someone or something is: *Some days, the temperature reaches over 40 degrees Celsius.* ◇ *a high/low temperature*
have a temperature to feel very hot because you are ill
take someone's temperature to see how hot someone is, using a special instrument called a **thermometer**

temple /ˈtempl/ *noun* a building where people go to say prayers to God or a god

temporarily /ˈtemprərəli/ *adverb* for a short time only: *The road is temporarily closed for repairs.* OPPOSITE **permanently**

temporary 🔑 /ˈtemprəri/ *adjective* Something that is temporary lasts for a short time: *She has a temporary job in an office.* OPPOSITE **permanent**

tempt /tempt/ *verb* (**tempts**, **tempting**, **tempted**) to make someone want to do something, especially something that is wrong: *He saw the money on the table and he was tempted to steal it.*

temptation /tempˈteɪʃn/ *noun* **1** (*plural* **temptations**) a thing that makes you want to do something wrong: *Don't leave the money on your desk – it's a temptation to thieves.* **2** (no plural) a feeling that you want to do something that you know is wrong: *I couldn't resist the temptation to eat another chocolate.*

tempting /ˈtemptɪŋ/ *adjective* Something that is **tempting** makes you want to do or have it: *That food looks very tempting!*

ten 🔑 /ten/ *number* 10

tenant /ˈtenənt/ *noun* a person who pays money to live in or use a place

tend 🔑 /tend/ *verb* (**tends**, **tending**, **tended**) to usually do or be something: *Men tend to be taller than women.*

tendency /ˈtendənsi/ *noun* (*plural* **tendencies**) something that a person or thing often does: *He has a tendency to be late.*

tender /ˈtendə(r)/ *adjective* **1** kind and gentle: *a tender look* **2 Tender** meat is soft and easy to cut or bite. OPPOSITE **tough** **3** If a part of your body is **tender**, it hurts when you touch it: *My knee still feels very tender.* ▶ **tenderly** *adverb* in a kind and gentle way: *He touched her arm tenderly.* ▶ **tenderness** /ˈtendənəs/ *noun* (no plural): *a feeling of tenderness*

tennis /ˈtenɪs/ *noun* (no plural) a game for two or four players who hit a small ball over a net using **rackets** (= equipment that they hold in their hands): *Let's play tennis.* ➲ Picture at **racket**.

tennis court /ˈtenɪs kɔːt/ *noun* a special place where you play **tennis**

tenor /ˈtenə(r)/ *noun* a male singing voice that is not the lowest (**bass**); a man with this voice: *He sings tenor in our choir.*

tense[1] /tens/ *adjective* (**tenser**, **tensest**) **1** worried because you are waiting for something to happen: *I always feel very tense before exams.* ℹ The noun is **tension**. OPPOSITE **relaxed** **2** pulled tightly: *tense muscles*

tense[2] /tens/ *noun* the form of a verb that shows if something happens in the past, present or future

tension /ˈtenʃn/ *noun* (no plural) being worried and not able to relax: *Tension can give you headaches.* ℹ The adjective is **tense**.

tent

tent 🔑 /tent/ *noun* a kind of a house made of cloth. You sleep in a tent when you go camping: *We put up our tent.*

tenth /tenθ/ *adjective, adverb, noun* **1** 10th **2** one of ten equal parts of something; 1/10

term /tɜːm/ *noun* **1** the time between holidays when schools and colleges are open: *We have important exams next term.* **2** a word or group of words connected with a special subject: *a computing term*

terminal /ˈtɜːmɪnl/ *noun* a building where people begin and end their journeys by bus, train, plane or ship: *Passengers for Nairobi should go to Terminal 2.*

termite /ˈtɜːmaɪt/ (also **white ant**) *noun* a small insect that eats wood

terrace /ˈterəs/ *noun* **1** steps that are cut into a hill so that crops can be grown there: *The villagers dug terraces in the hillside.* **2** a flat area outside a house or restaurant: *a sun terrace*

terrible 🔑 /ˈterəbl/ *adjective* very bad: *She had a terrible accident.* ◇ *Her spelling is terrible!*

terribly /ˈterəbli/ *adverb* **1** very: *I'm terribly sorry!* **2** very badly: *He played terribly.*

terrific /təˈrɪfɪk/ *adjective* **1** very good; wonderful: *What a terrific idea!* **2** very great: *a terrific storm*

terrified /ˈterɪfaɪd/ *adjective* very frightened: *Kamal is terrified of dogs.*

terrify /ˈterɪfaɪ/ *verb* (**terrifies**, **terrifying**, **terrified** /ˈterɪfaɪd/) to make someone very frightened: *Spiders terrify me!*

territory /ˈterətri/ *noun* (*plural* **territories**) the land that belongs to one country: *This island was once French territory.*

terror /ˈterə(r)/ *noun* (no plural) very great fear: *He screamed in terror.*

terrorism /ˈterərɪzəm/ *noun* (no plural) when a group of people hurt or kill other people, in order to make a government do what they want: *an act of terrorism*

terrorist /ˈterərɪst/ *noun* a person who frightens, hurts or kills people so that the government, etc. will do what they want: *The terrorists put a bomb in the station.*

test[1] 🔑 /test/ *verb* (**tests**, **testing**, **tested**) **1** to use or look at something carefully to find out how good it is or if it works well: *The doctor tested my eyes.* ◇ *These drugs are tested on monkeys before being sold.* **2** to ask someone questions to find out what they know or what they can do: *The teacher tested us on our spelling.*

test[2] 🔑 /test/ *noun* **1** an exam that you do in order to show what you know or what you can do: *a maths test* ◇ *Did you pass your driving test?* **2** when someone looks at something carefully to find out how good it is or if it works well: *She had a blood test.*

test tube /ˈtest tjuːb/ *noun* a long thin glass tube that you use in chemistry

test tubes

text[1] 🔑 /tekst/ *noun* **1** (no plural) the words in a book, newspaper or magazine: *That book has a lot of pictures but not much text.* **2** (*plural* **texts**) a book or a short piece of writing that you study: *Read the text and answer the questions.* **3** = **text message**

text[2] /tekst/ *verb* (**texts**, **texting**, **texted**) to send someone a message on a mobile phone

textbook /ˈtekstbʊk/ *noun* a book that teaches you about something: *a science textbook*

textile /ˈtekstaɪl/ *noun* cloth or material: *Kirezi works in the textile industry, making and exporting cloth.*

text message /ˈtekst mesɪdʒ/ (also **text**) *noun* a message that you send in writing from one mobile phone to another ➲ Look at **SMS**.

texture /ˈtekstʃə(r)/ *noun* the way that something feels when you touch it: *Silk has a smooth texture.*

than 🔑 /ðən; ðæn/ *conjunction, preposition* You use 'than' when you compare people or things: *I'm older than him.* ◇ *You cook much better than she does.* ◇ *We live less than a kilometre from the beach.*

thank 🔑 /θæŋk/ *verb* (**thanks**, **thanking**, **thanked** /θæŋkt/) to tell someone that you are pleased because they gave you something or helped you: *I thanked Hawa for the present.*

❖ **WORD FAMILY**

thank thanks thankful thankfully

thankful /ˈθæŋkfl/ *adjective* happy that something good has happened: *I was thankful for a rest after the long walk.*

▸ **thankfully** /ˈθæŋkfəli/ *adverb* You say **thankfully** when you are pleased about something: *There was an accident, but thankfully nobody was hurt.*

thanks /θæŋks/ *noun* (plural) words that show you are pleased because someone gave you something or helped you: *Please give my thanks to your sister for her help.* ➲ Look at **thank**.

thanks to someone or **something** because of someone or something: *We're late, thanks to you!*

thank you /ˈθæŋk juː/ *noun* You use 'thank you' to tell someone that you are pleased because they gave you something or helped you: *Thank you very much for your help.* ℹ You can also say **thanks**: *'How are you?' 'I'm fine, thanks.'*

no, thank you You use **no, thank you** to say that you do not want something: *'Would you like some more tea?' 'No, thank you.'* ℹ You can also say **no, thanks**.

that[1] /ðət/ *pronoun* which, who or whom: *An ostrich is a bird that can't fly.* ◇ *The people that I met were very nice.* ◇ *I'm reading the book that you gave me.*

that[2] /ðət/ *conjunction* a word that you use to join two parts of a sentence: *Fatma said that she was unhappy.* ◇ *I'm sure that he will come.* ◇ *I was so hungry that I ate all the food.* ℹ You can also use these sentences without **that**: *Fatma said she was unhappy.*

that[3] /ðæt/ *adjective, pronoun* (*plural* **those**) a word that you use to talk about a person or thing that is there or then: *'Who is that boy over there?' 'That's my brother.'* ◇ *She got married in 2006. At that time, she was a teacher.* ➲ Picture at **this**[1].

that[4] /ðæt/ *adverb* so: *The village is ten kilometres from here. I can't walk that far.*

thatch /θatʃ/ *noun* (no plural) a roof covering that is made of dried grass or branches

thaw /θɔː/ *verb* (**thaws**, **thawing**, **thawed** /θɔːd/) to warm something that is frozen so that it becomes soft or liquid; to get warmer so that it becomes soft or liquid: *The ice is thawing.* OPPOSITE **freeze**

the /ðə; ði; ðiː/ *article* **1** a word that you use before the name of someone or something when it is clear what person or thing you mean: *I bought a shirt and some trousers. The shirt is blue.* ◇ *The sun is shining.* **2** a word that you use before numbers and dates: *Monday the sixth of May* **3** a word that you use to talk about a group of people or things of the same kind: *the French* (= all French people) ◇ *Do you play the piano?* **4** a word that you use before the names of rivers, seas, etc. and some countries: *the Nile* ◇ *the Atlantic* ◇ *the United States of America*

> ❖ **GRAMMAR**
>
> Before the names of most countries, we do not use 'the': *I went to France.* **NOT**: *I went to the France.*

the…, the… words that you use to talk about two things happening together: *The more you read, the more you learn.*

theatre /ˈθɪətə(r)/ *noun* a building where you go to see plays: *I'm going to the theatre this evening.*

theft /θeft/ *noun* taking something that is not yours; stealing: *She was sent to prison for theft.* ◇ *I told the police about the theft of my car.* ➲ Look at **thief**.

their /ðeə(r)/ *adjective*

> ❖ **PRONUNCIATION**
>
> **Their** sounds just like **there** and **they're**.

of them: *What is their address?*

theirs /ðeəz/ *pronoun* something that belongs to them: *Our flat is smaller than theirs.*

them /ðəm; ðem/ *pronoun* (plural) **1** a word that shows more than one person, animal or thing: *I wrote them a letter and then I visited them.* ◇ *I'm looking for my keys. Have you seen them?* **2** him or her: *If anybody calls, tell them I'm busy.*

theme /θiːm/ *noun* something that you talk or write about: *The theme of his speech was 'The future of Africa'.*

themselves /ðəmˈselvz/ *pronoun* (plural) **1** a word that shows the same people, animals or things that you have just talked about: *They made themselves a meal.* **2** a word that makes 'they' stronger: *Did they paint the wall themselves?*

by themselves 1 alone; without other people: *The children went out by themselves.* **2** without help: *They cooked dinner by themselves.*

then /ðen/ *adverb* **1** at that time: *I became a teacher in 1999. I was single then, but now I'm married.* ◇ *I can't come next week. I will be on holiday then.* **2** next; after that: *We had dinner and then did the washing-up.* **3** if that is true: *'I don't feel well.' 'Then why don't you go to the doctor's?'*

theory /ˈθɪəri/ *noun* (*plural* **theories**) an idea that tries to explain something: *There are a lot of different theories about how life began.*

therapy /ˈθerəpi/ *noun* (no plural) a way of helping people who are ill in their body or mind, usually without drugs: *speech therapy*

there[1] /ðeə(r)/ *adverb* in, at or to that place: *Don't put the box there – put it here.* ◇ *Have you been to Lamu? I'm going there next week.*
there you are words that you say when you give something to someone: *'There you are,' she said, giving me a plate.*

there[2] /ðeə(r)/ *pronoun* **1** a word that you use with verbs like 'be', 'seem' and 'appear' to show that something is true or that something is happening: *There is a man at the door.* ◇ *Is there any more coffee?* ◇ *There aren't any shops in this village.* **2** a word that makes people look or listen: *There's the bell for my class! I must go.*

therefore /ˈðeəfɔː(r)/ *adverb* for that reason: *Kendi was busy and therefore could not come to the meeting.*

thermometer /θəˈmɒmɪtə(r)/ *noun* an instrument that shows how hot or cold something is

thermometer

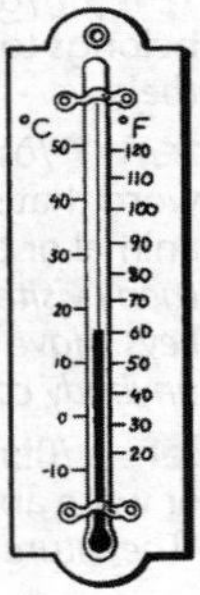

these /ðiːz/ *adjective, pronoun* (plural) a word that you use to talk about people or things that are here or now: *These books are mine.* ◇ *Do you want these?* ➲ Picture at **this**[1].

they /ðeɪ/ *pronoun* (plural) **1** the people, animals or things that the sentence is about: *Chebet and Boke came at two o'clock and they left at six o'clock.* ◇ *'Where are my keys?' 'They're* (= they are) *on the table.'* **2** a word that you use instead of 'he' or 'she': *Someone phoned for you – they said they would phone again later.* **3** people: *They say that this area is dangerous.*

they'd /ðeɪd/ **1** = **they had** **2** = **they would**

they'll /ðeɪl/ = **they will**

they're /ðeə(r)/ = **they are**

they've /ðeɪv/ = **they have**

thick /θɪk/ *adjective* (**thicker, thickest**) **1** far from one side to the other: *The walls are very thick.* OPPOSITE **thin** **2** You use 'thick' to say or ask how far something is from one side to the other: *The wall is ten centimetres thick.* **3** with a lot of people or things close together: *a thick forest* **4** If a liquid is thick, it does not flow easily: *This paint is too thick.* OPPOSITE **thin** **5** difficult to see through: *thick smoke* ▶ **thickness** /ˈθɪknəs/ *noun* (no plural): *The wood is 3 centimetres in thickness.*

thicket /ˈθɪkɪt/ *noun* a group of bushes or trees that grow closely together: *a dense thicket of bamboo*

thief /θiːf/ *noun* (*plural* **thieves** /θiːvz/) a person who steals something: *Most of the class had money stolen but we didn't know who the thief was.*

❖ **WORD BUILDING**

A **thief** is a general word for a person who steals things, usually secretly and with no violence. The name of the crime is **theft**.

A **robber** steals from a bank, shop, etc. and often uses violence.

A **burglar** takes things from your house, often when you are out or asleep.

thigh /θaɪ/ *noun* the part of your leg above your knee ➲ picture on page A13

thin /θɪn/ *adjective* (**thinner, thinnest**) **1** not far from one side to the other; not thick: *The walls in this house are very thin.* OPPOSITE **thick** **2** not fat: *My father is tall and thin.* **3** If a liquid is thin, it flows easily like water: *The soup was very thin.* OPPOSITE **thick** **4** not close together: *My father's hair is getting thin.* OPPOSITE **thick**

thing /θɪŋ/ *noun* **1** an object: *What's that red thing?* **2** what happens or what you do: *A strange thing happened to me yesterday.* ◇ *That was a difficult thing to do.* **3** an idea or subject: *We talked about a lot of things.* **4** **things** (plural) what you own: *Have you packed your things for the journey?*

think /θɪŋk/ *verb* (**thinks, thinking, thought** /θɔːt/, **has thought**) **1** to use your mind: *Think before you answer the question.* **2** to believe something: *I think it's going to rain.* ◇ *'Do you think Ajuma will come tomorrow?' 'Yes, I think so.'* (= I think that she will come.) ◇ *I think they live in Nakuru but I'm not sure.*
think about someone or **something** **1** to have someone or something in your mind: *I often think about that day.* **2** to try to

decide whether to do something: *Ereng is thinking about leaving the team.*
think of someone or **something 1** to have something in your mind: *I can't think of her name.* **2** to have an opinion about someone or something: *What do you think of this music?* **3** to try to decide whether to do something: *We're thinking of moving to the city.*

third /θɜːd/ *adjective, adverb, noun* **1** 3rd **2** one of three equal parts; ⅓

thirst /θɜːst/ *noun* (no plural) the feeling you have when you want to drink something

thirsty 🔑 /ˈθɜːsti/ *adjective* (**thirstier, thirstiest**) If you are thirsty, you want to drink something: *Salty food makes you thirsty.*

thirteen 🔑 /ˌθɜːˈtiːn/ *number* 13

thirteenth /ˌθɜːˈtiːnθ/ *adjective, adverb, noun* 13th

thirtieth /ˈθɜːtiəθ/ *adjective, adverb, noun* 30th

thirty 🔑 /ˈθɜːti/ *number* **1** 30 **2 the thirties** (plural) the numbers, years or temperature between 30 and 39
in your thirties between the ages of 30 and 39

this, that, these and those

this¹ 🔑 /ðɪs/ *adjective, pronoun* (*plural* **these**) a word that you use to talk about a person or thing that is here or now: *Come and look at this photo.* ◇ *This is my sister.* ◇ *I am on holiday this week.* ◇ *How much does this cost?*

this² /ðɪs/ *adverb* so: *The other film was not this good* (= not as good as this film).

thorn /θɔːn/ *noun* **1** a sharp point that grows on a plant: *Be careful, that bush has thorns.* **2** a tree or large plant that has **thorns**

thorough /ˈθʌrə/ *adjective* careful and complete: *We gave the room a thorough clean.*

thoroughly /ˈθʌrəli/ *adverb* **1** carefully and completely: *He cleaned the room thoroughly.* **2** completely; very or very much: *I thoroughly enjoyed the lesson.*

those 🔑 /ðəʊz/ *adjective, pronoun* (plural) a word that you use to talk about people or things that are there or then: *I don't know those boys.* ◇ *Her grandfather was born in 1850. In those days, there were no cars.* ◇ *Can I have those?* ➲ Picture at **this¹**.

though¹ 🔑 /ðəʊ/ *conjunction*

> ❖ **PRONUNCIATION**
> **Though** sounds like **go**.

1 in spite of something; although: *Though she was in a hurry, she stopped to talk.* **2** but: *I thought it was right though I wasn't sure.*
as though in a way that makes you think something: *The house looks as though nobody lives there.* ◇ *I'm so hungry – I feel as though I haven't eaten for days!*

though² 🔑 /ðəʊ/ *adverb* however: *I like him very much. I don't like his wife, though.*

thought¹ 🔑 /θɔːt/ *noun*

> ❖ **PRONUNCIATION**
> **Thought** sounds like **sort**.

1 (no plural) thinking: *After a lot of thought, I decided not to join the club.* **2** (*plural* **thoughts**) an idea: *Have you had any thoughts about what you want to do when you leave school?*

thought² *form of* THINK

thoughtful /ˈθɔːtfl/ *adjective* **1** If you are **thoughtful**, you are thinking carefully: *She listened with a thoughtful look on her face.* **2** A person who is **thoughtful** is kind, and thinks and cares about other people: *It was very thoughtful of you to come and help us.*

thousand ⚷ /ˈθaʊznd/ *number* 1000: *a thousand people* ◇ *two thousand and fifteen* ◇ *There were thousands of birds on the lake.*

thousandth /ˈθaʊznθ/ *adjective, adverb, noun* 1000th

thread[1] ⚷ /θred/ *noun*

> ❖ **PRONUNCIATION**
> **Thread** sounds like **red**.

a long thin piece of cotton, wool, etc. that you use with a **needle** for sewing: *Have you got a needle and thread I can borrow?* ➲ Picture at **sew**.

thread[2] /θred/ *verb* (**threads, threading, threaded**) to put **thread** through the hole in a needle

threat ⚷ /θret/ *noun* **1** a promise that you will hurt someone if they do not do what you want: *The government refused to give in to the terrorists' threats.* **2** a person or thing that may damage or hurt someone or something: *Pollution is a threat to the lives of animals and people.*

threaten ⚷ /ˈθretn/ *verb* (**threatens, threatening, threatened** /ˈθretnd/) **1** to say that you will hurt someone if they do not do what you want: *They threatened to kill everyone on the plane.* ◇ *She threatened him with a knife.* **2** to seem ready to do something bad: *The dark clouds threatened a storm.*

three ⚷ /θriː/ *number* 3

threw *form of* THROW

thrill[1] /θrɪl/ *noun* a sudden strong feeling of excitement

thrill[2] /θrɪl/ *verb* (**thrills, thrilling, thrilled** /θrɪld/) to make someone feel strong excitement

thrilled /θrɪld/ *adjective* very happy and excited: *We are all thrilled that you have won the prize.*

thriller /ˈθrɪlə(r)/ *noun* an exciting book, film or play about a crime

thrilling /ˈθrɪlɪŋ/ *adjective* very exciting: *a thrilling adventure*

throat ⚷ /θrəʊt/ *noun* **1** the front part of your neck: *The bird had a bright blue throat.* ➲ picture on page A13 **2** the part inside your neck that takes food and air down from your mouth into your body: *I've got a sore throat* (= my throat hurts).

throb /θrɒb/ *verb* (**throbs, throbbing, throbbed** /θrɒbd/) to beat quickly and strongly: *His thumb throbbed with pain when he hit it.*

throne /θrəʊn/ *noun* a special chair where a king or queen sits

through ⚷ /θruː/ *preposition, adverb*

> ❖ **PRONUNCIATION**
> **Through** sounds like **who**.

1 from one side or end of something to the other side or end: *We drove through the tunnel.* ◇ *What can you see through the window?* ◇ *She opened the gate and we walked through.* ➲ picture on page A7 **2** from the beginning to the end of something: *We travelled through the night.* **3** connected by telephone: *Can you put me through to Mrs Tuiyot, please?* ◇ *I tried to phone you but I couldn't get through.* **4** because of someone or something: *She passed the test through hard work.*

throughout /θruːˈaʊt/ *preposition, adverb* **1** in every part of something: *We painted the house throughout.* ◇ *She is famous throughout the world.* **2** from the beginning to the end of something: *They talked throughout the lesson.*

throw ⚷ /θrəʊ/ *verb* (**throws, throwing, threw** /θruː/, **has thrown** /θrəʊn/) **1** to move your arm quickly to send something through the air: *Throw the ball to Ereng.* ◇ *The boys were throwing stones at people.* **2** to do something quickly and without care: *She threw on her coat* (= put it on quickly) *and ran out of the house.* **3** to move your body or part of it quickly: *He threw his arms up.*

throw something away or **out** to get rid of rubbish or something you do not want: *Don't throw that box away.* ▸ **throw** *noun*: *What a good throw!*

thrust /θrʌst/ *verb* (**thrusts, thrusting, thrust, has thrust**) to push someone or something suddenly and strongly: *She thrust the money into my hand.* ▸ **thrust** *noun* a strong push

thud /θʌd/ *noun* the sound that a heavy thing makes when it hits something: *The book hit the floor with a thud.*

thug /θʌg/ *noun* a violent person

thumb 🔑 /θʌm/ *noun*

> ❖ **PRONUNCIATION**
>
> **Thumb** sounds like **come** because we do not say the 'b'.

the short thick finger at the side of your hand: *The baby was sucking her thumb.* ➲ picture on page A13

thumbnail /ˈθʌmneɪl/ *noun* the **nail** (= hard part) on your thumb

thump /θʌmp/ *verb* (**thumps, thumping, thumped** /θʌmpt/) **1** to hit something hard with your hand or a heavy thing: *He thumped on the door.* **2** to make a loud sound by hitting or beating hard: *Her heart was thumping with fear.*

thunder¹ /ˈθʌndə(r)/ *noun* (no plural) a loud noise in the sky when there is a storm

> ❖ **WORD BUILDING**
>
> The light that you see in the sky in a storm is called **lightning**.

thunder² /ˈθʌndə(r)/ *verb* (**thunders, thundering, thundered** /ˈθʌndəd/) **1** When it **thunders**, there is a loud noise in the sky during a storm: *It thundered all night.* **2** to make a very loud, deep noise: *The lorries thundered along the road.*

thunderstorm /ˈθʌndəstɔːm/ *noun* a storm with a lot of rain, **thunder** and flashes of light (called **lightning**) in the sky

Thursday 🔑 /ˈθɜːzdeɪ/ *noun* the fifth day of the week, next after Wednesday

thus /ðʌs/ *adverb* **1** in this way: *Hold the wheel in both hands, thus.* **2** because of this: *He was very busy and was thus unable to come to the meeting.*

tick¹ /tɪk/ *noun* **1** the sound that a clock or watch makes **2** a small mark like this ✓, that shows that something is correct, etc: *Put a tick by the correct answer.* **3** a very small animal that lives on the skin of sheep, cattle, etc. and drinks their blood

tick

tick² /tɪk/ *verb* (**ticks, ticking, ticked** /tɪkt/) **1** to make a mark like this ✓: *Tick the right answer.* **2** to make sounds like a clock or watch: *I could hear a clock ticking.*

ticket 🔑 /ˈtɪkɪt/ *noun* a small piece of paper or card that you must buy to travel or to go into a cinema, theatre, museum, etc: *How much is a ticket to Nyali?* ◇ *a bus/theatre ticket*

ticket office /ˈtɪkɪt ɒfɪs/ *noun* a place where you buy tickets

tickle /ˈtɪkl/ *verb* (**tickles, tickling, tickled** /ˈtɪkld/) **1** to touch someone lightly with your fingers to make them laugh: *She tickled the baby's feet.* **2** to have the feeling that something is touching you lightly: *My nose tickles.*

tide /taɪd/ *noun* the movement of the sea towards the land and away from the land: *The tide is coming in.* ◇ *The tide is going out.*

> ❖ **WORD BUILDING**
>
> **High tide** is when the sea is nearest the land, and **low tide** is when the sea is furthest from the land.

tidy¹ 🔑 /ˈtaɪdi/ *adjective* (**tidier, tidiest**) **1** with everything in the right place: *Her room is very tidy.* **2** If you are tidy, you like to have everything in the right place: *a tidy boy* OPPOSITE **untidy** ▶ **tidily** /ˈtaɪdɪli/ *adverb*: *Put the books back tidily when you've finished with them.* ▶ **tidiness** /ˈtaɪdinəs/ *noun* (no plural) being tidy

tidy² 🔑 /ˈtaɪdi/ (also **tidy up**) *verb* (**tidies, tidying, tidied** /ˈtaɪdid/) to make something tidy: *I tidied the house before my parents arrived.* ◇ *Can you help me to tidy up?*

tie¹ 🔑 /taɪ/ *verb* (**ties, tying, tied** /taɪd/) **1** to fasten two ends of string, rope, etc. together to hold someone or something in place: *The prisoner was tied to a chair.* ◇ *I tied a scarf round my neck.* **2** to end a game or competition with the same number of points for both teams or players: *Guinea tied with Kenya for second place.*

tie someone up to put a piece of rope around someone so that they cannot move: *The robbers tied up the owner of the shop.*

tie something up to put a piece of string or rope around something to hold it in place: *I tied up the parcel with string.*

tie² 🔑 /taɪ/ *noun* **1** (also **necktie**) a long thin piece of cloth that you wear round your neck with a shirt: *He wears a suit and tie to work.* ➲ Picture at **suit¹**.

2 when two teams or players have the same number of points at the end of a game or competition: *The match ended in a tie.* **3** something that holds people together: *Our country has close ties with Britain.*

tiger

tiger /ˈtaɪgə(r)/ *noun* a wild animal like a big cat, with yellow fur and black stripes. **Tigers** live in Asia.

tight /taɪt/ *adjective* (**tighter**, **tightest**)

> ❖ **PRONUNCIATION**
> **Tight** sounds like **white**.

1 fixed firmly so that you cannot move it easily: *a tight knot* ◇ *I can't open this jar – the lid is too tight.* **2** small, so that there is no space between it and your body: *These shoes are too tight.* ◇ *tight trousers* OPPOSITE **loose** ▸ **tight**, **tightly** *adverb*: *Hold tight!* ◇ *I tied the string tightly around the box.*

tighten /ˈtaɪtn/ *verb* (**tightens**, **tightening**, **tightened** /ˈtaɪtnd/) to become tighter or make something tighter: *Can you tighten this screw?* OPPOSITE **loosen**

tightrope /ˈtaɪtrəʊp/ *noun* a rope or wire high above the ground. **Acrobats** walk along tightropes in a **circus**.

tights /taɪts/ *noun* (plural) a thin piece of clothing that a woman or girl wears over her feet and legs: *a pair of tights*

tilapia /tɪˈlɑːpiə; tɪˈleɪpiə/ *noun* (*plural* **tilapia** *or* **tilapias**) a fish that lives in rivers in Africa and that you can eat

tile /taɪl/ *noun* a flat, usually square, thing. We use **tiles** for covering walls, floors, etc.

tiles

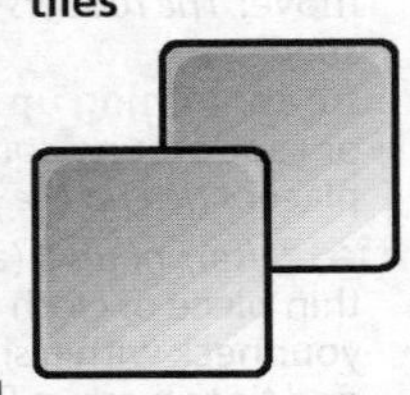

till¹ /tɪl/ *conjunction* up to the time when: *Let's wait till the rain stops.* ➲ Look at **until¹**.

till² /tɪl/ *preposition* **1** up to a certain time: *I'll be here till Monday.* **2** before: *I didn't arrive till six o'clock.* ➲ Look at **until²**.

till³ /tɪl/ *noun* a drawer or box for money in a shop: *She opened the till and gave me my change.*

tilt /tɪlt/ *verb* (**tilts**, **tilting**, **tilted**) to have one side higher than the other; to move something so that it has one side higher than the other: *She tilted the tray and all the glasses fell off.*

timber /ˈtɪmbə(r)/ *noun* (no plural) wood that we use for building and making things

time¹ /taɪm/ *noun* **1** (*plural* **times**) a certain point in the day or night, that you say in hours and minutes: *'What time is it?' 'It's twenty past six.'* ◇ *What's the time?* ◇ *Can you tell me the times of buses to Narok, please?* ❶ Look at page A17. **2** (no plural) all the seconds, minutes, hours, days, weeks, months and years: *Time passes quickly when you're busy.* **3** (no plural) an amount of minutes, days, etc: *They have lived here for a long time.* ◇ *I haven't got time to help you now – I'm late for school.* ◇ *It takes a long time to write a book.* **4** (*plural* **times**) a certain moment or occasion: *I've been to Mandera four times.* ◇ *Come and visit us next time you're in Kenya.* **5** (*plural* **times**) experience; something that you do: *We had a great time at the party.* **6** (*plural* **times**) certain years in history: *In my great-grandfather's time, Nairobi was just a small town.*

at a time together; on one occasion: *The lift can carry six people at a time.*

at one time in the past, but not now: *We were in the same class at one time.*

at the time then: *My family moved to this town in 2008– I was four at the time.*

at times sometimes: *A teacher's job can be very difficult at times.*

by the time when: *By the time we arrived they had eaten all the food.*

for the time being now, but not for long: *You can stay here for the time being, until you find a flat.*

from time to time sometimes; not often: *I see my cousin from time to time.*

have a good time to enjoy yourself: *Have a good time at the party!*

in a week's, etc. time after a week, etc: *I'll see you in a month's time.*

in good time at the right time or early: *I want to get to the station in good time.*

in time **1** not late: *If you hurry, you'll arrive in time for the film.* **2** at some time in the future: *You will find speaking English easier in time.*
it's about time words that you use to say that something should be done now: *It's about time you started studying if you want to pass the exam.*
it's time to it is the right time to do something: *It's time to go home.*
on time not late or early: *My train was on time.*
save time to do something quickly and not waste time: *You can save time in the morning by getting your books and clothes ready for school the night before.*
spare time; free time time when you do not have to work or study
spend time to use time to do something: *I spend a lot of time studying.*
take your time to do something slowly
tell the time to read the time from a clock or watch: *Can your children tell the time?*
time after time; time and time again many times: *I've told you time after time to hang your coat up.*

time² /taɪm/ *verb* (**times**, **timing**, **timed** /taɪmd/) **1** to plan something so that it will happen when you want: *The bomb was timed to explode at six o'clock.* **2** to measure how much time it takes to do something: *We timed the journey – it took half an hour.*

times¹ /taɪmz/ *noun* (plural) a word that you use to show how much bigger, smaller, more expensive, etc. one thing is than another thing: *Mount Kilimanjaro is three times bigger than Mount Kulai.*

times² /taɪmz/ *preposition* multiplied by: *Three times four is twelve.*

timetable /ˈtaɪmteɪbl/ *noun* a list of times when something happens: *A bus timetable shows when buses arrive and leave.* ◇ *A school timetable shows when lessons start.*

timid /ˈtɪmɪd/ *adjective* shy and easily frightened ▸ **timidly** *adverb*: *She opened the door timidly and came in.*

tin ⚷ /tɪn/ *noun* **1** (no plural) a soft white metal **2** (*plural* **tins**) a metal container for food and drink that keeps it fresh: *I opened a tin of beans.* SAME MEANING **can** ➲ Picture at **container**. ▸ **tinned** /tɪnd/ *adjective* in a tin so that it will stay fresh: *tinned fruit*

tin opener /ˈtɪn əʊpənə(r)/ *noun* a tool for opening tins

tiny /ˈtaɪni/ *adjective* (**tinier**, **tiniest**) very small: *Ants are tiny insects.*

tip¹ /tɪp/ *noun* **1** the pointed or thin end of something: *the tips of your fingers* **2** a small, extra amount of money that you give to someone who has done a job for you: *I left a tip for the waiter.* **3** a small piece of advice: *She gave me some useful tips on how to pass the exam.*

tip² /tɪp/ *verb* (**tips**, **tipping**, **tipped** /tɪpt/) **1** to move so that one side goes up or down; to move something so that one side goes up or down: *Don't tip your chair back.* **2** to turn something so that the things inside fall out: *She opened a tin of beans and tipped them into a bowl.* **3** to give a small, extra amount of money to someone who has done a job for you: *He paid for the meal and tipped the waiter.*
tip over to turn over; to make something turn over: *The boat tipped over and we all fell in the water.* ◇ *Don't tip your drink over!*

tiptoe /ˈtɪptəʊ/ *verb* (**tiptoes**, **tiptoeing**, **tiptoed** /ˈtɪptəʊd/) to walk quietly on your toes: *He tiptoed into the bedroom.*
on tiptoe/tiptoes on your toes: *She walked on tiptoe.*

tired ⚷ /ˈtaɪəd/ *adjective* If you are tired, you need to rest or sleep: *I've been working all day and I'm really tired.* ◇ *He's feeling tired.*
be tired of something to have had or done too much of something, so that you do not want it any longer: *I'm tired of studying – let's go out.*

tiring ⚷ /ˈtaɪərɪŋ/ *adjective* If something is tiring, it makes you tired: *a tiring journey*

tissue /ˈtɪʃuː/ *noun* a thin piece of soft paper that you use to clean your nose: *a box of tissues*

title ⚷ /ˈtaɪtl/ *noun* **1** the name of something, for example a book, film or picture: *What is the title of this poem?* **2** a word like 'Mr', 'Mrs' or 'Doctor' that you put in front of a person's name: *Give your name and title.*

tjanting tool /ˈtʃæntɪŋ tuːl/ *noun* a tool like a pen that you use to make patterns on cloth with hot **wax** (= a substance made from fat or oil) ➲ Look at **batik**.

to¹ ⚷ /tə; tu; tuː/ *preposition* **1** a word that shows where someone or something is going: *She went to Italy.* ◇ *Robi has gone to school.* ◇ *This bus goes to the town centre.* **2** a word that shows the person or thing that receives something: *I gave the book to Adisa.* ◇ *He sent a letter to his parents.* ◇ *Be* *kind to animals.* **3** a word that shows how many minutes before the hour: *It's two minutes to six.* ➲ Look at page A10. **4** a word that shows the last or the highest time, price, etc: *The museum is open from 9.30 to 5.30.* ◇ *Shoes cost from 800 to 1500 shillings in this shop.* **5** on or against something: *He put his hands to his ears.* **6** a word that shows how something changes: *The sky changed from blue to grey.* **7** a word that shows why: *I came to help.* **8** a word that you use for comparing things: *I prefer football to athletics.*

to² 🔑 /tə; tu/ a word that you use before verbs to make the **infinitive**: *I want to go home.* ◇ *Don't forget to write.* ◇ *She asked me to go but I didn't want to* (= to go).

toad /təʊd/ *noun* an animal like a big frog, with rough skin

toad

toast /təʊst/ *noun* (no plural) a thin piece of bread that you have cooked so that it is brown: *I had a slice of toast and jam for breakfast.* ▸ **toast** *verb* (**toasts, toasting, toasted**) to cook bread to make it brown: *toasted sandwiches* ▸ **toaster** *noun* a machine for making **toast**

tobacco /tə'bækəʊ/ *noun* (no plural) special dried leaves that people smoke in cigarettes, etc.

today 🔑 /tə'deɪ/ *adverb, noun* (no plural) **1** (on) this day: *What shall we do today?* ◇ *Today is Friday.* **2** (at) the present time; now: *Most schools today use computers.*

toe 🔑 /təʊ/ *noun* **1** one of the five parts at the end of your foot: *Can you touch your toes?* ➲ picture on page A13 **2** the part of a shoe or sock that covers the end of your foot: *There's a hole in the toe of my shoe.*

toenail /'təʊneɪl/ *noun* the **nail** (= hard part) on your toe ➲ picture on page A13

together 🔑 /tə'geðə(r)/ *adverb* **1** with each other or close to each other: *Adisa and Nduku usually walk home together.* ◇ *Stand with your feet together.* **2** so that they are joined to or mixed with each other: *Tie the ends of the rope together.* ◇ *Add these numbers together.* ◇ *Mix the eggs and sugar together.*

toilet 🔑 /'tɔɪlət/ *noun* a large bowl with a seat, that you use when you need to empty waste from your body. The room that it is in is also called a **toilet**: *I'm going to the toilet.*

toilet paper /'tɔɪlət peɪpə(r)/ *noun* (no plural) paper that you use in the toilet

toilet roll /'tɔɪlət rəʊl/ *noun* a roll of paper that you use in the toilet

token /'təʊkən/ *noun* **1** a small thing that you use to show something else: *This gift is a token of our friendship.* **2** a piece of paper, plastic or metal that you use instead of money to pay for something: *You can use these tokens to buy books.*

told *form of* TELL

tolerant /'tɒlərənt/ *adjective* If you are **tolerant**, you let people do things although you may not like or understand them: *You need to be very tolerant with young children.* OPPOSITE **intolerant** ▸ **tolerance** /'tɒlərəns/ *noun* (no plural) *tolerance of other religions* OPPOSITE **intolerance**

tolerate /'tɒləreɪt/ *verb* (**tolerates, tolerating, tolerated**) to let people do something that you may not like or understand: *He won't tolerate rudeness.*

tomato 🔑 /tə'mɑːtəʊ/ *noun* (*plural* **tomatoes**) a soft red fruit that you eat in salads or cook as a vegetable: *a cheese and tomato roll*

tomato

tomb /tuːm/ *noun* a thing made of stone where a dead person's body is buried

tomorrow 🔑 /tə'mɒrəʊ/ *adverb, noun* (no plural) (on) the day after today: *Let's go swimming tomorrow.* ◇ *I'll see you tomorrow morning.* ◇ *We are going home the day after tomorrow.*

ton /tʌn/ *noun* **1** a measure of weight (= 1016 kilograms) **2 tons** (plural) a lot: *He's got tons of money.*

tone /təʊn/ *noun* how something sounds: *I knew he was angry by the tone of his voice.*

tongue 🔑 /tʌŋ/ *noun*

> ❖ **PRONUNCIATION**
> **Tongue** sounds like **young**.

the soft part inside your mouth that moves when you talk or eat

tongue-twister /ˈtʌŋ twɪstə(r)/ *noun* words that are difficult to say together quickly: *'Red lorry, yellow lorry' is a tongue-twister.*

tonight 🔑 /təˈnaɪt/ *adverb, noun* (no plural) (on) the evening or night of today: *I'm going to do my homework tonight.*

tonne /tʌn/ *noun* a measure of weight. There are 1 000 **kilograms** in a tonne.

tonsil /ˈtɒnsl/ *noun* one of the two soft lumps in your throat at the back of your mouth: *She had to* ***have*** *her* ***tonsils out*** (= removed in a medical operation).

too 🔑 /tuː/ *adverb* **1** also; as well: *Green is my favourite colour but I like blue too.* **2** more than you want or need: *These shoes are too big.* ◇ *She put too much salt in the food.*

> ❖ **too** and **very**
>
> Look at these sentences. They mean the same: *I am very tired. I can't walk any further.* ◇ *I am too tired to walk any further.*

took *form of* TAKE

tool 🔑 /tuːl/ *noun* a thing that you hold in your hand and use to do a special job: *Hammers and saws are tools.*

> ❖ **WORD BUILDING**
>
> We use many different types of tools. Here are some of them: **drill, hammer, saw, spade, spanner**. Do you know any others?

tooth 🔑 /tuːθ/ *noun* (*plural* **teeth** /tiːθ/) **1** one of the hard white things in your mouth that you use for eating: *I brush my teeth every day.*

> ❖ **WORD BUILDING**
>
> A **dentist** is a person whose job is to look after teeth. If a tooth is bad, the dentist may **fill** it or **take** it **out**. People who have lost their own teeth can wear **false teeth**.

2 one of the long sharp parts of something such as a **comb** (= an object that you use to make your hair tidy)

toothache /ˈtuːθeɪk/ *noun* (no plural) a pain in your tooth: *I've got toothache.*

toothbrush /ˈtuːθbrʌʃ/ *noun* (*plural* **toothbrushes**) a small brush for cleaning your teeth

toothpaste /ˈtuːθpeɪst/ *noun* (no plural) stuff that you put on your **toothbrush** and use for cleaning your teeth

top[1] 🔑 /tɒp/ *noun* **1** the highest part of something: *There's a church at the top of the hill.* OPPOSITE **bottom** **2** a cover that you put on something to close it: *Where's the top of this jar?* **3** a piece of clothing that you wear on the top part of your body: *She was wearing jeans and a red top.* **4** the first part of something: *There's a new shop at the top of the road.* OPPOSITE **bottom**

at the top of your voice very loudly: *'Come here!' she shouted at the top of her voice.*

on top on its highest part: *The people got on the bus and their luggage went on top.*

on top of something on or over something: *A tree fell on top of my car.*

on top of the world very happy

top[2] 🔑 /tɒp/ *adjective* highest: *Put this book on the top shelf.* OPPOSITE **bottom**

top[3] /tɒp/ *verb* (**tops, topping, topped** /tɒpt/)

top something up 1 to fill something that is partly empty: *Let me top up your glass.* **2** to make a payment to buy more time for calls, etc. on your mobile phone: *I need to top up my phone.*

topic /ˈtɒpɪk/ *noun* something that you talk, learn or write about; a subject: *The topic of the discussion was school uniform.*

topping /ˈtɒpɪŋ/ *noun* the food that you put on the top of other food to decorate it or make it taste nicer: *pizza with a tomato and mushroom topping*

topsoil /ˈtɒpsɔɪl/ *noun* (no plural) the layer of soil that is nearest to the surface of the ground

top-up /ˈtɒp ʌp/ *noun* a payment that you make to buy more time for calls, etc. on your mobile phone

torch /tɔːtʃ/ *noun* (*plural* **torches**) a small electric light that you can carry

torch

tore, torn *forms of* TEAR[2]

tornado /tɔːˈneɪdəʊ/ *noun* (*plural* **tornadoes**) a violent storm with a very strong wind that blows in circles

tortoise /ˈtɔːtəs/ *noun* an animal with a hard shell on its back, that moves very slowly ℹ A **tortoise** lives on land, and a **turtle** lives in the sea.

torture /ˈtɔːtʃə(r)/ *verb* (**tortures, torturing, tortured** /ˈtɔːtʃəd/) to make someone feel great pain, often to make them give information: *They tortured the prisoner until he told them his plans.* ▶ **torture** *noun* (no plural): *the torture of prisoners*

toss /tɒs/ *verb* (**tosses, tossing, tossed** /tɒst/) **1** to throw something quickly and without care: *I tossed the paper into the bin.* **2** to move quickly up and down or from side to side; to make something do this: *The boat tossed around on the big waves.* **3** to decide something by throwing a coin in the air and seeing which side shows when it falls: *We tossed a coin to see who would play first.*

total[1] 🔑 /ˈtəʊtl/ *adjective* complete; if you count everything or everybody: *There was total silence in the classroom.* ◇ *What was the total number of people at the meeting?*

total[2] 🔑 /ˈtəʊtl/ *noun* the number you have when you add everything together: *50 points in maths and 35 in English gives you a total of 85.*

totally 🔑 /ˈtəʊtəli/ *adverb* completely: *I totally agree.*

touch[1] 🔑 /tʌtʃ/ *verb* (**touches, touching, touched** /tʌtʃt/) **1** to put your hand or finger on someone or something: *Don't touch the paint – it's still wet.* ◇ *He touched me on the arm.* **2** to be so close to another thing or person that there is no space in between: *The two wires were touching.* ◇ *Her coat was so long that it touched the ground.*

touch[2] 🔑 /tʌtʃ/ *noun* **1** (*plural* **touches**) when a hand or finger is put on someone or something: *I felt the touch of his hand on my arm.* **2** (no plural) the feeling in your hands and skin that tells you about something: *He can't see, but he can read by touch.*

be or **keep in touch with someone** to meet, telephone or write to someone often: *Are you still in touch with Karimi?* ◇ *Let's keep in touch.*

get in touch with someone to write to, or telephone someone: *I'm trying to get in touch with my cousin.*

lose touch with someone to stop meeting, telephoning or writing to someone: *I've lost touch with all my old friends from school.*

touch screen /ˈtʌtʃ skriːn/ *noun* a screen on a computer or mobile phone which shows information when you touch it

tough /tʌf/ *adjective* (**tougher, toughest**)

> ❖ **PRONUNCIATION**
>
> **Tough** sounds like **stuff**.

1 difficult to tear or break; strong: *Leather is tougher than paper.* **2** difficult: *This is a tough job.* **3** If meat is **tough**, it is difficult to cut and eat. OPPOSITE **tender** **4** very strong in your body: *You need to be tough to run a marathon.* **5** strict or firm: *a tough leader* OPPOSITE **soft**

tour 🔑 /tʊə(r)/ *noun* **1** a short visit to see a building or city: *They gave us a tour of the neighbourhood.* **2** a journey to see a lot of different places: *We went on a tour of the whole country.* ▶ **tour** *verb* (**tours, touring, toured** /tʊəd/): *We toured the country for three weeks.*

tourism /ˈtʊərɪzəm/ *noun* (no plural) the business of arranging holidays for people: *This country earns a lot of money from tourism.*

tourist 🔑 /ˈtʊərɪst/ *noun* a person who visits a place on holiday: *The city was full of foreign tourists.*

tournament /ˈtʊənəmənt/ *noun* a sports competition with a lot of players or teams: *The team has competed in tournaments all over the world.*

tow /təʊ/ *verb* (**tows, towing, towed** /təʊd/) to pull a car, etc. using a rope or chain: *The car was towed to a garage.*

towards 🔑 /təˈwɔːdz/ (also **toward** /təˈwɔːd/) *preposition* **1** in the direction of someone or something: *We walked towards the river.* ◇ *I couldn't see her face – she had her back towards me.* ➲ picture on page A7 **2** to someone or something: *The people in the village are always very friendly towards tourists.* **3** at a time near: *Let's meet towards the end of the week.* **4** to help pay for something: *Everyone in the class gave 10 shillings towards a present for the teacher.*

towel 🔑 /ˈtaʊəl/ *noun* a piece of cloth that you use for drying yourself: *I washed my hands and dried them on a towel.*

tower 🔑 /ˈtaʊə(r)/ *noun* a tall narrow building or a tall part of a building: *the Eiffel Tower ◇ a church tower*

tower block /ˈtaʊə(r) blɒk/ *noun* a very tall building with a lot of flats or offices inside

town 🔑 /taʊn/ *noun* a place where there are a lot of houses and other buildings: *Nyeri is a town near Nairobi. ◇ I'm going into town to do some shopping.*

> ❖ **WORD BUILDING**
>
> A **town** is bigger than a **village** but smaller than a **city**.

town hall /ˌtaʊn ˈhɔːl/ *noun* a building with offices for the people who control a town

toy 🔑 /tɔɪ/ *noun* a thing for a child to play with: *We were playing happily with our toys.*

trace[1] /treɪs/ *noun* a mark or sign that shows that someone or something has been in a place: *The police could not find any trace of the missing child.*

trace[2] /treɪs/ *verb* (**traces, tracing, traced** /treɪst/) **1** to look for and find someone or something: *The police have traced the stolen car.* **2** to put thin paper over a picture and draw over the lines to make a copy: *I traced the outline of a map.*

track[1] 🔑 /træk/ *noun* **1** a rough path or road: *We walked along the track to the next village.* **2 tracks** (plural) a line of marks that an animal, a person or a vehicle makes on the ground: *We saw his tracks in the mud.* **3** the metal lines that a train runs on ➲ Picture at **train**[1]. **4** a special road for races **5** one song or piece of music on a CD, tape, etc: *He played a track from their latest album.*

track[2] /træk/ *verb* (**tracks, tracking, tracked** /trækt/) to follow signs or marks to find someone or something
track down to find someone or something after looking: *I finally tracked her down.*

track event /ˈtræk ɪvent/ *noun* a sports event that is a race run on a track ➲ Look at **field event**.

tracksuit /ˈtræk suːt/ *noun* a special jacket and trousers that you wear for sport

tractor

tractor /ˈtræktə(r)/ *noun* a big strong vehicle that people use on farms to pull heavy things

trade[1] /treɪd/ *noun* **1** (no plural) the buying and selling of things: *trade between Kenya and Britain* **2** (*plural* **trades**) a job, especially one that needs special skills: *Are you learning a trade? ◇ Egesa is a plumber by trade.*

trade[2] /treɪd/ *verb* (**trades, trading, traded**) to buy and sell things: *Tanzania trades with many different countries.*

trademark /ˈtreɪdmɑːk/ *noun* a special mark or name that a company puts on the things it makes and that other companies must not use

trader /ˈtreɪdə(r)/ *noun* a person who buys and sells things, especially in a market

trade union /ˌtreɪd ˈjuːniən/ *noun* a group of workers who have joined together to talk to their managers about things like pay and the way they work

tradition 🔑 /trəˈdɪʃn/ *noun* something that people in a certain place have done or believed for a long time: *In many countries it's a tradition to give gifts at Christmas.* ▶ **traditional** /trəˈdɪʃənl/ *adjective*: *traditional East African food* ▶ **traditionally** /trəˈdɪʃənəli/ *adverb*: *Driving trucks is traditionally a man's job.*

traffic 🔑 /ˈtræfɪk/ *noun* (no plural) all the cars, etc. that are on a road: *There was a lot of traffic on the roads this morning. ◇ More traffic police are needed in cities.*

traffic jam /ˈtræfɪk dʒæm/ *noun* a long line of cars, etc. that cannot move very fast

trafficking /ˈtræfɪkɪŋ/ *noun* (no plural) buying and selling something illegally: *He spent 4 years in jail for drug trafficking.* ▶ **trafficker** /ˈtræfɪkə(r)/ *noun*: *a drugs trafficker*

traffic lights /ˈtræfɪk laɪts/ *noun* (plural) lights that change from red to orange to green to tell cars, etc. when to stop and start

tragedy /ˈtrædʒədi/ *noun* (*plural* **tragedies**) **1** a very sad thing that happens: *The child's death was a tragedy.* **2** a serious and sad play: *John Ruganda's 'The Burdens' is a tragedy.*

tragic /ˈtrædʒɪk/ *adjective* very sad: *a tragic accident* ▶ **tragically** /ˈtrædʒɪkli/ *adverb*: *He died tragically at the age of 25.*

trail[1] /treɪl/ *noun* **1** a line of marks that show which way a person or thing has gone: *There was a trail of blood from the cut in her leg.* **2** a path in the country: *We followed the trail through the forest.*

trail[2] /treɪl/ *verb* (**trails, trailing, trailed** /treɪld/) to pull something along behind you; to be pulled along behind someone or something: *Her long hair trailed behind her in the wind.*

trailer /ˈtreɪlə(r)/ *noun* **1** a vehicle with no engine that a car or lorry pulls along **2** a short piece from a film that shows you what it is like

train

train[1] /treɪn/ *noun* a vehicle that is pulled by an engine along a railway line: *I'm going to Mombasa by train.*
catch a train to get on a train to go somewhere: *We caught the 7.15 train to Nairobi.*
change trains to go from one train to another: *You have to change trains at Makadara.*

> ❖ **WORD BUILDING**
>
> You **get on** and **get off** trains at a **station**. A **goods train** or a **freight train** carries things and a **passenger train** carries people.

train[2] /treɪn/ *verb* (**trains, training, trained** /treɪnd/) **1** to teach a person or an animal to do something: *He was trained as a pilot.* **2** to make yourself ready for something by studying or doing something a lot: *Robi is training to be a doctor.* ◇ *He goes running every morning when he's training for a race.*

> ❖ **WORD FAMILY**
>
> **train** *verb*
> **trainer trainee training**

trainee /ˌtreɪˈniː/ *noun* a person who is learning how to do a job ➲ Look at **trainer**.

trainer /ˈtreɪnə(r)/ *noun* **1** a person who teaches other people to do a sport **2** a person who teaches people or animals to do something well: *teacher trainers* ➲ Look at **trainee**. **3** a soft shoe that you wear for running

trainers

a pair of **traine**

training /ˈtreɪnɪŋ/ *noun* (no plural) getting ready for a sport or job: *She is in training for the Olympic Games.*

traitor /ˈtreɪtə(r)/ *noun* a person who harms their country or friends to help another country or person

tram /træm/ *noun* an electric bus that goe along metal tracks (called **rails**) in a town

trample /ˈtræmpl/ *verb* (**tramples, trampling, trampled** /ˈtræmpld/) to walk on something and push it down with you feet: *Don't trample on the flowers!*

transfer /trænsˈfɜː(r)/ *verb* (**transfers, transferring, transferred** /trænsˈfɜːd/) to move someone or something to a different place: *Ngenzi's company is transferring him to their London office.* ▶ **transfer** /ˈtrænsfɜː(r)/ *noun*: *Mariga wants a transfer to another team.*

transform /trænsˈfɔːm/ *verb* (**transforms, transforming, transformed** /trænsˈfɔːmd/) to change someone or something so that they are or look completely different: *Electricity has transformed people's lives.* ▶ **transformation** /ˌtrænsfəˈmeɪʃn/ *nou* a complete change

transfusion /trænsˈfjuːʒn/ *noun* when new blood is put into someone's body because they are ill: *He needed a blood transfusion after the accident.*

transistor /trænˈzɪstə(r)/ *noun* a small part inside something electrical, for example a radio or television

translate 🔑 /træns'leɪt/ *verb* (**translates, translating, translated**) to say or write in one language what someone has said or written in another language: *This letter is in German – can you translate it into English for me?* ▶ **translation** /træns'leɪʃn/ *noun* **1** (no plural) translating: *translation from English into French* **2** (*plural* **translations**) something that someone has translated ▶ **translator** /træns'leɪtə(r)/ *noun* a person who translates

transparent 🔑 /træns'pærənt/ *adjective* **1** If something is transparent, you can see through it: *Glass is transparent.* **2** If information is transparent, it is easy to understand: *New documents were written to make matters more transparent.* ▶ **transparency** /træns'pærənsi/ *noun* (no plural) the quality of being easy to understand

transplant[1] /træns'plɑːnt; trænz'plɑːnt/ *verb* **1** to take out a part of a person's body and put it into another person's body **2** to move a growing plant and plant it somewhere else

transplant[2] /'trænsplɑːnt; 'trænzplɑːnt/ *noun* a medical operation in which a part is taken out of one person's body and put into another person's body: *My uncle needs a kidney transplant.*

transport 🔑 /'trænspɔːt/ *noun* (no plural) a way of carrying people or things from one place to another: *The bus is the cheapest form of transport.* ▶ **transport** /træn'spɔːt/ *verb* (**transports, transporting, transported**) to carry people or things from one place to another: *Most of the goods were transported by air.*

trap[1] /træp/ *noun* **1** a thing that you use for catching animals: *The mouse was caught in a trap.* **2** a plan to trick someone: *I knew the question was a trap, so I didn't answer it.*

trap[2] /træp/ *verb* (**traps, trapping, trapped** /træpt/) **1** to keep someone in a place that they cannot escape from: *They were trapped in the burning building.* **2** to catch or trick someone or something

travel 🔑 /'trævl/ *verb* (**travels , travelling, travelled** /'trævld/) to go from one place to another: *I would like to travel round the world.* ◇ *I travel to school by bus.* ◇ *She travelled 80 kilometres in one day.* ▶ **travel** *noun* (no plural) travelling: *Rail travel can be expensive.*

travel agency /'trævl eɪdʒənsi/ *noun* (*plural* **travel agencies**) a company that plans holidays and journeys for people

travel agent /'trævl eɪdʒənt/ *noun* a person who works in a **travel agency**

traveller /'trævələ(r)/ *noun* a person who is travelling

tray /treɪ/ *noun* a flat thing that you use for carrying food or drinks

tray

tread /tred/ *verb* (**treads, treading, trod** /trɒd/, **has trodden** /'trɒdn/) to put your foot down: *He trod on my foot.*

treason /'triːzn/ *noun* (no plural) the crime of doing harm to your country

treasure /'treʒə(r)/ *noun* gold, silver, jewellery or other things that are worth a lot of money

treasurer /'treʒərə(r)/ *noun* a person who looks after the money of a club or a group of people

treat[1] 🔑 /triːt/ *verb* (**treats, treating, treated**) **1** to behave towards someone or something: *How does your teacher treat you?* ◇ *Treat these glasses with care.* **2** to try to make a sick person well again: *The doctor is treating him for malaria.*
treat something as something to think about something in a certain way: *They treated my idea as a joke.*

treat[2] /triːt/ *noun* something very special that makes someone happy: *My father took me to a football match as a treat.*

treatment 🔑 /'triːtmənt/ *noun* **1** (no plural) the way that you behave towards someone or something: *The treatment of the animals was very cruel.* **2** (*plural* **treatments**) the things that a doctor does to try to make a sick person well again: *He is receiving treatment for cancer.*

treaty /'triːti/ *noun* (*plural* **treaties**) an agreement between countries: *The two countries signed a peace treaty.*

tree 🔑 /triː/ *noun* a big tall plant with a thick main part (called a **trunk**), branches and leaves: *an acacia tree* ◇ *Mangoes grow on trees.*

tree

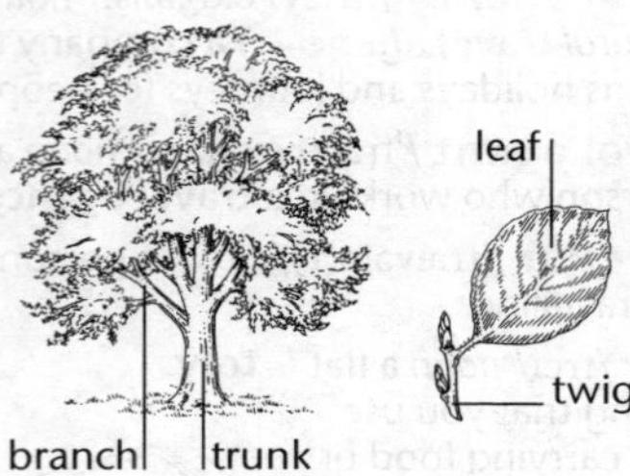

tremble /ˈtrembl/ *verb* (**trembles, trembling, trembled** /ˈtrembld/) to shake, for example because you are cold, afraid or ill: *She was trembling with fear.*

tremendous /trəˈmendəs/ *adjective* **1** very big or very great: *The new trains travel at a tremendous speed.* **2** very good: *The match was tremendous.* ▶ **tremendously** *adverb* very or very much: *The film was tremendously exciting.*

trench /trentʃ/ *noun* (*plural* **trenches**) a long narrow hole that you make in the ground

trend /trend/ *noun* a change to something different: *new trends in science*

trespass /ˈtrespəs/ *verb* (**trespasses, trespassing, trespassed** /ˈtrespəst/) to go on someone's land without asking them if you can: *A sign on the gate of the big house said 'No Trespassing'.* ▶ **trespasser** /ˈtrespəsə(r)/ *noun* a person who **trespasses**

trial 🔑 /ˈtraɪəl/ *noun* **1** the time when a person is in a **court of law** so that people (the **judge** and **jury**) can decide if they have done something wrong and what the punishment will be: *He did not receive a fair trial.* **2** using something to see if it is good or bad: *trials of a new drug*
on trial in a **court of law** so that people can decide if you have done something wrong: *She was on trial for murder.*

triangle 🔑 /ˈtraɪæŋgl/ *noun* a shape with three straight sides ➲ picture on page A12: *Draw a right-angled triangle.* ▶ **triangular** /traɪˈæŋgjələ(r)/ *adjective* with the shape of a triangle

tribe /traɪb/ *noun* a group of people who have the same language and customs: *the Zulu tribe of South Africa* ▶ **tribal** /ˈtraɪbl/ *adjective*: *tribal dances*

tributary /ˈtrɪbjətri/ *noun* (*plural* **tributaries**) a small river that flows into a larger river: *Many tributaries join the Congo River.*

tribute /ˈtrɪbjuːt/ *noun* something that you do, say or give to show that you respect or admire someone: *They built a statue as a tribute to Nelson Mandela.*

trick[1] 🔑 /trɪk/ *noun* **1** a clever plan that makes someone believe something that is not true: *He used a clever trick to get money from me.* **2** something that you do to make someone seem stupid: *The children hid their teacher's books to play a trick on her.* **3** something clever that you have learnt to do: *He can do amazing tricks with a football.*

trick[2] 🔑 /trɪk/ *verb* (**tricks, tricking, tricked** /trɪkt/) to do something that is not honest to get what you want from someone: *He tricked the old lady so that she gave him all her money.*

trickle /ˈtrɪkl/ *verb* (**trickles, trickling, trickled** /ˈtrɪkld/) to move slowly like a thin line of water: *Tears trickled down her cheeks.* ▶ **trickle** *noun*: *a trickle of blood*

tricky /ˈtrɪki/ *adjective* (**trickier, trickiest**) difficult; hard to do: *a tricky question*

tried, tries *forms of* TRY

trigger /ˈtrɪgə(r)/ *noun* the part of a gun that you pull with your finger to fire it

trim /trɪm/ *verb* (**trims, trimming, trimmed** /trɪmd/) to cut something to make it tidy: *He trimmed my hair.* ▶ **trim** *noun* (no plural): *My hair needs a trim.*

trip[1] 🔑 /trɪp/ *noun* a short journey to a place and back again: *We went on a trip to the mountains.*

trip[2] 🔑 /trɪp/ *verb* (**trips, tripping, tripped** /trɪpt/) to hit your foot against something so that you fall or nearly fall: *She tripped over the step.*
trip up to make someone fall or nearly fall: *He put out his foot and tripped me up.*

triple /ˈtrɪpl/ *adjective* with three parts or happening three times: *a triple world champion* ▶ **triple** *verb* (**triples, tripling, tripled** /ˈtrɪpld/) to become or make something three times bigger: *Sales have tripled this year.*

the triple jump /ðə ˈtrɪpl dʒʌmp/ *noun* (no plural) a sport where you try to jump as far as you can with three jumps. The first jump lands on one foot, the second on the other, and the third on both feet.

triumph /ˈtraɪʌmf/ *noun* great success; winning: *The race ended in triumph for the Kenyan team.*

trivial /ˈtrɪviəl/ *adjective* not important: *She gets angry about trivial things.*

trod, trodden *forms of* **TREAD**

trolley /ˈtrɒli/ *noun* (*plural* **trolleys**) a thing on small wheels that you use for carrying things: *The man was pulling a trolley loaded up with boxes.*

trombone /trɒmˈbəʊn/ *noun* a large musical instrument. You play it by blowing and moving a long tube up and down.

trombone

troops /truːps/ *noun* (plural) soldiers

trophy /ˈtrəʊfi/ *noun* (*plural* **trophies**) a thing, for example a silver cup, that you get when you win a competition: *a tennis trophy*

the tropics /ðə ˈtrɒpɪks/ *noun* (plural) the very hot part of the world ▶ **tropical** /ˈtrɒpɪkl/ *adjective* of or from the tropics: *tropical fruit*

trot /trɒt/ *verb* (**trots, trotting, trotted**) to run with short quick steps: *The horse trotted along the road.*

trouble¹ ⚷ /ˈtrʌbl/ *noun* **1** (*plural* **troubles**) difficulty, problems or worry: *We had a lot of trouble finding the book you wanted.* ◇ *She told me all her troubles.* **2** (no plural) extra work: *'Thanks for your help!' 'Oh, it was no trouble.'* **3** (*plural* **troubles**) when people are fighting or arguing: *He left his country to escape from the troubles during the war.* **4** (no plural) pain or illness: *He's got heart trouble.*

be in trouble to have problems, for example because you have done something wrong: *He's in trouble with the police.*

get into trouble to do something that brings problems because it is wrong: *You'll get into trouble if you don't do your homework.*

go to a lot of trouble to do extra work: *They went to a lot of trouble to make us feel welcome.*

trouble² /ˈtrʌbl/ *verb* (**troubles, troubling, troubled** /ˈtrʌbld/) to worry someone; to bring someone problems or pain: *I was troubled by the news.* ◇ *I'm sorry to trouble you, but you're sitting in my seat.*

trough /trɒf/ *noun*

> ❖ **PRONUNCIATION**
> **Trough** sounds like **off**.

a long open box that holds food or water for animals

troupe /truːp/ *noun* a group of actors, singers, etc. who work together

trousers ⚷ /ˈtraʊzəz/ *noun* (plural) a piece of clothing for your legs and the lower part of your body: *I got some new trousers today.* ➲ Picture at **suit¹**.

> ❖ **GRAMMAR**
> Be careful! You cannot say 'a trousers'. You can say **a pair of trousers**: *I bought a new pair of trousers.*

trout /traʊt/ *noun* (*plural* **trout**) a fish that lives in rivers in cool places and that you can eat

truant /ˈtruːənt/ *noun* a child who stays away from school when they should be there

play truant to stay away from school

truce /truːs/ *noun* when people or groups agree to stop fighting for a short time

truck ⚷ /trʌk/ *noun* **1** a big vehicle for carrying heavy things: *a truck driver* **2** an open part of a train where heavy things are carried: *coal trucks*

true ⚷ /truː/ *adjective* **1** right or correct: *Is it true that you are leaving?* ◇ *Casablanca is in Tunisia: true or false?* OPPOSITE **untrue, false** **2** that really happened: *It's a true story.* **3** real: *A true friend will always help you.* ❶ The noun is **truth**.

come true to happen in the way that you hoped: *Her dream of going to university came true.*

truly /ˈtruːli/ *adverb* really: *I'm truly sorry.*

Yours truly words that you write at the end of a formal letter

trumpet /ˈtrʌmpɪt/ *noun* a musical instrument that you blow

trumpet

trunk /trʌŋk/ *noun* **1** the thick part of

a tree, that grows up from the ground ➲ Picture at **tree**. **2** an elephant's long nose ➲ Picture at **elephant**. **3** a big strong box for carrying things when you travel

trunks /trʌŋks/ *noun* (plural) short trousers that a man or boy wears for swimming

trust¹ /trʌst/ *noun* (no plural) feeling sure that someone or something will do what they should do; feeling that someone is honest and good: *Put your trust in God.*

trust² /trʌst/ *verb* (**trusts, trusting, trusted**) to feel sure that someone or something will do what they should do; to believe that someone is honest and good: *You can trust Shayo to do the job well.* ◇ *You can't trust him with money.*

trustworthy /ˈtrʌstwɜːði/ *adjective* A **trustworthy** person is someone that you can trust. ▶ **trustworthiness** /ˈtrʌstwɜːðinəs/ *noun* (no plural) the quality of always being good and honest

truth /truːθ/ *noun* (no plural) being true; what is true: *There is no truth in what he says – he is lying.* ◇ *We need to find out the truth about what happened.*

tell the truth to say what is true: *Are you telling me the truth?*

truthful /ˈtruːθfl/ *adjective* **1** true: *a truthful answer* **2** A person who is **truthful** tells the truth. ▶ **truthfully** /ˈtruːθfəli/ *adverb*: *You must answer me truthfully.*

try /traɪ/ *verb* (**tries, trying, tried** /traɪd/) **1** to work hard to do something: *I tried to remember her name but I couldn't.* ◇ *I'm not sure if I can help you, but I'll try.* **2** to use or do something to find out if you like it: *Have you ever tried Chinese food?* **3** to ask someone questions in a **court of law** to decide if they have done something wrong: *He was tried for murder.*

try and do something to try to do something: *I'll try and come early tomorrow.*

try on to put on a piece of clothing to see if you like it and if it is the correct size: *I tried the trousers on but they were too small.*

▶ **try** *noun* (*plural* **tries**): *I can't open this door – will you have a try?*

tsetse fly /ˈtsetsi flaɪ/ *noun* (*plural* **tsetse flies**) (also **tsetse** *plural* **tsetse**) an insect that can fly and that drinks blood. You can get serious illnesses from tsetse flies.

T-shirt /ˈtiː ʃɜːt/ *noun* a kind of shirt with short sleeves and no **collar** (= the folded part round the neck)

T-shirt

tub /tʌb/ *noun* a round container: *a tub of ice cream* ➲ Picture at **container**.

tube /tjuːb/ *noun* **1** a long thin pipe for a liquid or a gas **2** a long thin soft container with a hole and a lid at one end: *a tube of toothpaste* ➲ Picture at **container**.

tuberculosis /tjuːˌbɜːkjuˈləʊsɪs/ (also **TB**) *noun* (no plural) a serious illness of the **lungs** (= the parts inside your body that you use for breathing)

tuck /tʌk/ *verb* (**tucks, tucking, tucked** /tʌkt/) to put or push the edges of something inside or under something else: *He tucked his shirt into his trousers.*

Tuesday /ˈtjuːzdeɪ/ *noun* the third day of the week, next after Monday

tuft /tʌft/ *noun* a group of hairs, grass, etc. growing together

tug¹ /tʌg/ *verb* (**tugs, tugging, tugged** /tʌgd/) to pull something hard and quickly: *I tugged at the rope and it broke.*

tug² /tʌg/ *noun* **1** a sudden hard pull: *The little girl gave my hand a tug.* **2** (also **tugboat** /ˈtʌgbəʊt/) a small strong boat that pulls big ships

tuition /tjuˈɪʃn/ *noun* (no plural) teaching: *A lot of students have extra tuition before their exams.*

tuktuk /ˈtʊktʊk/ *noun* (in some countries) a vehicle with three wheels that is used as a taxi: *Tuktuk drivers were waiting at the station.*

tumble /ˈtʌmbl/ *verb* (**tumbles, tumbling, tumbled** /ˈtʌmbld/) to fall suddenly: *He tumbled down the steps.*

tummy /ˈtʌmi/ *noun* (*plural* **tummies**) the part of your body between your chest and your legs; your stomach

tuna /ˈtjuːnə/ *noun* (*plural* **tuna**) a large fish that lives in the sea and that you can eat

tune¹ /tjuːn/ *noun* a group of musical notes that make a nice sound when you play or sing them together: *I know the tune but I don't know the words.*

tune² /tjuːn/ *verb* (**tunes, tuning, tuned** /tjuːnd/) to do something to a musical instrument so that it makes the right sounds: *She tuned her guitar.*

tunnel

tunnel /ˈtʌnl/ *noun* a long hole under the ground or sea for a road or railway

turban /ˈtɜːbən/ *noun* a long piece of material that you put round and round your head

turban

turbine /ˈtɜːbaɪn/ *noun* an engine or a machine that uses moving water or gas to work

turkey /ˈtɜːki/ *noun* (*plural* **turkeys**) a big bird that people keep on farms and that you can eat

turn¹ /tɜːn/ *verb* (**turns, turning, turned** /tɜːnd/) **1** to move round, or move something round: *The wheels are turning.* ◇ *Turn the key.* **2** to move in a different direction: *Turn left at the crossroads.* **3** to become different: *The weather has turned cold.* **4** to make someone or something change: *The sun turned the paper yellow.* **5** to find a certain page in a book: *Turn to page 97.*

turn down 1 to say no to what someone wants to do or to give you: *I offered her more cake but she turned it down.* **2** to move the switch that controls something like a radio or a heater so that it makes less sound, heat, etc: *The music's much too loud – can you turn it down?*

turn into something to become different; to change someone or something into something different: *Water turns into ice when it gets very cold.*

turn off to move the handle, switch, etc. that controls something, so that it stops: *Turn the tap off.* ◇ *Turn off the engine.*

turn on to move the handle, switch, etc. that controls something, so that it starts: *Could you turn the light on?*

turn out 1 to be something in the end: *Kamau was a small child, but he has turned out to be a very big man.* **2** to go to an event: *The whole school turned out for the match.*

turn out a light to switch off a light

turn over; turn something over to move, or move something, so that the other side is on top: *Turn over the page to find the answers.*

turn up 1 to arrive: *Has Nduku turned up yet?* **2** to move the switch that controls something like a radio or a heater so that it makes more sound, heat, etc: *Turn up the television – I can't hear it.*

turn² /tɜːn/ *noun* **1** turning something round: *Give the screw a few turns.* **2** a change of direction: *Take a left turn at the end of this road.* **3** the time when you can or should do something: *It's your turn to do the washing-up!*

in turn one after the other: *I spoke to each of the students in turn.*

take turns at something; take it in turns to do something to do something one after the other: *The two boys took it in turns to be goalkeeper.*

turning /ˈtɜːnɪŋ/ *noun* a place where one road joins another road: *Take the first turning on the right.*

turquoise /ˈtɜːkwɔɪz/ *adjective* with a colour between blue and green

turtle /ˈtɜːtl/ *noun* an animal that lives in the sea and has a hard shell on its back ➲ Look at **tortoise**.

turtle

tusk /tʌsk/ *noun* a long pointed tooth that grows next to the mouth of an elephant ➲ Picture at **elephant**.

tutor /ˈtjuːtə(r)/ *noun* a teacher who teaches one person or a small group

TV /ˌtiː ˈviː/ *short for* TELEVISION

tweet /twiːt/ *noun* **1** the short high sound that a small bird makes **2** a short message that you send using Twitter™ (= a service for sending regular messages over the Internet to tell people what you are doing or what interests you): *She's been sending tweets all day.* ▸ **tweet** *verb* (**tweets, tweeting, tweeted**): *Birds were tweeting in the trees.* ◇ *My brother tweeted to wish me luck.*

tweezers /ˈtwiːzəz/ *noun* (plural) a small tool made of two pieces of metal that are joined at one end. You use **tweezers** for holding or pulling out very small things: *She pulled the splinter out of her finger with a pair of tweezers.*

twelfth 🔑 /twelfθ/ *adjective, adverb, noun* 12th

twelve 🔑 /twelv/ *number* 12

twentieth 🔑 /ˈtwentiəθ/ *adjective, adverb, noun* 20th

twenty 🔑 /ˈtwenti/ *number* **1** 20 **2 the twenties** (plural) the numbers, years or temperature between 20 and 29 **in your twenties** between the ages of 20 and 29

twice 🔑 /twaɪs/ *adverb* two times: *I have been to Goma twice. ◇ He ate twice as much as I did.*

twig /twɪg/ *noun* a small thin branch of a tree ➲ Picture at **tree**.

twilight /ˈtwaɪlaɪt/ *noun* (no plural) the time after the sun has gone down and before it gets completely dark

twin /twɪn/ *noun* **1 Twins** are two people who have the same mother and who were born on the same day: *Opiyo and Ereng are twins. ◇ I have got a twin sister.* **2** one of two things that are the same: *twin beds*

twinkle /ˈtwɪŋkl/ *verb* (**twinkles, twinkling, twinkled** /ˈtwɪŋkld/) to shine with a small bright light that comes and goes: *Stars twinkled in the night sky.*

twist 🔑 /twɪst/ *verb* (**twists, twisting, twisted**) **1** to turn strongly: *Twist the lid off the jar.* **2** to change the shape of something by turning it in different directions; to turn in many directions: *She twisted the metal into strange shapes. ◇ The path twists and turns through the forest.* **3** to wind threads, etc. round and round each other: *This machine twists the sisal to make rope.*

twitch /twɪtʃ/ *verb* (**twitches, twitching, twitched** /twɪtʃt/) to make a sudden quick movement with a part of your body: *Rabbits twitch their noses.*

two 🔑 /tu:/ *number* 2

> ❖ **PRONUNCIATION**
>
> **Two** sounds just like **too**.

in two into two pieces: *The cup fell on the floor and broke in two.*

type[1] 🔑 /taɪp/ *noun* **1** (*plural* **types**) a group of things that are the same in some way; a sort or kind: *A cashew is a type of nut. ◇ What type of music do you like?* **2** (no plural) the letters that a machine makes on paper: *The type is too small – I can't read it.*

type[2] 🔑 /taɪp/ *verb* (**types, typing, typed** /taɪpt/) to make words on paper with a **typewriter** or computer: *Her secretary types all her letters. ◇ Can you type?*

typewriter /ˈtaɪpraɪtə(r)/ *noun* a machine with keys that you use to write words on paper: *an electric typewriter*

typhoid /ˈtaɪfɔɪd/ *noun* (no plural) a serious disease that can cause death: *a typhoid epidemic*

typical 🔑 /ˈtɪpɪkl/ *adjective* Something that is **typical** is a good example of its kind: *We had a typical Ugandan meal – matoke and meat stew.* ▸ **typically** /ˈtɪpɪkli/ *adverb* in a typical way: *East African athletes are typically strong at distance events.*

tyrant /ˈtaɪrənt/ *noun* a person with a lot of power who rules a country in a cruel way ▸ **tyrannical** /tɪˈrænɪkl/ *adjective*: *a tyrannical ruler*

tyre 🔑 /ˈtaɪə(r)/ *noun* a circle of rubber around the outside of a wheel, for example on a car or bicycle: *I've got a burst/flat tyre* (= a tyre without enough air inside). ➲ Picture at **bicycle, car**.

Uu

U, u /ju:/ *noun* (*plural* **U's, u's** /ju:z/) the twenty-first letter of the English alphabet: *'Ugly' begins with a 'U'.*

UFO /ˌju: ef ˈəʊ/ *noun* (*plural* **UFOs**) a strange object that some people think they have seen in the sky and that may come from another planet. **UFO** is short for 'unidentified flying object'.

ugali *noun* (no plural) (East African English) soft food that we make from **maize** or **millet** flour and hot water

ugly 🔑 /ˈʌgli/ *adjective* (**uglier, ugliest**) not beautiful to look at: *an ugly face*

❖ **SPEAKING**
It is not polite to say that someone is **ugly**.

ujamaa *noun* (no plural) (in Tanzania) a system in which people in each village work together and help each other

ulcer /ˈʌlsə(r)/ *noun* a painful area on your skin or inside your body: *a mouth/stomach ulcer*

umbrella /ʌmˈbrelə/ *noun* a thing that you hold over your head to keep you dry when it rains: *It started to rain, so I put my umbrella up.*

umpire /ˈʌmpaɪə(r)/ *noun* a person who controls a game such as **tennis** or **cricket**

un- /ʌn/ *prefix* You can add **un-** to the beginning of some words to give them the opposite meaning, for example: *unhappy* (= not happy) ◇ *undress* (= take your clothes off)

unable 🔑 /ʌnˈeɪbl/ *adjective* not able to do something: *Mwita is unable to come to the meeting because he is ill.* ℹ The noun is **inability**.

unanimous /juˈnænɪməs/ *adjective* with the agreement of every person: *The decision was unanimous.*

unarmed /ˌʌnˈɑːmd/ *adjective* If someone is **unarmed**, they do not have a gun or any weapon: *an unarmed police officer*

unattractive /ˌʌnəˈtræktɪv/ *adjective* not nice to look at: *an unattractive building*
OPPOSITE **attractive**

unavoidable /ˌʌnəˈvɔɪdəbl/ *adjective* If something is **unavoidable**, you cannot stop it or get away from it: *He had no money, so selling his car was unavoidable.*

unaware /ˌʌnəˈweə(r)/ *adjective* If you are **unaware** of something, you do not know about it: *I was unaware of the danger.*
OPPOSITE **aware**

unbearable /ʌnˈbeərəbl/ *adjective* If something is **unbearable**, you cannot accept it because it is so bad: *Everyone left the room because the noise was unbearable.* ▶ **unbearably** /ʌnˈbeərəbli/ *adverb*: *It was unbearably hot in the kitchen.*

unbelievable /ˌʌnbɪˈliːvəbl/ *adjective* very surprising or difficult to believe
OPPOSITE **believable**

unborn /ˌʌnˈbɔːn/ *adjective* not yet born: *an unborn child*

uncertain /ʌnˈsɜːtn/ *adjective* not sure; not decided: *I'm uncertain about what to do.* ◇ *The future of the school is uncertain.*
OPPOSITE **certain** ▶ **uncertainty** /ʌnˈsɜːtnti/ *noun* not being sure: *There is uncertainty about who will be the next prime minister.*

uncle 🔑 /ˈʌŋkl/ *noun* the brother of your mother or father, or the husband of your aunt: *Uncle Kisoso*

uncomfortable 🔑 /ʌnˈkʌmftəbl/ *adjective* not comfortable: *The chair was hard and uncomfortable.*
▶ **uncomfortably** /ʌnˈkʌmftəbli/ *adverb*: *The room was uncomfortably hot.*

uncommon /ʌnˈkɒmən/ *adjective* not common; that you do not see, hear, etc. often: *That disease is very uncommon nowadays.*

unconscious 🔑 /ʌnˈkɒnʃəs/ *adjective*
1 If you are unconscious, you are in a kind of sleep and you do not know what is happening: *She fell and hit her head and she was unconscious for three hours.*
2 If you are unconscious of something, you do not know about it: *Shema seemed quite unconscious of the danger he was in.*
OPPOSITE **conscious** ▶ **unconsciousness** /ʌnˈkɒnʃəsnəs/ *noun* (no plural) being unconscious

uncountable /ʌnˈkaʊntəbl/ *adjective* **Uncountable** nouns have no plural and cannot be used with *a* or *an*, for example *advice* or *furniture*. ➲ Look at **countable**.

uncover /ʌnˈkʌvə(r)/ *verb* (**uncovers**, **uncovering**, **uncovered** /ʌnˈkʌvəd/) to take something from on top of another thing: *Uncover the pan and cook the soup for 30 minutes.*

under 🔑 /ˈʌndə(r)/ *preposition, adverb*
1 in or to a place that is lower than or below something: *We sat down under a tree.* ◇ *The cat ran under the table.* ◇ *The boat filled with water, then went under.* ➲ picture on page A6 **2** less than something: *Tickets are free for children aged 5 and under.* **3** covered by something: *I'm wearing a vest under my shirt.* **4** controlled by someone or something: *The team are playing well under their new captain.*

under- /ˈʌndə(r)/ *prefix* **1** You can add **under-** to the beginning of some words to show that something is under another thing: *underwater* (= below the surface of the water) ◇ *underground* **2** You can add **under-** to the beginning of some words to show that something is not enough: *This mango is underripe.* ◇ *an underdose* (= not enough medicine to make someone better)

undergo /ˌʌndəˈɡəʊ/ *verb* (**undergoes**, **undergoing**, **underwent** /ˌʌndəˈwent/, **has undergone** /ˌʌndəˈɡɒn/) If you **undergo** something, it happens to you: *Awino is in hospital undergoing an operation.*

undergraduate /ˌʌndəˈɡrædʒuət/ *noun* a student at a university

underground 🔑 /ˌʌndəˈɡraʊnd/ *adjective, adverb* under the ground: *an underground car park*

undergrowth /ˈʌndəɡrəʊθ/ *noun* (no plural) bushes and other plants that grow under trees: *There was a path through the undergrowth.*

underline /ˌʌndəˈlaɪn/ *verb* (**underlines**, **underlining**, **underlined** /ˌʌndəˈlaɪnd/) to draw or print a line under a word or words: This sentence is underlined.

underneath 🔑 /ˌʌndəˈniːθ/ *preposition, adverb* under or below something: *The dog sat underneath the table.* ◇ *I was wearing a shirt with a vest underneath.*

undernourished /ˌʌndəˈnʌrɪʃt/ *adjective* not getting enough to eat

underpants /ˈʌndəpænts/ *noun* (plural) a piece of clothing that a man or boy wears under his trousers: *a pair of underpants*

understand 🔑 /ˌʌndəˈstænd/ *verb* (**understands**, **understanding**, **understood** /ˌʌndəˈstʊd/, **has understood**) **1** to know what something means or why something happens: *I didn't understand what the teacher said.* ◇ *He doesn't understand Kiswahili.* ◇ *I don't understand why you're so angry.* **2** to know something because someone has told you about it: *I understand that you're leaving this school.*
make yourself understood to make people understand you: *My French isn't very good but I can usually make myself understood.*

understanding[1] /ˌʌndəˈstændɪŋ/ *adjective* If you are **understanding**, you listen to other people's problems and you try to understand them: *My parents are very understanding.*

understanding[2] /ˌʌndəˈstændɪŋ/ *noun* (no plural) knowing about something, or knowing how someone feels: *He's got a good understanding of computers.*

understood *form of* UNDERSTAND

undertaker /ˈʌndəteɪkə(r)/ *noun* a person whose job is to organize **funerals** (= the time when dead people are buried or burned)

underwater 🔑 /ˌʌndəˈwɔːtə(r)/ *adjective, adverb* below the top of water: *an underwater camera* ◇ *Can you swim underwater?*

underwear 🔑 /ˈʌndəweə(r)/ *noun* (no plural) clothes that you wear next to your body, under your other clothes: *Put your clean underwear away.*

underwent *form of* UNDERGO

undo /ʌnˈduː/ *verb* (**undoes** /ʌnˈdʌz/, **undoing**, **undid** /ʌnˈdɪd/, **has undone** /ʌnˈdʌn/) to open something that was tied or fixed: *I undid the string and opened the parcel.* ◇ *I can't undo these buttons.*
➲ Look at **do up**.

undone /ʌnˈdʌn/ *adjective* not tied or fixed: *Your shoelaces are undone.*

undoubtedly /ʌnˈdaʊtɪdli/ *adverb* certainly; without doubt: *She is undoubtedly very intelligent.*

undress /ʌnˈdres/ *verb* (**undresses**, **undressing**, **undressed** /ʌnˈdrest/) to take clothes off yourself or another person: *He undressed and got into bed.* ◇ *She undressed her baby.* OPPOSITE **dress**
get undressed to take off your clothes: *I got undressed and had a shower.* OPPOSITE **get dressed**

uneasy /ʌnˈiːzi/ *adjective* worried that something is wrong: *I started to feel uneasy when the children didn't come home.* ▶ **uneasily** /ʌnˈiːzɪli/ *adverb*: *She looked uneasily around the room.*

unemployed /ˌʌnɪmˈplɔɪd/ *adjective* If someone is **unemployed**, they want a job but they do not have one.

unemployment 🔑 /ˌʌnɪmˈplɔɪmənt/ *noun* (no plural) when there are not enough jobs for the people who want to work: *If the factory closes, unemployment in the town will increase.* OPPOSITE **employment**

uneven /ʌnˈiːvn/ *adjective* not smooth or flat: *We had to drive slowly because the road was so uneven.* OPPOSITE **even**

unexpected 🔑 /ˌʌnɪk'spektɪd/ *adjective* surprising because you did not expect it: *an unexpected visit* ▸ **unexpectedly** *adverb*: *She arrived unexpectedly.*

unfair 🔑 /ˌʌn'feə(r)/ *adjective* Something that is unfair does not treat people in the same way or in the right way: *It was unfair to give homework to some of the children and not to the others.* OPPOSITE **fair** ▸ **unfairly** *adverb*: *She thought her mother had treated her unfairly.*

unfamiliar /ˌʌnfə'mɪliə(r)/ *adjective* that you do not know; strange: *I woke up in an unfamiliar room.* OPPOSITE **familiar**

unfashionable /ʌn'fæʃnəbl/ *adjective* not fashionable: *unfashionable clothes*

unfasten /ʌn'fɑ:sn/ *verb* (**unfastens**, **unfastening**, **unfastened** /ʌn'fɑ:snd/) to open something that was tied or fixed: *You can unfasten your seat belts now.* OPPOSITE **fasten**

unfit /ʌn'fɪt/ *adjective* **1** not healthy or strong: *She never takes any exercise – that's why she's so unfit.* **2** not good enough for something: *This house is unfit for people to live in.* OPPOSITE **fit**

unfold /ʌn'fəʊld/ *verb* (**unfolds**, **unfolding**, **unfolded**) to open something to make it flat; to open out and become flat: *Njoki unfolded the newspaper and started to read.* ◇ *The sofa unfolds to make a bed.* OPPOSITE **fold**, **fold up**

unfortunate /ʌn'fɔ:tʃənət/ *adjective* not lucky: *It's unfortunate that you were ill on the day of your exam.* OPPOSITE **fortunate**

unfortunately 🔑 /ʌn'fɔ:tʃənətli/ *adverb* a word that you use to show that you are not happy about something: *I would like to give you some money, but unfortunately I haven't got any.* OPPOSITE **fortunately**

unfriendly 🔑 /ʌn'frendli/ *adjective* not friendly; not kind or helpful to other people: *She gave me an unfriendly look.*

unfurnished /ʌn'fɜ:nɪʃt/ *adjective* with no furniture in it: *He rents an unfurnished flat.* OPPOSITE **furnished**

ungrammatical /ˌʌngrə'mætɪkl/ *adjective* not correct because it does not follow the rules of grammar: *The sentence 'They is happy' is ungrammatical.* OPPOSITE **grammatical**

ungrateful /ʌn'greɪtfl/ *adjective* If you are **ungrateful**, you do not show thanks when someone helps you or gives you something: *Don't be so ungrateful! I spent all morning helping you!* OPPOSITE **grateful**

unhappy 🔑 /ʌn'hæpi/ *adjective* (**unhappier**, **unhappiest**) not happy; sad: *He was very unhappy when he lost the race.* ▸ **unhappily** /ʌn'hæpɪli/ *adverb*: *'I failed the exam,' she said unhappily.* ▸ **unhappiness** /ʌn'hæpinəs/ *noun* (no plural): *Odoi has had a lot of unhappiness in his life.*

unhealthy /ʌn'helθi/ *adjective* (**unhealthier**, **unhealthiest**) **1** not well; often ill: *an unhealthy child* **2** that can make you ill: *unhealthy food* OPPOSITE **healthy**

unhelpful /ʌn'helpfl/ *adjective* not wanting to help someone; not useful: *The waiter was rude and unhelpful.* OPPOSITE **helpful**

unhygienic /ˌʌnhaɪ'dʒi:nɪk/ *adjective* not clean OPPOSITE **hygienic**

uniform 🔑 /'ju:nɪfɔ:m/ *noun* the special clothes that everybody in the same school, job, etc. wears: *What colour is your school uniform?*

unimportant /ˌʌnɪm'pɔ:tnt/ *adjective* not important

uninhabited /ˌʌnɪn'hæbɪtɪd/ *adjective* where nobody lives: *an uninhabited island*

unintentional /ɪn'tenʃənl/ *adjective* that you do by mistake OPPOSITE **intentional** ▸ **unintentionally** /ˌʌnɪn'tenʃənəli/ *adverb*: *I unintentionally hurt his feelings.* OPPOSITE **intentionally**

uninterested /ʌn'ɪntrəstɪd/ *adjective* If you are **uninterested** in someone or something, you do not want to know more about them. OPPOSITE **interested**

union 🔑 /'ju:niən/ *noun* **1** (*plural* **unions**) a group of workers who have joined together to talk to their managers about things like pay and the way they work: *the National Union of Teachers* **2** (*plural* **unions**) a group of people or countries that have joined together **3** (no plural) coming together: *The President hopes to establish a closer union between the two countries.*

unique /ju'ni:k/ *adjective* not like anyone or anything else: *Everybody in the world is unique.*

unit 🔑 /'ju:nɪt/ *noun* **1** one complete thing or group that may be part of something larger: *The book has twelve units.*

2 a measurement: *A metre is a unit of length.*

unite 🔑 /ju'naɪt/ *verb* (**unites, uniting, united**) to join together to become one; to put two things together: *East and West Germany united in 1990.* ▶ **united** /ju'naɪtɪd/ *adjective* joined together: *the United States of America*

unity /'ju:nəti/ *noun* (no plural) the situation in which people are in agreement and working together: *What we want is a feeling of unity and public spirit in the school.*

universal /ˌju:nɪ'vɜ:sl/ *adjective* of, by or for everybody: *This subject is of universal interest.*

the universe 🔑 /ðə 'ju:nɪvɜ:s/ *noun* (no plural) the earth and all the stars, planets and everything else in space: *The universe is still expanding.*

university 🔑 /ˌju:nɪ'vɜ:səti/ *noun* (*plural* **universities**) a place where people go to study more difficult subjects after they have left school: *I'm hoping to go to university next year.* ◇ *My sister is at university studying biology.*

> ❖ **WORD BUILDING**
> If you pass special courses at a university, you get a **degree**.
> Look at **graduate** and **undergraduate**.

unjust /ˌʌn'dʒʌst/ *adjective* not just; not fair or right: *This tax is unjust because poor people pay as much as rich people.*

unkind 🔑 /ˌʌn'kaɪnd/ *adjective* not kind; cruel: *It was unkind of you to laugh at her.*

unknown 🔑 /ˌʌn'nəʊn/ *adjective* **1** that you do not know: *an unknown face* OPPOSITE **familiar** **2** not famous: *an unknown actor* OPPOSITE **famous, well known**

unless 🔑 /ən'les/ *conjunction* if not; except if: *You will be late unless you leave now.* ◇ *Unless you work harder you'll fail the exam.*

unlike /ˌʌn'laɪk/ *preposition* not like; different from: *She is very good at sport, unlike her sister, who prefers drama.*

unlikely 🔑 /ʌn'laɪkli/ *adjective* (**unlikelier, unlikeliest**) If something is unlikely, it will probably not happen: *It is unlikely that it will rain today.* ◇ *He is unlikely to pass the exam.* OPPOSITE **likely**

unload /ʌn'ləʊd/ *verb* (**unloads, unloading, unloaded**) to take off or out the things that a car, lorry, ship or plane is carrying: *I unloaded the sacks from the pickup.* ◇ *They unloaded the ship at the dock.* OPPOSITE **load**

unlock /ʌn'lɒk/ *verb* (**unlocks, unlocking, unlocked** /ˌʌn'lɒkt/) to open something with a key: *I unlocked the door and went in.* OPPOSITE **lock**

unlucky /ʌn'lʌki/ *adjective* (**unluckier, unluckiest**) **1** If you are **unlucky**, good things do not happen to you: *The team were unlucky to lose because they played so well.* **2** Something that is **unlucky** brings bad luck: *Some people think that the number 13 is unlucky.* OPPOSITE **lucky**
▶ **unluckily** /ʌn'lʌkɪli/ *adverb* it is **unlucky** that: *Unluckily, I missed the bus.*

unmarried /ˌʌn'mærɪd/ *adjective* not married; without a husband or wife

unnatural /ʌn'nætʃrəl/ *adjective* different from what is normal or expected: *There was an unnatural silence in the room.* OPPOSITE **natural**

unnecessary /ʌn'nesəsəri/ *adjective* not necessary; not needed

> ❖ **SPELLING**
> Remember! You spell **unnecessary** with **nn**, one **c** and **ss**.

unofficial /ˌʌnə'fɪʃl/ *adjective* not of or from the government or someone who is important: *Unofficial reports say that thirty people were hurt in the earthquake.* OPPOSITE **official**

unpack /ˌʌn'pæk/ *verb* (**unpacks, unpacking, unpacked** /ˌʌn'pækt/) to take all the things out of a bag, suitcase, etc: *Have you unpacked your suitcase?* ◇ *When I got home I unpacked and washed all my clothes.* OPPOSITE **pack**

unpaid /ˌʌn'peɪd/ *adjective* not paid: *an unpaid bill*

unpleasant 🔑 /ʌn'pleznt/ *adjective* not pleasant; not nice: *There was an unpleasant smell of bad fish.*
▶ **unpleasantly** *adverb*: *Inside the room it was unpleasantly hot.*

unplug /ˌʌn'plʌg/ *verb* (**unplugs, unplugging, unplugged** /ˌʌn'plʌgd/) to take a lamp, a machine, etc. out of a place in a wall (called a **socket**) where there is electricity: *Could you unplug the TV?* OPPOSITE **plug in**

unpopular /ʌn'pɒpjələ(r)/ *adjective* not popular; not liked by many people: *He's unpopular at work because he's lazy.*

unreasonable /ʌn'ri:znəbl/ *adjective* not fair or right: *Some traders charge unreasonable prices.* OPPOSITE **reasonable**

unreliable /ˌʌnrɪ'laɪəbl/ *adjective* that you cannot trust or depend on: *Don't ask her for help – she's very unreliable.* OPPOSITE **reliable**

unsafe /ʌn'seɪf/ *adjective* not safe; dangerous: *Don't climb on that wall – it's unsafe.*

unsatisfactory /ˌʌnsætɪs'fæktri/ *adjective* not good enough; not satisfactory: *Chebet's work was unsatisfactory so she had to do it again.*

unscrew /ˌʌn'skru:/ *verb* (**unscrews**, **unscrewing**, **unscrewed** /ˌʌn'skru:d/) **1** to open or remove something by turning it: *I can't unscrew the top of the bottle.* **2** to remove the **screws** (= small metal things with a sharp end) from something OPPOSITE **screw**

unselfish /ʌn'selfɪʃ/ *adjective* thinking more about what other people want than what you want SAME MEANING **selfless** OPPOSITE **selfish**

unskilled /ˌʌn'skɪld/ *adjective* not good at something because you have not learnt about it: *unskilled workers* OPPOSITE **skilled**

unstable /ʌn'steɪbl/ *adjective* Something that is **unstable** may fall, move or change: *This bridge is unstable.* ◇ *an unstable government* OPPOSITE **stable**

unsteady /ʌn'stedi/ *adjective* If something is **unsteady**, it may move or shake. OPPOSITE **steady**

unsuccessful /ˌʌnsək'sesfl/ *adjective* If you are unsuccessful, you have not done what you wanted and tried to do: *I tried to repair the bike but I was unsuccessful.* ▶ **unsuccessfully** /ˌʌnsək'sesfəli/ *adverb*: *Ngenzi tried unsuccessfully to lift the box.*

unsuitable /ʌn'su:təbl/ *adjective* not suitable; not right for someone or something: *This film is unsuitable for children.*

unsure /ˌʌn'ʃɔ:(r)/ *adjective* not sure: *We were unsure what to do.*

unsympathetic /ˌʌnˌsɪmpə'θetɪk/ *adjective* If you are **unsympathetic**, you do not show that you understand other people's feelings when they have problems. OPPOSITE **sympathetic**

untangle /ˌʌn'tæŋgl/ *verb* (**untangles**, **untangling**, **untangled** /ˌʌn'tæŋgld/) to separate something like pieces of string or hair that have become mixed or twisted together OPPOSITE **tangle**

untidy 🔑 /ʌn'taɪdi/ *adjective* (**untidier**, **untidiest**) not tidy; not with everything in the right place: *Your room is always so untidy!* ▶ **untidiness** /ʌn'taɪdinəs/ *noun* (no plural): *I hate untidiness!*

untie /ˌʌn'taɪ/ *verb* (**unties**, **untying**, **untied** /ˌʌn'taɪd/) **1** to take off the string or rope that is holding something or someone: *I untied the parcel.* **2** to make a knot loose: *Can you untie this knot?* ◇ *I untied my shoelaces.*

until[1] 🔑 /ən'tɪl/ *conjunction* up to the time when: *Stay in bed until you feel better.* ➲ Look at **till**[1].

> ❖ **SPELLING**
>
> Be careful! You spell **until** with one **l** but **till** with **ll**.

until[2] 🔑 /ən'tɪl/ *preposition* **1** up to a certain time: *The shop is open until 6.30.* **2** before: *I can't come until tomorrow.* ➲ Look at **till**[2].

untrue /ʌn'tru:/ *adjective* not true or correct: *What you said was completely untrue.*

unusual 🔑 /ʌn'ju:ʒuəl/ *adjective* If something is unusual, it does not often happen or you do not often see it: *It's unusual to see a cat without a tail.* ▶ **unusually** /ʌn'ju:ʒuəli/ *adverb*: *She's unusually tall for her age.*

unwanted /ˌʌn'wɒntɪd/ *adjective* not wanted: *unwanted children*

unwelcome /ʌn'welkəm/ *adjective* If someone or something is **unwelcome**, you are not happy to have or see them: *an unwelcome visitor*

unwell /ʌn'wel/ *adjective* not well; ill

unwilling /ʌn'wɪlɪŋ/ *adjective* If you are **unwilling** to do something, you are not ready or happy to do it: *He was unwilling to lend me any money.* OPPOSITE **willing**

unwrap /ˌʌn'ræp/ *verb* (**unwraps**,

unwrapping, unwrapped /ˌʌnˈræpt/) to take off the paper or cloth that is around something: *I unwrapped the parcel.* OPPOSITE **wrap**

unzip /ˌʌnˈzɪp/ *verb* (**unzips, unzipping, unzipped** /ˌʌnˈzɪpt/) to open something that has a **zip**: *She unzipped her bag and took out a comb.* OPPOSITE **zip up**

up 🔑 /ʌp/ *preposition, adverb* **1** in or to a higher place: *We climbed up the mountain.* ◇ *Put your hand up if you know the answer.* OPPOSITE **down** ➲ picture on page A7 **2** from sitting or lying to standing: *Stand up, please.* ◇ *What time do you get up?* (= out of bed) **3** in a way that is bigger, stronger, etc: *The price of petrol is going up.* ◇ *Please turn the radio up – I can't hear it.* OPPOSITE **down** **4** so that it is finished: *Who used all the coffee up?* **5** along: *We walked up the road.* OPPOSITE **down** **6** towards and near someone or something: *She came up to me and asked me the time.* **7** into pieces: *Cut the meat up.*
be up to be out of bed: *'Is Bigogo up?' 'No, he's still asleep.'*
it's up to you you are the person who should do or decide something: *'What shall we do this evening?' 'I don't mind. It's up to you.'*
up to **1** as far as; until: *Up to now, she has worked very hard.* **2** as much or as many as: *Up to 300 people came to the meeting.* **3** doing something: *What is that man up to?*

upbringing /ˈʌpbrɪŋɪŋ/ *noun* (no plural) the way a child is treated and taught how to behave by their parents: *She had a strict upbringing.*

up-country /ˌʌp ˈkʌntri/ *adjective, adverb* used about a part of a country that is not near large towns: *My father is at our up-country farm.*

update /ˌʌpˈdeɪt/ *verb* (**updates, updating, updated**) to make something more modern or add new things to it: *The information on the computer is updated every week.* ▸ **update** /ˈʌpdeɪt/ *noun*: *We get regular updates on school news.*

uphill /ˌʌpˈhɪl/ *adverb* up, towards the top of a hill: *It's difficult to ride a bicycle uphill.* OPPOSITE **downhill**

upload /ˌʌpˈləʊd/ *verb* (**uploads, uploading, uploaded**) If you **upload** a computer program or information, you copy it from your computer to a larger computer system: *You can upload your photos to our website.* OPPOSITE **downloa**

upon /əˈpɒn/ *preposition* on ⓘ **On** is the word that we usually use.
once upon a time a long time ago (words that sometimes begin children's stories): *Once upon a time there was a beautiful princess …*

upper 🔑 /ˈʌpə(r)/ *adjective* higher than another; top: *the upper lip* OPPOSITE **lower**

upright /ˈʌpraɪt/ *adjective, adverb* standing straight up, not lying down: *Pu the ladder upright against the wall.*

upset[1] 🔑 /ˌʌpˈset/ *verb* (**upsets, upsetting, upset, has upset**) **1** to make someone feel unhappy or worried: *You upset Ali when you said he was stupid.* **2** t make something go wrong: *The injury to the goalkeeper upset our chances of winning the match.* **3** to knock somethin so that it turns over and things fall out: *I upset a bucket of water all over the floor.*

upset[2] 🔑 /ˌʌpˈset/ *adjective* **1** unhappy or worried: *The children were very upset when their dog died.* **2** ill: *I've got an upset stomach.* ▸ **upset** /ˈʌpset/ *noun* an illnes in your stomach: *Adisa has got a stomac upset.*

upside down /ˌʌpsaɪd ˈdaʊn/ *adverb* with the top part at the bottom: *The boy is upside down in the tree.*

upside down

upstairs 🔑 /ˌʌpˈsteəz/ *adverb* to or on a higher floor of a building: *I went upstairs to the second floor.* ▸ **upstairs** *adjective*: *An upstairs window was open.* OPPOSITE **downstairs**

up to date /ˌʌp tə ˈdeɪt/ *adjective* moder using new information: *Is this timetable up to date?*

upwards 🔑 /ˈʌpwədz/ (also **upward** /ˈʌpwəd/) *adverb* up; towards a higher place: *We climbed upwards, towards the top of the mountain.* OPPOSITE **downwards**

urban /ˈɜːbən/ *adjective* of a town or city: *urban areas*

urge[1] /ɜ:dʒ/ *verb* (**urges, urging, urged** /ɜ:dʒd/) to try to make someone do something: *I urged him to stay for dinner.*

urge[2] /ɜ:dʒ/ *noun* a strong feeling that you want to do something: *I had a sudden urge to laugh.*

urgency /ˈɜ:dʒənsi/ *noun* (no plural) the need to do something quickly because it is very important

urgent 🔑 /ˈɜ:dʒənt/ *adjective* so important that you must do it or answer it quickly: *The doctor received an urgent telephone call.* ▶ **urgently** *adverb*: *I must see you urgently.*

us 🔑 /əs; ʌs/ *pronoun* (plural) me and another person or other people; me and you: *The teacher asked us a lot of questions.* ◇ *Kirezi wrote to us.*

use[1] 🔑 /ju:z/ *verb* (**uses, using, used** /ju:zd/)

> ❖ **PRONUNCIATION**
>
> **Use** (verb) ends with a 'z' sound like **shoes** or **snooze**.

1 to do a job with something: *Could I use your telephone?* ◇ *Do you know how to use this machine?* ◇ *Wood is used to make paper.* **2** to take something: *Don't use all the milk.*

use up to use something until you have no more: *I've used up all the sugar, so I need to buy some more.*

> ❖ **WORD FAMILY**
>
> **use used user**
> **useful**: OPPOSITE **useless**

use[2] 🔑 /ju:s/ *noun*

> ❖ **PRONUNCIATION**
>
> **Use** (noun) ends with an 's' sound like **juice**.

1 (no plural) using something: *This library is for the use of students only.* **2** (*plural* **uses**) what you can do with something: *This tool has many uses.*

have the use of something to have the right to use something: *The school let us have the use of a classroom for our meeting.*

it's no use it will not help to do something: *It's no use telling her anything – she never listens.*

make use of something to find a way of using something: *If you don't want that box, I can make use of it.*

used[1] 🔑 /ju:zd/ *adjective*

> ❖ **PRONUNCIATION**
>
> In this meaning, **used** ends with a 'zd' sound like the end of **snoozed**.

not new: *The garage sells used cars.*

used[2] 🔑 /ju:st/ *adjective*

> ❖ **PRONUNCIATION**
>
> In this meaning, **used** ends with an 'st' sound like the end of **rest**.

be used to something to know something well because you have seen, heard, tasted, done, etc. it a lot: *I'm used to walking because I haven't got a bicycle.*

get used to something to begin to know something well after a time: *I'm getting used to my new school.*

used[3] /ju:st/ *verb*

> ❖ **PRONUNCIATION**
>
> In this meaning, **used** ends with an 'st' sound like the end of **rest**.

used to words that tell us about something that happened often or that was true in the past: *She used to act when she was young.* ◇ *I used to be afraid of my uncle, but now I like him.*

> ❖ **GRAMMAR**
>
> We make negatives with **didn't use to** or **never used to**: *I didn't use to like fish, but I do now.*
>
> To make questions, we use **did** with **use to**: *Did she use to hate fish?*

useful 🔑 /ˈju:sfl/ *adjective* good and helpful for doing something: *This bag will be useful for carrying my books.*

useless 🔑 /ˈju:sləs/ *adjective* **1** not good for anything: *A car is useless without petrol.* **2** that does not do what you hoped: *It was useless asking my brother for money – he didn't have any.*

user 🔑 /ˈju:zə(r)/ *noun* a person who uses something: *computer users*

username /ˈju:zəneɪm/ *noun* the name that you use so that you can use a computer program or system: *Please enter your username and password.*

usher /ˈʌʃə(r)/ *noun* a person who has special duties in a church, court, public hall, etc: *The ushers showed us where to sit.*

usual /ˈjuːʒuəl/ *adjective* that happens most often: *It's not usual for such a young baby to be able to walk.*
as usual as happens most often: *Teta was late, as usual.*

usually /ˈjuːʒuəli/ *adverb* in a way that is usual; most often: *I usually ride my bike to school, but today I'm walking.*

utensil /juːˈtensl/ *noun* a tool that you use in the home: *cooking utensils*

❖ **WORD BUILDING**

We use many different types of utensils. Here are some of them: **spoons, forks, pans, plates** and **whisks**.

utter[1] /ˈʌtə(r)/ *adjective* complete: *The room was in utter darkness and I couldn't see anything.*

utter[2] /ˈʌtə(r)/ *verb* (**utters, uttering, uttered** /ˈʌtəd/) to say something or make a sound with your mouth: *He uttered a cry of pain.*

utterly /ˈʌtəli/ *adverb* completely or very: *That's utterly impossible!*

V, v /viː/ *noun* **1** (*plural* **V's, v's** /viːz/) the twenty-second letter of the English alphabet: *'Voice' begins with a 'V'.* **2** V *short for* VOLT **3** v *short for* VERSUS

vacancy /ˈveɪkənsi/ *noun* (*plural* **vacancies**) **1** a job that nobody is doing: *We have a vacancy for a secretary in our office.* **2** a room in a hotel that nobody is using: *The sign outside the hotel said 'no vacancies'* (= the hotel is full).

vacant /ˈveɪkənt/ *adjective* empty; with nobody in it: *a vacant room*

vacation /vəˈkeɪʃn/ *noun* a holiday time when a university is not open: *the summer vacation*

vaccinate /ˈvæksɪneɪt/ *verb* (**vaccinates, vaccinating, vaccinated**) to make someone safe from a disease by putting a medicine (called a **vaccine**) into their arm or leg with a needle: *Children can be vaccinated against several diseases.* ▶ **vaccination** /ˌvæksɪˈneɪʃn/ *noun*: *Have you had your measles vaccination?*

vaccine /ˈvæksiːn/ *noun* a substance that is put into someone's arm or leg with a needle to stop them getting a disease

vacuum /ˈvækjuəm/ *noun* a space with no air, gas or anything else in it

vacuum cleaner /ˈvækjuəm kliːnə(r)/ *noun* a machine that cleans carpets by sucking up dirt

vague /veɪg/ *adjective* (**vaguer, vaguest**) not clear or not exact: *I couldn't find the house because he gave me very vague directions.* ▶ **vaguely** /ˈveɪgli/ *adverb*: *I vaguely remember what happened.*

vain /veɪn/ *adjective* (**vainer, vainest**) **1** too proud of what you can do or how you look ❶ The noun is **vanity**. **2** with no success; useless: *They made a vain attempt to save his life.*
in vain with no success: *I tried in vain to sleep.*

valid /ˈvælɪd/ *adjective* If something like a ticket or a cheque is **valid**, you can use it and other people will accept it: *Your bus ticket is valid for one week.*

valley

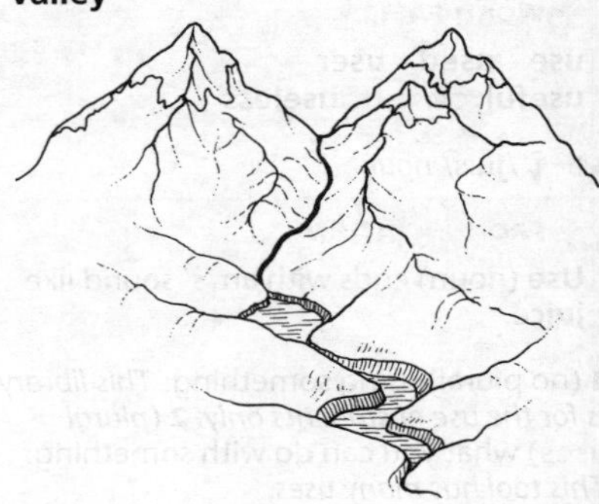

valley /ˈvæli/ *noun* (*plural* **valleys**) low land, usually with a river, between hills or mountains: *the Rift Valley*

valuable /ˈvæljuəbl/ *adjective* **1** worth a lot of money: *Is this ring valuable?* **2** very useful: *valuable information*

value¹ 🔑 /ˈvæljuː/ *noun* **1** (*plural* **values**) how much money you can sell something for: *What is the value of this property?* **2** (no plural) how useful or important something is: *Their help was of great value.* **3** (no plural) how much something is worth compared with its price: *The book was good value at only 50 shillings.* **4** (*plural* **values**) beliefs about what is the right and wrong way for people to behave: *moral values*

value² /ˈvæljuː/ *verb* (**values, valuing, valued** /ˈvæljuːd/) **1** to think that something is very important: *I value my freedom.* **2** to say how much money something is worth: *The property was valued at two million shillings.*

vampire /ˈvæmpaɪə(r)/ *noun* a dead person in stories who comes to life at night and drinks people's blood

van

van /væn/ *noun* a kind of big car or small lorry for carrying things

vandal /ˈvændl/ *noun* a person who damages and breaks things that belong to other people: *Vandals have damaged our classroom.*

vandalism /ˈvændəlɪzəm/ *noun* (no plural) the crime of damaging or breaking things that belong to other people: *Vandalism is a problem in this part of the city.*

vanilla /vəˈnɪlə/ *noun* (no plural) a plant that gives a taste to some sweet foods, for example white ice cream

vanish /ˈvænɪʃ/ *verb* (**vanishes, vanishing, vanished** /ˈvænɪʃt/) to go away suddenly; to disappear: *The thief ran into the crowd and vanished.*

vanity /ˈvænəti/ *noun* (no plural) being too proud of what you can do or how you look ❶ The adjective is **vain**.

vapour /ˈveɪpə(r)/ *noun* (no plural) very small drops of liquid that look like a gas: *water vapour*

varied 🔑 /ˈveərid/ *adjective* with a lot of different things in: *The activities in our English lessons are very varied.*

varied, varies *form of* VARY

variety 🔑 /vəˈraɪəti/ *noun* **1** (no plural) If something has variety, it is full of different things and changes often: *We all need variety in our daily lives.* **2** (no plural) a lot of different things: *There's a large variety of dishes on the menu.* ➲ Look at **vary**. **3** (*plural* **varieties**) a kind of something: *This variety of apple is very sweet.*

various 🔑 /ˈveəriəs/ *adjective* many different: *We sell this shirt in various colours and sizes.*

varnish /ˈvɑːnɪʃ/ *noun* (no plural) a clear paint with no colour, that you put on something to make it shine ▶ **varnish** *verb* (**varnishes, varnishing, varnished** /ˈvɑːnɪʃt/): *The doors were varnished.*

vary 🔑 /ˈveəri/ *verb* (**varies, varying, varied** /ˈveərid/, **has varied**) to be or become different from each other: *These shoes vary in price from 600 to 1200 shillings.* ➲ Look at **variety**.

vase /vɑːz/ *noun* a pot that you put cut flowers in

vase

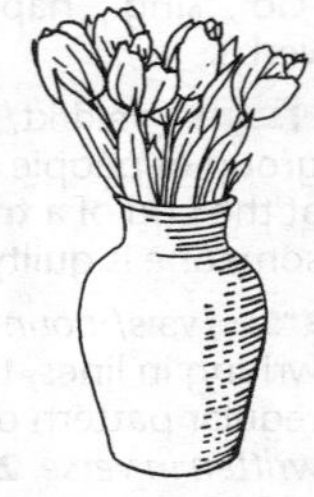

a **vase** of flowers

vast /vɑːst/ *adjective* very big: *Australia is a vast country.*

veal /viːl/ *noun* (no plural) meat from a young cow (a **calf**) ➲ Note at **cow**.

vegetable 🔑 /ˈvedʒtəbl/ *noun* a plant or part of a plant that we eat: *vegetable soup* ◇ *The children grow vegetables such as cabbages, carrots and beans.*

vegetarian /ˌvedʒɪˈteəriən/ *noun* a person who does not eat meat

vegetation /ˌvedʒɪˈteɪʃn/ *noun* (no plural) the trees and plants that grow in a place: *There is little or no vegetation in desert regions.*

vehicle 🔑 /ˈviːəkl/ *noun* any thing that carries people or things from one place to another: *We heard a vehicle approaching.*

❖ **WORD BUILDING**

There are many different types of vehicles. Here are some of them: **bus, car, motorbike** and **truck**.

veil /veɪl/ *noun* a piece of thin material that a woman puts over her head and face: *The bride wore a white veil.*

vein /veɪn/ *noun* one of the small tubes in your body that carry blood to the heart

ventilate /ˈventɪleɪt/ *verb* (**ventilates, ventilating, ventilated**) to allow air to move through something: *Keep the fruit in a cool, well-ventilated place.* ▸ **ventilation** /ˌventɪˈleɪʃn/ *noun* (no plural): *The only ventilation was one tiny window.*

venue /ˈvenjuː/ *noun* a place where people meet for an organized event: *The hall is a popular venue for weddings.*

veranda (also **verandah** /vəˈrændə/) *noun* an area like a room at the side of a house, with a roof and floor but no walls: *We sat on the veranda.*

verb /vɜːb/ *noun* a word that tells you what someone or something is or does. 'Go', 'sing', 'happen' and 'be' are all verbs.

verdict /ˈvɜːdɪkt/ *noun* what the **jury** (= a group of people in a court of law) decides at the end of a **trial** about whether someone is guilty or not

verse /vɜːs/ *noun* **1** (no plural) poetry; writing in lines, that has a **rhythm** (= a regular pattern of sounds): *The play is written in verse.* **2** (*plural* **verses**) a group of lines in a song or poem: *This song has five verses.*

version /ˈvɜːʃn/ *noun* **1** a form of something that is different in some way: *a new version of a well-known song* **2** what one person says or writes about something that happened: *His version of the accident is different from mine.*

versus /ˈvɜːsəs/ *preposition* on the other side in a sport; against: *There's a good football match on TV tonight – Kenya versus Brazil.* ℹ The short way of writing 'versus' is **v** or **vs**.

vertical /ˈvɜːtɪkl/ *adjective* Something that is **vertical** goes straight up, not from side to side: *a vertical line* ➲ picture on page A12 ➲ Look at **horizontal**.

very¹ 🔑 /ˈveri/ *adverb* You use 'very' before another word to make it stronger: *The Nile is a very long river.* ◇ *She speaks very quietly.* ◇ *I like athletics very much.* ◇ *I'm not very hungry.* ◇ *I'm very tired, but I'll help you with the work.* ➲ Note at **too**.

❖ **WORD BUILDING**

These words tell us how strong an adjective is:

very: *I'm very tired* (= I need a rest).

quite, fairly: *I'm quite tired* (= I can work a little longer before I rest).

slightly, a little, a bit: *I'm a bit tired* (= I can go on working for a while).

very² /ˈveri/ *adjective* same; exact: *You are the very person I wanted to see!* ◇ *We climbed to the very top of the mountain.*

vessel /ˈvesl/ *noun* a large ship or boat: *We could see large vessels far out at sea.*

vest /vest/ *noun* a piece of clothing that you wear under your other clothes on the top part of your body

vet /vet/ (also **veterinary surgeon** /ˈvetnri sɜːdʒən/) *noun* a doctor for animals

via /ˈvaɪə/ *preposition* going through a place: *We went from Nairobi to Sydney via Bangkok.*

vibrate /vaɪˈbreɪt/ *verb* (**vibrates, vibrating, vibrated**) to move very quickly from side to side or up and down: *The house vibrates every time a truck goes past.* ▸ **vibration** /vaɪˈbreɪʃn/ *noun*: *You can feel the vibrations from the engine when you are in the car.*

vice- /vaɪs/ *prefix* a word that you use before another word, to describe someone who is next to the leader in importance: *The vice-captain leads the team when the captain is ill.* ◇ *the Vice-President*

vicious /ˈvɪʃəs/ *adjective* cruel; wanting to hurt someone or something: *a vicious attack*

victim /ˈvɪktɪm/ *noun* a person or an animal that is hurt or killed by someone or something: *The victims of the car accident were taken to hospital.*

victory /ˈvɪktəri/ *noun* (*plural* **victories**) winning a fight, game or war

video 🔑 /ˈvɪdiəʊ/ *noun* (*plural* **videos**) **1** a short film made with **digital** technology that you can watch on a computer, mobile phone, etc: *The school made a short video for its website.* **2** (also **videotape** /ˈvɪdiəʊteɪp/) tape in a **cassette** (= a plastic box) on which a film, TV programme or real event is recorded: *You can get this film on video or on DVD.* **3** (also **video recorder**) a machine connected to a television, that you use for recording or showing programmes: *Have you set the video?*

view 🔑 /vjuː/ *noun* **1** what you can see from a certain place: *There is a beautiful view of the mountains from our window.* **2** what you believe or think about something: *What are your views on keeping pets?*
in view of something because of something: *In view of the heavy rain we decided to cancel the match.*
on view in a place for people to see: *Her paintings are on view at the museum.*

viewer /ˈvjuːə(r)/ *noun* a person who watches television

vigorous /ˈvɪgərəs/ *adjective* strong and active: *vigorous exercise* ▶ **vigorously** *adverb*: *She shook my hand vigorously.*

vile /vaɪl/ *adjective* (**viler**, **vilest**) very bad: *What a vile smell!* SAME MEANING **horrible**, **disgusting**

village 🔑 /ˈvɪlɪdʒ/ *noun* a small place where people live. A village is smaller than a town: *a village in the countryside* ➲ Note at **town**.

villager /ˈvɪlɪdʒə(r)/ *noun* a person who lives in a village

villain /ˈvɪlən/ *noun* a bad person, usually in a book, play or film

vine /vaɪn/ *noun* the plant that **grapes** (= small green or purple fruit) grow on

vinegar /ˈvɪnɪgə(r)/ *noun* (no plural) a liquid with a strong sharp taste. You put it on food and use it for cooking: *I mixed some oil and vinegar to put on the salad.*

vineyard /ˈvɪnjəd/ *noun* a piece of land where **vines** grow

violate /ˈvaɪəleɪt/ *verb* (**violates**, **violating**, **violated**) to break a rule, an agreement, etc: *to violate international law*

violence 🔑 /ˈvaɪələns/ *noun* (no plural) being violent: *Do you think there's too much violence on TV?*

violent 🔑 /ˈvaɪələnt/ *adjective* A person or thing that is violent is very strong and dangerous and hurts people: *a violent man* ◇ *a violent storm* ▶ **violently** *adverb*: *Did she behave violently towards you?*

violet /ˈvaɪələt/ *noun* a small purple flower ▶ **violet** *adjective* with a purple colour

violin /ˌvaɪəˈlɪn/ *noun* a musical instrument made of wood, with strings across it. You play a violin with a **bow**: *I play the violin.*

VIP /ˌviː aɪ ˈpiː/ *noun* a person who is famous or important. **VIP** is short for 'very important person': *The President is a VIP.*

virtually /ˈvɜːtʃuəli/ *adverb* almost: *The two boys look virtually the same.*

virtue /ˈvɜːtʃuː/ *noun* good behaviour; a good quality or habit: *Patience is just one of her virtues.*

virus /ˈvaɪrəs/ *noun* (*plural* **viruses**) **1** a very small living thing that can make you ill: *a flu virus* **2** a program that enters your computer and stops it working

visa /ˈviːzə/ *noun* a special piece of paper or mark in your passport to show that you can go into a country

visible /ˈvɪzəbl/ *adjective* If something is **visible**, you can see it: *Stars are only visible at night.* OPPOSITE **invisible**

vision /ˈvɪʒn/ *noun* **1** (no plural) the power to see; sight: *He wears glasses because he has poor vision.* **2** (*plural* **visions**) a picture in your mind; a dream: *They have a vision of a world without war.*

visit 🔑 /ˈvɪzɪt/ *verb* (**visits**, **visiting**, **visited**) to go to see a person or place for a short time: *Have you ever visited the National Museum?* ◇ *She visited me in hospital.* ▶ **visit** *noun*: *This is my first visit to Mwanza.* ◇ *He promised to pay us a visit next year.*

visitor 🔑 /ˈvɪzɪtə(r)/ *noun* a person who goes to see another person or a place for a short time: *The old lady never has any visitors.* ◇ *Millions of visitors come to East Africa every year.*

visual /ˈvɪʒuəl/ *adjective* of or about seeing: *Painting and cinema are visual arts.*

vital /ˈvaɪtl/ *adjective* very important; that

you must do or have: *It's vital that she sees a doctor – she's very ill.*

vitamin /ˈvɪtəmɪn/ *noun* one of the things in food that you need to be healthy: *Oranges are full of vitamin C.*

vivid /ˈvɪvɪd/ *adjective* **1** with a strong bright colour: *vivid yellow* **2** that makes a very clear picture in your mind: *I had a very vivid dream last night.* ▶ **vividly** *adverb*: *I vividly remember the first day we met.*

vocabulary /vəˈkæbjələri/ *noun* **1** (no plural) all the words in a language **2** (*plural* **vocabularies**) a list of words in a lesson or book: *We have to learn this new vocabulary for homework.* **3** (*plural* **vocabularies**) all the words that someone knows

voice 🔑 /vɔɪs/ *noun* the sounds that you make when you speak or sing: *Kisoso has a very deep voice.*
raise your voice to speak very loudly

volcano /vɒlˈkeɪnəʊ/ *noun* (*plural* **volcanoes**) a mountain with a hole in the top where fire, gas and hot liquid rock (called **lava**) sometimes come out ▶ **volcanic** /vɒlˈkænɪk/ *adjective*: *volcanic rocks*

volleyball /ˈvɒlibɔːl/ *noun* (no plural) a game where two teams try to hit a ball over a high net with their hands

volt /vəʊlt/ *noun* a measure of electricity ℹ The short way of writing 'volt' is **V**.

volume /ˈvɒljuːm/ *noun* **1** (no plural) the amount of space that something fills, or the amount of space inside something: *What is the volume of this box?* **2** (no plural) the amount of sound that something makes: *I can't hear the radio. Can you turn the volume up?*
3 (*plural* **volumes**) a book, especially one of a set: *The dictionary is in two volumes.*

volume

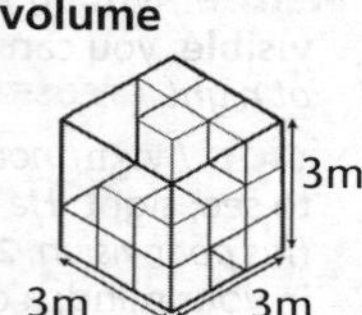

volume = 27m³ / 27 cubic metres

voluntarily /ˈvɒləntrəli/ *adverb* because you want to, not because you must: *She wasn't asked to leave – she went voluntarily.*

voluntary /ˈvɒləntri/ *adjective* **1** If something is **voluntary**, you do it because you want to, not because you must: *She made a voluntary decision to stay and help the teacher.* OPPOSITE **compulsory** **2** If work is **voluntary**, you are not paid to do it: *He does voluntary work at a children's hospital.*

volunteer¹ /ˌvɒlənˈtɪə(r)/ *verb* (**volunteers, volunteering, volunteered** /ˌvɒlənˈtɪəd/) to say that you will do something that you do not have to do: *I volunteered to do the washing-up.*

volunteer² /ˌvɒlənˈtɪə(r)/ *noun* a person who says they will do a job that they do not have to do, or without being paid: *They're asking for volunteers to help repair the road.*

vomit /ˈvɒmɪt/ *verb* (**vomits, vomiting, vomited**) When you **vomit**, food comes up from your stomach and out of your mouth. ℹ It is more usual to say **be sick**. ▶ **vomit** *noun* (no plural) the food that comes up from your stomach when you **vomit**

vote 🔑 /vəʊt/ *verb* (**votes, voting, voted**) to choose someone or something by putting up your hand or writing on a piece of paper: *Who did you vote for in the election?* ▶ **vote** *noun*: *There were 96 votes for the plan and 25 against.*

voter /ˈvəʊtə(r)/ *noun* a person who votes in a political election

voucher /ˈvaʊtʃə(r)/ *noun* a piece of paper that you can use instead of money to pay for something: *They received vouchers for uniforms and books.*

vow /vaʊ/ *verb* (**vows, vowing, vowed** /vaʊd/)

> ❖ **PRONUNCIATION**
>
> **Vow** sounds like **now**.

to make a serious promise: *We vowed we would stay friends for ever.* ▶ **vow** *noun*: *She made a vow never to go there again.*

vowel /ˈvaʊəl/ *noun* one of the letters *a, e, i, o* or *u*, or the sound that you make when you say it ➲ Look at **consonant**.

voyage /ˈvɔɪɪdʒ/ *noun* a long journey by boat or in space: *a voyage from London to New York*

vs *short for* VERSUS

vulture /ˈvʌltʃə(r)/ *noun* a large bird that eats dead animals. **Vultures** have no feathers on their head and neck.

vulture

Ww

W, w /ˈdʌblju:/ *noun* (*plural* **W's, w's** /ˈdʌblju:z/)the twenty-third letter of the English alphabet: *'Water' begins with a 'W'.*

wade /weɪd/ *verb* (**wades, wading, waded**) to walk through water: *Can we wade across the river, or is it too deep?*

wag /wæg/ *verb* (**wags, wagging, wagged** /wægd/) to move or make something move from side to side or up and down: *She wagged her finger at me.* ◇ *My dog's tail wags when he's happy.*

wages /ˈweɪdʒɪz/ *noun* (plural) the money that someone receives every week for the work that they do: *The workers' wages are paid every Friday.* ◇ *low wages*

wagon /ˈwægən/ *noun* **1** a vehicle with four wheels that a horse pulls **2** a part of a train where goods are carried

wail /weɪl/ *verb* (**wails, wailing, wailed** /weɪld/) to make a long sad cry or noise: *The little boy started wailing for his mother.*

waist /weɪst/ *noun* the part around the middle of your body ➲ picture on page A13

waistcoat /ˈweɪskəʊt/ *noun* a piece of clothing like a jacket with no sleeves

waistcoat

wait¹ /weɪt/ *verb* (**waits, waiting, waited**) to stay in one place until something happens or until someone or something comes: *If I'm late, please wait for me.* ◇ *We've been waiting a long time.*

I can't wait words that you use when you are very excited about something that is going to happen: *I can't wait to see you again!*

keep someone waiting to make someone wait because you are late or busy: *I'm sorry to have kept you waiting – my bus was late.*

wait and see to wait and find out later: *'What have you got in the box?' 'Wait and see!'*

wait up to not go to bed until someone comes home: *I will be home late tonight so don't wait up for me.*

wait² /weɪt/ *noun* a time when you wait: *We had a long wait for the bus.*

waiter /ˈweɪtə(r)/ *noun* a man who brings food and drink to your table in a restaurant

waiting room /ˈweɪtɪŋ ru:m/ *noun* a room where people can sit and wait, for example to see a doctor

waitress /ˈweɪtrəs/ *noun* (*plural* **waitresses**) a woman who brings food and drink to your table in a restaurant

wake /weɪk/ (also **wake up**) *verb* (**wakes, waking, woke** /wəʊk/, **has woken** /ˈwəʊkən/) **1** to stop sleeping: *What time did you wake up this morning?* **2** to make someone stop sleeping: *The noise woke me up.* ◇ *Don't wake the baby.*
ℹ It is more usual to say **wake up** than **wake**.

walk¹ /wɔ:k/ *verb* (**walks, walking, walked** /wɔ:kt/) to move on your legs, but not run: *I usually walk to school.* ◇ *We walked 20 kilometres today.*

walk out to leave suddenly because you are angry: *He walked out of the meeting.*

walk² /wɔ:k/ *noun* a journey on foot: *The beach is a short walk from our house.* ◇ *We had a nice walk.*

go for a walk to walk somewhere because you enjoy it: *It was a lovely day so we went for a walk in the park.*

walker /ˈwɔ:kə(r)/ *noun* a person who is walking

wall /wɔ:l/ *noun* **1** a side of a building or room: *There are two pictures on the wall.* ➲ Picture at **ceiling**. **2** a thing made of stones or bricks around a garden, field, town, etc: *There's a high wall around the prison.*

wallet

wallet /ˈwɒlɪt/ *noun* a small flat case for paper money, that you can carry in your pocket

wallpaper /ˈwɔ:lpeɪpə(r)/ *noun* (no plural) special paper that you use for covering the walls of a room

wananchi *plural of* MWANANCHI

wand /wɒnd/ *noun* a thin stick that people hold when they are doing magic tricks

wander /ˈwɒndə(r)/ *verb* (**wanders, wandering, wandered** /ˈwɒndəd/)

> ❖ **PRONUNCIATION**
>
> **Wander** sounds like **fonder**.

to walk slowly with no special plan: *We wandered around the town until the shops opened.*

want /wɒnt/ *verb* (**wants, wanting, wanted**) **1** to wish to have or do something: *Do you want a drink?* ◇ *I want to go to Italy.* ◇ *She wanted me to give her some money.*

> ❖ **SPEAKING**
>
> **Would like** is more polite than **want**: *Would you like something to eat?*

2 to need something: *The roof wants fixing.*

war /wɔː(r)/ *noun* fighting between countries or between groups of people: *the First World War*
at war fighting: *The two countries have been at war for five years.*
declare war to start a war: *In 1812 Napoleon declared war on Russia.*

ward /wɔːd/ *noun* a big room in a hospital that has beds for the patients

warden /ˈwɔːdn/ *noun* a person whose job is to look after a place and the people in it: *He is a game warden in the National Park.*

warder /ˈwɔːdə(r)/ *noun* a person who guards prisoners in a prison

wardrobe /ˈwɔːdrəʊb/ *noun* a cupboard where you hang your clothes

warehouse /ˈweəhaʊs/ *noun* (*plural* **warehouses** /ˈweəhaʊzɪz/) a big building where people keep things before they sell them: *a furniture warehouse*

warm[1] /wɔːm/ *adjective* (**warmer, warmest**) **1** a little hot: *It's warm in the sunshine.* ◇ *We went near the stove to keep warm.* **2** Warm clothes are clothes that stop you feeling cold: *It's cold in the mountains, so take some warm clothes with you.* **3** friendly and kind: *Nafula is a very warm person.* ⓘ The noun is **warmth**.
OPPOSITE **cold** ▶ **warmly** *adverb*: *The children were warmly dressed.* ◇ *He thanked me warmly.*

warm[2] /wɔːm/ *verb* (**warms, warming, warmed** /wɔːmd/)
warm up 1 to become warmer, or make someone or something warmer: *I warmed up some soup for lunch.* ◇ *It was cold this morning, but it's warming up now.* **2** to prepare to do an activity or sport by practising gently: *You must warm up before a race, or you might pull a muscle.*

warmth /wɔːmθ/ *noun* (no plural) **1** heat: *the warmth of the sun* **2** being kind and friendly: *the warmth of his smile* ➲ Look at **warm**[1].

warn /wɔːn/ *verb* (**warns, warning, warned** /wɔːnd/) to tell someone about danger or about something bad that may happen: *I warned him not to go too close to the fire.*

warning /ˈwɔːnɪŋ/ *noun* something that tells you about danger or about something bad that may happen: *There was a warning on the gate: 'Beware of the dog.'*

warthog /ˈwɔːthɒg/ *noun* a wild animal like a large pig with two very large teeth (called **tusks**)

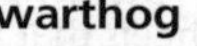

was *form of* BE

wash[1] /wɒʃ/ *verb* (**washes, washing, washed** /wɒʃt/)
1 to clean someone, something or yourself with water: *Have you washed the floor?* ◇ *Wash your hands before you eat.* ◇ *I washed and dressed quickly.* ➲ Look at **washing**. **2** (used about water) to flow somewhere: *The sea washed over my feet.* **3** to move something with water: *The house was washed away by the river.*
wash up to clean the plates, spoons, forks, etc. after a meal: *I washed up after dinner.*

wash[2] /wɒʃ/ *noun* (no plural) cleaning something with water: *I gave my hands a quick wash.*
have a wash to wash yourself: *I had a quick wash.*
in the wash being washed: *All my socks are in the wash!*

washbasin /ˈwɒʃbeɪsn/ *noun* the place in a bathroom where you wash your hands and face ➲ Picture at **plug**[1].

washing 🔑 /ˈwɒʃɪŋ/ *noun* (no plural) clothes that you need to wash or that you have washed: *Shall I hang the washing outside to dry?* ◇ *I've done the washing.*

washing machine /ˈwɒʃɪŋ məʃiːn/ *noun* a machine that washes clothes

washing powder /ˈwɒʃɪŋ paʊdə(r)/ *noun* (no plural) soap powder for washing clothes

washing-up /ˌwɒʃɪŋ ˈʌp/ *noun* (no plural) cleaning the plates, knives, forks, etc. after a meal: *I'll do the washing-up.*

washing-up liquid /ˌwɒʃɪŋ ˈʌp lɪkwɪd/ *noun* (no plural) liquid soap that you use for washing plates, pans, etc.

wasn't /ˈwɒznt/ = **was not**

wasp /wɒsp/ *noun* a yellow and black insect that flies and has a small sharp part that can hurt you (a **sting**) ➲ Picture at **insect**.

waste¹ 🔑 /weɪst/ *verb* (**wastes, wasting, wasted**) to use too much of something or not use something in a good way: *She wastes money on sweets.* ◇ *He wasted his time at school – he didn't do any work.*

waste² 🔑 /weɪst/ *noun* (no plural) **1** not using something in a useful way: *It's a waste to throw away all this food!* ◇ *This watch was a waste of money – it's broken already!* **2** things that people throw away because they are not useful: *A lot of waste from the factories goes into this river.*

waste³ 🔑 /weɪst/ *adjective* that you do not want because it is not good or useful: *waste paper* ◇ *waste ground*

waste-paper basket /ˌweɪst ˈpeɪpə bɑːskɪt/ *noun* a container where you put things like paper that you do not want

watch¹ 🔑 /wɒtʃ/ *verb* (**watches, watching, watched** /wɒtʃt/) **1** to look at someone or something for some time: *She watched the children playing in the yard.* ◇ *We watched television all evening.* ◇ *Watch how I do this.* ➲ Look at **see**. **2** to look after something or someone: *Could you watch my bag while I buy the tickets?*
watch out to be careful because of someone or something dangerous: *Watch out! There's a car coming.*
watch out for someone or **something** to look carefully and be ready for someone or something dangerous: *Watch out for animals on the road.*

watch² 🔑 /wɒtʃ/ *noun* **1** (*plural* **watches**) a thing that shows what time it is. You wear a watch on your arm: *She kept looking at her watch.* ➲ Look at **clock**. **2** (no plural) the action of watching something in case of danger or problems: *The soldier was keeping watch at the gate.*

watchman /ˈwɒtʃmən/ *noun* (*plural* **watchmen** /ˈwɒtʃmən/) a man whose job is to guard a building such as a bank or a factory, especially at night

water¹ 🔑 /ˈwɔːtə(r)/ *noun* (no plural) the liquid in rivers, lakes and seas that people and animals drink: *a glass of water*

water² /ˈwɔːtə(r)/ *verb* (**waters, watering, watered** /ˈwɔːtəd/) **1** to give water to plants: *Have you watered the plants?* **2** When your eyes **water**, they fill with tears: *The smoke made my eyes water.*

waterbuck /ˈwɔːtəbʌk/ *noun* a large **antelope** that lives near rivers and lakes

watercolour /ˈwɔːtəkʌlə(r)/ *noun* a picture that you make with paint and water

waterfall /ˈwɔːtəfɔːl/ *noun* a place where water falls from a high place to a low place

watering can /ˈwɔːtərɪŋ kæn/ *noun* a container that you use for giving water to plants

watermelon /ˈwɔːtəmelən/ *noun* a big round fruit with a thick green skin. It is pink inside with a lot of black seeds.

watermelon

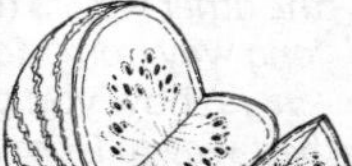

waterproof /ˈwɔːtəpruːf/ *adjective* If something is **waterproof**, it does not let water go through it: *a waterproof watch* ◇ *waterproof clothing*

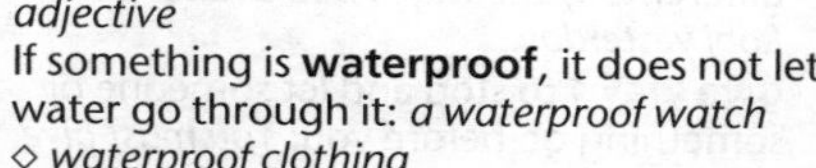

waterskiing /ˈwɔːtəskiːɪŋ/ *noun* (no plural) the sport of moving fast over water on long boards (called **waterskis**), pulled by a boat

wave¹ 🔑 /weɪv/ *verb* (**waves, waving, waved** /weɪvd/) **1** to move your hand from side to side in the air to say hello or goodbye or to make a sign to someone: *She waved to me as the bus left the station.* ◇ *Who are you waving at?* **2** to move something quickly from side to side in the air: *The children were waving flags as the*

President's car drove past. **3** to move up and down or from side to side: *The flags were waving in the wind.*

wave² 🔑 /weɪv/ *noun* **1** one of the lines of water that moves across the top of the sea: *Children were playing in the waves.* **2** moving your hand from side to side in the air, to say hello or goodbye or to make a sign to someone: *He gave a wave as the bus drove off.* **3** a gentle curve in hair **4** a movement like a wave on the sea, that carries heat, light, sound, etc: *radio waves*

wavy /ˈweɪvi/ *adjective* (**wavier, waviest**) Something that is **wavy** has small curves in it: *She has wavy hair.*

wavy

a **wavy** line

a **straight** line

a **dotted** line

wax /wæks/ *noun* (no plural) the stuff that is used for making **candles** (= tall sticks that you burn to give light) or for making things shine

way 🔑 /weɪ/ *noun* **1** (*plural* **ways**) a road or path that you must follow to go to a place: *Can you tell me the way to the station, please?* ◇ *I lost my way and I had to look at the map.* **2** (*plural* **ways**) a direction; where someone or something is going or looking: *Come this way.* ◇ *She was looking the other way.* **3** (no plural) distance: *It's a long way from Mombasa to Kitale.* **4** (*plural* **ways**) how you do something: *What is the best way to learn a language?* ◇ *He smiled in a very friendly way.*

by the way words that you say when you are going to talk about something different: *By the way, I had a letter from Robi yesterday.*

give way 1 to stop and let someone or something go before you: *You must give way to traffic coming from the right.* **2** to agree with someone when you did not agree before: *After a long argument, my parents finally gave way and said I could go out.* **3** to break: *The ladder gave way and Kisoso fell to the ground.*

in the way in front of someone so that you stop them from seeing something or moving: *I couldn't see the blackboard because the teacher was in the way.*

no way a way of saying 'no' more strongly: *'Can I borrow your bike?' 'No way!'*

on the way when you are going somewhere: *I stopped to have a drink on the way to school.*

out of the way not in a place where you stop someone from moving or doing something: *Can you move your bag out of the way? I can't get past.*

the right way up or **round** with the correct part at the top or at the front: *Is this picture the right way up?*

the wrong way up or **round** with the wrong part at the top or at the front: *Those two words are the wrong way round.*

way in where you go into a building: *Here's the museum. Where's the way in?*

way of life how people live: *Is the way of life in Europe different from America?*

way out where you go out of a place: *I can't find the way out.*

wazungu *plural of* MZUNGU

WC /ˌdʌbljuː ˈsiː/ *noun* a toilet ℹ **WC** is short for 'water closet'.

we 🔑 /wiː/ *pronoun* (plural) I and another person or other people; you and I: *Odoi and I quarrelled yesterday – we're friends again now, though.* ◇ *Are we late?*

weak 🔑 /wiːk/ *adjective* (**weaker, weakest**)

❖ **PRONUNCIATION**

Weak and **week** sound the same.

1 not powerful or strong: *She felt very weak after her long illness.* ◇ *a weak government* ➲ picture on page A5 **2** that can break easily: *The bridge was too weak to carry the heavy lorry.* **3** that you cannot see, taste, smell, hear or feel clearly: *weak tea* OPPOSITE **strong**

❖ **WORD FAMILY**

weak weaken weakness

weaken /ˈwiːkən/ *verb* (**weakens, weakening, weakened** /ˈwiːkənd/) to become less strong or to make someone or something less strong: *He was weakened by the illness.* OPPOSITE **strengthen**

weakness 🔑 /ˈwiːknəs/ *noun* **1** (no plural) not being strong: *I have a feeling of weakness in my legs.* **2** (*plural* **weaknesses**) something that is wrong or bad in a person or thing: *What are your strengths and weaknesses?* OPPOSITE **strength**

wealth /welθ/ *noun* (no plural) having a lot of money, land, etc: *He is a man of great wealth.* ▶ **wealthy** /ˈwelθi/ *adjective* (**wealthier**, **wealthiest**) rich: *a wealthy family*

weapon 🔑 /ˈwepən/ *noun* a thing that you use for fighting. Guns and bombs are weapons: *He was carrying a weapon.*

wear[1] 🔑 /weə(r)/ *verb* (**wears**, **wearing**, **wore** /wɔː(r)/, **has worn** /wɔːn/)

> ❖ **PRONUNCIATION**
>
> **Wear** and **where** sound the same.

to have clothes, etc. on your body: *She was wearing a red dress.* ◇ *I wear glasses.*
wear off to become less strong: *The pain is wearing off.*
wear out to become thin or damaged because you have used it a lot; to make something do this: *Children's shoes usually wear out very quickly.*
wear someone out to make someone very tired: *She wore herself out by working too hard.*

wear[2] /weə(r)/ *noun* (no plural) **1** clothes: *sportswear* **2** using something and making it old: *These boots are showing signs of wear – I need a new pair.*

weather 🔑 /ˈweðə(r)/ *noun* (no plural) how much sun, rain, wind, etc. there is at a certain time, or how hot or cold it is: *What's the weather going to be like tomorrow?* ◇ *bad weather*

weather forecast /ˈweðə fɔːkɑːst/ *noun* words on television, radio or in a newspaper that tell you what the weather will be like: *The weather forecast is good for tomorrow.*

weathervane /ˈweðəveɪn/ (also **wind vane**) *noun* an object on top of a building that turns in the wind and shows which direction the wind is blowing from

weathervane

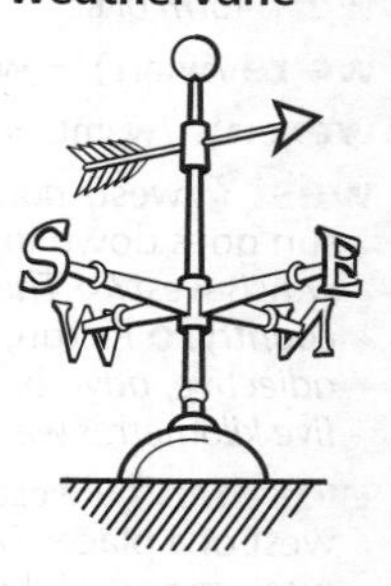

weave /wiːv/ *verb* (**weaves**, **weaving**, **wove** /wəʊv/, **has woven** /ˈwəʊvn/) to make cloth by putting threads over and under one another: *This cloth is woven by hand.*

weaver bird /ˈwiːvə bɜːd/ *noun* a small bird that builds a round nest, like a ball, with a small hole in it where the bird goes in and out

web /web/ *noun* **1** (*plural* **webs**) a thin net that a spider makes to catch flies ➲ Picture at **spider**. **2** (no plural) **the Web** the system that makes it possible for you to see information from all over the world on your computer SAME MEANING **World Wide Web**

website 🔑 /ˈwebsaɪt/ *noun* a place on the Internet that you can look at to find out information about something: *I found this information on the company's website.*

we'd /wiːd/ **1** = **we had** **2** = **we would**

wedding 🔑 /ˈwedɪŋ/ *noun* a time when a man and a woman get married: *Kendi and Rono invited me to their wedding.* ◇ *wedding guests*

Wednesday 🔑 /ˈwenzdeɪ/ *noun* the fourth day of the week, next after Tuesday

weed[1] /wiːd/ *noun* a wild plant that grows where you do not want it: *The garden is full of weeds.*

weed[2] /wiːd/ *verb* (**weeds**, **weeding**, **weeded**) to pull **weeds** out of the ground

week 🔑 /wiːk/ *noun* **1** a time of seven days, usually from Sunday to the next Saturday: *I'm taking the exam next week.* ◇ *I have English homework twice a week.* ◇ *I saw him two weeks ago.* ℹ A **fortnight** is the same as two weeks. **2** Monday to Friday: *He works during the week but not at weekends.*

weekday /ˈwiːkdeɪ/ *noun* any day except Saturday or Sunday: *She only works on weekdays.*

weekend 🔑 /ˌwiːkˈend/ *noun* Saturday and Sunday: *What are you doing at the weekend?*

weekly /ˈwiːkli/ *adjective*, *adverb* that happens or comes every week or once a week: *a weekly magazine* ◇ *He is paid weekly.*

weep /wiːp/ *verb* (**weeps**, **weeping**, **wept** /wept/, **has wept**) to cry
ℹ **Cry** is the word that we usually use.

weevil /ˈwiːvl/ *noun* an insect that has a very hard body and can destroy crops

weigh 🔑 /weɪ/ *verb* (**weighs**, **weighing**, **weighed** /weɪd/)

❖ **PRONUNCIATION**

Weigh and **way** sound the same.

1 to measure how heavy someone or something is using a machine called **scales**: *The shop assistant weighed the tomatoes.* **2** to have a certain number of kilograms, etc: *'How much do you weigh?' 'I weigh 55 kilograms.'*

weight /weɪt/ *noun*

❖ **PRONUNCIATION**

Weight and **wait** sound the same.

1 (no plural) how heavy someone or something is: *Do you know the weight of the parcel?* **2** (*plural* **weights**) a piece of metal that you use on **scales** for measuring how heavy something is: *a set of weights*
lose weight to become thinner and less heavy: *Fatma lost a lot of weight when she was ill.*
put on weight to become fatter and heavier

weird /wɪəd/ *adjective* (**weirder**, **weirdest**) very strange: *a weird dream*

welcome[1] /ˈwelkəm/ *adjective* If someone or something is welcome, you are happy to have or see them: *The cool drink was welcome on such a hot day.* ◇ *Welcome to our school!*
be welcome to to be allowed to do or have something: *If you come to Kenya again, you're welcome to stay with us.*
make someone welcome to show a visitor that you are happy to see them: *They made us very welcome.*
you're welcome polite words that you say when someone has said 'thank you': *'Thank you.' 'You're welcome.'*

welcome[2] /ˈwelkəm/ *verb* (**welcome**, **welcoming**, **welcomed** /ˈwelkəmd/) to show that you are happy to have or see someone or something: *He came to the door to welcome us.* ▶ **welcome** *noun* (no plural): *They gave us a great welcome when we arrived.*

weld /weld/ *verb* (**welds**, **welding**, **welded**) to join pieces of metal together using heat

welfare /ˈwelfeə(r)/ *noun* (no plural) the health and happiness of a person: *The school looks after the welfare of its pupils.*

we'll /wiːl/ **1** = **we will** **2** = **we shall**

well[1] /wel/ *adverb* (**better**, **best**) **1** in a good or right way: *You speak English very well.* ◇ *These shoes are very well made.* OPPOSITE **badly** **2** completely or very much: *I don't know Njoki very well.* ◇ *Shake the bottle well before you open it.*
as well also: *'I'm going out.' 'Can I come as well?'*
as well as something and also: *She has a flat in Nairobi as well as a house in Nyeri.*
do well to be successful: *He did well in his exams.*
may or **might as well** words that you use to say that you will do something, often because there is nothing else to do: *If you've finished the work, you may as well go home.*
well done! words that you say to someone who has done something good: *'I passed the exam!' 'Well done!'*

well[2] /wel/ *adjective* (**better**, **best**) healthy; not ill: *'How are you?' 'I'm very well, thanks.'*

well[3] /wel/ *exclamation* **1** a word that you often say when you are starting to speak: *'Do you like it?' 'Well, I'm not really sure.'* **2** a word that you use to show surprise: *Well, that's strange!*

well[4] /wel/ *noun* a deep hole for getting water or oil from under the ground: *an oil well*

well known /ˌwel ˈnəʊn/ *adjective* famous: *Her books are not well known.* ◇ *a well-known writer* OPPOSITE **unknown**

well off /ˌwel ˈɒf/ *adjective* rich: *They are very well off and they live in a big house.*

went *form of* GO[1]

wept *form of* WEEP

were *form of* BE

we're /wɪə(r)/ = **we are**

weren't /wɜːnt/ = **were not**

west /west/ *noun* (no plural) where the sun goes down in the evening: *Which way is west?* ◇ *They live in the west of the country.* ➲ Picture at **compass**. ▶ **west** *adjective, adverb*: *West Pokot* ◇ *The town is five kilometres west of here.*

western /ˈwestən/ *adjective* in or of the west of a place: *There will be storms in the western part of the country.*

wet /wet/ *adjective* (**wetter**, **wettest**) **1** covered in water or another liquid; not dry: *This towel is wet – can I have a dry one?* ◇ *wet paint* ➲ picture on page A5 **2** with a lot of rain: *a wet day* OPPOSITE **dry**

we've /wiv/ = **we have**

whale

whale /weɪl/ *noun* a very big animal that lives in the sea and looks like a fish

> ❖ **PRONUNCIATION**
> When a word begins with 'wh' we do not usually say the 'h'. So **whale** and **wail** sound the same.

what 🔑 /wɒt/ *pronoun, adjective* **1** a word that you use when you ask about someone or something: *What's your name?* ◇ *What are you reading?* ◇ *What time is it?* ◇ *What kind of music do you like?* **2** the thing that: *I don't know what this word means.* ◇ *Tell me what to do.* **3** a word that you use to show surprise or other strong feelings: *What a terrible day!* ◇ *What a beautiful picture!*
what about ...? words that you use when you suggest something: *What about going to the park today?*
what ... for? why?; for what use?: *What did you say that for?* ◇ *What's this machine for?*
what is ... like? words that you use when you want to know more about someone or something: *'What's her brother like?' 'He's very nice.'*
what's on? what film, television programme, etc. is being shown?: *What's on TV tonight?*
what's up? what is wrong?: *You look sad. What's up?*

whatever[1] 🔑 /wɒt'evə(r)/ *adjective* of any kind; any or every: *These animals eat whatever food they can find.*

whatever[2] 🔑 /wɒt'evə(r)/ *pronoun* **1** anything or everything: *I'll do whatever I can to help you.* **2** it does not matter what: *Whatever you do, don't be late.*

what's /wɒts/ **1** = **what is** **2** = **what has**

wheat /wi:t/ *noun* (no plural) a plant with seeds (called **grain**) that we can make into flour

wheat

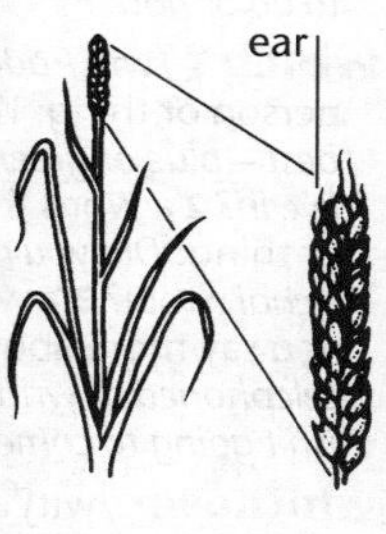

wheel[1] 🔑 /wi:l/ *noun* a thing like a circle that turns round to move something. Cars and bicycles have wheels: *His favourite toy is a dog on wheels.* ➲ Picture at **bicycle**, **car**.

wheel[2] /wi:l/ *verb* (**wheels, wheeling, wheeled** /wi:ld/) to push along something that has wheels: *I wheeled my bicycle up the hill.*

wheelbarrow /'wi:lbærəʊ/ (also **barrow**) *noun* a container with a wheel and two handles that you use outside to carry things

wheelbarrow

wheelchair /'wi:ltʃeə(r)/ *noun* a chair with wheels for someone who cannot walk

when 🔑 /wen/ *adverb, conjunction* **1** at what time: *When did she arrive?* ◇ *I don't know when his birthday is.* **2** at the time that: *I saw her in May, when she visited us.* ◇ *He came back when I called him.*

whenever 🔑 /wen'evə(r)/ *conjunction* **1** at any time: *Come and see us whenever you want.* **2** every time that: *Whenever I see her, she talks about her rich parents.*

where 🔑 /weə(r)/ *adverb, conjunction* **1** in or to what place: *Where do you live?* ◇ *I asked her where she lived.* ◇ *Where is she going?* **2** in which; at which: *This is the estate where I live.*

whereas 🔑 /weər'æz/ *conjunction* a word that you use between two different ideas: *Shema likes football, whereas I don't.*

wherever 🔑 /weər'eve(r)/ *adverb, conjunction* **1** at, in or to any place: *Sit wherever you like.* **2** a way of saying 'where' more strongly: *Wherever did I put my keys?*

whether 🔑 /'weðə(r)/ *conjunction* **1** if: *She asked me whether I spoke French.* **2** a word that we use to talk about choosing between two things: *I don't know whether to go or not.*

which /wɪtʃ/ *adjective, pronoun* **1** what person or thing: *Which colour do you like best – blue or green?* ◇ *Which flat do you live in?* **2** a word that shows what person or thing: *Did you read the poem (which) Achal wrote?* **3** a word that you use before you say more about something: *He hasn't telephoned or written, which means that he isn't going to come.*

whichever /wɪtʃˈevə(r)/ *adjective, pronoun* any person or thing: *Here are two books – take whichever you want.*

while[1] /waɪl/ *conjunction* **1** during the time that; when: *While I was coming home from school I started to feel ill.* **2** at the same time as: *I listen to the radio while I'm eating my breakfast.*

while[2] /waɪl/ *noun* (no plural) some time: *Let's sit here for a while.* ◇ *I'm going home in a while.*

whine /waɪn/ *verb* (**whines**, **whining**, **whined** /waɪnd/) to make a long high sad sound: *The dog was whining outside the door.*

whip[1] /wɪp/ *noun* a long piece of leather or rope with a handle, for hitting animals or people

whip[2] /wɪp/ *verb* (**whips**, **whipping**, **whipped** /wɪpt/) **1** to hit an animal or a person with a **whip**: *The farmer whipped the horse to make it go faster.* **2** to mix food very quickly with a fork until it is light and thick: *Whip the whites of two eggs.*

whirl /wɜːl/ *verb* (**whirls**, **whirling**, **whirled** /wɜːld/) to move round and round very quickly: *The dancers whirled round the room.*

whisk[1] /wɪsk/ *verb* (**whisks**, **whisking**, **whisked** /wɪskt/) **1** to mix eggs or cream very quickly **2** to move someone or something very quickly: *The President was whisked away in a helicopter.*

whisk[2] /wɪsk/ *noun* a tool that you use for mixing eggs or cream

whisker /ˈwɪskə(r)/ *noun* one of the long hairs that grow near the mouths of cats, mice and other animals ➲ Picture at **cat**.

whisper /ˈwɪspə(r)/ *verb* (**whispers**, **whispering**, **whispered** /ˈwɪspəd/) to speak very quietly: *He whispered so that he would not wake the baby up.* ▶ **whisper** *noun*: *She spoke in a whisper.*

whistle[1] /ˈwɪsl/ *noun* **1** a small musical instrument that makes a long high sound when you blow it: *The referee blew his whistle to end the match.* **2** the long high sound that you make when you blow air out between your lips

whistle[2] /ˈwɪsl/ *verb* (**whistles**, **whistling**, **whistled** /ˈwɪsld/) to make a long high sound by blowing air out between your lips or through a **whistle**: *I saw Pembe and whistled to attract his attention.*

white[1] /waɪt/ *adjective* (**whiter**, **whitest**) **1** with the colour of snow or milk: *She has perfect white teeth.* ➲ Look at **coffee**. **2** with a pale colour: *white grapes*

white[2] /waɪt/ *noun* **1** (no plural) the colour of snow or milk: *She was dressed in white.* **2** (*plural* **whites**) a person with pale skin **3** (*plural* **whites**) the part inside an egg that is round the yellow middle part ➲ Picture at **egg**.

white ant /ˌwaɪt ˈænt/ = **termite**

whiteboard /ˈwaɪtbɔːd/ *noun* a white board that a teacher writes on with a special pen ➲ Look at **interactive**.

whizz /wɪz/ *verb* (**whizzes**, **whizzing**, **whizzed** /wɪzd/) to move very quickly: *The bullet whizzed past his head.*

who /huː/ *pronoun*

> ❖ **PRONUNCIATION**
>
> The beginning of **who** sounds like the beginning of **hot** because we say the 'h' but not the 'w'.

1 what person or people: *Who is that girl?* ◇ *I don't know who did it.* **2** a word that shows what person or people: *He's the boy who sits next to me in school.* ◇ *The people (who) I work with are very nice.*

who'd /huːd/ **1** = **who had** **2** = **who would**

whoever /huˈevə(r)/ *pronoun*

> ❖ **PRONUNCIATION**
>
> The beginning of **whoever** sounds like the beginning of **hot** because we say the 'h' but not the 'w'.

1 the person who; any person who: *Whoever broke the window must pay for it.* **2** a way of saying 'who' more strongly: *Whoever gave you those flowers?*

whole¹ 🗝 /həʊl/ *adjective*

> ❖ **PRONUNCIATION**
> **Whole** sounds just like **hole**.

complete; with no parts missing: *I'm so hungry I could eat a whole cow!* ◇ *We are going camping for a whole week.*

whole² 🗝 /həʊl/ *noun* (no plural) **1** all of something: *I spent the whole of the weekend working.* **2** a thing that is complete: *Two halves make a whole.*
on the whole in general: *On the whole, I think it's a good idea.*

whole number /ˌhəʊl ˈnʌmbə(r)/ *noun* a number that has no **fractions** (= parts of a number less than one): *Give your answer as a whole number.*

wholesale /ˈhəʊlseɪl/ *adverb, adjective* used about buying and selling goods in large quantities, usually to sell them again for a higher price: *They got the building materials wholesale.* ➲ Look at **retail**.
▶ **wholesaler** /ˈhəʊlseɪlə(r)/ *noun* a person who sells large quantities of goods to people so that they can sell them again: *fruit and vegetable wholesalers*

who'll /huːl/ = **who will**

whom 🗝 /huːm/ *pronoun*

> ❖ **PRONUNCIATION**
> The beginning of **whom** sounds like the beginning of **hot** because we say the 'h' but not the 'w'.

1 what person or people: *To whom did you give the money?* **2** a word that you use to say what person or people: *She's the woman whom I met on the bus.*

> ❖ **GRAMMAR**
> **Who** is the word that we usually use. You can also use this sentence without **who** or **whom**: *She's the woman I met on the bus.*

whooping cough /ˈhuːpɪŋ kɒf/ *noun* (no plural)

> ❖ **PRONUNCIATION**
> The beginning of **whooping** sounds like the beginning of **hot** because we say the 'h' but not the 'w'.

a serious illness, especially of children. If you have **whooping cough**, you make a loud noise when you breathe in after every cough.

who're /ˈhuːə(r)/ = **who are**

who's /huːz/ **1** = **who is** **2** = **who has**

whose 🗝 /huːz/ *adjective, pronoun*

> ❖ **PRONUNCIATION**
> The beginning of **whose** sounds like the beginning of **hot** because we say the 'h' but not the 'w'.

of which person: *Whose key is this?* ◇ *That's the boy whose sister is a singer.*

> ❖ **SPELLING**
> Be careful! **Whose** is not the same as **who's** although they sound the same: *The boy whose bike you borrowed is here.* ◇ *Here's the boy who's* (= who is) *cycling round Africa.*

who've /huːv/ = **who have**

why 🗝 /waɪ/ *adverb* for what reason: *Why are you late?* ◇ *I don't know why she's angry.*
why not words that you use to say that something is a good idea: *Why not ask Kirezi to go with you?*

wicked /ˈwɪkɪd/ *adjective* very bad: *Stealing is a wicked thing to do.*

wide¹ 🗝 /waɪd/ *adjective* (**wider**, **widest**) **1** far from one side to the other: *a wide road* OPPOSITE **narrow** **2** You use 'wide' to say or ask how far something is from one side to the other: *The table was 2 metres wide.* ◇ *How wide is the river?* ➲ picture on page A12 **3** completely open: *wide eyes* ⓘ The noun is **width**.

wide² /waɪd/ *adverb* completely; as far or as much as possible: *Open your mouth wide.* ◇ *I'm wide awake!*
wide apart a long way from each other: *She stood with her feet wide apart.*

widen /ˈwaɪdn/ *verb* (**widens**, **widening**, **widened** /ˈwaɪdnd/) to become wider; to make something wider: *They are widening the road.*

widespread /ˈwaɪdspred/ *adjective* If something is **widespread**, it is happening in many places: *The disease is becoming more widespread.*

widow /ˈwɪdəʊ/ *noun* a woman whose husband is dead

widower /ˈwɪdəʊə(r)/ *noun* a man whose wife is dead

width /wɪdθ/ *noun* how far it is from one side of something to the other; how wide something is: *The room is five metres in width.* ➲ picture on page A12

wife 🔑 /waɪf/ *noun* (*plural* **wives** /waɪvz/) the woman that a man is married to: *He met his wife in Paris.*

wig /wɪg/ *noun* a covering for your head made of hair that is not your own

wild 🔑 /waɪld/ *adjective* (**wilder**, **wildest**) **1** Wild plants and animals live or grow in nature, not with people: *wild pigs* ◇ *wild flowers* **2** excited; not controlled: *She was wild with anger.*

wildebeest

wildebeest /ˈwɪldəbiːst/ *noun* (*plural* **wildebeest**) a large **antelope** with a long head and a beard

wildlife /ˈwaɪldlaɪf/ *noun* (no plural) animals and plants in nature

will[1] 🔑 /wɪl/ *modal verb*

> ❖ **GRAMMAR**
>
> The negative form of **will** is **will not** or the short form **won't** /wəʊnt/: *They won't be there.*
>
> The short form of **will** is **'ll**. We often use this: *You'll* (= you will) *be late.* ◇ *He'll* (= he will) *drive you to the station.*

1 a word that shows the future: *Do you think she will come tomorrow?* **2** a word that you use when you agree or promise to do something: *I'll* (= I will) *carry your bag.* **3** a word that you use when you ask someone to do something: *Will you open the window, please?* ➲ Look at **modal verb**.

will[2] 🔑 /wɪl/ *noun* **1** (no plural) the power of your mind that makes you choose, decide and do things: *She has a very strong will and nobody can stop her doing what she wants to do.* **2** (no plural) what someone wants: *The man made him get into the car against his will* (= when he did not want to). **3** (*plural* **wills**) a piece of paper that says who will have your money, house, etc. when you die: *My grandmother left me some money in her will.*

willing /ˈwɪlɪŋ/ *adjective* ready and happy to do something: *I'm willing to lend you some money.* OPPOSITE **unwilling**
▸ **willingly** *adverb*: *I'll willingly help you.*
▸ **willingness** /ˈwɪlɪŋnəs/ *noun* (no plural): *willingness to help*

win 🔑 /wɪn/ *verb* (**wins**, **winning**, **won** /wʌn/, **has won**) **1** to be the best or the first in a game, race or competition: *Who won the race?* ◇ *Nafula won and I was second.* OPPOSITE **lose** **2** to receive something because you did well or tried hard: *I won a prize in the competition.* ◇ *Who won the gold medal?*

> ❖ **WORD BUILDING**
>
> Be careful! A person **earns** (not **wins**) money by working.

▸ **win** *noun*: *Our team has had five wins this year.*

> ❖ **WORD FAMILY**
>
> **win** **winner** **winning**

wind[1] 🔑 /wɪnd/ *noun*

> ❖ **PRONUNCIATION**
>
> **Wind** (noun) sounds like the beginning of **window**.

air that moves: *The wind blew his hat off.* ◇ *strong winds*

wind[2] /waɪnd/ *verb* (**winds**, **winding**, **wound** /waʊnd/, **has wound**)

> ❖ **PRONUNCIATION**
>
> **Wind** (verb) sounds like **kind**.

1 to make something long go round and round another thing: *The nurse wound the bandage around my arm.* **2** to turn a key or handle to make something work or move: *Wind the handle as fast as you can.* **3** A road or river that **winds** has a lot of bends and turns: *The path winds through the forest.*

wind farm /ˈwɪnd fɑːm/ *noun* a place where there are a lot of **wind turbines** for producing electricity

windmill /ˈwɪndmɪl/ *noun* a tall building with long flat parts (called **sails**) that turn in the wind

window 🔑 /ˈwɪndəʊ/ *noun* **1** an opening in a wall or in a car, etc. with glass in it: *She looked out of the window.* **2** an area o a computer screen that has a particular type of information in it: *You can close the window by clicking on the X.*

window ledge /ˈwɪndəʊ ledʒ/ = **windowsill**

windowpane /ˈwɪndəʊpeɪn/ *noun* a piece of glass in a window

window-shopping /ˈwɪndəʊ ʃɒpɪŋ/ *noun* (no plural) looking at things in shop windows when you do not intend to buy anything: *I went window-shopping.*

windowsill /ˈwɪndəʊsɪl/ (also **window ledge**) *noun* a shelf under a window

windscreen /ˈwɪndskriːn/ *noun* the big window at the front of a car ➲ Picture at **car**.

windscreen wiper /ˈwɪndskriːn waɪpə(r)/ *noun* a thing that cleans rain and dirt off the **windscreen** while you are driving

windsock /ˈwɪndsɒk/ *noun* a piece of light material that hangs on a pole and shows the direction of the wind

windsurfer /ˈwɪndsɜːfə(r)/ *noun* **1** a special board with a sail. You stand on it as it moves over the water. **2** a person who rides on a board like this

windsurfing

windsurfing /ˈwɪndsɜːfɪŋ/ *noun* (no plural) the sport of moving over water on a special board with a sail
ⓘ You can say **go windsurfing**.

wind turbine /ˈwɪnd tɜːbaɪn/ *noun* a tall structure with three long parts (called **sails**) that turn in the wind, used for producing electricity

wind vane /ˈwɪnd veɪn/ = **weathervane**

windy /ˈwɪndi/ *adjective* (**windier**, **windiest**) with a lot of wind: *It's very windy today!*

wine /waɪn/ *noun* an alcoholic drink. Wine is made from **grapes**: *red wine* ◇ *white wine*

wing /wɪŋ/ *noun* the part of a bird, an insect or a plane that helps it to fly: *The duck flapped its wings and flew off.* ➲ Picture at **bird**.

wink /wɪŋk/ *verb* (**winks**, **winking**, **winked** /wɪŋkt/) to close and open one eye quickly to make a friendly or secret sign: *She winked at me.* ▶ **wink** *noun*: *He gave me a wink.*

winner /ˈwɪnə(r)/ *noun* a person or animal that wins a game, race or competition: *The winner was given a prize.* OPPOSITE **loser**

winning /ˈwɪnɪŋ/ *adjective* that wins a game, race or competition: *the winning team*

winter /ˈwɪntə(r)/ *noun* in cool countries, the coldest part of the year: *It often snows in winter in the mountains.*

wipe[1] /waɪp/ *verb* (**wipes**, **wiping**, **wiped** /waɪpt/) to make something clean or dry with a cloth: *The waitress wiped the table.* ◇ *I washed my hands and wiped them on a towel.*
wipe off to take away something by wiping: *She wiped the writing off the blackboard.*
wipe out to destroy a place completely, or kill a lot of people: *The bombs wiped out many villages.*
wipe up to take away liquid by wiping with a cloth: *I wiped up the milk on the floor.*

wipe[2] /waɪp/ *noun* **1** the action of **wiping** something: *He gave the table a quick wipe.* **2** a piece of paper or thin cloth with a special liquid on it, that you use for cleaning things: *a box of face wipes* (= for cleaning your face)

wire /ˈwaɪə(r)/ *noun* a long piece of very thin metal: *electrical wires* ◇ *a piece of wire*

wireless /ˈwaɪələs/ *adjective* not using wires: *wireless technology*

wisdom /ˈwɪzdəm/ *noun* (no plural) knowing and understanding a lot about many things: *It is said that age brings wisdom.* ⓘ The adjective is **wise**.

wise /waɪz/ *adjective* (**wiser**, **wisest**) A person who is **wise** knows and understands a lot about many things: *a wise old man* ◇ *You made a wise c hoice.* ▶ **wisely** *adverb*: *Many people wisely stayed at home in the bad weather.*

wish[1] /wɪʃ/ *verb* (**wishes**, **wishing**, **wished** /wɪʃt/) **1** to want something that is not possible or that probably will not happen: *I wish I could fly! ◇ I wish I had passed the exam! ◇ I wish I were rich.*

❖ **GRAMMAR**

Look carefully at the tenses we use after **wish**: *Nduku can't come with us this afternoon. I wish she* ***could****. ◇ I wish I* ***had done*** *my homework yesterday. Then I would have passed the test.*

2 to say that you hope someone will have something: *I wished her a happy birthday.* **3** to want to do or have something: *I wish to see the manager.*

❖ **SPEAKING**

It is more usual to say **want** or **would like**.

wish for something to say to yourself that you want something and hope that it will happen: *You can't have everything you wish for.*

wish[2] 🔑 /wɪʃ/ *noun* (*plural* **wishes**) a feeling that you want something: *I have no wish to go.*
best wishes words that you write at the end of a letter, before your name, to show that you hope someone is well and happy: *See you soon. Best wishes, Tanei.*
make a wish to say to yourself that you want something and hope that it will happen: *Close your eyes and make a wish!*

wit /wɪt/ *noun* (no plural) speaking or writing in a clever and funny way

witch /wɪtʃ/ *noun* a woman in stories who uses magic to do bad things

witch doctor /ˈwɪtʃ dɒktə(r)/ *noun* a person that people believe has magic powers

with 🔑 /wɪð/ *preposition* **1** having or carrying: *a man with grey hair ◇ a house with a garden ◇ a woman with a suitcase* **2** a word that shows people or things are together: *I live with my parents. ◇ Mix the flour with milk. ◇ I agree with you.* **3** using: *I cut it with a knife. ◇ Fill the bottle with water.* **4** against: *I played a game with my sister.* **5** because of: *Her hands were shaking with nerves.*

withdraw /wɪðˈdrɔː/ *verb* (**withdraws, withdrawing, withdrew** /wɪðˈdruː/, **has withdrawn** /wɪðˈdrɔːn/) **1** to take something out or away: *He withdrew some money from his bank account.* **2** to move back or away: *The army withdrew from the town.* **3** to say that you will not take part in something: *Malika has withdrawn from the race.* ▶ **withdrawa** /wɪðˈdrɔːəl/ *noun*: *a withdrawal form* (= a form you use to take money out of your bank account)

wither /ˈwɪðə(r)/ *verb* (**withers, withering, withered** /ˈwɪðəd/) If a plan **withers**, it becomes dry and dies: *The plants withered in the hot sun.*

within 🔑 /wɪˈðɪn/ *preposition* **1** inside: *There are 400 prisoners within the prison walls.* **2** before the end of: *I will be back within an hour.* **3** not further than: *We liv within a kilometre of the school.*

without 🔑 /wɪˈðaʊt/ *preposition* **1** not having, showing or using something: *Don't go out without a coat on. ◇ a cup of coffee without milk* **2** not being with someone or something: *He left without me.*
do without to manage when somethin is not there: *There isn't any tea so we will have to do without.*
without doing something not doing something: *They left without saying goodbye.*

witness /ˈwɪtnəs/ *noun* (*plural* **witnesses**) **1** a person who sees something happen and can tell other people about it later: *There were two witnesses to the accident.* **2** a person in a **court of law** who tells what they saw ▶ **witness** *verb* (**witnesses, witnessing, witnessed** /ˈwɪtnəst/) to see something happen: *Sh witnessed a murder.*

witty /ˈwɪti/ *adjective* (**wittier, wittiest**) clever and funny: *a witty answer*

wives *plural of* WIFE

wobble /ˈwɒbl/ *verb* (**wobbles, wobbling, wobbled** /ˈwɒbld/) to move little from side to side: *That chair wobbles when you sit on it.* ▶ **wobbly** /ˈwɒbli/ *adjective* If something is **wobbly**, it moves a little from side to side: *a wobbly table*

woke, woken *forms of* WAKE

woman 🔑 /ˈwʊmən/ *noun* (*plural* **women** /ˈwɪmɪn/) an adult female person: *men, women and children*

womb /wuːm/ *noun* the part inside a woman or a female animal where a baby grows before it is born

won *form of* WIN

wonder[1] /ˈwʌndə(r)/ *verb* (**wonders, wondering, wondered** /ˈwʌndəd/)

❖ **PRONUNCIATION**
Wonder sounds like **thunder**.

to ask yourself something; to want to know something: *I wonder what that noise is.* ◇ *I wonder why he didn't come.*
I wonder if words that you use to ask a question politely: *I wonder if you could help me.* ➲ Note at **wander**.

wonder[2] /ˈwʌndə(r)/ *noun* **1** (no plural) a feeling that you have when you see or hear something very strange, surprising or beautiful: *The boy looked up in wonder at the elephant.* **2** (*plural* **wonders**) something that gives you this feeling: *the wonders of modern medicine*
it's a wonder it is surprising that: *It's a wonder you weren't killed in the accident.*
no wonder it is not surprising: *She didn't sleep last night, so no wonder she's tired.*

wonderful /ˈwʌndəfl/ *adjective* very good; excellent: *What a wonderful present!* ◇ *This food is wonderful.*

won't /wəʊnt/ = **will not**

wood /wʊd/ *noun* **1** (no plural) the hard part of a tree: *The table is made of wood.* **2** (also **woods**) a big group of trees, smaller than a forest: *We went for a walk in the woods.* ➲ Note at **forest**.

wooden /ˈwʊdn/ *adjective* made of wood: *a wooden box*

wool /wʊl/ *noun* (no plural) **1** the soft thick hair of sheep **2** thread or cloth that is made from the hair of sheep: *a ball of wool* ◇ *This blanket is made of wool.* ➲ Picture at **knit**.

woollen /ˈwʊlən/ *adjective* made of wool: *woollen socks*

woolly /ˈwʊli/ *adjective* made of wool, or like wool: *a woolly hat*

word /wɜːd/ *noun* **1** (*plural* **words**) a sound that you make or a letter or group of letters that you write, that has a meaning: *What's the French word for 'dog'?* ◇ *Do you know the words of this song?* **2** (no plural) a promise: *She gave me her word that she wouldn't tell anyone.*
have a word with someone to speak to someone: *Can I have a word with you?*
in other words saying the same thing in a different way: *Mwita doesn't like hard work – in other words, he's lazy!*
keep your word to do what you promised: *Tanei said she would come, and she kept her word.*
take someone's word for it to believe what someone says
word for word using exactly the same words: *Shema repeated word for word what you told him.*

wore *form of* **WEAR**[1]

work[1] /wɜːk/ *noun* **1** (no plural) doing or making something: *Digging is hard work.* ◇ *She's lazy – she never does any work.* **2** (no plural) what you do to earn money; a job: *What time do you start work?*

❖ **GRAMMAR**
Be careful! You cannot say 'a work' or 'works'. You can say: *'He's looking for work.'* or use **a job** or **jobs**: *He's looking for a job.*

3 (no plural) the place where you have a job: *I phoned him at work.* ◇ *She's not going to work today.* **4** (no plural) something that you make or do: *The teacher marked our work.* ◇ *The artist only sells her work to friends.* **5** (*plural* **works**) a book, painting or piece of music: *the works of Shakespeare* ◇ *a work of art* **6** **works** (plural) a place where people make things with machines: *the steelworks* (= where steel is made)
at work doing some work: *The group are at work on* (= making) *a new album.*
get to work start doing something: *Let's get to work on this washing-up.*
out of work If someone is **out of work**, they do not have a job that they are paid to do: *How long has Kendi been out of work?*

work[2] /wɜːk/ *verb* (**works, working, worked** /wɜːkt/) **1** to do or make something; to be busy: *You will need to work harder if you want to pass the exam.* **2** to do something as a job and get money for it: *Hawa works for a national newspaper.* ◇ *He works at the car factory.* **3** to go correctly or do something correctly: *We can't listen to the radio – it isn't working.* ◇ *How does this computer work?* **4** to make something do something: *Can you show me how to work this machine?* **5** to have the result you wanted: *I don't think your plan will work.*

work out to have the result you wanted: *I hope your plans work out.*
work something out to find the answer to something: *We worked out the cost of the new equipment.* ◇ *Why did she do it? I can't work it out.*

workbook /ˈwɜːkbʊk/ *noun* a book where you write answers to questions, that you use when you are studying something

worker 🔑 /ˈwɜːkə(r)/ *noun* a person who works: *factory workers* ◇ *an office worker*

worker bee /ˈwɜːkə biː/ *noun* a female **bee** (= a small insect that flies and makes honey) that helps do the work for a group of bees but does not have young ones

workman /ˈwɜːkmən/ *noun* (*plural* **workmen** /ˈwɜːkmən/) a man who works with his hands to build or repair something

worksheet /ˈwɜkʃiːt/ *noun* a piece of paper where you write answers to questions, that you use when you are studying something

workshop /ˈwɜːkʃɒp/ *noun* **1** a place where people make or repair things **2** a time when people meet and work together to learn about something

world 🔑 /wɜːld/ *noun* **1** (no plural) the earth with all its countries and people: *a map of the world* ◇ *Which is the biggest city in the world?* **2** (*plural* **worlds**) all the people who do the same kind of thing: *the world of politics*
think the world of someone or **something** to like someone or something very much: *She thinks the world of her grandchildren.*

world-famous /ˌwɜːld ˈfeɪməs/ *adjective* known everywhere in the world: *a world-famous writer*

worldwide /ˌwɜːldˈwaɪd/ *adjective* that you find everywhere in the world: *Pollution is a worldwide problem.*

the World Wide Web /ðə ˌwɜːld waɪd ˈweb/ *noun* (no plural) the system that makes it possible for you to see information from all over the world on your computer ℹ The short form is **WWW**.

worm /wɜːm/ *noun* a small animal with a long thin body and no legs. **Worms** live in the ground or in other animals.

worn *form of* **WEAR**[1]

worn out /ˌwɔːn ˈaʊt/ *adjective* **1** old and completely finished because you have used it a lot: *I threw the shoes away because they were worn out.* **2** very tired: *He's worn out after his long journey.*

worried 🔑 /ˈwʌrid/ *adjective* unhappy because you think that something bad will happen or has happened: *Kendi is worried that she's going to fail the exam.* ◇ *I'm worried about my brother – he looks ill.* ➲ Look at **worry**[1].

worry[1] 🔑 /ˈwʌri/ *verb* (**worries, worrying, worried** /ˈwʌrid/, **has worried**) **1** to feel that something bad will happen or has happened: *I worried when Odoi didn't come home at the usual time.* ◇ *Don't worry if you don't know the answer.* ◇ *There's nothing to worry about.* **2** to make someone feel that something bad will happen or has happened: *Pembe's illness is worrying his parents.* ➲ Look at **worried**.

worry[2] 🔑 /ˈwʌri/ *noun* **1** (no plural) a feeling that something bad will happen or has happened: *Her face showed signs of worry.* **2** (*plural* **worries**) a problem; something that makes you feel worried: *I have a lot of worries.*

worse 🔑 /wɜːs/ *adjective, adverb* (**worse, worst**) **1** more bad; less good: *The weather today is worse than yesterday.* ◇ *His singing is bad but his dancing is even worse.* **2** more ill: *If you get worse, you must go to the doctor's.* OPPOSITE **better**

worship /ˈwɜːʃɪp/ *verb* (**worships, worshipping, worshipped** /ˈwɜːʃɪpt/) **1** to show that you believe in God or a god by saying prayers: *Christians worship in a church.* **2** to love someone very much or think that someone is wonderful: *She worships her grandchildren.* ▸ **worship** *noun* (no plural): *A mosque is a place of worship.*

worst[1] 🔑 /wɜːst/ *adjective, adverb* (**worse, worst**) most bad; the least well: *He's the worst player in the team!* ◇ *the worst day of my life* ◇ *Bigogo played badly, but I played worst of all.* OPPOSITE **best**

worst[2] 🔑 /wɜːst/ *noun* (no plural) the most bad thing or person: *I'm the worst in the class at grammar.* OPPOSITE **best**
if the worst comes to the worst

if something very bad happens: *If the worst comes to the worst and I fail the exam, I'll take it again next year.*

worth[1] /wɜːθ/ *adjective* **1** with a value of: *That house is worth a lot of money.* **2** good or useful enough to do or have: *Is this film worth seeing?* ◇ *It's not worth asking Awino for money – she never has any.*

worth[2] /wɜːθ/ *noun* (no plural) value: *This painting is of little worth.*
worth of how much of something an amount of money will buy: *I'd like 1000 shillings' worth of petrol, please.*

worthless /ˈwɜːθləs/ *adjective* with no value or use: *The ring was worthless because it wasn't made of real gold.*

worthwhile /ˌwɜːθˈwaɪl/ *adjective* good or useful enough for the time that you spend or the work that you do: *The hard work was worthwhile because I passed the exam.*

would /wʊd/ *modal verb* **1** the word for 'will' in the past: *He said he would come.* **2** a word that you use to talk about a situation that is not real: *If I had as much money as I wanted, I would buy a big house.* **3** a word that you use to ask something in a polite way: *Would you close the door, please?* **4** a word that you use to talk about something that happened many times in the past: *When I was young, I would go to the river nearly every day.*
would like want; words that you use when you ask or say something in a polite way: *Would you like a cup of tea?* ◇ *I would like to go to America.* ➲ Note at **modal verb**.

> ❖ **GRAMMAR**
>
> The negative form of **would** is **would not** or the short form **wouldn't** /ˈwʊdnt/: *He wouldn't help me.*
>
> The short form of **would** is **'d**. We often use this: *I'd* (= I would) *like to meet her.* ◇ *They'd* (= they would) *help if they had the time.*

would've /ˈwʊdəv/ = **would have**

wound[1] *form of* WIND[2]

wound[2] /wuːnd/ *verb* (**wounds**, **wounding**, **wounded**) to hurt someone: *The bullet wounded him in the leg.*

wound[3] /wuːnd/ *noun* a hurt place in your body made by something like a gun or a knife: *a knife wound*

wove, woven *forms of* WEAVE

wow /waʊ/ a word that shows surprise and pleasure: *Wow! What a lovely car!*

wrap /ræp/ *verb* (**wraps**, **wrapping**, **wrapped** /ræpt/) (also **wrap up**)

> ❖ **PRONUNCIATION**
>
> Be careful. We do not say the **w** in words beginning with **wr**, so **wrap** sounds like **rap**, and **wring** sounds like **ring**.

to put paper or cloth around someone or something: *The baby was wrapped in a blanket.* ◇ *She wrapped the glass up in paper.* OPPOSITE **unwrap**

wrapper /ˈræpə(r)/ *noun* a piece of paper or plastic that covers something like a sweet or a packet of biscuits: *Don't throw your wrappers on the floor!*

wrapping /ˈræpɪŋ/ *noun* (no plural) a piece of paper or plastic that covers a present or something that you buy: *I took the new shirt out of its wrapping.*

wrapping paper /ˈræpɪŋ peɪpə(r)/ *noun* (no plural) special paper that you use to wrap presents

wreath /riːθ/ *noun* a circle of flowers or leaves: *She put a wreath on the grave.*

wreck[1] /rek/ *noun* a ship, car or plane that has been very badly damaged in an accident: *The car was a wreck after the crash.*

wreck[2] /rek/ *verb* (**wrecks**, **wrecking**, **wrecked** /rekt/) to break or destroy something completely: *The fire wrecked the hotel.*

wreckage /ˈrekɪdʒ/ *noun* (no plural) the broken parts of something that has been badly damaged: *They found a child in the wreckage of the plane.*

wrestle /ˈresl/ *verb* (**wrestles**, **wrestling**, **wrestled** /ˈresld/) to fight by trying to throw someone to the ground. People often **wrestle** as a sport. ► **wrestler** /ˈreslə(r)/ *noun* a person who wrestles as a sport ► **wrestling** /ˈreslɪŋ/ *noun* (no plural) the sport where two people fight and try to throw each other to the ground: *a wrestling match*

wriggle /ˈrɪgl/ *verb* (**wriggles, wriggling, wriggled** /ˈrɪgld/) to turn your body quickly from side to side: *The teacher told the children to stop wriggling and sit still.*

wring /rɪŋ/ *verb* (**wrings, wringing, wrung** /rʌŋ/, **has wrung**) to press and twist something with your hands to make water come out: *He wrung the towel out and put it outside to dry.*

wrinkle /ˈrɪŋkl/ *noun* a small line in something, for example in the skin of your face: *My grandmother has a lot of wrinkles.* ▶ **wrinkled** /ˈrɪŋkld/ *adjective* with a lot of wrinkles: *His face is very wrinkled.*

wrist /rɪst/ *noun* the part of your body where your arm joins your hand: *I broke my wrist.* ➲ picture on page A13

write 🔑 /raɪt/ *verb* (**writes, writing, wrote** /rəʊt/, **has written** /ˈrɪtn/) **1** to make letters or words on paper using a pen or pencil: *Write your name at the top of the page.* ◇ *He can't read or write.* **2** to write and send a letter to someone: *My mother writes to me every week.* ◇ *I wrote her a postcard.* **3** to make a story, book, etc: *Meja Mwangi writes books.*
write down to write something on paper, so that you can remember it: *I wrote down his telephone number.*

writer 🔑 /ˈraɪtə(r)/ *noun* a person who writes books, stories, etc: *Barbara Kimenye was a famous writer.*

writing 🔑 /ˈraɪtɪŋ/ *noun* (no plural)
1 words that someone puts on paper: *I can't read your writing – it's so small.*
2 putting words on paper: *Writing is slower than phoning.*
in writing written on paper: *I'll confirm the offer in writing next week.*

writing paper /ˈraɪtɪŋ peɪpə(r)/ *noun* (no plural) paper for writing letters on

written *form of* WRITE

wrong¹ 🔑 /rɒŋ/ *adjective*

> ❖ **PRONUNCIATION**
> We do not say the 'w' in **wrong**.

1 not true or not correct: *She gave me the wrong key, so I couldn't open the door.* ◇ *This clock is wrong.* OPPOSITE **right** **2** bad, or not what the law allows: *Stealing is wrong.* ◇ *I haven't done anything wrong.* OPPOSITE **right** **3** not the best: *We're late because we took the wrong road.* OPPOSITE **right** **4** not as it should be, or not working well: *There's something wrong with my bike – it's making a strange noise.* ◇ *'What's wrong with Mrs Karomo?' 'She's got a bad headache.'*

wrong² 🔑 /rɒŋ/ *adverb* not correctly; not right: *You've spelt my name wrong.*
go wrong 1 to stop working well: *The television has gone wrong – can you mend it?* **2** to not happen as you hoped or wanted: *All our plans went wrong.*

wrong³ /rɒŋ/ *noun* (no plural) what is bad or not right: *Babies don't know the difference between right and wrong.*

wrongly /ˈrɒŋli/ *adverb* not correctly: *The letter didn't arrive because it was wrongly addressed.*

wrote *form of* WRITE

wrung *form of* WRING

WWW /ˌdʌblju: dʌblju: ˈdʌblju:/ *short for* **World Wide Web**

X, x /eks/ *noun* (*plural* **X's, x's** /ˈeksɪz/) the twenty-fourth letter of the English alphabet: *'X-ray' begins with an 'X'.*

Xmas /ˈeksməs/ = **Christmas**

> ❖ **SPEAKING**
> **Christmas** is used mainly in speaking and **Xmas** mainly in writing: *Happy Xmas and New Year!* (= on a card)

X-ray /ˈeks reɪ/ *noun* a photograph of the inside of your body that is made by using a special light that you cannot see: *The doctor took an X-ray of my arm to see if it was broken.* ▶ **X-ray** *verb* (**X-rays, X-raying, X-rayed** /ˈeks reɪd/) to take a photograph using an **X-ray** machine: *She had her leg X-rayed.*

Yy

Y, y /waɪ/ *noun* (*plural* **Y's, y's** /waɪz/) the twenty-fifth letter of the English alphabet: *'Yawn' begins with a 'Y'.*

-y /i/ *suffix* with a lot of: *dusty* ◇ *hairy*

yacht /jɒt/ *noun*

> ❖ **PRONUNCIATION**
>
> **Yacht** sounds like **not**.

1 a boat with sails that is used for racing ➲ Picture at **sail**[1]. **2** a big boat with an engine: *a millionaire's yacht*

yam /jæm/ *noun* a vegetable that grows under the ground

yard /jɑːd/ *noun* **1** a measure of length (=91 centimetres). There are three **feet** or thirty-six **inches** in a yard. ❶ The short way of writing 'yard' is **yd.** ➲ Look at **foot**. **2** a piece of hard ground next to a building, with a fence or wall around it: *The children were playing in the school yard.* ◇ *a farmyard*

yawn /jɔːn/ *verb* (**yawns, yawning, yawned** /jɔːnd/) to open your mouth wide because you are tired or bored ▸ **yawn** *noun*: *'I'm going to bed now,' she said with a yawn.*

yaws /jɔːz/ *noun* (no plural) a serious illness that makes you get large red lumps on your skin. You can get **yaws** if you touch a person who has got it.

yd *short for* YARD

yeah /jeə/ yes ❶ This is an informal word.

year ⚷ /jɪə(r)/ *noun* **1** a time of 365 or 366 days from 1 January to 31 December. A year has twelve **months**: *'In which year were you born?' 'In 2004.'* ◇ *He left school last year.* **2** any time of twelve months: *I have known Katee for three years.* ◇ *Her son is five years old.* ◇ *She has a five-year-old son.* ◇ *a two-year-old* ➲ Note at **age**.

all year round through all the year: *The swimming pool is open all year round.*

yearly /ˈjɪəli/ *adjective, adverb* that happens or comes every year or once a year: *a yearly visit* ◇ *We meet twice yearly.*

yeast /jiːst/ *noun* (no plural) a substance that you use for making bread rise

yell /jel/ *verb* (**yells, yelling, yelled** /jeld/) to shout loudly: *'Look out!' she yelled as the car came towards them.* ▸ **yell** *noun*: *He gave a yell of pain.*

yellow ⚷ /ˈjeləʊ/ *adjective* with the colour of a lemon or of butter: *She was wearing a yellow skirt.* ▸ **yellow** *noun*: *Yellow is my favourite colour.*

yellow fever *noun* /ˈjeləʊ fiːvə(r)/ (no plural) an illness that makes your eyes yellow and makes you feel very hot. You get **yellow fever** from the bite of a small flying insect (called a **mosquito**).

yellow line /ˌjeləʊ ˈlaɪn/ *noun* (in Britain) a yellow line painted at the side of a road to show that you can only park your car there at particular times or for a short time: *double yellow lines* (= two lines that mean you cannot park there at all)

yes ⚷ /jes/ a word that you use for answering a question. You use 'yes' to agree, to say that something is true, or to say that you would like something: *'Have you got the key?' 'Yes, here it is.'* ◇ *'Would you like some tea?' 'Yes, please.'* OPPOSITE **no**

yesterday ⚷ /ˈjestədeɪ/ *adverb, noun* (no plural) (on) the day before today: *I saw Ali yesterday.* ◇ *I phoned you yesterday afternoon but you were out.* ◇ *I sent the letter the day before yesterday.*

yet[1] ⚷ /jet/ *adverb* **1** until now: *I haven't finished the book yet.* ◇ *Have you seen that film yet?* ➲ Note at **already**. **2** now; as early as this: *You don't need to go yet – it's only seven o'clock.* **3** in the future: *They may win yet.*

as yet until now: *As yet, I haven't met her.*

yet again once more: *Robi is late yet again!*

yet[2] ⚷ /jet/ *conjunction* but; however: *We arrived home tired yet happy.*

yogurt /ˈjɒgət/ *noun* thick liquid food made from milk: *apricot yogurt* ◇ *Do you want a yogurt?* ❶ When we say 'a yogurt', we mean 'a pot of yogurt'.

yolk /jəʊk/ *noun*

> ❖ **PRONUNCIATION**
>
> **Yolk** sounds like **smoke** because we do not say the 'l'.

the yellow part in an egg ➲ Picture at **egg**.

you 🔑 /juː; ju/ *pronoun* **1** the person or people that I am speaking to: *You are late.* ◇ *I saw you yesterday.* **2** any person; a person: *You can buy stamps at a post office.*

you'd /juːd/ **1** = **you had** **2** = **you would**

you'll /juːl/ = **you will**

young[1] 🔑 /jʌŋ/ *adjective* (**younger** /ˈjʌŋgə(r)/, **youngest** /ˈjʌŋgɪst/) in the early part of life; not old: *They have two young children.* ◇ *You're younger than me.* OPPOSITE **old** ➲ Look at **youth**.

young[2] /jʌŋ/ *noun* (plural) **1** baby animals: *Birds build nests for their young.* **2 the young** children and young people: *school books for the young*

your 🔑 /jɔː(r)/ *adjective* of you: *Where is your bag?* ◇ *Do you all have your books?* ◇ *Show me your hands.*

you're /jɔː(r)/ = **you are**

yours 🔑 /jɔːz/ *pronoun* **1** something that belongs to you: *Is this pen yours or mine?* **2 Yours** a word that you write at the end of a letter: *Yours sincerely …* ◇ *Yours faithfully …*

yourself 🔑 /jɔːˈself/ *pronoun* (*plural* **yourselves** /jɔːˈselvz/) **1** a word that shows 'you' when I have just talked about you: *Did you hurt yourself?* ◇ *Buy yourselves a drink.* **2** a word that makes 'you' stronger: *Did you make this cake yourself?* ◇ *'Who told you?' 'You told me yourself!'*
by yourself; by yourselves **1** alone; without other people: *Do you live by yourself?* **2** without help: *You can't carry all those bags by yourself.*

youth 🔑 /juːθ/ *noun* **1** (no plural) the part of your life when you are young: *He spent his youth in Tanzania and came to Kenya when he was 18.* ◇ *She was very poor in her youth.* OPPOSITE **old age** **2** (*plural* **youths** /juːðz/) a boy or young man **3 the youth** (plural) young people: *the youth of this country*

you've /juːv/ = **you have**

Zz

Z, z /zed/ *noun* (*plural* **Z's, z's** /zedz/) the twenty-sixth and last letter of the English alphabet: *'Zoo' begins with a 'Z'.*

zebra

zebra /ˈzebrə/ *noun* an African wild animal like a horse, with black and white lines on its body

zebra crossing /ˌzebrə ˈkrɒsɪŋ/ *noun* a black and white path across a road. Cars must stop there to let people cross the road safely.

zebu /ˈziːbuː/ *noun* a kind of cattle. A zebu has long horns and a high part (called a **hump**) on its back.

zero 🔑 /ˈzɪərəʊ/ *noun* **1** (*plural* **zeros**) the number 0 **2** (no plural) the point between + and – on an instrument that measures how hot or cold something is (a **thermometer**): *The temperature is five degrees below zero.*

zero grazing /ˌzɪərəʊ ˈgreɪzɪŋ/ *noun* (no plural) when farm animals are kept in buildings and eat grass that is cut and brought to them

zeze

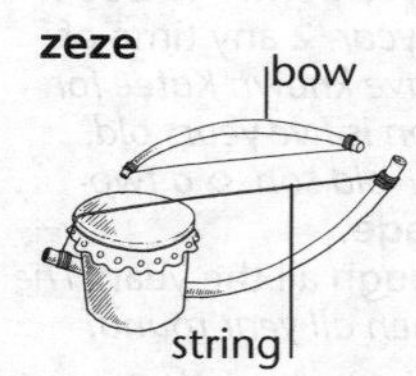

zeze *noun* (East African English) a musical instrument with strings

zigzag

zigzag /ˈzɪɡzæɡ/ *noun* a line that goes up and down like a lot of letter Ws

zip

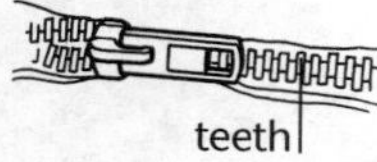

zip¹ /zɪp/ *noun* a long metal or plastic thing with a small part that you pull to close and open things like clothes and bags

zip² /zɪp/ *verb* (**zips**, **zipping**, **zipped** /zɪpt/)

zip up to close something with a **zip**: *She zipped up her dress.* OPPOSITE **unzip**

zone /zəʊn/ *noun* a place that is different from others near it, or where something special happens: *The city is divided into three zones.* ◇ *Do not enter the danger zone!*

zoo /zuː/ *noun* (*plural* **zoos**) a place where wild animals are kept behind fences or bars and you can go and see them

zoom /zuːm/ *verb* (**zooms**, **zooming**, **zoomed** /zuːmd/) to move very fast: *Katee zoomed past on his bike.*

STUDY PAGES

Contents

GRAMMAR

Words can be put into sets called parts of speech. The main ones are: **noun**, **pronoun**, **verb**, **adjective**, **adverb**, **preposition**, **conjunction**, **interjection**.

Nouns

Nouns are words that are the names of things or persons, such as **child**, **danger**, **tree**. Nouns divide up into **common nouns** and **proper nouns**.

common nouns	*dog, stream, mystery, bone, fire, danger ...*
proper nouns	*Nzula, Africa, Mandela ...*

Common nouns divide into those which stand for objects (**concrete nouns**) and those which stand for ideas (**abstract nouns**).

concrete nouns	*dog, stream, fire, water, bread, car ...*
abstract nouns	*mystery, danger, happiness, beauty ...*

Nouns also divide into those which can be made plural (**countable nouns**) and those which cannot be made plural (**uncountable nouns**).

countable nouns	*stream, bone, car ...*
uncountable nouns	*bread, water, air, clothing ...*

Pronouns

Pronouns are words used to replace a noun, such as **it**, **me**, **they**.

Nassir likes fish. ***He*** *eats* ***it*** *every day.*

Verbs and their tenses

Some verbs express actions, for example:

I **came**. *She* **eats**. *They* **sing**.

Some verbs express a state, for example:

He **is** *sick. She* **is** *sad.*

Other verbs express feelings, for example:

I **hate** *carrots. She* **loves** *her sister.*

Verbs have several different forms, depending on their **tense**, for example:

present tense:	I speak, she speaks, they are speaking
past tenses:	I spoke, she has spoken, you had spoken, they have been speaking
future tense:	I will be speaking, they will be speaking

The forms of verbs are given in the dictionary in the same order every time:

speak *verb*	(**speaks**, **speaking**, **spoke**, **has spoken**)
speak	present tense after **I, you, they**
speaks	present tense after **he**, **she** or **it**
speaking	present participle (used after **is, are, was, has been**, etc.)
spoke	simple past tense
spoken	past participle (used after **has, had**, etc.)

Some verbs are **regular**, which means that they follow a rule in the way they form their tenses, for example:

kick *verb* (**kicks**, **kicking**, **kicked**)

Other verbs are **irregular** and have rules of their own, for example:

throw *verb* (**throws**, **throwing**, **threw**, **thrown**)

The connecting verb **be** is the most irregular of all:

present tense:	*singular*	I **am**, you **are**, he/she **is**; plural, we/you/they **are**;
present participle:	*singular*	I **am**, you **are**, he/she is **being**;
	plural	we/you/they **are being**;
past tense:	*singular*	I/he/she **was**, you **were**; plural, we/you/they **were**;
past participle:	*singular*	I/you **have been**, he/she **has been**;
	plural	we/you/they **have been**

Adjectives

Adjectives are words that describe a noun and add to its meaning, such as **happy**, **important**, **old**.

*a **happy** girl   an **important** event   an **old** dog*

Adverbs

Adverbs are words that tell you how, when, where or why something happens, such as **quickly**, **again**, **here**, **together**, **yesterday**, **very**.

*She ran **quickly**.   He came **yesterday**.   They are **very** happy.*

Comparison of adjectives and adverbs

Adjectives and adverbs can be made **comparative** or **superlative** in the following ways:

positive	comparative	superlative	positive	comparative	superlative
stiff	stiffer	stiffest	funny	funnier	funniest
quick	quicker	quickest	fast	faster	fastest

For longer adjectives, and for most adverbs, the comparative and superlative are formed by putting **more** or **most** in front of them.

positive	comparative	superlative
terrible	more terrible	most terrible
quickly	more quickly	most quickly

But watch out for exceptions:

bad	worse	worst	good	better	best
badly	worse	worst	little	less	least

If in doubt, look them up in the dictionary.

Prepositions

Prepositions are words put in front of nouns or pronouns to show how the nouns and pronouns are connected with other words, such as **against**, **in**, **on**, **next to**, **in front of**.

*Put the plate **on** the table.   She stood **in front of** the door.*

Conjunctions

Conjunctions are joining words, such as **and**, **but** or **whether**.

*I bought oranges **and** mangoes.   You can have fish **or** chicken.*

Interjections

Interjections are words that express surprise, pain, delight, etc., such as **oh**, **ouch**, **hooray**.

***Ouch**! I hurt my toe.   **Hooray**! We have won.*

WORDS THAT GO TOGETHER

a **pair** of shoes

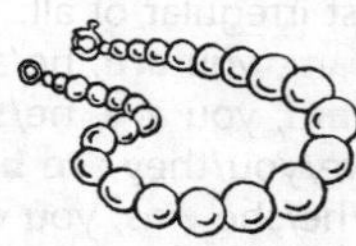
a **string** of beads

a **bar** of chocolate

a **row** of houses

a **bundle** of newspapers

a **drop** of water

a **ball** of string

a **bunch** of flowers

a **crowd** of people

a **slice/piece** of bread

a **pile** of books

a **queue** (of people)

a **lump** of coal

This dictionary tells you about words that often go together. There are special words for groups of animals that go together. Do you know what word is missing in each of these expressions? You can use the dictionary (look up **flock**, **herd**, **litter**, **pack** and **swarm**, and read the example sentences) to find out.

a **flock** of ?

a **herd** of ?

a **litter** of ?

a **pack** of ?

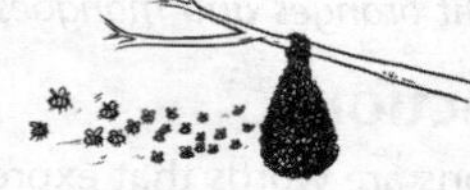
a **swarm** of ?

Opposites

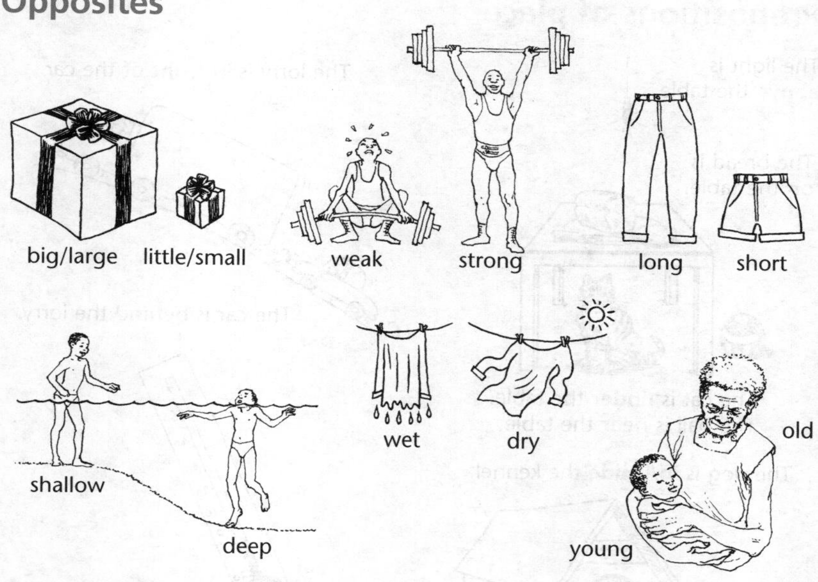

We give opposites for many of the words in this dictionary. If you look up **tidy**, for example, you will find OPPOSITE **untidy**. Look at these words to find their opposites:

hot	cheap	open	loud	tight	soft
clean	fat	high	tall	thick	wide

Order of adjectives

Adjectives tell you what things are like:

*The weather is **hot** and **dry**.* *He drives a **big old yellow** car.*

We use adjectives in this order before a noun:

Opinion	Size/ shape	Age	Colour	Origin (where it comes from)	Material (what it's made of)	Purpose or use	Noun
	a big	old		American			**car**
a lovely		new	green		cotton	school	**dress**

You can practise making up sentences about things you own:

I ate a delicious big red apple.

Tip: You can remember the order of adjectives by saying '**OPSHACOMP**' (**Op**inion, **S**ize/**Sh**ape, **A**ge, **C**olour, **O**rigin, **M**aterial, **P**urpose).

PREPOSITIONS

Prepositions of place

The light is **above** the table.

The bread is **on** the table.

The cat is **under** the table.
The ball is **near** the table.

The dog is **in/inside** the kennel.

The puppies are **outside** the kennel.

Kim is **between** Amo and Ali.

Amo is **next to/beside** Kim.

Amo is **opposite** Kim.

The lorry is **in front of** the car.

The car is **behind** the lorry.

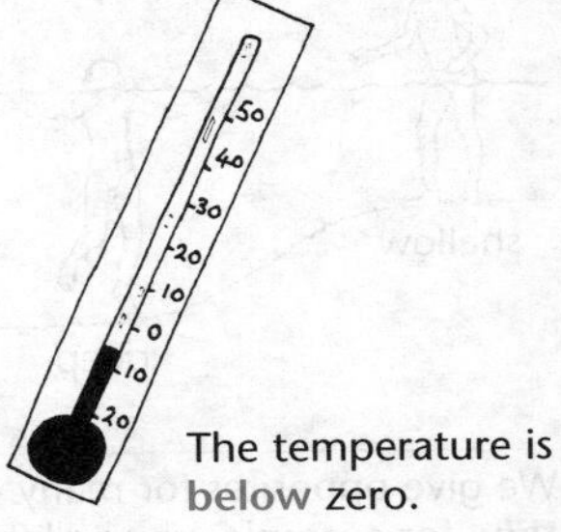

The temperature is **below** zero.

The girl is leaning **against** the wall.

The house is **among** the trees.

The trees are **around** the house.

Prepositions of movement

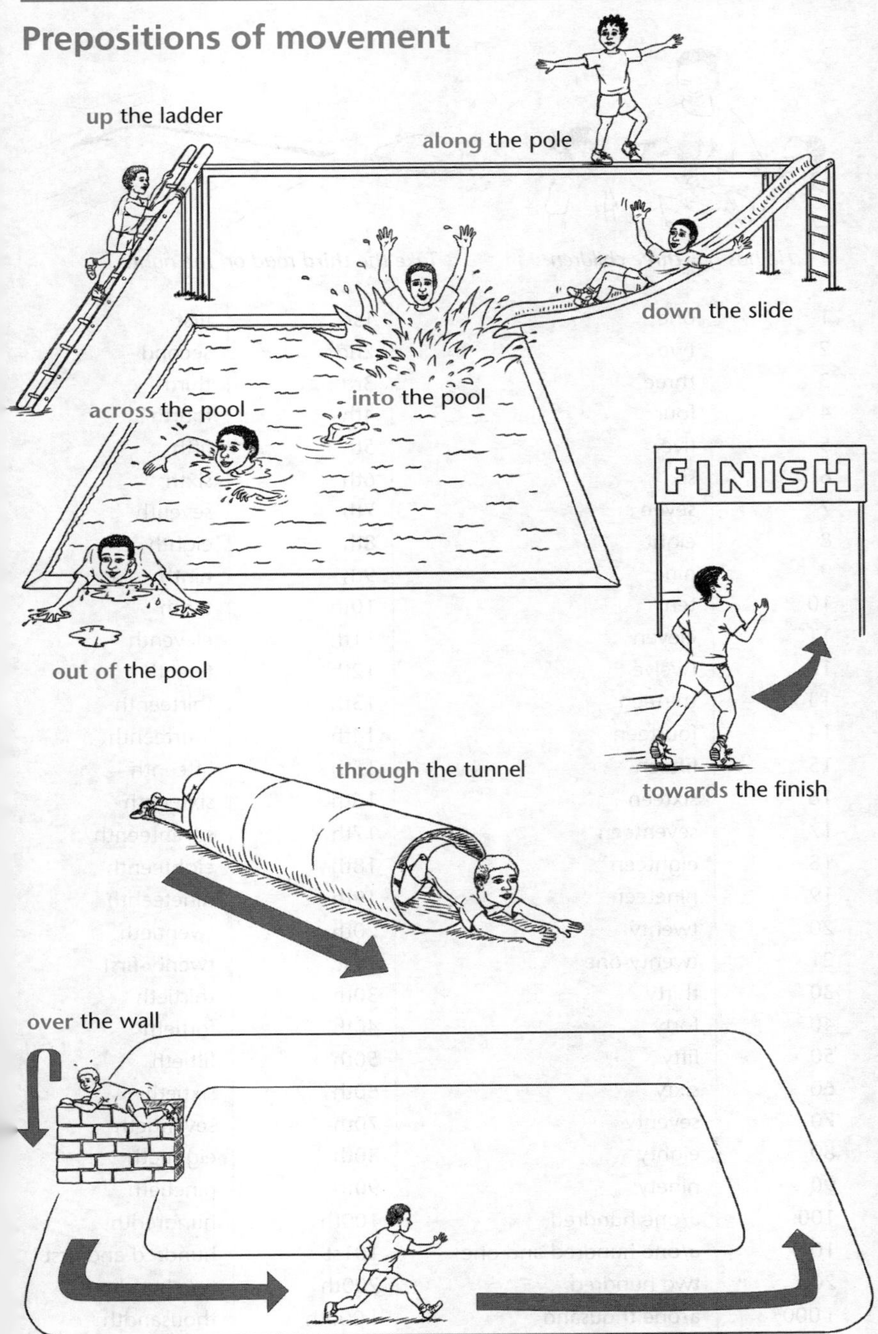

NUMBERS

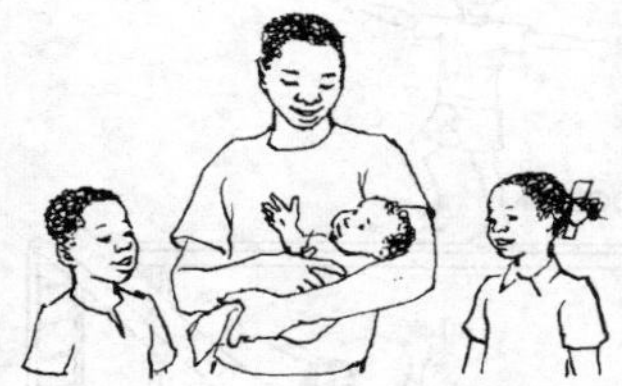

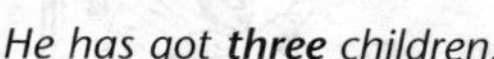

*He has got **three** children.*

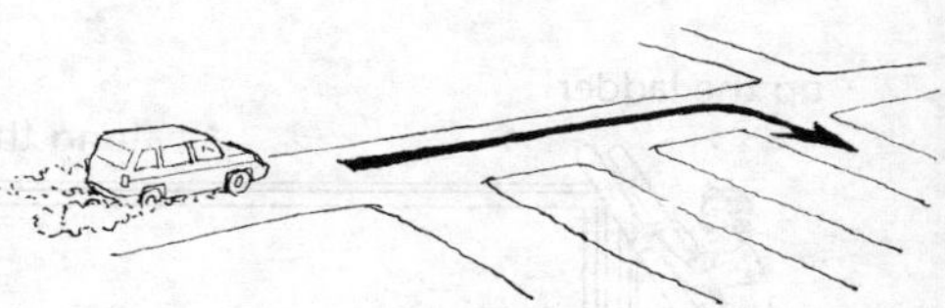

*Take the **third** road on the right.*

1	one	1st	first
2	two	2nd	second
3	three	3rd	third
4	four	4th	fourth
5	five	5th	fifth
6	six	6th	sixth
7	seven	7th	seventh
8	eight	8th	eighth
9	nine	9th	ninth
10	ten	10th	tenth
11	eleven	11th	eleventh
12	twelve	12th	twelfth
13	thirteen	13th	thirteenth
14	fourteen	14th	fourteenth
15	fifteen	15th	fifteenth
16	sixteen	16th	sixteenth
17	seventeen	17th	seventeenth
18	eighteen	18th	eighteenth
19	nineteen	19th	nineteenth
20	twenty	20th	twentieth
21	twenty-one	21st	twenty-first
30	thirty	30th	thirtieth
40	forty	40th	fortieth
50	fifty	50th	fiftieth
60	sixty	60th	sixtieth
70	seventy	70th	seventieth
80	eighty	80th	eightieth
90	ninety	90th	ninetieth
100	a/one hundred	100th	hundredth
101	a/one hundred and one	101st	hundred and first
200	two hundred	200th	two hundredth
1 000	a/one thousand	1 000th	thousandth
1 000 000	a/one million	1 000 000th	millionth

Saying numbers

267 two hundred and sixty-seven

4302 four thousand, three hundred and two

Saying '0'

We usually say **zero**:
zero point five (0.5)
My telephone number is 0728607594 (zero seven two eight six zero seven five nine four).
It was very cold – the temperature was below zero.

When we are telling the time, we say **o** (you say it like **oh**) when the minutes are between one and nine:
10:01 (ten oh one)
11:05 (eleven oh five)

In scores of games like football, we say **nil**:
The score was two–nil.

Writing numbers

We put a small space or a comma (**,**) between *thousands* and *hundreds* in numbers, for example:

15 000 or 15,000

Fractions

1/2 a half

1/3 a/one third

1/4 a/one quarter

1/8 an/one eighth

1/16 a/one sixteenth

3/4 three quarters

1 1/4 one and a quarter

To find out how to say and write **numbers in dates**, look at page A11.

We use **.** (NOT **,**) in **decimals**.

Symbols		We write:	We say:
.	point	3.2	three point two
+	plus	5 + 6	five plus six
-	minus	10 - 4	ten minus four
x	multiplied by / times	4 x 6	four multiplied by six / four times six
÷	divided by	4 ÷ 2	four divided by two
%	per cent	78%	seventy-eight per cent
=	equals	1 + 3 = 4	one plus three equals four
>	greater than	5 > 4	five is greater than four
<	less than	4 < 5	four is less than five

TIME

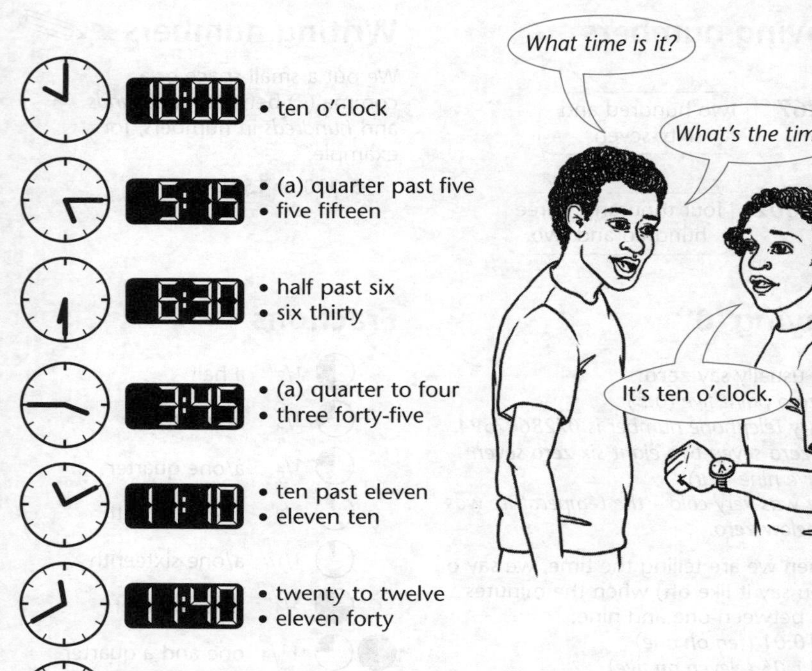

To show what part of the day we mean, we can use:

a.m. *or* **in the morning**

The lesson is at 11 a.m.
The telephone rang at four o'clock in the morning.

p.m. *or* **in the afternoon**
in the evening
at night

We went to the park in the afternoon.
The shop closes at 6 p.m.
She came home at eight o'clock in the evening.
Nurses often have to work at night.

60 seconds = 1 minute
60 minutes = 1 hour
24 hours = 1 day

* We do not often use the 'twenty-four hour clock' when we talk about the time (so we do not say 'fourteen **oh** seven').

What's the date?

Saying dates

How do you say … ?:

the twenty-fourth of September, two thousand and fifteen

or September **the** twenty-fourth, two thousand and fifteen

We also say years like this:

1706 seventeen oh six

1800 eighteen hundred

1999 nineteen ninety-nine

2015 twenty fifteen

Writing dates

Here are some ways of writing the date:

24 September
September 24
24th September
September 24th

Sometimes we just write numbers:

24 September 2015

24/9/15 (*in Britain*)

9/24/15 (*in the USA*)

Talking about days:

If **today** is Wednesday, **yesterday** was Tuesday and **tomorrow** is Thursday.

on, in *or* **at**?

on	5 August Monday Wednesday morning my birthday
in	August 2015 the rainy season the morning/afternoon/evening
at	the beginning of June the weekend Christmas night six o'clock

MONTHS

January
February
March
April
May
June
July
August
September
October
November
December

DAYS

Sunday
Monday
Tuesday
Wednesday
Thursday
Friday
Saturday

SHAPES AND SIZES

Shapes

square circle triangle rectangle/oblong oval

cube sphere pyramid cone cylinder

star crescent

circumference diameter radius

angle right angle

parallel lines vertical line horizontal line diagonal line

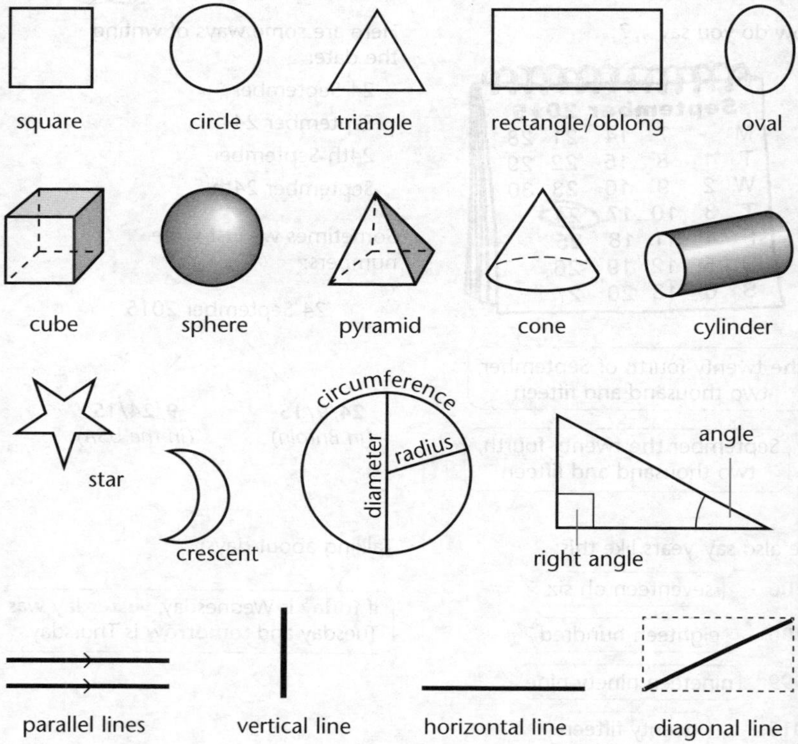

Size

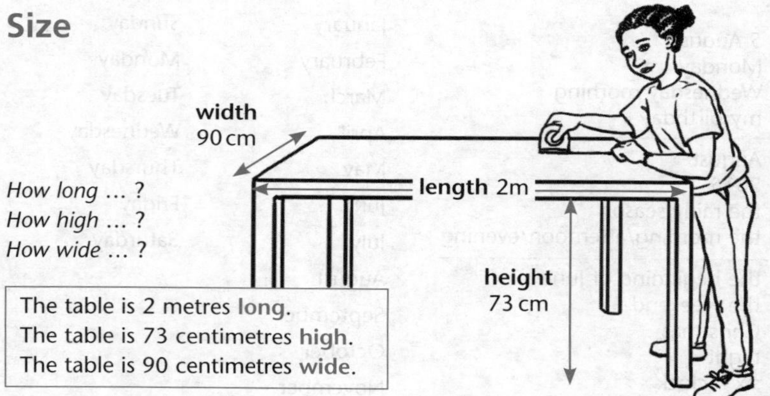

How long ... ?
How high ... ?
How wide ... ?

The table is 2 metres **long**.
The table is 73 centimetres **high**.
The table is 90 centimetres **wide**.

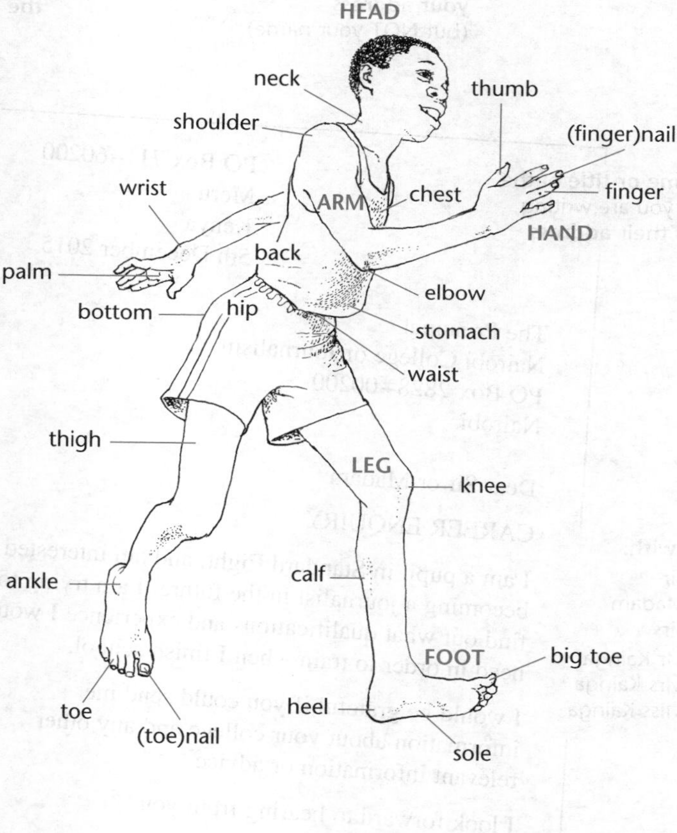

HEAD
neck
shoulder
thumb
(finger)nail
wrist
ARM
chest
finger
HAND
back
palm
elbow
bottom
hip
stomach
waist
thigh
LEG
knee
ankle
calf
FOOT
big toe
toe
heel
(toe)nail
sole

hair
forehead
eyebrow
eyelashes
eye
ear
nose
nostril
cheek
mouth
lip
jaw
chin
throat

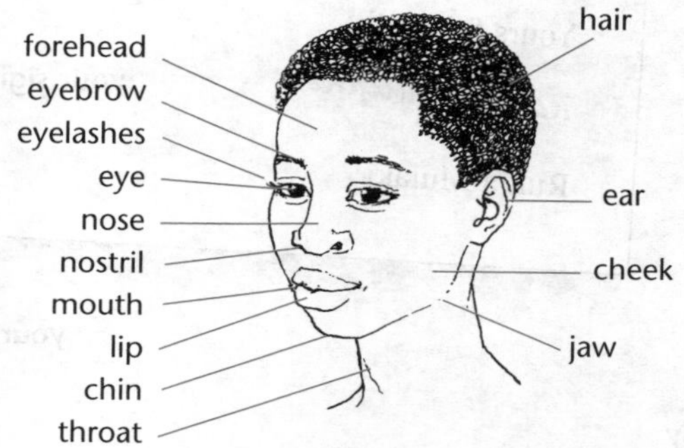

Formal letters

your address (but NOT your name)

the date

the name or title of the person you are writing to, and **their address**

PO Box 711–60200
Meru
Kenya
5th December 2015

The Principal
Nairobi College of Journalism
PO Box 2828–00200
Nairobi

Dear Sir or Madam

CAREER ENQUIRY

I am a pupil in Standard Eight, and am interested in becoming a journalist in the future. I am trying to find out what qualifications and experience I would need in order to train when I finish school.

I would be grateful if you could send me information about your college and any other relevant information or advice.

I look forward to hearing from you.

Yours faithfully

Rukia Mulaki

Rukia Mulaki

begin with:
Dear Sir
Madam
Sirs
Dear Mr Kainga
Mrs Kainga
Miss Kainga

your signature

your full name

end with:
Yours faithfully
(when you begin with *Dear Sir*, etc.)
Yours sincerely
(when you begin with *Dear Mr Kainga*, etc.)

Informal letters

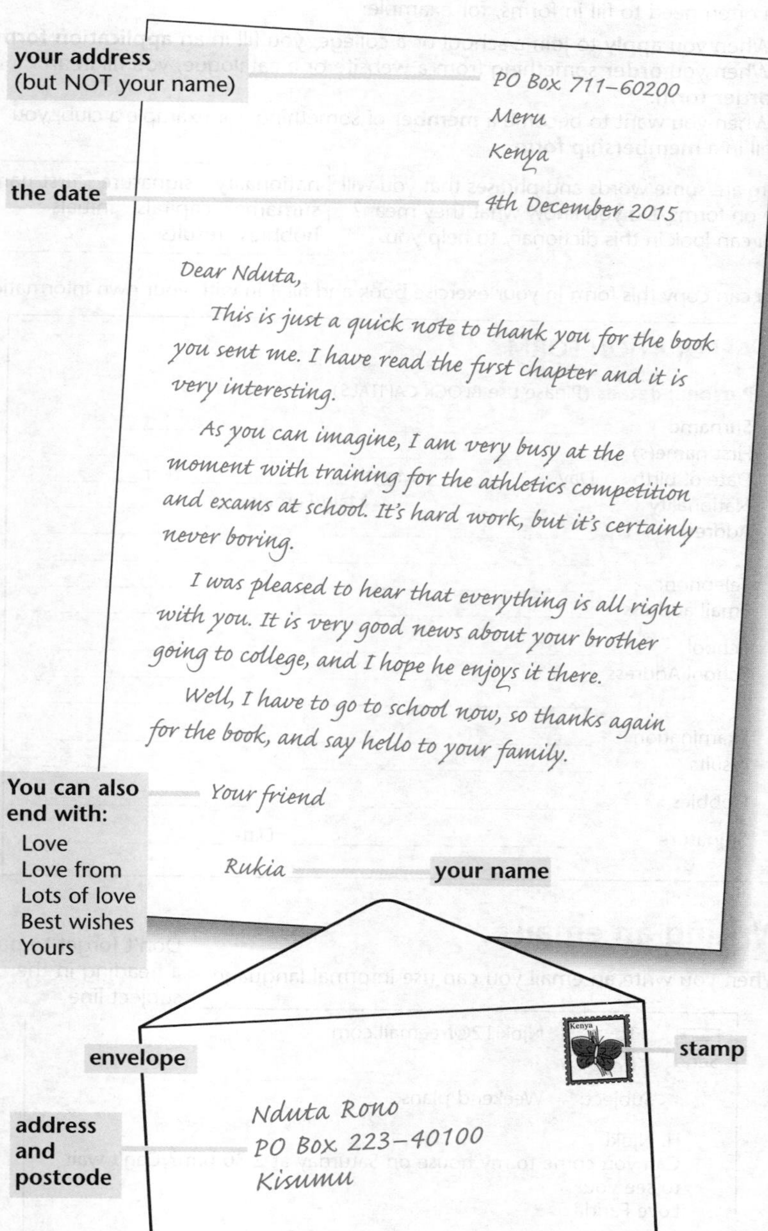

EMAILS AND FORMS

Filling in a form

We often need to fill in forms, for example:

When you **apply** to join a school or a college, you fill in an **application form**.
When you **order** something from a website or a catalogue, you fill in an **order form**.
When you want to become a **member** of something, for example a club, you fill in a **membership form**.

Here are some words and phrases that you will see on forms. Do you know what they mean? You can look in this dictionary to help you.

nationality signature first name
surname capitals initials
hobbies results

You can copy this form in your exercise book and fill it in with your own information.

APPLICATION FORM

Personal details (Please use BLOCK CAPITALS)

Surname ______
First name(s) ______
Date of birth Day ______ Month ______ Year ______
Nationality ______ Male/Female ______
Address ______

Telephone ______
Email address ______
School ______
School Address ______

Examination results ______
Hobbies ______
Signature ______ Date ______

Writing an email

When you write an email you can use informal language.

Don't forget to put a heading in the subject line.

Send
To: Njoki12@freemail.com
Cc:
Subject: Weekend plans

Hi Njoki
Can you come to my house on Saturday at 2.30 p.m? Can't wait to see you!
Love Farida

You can write 'Hello ...' or 'Hi ...', or you can leave this out if you wish.

You do not have to sign your name, but most people put a friendly greeting at the end.

Punctuation marks help us read with the correct meaning.

A, B, C... We use a **capital letter** at the start of each new sentence. We also use capital letters for proper nouns (names of people and places), titles of books, films, etc:

My brother Sewe works in Nairobi, the capital of Kenya.

. A **full stop** shows the end of a sentence:

Adila went to school.

It is also often used after initials and in abbreviations:

e.g. *a.m.*

! An **exclamation mark** is used at the end of a sentence to show surprise, joy, anger or shock:

I can't believe it!

Be quiet!

? We use a **question mark** at the end of a direct question:

How old are you?

, A **comma** separates words in a list:

We bought oranges, bananas, pears and mangoes.

We also use a comma to separate parts of a sentence or show extra information:

You have done your homework, haven't you?

Can I help you, Mrs Odinga?

I have two brothers, both of whom work in Dodoma.

' An **apostrophe** replaces a missing letter or letters:

I'd (= I had) *isn't (= is not)*
we'll (= we will) *won't (= will not)*

We also use an apostrophe to show who or what something belongs to:

Omba's book

Rwanda's capital city

' ' Single quotation marks are used for titles: *Omugave Ndugwa wrote 'The Traffic Jam'.*

– A **dash** is used when an extra comment or extra information is added:

Okeno is usually – but not always – early for school.

- A **hyphen** is used in many cases where two words have joined together into one:

self-service *mother-in-law*

: A **colon** tells the reader that something is coming next, for example in a list:

She speaks several languages: Kiswahili, English and French.

; A **semicolon** is used to separate two parts of a sentence:

We had to walk everywhere; the bus drivers were on strike.

" " **Speech marks** or **quotation marks** are used to show the exact words that somebody says. They go before and after the words spoken. The spoken words are divided from the reporting verb by a comma and a full stop comes at the end:

"I'm scared," said Wambui.

Wambui said, "I'm scared."

( ) **Brackets** are used to separate extra information from the rest of a sentence:

Mount Kilimanjaro (5 895 metres) is the highest mountain in Africa.

Brackets are also used around numbers or letters:

The library rules are:
(a) No talking
(b) No eating or drinking

/ A **slash** is used to separate words that are alternatives:

You can have water/juice with your meal.

A slash is also used when dates are written in numbers:

Today is 7/11/2015.

SAYINGS AND PROVERBS

Here are some well-known sayings and proverbs. They are fixed phrases or sentences that give advice or say something that is generally true. After each saying or proverb there is a short explanation to help you understand what it means.

Many hands make light work.

actions speak louder than words
what a person usually does means more than what they say they will do

the early bird catches the worm
the person who takes the opportunity to do something before other people will have an advantage over them

every cloud has a silver lining
every sad or difficult situation has a positive side

many hands make light work
a job is easier if a lot of people help

two heads are better than one
two people can achieve more than one person working alone

don't judge a book by its cover
you should not form an opinion of someone or something from their appearance only

better late than never
it is better to arrive late, or for something to happen late, than not to come or happen at all

a leopard cannot change its spots
people cannot change their character, especially if they have a bad character

once bitten, twice shy
after an unpleasant experience you are careful to avoid something similar

the pen is mightier than the sword
people who write books, poems, etc. have a greater effect on human affairs than soldiers and wars

Practice makes perfect.

practice makes perfect

if you do an activity regularly, you will improve and become very good at it

prevention is better than cure

it is better to stop something bad from happening than to deal with the problems after it has happened

better safe than sorry

it is better to be too careful than to act too quickly and do something that you may later wish you had not done

let sleeping dogs lie

you should avoid mentioning something that happened in the past, in order to avoid any problems now

a stitch in time saves nine

it is better to deal with a problem immediately, because if you wait it may become worse and cause extra work

you can't teach an old dog new tricks

you cannot successfully make people change their ideas or how they do things when they have been like that for a long time

one good turn deserves another

you should help someone who has helped you

waste not, want not

if you never waste anything, especially food or money, you will always have it when you need it

a watched pot never boils

when you are impatient for something to happen, time seems to pass very slowly

two wrongs don't make a right

if somebody does something bad to you, the situation will not be improved by doing something bad to them

COUNTRIES AND NATIONALITIES

COUNTRY	ADJECTIVE
Afghanistan	Afghan
Africa	African
Albania	Albanian
Algeria	Algerian
America	American
Angola	Angolan
Antigua and Barbuda	Antiguan, Barbudan
Argentina	Argentinian
Armenia	Armenian
Asia	Asian
Australia	Australian
Austria	Austrian
Azerbaijan	Azerbaijani, Azeri
the Bahamas	Bahamian
Bahrain	Bahraini
Bangladesh	Bangladeshi
Barbados	Barbadian
Belarus	Belarusian
Belgium	Belgian
Belize	Belizean
Benin	Beninese
Bhutan	Bhutanese
Bolivia	Bolivian
Bosnia-Herzegovina	Bosnian, Herzegovinian
Botswana	Botswanan Motswana (person) Batswana (people)
Brazil	Brazilian
Britain → the United Kingdom	
Bulgaria	Bulgarian
Burkina Faso	Burkinan, Burkinabe
Burma (now officially Myanmar)	Burmese
Burundi	Burundian
Cambodia	Cambodian
Cameroon	Cameroonian
Canada	Canadian
the Caribbean	Caribbean
Central African Republic	Central African
Chad	Chadian
Chile	Chilean
China	Chinese
Colombia	Colombian
Congo	Congolese
the Democratic Republic of the Congo (DR Congo)	Congolese
Costa Rica	Costa Rican
Côte d'Ivoire	Ivorian
Croatia	Croatian
Cuba	Cuban
Cyprus	Cypriot
the Czech Republic	Czech
Denmark	Danish
Djibouti	Djiboutian
East Timor	East Timorese
Ecuador	Ecuadorian
Egypt	Egyptian
El Salvador	Salvadorean
England	English
Equatorial Guinea	Equatorial Guinean
Eritrea	Eritrean
Estonia	Estonian
Ethiopia	Ethiopian
Fiji	Fijian
Finland	Finnish
France	French
FYROM (the) Former Yugoslav Republic of Macedonia	Macedonian
Gabon	Gabonese
the Gambia	Gambian
Georgia	Georgian
Germany	German
Ghana	Ghanaian
Great Britain	British
Greece	Greek
Grenada	Grenadian
Guatemala	Guatemalan
Guinea	Guinean
Guinea-Bissau	Guinean
Guyana	Guyanese
Haiti	Haitian
Holland → the Netherlands	
Honduras	Honduran
Hungary	Hungarian
Iceland	Icelandic
India	Indian
Indonesia	Indonesian
Iran	Iranian
Iraq	Iraqi
the Republic of Ireland	Irish
Israel	Israeli
Italy	Italian
the Ivory Coast → Côte d'Ivoire	
Jamaica	Jamaican
Japan	Japanese
Jordan	Jordanian

COUNTRY	ADJECTIVE
Kazakhstan	Kazakh
Kenya	Kenyan
Korea, North	North Korean
Korea, South	South Korean
Kuwait	Kuwaiti
Kyrgyzstan	Kyrgyz
Laos	Laotian
Latvia	Latvian
Lebanon	Lebanese
Lesotho	Sotho Mosotho (person) Basotho (people)
Liberia	Liberian
Libyan	Libya
Lithuania	Lithuanian
Luxembourg	Luxembourg
Macedonia	Macedonian
Madagascar	Madagascan Malagasy
Malawi	Malawian
Malaysia	Malaysian
Mali	Malian
Mauritania	Mauritanian
Mexico	Mexican
Moldova	Moldovan
Mongolia	Mongolian Mongol
Montenegro	Montenegrin
Morocco	Moroccan
Mozambique	Mozambican
Myanmar → Burma	
Namibia	Namibian
Nepal	Nepalese
the Netherlands	Dutch
New Zealand	New Zealand
Nicaragua	Nicaraguan
Niger	Nigerien
Nigeria	Nigerian
Northern Ireland	Northern Irish
Norway	Norwegian
Oman	Omani
Pakistan	Pakistani
Panama	Panamanian
Papua New Guinea	Papua New Guinean
Paraguay	Paraguayan
Peru	Peruvian
the Philippines	Philippine
Poland	Polish
Portugal	Portuguese

COUNTRY	ADJECTIVE
Puerto Rico	Puerto Rican
Qatar	Qatari
Romania	Romanian
Russia	Russian
Rwanda	Rwandan, Rwandese
Samoa	Samoan
Saudi Arabia	Saudi Arabian
Scotland	Scottish
Senegal	Senegalese
Serbia	Serbian
Sierra Leone	Sierra Leonean
Singapore	Singaporean
Slovakia	Slovak, Slovakian
Slovenia	Slovenian
Somalia	Somali
South Africa	South African
South Sudan	South Sudanese
Spain	Spanish
Sri Lanka	Sri Lankan
Sudan	Sudanese
Suriname	Surinamese
Swaziland	Swazi
Sweden	Swedish
Switzerland	Swiss
Syria	Syrian
Tajikistan	Tajik
Tanzania	Tanzanian
Thailand	Thai
Togo	Togolese
Trinidad and Tobago	Trinidadian, Tobagan
Tunisia	Tunisian
Turkey	Turkish
Turkmenistan	Turkmen
Uganda	Ugandan
Ukraine	Ukrainian
the United Arab Emirates	Emirati
the United Kingdom	British
the United States of America (also the USA, the US)	American
Uruguay	Uruguayan
Uzbekistan	Uzbek
Venezuela	Venezuelan
Vietnam	Vietnamese
Wales	Welsh
Yemen	Yemeni
Zambia	Zambian
Zimbabwe	Zimbabwean

IRREGULAR VERBS

INFINITIVE	PAST TENSE	PAST PARTICIPLE
arise	arose	arisen
babysit	babysat	babysat
be	was/were	been
bear	bore	borne
beat	beat	beaten
become	became	become
begin	began	begun
bend	bent	bent
bet	bet	bet
bid	bid	bid
bind	bound	bound
bite	bit	bitten
bleed	bled	bled
blow	blew	blown
break	broke	broken
breed	bred	bred
bring	brought	brought
broadcast	broadcast	broadcast
build	built	built
burn	burnt, burned	burnt, burned
burst	burst	burst
buy	bought	bought
catch	caught	caught
choose	chose	chosen
cling	clung	clung
come	came	come
cost	cost	cost
creep	crept	crept
cut	cut	cut
deal	dealt	dealt
dig	dug	dug
do	did	done
draw	drew	drawn
dream	dreamt, dreamed	dreamt, dreamed
drink	drank	drunk
drive	drove	driven
eat	ate	eaten
fall	fell	fallen
feed	fed	fed
feel	felt	felt
fight	fought	fought
find	found	found
flee	fled	fled

INFINITIVE	PAST TENSE	PAST PARTICIPLE
fling	flung	flung
fly	flew	flown
forbid	forbade	forbidden
forget	forgot	forgotten
forgive	forgave	forgiven
freeze	froze	frozen
get	got	got
give	gave	given
go	went	gone
grind	ground	ground
grow	grew	grown
hang	hung, hanged	hung, hanged
have	had	had
hear	heard	heard
hide	hid	hidden
hit	hit	hit
hold	held	held
hurt	hurt	hurt
keep	kept	kept
kneel	knelt, kneeled	knelt, kneeled
know	knew	known
lay	laid	laid
lead	led	led
lean	leant, leaned	leant, leaned
leap	leapt, leaped	leapt, leaped
learn	learnt, learned	learnt, learned
leave	left	left
lend	lent	lent
let	let	let
lie	lay	lain
light	lit, lighted	lit, lighted
lose	lost	lost
make	made	made
mean	meant	meant
meet	met	met
mislead	misled	misled
mistake	mistook	mistaken
misunderstand	misunderstood	misunderstood
mow	mowed	mown

INFINITIVE	PAST TENSE	PAST PARTICIPLE
overcome	overcame	overcome
overhear	overheard	overheard
oversleep	overslept	overslept
overtake	overtook	overtaken
pay	paid	paid
prove	proved	proved, proven
put	put	put
read	read	read
repay	repaid	repaid
rewind	rewound	rewound
ride	rode	ridden
ring	rang	rung
rise	rose	risen
run	ran	run
saw	sawed	sawn
say	said	said
see	saw	seen
seek	sought	sought
sell	sold	sold
send	sent	sent
set	set	set
sew	sewed	sewed, sewn
shake	shook	shaken
shed	shed	shed
shine	shone	shone
shoot	shot	shot
show	showed	shown, showed
shrink	shrank, shrunk	shrunk
shut	shut	shut
sing	sang	sung
sink	sank	sunk
sit	sat	sat
sleep	slept	slept
slide	slid	slid
sling	slung	slung
slit	slit	slit
smell	smelt, smelled	smelt, smelled
sow	sowed	sown, sowed
speak	spoke	spoken
speed	sped, speeded	sped, speeded
spell	spelt, spelled	spelt, spelled
spend	spent	spent
spill	spilt, spilled	spilt, spilled
spin	spun	spun
spit	spat	spat
split	split	split
spoil	spoilt, spoiled	spoilt, spoiled
spread	spread	spread
spring	sprang	sprung
stand	stood	stood
steal	stole	stolen
stick	stuck	stuck
sting	stung	stung
stink	stank	stunk
stride	strode	–
strike	struck	struck
swear	swore	sworn
sweep	swept	swept
swell	swelled	swollen, swelled
swim	swam	swum
swing	swung	swung
take	took	taken
teach	taught	taught
tear	tore	torn
tell	told	told
think	thought	thought
throw	threw	thrown
thrust	thrust	thrust
tread	trod	trodden
undergo	underwent	undergone
understand	understood	understood
undo	undid	undone
upset	upset	upset
wake	woke	woken
wear	wore	worn
weave	wove	woven
weep	wept	wept
win	won	won
wind	wound	wound
withdraw	withdrew	withdrawn
wring	wrung	wrung
write	wrote	written

QUIZ

Using the study pages

The study pages in this dictionary will help you get things right.

1 Look at pages **A4**, **A6** and **A11** and choose the best answers.

1 I'd like a **bundle/bunch** of flowers, please.
2 The cat is **under/below** the table.
3 My birthday is **at/on** May 4th.

The study pages can also help you learn more words.

2 Words for parts of the body have been jumbled up. What are they? You can look at page **A13** to help you.

stawi	mapl	fering	klean	holderus	listron
______	______	______	______	______	______

The study pages also show you the right phrases and expressions to use.

3 Look at pages **A14 – A16** and answer these questions:

1 Do you use **'Yours faithfully'** in a formal/informal letter?
2 Do you put your name at the top of a letter?
3 Can you use **'Best wishes'** at the end of an informal letter?
4 Can you use informal language when you write an email?

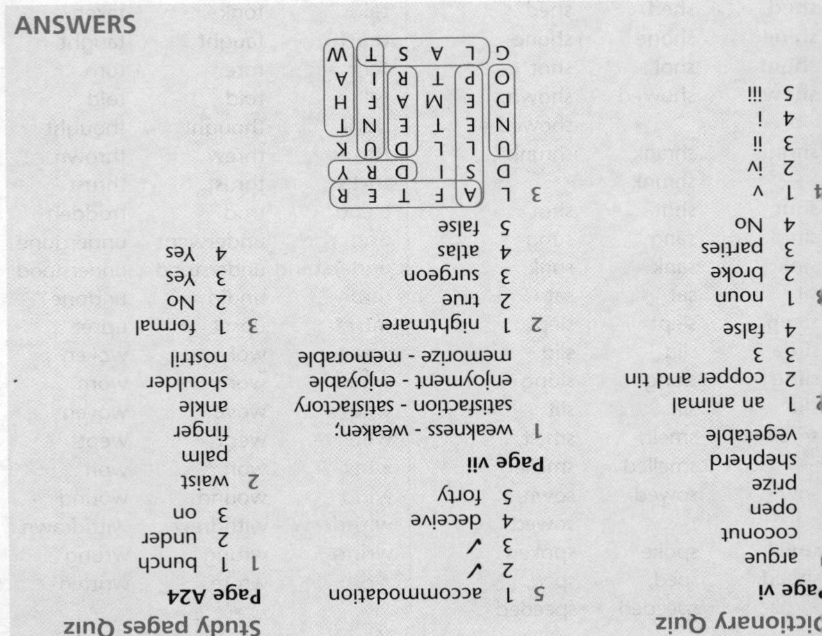

ANSWERS

Dictionary Quiz

Page vi

argue
coconut
open
prize
shepherd
vegetable

1 an animal
2 copper and tin
3 3
4 false

1 noun
2 broke
3 parties
4 No

1 v
2 iv
3 ii
4 i
5 iii

5
1 accommodation
2 ✓
3 ✓
4 deceive
5 forty

Page vii

1 weakness - weaken; satisfaction - satisfactory enjoyment - enjoyable memorize - memorable

2
1 nightmare
2 true
3 surgeon
4 atlas
5 false

3
L A F T E R
D S I D R Y
U L L D U K
N E T E N T
D E M A F H
O P T R I A
G L A S T W

Study pages Quiz

Page A24

1
1 bunch
2 under
3 on

2 waist
palm
finger
ankle
shoulder
nostril

3
1 formal
2 No
3 Yes
4 Yes